INTERNATIONAL FINANCIAL MANAGEMENT

(TEXT AND CASES)

INTERNATIONAL FINANCIAL MANAGEMENT

(TEXT AND CASES)

V.K. BHALLA
Professor
Faculty of Management Studies
University of Delhi
DELHI

S Chand And Company Limited

(ISO 9001 Certified Company)

S Chand And Company Limited

(ISO 9001 Certified Company)

Head Office: Block B-1, House No. D-1, Ground Floor, Mohan Co-operative Industrial Estate, New Delhi – 110 044 | Phone: 011-66672000

Registered Office: A-27, 2nd Floor, Mohan Co-operative Industrial Estate, New Delhi – 110 044 Phone: 011-49731800

www.schandpublishing.com; e-mail: info@schandpublishing.com

Branches

Ahmedabad	:	Ph: 27542369, 27541965; ahmedabad@schandpublishing.com
Bengaluru	:	Ph: 22354008, 22268048; bangalore@schandpublishing.com
Bhopal	:	Ph: 4274723, 4209587; bhopal@schandpublishing.com
Bhubaneshwar	:	Ph: 2951580; bhubaneshwar@schandpublishing.com
Chennai	:	Ph: 23632120; chennai@schandpublishing.com
Guwahati	:	Ph: 2738811, 2735640; guwahati@schandpublishing.com
Hyderabad	:	Ph: 40186018; hyderabad@schandpublishing.com
Jaipur	:	Ph: 2291317, 2291318; jaipur@schandpublishing.com
Jalandhar	:	Ph: 4645630; jalandhar@schandpublishing.com
Kochi	:	Ph: 2576207, 2576208; cochin@schandpublishing.com
Kolkata	:	Ph: 23357458, 23353914; kolkata@schandpublishing.com
Lucknow	:	Ph: 4003633; lucknow@schandpublishing.com
Mumbai	:	Ph: 25000297; mumbai@schandpublishing.com
Nagpur	:	Ph: 2250230; nagpur@schandpublishing.com
Patna	:	Ph: 2260011; patna@schandpublishing.com
Ranchi	:	Ph: 2361178; ranchi@schandpublishing.com
Sahibabad	:	Ph: 2771238; info@schandpublishing.com

First Edition 2014
Reprint 2018

ISBN: 978-81-219-4291-1

Product Code: H8IFM60FINC10ENAA14O

By Vikas Publishing House Private Limited, Plot 20/4, Site-IV, Industrial Area Sahibabad, Ghaziabad – 201 010 and Published by S Chand And Company Limited, A-27, 2nd Floor, Mohan Co-operative Industrial Estate, New Delhi – 110 044

PREFACE

A perennial challenge facing all of the world's countries, regardless of their level of economic development, is achieving a financial stability, economic growth, and higher living standards. There are many different paths that can be taken to achieve these objectives, and every country's path will be different given the distinctive nature of national economies and political systems. Yet, based on experience throughout the world, several basic principles seem to underpin greater prosperity. These include investment (particularly foreign direct investment), the spread of technology, strong institutions, sound macroeconomic policies, an educated workforce,and the existence of market economy. Furthermore, a common denominator which appears to link nearly all high-growth countries together in their participation in, and integration with,the global financial markets.

Financial globalisation is a catalyst for economic growth and stability. The world's financial markets have experienced a dramatic increase in globalisation in recent years. The most rapid increase has been experienced by advanced economies, but emerging markets and developing countries have also become more financially integrated. Emerging market risks have also risen, as the prospects for these economies appear increasingly linked to the global cycle. In recent years, the resilience of emerging market economies amid the high-risk global environment has been evident in persistent investor flows seeking the relative safety of the sector's fixed-income assets. However, a further escalation of euro area stresses poses risks, especially for the countries in central and eastern Europe. A slowdown in economic activity heightens these risks, as some emerging market economies have only limited policy space to provide countercyclical stimulus and safeguard against external shocks. While the advanced economies face cold headwinds, the emerging markets and developing countries face too much heat.

The global economy has entered a dangerous new phase. While the recovery continues, it looks weaker, bumpier, and more uneven. If anything, it is getting starker. Financial stress has risen substantially. The world is suffering from a collective crises of confidence, which is holding back consumption, investment, and job creation. This imposes not only economic, but also social costs. And uncertainty has been exacerbated by the policy indecision and political dysfunction across the advanced economies. Confidence in policymaking has faltered, despite significant and continuing efforts by European policymakers, which have been essential in addressing investors' biggest fears, the principal risk remains the euro area crisis. A key problem is too much debt in the system. Uncertainty hovers over sovereigns across the advanced economies., banks in Europe, and households in the United States. Adverse feedback loops between the real economy and the financial sector are gaining strength. Concerns about public debt sustainability in the euro area have intensified, leading to fear about the health of the area's banks. Credit risks remain largely unchanged, albeit at high levels, as the renewed deterioration in the banking sector and growing deleveraging and credit pressures in the euro area periphery have been offset by some improvements in corporate and household balance sheets in advanced economies. Within the euro area, the combination of lower risk appetite, a weakened outlook for growth, and persistently volatile and wide spreads in the euro area periphery has led to an increase in macroeconomic risks. Capital has continued to move out of the periphery, both to the core and to countries outside of the euro area altogether, as official measures to safeguard integration have so far proved insufficient to offset strong private sector forces for fragmentation. A further deterioration in the euro area crisis is the biggest risk to global financial stability, but rising imbalances elsewhere are also a cause for concern. Incremental policy- making has been insufficient to fully allay market tensions. Notwithstanding recent market improvements in response to policy actions, conditions remain fragile after a prolonged deterioration in underlying trends. Imbalances in the United States and Japan are amenable to medium-term adjustment, but clarification now of necessary policy actions to be taken over the medium term would sustain confidence and preempt potential future market pressures. Flows into global bond funds have jumped since the April 2012, with investors favouring safe-haven sovereign bonds and investment-grade corporate bonds amid concerns about tail risk outcomes.

This new phase of monetary policy accommodation in the major currency areas spilled over to financial markets around the world. The prospect of low yields in core bond markets contributed to investors searching for yield in lower-rated European bonds and emerging market paper as well as in corporate debt. This drove spreads even lower while issuance in riskier credit market segments strengthened. Abundant liquidity and low volatility fostered an environment favouring risk-taking and carry trade activity. Risky assets extended their rally as further monetary easing helped market participants tune out signs of a global growth slowdown. The spate of negative economic news between mid-March, 2013 and mid-April, 2013 did little to interrupt the rise of equity prices in advanced economies. The growth jitters left more of a dent on commodity prices while emerging market equities continued to underperform. Further, policy easing, followed promptly by an improved US outlook in early May, boosted market sentiment and lifted the main equity indices to new highs. Central banks stepped up their expansionary monetary policies from an already accommodative stance. In April, 2013 the Bank of Japan (BOJ) outlined its new monetary easing policy framework, and in May, 2013 the ECB lowered its policy rate to 0.5% while the Federal Reserve reassured markets of continued asset purchases and a low federal funds rate going forward. The United Kingdom and Switzerland left their policy stances unchanged. Partly in response to monetary easing in the major currency areas, a number of central banks subsequently lowered their policy rates, including in Australia, Denmark, India, Israel, Korea, Mexico, Poland and Turkey.

Major central banks further eased their monetary stance from already accommodative levels that had pushed nominal yields to record lows, the ECB cut its policy rate, and the Federal Reserve provided forward guidance while reaffirming its commitment to further asset purchases. The Bank of Japan had surprised markets with its ambitious new monetary easing framework. The announcement triggered sharp price movements in the Japanese government bond (JGB) market as investors weighed the yield implications of official purchases against future inflation expectations. Renewed monetary stimulus and ample liquidity in the reserve currency areas also helped boost speculative activity in currency markets. A popular trading strategy was the carry trade, in which positions in higher-yielding currencies are funded via positions in lower-yielding ones. Carry-to-risk, a gauge of risk-adjusted ex ante returns on foreign currency-denominated investments, was elevated in recent months, in particular for several emerging market currencies. While global interest rate differentials (carry) have narrowed compared to the 2003–07 episode, they remain relatively high. This environment of persistent interest rate differentials coupled with low foreign exchange volatility fostered the attractiveness of carry trades since mid-2012, especially for leveraged investors.

In global financial markets, the countries which have strengthened their capital markets will attract more investment capital and, thus, enable a broader entrepreneurial class to develop, facilitate more efficient allocation of capital, encourage international risk sharing, and foster economic growth. However, countries must carefully weigh the risks and benefits of unfettered capital flows. Certain factors are likely to influence the effect of financial globalisation on economic volatility and growth : countries with well-developed financial sectors, strong institutions, sound macroeconomic policies, and substantial trade openness are more likely to gain from financial liberalisation and less likely to risk increased macroeconomic volatility and to experience financial crises. For example, well-developed financial markets help moderate boom-bust cycles that can be triggered by surges and sudden stops in international capital flows, while strong domestic institutions and sound macroeconomic policies help attract "good" capital, such as portfolio equity flows and FDI. However, there are also costs associated with being overly cautious about opening to capital flows. These costs include lower international trade, higher investment costs for firms, poorer economic incentives, and additional administrative /monitoring costs. Opening up to foreign investment may encourage changes in domestic economy that eliminate these distortions and help foster growth. However, capital account liberalisation should be pursued as a part of a broader reform package encompassing a country's macroeconomic policy framework, domestic financial system, and prudential regulation. Moreover, long-term,non-debt-creating flows, such as FDI, should be liberalised before short-term, debt-creating flows. Countries should still weigh the possible risks involved in opening up to capital flows against the efficiency costs associated with controls, but under certain conditions (such as good institutions, sound domestic and foreign policies, and developed financial markets), the benefits from financial globalisation are likely to outweigh the risks.

The new millennium is likely to pose new challenges for the international financial managers as the demand for investment capital by the new entrants into the international market economy and the escalating costs of innovations place enormous pressures on the global demand for finance capital and its main supplying agents. In fact, present inadequacy of national capital markets and financial intermediaries, differences in tax regulations, inability of individuals to obtain foreign financial leverage, varying national attitudes toward risk, different rates of inflation, etc. have forced the financial managers of international firms, their bankers, and financial consultants to rethink on domestic oriented concepts which have traditionally influenced the corporate financial decision-making. The determinants of the way in which multinational firms acquire, organise and manage these assets is of critical importance, not only to the success of these firms, but also to the development and industrial restructuring of nation states.

This is one of the most important reasons why a basic understanding of the management of the business transactions of companies is so important. However, the communication of the new ideas in international business has been hampered by the fact that the important material is scattered among various journals. The most significant contributions were to be brought together and synthesised to make them readily available to the students. Towards this end, an attempt is made to provide a thorough exposition of the developments in international business both at macro and micro level. Analytical techniques help translate the often vague rules of thumb used by global managers into specific decision criteria. In the text, designed in Six Parts: 41 chapters, readers are asked to insert themselves in the role of the global manager. From this vantage point, they can then envision the entire panorama of the financial setting and the problems and consideration therein. In placing emphasis on the importance of ideas and theories in structuring expectation and action, an attempt is made to show that conflicts of values are internal to the operations of the international organisations. The aim of the book is to help and enable readers in developing an understanding of the operations of the multinational firm with the aid of solid theoretical foundation.

The detailed knowledge gained by the reader should make him more conversant with the discipline and should provide a strong conceptual foundation on which to build his future financial activities and decisions. The text is based on the courses we have taught in the past two decades at the Faculty of Management Studies, Delhi University. Keeping in view the requirements of the students of MBA/Commerce/ Business Economics at various Universities/Institutes, Chartered Accountants, Company Secretaries and other professional courses, the text is designed to fill the gap and also transmit some of the excitement of current thinking and controversy. Since the book is synthesis, I am indebted to all writers who have contributed to the area of finance. I hope that I have interpreted their views correctly. I have made acknowledgement of every idea whose source I have been able to identify, but some writers may have been missed unintentionally. I have benefited greatly form feedback from students and colleagues. Finally, I wish to express thanks and appreciate the diligent support provided by the members of the S. Chand & Company Pvt. Ltd. whose high performance standards and in- depth knowledge of publishing have been invaluable in the development of the text.

V.K. BHALLA

CONTENTS

PART III

PART IV

PART V

This Page has been intentionally left blank

PART I

This Page has been intentionally left blank

1

INTERNATIONAL FINANCIAL MANAGEMENT: AN OVERVIEW

INTRODUCTION

The importance of multinational corporations and the globalisation of production are now well recognised. Multinational corporations have become central actors of the world economy and, in linking foreign direct investment, trade, technology and finance, they are a driving force of economic growth. Since the world is reduced to an electronic village and global finance has become a reality, therefore in a contemporary global corporation financial capital is one of the most fungible assets to cross national boundaries. The determinants of the way in which transnational corporation acquire, organise and manage those assets is of critical importance, not only to the success of those corporations, but also to the development and industrial restructuring of nation states. The task of international financial manager is to make the best possible tactical decision that the market has to offer on liabilities, within the strategic funding constraints set by currency denomination, maturity, and capital structure.

THEORETICAL DEVELOPMENTS IN THE INTERNATIONAL FINANCIAL MANAGEMENT

From the perspective of international corporate financial management, the definition of international business and—by implication—the international firm, is quite comprehensive: it includes all business activities on which management must make financial decisions, taking into account simultaneously: (1) the conditions prevailing in *two or more financial markets,* (2) regulatory and institutional *barriers* to the international movement of funds, and (3) the changes in the *exchange rates* of national monies. To illustrate, instead of taking into account one set of national tax rules, one rate of inflation, one set of interest rates, one integrated system of money and capital markets and the assorted institutions, management must now take into account the complex interactions of at least two tax systems, two interest rate structures, and two sets of financial institutions when making decisions. Obviously, this entails additional complications and risks. However—and this represents the other side of the coin—management has available more alternatives and, therefore, better opportunities to attain the firm's objectives: to enhance the value of the business enterprise by minimising the cost of funds and the risk to the firm.

Thus the range of enterprises for which the practice and theory of international financial management is relevant is much more inclusive than the traditional concepts of the multinational corporation (MNC), which is defined typically as a firm having a substantial portion of its activities and assets deployed in different countries. The concept relevant for financial management comprises all firms that are involved in international business, directly or indirectly, to such an extent that the managerial process must take into account the complexities of a *multimarket, multicurrency environment.* The objective of international financial management is the same as that of domestically oriented financial management i.e. the maximisation of the value of the firm. The differences arise because of the term's exposure to international and multinational environments. The common thread of international aspects of financial management is found in the following: What aspects of the issue are peculiarly international, and what opportunities does a firm have by virtue of its being international? The clues to an answer lie in the basic understanding of the management of the cross border financial assets and liabilities and cash flows. From a corporate perspective, the most important theoretical developments in international financial management can be captured by concentrating on the following areas:

The Foreign Exchange Markets

What is foreign exchange? Foreign exchange is simply a *payment or a deposit* in some national currency (or artificial currency) that is exchanged for a payment in another currency. Thus any money can become foreign exchange by surprise and the moment after it has been exchanged it forgets it was foreign exchange. Once more, it is national money.

Unlike the money and capital markets, the foreign exchange market deals not in *credit* but in *means of payment*. This brings one to a fundamental point: While foreign exchange deals frequently take place between residents of different countries, the money being traded never actually leaves the country of the currency. Thus when German deutsche marks are exchanged for U.S. dollars in London, the deutsche marks and dollars stay in Germany and the United States respectively. The act of trading only effects a *change of ownership* of the money. The money itself, in the form of bank deposits, merely gets shifted from one deposit to another through the country's interbank payments system.

In contrast to a *spot transaction, a forward foreign exchange contract* calls for delivery at a fixed future date of a specified amount of one currency for a specified amount of another currency. By *borrowing* money in one currency, buying a second currency *spot*, placing the funds in a *deposit* in the foreign currency, and simultaneously selling the foreign currency forward, an arbitrageur can profit if the domestic interest rate does not equal the foreign interest rate, adjusted for the *forward premium or discount* (the difference between the spot and forward exchange rate, expressed as an annualised percentage). This means that arbitrage will insure *interest rate parity—the* forward premium or discount always equals the interest rate differential between two currencies.

Covered interest arbitrage of this kind represents the fundamental link between Euro currency deposits or loans denominated in different currencies, and also between national capital markets—though, as will be shown, the last are imperfectly linked because of national controls on financial markets and because of exchange controls.

Doing business across national boundaries means dealing with more than one currency and therefore involves exchange risk. *Exchange risk* is the additional systematic risk to a firm's flows arising from exchange rate changes. The three main types of foreign exchange-risk management which are of special interest to MNCs fall under the heading of *economic, transaction* and *translation*—exposure management. The foreign exchange economic exposure is defined as the likelihood that the net present value of a firm's future cash flows will change due to an unexpected change in exchange rates. When exchange rates change unexpectedly, a transnational corporation's sales volume, price and costs are likely to be affected.

Effort by the firm to manage exchange rate changes are really the macroeconomic version of what is happening at the macroeconomic level. International economics literature is rich in discussions of how countries adjust to exchange rate changes. For example, the concept of a "real (inflation-adjusted) exchange rate" is well understood in economics literature and by government policy makers. However, neither economic exposure nor the real effective exchange rate are well understood by top management. Instead, they often assume that any foreign exchange issue is the responsibility of the treasurer or financial vice president. In reality, managing economic exposure is best accomplished by internationally diversifying sales, production and financing by currency. These are strategic decisions that must be approved by top management and the board of directors, as well as by the financial officers.

Foreign exchange transaction exposure is defined as the change in domestic (reporting) currency value of outstanding financial accounts which are denominated in a foreign currency. Typical accounts which are exposed are foreign currency denominated accounts receivable, accounts payable and dividends which have been declared but not yet paid from foreign affiliates. Transaction exposure can be managed by both operating policies, such as leads and lags in payments, and by contractual hedging instruments such as forward contracts, money market hedges, swaps and foreign currency future and option contracts.

Exchange rate determination and the use of contractual hedges have long been the domain of the international economics literature. Therefore the corporate finance literature has focused more on a derivative question: are exchange rate changes predictable and, if so, can a firm (engaged in international transactions) benefit from the prediction? The answer to that question depends on whether or not foreign exchange markets are efficient and how much risk aversion management can tolerate. Reported hedging of all transaction exposure can be more costly than the expected loss or gain from remaining unhedged, especially if foreign exchange markets are efficient. However, if the markets are inefficient, and the size of a transaction exposure is large compared to the size of the firm, most managers would probably hedge all or some of the exposure in order to reduce variability of cash flows and earnings.

International Financial Markets

The capital markets of the world consist of sources of finance, and uses for finance, in a number of different countries. Each of these is a capital market on its own. On the other hand, *national capital markets* are partially linked, and partially segmented.

This fact is what makes international finance so exciting. Because national capital markets are of very different stages of development and size and depth, they have very different prices and availability of capital. Hence, the international financier has great opportunities for *arbitrage*—finding the cheapest source of funds, and the highest return, without adding to risk. And because markets are imperfectly linked, the means and channels by which foreigners enter domestic capital markets, and domestic sources or users of funds go abroad, are the essence of this aspect of international financial management. The other aspect is the fact that domestic claims and liabilities are denominated in national currencies. These must be exchanged for one another for capital to flow internationally; since relative values depend on supply and demand, the international financier faces *exchange risk.* Finally, the past few decades have seen a new phenomenon: the separation of *currency of denomination* of assets and liabilities from *country of jurisdiction.* This removal of currencies from their home countries is the *Euromarket* phenomenon.

Exhibit-1 illustrates *the three sets* of markets—home, foreign and Euromarket—faced by every investor or borrower, plus the fourth market, the foreign currency market, which must be crossed as one enters the world of finance. Each country has more or less imperfect linkages with every other country and with the Euromarket, both the segment in its own currency and Euromarket segments in other currencies. The *linkages of each country with its Euromarket* segment are very important, since domestic and Euromarket instrument are close substitutes and no foreign exchange

EXHIBIT-1

MARKETS OF INTERNATIONAL FINANCE

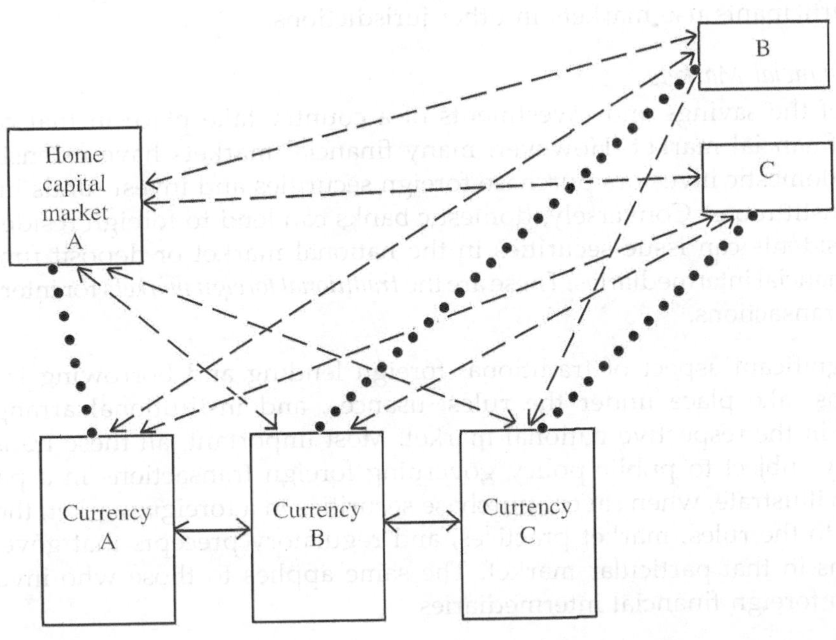

Key: Solid lines, prefect linkages; dotted lines, partial linkages; arrow, foreign exchange linkages.

market comes between them. The *links among segments of the Euromarket* are also very important, since no national controls come between them—in other words, linkages within the Euromarket are perfect, being differentiated only by currency of denomination. They are linked through the *spot* and *forward foreign exchange markets.*

This scheme provides a picture of the contents herein *as* well as that of the environment of international finance. International finance is thus concerned with:

Domestic capital markets and their linkages with Euromarkets and other domestic markets.

Euromarkets and their linkages' with other Euromarkets and domestic markets.

Foreign exchange markets that link domestic markets and Euromarkets in different currencies.

The *techniques* of borrowing, investing, moving; and exchanging funds internationally: international financial management.

Domestic Capital Markets and their Linkages

The *international role* of a capital market and. the *regulatory climate* that prevails are closely related. Appropriate regulation can and does make markets more attractive (e.g., by minimising the risk of losses through fraud, through conflicts of interest, and through a lack of adequate disclosure). However, the dividing line between regulatory measures that improve markets and those that have just the opposite effect is very thin. When governments pursue other objectives, such' as *credit allocation* according to political criteria, or when they discriminate against non-residents, markets can quickly become inefficient. The result is that both foreign and domestic market participants use markets in other jurisdictions.

Foreign Financial Markets

Most of the savings and investments of a country take place in that country's domestic financial market. However, many financial markets have extensive links abroad—domestic investors purchase foreign securities and invest funds in foreign financial institutions. Conversely, domestic banks can lend to foreign residents, and foreign residents can issue securities in the national market or deposit funds with resident financial intermediaries. These are the *traditional foreign markets* for international financial transactions.

The significant aspect of traditional foreign lending and borrowing is that all transactions take place under the rules, usances, and institutional arrangements prevailing in the respective national market. Most important, all these transactions are directly subject to public policy governing foreign transactions in a particular market. To illustrate, when savers purchase securities in a foreign market, they do so according to the rules, market practices, and regulatory precepts that govern such transactions in that particular market. The same applies to those who invest their funds with foreign financial intermediaries.

Likewise, foreign borrowers who wish to issue securities in a national market must follow the rules and regulations of that market. Frequently, these rules are *discriminatory* and *restrictive.* The same is true with respect to financial intermediaries; the borrower who approaches a foreign financial institution for a loan obtains funds at rates and conditions imposed by the financial institutions of the foreign country and is directly affected by the authorities' policy towards lending to foreign residents.

The Euromarkets and their Linkages

Eurocurrencies—which are neither currencies (they are deposits, loans, or securities) nor are they necessarily connected with Europe—represent the separation of currency of denomination from the country of jurisdiction.

Banks and clients make this separation simply by locating the market for credit denominated in a particular currency outside the country where that currency is legal tender (i.e. the locus is in a jurisdiction that offers a more hospitable regulatory climate for such transactions).

To illustrate, markets for dollar-denominated loans, deposits, and securities in jurisdictions other than in the United States effectively avoid U.S. banking and securities regulations. These markets are referred to as "Euro" or, more properly, as "external" markets in order to indicate that they are not part of the domestic or national financial system. Thus the essence of this classification criterion is the nature of regulation. Differences in interest rates, practices and regulations that exist between domestic and external markets arise primarily from the extent to which regulatory constraints are different.

As in the domestic markets, the Euromarket consists of *intermediated funds* and *direct funds.* Intermediated credit in channel through banks is called the "Eurocurrency market". Direct credit—in particular, bonds—can be arranged by banks but it represents the direct liability of the borrower. The Eurobond market is such a market.

Exhibit-2 summarises the three-tiered structure of capital markets. Capital markets consist of:

A *domestic market,* usually with special and unique aspects and institutions stemming from historical and regulatory differences.

A *foreign segment* attached to the national market, where non-residents participate as suppliers and takers of funds, frequently playing both roles simultaneously, but always under the specific conditions, rules and regulations established for foreign participants in a particular national market.

An *external segment* that is characterised by being in a different political jurisdiction, with only the currency used to denominate the financial claims being the essential link to the national market.

As a result, the various external markets have more features in common with each other than with the respective national markets. Therefore, they are properly discussed as a common, integrated market where claims denominated in different currencies are exchanged.

International business is subject to *capital and credit controls.* International managers should know how to respond to governments' attempts to restrict the movement of funds into or out of countries and to manipulate the allocation of funds in domestic capital markets.

EXHIBIT - 2
INTERNATIONAL CREDIT MARKETS
A SCHEMATIC PRESENTATION

	National	International	
Credit Channel	Domestic	Foreign	Euro
Intermediated (banks)			
Direct (securities markets)			
	Internal		External

The multinational enterprise, by virtue of its foreign origin and international character, has special *monopolistically held advantages* that enable it to create and take advantage of imperfections in markets for factors, products and financial capital.

As the last suggests, much of what international financial management is about is taking advantage of the international firm's ability to exploit market imperfections. The crux of this is the ability to distinguish between situations where market imperfections truly exist and those where the profit opportunities have been eliminated by the workings of the market. A prime example is in the foreign exchange forecasting area—in currency markets that are likely to be efficient, no gain is to be had from exchange rate forecasting. The task is therefore to judge where the markets are inefficient and where the firm has a special advantage.

In general, where the market works the firm is better off accepting market prices as signals rather than searching out additional information. A framework against which market imperfections can be judged is corporate funding decisions. From the standpoint of the individual operating unit, for example, a foreign affiliate that is typically in the legal form of a subsidiary and undertakes the asset commitment, two basic alternatives present themselves. First, funds can be obtained from within the corporate group. This includes the use of the affiliate's own funds through a reduction of cash or the liquidation of other assets. Alternatively, funds can be obtained from either the parent or one of the sister affiliates who use their own resources. Second, funds can be obtained from outside sources, either directly, from the financial markets, or via the parent and other affiliates.

Unless the foreign affiliate uses its own means, a basic decision has to be made in which form to inject the funds into this entity that employs them. And while these decisions are all the same in a formal sense, multinational enterprise financing requires careful *distinction between outside relations and intragroup transactions.* This while the labels might look alike, the economic significance of the decision is quite different, except when joint ventures are involved. In this case, complex managerial and financial control issues result that are typical for joint ventures. And while both corporate managements are normally unwilling to tackle such problems, strong nationalistic tendencies in many countries make this form of foreign operation much more prevalent than business conditions would suggest.

Limiting the discussion to wholly owned affiliates, it must be pointed out that unlike the case of transactions, the distinction between inside and outside funds is of limited significance. This is because ultimately all funds are outside funds *in an opportunity cost sense;* the alternative use for retained profits is always to repay loans and/or to increase dividends to stockholders. Thus the only difference between the cost of external and internal funds (capital) can be attributed to agency costs (issuing and underwriting fees), restrictive covenants, and/or tax-related costs. To illustrate, a number of countries apply a lower tax rate to distributed earnings than to funds retained within the corporation. In the absence of specific institutional costs or incentives, the cost of internally generated funds in a multinational firm and its affiliates is equal to the cost of capital for the group as a whole.

Cost of Capital

A number of transnational corporations have been able to lower their cost of capital by raising funds in international capital markets and by cross-listing on foreign stock exchanges. As a result of the efforts of those firms to internationalise their cost of capital, segmented capital markets have gradually become more integrated and international portfolio investment has flourished. In addition, the investors may purchaser the shares of firms which are resident in segmented capital markets. This could further lower the cost of capital of transnational firms.

If capital markets are partially segmented, investors cannot gain the full benefit from international portfolio diversification, and firms cannot fully lower their cost of capital by selling their securities to foreign investors. A national capital market can be segmented because of government interference and/or because of investor perceptions. An example of government interference is restrictions on the free movement of capital, either by limiting what domestic securities foreign investors can buy, or by limiting what foreign securities domestic investors can buy. Other examples are discriminatory tax policies, rationing of foreign exchange, and policies which increase transactions costs in domestic securities markets. Investor perceptions are shaped by the quality of financial disclosures, familiarity with foreign securities markets and institutions, alternative portfolio possibilities, foreign exchange risk and political risk.

If a country's capital market is segmented, investors resident in that country may not be able to hold an efficient internationally diversified portfolio, and firms resident in that country may not enjoy the lowest possible cost of capital. However, with the proper strategies, transnational firms may be able to raise their funds abroad and gain an international pricing of their securities even though their home market remains segmented. On the other hand, firms which are too small to tap international capital markets are forced to continue to accept the higher cost of capital typical of their domestic markets.

The "small firm" bias is even more of a deterrent when it comes to interesting international equity investors in holding the shares of a small firm. Most institutional investors are very concerned about their ability to sell as well as to buy a firm's shares. The market for shares in a small firm is perceived as being illiquid, whether that firm is transnational or domestic.

To what extent can the shares of a transnational corporation serve as a substitute for investors who wish to diversify their portfolios internationally but cannot find or purchase the shares of firms which are resident in segmented capital markets? Considerable evidence exists to suggest that transnational firms should have a lower cost of capital than their domestic counterparts. Because of that, they may receive a higher valuation by investors who are using their shares for international diversification into segmented markets that they cannot tap themselves. Listing on foreign securities exchanges has a favourable liquidity effect because more investors are available to buy the limited number of a firm's shares outstanding. Tapping foreign markets is also a way for firms which are resident in segmented markets to escape the lower valuation of their shares in that market. Normally a firm must be transnational, or at least extremely visible abroad, to succeed in attracting a significant following of foreign investors.

Financial Structure

Modigliani and Miller launched the great debate about whether or not an optimal financial structure for a firm exists. Their original contention was that, under certain very restrictive assumptions about perfect competition, financial structure was irrelevant. They later modified this assertion by recognising that the tax advantages of debt biases the firm towards a much higher use of debt. Later theorists suggested that agency and bankruptcy costs place an upper limit on the desirable portion of debt.

The "traditionalists" always felt that an optimal debt ratio exists in the form of a U-shaped cost of capital curve. As a firm takes on debt, the weighted average cost of capital is reduced due to the tax advantages of debt; but when the debt ratio becomes too high, agency and bankruptcy costs, as well as the reticence of lenders, raises the cost of capital. Therefore, the optimal debt ratio is a flat range at the bottom of the U-shaped cost of capital curve.

Capital structure decisions are particularly important when financial structure decisions dealing with leverage (or gearing) must be made. To the extent that any priorities can be established among the complex, interrelated steps of a funding decision in MNC, such strategic considerations probably take first place. Of course, the reason why the debt/equity ratio matters so much is that it determines the financial risk of the enterprise. because of the contractually fixed nature of payments to debt holders, returns to the owners of equity will fluctuate more in response to given, unanticipated fluctuations of operating returns the higher the proportion of debt relative to equity. Thus a positive partial relationship between the risk of equity returns and leverage ratios can be documented. Because of nontrivial default costs one can also find that a firm's leverage ratios and enterprise risk are negatively related. The interaction between the tax shield provided by debt and the various costs associated with default provide the theoretical support for an optimal capital structure. And to the extent that these factors are influenced by environmental factors such as tax laws and factors affecting the cost and probability of bankruptcy. one finds significant country factors in the capital structure of MNCs based in various countries.

This rationale is often mistakenly applied in the analysis of funding decisions involving individual, wholly owned affiliates. What is usually overlooked is the fact that such wholly owned affiliates of MNC's have a distinct and separate debt/equity ratio only if the parent is prepared to allow the affiliate in question to default on its debt without coming to its rescue. On the other hand, as long as the rest of the MNC group has a *legal* (loan guarantees) or an effective *moral obligation* to prevent the affiliate from defaulting—even if this threatens the survival of the remainder of the group—the individual affiliate has *no independent debt/equity ratio.* Its true leverage ratio is equal to that of the consolidated group.

Since virtually all MNC's feel obliged to their wholly owned (and sometimes even partially owned) affiliates, simply because they cannot afford to lose their financial respectability, the debt/equity ratio of the affiliate is determined by purely institutional factors. Most prominent among such are (i) *Statutory laws,* which prescribe a required minimum equity level in many countries; (2) *tax laws,* which often treat interest payments differently than payments on equity (dividends): (3) *exchange control regulations,* which are usually less restrictive when interest payments are concerned: (4) expropriation risk, *which can be lessened if the parent expects to default on its local debt in the specific case that the lending institutions have also been taken over by the government in question, or the lending institutions are state-owned already.*

Thus the debt/equity decision for foreign affiliates is either a purely legal one—as opposed to a financial decision—or it involves *strategic questions of ownership* to the extent that third-party investors, local or otherwise, own a part of the affiliate's equity.

When it comes to making debt/equity decisions for the parent, or rather the group as a whole, a very difficult issue arises: which market's standards will govern its "acceptable" debt/equity ratio? For domestic firms, the answer is usually quite clear. In different national capital markets, certain target debt/equity ratios have been established by market forces for different kinds of firms. These acceptable debt/equity ratios are influenced by the nature of the firm. To illustrate, public utilities, whose operating risk is relatively low, are permitted to have a much higher proportion of debt before the market begins to penalise these enterprises by increasing the required rate of return on equity or the interest on their debt relative to for example, capital goods producers, whose return on assets is very much subject to the vagaries of the business cycle. The problem for the multinational firm is that different national markets differ quite a bit in terms of standards for acceptable debt/equity ratios, and to the extent that MNCs sell their equity or borrow funds in many countries they must choose a reference market.

Theoretically, this question is largely unsolved because empirical work in finance has not sufficiently progressed to answer the question. "Precisely how are financial assets priced internationally?" That is, which is a more correct approximation of reality, that markets are separated or that they are integrated? In practice, most MNCs do not have to face this problem head on because the great bulk of the equity is usually held by investors of a national market whose standards dominate the applicable debt/equity ratio. However, as more and more companies make an effort to broaden their stockholder base internationally (e.g., by listing their stock on the exchanges of two or more countries) this issue will become more and more acute.

Next to capital structure decisions, the issue of *debt denomination* is probably the most important strategic aspect of the funding decision. In the absence of specific and identifiable market imperfections, currency decisions cannot be made on the basis of financial market factors alone. They must be coordinated with an analysis of the impact of *currency fluctuations* on the firm's operating cash flows (i.e., *corporate exchange risk*).

Intracompany Transfers

The problems encountered in the financial structure decision of a multinational firm and its individual affiliates turn up again when tactical questions of funding international operations are being considered. By their nature MNCs have complicated legal structures, such as that depicted in Exhibit-3.

EXHIBIT-3

LEGAL STRUCTURE OF A MULTINATIONAL CORPORATION

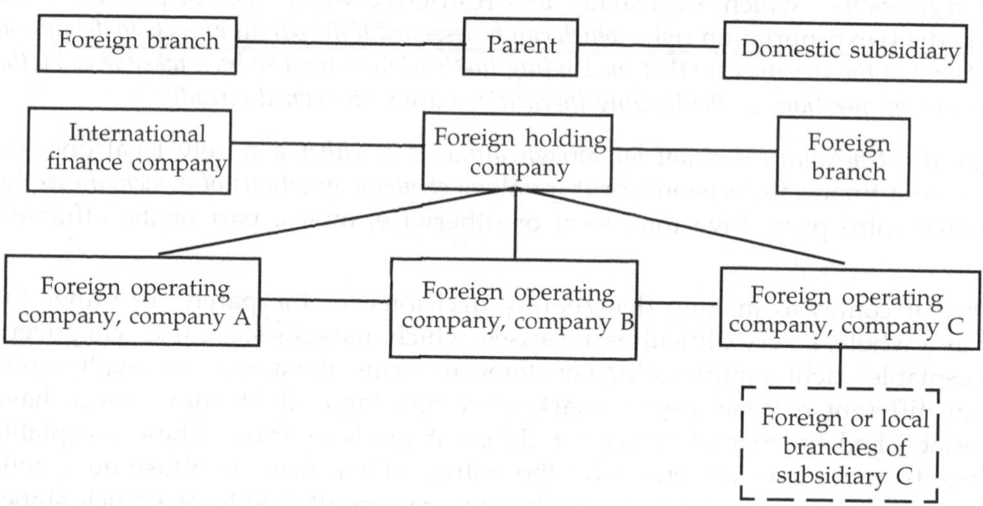

Of course, Exhibit-3 is a schematic presentation only and in reality an almost infinite number of combinations are possible. For financial management, this raises the question as to which one of the entities should contract with providers of funds. In respect to equity, this is almost invariably the parent company, especially if the firm has a policy of maintaining wholly owned affiliates. With respect to debt, however, there are many possibilities. And unless the answer to the question is. "The same affiliate that needs the funds," another decision must be made right away—

how to move the funds through the various corporate entities to their final destination. In turn this decision is directly related to yet another question: In what legal form and in which currency should funds be injected in the affiliate that acquires productive assets?

Having affiliates in many financial markets provides the MNF with opportunities to *minimise the cost of funds* for the corporation by borrowing wherever the effective cost is least. In practice, however, there are serious constraints that limit these opportunities. After all, it is because of the government restrictions, and to a certain extent institutional arrangements, that the cost of funds in various markets will not be equalised through direct arbitrage.

The only real advantage that the MNC has in this respect is that it can somewhat more easily circumvent such restrictions because of its particular structure of centrally coordinated, but legally separate entities. To illustrate, many countries have tight controls on direct lending to borrowers abroad. Theoretically, then, a multinational firm can get around this restriction by having its local affiliate borrow the funds and subsequently transfer them in some form to its parent or sister affiliates. Governments, of course, are aware of such operations, too, and they have usually issued all kinds of rules and regulations to prevent such internatioal *intracorporate transfers of funds.* However, if these regulations were written and administered too tightly, they would strangle international trade and investment. Thus firms usually have some leeway in transferring funds, although their flexibility is much more limited than is usually implied by critics of multinational firms.

In an integrated MNC, where each affiliate has dealings with the others, transfer of funds can usually be effected because most are simply necessary to run the operation, regardless of the existence of restrictions. Thus the question is not one of whether or not to shift funds among the MNC's affiliates, but how much and in which direction. This also highlights the fact that it is often impossible to determine the "correct" arm's length transaction, not only for government but even the corporate controller. To illustrate, economists and accountants still argue about correct cost allocation, transfer prices, and interest charges in multidivision operations that are closely integrated. Interestingly, many financial executives in multinational firms point to the fact that their ability to move funds within the corporate family is severely restricted not only by government, but by the disadvantage of distorting their internal control system.

That MNC's do have some freedom to move funds internationally is simply based on the fact that funds flows can be effected in very many ways, as depicted in Exhibit-4.

Analytically, it is very important to generalise on a point that is made above in respect to the debt/equity ratios: Intracompany transfers of funds do not give rise to any change in the cost of funds or the risk of the multinational firms as such. These transfers have an impact only in terms of taxes, exchange controls, and other regulatory aspects. The cost of funds and financial risk is affected only when there is a change in the kind or amount of *outside sources of funds.* Thus the determinants of such inside transactions are to be found in tax and regulatory matters only.

EXHIBIT-4

FINANCIAL AND REAL FLOWS IN THE MULTINATIONAL FIRM

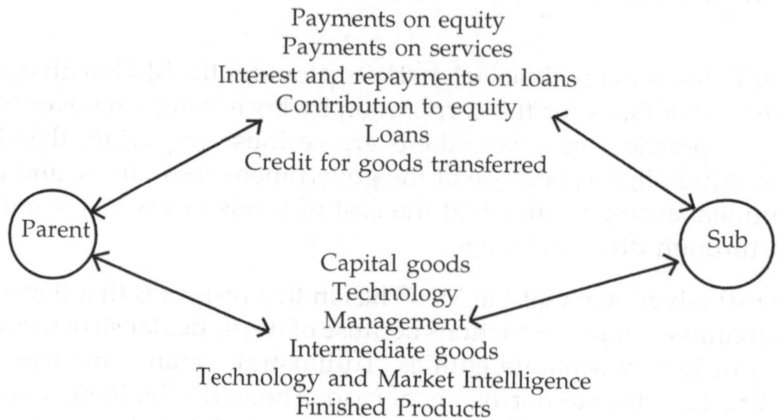

While all this sounds very complex—and in reality it is complex because of all the environmental factors that impinge upon the decision (tax effects, exchange regulations, financial market regulations and practices, banking relations, etc.)—the basic conceptual framework is quite simple and can be summarised as follows. If an MNC requires additional funds, it can raise these funds directly or through any one of its affiliates. The conditions on which the funds are obtained from outside sources (i.e., debt vs. equity, short-term vs. long-term funding, currency of denomination, and restrictive covenants) will have an impact on the basic cost of funds and the financial risk faced by the group as a whole. And it is these relationships that determine the weighted average cost of funds that must be minimised.

Capital Budgeting

The return of most industrial countries to currency convertibility in the 1950's, and the formation of the European Community and EFTA, led to large new capital movements in the form of foreign direct investment. The strategic, economic and behavioural motives for foreign direct investment enjoy an immense rich literature. However, the analytical methods used to evaluate specific new foreign direct projects, or reinvestment in existing projects, is the subject of capital budgeting, which is an important topic in the corporate financial management literature.

Capital budgeting for a foreign project uses the same discounted cash-flow techniques as are used to evaluate domestic projects. In a true transnational corporation, all projects, foreign and domestic, compete on an equal footing for a piece of the capital budget. However, the analysis of a foreign project is considerably more complex than for a domestic project for the following reasons:

i) Parent cash flows must be distinguished form project cash flows. Each of these two types of flow contributes to a different view of value.

ii) Parent cash flows often depend on the form of financing. Thus cash flows cannot be clearly separated from financing decisions, as is done in domestic capital budgeting.

iii) Remittance of funds to the parent must be explicitly recognised because of differing tax systems, legal and political constraints on the movement of funds, local business norms, and differences in how financial markets and institutions function.

iv) Cash flows from affiliates to parent can be generated by an array of non-financial payments, including payment of license fees and payments for imports from the parent.

v) Differing rates of national inflation must be anticipated because of their importance in causing changes in competitive position, and thus in cash flows over a period of time.

vi) The possibility of unanticipated foreign exchange rate changes must be remembered because of possible direct effects on the value to the parent of local cash flows, as well as an indirect effect on the competitive position of the foreign affiliate.

vii) Use of segmented national capital markets may create an opportunity for financial gains or may lead to additional financial costs.

viii) Use of host government subsidised loans complicates both capital structure and the ability to determine an appropriate weighted average cost of capital for discounting purposes.

ix) Political risk must be evaluated because political events can drastically reduce the value or availability of expected cash flows.

x) Terminal value is more difficult to estimate because potential purchasers from the host, parent, or third countries, or from the private or public sector, may have widely divergent perspectives on the value to them of acquiring the project.

Since the same theoretical capital budgeting framework is used to choose among competing foreign and domestic projects, a common standard is critical. Thus all foreign complexities must be quantified as modifications to either expected cash flow or the rate of discount. Although in practice many firms make such modifications arbitrarily, readily available information, theoretical deduction, or just plain common sense can be used to make less arbitrary and more reasonable choices.

Though some inputs were made to introduce the complexities of capital budgeting for a foreign project into the corporate finance literature of the late 1960s, but it was many years before mainline financial theories considered the problem worthy of further study. It was suggested that a foreign project be evaluated from the viewpoint both of the parent firm and of the foreign project itself. In order to be acceptable, a project should pass muster on both counts. Further, the financial cash flows must be considered rather than just operating cash flows since project cash flows were not necessarily immediately available to the parent. Moreover, when they would be repatriated in the future, contingent tax and foreign exchange cost could be expected. In addition, an allowance for political and foreign exchange risks should be made by charging cash flows the cost of a programme of uncertainty absorption, whether or not is actually carried out. Uncertainty could be absorbed by purchasing more *information*, borrowing most of the investment locally, buying, hedging and investment insurance if available and negotiating the environment with the host-country government. Arbitrarily raising the discount rate for a foreign project was rejected because that does not take account of the actual amounts at risk, or for variations in the degree of risk of the project over time. It should be noted, however, that capital budgeting was at an early stage of acceptance even for domestic projects. During the 1970s, capital budgeting for foreign projects attracted a respectable number of scholars' attention to expand the analysis to include more variables, in particular, the tax treatment of foreign income, the risk of expropriation, blocked hinds, inflation and segmented capital markets. They advocated that all foreign risks should be incorporated as adjustments to cash flow rather than adjusting the discount rate.

In 1985, Lessard contributed an adjusted present-value approach to foreign project evaluation. The main difference between this approach and the traditional one lies in its separation of contractual and non-contractual cash flows. For example, the tax advantages of debt are treated separately and explicitly as is the effect of expropriation, exchange risk and other foreign complexities. The present value of each of these components can be determined separately, perhaps even with different discount rates to reflect varying risks, and then all the resulting present values are added together. The main advantage of this approach is its simplicity because it breaks up a complex simulation into more manageable prices. Its main disadvantage is that a whole generation of managers has finally learned capital budgeting in the traditional manner, and it is difficult for them to simultaneously learn both the foreign complexities and a new approach to analysis.

INTERNATIONAL FINANCIAL MANAGEMENT AND IMPERFECTIONS IN FINANCIAL MARKETS

The equilibrium relationships and market linkages provide a point of departure for decision making. One can think of the expected relationships—in particular, the *unbiased forward rate* theory—as providing *market-based forecasts* of the exchange rate and other conditions.

Such forecasts can be used as a *benchmark* against which to judge the firm's own ability to forecast or to exploit market imperfections. Given the market-based forecasts, one can distinguish three situations, each with distinct implications for the currency aspects of financial planning:

1. *When the financial markets in question are reasonably efficient, and financial planners know of no systematic biases or constraints on market rates, then market-based forecasts should be accepted as valid.* Under these conditions, which probably hold for most financial decisions involving the U.S. and major international financial markets, no expected gain will result from manipulating the timing or currency of borrowing or investing, and financial management's energies should be directed toward matching borrowings and investments with the timing and currency of the funds needed or generated by the firm's operations. The use of market-based forecasts then implies planning for the deviations, or forecasting errors, that will probably occur.

Specifically, what one wants to know is how cash flows from operations (return on assets) will change for any given deviation of the interest or exchange rate from the value predicted. As long as the return on assets is contractually fixed and denominated in a particular currency, as would be a portfolio of bonds or loans, the analysis is quite straightforward. A rise in interest rates will cause a proportional fall in the value of such a fixed-interest portfolio; a given fall in the exchange rate will lead to an equal drop in the dollar value of the portfolio. Protecting the value of such assets, therefore, requires funding the liabilities of the firm in the same currency and maturity as the assets.

This *efficient market financial planning framework* assumes the market's forecasts unbiased predictions of future exchange rates. Often, specific market imperfections will not allow this assumption to hold. The next two situations consider the Implications of such biases.

2. *When the term structure of interest or exchange rates deviates in a systematic way from the market's actual expectations because of government controls, or because of other specific market imperfections, financial management has profit opportunities.* The exploitation of these opportunities requires first, a flexible legal and operational structure, and second, *an* explicit trade-off function that permits management to decide whether the gains are worth the increase in risk and the exploitation of market imperfections might involve.

Government controls tend to be always partial, never comprehensive. The reason is simple; controls on all borrowing or lending, and all international transfers of funds, would cause economic activity to come to a grinding halt. Therefore, with regulations permitting certain transactions, and funds being fungible, international firms with diverse legal structures and a multitude of intercompany links usually are in a privileged position to *exploit the financial windfalls that government distortions provide* by keeping interest rates low and preventing exchange rates from adjusting to market pressures.

3. *When the market-based forecasts deviate from forecasted rates, not because of* market *imperfections but because the firm has some proprietary information or unusual forecasting ability, then financial managers should act on their forecasts only when the risks of doing so are offset by the expected gains.* When financial planners can confidently answer the questions, "Why do we believe we can predict interest or exchange rates better than the market"? Their focus should be on the proper perspective on the risks involved in speculative actions, and on a rapid response to opportunities when action is warranted.

Few financial managers can consistently resist the temptation to base financing decisions on their own judgements rather than those of the market. In most cases little harm is done, for unless the firm really goes out on a limb, position and negative forecasting errors tend to cancel out over time. But the mark of a good financial manager is not a knack for occasionally outguessing the market's forecasts, but rather an ability to obtain the highest return on invested assets, for a given level of risk, and the best long-run terms and conditions on debt, irrespective of the tend of interest rates or exchange rates. It is important for the integrity of the financial management process to keep these aspects of the function strictly separate. Otherwise, the inability of financial management out perform the markets tends to be hidden in the results of the risk management function.

The imperfections and linkages of domestic financial markets, Euromarkets, and foreign exchange markets provide both risks and opportunities for the international financial management. Management attention should be concentrated on those markets and channels in which the firm has a competitive advantage, and should rely on banks, partners, and markets themselves to do what they can do more cheaply and efficiently. In the area of foreign exchange risk management, the market's forecasts of future exchange rates are readily available in the form of the forward exchange rates. On the other hand, where financial managers feel they have a peculiar advantage in financial markets, resulting from the firm's legal structure, geographical locations, or because of an unusual forecasting ability, then the timing, maturity, and currency of borrowing and investment decisions should be based on the firm's own forecasts whenever the expected gains justify the risks.

ROLE OF THE INTERNATIONAL FINANCIAL MANAGER

The chief tasks of the international financial manager are summarised as under:

Forecasting the financial environment—prices, inflation rates, interest rates and exchange rates.

Management of assets—from cash management to international capital budgeting, at home and abroad, in domestic and foreign currencies.

Management of liabilities—borrowing relationships and decisions, in domestic and foreign currencies and markets, short-term and long-term.

Exchange risk management—measuring the effect of exchange rate changes on balance sheets, income, and cash flows, and managing these risks.

Performance evaluation and control—accounting for outsiders, the tax authorities, and for management, and doing so across countries and currencies without distortion.

Sounds like a Herculean agenda? Yes, but domestic financial management is difficult too, and many of the techniques are transferable. The place to start learning about international financial management is therefore to gain a basic understanding of what and how financial decisions affect the value of the firm.

ECONOMIC FRAMEWORK OF INTERNATIONAL FINANCIAL MANAGEMENT

Much of received international financial management doctrine consists of techniques for borrowing, investing, or hedging decisions in one currency or another. However, many of these techniques work only under certain macroeconomic conditions, and the rules of thumb do not apply under other, quite plausible, conditions. In order to see how a number of the techniques of international finance are applicable only under conditions of disequilibrium. Exhibit-5 illustrates a framework showing the linkages among prices, exchange rates, interest rates, and other variables.

EXHIBIT-5

DISEQUILIBRIUM CONDITIONS

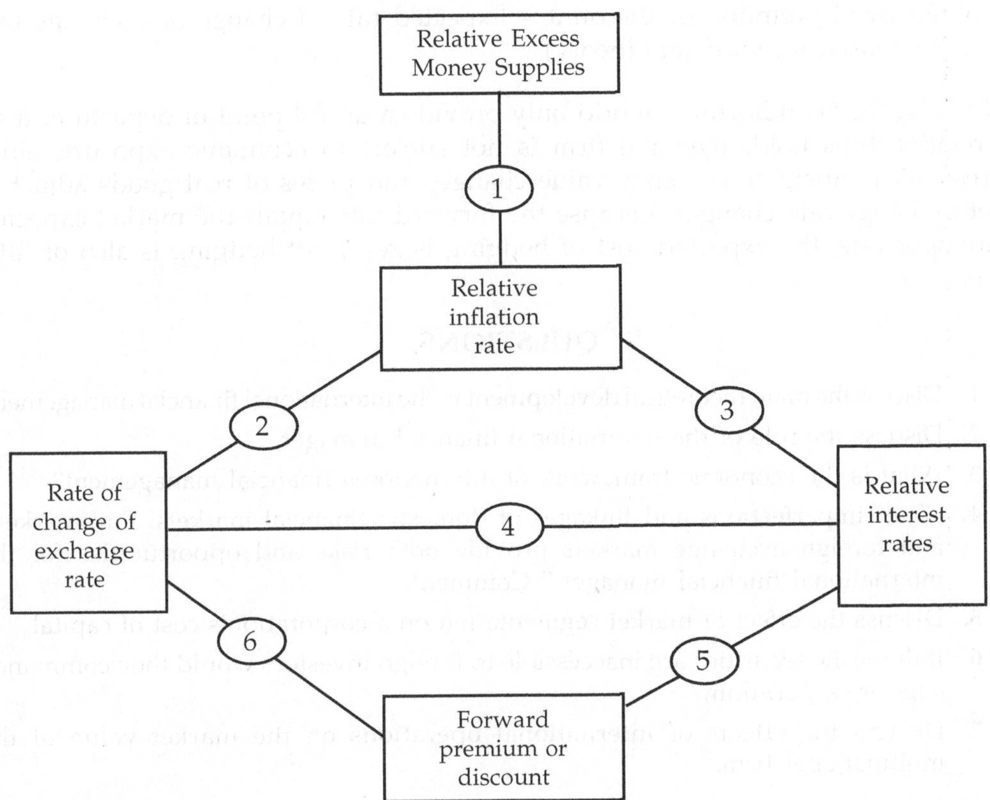

Exhibit-5 is interpreted as follows International differences in the extent to which the growth of the money supply exceeds the growth of real income result in international differences in inflation rates. Through the purchasing power parity relationship the inflation rate differential causes a corresponding rate of change of the exchange rate. If the foreign exchange market is efficient, the forward exchange rate equals the market's expected future exchange rate. Hence, the expected rate of change of the exchange rate equals the forward premium or discount, which in turn equals the interest rate differential while the interest rate differential equals the expected inflation rate differential.

These six relations are stated more explicit:

1. Inflation rate = rate of growth of money supply—rate of growth of real gross national product (too much money chasing too few goods).
2. Rate of change of exchange rate = Inflation rate differential (Purchasing power parity theory).
3. Interest rate = "Real " interest rate + Expected inflation rate (Fisher effect: one country).
4. Expected rate of change of exchange rate = Interest rate differential (International Fisher effect).

5. Forward exchange premium or discount = Interest rate differential (Interest rate parity theorem).

6. Forward premium or discount = Expected rate of change of exchange rate (unbiased forward rate theory).

Clearly, the "equilibrium" world only provide a useful point of departure. If all the relationships hold, then the firm is not subject to economic exposure, since interest rates anticipate currency value changes and prices of real goods adjust to offset exchange rate changes. Because the forward rate equals the market-expected future spot rate, the expected cost of hedging is zero; but hedging is also of little value.

QUESTIONS

1. Discuss the main theoretical development in the international financial management.
2. Disucss the role of the international financial manager.
3. What is the economic framework of international financial management?
4. "The imperfections and linkages of domestic financial markets, Euromarkets, and foreign exchange markets provide both risks and opportunities for the international financial manager." Comment.
5. Discuss the effect of market segmentation on a corporation's cost of capital.
6. If domestic securities are inaccessible to foreign investors would they commands super-risk permium?
7. Disucss the effects of international operations on the market value of the multinational firm.

2

THE INTERNATIONAL MONETARY SYSTEM

INTRODUCTION

The completion of a business contract implies that each party has obtained a value at least equal to the value it has surrendered, otherwise the deal would not have been completed. Before the introduction of the common currency of money a deal was completed by swapping goods or Services of at least equivalent value. The introduction of money introduced a small complication into the bargaining process since one party to the deal received money instead of goods. The money would be held for a period of time before being exchanged for goods of equivalent value. The small complication arose because the party who received money had to be convinced that the money was a genuine store of value which would hold its value through time so that it could be exchanged for goods of equivalent value at a later date.

The earliest form of money solved the store-of-value problem by using relatively scarce metals such as gold, silver or copper. However, an international payments system based on precious metals was by no means a perfect system. For example, the purity of the gold could be diluted with other metals making it difficult for a trader to assay the precise amount of gold in the coin. Precious metals are heavy and so difficult to transport. The volume of precious metals is limited and a sudden scarcity might provide insufficient funds to finance the desired rate of trade, and so on. The 19th century economic literature on international finance is almost exclusively devoted to a discussion of these deficiencies, but such a system has one outstanding advantage, namely that the value of a unit of international money, i.e. gold, is underpinned by the market valise of the metal. It is not determined by international confidence in the government stamping out the gold coins.

BRETTON WOODS

Towards the end of World War II the governments of the leading trading nations of the free world decided that the chaotic financial conditions of the inter-war period could not be tolerated after the war had ended. An International Monetary and Financial Conference of the United and Associated Nations was convened at Bretton Woods, New Hampshire on I July 1944.

The main goal of the architects of the Bretton Woods system was to establish an international economic order that would prevent another political and economic collapse. In the Issue-area of international monetary relations two interests remained uppermost: *First*, the provision of adequate liquidity so that countries experiencing short-term balance of payments problems would not resort to nationalistic measures (it was feared that countries temporarily in payments crisis might curtail imports or impose restrictions on trade); *Secondly,* the creation of an adequate mechanism for international adjustment. Underlying the monetary arrangements lay a commitment to free trade and an open international economy. This new order under the leadership of the United States aimed to prevent a return to economic nationalism by fostering free trade and high level of international interaction.

INTERNATIONAL MONETARY FUND (IMY)

The prime goal of the IMF agreed at Bretton Woods was to assist its members in resolving short-term balance of payments problems under a regime of fixed exchange rates, thus permitting the orderly expansion of international trade. The Fund was created as an international institution to supervise and promote an open and stable international monetary system. Exchange rate supervision and balance of payments surveillance presaged a movement away from sole national control of economic policy and the acceptance of a degree of international interference in domestic economies. The purposes of the International Monetary Fund are stated in Article I of the IMF's constitutive document. These are:

(i) To promote international monetary cooperation through a permanent institution which provides the machinery for consultation and collaboration on international monetary problems.

(ii) To facilitate the expansion and balanced growth of international trade, and to contribute thereby to the promotion and maintenance of high levels of employment and real income and to the development of the productive resources of all members as primary objectives of economic policy.

(iii) To promote exchange stability, to maintain orderly exchange arrangements among members, and to avoid competitive exchange depreciation.

(iv) To assist in the establishment of a multilateral system of payments in respect of current transactions between members and in the elimination of foreign exchange restrictions which hamper the growth of trade.

(v) To give confidence to members by making the general resources of the Fund temporarily available to them under adequate safeguards, thus providing them with opportunity to correct maladjustments in their balance of payments without resorting to measures destructive of national or international prosperity.

(vi) In accordance with the above, to shorten the duration and lessen the degree of disequilibrium in the international balance of payments of members.

ORGANISATIONAL STRUCTURE

The IMF, organisational structure is set out in its Articles of Agreement, which entered into force in December, 1945, The Articles provide for a Board of Governors, an Executive Board, a Managing Director, and a staff of international civil servants.

The *Board of Governors,* the highest decision-making body of the IMF, consists of one governor and one alternate for each member country. The governor, appointed by the member country, is usually the minister of finance or the central bank governor. The Board of Governors has delegated to the Executive Board all except certain reserved powers. It normally meets once a year.

The *Executive Board* (the Board) is responsible for conducting the business of the IMF. It is composed of 24 directors, who are appointed or elected by member countries or groups of countries. The Managing Director serves as its chairman. Meeting several times a week, the Board deals with a wide variety of policy, operational, and administrative matters, including surveillance of members' exchange rate policies, provision of IMF financial assistance to member countries, and discussion of systemic issues in the global economy.

Selected by the Executive Board, the IMF's *Managing Director* serves as the head of the organisation's staff. Under the Board's direction, the Managing Director is responsible for conducting the ordinary business of the IMF. The Managing Director serves a five-year term and may be reelected to successive terms.

The *International Monetary and Financial Committee of the Board of Governors* (formerly the Interim Committee of the Board of Governors on the International Monetary System) is an advisory body composed of 24 IMF governors, ministers, or other officials of comparable rank and represents the same constituencies as the IMF's Executive Board. It normally meets twice a year, in April or May and at the time of the Annual Meeting of the Board of Governors in September or October. Among its responsibilities are to guide the Executive Board and to advise and report to the Board of Governors on issues related to the management and adaptation of the international monetary and financial system— including sudden disturbances that might threaten the international monetary system—and on proposals to amend the IMF's Articles of Agreement.

The *Development Committee* (the Joint Ministerial Committee of the Boards of Governors of the World Bank and the IMF on the Transfer of Real Resources to Developing Countries) also has 24 members— finance ministers or other officials of comparable rank—and generally meets at the same time as the International Monetary and Financial Committee. It advises and reports to the Boards of Governors of the World Bank and the IMF on development issues.

FUNCTIONS OF THE IMF

The Fund is designed to perform three important roles in the international monetary system. *First*, to regulate the financial relations of its members. This regulatory function includes an element of rule supervision and law enforcement with respect to exchange rates and balance of payments restrictions. *Secondly*, to provide financial assistance to members experiencing balance of payments difficulties. The Fund has acted as a lender of the last resort to countries with chronic payments problems. The regulatory and financial roles are closely entwined with access to the Fund's resources being made dependent on following the code of conduct devised by the Fund. *Thirdly*, to act as a consultative organ. The IMF's role is to create a climate in which governments are persuaded to dismantle exchange controls and to permit free trade and the free movement of capital.

Although 28 of the 44 nations represented at the Bretton Woods Conference can be classified as underdeveloped, these countries exerted minimal influence on the negotiations and the final outcome. The negotiations at Bretton Woods reflected the prevailing distribution of political and economic power in the international system. The deliberations were based around the plans developed by John Maynard Keynes (UK) and Harry Dexter White (US). American hegemony ensured that the final agreement bore a greater resemblance to the White Plan than the Keynes Plan. The developing countries were in a subordinate position and closely linked through imperial ties to the leading European states. Nevertheless, some developing countries, notably India, attempted to influence the final outcome of the conference. India called on the IMF to *assist in the fuller utilisation of the resources of the underdeveloped countries* and was supported in this request by Ecuador. An amended version of this request which called for *the development of the resources and productive power of all member countries with due regard to the needs of the economically backward countries* also failed. The developed countries insisted that development was within the terms of reference of the World Bank and not the IMF. Thus from the outset the concern of the Fund was with short-term balance of payments financing and not development.

This has led to charges that the IMF is anti-development and sacrifices development for stability. The Fund's retort is that a stable economic environment is a necessary prerequisite for the achievement of economic development. It has been argued, however, that since the Articles of Agreement of the IMF acknowledged the 'development of the productive resources of all members' as a salient objective, this is an indication that some importance was given to the special problem of development. However, this rather cursory reference to development, when taken in the context of the Fund's overall approach at its inception, which was to treat countries in an undifferentiated manner, did not suggest that the Fund would be sensitive to the special needs of the developing countries.

This review of the origins of the IMF shows that the main purposes of the Fund at its inception were to foster international cooperation and promote stability. Economic development was not a prime goal of the international regime established at Bretton Woods. The efforts of the Third World states to increase their participation in the international monetary system led them to demand changes in the IMF. The concerted campaign by the developing countries for a recognition of their particular interests has, to date, achieved limited success.

RECENT STRUCTURAL CHANGES IN THE IMF

IMF QUOTAS

Quota subscriptions are a central component of the IMF's financial resources. Each member country of the IMF is assigned a quota, based broadly on its relative position in the world economy. A member country's quota determines its maximum financial commitment to the IMF, its voting power, and has a bearing on its access to IMF financing.

Doubling of Quotas and Major Realignment of Quota Shares

On December 15, 2010, the Board of Governors, the Fund's highest decision-making body, approved a package of far-reaching reforms of the Fund's quotas and governance, completing the 14th General Review of Quotas. Once the reform package is approved by member countries (it includes an amendment to the Articles of Agreement that requires acceptance by three-fifths of the members having 85 percent of the total voting power) and implemented, it will result in an unprecedented 100 percent increase in total quotas and a major realignment of quota shares to better reflect the changing relative weights of the IMF's member countries in the global economy.

The reform package builds on the 2008 reforms, which became effective on March 3, 2011. The 2008 reforms strengthen the representation of dynamic economies, many of which are emerging market countries, through ad hoc quota increases for 54 member countries, and enhance the voice and participation of low-income countries through a near tripling of basic votes.

The 14th General Review of Quotas will: (i) double quotas from approximately SDR 238.4 billion to approximately SDR 476.8 billion, (about US$767 billion at current exchange rates); (ii) shift more than 6 percent of quota shares from over-represented to under-represented member countries; (iii) shift more than 6 percent of quota shares to dynamic emerging market and developing countries (EMDCs); (iv) significantly realign quota shares. China will become the 3rd largest member country in the IMF, and there will be four EMDCs (Brazil, China, India, and Russia) among the 10 largest shareholders in the Fund; and (v) preserve the quota and voting share of the poorest member countries. This group of countries is defined as those eligible for the low-income Poverty Reduction and Growth Trust (PRGT) and whose per capita income fell below US$1,135 in 2008 (the threshold set by the International Development Association) or twice that amount for small countries.

A comprehensive review of the current quota formula, which formed the basis to work from during the 14th General Review, will be completed by January 2013. Completion of the 15th General Review of Quotas will be brought forward by about two years to January 2014.

How Member Countries' Quotas are Determined

When a country joins the IMF, it is assigned an initial quota in the same range as the quotas of existing members that are broadly comparable in economic size and characteristics. The IMF uses a quota formula to guide the assessment of a member's relative position.

The current quota formula is a weighted average of GDP (weight of 50 percent), openness (30 percent), economic variability (15 percent), and international reserves (5 percent). For this purpose, GDP is measured as a blend of GDP based on market exchange rates (weight of 60 percent) and on PPP exchange rates (40 percent). The formula also includes a "compression factor" that reduces the dispersion in calculated quota shares across members.

Quotas are denominated in Special Drawing Rights (SDRs), the IMF's unit of account. The largest member of the IMF is the United States, with a current quota of SDR 42.1 billion (about $68 billion), and the smallest member is Tuvalu, with a current quota of SDR 1.8 million (about $2.9 million).

Quotas Play Several Key Roles in the IMF

A member's quota delineates basic aspects of its financial and organizational relationship with the IMF, including:

(i) *Subscriptions (quota share)*: A member's quota subscription determines the maximum amount of financial resources the member is obliged to provide to the IMF. A member must pay its subscription in full upon joining the Fund: up to 25 percent must be paid in SDRs or widely accepted currencies (such as the U.S. dollar, the euro, the yen, or the pound sterling), while the rest is paid in the member's own currency;

(ii) *Voting power (voting share):* The quota largely determines a member's voting power in IMF decisions. Each IMF member's votes are comprised of basic votes plus one additional vote for each SDR 100,000 of quota. The 2008 reform fixed the number of basic votes at 5.502 percent of total votes. The current number of basic votes represents close to a tripling of the number prior to the effectiveness of the 2008 reform;

(iii) *Access to financing:* The amount of financing a member can obtain from the IMF (its access limit) is based on its quota. For example, under Stand-By and Extended Arrangements, a member can borrow up to 200 percent of its quota annually and 600 percent cumulatively. However, access may be higher in exceptional circumstances.

How Quota Reviews Work

The IMF's Board of Governors conducts general quota reviews at regular intervals (usually every five years). Any changes in quotas must be approved by an 85 percent majority of the total voting power, and a member's quota cannot be changed without its consent. There are two main issues addressed in a general quota review: the size of an overall increase and the distribution of the increase among the members. First, a general quota review allows the IMF to assess the adequacy of quotas both in terms of members' balance of payments financing needs and in terms of its own ability to help meet those needs. Second, a general review allows for increases in members' quotas to reflect changes in their relative positions in the world economy. Ad hoc increases outside general reviews do not occur often, but the increases in quotas for 54 member countries approved under the 2008 Reform are a recent example.

GOLD IN THE IMF

Gold played a central role in the international monetary system until the collapse of the Bretton Woods system of fixed exchange rates in 1973. Since then, the role of gold has been gradually reduced. However, it is still an important asset in the reserve holdings of a number of countries, and the IMF remains one of the largest official holders of gold in the world. Consistent with the new income model for the Fund agreed in April 2008, on September 18, 2009, the IMF Executive Board approved gold sales strictly limited to 403.3 metric tons, representing one eighth of the Fund's total holdings of gold at that time. Resources linked to these gold sales will also help boost the Fund's concessional lending capacity. The approved sales programme was completed in late December 2010.

The IMF held 90.5 million ounces (2,814.1 metric tons) of gold at designated depositories at end February 2012. The IMF's total gold holdings are valued on its balance sheet at SDR 3.2 billion (about $4.9 billion) on the basis of historical cost. As of February 29, 2012, the IMF's holdings amounted to $160.1 billion at current market prices.

The IMF acquired its current gold holdings prior to the Second Amendment through four main types of transactions.

(i) First, when the IMF was founded in 1944 it was decided that 25 percent of initial quota subscriptions and subsequent quota increases were to be paid in gold. This represents the largest source of the IMF's gold.

(ii) Second, all payments of charges (interest on member countries' use of IMF credit) were normally made in gold.

(iii) Third, a member wishing to acquire the currency of another member could do so by selling gold to the IMF. The major use of this provision was sales of gold to the IMF by South Africa in 1970–71.

(iv) And finally, member countries could use gold to repay the IMF for credit previously extended.

The IMF's legal framework for gold

Role of gold

The Second Amendment to the Articles of Agreement in April 1978 fundamentally changed the role of gold in the international monetary system by eliminating the use of gold as the common denominator of the post-World War II exchange rate system and as the basis of the value of the Special Drawing Right (SDR). It also abolished the official price of gold and ended the obligatory use of gold in transactions between the IMF and its member countries. It furthermore required that the IMF, when dealing in gold, avoid managing its price or establishing a fixed price.

Transactions

Following the Second Amendment, the Articles of Agreement limit the use of gold in the IMF's operations and transactions. The IMF may sell gold outright on the basis of prevailing market prices, and may accept gold in the discharge of a member country's obligations (loan repayment) at an agreed price, based on market prices at the time of acceptance. Such transactions require Executive Board approval by an 85 percent majority of the total voting power. The IMF does not have the authority under its Articles to engage in any other gold transactions—such as loans, leases, swaps, or use of gold as collateral—nor does it have the authority to buy gold.

Restitution

The Articles also provide for the restitution of the gold the Fund held on the date of the Second Amendment (April 1978) to those countries that were members of the Fund as of August 31, 1975. Restitution would involve the sale of gold to this group of member countries at the former official price of SDR 35 per ounce, with such sales made to those members who agree to buy it in proportion to their quotas on the date of the Second Amendment. A decision to restitute gold requires support from an

85 percent majority of the total voting power. The Articles do not provide for the restitution of gold acquired by the IMF after the date of the Second Amendment.

How and when the IMF has used gold in the past

Outflows of gold from the IMF's holdings occurred under the original Articles of Agreement through sales of gold for currency, and via payments of remuneration and interest. As it is pointed out in the Second Amendment of the Articles of Agreement, outflows of gold can only occur through outright sales. Key gold transactions included:

(i) *Sales for replenishment (1957–70):* The IMF sold gold on several occasions to replenish its holdings of currencies.

(ii) *South African gold (1970–71):* The IMF sold gold to member countries in amounts roughly corresponding to those purchased from South Africa during this period.

(iii) *Investment in U.S. government securities (1956–72):* In order to generate income to offset operational deficits, some IMF gold was sold to the United States and the proceeds invested in U.S. government securities. Subsequently, a significant buildup of IMF reserves prompted the IMF to reacquire this gold from the U.S. government.

(iv) *Auctions and "restitution" sales (1976–80):* The IMF sold approximately one-third (50 million ounces) of its then-existing gold holdings following an agreement by its member countries to reduce the role of gold in the international monetary system. Half of this amount was sold in restitution to member countries at the then-official price of SDR 35 per ounce; the other half was auctioned to the market to finance the Trust Fund, which supported concessional lending by the IMF to low-income countries.

(v) *Off-market transactions in gold (1999–2000):* In December 1999, the Executive Board authorized off-market transactions in gold of up to 14 million ounces to help finance the IMF's participation in the Heavily Indebted Poor Countries (HIPC) Initiative. Between December 1999 and April 2000, separate but closely linked transactions involving a total of 12.9 million ounces of gold were carried out between the IMF and two members (Brazil and Mexico) that had financial obligations falling due to the IMF. In the first step, the IMF sold gold to the member at the prevailing market price and the profits were placed in a special account invested for the benefit of the HIPC Initiative. In the second step, the IMF immediately accepted back, at the same market price, the same amount of gold from the member in settlement of that member's financial obligations. In the end, these transactions left the balance of the IMF's holdings of physical gold unchanged.

The IMF's Strictly Limited Gold Sales

On September 18, 2009, the Executive Board approved the sale of 403.3 metric tons of gold (12.97 million ounces), which amounted to one-eighth of the Fund's total holdings of gold at that time. The gold authorized for sale was acquired after the Second Amendment of the IMF's Articles of Agreement in April 1978 and thus not subject to restitution to IMF member countries, unlike gold the IMF acquired before

1978. The Executive Board adopted modalities for the gold sales consistent with the priority of avoiding disruption of the gold market.

This decision to sell gold was a key step in implementing the new income model agreed in April 2008 to help put the IMF's finances on a sound long-term footing. A central component of the new income model is the establishment of an endowment funded by the profits from the sale of a strictly limited portion of the IMF's gold, being the gold the Fund had acquired after the Second Amendment of the Articles. In July 2009, the Executive Board agreed that resources linked to gold sales would also help boost the IMF's concessional lending capacity. The Executive Board subsequently approved a distribution of SDR 700 million in reserves attributed to a portion of the gold windfall profits, with the expectation that members would transfer or return equivalent amounts to support concessional lending to low income countries. The distribution will be effected only when the membership provides satisfactory assurances of PRGT subsidy contributions equivalent to at least 90 percent of the amount distributed—i.e. SDR 630 million.

In August 2009, the European Central Bank and other central banks announced the renewal of their agreement (Central Bank Gold Agreement) on gold sales, which are not to exceed 400 metric tons annually and 2,000 metric tons over the five years starting on September 27, 2009. The announcement noted that sales of 403 tons of gold by the IMF could be accommodated within these ceilings. This ensured that gold sales by the Fund would not add to the announced volume of sales from official sources.

The first phase in the Fund's gold sales was set aside exclusively for off-market sales to interested central banks and other official holders, which were conducted at market prices at the time of the transactions. In October and November 2009, the Fund sold 212 metric tons of gold in separate off-market transactions to three central banks: 200 metric tons were sold to the Reserve Bank of India during October 19-30; 2 metric tons to the Bank of Mauritius on November 11; and 10 metric tons to the Central Bank of Sri Lanka on November 23.

The IMF announced in February 2010 the beginning of sales of gold on the market. At that time, a total of 191.3 tons of gold remained to be sold. In accordance with the priority of avoiding disruption of the gold market, the on market sales were to be conducted in a phased manner over time. This followed the approach adopted successfully by the central banks participating in the Central Bank Gold Agreement. The initiation of on market sales did not preclude further off-market gold sales directly to interested central banks or other official holders. On September 7, 2010, the Fund sold 10 metric tons to the Bangladesh Bank. Such sales reduced the amount of gold to be placed on the market.

In December 2010 the IMF concluded the gold sales program with total sales of 403.3 metric tons of gold (12.97 million ounces), as authorized by the Executive Board. Total proceeds amounted to SDR 9.5 billion (about $15 billion).

IMF's LENDING CAPACITY

IMF can use its quota funded holdings of currencies of financially strong economies to finance lending. The IMF's Executive Board selects these currencies every three months. Most are issued by industrial countries, but the list also has included currencies of lower income countries such as Botswana, China, and India. The IMF's holdings of these currencies, together with its own SDR holdings, make up its own usable resources. If needed, the IMF can supplement its own usable resources by borrowing.

The amount the IMF has readily available for new (non-concessional) lending is indicated by its one-year forward commitment capacity. This is determined by its usable resources, plus projected loan repayments over the subsequent twelve months, less the resources that have already been committed under existing arrangements, less a prudential balance

BORROWING ARRANGEMENTS

The IMF maintains two standing multilateral borrowing arrangements—the New Arrangements to Borrow (NAB) and the General Arrangements to Borrow (GAB)—with a total borrowing capacity of SDR 34 billion (about $50 billion). If the IMF believes that its forward commitment capacity might fall short of its members' needs—for example, in the event of a major financial crisis—it can activate these arrangements. Supplementary resources available under these arrangements will help to ensure that the Fund can continue to provide timely and effective balance of payments assistance to its members.Their renewal was approved in 2007 for another five years starting in 2008. In February 2009, the IMF signed a bilateral borrowing agreement with Japan to temporarily bolster its capacity to support members during the current global economic and financial crisis. Under this agreement Japan committed to lend up to US$100 billion (about SDR 68 billion) to the IMF.

ECONOMIC SURVEILLANCE

When a country joins the IMF, it agrees to subject its economic and financial policies to the scrutiny of the international community. It also makes a commitment to pursue policies that are conducive to orderly economic growth and reasonable price stability, to avoid manipulating exchange rates for unfair competitive advantage, and to provide the IMF with data about its economy. The IMF's regular monitoring of economies and associated provision of policy advice is intended to identify weaknesses that are causing or could lead to financial or economic instability. This process is known as surveillance.

The legal framework for surveillance was updated in June 2007 with the adoption of the Decision on Bilateral Surveillance over Members' Policies. The Decision clarified that country surveillance should be focused on assessing whether countries' policies promote domestic and external stability. This means surveillance should cover *cover a range of economic policies, with the emphasis varying in accordance with a country's individual circumstances.*

(i) Exchange rate, monetary, and fiscal policies. The IMF provides advice on issues such as the choice of exchange rate policies and ensuring consistency between the regime and fiscal and monetary policies.

(ii) Financial sector issues are receiving elevated coverage in surveillance reports, building on the achievements under the Financial Sector Assessment Program (FSAP), which enables the IMF and the World Bank to gauge the strengths and weaknesses of countries' financial sectors.

(iii) Assessment of risks and vulnerabilities stemming from large and sometimes volatile capital flows has become more central to IMF surveillance in recent years.

(iv) Institutional and structural issues have also gained importance in the wake of financial crises and in the context of some countries' transition from planned to market economies. The IMF and the World Bank play a central role in developing, implementing, and assessing internationally recognized standards and codes in areas crucial to the efficient functioning of a modern economy such as central bank independence, financial sector regulation, and policy transparency and accountability.

In 2010, the IMF undertook a review of its surveillance mandate. This resulted in measures to integrate all dimensions of IMF surveillance—multilateral, bilateral and financial—and make it more effective. These measures helped address some of the weaknesses identified in pre-crisis surveillance which were set out in the report by the IMF's Independent Evaluation Office on IMF Performance in the Run-up to the Financial and Economic Crisis.

In October 2011, the latest comprehensive review of the effectiveness of its surveillance, or Triennial Surveillance Review, was completed. The review highlighted progress since the beginning of the global financial crisis but also found remaining gaps in the IMF's surveillance. In particular, surveillance was seen as too fragmented, with risk assessments lacking depth and insufficient focus on interconnections and the transmission of shocks. Surveillance was also found to have less impact for larger member countries. The subsequent recommended actions include improvements in six key areas: interconnectedness, risk assessments, external stability, financial stability, traction and the legal framework. The IMF is working on concrete proposals for a new, integrated surveillance decision—covering both bilateral and multilateral surveillance—that will foster a broader approach to global stability.

CONDITIONALITY

Conditionality in its broad sense covers both the design of IMF-supported programs—that is, the macroeconomic and structural policies—and the specific tools used to monitor progress toward the goals outlined by the country in cooperation with the IMF.

Conditionality helps countries solve balance of payments problems without resorting to measures that are harmful to national or international prosperity. At the same time, the measures are meant to safeguard IMF resources by ensuring that the country's balance of payments will be strong enough to permit it to repay the loan. All conditionality under an IMF-supported program must be "macro-critical"—that is, either critical to the achievement of macroeconomic program goals or necessary for the implementation of specific provisions under the IMF's Articles of Agreement.

Over the years, the IMF has developed a number of loan instruments, or "facilities," that are tailored to address the specific circumstances of its diverse membership (See Box-1).

BOX-1

HOW THE IMF LENDS: TERMS AND CONDITIONS OF FINANCIAL FACILITIES

STAND-BY ARRANGEMENT AND EXTENDED FUND FACILITY

STAND-BY ARRANGEMENT (1952)

Addresses balance of payments difficulties that are short term; the arrangement is typically 12–18 months with a legal maximum of 3 years.

Access limits: Annual: 100 percent of quota; cumulative: 300 percent of quota for all use of IMF resources in the General Resources Account.

Maturities (expected repayment)/(obligatory repayment): 2¼–4 years/3¼–5 years.

Charges: Basic rate of charge + level-based surcharges of 100 basis points on amounts above 200 percent of quota and 200 basis points on 300 percent of quota.

Conditions: Member adopts policies that provide confidence that its balance of payments difficulties will be resolved within a reasonable period.

Cumulative access: Above 25 percent of quota is subject to stricter conditions (known as upper credit tranche conditionality).

Phasing and monitoring: Quarterly disbursements contingent on observance of performance criteria and other conditions.

EXTENDED FUND FACILITY (1974)

Provides longer-term assistance in support of structural reforms that address longer-term balance of payments difficulties.

Access limits: Annual: 100 percent of quota; cumulative: 300 percent of quota for all use of IMF resources in the General Resources Account.

Maturities (expected repayment)/(obligatory repayment): 4½–7 years/4½–10 years.

Charges: Basic rate of charge + level-based surcharges of 100 basis points on amounts above 200 percent of quota and 200 basis points above 300 percent of quota.

Conditions: Member adopts 3-year programme, with structural agenda, and provides annual detailed statement of policies for the next 12 months.

Phasing and monitoring: Quarterly or semiannual disbursements contingent on observance of performance criteria and other conditions.

SPECIAL LOANS

SUPPLEMENTAL RESERVE FACILITY (1997)

Provides short-term assistance to members with balance of payments difficulties related to a sudden and disruptive loss of market confidence. Available only as a supplement to a regular arrangement.

Access limits: None; this facility is available only when access under an associated regular arrangement would otherwise exceed either annual or cumulative limit.

Maturities (expected repayment)/(obligatory repayment): 2–2½ years/2½–3 years.

Charges: Basic rate of charge + 300 basis points rising to a maximum of 500 basis points after 2½ years.

Conditions: Programme under an associated arrangement, with strengthened policies to address a loss of market confidence.

Phasing and monitoring: Facility available for one year; front-loaded access with two or more disbursements.

COMPENSATORY FINANCING FACILITY (1963)

Covers a shortfall in a member's export earnings and services receipts or an excess in cereal import costs that is temporary and arises from events beyond the member's control.

Access limits: Maximum 45 percent of quota for each element—export shortfall and excess cereal import costs—and a combined limit of 55 percent of quota.

Maturities (expected repayment)/(obligatory repayment): 2¼–4 years/3¼–5 years.

Charges: Basic rate of charge; not subject to surcharges.

Conditions: Usually available only when a member already has a Stand-By Arrangement or when its balance of payments position, apart from its export shortfall or import excess, is otherwise satisfactory.

Phasing and monitoring: Typically disbursed over a minimum of six months and in accordance with the phasing provisions of the arrangement.

EMERGENCY ASSISTANCE

Natural disasters (1962): Provides quick, medium-term assistance to members with balance of payments difficulties related to natural disasters.

Postconflict (1995): Provides quick, medium-term assistance for balance of payments difficulties related to the aftermath of civil unrest or cross-border armed conflict.

Access limits: 25 percent of quota, although larger amounts can be made available in exceptional cases.

Maturities (expected repayment)/ (obligatory repayment): No early repayment expectation/ 3¼–5 years.

Charges: Basic rate of charge; not subject to surcharges; possibility of interest subsidy for low-income countries if resources are available.

Conditions: Reasonable efforts to overcome balance of payments difficulties and focus on institutional and administrative capacity building to pave the way toward an upper credit tranche arrangement or an arrangement under the Poverty Reduction and Growth Facility. The conditions for emergency postconflict assistance also include that IMF support would be part of a concerted international effort to address the aftermath of the conflict.

Phasing and monitoring: Typically none.

LOANS FOR LOW-INCOME MEMBERS

POVERTY REDUCTION AND GROWTH FACILITY (PRGF) (1999)

Provides longer-term assistance for deepseated, structural balance of payments difficulties; aims at sustained, povertyreducing growth.

Access limits: 140 percent of quota; exceptional maximum, 185 percent.

Maturities (expected repayment)/(obligatory repayment): No early repayment expectation/ 5½–10 years.

Charges: Concessional interest rate: ½ of 1 percent a year; not subject to surcharges.

Conditions: Based on a Poverty Reduction Strategy Paper prepared by the country in a participatory process, and integrating macroeconomic, structural, and poverty reduction policies.

Phasing and monitoring: Semiannual (or occasionally quarterly) disbursements contingent on observance of performance criteria and completion of reviews.

EXOGENOUS SHOCKS FACILITY (ESF) (2005)

Approved but not yet fully funded. Would provide policy support and financial assistance to low-income countries facing exogenous shocks (such as commodity price changes, natural disasters, and trade disruptions caused by events in a neighboring country). Available to countries eligible for the PRGF but without a PRGF-supported programme in place; ESF programmes would be one to two years in length.

Access limits: 25 percent of quota; cumulative access limit of 50 percent of quota.

Maturities (expected repayment)/ (obligatory repayment): No early repayment expectation/ 5½–10 years.

Charges: ½ of 1 percent a year; not subject to surcharges.

Conditions: Poverty reduction strategy must be in place, and comprehensive economic programme must be formulated.

Phasing and monitoring: Semiannual or quarterly disbursements contingent on observance of performance criteria and, in most cases, completion of a review.

Nonconcessional loans are provided through four main facilities: Stand-By Arrangements (SBAs), the Extended Fund Facility, the Supplemental Reserve Facility, and the Compensatory Financing Facility. Low-income countries may borrow at a concessional interest rate through the Poverty Reduction and Growth Facility (PRGF) and, if hit by a shock beyond their control, through the Exogenous Shocks Facility (ESF). The ESF is designed for countries without a PRGF supported programme or with a Policy Support Instrument (PSI) programme. An on-track PSI could provide the basis for rapid access to ESF financing if a shock occurs, although access would not be automatic. Members recovering from natural disasters and armed conflicts can also request emergency assistance from the IMF—possibly at concessional rates for low income countries.

As part of a wide-ranging reform of its lending, the IMF introduced in 2009 a new lending facility—the Flexible Credit Line (FCL)—that does not rely on traditional program conditionality, but instead involves rigorous pre-qualification criteria (also referred to as "ex-ante conditionality"). In situations where a full-fledged economic program is either not necessary (for instance, because of the transitory and limited nature of the shock) or not feasible (for instance, because the need is urgent or policy implementation capacity is limited, including due to fragilities), IMF financial assistance is offered under the Rapid Financing Instrument (RFI) and Rapid Credit Facility (RCF). These also do not involve traditional program conditionality, except for prior actions which may be required where warranted. In all other Fund financing facilities, disbursements are conditional on successfully completing reviews of program implementation (known as "ex-post conditionality"). The Precautionary and Liquidity Line (PLL)—which was introduced in 2011 and broadens the scope of the former Precautionary Credit Line (PCL)—combines elements of both ex-ante and (light) ex-post conditionality.

The member country has primary responsibility for selecting, designing, and implementing the policies that will make the IMF-supported program successful. The program is described in a letter of intent(which often has a memorandum of economic and financial policies attached to it). The program's objectives and policies depend on country circumstances. But the overarching goal is always to restore or maintain balance of payments viability and macroeconomic stability, while setting the stage for sustained, high-quality growth and, in low-income countries, for reducing poverty.

When a member does not face a pressing balance of payments need, it may treat an IMF arrangement as precautionary, which provides the right—conditional on implementation of specific policies—to make drawings should the need arise. In recent years, the largest number of loans has been made through the PRGF. The largest amount of funds is provided through SBAs, however. In the context of the IMF's mediumterm strategy further consideration is being given to a possible new instrument to provide high- access contingent financing for emerging market economies that have strong macroeconomic policies, sustainable debt, and transparent reporting but remain vulnerable to shocks.

Nonconcessional facilities are subject to the IMF's marketrelated interest rate, known as the "basic rate of charge." This rate of charge is based on the Special Drawing Right (SDR) interest rate, which is revised weekly to take into account changes in short-term interest rates in the major international money markets. Large loans carry an interest rate premium, or "surcharge." The amount that a country can borrow varies with the type of loan and is expressed as a multiple of the country's IMF quota. To finance an exceptional balance of payments need, the IMF may also lend beyond the access limits. The IMF encourages early repayment of loans. Although it has a standard repayment obligations schedule, members are expected to repay according to a faster schedule when possible.

Conditionality in IMF Lending

When a country faces serious medium-term balance of payments problems because of structural weaknesses that require time to address, the IMF can assist with the adjustment process under an Extended Fund Facility (EFF). Compared to assistance provided under the more common Stand-by Arrangement, assistance under an extended arrangement features longer program engagement—to help countries implement medium term structural reforms—and a longer repayment period.

Strong focus on structural adjustment: When a country borrows from the IMF, it commits to undertake policies to overcome the economic and structural problems. These commitments, including specific conditionality, are expected to have a strong focus on structural reforms, in addition to policies that maintain macroeconomic stability. Program performance is assessed regularly by the IMF's Executive Board which also allows the program to adapt to economic developments. The EFF has flexibility in the frequency of reviews based on the strength of the country's policies and the nature of its financing needs.

How much can a country borrow under the EFF and how expensive is it? As with the SBA, the size of borrowing under the EFF is guided by a member country's need for financing, capacity to repay, and track record with use of IMF resources.

Normal access

Borrowing under the EFF is subject to the normal limits of up to 200 percent of a country's IMF quota annually and 600 percent of quota of total credit outstanding (net of scheduled repayments).

Exceptional Access

The Fund may grant loan amounts above these limits on a case-by-case basis in exceptional circumstances provided that the country satisfies the exceptional access criteria.

In addition, EFFs generally are not formulated on a precautionary basis in anticipation of a future balance of payments problem.

The EFF is subject to the same charges as other non-concessional factilities. The lending rate is tied to the IMF's market-related interest rate, known as the basic rate of charge, and large loans (above certain limites) carry a surcharge. The rate of charge is based on the SDR interest rate, which is revised weekly to take acount of changes in short-term interest rates in major international money markets.

Like the SBA, resources committed under the EFFs are subject to a commitment fee leivied at the beginning of each 12-month period on amounts that could be drawn in the period (15 basis points for amounts up to 200 percent of quota, 30 basis points on amounts between 200 and 1,000 percent of quota, and 60 basis points on amounts exceeding 1,000 percent of quota). These fees are refunded if the amounts are borrowed during the course of the relevant period. A service charges of 50 basis points is also applied on each amount drawn.

How is Compliance Assessed?

Most IMF loans feature phased disbursements. This allows the IMF to verify that a country is continuing to adhere to its commitments before successive installments are disbursed. Programme monitoring relies on several different tools:

(i) **Prior actions** are measures that a country agrees to take before the IMF's Executive Board approves a loan or completes a programme review (see below). Such measures ensure that the programme has the necessary foundation to succeed or is put back on track following deviations from the agreed policies. Prior actions could include, for example, adjustment of the exchange rate to a sustainable level, elimination of price controls, or formal approval of a government budget consistent with the programme's fiscal framework.

(ii) **Performance criteria** are specific conditions that have to be met for the agreed amount of credit to be disbursed. There are two types of performance criteria: quantitative and structural. ***Quantitative criteria*** typically refer to macroeconomic policy variables such as international reserves, monetary and credit aggregates, fiscal balances, or external borrowing. For example, a programme might include a minimum level of net international reserves, a maximum level of central bank net domestic assets, or a maximum level of government borrowing. ***Structural criteria*** are used for structural measures that are critical to the success of the economic programme. These vary widely across programmes but could, for example, include specific measures to improve financial sector operations, reform social security systems, or restructure key sectors such as energy.

(iii) Quantitative criteria may be supplemented with **indicative targets**. These are often set for the later months of a programme and are then turned into performance criteria, with appropriate modifications, as economic trends firm up.

(iv) **Structural benchmarks** are used for measures that cannot be monitored specifically enough to be performance criteria, or for small steps in a critical reform process; breach of these would not individually warrant an interruption of IMF financing.

(v) Another important monitoring tool is the **programme review**, which serves as an opportunity for a broad-based assessment by the Executive Board of progress toward the programme's objectives. Reviews are used to discuss policies and introduce changes that may be necessary in light of new developments. In some cases, a country might request a waiver for a breached performance criterion—for example, when its authorities have already taken measures to correct the deviation.

Conditions for IMF financial support may range from general commitments to cooperate with the IMF in setting policies, to the formulation of specific, quantified plans for financial policies. IMF financing from its general resources in the "upper credit tranches" (that is, where larger amounts are provided in return for implementation of remedial measures) is disbursed in stages. The IMF requires a "letter of intent" or a "memorandum of economic and financial policies," in which a government outlines its policy intentions during the period of the adjustment program; the policy changes it will make before the arrangement can be approved; performance criteria, which are objective indicators for certain policies that must be satisfied on a quarterly, semiannual, or in some instances monthly basis in order for drawings to be made; and periodic reviews that allow the Executive Board to assess whether the member's policies are consistent with the program's objectives.

TRANSPARENCY AT THE IMF

The IMF has also focused on improving its own accountability by establishing in 2001 the Independent Evaluation Office and by increasing over the past decade the transparency of its operations and decision making. The IMF has become a more open and accountable institution and a major source of information for the general public and capital market participants while preserving its role as confidential advisor to its member countries.

TECHNICAL ASSISTANCE AND TRAINING

The IMF provides technical advice and training to help strengthen the design and implementation of macroeconomic and financial sector policies in member countries and boost the institutional capacity of their governments. Sound economic policymaking and implementation require know-how and effective government institutions. Many developing countries, in particular, need help to build up expertise in economic management and advice about what policies, reforms, and institutional arrangements are appropriate and have worked well elsewhere. The IMF gives priority to providing assistance where it complements and enhances its other key activities—surveillance and lending.

SPECIAL DRAWING RIGHTS (SDRs): AN INTERNATIONAL RESERVE ASSET

Special Drawing Rights (SDRs)

The SDR was created by the IMF in 1969 to support the Bretton Woods fixed exchange rate system. A country participating in this system needed official reserves—government or central bank holdings of gold and widely accepted foreign currencies—that could be used to purchase the domestic currency in foreign exchange markets, as required to maintain its exchange rate. But the international supply of two key reserve assets—gold and the U.S. dollar—proved inadequate for supporting the expansion of world trade and financial development that was taking place. Therefore, the international community decided to create a new international reserve asset under the auspices of the IMF.

However, only a few years later, the Bretton Woods system collapsed and the major currencies shifted to a floating exchange rate regime. In addition, the growth in international capital markets facilitated borrowing by creditworthy governments. Both of these developments lessened the need for SDRs.

The SDR is neither a currency, nor a claim on the IMF. Rather, it is a potential claim on the freely usable currencies of IMF members. Holders of SDRs can obtain these currencies in exchange for their SDRs in two ways: first, through the arrangement of voluntary exchanges between members; and second, by the IMF designating members with strong external positions to purchase SDRs from members with weak external positions. In addition to its role as a supplementary reserve asset, the SDR, serves as theunit of account of the IMF and some other international organizations.

Basket of Currencies Determines the Value of the SDR

The value of the SDR was initially defined as equivalent to 0.888671 grams of fine gold—which, at the time, was also equivalent to one U.S. dollar. After the collapse of the Bretton Woods system in 1973, however, the SDR was redefined as a basket of currencies,today consisting of the euro, Japanese yen, pound sterling, and U.S. dollar. It is calculated as the sum of specific amounts of the four basket currencies valued in U.S. dollars, on the basis of exchange rates quoted at noon each day in the London market.

The basket composition is reviewed every five years by the Executive Board, or earlier if the Fund finds changed circumstances warrant an earlier review, to ensure that it reflects the relative importance of currencies in the world's trading and financial systems. In the most recent review (in November 2010), the weights of the currencies in the SDR basket were revised based on the value of the exports of goods and services and the amount of reserves denominated in the respective currencies that were held by other members of the IMF. These changes became effective on January 1, 2011. The next review will take place by 2015. In October 2011, the IMF Executive Board discussed clarifications and possible reform options of the existing criteria for broadening the SDR currency basket. Most directors held the view that the current criteria for SDR basket selection remained appropriate.

The SDR Interest Rate

The SDR interest rate provides the basis for calculating the interest charged to members on regular (non-concessional) IMF loans, the interest paid to members on their SDR holdings and charged on their SDR allocation, and the interest paid to members on a portion of their quota subscriptions. The SDR interest rate is determined weekly and is based on a weighted average of representative interest rates on short-term debt in the money markets of the SDR basket currencies.

SDR Allocations to IMF Members

Under its Articles of Agreement (Article XV, Section 1, and Article XVIII), the IMF may allocate SDRs to member countries in proportion to their IMF quotas. Such an allocation provides each member with a costless, unconditional international reserve asset on which interest is neither earned nor paid. However, if a member's SDR holdings rise above its allocation, it earns interest on the excess. Conversely, if it holds fewer SDRs than allocated, it pays interest on the shortfall. The Articles of Agreement also allow for cancellations of SDRs, but this provision has never been used. The IMF cannot allocate SDRs to itself or to other prescribed holders.

General allocations of SDRs have to be based on a long-term global need to supplement existing reserve assets. Decisions on general allocations are made for successive basic periods of up to five years, although general SDR allocations have been made only three times. The first allocation was for a total amount of SDR 9.3 billion, distributed in 1970-72, and the second allocated SDR 12.1 billion, distributed in 1979-81. These two allocations resulted in cumulative SDR allocations of SDR 21.4 billion. To help mitigate the effects of the financial crisis, a third general SDR allocation of SDR 161.2 billion was made on August 28, 2009.

Separately, the Fourth Amendment to the Articles of Agreement became effective August 10, 2009 and provided for a special one-time allocation of SDR 21.5 billion. The purpose of the Fourth Amendment was to enable all members of the IMF to participate in the SDR system on an equitable basis and correct for the fact that countries that joined the IMF after 1981—more than one fifth of the current IMF membership—never received an SDR allocation until 2009. The 2009 general and special SDR allocations together raised total cumulative SDR allocations to about SDR 204 billion (equivalent to about $ 328.3 billion, converted during the rate of August 31, .2009).

Buying and Selling SDRs

IMF members often need to buy SDRs to discharge obligations to the IMF, or they may wish to sell SDRs in order to adjust the composition of their reserves. The IMF may act as an intermediary between members and prescribed holders to ensure that SDRs can be exchanged for freely usable currencies. For more than two decades, the SDR market has functioned through voluntary trading arrangements. Under these arrangements a number of members and one prescribed holder have volunteered to buy or sell SDRs within limits defined by their respective arrangements. Following the 2009 SDR allocations, the number and size of the voluntary arrangements has been expanded to ensure continued liquidity of the voluntary SDR market. The number of voluntary SDR trading arrangements now stands at 32, including 19 new arrangements since the 2009 SDR allocations.

In the event that there is insufficient capacity under the voluntary trading arrangements, the Fund can activate the designation mechanism. Under this mechanism, members with sufficiently strong external positions are designated by the Fund to buy SDRs with freely usable currencies up to certain amounts from members with weak external positions. This arrangement serves as a backstop to guarantee the liquidity and the reserve asset character of the SDR.

WORLD BANK

Like the IMF, the World Bank was created at Bretton Woods in July 1944, the culmination of wartime discussions between the United States and the United Kingdom on the shape of the post-World War II international economic order. The flank that emerged was essentially an American creation. The IMF was established to provide funds for short-term balance of payments relief and the role of the International Bank for Reconstruction and Development was the provision of longer-term finance for the development of productive resources. The initial priority of the IBRD, which opened for business on 25 June 1946, was reconstruction. Box-3 provides the basic difference between these two internatinal twins.

BOX-3

THE IMF AND THE WORLD BANK—WHAT'S THE DIFFERENCE?

The IMF and the World Bank were conceived at the Bretton Woods conference in July 1944 to strengthen international economic cooperation and to help create a more stable and prosperous global economy. Although these goals have remained central to both institutions, their mandates and functions differ, and their work has evolved in response to new economic developments and challenges. The IMF promotes international monetary cooperation and provides member countries with policy advice, temporary loans, and technical assistance so they can establish and maintain financial stability and external viability, and build and maintain strong economies. The IMF's loans are provided in support of policy programmes designed to solve balance of payments problems—that is, situations in which a country cannot obtain sufficient financing on affordable terms to meet international payment obligations. Some IMF loans are relatively short term and funded by the pool of quota contributions provided by its members. Others are for longer periods, including concessional loans provided to low-income members on the basis of subsidies financed by past IMF gold sales and members' contributions. In its work in low-income countries, the IMF's main focus is on how macroeconomic and financial policies can contribute to laying a basis for sustainable growth and poverty reduction. Most IMF professional staff are economists.

The World Bank promotes long-term economic development and poverty reduction by providing technical and financial support, including by helping countries reform particular sectors or implement specific projects—for example, building schools and health centers, providing water and electricity, fighting disease, and protecting the environment. World Bank financial assistance is generally long term and is funded both by member country contributions and through bond issuance. World Bank staff have qualifications that embrace a broader range of disciplines than those of IMF staff.

The IMF and the World Bank collaborate in a variety of areas, particularly in supporting governments in implementing poverty reduction strategies in low-income countries, providing debt relief for the poorest countries, and assessing the financial sectors of countries. The two institutions hold joint meetings twice a year.

The Bank that emerged from the Bretton Woods conference was mainly conceived in terms of the economic problems of the immediate post-war period. It was the tasks of reconstruction rather than the challenge of development which ranked uppermost in the minds of its major proponents. The developing countries attending the conference were concerned that if too high a priority was placed on reconstruction limited resources would be available for development. The Latin American countries therefore proposed that in the Articles of Agreement equal emphasis should be given to reconstruction and development. The United States conceded the inclusion of development functions in the Articles of Agreement so that Latin American countries would agree to join the IMF, access to the Bank's lending being tied to membership of the Fund. It was decided that the resources and facilities of the Bank shall be used exclusively for the benefit of members with equitable consideration to projects for development and projects for reconstruction alike. Nevertheless, the provision of capital for reconstruction of the war-damaged economies dominated the concerns of the organisation. It was envisaged that the flank would fulfil its role in reconstruction largely by channelling US private investment to Europe through its guarantee of these loans. In the absence of private investment on reasonable terms the Bank was mandated to provide finance for investment purposes out of its own financial resources.

IDA, IFC AND MIGA

As its mission has expanded, the World Bank has cueted these affiliated organisation: International Development Association (IDA), International Finance Corporation (IFC) and Multilateral Investment Guarantee Agency (MIGA). The IDA established in 1960 as the soft-loan affiliate of the IBRD has its own constitution but shares the same offices and staff as the IBRD. In organisational terms the IDA isan 'elaborate fiction.' Though Membership is open to all members of the IBRD, but some IBRD members have chosen not to join the IDA. The IDA is essentially an instrument for resource transfer. The criteria for project selection, scrutiny of projects, implementation and financial and economic rates of return are identical to the IBRD but IDA credits are reserved for developing countries not capable of borrowing from the IBRD. Some countries, the so-called 'blend countries' are eligible for both IDA credits and IBRD loans. Eligibility for IDA loans—called credits-is based on per capita national income. IDA loans are interest-free but carry an annual service charge of 0.75 per cent. The maturity on an IDA credit is 35 to 40 years with a grace period of 10 years. Unlike the IBRD, the IDA is almost wholly dependent on member countries for its finances. The primary source of funding comes directly from grants made by its members in three-yearly replenishments. Further, income accrues from transfers of IBRD income from its retained profits, repayment of principal and special supplementary contributions from members. The dependence of the IDA on the industrialised countries for the periodic replenishment of its resources makes it vulnerable to the changing development assistance priorities of these countries and ensures the existence of a permanent negotiating process between the Bank and donor governments.

The IFC, founded in 1956, is legally a separate entity from the Bank although membership in the IFC is not open to non-members of the IBRD. Membership of the IFC stood at 146 in 1992. The IFC has its own legal and operating staff but draws on the Bank for administrative and other services. The IFC functions like an investment bank. It participates directly in equity as well as loan investments. It participates only in private ventures and its loans are not dependent on government guarantees.

Created in 1988, the MIGA offers investment insurance to mitigate political risk through its guarantee programme and provides promotional and advisory services 10 assist member countries in their efforts to attract or retain direct foreign investment. MIGA is a legally distinct entity from the Bank or the IFC and has its own Executive Board.

REFORMING THE INTERNATIONAL MONETARY SYSTEM

The outbreak of the current crisis and its spillover in the world have confronted us with a long-existing but still unanswered question,i.e., what kind of international reserve currency do we need to secure global financial stability and facilitate world economic growth, which was one of the purposes for establishing the IMF? There were various institutional arrangements in an attempt to find a solution, including the Silver Standard, the Gold Standard, the Gold Exchange Standard and the Bretton Woods system. The above question, however, as the ongoing financial crisis demonstrates, is far from being solved, and has become even more severe due to the inherent weaknesses of the current international monetary system.

Theoretically, an international reserve currency should first be anchored to a stable benchmark and issued according to a clear set of rules, therefore to ensure orderly supply; second, its supply should be flexible enough to allow timely adjustment according to the changing demand; third, such adjustments should be disconnected from economic conditions and sovereign interests of any single country. The acceptance of credit-based national currencies as major international reserve currencies, as is the case in the current system, is a rare special case in history. The crisis again calls for creative reform of the existing international monetary system towards an international reserve currency with a stable value, rule-based issuance and manageable supply, so as to achieve the objective of safeguarding global economic and financial stability.

I. The outbreak of the crisis and its spillover to the entire world reflect the inherent vulnerabilities and systemic risks in the existing international monetary system. Issuing countries of reserve currencies are constantly confronted with the dilemma between achieving their domestic monetary policy goals and meeting other countries' demand for reserve currencies. On the one hand, the monetary authorities cannot simply focus on domestic goals without carrying out their international responsibilities; on the other hand, they cannot pursue different domestic and international objectives at the same time. They may either fail to adequately meet the demand of a growing global economy for liquidity as they try to ease inflation pressures at home, or create excess liquidity in the global markets by overly stimulating domestic demand. The Triffin Dilemma, i.e., the issuing countries of reserve currencies cannot maintain the value of the reserve currencies while providing liquidity to the world, still exists.

When a national currency is used in pricing primary commodities, trade settlements and is adopted as a reserve currency globally, efforts of the monetary authority issuing such a currency to address its economic imbalances by adjusting exchange rate would be made in vain, as its currency serves as a benchmark for many other currencies. While benefiting from a widely accepted reserve currency, the globalization also suffers from the flaws of such a system. The frequency and increasing intensity of financial crises following the collapse of the Bretton Woods system suggests the costs of such a system to the world may have exceeded its benefits. The price is becoming increasingly higher, not only for the users, but also for the issuers of the reserve currencies. Although crisis may not necessarily be an intended result of the issuing authorities, it is an inevitable outcome of the institutional flaws.

II. The desirable goal of reforming the international monetary system, therefore, is to create an international reserve currency that is disconnected from individual nations and is able to remain stable in the long run, thus removing the inherent deficiencies caused by using credit-based national currencies. Though the super-sovereign reserve currency has long since been proposed, yet no substantive progress has been achieved to date. Back in the 1940s, Keynes had already proposed to introduce an international currency unit named "Bancor", based on the value of 30 representative commodities. Unfortunately, the proposal was not accepted. The collapse of the Bretton Woods system, which was based on the White approach, indicates that the Keynesian approach may have been more farsighted. The IMF also created the SDR in 1969, when the defects of the Bretton Woods system initially emerged, to mitigate the inherent risks sovereign reserve currencies caused. Yet, the role of the SDR has not been put into full play due to limitations on its allocation and the scope of its uses. However, it serves as the light in the tunnel for the reform of the international monetary system.

A super-sovereign reserve currency not only eliminates the inherent risks of credit-based sovereign currency, but also makes it possible to manage global liquidity. A super-sovereign reserve currency managed by a global institution could be used to both create and control the global liquidity. And when a country's currency is no longer used as the yardstick for global trade and as the benchmark for other currencies, the exchange rate policy of the country would be far more effective in adjusting economic imbalances. This will significantly reduce the risks of a future crisis and enhance crisis management capability.

III. The reform should be guided by a grand vision and begin with specific deliverables. It should be a gradual process that yields win-win results for all. The reestablishment of a new and widely accepted reserve currency with a stable valuation benchmark may take a long time. The creation of an international currency unit, based on the Keynesian proposal, is a bold initiative that requires extraordinary political vision and courage. In the short run, the international community, particularly the IMF, should at least recognize and face up to the risks resulting from the existing system, conduct regular monitoring and assessment and issue timely early warnings.

Special consideration should be given to giving the SDR a greater role. The SDR has the features and potential to act as a super-sovereign reserve currency. Moreover, an increase in SDR allocation would help the Fund address its resources problem and the difficulties in the voice and representation reform. Therefore, efforts should be made to push forward a SDR allocation. This will require political cooperation among member countries. Specifically, the Fourth Amendment to the Articles of Agreement and relevant resolution on SDR allocation proposed in 1997 should be approved as soon as possible so that members joined the Fund after 1981 could also share the benefits of the SDR. On the basis of this, considerations could be given to further increase SDR allocation.

The scope of using the SDR should be broadened, so as to enable it to fully satisfy the member countries' demand for a reserve currency. SDR, which is now only used between governments and international institutions, could become a widely accepted means of payment in international trade and financial transactions. Further the use of the SDR in international trade, commodities pricing, investment and corporate book-keeping should be actively promoted. This will help enhance the role of the SDR, and will effectively reduce the fluctuation of prices of assets denominated in national currencies and related risks. In addition, financial assets denominated in the SDR to increase its appeal. should be created. The introduction of SDR-denominated securities, which is being studied by the IMF, will be a good start. Moreover, to improve the valuation and allocation of the SDR, the basket of currencies forming the basis for SDR valuation should be expanded to include currencies of all major economies, and the GDP may also be included as a weight. The allocation of the SDR can be shifted from a purely calculation-based system to a system backed by real assets, such as a reserve pool, to further boost market confidence in its value.

IV. Entrusting part of the member countries' reserve to the centralized management of the IMF will not only enhance the international community's ability to address the crisis and maintain the stability of the international monetary and financial system, but also significantly strengthen the role of the SDR: Compared with separate management of reserves by individual countries, the centralized management of part of the global reserve by a trustworthy international institution with a reasonable return to encourage participation will be more effective in deterring speculation and stabilizing financial markets. The participating countries can also save some reserve for domestic development and economic growth. With its universal membership, its unique mandate of maintaining monetary and financial stability, and as an international "supervisor" on the macroeconomic policies of its member countries, the IMF, equipped with its expertise, is endowed with a natural advantage to act as the manager of its member countries' reserves.

The centralized management of its member countries' reserves by the Fund will be an effective measure to promote a greater role of the SDR as a reserve currency. To achieve this, the IMF can set up an open-ended SDR-denominated fund based on the market practice, allowing subscription and redemption in the existing reserve currencies by various investors as desired. This arrangement will not only promote the development of SDR-denominated assets, but will also partially allow management of the liquidity in the form of the existing reserve currencies. It can even lay a foundation for increasing SDR allocation to gradually replace existing reserve currencies with the SDR.

DOES THE WORLD NEED A UNIVERSAL FINANCIAL INSTITUTION ?

When the Soviet Union disintegrated in 1991 and all of the newly emergent countries joined the membership of the International Monetary Fund, the IMF almost overnight became a nearly universal financial institution.

Universalism is not only a question of membership. Several official international agencies now have universal, or near-universal, membership, including the United Nations and many of its specialized agencies as well as both the IMF and the World Bank (but not yet the World Trade Organization). Membership in the IMF is not quite as universal as that of the United Nations. Throughout the Cold War, most states with Communist governments elected not to join the IMF. Since 1990, nearly all of those formerly in that category have joined, but neither Cuba nor North Korea has done so. Five tiny countries that are members of the UN also have not applied to join the IMF: three in Europe (Andorra, Liechtenstein, and Monaco) and two in the South Pacific (Nauru and Tuvalu). World Bank membership currently is identical to that of the IMF.Thus, having a very broad and inclusive membership is obviously a necessary condition, but it is not sufficient. More fundamentally, it is a question of focus. The World Bank lends only to developing and transition countries: to middle-income countries through its original body, the International Bank for Reconstruction and Development (IBRD), and to low-income countries through its concessional-lending arm, the International Development Association (IDA). In contrast, any of the member countries can borrow from the IMF: the only financial institution in the world with this universal approach to lending.

A broad implication of this fact is that the IMF is designed to function as a cooperative, or a club of peers. In principle, each member country might be a creditor part of the time and a borrower at other times. Since the early years of the IMF (which started lending in 1947), revolving-fund aspect has been important. Canada, Denmark, France Italy and the United Kingdom are all countries that are now financial and industrial power but that have in the past cycled between being creditors and debtors of the IMF. Even Japan and the United States had stand-by arrangements with the IMF in the early years And this distinguishing feature of the Fund has not vanished. More recently, China the Czech Republic, Estonia, and the Republic of Korea have been borrowers for a time and are now creditors and Russia is on the threshold of making that transition for the first time.

Universal lending by the IMF is an adjunct to the even more comprehensive use of surveillance. The Fund is the only financial institution that conducts routine (usually annual) consultations with all countries. These consultations focus primarily on macroeconomic policies but also cover related structural issues such as the soundness of the financial sector and the country's adherence to a variety of internationally accepted standards and codes. When and if a member country applies to borrow from the Fund, the knowledge that the staff has gained through these consultations, and the policy advice that it has given, make a useful starting point for discussion of lending terms and policy conditions. More generally the consultations are a platform for the Fund to develop and disseminate a comprehensive and consistent policy framework covering all regions and economies.

Financial Classification of Countries

As a basis for analyzing the contribution that IMF financial assistance might make for various groups of countries, the usual distinctions based on income level are not very helpful. What distinguishes countries with regular, intermittent, or rare demands for official assistance is the strength and stability of their national or fiscal finances, not the level of their per capita incomes. The correlation between the two is certainly positive, but it is far from perfect. An alternative taxonomy based on financial strength may be more informative.

In this scheme, the first group of countries includes those that have adequate domestic saving, supplemented by a steady, reliable access to private international capital markets, and usually with an ability to borrow in their own currencies with little or no premium for default or exchange risk. These advanced financial economies are very unlikely to face a need for IMF financing, although a marked deterioration in conditions could push them out of this box (as happened to Korea in 1997). This group currently would include most of the 30 members of the OECD and a scattering of other countries, but the membership at the margins is fairly unstable. South Africa, for example, has been more successful at borrowing abroad in its own currency than have OECD members Korea and Mexico. Sweden is far behind Australia in the portion of its public external debt denominated in its own currency. Saudi Arabia and some other major oil exporters presumably could borrow in their own currencies with little premium if they chose to do so, regardless of their level of industrialization or economic development.

The second category comprises the *emerging market economies*. These countries have a substantial ability to mobilize domestic savings and to supplement them with private international capital, both in debt instruments and in equity claims, but their access to international capital is not assured. These countries may face a significant credit risk premium and are unlikely to borrow in their own currency: the source of the "original sin" concept introduced to the finance literature by Eichengreen and Hausmann. Access to international capital is thus both expensive and unreliable, which makes these countries good candidates as applicants for occasional and intermittent financial assistance from the IMF.

The third category includes the rest of the world: the countries that we might call *pre-emergent market economies*. These countries—which could be low- or middle-income and would include many of the countries that are still in transition from centrally controlled to market economies—have little or no access to private-sector international capital. They also generally have insufficient domestic savings to finance the capital investment and social services that are prerequisites for economic growth. Even if capital were available, many governments of pre-emergent economies cannot afford to take on unsubsidized debt, so they are almost entirely dependent on official development assistance and concessional borrowing from multilateral creditors. In terms of the number of countries, this third group is the most numerous but countries do slide between this category and the emerging market group.

Modern Role of the IMF

If the IMF is to be a universal institution, how can it best serve the needs of each of these three groups of countries? To answer this question, it is essential to keep in mind that the purpose of the institution—indeed, the purpose of the international financial system—is not just to help countries avoid and deal with mishaps, to help them run in place without stumbling. The purpose, at least for the latter two groups, is to help them grow. Over time, pre-emergent economies should emerge, and emerging markets should mature.

The main challenge facing most pre-emergent countries is development: economic, social, and institutional development. Among other challenges, these countries need better health systems, especially in the age of HIV/AIDS. According to the World Health Organization, the least-developed countries spend an average of $US13 per person per year on health, a sum that cannot possibly begin to reduce their enormous deficiencies in access to health care. Pre-emergent countries also need better education systems: more and better schools, more and better teachers, more pencils and books, better transportation systems for getting children to schools, more awareness of the value of educating girls as much as boys. At the same time, they need better access to clean water and sanitation facilities and better protection of the natural environment. Many of them need to diversify production so as to reduce dependence on one or two export commodities, but they need to diversify in ways that are consistent with their resource endowments and comparative advantages, and they need greater access to world markets. These are serious challenges that override and dominate the stabilization challenges on which the IMF generally focuses.

To meet these challenges, pre-emergent countries need more and better external support, predominantly in the form of reliable and effectively directed grants and highly concessional and long-term finance from donors. Because the IMF does not have, and cannot provide, that type of support, it is tempting to conclude that the institution is of little value for this group of countries. But pre-emergent countries also need to implement better policies, both for their own sake and to qualify for and attract development finance from donors. In that regard, in general terms, they need to improve their institutional structures, their systems of governance, their ability to raise tax revenues and control government spending, and—not least—their macroeconomic policies: fiscal, monetary, and exchange rate policies.

Several of these key targets for policy reform are within the IMF's mandate and field of expertise: macroeconomic policies, economic and financial governance, tax reform, and improved expenditure management. The IMF can help countries to make and adhere to policy commitments in these areas, and it can signal to donors that countries are making progress and are serious about reform. In practice, because Fund-supported programmes in low-income countries usually include a broad array of structural as well as macroeconomic policy reforms, the signaling role of IMF support may be diluted as programmes are suspended despite adequate progress on macroeconomic policies. Effectiveness requires that signals are clear and are not distorted by political pressures. The financial role of the IMF is to commit enough money for a limited, but sufficient time to enable a country to undertake reforms without endangering financial stability, and enough to ensure that the accompanying policy advice and conditionality will be taken seriously by both sides. Although this role might lead to a continuing indebtedness to the IMF over a period of several years in cases where an ongoing relationship is beneficial to the country, the amounts will normally be quite small in relation to the country's overall development needs. The temporary nature of the financing, its dependence on macroeconomic policy reforms, and its limited size are the key components that distinguish the IMF's role from that of official development banks.

For emerging market economies, the overarching challenge is to develop an economic and financial strength comparable to that of the more advanced countries. In contrast to pre-emergent countries, where IMF financing is expected to be small but possibly of some persistence, here IMF financing is expected to be intermittent and quickly repaid, but possibly quite large. Korea provides a good illustration of a country that began as a pre-emergent borrower and was indebted continuously from 1974 to 1987, and then developed into a country that needed the IMF only as an emergency backup in 1997-2000.

Whereas the effectiveness of the Fund's role in pre-emergent economies depends on its ability to encourage and induce policy improvements and to catalyze support from other official creditors and donors, the effectiveness of lending to emerging market economies depends largely on the country's ability to restore stability quickly and on the ability of the process to restore market confidence and thus catalyze inflows from private capital markets.

For the advanced economies, there is a strong expectation—but no guarantee—that they will never have to borrow from the IMF. Nonetheless, the IMF's charter gives every member country the right to borrow under specified conditions to meet a balance of payments need. The IMF recognizes this right by maintaining a prudential balance of usable resources equal to 20 percent of the quotas of its creditor countries. Although most of these countries never will borrow, a few of them may. In any event, the existence of the IMF as a standby lender is an integral part of its contribution to global financial stability.

What links these various financial roles together is the policy advice that the IMF proffers regularly to all members, whether they are active borrowers, strong creditors, or in between. Because that advice always focuses primarily on the policy requirements for achieving and maintaining macroeconomic and financial stability, its *elements* include some recurring and dominant themes. What varies more is the *context*. Hence, while it is important for all countries to take such advice, the reasons differ. For pre-emergent markets such as Uganda's, macroeconomic stability has to be formulated in the context of—and in support of—a longer-run strategy aimed at achieving key development goals. Otherwise, conflicts will arise between development and stability (for example, cutting spending on health and education services could help reduce a fiscal deficit, but at the expense of the country's development goals), and stability will be squeezed out as the lower priority. Hence, advice to Uganda focuses squarely on optimizing the budget "as a development tool. For the emerging-market country, Uruguay, the advice is aimed at maintaining market confidence. For the advanced economy, the United States, the advice is aimed at putting the federal budget on a course that can be sustained over the longer term, thus avoiding the need for a belated and disruptive policy reversal.

How realistic is this approach? Getting the words right is one achievement, and generating real economic progress is another. For a practical answer to this question, it is necessary first to acknowledge two obvious but not innocuous points. *First,* there is no ideal international financial system, simply because we do not live in an ideal world. The current system has flaws and weaknesses, as do all the alternatives that have been or might be proposed. *Second,* no agency can solve or even marginally alleviate all of the economic and financial problems in the world: development and stabilization, for all types of countries. Specialization is essential and inevitable.

Some multilateral agencies specialize *horizontally,* by country type: the OECD (rich countries), the IBRD (middle-income), or IDA (low-income). While this horizontal specialization has the advantage of enabling a holistic approach to the agencies' policy advice, no institution can be expected to address the full range of problems that a country—especially the least developed—might face. Moreover, allowance must be made for the tendency of countries to shift between categories. Alternatively, agencies can specialize *vertically,* by the type of problem, and stand ready to help any country that faces that type of problem. That is the logic behind the IMF.

Vertical specialization, however, has its own limitations. In particular, it requires a sophisticated understanding of the context in which policy advice and policy conditions are formulated. It also requires effective collaboration, both with the affected countries and with other specialized agencies. The IMF cannot help pre-emergent countries unless it embeds its advice in a broader development strategy. That, in turn, requires working with the country to ensure that a solid strategy is in place, and it requires working with multilateral development banks and donor countries in support of that strategy.

What underpins the IMF's role in this dynamic process is an understanding that (1) the purpose of the international financial system (of which the IMF is a key component) is to help countries develop and move up the ladder and (2) that all countries need to pursue sound macroeconomic policies in order to succeed economically. Moreover, sustaining sound macroeconomic policies is neither easy nor free of cost.

Even though the IMF does not and should not provide development finance, it does aim to contribute to the development process within its mandate, by providing temporary financing in support of countries' efforts to strengthen their policies and their balance of payments. Rather than specializing *horizontally* by providing assistance to a select section of countries, the IMF specializes *vertically* by offering to help all countries that are trying to *improve* macroeconomic policymaking. This vertical specialization is underlying rationale for the IMF as a universal financial institution.

The dynamic nature of the world economy, through which countries develop at different rates and shift—or at least know that they might shift—between providing and using the financial resources of the IMF, has, in the past, helped to ensure a measure of balance in the institution's governance. Maintaining and strengthening that balance is a key challenge in preserving the future value of the IMF as a universal financial institution. As more and more countries advance to the point where they stop viewing themselves as potential borrowers, and as others borrow continuously for long periods and lose sight of the possibility of graduating from this dependence, the dangers of polarization of the membership and marginalization of the influence of borrowers become increasingly acute.

Today, all countries that have not already achieved all of their devgelopment objectives are urged to specify quantitative and time-bound goals, set out a realistic strategy and tactics for reaching those goals, and carry out the necessary institutional and policy reforms. Developed countries have a responsibility to ensure that the global economy is conducive to development and to provide the necessary financial and other support to developing countries. An internal agencies have a responsibility to work together and with national governments to provide additional support, advice, and coordination.

QUESTIONS

1. Discuss the organisational structure and function of International Monetary System.
2. Critically examine the terms and condition of financial facilities provided under various IMF's lending schemes.
3. Define the principle of "conditionality" as applied by the IMF. Is the IMF still applying this principle under the current international monetary system? Why do a large number of countries find it difficult to accept the IMF prescription as a cure for their ailments?
4. "Quotas define members' voting and borrowing rights with IMF." Discuss.
5. Discuss the response of the IMF/World Banks to the Third World's demands.

6. Discuss the evolution of the IMF/the World Bank. Critically examine the role and ideologies of the IDA, IFC and MIGA institution.
7. Discuss the cooperative efforts to strengthen the international monetary system.
8. Discuss the social dimensions of IMF-supported programmemes.
9. "The IMF is a financial co-operative, in some ways like a credit union." Do you agree?
10. Discuss the use of SDRs as an international reserve asset.
11. Critically examine the IMF's sources of supplementary financing.
12. Critically analyse othe IMF's approval of a new 28 billion loan for Greece as part of the overall financial package agreed by Athens and its partners in eurozone.
13. Critically examine the IMF financing facilities and policies to help members to correct balance of payments problems in a manner that promotes sustained growth.
14. Discuss the IMF's legal framework for gold. How has the IMF acquired its current gold holdings prior to the Second Amendment.
15. Does the world need a universal financial institution ?

3

EUROPEAN MONETARY SYSTEM

INTRODUCTION

Economic and Monetary Union (EMU) in Europe can be described as an unprecedented, imaginative and successful model for economic integration. The objectives initially pursued by European integration -ensuring peace and prosperity in what had historically been a conflict-ridden part of the world—have thus far been fulfilled. This is proof of how successful the European Union (EU) has been in adjusting to the manifold challenges of its more than 50-year history. Such is its attractiveness that there are now many non-EU countries eager to join EMU.

HISTORICAL OVERVIEW

A cursory glance at European history over the past few decades clearly shows that progress in European integration has been a lengthy and gradual process with many obstacles, detours and setbacks on the way. The first attempts at European integration were in the economic field with the setting up of the European Coal and Steel Community (ECSC) in 1951. This institution had already had a supranational High-Authority which was consistent with the desire for political integration to go beyond purely economic relations. This goal was even more evident in the Treaty on the Establishment of the European Defence Community (EDC), signed in 1952. At the same time, plans to establish a European Political Union were being drafted. However, these initiatives ended abruptly in the summer of 1954 when the French National Assembly failed to ratify the Treaty on EDC. This refusal reflected the underlying mood that it was not the right moment to move towards political union. However, this period of disappointment was soon forgotten, thanks to the strong desire of the leading political figures in Europe of the time to learn from the past by concentrating on economic integration in the future.

The process of economic and monetary integration in the EU parallels the history of the Union itself. When the EU was founded in 1957, the Member States concentrated on building a 'common market'. However, over time it became clear that closer economic and monetary co-operation was desirable for the internal market to develop and flourish further. But the goal of achieving the EMU including a single currency was not enshrined until the 1992 Maastricht Treaty (Treaty on European Union), which set out the ground rules for its introduction. These state what the objectives of EMU are, who is responsible for what, and what conditions Member States must meet in order to adopt the euro. These conditions are known as the 'convergence criteria' (or 'Maastricht criteria') and include low and stable inflation, exchange rate stability and sound public finances.

All EU Member States form part of Economic and Monetary Union (EMU), which can be described as an advanced stage of economic integration based on a single market. It involves close co-ordination of economic and fiscal policies and, for those countries fulfilling certain conditions, a single monetary policy and a single currency – the euro.

The euro is the single currency shared by (currently) 17 of the European Union's Member States, which together make up the euro area. The introduction of the euro in 1999 was a major step in European integration. It has also been one of its major successes: around 330 million EU citizens now use it as their currency and enjoy its benefits, which will spread even more widely as other EU countries adopt the euro.

When the euro was launched on 1 January 1999, it became the new official currency of 11 Member States, replacing the old national currencies – such as the Deutschmark and the French franc – in two stages. First the euro was introduced as an accounting currency for cash-less payments and accounting purposes, while the old currencies continued to be used for cash payments. Since 1 January 2002 the euro has been circulating in physical form, as banknotes and coins. The euro is not the currency of all EU Member States. Two countries (Denmark and the United Kingdom) have 'opt-out' clauses in the Treaty exempting them from participation, while the remainder (several of the more recently acceded EU members plus Sweden) have yet to meet the conditions for adopting the single currency. Table-1 shows the timing of the countries which have adopted the euro.

TABLE-1

1999	Belgium, Germany, Ireland, Spain, France, Italy, Luxembourg, the Netherlands, Austria, Portugal and Finland
2001	Greece
2002	Introduction of euro banknotes and coins
2007	Slovenia
2008	Cyprus, Malta
2009	Slovakia
2011	Estonia

ORGANISATION OF THE EUROPEAN SYSTEM OF CENTRAL BANKS (ESCB): AN INSTITUTIONAL FRAMEWORK FOR THE EURO

The European System of Central Banks (ESCB) is composed of the **European Central Bank (ECB)** and the national central banks (NCBs) of all EU Member States. The "**Eurosystem**" is the term used to refer to the ECB and the NCBs of the Member States which have adopted the euro. The primary objective of the Eurosystem is to maintain price stability by performing follwing basic tasks: (i) to define and implement the monetary policy of the euro area; (ii) to conduct foreign exchange operations; (iii) to hold and manage the official foreign reserves of the Member States; and (iv) to promote the smooth operation of payment systems. The Eurosystem contributes to the smooth conduct of policies pursued by the competent authorities relating to the prudential supervision of credit institutions and the stability of the financial system.

The **Eurosystem is independent**. When performing Eurosystem-related tasks, neither the ECB, nor an NCB, nor any member of their decision-making bodies may seek or take instructions from any external body. The Community institutions and bodies and the governments of the Member States may not seek to influence the members of the decision-making bodies of the ECB or of the NCBs in the performance of their tasks. The Statute of the ESCB makes provision for the following measures to ensure security of tenure for NCB governors and members of the Executive Board: (i) a minimum renewable term of office for governors of five years; (ii) a minimum non-renewable term of office for members of the Executive Board of eight years (it should be noted that a system of staggered appointments was used for the first Executive Board for members other than the President in order to ensure continuity); and (iii) removal from office is only possible in the event of incapacity or serious misconduct; in this respect the Court of Justice of the European Communities is competent to settle any disputes.

EURO: A SUCCESS STORY TILL THE FINANCIAL CRISIS

The Euro, the promise of a single and stable currency for Europe – from its inception – has been both a political and economic project. With the establishment of the ECB fifteen years ago and the creation of the euro on 1 January 1999 monetary policy was centralised and safeguarding the euro's stability was delegated to a strong and independent central bank. The ECB has delivered on its primary objective of price stability and will continue to do so. By contrast, responsibilities for fiscal policy, economic policies and supervision remained located at national level, while being subject to common rules and procedures. In the end this arrangement has proved insufficient in preventing the build-up of financial and economic imbalances in the euro area, associated with divergence in competitiveness as well as unsustainable trends in public and private debt and associated banking crises.

Before the euro was created, there was an academic debate turning on the theory of optimal currency areas, which questioned whether a single interest rate and, therefore, *a* single monetary policy could possibly be appropriate for such diverse countries. Ten years after the birth of the euro those who joined EMU, and many of those who did not, acknowledge the enormous advantages of being inside the monetary union. Any assessment of the first ten years of the euro should consider what the objectives were at the start of Monetary Union. Some of the **objectives** of the euro and the expectations it gave rise to discussed below:

The first, main objective of the euro was to create an area of monetary stability in Europe. This has been achieved. The average inflation rate between 1999 and 2008 was 2.2%, about 1 percentage point less than in the 1990s. It was also lower than the best performing countries, like Germany, before the euro. Monetary stability was reflected also in the low level of interest rates, which was also an improvement compared with the previous decade. This suggests that monetary stability was well entrenched in expectations.

A second objective was to ensure that this monetary stability was not attained at the expense of economic growth and stability. This too had been achieved. The GDP growth rate of the euro area over the first decade has been similar, by and large, to that of the previous decade, both in absolute and in per capita terms. Unemployment had been lower on average and employment growth stronger. All this had been achieved in spite of the more rigorous budgetary policies of the Member States, at least compared with the previous decade. It may be argued that other countries, in particular EU countries which do not have the euro, have performed even better than the euro area. The UK had had a higher average inflation rate than the euro area but also a higher growth rate; Sweden had a comparable inflation rate and higher growth. But then one has to compare like with like. In the euro area there were countries of a comparable size to the UK, like Spain, which had even stronger growth during these years, others though have grown less.Again,the euro area and the US are often compared, and these two monetary areas are of a size that can be compared. Over the last decade the US has recorded higher average GDP growth than the euro area only because of its higher population growth. GDP per capita has increased at exactly the same pace in the two areas. As for employment growth over the last ten years, it has been stronger in the euro area than in the US, and the rate of unemployment has decreased to a substantially greater extent. However it would be incorrect to claim that the strong employment results achieved over the last ten years are exclusively due to the euro. The improvement is more likely to stem from the structural reforms implemented in the Member States over the years.

A third objective of the euro was to move forward the integration of the financial markets. The results in this field are positive, but also uneven, depending on the market segment. Integration is more advanced in the areas close to the single monetary policy, but it also depends on the degree of integration of the underlying market infrastructure. The euro area money market, the segment closest to the single monetary policy, reached a stage of "near perfect" integration almost immediately after the introduction of the euro. The malfunctioning of recent months is common to all currencies. On the other hand, short-term debt securities (i.e. commercial paper and certificates of deposit) have remained much more fragmented. Financial integration has been fastest in the government bond market, where yields have converged and are increasingly driven by common factors, although local factors and perceived differences in credit risk continue to play a role. Likewise, the corporate bond segment is also more integrated as the various markets have merged into a single, yet diversified euro market. As a result, country-specific factors have become less important in determining corporate bond prices and spreads. Cross- border holdings of long-term debt securities of monetary financial institutions grew from about 15% in 1999 to nearly 40% in 2007. Integration in the equity markets is less advanced but shows signs of improvement. Between 1997 and 2006, euro area investors doubled their holdings of equity issued in other euro area countries to 29% of their total portfolio of euro area equity assets.

The retail banking segment has remained more fragmented. In particular, the euro area cross-country dispersion of bank interest rates, especially of interest rates on consumer loans, has remained relatively high. This reflects different conditions in national economies (e.g. credit and interest rate risk, size of firms, industrial structure and degree of capital market development), institutional factors (e.g. taxation, regulation, supervision and consumer protection) and financial structures (e.g. degree of bank/ capital market financing and competitiveness). It was probably overoptimistic to expect a faster convergence in this segment.

The creation of the euro also gave rise to expectations of a broad based convergence of underlying economic developments. These expectations were quite varied, in fact. Some people expected greater divergence as a consequence of specialisation. Others expected greater convergence. The result is mixed. Some convergence has been observed, in particular in terms of business cycle and dispersion across countries, which is comparable with that among the US states. The degree of business cycle synchronisation has remained at the same levels reached in the second half of the 1990s. On the other hand, some underlying variables have diverged, in particular cost and price competitiveness, leading to an accumulation of payments imbalances within the euro area. Some countries have accumulated large current account deficits, while others have growing surpluses. It can be argued that imbalances do not matter in a monetary union, because they are automatically financed. But such imbalances might make countries more vulnerable to external shocks and their financing might become more difficult in the midst of a financial crisis, even within a monetary union.

Finally,the euro has contributed to the completion of the single European market. The advantages of the single market could be better exploited by the common currency. Trade and capital ties between euro countries have grown. In this context, few examples are listed below:

a. The cross-border trade in goods and services in the euro area has increased by about 10 percentage points in relation to GDP since the introduction of the single currency. This can be partly attributed to the euro. Trade between individual euro countries now accounts for about half of their total exports and imports. At the same time, extra euro area trade developed very dynamically as well. Increasing trade integration within the monetary union did not come at the expense of trade with third countries. Hence, there is no "fortress Europe".
b. The euro has promoted competition, price transparency and the convergence of prices, and has lowered transaction costs and eliminated exchange rate risk.
c. The euro has boosted direct investment within the euro area. Mergers between companies in the euro area have risen noticeably.
d. The euro has also led to a marked increase in cross-border security investments within the euro area. This is only one example of the contribution made by the single currency to the integration of the financial markets in Europe. It's not over yet. The ECB and the Eurosystem strongly support a further integration of Europe's financial markets.

These developments show that the euro is an important catalyst for the completion of the single European market. The logic of "one market, one currency" was a substantial impetus for monetary integration in Europe. It has proved to be correct.

THE ROLE OF THE EURO AMID THE CURRENT FINANCIAL MARKET TURBULENCE

The global environment has completely changed in last few years. It is marked by an intensification and broadening of the global financial market turbulence and a sharp downturn in the world economy. The tensions have increasingly spilled over from the financial sector to the real economy. Their negative effects can be felt worldwide. Since the end of 2008 virtually all economies - both of the industrialised countries and the emerging markets - have been moving in the same direction. This considerably contributes to the scale of the present downturn.

THE ORIGINS OF THE CRISIS IN THE EURO AREA

In the euro area, the extraordinary success of the single currency concealed for years the risks that were building up. The governments of the Member States considered themselves free from previous constraints: with the exception of Germany and a few other countries, they delayed structural reforms that could have redressed the competitiveness of obsolete economic structures to meet the challenges of relentless globalisation; they undermined the limits introduced in the Stability and Growth Pact, jeopardising their own credibility as partners in a Monetary Union.

In the years preceding the crisis, this Union began to divide countries with positive trade balances and sound budgets from those with growing budget deficits and external deficits financed by private credit flows increasingly sourced from the first group of countries and not used for investments to increase competitiveness, but rather to finance unproductive spending, or property bubbles. No one ever imagined that the Monetary Union could become a union divided between permanent creditors and permanent debtors, where the former would perpetually lend money and credibility to the latter.

A profound change in the governance of the Union became necessary, with new rules whereby the solidarity clamoured for had as its counterpart the transfer of national powers. But this too was delayed and its urgency was downplayed in the face of the requirements of a purported national sovereignty which was in reality weakened by globalisation and growing levels of public debt.

The global financial crisis, which swiftly and dramatically increased market perceptions of risk, rudely awakened all the actors from this long, complacent amnesia. The external deficits, budget deficits and levels of public debt of the countries in the second group fast became unsustainable once they were no longer financed externally and in particular by the rest of the Union, the inadequate governance of which was then laid bare.

The Crisis and the ECB's Monetary Policy

The epicentre of the crisis in the initial phase was liquidity, an economic measure that had been neglected by the theory for many years since a lack thereof seemed so unlikely. The day after Lehman Brothers collapsed, the money markets stopped functioning. The liquidity required by banks to refinance their maturing assets suddenly became extremely scarce.

Generally speaking, banks borrow at short-term or very short-term from savers with a strong preference for the immediate availability of funds, or for "liquidity". If savers suddenly refuse to roll over their deposits with the banks, the banks then attempt to discontinue the credit that they supply to the economy. If this is not possible owing to long maturities, banks seek to liquidate first of all those assets in their portfolio that are traded on the market at known and verifiable exchange prices, in an effort to avoid insolvency. But a sudden financial retreat by many financial institutions simultaneously cannot occur without generalised financial suffering, and without banks incurring substantial capital losses.

Asset prices fall rapidly and bank capital declines. The interbank markets dry up. The economy loses an indispensable mechanism for generating income and allocating resources, namely the intermediation of savings.

In a second phase beginning in 2011, the lack of credit to the more vulnerable sovereign issuers became the centre point of the crisis. The euro area governments responded with actions that, while individually effective, revealed the political unsustainability of a Union in which the countries that pay and the countries that receive are always the same. Sovereign debt in the euro area is no longer risk-free: it depends on the sovereign and the quality of its policies. This process, beneficial in and of itself, revolutionised the risk structure on which the functioning of the European financial markets was based for so many years. In addition, without a single Union government and economic policy, it led to an abnormal increase in risk premia, which reached systemic proportions. Premia were no longer based on the creditworthiness of borrowers, which was admittedly shaky for reasons already mentioned, but rather could only be explained by the manifestation of expectations regarding the end of the euro.

Risk Premia and Non-standard Measures

But what are risk premia? The compensation required on a long-term financial contract must be at least equal to what could be obtained with a short-term contract that is continuously renewed until the end of the term. Long-term investors require a return that, at the very least, establishes financial equivalence between the two strategies. But, in general, equivalence is not enough. Creditors expect additional compensation for the risks they take on relating to not being paid back promptly. These risks are varied and the markets attach a price – or risk premium – to each one. The pure risk relating to postponing the availability of capital for a period of time is compensated by a term risk premium. The risk that a creditor is forced to liquidate a long-term financial investment before maturity in difficult market circumstances is compensated by a liquidity risk premium. Finally, the risk that the borrower does not meet his/her repayment obligations at the end of the contractually-agreed term is compensated by a credit risk premium.

In a period of deep financial crisis, the increase in all risk premia is, out of proportion because market participants are no longer willing or able to bear them. The non-standard measures adopted by the central banks in the larger countries in the five years since the start of the financial crisis can be identified according to the type of risk premia they were intended to tackle.

For example, the large-scale purchasing of assets, or quantitative easing, carried out by the Federal Reserve System affects the term risk premium. The main aim of quantitative easing is to reabsorb the quantity of term risk held in the economy as a whole and thereby compress its price – the corresponding risk premium.

The ECB initially adopted non-standard measures primarily aimed at cutting the financial premium linked to liquidity risk. At the dawn of the crisis, shortly after the collapse of Lehman Brothers in 2008, the liquidity risk in the interbank market shook to its foundations the very structure of the payment system. This catastrophic risk led to an exceptional reassessment of the liquidity risk premium on credit between transactors. In this context, the ECB took the place of the interbank market, which had cut off its supply of short-term and very short-term credit to banks. The ECB subsequently changed its own instrument for providing banks with liquidity, adopting a system whereby it supplied unlimited credit at a fixed interest rate – known as the fixed rate full allotment policy. In this way, the ECB allowed banks to refinance their assets using its own credit, rather than through asset fire sales in the market. A situation in which sound and solvent banks became insolvent was thus avoided.

In order to reassure banks that access to central bank liquidity would indeed be extended in line with their refinancing needs in the medium term, ECB extended the maturity of credit lending from the standard three months pre-crisis, to six months after the collapse of Lehman Brothers, to one year by mid-2009 and, finally, to three years at the end of 2011.

From the second half of 2011, the emergence of a new source of stress, which has been defined as the risk of "redenomination", resulting from the potential exit of a country from the euro or even from the potential collapse of the single currency was witnessed. A particular form of credit risk premium was associated with these possibilities, which was unrelated to the assessment of a borrower's solvency but which, in fact, came about owing to unfounded concerns regarding a systemic breakdown in the euro area. The ECB therefore launched the OMTs (Outright Monetary Transactions), a monetary policy instrument aimed at eliminating the financial risk premium caused by this specific systemic risk.

OMTs allow the ECB to buy sovereign bonds with a remaining maturity of up to three years in the secondary market, where necessary in order to remove the risk of "redenomination" (i.e. the risk related to concerns about the end of the euro) from the financial markets. The bond-issuing governments which request the activation of OMTs agree, in conjunction with the European authorities and, if possible, with the International Monetary Fund, on a recovery programme to address macroeconomic and structural weaknesses. This is a necessary, but not sufficient, condition as the ECB has full discretion to decide on the start, continuation or suspension of OMTs. Furthermore, the excess liquidity created by these purchases will be reabsorbed by the ECB.

The conditionality associated with the programme to which governments and the European authorities agree is a crucial element in being able to preserve monetary policy independence. It is important in providing the ECB with adequate assurance that interventions supporting sovereign debt bond prices do not mutate into financial subsidies for unsustainable national policies in the medium term.

By way of drawing a parallel between OMTs and ECB standard liquidity operations: as the credit provided to banking counterparties cannot be, and must not be, interpreted as an injection of capital into failing banks; in the same vein, under OMTs, in compressing the premium for the risk of "redenomination", the ECB cannot and does not intend to provide financial support to governments which reinstate solvency conditions which have not already been approved ex ante. In both cases, the ECB's non-standard measures were triggered by the need to restore the functioning of monetary policy transmission channels, first by reducing liquidity premia and then by reducing the redenomination risk premium.

Diverging Financing Conditions in the Euro Area

Throughout the two phases of the crisis – the banking crisis and the sovereign debt crisis – approach to liquidity provision was elastic, with adjustments made in response to demand for support from banks more severely affected by market pressures. At first, this demand was widespread across large parts of the euro area. In 2008 and 2009, those banks more exposed to sectors and activities under stress were ostracised by the market, no matter where they were based. Then, in the second phase of the crisis, the obstacles to liquidity provision became linked to territory. The banking sector and financial market in the euro area gradually fragmented along national borders. These borders separate banking sectors which, irrespective of the intrinsic quality of their intermediaries, are considered robust, because the country in which they are based is able to cope with a banking crisis, from those considered to be fragile, where the markets consider this capacity to be lacking. These borders thus separate countries that are competitive and have sound balance sheets from those characterised by fragile balance sheets and a lack of capacity for growth.

The measures decided on by the ECB (fixed rate full allotment, LTROs, OMTs, assessment and quality of collateral, guidance on the duration of fixed rate full allotment) helped to overcome, to a large extent, this fragmentation that characterised the funding of the banking system until mid-2012. The dispersion in the growth rate of bank deposits has now returned to 2007 levels.

Progress on the lending front has been much slower. In the first group of countries, there has been normal or accommodative financing conditions for firms and households. In the second group, a persistent tightening of credit, possibly decreasing in intensity in some countries has been seen with retail bank loan rates that are much higher than those applied by banks located in the first group of countries and more stringent collateral requirements for loans.

Access to finance of small and medium enterprises (SMEs) in the euro area"provides a clear picture of the difficulties this sector, so crucial for the euro area economy, finds itself in. Among the principal causes for concern cited by the SMEs interviewed, access to credit was second only to the difficulties encountered in finding customers for their products. The obstacles to obtaining credit (linked to the refusal to grant credit) persist, and represent one of the main factors of heterogeneity between countries in the euro area, though they are not confined to those countries under stress. In fact, in addition to SMEs in Greece, Ireland and Spain, a large number of SMEs operating in The Netherlands are encountering significant obstacles (around

45% of the firms surveyed). These figures reflect the considerable heterogeneity in borrowing conditions, as also shown by the most recent bank lending survey.

This fragmentation is all the more troublesome in an economy such as that of the euro area, in which financial intermediation is bank-based for at least three-quarters of firms' financing. And it penalises all the more those enterprises, often of a small or medium size, which depend more heavily on the banking system. This is particularly serious considering that this sector employs around two-thirds of workers in the euro area.

Banks are not lending for a number of reasons: *lack of funding, investment alternatives, lack of capital, risk aversion.* The ECB has done a great deal on the first two fronts, providing liquidity and reducing the redenomination risk premium on government bonds. However, it cannot subsidise governments by buying their bonds, and it cannot subsidise bank shareholders by removing the need for them to strengthen their balance sheets by means of necessary recapitalisation measures. ECB can do little directly to reduce the risk aversion which is holding back bank lending. In other financial systems, a large share of credit is transmitted to the economy via capital markets; financial assets are traded on the basis of known, verifiable prices and are often subject to ratings. A central bank that wished to try to reduce the risk premia on such assets would not face great operational obstacles. In the euro area, the capital market is much smaller, and a central bank that wished to intervene would have to purchase from the banking system the loans the latter had made to the economy, for which there is only a very limited market. This would be a very complex undertaking, even without taking into account the institutional context which would necessarily involve intervention in 17 countries.

But the ECB has taken a number of measures on this front too. Banks have for some time been able to use credit claims as collateral when obtaining funding from the ECB. And one should not underestimate the effectiveness of traditional monetary policy when general conditions change. The Governing Council of the ECB cut interest rates macroeconomic weakness is now also affecting parts of the euro area in which the transmission of monetary policy had never been an issue, and also because some signs that fragmentation is receding with regard to lending in some of the euro area countries experiencing stress are observed. In this regard, national measures can also be effective, as already put into practice in some countries, with the involvement of governments, public banks and development agencies. The ECB has launched initiatives with the EIB and the European Commission with the aim of reducing the fragmentation of lending in the euro area. Extraordinary progress has been made on this front by the European Council in bringing together the national supervisory systems in a single European mechanism – the management of which has been assigned to the ECB – and in creating a European mechanism for the resolution of banks. These initiatives will go the furthest in breaking the link between banks and sovereign debt which is behind the current fragmentation. However, the growth is currently weaker in some countries than in others, and not just because credit is scarce. It was weaker even before the crisis, notwithstanding often turbulent growth in public spending, because structural weaknesses were not tackled. In the wake of the crisis, the burden of this failure is now being felt by all members

Structural Reforms for Growth and More Solidarity in Society

The reforms aim to untie the knots that curb competitiveness and suffocate growth. Effective promotion and safeguarding of competition; an adequate degree of flexibility in the labour market that is properly distributed across the generations; the cutting of government red tape that is an obstacle to growth; human capital that is equipped to face the challenges posed by global competition; and a better environment – these are all fronts on which, despite recent progress, much remains to be done, albeit to varying degrees across individual countries.

Fiscal policies must follow a sustainable path, separate and distinct from cyclical fluctuations. Without this prerequisite, lasting growth is not possible. Particularly for countries with structurally high levels of public debt, rather than temporarily high levels as a result of the current crisis, this means not slipping back from the goals already achieved. It is important to note that in an institutional context in which the solvency of sovereign states is no longer an established fact and the governance of the Union is still incomplete, when a country's public finances lack credibility its banks are quickly cut off from the rest of the euro financial market in the absence of private sector credit in that country: this is what being now observed. However, to mitigate the inevitable recessionary effects of fiscal consolidation, the composition of such measures must favour the reduction of current public spending and of taxes, particularly in a context such as in Europe where taxation is already high by international standards.

Output growth was essential for the success of the European social model. The extraordinary economic growth during the so-called "Golden Age" – namely the thirty years that followed the Second World War – allowed a significant improvement in the material wealth of a large portion of the European population. At the same time, this wealth strengthened the growth process. At that time the foundations were laid in Europe for modern welfare systems aimed at protecting individuals against the risk that unemployment, illness or old age could lead to a deterioration in their living standards. It is in part thanks to these instruments that the financial crisis and the recession have not had the same devastating social effects as the Great Depression.

Many years ago Rudi Dornbusch said, exaggerating rather, that Europeans were so rich they could afford to pay everybody for not working. This is no longer the case. In some European countries unemployment has reached levels that damage people's faith in prospects for a decent life and which risk giving rise to extreme and destructive forms of protest. Therefore, today with the changes that demographic dynamics and the new environment of global competition demand, initiative are required to reduce youth unemployment, increase consumption and preserve the very essence of welfare.

THE ECB'S RELATIONS WITH INTERNATIONAL ORGANISATIONS AND FORA

The establishment of the ECB made it necessary to devise arrangements that permit its involvement in international co-operation, both from an institutional and from a policy perspective. Devising such arrangements has been and remains a unique task for three main reasons. *First*, the existing array of international organisations and fora was designed to promote co- operation among sovereign states that have full competence for the conduct of their economic, monetary and financial policies. The increase in membership of international organisations and fora during the post-war period could easily be accommodated within the prevailing institutional settings. By contrast, the decision by the euro area countries to transfer their monetary sovereignty to the ECB, as a supranational institution, posed some highly novel questions in the present institutional framework for international relations. *Second,* individual euro area countries remain responsible for the economic policies other than monetary and exchange rate policies, even though co-ordination mechanisms have been strengthened at the European Community level (e.g. in the areas of fiscal and structural policy). This means that the involvement of the ECB, the European Community and individual EU Member States in the process of international co-operation varies depending on the mandates of the relevant international organisations and fora. *Third,* not only the ECB, but also the other components of the Eurosystem, namely national central banks (NCBs) take part to varying degrees international organisations and fora, depending on the participation in the latter of their respective countries. Therefore, achieving a consistent representation of the Eurosystem presented unique challenges.

ECB AND THE INTERNATIONAL MONETARY FUND

The Articles of Agreement of the International Monetary Fund entrust it with the task of promoting, inter alia, international monetary co-operation, exchange rate stability, international trade and economic growth. The standing invitation to the ECB to attend IMF Executive Board meetings as an observer relates to the following agenda items: i) Article IV consultations on the monetary and exchange rate policies of the euro area; ii) Article IV consultations with individual euro area Member States; iii) the role of the euro in the international monetary system; and, iv) multilateral surveillance, i.e. biannual discussion of the World Economic Outlook and the International Capital Markets Report and regular discussions on world economic and market developments.

In all these discussions of the IMF Executive Board, representatives of the euro area member countries respect the allocation of competences provided for by the Treaty. In practical terms this means, first, that insofar as the monetary policy of the euro area is concerned the ECB observer presents the policy positions of the European Community, and, second, that with regard to exchange rate matters, the Executive Director representing the Eurogroup Presidency and the ECB observer both present the Community position, reflecting the regular exchange of views which takes place at the euro area level, e.g. at meetings of the Eurogroup.

Apart from the standing invitation, the ECB observer may be invited to attend on an ad hoc basis for agenda items which both the ECB and the IMF consider to be of mutual interest for the performance of their respective mandates. It has now become common practice for the ECB observer to be invited to attend Article IV discussions concerning EU Member States which have not yet adopted the euro, given that the ECB is involved in monetary policy co-ordination procedures with the NCBs of these Member States. Another example of ad hoc participation was the last quinquennial review by the IMF Executive Board of the valuation of the Special Drawing Rights (SDRs), which resulted in a change from a country-based to a currency-based approach in order to take fully into account the introduction of the euro.

The ECB is also involved in certain IMF initiatives to strengthen the international financial architecture whenever these concern the areas of competence of the ECB. This was the case for the Code on Good Practices on Transparency in Monetary and Financial Policies. Similarly, the ECB is involved in the current process at the IMF of developing guidelines on the management of foreign exchange reserves. These guidelines will also be aimed at reducing the vulnerability of emerging market countries to financial crises.

The ECB has developed working relationships with the IMF in other areas. In particular, the ECB actively participates in the application and development of international statistical standards, such as the IMF's Balance of Payments Manual (5th edition), within the framework of the System of National Accounts 1993. Working relationships have also been developed in the framework of the Special Data Dissemination Standard (SDDS), which was established in 1996 to ensure the provision of timely, reliable, and comprehensive data by member countries to the public and to the IMF for surveillance purposes.

ECB AND THE ORGANISATION FOR ECONOMIC CO-OPERATION AND DEVELOPMENT (OECD)

The OECD, an intergovernmental organisation which currently comprises 29 countries, provides a forum for its members to consult each other, compare experiences and co-operate in order to achieve the highest possible sustainable growth and to improve economic and social well-being in line with the principles of a market economy. In pursuing these tasks, the OECD covers all areas of public policy, including monetary and other economic policies. The ECB takes part in any OECD activities which concern the tasks of the Eurosystem.

The OECD Committees and Working Parties in which the ECB participates include the following: i) Economic and Development Review Committee; ii) Economic Policy Committee and its working parties; and, iii) Financial Markets Committee.

The Economic and Development Review Committee (EDRC), established in 1961, the economic situation and policies of each OECD member country. Such reviews lead to the publication, under the direct responsibility of the EDRC, of economic surveys which include a number of policy recommendations. Member countries may then take these policy recommendations into account on the basis of the principle of self-assessment. The Economic Policy Committee (EPC) focuses on the global economic situation, with particular emphasis on the implications of developments in three major OECD regions (the United States, the euro area and Japan). By examining a wide range of issues related both to economic outlooks and to policy requirements in the OECD area, the EPC provides OECD members with a comprehensive assessment. Finally, the ECB's involvement in OECD activities also includes participation in the Financial Markets Committee (FMC) which examines structural developments in OECD financial markets.

ECB AND THE BANK FOR INTERNATIONAL SETTLEMENTS (BIS)

A major objective of the BIS is to promote the co-operation of central banks, as laid down in Article 3 of the Statute of the BIS. The ECB takes part in all BIS-based co-operaiion activities, including associated statistical work. Four permanent committees in which the ECB takes part are of particular relevance: the Basel Committee on Banking Supervision; the Committee on Payment and Settlement Systems (CPSS); the Committee on the Global Financial System (CGFS); and the Gold Committee.

The Basel Committee on Banking Supervision (BCBS) countries is an internationally recognised standard setter for banking regulation, supervision and best practices. Given the importance of the work carried out by the BCBS for the activities of the ECB and the Eurosysiem in the field of prudential supervision and financial stability, the ECB participates in some of the BCBS Working Groups, such as the Electronic Banking Group, the Capital Group, the Research Task Force and the Risk Management Group. The last three of these are currently involved in the preparation of the new capital framework. The CPSS is at the forefront of efforts to promote efficient and robust payment and settlement arrangements. This is to be achieved by fostering an awareness of risks, by developing minimum standards or best practices and by providing a forum for co-operation among central banks in the field of oversight. Co-operation with other groups including the International Organisation of Securities Commissions (IOSCO) and other G 10 committees takes place regularly in order to deal with issues of common concern. The ECB is also a member of the CGFS designed to identify and assess potential sources of stress in the global financial environment, to understand the functioning of financial markets and to promote their efficiency and stability. The CGFS also contributes to the transparency of financial markets by designing, producing and publishing financial statistics with the support of the BIS.

Finally, the ECB is a member of the Gold and Foreign Exchange Committee (GFEC), a group of senior central bank representatives which regularly reviews developments in financial markets, focusing in particular on foreign exchange markets. the store-of-value role. In the last case, diversification arguments can be invoked in the name of the individual investor if not the system as a whole.

By contrast, the second school of thought is of the view that the euro's role would match that of the dollar a decade after monetary union. This is based on the relative size of the euro area economy and its importance in global trade, as well as a view that EMU would spur the growth of euro area financial markets. It has also been argued that the euro would benefit from monetary stability, grounded on the Maastricht treaty. However, a significant role for the euro would require a protracted current account deficit of the euro area. The euro would eventually have a role comparable to that of the dollar, since an international investor should diversify to hedge their exposure to macroeconomic risks, resulting in a "multiplicity" of reserve currencies. The euro will challenge the dollar as the world's leading international reserve currency on the strength of the relative size of the economy and financial markets. The euro may surpass the dollar as the leading international reserve currency by 2020, if the United Kingdom and other non-euro area EU members join EMU by 2020, or the recent depreciation trend of the dollar persists into the future.

QUESTIONS

1. Discuss the organisation of the European System of Central Banks (ESCB) and the basic tasks carried out by the Eurosystem.
2. Discuss the institutional setting and policy content of the European Central Bank's international relations.
3. Critically examine the factors suggesting that the euro would become a leading international currency.
4. Discuss the use of euro in international banking. Is there any significant change in the pattern of net cash flows through the banking system?
5. Critically examine the role of European Union, the European Central Bank and the Eurosystem in the world economy.
6. By making use of the insight gained from examining the history of the European integration and by observing the behavioural and institution patterns established over the past decades, identify the challenges ahead and assess the Europe's capacity to deal with these.
7. Critically examine the diverging financing conditions in the Euro Area.
8. Discuss the monetary policy strategy of the European Central Bank and the operational framework of the Eurosystem.
9. Critically examine the role of the Euro and the current financial market turbulence.
10. Discuss the functions of an international currency. Can euro assure the role of the parallel currency in countries which don't have a stable money?
11. "An important feature of the main determinants of a currency's international status is that they tend to change slowly, inducing inertia. Network externalities exacerbate this inertia and create strong path-dependence." Comment.
12. Discuss the ECB's relations with international organisations.
13. Critically examine the key systematic problems in its euro area.

4

THE GLOBAL LIQUIDITY

INTRODUCTION

Global liquidity, a buzzword in discussions about the international monetary system, reflects a broad, though often vague, perception that it is an important driver of capital flows, global asset price dynamics and inflation, and that international monetary arrangements – including exchange rate regimes, capital account policies and financial safety nets – have a major bearing on global liquidity.

It is used in a variety of ways. Sometimes it has been used to refer to the stance of monetary policy in major currency areas. Surges in global liquidity may be associated with strong asset price increases, rapidly rising credit growth and – in extreme cases – excessive risk-taking among investors. Shortages of global liquidity may lead to disruptions in the functioning of financial markets and –in extreme cases – depressed investor risk appetite, leading to malfunctioning markets. Thus, the global liquidity, both in times of abundance and shortage, has a range of implication for financial stability.

This view of global liquidity typically reflects the recognition that the availability of ample and low-cost funding in global financial markets can contribute to the build-up of financial system vulnerabilities in the form of leverage and large mismatches across currencies, maturities and countries.

The global economy is characterised by two largely unprecedented phenomena since the late 1990s. The first is the benign financial market environment, low long-term interest rates, low risk aversion, the hunt for yield, and the perceived abundance of global liquidity, all of which prevailed at least until the turmoil episode that his global financial markets during the summer of 2007. The second is the widening of external imbalances, in particular the increasing current account deficit in the United States and the corresponding pick-up in current account surpluses of emerging Asian economies. While widening external imbalances have been extensively studied in the literature, global liquidity has been more loosely defined, for example as the total stock of foreign exchange reserves or monetary aggregates in the major economies, and has received relatively limited coverage.

One challenge in assessing trends in global liquidity and widening imbalances is the identification of underlying structural drivers. Are global liquidity and imbalances policy-driven phenomena, and are they in particular related to the path of monetary policy in major economies? Are they driven by real economy shocks, such as increased savings in oil exporting and Asian economies? What is the role of financial market structures, in particular the incomplete nature of those markets in emerging economies?

The lack of a coherent conceptual framework hinders diagnosis of global liquidity conditions and the development and implementation of effective policy responses. For instance, a focus on the collapse of interbank markets during the recent crisis may lead to calls for an expansion of safety nets, but may miss the importance of appropriate measures to prevent the build-up of vulnerabilities because of ample liquidity. Similarly, an exclusive focus on monetary policy as a driver of global liquidity may miss the role of risk-taking incentives in the private sector and how these relate to economic policies. The chapter discusses elements of a conceptual framework for global liquidity, and highlights the analytical challenges involved in assessing the global liquidity, involving a broad set of indicators and measures. Building on this framework, the policy responses to global liquidity developments from a financial stability viewpoint have been discussed.

TERMS AND CONCEPTS

In general terms, liquidity is the ease with which an asset can be converted into a means of payment. One way in which conversion may occur is through the selling of the asset. The less such a sale moves the price of the asset, the greater is market liquidity. Borrowing, in turn, can be seen as an alternative way of converting assets into cash, either by pledging assets as collateral or by issuing unsecured claims against those assets. The less borrowing moves the price of funding, the greater is funding liquidity.

These basic considerations have two important implications for the concept of global liquidity. First, at the aggregate level, liquidity depends on the interaction of funding and market liquidity. For instance, in the run-up to the financial crisis, securitisations such as mortgage-backed securities were perceived as highly liquid. This, in turn, allowed banks and other financial instutions to use these securities as collateral in repo transactions or similar activities, which increased funding liquidity. Hence, global liquidity should be understood as the overall "ease of financing" in the international financial system.

Second, this overall "ease of financing" (or perceptions thereof) depends on the actions of both private investors and financial institutions as well as the public sector. The securitisation example illustrates how liquidity is being created through interactions among private market participants. In addition, central banks supply the means of payment in the form of base money. The terms and conditions on which they do so, in turn, affect funding and market liquidity in private markets. The distinction between liquidity created by private and public sector market participants, for its part, is key to understanding the sources of global liquidity and its dynamics.

PRIVATE LIQUIDITY

Private liquidity is created by private sector market participants, including international banks, institutional investors, non-bank financial institutions (including shadow banks) and so on. For instance, financial institutions provide funding liquidity by lending in the interbank market. Or money market mutual funds provide liquidity to corporations by buying commercial paper.

The availability of private liquidity is a key factor behind the build-up of exposures in the global financial system. Movements in private liquidity are transmitted internationally through the cross-border and/or cross-currency operations of bank and non-bank financial institutions. These effects can go both ways: domestic liquidity conditions can spill over to global markets and, conversely, global developments can amplify movements in domestic financial conditions and intensify domestic imbalances.

Private liquidity is *endogenous* to the conditions in the global financial system. It depends on the willingness of market participants to supply funding or trade in securities markets. For instance, the conditions under which banks can fund their own balance sheets depend, in turn, on the willingness of other private sector participants – such as money market funds or institutional investors – to provide funding or market liquidity. These funding conditions, in turn, determine the ability of banks to provide liquidity. This example illustrates that perceptions of counterparty risk or, more generally, the degree of confidence in the financial system are an important determinant of global private liquidity.

OFFICIAL LIQUIDITY

Official liquidity is funding provided by the public sector. The central bank supplies official liquidity in domestic currency in the form of reserve balances or central bank money, on terms and conditions that do not depend on the availability of funding in financial markets. Official liquidity is therefore *exogenous*.

Central banks create official liquidity in their domestic currency through regular monetary operations and, in periods of stress, through emergency liquidity assistance (ELA). Other public entities, including treasuries or state- owned commercial banks, can also provide liquidity. But their ability to do so depends in principle on the conditions under which they can fund themselves in private markets – unless they have access to central bank liquidity. Ultimately, official liquidity is therefore the funding that central banks provide.

The capacity of monetary authorities to supply official liquidity depends on domestic monetary policy frameworks and the international monetary system. The exchange rate regime or currency backing requirements may constrain the ability of national authorities to issue their domestic currency. At the international level, an external anchor – such as the quantity of official gold holdings under the gold standard – could impose an absolute limit on official liquidity supply. In a pure fiat money system, by contrast, central banks can technically create any amount of official liquidity. Ultimately, however, their ability to do so will depend on the level of confidence in the value of their currencies.

Various instruments and mechanisms can provide domestic authorities and financial institutions with access to official liquidity in foreign currency. The first is by selling foreign exchange reserves. Second, swap lines between central banks and similar facilities provide direct access to central bank money. Such swap lines between the US and European monetary authorities were critically important during the recent financial crisis, particularly in the months following the collapse of Lehman Brothers . A third possibility are facilities offered by international financial institutions or regional financing arrangements, including IMF programmes or Special

Drawing Rights (SDR). Ultimately, all these instruments give the domestic financial system access to official liquidity created by a foreign central bank, though subject to different costs and conditions ("conversion costs"). This suggests that any measure of official liquidity would have to weigh different components of the liquidity concept in ways that reflect the different degrees to which they allow access to central bank liquidity in foreign currency ("conversion costs"), similar to the so-called Divisia monetary aggregates.

Since 2008, central banks in major advanced economies have massively expanded the provision of official liquidity. Their balance sheets have swollen as central banks have created liquidity in domestic currency on a large scale. The central bank balance sheets in major advanced economies as a percentage of GDP have doubled since 2007. At the same time, nominal policy rates have fallen to near-zero levels.

CONVERSION COSTS: THE CASE OF FOREIGN EXCHANGE RESERVES

Foreign exchange reserves are the traditional means for accessing official liquidity in foreign currency and are typically viewed as a core component of official liquidity. Indeed, foreign exchange reserves have been used to alleviate foreign currency funding pressures in domestic financial systems, for example in Korea and Brazil during the recent financial crisis. However, the degree of self-insurance afforded by such stocks of reserves depends on the size and source of the shock hitting the domestic financial system as well as the instruments and currencies the reserves are invested in. Hence, the use of foreign exchange reserves is subject to various forms of conversion cost.

First, there are costs at the level of the individual reserve holder. Only a small fraction of foreign exchange reserves is held in the form of deposits with central banks or as (term) deposits with private banks (about 5% in each case), whereas the bulk is invested in securities, mostly US Treasuries and government bonds of euro area sovereigns. Converting these foreign assets into funds that can be used to settle foreign currency claims involves costs that depend on market conditions. Such costs may be low in the case of a country-specific shock, when global interbank and securities markets remain liquid. But it may not be so easy to deploy reserves quickly in the event of a global liquidity shock, as drawdowns of such reserves by multiple countries at the same time could depress the prices of foreign reserve assets.

Second, deploying foreign exchange reserves may also involve more indirect costs in the form of higher country risk premia in financial markets and depreciation pressure on the domestic currency (which could result from lower reserve levels). This can aggravate the very foreign currency funding pressures that the use of foreign exchange reserves is supposed to alleviate. Indeed, concerns that only a fraction of the stock of foreign exchange reserves can be used without triggering adverse confidence effects have reinforced calls for alternative mechanisms for insuring against liquidity shortages.

Third, mobilising foreign exchange reserves may also impose costs on international financial markets and institutions by adversely affecting liquidity conditions at the global level. For instance, drawing down reserves that are deposited with commercial banks would reduce funding liquidity. This can have knock-on effects on the financial system more broadly – for instance, if the affected banks struggle to replace their corresponding foreign currency funding, as experienced during the Lehman crisis. Only foreign reserves held in the form of central bank money will tend to avoid such effects.

THE INTERACTION BETWEEN PRIVATE AND OFFICIAL LIQUIDITY

In a world with high international capital mobility and a well developed financial system, private sources of liquidity quantitatively dominate public ones. But the two can, and do, behave quite differently over time. Private liquidity is procyclical, driven by changes in a variety of factors, including growth rates, growth differentials, monetary policies, regulatory frameworks and, above all, investors' attitude towards risk. Furthermore, structural developments that help shape the way international banks operate, such as financial innovation and integration, also play a role. This multitude of factors and their interdependence underline the endogenous character of private liquidity.

Official and private liquidity interact in various ways. One way to think about this interaction is the traditional money multiplier concept: by determining the risk-free short-term interest rate and the amount of funds available to settle payments through the central bank, official liquidity is the basis for private liquidity creation. In times of crisis, however, private liquidity tends to evaporate and global liquidity collapses into its official component – or, to use the money multiplier analogy, the multiplier falls to zero. In those circumstances, global liquidity will crucially depend on individual banks' access to official sector funding. This is particularly relevant when banks' funding needs are in a foreign currency, constraining the ability of the domestic central bank to address liquidity shortages, as observed in late 2008.

But the interactions between private and public liquidity are arguably more complex than this conventional view suggests. For instance, private capital flows may lead to foreign exchange reserve accumulation (increasing official liquidity), and the reinvestment of these reserves in the liquid assets of other countries may help to further ease financial conditions (increasing private liquidity). There are signs, for example, that the channelling of large reserve holdings into government securities can contribute to global liquidity conditions through its effect on yield levels.

INDICATORS AND MEASURES OF GLOBAL LIQUIDITY

In spite of increased attention to global liquidity in recent years, a clear-cut definition is still missing. Liquidity is a multifaceted concept and, if anything, the common element in all of the definitions appears to be "ease of financing". From a global perspective, an essential distinction is made between central bank liquidity and liquidity created outside the public sector. Central bank liquidity can be considered as the amount of funds unconditionally available to settle claims through monetary authorities. Liquidity generated outside the public sector refers to liquidity provided by the financial and non-financial sectors, and is considered a key determinant of funding conditions globally.

Traditionally, global liquidity has been defined as the sum of narrow money created by central banks and international reserves within advanced economies. Such a monetary liquidity measure is, however, less suitable today owing to global financial integration, new financial innovations that have led to alternative channels of access to credit and the growing importance of emerging markets. On the former point, a broader definition of money – including "close substitutes" for money – helps to capture global liquidity. On the latter point, real broad money growth has been higher in emerging economies compared with advanced economies over the past decade. This suggests that traditional measures that only include advanced economies do not fully measure overall global liquidity. These measures also fail to take into account the increasing role of liquidity generated by the financial and non-financial sectors.

Not only is it difficult to arrive at a unanimous definition of the concept of global liquidity, but it is equally difficult to derive a quantitative threshold to identify an excess or a shortage of global liquidity. Nevertheless, a number of specific indicators of global liquidity are discussed below which help to address the shortcomings of the traditional measures and provide a picture of when liquidity may be abundant or scarce. Depending on the policy question at hand, these indicators can be divided into four broad categories. Each is assessed below. Given the difficulties in determining to what extent global liquidity is excessive or scarce, it is important to stress that any conclusion should be based on a broad set of indicators.

Short-Term Interest Rates and Global Liquidity Conditions

A first set of indicators which can provide a measure of global liquidity conditions relates to short-term interest rates in advanced and emerging market economies. Short-term interest rates, mostly determined by central banks, are a crucial determinant of households', banks' and non-financial firms' financing costs and thus is an essential element in understanding global liquidity conditions as a precondition to gauging financial stability risks from extreme liquidity conditions. Domestic short-term interest rates, through expectations about the future path of policy rates, also influence risk-free (nominal) yield curves. Interbank market rates and those for other financial assets, in turn, are set on the basis of these risk-free rates, adding risk premia for liquidity and counterparty risks that reflect market-specific characteristics (such as depth of markets or risk management practices) as well as risk appetite. The level of interest rates, in turn, affects the growth rate of credit and overall liquidity conditions throughout the economy.

An alternative means by which to demonstrate the role of central bank interest rates in determining global liquidity conditions would be to make use of Taylor rules. Taylor rules can show how central banks have historically adjusted their policy rates to changes in the macroeconomic environment (i.e. inflation and output). It should be noted that results will differ, depending on the way the Taylor rules are estimated (backward looking, forward looking, the inclusion of an interest smoothing component, how the output gap measure is calculated, etc.). Moreover, estimates are based on average central bank behaviour over the sample under consideration. Structural changes in the macro series, changes in central banks' objectives and market participants' behaviour are not fully taken into account. Keeping these caveats in mind, by aggregating the estimates for a large set of economies, Taylor rules can still help policy-makers to form a rough view about global liquidity conditions.

A simple rule of thumb says that liquidity is neither too high nor too low if policy rates are broadly in line with the policy rates implied by the Taylor rule. While subject to numerous caveats, not least that unconventional monetary policy measures are not taken into account, aggregated Taylor rules can nonetheless provide an illustrative cross-country quantitative benchmark for evaluating global liquidity.

Asset Price Valuation

Alternatively, global liquidity conditions can indirectly be measured by asset price valuation indicators. Misaligned asset prices may partly reflect excessive liquidity conditions with negative consequences for financial stability. For instance, excess liquidity and loose financing conditions may induce investors to take on too much risk, thereby compressing the risk premium on financial and real estate assets. As a result, asset prices may rise to levels elevated from their fundamentals, which in turn may lead to costly asset price booms and busts. Empirical research on global liquidity and asset prices has mostly focused on the impact on equity, commodity and house prices. The IMF has recently examined the linkages between global liquidity expansion, asset prices and capital inflows in emerging economies. It has been found that rising global liquidity is associated with rising equity returns and declining real interest rates in 34 "liquidity-receiving" economies.

A standard valuation metric for stock markets is the price/earnings (P/E) ratio. In general, the P/E ratio tends to display mean-reverting behaviour over time. The reversion back to its mean usually emanates from its price component and, to a lesser extent, reflects a correction of the earnings component. Thus, if the P/E ratio is hovering at levels much above its mean, this could indicate it has risen above the levels suggested by its "fundamentals". During 2011 P/E ratios in emerging markets have remained rather stable, broadly in line with their long-term averages, whereas P/E ratios in advanced economies have dropped to levels slightly below their long-term averages.

Uncertainty, Risk Appetite and Financial Market Liquidity Indicators

A third set of indicators to measure global liquidity relates to estimates of uncertainty, risk appetite and financial market liquidity indicators. For instance, the search for yield (or lack thereof) can have important implications for global financial stability through misallocations of financial and economic resources and the associated financial stability risks. Policy-makers should also view global liquidity in relation to market uncertainty and risk aversion. There is empirical evidence that during periods of ample liquidity, asset price volatility tends to be low. Abnormally low asset price volatility can have the effect that market participants take on too much risk in their portfolio decisions, which in turn can have adverse consequences for financial stability in the form of misallocations and costly asset price booms and busts.

The implied volatility derived from option prices on the US S&P 500 index (i.e. the VIX index) is an indicator of risk monitored by most policy-makers and financial market commentators. This measure is theoretically appealing as it measures the expected volatility in the eyes of investors. If expected volatility measures across major markets remain well below their average for a prolonged period, this can indicate that global liquidity is too ample.

Financial market liquidity can also be used to assess global liquidity conditions. For instance, substantial concerns over liquidity risk in September 2008 triggered looser global financing conditions, and a subsequent rise in global liquidity. Arbitrage would imply a zero spread in interbank term spreads at a three-month maturity, while a non-zero spread is indicative of tension in the interbank market. This indicator can provide policy-makers with insights into the degree of liquidity risk faced by the banking sector as a whole across major markets.

Developments in carry trades are also of interest in the context of global liquidity as carry trades are more likely to occur in an environment of favourable financing conditions and low financial market volatility, while they tend to retract in use during global liquidity shortages. Carry-trade opportunities mainly arise owing to differences in the monetary policy stance across regions. A carry trade consists of an unhedged bet where an investor borrows in low-yielding currencies and invests in high-yielding currencies. If the bilateral exchange rate between the two countries remains unchanged over the investment horizon, the investor makes a profit equal to the interest rate differentials.

No direct data on carry trades exist so policy-makers have to rely on indicators such as ex post returns from carry trade strategies, currency flows in the international banking system or net open positions of non-commercial traders in different currency futures. In addition, one ex ante approach is to compute a "carry trade attractiveness indicator". This is computed as the interest rate differential between a high-yielding currency and a low-yielding currency, divided by the exchange rate volatility between the two currencies. A "high" ratio between two currencies would imply, everything else held equal, a favourable carry trade environment. By averaging carry trade attractiveness indicators for a number of well-known bilateral funding and investment currency strategies, it is possible to gauge carry trade attractiveness on a global scale.

This global carry trade attractiveness indicator suggests less favourable conditions for carry trades since 2007/08 mainly owing to higher foreign exchange volatility. From a global liquidity perspective, the low attractiveness of carry trades possibly reflects less favourable funding conditions and global liquidity shortages.

All in all, financial market liquidity indicators have the common theme of being volatile and should thus be treated with utmost caution. Notwithstanding the obvious caveats, a close monitoring and analysis of a broad range of financial market indicators can be helpful if a policy-maker wishes to better understand the interaction between global liquidity conditions and the functioning of financial markets.

Capital Flows, International Reserves and Cross-Border Credit Growth

A fourth and last set of indicators to measure global liquidity relates to capital flows, international reserves and cross-border credit growth. The potential for sudden stops and reversals in such flows represents an important financial stability risk. Given that the quality of the data used to calculate these indicators can sometimes be questionable, a broad set of indicators should be monitored before any policy actions can be taken.

Over recent decades, emerging markets have become increasingly important for the world economy. Strong economic growth coupled with rising asset prices and relatively high credit growth means that these economies should also be closely monitored from a global liquidity perspective.

The combination of the increased importance of emerging markets and improved opportunities to seek finance abroad suggests that measures of cross-border credit should be closely monitored by policy-makers. In fact, the growth in international bank credit exhibits boom-and-bust cycles that correspond closely to episodes of financial distress. Moreover, periods of particularly strong growth in cross-border credit often coincide with episodes of elevated risk appetite and compressed risk premia.

Furthermore, developments in various measures of capital flows (net, gross and the composition of flows), stock prices, credit growth and foreign reserves in emerging markets are particularly important.

An environment of excessive global liquidity may be characterised by abnormally high capital inflows to emerging markets, stock prices surging to levels much above firms' earnings growth, credit growth rising much faster than nominal GDP growth and foreign reserves increasing to levels beyond what would satisfy the traditional motives for holding reserves.

Global liquidity and capital flows are closely connected. Push factors, such as accommodative monetary policy and quantitative easing strategies in advanced economies, may drive capital into emerging market assets. Apart from potentially being a reflection of excess liquidity, elevated capital inflows may have a number of adverse consequences for financial stability. *First,* strong inflows can place further upward pressure on assets in countries where valuations are already high, therefore leading to substantial deviations of prices from fundamental values. *Second,* strong net inflows can produce undesired real exchange rate appreciation, leading to overshooting and an undermining of the competitiveness of the economy. *Third,* an environment of high appetite for emerging market securities in combination with low interest rates in advanced economies increases the incentive for emerging markets to issue debt in foreign currency, especially in countries with exchange rate regimes that are not fully flexible. This could lead to excessive exposure to foreign exchange risk.

Foreign reserve accumulation in emerging markets warrants further discussion, given the substantial increase in reserve holdings in these economies, particularly since 2007. Foreign reserves are partially accumulated by these economies for precautionary purposes, as a liquidity buffer to self-insure against future crises. The build-up of reserves has been used in some cases as a tool for maintaining export competitiveness by controlling the pace of appreciation of the domestic currency.

The accumulation of reserves can contribute to global liquidity through its impact on global bond yield configurations, as flows of capital to emerging markets are channelled back to advanced economies, mainly *via* purchases of US Treasury bonds. As global liquidity in a broad sense can be seen as (and measured by) the "ease of financing", strong foreign demand for US Treasuries exerts a downward pressure on yields and thus has a marked impact on global liquidity.

Rule-of-thumb measures to assess a benchmark level of reserves include three months of import coverage, 20% of broad money, or 100% of short-term debt. Levels of reserves beyond these benchmarks provide an indication of excess reserves. Accumulation of reserves for non-precautionary purposes can affect global liquidity conditions by contributing to an artificially low yield environment. The level of reserve holdings in emerging markets has been in excess of all three rule-of-thumb benchmark levels since 2003.

The conceptual considerations above suggest that measures of global liquidity should capture the evolution of both private and official liquidity as well as the ease of financing in the global financial system. The former would call for indicators that track the quantity of liquidity in the system, while the latter would tend to emphasise measures of the availability of market and funding liquidity. Ideally, such measures should also provide early indications of financial system vulnerabilities.

CREDIT AGREEGATES AND THE EVOLUTION OF GLOBAL LIQUIDITY

Global credit aggregates allow an analysis of global liquidity.However,a potential problem in using credit aggregates as measures of global liquidity is that they do not focus on liquidity or financing conditions as such, but rather on one of the *outcomes* of these conditions. This may complicate interpretation, because credit aggregates may change irrespective of any developments in financing conditions.Several arguments speak in favour of using credit aggregates as a proxy for global liquidity.

First, private sector credit stands at the end of the financial intermediation chain and captures the interaction of market and funding liquidity. Credit measures also provide broad coverage of private liquidity sources, including banks and securities markets. Moreover, credit aggregates have been shown to behave as early warning indicators, especially when combined with measures such as asset prices. Cross-border positions, particularly those in interbank markets, will be important when the focus is on how changes in liquidity conditions are transmitted internationally and affect domestic financial stability in the target economies. This places a premium on measures that capture such interlinkages.

Second, international credit aggregates facilitate the analysis of global liquidity conditions from various vantage points. One such perspective suggests that, worldwide, bank credit continued to expand throughout the recent crisis .

A complementary, *"recipient economy"* perspective focuses on the evolution of borrowing by non-banks in individual economies. This perspective can, for instance, inform assessments of whether cross-border credit flows are associated with a build-up of vulnerabilities in the recipient country's financial system. Differences in credit growth across countries and regions are considerable . While total bank credit to non-banks in the United States and the euro area has levelled off since the start of the crisis, Asia- Pacific has seen a particularly strong rebound in cross-border credit. This is in line with the observation that cross-border and foreign currency credit tend to grow especially strongly within countries that are experiencing a domestic credit boom – such as China.

This could be because banks that lend cross-border may have less information than local lenders on the quality of borrowers. Therefore, these banks may have been over-optimistic about the strength of borrowers in foreign markets in the upswing, to then change their assessment in the downswing. Another possibility is that internationally active banks may regard foreign markets as less important to their business than is the case for domestic banks, which might affect their willingness to expand or contract their international activities in a procyclical fashion. It is also possible that internationally active banks faced bigger negative shocks in their home markets and that these banks relied more on wholesale funding than domestic banks.

Yet another perspective is that of the credit originator. Here, it is important to distinguish the economy that issues the currency – the *"currency of denomination"* perspective – from the intermediaries that extend credit, possibly in foreign currency – the *"lender"* perspective.

The *"currency of denomination"* perspective considers global credit provided in a particular currency, and may help to answer the question to what extent funding conditions in one particular currency contribute to global liquidity. Most international credit is denominated in US dollars, euros, yen, sterling and Swiss francs.

The *lender perspective* sheds light on the evolution of the international credit and funding exposures of banks (and other intermediaries). Growth in funding exposures and the currency and/or maturity mismatches of banks are an indication of financial vulnerability and may force a contraction of global liquidity if bank balance sheets come under stress. Current deleveraging pressures in the European banking sector should be seen in this light.

ASSESSING THE EASE OF FINANCING BY COMBINING QUANTITY AND PRICE-BASED INDICATORS

The combination of price and quantity measures supports assessments of the ease of financing. Price-based indicators provide information about liquidity supply conditions in different markets, while quantity-based indicators capture how far such conditions translate into changes in exposures and risks. Key indicators in this regard are proxies of risk appetite, which is a major driver of the willingness of private investors to provide funding and, therefore, of private liquidity (Table 1).

TABLE 1

SELECTED COMPLEMENTARY INDICATORS

Quantities	*Prices*		
Monetary liquidity	Base money and broader monetary aggregates		
Foreign exchange reserves	Policy and money market interest rates	Monetary conditions indices	
Funding liquidity	Bank liquidity ratios	Maturity mismatch measuresCP market volumes	Libor-OIS spreads FX swap basis Bond-CDS basisSurveys of funding conditions
Market liquidity	Transaction volumes	Bid-ask spreads on selected global assetsQualitative fund manager surveys	
Risk-taking and valuation	Bank leverage ratios	VIX index and other risk appetite measures	Sharpe and carry-to-risk ratios Asset prices and spreads Price/earnings ratios

OPEN TECHNICAL AND ANALYTICAL ISSUES

Assessment of global liquidity faces a number of challenges. The first is aggregation. The appropriate credit aggregate may depend on the analytical question at hand. For example, when assessing financial exposures of households and corporates, information on the currency composition of creditis of particular importance.

In contrast, when assessing the role of different intermediation channels in the provision of liquidity, distinguishing between bank and non-bank providers of credit is essential. In France, Germany, the United Kingdom and the United States, for example, non-banks supply roughly half the total. In contrast, banks are the main suppliers of funds in Japan and Spain. In most emerging market economies (not shown), banks provide the bulk of credit to non-bank borrowers, although in several (eg the Czech Republic, Hungary and Poland) the share of total credit provided by non-banks is similar to that in advanced economies.

A second issue is data gaps. More granular information on creditor-side data in individual sectors would help improve the monitoring of global liquidity conditions. For instance, more comprehensive data on currency composition and maturity of international claims would enhance the diagnosis of the build- up of financial system risks associated with ample global liquidity. The same applies more generally for data on the shadow banking sector and derivatives market activities.

A third, related issue is the need for analytical work to better understand the dynamics of global liquidity and its impact on financial markets and institutions. For example, the interaction of private and public liquidity is not fully understood. Private sector perceptions that central banks will support liquidity in times of stress may affect risk-taking and the ease of financing.

Other linkages between private and official liquidity may result from the use of private financial instruments when providing or managing official liquidity. For instance, the collateral policies of central banks may influence the terms and conditions of secured funding in private markets. Another example is, as mentioned above, the impact of foreign exchange reserves on the markets of those assets where the reserves are invested.

POLICY ISSUES

Armed with signals from these methods for measuring global liquidity, a key question is how public sector authorities respond when the measures signal important aberrations. In this vein, the ongoing discussions regarding policy responses to global liquidity developments can be summarised in terms of two broad needs. *First,* there is a need to agree on measures that can deal with liquidity surges and the associated build-up of risks. *Second,* policy-makers need to improve the ability to handle situations of liquidity shortages and the ensuing potential disruptions.

Global capital and liquidity regulations discussed within the Basel Committee on Banking Supervision are at the core when it comes to dealing with liquidity surges. Regarding capital regulations, there is a need for banks to hold more capital as well as counter-cyclical capital buffers and additional capital to further enhance their loss-absorption capacity. This is particularly crucial for institutions that are deemed systemically important. Furthermore, strengthened liquidity regulation should help to constrain the ability of the banking system to provide maturity transformation services, which should then reduce the amplitude of boom-bust cycles in global liquidity provision. These reforms are, however, not enough by themselves to avoid costly asset price booms and busts; they need to be complemented with further macroprudential policy initiatives.

When it comes to addressing liquidity shortages, they can be divided into domestic and foreign currency liquidity shortages. Domestic shortages are usually handled by the central banks in the form of changes in liquidity operations and, in some cases, via purchases of assets. It is important to note that the central bank is the only institution which can supply domestic liquidity in an unlimited quantity.

To address foreign currency shortages, the main sources of public sector liquidity at the international level include: foreign exchange reserves, various IMF lending facilities (including new IMF instruments which increase the scale and flexibility for responding to global liquidity shortages), regional arrangements, special drawing rights and currency swaps and related arrangements between central banks. While foreign reserves helped to insulate some emerging market economies from funding difficulties in the course of 2008, the level of these reserves remain, as indicated above, beyond a level which could be considered to be precautionary.

Central bank currency swap arrangements have been an effective tool for addressing foreign currency liquidity shortages. While it is important that there are no technical obstacles to establishing these swap lines in times of need, it is of even more importance that the provision of liquidity under such arrangements is subject to "constructive ambiguity". Central banks should hence not commit *ex ante* to the provision of international liquidity in a crisis. This is necessary in order to: (i) preserve monetary policy autonomy; (ii) respect the mandate, resources, expertise and, ultimately, nature of these institutions; and (iii) minimise the risk of moral hazard behaviour at the global level on the part of the recipients of the liquidity. The unique ability of the central bank to provide unlimited liquidity in the currencies that are demanded globally means that its role in addressing global liquidity shocks is key. That said, the financial risks for the liquidity-providing central banks need to be kept to a minimum. To enable central banks to continue to fulfil their mandate, it will be necessary for liquidity-providing mechanisms to protect the soundness of central banks' balance sheets. This implies an appropriate design which includes the use of risk-mitigating mechanisms. While central bank policies are the key avenue for influencing public sector liquidity, the regulatory and macroprudential policy framework has a central role in influencing liquidity provision by the financial and non-financial sectors.

Thus the policy responses to surges in global liquidity are closely associated with the financial reform agenda. Microprudential measures that prevent excessive maturity phenomenon – such as liquidity coverage ratio (LCR) under Basel III – and that enhance the resilience of financial institutions more generally – such as the new, higher capital ratios – will tend to reduce the size and frequency of abrupt changes in liquidity provision due to banking sector strains. And measures that help to counter the procyclicality of credit (such as leverage ratios and capital conservation buffers) will tend to dampen cyclical fluctuations in private liquidity.

Macroprudential tools can also be used to address global liquidity surges. The new Basel III framework goes some way in this direction by providing a macroprudential overlay targeting both the cross-sectional dimension of systemic risk (eg capital surcharges for systemically important institutions) and ts time dimension (eg the countercyclical capital buffer). In addition, macroeconomic policy has an important part to play. Fiscal, monetary and exchange rate policies are ultimately and necessarily set to meet domestic policy objectives. At the same time, macroeconomic policy settings can be a key influence on global liquidity and the international transmission of liquidity cycles. Policy settings that help to avoid the build-up of domestic financial imbalances can, hence, also help to prevent unwanted surges in global liquidity. For instance, greater exchange rate flexibility may be consistent with domestic macroeconomic objectives, while helping to dampen global liquidity spillovers. In particular, such flexibility can reduce private sector incentives to establish unmatched foreign currency funding and investment positions.

The possible need to respond to liquidity shortages raises the issue of when and how the official sector should step in to fill the gap. To be sure, successful prevention of unsustainable surges in liquidity could substantially reduce the frequency and size of liquidity shortages. Even so, additional policy measures may still be needed.

Designing policies to address liquidity shortages involves questions about the effectiveness of self-insurance mechanisms, including precautionary accumulation of reserves and financial safety nets. Key considerations in this context are the nature of the shock and the degree of pre-commitment and moral hazard risk. When assessing the role of different intermediation channels in the provision of liquidity, distinguishing between bank and non-bank providers of credit is essential. In France, Germany, the United Kingdom and the United States, for example, non-banks supply roughly half the total. In contrast, banks are the main suppliers of funds in Japan and Spain. In most emerging market economies (not shown), banks provide the bulk of credit to non-bank borrowers, although in several (eg the Czech Republic, Hungary and Poland) the share of total credit provided by non-banks is similar to that in advanced economies. A second issue is data gaps. More granular information on creditor-side data in individual sectors would help improve the monitoring of global liquidity conditions. For instance, more comprehensive data on currency composition and maturity of international claims would enhance the diagnosis of the build- up of financial system risks associated with ample global liquidity. The same applies more generally for data on the shadow banking sector and derivatives market activities. A third, related issue is the need for analytical work to better understand the dynamics of global liquidity and its impact on financial markets and institutions. For example, the interaction of private and public liquidity is not fully understood. Private sector perceptions that central banks will support liquidity in times of stress may affect risk-taking and the ease of financing. Other linkages between private and official liquidity may result from the use of private financial instruments when providing or managing official liquidity. For instance, the collateral policies of central banks may influence the terms and conditions of secured funding in private markets. Another example is the impact of foreign exchange reserves on the markets of those assets where the reserves are invested.

The appropriate policy responses will have to be calibrated to the possible size and nature of the liquidity shock. In the case of idiosyncratic and smaller- scale regional shocks, self-insurance in the form of precautionary foreign reserves holdings and supply of liquidity through mechanisms for redistributing official liquidity, such as IMF programmes, SDR allocations and regional support arrangements, will typically be sufficient. In the case of a global liquidity shock, however, drawing on such prearranged mechanisms may not suffice. For instance, a freezing of interbank markets in major funding currencies, as during the recent crisis, may require the ability to supply official liquidity in major currencies in an elastic manner. Only the currency-issuing central banks have this ability.

Finally, since the concept of global liquidity is very broad, the focus has to be on a core sub-set of definitions and measures. It has been argued that policy-makers should aim to monitor a broad set of indicators and that the indicators may differ depending on the policy question at hand. The financial stability implications of global liquidity may differ according to the indicator used to measure it. In broad terms, however, global liquidity affects financial stability through its impact on asset prices and overall financing and credit conditions. Global liquidity generated by the financial and non-financial sectors is strongly cyclical, and closely related to investor risk appetite and (de)leveraging by financial institutions. In times of easy funding conditions, there may be global liquidity surges associated with strong asset price rises, rapidly rising credit growth and higher risk-taking among investors. Such liquidity-surging cycles may reverse in times of financial distress through deleveraging. As a result, addressing global liquidity cycles and surges in global liquidity require an appropriate macro-prudential policy framework to mitigate the risks to financial stability. In times of global liquidity shortages, the central bank plays a crucial role in the provision of public sector liquidity. It is important to stress, however, that this should be seen as part of a multi-layered approach whereby no single player has overall responsibility for handling a global liquidity crisis.

QUESTIONS

1. Explain the concept of global liquidity. What are the various instruments and mechanisms that provide domestic authorities and financial institutions access to official liquidity?
2. Critically examine the indicators and measures to assess the global liquidity.
3. Critically examine the dominant role of the choices and decisions of financial institutions and other economic agents in determining global liquidity which has important implications for the design of policy frameworks aimed at ensuring financial stability.
4. Discuss the coversion costs with reference to foreign exchange reserves.
5. Critically examine the policy responses to global liquidity developments in recent times.

5

INTERNATIONAL FINANCIAL SYSTEM

INTRODUCTION

Financial markets play a central role in promoting economic well being by bringing buyers and sellers together. Market prices, which result from this interaction, promote economic efficiency by providing signals to both producers and consumers about the size of the demand or supply of the traded commodity. When markets function smoothly, market participants can improve their welfare by trading: endowments or assets that fail to promote one owner's objectives can be traded for other goods or assets with more desirable characteristics.

ROLE OF FINANCIAL MARKETS

Financial markets facilitate trade between buyers and sellers of financial assets. Smoothly functioning financial markets allow traders to exchange one set of financial characteristics for another in the same way that efficient commodity markets permit the exchange of goods that embody different productive and consumption possibilities.

Financial markets allow individuals and institutions to trade loanable funds. Traders can select the set of financial asset characteristics that best meet their objectives. In complete markets investors and borrowers can complete multiple transactions to obtain some preferred combination of characteristics. In a sense they can custom design their own financial instruments by combining available instruments.

In domestic financial markets two basic asset characteristics are traded. The first is investment maturity. Borrowers exchange a promise to return cash in future for investable funds received in the present. The future might be two days or twenty years hence, and a borrower can often combine borrowing and lending transactions to achieve a particular maturity not directly available in the market place.

The other basic characteristic is the expectation of *asset risk* and *return*. Borrowers can choose to increase the risk attached to their commitment by making the future payment contingent on some economic outcome. For example, a borrower who issues equity is selling some of the risk attached to the underlying investment project because the lender's return in dividends and capital gains will depend on the success of the project.

In forward or futures markets the risk is isolated and traded separately from the underlying asset or commodity. For example, an investor can use futures contracts to insure the expected return on an asset.

In combination, these two characteristics, risk/return and maturity, can be used to smooth the flow of funds available for investment as well as funds that represent returns on investment. Financial markets should supply signals (interest rates, capital costs, or rates of return) so that investors and borrowers efficiently allocate funds to the end uses of capital consumption and investment.

Well-functioning and complete markets increase welfare by promoting allocative efficiency. Available funds are utilized effectively. In addition, both the overall supply of and demand for lendable funds increase as borrowers and lenders create the combination of maturity and risk characteristics that are most appropriate to their particular circumstances.

MARKET PARTICIPANTS

The markets are the channels through which funds flow from one market participant to another. There are three types of market participants: ultimate *borrowers*, ultimate *lenders*, and *financial intermediaries*. Investors attempt to accumulate wealth, to alter or smooth their pattern of consumption, or to change the risks attached to their consumption or portfolios of assets. Borrowers transact to gain investable funds, to consume or to alter the risks attached to their liabilities. Financial intermediaries earn a return by packaging financial assets for borrowers or lenders-increasing the variety of securities directly available in the market. They can also act as brokers by arranging deals between borrowers and lenders.

In recent years government agencies and institutions have become increasingly active as intermediaries in domestic financial systems. However, their stated goals are not regulatory, but the redistribution of wealth or income. These agencies can borrow directly in the capital market and lend to qualified beneficiaries at reduced rates; they can also provide an indirect subsidy by guaranteeing the beneficiaries debt. Beneficiaries include groups or individuals whose objectives are considered socially desirable, but insupportable at free-market costs of capital. For obvious reasons this method of income redistribution has become an extremely popular policy tool in many countries; in consequence, the relative presence in the capital markets of government agencies and institutions has increased enormously.

Private and public institutions can facilitate the growth and strength of the financial system. Government agencies such as the SEBI perform both regulatory and market development functions. Rules that insure the smooth functioning of the markets are developed and enforced. In addition these agencies can develop markets for new types of securities.

THE INTERNATIONAL FINANCIAL SYSTEM: *UNIQUE ELEMENTS*

In many countries domestic financial markets are inadequate. Borrowers and investors in countries with inefficient or incomplete capital markets are often forced to use foreign markets to meet financial needs.

Borrowers and lenders from countries with fully developed financial systems can also choose to transact in foreign markets; they can act from any of several possible motives. One of the most important motive is the financial support of direct foreign investment. Many investors find that foreign operations can be financed by foreign debt at a lower cost or with lower risk. Portfolio considerations also encourage investors to lend abroad in pursuit of more attractive combinations of risk, return, maturity, and liquidity. Finally, funds can flow between different capital markets in response to speculative expectations or to equate the supplies and demands for loanable funds.

One unique element of this decision to finance or invest abroad is that foreign financial contracts are denominated in a foreign currency. As a consequence, the market for the exchange of currencies, the forex market, is a basic and unique element of the international financial system. A second characteristic that differentiates international from domestic transactions is that some market participants are operating outside their national boundaries. In summary, the international financial system is distinguished by two elements. *First,* some parties might be transacting in currencies that are foreign to them. *Second,* participants are financing or investing outside their national boundaries.

These elements are shown on Exhibit-1 which is a diagram of the international financial system. The domestic financial systems—markets and participants—are subsets of the international system. In the past the domestic financial markets were thought to be segregated or independent of each other. Whatever the past reality of capital market independence, domestic markets are now generally integrated into the world financial system. The unique elements of the international system are shown at the centre section on the diagram in Exhibit-1.

EXHIBIT-1

THE INTERNATIONAL FINANCIAL SYSTEM

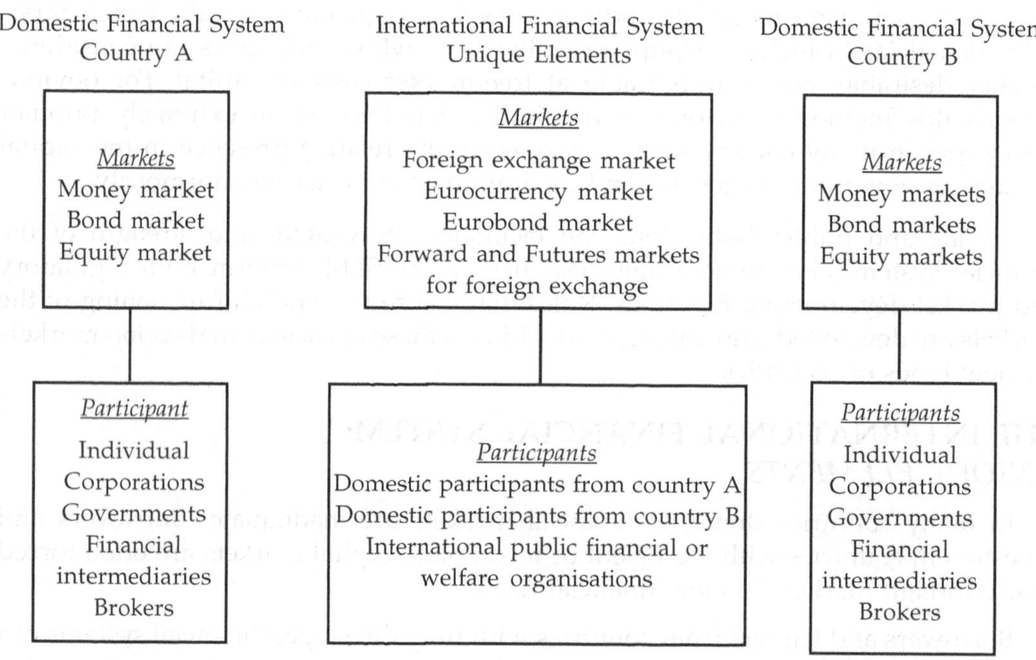

The international financial system is similar to the domestic systems because it embodies all of the elements of the domestic financial systems. As in domestic financial markets, risk, in this case international risk or the risk of variation in the rates at which currencies can be exchanged, can be isolated from other elements of the financial transaction. This risk can be traded directly in forward or futures markets for foreign exchange, or indirectly through other markets.

An additional similarity is the presence of financial intermediaries and public agencies. Many domestic financial intermediaries transact directly with foreigners and the financial sectors of most countries are heavily international by virtue of the extensive branch networks of major financial institutions. While international organizations do not generally perform a regulatory function, several other institutions actively redistribute wealth from developed to developing countries. Such institutions include the International Monetary Fund and the World Bank.

EXHIBIT-2

THE INTERNATIONAL FINANCIAL SYSTEM-A CHANNEL BETWEEN DOMESTIC MARKETS

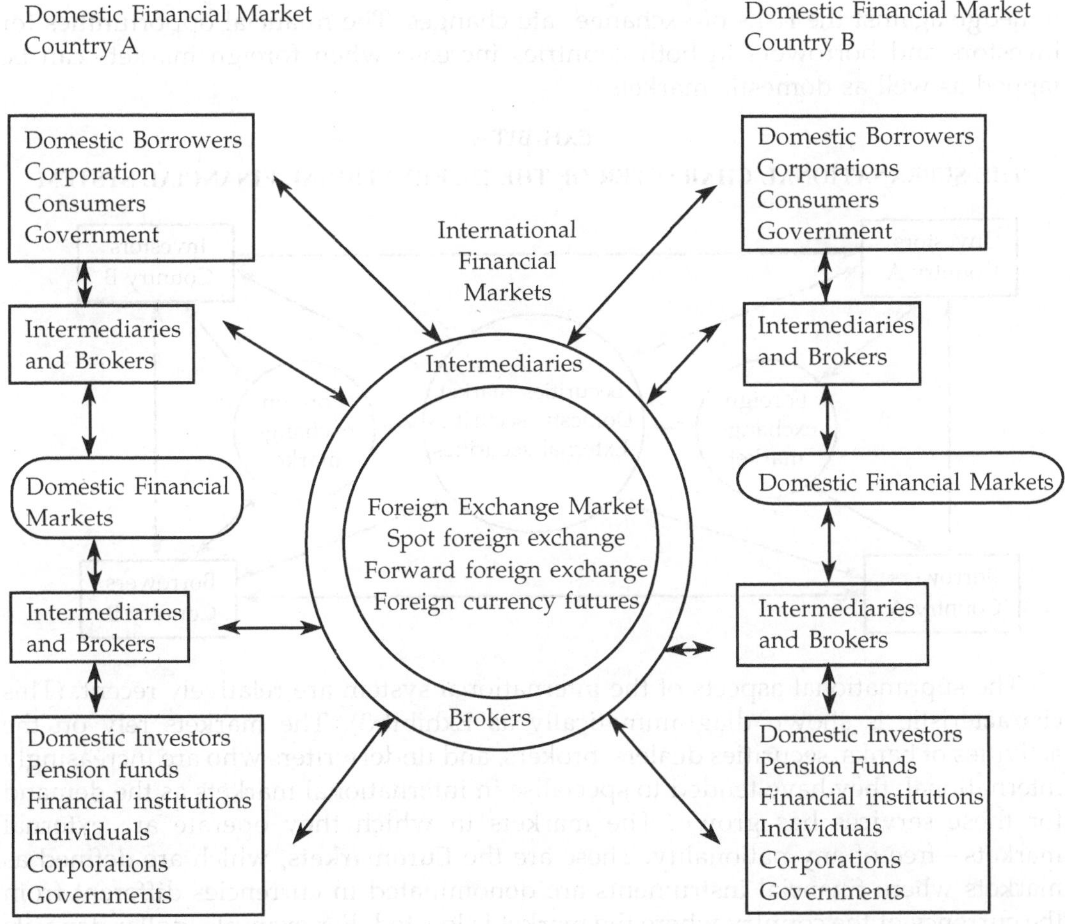

The international financial system fulfills two major roles. *First,* it serves to integrate the separate domestic systems. As a result the international financial system *has grown to* accommodate large and more numerous domestic financial systems. *Second,* it acts as a system in its own fight by supporting financial transactions that are supranational. Increasing numbers of borrowers and investors prefer to operate outside of domestic financial markets or are located in countries where financial markets are limited or nonexistent.

The foreign exchange market is the channel by which the first function is accomplished; it links domestic financial systems. (The linkage is diagrammed an Exhibit-2). In this market, borrowers and lenders can literally change the currency denomination of securities. For example, a Japanese investor can purchase a bond in the U.S. domestic market after exchanging yen for U.S. dollars in the foreign exchange market. The principal and interest payments, made in U.S. dollars, can be exchanged for yen at the time of payment. The risk that the exchange rate will vary in the interim can be hedged in the market *for forward foreign exchange.* In essence, the foreign exchange market opens the domestic financial markets to foreign investors and borrowers because it allows them to move funds from one currency to another and to hedge against the risks of exchange rate changes. The financial opportunities for investors and borrowers in both countries increase when foreign markets can be tapped as well as domestic markets.

EXHIBIT-3

THE SUPRANATIONAL CHARACTER OF THE INTERNATIONAL FINANCIAL SYSTEM

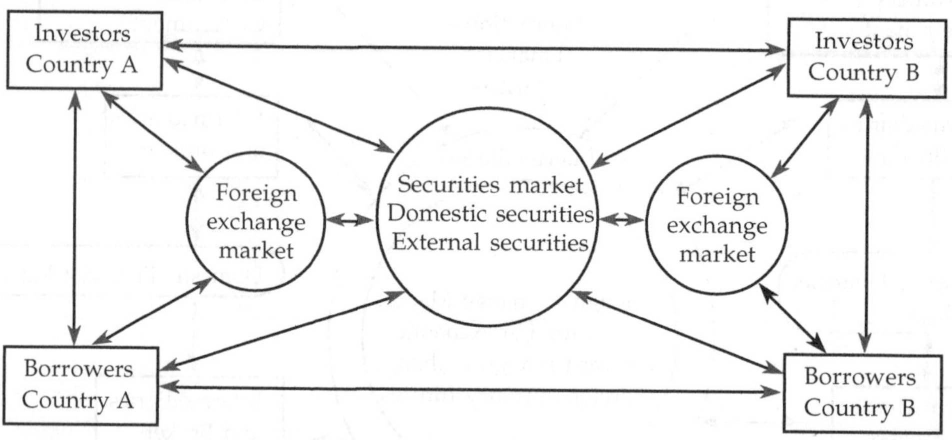

The supranational aspects of the international system are relatively recent. (This characteristic is shown diagrammatically as Exhibit-3). The markets rely on the activities of banks, securities dealers, brokers, and underwriters who are increasingly international; they have tended to specialise in international markets as the demand for these services has grown. The markets in which they operate are external markets—free of any nationality. These are the **Euromarkets,** which are defined as markets where financial instruments are denominated in currencies different from the currency of the country where the market is located. For example, dollar deposits that are accepted by the London branch of Citibank are Eurodollars. Euro-Swiss Franc bonds might be issued and placed in Frankfurt.

The supranational character of these transactions is the source of their advantage. Since no national authority generally regulates the activities of intermediaries in these markets, intermediation costs can be very low in comparison to domestic markets. This reduced cost translates into smaller spreads and ultimately into higher investor returns and lower borrowing costs.

Some investors also believe that external markets offer reduced risk of expropriation. The reasoning is that governments might not have the authority to impose capital controls on funds deposited in a foreign country. While this might not be true for foreign branches of domestic banks, foreign banks that accept deposits in a foreign currency are almost certainly immune from such control.

Transactions in external markets can be linked to foreign exchange transactions. A U.S. borrower can transform the proceeds of a Euro-Deutsche mark issue into dollars via the foreign exchange market. On the other hand, many participants in the system have no need to transfer funds between currencies. Truly, international corporations, banks, international and national institutions, and wealthy individuals enjoy a great deal of flexibility in their choice of currency denomination. For example, governments of oil-exporting companies might complete all transactions in U.S. dollars—from the sale of oil to the payment for imported goods and services. Most economists believe that the international markets have grown along with these international borrowers and lenders.

FINANCIAL MARKETS INTERDEPENDENCE AND SECURITISATION

With growing international linkages and gathering momentum of the transaction from guided or controlled economies to deregulated and decentralised ones- not only in the industrial world but also in a number of developing countries, the liberalisation has been in the making over the years in an increasingly interdependent, open and competitive, world. The trends towards globalisation and liberalisation are seen mostly in the financial flows and direct investment. Taken together, innovation, technology and deregulation have smashed the barriers both within and among national financial markets.

The chief factors behind the advancement of globalisation are: (i) the worldwide flow of funds has increased due to expanding world trade and an increasing imbalance in the international balance of payments: (ii) technological advances in communications and data processing have made possible the real-time transmission of information and settlement data, prerequisites for global transactions. Finance, too; has gone 'hi-tech'; (iii) drawn into entering foreign markets as local controls and restrictions on foreign exchange, interest rates, rules creating barriers between financial institutions, withholding taxes on interest income and so on, have been eased or abolished. As a result, the connections between markets have been strengthened. There is now a blurring of the dichotomy between banks and other financial firms. Future contracts and currency options are traded on organised markets. The development of swaps, some of which have become so standardised that they are traded as commodities, has created opportunities for trade in almost any -contingent asset that market participants can invest. Such trade is increasingly commonplace among firms engaged in international business. Trade in equities of firms permits indirect access to global markets for investors. Increasingly, they tend to bypass local banking system for the management of surplus assets, unless competitive rates and other conditions are offered; and official controls likely to be less effective due to the difficulty in enforcing them. The governments increasingly compete in the same market for the savings of their citizens as well as for access to foreign capital.

Integration of financial markets has resulted in the demise of financing along the predominantly national lines. The concept of the "family doctor" has been replaced. In days gone by, if companies needed money they went, as it were, to the "family banker". Nowadays not just one bank approaches companies regularly; instead many banks from different countries complete at corporate level for favours. This competition between financial intermediaries resulted from liberalisation and globalisation of financial markets. This trend has increased competition on a global scale and led to concentration of the parties in the financial markets.

The liberalisation of international capital account transactions in most major countries over the past decade or so has given rise to the rapid development of an integrated international capital market. This development has enhanced capital mobility and substitutability between domestic and foreign bonds. Euro and domestic interest rates have converged for most major currencies. Furthermore, there appears to be a tendency for real interest rate differentials between countries, averaged over periods of several years, to be smaller, although with considerable volatility of these differentials over shorter time periods (especially at the short and medium term part of the spectrum). Increased international capital transactions have also strengthened the interaction between real interest rates and real exchange rates with important long and short-term implications.

The internationalisation of financial markets exert important effects on the efficiency of macro-economic policy. If domestic real interest rates are affected more by the development of the world real interest rate than in the past, the efficacy of monetary policy in influencing domestic private investment might be reduced. On the other hand, monetary policy may have stronger effects on exports (exchange rate crowding out) and prices via the exchange rate. The impact of fiscal policy on real output might also change; the more closely linked are financial markets, the stronger are the exchange rate crowding out effects and the weaker are the interest rate crowding out effects, i.e., the stronger the link between fiscal policy changed and current account imbalances together with corresponding capital flows. Since all these changes tend to strengthen the effect of macro-economic policy instruments on the exchange rate and the current balance, better international co-ordination of macro policies is indispensable for stable exchange rates and for the sustainable international configuration of balance of payments.

These developments raise the question of various effects of the internationalisation of financial markets. The main questions to be considered are: *how did the removal of exchange controls affect the determinants of domestic interest rates in relation to Euro-currency market? How strong is the tendency towards convergence of real interest rates, especially among countries and adding them to deficit countries?*

International integration of financial markets also has implications for the international allocation of capital. Provided there are no other distortions, how does the tendency towards convergence effect financially open countries? *How does the internationalisation of financial markets effect the efficacy of macro-economic policy instruments? To what extent does the increased integration of financial markets improve the international allocation of capital? What are the effects of domestic tax incentives for investment when capital is highly mobile?*

During the past twenty-five years or so, increasing capital market integration has strengthened convergence between domestic and Euro market interest rates. Internationalisation of capital markets has produced convergence of real returns on financial assets across countries through various mechanisms. An important mechanism for the real interest rate convergence is a long-run tendency of exchange rates to fluctuate around purchasing power parity (PPP). Of course, exchange rates diverse some PPP levels and, correspondingly, expected changes in exchange rates can differ from expected inflation differentials. If such changes in real exchange rates take place, current account positions will be affected, with corresponding effect on net capital flows. Such capital flows will tend to reduce real interest rate differentials though subtracting savings from surplus of real interest rates though international capital movements would improve the allocation of resources and raise the level of welfare. However, the corporate and personal tax system of each country penetrates wedges specific to that country between market real interest rates and the real after tax cost of capital for corporate investments. Since tax systems are usually not indexed to prices, these tax wedges depend not only on tax parameters but also on the rate of inflation. It may be pointed that the countries with tax incentives for investment and/or with high inflation tend to have wide tax wedges. Therefore, even if market real-interest rates are equalised across countries, real costs of capital would differ significantly among them penetrating a distorted allocation of capital. If resource allocation is to be improved on a world-wide basis, international financial integration may call for international harmonisation of those aspects of tax systems that relate to investment and saving.

Private capital flows can be expected to yield an efficient allocation of savings across countries only if global capital markets operate with stability and efficiency, and generate prices which appropriately reflect underlying risks and returns. Indeed one factor motivating the process of financial liberalisation and the removal of capital controls in the industrialised countries has been the desire to increase the market efficiency by dismantling market-distorting regulations. While these reforms have increased market competition and efficiency, there have been concerns that financial liberalisation, and the accompanying financial innovations, may have given rise to institutional weaknesses that may threaten the stability of the international financial system. Nowadays, besides the increasing number of parties in the market and the related trends of competition and concentration, there is a second major development, namely the changing role of financial instruments. The traditional distinction between debt and equity has become less clear for various reasons.

Securitisation of financial means is the result of selection made in assessing private profit from the points of view of maintaining profit, growth and fluidity, and the risk bearing by individual borrowers, investors or financial institutions, constitutes a practice of individual economic entities. And, when this accompanies the emergence of new instruments (new financial means), this practice comes to be described as "innovative". For example, Corrigan Report puts it thus:

> *There are two background factors behind securitisation. First, the cost of fund raising on the securities has become lower than that the cost of bank borrowing for many bank borrowers. Second, for the financial institutions, securitisation has become desirable from the point of view of securing greater liquidity or the possibility of a more flexible response under the imposed restrictions on the capital." The advent of such a new behaviour and the emergence of financial innovations presupposes changes in the environmental conditions surrounding financial institutions and investors. There is no doubt that changes in economic and technological conditions have indirect effects on securitisation."*

The issue in this connection, as a parameter connecting environmental changes to reform, is to what extent factors such as administrative strategies of the individual financial institutions and investors and the conditions of competition in the financial market and the financial services sector are given priority. With changes in the environment, financial institutions can no longer meet their customer's requirements with existing financial means alone, and financial disintermediation takes place with respect to these customers. Alternatively, if the financial institutions rely on traditional financial means alone, their business itself may be jeopardised. This is all the more reason for new behaviours and financial innovations. Why does this occur? *Is it due to faulty management on the part of the financial institutions? Or were there problems in the structure of the financial services industry? Or perhaps the regulations imposed on the financial institutions were too stringent.* The problem can be approached from various aspects. For this reason, it would be unreasonable to conclude that securitisation is simply the trend of the times. In thinking of securitisation of financial means, one must ask why the past limitations on the functions of financial institutions such as banks (reduced adaptability) which brought about this securitisation arose. This is a question which must be approached since the characteristics of the financial system are ultimately determined by the respective (combined) characters of fund demand (final borrowers), fund supply (final lenders) and financial mediation/distribution (the financial service industry). *In what way do the two-kinds of securitisation differ?* First of all, in the case of securitisation of financial means, this securitisation either moves forward or stagnates depending on the investment and fund raising strategies of institutions, investors, and lenders, and on the status of competition in the financial markets and financial service industry. For this reason, the factors inherent in the financial system become vital parameters in the progress of securitisation. In the case of securitisation of the financial system, however, because the strategies of the financial institutions and investors and the status of competition in the financial markets and the financial services industry change with this progress, primary factors such as the financial behaviour of individual economic entities and the nature of market competition are the result of securitisation, not the cause of it. Nor are they parameters linking certain causes to the phenomenon of securitisation. It is particularly important to bear this point to mind when comparing the securitisation in the international financial markets. Securitisation is not necessarily a natural consequence of financial expansion. As we have seen, securitisation can be roughly classified into two types. *Why is such a classification necessary?* To cite an example, such classification prepares the way for dealing with the problems of whether or not securitisation is a natural outgrowth of financial expansion and what its effects on the future financial system will be. To begin with, in the case of securitisation of the financial system, which is highly heteronomous in character, the factors promoting the securitisation can be considered under given conditions, so the way these factors change in the future can be considered to the relatively independent from the ideal state of finance. Although there is no doubt that the trend of securitisation is greatly affected by these factors, one cannot conclude that the securitisation is a phenomenon of financial expansion. The character of the financial system changes due to forces originating within finance itself and to the extent that financial performance is increased, one can speak of a natural financial expansion.

On the other hand, when we use the expression "securitisation of financial means", two cases can be postulated. To the extent that they submit to existing restrictions (particularly regulations), financial institutions cannot adapt to new environment, they miss opportunities for profit and growth, and they are forced to bear excessive risks (the danger increases). For this reason, they are taking bold action in innovations to breakthrough or avoid these existing regulations. *Can securitisation which proceeds in this manner be a natural outgrowth of a financial expansion?* No. However, the use of new technologies in particular has the effect of developing and creating new unprecedented financial means, alleviating the expense of existing financial transactions. With respect to this type of innovation in its turn, securitisation could clearly be referred to as a natural outgrowth of financial expansion. Such securitisation of financial means can be decided into the regulation-avoiding type and the technology-led type.

Among the types of securitisation currently taking place worldwide, which constitute securitisation of the financial system and which are securitisation finance means? And of the latter, which are the regulation - avoiding type and which are technology - led type? Logically speaking there are problems involved with seeing all types of securitisation as a natural outgrowth of financial expansion. The phenomenon of securitisation of financial means must be seen as an accumulation of micro-economic phenomena, the phenomenon referred as securitisation of the financial system has more of a micro-economic character. What this means is that rather than taking both autonomously from the financial system or financial markets, this phenomenon is rather strongly heteronomous in character. To be more specific, the direct cause of securitisation of the financial system does not lie within the system itself but is to be found in changes in the external economic environment. Japan is an excellent example of this. This can be summed up in the working of the following theory. Mass quantities of negotiable financial instruments (government bonds) injected into the financial system from outside promote the formation of an open market, which it has not been possible to achieve to a sufficient degree in the past. At the same time, moreover, factors such as diversified preferences of asset holders and technological progress, which make increasing sophistication of financial technology possible, facilitate the appearance of new instruments which take advantage of the open market and the emergence of new markets.

Once a broad and deep open market has been formed, financial innovation within the financial system results in the accumulation of incentives to secure and expand private profit. Moreover, there are regulations, particularly on interest rates, and if the management of these regulations is rigid due to the government or other reasons, the incentives for new instruments and markets also become greater, and the probability that these will be actualised increases. Of course, it goes without saying that market conditions such as the level of the economy and interest rates are also decisive factors in substantiating these incentives. By any definition, however, the formation of a deep open market through securitisation of the financial system is an indispensable prerequisite for the emergence of new instruments and new markets. These changes are nothing less than the phenomenon referred as securitisation of the financial system proceeds. Securitisation of financial means also becomes apparent in the form of financial innovations carried out by financial institutions, etc.

GLOBAL BENEFITS FROM A WELL-FUNCTIONING INTERNATIONAL FINANCIAL SYSTEM

The concept of an international financial system was historically equated to the foreign exchange or international monetary system. As a result, economic and political gains attributed to the system emphasized the gains attributed to trade between countries. A complete, efficient, and stable foreign exchange market supports and encourages trade between nations; the economic gains from production specialisation are shared by all. For the same reason, short-term trade financing that supports trading activity contributes to world economic welfare.

A related benefit is the foreign direct investment that is encouraged by the availability of foreign financing. Clearly, such investment activity brings capital to undercapitalised regions with concomitant economic and political benefits. These benefits parallel the benefits of allocative efficiency promoted by the domestic financial systems.

Increased financial opportunities also increase the supply and demand for loanable funds. Saving and investment are encouraged as risk, liquidity and maturity options are increased by access to international markets.

The international system also reduce variability and turnout in the underlying economic system. In a closed domestic system, economic sub-sectors can reduce economic variability by borrowing and lending from each other. The international system augments the domestic system by smoothing the effects of economic shocks across countries. The dramatic transfers of national wealth that were caused by changes in energy pricing are a prime example. Without the international finance system, the political upheaval resulting from the shocks would have been enormous. The adjustments forced on many developing countries would have destroyed decades of economic progress. Instead, oil exporting countries and, to some extent, developed countries that were relatively less energy dependent financed the developing countries during the adjustment process. The reduction in wealth was spread over a longer period of time, allowing a more rational and less painful adjustment of development activity.

The effects of many other economic and political shocks are lessened by the activity of the international financial system. The most obvious shock is that of wartime, when international loans are extended to reduce the -current economic drains on the combative countries. Other sources of economic variability include domestic business cycles and the effects of weather on agricultural yields.

A well functioning system also supports the objective of international political stability and humanitarian goals. International institutions can draw funds for such purposes from international financial markets; when these markets operate smoothly, objectives can be achieved more effectively at lower cost.

Finally, the development of an international system that increase the interdependence of domestic system has an important, hidden benefit-the financial discipline required of members of the system, the force of economic discipline was obvious during the periods when the international monetary system operated under the rules of the gold standard and Bretton Woods system. In these periods, national economic policies were subjected to the discipline of the international community in the interest of maintaining the foreign exchange rate. Much of the discipline has remained under the present system of management floating rates, but has been replaced somewhat by stringent conditions that can be attached to international loans.

QUESTIONS

1. Discuss the unique elements of the international financial system.
2. Discuss the role of financial markets in international financial market smooth functioning.
3. Discuss the interdependencies between global financial institutions and markets. What are the limits to international financial markets diversification?
4. Explain the global benefits from a well-functioning international financial system.
5. What is securitisation ? Why does this occur ?
6. "If financial institutions city on traditional financial instruments alone, their business itself may be jeoparadised." In the light of this statement, explain the role of financial innovations.

6

FINANCIAL GLOBALISATION AND THE CRISIS

INTRODUCTION

After a long period of relative calm in the international financial system, the global crisis has provided a severe test of financial globalisation. At a global level, the rapid growth in cross-border financial trade in the decade before the crisis contributed to the excessive growth in credit markets that was at the centre of the initial phase of the crisis. Moreover, financial globalisation fuelled the asymmetries in credit growth and external positions across countries that have played a critical role in determining the cross-country incidence and propagation of the crisis.

Once the crisis occurred, financial globalisation provided a buffer against the crisis for some countries, whereas it amplified the crisis for others. By and large, the structure of the international balance sheets of emerging economies provided valuable insulation against the crisis. In contrast, the "long equity, short debt" profile of many advanced economies was a risky profile in the face of declining equity markets and disruption in credit markets. However, currency depreciation for some advanced economies did improve external positions during the crisis.

Moreover, the global crisis has powerfully demonstrated that international financial integration amplifies the costs of policy and regulatory failures, both in terms of crisis prevention and crisis management. Although there has been an array of policy reforms in the wake of the crisis, much more remains to be done in terms of designing global, regional and national policy frameworks that can cope with high levels of international financial integration.

If the appropriate international and national institutions are put in place, financial globalisation retains its potential to positively contribute to risk diversification, consumption smoothing and efficient capital allocation. Indeed, under an improved institutional framework, a lower volume of cross-border financial trade might deliver more genuine benefits from financial globalisation, if "smart" international asset trade is enhanced at the expense of "distorting" international asset trade. The chapter examines the contrasting experiences of advanced and emerging market economies (EMEs) during the global crisis which can be directly related to their very different modes of engagement with financial globalisation during the pre-crisis period. In this context, the current European crisis provides important lessons for the rest of the world, in view of the extremely high levels of cross-border financial integration within Europe (especially within the euro area).

DEFINING FINANCIAL GLOBALISATION

Financial globalisation has two main aspects: i) Free flow of capital into and out of the domestic economy; ii) High foreign participation in domestic financial system. Both aspects can be measured in many ways: *Capital mobility:* holdings of cross-border financial assets and liabilities, magnitude of cross-border flows into and out of the financial system. Foreign participation: foreign share of domestic banking assets and liabilities, ease of entry for foreign financial institutions into domestic market.

Financial globalisation along both dimensions, if well managed, can yield benefits for the economy. The purported benefits of open capital markets are well known, even if there is controversy around the significance of these benefits. For EMEs, the strongest benefit is the access that it provides to international capital. As for openness to foreign financial institutions, they play a critical function in credit intermediation, and maturity and risk transformation across national borders. They promote competition and innovation and introduce new technologies and best practices.

MEASURING FINANCIAL GLOBALISATION

The sum of foreign assets and foreign liabilities (expressed as a ratio to GDP and termed the IFI ratio) is a useful measure of the de facto scale of cross-border financial integration. While financial globalisation also operates through the determination of asset prices and the responsiveness of international capital flows to shocks, the accumulated stocks of foreign assets and foreign liabilities reflect the history of past capital flows, plus the impact of valuation adjustments on previous positions. In addition, the level and composition of the international balance sheet matter for the exposure of individual countries to shocks to underlying asset prices and exchange rates. Finally, the net international investment position is a key state variable in many dynamic macroeconomic models. In addition to the structural factors, it is also important to take into account the market shift in emerging-market strategies in the wake of the 1990 financial crises. These countries reduced net external liabilities by running current account surpluses, improved liquidity by accumulating foreign-exchange reserves and lowered debt-equity ratios in the composition of external liabilities.

The IFI ratio only captures the aggregate scale of international balance sheets. It is especially important to consider the debt-equity mix, in view of the different risk-bearing properties of debt and equity instruments. The "long equity, short debt" strategy pursued by many advanced economies clearly carried risks. While this mix might earn a positive net return during normal times, it is destabilising during a crisis period since a decline in equity values reduces the net worth of domestic investors at the same time that tighter conditions in credit markets increases funding risks for debt liabilities.

By way of contrast, the "long debt, short equity" profile of emerging economic provided substantial protection. The buffer provided by holding liquid foreign-currency foreign debt assets covered in the event of disruption in credit markets or currency depreciation, while the high equity component in external liabilities provided considerable outward risk transfer in the event of a decline in domestic asset prices. Still, as the same time, this profile also contained vulnerabilities, since foreign debt assets are exposed to default risk during crisis periods. In addition, the funding of equity liabilities and the value of domestic assets can be compromised by international financial multiplier effects, by which foreign investors that face a tougher domestic financial environment may be forced to sell foreign positions through a variety of mechanisms.

FINANCIAL GLOBALISATION AND SOURCES OF THE CRISIS

Did the rise in cross-border financial trade contribute to the origination of the global financial crisis? It is possible to identify main channels by which financial globalisation contributed to the financial conditions that ultimately gave rise to the crisis. First, the participation of foreign investors (especially foreign banks) fuelled the accelerated growth of the asset-backed securities markets in the United States that were central in the original market panic in 2007-2008. As European banks were major purchasers of asset-backed securities. In large part, these banks also obtained dollar funding in the US money markets. For this reason, the role of European banks in enabling the expansion of the US ABS markets did not jump out of the balance of payments data, although the implicit risk exposure of European parent banks grew in line with these US activities. Second, financial globalisation permitted rapid growth in the balance sheets of many banks. This took place at two levels. In relation to globally-active banks, the size and complexity of these banks grew rapidly, making it difficult for national regulators to adequately police risk profiles. In addition, the capacity of local banks to expand lending by tapping international wholesale markets fuelled credit growth in a number of countries. Third, the growing role of emerging markets in the world financial system may also have contributed to the build-up of weaknesses in credit markets. In particular, the general-equilibrium impact of the demand for low-risk debt assets from emerging-market official sources and the increased supply of equity opportunities in these countries may have added fuel to the securitisation boom.

In these ways, although there is no easy way to quantify its importance relative to other factors, financial globalisation plausibly contributed to the credit market vulnerabilities that were at the origin of the global financial crisis. In essence, financial globalisation magnified the impact of underlying distortions, such as inadequate regulation of credit markets and banks, by allowing the scaling-up of financial activities that might have faced capacity limits in autarkic financial systems.

Going further, the variation in the cross-country incidence and propagation of the global crisis may be linked to differential levels and types of participation in cross-border financial trade. The rate of pre-crisis credit growth and the scale of pre-crisis current account deficits are important correlates of the scale of the decline in output and domestic expenditure during 2009. More generally, credit growth is an important leading indicator of subsequent financial crises. In related fashion, the scale of pre-crisis " excess" current account deficits has been associated with larger current account turnarounds over 2008-2010, which were mostly accomplished through reductions in domestic absorption.

Financial globalisation plausibly contributed to rapid domestic credit growth by operating on both supply factors and demand factors. In relation to credit supply, domestic banks and the affiliates of foreign banks can raise various types of wholesale funding, on international markets, with foreign investors also an important source of bank equity (both through portfolio equity and FDI). In relation to credit demand, capital inflows can contribute to a low interest rate environment and improve the net worth of domestic borrowers by pushing up domestic asset prices.

International capital inflows were indeed correlated with domestic credit growth during the 2003-2008 pre-crisis period. In particular, a high level of net debt inflows was associated with more rapid domestic credit growth. This is consistent with the funding channel by which domestic banks were able to expand lending capacity by raising wholesale funding on international markets. The flip side is that high rates of net debt outflows were associated with lower domes credit growth in key source countries. It is also plausible that financial globalisation facilitated the emergence of large and persistent current account imbalances.

However, the factors driving current account balances varied across different phases. Still, international financial integration surely increased the elasticity of capital flows to these underlying forces, both in relation to welfare-increasing factors (such as differences in demographics or productivity) and welfare-reducing factors (asset bubbles, overborrowing distortions).

FINANCIAL GLOBALISATION: CRISIS AMPLIFIERS AND CRISIS BUFFERS

Regardless of whether financial globalisation contributed to the origination of the crisis, it is important to investigate the mechanisms by which cross-border financial integration either amplified crisis dynamics or provided a buffer that mitigated crisis shocks. For this, it is useful the divide the analysis between "flow" effects and "balance sheet" effects in relation to the behaviour of capital flows during the crisis. At a general level periods of enhanced global risk are associated with much smaller volumes of gross capital flows, as investors refrain from making international commitments and seek to pull back from accumulated positions that were built up during normal times but look outsized in a higher-risk environment. The most dramatic turnaround took place in relation to banking-sector flows, with foreign investors draining liquid liabilities (deposits, short-term wholesale funding) from stressed banks and domestic investors similarly repatriating foreign liquid assets. In both directions, banks were the main proximate investors in other banks, so the cross-border retrenchment was part of the general breakdown in inter-bank markets during the crisis. While individually rational, the collective exit from these markets contributed to the illiquidity problems that defined the acute phase of the crisis. Given the lack of an adequate international regulatory framework, cross-border liquidity runs were more difficult to forestall than domestic liquidity runs.

It is worth noting that the exit from foreign markets was far from uniform, with the composition of the investor base mattering for the scale of the capital flow reversal. Banks were most likely to pull back from destinations that were more geographically distant from the home market. In similar fashion, foreign investors were more likely to reduce portfolio equity and portfolio debt positions in further-distant host countries.

It might be expected that some types of capital flows could be a stabilising force during a crisis. For instance, in the wake of a decline in domestic asset prices, bargain-seeking foreign investors could be a source of new capital inflows in the forms of portfolio investment and foreign direct investment. While this mechanism has partially operated during the crisis, it has less force in the context of a banking crisis, in view of the opacity of banking-sector balance sheets and the risks of subsequent regulatory interventions that could harm foreign investors in distressed domestic banks.

For those countries suffering the most severe domestic crises, the opportunity to repatriate foreign assets might assist in domestic recovery. This has most force if there is a low (or even negative) correlation between foreign asset returns and domestic asset returns and if foreign assets are selected to provide diversification against domestic risks. However, the effectiveness of this mechanism is weaker during a global downturn in asset prices; it also is less helpful if foreign asset purchases acted to concentrate risk rather than to diversify risk. For instance, domestic speculators who had done well during the real estate boom in Ireland doubled down by making aggressive purchases in the property sector in other hot markets (Central and Eastern Europe, United Kingdom, United States). This pattern boosted levered returns during the global real estate boom but exacerbated the losses once the global property prices went into reverse.

Turning to the role of "international balance sheet" effects, the rise in foreign holdings has magnified the quantitative importance of the valuation channel of external dynamics. All else equal, capital gains on foreign assets and capital losses on foreign liabilities improve the net international investment position and such gains in external wealth can provide a stabilising force if excess returns are earned during crisis periods. However, it is also possible to envisage scenarios in which valuation losses occur during a crisis, which is a destabilising pattern. In fact, this was the classic pattern in traditional emerging-market crises, with the toxic pattern of exchange rate depreciation in combination with high levels of foreign-currency debt delivering negative valuation effects that amplified crisis dynamics.

In working out the role played by the valuation channel during the current crisis, a number of factors have to be taken into consideration. First, the strong global co-movement in equity prices during the crisis meant that the overall net equity position of each country was very important in determining the distribution of gains and losses. In this regard, the general pattern was that advanced economies lost and emerging markets gained, in view of the asymmetric positions of the two groups in relation to portfolio equity and FDI net positions. Second, it is important to differentiate across different debt categories. In relation to the 2008 US-centred phase of the crisis, the foreign investors in loss-making, asset-backed securities were primarily from other advanced economies. In contrast, investors from emerging markets (mainly official investors) held safe government-backed securities and so were not exposed to the meltdown in the ABS markets.

Taking a longer and broader view of the crisis, the full attribution of losses on debt positions is incomplete, since there are typically long delays before losses on bank loan books are fully acknowledged, while the distinction between " hold to maturity" securities and " trading" securities means that the accounting treatment of bank holdings of sovereign debt only partially reflects mark-to-market principles. Still, the writing down of 107 billion in Greece's sovereign debt obligations to private-sector investors (corresponding to 50 percent of Greek GDP) will primarily fall on foreign investors, substantially improving its net international investment position. On a more minor scale, the write down of 14 billion on the subordinated debt issued by Irish banks corresponds to about 9 percent of Irish GDP and will also overwhelmingly fall on foreign investors. Over time, the scale of national and sectoral debt burdens in Europe makes it likely that external balance sheet adjustment will partly take place through further debt write downs.

Third, exchange rate movements have a primary role in determining valuation effects, since foreign assets are typically denominated in foreign currency and, especially for advanced economies, foreign liabilities typically have a large domestic-currency component. During 2008, the appreciation of the US dollar constituted a capital loss for the United States but a capital gain for the many emerging markets that maintained "long dollar" positions, largely consisting of high levels of dollar-denominated official reserves. In contrast, the sizeable depreciation of Sterling during 2008 provided a valuation gain to the United Kingdom, while Australia and New Zealand also enjoyed sizeable currency-related valuation gains during 2008. Within the euro area, both foreign assets and foreign liabilities are mainly denominated in euro, so that the exchange rate component of the valuation channel is weaker for these countries than for countries with independent exchange rates.

The currencies of many emerging markets also depreciated during 2008. Historically, this would have been problematic due to high levels of foreign-currency debt. However, the accumulation of large foreign-currency reserves meant that domestic currency depreciation now was associated with a capital gain on foreign assets, while the shift from foreign-currency debt to equity-type instruments reduced the impact on the liability side of the international balance sheet.

Finally, the overall return on foreign assets and foreign liabilities is determined by international investment income flows as well as by capital gains and losses. The general decline in interest rates in the advanced economies during the crisis constituted a reduction in net international payments on the "short debt" positions of these economies. Since 2010, a partial exception has been the euro area periphery, to the extent that rising spreads on sovereign debt liabilities have offset the lower policy interest rates.

FINANCIAL GLOBALISATION: CRISIS MANAGEMENT

Financial globalisation also affected crisis management along a number of dimensions. At a basic level, the very high levels of cross-border financial positions mark the current crisis as quantitatively different from previous crisis episodes in terms of the scale of international financial linkages. In turn, this has constrained the intervention capacity of national governments, while increasing the importance of different types of international policy responses.

In relation to the international banking system, the contagion risks associated with the vulnerabilities of global systemically-important financial institutions (G-SIFIs) highlighted the inadequacy of national-level financial regulatory systems. In turn, this prompted the upgrading of the activities of the Financial Stability Board (FSB), even if this remains far from acting as a global regulator.

At a European level, a new European System of Financial Supervision (ESFS) was created, including the establishment of the European Systemic Risk Board (ESRB) and three new pan-European sectoral agencies (the European Banking Authority; the European Insurance and Occupational Pensions Authority; and the European Securities and Markets Authority). Still, even within Europe, the primary responsibility for financial supervision remains at the national level.

In terms of the provision of central bank liquidity, the high reliance of international banks (especially European banks) on dollar funding exposed the limitations of relying on home central banks as a source of non-market liquidity. In part, foreign-currency liquidity was obtained by the ability of the local affiliates of international banks to tap the liquidity facilities offered by national central banks. In addition, foreign-currency liquidity was made available through a remarkable series of ad-hoc currency swap arrangements among the world's major central banks. Still, in terms of institutional design, the absence of a long-term standing currency-swap agreements limit the capacity of the international system to deal with financial shocks.

The resolution of failing banks is also made more challenging by financial globalisation. First, the cross-country issues involved in the Lehmans bankruptcy process illustrate the complexity of liquidating internationally-active banks. Second, cases such as Dexia show the difficulties involved in sharing the fiscal costs involved in the resolution of multi-country banking groups. Third, (actual or prospective) losses concentrated in overseas affiliates might tempt a home government to cut loose these affiliates in order to protect the parent bank. While this risk remains non-trivial, it is important to recognise that some home governments have accepted substantial fiscal costs in order to support the foreign affiliates of domestic banks. Finally, ad-hoc financial diplomacy may also have deterrred some parent banks from abandoning troubled affiliates. The most notable example is the Vienna Initiative by which Western European parent banks agreed to maintain commitments vis-a-vis affiliates in Central and Eastern Europe during the initial stages of the global financial crisis.. This coordinated approach solved the "race to the exit" problem by which individual parent banks might fail to internalise the systemic impact of pulling funding from affiliates in host countries, especially those host countries in which foreign-owned banks were the bedrock of the local financial system.

While such a coordinated approach might have been effective in forestalling a panic-driven suboptimal equilibrium during the most intense phase of the crisis, it does not remove the underlying tensions between home and host countries in relation to the relative financial health of parent banks and affiliate banks and differing regulatory incentives.

The very high level of cross-border financial integration within the euro area has posed particular difficulties in managing the banking crisis. A remarkable feature of the European crisis has been the replacement of private-sector capital flows to the periphery with quasi-automatic official flows in the form of ECB liquidity flows. Relative to countries with independent currencies and/or with foreign-currency liabilities, ECB liquidity flows have been a stabilising force during the crisis, ameliorating the impact of the large-scale private-sector reversal in capital flows. For instance, liquidity inflows grew from virtually zero during the pre-crisis period to 2010 values of 54 percent of GDP for Ireland, 22 percent for Greece and 17 percent for Portugal. In related fashion, cross-border liquidity flows are the source of the large Target 2 imbalances that have emerged since the onset of the crisis. Still, even with the over-collateralisation of refinancing operations, the ECB takes on credit risk in providing liquidity funding. In turn, this gives rise to the possibility of cross-border transfers if banks in a given country default on ECB obligations and the underlying collateral proves to be inadequate, since the losses are shared among the member countries in proportion to their share in the capital key of the ECB.

In order to manage this risk, liquidity needs can be reduced by scaling down bank balance sheets through an asset disposal programme. In addition, a primary policy prescription is to require banks to hold a sufficient level of capital to absorb expected losses, thereby increasing the ability of banks to raise wholesale funding and reducing the risk of defaulting on central bank obligations. If current capital levels are too low to cover prospective loan losses, this entails a bank recapitalisation programme.

The composition of asset disposal programmes may also involve cross-country asymmetries. In particular, home regulators may push banks to dispose of foreign assets, in order to avoid the impact of domestic asset sales. While this may represent a form of financial protectionism, the prioritisation of foreign asset sales may be desirable to the extent that the original acquisition of foreign assets was driven by distorted over-expansion of the balance sheets of domestic banks. Under this scenario, foreign asset sales represent the shrinkage of "non-core" operations, allowing these banks to focus on their core activities.

It is difficult to set the optimal speed of deleveraging through asset disposals, especially in relation to long-lived assets such as mortgages and other property-backed loans where the value of the underlying collateral would be driven down in the event of overly-rapid deleveraging. In this regard, there is a clear collective-action problem if deleveraging programmes are not coordinated across countries, especially when banks under different national regulators have outstanding positions in common loan markets.

In addition to the fire-sale problem, non-coordinated deleveraging programmes also pose problems for macroeconomic policy, in view of the negative impact of deleveraging on the current level of aggregate demand. A slower pace of deleveraging may necessitate a longer period of reliance on central bank liquidity. A faster pace raises expected losses on asset disposals, requiring a greater degree of recapitalisation. This trade off can give rise to cross-border tensions in view of the different distribution of risk across these two margins.

Banks can be recapitalised from a variety of sources. Equity injections from private-sector investors are difficult to obtain, especially if there are large non-crystallized prospective losses. Even in scenarios in which private-sector interest might be envisaged, the entry of foreign equity investors is hampered by asymmetric information problems by which the quality of domestic loans might be especially hard to assess by non-local investors. By way of counter-example, .one of the main Irish banks (Bank of Ireland) was able to raise foreign private-sector equity as part of its recapitalisation programme only after the quality of its loan books had been subjected to a rigorous granular stress test that was managed by an external agency. In the other direction, the disposal of foreign affiliates can be a source of extra capital if these are profitable and the sale generates a capital gain. This can be the case if the domestic loan book is the main source of losses, while foreign affiliates operate in better-performing markets.

In cases where existing shareholders are virtually wiped out, capital may also be obtained by achieving write downs on subordinated debt obligations. Going further, it is arguable that it is desirable to extract concessions on senior bonds (at least in the case of extreme losses). However, senior bonds have so far remained untouched in the euro area, even if recent proposals from the European Commission recommend that senior bonds should form part of the loss-absorbing component of the capital structure in the future.

If these market-based options prove insufficient, the taxpayer is the final source of fresh capital for banks. If foreign investors hold a large proportion of bank bonds, there is a clear conflict of interest between domestic taxpayers and foreign bondholders in relation to recapitalisation options: the more can be obtained through writedowns of bonds, the lower the fiscal cost. Moreover, to the extent that the protection of bondholders is motivated by financial stability concerns, there is an externality in relation to international financial stability. While this applies at a global level, it is even stronger within a currency union, in view of the high degree of integration of common-currency bond markets. In the presence of this externality, national governments will undervalue the public good of international financial stability.

One way to address the externality issue is to provide directly recapitalise banks through a common international fund. Of course, international bank recapitalisation would have to be accompanied by parallel international regulatory control of such banks. Furthermore, this would break the "diabolic loop" between national banking systems and national sovereigns in relation to the heavy fiscal costs of resolving deeply-troubled banking systems. Again, the importance of breaking this link applies most strongly inside the euro area, in view of the greater scope for cross-border contagion across banks and across national governments.

Such international cooperation in the provision of risk-bearing funding is not yet in place. Rather, official funding during the crisis has taken the traditional form of plain-vanilla loans and lines of credit to national governments. After a period of quietude, the IMF has become an active lender again during this crisis, committing more than $300 billion in loans to member countries since 2007. This has required a major increase in the IMF's funding capacity, with further expansion planned.

In addition to its traditional role of acting as a source of foreign-currency funding for emerging-market economies that have been shut out of international markets, the IMF has taken on a major role in lending to high-income members of the euro area. In view of the scale of official funding needs in Europe, the IMF has entered joint loan agreements with the European Union, with the IMF providing only a minority of the required funding.

At one level, the marriage of IMF and regional funding is an appealing combination. In particular, the greater financial and trade linkages at the regional level mean that contagion risks are higher at a regional level than at a global level. However, there is a limit to the effectiveness of regional funding in the case of a common shock that negatively affects the fiscal positions of all countries in a given region. Moreover, cross-country political sensitivities at a regional level make it more difficult to implement standard adjustment programmes, since both creditor and debtor countries may seek to obtain politically-attractive exceptions to normal official loan conditions.

In view of the very large increase in financial balance sheets and the scale of cross-border financial positions, it is not too surprising that the scale of official funding requirements has grown dramatically. The macroeconomic and financial impact of a sudden stop in capital flows and/or the funding of fiscal deficits is increasing in the scale of balance sheet exposures. Moreover, the scope for cross-country contagion is also increasing the extent of cross-border financial positions.

The importance of official funding is even stronger inside a currency union. First, the inability to devalue means that fiscal policy is the main macroeconomic stabilisation instrument at a national level, so that swings in fiscal positions during a crisis are larger and more persistent than under an independent currency regime. Second, investor demand for national sovereign debt is more elastic, since alternative sovereign debt assets from other member governments are available without having to take on currency risk. During the crisis, this "flight to safety" effect within the euro area has generated substantial cross-border capital flows, with a reduction in demand for peripheral sovereign debt and sharp reductions in the yields on the main safe asset, the German bund. Third, there is considerable contagion among sovereign spreads inside the currency union during the crisis, with a jump in the spread for one vulnerable country quickly spreading to other member countries with similar fiscal characteristics.

Financial globalisation also affected macroeconomic policy management during the crisis. In terms of global policy coordination, the world's major central banks announced coordinated interest rate cuts in October 2008, while coordinated fiscal expansions were announced at the G-20 summit in November 2009. After this most intense phase of the crisis in Autumn 2008, explicit macroeconomic policy coordination has not been maintained.

The limited role for global policy coordination has obvious explanations in view of the domestic mandates under which macroeconomic policy is determined. Still, the international spillovers from macroeconomic policy choices highlight the inefficiencies embedded in a non-coordinated approach. In addition to traditional spillovers from interest rate choices and fiscal choices, there are also international spillovers from the non-standard monetary instruments activated by central banks.

Again, the potential gains from policy coordination are largest within the euro area, in view of the strong financial and trade linkages across the member countries. Relative to alternative monetary arrangements, a common central bank certainly delivers a coordinated interest rate policy. The ECB main refinancing rate was cut substantially during the crisis, from 4.25 percent in June 2008 to 1.0 percent by April 2009. It is an open question whether similarly-low policy interest rates could have been delivered by all member countries under a system of independent national currencies, in view of the risk premia and liquidity premia traditionally faced by the smaller member countries under previous systems.

At the same time, the ECB's traditional focus on area-wide aggregates in making its monetary policy decisions may be inadequate under conditions in which fundamental asymmetries exist among the member countries. In particular, cross-border financial integration was associated with the emergence of large net external imbalances among the member countries. In turn, the process of external adjustment among the member countries necessitates substantial shifts in intra-area real exchanges, which can only take the form of intra-area inflation differentials. In view of the considerable evidence of downward wage rigidities, a temporarily-higher inflation target could facilitate external adjustment at a lower cost in terms of the shortfall of aggregate output and employment relative to potential.

Furthermore, fiscal policy coordination within the euro area is quite weak, despite the fiscal spillovers across the member countries. In particular, the European economic governance system is primarily directed at monitoring fiscal sustainability at a national level., even if the guidelines in principle do recognise the importance of taking into account the overall European macroeconomic situation in determining fiscal policies. Still, the primary emphasis placed on national-level fiscal targets means that insufficient attention is given to the implications for the area-wide fiscal stance. Moreover, hard-wired fiscal coordination through the European-level joint fiscal budget is currently very small (at about one percent of aggregate GDP), especially relative to other monetary unions (such as the United States). This lack of fiscal coordination is especially problematic during a crisis period in view of the inherent fragility of national-level fiscal positions inside a currency union.

These factors indicate how financial integration reinforces the importance of fiscal reforms to improve the stability of the euro area. Of course, more prudent national fiscal policies during normal times would reduce the vulnerability of member countries during crisis periods by reducing average debt levels and improving the cyclical conduct of fiscal policy.

However, joint fiscal initiatives are also important. The issuance of European-level tranched bonds can delink the "flight to safety" effect and cross-border flows, even if each national government remains fully liable for its own debt. The various proposals for eurobonds that involve joint-and-several liability can also accomplish this goal, although with a deeper level of fiscal union required in view of the moral hazard problems associated with jointly-guaranteed debt. A larger European-level fiscal budget can also relieve the pressure on national sovereigns. Here, two routes can be envisaged. First, a limited form of fiscal union would be involved in the creation of a common fiscal reserve fund that would be able to finance area-wide stimulus programmes in the event of an aggregate negative shock. As is the case with a common banking resolution fund and the European Stability Mechanism, this type of fiscal fund would only target the tail risks associated with crisis periods, such that fiscal policy primarily remains national in scope during normal times. However, a deeper level of fiscal union would require a greater pooling of area-wide tax revenues in order to finance cyclically-sensitive expenditure lines (such as unemployment insurance) or distribute resources to member states in line with area-wide GDP rather than national-level GDP. Since such schemes could entail permanent net transfers across member countries in the event of permanent asymmetric shocks, a high level of political integration would be required to ensure the sustainability of this type of deep fiscal union:

Accordingly, the current intense debate about constructing European-level banking and fiscal institutions serves to illustrate the implications of a high level of financial integration for macroeconomic and financial stability, especially when financial globalisation amplifies the costs of various underlying distortions (such as inadequately-regulated banks and overborrowing incentives in different sectors). By way of contrast, the much weaker state of global governance (relative to even existing intra-European governance arrangements) suggests that a similar level of financial integration among a broader set of countries would not be remotely sustainable.

FINANCIAL GLOBALISATION AND EMERGING MARKET ECONOMIES (EMEs)

For most EMEs, financial globalisation is not costless and its benefits are not compelling. For instance, there have been second thoughts about the benefits of unfettered capital flows. However, financial openness in itself does not bring about a crisis. Inappropriate monetary policies have played a big part in causing financial crises. Excessive credit expansion is a key causal factor.

But financial globalisation is the channel through which crisis contagion takes place. It raises risk of spillovers. Crisis contagion is so disruptive because in the absence of a proper system of international deposit guarantees and a global regime for bankruptcy and resolution. International trade has a WTO to set and enforce the rules of the game. International finance does not. The periodic transmission of financial crises tends to roll back the benefits from greater financial globalisation. There has been a positive correlation between banking crises and cross-border capital mobility. This is due in part to the procyclical nature of financial markets. Existing informational and institutional structure for global policymaking remains woefully inadequate to the challenge of financial globalisation.

What about foreign participation in the domestic financial system? The basic direction should be towards opening up financial sector, allowing for the presence of global players in domestic markets, but also putting in place appropriate financial stability safeguards. Many of these safeguards are well known and universally accepted – sound regulation and rigorous supervision of financial institutions, having in place adequate capital and liquidity buffers, and improving transparency and corporate governance. But two additional areas where more thought is required are:

First, to what extent should foreign banks be allowed to take deposits, especially retail deposits, and especially through branches? The universal branching model where branches of foreign banks are permitted to undertake a combination of retail, commercial and investment banking activities, without a need to legally separate these activities, has significant efficiency benefits for banks. It allows them to take advantage of economies of scale by sharing management resources and capital across its business lines, and to pool risks across the banking group globally. For commercial and investment banking business, financial globalisation generally works well. But when foreign bank branches have a significant share of domestic retail deposits, financial globalisation can be risky. During periods of severe stress, the provision of essential services by a branch – especially to retail customers – could be disrupted. Local retail depositors would be exposed to possible contagion or a crisis of confidence arising from problems in the bank's home market. There is, therefore, a case for additional safeguards for retail deposit-taking by foreign banks – through limits on branching privileges or by imposing local incorporation requirements.

Second, to what extent should financial openness be limited by the prudential need for strong domestically anchored banks, whose interests are aligned with those of the domestic economy? There is a proposition that banks with long-term interests aligned with the domestic economy will be more likely to act in support of the country's financial and economic stability. In a crisis, strong, domestically anchored banks may be needed to undertake various roles. First, they may be needed to acquire distressed financial institutions whose failure could have a systemic impact. The 2008 crisis provides some examples of this. In the United States, Bank of America took over Merrill Lynch, and JP Morgan took over Bear Stearns. And in the UK, Lloyds took over HBOS. Second, strong and anchored banks may be needed to increase their role as key credit intermediaries in a crisis. This may include collaborating with the government to sustain lending to businesses in the real economy, where a credit freeze could result in business failures, job losses, and a more severe downturn.

From EMEs perspective, liberalising and deepening the financial markets is an important element in economic rebalancing and restructuring. The new global economic landscape over next decade will be shaped by three fundamental forces: i) Deleveraging in advanced economies (AEs) – this will mean slower economic growth in AEs; ii) Re-regulation globally – this could mean less financial intermediation globally; iii) Demographic change globally: population ageing in AEs and rise of affluent middle class in Asia will mean a shift in consumption demand from AEs to EMEs in general, and within Asia in particular.

Net exports will no longer contribute as significantly to EMEs growth in the next decade as they have in the past. To counter a potentially significant decline in overall growth, EMEs needs to boost domestic and regional sources of growth. This calls for policies to encourage greater consumption spending in some countries and more investment spending in others. In particular, Asia continues to lag in infrastructure capacity and needs to invest significantly more in the years ahead.

Successful rebalancing involves a multi-faceted economic restructuring process that entails macro and micro adjustments: i) Fiscal reforms are crucial. A more developed social safety net can reduce the need for high individual savings. ii) Appropriate macroeconomic policies are also important. Real exchange rate appreciation will facilitate expenditure switching towards the non-tradable (domestic) sector.

If appropriately carried out, financial sector reforms can complement and accelerate the process of economic restructuring in EMEs by improving the intermediation of savings and raising the efficiency of investment spending. The deepening of capital markets, in particular, is of critical importance.

The ongoing consolidation by European banks and changes in regulatory and prudential requirements mean that there is an increased need to develop alternative sources of long-term financing to traditional bank loans. Households will also benefit from financial liberalisation because their savings can be put to better use, thus generating higher returns.

By fostering financial innovation, liberalisation provides savers with a broader menu of investment and insurance products, thus lessening the motive for precautionary saving. Improved household access to financial services provides a net boost to consumption. For China, further financial reforms would raise private consumption by about 5% of GDP. The Mexico and Thailand saw an increasing trend in consumption after liberalising their domestic financial sectors in the 1980s and 1990s.

Financial globalisation is eventually necessary to maximise the benefits of domestic financial reform but it should not be rushed and it should be carefully sequenced. In the longer run, greater financial integration and globalisation can potentially yield additional benefits for EMEs. However, certain pre-requisites or "threshold" factors have to be met before a country can be expected to benefit from financial globalisation. Otherwise, the country could experience more crises and lower growth.

Only countries with reasonably good public institutions, adequate control of corruption, and a minimum level of human capital would be able to translate greater financial openness into higher investment and growth on a sustained basis. Greater benefits from financial globalisation were reaped when domestic financial markets were more developed and well supervised. Indeed, domestic financial deepening, along with merchandise trade expansion, makes capital controls more difficult to enforce.

Domestic financial reforms should precede financial globalisation in EMEs. First, long-term capital flows and trade-related flows be removed to facilitate economic growth and development. Next, controls on short-term flows can be removed after interest rates have been liberalised and government finances put on a sound footing. Finally, when domestic banks are sufficiently strong and a sound system of banking regulation and supervision is in place, free entry and exit of foreign banks can be allowed.

FINANCIAL GLOBALISATION AFTER THE CRISIS: POLICY REFORMS

The global crisis has reinforced the importance of an array of policy reforms at international and national levels. There are two broad categories - reforms that can reduce the likelihood and severity of future crises and reforms that can improve macroeconomic and financial resilience in the event of a crisis.

At the international level, the most direct challenge is to improve the regulation of the global financial system. Here, the reform agenda includes the coordinated, effective regulation of the group of global banks that form the backbone of the international financial system. At a basic level, this would be facilitated by a much deeper knowledge base about the international activities of these banks, which in turn requires much richer data collection, including the full integration of offshore international financial centres into the data matrix on cross-border financial activities. In related fashion, better analytical models of international systemic risk are needed in order to usefully interpret such data and develop appropriatae preventive policy responses.

At the same time, regulatory oversight cannot be an adequate substitute for ensuring that these banks have sufficient incentives to avoid excessive risk taking, while market discipline can also be enhanced through the design of capital structures that increase the incentives for investor monitoring. In addition to enhancing bank safety, it is essential to develop international resolution regimes that can handle failures among this group of banks.

The other main element in international policy reform is the construction of stronger international safety nets. Even with the recent increases in its resources, the lending capacity of the IMF has not kept pace with the growth in cross-border financial positions. Given the costliness of avoidable defaults to the debtor country and, through contagion effects, to the global system, international liquidity provision has to remain a fundamental component in the international financial architecture.

At the same time, the growing size of international balance sheets and the fiscal costs of back stopping international liquidity facilities reinforces the importance of designing bailout systems that limit moral hazard problems. In related fashion, the international system has to be better prepared to deal with insolvency cases, whether it is bankrupt sovereigns or bankrupt banking systems. To this end, the potential gains from establishing an international bankruptcy court could be revisited.

In additional to global-level institutional reform, the very high level of financial integration in Europe (especially within the euro area) calls for the development of regional-level institutions that can help to improve macroeconomic and financial stability. It may be noted that an important differentiating factor between global-level and European-level reform is the much closer degree of political integration at the European level, even if it remains to be seen whether there is sufficient political will to deliver the required European-level institutional reforms.

Still, even if the global and regional financial architectures were much improved, it would remain the case that domestic residents bear the largest costs in the event of a financial crisis. Accordingly, the main responsibility for adapting policy regimes to cope with financial globalisation lies with national governments. In general, domestic policy reforms should be complementary to parallel reforms at the international level.

While operating under the general auspices of international or regional regulatory frameworks, the implementation of financial regulation is set to remain primarily local (with the possible exception of very large financial institutions). A key step is the development of national bank resolution regimes that limit the systemic and fiscal costs of failing banks. In addition, as is well understood, a primary challenge is to develop effective macro-prudential instruments that limit systemic risk. Even more important, national governments have to be willing to actively implement a rigorous macro-prudential framework, even at the risk of committing Type II errors that forestall sustainable expansions in credit growth. A broad macro-prudential framework can include a role for capital controls. Finally, excessive leverage in the non-financial sector (corporates and households) can be further deterred through tax and regulatory policies that do not favour debt financing over equity financing.

In terms of national macroeconomic policy frameworks, two key principles should guide the implementation of monetary and fiscal policies. First, the global crisis has provided further evidence of the costs of excessive imbalances (whether excessive domestic credit growth or excessive external deficits). While accepting that it is difficult to draw the line between sustainable and excessive imbalances, a prudential approach would suggest greater activism to lean against the wind. This includes operating a countercyclical fiscal policy that takes into account financial cycles as well as the output cycle. Second, it is important to have in place national buffers that can cope with adverse shocks. In terms of monetary regimes for countries with independent currencies, the crisis has revised upwards the prudential level of foreign-currency reserves, even if that level remains far below the scale of reserves currently maintained by some countries. In relation to fiscal policy, a basic message is that the crisis has revised downwards the level of public debt that can be considered "safe" in normal times, in view of the scope for rapid growth in public debt during financial crises. Moreover, the crisis has shown the importance of a strong public balance sheet in order to adequately address balance sheet problems in other domestic sectors (households, corporates, banks). In addition to maintaining a sufficiently-low public debt, this can involve the accumulation of a liquid rainy-day fund, since even a low-debt government may find it difficult to borrow during crisis periods.

For those countries still operating under binding financial account controls, the importance of a robust domestic institutional and policy framework in effectively managing cross-border financial integration strengthens the case for a gradualist approach to financial account liberalisation. At the same time, the classic tension remains - external account restrictions protect the monopoly power of domestic financial institutions, at the possible cost of lower efficiency and lost growth opportunities. Managing this trade-off remains a primary challenge for policy officials in emerging and developing economies.

Finally, there are international externality effects from national policy choices, especially in areas such as the implementation of financial regulation, reserve accumulation and capital controls. In related fashion, there are international externality effects from national systemic imbalances (banking-system fragilities, external imbalances). Accordingly, an additional role for international institutions is to flag such externalities through monitoring and surveillance frameworks, even if such "soft" financial diplomacy faces natural limits.

WILL FINANCIAL GLOBALISATION SURVIVE?

In the same way that a deep and well-functioning financial system is useful and desirable for an individual country, financial globalisation is useful for all the benefits that have been widely recognised in the literature and in policy circles. Nonetheless, as in the case of individual financial systems, financial globalisation entails risks and challenges that derive from three features of financial markets:

i) They are prone to suffer from information imperfections and asymmetries that create poor incentives and induce excessive risk-taking.

ii) Failure of some of their institutions or segments may have systemic and macroeconomic consequences.

iii) They behave procyclically, propagating and exacerbating macroeconomic shocks.

These features give rise to financial crises and to deep and protracted recessions that follow a period of excessive leveraging and risk-taking. And, financial globalisation amplifies the scale and the scope of these problems while making their solution more difficult due to their size, complexity, and the need for coordination between different countries.

Hence, if some degree of financial globalisation is desirable, it must be made sustainable by appropriate "global" supervision and macro- and microeconomic regulation in the same fashion that a healthy financial system is sustained in each individual country. This would probably be part of the "first best" solution. However, it is not a practical one in the current state of affairs. Not even Europe, with a commitment to a long-term economic and political project, has been able to institute such an arrangement.

Therefore, we must move to the world of the "second best" solutions, in which a more restricted but sustainable financial globalisation is obtained. The degree of cross-border financial integration between countries depends on the institutional capacity of each country. World's institutional capacity to deal with financial integration is rather limited.

This applies not only to the world's inability to coordinate adequate crisis resolutions, liquidity or capital regulation and supervision, but it also may be understood in a wider sense as the absence of general macroeconomic policy frameworks that would mitigate the probability of financial imbalances and crises. Unlike emerging economies in the past decade, advanced economies generally did not conduct countercyclical fiscal policies or build buffers in good times. Will they in the future? Unlike some emerging economies that were badly hit by previous financial crises, advanced economies did not pay enough attention to credit growth in their monetary and financial policy strategies. Will they from now on?

Thus, as long as neither of these two factors – liquidity provision and crisis prevention/resolution mechanisms – are sufficiently coordinated between countries, and as long as appropriate fiscal/monetary policy frameworks are lacking in relevant advanced and emerging economies, it could be better to proceed on a gradual path of financial globalisation under the following conditions:

i) Limited bank and private sector leverage: this would cut credit supply and increase the cost of finance but would reduce the size and contagion of financial market disruptions.

ii) Stricter FX and local currency liquidity requirements: this is key, especially in the absence of coordinated liquidity provision plans between countries.

iii) International banks should preferably work as fully incorporated local institutions wherever they are present, subject to the domestic capital and liquidity regulations, and covered by the domestic financial safety net. Again, this could make credit more expensive, but it would limit contagion and rely on supervision and regulation by agencies that are probably more familiar with the local risks and environment.

iv) Financial innovation should not be discouraged, but new products should carry large capital requirements whenever their risks or valuation are not fully understood by the authorities.

v) Large countercyclical capital and provisioning requirements (with respect to the credit cycle) should be embedded as part of the existing rules. This way, an excessive credit expansion is not only more easily curbed, but it is also made less likely since banks can expect that the costs of feeding it will increase.

Elements along these lines are included in the Basel III initiative. It will be desirable for them to be shared by many financially relevant economies, so that regulatory arbitrage is limited and the effectiveness of the regulation is not significantly weakened. This would be the minimum of international coordination that is necessary for financial globalisation to be sustainable. Some may argue that this is a return to financial repression. That is one way to put it. Another is that financial globalisation went too far in the first place given the "institutional capacity" of the world as a whole, so it is necessary to step back somewhat.

Yet, although a movement in this direction is clearly a retrenchment of financial liberalisation for a number of advanced countries, for many emerging economies there is still ample room to continue adopting financial products and deepening their financial systems within this more prudent framework.

Finally, on financial globalisation and macroeconomic resilience in some emerging economies in the face of the shocks observed since 2008 illustrate the benefits of flexible exchange rate regimes (among other policy response elements). The shock absorber role played by the exchange rate and the fact that flexible regimes enabled countercyclical monetary policy responses suggest that for many emerging economies, this will continue to be a useful part of their policy framework. But a properly working flexible exchange rate regime requires limits on currency and FX maturity mismatches, limited financial dollarisation and other related regulation. Hence, from the point of view of these economies, sustainable financial and trade globalisation imply the presence of such restrictions on some financial activities and exposures.

INTERNATIONAL DIMENSIONS OF THE RISK-TAKING CHANNEL

The decade before the global financial crisis was marked by very rapid growth in cross-border financial positions. While the 1990s Mexican and Asian crises had certainly induced greater caution among emerging economies, most advanced economies fully embraced the financial globalisation model. Although the potential risks from these developments were much discussed, by and large there was relatively little by way of policy responses to the structural changes generated by financial globalisation.

The relative calm in the global economy during this period meant that the full implications of financial globalisation could not be evaluated. First, it is only in retrospect that the build-up of vulnerabilities in the pre-crisis phase can be fully appreciated. Second, the cross-country and cross-group variation in the scale of international financial integration might deliver very different outcomes in the heat of a financial crisis than during non-crisis times. Third, the capacity of national governments and the international system to effectively manage a financial crisis in an environment of very high international financial linkages was not challenged during this period.

Accordingly, the global financial crisis provides an important testing ground for the financial globalisation model. While the market-panic phase of the global crisis was most intense during Autumn 2008 and Spring 2009, subsequent crisis stages are still playing out, with Europe at the centre of the current phase of the crisis.

A long period of low interest rates in advanced economies induces cross border lending by international banks and this reduces the cost of funds for emerging countries' banks and their respective customers (firms and households). At the same time, it causes the emerging country's currency to appreciate. The latter effect increases the net worth of the emerging country residents, thereby reducing their perceived risk and opening additional room for more cross-border lending. Moreover, the new capital flows stabilise the exchange rate and further enhance the scope for cross-border lending. The trouble is that these cycles feed excessive risk-taking in the emerging economy and exacerbate the build-up in both credit and spending. This makes the reversal of the external conditions traumatic.

This is a relevant channel of transmission and poses a serious challenge to monetary policymakers in emerging economies. In this context, the advanced countries position is rather fortunate because there is a substantial non-tradable sector and they are net commodity exporters. This means *first*, that the pass-through from the exchange rate to domestic prices is low, and second, that large capital inflows tend to coincide with external conditions that enhance national income and aggregate demand. Hence, policy interest rates have been generally raised during periods of large capital inflows, thus reducing the impact of the risk-taking channel. In addition, the policy framework itself has features that dampen the effects of this channel. To begin with, the flexible exchange rate regime and an increasingly credible inflation target have further weakened the pass-through. The downward pressure on policy rates stemming from the appreciation of the currency has thereby been reduced. *Second,* exchange rate flexibility also discourages the emergence of currency mismatches (due to the greater volatility of the exchange rate) and reduces the incentives of local borrowers to use cross-border, euro-dollar-denominated funds. *Third,* advanced countries have strict regulation preventing financial dollarisation and restricting currency and FX maturity mismatches by banks. In practice, this means that all cross-border financing must be provided internally in the same currency and with terms that are no longer than those of the original foreign funds.

Thus, the scope for a substantial expansion of local credit following a reduction in external interest rates is rather limited. Intermediated cross-border flows are low relative to the total credit supply. However, in some instances it is possible that the collateral valuation effects could be too strong, or currency mismatches in the real sector might rise significantly, or overall real sector leverage increase too fast, or the appreciation pressures could become strong enough to keep policy rates too low for too long. In these cases, advanced economies are willing to use and have used temporary capital controls in the form of unremunerated reserve requirements on external loans. These are also sometimes coupled with the imposition of temporary marginal reserve requirements on domestic deposits.

Is this policy response to the risk-taking channel easily applied in other emerging countries? Probably not, especially in more open economies, where the pass-through is larger and the possibility of raising policy interest rates in the face of declining external interest rates is more restricted. In these cases, conflicts between price and financial stability may be more common and could require more frequent deviations from the inflation target (with the corresponding communication effort) or more frequent use of capital controls.

SOME IMPLICATIONS OF ADVANCED ECONOMY DELEVERAGING FOR EMERGING COUNTRIES

As part of their deleveraging process, financial institutions in advanced economies are selling a number of assets and businesses they hold in emerging countries. The buyers in many cases have been financial institutions from emerging economies. This poses a risk and a challenge for financial regulators and supervisors in the emerging world. For example, Colombian conglomerates are now in control of several banking and pension businesses across Latin America.

This is an issue that must be closely monitored since the ownership of many financial institutions across the emerging world may now be in the hands of agents whose home regulatory and supervisory agencies may not have sufficient expertise or resources to deal with systemic problems at the regional level (as opposed to the national level).

Of course, this is relevant to both the host and home countries. For the host countries, it is key to gauge the risk control, liquidity/capital provision facilities, and resolution mechanisms of important parts of their financial systems. For home countries, it is crucial to assess the vulnerability of their financial system and the fiscal, exchange rate, and monetary implications of this new exposure. For both, it is a contagion channel that must be understood and monitored.

QUESTIONS

1. Define financial globalisation. Did financial globalisation materially contribute to the origination of the global financial crisis?
2. Once the crisis occurred, how did financial globalisation affect the incidence and propagation of the crisis across different countries?
3. How has financial globalisation affected the management of the crisis at national and international levels?
4. Critically examine the sources of global financial crisis.
5. Discuss the mechanisms by which cross-global financial integration either amplified crises dynamics or provided a buffer that mitigated crises shocks.
6. Critically examine the various dimensions of crisis management which were affected by financial globalisation.
7. Discuss the policy response and global financial globalisation after the crisis.
8. Will financial globalisation survive? Discuss the influence that monetary policy responses in advanced economies may have on credit supply and risk-taking in emerging economies.

7

THE FINANCIAL ACCOUNTING AMONG COUNTRIES AND INTERNATIONAL ECONOMIC LINKAGES

INTRODUCTION

The balance of payments is a comprehensive record of economic transactions of the residents of a country with the rest of the world. The record is so prepared as to provide meaning and measure to the various components of the country's external economic transactions. Thus, it aims at presenting an account of all receipts and payments on account of goods exported, services rendred and capital received by residents of the country and goods imported, services received and capital transferred by residents of the country.

THE CONCEPT OF BALANCE OF PAYMENT

The balance of payments record the *flow* of economic transactions between the *residents* of a given country and the *residents* of other countries during a certain *period of time.* In other words, it is a statistical statement for a given period showing (a) transactions in goods, services and income between an economy and rest of the world, (b) changes of ownership and other changes in that economy's monetary gold. Special Drawing Rights (SDRs) and claims on the liabilities to the rest of the world, capital transfers and (c) unrequited transfers and counterpart entries that are needed to balance, in the accounting sense, any entries for the foregoing transactions and changes which are not mutually offsetting.

The 'economy' referred to above is conceived as comprising economic entities that have a closer association with a given territory than with any other territory. Such an economic entity is called a resident. Balance of payments of a given economy will record an economic entity's transactions with the rest of the world, if the entity is a resident of the economy, or any economic entity's transactions with the given economy if the entity is considered a non-resident.

An economic entity which is not a resident entity by the above criterion, is a non-resident. The resident economic entities are classified into three categories. They comprise (i) general government and individuals, (ii) enterprises and (iii) private non-profit making bodies serving individuals. The 'general government' includes all departments, establishments and bodies of Central, State and Local Governments located in the territory of a given economy and also includes embassies, consulates, military establishments and other entities of general government located elsewhere. The latter institutions are treated as residents of that economy because firstly, they are extra-territorial to the economy where they are physically located and secondly, they have a closer affinity with the government they represent. Similarly, embassies, consulates, etc., of foreign countries located in the given economy are treated as residents of the foreign economy and hence a non-resident for the given economy. The conceptual basis relevant for determining the resident status of an individual is whether he is regarded to have been involved in the productive and consumptive process of a given economy with some degree of permanence. The rule of thumb generally adopted for recognition of permanence is a stay for one year or more. This implies that persons visiting the territory of an given economy and staying there for a year or more are to be treated as residents while those visitors who stay for less than a year would be treated as non-residents. Exception to this rule is the given economy's diplomatic or consular representatives and other government personnel stationed abroad. These persons are treated as residents of the given economy and not of the economy where they stay, irrespective of length of their stay. 'Enterprises' include all enterprises engaged in (a) the production of goods and services, (b) transactions in land, etc., or (c) leases, rights, etc., on a commercial or equivalent basis, within the territory of a given economy. 'The private non-profit making bodies serving individuals' are treated on whose territory they are functioning.

The 'transaction' referred to above is an economic transaction. A transaction presupposes two parties or transactors. An economic transaction takes place when something is exchanged between one party and another for economic value. There are, however, few exceptions to the rule that there must be two parties to every transaction. One such exception is a transaction between a branch and its office, as a branch has no separate legal existence. Similarly, when a migrating individual transfers his assets from the old country to the new country, no two parties are involved in the movement of resources. The latter example also serves as an exception to the rule that an economic transaction provides for *quid pro quo.* This is a one sided transaction. Such a transaction is known as an 'unrequited transfer'.

Transactions that enter balance of payments are usually between a resident and a non-resident. A notable exception to this are transactions in gold between a Central Monetary Authority and other residents, both being 'residents'. Certain transactions involving claims on and liabilities to the rest of the world also get covered here even if they are between two residents or between two non-residents. The transactions relating to claims on and liabilities to the rest of the world involve financial flows and these flows are recorded under different economic sectors under capital account. A sale of foreign exchange by the central bank to a commercial bank (both residents) in the same country would be recorded as a reduction in the foreign assets of the official sector matched by a corresponding increase in banking sector's foreign assets. The other types of transactions which form part of balance of payments are the 'unrequited transfers' referred to above and imputed transactions for undistributed income of direct investment enterprises attributable to direct investors.

Allocation (or Cancellation) of Special Drawing Rights (SDRs)

The allocation or cancellation of SDRs by the IMF involves the creation or extinction by the IMF of reserve assets which form part of a country's holdings of official reserve assets. The allocation of SDRs results in increase (debit) in SDR holdings while cancellation results in decrease (credit). The SDR holdings is a component of official reserve assets. In the balance of payments, the offsetting entry to increase in SDR holdings is provided by the item allocation (credit) while cancellation (debit) serves as an offsetting entry to decrease in SDR holdings.

Monetisation/Demonetisation of Gold

Gold is both a commodity and a financial asset. When it is held by the Central Monetary Authority (in India, it is the Reserve Bank of India), as a part of its international reserves, it is treated as a financial asset and it referred to as monetary gold. When it is held by any other party including the government, it is treated like any other commodity. When the Central Monetary Authority acquires gold with a view to strengthening its international reserves, from a non-monetary sector, either from a resident or from a non-resident, it is referred to as monetisation of gold. Demonetisation refers to the reverse transfer of gold from monetary sector to non-monetary sector. It occurs when the Central Monetary Authority releases monetary gold from the holdings of official reserve assets for non-monetary purposes.

Unrequited Transfers

The unrequited transfers cover gifts, grants, migrants' transfers, taxes, etc. where one transactor provides something of an economic value to another without a *quid pro quo* i.e., anything in return. The country receiving the grant or gift neither transfers nor promises to transfer anything in exchange. The lack of economic values on one side is compensated for by an entry which is referred to unrequited transfers. In India's balance of payments, the term 'transfers' is used in the same sense as unrequited transfers.

Migrants' transfers represent a particular type of unrequited transfer. When a person migrates from an economy to a new economy, the property (real and financial resources) owned by the migrant also gets transferred to the new economy. As this is a one sided transaction, it is treated as an unrequited transfer. In principle, this transaction includes all the migrants' property whether or not it accompanies him.

Undistributed Income Attributable to Direct Investors

Retained earnings of an enterprise are owned by its equity holders. The retained earnings are reinvested in the enterprise. That part of such earnings which is attributable to non-resident equity holders need to be recorded in balance of payments. Such retained earnings/reinvested earnings are conceived as a payment of income to the foreign investor and a simultaneous reinvestment of that income by the foreign investor in the same enterprise. In the balance of payments statistics, such retained earnings attributable to direct investors are recorded as a component of foreign investment income receipts/payments in the current account matched by an outflow/inflow of direct foreign investment in the capital account.

Double Entry System of Recording

The balance of payments is built on double entry system of book-keeping. Similar to that used in business accounting. This is an internationally accepted convention for balance of payments compilation. Transactions in a double entry accounting system are recorded in pairs of credit and debit entries of equal value. In an accounting sense, therefore, a country's balance of payments is always in balance. As most of the entries in the balance of payments refer to transactions which have economic values, the counterpart entries for credits or debits are automatically paired.

Valuation

As every transaction has a credit and a debit aspect due to adoption of double entry recording assumes significance. If they are not valued at the same price, the balance of payments statement would not balance. Need for uniform valuation arises *firstly* because the credit and debit aspects are often derived independently from separate sources. *Secondly,* without the uniform valuation system, different items in the balance of payments cannot be compared with each other. *Thirdly,* balance of payments statements of different countries will not be comparable unless every country adopts a uniform valuation procedure. The IMF has, therefore, recommended in the *Balance of Payments Manual* that "market prices" be used for valuing transactions.

Generally, the value of merchandise transactions recorded in India's balance of payments represents the actual price paid through the banking channel, as required under the *Exchange Control Manual* of the Reserve Bank of India. However, it may not always be possible to value transactions at market price. For example, valuation of issue of shares against import of machinery and technical knowhow may not be at the market price. Transactions between a branch and its parents office may not necessarily be at a market price. Further, exports could be undervalued or imports overvalued. Alternatively, exports could also be overvalued (to take advantage of export incentives) or imports undervalued (to benefit from import duty on lower base value). In all such cases, it may not be possible to ascertain the market price. In the case of non-merchandise items, transactions are recorded in balance of payments at the price reported by transactors to authorised dealers while putting through the financial transactions.

Another aspect of the valuation of merchandise transactions is that both exports and imports are to be valued f.o.b. at the customs frontier of the exporter's country. In India's balance of payments statistics, exports are valued on f.o.b. basis at the port of shipment. In the case of imports, they are valued on c.i.f. basis, which also covers cost of insurance and freight borne by the importer, as it is not possible to segregate cost of shipment services.

Still another problem arises in regard to valuation of transactions originally denominated in foreign currencies. While such transactions are to be converted into domestic currency at the market rates of exchange prevailing on the date of transaction, in India's balance of payments statistics, the procedure adopted for conversion into domestic currency is as follows:

> Most of the foreign exchange transactions during a given month, such as exports, imports, trade in service, commercial borrowings and loans received

by the private sector including those from foreign official sources, utilisation of foreign official grants and loans and imports thereof by ways of direct payments to suppliers abroad, in respect of PL 480 Title II grants and transactions passing through banking channels, are converted at the average exchange rate for the month. The procedure is as under:

The pound sterling transactions are converted at the average of the rupee sterling middle rate [average of spot buying and selling rates fixed by Reserve Bank of India (RBI)] for all the working days in a month; in respect of the other currency transactions, the conversions are based on the monthly averages of cross rates of non-sterling currencies to sterling, based on London market, with the average of the rupee sterling rate mentioned above.*

In regard to IBRD/IDA loans and other grants and loans, with effect from April-June 1985 quarter, spot buying rates as on the date of transaction are applied. Prior to April-June 1985 quarter, spot buying rates as on the date of transaction are applied. Prior to April-June 1985, these transactions also were converted at the average exchange rates referred to above.

Until 1984-85, transactions with the IMF were converted at the rupee SDR representative rate. As from April-June 1985 quarter, the SDR/rupee rate prevailing on the date of transaction is used.

The procedure adopted for calculation of foreign exchange reserves is as under:

The Bank's foreign currency assets are valued at month-end average of the spot buying and selling rates. SDR holdings, which were converted at the representative rate upto March 1985, are worked out at the actual rupee-SDR rate prevailing at the end of the moth. However, in the date on foreign exchange reserves published in the RBI's Monthly Bulletin, the SDR balances, even for the past period, have been converted at the actual rates at the end of the month. Gold was valued at ₹18.21 per ten grams up to 1949-50, ₹53.58 per ten grams up to 1965-66 and at ₹84.39 per ten grams up to October 16, 1990 on the basis of the changes in parity value from time to time consequent on devaluation. The value of gold was revised further on October 17, 1990 on the basis of the change in the statutory price of gold effected on that date based on the new procedure, under which the gold is valued close to international market price. The movement in RBI's foreign exchange holdings and SDRs are corrected for valuation changes in the balance of payments statistics.

Timing

In order to avoid discrepancies in the two sides of balance of payments statements, both sides of the transaction that may be registered using different data sources, are required to be recorded in the same period in the balance of payments statistics. In accordance with this principle, the uniform time of recording the current account transactions is conceived of as the time when legal ownership of goods of services change. In the case of capital account transactions, by convention, the change of

* With effect form March 1, 1992 the RBI revised its intervention currency from Pound sterling to US dollar.

ownership takes place at the time when transactions are effected through banking channel.

In India's balance of payments statistics, beginning from October 1, 1983, exports are recorded when they are cleared by the customs authorities for shipment. Prior to this date, exports were recorded when the export documents were negotiated or sent for collection by authorised dealers, which represented change in the ownership of goods. Imports, by and large, are recorded when payments are made. On this basis, advance payments for imports, which create a financial asset for the importing country, get recorded as imports but for which timing adjustments are not made. Transportation and insurance services are recorded when the services are rendered. Other services are recorded at the time of receipt or payment for the services. Undistributed income of direct investment enterprises is recorded on the basis of period in which it is earned and unrequited transfers are recorded when the transactions, to which they are offsets, are recorded. Capital account transactions are recorded when the parties involved effect the transactions through the banking channel.

METHODS OF COMPILATION OF STATISTICS OF BALANCE OF PAYMENTS

Balance of payments statistics by their very nature involve recourse to a variety of sources of information. The methods of collecting the information vary from country to country depending on the nature and availability of statistics. The methods of compilation of statistics for countries which have imposed exchange control differ from those which have not. An exchange control system provides a a continuous record of the foreign exchange transactions of the public, providing valuable information for the compilation of balance of payments. The main advantage of relying on exchange control rely on customs statistics for merchandise transactions and for the remaining items resort to special arrangements using, wherever possible, the available statistical data. Some of the items have to be estimated by means of sample surveys either on a continuous basis or at periodic intervals involving concentrated work.

Data on India's balance of payments statistics are published regularly in the *RBI's Monthly Bulletin* and are presented as per the format in Table 1. The data are presented for a calendar quarter and for a fiscal year. The data published are on a gross (credit/debit) and a net basis. The items are divided into two broad sections—the *Current Account* and the *Capital Account*.

The current account, which may also be called the income account, shows a country's receipts and payments on account of goods and services sold to and purchased from the rest of the world. The capital account indicates how these transactions affect the country's investment position abroad. A surplus on current account leads to an acquisition of assets or repayment of debts previously contracted. Similarly, a deficit involves a withdrawal of previously accumulated assets or borrowing from abroad.

The capital account cannot be dismissed as unnecessary on the ground that it is merely a reflection oft he current account. A study of a country's balance of payments calls for an analysis of the pattern of changes in its foreign assets and liabilities. It is a matter of considerable significance whether a country met its external obligations by borrowing from abroad or by drawing down its assets. The changes in the composition of the assets and liabilities which may be brought about by shifts among different types of obligations or among different agencies holding them, even when there is no change in the overall creditor/debtor position of the country, are also of practical interest. A country which holds a large proportion of its foreign assets in a readily realisable (or usable) form is often in a much better position to withstand balance of payments difficulties than another whose assets are not so liquid.

It is also necessary to know the part of the readily reliable assets held by official and official controlled institutions. This part of the assets, called foreign exchange reserves is a guide to policy in as much as it is these reserves which bear the initial impact of a country's balance of payment surpluses or deficits. The foreign exchange reserves cannot, however, be studied independently of certain liquid obligations abroad, termed foreign exchange liabilities. Changes in foreign exchange reserves might give a deceptive impression of the underlying forces when, for instance, a country meets its foreign obligations by piling up short-term debts abroad. Short-term debts are merely a postponement of the pressures on the reserves to a later date as the liabilities will sooner or later have to be paid off.

TABLE - 1

NET CREDIT (+), NET DEBIT (-)

(₹ CRORE)

Item	*Credits*	*Debits*	*Net*
CURRENT ACCOUNT			
I. Merchandise			
(i) Private			
(ii) Government			
II. Invisibles			
1. Travel			
2. Transportation			
3. Insurance			
4. Investment			
5. Government, not included elsewhere			
6. Miscellaneous			
7. Transfer payments			
(i) Official			
(ii) Private			
A. TOTAL CURRENT ACCOUNT (I+II)			
CAPITAL ACCOUNT			
I. Private			
(i) Long-term			
(ii) Short-term			

II. Banking

III. Official

(i) Loans

(ii) Amortisation

(iii) Miscellaneous

B. TOTAL CAPITAL ACCOUNT (I + II + III)

C. IMF

D. SDR Allocation

E. Capital Account, IMF and SDR ALLOCATION (B + C + D)

F. TOTAL CURRENT ACCOUNT, CAPITAL ACCOUNT, IMF AND SDR ALLOCATION (A + E)

G. ERRORS AND OMISSIONS

H. RESERVES AND MONETARY GOLD

The changes in the composition of a country's assets and liabilities have repercussions also on the current account. For instance, a shift in the holding of assets which yield a certain return to those yielding a higher return will lead to an increase in a country's earnings on investment income.

Current Account

The current account of the balance of payments records India's total transactions, both, visible and invisible (i.e. merchandise, services and transfers) with the rest of the world. The basic data on most of the official transactions not put through ADs, are drawn form Government agencies. For transactions put through ADs, the basic data are taken from the records of the Exchange Control Department of the Reserve Bank.

Visibles

In principle, items included under merchandise trade should cover all transactions relating to movable goods with a few exceptions,* where the (i.e. merchandise trade) should cover all ownership of goods changes from residents to non-residents (exports) and from non-residents to residents (imports). The recording needs to be done at the time of change of ownership, at transaction value and on a 'free on board' (f.o.b.) basis which includes the value of distribution services up to the customs frontier. The use of f.o.b. valuation basis for balance of payments items conform to the recommendations of the *IMF Manual* and has the advantge that exports and imports are treated similarly in their valuation and that international freight and insurance of goods are treated as distinct services—(international freight and insurance come

---

* These exceptions are: goods (such as ships and airline—stores and bunkers) purchased by non-resident transport operators in a given country and similar purchases overseas by that country's transport operators, goods purchased by foreign travellers, purchases of goods by diplomatic and consular agencies.

within the scope of 'transportation' and 'insurance'. However, in the Indian balance of payments statistics, exports are valued f.o.b. while imports are valued c.i.f.

Exports Credits

Under the Foreign Exchange Regulation Act (FERA), 1973 exporters are required to submit declarations in the prescribed forms to the designated authority. GR forms are to be submitted by exporters to the customs in the case of exports by road, sea or air and PP forms are to be submitted to the postal authorities in the case of exports by parcel post. Exports enumerated in these forms include exports on outright sale basis, exports on consignment basis, i.e., exports intended for sale that have not actually been sold at the time they crossed the frontier, full value of exports on deferred payments basis, exports for which consideration is received other than in cash, such as, against equity participation in joint ventures abroad, a exports in respect of which proceeds have already been realised.

Exports of goods sold to overseas buyers on an outright basis, are valued at f.o.b. basis equivalent at the port of shipment at the actual price received/receivable by the exporters. For exports for shipment on consignment basis, the value on f.o.b. basis, equivalent of the expected value on sale of goods in the overseas market to which they are despatched is recorded. In the case of exports on deferred payments basis, full value of exports on f.o.b. basis is recorded at the time of exports.

Exports by Government departments are included under 'Government' exports. All other exports are included under 'Private' exports.

Imports (c.i.f.): Debits

Data for recording imports in India's balance of payments are largely derived from the exchange control records supplemented by information obtained from other sources, primarily government agencies. The exchange control records are based on 'R' returns and the supporting forms. In respect of outward remittances for imports Al forms are submitted by the ADs to the ECD. The value of imports recorded in these forms relates to the invoice value which could be on either c.i.f./c.f. or f.o.b. basis depending upon the terms of contract. Imports invoiced on c.i.f./c.f. basis represent both the merchandise value and payments made for insurance and freight or only for freight as the case may be. In the data on imports obtained from certain official sources, payments for freight and insurance are not distinguished from the cost of merchandise. Consequently, imports in balance of payments are not recorded at f.o.b. values at the customs frontier of the exporting countries as suggested by the *IMF Manual*. Since exchange control records cover imports for which remittances have been effected through the ADs, these would exclude imports that are not paid for at all or imports that are not paid for through the ADs. Coverage adjustment, therefore, is required to be made to include such other imports in the balance of payments statistics.

Imports by Government departments as well as those by public sector undertakings are included under 'Government' imports. All other imports are included under 'Private' imports.

Non-monetary Gold Movement

The monetisation refers to transfer of gold from non-monetary stocks to monetary stocks and demonetisation denotes transfer from monetary stocks to non-monetary stocks. Monetisation adds to the reserve assets while demonetisation effects a reduction. The counterpart entries to the increase (debit) in official reserve assets as a result of monetisation of gold were recorded as credit in the category of "Non-monetary Gold Movement."

The fourth edition of IMF's *Balance of Payments Manual* states that any increase in monetary gold holdings that results from monetisation is shown as a debit in the item for total changes in gold holdings, offset by a credit in the counterpart item for monetisation and *vice versa.*' The *Manual* states further, 'if a change of ownership between economies has also taken place, that change should be recorded, in addition to the entries required to show the monetisation (demonetisation), as an import (export of merchandise in the current account and as a credit (debit) in the capital account, assuming that a financial item was used (received) to pay for that import (export). It should be noted that the gold need not have the same value as a financial asset which it has as a commodity.'

Invisibles

Travel

The *credit* item under travel covers expenditure incurred by non-resident travellers during their stay in the country. It excludes international passenger services, which are included in 'transportation.' Credits cover (i) receipts in foreign exchange in amounts individually equivalent of above ₹ 10,000 and reported by ADs as travel receipts plus amount allocated to travel out of unclassified receipts, i.e., individual receipts equivalent of ₹ 10,000 or below on the basis of the results of the survey of unclassified receipts, (ii) foreign tourists' expenditure in India financed from rupee balances in PL 480 accounts maintained by the US Embassy in India with RBI, New Delhi. However, the credit represent only provisional estimates, as details of purpose-wise classification of travel credits are not called for. In regard to *debits,* detailed classification of the data is available and cover sales of foreign exchange for the purpose of (i) business, (ii) expenses of Indians studying abroad or receiving training abroad, (iii) official business travel, (iv) expenses incurred on medical treatment abroad, (v) tourists and (vi) others. They, however, exclude remittances by foreign nationals in India for meeting educational expenses of their children abroad and for correspondence courses overseas. These are covered under private transfer payments.

Transportation

This item covers all receipts and payments attributable to international transportation services on freight and shipping account except for the freight on imports invoiced c.i.f. or c.f. which is included under imports. These data are derived form transportation transactions reported in exchange control records. Estimated freight on exports invoiced on c.i.f./c.f. basis is separately recorded.

Credits (i) cover reimbursement of estimated freight on exports invoiced on c.i.f./ c.f. basis. Surplus funds remitted by foreign steamship/airline companies in respect of exports carried by them are required to be netted out of the estimated freight on exports, (ii) remittances received by Indian steamship/air-line companies against surpluses arising out of their freight and passage earnings abroad adjusted for the expenses like port charges, bunker charges incurred by their agents abroad, (iii) operating expenses of foreign steamship and airline companies in India netted out of their agents' earnings of freight and passage fares in India and remittances received from their principals abroad to meet the shortfall in expenses and (iv) amounts reallocated form unclassified receipts. A substantial portion of transportation receipts belongs to category (i).

Debits cover (i) remittances made by Indian shipping and airline companies to cover their operating expenses abroad. Similar expenses are also met from collection of freight and passage fare abroad. These data are available from the statements filed by the Indian shipping and airline companies on their foreign exchange collections and disbursements; (ii) remittances made abroad by branches/agents of foreign steamship/airline companies in India to their principals abroad of surplus funds left out of freight and passage fare collections in India after adjusting local expenditure incurred in rupees, (iii) remittances abroad by foreign companies in India to meet the operating expenses in third countries on behalf of their principals; (iv) charter hire payments by Indian companies to the foreign steamship and aircraft owners and (v) freight separately paid to foreign steamship/airline companies directly in respect of imports invoiced on f.o.b. basis.

Insurance

The entries against this item cover all receipts and payments on life and general insurance and re-insurance excepting payments for marine insurance, in respect of imports invoiced c.i.f., which are booked under import payments. *Credits* also include estimates of marine insurance receipts as derived as an element of value of exports, just as in the case of freight estimates. They also include estimated amounts reallocated form 'unclassified' receipts. Remittances out of foreign insurance companies' various insurance funds are treated as capital payments and are not included under this item.

Investment Income

Credits represent income received by Indian residents form the ownership of foreign financial assets. They cover mainly (i) current profits remitted by branches of Indian companies functioning abroad, (ii) dividends received on foreign shares held by residents, (iii) interest on foreign government securities held by residents, (iv) interest on loans extended to non-residents by official and semi-official institutions, (v) interest subsidy form the IMF, (vi) interest on holdings of SDRs, (vii) unclassified receipts re-allocated and (viii) interest and discount earnings on foreign currency assets of Reserve Bank of India. The last item accounts for a predominant share of total investment income receipts.

Debits represent income paid to non-residents accruing form their ownership of financial assets in India. They cover (a) remittances of current profits by Indian branches of foreign companies and of dividends abroad both to direct investors and to portfolio investors; (b) retained earnings (undistributed profits of the current year) of the foreign controlled Indian joint stock companies. These data are recorded only at the revision stage; (c) interest on long-term loans received form non-residents (including international institutions, other than the IMF) by official as well as private sector; (d) interest paid on loan from the IMF (including the Trust Fund loan) under various facilities and charges on utilisation of SDRs and (e) interest paid on rupee balances held by non-resident banks and official institutions in India.

Government, Not Included Elsewhere

Official transactions in goods and services which are not classified in the current account transactions elsewhere, are included here. *Credits* cover funds received from foreign governments for the maintenance of their embassies, consulates and diplomatic missions stationed in India and from international institutions for the maintenance of their offices in India. Payments made out of these funds for upkeep of missions in neighbouring countries are netted out. *Debits* cover remittances made by the Government of India for maintenance of Indian embassies and diplomatic missions abroad.

Miscellaneous

Miscellaneous transactions include all residual service transactions on current account. The major components, covered both under *credit* and *debits,* comprise receipts and payments respectively in respect of payment to technicians, professional services, royalties and management fees. The item also covers fees for agency services, film rentals, royalties, subscriptions for periodicals and refunds. Further, the item includes on both side large amounts for which purpose-wise classification was not available to the ADs at the time of reporting to the ECD. Moreover, travellers' cheques/foreign currency notes encashed by non-resident Indians on temporary visit to India are included here. On the other hand, the entire residual debits have been entered in the item, because most of them probably represent payments for services.

Transfer Payments

The entries represent all receipts and payments without a *quid pro quo.* These are classified into official and private:

Official: The item covers unrequited transfers between resident official sector and non-residents. It represents offsetting entries for inward remittances for donations, etc., in cash or in the form of import of commodities or outward remittances in cash or in kind by way of gifts.

Credits cover (i) grants received by the Government of India, (ii) India's share of profits form the sale of gold held by the IMF, (iii) interest subsidy relating to Oil Facility (1975) of the IMF received by the Government of India, (iv) US aid to Nepal under Title I of PL 480, of ₹8.4 crore for 1960-61 (as foreign exchange transactions of Nepal were merged with those of India as there was no exchange control between the two) and (v) commodity assistance received from the US Government under PL 480 Title II assistance.

Debits cover (i) remittances in cash by way of gifts and for technical assistance, scholarship grants to non-residents by the official sector in India, (ii) grants by way of supply of commodities and technical assistance provided by the Government of India to non-residents and (iii) contributions to international institutions such as the UN, the UNESCO, the regional institutions and pension paid to non-residents on Government of India account.

Private: The item covers all unilateral transfers between residents, other than the official sector, and non-residents. Offsetting entries to the private unilateral transfers, viz., the provision of things of economic value by non-residents to residents and by residents to non-residents for which no corresponding exchange value is provided for, are recorded here.

Credits cover mainly (i) repatriation of savings by Indian residents abroad, (ii) receipts for family maintenance, (iii) gifts and donations to religious organisation, (iv) one time receipt of compensation received for Bhopal Gas tragedy and (v) receipts re-allocated from unclassified category. A substantial portion of total credits, sometimes even more than half, under this head are estimated receipts based on the Survey of Unclassified Receipts. A significant art of the receipts represent remittances of savings or for family maintenance by Indian residents abroad. *Debits* comprise mainly (i) remittances for family maintenance, (ii) remittances of savings by foreign nationals and (iii) migrants' transfers by foreign nationals. The magnitude of items under debits is very low in India's balance of payments.

Capital Account

The capital account represents transfers of money and other capital items and changes in the country's foreign assets and liabilities resulting form the transactions recorded in the current account. Flows recorded in the capital account are divided into three sectors private, banking and official. The transactions with the IMF, SDR allocation by the IMF and movement in reserves are shown separately.

Private Capital

This item includes capital transactions of resident individuals, firms, privately owned non-financial corporate enterprises and non-bank financial enterprises, with non-residents including international institutions. Private capital is sub-divided into (i) long-term and (ii) short-term.

(i) Long-term

Credits cover mainly (a) foreign investment in shares of Indian joint stock companies, both foreign controlled and non-foreign controlled, (b) investment (including loans and overdrafts) by Head Offices abroad in their Indian branches (c) repatriation/sale proceeds of Indian investments abroad, (d) funds received from abroad for investment in real estate by non-residents (including diplomatic missions, etc., located in India), (e) long-term loans received by private individuals/enterprises/institutions, other than banking institutions, in India, from foreign companies and official sources abroad. They also include commercial borrowings raised abroad by non-banking private sector entitles/financial institutions, (f) repayments, by non-residents, of long-term loans obtained from private individuals, etc, in India, credits also cover non-cash inflow in the form of supply of plant and machinery by parent companies in exchange for issue of shares by the Indian companies as well as undistributed profits attributable to direct investors (notionally treated as investment income paid out and reinvested by the direct investor), (h) deposits received from non-resident Indians into Non-Resident (External) Rupee [NR (E) R] Accounts and Foreign Currency Non-Resident (FCNR) Accounts and (i) estimated portion of unclassified receipts allocated to capital account.

Debits comprise generally repatriation/out flow of funds corresponding to items (a to c) covered under credits. Further, it also covers (a) long-term loans including deferred credits extended to non-residents by individuals and private institutions other than banking institutions, (b) repayment of long-term loans/external commercial borrowings raised abroad, etc., corresponding to the item (e) under credits and (c) repatriation of balances in [NR (E) R] and FCNR accounts on maturity. These outflows may include both principal and interest.

(ii) Short-term

Private short-term capital receipts and payments cover transactions in the nature of short-term borrowings and repayments. Short-term loans are loans with an original maturity of one year or less. *Credits* cover mainly (i) loans secured form foreigners, (ii) advance payment on deferred credit exports and (iii) miscellaneous capital receipts. *Debits* cover (a) loans repaid to foreigners and (b) miscellaneous capital payments.

Banking Capital

This item covers changes in the foreign financial assets and liabilities of deposit money banks, comprising commercial banks, whether privately owned or state owned, and such co-operative banks which are authorised to deal in foreign exchange. There are five constituents of foreign financial assets and liabilities of deposit money banks and changes in these items are recorded in banking capital. The five items are recorded in banking capital. The five items are (1) foreign currency holdings of authorised dealers (ADs), (2) rupee overdrafts, i.e. overdrafts granted by Indian ADs to branches of overseas banks, (3) foreign currency liabilities of the ADs, (4) changes in rupee balances of non-resident official and semi-official institutions held with ADs in India and (5) rupee liabilities to non-resident banks.

(1) Foreign currency holdings comprise credit balances in the form of current accounts or fixed deposit accounts held by the ADs in India with their foreign branches or correspondents (NOSTRO accounts) and investments in foreign currency securities, (2) rupee overdrafts relate to the debit balances held by foreign branches or foreign banking institution with the ADs in India representing overdraft facilities granted by the latter, (3) foreign currency liabilities are the debit balances in the accounts held by the ADs in India with their foreign branches and correspondents representing overdraft facilities obtained or loans taken by the ADs in India from their foreign branches or correspondents representing overdraft facilities obtained or loans taken by the ADs in India from their foreign branches or correspondents, (4) rupee balances of non-resident official and semi-official institutions (excluding

international institutions) held with the ADs in India, (5) rupee liabilities on account of non-resident banks and correspondents relate to credit balances in the accounts with the Indian ADs held by foreign branches and correspondents.

Items (1) and (2) constitute the assets and item (3) to (5) the liabilities of the banking sector. An increase in assets or decrease in liabilities represents an outflow of capital or debit. Similarly, a decrease in assets or an increase in liabilities represents an inflow of capital or credit. The net credits or debits under each of the above heads are compiled separately and then the sum of credit/debits entries so recorded in respect of the above five items is shown as *credits* and *debits* under the banking capital.

Official Capital

The official capital comprises transactions affecting foreign financial assets and liabilities of the Government of India and the Reserve Bank of India. This item, however, excludes transactions with the IMF (except Trust Fund loans), SDR allocation and movement in reserves. Reserve Bank of India's transactions covered in official capital relate to transactions in assets other than the official reserve assets (which are shown separately) and its transactions in rupee liabilities.

The capital transactions thus covered under this item are classified into (i) loans, (ii) amortisation and (iii) miscellaneous.

Loans: Credit cover drawals of loans/credits granted by foreign governments, international institutions to Government of India and State Governments. Similar drawals of loans/credits granted to entities other than the Central and State Governments and public sector undertakings and which are guaranteed by the Government of India are treated as loans by the private sector and recorded in private long-term capital. Drawals by public sector undertakings against external commercial borrowings are included under this item. *Debits* represent disbursements of loans granted by the Government of India to foreign governments.

Amortisation: Credits cover repayments of principal received by the Government of India and Exim Bank in respect of loans granted by her to foreign governments while *debits* represent similar payments by the Government of India in respect of loans/credits extended to her by foreign governments and international institutions and in respect of commercial borrowings by public sector undertakings.

Miscellaneous: This item relates to rest of the transactions on capital receipts and payments on official account, other than those covered under loans and amortisation payments. The item comprises (i) changes in balances in central clearing accounts in non-convertible rupees maintained with the Reserve Bank of India by central banks or foreign trade banks of countries having rupee payment agreements, (ii) extension/ repayment of technical credits to this group of countries, (iii) changes in rupee balances in accounts of non-resident government and non-government institutions including the increase in liabilities resulting from the creation of non-negotiable securities in favour of the IMF representing the local currency portion of the increased subscription, (iv) increase/decrease in investments in treasury bills depending upon availability of funds in any of the rupee accounts referred to above, (v) movement in balances of the US embassy in India maintained with the Reserve Bank of India in various accounts, viz., rupee account, dollar denominated account and Cooley account, (vi) movement in working balances in the accounts maintained abroad by India Supply Mission, Washington, the High Commission of India, London and the Indian Embassy, Tokyo, (vii) contribution to capital made by Government of India to international institutions including quota payment to IMF; contribution in the nature of grants is shown under official transfer payments, (viii) movement in funds held abroad by public sector undertakings out of foreign currency loans raised by them and (ix) contra entry for monetisation of gold.

IMF

This item represents purchases and repurchases of SDRs under various IMF facilities. However, drawals and repayments under Trust Fund loan are not included here but included under official loans.

SDR Allocation

This item represents India's share of net SDR allocation as and when IMF allocates SDRs to its members.

Movement in Reserves

Comprise changes in the official reserve holdings in foreign currencies, gold and SDRs.

INTERNATIONAL ECONOMIC LINKAGES

The analytical framework that links the international flow of goods, services, and capital to domestic economic behaviour consists of a set of basic *macroeconomic accounting identities.* These basic identities linking national economic activity with balance-of-payments account shows that a nation produces more than it spends will save more than it invests, export more than it imports, and wind up with a capital outflow. A nation that spends more than it produces will invest more than it saves, import more than it expors, and wind up with a capital inflow. Exhibit-1 show the

EXHIBIT-1

BASIC MACROECONOMIC ACCOUNTING IDENTITIES: LINKING NATIONAL ECONOMIC ACTIVITY WITH BALANCE-OF-PAYMENTS ACCOUNTS

	National Product (Y)	–	Total spending (E)
Minus	Spending for Consumption	minus	Spending for consumption
=	National Saving (S)	—	Investment in new real assets (I_d)
=	Net foreign investment, or net increase in claims on foreigners and official reserve assets, e.g., gold (I_d)		
	National products (Y)	—	Total spending (E)
minus	Spending on domestic goods and services		minus Spending on domestic goods and services
=	Export of goods and services (X) – Import of goods and services (M)		
=	Balance on current account		
=	(Balance on capital and official reserves accounts)		

$$Y - E = S - I_d = X - M = I_f$$

macroeconomic accounting identities that links domestic spending and production to savings, consumption, and investment behaviour, and hence to the current-account and capital-account balances. By manipulating the equation shown in Exhibit-1, we can identify the nature of links between the Indian economy and the world economy and assess the effects on the domestic economy of international economic policies, and vice versa.

COPING WITH THE CAPITAL INFLOWS: ADJUSTMENT MIX POLICY

In recent years, capital inflows to some developing countries have increased sharply. This increase in capital inflows has provided much needed financing to increase the use of existing capacity and to increase investment level. Though it appears paradoxical but *too much* capital inflows to developing countries is a matter of concern because of the macroeconomic and other related effects that capital inflows could have on the recipient countries. Indeed, capital inflows could potentially be a problem if they are of a short-term nature and highly volatile. This type of inflow, also called hot money, is usually attracted by some imperfections or policy mistakes that create a large gap between domestic and expected devaluation-augmented foreign interest rates. This type of inflow could create undue instability in inflation rates and in the nominal and real exchange rates. If there are imperfections in capital markets and hysterisis type of effects in the export and import competition sectors, or real bankruptcy and reallocation costs, then these fluctuations could have important economic costs.

Not surprisingly, in many countries the economic authorities try to discourage hot money by lifting the imperfections that encourage them in the first place, or by controlling the side effects of capital inflows through different types of government intervention. Capital inflows of a more cyclical variety could also create cyclical fluctuations in the real exchange rate. The later could create difficulties to the tradable sectors and to overall macroeconomic management. This type of flow creates problems similar to the traditional Dutch disease problem of a mineral discovery.

What can be done to deal with the side effects of Capital Inflows? Many countries have tried to gain access to international capital flows while simultaneously protecting the macroeconomic situation from a large real appreciation and/or acceleration of inflation. To deal with these potential problems caused by capital inflows, countries can use either indirect methods, direct methods, or both.

Direct Methods

If capital inflows (due to their size or composition) are considered to create macroeconomic problems and are motivated by imperfections in the domestic financial markets, countries may try to eliminate the distortion causing the capital inflow. A type of distortion that encourages short-term capital inflows is, for example, keeping a high domestic interest rate while at the same time offering free currency risk protection through a swap facility at the central bank. Offering free deposit insurance at domestic commercial banks, along with a high domestic interest rate and a fixed nominal exchange rate, may also cause an increase in capital inflows.

Short-term speculative capital inflows (hot money) could also result from a restrictive monetary policy that accompany an expansionary fiscal policy. In the latter case, changing the policy mix toward a more restrictive fiscal policy and a less restrictive monetary policy by reducing domestic interest rates to a level closer to the sum of international interest rates and the expected rate of devaluation (that is, getting closer to the interest rate parity condition) reduces the incentives for the type of capital inflows that respond mainly to interest rate differentials and/or to the expectation of a future drop in domestic interest rates, that is, bank loans and portfolio investment.

If the ultimate cause of the increase in capital inflows could not be dealt with, and the country is concerned with the macroeconomic effects of capital inflows, it could try direct methods to control their size. Direct methods consist of imposing restrictions on capital inflows in order to reduce their amount. Measures include ceiling on foreign borrowing, minimum reserve requirements on foreign loans, and ceiling on foreign direct investment. The authorities could also try to reduce the size of the inflows through taxation of the flows with a Tobin-type interest rate equalisation tax. This measure works only in the short run as it is very difficult to have effective ways to control capital flows in the long run.

Indirect Methods

Indirect methods comprise the following:

i) Intervention

Intervention is the purchase of foreign currency by the central bank in order to support the nominal exchange rate. It can be of two types: *sterilised* and *nonsterilised*. In the case of sterilised intervention, the central bank also carries out open market operations to mop up the liquidity created by the initial purchase of foreign exchange. The sterilisation could also be done by imposing other restrictions that work through a reduction in the money multiplier—such as an increase in commercial banks' required reserves or a ceiling in total commercial effect of the purchase of foreign currency (that is, limits the increase in the money supply). However, the room in this area is limited by the degree of substitution between foreign and domestic assets. In a fixed exchange rate or preannounced nominal exchange rate regime, the more open the capital account is and the higher the degree of substitution between domestic and foreign assets is, the less effective is this policy. This policy also usually increases the quasi-fiscal deficit of the central bank. In countries with a level of output close to the potential output, nonsterilised intervention is usually implemented with another policy to restrain aggregate demand.

ii) Fiscal adjustment

A restrictive fiscal policy is intended to have a macro effect and a composition effect. The first effect *(ceteris paribus)* attempts to counteract for the increase in aggregate demand created by capital inflows. The second effect helps to keep a higher real exchange rate than otherwise, as government consumption is most likely more intensive in tradable goods than private expenditures.

iii) Current account liberalisation

The liberalisation of the current account helps to ease the pressure on the domestic economy by shifting consumption toward tradable (that is, importable and exportable) goods. Like a restrictive fiscal policy, it has a composition effect and helps to keep a higher real exchange rate than otherwise possible.

iv) Capital outflow liberalisation

The liberalisation of capital outflows may induce domestic investors, to take their capital abroad. This may partially compensate for the effects of capital inflows.

v) Move toward a floating exchange rate system

By moving closer to a floating exchange rate regime, such as widening the band in a target-zone exchange-rate system, the exchange-rate risk faced by market participants increases. Therefore, there will be less interest in bringing short-term capital inflows.

USES OF THE BALANCE OF PAYMENTS

In recent years, the balance of payments has emerged as a major branch of economic enquiry. The interest in this subject is, in part, a reflection of the complex payments problems of the postwar years and, in part, the result of a greater appreciation of the implications of national economic measures of the external financial position of a country. Developments in the balance of payments are, therefore, of special concern to all those interested n the formulation of correct national economic policies.

The practical uses of a balance of payments statement are many. Apart from lending precision to a country's external transactions, it gives an idea of the historical influences governing the balance of payments. Data presented over a period of time provide a reliable basis for estimating the kind of relationship that exists between the balance of payments and the national income, and help to provide answers to such other questions as the seasonal and cyclical trends, and regional features of the transactions. The usefulness of a balance of payments statement as a guide to monetary, fiscal, trade and other policies cannot, therefore, be over-emphasised. A decision to raise the Bank Rate, for instance, inevitably involves an examination of the balance of payments. A tax measure on exports or on imports may affect the balance of payments similar to direct regulations of trade. Public investment policies too, have an important bearing on, and are, therefore, framed with reference to balance of payments. A decision to expand the capacity of an export industry has necessarily to be based, *inter alia,* on the foreign exchange earnings of the industry. Similarly, development of facilities for foreign tourists requires a knowledge of their expenditure patterns and the contribution of tourism to the economy of the country providing the facilities. The balance of payments also assists in assessing a country's ability to pay for current goods and services and of its credit-worthiness to borrow abroad and repay the loans.

A major contribution to the development of standard compilation techniques for balance of payments statistics came from the International Monetary Fund, a specialised agency of the UN operating in the monetary and exchange field. India is one of the members of the IMF. Among the various obligations imposed by the membership of the institution is one which requires every member to submit periodic reports on the balance of payments to the IMF. To facilitate a consistent system of international reporting, the IMF, has also developed a "Balance of Payments Manual."

Compilation of balance of payments was not entirely a new technique to India. During the per-war years, India had, in fact, compiled certain estimates of balance of payments for the use of the League of Nations which had assumed responsibility for the dissemination of data on the international transactions of the individual countries before the setting up of the IMF. In the pre-war estimates of India's balance of payments, a large part of the invisible transactions remained unrecorded and the compilations lacked certain essentials of a modern balance of payments statement. A systematic compilation of India's balance of payments commenced only in 1948 for meeting the growing official demands for statistics in this field and for fulfilling the country's obligations to the IMF.

There is an obvious relationship between the balance of payments and the national income, since the latter, providing as it does a measure of a country's total economic transactions, includes also the activities of the residents transcending the national boundaries. The contribution of the balance of payments to, or its draft on the flow of national income will equal the difference between the exports and imports of goods and services. Other relationships between the balance of payments and the national income have also been gaining increasing attention in recent years. Mention may be made here, in passing, of such relationships as the propensity to import, the income elasticity of imports, the foreign trade multiplier and the foreign trade accelerator. In the context of the development that has been planned in India, studies of these relationships would gain in importance.

BALANCE OF PAYMENT (BOP)

As per the Balance of Payment Manual (Fifth Edition), BoP comprises current account, capital account, errors and omissions, and change in foreign exchange reserves. Under current account of the BoP, transactions are classified into merchandise (exports and imports) and invisibles. Invisible transactions are further classified into three categories. The first component is Services comprising travel, transportation, insurance, government not included elsewhere (GNIE), and miscellaneous. Miscellaneous services include communication, construction, financial, software, news agency, royalties, management, and business services. The second component of invisibles is income. Transfers (grants, gifts, remittances, etc.) which do not have any *quid pro quo* form the third category of invisibles.

Under capital account, capital inflows can be classified by instrument (debt or equity) and maturity (short- or long-term). The main components of capital account include foreign investment, loans, and banking capital. Foreign investment comprising foreign direct investment (FDI) and portfolio investment consisting of foreign institutional investor (FIIs) investment and American depository receipts /global depository receipts (ADRs/GDRs) represents non-debt liabilities. Loans (external assistance, external commercial borrowings [ECB], and trade credit) and banking capital including non-resident Indian (NRI) deposits are debt liabilities.

No country in today's globalized world can be fully insulated from what happens in the global economy and India is no exception to the rule. As the country is increasingly integrated into the world, it cannot remain impervious to developments abroad. The unfolding of the euro zone crisis and uncertainty surrounding the global economy have impacted the Indian economy causing drop in growth, higher current account deficit (CAD) and declining capital inflows. As in 2008, the transmission of the crisis has been mainly through the balance-of-payments (BoP) channel.

India's external sector exhibited resilience during the global financial crisis of 2008. The balance of payments has been under increasing stress recently. Exports have declined while imports have not fallen significantly, resulting in increasing trade and current account deficits. Though capital flows are bridging the gap, the nature of portfolio capital may lead to greater potential financial fragility and also rupee volatility. India's growing external exposures can also be attributed to the increasing integration of the Indian economy with the rest of the world, which is reflected in both current and capital account transactions. The combined share of exports and imports of goods increased from 14.2 per cent of GDP in 1990-91 to about 43.0 per cent in 2011-12. Two way external sector transactions (i.e, gross current account plus gross capital account flows) have risen from 30.6 per cent of GDP in 1990-91 to about 108.0 per cent in 2011-12. Therefore, while the globalization of Indian economy has helped raise growth, it has also meant greater vulnerability to external shocks.

Table 2 shows that India's balance of payments continued to be under stress. This is reflected in the higher current account deficit in H1 (April-September) of 2012-13 than the corresponding period of the previous year, mainly due to worsening of trade deficit reflected in sharper decline in exports than the imports and lower invisibles surplus. The net capital flows in absolute term, were also lower during H1 of 2012-13 vis-a-vis the corresponding period of 2011-12.

TABLE 2

BALANCE OF PAYMENTS : SUMMARY (US$ MILLION)

Sl. No.	*Item*	*2007-08*	*2008-09*	*2009-10*	*2010-11[PR]*	*2011-12[P]*	*2011-12 H1 (April-Sept. 2011)PR*	*2012-13 H1 (April-Sept. 2012)P*
1	2	3	4	5	6	7	8	9
I.	Current Account							
	1. Exports	166,162	189,001	182,442	256,159	309,774	158,202	146,549
	2. Imports	257,629	308,520	300,644	383,481	499,533	247,739	237,221
	3. Trade Balance	-91,467	-119,519	-118,203	-127,322	-189,759	-89,537	-90,672
	4. Invisibles (net)	75,731	91,604	80,022	79,269	111,604	53,103	51,699
	A Non-factor Services	38,853	53,916	36,016	44,081	64,098	30,409	29,572
	B Income	-5,068	-7,110	-8,038	-17,952	-15,988	-7,587	-10,510
	C Transfers	41,945	44,798	52,045	53,140	63,494	30,281	32,637
	5. Goods and Services Balance	-52,614	-65,603	-82,187	-83,241	-125,661	-59,128	-61,100
	6. Current Account Balance	-15,737	-27,914	-38,181	-48,053	-78,155	-36,433	-38,973

II Capital Account							
Capital Account Balance	106,585	7,395	51,634	63,740	67,755	43,490	39,989
i. External Assistance (net)	2,114	2,439	2,890	4,941	2,296	640	15
ii. External Commercial Borrowings (net)	22,609	7,861	2,000	12,160	10,344	8,388	1,726
iii. Short-term debt	15,930	-1,985	7,558	12,034	6,668	5,940	9,511
iv. Banking Capital (net)]	11,759	-3,245	2,083	4,962	16,226	19,714	14,899
of which:							
Non-Resident Deposits (net)	179	4,290	2,922	3,238	11,918	3,937	9,397
v. Foreign Investment (net)	43,326	8,342	50,362	42,127	39,231	17,087	18,608
of which:							
A FDI (net)	15,893	22,372	17,966	11,834	22,061	15,741	12,812
B Portfolio (net)	27,433	-14,030	32,396	30,293	17,170	1,346	5,796
vi. Other Flows (net)	10,847	-6,016	-13,259	-12,484	-7,008	-8,278	-4,769
III Errors and Omission	1,316	440	-12	-2,636	-2,432	-1,338	-653
IV Overall Balance	92,164	-20,080	13,441	13,050	-12,831	5,719	363
V Reserves change [increase (-) / decrease (+)]	-92,164	20,080	-13,441	-13,050	12,831	-5,719	-363

Source: RBI. PR : Partially Revised. P : Preliminary.

Current Account

The current account of the BoP includes all the transaction (other than those in financial items) involving exchange of economic value which takes place between resident and non-resident entities. During 2011-12, exports crossed the US$ 300 billion mark for the first time. The rate of growth however, declined to 20.9 per cent to US$ 309.8 billion against 40.5 per cent (US$ 256.2 billion) in 2010-11. Exports at US$ 158.2 billion performed well in first half (H1–April-September 2011) of 2011- 12 vis-a-vis exports of US$112.0 billion in H1 of 2010- 11. There was, however, significant deceleration in exports during second half (H2- October 2011 – March 2012) of 2011-12 to US$ 151.6 billion (US$ 144.2 billion in H2 of 2010-11). This was on account of deterioration in global trading conditions reflecting weakening of world demand inter-alia caused by euro zone crisis. Imports valued at US$ 499.5 billion, recorded 30.3 per cent increase in 2011-12 over US$ 383.5 billion in 2010-11. The growth in imports during 2011-12 was mainly due to higher growth in imports of petroleum, oil and lubricants (POL), gold and silver and machinery. Oil imports grew by about 47 per cent, while gold and silver registered a growth of 49 per cent in 2011-12. Imports of oil and precious metal (gold and silver) together accounted for nearly 45 per cent of total imports in 2011-12. The trade deficit increased to US$ 189.8 billion (10.2 per cent of GDP) in 2011-12 as compared to US$ 127.3 billion (7.4 per cent of GDP) during 2010-11. Higher growth in imports than exports was responsible for the widening of the trade deficit in 2011-12.

The net invisible balances showed significant improvement, registering 40.7 per cent increase to US$ 111.6 billion during 2011-12 from US$ 79.3 billion in 2010-11, due to increase in invisibles receipts while invisible payments witnessed a decline. The invisible receipts increased by 15.1 per cent to US$ 219.2 billion in 2011-12 as compared to US$ 190.5 billion during 2010-11, mainly driven by services exports (comprising travel, transportation, insurance, Government not included elsewhere (GNIE), software and non-software), which recorded a growth of 14.2 per cent during 2011-12 (as against of 29.8 per cent in 2010-11). Invisibles payments decreased by 3.2 per cent to US$ 107.6 billion during 2011-12 (US$ 111.2 billion during 2010-11), mainly reflecting lower services payments.

Services exports increased to US$ 142.3 billion in 2011-12 from US$ 124.6 in 2010-11. Though the increase in services exports was broad-based, it was more prominent in case of insurance, transportation, travel and software services. Receipts on account of software services witnessed a rise, mainly on account of improved efficiency and diversified exports destinations. Software receipts at US$ 62.2 billion, accounting for nearly 43.7 per cent of total services receipts, showed an increase of 17.1 per cent in 2011-12. Payment on account of services imports witnessed a decline from US$ 80.6 billion in 2010-11 to US$ 78.2 billion in 2011-12, primarily on account of decline in the imports of business and software services.

Among other components of invisibles, transfers, mainly representing private transfers (secondary income as per BPM 6) recorded a significant increase while income (primary income as per BPM 6) showed a decline. Net private transfer receipts, which basically comprise remittances from Indians working overseas increased by 18.9 per cent to US$ 66.1 billion in 2011-12 from US$ 55.6 billion in the previous year. Increase in private transfers could be attributed to depreciation of rupee in the recent period. In contrast, income (net) showed an outflow of US$ 16.0 billion albeit marginally lower than the preceding year. Overall, gross invisible receipts, showed a sharp rise of 15.1 per cent in 2011-12. Invisible payments declined by 3.2 per cent to US$ 107.6 billion in 2011-12 from US$ 111.2 billion in 2010-11. The decline in payments was mainly on account of lower imports of software and business services and investment income payments. Net invisible balance as per cent of GDP improved to 6.0 per cent in 2011-12 from 4.6 per cent in 2010-11.

The Goods and Services deficit (i.e. Trade Balance plus Services) increased substantially by 51.1 per cent to US$ 125.7 billion (6.7 per cent of GDP) during 2011-12 as compared to US$ 83.2 billion (4.9 per cent of GDP) during 2010-11. The CAD widened to its highest ever level both in absolute terms as well as a proportion of GDP in 2011-12. The CAD in 2011-12 at US$ 78.2 billion was 4.2 per cent of GDP as compared with US$ 48.1 billion or 2.8 per cent of GDP in 2010-11.

In the first Half (H1 - April-September 2012) of 2012-13, there was a steep decline in exports to US$ 146.5 billion, registering a 7.4 per cent decline over US$ 158.2 billion in H1 of 2011-12. Commodity-wise data show that growth in exports of engineering goods, petroleum products, textile products, gems & jewellery and chemical & related products were severely affected as the demand conditions in key markets like the US and Europe continued to remain sluggish. During H1 of 2012-13, EU accounted for nearly 27 per cent of the total decline in merchandise exports, followed by Singapore (19 per cent), China (13 per cent) and Indonesia (6 per cent). Lower growth in export oriented Asian economies caused by setbacks to the global recovery has clearly weighed on India's external demand from these economies. Detailed analysis is given in the chapter on international trade. Like exports, there was decline of 4.2

per cent in imports to US$ 237.2 billion in H1 of 2012-13 from US$ 247.7 billion during the corresponding period in previous year. The steep fall in exports than that in imports was responsible for widening of trade deficit to US$ 90.7 billion (10.8 per cent of GDP) in H1 of 2012-13 vis-à-vis US$ 89.5 billion (9.9 per cent of GDP) in H1 of 2011-12.

During H1 (April-September 2012) of 2012-13, net surplus under invisibles showed a decline of 2.6 per cent as outflows on account of payments under invisibles increased considerably. Growth in invisible receipts decelerated to 4.7 per cent, mainly due to lower growth in exports of services, private transfers and decline in investment income. Lower growth in exports of software services accompanied by decline in exports of travel, transport and insurance services led to a growth of 4.3 per cent in service exports in H1 of 2012-13, substantially lower than 22.7 per cent in the corresponding period of 2011-12. Lower growth in receipts under invisibles was also caused by lower growth in private transfers and decline in income receipts. Within income receipts, investment income declined by 19.1 per cent to US$ 3.5 billion during H1 of 2012-13 reflecting the lower level of interest rates abroad. In contrast to lower growth in receipts under invisibles, payments under invisibles recorded an increase of 12.3 per cent in H1 of 2012-13, as against a decline of 0.8 per cent in H1 of 2011-12. In particular, payment on account of business services showed a sharp increase as compared with a decline in H1 of 2011-12. Investment income payments rose by 17.6 per cent to US$ 14.5 billion during H1 of 2012-13 on account of rising external liabilities. Net secondary income receipts, which primarily comprise private transfers, increased by 8.2 per cent to US$ 32.9 billion during H1 of 2012-13 compared to US$ 30.4 billion a year ago. During H1 of 2012-13, net invisible balance declined to US$ 51.7 billion (6.2 per cent of GDP) from US$ 53.1 billion (5.9 per cent of GDP) in H1 of 2011-12.

Goods and Services deficit at US$ 61.1 billion in H1 of 2012-13 recorded an increase of 3.4 per cent from US$ 59.1 billion during H1 of 2011-12. India's CAD worsened further in H1; CAD was US$ 39.0 billion (4.6 per cent of GDP) during H1 of 2012-13 as compared to US$ 36.4 billion (4.0 per cent of GDP) in H1 of 2011-12. Besides global factors, the increase in the CAD to GDP ratio was also because of slower GDP growth and its contraction in dollar terms due to the depreciation of rupee. Exports of US$ 214.1 billion during April-December 2012, registered a decline of 5.5 per cent over export of US$ 226.6 billion during the same period in 2011-12. Imports of US$ 361.3 billion recorded a marginal decline of 0.7 per cent during April-December 2012 over the figure of US$ 363.9 billion during the corresponding period of previous year. As a result of steeper decline in exports than imports, trade deficit increased by 7.2 per cent to US$ 147.2 billion during April-December 2012 as compared to US$ 137.3 billion in April December 2011.

Capital Account and Financial Account

The capital account comprises capital transfers receivable and payable between residents and non-residents and the acquisition and disposal of non-produced non-financial assets between residents and nonresidents. The financial account records transactions relating to financial assets and liabilities and that take place between residents and non-residents. Some of the major components of financial accounts include direct investment, portfolio investment, financial derivates (other than reserves) and employees stock options, other investments, reserve assets (monetary gold), equity and investment fund shares, debt instruments and other financial assets and liabilities. The overall balance on the financial account is called net lending/net borrowing depending on the outflow or inflow of resources. The capital account showed a small outflow of US$ 0.06 billion in 2011-12 vis-à-vis inflow of US$ 0.04 billion in 2010-11. In the first half of 2012-13, there was also an outflow of US$ 0.5 billion. During 2011-12, both gross inflows of US$ 478.8 billion and outflows of US$ 411.1 billion under the capital account (old format) were lower than those of US$ 503.7 billion and US$ 439.9 billion in the preceding year 2010-11. However, net inflows of US$ 67.8 billion under the capital account (bifurcated into capital account and financial account under BPM6) were moderately higher than that of US$ 63.7 billion in 2010-11. This was primarily on account of a revival in FDI flows to India, a surge in NRI deposits and higher overseas borrowings by banks. However, there was a decline in inflows under FII investments, ADRs/ GDRs, external assistance, ECBs and short term trade credit. Risk on/risk off behaviour significantly influenced capital flows to India.

Even though the FDI to India (inward FDI) of US$ 33.0 billion in 2011-12 was significantly higher than US$ 29.0 billion in the preceding year, net inflows on account of portfolio investments at US$ 17.4 billion were lower as compared to US$ 31.5 billion in 2010-11 reflecting trend towards risk aversion among FIIs due to global economic uncertainty. Rise in inward FDI reflected flows received under BPReliance deal of US$ 7.0 billion in 2011-12. Sectorwise, manufacturing, construction, financial services, business services and communication services received significant amount of inflows. Country-wise, investment routed through Mauritius remained, as in the past, the largest component, followed by Singapore and the UK. FDI by India (i.e., outward FDI) in net terms moderated by 37.0 per cent to US$ 10.9 billion in 2011-12 compared to US$ 17.2 billion a year ago. Sector-wise, moderation in outward FDI was observed in agriculture, hunting, forestry & fishing, financial insurance, real estate & business services, manufacturing and wholesale, retail trade, restaurants & hotels. Furthermore, sectors, viz. financial, insurance, real estate & business services and manufacturing continued to account for more than 50 per cent of total outward FDI during 2011-12. Net FDI (inward FDI minus outward FDI) at US$ 22.1 billion in 2011-12 showed a significant increase of about 87.0 per cent as against US$ 11.8 billion in 2010-11.

Among the debt creating capital flows, net flows under NRI deposits of US$ 11.9 billion surged more than three-fold in 2011-12 vis-à-vis US$ 3.2 billion in 2010-11 because of the higher interest rates prevailing in India. Net flows under external commercial borrowing and trade credit showed a decline in 2011-12 vis-à-vis 2010-11. In net terms, capital inflows increased moderately by 6.4 per cent to US$ 67.8 billion (3.6 per cent of GDP) in 2011-12 as compared with US$ 63.7 billion (3.7 per cent of GDP) during 2010-11. Since net capital inflows were inadequate to finance the higher CAD recorded during 2011-12, there was a net drawdown of foreign exchange reserves to the extent of US$ 12.8 billion during the same period.

Both gross inflows of US$ 219.5 billion and outflows of US$ 179.5 billion under the financial account were lower in H1 of 2012-13 as compared with gross inflow of US$ 246.4 billion and outflow of US$ 202.9 billion in the same period a year ago. In net terms also, financial inflows declined to US$ 40.0 billion in H1 of 2012-13 as against US$ 43.5 billion in H1 of 2011-12. As regards the pattern of capital inflows during H1 of 2012-13, there has been a mixed trend. Inward FDI to India at US$ 16.2 billion during H1 of 2012-13 decreased by 26.0 per cent compared to US$ 21.9 billion in H1 of 2011-12. Outward FDI by India was US$ 3.4 billion in April-September 2012 as against the US$ 6.1 billion in April-September 2011. The net FDI (inward minus outward) to India was US$ 12.8 billion during first half of 2012-13 vis-avis US$ 15.7 billion during the corresponding period of previous year. However, recent measures taken by Government regarding liberalisation of FDI limits are likely to improve investment sentiment and to boost FDI flows into the Indian economy. Scope for further liberalization of FDI norms however remains.

Net portfolio flows including FIIs showed a quantum jump to US$ 5.8 billion during H1 of 2012-13 as against US$ 1.3 billion in H1 of 2011-12. Among debt creating flows, NRI deposits remained robust at US$ 9.4 billion in H1 of 2012-13 (US$ 3.9 billion in H1 of 2011-12) but net flows under ECBs declined sharply by about 80.0 per cent to US$ 1.7 billion during H1 of 2012-13 from US$ 8.4 billion in H1 of 2011-12. However, unlike in H1 of 2011-12, net flows under trade credit showed an increase of nearly 60 per cent to US$ 9.5 billion during April-September 2012 as against US$ 5.9 billion during the corresponding period of 2011-12. Net accretion to reserves (on a BoP basis) during H1 of 2012-13 at 0.4 billion was substantially lower as compared to US$ 5.7 billion in H1 of previous year.

As per the latest available information on capital inflows, FDI flows to India stood at US$ 22.2 billion during April-December 2012, which is 22.1 per cent lower than US$ 28.5 billion during April-December 2011. Up to December 2012, net FII flows amounted to at US$ 16.0 billion (US$ 2.7 billion during the corresponding period of 2011-12). FII flows in recent months witnessed improvement, reflecting the impact of various reform measures announced by the Government.

ILLUSTRATIVE PROBLEMS

1. Below there is a series of transactions between country *A* and country *B* (the rest of the world). Assume the point of view of country *A* and that *A*'s currency is dollars($). Do the following:

i) Indicate the accounts to be debited and credited in each transaction.

ii) Enter these transactions in the appropriate "T-accounts" provided for that purpose in Exhibit-1.

iii) Prepare the balance of payments for country *A*. Assume that all the short-term capital movements are of a compensating nature.

TRANSACTIONS

1. a. *A* exports goods to *B* for $1,000. *B*'s importers sign a bill of exchange for the goods they imported from *A*.

b. *A's* exporters discount the bill of exchange with their bank which in turn keeps the bill until maturity. (Assume 10% discount.)

c. On the bill's maturity *A's* bank receives payment for the bill in *B's* currency (as it was originally drawn). *A's* bank deposits *B's* currency in *B's* bank. The interest accrued on the bill is $50.

2. *A* imports goods from *B* for $800. *A's* importers pay *B's* exporters for the $800 with a loan in *B's* currency which they get from *A's* bank.
3. A resident of country *A*, Mr. X, goes on vacation to country *B*. He spends all the money the had with him, $5,000, for services received while on his vacation in country *B*.
4. Mr. X is lucky, however, because on the last day of his vacation he finds in the street a purse with $100 in *B's* currency. He brings the money home and declares his finding to custom authorities.
5. Another resident of *A* who has migrated from *B* a few years ago decides to send $1000 to his family. His father uses this money to buy a bond from another citizen of *A*.
6. A businessman of *A*, Mr. Y, decides to build a subsidiary plant in *B*. Therefore, he ships to *B* all necessary materials for this purpose, which cost $50,000.
7. Mr. Y very soon finds out that he needs another $20,000 for the completion of the plant. Thus, he issues bonds on the parent company for this amount and sells them to the citizens of *B*.
8. Mr. Y makes $10,000 profit during the first year of operation, which Mr. Y uses to enlarge his business in *B*. *A's* citizens are very impressed by the successful operation of Mr. Y's plant in *B*. Therefore, *A's* citizens buy from *B's* citizens half of the bonds issued by Mr. Y.
9. *A* resident of *B*, Mr. Z, migrates to *A*. His only property is $1,000 in B's currency which he carried with him to *A*, and his house in *B* which he rented to a friend of his for $100 a month. The house is worth $8,000. No rent payment, however, has been received.
10. Mr. Z decides to sell his house to his friend for $8,000. Payment is arranged as follows: $4,000 in cash and $4,000 in 5 years. Mr. Z deposits this money with his old bank in *B*. (Everything here is in terms of B's currency.)
11. Mr. Z, however, thinks he should give back to the church of his village $1,000. Therefore $1,000 is transferred from Mr. Z's account in *B's* bank to the account of the church.
12. *B* is a producer of gold. During the period of time for which the balance of payments is compiled, *B* produced $1 million. Half of this is consumed at home. However 20% is sold to B's central bank, 20% is sold to *A's* central bank, and 10% is exported to *A* for industrial use. For the amount of gold exported to *A*, *B* accepts a deposit with the central bank of country *A*.
13. A citizen of *A*, Mr. M, who migrated there from *B* a long time ago, finds out that he inherited the property of his uncle which consists of a farm worth $2,000 and a deposit of $1,000 in *B's* bank.
14. Mr. M Keeps the money with *B's* bank but he buys a designer's dress for $200 which he sends to his sister in *B* as a gift. The dress is purchased in *A* with *A's* currency.
15. Finally, Mr. M sells the farm for $2,000. He uses the proceeds along with his deposit in *B's* bank to buy bonds issued by *B's* government.
16. Mr. M makes a gift to his brother in *B*. This gift consists of a watch which costs $500 and a check for $100. The watch is purchased in country *A* with *A's* currency.

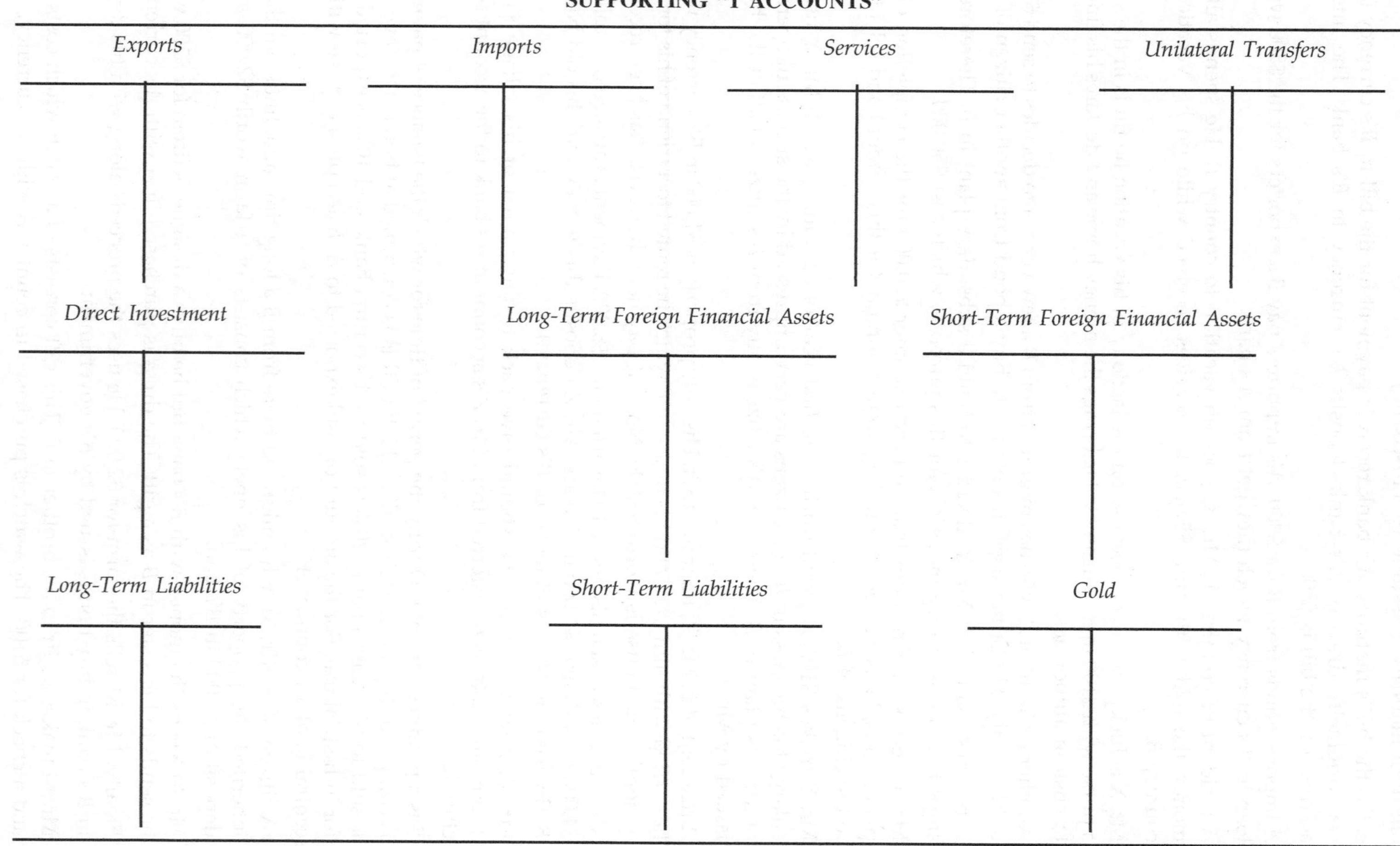
EXHIBIT-1
SUPPORTING "T ACCOUNTS"
Exports
Imports
Services
Unilateral Transfers
Direct Investment
Long-Term Foreign Financial Assets
Short-Term Foreign Financial Assets
Long-Term Liabilities
Short-Term Liabilities
Gold

Solution

A. *Accounts Debited and Credited*

	Dr.	Cr.
1. a. Increase in short-term foreign assets (bill of exchange)	1,000	
Exports		1,000
b. No entry. Foreign assets' ownership remains in the hands of *A's* residents.		
c. Increase in short-term foreign assets (the bank deposits in *B*)	1,050	
Decrease in short-term foreign assets (bill of exchange)—a capital inflow		1,000
Interest		50
2. Imports	800	
Decrease in short-term foreign assets—(assume *A's* bank had deposits with a correspondent in *B*)		800
3. Travel and tourist expenses abroad	5,000	
Increase in short-term liabilities to foreigners (dollars spent to purchase *B's* currency)		5,000
4. Increase in short-term foreign assets—	100	
Unilateral transfers		100

But who will know about the unilateral transfer? It will very likely end up in "errors and omissions."

	Dr.	Cr.
5. Unilateral transfers	100	
Increase in long-term liabilities to foreigners		100
6. Direct investment abroad	50,000	
Exports		50,000
7. Direct investment abroad	20,000	
Increase in long-term liabilities to foreigners		20,000

8. Profits of a foreign *subsidiary* (in contrast to a foreign branch) do not enter the balance of payments if these profits are reinvested in the foreign subsidiary. If dividends are declared, then the service account would be credited.

	Dr.	Cr.
Decrease in long-term liabilities to foreigners (the bonds)	10,000	
Increase in short-term liabilities to foreigners (the dollars used to pay)		10,000
9. Direct investment (the house)	8,000	
Increase in short-term foreign assets (*B's* balances)	1,000	
Unilateral transfers		9,000
10. Increase in short-term foreign assets (cash)	4,000	
Increase in long-term foreign assets (5-year note)	4,000	
Direct investment		8,000
11. Unilateral transfers	1,000	
Decrease in short-term foreign assets		1,000
12. Gold	200,000	
Imports	100,000	
Increase in short-term liabilities to foreigners		300,000

13. Direct investment	2,000	
Increase in short-term foreign assets	1,000	
Unilateral transfers		3,000
14. Unilateral transfers	200	
Exports		200
15. Increase in short-term foreign assets (proceeds from sale)	2,000	
Direct investment		2,000
Increase in long-term foreign assets (the purchase of bonds)	3,000	
Decrease in short-term foreign assets (payment for bonds)		3,000
16. Unilateral transfers	600	
Exports		500
Increase in short-term liabilities to foreigners		100

COUNTRY A

BALANCE OF PAYMENTS FOR THE PERIOD IN THE EXERCISES

Exports	$ 51,700	
Imports	100,800	
Balance of Trade		$ (49,100)
Balance of Invisibles		(4,950)
Unilateral Transfers		10,200
Balance on the Current Account		$ (43,850)
Long-Term Capital Account		
Direct Investment	$ (70,000)	
Increase in Long-Term Foreign Assets	(7,000)	
Increase in Long-Term Liabilities to Foreigners	10,100	
Basic Balance		(66,900)
		$ (110,750)
Short-Term Capital Account		
Increase in Short-Term Foreign Assets	$ (4,350)	
Increase in Short-Term Liabilities to Foreigners	315,100	310,750
Increase in Gold Stock		(200,000)
		$ 110,750

QUESTIONS AND PROBLEMS

1. Discuss the concept of balance-of-payments. Critically examine the various methods of compilation of statistics of balance-of-payments.
2. Why should a government concern about the increase in capital inflows?
3. Discuss the analytical framework that links international flow of goods, services, and capital to domestic economic behaviour.
4. Distinguish between balance of trade and balance of payments. Discuss the macroeconomic and other related effects of capital inflows.
5. Discuss some of the selected key economic indicators of Indian external sector and fastest growing export and import commodities.
6. Dissuss the various uses of the balance of payments in economic enquiry.
7. Discuss the rationale of policy adjustment mix to capital inflows.

B. *Supporting "T Accounts"*

Exports

		(1a)	1,000
		(6)	50,000
		(14)	200
		(16)	500
			51,700

Imports

(2)	800		
(12)	100,000		
	100,800		

Services

(3)	5,000	(1c)	50
	5,000		50

Unilateral Transfers

(5)	100	(4)	100
(11)	1,000	(9)	9,000
(14)	200	(13)	3,000
(16)	600		
	1,900		12,100

Direct Investment

(6)	50,000	(10)	8,000
(7)	20,000	(15)	2,000
(9)	8,000		
(13)	2,000		
	80,000		10,000

Long-Term Foreign Financial Assets

(10)	4,000		
(15)	3,000		
	7,000		

Short-Term Foreign Financial Assets

(1a)	1,000	(1c)	1,000
(1c)	1050	(2)	800
(4)	1000	(11)	1,000
(9)	1,000	(15)	3,000
(10)	4,000		
(13)	1,000		
(15)	2,000		
	10,150		5,800

Long-Term Liabilities

(8)	10,000	(5)	100
		(7)	20,000
	10,000		20,100

Short-Term Liabilities

		(3)	5,000
		(8)	10,000
		(12)	300,000
		(16)	100
			315,100

Gold

(12)	200,000		

PART II

This Page has been intentionally left blank

8

FOREIGN EXCHANGE MARKETS

INTRODUCTION

The foreign exchange market is the market where one currency is traded for another. This market is somewhat similar to the over- the-counter market in securities. The trading in currencies is usually accomplished over the telephone or through the telex. With direct dialing telephone service anywhere in the world, foreign exchange markets have become truly global in the sense that currency transactions now require only a single telephone call and take place twenty-four hours per day. As banks end their regular business day in San Francisco and Los Angeles, they open in Singapore, Hong Kong, Sydney and Tokyo, and by the time the latter wind down their regular business day, banks open in London, Paris, Zurich, Frankfurt, and Milan; and before the latter close, New York and Chicago banks open. The different monetary centres are connected by a telephone network and video screens and are in constant contact with one another, thus forming a single international foreign exchange market. However, the currencies and the extent of the participation of each currency in this market depend on local regulations which vary from country to country.

MARKETS AND MARKET PARTICIPANTS

From ladder of transactions the participants can be identified in foreign exchange markets. At the base, or at the first level, are traditional users (such as tourists, importers, exporters and investors, who exchange domestic currency for foreign currencies and vice versa) as well as traders and speculators (individuals, investment managers, and corporate treasurers who trade currencies seeking short-term profits by betting on the direction of changes in their relative price). At the next or second level are the commercial banks, which act as clearing house between users and earners of foreign exchange. At third level are foreign exchange brokers, through whom the nation's commercial banks even out their foreign exchange inflow and outflows among themselves (the so-called interbank or wholesale market). Finally, at the top is the nation's central bank which acts as a seller or buyer of last resort when the nation's total foreign exchange earnings and expenditures are required. When the market rate of the currency reaches the upper lines ("upper intervention point") of the band, the central bank of that country must increase sales of its currency in exchange for other currencies. Similarly, the central bank must sell foreign exchange and buy its own currency when the market rate reaches the "lower intervention point".

FOREIGN EXCHANGE TRANSACTIONS

The most common type of foreign exchange transaction involves the payment and receipt of the foreign exchange within two business days after the day the transaction is agreed upon. The two-day period gives adequate time for the parties to send instructions to debit and credit the appropriate bank accounts at home and abroad and complete requirements under the forex regulations. This type of transaction is called a *spot transaction,* and the exchange rate at which the transaction takes place is called the *spot rate.* Besides spot transaction, there are *forward transactions.* A forward transaction involves an agreement today to buy or sell a specified amount of a foreign currency at a specified future date at a rate agreed upon today (the forward rate). The typical forward contracts is for one month; three months; or six months, with three months being most common. Forward contracts for longer periods are not as common because of the great uncertainties involved. However, forward contract can be renegotiated for one or more periods when they become due.

The equilibrium forward rate is determined at the intersection of the market demand and supply forces of foreign exchange for *future delivery.* The demand for and supply of forward foreign exchange arise in the course of hedging, from foreign exchange speculation, and from covered interest arbitrage.

THE FORWARD CONTRACT

A forward foreign-exchange contract, used to hedge a future payment in a foreign currency, entails delivery of a certain amount of one currency in exchange for a certain amount of another currency at a certain future date. A more general definition of a *forward-exchange contract* is a fixed-price contract made today for delivery of a certain amount of a currency at a specified future date. The specified date is the *settlement date.*[1] The agreed-upon price is termed the *forward rate.*

Typically in such contracts, *no money changes hands today.*[2] The exchange takes place on a future date. Also typically, the forward contract stipulates that the full amount need not be exchanged on the settlement date. Instead, because the purpose is to hedge against change in the exchange rate, only the difference between the forward rate and the spot rate prevailing on the settlement date will be paid.

Forward-exchange contracts may be used, to *hedge* a future import payment or export receipt. A forward contract can also be used selectively, by companies and others, to implement a view on a currency's direction—in other words, for *speculation.* A bank may engage in a forward contract as a service to a customer the bank will

---

1. No money need change hands because the contract is done at an agreed-upon forward rate that both parties think is fair—as long as it's done at the prevailing market rate. If for some reason they arrange to do it at a rate different form the prevailing market rate. If for some reason they arrange to do it at a rate different form the prevailing market rate, an up-front payment will be required. This arrangement may be made, for example, to "unwind" a pre-existing forward contract.
2. By convention, the settlement date for spot transactions is two business days after the trade date. The settlement date for a forward contract is a certain number of days or months *after the spot date.* Thus a three-month forward contract settles in three months plus two business days' time.

then offset the forward, seeking to profit form the spread between currency bought and currency sold. A money-market trader may use forwards to *arbitrage* between instruments denominated in one currency and similar instruments denominated in another currency. And a forward combined with a financial asset or liability can effectively transform the currency of denomination of that asset or liability, thus creating *synthetic securities*. The financial-market participants seek to take advantage of an apparent inefficiency in the currency or money markets.

Forward-exchange contracts are amazingly versatile. They are available in two dozen or more currencies, and for maturities ranging from one week to several years. Yet many market participants shun them. Bond issuers and investors prefer currency swaps because, they're tailored to coupon-bearing instruments. Banks prefer to hedge with short-term foreign-exchange swaps, because they're more liquid. And many individuals and even institutions are drawn to the currency-futures market, because it entails far less default risk.

Default risk in forward contracts arises because such a contract is commitment for future performance, and one or the other party may be unwilling or unable to honour that commitment. What would either party have to gain from nonperformance? The answer is that on the settlement date, one party in effect owes the other party a net amount. The net amount, and who owes whom, cannot be determined in advance—it depends on the direction and extent to which the currency has moved in the interim. To see this effect more clearly, let's use a simplified example.

On March 1, *A* agrees to buy one pound sterling form *B* three months forward at a price of \$ 1.75. *A* is doing this to hedge against any movement in the pound during the next quarter. As a convenience to both, they agree that on the settlement date (June 3) only the **net amount** will be exchanged. The net amount is defined to be the difference between the forward rate (\$ 1.75) and the spot rate, whatever it is, in three months' time (June 1). If the pound is above \$ 1.75, *B* pays *A* the difference; if the spot rate turns out to be below \$ 1.75, *A* pays *B* the difference. Either way, the payment will take place in dollars—again, as a convenience. Table 1 shows the possible outcomes.

Today's three-month forward rate is F_o, in domestic units per unit of foreign currency, and S_t, is the spot rate on day *t*.[3] The principal amount of the transaction is Q units of the foreign currency.

On the settlement date *B* owes *A* $(S_t - F_o)$ Q or *A* owes *B* $(F_o - S_t)Q$, depending on whether the spot rate is above or below the prearranged forward. If the latter, and if *A* is a company and *B* a bank, it's just as though the bank had loaned *A* some money that was now due for repayment. The risk of default on the amount $(F_o - S_t)$ Q is the same as though it were a maturing loan. So it is easy to see why bankers think of forward contracts as involving "credit risk," and why they evaluate and limit the extent to which they are willing to expose themselves to default by the counterpart in any forward-exchange agreement.

TABLE-1

THE FORWARD CONTRACT

Time	Agreement between A and B		General forward contract	
Today (time 0); Trade date	*A* buys £1 forward form *B* at $ 1.75		*A* buys Q units forward from *B* at Forward rate F_o	
↓	↓		↓	
In 3 months (time t)	If spot $ 1.79	If spot = $ 1.72	If $S_t > F_o$	If $S_t < F_o$
↓				
In 3 months and 2 days (time *t* + 2); Settlement date	Then *B* pays *A* $ 0.04	Then *A* pays *B* $0.03	Then *B* pays *A* $(S_t - F_o)Q$	Then *A* pays *B* $(F_o - S_t)Q$

Nontransferability and Reversal of Forward Contracts

In principle, forward-exchange contracts could be "securitised" like so many other financial instruments, so that they could be traded in a secondary market. All one would have to do is include a clause in the original agreement stating that the rights and obligations of the contract could be assigned to a third party. This has not happened, for a simple reason: default risk. No bank wants to get up one morning and find that Escort's forward contracts have been sold to Novex Group, a fly-by-night outfit. Transferability without the hazard of deteriorating counterparty creditworthiness would require the other party's approval—that is, establishment of a line of credit, before any transfer could be made effective. This arrangement would be more cumbersome than simply engaging a new contract with the buying party.

On the other hand, corporations do want to get out of forward contracts from time to time, so their master agreement generally specifies how this can be done and at what cost. Briefly, what happens is that the two parties agree on the "net value" of the out-standing forward contract, and a payment is made form one party to the other. Assume, for example, that *A* and *B* have entered into a forward contract to sell SF 25 million to *B* at a price of F_o. Sometime before maturity *A* wishes to cancel the contract. The prevailing forward rate for the same settlement date has risen to F_m. From *B*'s point of view, the contract is "in the money," and he will have to be compensated for canceling it now. The minimum net amount that *A* will have to pay *B* is the present value of the difference between the two rates, or $PV(F_m - F_o)$.

If *B* still grumbles, or if the forward contract lacked cancelation provisions, *A* can still achieve an *effective cancellation* of the contract without *B*'s cooperation. He does this by going to another bank, say *C*, and buying SF 25 million forward at the going rate, F_m. The forward contract has been *reversed.* He has now locked in a future purchase at F_m and sale at F_o, guaranteeing a loss of F_m - F_o. Today's cost of reversing the forward contract is $PV(F_m = F_o)$.

Quoting Foreign Exchange Rates

Foreign exchange rates can be quoted in one of two ways. The first way, the *indirect quote,* is to quote one unit of local currency as equal to *n* units of the foreign currency. The second way, the *direct quote,* is to quote *n* units of the local currency as equal to one unit or 100 units of the foreign currency.

London invariably uses the first method of quotation. For example in London:

Indirect Quote (London):

₹ 68.05/£

¥ 185/£

$ 1.58/£

£ 1 is worth 68.05 Indian rupees

£ 1 is worth 185 Japanese yen

£ 1 is worth 1.58 US dollars

Direct Quote (Paris):

France uses the second method of quotation. For example, in Paris:

100 Swiss Franc are worth 24.39 French Franc

100 Japanese Yen are worth 19.21 French Franc

100 Indian ₹ are worth 14.84 French Franc

Care must be taken when reading exchange rates to see which method is being employed. To make explicit the role of each currency in an exchange quote, it is helpful to write down the names of each currency in its appropriate position. The currency used as a unit of account is placed in front of the quote. The unit of currency being priced follows the quote. For example, in the following quote of:

$ 0.60/DM

The unit of account is the U.S. dollar and the unit of currency being priced is one mark. A foreign exchange dealer will usually quote two rates to a potential customer - a *bid* and an *offer* rate. The dealer is willing to buy at the bid rate and sell at the offer or ask rate. In either case, the currency for which the end or offer price is given is the unit of item price. When he makes the quotation, he does not know whether the customer is a buyer or a seller of currency.[3] For instance, in the example quoted in Table-2, the foreign exchange dealer is quoting a spread ₹ 43.1514 to ₹ 43.2219 to the U.S. dollar. This means that he is prepared to buy dollars at ₹ 43.1514 to the dollar and sell dollars at ₹ 43.2219 to the dollar.

3. The gross returns from arbitrage must exceed transactions costs, otherwise arbitrage would not occur. In ascertaining the syntehtic forward price, account must be taken of the fact that currency is bought at an offer and sold at a bid price (and that the offer price is higher than the bid price). Likewise, money is borrowed at the offer (high) interest rate and deposited at the bid (low) rate. As a result, syntehtic long and short positions have different prices. Specifically synthetic purchases will be at a relatively high price and synthetic sales at a lower price. The different between the price will reflect the bid-offer spreads on currencies and interest rates.

TABLE-2

QUOTATION RATES BY FOREIGN EXCHANGE DEALER

Bid	*Offer*	
₹43.1514	43.2219	$
₹68.0013	68.2006	pound
₹ 22.4056	22.9058	DM
₹ 27.6543	27.7009	Sw. Fr.
₹ 44.1905	44.1925	Euro

FOREIGN EXCHANGE RATES

Under the flexible exchange rate system, the price of a currency is determined just like the price of any commodity, by the intersection of the market demand and the supply curves for currencies. This is shown in Figure-1, while the vertical axis measures the rupee price of pound, or the exchange rate, and the horizontal axis measures the quantity of pounds. The market demand and supply curves for pounds intersect at point K, determining the equilibrium exchange rate of ₹ 70/ pound, at which the quantity of pounds demanded and the quantity supplied are equal at pound 40 million per day. At higher exchange rate, the quantity of pound is not equal to its equilibrium level (as under the fixed exchange rate system that prevailed until March 1973), then either restrictions would have -to be imposed on the demand for pounds of Indian residents, or the central bank (the Reserve Bank of India) would have to fill the excess demand for pounds out of its reserves.

FIGURE - 1

EXCHANGE RATE UNDER A FLEXIBLE EXCHANGE RATE SYSTEM

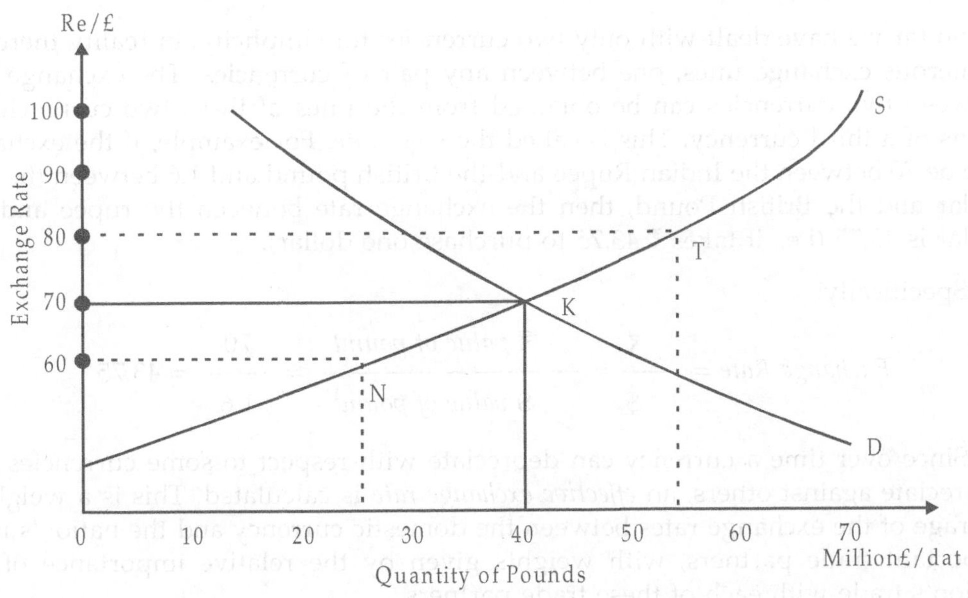

Indian demand for pounds is negatively inclined, indicating that the lower the exchange rate, the greater the quantity of pounds demanded. The reason being that lower the exchange rate (i.e. fewer the rupees required to purchase one pound), cheaper it is for the Indians to import from and to invest in the United Kingdom, and thus greater is the quantity of pounds demanded by Indians. On the other hand, the Indian supply of pounds exceeds the quantity demanded, and thus the exchange rate falls towards the equilibrium rate of ₹ 70/- pound. At an exchange rate lower than ₹ 70/- pound, the quantity of pounds demanded exceeds the quantity supplied, and hence the exchange rate lid up toward the equilibrium rate of ₹ 70/- pound. If the exchange rate is not allowed to rise in the domestic price of the foreign currency. On the other hand, if the Indian supply curve for pounds shifts at point N, the equilibrium exchange rate would fall to ₹ 60/- pound and the rupee is said to have appreciated (because fewer rupees are required to purchase one pound). Appreciation thus refers to a decline in the domestic price of the foreign currency. An appreciation of the domestic currency means a depreciation of the foreign currency and vice versa. Shifts in the Indian supply curve for pounds would similarly affect the equilibrium exchange rate and the equilibrium quantity of pounds is usually positively inclined, indicating that higher the exchange rate, greater the quantity of pounds earned by or supplied to India. The reason being that at higher exchange rates, Indian residents receive more rupees for each of their pounds. As a result they find Indian goods and investments cheaper and more attractive and spend more in India, thus supplying more pounds to India.

If the Indian demand curve for pounds shifts up (for example, as a result of increased Indian demand for British pounds) and it intersects the Indian supply curve for pounds at point T, the equilibrium exchange rate would be ₹ 80/- and the equilibrium quantity of pounds would be more than £50 million per day. The rupee is then said to have depreciated since it now requires ₹ 80 (instead of ₹ 70) to purchase one pound.

So far we have dealt with only two currencies for simplicity, in reality there are numerous exchange rates, one between any pair of currencies. The exchange rate between two currencies can be obtained from the rates of these two currencies in terms of a third currency. This is called the *cross-rate.* For example, if the exchange rate be 70 between the Indian Rupee and-the British pound and 1.6 between the U.S. dollar and the British Pound, then the exchange rate between the rupee and the dollar is 43.75 (i.e., it takes ₹ 43.75 to purchase one dollar).

Specifically:

$$\textit{Exchange Rate} = \frac{₹}{\$} = \frac{₹ \textit{ value of pound}}{\$ \textit{ value of pound}} = \frac{70}{1.6} = 43.75$$

Since over time a currency can depreciate with respect to some currencies and appreciate against others, an *effective exchange rate* is calculated. This is a weighted average of the exchange rates between the domestic currency and the nation's most important trade partners, with weights given by the relative importance of the nation's trade with each of these trade partners.

ECONOMIC FORCES IN EXCHANGE MARKETS

GEOGRAPHICAL ARBITRAGE

The exchange rate between any two currencies is kept the same in different monetary centres by *arbitrage.* This refers to the purchase of a currency in the monetary centre where it is cheaper, for immediate resale in the monetary centre where it is more expensive, in order to make a profit. For example, assume that the quotes of the rupee against the pound sterling in Bombay and London are as follows:

Bombay	*London*
₹ 70.021511	₹ 70.021523

The rupee commands a higher price against the pound sterling in Bombay than in London. It will attract arbitrageurs. They will purchase pounds with rupees in Bombay and convert pounds in rupees in London to make profit. As arbitrage takes place, the purchase of pound in Bombay will tend to increase the price of the pound against the rupee in that market. In London, reverse will happen with the sale of pound sterling and hence the fall in the price of the pound against rupee. This arbitrage process tends to equalise the exchange rate between the two currencies in both the markets. This is of course assuming that both are totally free markets.

Example-1

1. Assume the buying rate for deutsche mark spot in New York is $0.40.
   a. What would you expect the price of the U.S. dollar to be in Germany?
   b. If the dollar were quoted in Germany at DM 2.60, how is the market supposed to react?

Ans.

1. a. DM 2.50/\$ = $\frac{1}{.40}$

N.Y. prices	*Frankfurt prices*
$.40 / Dm	$0.385 / DM[1]
DM 2.50/$[2]	DM 2.60/$

Buy dollars in New York with DMs and sell dollars in Frankfurt for DMs; which is the same as buying DMs in Frankfurt with dollars and selling DMs in New York for dollars. (This calculation ignores buying-selling spreads.) This will tend to increase the price of dollars in New York and decrease the price in Frankfurt until the prices are the same in both locations.

1 $\frac{1}{2.60}$ = \$0.385/DM

2 from part (a) of this problem

Example-2

On the same date that the DM spot was quoted \$0.40 in New York, the price of the pound sterling was quoted \$1.80.

(a) What would you expect the price of the pound to be in Germany?

(b) If the pound were quoted in Frankfurt at DM 4.40/£, what would you do to profit from the situation?

Ans.

2. (a) We want DM/£

We know in New York DM/\$ = 2.50 (from example-2)

\$/£ = 1.80;

$$\text{then } £/\$ = \frac{1}{1.80} = £\ .556$$

$$\text{Therefore } \frac{\text{DM}/\$}{£/\$} = \frac{2.50}{.556} = \text{DM } 4.496/£$$

b.

New York prices	Frankfurt prices
DM 4.496 / £ (from part 2a)	DM 4.40 / £

Buy pounds with DMs in Frankfurt and sell pounds in exchange for DMs in New York where the pound commands a higher price in terms of DMs. This will tend to increase the price of £'s against DM's in Frankfurt and decrease the price of £'s against DMs in New York, until the price of £s (and therefore DMs) is the same in both locations. If the dollar quotations continue being \$.40/DM and \$1.80/£, the equilibrium price will be DM 4.496/£. Otherwise, there will still be opportunities to move funds from one trading center to the other. With modern communication equipment, the opportunities for this type of arbitrage are rather small.

When only two currencies and two monetary centres are involved in arbitrage, we have *two-point arbitrage,* when three currencies and three monetary centres are involved, we have *triangular,* or *three-point* arbitrage. While traingular arbitrage is not very common, it operates in the same manner to ensure *consistent* indirect, or *cross, exchange rates* between the three currencies in the three monetary centres. For example, if on April 1, 1999, the DM was quoted \$ 0.708707/DM and the Indian rupee was quoted ₹ 42.956325/\$ in Bombay and if on the same date New York happened to quote ₹ 30.415265/DM and ₹ 42.956325/\$, what are the incentives for arbitrage?

	Bombay	*New York*
$\frac{₹}{\$}$	$\frac{42.956325}{\$}$	$\frac{42.956325}{\$}$
$\frac{\$}{DM}$	$\frac{0.708707}{DM}$	$\frac{0.708025}{DM}$ (a)

$\frac{₹}{\$}$	$\frac{30.443456}{DM}$ (b)	$\frac{30.415625}{DM}$

(a) To find $/DM in New York:

We know $\frac{₹}{\$} = \frac{₹\ 42.956325}{\$}$

then $\$/₹ = 1/42.956325 = \$0.023279$

$$\frac{₹}{DM} = \frac{₹\ 30.415625}{DM}$$

then $\frac{DM}{₹} = \frac{1}{30.415625} = DM\ 0.032878/₹$

$$\text{So, } \frac{\$}{DM} = \frac{\frac{\$}{₹}}{\frac{DM}{₹}} = \frac{0.023279}{0.032878} = 0.708042$$

(b) To find Re/Dm in Bombay

$$\frac{\$}{Dm} = 0.708707$$

Then $DM = \frac{1}{0.708707}/\$$

$$DM = \frac{1.411020}{\$}$$

$$₹/\$ = ₹\ 42.956325/\$;$$

therefore,

DM 1.411020/$ = ₹ 42.956325

$$₹/DM = \frac{Re/\$}{DM/\$} = \frac{42.956325}{1.411020}$$

$$= 30.443456$$

By reading various quotes in two markets, we can say:

(i) The DM in terms of dollar is cheaper in New York than in Bombay.

(ii) The dollar and the rupee are at parity in both markets;

(iii) The DM fetches more, rupee is cheaper in Bombay than in New York.

Therefore buy DMs against dollars in New York; sell DMs against ₹ in Bombay; and convert ₹ in dollars in either Bombay or New York.

If we express spot rates as S(Re/$), S($/Dm) and S(Dm/Re) then the arbitrage possibilities exist only when S(Re/$). S($/Dm). S(Dm/Re) $\neq$ 1 i.e. when the product of inverse and cross rates is not equal to units, the arbitrage possibilities exist.

Example-3

On August 2, 1994 the DM was quoted \$0.3876/DM, and the French franc was quoted \$0.2133/FF, in New York. If on this same date Paris was quoting FF1.7500/DM, and FF4.6875/\$, what are the incentives for arbitrage?

Ans.

3.

In terms of		*New York*	*Paris*
	S/FF	\$0.2133/FF	\$0.2133/FF[a]
	\$/DM	\$0.3876/DM	\$0.3733/DM[b]
	FF/DM	FF1.8171/DM[c]	FF1.7500/DM

(a) To find \$/DM in Paris:

We know FF/\$ = 4.6875

$$\text{then S/FF} = \frac{1}{4.6875} = \$0.2133/\text{FF}$$

(b) In Paris

We know: \$/FF = \$0.2133/FF (from footnote a)

FF/DM = FF1.7500/DM

$$\text{Then DM/FF} = \frac{1}{1.7500} = \text{DM } 0.5714/\text{FF}$$

$$S_o = \frac{.2133}{0.5714} = \frac{\$/\text{FF}}{\text{DM}/\text{FF}} = .3733$$

(c) In New York

$$\$/\text{DM} = \$0.3876/\text{DM}; \text{ then DM } \frac{1}{0.3876}/\$ = \text{DM } 2.5800/\$$$

$$\$/\text{FF} = \$0.2133/\text{FF}; \text{ then FF } \frac{1}{0.2133}/\$ = \text{FF } 4.6882/\$$$

therefore DM 2.5800/\$ = FF 4.6882/\$

$$\text{FF/DM} = \frac{\text{FF}/\$}{\text{DM}/\$} = \frac{4.6882}{2.5800} = 1.8171$$

Reading down the various quotes:

(1) the DM in terms of dollars is cheaper in Paris than in New York;

(2) the dollar and the FF are at parity in both markets;

(3) the DM in terms of FF is cheaper in New York than in Paris.

Therefore buy DMs against dollars in Paris; sell DMs against FFs in New York; and convert FFs into dollars in either New York or Paris.

As in the case of two-point arbitrage, triangular arbitrage increases the demand for the currency in the monetary centre where the currency is cheaper, increases the supply of the currency in the monetary centre where the currency is more expensive, and quickly eliminates inconsistent cross rates and the possibility of further arbitrage. As a result, arbitrage quickly equalises exchange rates for each pair of currencies and results in consistent cross rates among all pairs of currencies, thus unifying all international monetary centres into a single market.

The quotation for forward rate can be made in two ways. They can be expressed in terms of the amount of local currency at which the quoter will buy and sell a unit of foreign currency. This is called the *outright rate* and is used by the traders in prompting to customers. The forward rates can also be quoted in terms of points, called the forward points, and used in interbank quotations. The points are added to the spot price if the foreign currency is traded at a premium; if trading at a discount, the forward points are subtracted from the spot price. The resulting number is the outright forward rate. In other words, the outright rate is the spot rate adjusted for forward points.

How to know whether a currency is at a premium or discount? There are two simple rule of thumb to decide if a currency is at a premium or discount, and what to do with forward points. Assuming that the quote is direct, if forward point decline from left to right, the foreign currency is at a premium and the forward points are deducted from the spot rate. If the forward points vary from left to right, the foreign currency is at a discount and forward points are added. In the case of indirect quotes the rule works exactly in the opposite way. For instance suppose you have called your foreign exchange trader and asked for quotations on the U.S. dollar spot, one-month, three-month and six-month. The trader has reported the following:

TABLE-3

Maturity	*Bid*	*Offer*	*Spread (%)*
Spot	0.024122	0.024128	
1-month	0.024130	0.024138	
3-month	0.024145	0.024123	
6-month	0.024132	0.024140	

It shows that the one and six-month forwards are at premium whereas the three-month forward is at discount.

The value of a currency is often expressed as a single figure, i.e., $ 0.024125 is worth Re.1, rather than being quoted as both a bid and offer rate. The single rate is the *middle rate* arrived at by adding the bid and offer rate together and dividing by two. For example, if the dollar bid rate be 0.024122 and the dollar offer rate be 0.024128, then the middle rate is given by (0.024122 + 0.024128)/12 = 0.024125. The difference between the bid price and the offer price is known as the spread and it represents the service charges of the trader. Spreads in the forward market are a function of both the breadth of the market (the volume of transactions/in a given currency and the risk associated with forward contracts. The risk, in turn, are based on the variability of future spot rates. Even if the spot market is stable, there is no guarantee that future rates will remain invariant. This uncertainty will be reflected in the forward markets.

In a foreign exchange market, dealers quote the forward rate in terms of forward points. If the forward rate is below the present spot rate, the foreign currency is said to be at a discount in relation to the domestic currency. On the other hand, if the forward rate is above the present spot rate, the foreign currency is said to be at a premium. To illustrate, if the spot rate is ₹ 70/- pound and three-month forward rate is ₹ 73.50 per pound, we say that the pound is at a three-month forward discount of ₹ 3.50 or 5 per cent for three months (or at a 20 per cent forward discount per year) with respect to the pound. On the other hand, if the spot rate is still ₹ 70 per pound, but the three-month forward rate is ₹ 71.75 per pound, the pound is said to be a forward premium of ₹ 1.75 or 2.50 per cent for three months, or 10 per cent per year.

Forward discounts or premiums can be expressed as percentages per year from the corresponding spot rate and can be calculated using the following formula:

$$ForwardPreium = \frac{Forward\ Rate - Spot\ Rate}{Spot\ Rate} \times \frac{12 \times 100}{Forward\ Contract\ length\ in\ months}$$

Thus, when the spot rate of the rupee/pound is ₹ 70 per pound and the forward rate is ₹ 66.50 per pound, we get:

$$\text{Forward Discount} = \frac{₹66.50 - ₹70.00}{₹70.00} \times \frac{12}{3} \times 100$$

$$= \frac{₹3.50}{₹70.00} \times 4 \times 100$$

$$= -20\% \text{ p.a.}$$

which is same as found earlier without the formula.

Similarly if the forward rate is ₹ 73.50/£

$$Forward\ Premium = \frac{₹73.50 - ₹70.00}{₹70.00} \times \frac{12}{3} \times 100$$

$$= \frac{₹3.50}{₹70.00} \times 4 \times 100 = 20\% \text{ p.a}$$

Example-4

You have called your foreign exchange trader and asked for quotations on the Belgian franc spot, one-month, three-month, and six-month. The trader has responded with the following:

$0.02479/81 3/5 8/7 13/10

a. What does this mean in terms of dollars per Belgian franc?

b. If you wished to buy spot Belgian francs, how much would you pay in dollars?

c. If you wanted to purchase spot U.S. dollars, how much would you have to pay in Belgian francs?

d. What is the premium or discount in the one-, three-, and six-month forward rates in annual percentages? (Assume you are buying Belgian francs.)

Ans.

4. a.

Maturity	*Bid*	*Ask*
spot	$0.02479/BF	$0.02481/BF
1 month	0.02482	0.02486
3 months	0.02471	0.02474
6 months	0.02466	0.02471

b. $0.02481/BF

c. $0.02479/BF

d. $$\frac{(\text{forward rate} - \text{spot rate})}{\text{spot rate}} \times \frac{12}{\text{No. months forward}}$$

= Forward premium (+) of discount (–)

1-month

$$\frac{(.02486 - .02481)}{.02481} \times \frac{12}{1} = 2.42\% \text{ (premium)}$$

3-months

$$\frac{(.02474 - .02481)}{.02481} \times \frac{12}{3} = -1.13\% \text{ (discount)}$$

6-months

$$\frac{(.02471 - .02481)}{.02481} \times \frac{12}{6} = -0.81\% \text{ (discount)}$$

INTEREST ARBITRAGE

Interest arbitrage refers to the international flow of short-term liquid capital to earn high returns abroad. Since the transfer of funds abroad to take advantage of higher returns in foreign monetary centres involves the conversion of the domestic to the foreign currency to make the investment, and the subsequent reconversion of the funds (plus the interest earned) from the foreign currency to the domestic currency at the time of maturity, a foreign exchange risk is involved due to the possible depreciation of the foreign currency during the period of the investment.

Suppose that the interest on risk-free security XYZ, is 5 per cent per annum in Singapore and 9 per cent in India on risk-free security ABC. It may then pay for a Singapore investor to exchange dollars for rupees at the current spot rate and invest in India to earn the extra 4 per cent on risk-free security or earn extra interest of 1% for three months on risk- free security in India. When the Indian risk-free security, ABC matures, the Singapore investor may want to exchange the rupees he invested plus the interest he earned back into dollars. However, by that time the rupee may have depreciated so that he would get back fewer dollars for rupee than he paid, if the rupee depreciates by 1/2 of the I per cent during the maturity period, say of 3-month, of the investment the Singapore investor nets only about 1/2 of 1 per cent from his foreign investment (the extra I per cent interest he earns minus the 1/2 of 1 per cent that he loses for the depreciation of the rupee). If the rupee depreciates by I per cent during the three months, the Singapore investor gains nothing, and if the rupee depreciates by more than 1 per cent, the Singapore investor loses. Of course, if the rupee *appreciates,* the Singapore investor gains both from the extra interest he earns and from the appreciation of the rupee. This is a case of uncovered interest arbitrage. But as the investors of short-term funds abroad generally want to avoid the foreign exchange risk, interest arbitrage is usually covered

Covered interest arbitrage refers to the spot purchase of the foreign currency to make the investment and the offsetting simultaneous forward sale (swap) of the foreign currency to cover the foreign exchange risk. When the risk-free security, say treasury bills, mature, the investor can then get the domestic currency equivalent of the foreign investment plus the interest earned without a foreign exchange risk. Since the currency with the higher interest rate is usually at a forward discount, the net return on investment is roughly equal to the positive interest differential earned abroad minus the forward discount on the foreign currency. This reduction in earnings is the cost of insurance against the foreign exchange risk. Now we will show the condition under which the covered interest rate arbitrage exists.

To compare the rate of return from two markets one domestic and the other international, assume that in the spot market, Indian rupee is selling for $ 0.15785, and the three-month forward is selling for $ 0.15725. If the three-month risk-free security rate in the U.S. is 7.50% and in India 8.75%

(a) Are the forward rates and interest rates in equilibrium? Why?

(b) If not, what would you do to take advantage of the situation?

(c) If a large number of individuals take similar action, what will be the impact in the market? (Assume interest rates remain constant.)

Following steps are to be followed to compare the rate of return from two markets:

(a) Interest differential in favour of ABC Company 8.75-7.50 = 1.25%

$$\text{Forward premium or discount} = \frac{\textit{Forward Rate} - \textit{Spot Rate}}{\textit{Spot Rate}} \times \frac{12}{3}$$

$$= \frac{.15750 - .1585}{.15785} \times 4$$

$$= -0.5204$$

Since there is an incentive for covered interest arbitrage

1.5204-1.25 = 0.27704 in favour of the U.S., the forward rates and interest rates are not in equilibrium.

(b) Borrow ABC currency at 8.75%, convert into dollars at $ .15785/Re

Invest proceeds in U.S. at 7.50%, sell dollars forward at $ .15750/Re

April 1

(1) Borrow ABC currency ₹ 63,35,128 at 8.75%
convert into $ 1000000 at .15785

(2) Buy U.S. risk-free security at 7.50%
Expected interest 18750 (1000000 × .075 × .25)

(3) Sell $ 10,18,750 on forward at .15750 = ₹ 64,78,537

July 1

(4) Receive proceeds on U.S. risk-free security $ 10,18,750

(5) Deliver $ 10,18,750 on forward contract and receive ABC currency. 33,33726.7

(6) Pay loan ABC Currency 63,35,128 puls interest 63,35,128 × .0875 × 25 = 64,73,709

Total Gain:	=	64,78,537
Proceeds from investment		
Cost of borrowing	=	64,73,709
Annual Gain	=	4828

$$= \frac{4828 \times 4}{64,73,709} = 0.2983\%$$

(c) The spot rate of ABC currency will decrease, as the supply of spot rupee increass. The 3-month forward rate will tend to decline as the demand for forward ABC Currency increases.

THE DEALER'S BOOK

To keep track of its various transactions and the risks they entail, the foreign-exchange dealing room maintains a "Book" or accounting of outstanding positions. A simplified position book representing a dealer's French-franc position is shown below.

TABLE-4

DEALING ROOM: FRENCH-FRANC POSITION

Long		*Short*	
FF-deposits owned	XX	FF-deposits issued	XX

FF bought spot	XX	FF sold spot	XX
FF bought forward	XX	FF sold forward	XX
Total Long	**XX**	**Total Short**	**XX**

From the table one can see that a "Long" position is like an asset, and a "short" position is like a liability. When you own something you gain if its price rises; when you owe something, you gain when its price falls. Thus we can define the two positions as follows:

> ***A long position*** *is any contract whose value rises when the underlying instruments price rises, and vice versa.*
>
> ***A short position*** *is any contract whose value rises when the underlying instruments price falls, and vice versa.*

Any short position can be used to offset any long position of equal amount, to provide a rough hedge. Of course, a three-month deposit owned is not going to behave exactly like French francs sold spot, so one is not perfectly hedged simply by matching long and short positions in French francs. The relative movements of different long or short positions depend in large part on movements in interest rates. Matching hedges the gross movements in the spot value of the currency. The spot movement accounts for most of the risk in a currency position that entails future delivery.

A useful way to look at the dealer's position in any particular instrument, including spot; forward, deposit, futures, and options positions, is the *profit-profile diagram.* Figure-2 profiles the potential gains or losses from a long forward contract

FIGURE - 2

PROFIT-PROFILE DIAGRAM

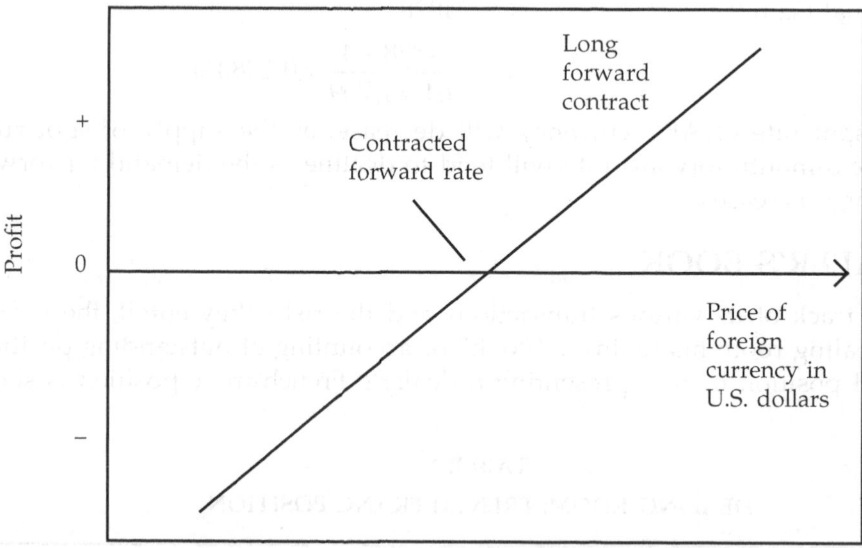

This graph shows the gains and losses on a forward contract arising from currency movements.

in French francs. If the market forward rate is above the contracted forward rate, the dealer has a profit; if below, a loss. The amount of gain or loss is the present value of the difference between the contracted forward rate and the prevailing forward rate for the same delivery date.

FORWARDS IN HEDGING

Hedging foreign-exchange risk means doing something that reduces one's **foreign-exchange exposure,** or risk of loss form currency fluctuations. The forward-exchange contract is the classic way to do this, but it is by no means the only one. Money-market instrument, futures, options, and swaps can also be used. As long as the market is efficient, they will all cost about the same. But when imperfections do prevail, the forward-exchange market usually turns out to be the cheapest way to hedge exchange risk. Trans-actions costs are low, the market is reasonably liquid, and only one cash flow is necessary. There are three kinds of hedging applications:

1. *Hedging transaction exposure* in the forward market simply entails buying or selling foreign exchange for future delivery to match a *known foreign currency payment or receipt.* This kind of hedging can also be termed monetary, or contractual, hedging. Both terms convey the idea that the forward sale or purchase is designed to match and offset a foreign -currency cash flow of known amount and date. The forward contract guarantees conversion at a known rate, locking in the amount of domestic curency to be paid or received.

2. *Hedging balance-sheet exposure* means using short-term forward contracts to offset "paper" gains and losses on the long-term assets and liabilities of foreign subsidiaries. The balance sheets, the assets and liabilities, of foreign subsidiaries are valued according to accounting principles applied fairly uniformly across companies, but differing between countries. Depending on the type of business the company is in, the balance sheet may not be a good reflection of the true gains and losses arising from foreign-exchange fluctuations. Nevertheless, these do get recorded as gains or losses in year-end financial statements, and so corporate foreign-exchange managers frequently must hedge part or all of this exposure.

3. *Hedging economic exposure* is trickier than either of the above. It entails estimating neither immediate transactions nor the accounting exposure but rather the effect of an exchange-rate change on the firm's overall profitability. Only that risk then gets hedged. The economic purpose of an exchange-rate change is to alter consumers' and producers' incentives. Thus a devaluation could stimulate exporters' revenues and those of import-companies, *regardless of the currency of denomination of their short-term assets and liabilities.*

FORWARDS IN SPECULATION

Anyone involved in international financial transactions must sooner or later make a decision as to whether and when an exposed position should be covered in the forward market. Forward contracts are thus being used selectively to gain from anticipated rises or falls in a currency's value. To illustrate, assume that a given textile firm's "natural" exposure, such as payables form the import of raw materials and receivables from the export of textiles, the firm's treasury department may decide to leave the exposure unhedged on the grounds that the cost of hedging is too high. This means that an asset is denominated in a foreign currency whose forward rate is at a discount, or a liability is denominated in a currency trading at a premium in the forward market. In effect, the corporate official is saying that he disagrees with the forward market's assessment of the currency's future. He thinks that the actual rate will be above the forward rate (if he has an asset in the currency) or he thinks the spot will end up below today's forward rate (if he has a liability denominated in the currency). The decision to add or remove forward cover is simply a decision to go long, short, or neutral on the currency, just as one would do if only forward contracts were traded.

Banks claim they do not assume exposure in the forward market the way corporations do since they match asset and liability positions, purchases, and sale of forward foreign exchange every day. True; but during the day, perhaps only for minutes at a time, currency dealers are of necessity speculators, deciding when and how to hedge an exposed position. The differnece lies in their time horizon—and in the fact that they break exposure down into finer components, such as spot risk and swap risk, than do their corporate counterparts.

FORWARDS IN ARBITRAGE

The forward rate is kept in place by those who detect any exploitable deviation from interest-rate parity, in particular those banks whose lines with one another allow them to undertake large forward-exchange trnasactions rapidly. These transactors can borrow in one currency, convert the funds into the other curency in the spot market, and invest in the other currency. To eliminate exchange risk, they sell the proceeds of the foreign-currency investment forward. If they can do this at a profit they've conducted true arbitrage. *True arbitrage* is a self-contained, profitable set of transactions, which in combination is free of market risk (but perhaps not free of default risk). This technique of arbitrage is illustrated below:

Borrow in dollars at interest rate $i_\$$ for n days

$$Cost: 1+\frac{i_\$}{360/n}$$

and then:

- change the dollars into deutschemarks at the spot rate S_o
- invest the DM in an n-day instrument at rate $r_{DM.}$
- sell the DM principal and interest forward for settlement in n days' time at forward rate F_0.

$$Revenue: \frac{1}{S_o}\left(1+\frac{i_{DM}}{360/n}\right)F_0$$

At maturity, use the dollar proceeds of the forward sale of DM to repay the dollars borrowed. If the arbitrage is successful, there will be a profit left over.

The profit from the above transaction will be the investment proceeds minus the debt repayment:

$$\Pi = \frac{F_o}{S_o}\left(1+\frac{i_{DM}}{360/n}\right) - \left(1+\frac{i_\$}{360/n}\right)$$

At a second level, international investors and borrowers use forward contracts to undertake arbitrage of a different kind: choosing among fixed-income investments or debt denominated in different currencies, made equivalent by covering the foreign-currency cash flows in the forward market. If one is better than the other, a kind of arbitrage profit has been made. But this does not mean anyone can do it; this kind of arbitrage depends on an existing asset or liability being improved upon. It is not a stand-alone transaction entailing both borrowing and lending; rather it is a substitution of one kind of lending or borrowing for another. For this reason we can call it *quasi-arbitrage.*

COMPREHENSIVE EXAMPLE

Consider that the dealer at XYZ Bank who entered into a forward contract with ABCL to hedge the company's Norwegian krone exposure decides to use it in a profitable covered-interest-arbitrage transaction. He is able to fund the arbitrage with one-month interbank NKr deposits at 11.14 per cent per annum. Using the covered-interest-arbitrage method given above, the dealer's cost in kroner is

$$1+\frac{.1114}{12} = 1.009283$$

The borrowed kroner are converted into U.S. dollars at the best spot rate he is able to obtain in the market, namely 6.019 kroner per dollar. (Observe that this is his home-currency price for one unit of foreign currency. The funds are placed in the Eurodollar market for one month at 8 per cent per year, and at maturity converted back at the forward rate he quoted Sen, 6.04. The proceeds for this are

$$\frac{6.04}{6.019}\left(1+\frac{.08}{12}\right) = 1.010179$$

The net profit is 0.000896 per krone, or about NKr 22,388 for a 25-million-kroner transaction. This is about $ 3700 in U.S. dollars. Not a fortune, but not bad for ten minute's work.

Assume that Sen has been placing ABCL's surplus cash in the U.S.-Treasury-bill market. Recently he noticed that U.K.-Treasury-bill rates are much higher. At the three-month maturity, for example, U.K. bills pay 14-3/8 compared to 7.36 for U.S. bills. The best post quotes he has been able to get are 1.8890-1.8900, and the best forward quotes are 1.8564-1.8698. As usual, sterling is quoted in dollars per pound. *Is there an opportunity to improve his profit without additional risk?*

For a correct comparison, Sen must assume money that would otherwise earn

7.36 per cent per annum in the United States would instead be converted into pounds at $ 1.89, invested at 14.375 per cent, and reconverted forward at $ 1.8564. If left in the United States, each dollar would be worth $ 1.0184 at maturity. If invested in U.K. bills and hedged in the forward market, it would be worth $ 1.01752 at maturity. So there's no advantage to the switch this time.

EXCHANGE RATE MOVEMENT: *THE FACTS*

Volatility is an unavoidable feature of all financial markets and heightened volatility in the forex market that we witness today is neither unprecedented nor unexpected. All economic agents with currency risk will have to frame a conscious risk management policy to cope with the impact of the volatility on their cost, revenue and profit. Even as the Reserve Bank strives to maintain orderly conditions in the forex market, certain behavioral issues that tend to accentuate volatility have to be understood by all market participants and factored into their response and risk management strategy

India, around the onset of the crisis, inundated with capital flows and the Rupee had appreciated. It had touched a high of 39.27 in Nov 2007. As the crisis unfolded, the trend reversed and Rupee started depreciating and reached 52.06 in March 2009. The Rupee started correcting soon and for almost two years between Nov 2009 and Aug 2011, remained range-bound at 44-47 levels. Overall the movement of the exchange rate in 2011-12 indicates that the average monthly exchange rate of rupee against the US dollar depreciated by 10.6 per cent from ₹ 44.97 per US dollar in March 2011 to ₹ 50.32 per US dollar in March 2012. Similarly, on point-to-point basis, the average exchange rate of rupee (average of buying and selling rate of FEDAI) depreciated by 12.7 per cent from ₹ 44.65 per US dollar on 31 March 2011 to ₹ 51.16 per US dollar on March 30, 2012. The monthly average exchange rate of rupee vis-a-vis pound sterling, euro and Japanese yen also depreciated in 2011-12. The monthly average exchange rate of rupee vis-a-vis pound sterling depreciated by 8.7 per cent from ₹ 72.71 per pound sterling in March 2011 to ₹ 79.65 in March 2012. Similarly, monthly average exchange rate of rupee depreciated by 5.3 per cent from ₹ 62.97 in March 2011 to ₹ 66.48 in March 2012 against the euro and against the Japanese yen by 9.9 per cent from ₹ 54.98 per 100 Japanese yen in March 2011 to ₹ 61.03 per 100 Japanese yen in March 2012.

On an annual average basis, rupee depreciated against major international currencies in fiscal 2011-12. The annual average exchange rate of rupee was ₹ 45.56 per US dollar in 2010-11 that depreciated by 4.9 per cent to ₹ 47.92 per US dollar in 2011-12. Similarly, the annual average exchange rate of rupee in 2010-11 was ₹ 70.87 per pound sterling, ₹ 60.21 per euro, and ₹ 53.27 per 100 Japanese yen which depreciated by 7.2 per cent to ₹ 76.38 per pound sterling, 8.6 per cent to ₹ 65.88 per euro and 12.3 per cent to ₹ 60.73 per 100 Japanese yen respectively in 2011-12.

The sharp fall in value of rupee can be explained by the supply-demand imbalance in the domestic foreign exchange market on account of slowdown in FII inflows, strengthening of US dollar in the international market due to the safe haven status of US Treasuries and heightened risk aversion and deleveraging due to the euro area crisis that impacted financial markets across emerging market economies. Apart from the global factors, there were several domestic factors that have added to the weakening trend of the rupee, which include increasing current account deficit, high inflation (Box 1). In order to reduce the volatility of exchange rate value of the rupee, the RBI intervened in the foreign exchange market through sale of US dollars amounting to US$ 20.1 billion in 2011-12. Further, in view of the sharp depreciation of the rupee in 2011-12, the RBI announced various policy measures that were aimed at curbing speculative behaviour of banks and corporate in the foreign exchange market. A number of steps were also taken to facilitate capital flows and boost exports to augment supply of foreign exchange.

BOX 1

REASONS FOR HIGH VOLATILITY IN RUPEE EXCHANGE RATE

The rupee has experienced unusually high volatility in the past few months. The currency touched the low of ₹ 57.22 per US dollar on 27th June, 2012, before appreciated to ₹ 51.62 per US dollar on October 05, 2012. It again began declining thereafter and has since been in the range of ₹ 53-54 per US dollar. Such volatility has introduced a measure of uncertainty in the domestic market and has impacted business confidence.

The rupee has been under pressure since August 2011, when US sovereign rating was downgraded and the euro zone crisis escalated. The currency went steadily downhill till the end of July, 2012, except for intermitted respite and appreciation in January-February 2012, mainly due to European Central Banks Long Term Refinancing Operation (LTRO) that injected more than euro 1 trillion in three-year loans to banks and created a risk-on environment.

The rupee fell due to decline in exports on account of euro-zone crisis and widening of trade deficit, as imports remained resilient due to high oil prices and gold imports. The widening of trade deficit to 10.2 per cent of GDP in 2011-12 had upset the supply-demand balance in the domestic foreign exchange market, placing downward pressure on the currency. The trade deficit has remained high at 10.8 per cent of GDP in the first six months of the current financial year (April-September 2012), with current account deficit at 4.6 per cent of GDP.

Improved capital flows in recent months, particularly FII flows, however have dampened the downward pressure on the rupee. Such an increase in portfolio flows is partly due to the risk-on behaviour of investors, following series of policy initiatives in the euro zone that lowered the `tail risk' of euro zone disintegration. The launch of quantitative easing (QE3) by the US Federal Reserve further helped the process. Capital flows have also been attracted by the confidence -inducing effects of major policy reforms that have been announced recently. The resulting increase in capital flows has more than balanced the widening current account deficit in recent months, curbing the rupee slide. Volatility however remains high because of high share of FII flows in total capital flows, and the week-to-week variation in such flows.

Another contributory factor is the fluctuation in the dollar exchange rate vis-a-vis other international currencies. Since bulk of global trade is invoiced and settled in US$ and most capital flows are denominated in US dollar, the volatility in the value of US dollar exchange rate in the international market has an immediate impact on rupee-US dollar exchange rate. Thus, the fall in the US dollar exchange rate in the international market leads to rupee appreciation, unless offset by widening trade deficit/ changes in the volume of capital flows and vice-versa.

In the current fiscal, the exchange rate value of rupee has so far undergone many ups and downs. The monthly average exchange rate of rupee per US dollar mostly remained in the range of ₹ 54-56 per US dollar except in the month of April 2012 when the rate was ₹ 51.81 and ₹ 53.02 in October 2012. In the first quarter of current fiscal 2012-13, monthly average exchange rate of rupee showed depreciating trend, going down by 2.9 per cent in April 2012, 4.9 per cent in May and 2.8 per cent in June 2012 over the previous month. In the month of June 2012, the rupee touched all-time low of ₹ 57.22 per US dollar (RBI's reference rate) on June 27, 2012 indicating 10.6 per cent depreciation over ₹ 51.16 per US dollar on March 30, 2012. In the second quarter of 2012-13, monthly average exchange rate of rupee has appreciated by 1.0 per cent in July 2012 and 1.7 per cent in September 2012 over the previous month, while in the month of August 2012 it has marginally depreciated by 0.1 per cent. In the third quarter, it appreciated by 3.0 per cent in October 2012 and 0.2 per cent in December 2012 while in month of November 2012 it depreciated by 3.2 per cent over the previous month level.

The Government of India and the RBI have taken a number of steps to boost exports and facilitate capital inflows so as to reduce external vulnerability. Under the Annual Supplement 2012-13 to Foreign Trade Policy 2009-14, the Government has announced initiatives to boost exports. The government has further liberalised FDI policy, including allowing foreign direct investment in multibrand retail. Other measures to boost capital inflows include a hike in FII investment in debt securities (both corporate and Government), enhancement of all-in-cost ceiling for external commercial borrowings (ECBs) between 3-5 year maturity, higher interest rate ceiling for foreign currency non-resident deposits, deregulation of interest rates on rupee denominated NRI deposits, and administrative steps to curb currency speculation.

TABLE 1

EXCHANGE RATES OF RUPEE PER FOREIGN CURRENCY AND RBI'S SALE/PURCHASES OF DOLLAR IN THE EXCHANGE MARKET DURING 2012-13

	Average exchange rates (₹ per foreign currency)[a]				
Month	*US Dollar*	*Pound sterling*	*Euro*	*Japanese Yen*[b]	*RBI Net sale (-) / purchase (+) (US$ million)*
1	2	3	4	5	6
2011-12					
(annual average)	47.9190 (-4.9)	76.3809 (-7.2)	65.8761 (-8.6)	60.7257 (-12.3)	(-) 20,138
March 2012	50.3213 (-2.3)	79.6549 (-2.5)	66.4807 (-2.1)	61.0259 (2.8)	-
2012-13					
(monthly average)					(-) 3123.0
April 2012	51.8121 (-2.9)	82.9119 (-3.9)	68.1872 (-2.5)	63.7934 (-4.3)	-275.0
May 2012	54.4736 (-4.9)	86.7323 (-4.4)	69.6991 (-2.2)	68.3286 (-6.6)	-485.0
June 2012	56.0302 (-2.8)	87.1349 (-0.5)	70.3087 (-0.9)	70.6743 (-3.3)	-50.0

July 2012	55.4948 (1.0)	86.5173 (0.7)	68.2520 (3.0)	70.2809 (0.6)	-785.0
August 2012	55.5594 (-0.1)	87.3444 (-0.9)	68.8750 (-0.9)	70.6814 (-0.6)	-452.0
September 2012	54.6055 (1.7)	87.8663 (-0.6)	70.1263 (-1.8)	69.9084 (1.1)	- 10.0
October 2012	53.0239 (3.0)	85.2128 (3.1)	68.7522 (2.0)	67.2305 (4.0)	- 95.0
November 2012	54.7758 (- 3.2)	87.5374 (- 2.7)	70.3665 (- 2.3)	67.6032 (- 0.6)	- 921.0
December 2012	54.6478 (0.2)	88.1910 (- 0.7)	71.6671 (- 1.8)	65.2805 (3.6)	-50.0

Source: RBI.

Notes: a. Per 100 Yen; Figures in parentheses indicate appreciation (+) and depreciation (-) over the previous month/year in per cent. Figures may not tally due to rounding off.

b. FEDAI market indicative rates. Data from May 2012 onwards are RBIs reference rates,

Domestic policy measures for attracting FDI, coupled with the announcement of quantitative easing by the US Federal Reserve and Bank of Japan in September 2012 contributed to increase in capital inflows to India leading to strengthening of the rupee. Besides, the RBI sold nearly US$ 3.1 billion during 2012-13 (April-December 2012). As a result, the rupee recovered to ₹ 51.62 per US dollar on October 05, 2012. However, since the second week of October 2012, rupee again showed depreciating trend on account of concerns relating to high CAD and the demand for dollars from oil importing firms and continued uncertainty in the global financial markets. In December 2012, rupee remained range bound (₹ 54.20-55.09 per US dollar) as FIIs continued to be largely buoyant except on December 21, 2012 when rupee touched a low of ₹ 55.09 per US dollar. The month-wise exchange rate of the rupee against major international currencies and the RBI's sale/purchase of foreign currency in the foreign exchange market during 2012-13 are shown in Table 1.

It may be noted that a depreciating exchange rate in 2012-13 is not specific to India. The currencies of other emerging economies, such as Brazilian real, Argentina peso, Russian rouble, and South Africa's rand also depreciated against the US dollar reflecting the increased demand for dollar as a safe haven asset in the wake of sovereign debt crisis in the euro zone and due to uncertain global economic environment. On a point-on-point basis between March 30,2012 and December 28, 2012, the Argentina peso has depreciated by 10.9 per cent, Brazilian real by 10.5 per cent, South African rand by 9.7 per cent, Indian rupee by 6.7 per cent, Indonesian rupiah by 5.1 per cent and Russian rouble by 3.4 per cent.

NOMINAL EFFECTIVE EXCHANGE RATE AND REAL EFFECTIVE EXCHANGE RATE

Nominal rupee depreciation, while having some adverse effects such as greater imported inflation, is also useful over time in offsetting higher domestic inflation and ensuring Indian exports remain competitive. The nominal effective exchange rate (NEER) and real effective exchange rate (REER) indices are used as indicators of external competitiveness of the country over a period of time. NEER is the weighted average of bilateral nominal exchange rates of the home currency in terms of foreign currencies, while REER is defined as a weighted average of nominal exchange rates, adjusted for home and foreign country relative price differentials. REER captures movements in cross-currency exchange rates as well as inflation differentials between India and its major trading partners and reflects the degree of external competitiveness of Indian products. The RBI has been constructing six currency (US dollar, euro for euro zone, pound sterling, Japanese yen, Chinese renminbi and Hong Kong dollar) and 36 currency indices of NEER and REER.

The 6-currency trade-based NEER (base: 2004-05=100) depreciated by 9.6 per cent between March 2011 and March 2012 and by 8.0 per cent between March 2012 to December 2012. As compared to this, the monthly average exchange rate of rupee depreciated by 10.6 per cent between March 2011 and March 2012, while in current fiscal it depreciated by 7.9 per cent against the US dollar from ₹ 50.32 per US dollar in March 2012 to ₹ 54.65 per US dollar in December 2012. The 6-currency trade-based REER (base: 2004-05=100) of the Rupee depreciated by 5.5 per cent from 115.97 to 109.59 between March 2011 and March 2012. During 2012- 13 so far (up to December 2012), the 6 currency index of 104.56 showed depreciation of 4.6 per cent over March 2012 index of 109.59 largely reflecting depreciation of rupee in nominal terms (Table 2).

US Dollar Exchange Rate in International Market

In so far as international currencies are concerned, the US dollar appreciated by 2.2 per cent against the pound sterling, 6.0 per cent against the euro, and 0.8 per cent

TABLE 2

INDICES OF NEER AND REER OF THE INDIAN RUPEE (SIX-CURRENCY TRADE-BASED WEIGHTS) BASE 2004-05 (APRIL-MARCH) = 100

Month average	*NEER*	*Appreciation (+)/ depreciation (-) NEER over previous period/month*	*REER*	*Appreciation (+) depreciation (-) REER over previous period/month*
1	2	3	4	5
March 2011	90.29	115.97		
March 2012	81.60	-9.6	109.59	-5.5
2012-13				
April 2012 (P)	79.24	-2.9	107.57	-1.8
May 2012 (P)	76.10	-4.0	104.12	-3.2
June 2012 (P)	74.67	-1.9	102.24	-1.8
July 2012 (P)	75.95	1.7	104.16	1.9
August 2012 (P)	75.53	-0.6	104.76	0.6
September 2012 (P)	75.67	0.2	105.75	0.9
October 2012 (P)	77.55	2.5	107.86	2.0
November 2012 (P)	75.33	- 2.9	105.11	- 2.5
December 2012 (P)	75.05	- 0.4	104.56	- 0.5

Source: RBI. P: Provisional.

against the Japanese yen during between March 2011 and March 2012. However, it depreciated by 4.2 per cent against Australian dollar during the same period. In current fiscal (up to end-December 2012), the US dollar appreciated by 0.7 per cent against euro, 1.4 per cent against Japanese yen and 0.6 per cent against Australian dollar between March 2012 and December 2012. However, US dollar depreciated by 2.0 per cent against pound sterling (Table 3).

TABLE 3

EXCHANGE RATE OF US DOLLAR AGAINST INTERNATIONAL CURRENCIES

Month/Year	*USD/ GBP*	*USD/Euro*	*JPY/USD*	*USD /AUD*
1	2	3	4	5
March 2010	1.5082	1.3543	90.8850	0.9095
March 2011	1.6168	1.3999	81.7936	1.0102
March 2012	1.5817	1.3201	82.4348	1.0543
US$ Appreciation (+) / Depreciation (-) (March 2011- March 2012) in percent	2.22	6.04	-0.78	-4.18
2012-13				
April 2012	1.6009	1.3162	81.4895	1.0350
May 2012	1.5906	1.2800	79.7084	0.9982
June 2012	1.5564	1.2526	79.3214	0.9986
July 2012	1.5589	1.2276	78.9830	1.0293
August 2012	1.5713	1.2400	78.6648	1.0468
September 2012	1.6119	1.2871	78.1678	1.0401
October 2012	1.6083	1.2975	78.9686	1.0293
November 2012	1.5966	1.2820	80.7920	1.0412
December 2012	1.6144	1.3109	83.5778	1.0477
US$ Appreciation (+) /Depreciation (-) (March 2012-December 2012) in percent	-2.03	0.70	1.39	0.63

Source: Reserve Bank of India. Note: Exchange rate is based on monthly average.

ISSUES INVOLVED IN INDIAN RUPEE DEPRECIATION AND VOLATILITY

There are two issues involved here – depreciation and volatility. As far as depreciation is concerned, the facts are well known. India has always had current account deficit which has increased significantly during the past few years in view of strong petroleum prices, increased gold imports coupled with strong gold prices and deceleration in the growth of exports on the back of faltering or even falling growth in most of the developing/developed countries which also happen to be the major trading partners. On the other hand, autonomous capital flows also seem to have slowed down because of several factors including global risk aversion, slowdown of investment in the Indian economy and several structural issues including inadequate infrastructure. In such a situation Rupee exhibiting a depreciating bias is no surprise. A depreciating currency is often seen to act as an instrument for correction of imbalances in the BoP. However, a sharp depreciation within a short period of time has a destabilising impact inasmuch as it provokes panic reaction amongst market participants which apart from leading to sub-optimal economic decision making further accentuates the price process. While the policy response to structural as well as exogenous factors that lead to mismatch between inflows and outflows and consequent depreciation (or appreciation) of the currency take time to yield results, Reserve Bank has a mandate to maintain orderliness in the foreign exchange market.

In forex markets, volatility essentially means unpredictability. Unpredictability not only of the extent of change over any given time period but also the direction of change. It affects all as the decisions are to be taken today that will fructify at a future point in time. Because all financial prices are inherently forward looking in the sense that they incorporate the participants' future view, it is no wonder that volatility is their most important attribute. It is further complicated by the fact that usually future view is informed by past experience. It may be interesting to recall that in 2007-08 when Rupee was at 39 levels, informed participants were forecasting 35-36 levels by the end of 2008 and very recently, during end-June this year, when Rupee reached 57, market was looking at 58-60 or even 60-65 as inevitable. It is to be emphasised that when economic agents take decision based on such a view of the future, it certainly does not bode well either for them or for the economy as a whole. This raises a related issue. If we accept that market makers/analysts who often are in a position to influence the market sentiment tend to be either euphoric or despondent, what is the accountability if their forecasts turn out to be widely wrong but meanwhile some participants in the market do get taken in by these forecasts and their decisions then turn out to be sub-optimal or inappropriate?

Thus, it needs to be recognised that increased volatility in the financial markets has become a way of life- a kind of new normal-and it has to be accepted as such. Capital account liberalisation during last few decades and enormous increase in the scale and variety of cross border financial transactions has increased the magnitude of exchange rate movements, particularly in the emerging market economies. Of course, volatility may be moderate for some stretch of time – recall that in 2006 people were seeking explanations for low volatility in the forex market – and heightened at other times, as now. The question is: *What should be the response to volatility?* For ease of exposition, may be discussed the issue in the context of two sets of market participants. The real sector agents – exporters, importers, foreign currency borrowers and so on and the banks or authorised dealers.

Real Sector or Real Culprits?

First, the real sector. In view of the extant capital account restrictions, exposure of residents to assets denominated in foreign currency (other than overseas direct investment) is marginal. Whenever a contract is denominated in a foreign currency, the contracting party faces uncertainty in its cost or revenue and ultimately profit on account of fluctuations in the exchange rate. It is to be particularly emphasised in the case of exporters, who in the face of stiff global competition and absence of any significant pricing power, have to reckon with rather thin margins which can be easily eroded because of fall in the value of the foreign currency before the payment is received. The same applies to importers as well when they are handicapped by incomplete pass-through of the increase in their input cost. The foreign currency borrower, who has to carry the exposure for a much longer period than the exporter or the importer, can find his cash flows and the bottom line seriously impaired because of depreciation of the home currency.

How do the corporates manage this risk? There are basically two routes available: non-hedging techniques and hedging techniques. Non-hedging techniques include:

(a) Settlement of transaction through advance payment, which though beneficial for an exporter, carries a cost for the importer and is impossible for a borrower. Even for the exporter, it is doubtful, in how many cases an exporter can demand and obtain advance payment without the risk of losing the order.

(b) Invoicing in the home currency has been discussed a great deal in recent times, which, however is quite sometime away before it can be effectively implemented. In the current state of global slowdown declining exports, exporters simply are not in a position to dictate terms.

Now, when it comes to hedging , are the corporates taking a well- deliberated and calculated call? To this , 'no' would have to be the answer in most cases. The reason is obvious. The rupee was rock solid in the range of 44 to 46 for about 2 years from 2009 to 2011. That lulled the corporates into a sense of complacency that nothing can go wrong. They started believing that this is the eternal range for rupee. A good bit of sales talk from various analysts (and some bankers too) convinced then that hedging is an unwarranted cost imposed on the business when the rupee is so well-behaved. It is like saying that life insurance is of no value since you are alive today !! This is where the answer to the earlier question comes in. If India is a high inflation country in comparison to the US, then the classical theory of foreign exchange states that rupee has to depreciate against the dollar to the extent of inflation differential. But there seems to have been an optimism among the corporates that the rupee will continue to be stable even if India is a high inflation country and that the financing of the CAD will never be a problem since India will continue to attract flows!

Over the years, a wide range of derivative products have been made available to enable those with foreign currency exposure to effectively manage their risk. The products include forwards, options and futures. The OTC forex markets and the Currency Futures are two different market segments for the same product. Both are governed by two different regulatory framework in terms of requirement of underlying, delivery and the extent of position taking by participants. We can no doubt have competing market segments as competition will bring in more efficiency. But, how can the competition be fair when the playing fields are completely asymmetric? This is an important issue warranting further public debate. But it need to be underscore the fact that exchange rate is a critical macro-economic variable particularly for countries having capital controls, perhaps no less sacrosanct than the policy interest rates which are targeted by the central banks, the world over. We also need to bear in mind that excessive overshooting and volatility in such a critical variable can have adverse financial stability implications. There is a paramount need for aligning these market segments, perhaps with a road map over an acceptable time span. One of the motivations for introduction of derivative products like exchange traded futures or options was to enable the small and medium enterprises to access the derivative market at competitive cost. But the use of these products depends on the agents themselves. But, unfortunately, even these hedging instruments have become weapons in the hands of corporates to trigger market instability. Whether it is past-performance based booking or cancellation and rebooking, or EEFC accounts, the corporate deemed these instruments as unfailing profit channels rather than flexible operational tools to manage real- life business events. These instruments have a tendency to exacerbate volatility in the markets and create a constant undercurrent of instability. That is why Reserve Bank had to step in to moderate volatility and cushion the rupee fall.

ILLUSTRATIVE PROBLEMS

1. Assume that the following spot exchange rates exist today:

DM = \$.60
FF = \$.15
DM = FF4.

Assume no transaction costs. Based on these exchange rates, can triangular arbitrage be used to earn a profit? Explain.

Ans.

No. The cross exchange rate between the mark and the franc is appropriate, based on the other exchange rates. There is no discrepancy to capitalise on.

2. Assume the following information:

Spot rate of £ = \$1.60
180-day forward rate of £ = \$1.56
180-day British interest rate = 4%
180-day U.S. interest rate = 3%

Based on the information, is covered interest arbitrage by U.S. investors feasible? Explain.

Ans.

No. Covered interest arbitrage involves the exchange of \$ for £. Assuming the investors begin with \$ 1 million, the \$ would be converted to £ as shown below

\$1 million/\$1.60 per £ = £ 625,000.

The British investment would accumulate interest over the 180-day period, resulating in:

£625,000 × 1.04
= £ 650,000

After 180 days, the £ would be convered to $:

£650,000 × $ 1.56 per pound
= $ 1,014,000

This amount reflect a return of 1.4% above the current U.S. investors initially started with. The investors could simply invest the funds in the U.S. at 3%. Thus, U.S. investors would earn less using the covered interest arbitrage strategy than investing in the U.S.

3. Suppose that the interest rate in XYZ Country is 24 per cent per annum, whereas it is only 8 per cent per annum in the United States. You are considering investing $10,000 for 180 days in XYZ's securities but are concerned about the exchange risk. XYZ's currency is *crown.* You find the following quotations in the newspaper in U.S. dollar terms:

XYZ Country (crown)	$0.1000
30-day forward	0.0980
90-day forward	0.0970
180-day forward	0.0950

a. Calculate the forward premium (discount) of the crown against the U.S. dollar (based on the 180-day quotation).
b. What is the net gain in U.S. dollars from investing in XYZ's securities relative to U.S. securities if it is assumed that the exchange rate in 180 days equals today's spot rate?
c. Suppose the crown depreciates by 10 per cent relative to the dollar in the next 180 days; what is your net gain (or loss) from an uncovered position relative to investment in the United States?
d. What is your net gain (or loss) from a covered position? (Ignore transaction cost.)

Ans.

(a) Forward premium (discount) $= \frac{0.950-0.1000}{0.1000} \times \frac{12}{6} \times 100$

$= -10\%$

(b) $10,000 (.12 – .04) = $800

(c) $\frac{\$10,000}{\$0.1000}$ = crown 100,000

Crown 100,000 (1.12) = crown 112,000
(112,000) × $0.0900 = $10,080
($10,000) (1.04)= $10,400
10,400 - 10,080 = $320 in favour of investment in the U.S.

(d) (112,000) × \$0.950 = 10,640
\$10,640 – 10,400 = \$240 in favour of investment in XYZ Country.

4. Consider the following data:

Spot £1=\$1.9510—1.9520

Three-month forward rate is £1=\$1.9257—1.9270

Three-month forward premium =2.53—2.50 cents (spot minus forward)

Calculate the rate of dollar premium against sterling (sterling discount against the dollar).

Ans.

Rate of premium (% p.a.)

For seller of sterling

$$\frac{0.0253}{1.9510}\times 4 = 0.0519 \text{ (5.19\% p.a.)}$$

For buyer of sterling

$$\frac{0.0250}{1.9520}\times 4 = 0.05125 \text{ (5.12\%) p.a.)}$$

Mid-price quote

$$\frac{0.02515}{1.9515}\times 4 = 0.0516 \text{ (5.16\% p.a.)}$$

5. The spot DM/£ exchange rate is £1 = DM2 .5000 – 2.4990. Six-month interest rates are:

DM	£
7-7/8-8% p.a.	5-7/8-6% p.a.

(a) Within what range should the six-month forward exchange rate fall?

(b) If a 1% rise in sterling interest rates causes a DM0-1 rise in the spot price of the pound, what should happen to the forward price of the pound?

Ans.

(a) *Borrow DM, sell DM, deposit £, buy DM forward:*

$$\frac{0.04-0.029375}{1.029375}=\frac{F-2.5}{2.5}$$

$$(0.010322 \times 2.5) + 2.5 = F = 2.5258$$

Borrow £, buy DM, deposit DM, sell DM forward:

$$\frac{0.039375-0.03}{1.03}=\frac{F-2.499}{2.499}$$

$(0.009102 \times 2.499) + 2.499 = F = 2.5217$

The range is DM2.5258—DM2.5217/£

(b) *The spot exchange rate becomes £1 = DM2.6000—2.5990 with interest rates at:*

DM	£
7-7/8-8% p.a.	6-7/8-6% p.a.

Borrow DM, sell DM, deposit £, buy DM forward:

$$\frac{0.04-0.034375}{1.034375} = \frac{F-2.6}{2.6}$$

$(0.005438 \times 2.6) + 2.6 = F = 2.6141$

Borrow £, buy DM, deposit DM, sell DM forward:

$$\frac{0.039375}{1.035} = \frac{F-2.599}{2.599}$$

$(0.004227 \times 2.599) + 2.599 = F = 2.61$

The new range should be DM2.6141–DM2.61/£

6. A foreign exchange dealer quoted the following rates for the pound sterling on Friday, November 30, 1995.

Spot	\$1.4710/\$1.4810
30-day forward	65/44
90-day forward	145/123
180-day forward	290/222

a. Determine the outright quotations for the pound sterling.

b. Was the pound sterling selling at a forward premium or a forward discount on that date? Calculate the forward premium (or discount) on the 90-day forward contract. Use ask (offer) rate to answer this question.

c. How many U.S. dollars would it cost you to buy £1,000,000 on November 30, 1995?

d. If you expect to receive £1,000,000 in 180 days from the quotation date, how many U.S. dollars would you expect to realise by selling them forward?

e. Assuming that the yield on a six-month CD of major banks in the United States is 9 per cent, what should be the yield on a comparable CD in the United Kingdom to insure interest parity between the two countries? Are covered yield differentials likely to persist under efficient money and exchange markets?

Ans.

1. (a)

Bid/Ask	Bid/Ask	Bid/Ask	Bid/Ask
\$1.4710/\$1.4810	\$1.4645/\$1.4766	\$1.4565/\$1.4687	\$1.4420/\$1.4588

—Spot— 30 day forward 90 day forward 180 day forward

(b) At a forward discount (swap points are in descending order and must, therefore, be subtracted from the spot rate to obtain the outright forward (quotations).

$$\text{Forward premium (discount)} = \frac{(\text{forward rate} - \text{spot rate})}{\text{spot rate}} \times \frac{12}{n} \times 100$$

$$= \frac{1.4687 - 1.4810}{1.4810} \times \frac{12}{3} \times 100$$

$$= -3.32\%$$

(c) 1,000,000 × 1.4810 = $1,481,000

(d) 1,000,000 × 1.4420 = $1,442,000

(e) $$\text{Forward premium (discount)} = \frac{1.4588 - 1.4810}{1.4810} \times \frac{12}{6} \times 100$$

$$= -3.00\%$$

The yield on a U.K. CD should be 12% per annum.

7. A U.S. distributor purchases goods from France in the amount of French francs (FF) 50 million. Payment in French francs is due in three months. Market data is as follows:

Exchange rates ($/FF) French francs

Spot	$0.118850
3-month forward	$0.118140

Interest rates (per cent per annum)

United States	9.00%
France	10.25%

a. What is the premium or discount on the forward franc? Is there an incentive for interest arbitrage? Explain how arbitrage operations will eventually eliminate profit opportunities.

b. Assume that the interest rate in France is 11.4 per cent instead of 10.25 per cent, that is, a condition of virtual interest parity. Show how the U.S. firm can hedge this transaction in (1) the money market, (2) the forward market. (Show all calculations, ignoring transaction cost.)

c. If actual spot rate in 90 days turned out to be $0.160735, how did the U.S. firm fare under the options listed in section (b) compared to an unhedged position? (Show all calculations, ignoring transaction cost.)

d. Which hedging technique in section (b) would you prefer to execute if you take into account transaction cost? What transaction costs are involved in either technique? Are transaction costs likely to be higher in one technique than the other?

Ans.

$$\text{Forward Premium (discount)} = \frac{0.118140 - 0.118850}{0.118850} \times \frac{12}{3} \times 100$$

$$= -2.39\%$$

There is incentive to borrow funds in France, invest these funds for 90 days in the United States, and buy the francs 90-day forward to settle the obligation in France. These transactions will result in a profit of 2.39%—1.25% (or 1.14%) of the amount borrowed in France (disregarding transaction costs).

(b) Forward market hedge will fix the cost of goods today at:

FF 50 million × \$0.118140 = \$5,907,000

Money market hedge:

$$\frac{\text{FF } 50{,}000{,}000}{1.0285} = \text{FF } 48{,}614{,}487$$

48,614,487 × 0.118850 = \$5,777,832

\$5,777,832 (1.0225) = \$5,907,833

(c) Under this highly unlikely scenario of a sharp appreciation of the French franc, the cost of imported goods for an unhedged position would have been \$8,036,750, some \$2,129,750 in excess of their cost using the forward market hedge or the money market hedge. The small difference between the cost of imported goods hedged in the forward market and in the money market is due to rounding. At the point of interest rate parity, the cost of the two hedges is equated (ignoring transaction costs). The money market hedge involve more transactions than the forward market hedge. Transaction costs are, therefore, likely to be higher in the former.

8. Given the following data:

\$ 12–11$\frac{7}{8}$% p.a. (for one-month money)

£ 6$\frac{1}{8}$-6% p.a. (for one-month money)

£/\$ spot \$1.7990–1.8000

Calculate the no-arbitrage range of futures prices for contracts maturing in one month. If the futures were trading at £1 = \$1.82, how could an arbitrage profit be made?

Ans.

Borrow \$, buy £, invest £, sell £ futures:

$$\frac{0.01 - 0.005}{1.005} = \frac{F - 1.8000}{1.8000}$$

$$\left[\frac{0.005}{1.005}\times 1.8\right]+1.8 = F = 1.8090$$

Borrow £, sell £, invest \$, buy £ futures:

$$\frac{0.0099-0.0051}{1.0051}=\frac{F-1.7990}{1.7990}$$

$$\left[\frac{0.0099-0.0051}{1.0051}\times 1.7990\right]+1.7990 = F = 1.8076$$

At a price of £1 = \$1.82, the sterling currency futures would be overpriced. The arbitrage strategy would therefore involve selling futures. So the appropriate arbitrage is:

borrow \$, buy £, invest £, sell £ futures

9. Pankaj Roy is convinced that the Japanese yen is presently undervalued. He wants to profit from his analysis.

Spot rate—day 1	\$0.003600
Forecast rate—day 30	0.004000
30-day forward	0.003620
Interest rates—1 month	
United States	7.50%
Japan	6.30%

a. What is the premium or discount on the forward yen?

b. What choices does Roy have to profit from his forecast of the future value of the yen?

c. What are the potential costs and gains of each alternative?

	Case A	*Case B*	*Case C*
Spot rate—Day 30	\$0.003600	\$0.004000	\$0.004200

d. What course of action would you advise Roy to follow?

Ans.

a. Forward premium or discount $= \dfrac{(\text{forward rate} - \text{spot rate})}{\text{spot rate}} \times \dfrac{12}{1}$

$$= \frac{.00362-.00360}{.00360} \times 12$$

Premium $= 6.7\%$

b. He can speculate either on the forward market or through the money market.

i. In the forward market Roy can buy 30-days forward yen at \$.003620 in the hope that at the end of the period he would be able to resell the yen at a higher price.

ii. In the money market, Roy will borrow funds in the U.S. at 7.50% and invest them in Japan at 6.30%. He would expect the interest differential to be more than compensated by the appreciation of the yen asset.

c. *Costs of speculating in the forward market:*

	Case A	*Case B*	*Case C*
Spot rate—Day 30 (selling price)	\$0.003600	\$0.004000	\$0.004200
Forward rate (buying price)	0.003620	0.003620	0.003620
Speculative gain or loss (–) per yen	–\$0.000020	\$0.000380	\$0.000580

Costs of speculating in the money market:

	Case A	*Case B*	*Case C*
(1) Spot rate-Day 30	\$0.003600	\$0.004000	\$0.004200
(2) Spot rate—Day 1	0.003600	0.003600	0.003600
(3) Gain or loss (–) per yen	—	\$0.000004	\$0.000600
(4) Interest differential			
$[(0.750 - 0.630) \div 12] \times .003600$	–0.000004	–0.000004	–0.000004
(5) Foreign exchange gain on interest received on yen security			
$0.0630 \times \frac{1}{12} \times$ (line 3)	—	0.000002	0.000003
(6) Gain or loss (–) per yen	– .000004	.000398	.000599

d. $1 + \frac{(0.75 - 0.63)}{12} \times .003600 = .003604$

Such differentials could occur because of restrictions among entrants to the markets, frictions in equilibrating between the two markets, spreads between bid and ask prices, etc.

e. Use the money market.

10. A company has purchased equipment from an American firm for \$6,000,000, payable in 4 annual instalments. The first instalment is payable immediately. The US company allows, credit at 6% p.a. The purchaser, whose revenues are in sterling, is at risk from an appreciation of the US dollar against sterling. The purchaser shops around for forward contracts and finds that the UK subsidiary of a US bank is prepared to offer one-, two—and three-year forward contracts at £1 = \$1.47, £1 = \$1.44 and £1 = \$1.41 respectively. The spot rate is £1 = \$1.50. Should the forwards be used to restructure the debt?

Ans.

The purchaser should agree to buy forward dollars as follows:

1 year hence	\$1,590,000 for £1,081,632
2 years hence	\$1,685,400 for £1,170,416
3 years hence	\$1,786,524 for £1,267,038

The future sterling cash flows are thus predetermined and exchange rate risk is eliminated. Effectively, the 6% p.a. dollar liability is converted to a sterling liability of about 8% p.a.

11. Nasir Hussain, a trader at one of the major banks in New York, has received information from the economic research department of his bank that short-term interest in the United States are bound to increase by 100 basis points within a month. (100% points equal 1%).

1-year treasury bill rates

United States	6.45%
Canada	4.46%
Spot rate:	\$0.996800/Canadian dollar
Forward rate:	
1 year	\$1.016636
1 month	\$0.998453

a. What is the premium or discount on the Canadian dollar?

b. What does the new information mean in terms of future rates? If the trader is bound by the rule "buy equals sell," what opportunities does he have to profit for the information given to him by his economic research department?

c. What are the costs or gains of such alternatives:

   i. if the U.S. interest rate increases to 7.45% within a month?

   ii. if interest rates remain constant?

   iii. if spot Canadian dollars on day 30 were \$0.9500?

d. What course of action would you advise the trader to follow?

Ans.

a. Premium or discount $= \dfrac{(\text{forward rate} - \text{spot rate})}{\text{spot rate}} \times \dfrac{12}{12}$

$$= \frac{1.016636 - 0.996800}{0.996800}$$

Premium = 1.99% equal to interest differential (6.45–4.46)

b. If the economist's forecast is correct (assuming everything else remains constant) in one month the following rates will prevail:

1-year treasury bills	*Spot Rate*
U.S. 7.45%	$0.996800
Canada 4.46%	

New 1 – year forward rate

$$\frac{X - 0.996800}{0.996800} = .0299$$

X = 1.026604

In terms of points discount/month:

Spot rate = .996800

	Fwd. rate	*12 month point premium*	*Points premium per month*
1 year – 1.99% premium	1.016636	.019836	.0016530
2.99% premium	1.026604	.029804	.0024836
	Difference	per month	.0008306

The trader can take advantage of this information in either of the following ways:

In the forward market:

Day 1 Sell 1-month C$ at	0.998453[a]	Buy 12-month C$ at	$1.0166360
Day 30 Buy spot C$ at	0.996800	Sell 11-month C$ at	1.0241196[b]
Gain	0.001653		0.0074836

Net profit/C$ = .0074836 + .001653 = .0091306[c]

In the money market:

Day 1—Borrow U.S. $ at 6.45% for one year, invest for a month.

Day 30—Reinvest proceeds of investment in 11-month security at 7.45%.

c. *Cost of speculating in the forward market:*

i. If forecast comes true, the computation above shows profit.

ii. If interest rates remain constant:

Day 1 Sell 1 month C$ at	0.998453	Buy 12-month C$ at	1.016636
Buy C$ spot at	0.996800	Sell 11-month C$ at	1.014983[d]
Gain	0.001653	= Loss	0.001653

iii. A devaluation will not affect the results because the gain or loss depends on the spread which is a function of interest rate differentials.

Costs of speculating in the money market:

i. If the forecast comes true, he makes 1% for eleven months.

ii. If the forecast does not come true, there is no gain or loss.

iii. Spot rates are irrelevant in this case.

(a) .996800 + .0016530 = .998453

(b) .996800 + 11 (.0024836) = 1.0241196

(c) (.0008306) 11 = .0091306

(d) (11 × .001653) + .996800 = 1.014983

12. MNC Corp. will have a net liability position in Switzerland in the amount of 163 million Swiss francs (approximately $50 million).

Exchange rates	
Spot rate—Day 1	$0.308500
Expected future spot rate	0.333180
1-year forward	0.320840
Interest rates—1 year	
United States	7.20%
Switzerland	2.00%

a. What is the premium or discount in the forward Swiss franc?

b. What would be the consequences of the Swiss net liability position if the forecast changes in the spot rate take place? What are the choices that MNC Corp. has to hedge its liability position in Switzerland?

c. What is the cost of each of these alternatives if the actual spot rate at the end of the period is as follows:

Spot rate–Day 360	*Case A*	*Case B*	*Case C*
	$0.308500	$0.320840	$0.339350

d. What course of action would you advise MNC Corp. to take?

Ans.

a. Forward premium or discount $= \dfrac{(\text{forward rate} - \text{spot rate})}{\text{spot rate}} \times \dfrac{12}{12}$

$$= \frac{.52 - .50}{.50} \times \frac{12}{12}$$

Premium = 4.00%

b. Consequences of liability position:

Liabilities at present rate in $ $80.0M

SF 160 x $ .50/FF

Liabilities if expected appreciation takes place	
SF 160 × \$.54	86.4
Loss in exposed position	(6.4M)

The simpler answers are that MNC can hedge its position either by:

i. Buying forward SF in which it can realise a gain when resold in the spot market.
ii. Borrowing funds in the U.S. and investing them in Switzerland. Gain on upvaluation of asset is expected to compensate for the loss in the exposed position.

(More involved transactions are shown below)

c. *Cost of Covering in the Forward Market:*
(forward amount) × (forward rate– expected spot rate) = Loss on exposed liabilities
(F) × (.52 – .54) = –6.4 million

$$F = \frac{6.4}{.02} = \text{SF 360 Million}$$

	Case A	*Case B*	*Case C*	*Forecast*
(1) Spot rate at end of period (sell)\$	.50 \$	.52 \$	.55	.54
(2) Forward rate (buy)	.52	.52	.52	.52
(3) Gain or loss per SF	(.02)	—	.03	.02
(4) Initial foreign exposure	\$80.0M	\$80.0M	\$80.0M	\$80.0M
(5) New exposure value				
160 × (line 1)	80.0	83.2	88.0	86.4
Gain or loss on exposure	—	(3.2)	(8.0)	(6.4)
Gain or loss on hedging				
320 × (line 3)	(6.4)	—	9.6	6.4
	(6.4M)	(3.2M)	1.6M	\$ 0

The cost or gain in the operation depends on the forward rate, as well as the eventual spot rate.

If the firm wishes *to lock in its loss with certainty,* (the simple answer (i) above), it may do so by buying 160M Swiss francs forward at the rate of \$.52/SF. Instead of the \$6.4M loss if the expected appreciation occurs, the firm would offset this appreciation by the forward purchase of the same amount in the same currency, SF 160M. This action neutralises the firm, locking in the difference in today's market price (\$.50/SF) and the forward market price (\$.52/SF), or \$.02×SF160M, or \$3.2M. Thus, even under Case C, the loss is the same throughout:

	Case C with SF160M forward contract
(1) Spot rate at end of period (sell)	$.55/SF
(2) Forward rate (buy)	.52
(3) Gain per SF	$.03/SF
(4) Initial exposure valuation	$80.0M
(5) New exposure valuation	88.0M
Loss on exposed liability	(8.0M)
SF160M×line 3 (Hedge)	4.8M
Loss after hedging	(3.2M)

Covering in the Money Market:

Interest rate parity suggests the SF should appreciate by (7.5%—2%=) 5.5% versus a forward market premium of 4% (see 1a). A rough calculation indicates the firm can make 1.5% on a money market hedge with a locked-in forward rate. So, if interest and foreign exchange gains/losses are netted, the money market hedge would involve $6.4M/.015, or $426.67M borrowed/invested. *The firm would borrow SF and invest in $, selling $ forward at the $.52/SF rate.* Total gains and losses would then be:

	Case A	*Case B*	*Case C*	*Forecast*
Loss on exposed liability	—	($3.2M)	($8.0M)	($6.4M)
Money market, net	$6.4	6.4	6.4	6.4
Total	6.47	3.2	(1.6)	0

If the rates are guessed incorrectly, again the money market generates the fixed amounts (assuming the money market/forward market disequilibrium prevails) but the gains or losses from the net exposure change sharply. In contrast, the forward market example volatility comes from both the net liability position of the firm and the forward market activity.

This same multiple interaction can be seen if the treasurer wishes to assume his/her forecast of $.54/SF will prevail, for an 8% appreciation of the SF. In this case, the treasurer would *borrow $* and *lend SF*, for the effective rate on SF (2% + 8% = 10%) exceeds the effective rate on dollars of 7.5%. This difference of 2.5% requires $6.4/.025 or $256M. *No forward contract is entered.*

Ignoring the adjustment on interest payments for exchange rate changes and netting accounts,

	Case A	*Case B*	*Cast C*	*Forecast*
(1) Loss on exposed liability	—	($3.2M)	($8.0M)	($6.4M)
(2) Interest differential	($14.0)	(14.0)	(14.0)	(14.0)

(3) Percentage gain over spot rate of \$.50/SF	0%	4%	10%	8%
(4) \$256M × line 3	0	\$10.2M	\$25.6M	\$20.5M
Net gain (approximately)	(\$14M)	(\$7.0M)	\$ 3.6M	~0

If the firm wishes to lock in its losses with certainty (the simple answer (ii) above), in the money market it obtains an asset offsetting the SF liability of SF 160M. Its cost is roughly the interest differential of 5.5%. At the end of the period, the SF asset and liability offset each other no matter what happens to the SF/\$ rate. The cost is the interest differential of .055 × \$80M, or *\$4.4M.*

13. A company wishes to borrow 10 million Finnish markka for 2 years, but can only borrow on a six-month floating rate basis. The company can borrow 2 million eurodollars for 2 years at 6% p.a. The spot exchange rate is \$1=5 markka and the two-year forward rate is \$1 = 5.10 markka. Can forward contracts be used to create a liability on a fixed rate basis?

Ans.:

The company buys 10 million markka spot and agrees to a forward sale of markka as follows:

2 years hence 11,460,720 markka for \$2,247,200

To repay the 2 million eurodollar loan, US\$2,247,200 is required. The company has guaranteed that 11,460,720 markka will be required at the end of the 2 years. This sum is equivalent to a fixed annual rate of about 7% on the initial 10 million markka.

14. A UK fund manager decides to increase exposure to the US stock market at the expense of UK equity investments. It is desired that £1 million of exposure be reallocated immediately with stock selection (for both sales and purchases) to take place during the following 2 weeks. It is 20 March and the current price data include:

June FTSE 100 futures = 2500

\$/£ exchange rate = \$2.00/£1

June S&P 500 futures = 200

Design a strategy that might be followed and calculate the numbers of futures contracts involved.

Ans.

The UK equity exposure is reduced by selling FTSE 100 futures. The US stock exposure is increased by buying S&P 500 futures. The US dollar currency exposure implicit in a US stock holding is obtained by selling sterling currency futures. The futures positions are progressively closed out as the cash market transactions take place.

Numbers of futures contracts

£1,000,000/(£25 × 2500) = 16 FTSE 100 futures contracts

£1,000,000/(£62,000 = 16 sterling currency futures contracts

$2,000,000/($500 × 200) = 20 S&P 500 futures contracts

QUESTIONS AND PROBLEMS

1. Define foreign exchange market. Who are the major participants in these markets? How are the exchange rates determined?
2. Discuss the economic forces in the foreign exchange markets.
3. Assume the following information:

	Bank X	*Bank Y*
Bid price of French francs	$.401	$.398
Ask price of French francs	$404	$.400

Given this information, is locational arbitrage possible? If so, explain the steps that would reflect locational arbitrage, and compute the profit from this arbitrage if you had $1,000,000 to use.

4. Based on the information in the previous question, what market forces would occur to eliminate any further possibilities of locational arbitrage?
5. Define the forward contract. Critically examine the role of forwards in speculation.
6. Explain the concept of triangular arbitrage and the scenario necessary for it to be plausible.
7. Assume the following information for a particular bank

	Quoted Price
Value of Canadian dollar in U.S. dollars	$.90
Value of German mark in U.S. dollars	$.55
Value of Canadian dollar in German marks	DM 1.65

Given this information, is triangular arbitrage possible? If so, explain the steps that would reflect triangular arbitrage, and compute the profit form this strategy if you had $ 1,000,000 to use.

8. Based on the information in the previous question, what market forces would occur to eliminate any further possibilities of triangular arbitrage?
9. Critically examine the impact of developments in the foreign exchange markets on emerging markets.
10. Explain the concept of covered interest arbitrage and the scenario necessary for it to be plausible.
11. Write a note on Dealer's book in the forex transactions.

12. Assume that the British pound's one-year forward rate exhibits a discount. Assume also that interest rate parity continually exists. Explain how the discount on the British pound's one-year forward discount would change if British one-year interest rates rose by 3 percentage points while U.S. one-year interests rates rose by 2 percentage points.
13. As of today, assume the following information is available:

	U.S.	*France*
Real rate of interest required by investors	2%	2%
Nominal interest rate	11%	15%
Spot rate	—	$.20
One-year forward rate	—	$.19

(a) Use the forward rate to forecast the percentage change in the French franc over the next year.

(b) Use the differential in expected inflation to forecast the percentage change in the French franc over the next year.

(c) Use the spot rate to forecast the percentage exchange in the French franc over the next year.

14. Assume that the spot exchange rate of the British pound is $1.73. How would this spot rate adjust according to purchasing power parity if Great Britain experiences an inflation rate of 7 per cent while the United States experiences an inflation rate of 2 per cent.
15. Assume the spot exchange rate of the Swiss franc is $.70. The one-year interest rate is 11 per cent in the United States and 7 per cent in Switzerland. What would be the spot rate in one year according to the international fisher effect?
16. Discuss the sources of competitive pressure on Asian currencies.
17. A.U.S. importer of Japanese computer supplies pays for the supplies in yen. The importer is not concerned about the possible increase in Japanese prices charged in yen) because of the likely offsetting effect caused by purchasing power parity (PPP). Explain what this means.
18. Evaluate the broad movements of the main currencies in recent years.
19. Before the 1990s, currencies of the Eastern Bloc countries were not convertible into dollars. Assume that these currencies are set against the dollar, but that large inflation occurs in these countries over time. use purchasing power parity to explain how the values of these currencies will be affected.
20. Discuss the Intre-European exchange rates and foreign exchange markets after the introduction of Euro.
21. Assume that the Canadian dollar's spot rate is $.85 and that the Canadian and U.S. inflation rates are similar. Then assume that the Canadian experiences 6 per cent inflation, while the U.S. experiences 4 per cent inflation. According to purchasing power parity, what will be the new value of the Canadian

dollar after it adjusts to the inflationary changes? (You may use the approximate formula to answer this question).

22. Write a short note on the deeper's book.

23. Forward-contracts entail a default risk because either party could walk away from its obligation at the contract's maturity. From a bank's point of view, is this default risk greater or less than a loan of the same face amount?

24. How are forward contracts nontransferable? How can one get out of a forward contract?

25. Why do traders use two transactions instead of just one to hedge a forward exchange contract?

26. Identify the different ways in which foreign-exchange dealer can hedge a forward transaction.

27. A U.S. firm about to issue an order to import 1000 widgets received the following C.I.F. quotations in local currency. Delivery from all suppliers would take three months (terms of payment: sight draft upon delivery).

	Italy	*Switzerland*	*France*
Local cost	Lit8,000,000	SF10,500	FF40,000
So ($/j)	0.000627	0.4712	0.1256
S¼ ($/j)	0.000600	0.4800	0.1240
F¼ ($/j)	0.000590	0.4850	0.1200
S¼ ($/j)	0.000575	0.4650	0.1250

a. Which country would you import from if you based your decision on today's rates?

b. Which country would you import from if you decided on forward hedging?

c. Which country actually provided the best price at the time of delivery?

d. If you were a speculator, in which currency or currencies would you go long? In which currency or currencies would you go short? What is the overall profit/loss from your positions per *one million units* of foreign currencies? (Ignore transaction cost.)

28. Given the following data about countries A and B, and given that interest rate parity, purchasing power parity, and the international Fisher Effect hold for both countries.

	Country A	*Country B*
Spot exchange rate	1A = 5B	1B = .20A
Yield on 12-month Treasury bills	7.5%	
Expected inflation rate during the next 12 months	4%	6%

a. Calculate the yield on 12-month Treasury bill in country B.

b. Calculate the 12-month forward exchange quote for currencies of both countries.

c. How is the differential in the rate of inflation related to the forward premium (discount) expressed in percentage per annum?

d. If the yield on 12-month Treasury bills in country B were given as 10 per cent, which of the parity equilibria given above would be violated? Under what circumstances would you expect such a situation to prevail?

29. The following prices of the U.S. dollar in terms of the Belgian franc, French franc, the Italian lira, and the Japanese yen has been published in a financial daily for January 3, 2001.

Spot Rates

Belgium	*France*	*Italy*	*Japan*
31.83	5.3390	1622.25	99.60

a. How much, in U.S. dollars, would it cost to buy 1,000 lira?

b. How much, in U.S. dollars, would it cost to buy 100 yen?

c. What are the prices of the French franc in yen and the Italian lira in Belgian francs?

30. The *London Times* bid-ask price quotations for the Swiss franc are 2.1775-2.1875 SFr/ £. The prices of gold in London and Zurich are, respectively, 233.75£/ oz, and 508.85 SFr/oz. Are these prices consistent with the theory of absolute purchasing power parity? Explain your answer.

31. The price of the British pound at the end of 2000 was $1.5650. In 2000, I expect U.S. inflation to be 3.5 percent and British inflation to be 6 percent. What is an appropriate forecast for the price of the pound at the end of this year based on these expectations and the theory of relative purchasing power parity?

32. Suppose that the expected rates of inflation in Chile and the United States are 33.1 percent and 10 percent, respectively, and the spot price of the Chilean peso is $0.0025.

a. What are the nominal interest rates necessary to produce expected real interest rates of 5 percent in each country?

b. What expected value of the peso one year from now does the purchasing power parity theory imply?

c. If someone offers to sell you pesos for delivery in one year, what will you be willing to pay?

33. The data in the table below report the foreign currency prices of the pound.

a. Identify all currencies that are at a discount to the British pound and all currencies that are at a premium to the pound.

b. Calculate the one-month, three-month and one-year premiums or discounts as percentages per annum.

FOREIGN EXCHANGE PRICE QUOTATIONS

	Spot Closing Mid-point	*Forward One-Month Rate**	*Forward Three-Months Rate**	*Forward One-Year Rate**
Canada	2.2500	2.2504	2.2512	2.2536
France	8.3502	8.3498	8.3490	8.3466
Germany	2.3610	2.3615	2.3625	2.3660
Japan	157.100	156.905	156.680	155.900

*percentage per annum

34. Given the following data, calculate the implied one-year forward price of each currency in U.S. dollars.

Country	*Spot Rate*	*One-Year Interest Rate*	*Implied One-Year Forward Rate*
Canada	$0.7534	5.25%	
Germany	0.6165	6.00	
Japan	0.009551	2.69	
Switzerland	0.7018	4.38	
United Kingdom	1.5274	5.69	
United States		3.44	

35. Below are exchange rate and consumer price indices (CPI) data from the U.S. and Chile for the years 1995-2000.

	1995	*1996*	*1997*	*1998*	*1999*	*2000*
Peso/$	8.5	17.4	28.0	34.0	39.0	39.0
Chilean CPI	100.0	312.0	599.0	838.0	1,118.0	1,511.0
U.S. CPI	161.2	170.5	181.5	195.4	271.4	257.0

Based on these data, would you argue that the peso is over- or undervalued at the end of 2000?

36. Trinity Forge is a small company with little international experience. It has agreed to buy two forging machines from a manufacturer in Germany. The price is DM 2,000,000 with delivery and payment in 0.5 years. The spot price of the mark is ₹ 25.00. The 180-day forward price is ₹ 24.50. Trinity is currently earning 7.50 percent per year on its short-term deposits. Its banker has offered Trinity the opportunity to earn 8.50 percent per year on short-term mark deposits.

a. If Trinity Forge wants to eliminate its mark exposure with a forward hedge, what transaction should it make?

b. What is the rupee cost of the machines if Trinity Forge hedges its mark exposure in the forward market?

c. If Trinity Forge wants to eliminate its mark exposure with a money market hedge, what transactions should it make?

d. What is the rupee cost of the machines if Trinity Forge hedges its mark exposure with a money market hedge?

e. Holding the other information unchanged, for what forward price would the two hedges yield identical costs for the machines?

37. Citigroup quotes French francs on European terms as "FF5.62/$ Bid and FF5.87/$ Ask."

a. Which currency is Citigroup buying at the FF5.62/$ bid rate, and which currency is Citigroup selling at the FF5.87/$ offer rate?

b. What are the bid and ask prices in American terms? Which currency is Citigroup buying at these prices and which currency is Citigroup selling?

c. With the foreign currency in the numerator, the "FF5.62/$ Bid and FF5.87/$ Ask" quotes are indirect quotes for a U.S. resident. What are the bid and ask prices in direct terms for a U.S. resident? At these prices, which currency is Citigroup buying and which currency is Citigroup selling?

d. If you sell $1 million to Citigroup at their bid price of FF5.62/$ and simultaneously buy $1 million at their offer price of FF5.87/$, how many French francs will you make or lose? What is Citigroup's franc profit or loss on the transaction?

38. You are interested in buying Swedish krona (SK). Your bank quotes "SK7.5050/$ Bid and SK7.5150/$ Ask." What would you pay in dollars if you bought SK10,000,000 at the current spot rate?

39. The following outright quotations are given for the Canadian dollar

	Bid (C$/$)	*Ask (C$/$)*
Spot rate	1.2340	1.2350
One month forward	1.2345	1.2365
Three months forward	1.2367	1.2382
Six months forward	1.2382	1.2397

Assume you reside in the United States. Calculate forward quotes for the Canadian dollar as an annual percentage premium or discount. Would a foreign exchange trader in Canada get a different answer if asked to calculate the annual percentage premium or discount on the U.S. dollar for each forward rate? Why?

40. Given the following spot and forward quotes, calculate forward premiums on Japanese yen as (a) a basis point premium or discount, and (b) an annualized percentage premium or discount.

Spot ($/¥)	*Forward ($/¥)*	*Days Forward*
0.009057355	0.008968408	30
0.009057355	0.008772945	90
0.009057355	0.008489101	180
0.009057355	0.007920290	360

41. In 1984, the number of German marks required to buy one U.S. dollar was 1.80. In 1987, the U.S. dollar was worth 2.00 marks. In 1992, the dollar was worth 1.50 marks. In 1997, the dollar was again worth 1.80 marks.

a. What was the percentage appreciation or depreciation of the dollar between 1984 and 1987? Between 1987 and 1992? Between 1992 and 1997?

b. What was the percentage appreciation or depreciation of the mark between 1984 and 1987; between 1987 and 1992; and between 1992 and 1997?

42. A foreign exchange dealer provides quotes for spot and one-month, three-month, and six-month forward rates for the U.S. dollar against the Finnish markka.

	Bid (FM/$)	*Ask (FM/$)*
Spot	4.0040	4.0200
One month forward	3.9920	4.0090
Three months forward	3.9690	3.9888
Six months forward	3.9360	3.9580

a. What would you receive in dollars if you sold FM5 million at the spot rate?

b. What would it cost you in dollars to purchase FM20 million forward three months? When would you make payment?

43. A foreign exchange dealer in Tokyo provides the following quotes for spot exchange and one-month, three-month, and six-month forward exchange.

	Bid (FM/$)	*Ask (FM/$)*
Spot	4.0040	4.0200
One month forward	3.9920	4.0090
Three months forward	3.9690	3.9888
Six months forward	3.9360	3.9580

a. In New York, three-month U.S. Treasury bills yield 7 percent per annum. What should be the annualized yield on three-month Finnish government bills? Use the Finnish markka ask quotes for simplicity,

b. Verify your answer to part a with a hypothetical investment of $10 million for three months in each country. Use only ask quotes for simplicity and ignore other fees, charges, and taxes.

44. You have sold ¥104 million (and purchased dollars) at a spot price of ¥1.04/$. One year later, you pay dollars to buy back the ¥104 million at the prevailing exchange rate of ¥1.00/$. How much have you gained or lost in dollars?

45. Dollar bid and ask prices on the Spanish peseta are quoted direct in New York at $0.007634/Pts Bid and $0.007643/Pts Ask. What should be the corresponding indirect quote for dollars?

46. Calculate appreciation or depreciation in each of the following:

a. If the dollar depreciates 10% against the yen, by what percentage does the yen appreciate against the dollar?

b. If the dollar appreciates 1,000% against the ruble, by what percentage does the ruble depreciate against the dollar?

47. In what way are the following two quotes equivalent?

a. "\$0.5841/DM Bid and \$0.5852/DM Ask"

b. "\$0.5852/DM Bid and \$0.5841/DM Ask"

48. The French franc is quoted in New York at \$0.18536/FF spot, \$0.18519/FF 30 days forward, \$0.18500/FF 90 days forward, and \$0.18488/FF 180 days forward. Calculate the forward discounts or premiums on the franc.

49. Suppose that at time t = 0 the dollar per yen spot rate is \$0.0100/¥ and that the yen appreciates 25.86 percent during the next period.

a. What is the closing spot rate in dollars per yen S1\$/¥?

b. By what percentage does the dollar depreciate against the yen?

50. The following quotations are available to you. (You may either buy or sell at the stated rates.)

Singapore bank: Singapore dollar quote for Korean won	Won 714.00/S\$
Hongkong bank: HK \$ quote for Singapore dollars	HK\$4.70/S\$
Korean bank: Korean Won quote for Hong Kong dollars	Won 150.00/HK\$

Assume you have on initial S\$ 1,000,000. Is triangular arbitrage possible? If so, explain the steps and compute your profit.

51. Quotes for the U.S. dollar and Thai baht (Bt) are as follows:

Spot contract midpoint	$S_0^{Bt/\$}$	= Bt24.96/\$
One-year forward contract midpoint	$F_1^{Bt/\$}$	= Bt25.64/\$
One-year Eurodollar interest rate	$i^{\$}$	= 6. 125% per year

a. Your newspaper does not quote one-year Eurocurrency interest rates on Thai baht. Make your own estimate of i^{Bt}.

b. Suppose that you can trade at the prices for $S^{Bt/S}$, $F^{Bt/S}$ and i^{S} just given and that you can also either borrow or lend at a Thai Eurocurrency interest rate of i^{Bt} = 10% per year. Based on a \$1 million initial amount, how much profit can you generate through covered interest arbitrage?

52. You have \$100,000 that you are free to invest in any currency. You can trade at the following prices:

Spot rate, Argentinean australs per dollar	AA20/\$
Six-month forward rate for australs	AA22/\$

Six-month Argentinean interest rate	18%
Six-month U.S. interest rate	6%

Is covered interest arbitrage worthwhile? If so, explain the steps and compute the profit based on your initial $100,000.

53. Currency exchange rates and Eurocurrency interest rates are as follows:

Current Singapore dollar (S$) spot rate	$0.50/S$
One-year Singapore dollar (S$) forward rate	$0.51/S$
One-year Singapore dollar (S$) interest rate	4.0%
One-year U.S. interest rate	6.0%

In what direction will covered interest arbitrage force the quoted rates to change? Explain the steps and compute the profit based on a $1 million initial position.

54. Consider the balance sheet of a U.S. firm that exports to Europe. Euro-denominated accounts have been translated into U.S. dollars at the current exchange rate.

Cash (in $)	$40,000	Wages payable (in $)	$40,000
Accts receivable (in $)	$30,000	Accts payable (in $)	70,000
Accts receivable (in €)	$60,000	Bank note due (in €)	10,000
Inventory	$20,000	Current liabilities	$120,000
Current assets	$130,000	Bank note (in €)	$50,000
Plant & Equipment	$50,000	Common equity	$30,000
Total assets	$200,000	Total liabilities & equity	$200,000

This firm considers inventory to be a real, rather than a monetary, asset

a. What is the dollar value of the firm's monetary assets? What is the dollar value of the firm's monetary liabilities? What is the dollar value of net monetary assets?

b. What is the dollar value of the firm's monetary assets exposed to currency risk? Exposed monetary liabilities? Net exposed monetary assets (exposed monetary assets less exposed monetary liabilities)?

c. Is the operating performance of a U.S. exporter such as this likely to be improved or worsened by a real appreciation of the euro? Explain.

d. This firm has a bank note denominated in euros. Does this foreign currency liability increase or reduce the firm's net monetary exposure to currency risk? Explain

55. Indicate whether each of the following individuals uses technical or fundamental analysis in forecasting currency values.

a. An investor uses charts of historical exchange rate movements to predict future exchange rate movements.

b. A hedger uses a computer programme called a neural network to identify patterns in exchange rates. The neural network uses past price information to generate a signal indicating whether a particular currency exposure should be hedged.

c. A speculator gathers the most recent balance-of-payments data from countries participating in European Monetary Union. She uses this data to make long-term forecasts of the value of the euro against the U.S. dollar.

d. A currency has been trading in a narrow range during the last several months. The currency falls in value days after the government announces it has suspended payments on dollar-denominated loans. A hedge fund manager sells the currency after comparing the size of the dollar-denominated loans to the country's foreign exchange reserves.

e. A currency has been trading in a narrow range during the last several months. The currency falls in value after the government announces it has suspended payments on dollar-denominated loans. A hedge fund manager sells the currency after noticing that the currency has fallen in value for three successive days.

56. Does the experience of the eurozone so far suggest that the difficulties inherent in corralling different and divergent economies into a single currency would be magnified and possibly disastrous if carried out worldwide?

57. Critically evaluate the theory of a single currency.

58. "Despite trend towards fewer currencies, a single world currency seems unlikely in near future." Do you agree?

9

MANAGING FOREIGN EXCHANGE RESERVES

INTRODUCTION

The foreign exchange reserves has received renewed interest in recent times in the context of increasing globalisation, acceleration of capital flows and integration of financial markets. The debt-banking-financial crises in several countries have also necessitated the need for an international financial architecture in which the management of foreign exchange reserves has emerged as one of the critical issues.

Contextually, the subject of foreign exchange reserves may be broadly classified into two inter-linked areas, *viz.*, the theory of reserves and the management of reserves. The theory of reserves encompasses issues relating to institutional and legal arrangements for holding reserve assets, conceptual and definitional aspects, objectives for holding reserve assets, exchange rate regimes and conceptualisation of the appropriate level of foreign reserves. In essence, a theoretical framework for reserves provides the rationale for holding foreign exchange reserves. Reserve management is mainly guided by the portfolio management consideration, i.e., how best to deploy foreign reserve assets subject to statutory stipulations? The portfolio considerations take into account *inter alia,* safety, liquidity and yield on reserves as the principal objectives of reserve management. The institutional and legal arrangements are largely country specific and these differences should be recognised in approaching the critical issues relating to both reserve management practices and policy-making.

MOTIVES FOR HOLDING FOREIGN EXCHANGE RESERVES

The motives for holding reserves may be broadly classified under three categories, viz, transaction, speculative and precautionary. International trade gives rise to currency flows, which are assumed to be handled by banks driven by the transaction motives. Similarly, speculative motives is left to individuals or corporates. Central banks reserves, however, are characterised primarily as a last resort stock of foreign currency for unpredictable flows, which is consistent with precautionary motives for holding foreign assets. Precautionary motive for holding foreign currency, like the demand for money, can be positively related to wealth and the cost of covering unplanned deficit, and negatively related to the return from alternative assets. Furthermore, foreign exchange reserves are instruments to maintain or manage the exchange rate, while enabling orderly absorption of international capital flows. Official reserves are mainly held for precautionary and transaction motives keeping in view the aggregate of national interests, to achieve balance between demand for and supply of foreign currencies, for interventin, and to preserve confidence in the county's ability to carry out external transactions.

The objectives for maintaining reserves are: (i) maintaining confidence in monetary and exchange rate policies; (ii) enhancing capicity to invervence in foreign exchange markets; (iii) limiting external vulnerability by maintaining foreign currency liquidity to absorb shocks during times of crisis including national disasters or emergencies; (iv) providing confidence to the markets, including credit cating agencies, that external obligations can always be met (thus reducing the overall costs at which foreign exchange resources are available to all the market participants); and (v) adding to the comfort of the market participatns, by demonstrating the backing of domestic currency by external assets.

FOREIGN EXCHANGE RESERVE ACCUMULATION

Foreign exchange reserves are an important component of the balance of payments and an essential element in the analysis of an economy's external position. Rapid reserve accumulation has significant implications for a central bank's balance sheet. While capital inflows—particularly portfolio inflows - have often been seen as temporary (perhaps justifying intervention), current account surpluses tend to endure and have persistent effects on the exchange rate. Moreover, there has been a tendency among investors and currency traders to identify persistent current account surpluses with an appreciation of the long-run equilibrium exchange rate. Resisting this may cause even larger capital inflows, potentially perpetuating a vicious circle of increased appreciation pressure and yet more intervention. Table 1 presents a stylised version of a monetary authority's balance sheet. Its assets consist of foreign currency and domestic assets; its liabilities comprise currency, bank reserves (taken together as monetary liabilities), its own securities, other liabilities (taken together as non-monetary liabilities) and equity capital. Of these, currency is largely determined by the public's demand for cash balances. Equity capital represents government transfers to the central bank (plus accumulated profits and losses). The remaining liabilities are within the control of the central bank.

An injection of equity capital in order to finance reserve accumulation would not result in monetary expansion, provided that the government did not finance this by drawing on deposits or using an overdraft facility at the central bank. Without increased equity capital, and assuming other things (ie the demand for cash) equal, the accumulation of reserves requires financing in some form. One simple measure of such a financing need is the excess of foreign currency reserves over currency in circulation. Up until the late 1990s, such a financing gap was either small or negative in many developing countries. In other words, forex reserve assets and currency in circulation were of a similar order of magnitude. However, the gap has widened appreciably over the past five years as a percentage of GDP in many emerging market economies, especially in Asia. In many countries, such a gap is also large in relation to the stock of public debt securities.

As intervention takes place, the central bank can finance this gap by issuing domestic monetary liabilities (typically commercial bank monetary reserves). Should these increased monetary reserves be allowed to put downward pressure on the short-term interest rate (unsterilised intervention), bank credit would tend to expand and inflationary pressures would eventually mount. If central banks have a target for the short-term rate (usually the policy rate), they would attempt to offset increases in bank reserves through changes in other balance sheet items (usually selling domestic assets or issuing their own securities) over which they have control (sterilised intervention).

TABLE-1

A CENTRAL BANK'S BALANCE SHEET

Assets	*Liabilities*
Net foreign assets	Monetary liabilities
Net domestic assets	• Currency
	• Bank reserves
	Non-monetary liabilities
	• Central bank securities
	• Others
	Equity capital

Challenges from Sterilised Intervention

Fully sterilising reserve accumulation can be challenging. Even when fully sterilised, intervention can have other unwelcome implications that can limit its usefulness as a policy instrument. The four possible and unwelcome implications are:

(i) The Fiscal Costs of Intervention

An earlier presumption was that intervention by central banks, in countries where local interest rates were well above international levels, entailed large carrying costs, and it was often these rising costs which led to policy reversals in the past. Nonetheless valuation losses do not reduce the central bank's ability to intervene (ie to sell local currency to limit further appreciation), nor do they reduce the purchasing power of its foreign currency reserves in terms of foreign goods. To the extent that the private sector and the government are net borrowers in foreign currency, appreciation reduces their net debt burden. Valuation losses might matter, however, if they were to undermine a central bank's credibility or independence.

(ii) Future Monetary Imbalances

The long-term effectiveness of sterilised intervention in dealing with excess liquidity depends on the instruments used for sterilisation and which sector ends up holding such paper. Large-scale reserve accumulation typically raises the underlying liquidity position of the banking system. This can be partly neutralised by selling long-term government bonds to banks. If such bonds are then sold to non-banks, sterilisation can be thought to be reasonably complete: households or non-bank firms lower their holding of monetary assets and increase that of non-monetary assets such as government bonds.

(iii) Financial Sector Imbalances

Intervention to prevent a rise in the exchange rate can accentuate macroeconomic and financial imbalances. There are several possible channels for this. Increased bank lending resulting from partial or ineffective sterilisation could finance excessive investment in certain sectors such as property markets. Such effects could also be associated with a persistently low inflation and low interest rate environment. Another possible channel is that expectations of future currency appreciation could attract large short-term capital inflows, pushing up equity prices. Such an effect could be reinforced by perception of a one-way currency bet, leading to increased currency substitution and unhedged foreign currency borrowing.

There are no simple indicators to show how far exchange rates might have become misaligned, or the extent to which investor expectations about future exchange rate movements might have been influenced, by continued sterilised intervention. Nevertheless, real exchange rates have not risen significantly in many countries with large and persistent current account surpluses. In some cases, real effective exchange rates are actually below what they were at the beginning of the decade, when current account surpluses were small.

(iv) Implications for Financial Intermediation

The difficulties experienced in sterilising large-scale intervention can lead to recourse to non-market instruments to drain excess liquidity, which may have adverse implications for the financial system. Prolonged sterilised intervention could alter the behaviour of banks: easy profits from large holdings of treasury securities could weaken pressures on banks to become more efficient. Moreover, large-scale issuance of sterilisation-related debts might also hamper the development of a private bond market, as a large supply of risk-free government and central bank paper crowds out private sector issuance. In contrast, in countries where the stock of initial public debt securities is relatively low, the issuance of sterilisation-related debt could actually help develop a domestic bond market.

INTERNATIONAL RESERVES AND OPTIMALITY

The policy of accretion to reserves to meet the transactions and precautionary needs generally involves both financial and economic cost to the country. In the absence of any unique definition of the opportunity cost, one comes across several interpretations in the literature, the applicability of which depends on the particular economic context. When an economy is both foreign exchange and saving constrained, the opportunity cost could be the rate of return on domestic investment (assuming that the foreign exchange used to finance unsatiated investment demand would have fetched the return on domestic investment). When an-economy is only foreign exchange constrained, the opportunity cost could be in terms of foregone consumption. When an economy is not foreign exchange constrained (*i.e.*, all productive forex demand are met beforethe reserves are built up), the opportunity cost would depend on the difference between the cost of borrowing and the return on reserve assets. If high cost borrowings are used to build reserves on which modest returns are obtained because of the emphasis on safety and liquidity of reserve assets, such reserve build-up policies may prove more costly. Another form of cost—often known as the quasi-fiscal cost - arises from the higher rate of return on domestic assets vis-a-vis foreign assets, Since sterilised intervention gives rise to an offsetting change in the domestic asset holding of a central bank when its foreign assets increase, the overall profits arising from the total asset portfolio of the Central Bank's balance sheet may decline. As a result, the profits transferred—to the Government-which represents a major source of non-tax revenue for the Government may decline. For countries operating with large fiscal imbalances, such a decline in non-tax revenue could prove more costly, forcing a higher mobilisation of tax revenue or a cut in expenditure that may affect growth and development.

The development of money demand theory along, the lines of optimal inventory control or buffer stock model provides a natural theoretical benchmark for the study of optimal reserve accumulation and has spurred a large body of empirical literature in the late 1960s and early 1970s. Heller used a cost-benefit approach and stressed that the issue is one of choosing an optimal level of reserves at which the central bank minimises the total expected cost i.e., the sum of the adjustment cost that is incurred when reserves reach some lower bound and the opportunity cost. Heller's estimation indicated that optimal reserves are directly proportional to the variability of exports and are inversely related to the opportunity cost variable (defined as foregone earnings or economic welfare). Frankel and Jovanovic and Landell-Mills also found a negative relationship between the demand for reserves and its opportunity cost. Flood and Marion, however, did not find any, relationship between reserves and opportunity cost. The sign of the propeinsity to import has also turned out to be ambiguous in the literature. Several studies have found an inverse relationship, while some others found a positive relationship between import propensity and reserves. While the inverse relationship between reserves and the propensity to import has been interpreted as the extent of adjustment to an external shock, the direct relationship is an indicator of the degree of openness. Eaton and Gersovitz formally introduced the concept of transactions demand for reserves. In addition to the 'conventional' variables, Ben-Bassat and Gottlieb introduced risk of default or sovereign risk into the assessment of precautionary demand for reserves. Lane and Burke adopted a broad approach to identify the potential determinants of reserves and found: (i) trade openness to be the most important variable along with financial deepening; (ii) smaller and more volatile industrial countries hold larger reserves than their larger, less volatile counterparts; and (iii) more indebted developing countries had smaller reserve ratios. The traditional determinants identified in the empirical literature on foreign exchange reserve holdings are presented in Table-2.

TABLE-2

DETERMINANTS OF THE DEMAND FOR RESERVES

Variables	*Description*
Scalar variable	Imports, per capita income, GDP, population
Propensity to import	Marginal/average propensity to import
Variability measure	Exports, imports, terms of trade, receipts, payments, nominal effective exchange rate, balance of payments, reserves
Opportunity cost	Marginal product of capital (MPK) or in the absence of MPK, per capita output (as an inverse proxy for marginal product of capital), marginal utility of consumption, rate of interest on borrowing from abroad, net foreign indebtedness, the government bond yield, the spread between the government bond yield and short-term international interest rates, marginal productivity of social capital, one-year deposit rate.

Analytically and empirically, reserve holding appears to be an under-researched area. Clear standard methodologies have yet to evolve on. this subject. However, relatively high demand for international reserves by countries in Far East and relatively low demand by some other countries has attracted attention. Aizenman and Marion recently showed that for 125 developing countries, reserve-holding over 1980-1996 period could be predicted by the size of international transactions, their volatility, the exchange rate arrangement and political- considerations. Sovereign risk and fiscal liabilities led to relatively large precautionary demand for reserves.

Aizenman and Marion showed that there has been a structural break in the equation for the demand for reserves in several Asian countries that were affected by crisis in 1997. Using a standard estimating equation, they found that over the period 1960-96, their model over-predicted the reserve holdings of countries such, as China, Taiwan, Hong Kong, South Korea and Singapore implying thereby that their reserves were low in relation to what was estimated as desirable in the model. Out of sample forecasts of desirable levels generated for 1997-99, however, under predicted the reserve holding (i.e., actual reserves holdings exceeded the predicted desirable level). Such a result has to be assessed in the context of the overall change in policy stance of the emerging market economies in the aftermath of the financial crisis that viewed high reserves as an appropriate policy of "self-insurance".

In India, the determinants of reserve holdings appear to have changed considerably and evolved over the recent years with the gradual opening up of the capital accovmt. The substantial growth in reserves since 2001-02 has generated a debate regarding the cost of holding reserves. While the cost of reserves is secondary to properly meeting the overall objective behind holding reserves, it is important to note that in India, in the last few years, almost the whole addition to reserves has been made without increasing the overall level of external debt, which has hovered around US $ 100 billion during the previous five years. The increase in reserves largely reflects higher remittances, quicker repatriation of export proceeds and non-debt flows. Even after taking into account foreign currency denominated NRI flows (where interest rates are linked to LIBOR), the financial cost of additional reserve accretion in India in the recent period is low.

MONETARY IMPACT OF FOREIGN EXCHANGE RESERVES

While the reserve build up policies of the emerging market economies like India reflect the importance of appropriate reaction to the vastly altered conditions prevailing at both national and global levels, high reserve policies also entail several other implications, particularly for monetary management and in terms of the quasi-fiscal costs, both of which poses different type of challenge to the policy makers.

Cross-country experiences of surges in capital inflows indicate that in the context of the limited capacity of the econorrv to absorb capital flows in the form of higher productive investment and the resultant implications for the exchange rate, monetary authorities often intervene in the foreign exchange market to absorb the surplus in the market and thereby avoid nominal appreciation of the exchange rate. A non-sterilised (or partially sterilised) intervention can, however, cause a sharp rise in the monetary base and hence higher inflation. Real appreciation resulting from higher inflation could erode external competitiveness; lower interest rates could also fuel lending and consumption boom, that can potentially lead to a sharp deterioration in the current account balance and culminate in a possible currency crisis. When the conflict between the policy objectives of checking nominal appreciation and limiting inflation emerges, central banks attempt to counter inflation through sterilised intervention, which by nature appears money supply neutral.

Among the instruments available for sterilisation, recourse to open market operations (OMOs) is particularly effective if inflows are temporary and there exists a near perfect elastic demand for domestic government securities. However, if the demand for government securities is not perfectly elastic in view of the limited absorptive capacity of market participants and the underdeveloped nature of the financial markets, OMOs can cause domestic interest rates to rise, nullifying the impact of sterilisation as higher interest rates could attract larger capital inflows. Sterilisation typically involves exchanging high-yielding domestic assets for low-yielding foreign assets and, therefore has quasi-fiscal costs. The degree of effectiveness of sterilised intervention would therefore depend on: (i) the sensitivity of domestic interest rates to OMOs and (ii) the degree to which foreign capital flows respond to such interest rate variations. The combined effect, which is captured through the estimated "offset coefficient", indicates that the value of the coefficient may range between 0 and (-) 1, with values close to zero indicating "effectiveness of sterilisation" and values close to (-) 1 indicating "ineffective sterilisation". Sterilisation induced increase in interest rates, however at times, may be more than offset by the change in the stance of monetary policy. When capital flows are persistent and sterilisation proves ineffective cross-country studies show that countries often attempt a few options available to them. These include: fiscal adjustment, easing of restrictions on capital outflows, accelerated trade liberalisation, lower interest rates on foreign currency deposits, prepayment of costly debt, adoption of new sterilisation techniques such as" foreign exchange swaps, switching of government deposits from the banking system to the central bank, imposition of taxes on domestic assets purchased by foreigners, fixing of ceilings on foreign borrowings by domestic residents, and recourse to indirect capital controls, such as variable unremunerated reserve requirements on certain categories of foreign borrowing. In the Indian case, capital flows have had a softening effect on interest rates and positive effect on broad money growth.

Capital inflows have served the twin purpose of meeting India's domestic investment-saving gap and the need for reserve accretion consistent with the standard indicators of reserve adequacy. Nonetheless, the surge in capital flows often poses a challenge to the conduct of monetary and exchange rate policy. As a result of large accretion to reserves resulting from surges in capital flows in the face of low domestic absorption, there has been a substantial increase in net foreign exchange assets (NFA) of the Reserve Bank. There is hardly any formal analysis available for emerging market economies (including India) to evaluate the monetary impact of large capital flows econometrically. One way to assess the impact is to simulate the emerging monetary condition in counterfactual scenarios where reserve accretion is placed at lower levels. For this purpose, an interest rate reaction function has been estimated that relates domestic interest rate to its possible determinants like inflation, output and capital flows along with a conventional money demand equation in terms of income and interest rate. Controlling for the impact on interest rates from the accretion to reserves, the counterfactual path generated through a simulation exercise under lower reserves accumulation points towards a perceptible monetary impact of reserves in terms of higher broad money demand.

In the period of surge in capital flows and significant accretion to foreign exchange reserves with the monetary authority, the literature points to the emergence of newer channels of monetary expansion, especially, if there is a disassociation between the growth of broad money and reserve money. In India, notwithstanding a fall in reserve money growth broad money grew almost at the same level in the two decades, which may be symptomatic of such a disassociation. There is an attempt to explore the likely mechanism that characterises the underlying process of monetary expansion. It is suggested that had there been a lower reserve accumulation with the RBI, the interest rate would perhaps have been higher, thus, possibly signifying that the liquidity effect of reserve accumulation would have outweighted the sterlization effect in the Indian context. Composition of reserve money expansion has shifted from domestic assets to foreign assets reflective of the surge in capital flows, accumulation of reserves and sterilisation operations of the Reserve Bank. Sterilisation operations have so far been successful in arresting reserve money growth to levels where the inflationary potential of capital flows has been kept in control. However, future concerns on monetary management may arise, among others, from the following factors: (i) need to ensure sufficient stock of Government securities at the hands of the Reserve Bank for sterilisation operations of the required magnitude; (ii) the absorption capacity of the financial system for Government securities once the credit demand picks up; and (iii) the upward drift in money multiplier arising partly from fall in currency-deposit ratio and CRR has sustained higher growth of broad money in the face of declining reserve money growth. With financial liberalisation and market-determined interest rates, there is evidence that innovations to money multiplier emanate from interest rates and other macroeconomic variables (such as growth) apart from the conventional proximate determinants. To the extent that these newer determinants of money multiplier are not entirely under the control of the monetary authority, it poses a challenge for the Reserve Bank to manage the emerging monetary conditions.

CAPITAL INFLOWS, FOREIGN EXCHANGE RESERVES AND GROWTH

The coexistence of slowdown in the growth rate of the Indian economy in the recent period and the sharp build-up of foreign exchange reserves, has fuelled the debate on their possible inter-relationship and has called into question, in some quarters, the extant policy of reserve accretion. A recent study (see Box-1) for example, has contended that India could have attained a higher growth trajectory had capital inflows been allowed to be absorbed by the economy (instead of accumulating them as foreign exchange reserves of the central bank) and had fiscal deficits not been incurred. According to the study, the entire foreign capital can be absorbed by allowing the real exchange rate to appreciate. The real appreciation could be engendered either by allowing the nominal exchange rate to appreciate or by allowing prices to increase (*i.e.*, non-sterilised reserve build-up which will increase the money supply and thereby give rise to both higher inflation and lower interest rates - both of which can increase absorption). An econometric exercise shows that the growth rate could have been higher by about 1 to 6 per cent in different years in the 1990s. The study makes the following policy recommendations: (i) the reserve management policy should be replaced by appropriate monetary and exchange rate policies that could boost growth; (ii) have a tighter fiscal policy (to contain the crowding out effect) and an easier monetary policy (by non-sterilisation of reserves - that,could increase prices and lower interest rates); (iii) high reserves and low domestic inflation provide the right environment against which the Rupee can be made fully convertible on the capital account; and (iv) replace on the managed exchange rate regime by full float.

BOX-1

Is Foreign Exchange Reserves Build-up Inimical to Growth?

A study by Lal, Bery and Pant has contended that the growth rate in the Indian economy would have been much higher had capital inflows been absorbed by the economy instead of being accumulated as foreign exchange reserves. The Study bases its conclusion on the relationship between the real exchange rate, capital inflows, excess demand and the growth rate. The Study estimates the real exchange rate (er) as the ratio of the prices of traded goods to non-traded goods, as obtained from the WPI series. Net capital flows (B) are taken to include transfers (mainly workers' remittances). The 'excess demand' variable (ED) (reflecting the fiscal and monetary impact) is constructed from the national income accounting identities, as the difference between the trade deficit and capital inflows, inclusive of remittances. The relationship between the three variables is estimated thus:

$$er_i = 87.6\, B_t + 3.05\, ED_t$$
$$(1.62) \quad (2.25)$$
$$R^2 = 0.26, \text{ adj. } R^2 = 0.18, F = 3.119, N = 20$$

The growth estimates consistent with full absorption of capital flows have been derived essentially by estimating the degree to which 'er' would have been misaligned with full market absorption of capital flows. The higher (S-l) gap resulting, from full absorption can increase the capital stock, which would yield higher growth through a production function having two factors of production (*i.e.* labour and capital).

A few technical anomalies are apparent in the above formulation.

First, R^2 is too low and the DW is not stated. Reworking on their data shows the presence of serious autocorrelation with a DW of 1.18. Furthermore, the Cusum Square criterion shows that the equation is highly unstable. Consequently, any estimation/Inference based on the above exercise would be highly tentative. In a separate exercise, a correction for autocorrelation using the Cochrane-Orcutt method brought about *a* reversal of the signs of both the excess demand (ED) and the capital inflow (B) coefficients.

Second, it is not clear how the 'er' series generated in the study can explain the impact of full absorption of foreign capital. Since the 'er' series is the relative price of tradebles and non-tradeables taken separately from the disaggregated WPI data for India, it may only explain the relative profitability of tradeable and non-tradeable sectors within the economy. The prices prevailing in the external markets (*i.e.* export markets and the markets from where the import originates) are, however, of significance to exporters and importers. The real appreciation cannot increase absorption, because 'er' cannot explain how the relative prices of domestic tradeables will change *vis-&-vis* international prices as a result of domestic nominal appreciation. In the absence of information on the latter, it is difficult to assess how the CAD would widen as a result of real appreciation. The most striking aspect of the 'er' series is that it shows very modest misalignment over the entire period 1981-2000. The series is not only smoother than the series published by the Reserve Bank but it also lies above the RBI series throughout the twenty year period covered in the study. It almost suggests that the prices of tradeables and non-tradeables moved in tandem, irrespective of the behaviour of the nominal exchange rate (which depreciatedduring this period) and inflation differentials (which remained positive throughout). The Study mentions that domestic prices of tradeables in rupees are the same as foreign prices of tradeables converted at the nominal exchange rate. This theoretical identify has not been verified empirically and since the Study uses only the tradeable prices from WPI, it does not explain how the effects of any change in nominal exchange rate can get transmitted to tradeable prices. In the absence of a transmission channel, even if nominal exchange rate appreciates due to full absorption of capital flows in the market, REER may not appreciate.

Third, the 'er' equation - that is used to determine the misaligned rate under full absorption - has net capital flows plus remittances *(i.e. B)* and excess demand (i.e. ED) on the right hand side. Since ED has been derived as (ED=(M-X) -B], if both B and ED are taken in the same equation, there could be the problem of multi-collinearity. Furthermore, the coefficient of B in the equation is statistically insignificant (i.e. not different from zero). The authors, however, use the B coefficient to estimate the misaligned 'er'. Also, as already mentioned, a part of § gets absorbed in financing the deficit in the goods and services account and therefore, something less than B could be taken to estimate the 'er' consistent with full absorption. Most importantly, it is not clear why the estimated 'or' from a regression of 'er' on B can be viewed as the proxy for the 'er' that would have prevailed under condition of full absorption. Given that a large part of B was already used for reserve buildup, that would have prevented major change in 'er' (both by preventing nominal appreciation and by sterilising the monetary impact of reserves). The empirical relationship between the two, therefore, should be negligible, which is also obtained in the regression equation as evidenced by the statistical insignificance of the B-coefficient. In the absence of any argument explaining why the estimated 'er' would approximate the full absorption-'er', it is not evident whether the channel suggested for increasing the absorption of foreign capital would help in raising growth. The estimated 'er' series that fully captures the impact of full absorption shows only very modest appreciation over the period 1981 - 2001 (a cumulative real appreciation of only 8 per cent over a 20 year period). With full absorption, however, one would nave expected a much larger real appreciation.

Fourth, in the production function equation, full absorption impact enters only through a change in the capital stock. In a sense, it does not use the estimated *'er'*. It only mentions about the factor A, which depends on the elasticity of substitution in both demand and supply between tradeables and nontradeabtes. The manner in which A is derived in the production function is critical, since the value of A can greatly influence the projected growth rate for any given level of capital and labour. It appears that the estimated values of A have a strong upward bias, and in the absence of any convincing justification supporting the determination of the value A, the entire exercise appears to be the result of discretionary adjustments.

Fifth, the reason why the Study obtains a high growth rate from the full absorption of capital flows is that "net capital flows and remittances' have been taken as the proxy for extra capital that is available under their hypothetical situation for addition to capital stock. It should, however, be recognised that these inflows would have already been partly utilised for financing the deficit in the goods and services account. After the partial absorption, only the remaining amount under "net capital flows plus remittances" should have been viewed as the proxy for extra absorption. Since the surplus capital flows used as proxy for extra absorption has been overestimated by dose to 40 per cent, the growth estimates also turn out to be higher. Moreover, even if one uses the correct figure on surplus capital flows, the production function used in the model may still yield a higher growth than what one would obtain through simple application of Incremental Capital-Output Ratio (ICOR). Since the authors do not mention anything about the productivity gains associated with capital flows and because that they only rely on increase in capital stock resulting from full absorption of foreign capital in the production function, it remains completely unclear as to why the growth could be higher than what the conventional ICOR would suggest.

Finally, even assuming that the entire capital flows would have been allowed to supplement domestic saving to ensure higher investment, then the annual investment could have increased (say) by about 2 percentage points (with capital flows of about 3 percent of GDP in the 1990s, 1 per cent was already used to finance current account deficit). Given the incremental capital output ratio of close to 4, additional growth of about 0.5 per cent could have been achieved (not 1 to 6 per cent as has been estimated in the paper).

Lal, D.; S. Bery and D.K. Pant: 'The Growth Slowdown: Real Exchange Rate Management, Fiscal Deficits and Capital Flows". Mines, New Delhi: NCAER, January. 2003.

The above results and policy prescriptions, however, need to be viewed with a great deal of circumspection. First, it needs to be recognised that high reserves reflect the lack of absorption/demand, and prescribing real appreciation as a means to raise domestic absorption completely disregards the importance of the trade-off between growth and stability and the role of a central bank in ensuring stability as a means to higher growth.

Second, the experience of the emerging market crises in the last decade shows that with low reserves and appreciated real exchange rate, India would have also faced a similar (or even more severe) crisis. On an average, the crisis years witnessed a sizeable growth reversal of the order of 6 to 7 per cent in all the crisis affected countries which could have offset the perceived 'first round' gains to the growth rate.

Third, it also needs to be recognised that even if REER appreciation is allowed to ensure full absorption of foreign capital, it is important to examine whether the full absorption (*i.e.* higher current account deficit) would result from an increase in imports or a major fall in exports. Given the asymmetric response of exports and imports to price changes brought about by REER appreciation, it is possible that a higher CAD. It would be attained more by a fall in exports than an increase in imports. It needs no emphasis that the external sector sustainability hinges critically on the performance of the export sector, and in the face of zero incremental reserves resulting from full absorption, weak export growth could be a strong source of vulnerability to crisis. On the other hand, even if imports increase in response to exchange rate appreciation, it is possible that import demand may just replace domestic demand, and as a result aggregate demand may remain unaltered. In other words, when imports are not driven by overall demand conditions (as is the case now) but are encouraged through a policy of exchange rate appreciation, imports may only compete with domestic supply and in the face of no increase in aggregate demand, the higher absorption through cheaper imports could displace some of the domestic manufacturers and thereby lower growth. Thus, growth gained through full absorption could be offset by lower growth resulting from displacement of domestic producers.

Fourth, the contention that full absorption of capital flows would significantly reduce the extent of crowding out by allowing a larger part of the fiscal deficit to be monetised, ignores the possibility of *crowding in* effects by certain types of government expenditure which at times may dominate the crowding-out effects.

Finally, it needs to be recognised that foreign capital should not be allowed either to give rise to excessive consumption or excessive investment just to ensure full absorption. When foreign capital finances consumption demand (as in Mexico) or sustains an investment driven overheating (as in South East Asia), higher growth can be obtained only at the cost of a severe financial crisis. High reserves, a flexible exchange rate regime, and cautious liberalisation of the capital account, together aim at preventing a crisis. Sterilisation is a strong instrument to regain monetary independence that allows a policy of reserve build-up without any adverse monetary implications. Sterilisation has beep used successfully so far in India and limits to sterilisation are yet to be reached.

Monetary policy has already, been eased to attain the objective of business cycle stabilisation without sacrificing the overriding inflation objective. The degree of manoeuvrability in fiscal policy is not very high because of the extent of fiscal imbalances prevailing today in India. During the phase of global slowdown, exchange rate appreciation could weaken exports and thereby have implication for external sector sustainability. The *Dutch disease* problem is at best a very distant reality for India. Real appreciation has been prevented both through reserves build-up and sterilisation (the former preventing nominal appreciation and the latter preventing higher inflation). Excessive consumption/investment has been prevented by maintaining the CAD within sustainable levels. Thus, both the channels through which the *Dutch disease* can spread, have been effectively regulated and their impact on the economy has been contained. With stronger recovery in demand, the surplus condition created by strong growth in remittances and software exports as well as capital flows would be absorbed automatically, reducing the scope for any *Dutch disease* effect and the need for any larger than desirable level of reserve build-up.

FOREIGN EXCHANGE RESERVE MANAGEMENT IN INDIA

The guiding objectives of foreign exchange reserves management in India are similar to those of many central banks in the world. The demands placed on the foreign exchange reserves may vary widely depending upon a variety of factors including the exchange rate regime adopted by the country, the extent of openness of the economy, the size of the external sector in a country's GDP and the nature of markets operating in the country. Even within this divergent framework most countries have adopted the primary objective of reserve management as preservation of the long-term value of the reserves in terms of purchasing power and the need to minimise risk and volatility in returns. India is not an exception in this regard. While safety and liquidity constitute the twin objectives of reserve management in India, return optimisation becomes an embedded strategy within this framework.

STATUTORY PROVISIONS AND MOVEMENT OF RESERVES

Legal Framework and Policies

The Reserve Bank of India Act, 1934 provides the overarching legal framework for deployment of the foreign currency assets (FCA) and gold defining the broad parameters in respect of currencies, instruments, issuers and counterparties. The essential legal framework for reserves management is provided in sub-sections 17 (6A), 17(12), 17(12A), 17(13) and 33 (6) of the above Act. In brief, the law broadly permits the following investment categories:

(i) deposits with other central banks and the Bank for International Settlements (BIS);

(ii) deposits with foreign commercial banks;

(iii) debt instruments representing sovereign/sovereign-guaranteed liability with residual maturity for the debt papers not exceeding 10 years;

(iv) other instruments / institutions as approved by the Central Board of the Reserve Bank in accordance with the provisions of the Act; and

(v) dealing in certain types of derivatives.

RBI has framed appropriate guidelines stipulating stringent criteria for issuers / counterparties / investments with a view to enhancing the safety and liquidity aspects of the reserves.

Growth in Foreign Exchange Reserves

India's foreign exchange reserves comprise foreign currency assets (FCA), gold, special drawing rights (SDRs), and reserve tranche position (RTP) in the International Monetary Fund (IMF). The level of foreign exchange reserves is largely the outcome of the RBI's intervention in the foreign exchange market to smoothen exchange rate volatility and valuation changes due to movement of the US dollar against other major currencies of the world. Foreign exchange reserves are accumulated when there is absorption of the excess foreign exchange flows by the RBI through intervention in the foreign exchange market, aid receipts, and interest receipts and funding from the International Bank for Reconstruction and Development (IBRD), Asian Development Bank (ADB), International Development Association (IDA), etc.

FCAs are maintained in major currencies like the US dollar, euro, pound sterling, Australian dollar, and Japanese yen. Both the US dollar and euro are intervention currencies; however, reserves are denominated and expressed in the US dollar only, which is the international numeraire for the purpose. The movement of the US dollar against other currencies in which FCAs are held therefore impacts the level of reserves in US dollar terms. The level of reserves declines when the US dollar appreciates against major international currencies and vice versa. The twin objectives of safety and liquidity have been the guiding principles of foreign exchange reserves management in India with return optimization being embedded strategy within this framework.

Beginning from a low level of US$ 5.8 billion at end-March 1991, India's foreign exchange reserves increased gradually to US$ 25.2 billion by end-March 1995, US$ 38.0 billion by end-March 2000, US$ 113.0 billion by end-March 2004 and US$ 199.2 billion by end-March 2007. The reserves stood at US$ 314.6 billion at end-May 2008 before declining to US$ 252.0 billion at the end of March 2009. The decline in reserves in 2008-09 was inter alia a fallout of the global crisis and strengthening of the US dollar vis-à-vis other international currencies. Foreign exchange reserves increased to US$ 279.1 billion at end-March 2010, mainly on account of valuation gain as the US dollar depreciated against most of the major international currencies. In fiscal 2010-11, the reserves again showed an increasing trend, reaching US$ 304.8 billion at end-March 2011. In fiscal 2011-12, they reached all-time high of US$ 322.0 billion at end-August 2011. However, they declined thereafter and stood at US$ 294.4 billion at end-March 2012.

In 2012-13, the reserves increased marginally by US$ 0.4 billion from US$ 294.4 billion at end-March 2012 to US$ 294.8 billion at end September 2012. Of this total increase, US$ 0.3 billion was on BoP basis and US$ 0.1 billion was on account of valuation effect. A summary of changes in the foreign exchange reserves since 2007-08, with a breakdown into increase / decrease on BoP basis and valuation effect is presented in Table-3.

TABLE-3

SUMMARY OF CHANGES IN FOREIGN EXCHANGE RESERVES (US$ BILLION)

Sl. No.	*Year*	*Foreign exchange reserves at the end of financial year (end March)*	*Total Increase (+)/ decrease (-) in reserves*	*Increase/decrease in reserves on a BoP basis*	*Increase/decrease in reserves due to valuation effect*
1	2	3	4	5	6
1	2007-08	309.7	110.5	92.2 (83.4)	18.3 (16.6)
2	2008-09	252.0	- 57.7	-20.1 (34.8)	- 37.6 (65.2)
3	2009-10	279.1	27.1	13.4 (49.4)	13.7 (50.6)
4	2010-11	304.8	25.7	13.1 (51.0)	12.6 (49.0)
5	2011-12	294.4	- 10.4	- 12.8 (123.0)	2.4 (-23.0)
6	2012-13 (up to Sept. 2012)	294.8	0.4	0.3 (75.0)	0.1 (25.0)

Source: RBI.

Note: Figures in parentheses indicate percentage shares of total change.

In the current fiscal, foreign exchange reserves on month-on-month basis remained in the range of US$ 286.0 billion (at end-May 2012) to US$ 295.6 billion (at end-December 2012). At end December 2012, reserves stood at US$ 295.6 billion, indicating a marginal increase of US$ 1.2 billion from US$ 294.4 billion at end-March, 2012. At this level, reserves provided about seven months of import cover. Issues relating to build up of foreign exchange reserves are summarized in Box 2.

BOX-2

Building up Foreign Exchange Reserves

The distinction between convertible and non-convertible currencies is important for emerging economies, as most transactions with the rest of the world are in convertible currencies like US dollar, euro, pound sterling, yen, Swiss Franc etc. The need for increasing the availability of convertible currency for self-insurance has also been behind the race to build-up foreign exchange reserves (FER) in emerging economies after the Asian Crisis of 1997. Such FER accumulation, however, is constrained by the fact that it is possible only in times of currency appreciation.

Following the BoP crisis of 1990-91 that was essentially due to depletion of foreign exchange reserves, there was a conscious effort by the RBI to build up FER. This was done through buying foreign currency in the market during periods of surge in capital flows. As a result, FER levels increased from US$ 5.8 billion in 1990-91 to US$ 314.6 billion at end May 2008. The RBI is however following a hands-off policy in foreign exchange market after the 2008 global crisis, with intervention limited to curbing excess rupee volatility. As a result, during 2009-10 and 2010-11, when rupee was appreciating due to increase in capital flows, there was virtually no intervention to build up FER.

The sharp decline in rupee in 2011-12 however led the RBI to inject foreign exchange to the extent of US$ 20.1 billion to stem the rupee slide. The pressure on currency has continued in the financial year 2012-13 because of the ongoing euro-zone crisis. The import cover of FER, as a result, has declined from 14.4 months of imports in 2007-08 to 7.1 months in 2011-12. There are costs to intervention. The main cost is the release of corresponding rupee liquidity, when RBI intervenes in the market to buy foreign exchange. This may stoke inflation, which may not appeal in the current inflationary situation.

Past experience however shows that measures like Market Stabilization Scheme (MSS) have been effective in draining excess liquidity from the system. Countries like China and Turkey use cash reserve ratio (CRR) for the same purpose. The cost of a particular policy, however, has to be weighed against the benefits, which are manifold. First, intervention to buy FER during surge in capital leads to build-up of reserves, which provides self-insurance against external vulnerability. Second, the higher reserve levels restore investor confidence and may lead to an increase in foreign direct and portfolio investment flows that spurs growth and helps bridge the current account deficit. Third, in a scenario of high trade and CAD, as in India, allowing the currency to appreciate through non-intervention during times of surge in capital, could have further negative fallout for the BoP by making exports less competitive and imports cheaper. Lastly, buying foreign exchange provides more ammunition for intervention when the currency is declining, which could potentially lower currency volatility.

Foreign Currency Assets (FCAs)

FCAs are the major constituent of India's foreign exchange reserves. FCAs increased by US$ 1.7 billion from US$ 260.7 billion at end March 2012 to US$ 262.4 billion at end-December 2012. In line with the principles of preserving the long-term value of the reserves in terms of purchasing power, minimizing risk and volatility in returns and maintaining liquidity, the RBI holds FCAs in major convertible currencies instruments. These include deposits of other country central banks, the Bank for International Settlements (BIS) and top-rated foreign commercial banks, and in securities representing debt of sovereigns and supranational institutions with residual maturity not exceeding 10 years, to provide a strong bias towards capital preservation and liquidity. The annualized rate of return, net of depreciation, on the multi-currency multi-asset portfolio of the RBI has shown declining trend over the years. It declined from 4.2 per cent in 2008-09 to 2.1 per cent in 2009-10, 1.7 per cent in 2010-11 and further to 1.5 per cent in 2011-12.

Foreign Exchange Reserves of Other Countries

India continues to be one of the largest holders of foreign exchange reserves. Country-wise details of foreign exchange reserves reveal that India is the eighth largest foreign exchange reserves holder in the world, after China, Japan, Russia, Switzerland, Brazil, Republic of Korea and China P R Hong Kong (Table-4) at end-December 2012.

TABLE-4

FOREIGN EXCHANGE RESERVES OF SOME MAJOR COUNTRIES

Sl. No.	*Country*	*Foreign exchange reserves (end Dec. 2012) (US$ billion)*
1	2	3
1	China	3310.0 [a]
2	Japan	1304.1
3	Russia	538.6
4	Switzerland (November 2012)	531.7
5	Brazil	373.1
6	Republic of Korea (November 2012)	326.2
7	China P R Hong Kong (November 2012)	305.2
8	India	295.6 [b]
9	Germany (November 2012)	259.4
10	France (November 2012)	211.0
11	Italy	185.6
12	Thailand	184.2

Source: IMF

a: As per PBC, at end-December 2012, China's foreign exchange reserves stood at US$ 3.31 trillion (source: http:/www.pbc.gov.cn).

b: RBI

In additional foreign exchange reserves of Taiwan are shown at US$ 403.2 billion (Q4) as per The Economist January 31, 2013.

RISK MANAGEMENT AND FOREIGN EXCHANGE RESERVES

Sound risk management is an integral part of efficient foreign exchange reserves management. The strategy for reserves management places emphasis on managing and controlling the exposure to financial and operational risks associated with deployment of reserves. The broad strategy for reserve management including currency composition and investment policy is decided in consultation with the Government of India. The risk management functions are aimed at ensuring development of sound governance structure in line with the best international practices, improved accountability, a culture of risk awareness across all operations and efficient allocation of resources for development of in-house skills and expertise. The risks attendant on deployment of reserves, *viz.*, credit risk, market risk, liquidity risk and operational risk and the systems employed to manage these risks are discussed below:

Credit Risk

Credit risk is defined as the potential that a borrower or counterparty will fail to meet its obligation in accordance with agreed terms. The Reserve Bank has been extremely sensitive to the credit risk it faces on the investment of foreign exchange reserves in the international markets. Investments in bonds/treasury bills, which represent debt obligations of highly rated sovereigns and supranational entities, do not give rise to any substantial credit risk. Placement of deposit with BIS and other central banks is also considered credit risk-free. However, placement of deposits with commercial banks as also transactions in foreign exchange and bonds/treasury bills with commercial banks/investment banks and other securities firms give rise to credit risk.

Credit risk has been in focus since the onset of the credit crisis in the US financial markets and its contagion effect on other economies leading to global financial crisis during the second half of 2008 and during 2009. The Reserve Bank continues to apply stringent credit criteria for selection of counterparties. Credit exposure *vis-a-vis* sanctioned limit in respect of approved counterparties is monitored continuously. Besides, the financial strength of counterparties is constantly under watch. The basic objective of such an on-going exercise is to assess whether counterparty's credit quality is under potential threat.

Market Risk

Market risk arises on account of exchange rate and interest rate movements. These are detailed as under:

Currency Risk

Currency risk arises due to uncertainty in exchange rates. Decisions are taken regarding the long-term exposure on different currencies depending on the likely movements in its exchange rate and other considerations in the medium and long-term (eg., maintenance of major portion of reserves in the intervention currency, the approximate currency profile of the reserves in line with the changing external trade profile of the country, benefit of diversification, etc.). The decision making procedure is supported by reviews of the strategy on a regular basis.

Interest Rate Risk

The crucial aspect of the management of interest rate risk is to protect the value of the investments as much as possible from the adverse impact of the interest rate movements. The interest rate sensitivity of the reserves portfolio is identified in terms of benchmark duration and the permitted deviation from the benchmark. The focus of the investment strategy revolves around the overwhelming need to keep the interest rate risk of the portfolio reasonably low with a view to minimising losses arising out of adverse interest rate movements, if any. This approach is warranted as reserves are viewed as a market stabilising force in uncertain environment.

Liquidity Risk

Liquidity risk involves the risk of not being able to sell an instrument or close a position when required without facing significant costs. The reserves need to maintain a high level of liquidity at all times in order to be able to meet any unforeseen and emergency needs. Any adverse development has to be met with reserves and, hence, the need for a highly liquid portfolio is a necessary constraint in the investment strategy. The choice of instruments determines the liquidity of the portfolio. For example, in some markets, treasury securities could be liquidated in large volumes without much distortion to the price in the market and, thus, can be considered as liquid. In fact, excepting fixed deposits with the foreign commercial banks and the central banks and securities issued by supranationals, almost all other types of investments are in highly liquid instruments which could be converted into cash at short notice. The Reserve Bank closely monitors the portion of the reserves which could be converted into cash at a very short notice to meet any unforeseen / emergent needs.

Operational Risk and Control System

In tune with the global trend, considerable attention is paid to strengthen the operational risk control arrangements. Key operational procedures are documented. Internally, there is total separation of the front office and back office functions and the internal control systems ensure several checks at the stages of deal capture, deal processing and settlement. There is a separate set-up responsible for risk measurement and monitoring, performance evaluation and concurrent audit. The deal processing and settlement system is also subject to internal control guidelines based on the principle of one point data entry and powers are delegated to officers at various levels for generation of payment instructions. There is a system of concurrent audit for monitoring compliance in respect of all the internal control guidelines. Further, reconciliation of accounts is done regularly. In addition to annual inspection by the internal machinery of the Reserve Bank for this purpose and statutory audit of accounts by external auditors, there is a system of appointing special external auditors to audit the dealing room transactions. The main objective of the special audit is to ensure that risk management systems and internal control guidelines are adhered to. There is a comprehensive reporting mechanism covering significant areas of activity / operations relating to reserve management. These are being provided to the senior management periodically, *viz.*, on daily, weekly, monthly, quarterly, half-yearly and yearly intervals, depending on the type and sensitivity of information. The Reserve Bank uses SWIFT as the messaging platform to settle its trades and send financial messages to its counterparties, banks with whom *nostro accounts* are maintained, custodians of securities and other business partners.

Going forward, capital inflows to India during 2010-11 are expected to be stronger driven by both push and pull factors. While the push factors for surge in capital inflows include excess global liquidity accompanied by low interest rates leading to search for higher yield, the pull factors include the buoyant growth prospects, favourable interest rate differential and relaxation of ECB norms for 3G spectrum. Higher expected capital inflows, however, may exert pressures on asset prices and exchange rate.

India has followed a consistent policy on allowing capital inflows in general and on capital account management in particular. RBI position is that capital account convertibility is not a stand alone objective but a means for higher and stable growth. Indian economy should traverse towards capital convertibility along a gradual path - the path itself being recaliberated on a dynamic basis in response to domestic and global developments. In other words, continue to move towards liberalizing our capital account, but to revisit the road map to reflect the lessons of the crisis.

Among the components of capital flows, India prefer long term flows to short-term flows and non-debt flows to debt flows. The logic for that is self-evident. The policy on equity flows has been quite liberal, and in sharp contrast to other EMEs which liberalized and then reversed the liberalization when flows became volatile, India's policy has been quite stable.

Historically, India has used policy levers on the debt side of the flows to manage volatility. Contrary to popular perception, the policy is to use both quantity and price based variables to moderate debt flows. There is a ceiling on the extent of FII investment in sovereign and corporate debt (quantity variable) and there is also a withholding tax (price variable). External commercial borrowings (ECB) by corporates come in through both an automatic route and an approval route. ECB flows under both the automatic and approval routes are moderated by interest rate ceilings (a price variable) and those under the automatic route through an additional ceiling on total quantity (quantity variable). Non-Resident Indians (NRI) deposits are monitored through an interest rate ceiling, a price variable.

Although India does not have a deliberate strategy of building up reserves for self-insurance, the reserves got built up as a result of relatively flexible exchange rate policy. The reserves so built up have been used to contain volatility in the event of capital flows reversals.

QUESTIONS

1. Discuss the forex market structure in India.
2. Critically examine the initiatives taken to widen and deepen the forex market in India.
3. Evaluate the recent developments in the forex marekts in India.
4. Critically examine the recommendations of the Report of the High Level Committee on Balance of Payments and the Report of the Expert Group on Foreign Exchange Markets on measures to integrate the Indian forex market with global forex markets.
5. "Liberalisation of capital account should be viewed as a process and not as a single event." Comment.

6. Discuss the report of the Committee on Capital Account Convertibility.
7. Comment on the changing composition of the foreign exchange reserves in India.
8. Critically examine the forex market turnover during the post-reform period.
9. Discuss the motives for holding foreign exchange reserves. Is foreign exchange reserves build-up immical to growth?
10. Critically examine the renewed interest in recent times in foreign exchange reserves in the context of increasing globalisation, acceleration of capital flows and integration of financial market.
11. Discuss the challenges posed by the surge in capital flows to the conduct of monetary and exchange rate policy.
12. Critically examine the determinants of the demand for foreign exchange reserves.

10

EXCHANGE RATE THEORIES

INTRODUCTION

The relative atrophy of the financial resources at the disposal of the financial institutions both national and international, has had implications that go beyond the sources, distribution and magnitude of payments-finance. This atrophy has also been closely associated with the evolution of the exchange rate regime. The abandonment of attempts to re-establish a viable system of par values, in the following two years following the suspension by the U.S. in 1971 of the convertibility of the dollar into gold, reflected recognition by monetary officials that their diminished shares in total international liquidity made it impossible for them to influence decisively the course of exchange rates in the face of massive movements of private flows across foreign exchange markets. The norms to float exchanges, however, also reflected past shortcomings in the operation of the adjustable pay system, which had provided private markets relatively costless and risk-free opportunities for profitable speculation.

The regime of the floating rates gave rise to a substantial increase in the instability of exchange rates. Exchange markets reacted quickly to changes in current account surplus or deficits, but goods markets reacted strongly to changes in exchange market. Further, the movements in capital transaction which had been of a large order had dwarfed the current account transactions and had complicated the determination of exchange rates. In this chapter, we present an introduction to exchange rate theories. We first examine the traditional theories based on trade flows and purchasing power parity, which are more important in explaining exchange rates movements in the long run. Then we present an overview of modern exchange rate theories, which focus instead on the importance of capital markets and international capital flows, and seek to explain the short-run volatility of exchange rates and their tendency to overshoot their long-run equilibrium level. While both traditional or long-run and modern or short-run forces are clearly important, a comprehensive theory that integrates them into a single unified exchange rate theory has not yet been fully developed.

TRADITIONAL (TRADE OR ELASTICITIES) APPROACH

One traditional and crucial exchange rate model is based on flows of goods and services and is, therefore, referred to as the *trade or* elasticities approach. According to this approach, the equilibrium exchange rate is the one that balances the value of the nation's imports and exports. If the value of the nation's imports exceeds the value of the nation's exports (i.e., if the nation faces a trade deficit), then the exchange rate will fall (i.e., the domestic currency will depreciate) under a flexible exchange rate system. This makes the nation's exports cheaper to foreigners and imports more expensive to domestic residents. The result is that the nation's exports rise and its imports fall until trade is balanced.

Since the speed of adjustment depends on how responsive (elastic) imports and exports are to price (exchange rate) changes, this approach is referred to as the elasticity approach. If the nation is at or near full employment, a larger depreciation of the nation's currency is required to shift domestic resources to the production of more exports and import substitutes than if the nation has unemployed resources. Alternatively, domestic policies may be required to reduce domestic expenditure (absorption) to release domestic resources to produce more exports and import substitutes, and thus allow the elasticities approach to operate.

What is important to keep in mind here is that the elasticities approach stresses trade or the flow of goods and services in the determination of exchange rates. International capital flows are important only as passive responses (i.e., to cover or pay) for temporary trade imbalances. This trade or elasticities approach is certainly important, but it can explain neither the large volatility (fluctuation) of exchange rates, nor the sharp increase of trade deficits when the currency sharply depreciates. However, this does not mean that the trade elasticity approach to exchange rate determination is wrong, but that it provides a fundamental part of the explanation of exchange rate determination on in the long run than in the short run and that there must, therefore, be other important determination of exchange rates, especially in the short run.

PURCHASING POWER PARITY (PPP)

One of the most popular and controversial theories in international finance is the *purchasing power parity (PPP) theory,* which focuses on the inflation-exchange rate relationship. There are various forms of PPP theory. The *absolute from,* also called the "law of one price," suggests that prices of similar products of two different countries should be equal when measured in a common currency. If a discrepancy in prices as measured by a common currency exists, the demand should shift so that these prices should converge. For example, if the same products is produced by the India and the China, and the price in the China is lower when measured in a common currency, the demand for that product should increase in the China while it declines it the India. Consequently, the actual price charged in each country may be affected and / or the exchange rate may adjust. Both forces would cause the prices of the products to be similar when measured in a common currency. Realistically, the existence of transportation costs, tariffs, and quotas may prevent the absolute form of PPP. If transportation costs were high in this example the demand for the products might not shift in the manner suggested. Thus the discrepancy in prices would continue.

The *relative form* of PPP is an alternative version that accounts for the possibility of market imperfections such as transportation costs, tariffs, and quotas. This version acknowledges that because of these market imperfections, prices of similar products of different countries will not necessarily be the same when measured in a common currency. However, it states that the rate of change in the prices of products should be somewhat similar when measured in a common currency, as long as the transportation costs and trade barriers are unchanged. To illustrate the relative form of PPP, assume that two countries initially have zero inflation. Also assume that the current exchange rate between the two countries' currencies is in equilibrium. As time passes, both countries may experience inflation; for PPP to hold, the exchange rate should adjust to offset the differential in the inflation rates of the two countries. If this occurs, the prices of goods in either country should appear similar to consumers. That is, consumers should note little difference in their purchasing power in the two countries.

In equilibrium form

$$S = \alpha \frac{P_D}{P_F} \tag{1}$$

where

S (Rs/$) = S is the spot rate

P_D is the price level in India, the domestic market

and P_F is the price level in the foreign market, the U.S. in this case.

and $\alpha = \alpha$ (Sectoral price and Sectoral Shares)

Assuming α to be constant then S (Rs./$)

$$S = \alpha \frac{P_D}{P_F}$$

where A is constant

This equation implies that as the price level in India rises, Rupee depreciates against $, because for each $ an increased number of $s are to be paid.

This PPP theory, however, is based on the implicit assumption that there are no transportation costs, tariffs, or other obstructions to the free flow of trade; that all commodities are traded internationally; and that no structural changes (such as wars) take place in either nation. Since these assumptions are not true, the absolute version of PPP cannot be taken seriously. The relative version of the PPP theory is potentially more useful. It states that the change in exchange rates is equal to inflation rate differentials.

Suppose that S_o (Rs./$) = $\frac{P_{Do}}{P_{Fo}}$ is the spot rate at period 'O.' Suppose that the rate of change of spot rate is given by ΔS and the price levels in the domestic and foreign markets change at the rate of ΔP_D and ΔP_F respectively.

$$S_1 = S_0 (1 + \Delta S)$$

and the price levels in domestic and foreign market are given by

$$P_{D1} = P_{D0}\ (1+\Delta P_D) \text{ and } P_{F1} = P_{F0}\ (1+\Delta P_F)$$

Spot exchange rate at the end of unit period is given by

$$S_1 = \frac{P_{D1}}{P_{F1}} \text{ or } S_0(1+\Delta S) = \frac{P_{D0}\ (1+\Delta P_D)}{P_{F0}\ (1+\Delta P_F)} \tag{2}$$

$$\text{or } (1 + \Delta S) = \frac{(1+\Delta P_D)}{(1+\Delta P_F)} \quad \text{because } S_0 = \frac{P_{D0}}{P_{F0}}$$

subtracting 1 from both the sides

$$(1 + \Delta S) - 1 = \frac{(1+\Delta P_D)}{(1+\Delta P_F)} - 1$$

$$\text{or} \quad \Delta S = \frac{(\Delta P_D - \Delta P_F)}{(1+\Delta P_F)}$$

Supposing that the inflation rate in the foreign economy is low in relation to 1 then $1 + \Delta P_F \rightarrow 1$

Then equation (2) can be written as:

$$\Delta S = \Delta P_D - \Delta P_F \tag{3}$$

i.e. in equilibrium the rate of change in exchange equals interest rate differ-ential. This equation is an equilibrium relationship and not the causal relationship.

The equation (3) can be represented by following diagram:

FIGURE-1

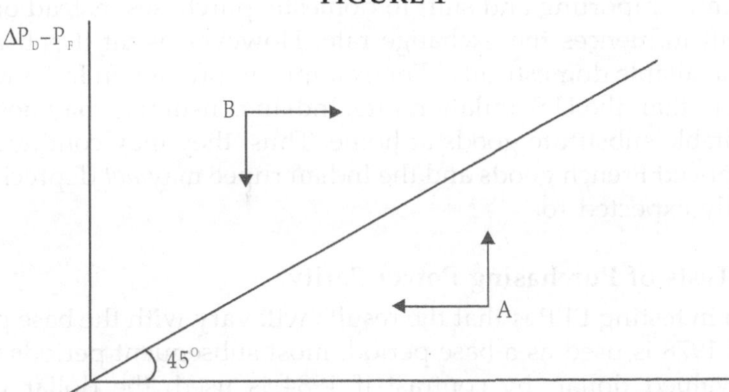

In the diagram OE represent parity line. Any point on this line is equidistant form both the axis, therefore on this line equation (3) holds. Any exogenous shock can disturb this equilibrium and send the point to A or B. On point 'A' $\Delta S > \Delta P_D - \Delta P_F$. Therefore the domestic currency is expected to depreciate in future. Therefore, the currency holder will shed off domestic currency in favour of appreciating currency. Thus depreciating the domestic currency more which brings equilibrium between $\Delta P_D - \Delta P_F$ and ΔS. A coverse process will take place when equilibrium point shifts to B. As long as there are no changes in transportation costs, obstructions to trade, or the ratio of traded to non-traded goods, and no structural changes in the two economies, the change in the exchange rate should be roughly proportional to the change in the ratio of the two countries' general price levels.

Two of the most commonly proposed reasons that PPP does not consistently occur follows:

1. *Other influential factors.* Exchange rates are affected by other factors in addition to the inflation differential. Recall the differentials in interest rate and income levels as well as government controls are important. To illustrate, assume the inflation rate in India is 5 per cent above the U.S. inflation rate. From this information, PPP theory would suggest the Indian rupee should depreciate by 5 per cent against the U.S. dollar. Yet, if the Indian government imposed trade barriers on imports from U.S., Indian consumers and firms could not adjust their spending in reaction to the inflation differential. Therefore, the exchange rate will not adjust.

   In the early 1990s, some European countries experienced higher inflation than the U.S. Yet, the currencies of these countries did not depreciate against the dollar because their high interest rates attracted large capital flows form U.S. investors. During the same period, Hong Kong, Singapore, and South Korea experienced relatively high inflation. However, the currencies of these countries did not depreciate against the dollar because of the large capital flows form U.S. firms and investors to capitalise on the higher interest rates and to invest in privatised businesses.
2. *No substitutes for traded goods.* The idea behind PPP theory is that as soon as the prices become relatively higher in one country, the other country will discontinue importing and shift to domestic purchases instead of importing. This shift influences the exchange rate. However, what if substitute goods are not available domestically? For example, if inflation in India was by 5 per cent more than the U.S. inflation rate, Indian consumers may not necessarily find suitable substitute goods at home. Thus, they may continue to buy the highly priced French goods and the Indian rupee may *not* depreciate as it was originally expected to.

Limitation in Tests of Purchasing Power Parity

A limitation in testing PPP is that the results will vary with the base period used. For example, if 1978 is used as a base period, most subsequent periods will show a relatively overvalued dollar; by contrast if 1984 is used, the dollar may appear undervalued in subsequent periods.

The base period chosen should reflect an equilibrium position, since subsequent periods are evaluated in comparison to it. Unfortunately, it is difficult to choose such a base period. In fact, one of the main reasons for abolishing fixed exchange rates was the difficulty in identifying an appropriate equilibrium exchange rate.

Once again, however, since trade and commodity arbitrage respond sluggishly, purchasing-power parity (PPP) is more closely approximated in the long run than in the short run and when disturbances are purely monetary in character. In the short run (and sometimes even in the long run—as during the 1980's), however, exchange rates have been found to deviate sharply from those predicted by the PPP theory. Therefore, other forces and theories must be introduced to explain the short-run volatility of exchange rates and their tendency to overshoot their long-run equilibrium level.

INTEREST RATE PARITY (IRP)

Once market forces cause the interest rates and exchange rates to be such that covered interest arbitrage is no longer feasible, we are in an equilibrium state referred to as *interest rate parity (IRP)*. In other words, the interest rate parity (IRP) is a theory which states that the size of the forward premium (or discount) should be equal to the interest rate differential between the two countries of concern. When IRP exists, covered interest arbitrage is not feasible, because any interest rate advantage in the foreign country will be offset by the discount on the forward rate. Thus, the act of covered interest arbitrage would generate a return that is no higher than what would be generated by a domestic investment. It also has two forms:

(a) Covered Interest Rate Parity

(b) Uncovered Interest Rate Parity.

The Covered interest rate parity equation is given by

$$(1+r_D)=\frac{F}{S}(1+r_F) \tag{4}$$

where $(1 + r_D)$ = Amount that an investor would get after a unit period by investing a rupee in the domestic market at r_D rate of interest and $\frac{F}{S}(1+r_F)$ is the amount that an investor would get after a unit period by investing a rupee in the foreign market at r_F rate of interest. The equation (4) asserts that the investment of one rupee yields same return in the domestic as well as in the foreign market. We shall try to find out under which conditions it will be so. Equation (5) can be written as:

$$\left(\frac{1+r_D}{1+r_F}\right)=\frac{F}{S}$$

Substracting one from both the sides we have

$$\left(\frac{1+r_D}{1+r_F}\right)-1=\frac{F}{S}-1$$

$$\frac{r_D-r_F}{1+r_F}=\frac{F-S}{S}$$

or $\quad r_D - r_F = D/P$

where D = Discount, P = Premium in the 1 + r_F is low in relation to 1. The above equation (5) can be represented by a diagram shown below:

In this diagram OE represents parity line. Any r_D - r_F > D/P. In the light of this observation the economic agents expect further depreciation of domestic currency. Therefore, they will try to shed of domestic currency for foreign currency, thus raising the demand for foreign currency and increasing the supply of domestic currency leading to appreciation of foreign currency on one side and depreciation of domestic currency on the other.

FIGURE-2

INTEREST RATE DIFFERENTIALS, DISCOUNT/PREMIUM RATES AND COVERED INTEREST ARBITRAGE

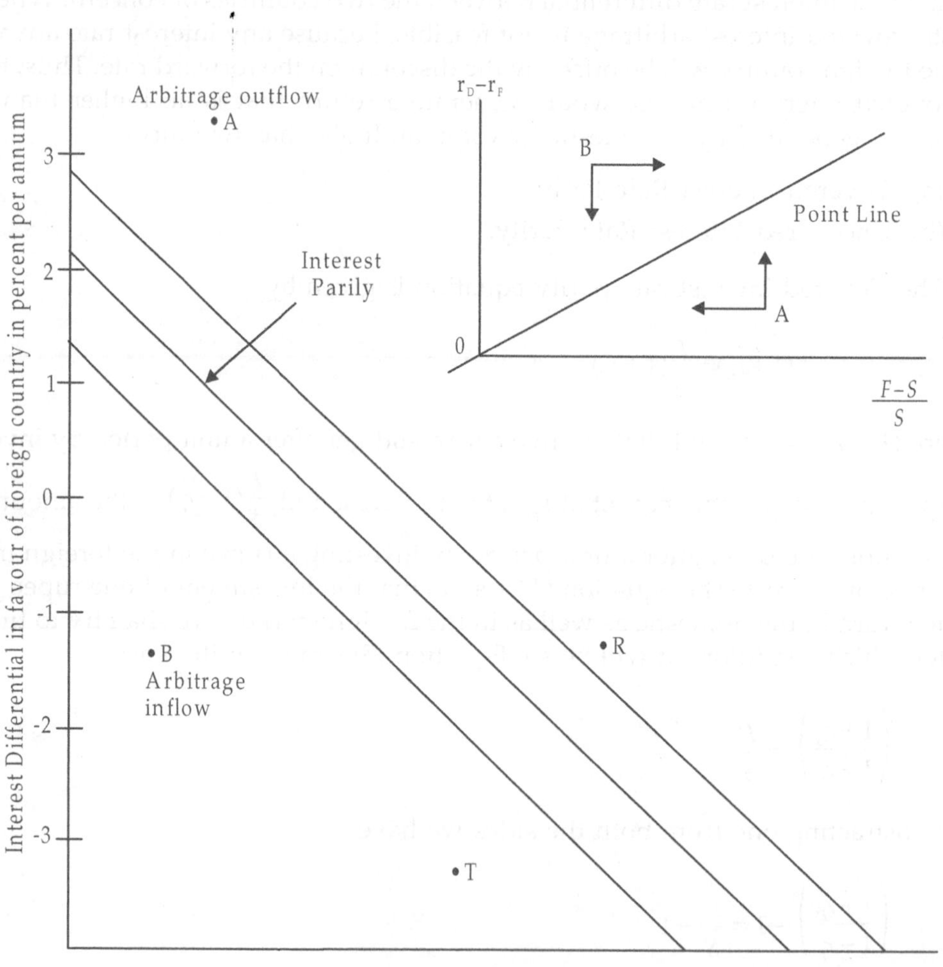

The equation (5) indicates that the yield in two markets will be equal when interest rate differentials are compensated by discounts and premiums.

In the case of uncovered interest rate parity, the equation (1) reduces to

$$(1+r_D)=\frac{S_1}{S}(1+r_F) \tag{6}$$

where S_1 = Expected future spot rate when the receipts denominated in foreign currency is converted into domestic currency. Equation (4) and (5) will be equal when:

$$F = S_1$$

i.e. forward rate equals the expected future spot rate i.e. the expectation on future spot rate and forward rate match. Of those do not much there will be lower/higher demand for forward contracts and because of the change in demand the forward rate will change to match expectations.

Figure 2 illustrates rigorously the relationship, through covered interest arbitrage, between the interest rate differentials between two nations and the forward discount or premium on the foreign currency. The vertical axis measures interest differentials expressed in percentages per year. Positive values indicate the interest rates are higher in domestic markets. The horizontal axis measures the forward discount on domestic currency or forward premium (+) on the foreign currency expressed in percentages per year.

$F > S$ indicates discount on domestic currency and premium on foreign currency i.e. if $\frac{F-S}{S} > 0$ then domestic currency is at discount therefore $r_D - r_F$ should also be positive to equalise. This implies that whenever the domestic currency is at discount the domestic interest rates should rule higher than foreign interest rates to compensate for depreciated currency.

The solid diagonal line indicates interest parity. Thus, when the positive interest differential is 1 per cent per year in favour of the domestic nation, the foreign currency is at a forward premium of 1 per cent per year. When the interest differential is zero, the foreign currency is neither at a forward discount nor at a forward premium (i.e., the forward rate on the foreign currency is equal to its spot rate).

The point A means that $\frac{F-S}{S}$ = Dis > $r_D - r_F$, the covered interest rate possibilities exist so arbitragers jump in and will push the point A towards point line. At point B the interest rate differential $r_D - r_F > \frac{F-S}{S} = Dis$ in this case also the arbitrage possibilities exist and arbitragers will push the point towards parity line.

Above the interest line, either the positive interest differential exceeds the forward discount or the forward premium exceeds the negative interest differential. In either case, there will be a net gain from an arbitrage outflow equal to their difference. For example, at point A, the positive interest differential is 1.5 per cent per year in favour of the foreign nation, while the foreign currency is at a forward discount of 0.5 per cent per year. Thus, there is a covered interest arbitrage margin of I per cent per year in favour of the foreign nation, leading to a capital outflow. On the other hand, point T involves a forward premium of 2 per cent on the foreign currency and a negative interest differential of only I per cent. Thus, investors have an incentive to invest abroad because they would gain 2 per cent on the exchange transaction and lose only 1 per cent in interest.

As the arbitrage outflow continues, the net gain diminishes and tends to disappear. Starting from point A, the transfer of funds abroad reduces the positive interest differential (say, from + 1.5 to + 1) and increases the forward discount (say, from -0.5 to - 1) so as to reach the interest parity line (see the figure). Starting from point T the transfer of funds abroad will increase the negative interest differential (say from -l to -1.5) and reduce the forward premium (say, from +2 to +1.5) so as to once again reach the interest parity line. Specifically, as funds move abroad, interest rates tend to rise at home and decline abroad. Since interest rates were already higher at home, the negative interest differential increases. On the other hand, as investors purchase the foreign currency to invest abroad, the spot rate rises. As they sell the foreign currency forward to cover their foreign exchange risk, the forward rate declines. Thus, the forward premium (i.e., the excess of the forward rate over the spot rate) diminishes. With the negative interest differential increasing and the forward premium decreasing, the net gain from arbitrage outflow diminishes until it becomes zero on the interest parity line and the arbitrage outflow comes to an end.

Below the interest parity line, either the forward discount exceeds the positive interest differential (point B in the figure) or the negative interest differential exceeds the forward premium (point R). In either case, it pays for investors to invest in India and there will be an arbitrage inflow. However, as the arbitrage inflow continues, the net gain diminishes and then disappears when the interest parity line is reached. In reality, interest arbitrage (inflow and outflow) will come to an end when the net gain reaches about 1/4 of 1 per cent per year (1/16 of I per cent for three months).

Does Interest Rate Parity Hold?

In general, under covered interest arbitrage, there is an incentive to invest in the higher-interest currency to the point where the discount of that currency in the forward market is less than the interest differential. If the discount on the forward market of the currency with the higher interest rate becomes larger than the interest differential, then it pays to invest in the lower-interest currency and take advantage of the excessive forward premium on this currency.

In the real world, significant covered interest arbitrage margins are often observed for long periods. The reason for this is not necessarily that covered interest arbitrage does not work. Rather, it is likely to be the result of other forces at work not accounted for by the pure theory of covered interest arbitrage. Some of these other forces are the different real growth rates among nations; differential growth in their money supplies; and differences in expectation, in liquidity preferences, in inflation rates, and in fiscal and trade policies. Lack of adequate information and government restrictions on short-term international capital flows can also sometimes account for the persistence of wide covered interest arbitrage margins.

Finally, it must be remembered that behind the demand and supply curves of foreign exchange are not only traders and investors, but also hedgers, speculators, and interest arbitrageurs. Governments also operate in foreign exchange markets, both in their normal function of making and receiving foreign payments and in their effort to affect the level and the movement of exchange rates. It is all of these forces together that determine exchange rates at the intersection of the nation's aggregate demand and supply curves for each foreign currency under a flexible exchange rate system.

To correctly determine whether IRP holds, it is necessary to compare the forward rate (or discount) and interest rate quotations that occur at the same time. If the forward rate and interest rate quotations do not reflect the same time of day, then results could be somewhat distorted. Due to limitations in access to data, it is difficult to get quotations that reflect the same point in time. Consequently, the testing of IRP is subject to some error. Yet, that should not discourage attempt to determine whether IRP exists. The actual relationship between the forward rate premium and interest rate differentials generally support IRP. While there are deviations, they are often not large enough to make covered interest arbitrage worthwhile.

These deviations may be due to potential costs that arise form foreign investments but not form domestic investments. Such costs could include transaction costs, currency restrictions, and differential tax laws.

If an investor wishes to account for transaction costs, the actual point reflecting the interest rate differential and forward rate premium must be farther from the IRP to make covered interest arbitrage worthwhile.

Even if covered interest arbitrage appears feasible after accounting for transaction costs, the act of investing funds overseas is subject to political risk. While the forward contract locks in the rate at which the foreign funds should be reconverted, there is no guarantee that funds will be allowed to be reconverted. A crisis in the foreign country could cause its government to restrict any exchange of the local currency for other currencies. In this case, the investor would be unable to use these funds until the foreign government eliminated the restriction. Investors may also perceive a slight default risk on foreign investments such as foreign Treasury bills, since they might not be assured that the foreign government will guarantee full repayment of interest and principal upon default.

Firms and investors recognise the impact that taxes may have on income. Because tax laws vary among countries, investors and firms that set up deposits in other countries must be aware of the existing tax laws. It is possible that covered interest arbitrage could be feasible when considering before-tax returns but not necessarily when considering after-tax returns. Such a scenario would be due to differential tax rates.

If IRP does not hold, the possibility of covered interest arbitrage deserves consideration. However, the existence of all these factors could eliminate the possibility of abnormal returns form covered interest arbitrage. Covered interest arbitrage should be attempted only if abnormal returns remain after considering transaction costs, potential currency restrictions, and taxes.

INTERNATIONAL FISHER EFFECT (IFE)

Along with PPP theory, another major theory in international finance is the *international Fisher effect (IFE)* theory. It uses interest rate rather than inflation rate differentials to explain why exchange rates change over time, but it is closely related to the PPP theory because interest rates are often highly correlated with inflation rates. According to the so-called *Fisher effect,* nominal risk-free interest rates contain a real rate of return and anticipated inflation. If investors of all countries require the same real return, interest rate differentials between countries may be the result of differentials in expected inflation.

Recall the PPP theory suggests that exchange rate movements are caused by inflation rate differentials. If real rates of interest are the same across countries, any difference in nominal interest rates could be attributed to the difference in expected inflation. The IFE theory suggests that foreign currencies with relatively high interest rates will depreciate because the high nominal interest rates reflect expected inflation. The nominal interest rate would also incorporate the *default risk* of an investment.

The precise relationship between the interest rate differential of two countries and the expected exchange rate change according to IFE can be derived with the help of relative form of PPP and IRP equation. This equation says that if there are no barriers to capital flows the investment will flow in such a manner that the real rate of return on investment will equalise. In fact, the Fisher's equation is to represent the interaction between real sector, monetary sector and foreign exchange market. As per open interest rate parity, we know:

$$(1+r_D) = \frac{S_1}{S}(1+r_F)$$

where S_1 = Future spot rate, S is the current spot rate; r_D = Domestic interest rate and r_F = Foreign interest rate.

The above equation can be written as:

$$\frac{1+r_D}{1+r_F} = \left(\frac{S_1}{S}\right)$$

Subtracting one form both the sides, we have

$$\frac{1+r_D}{1+r_F} - 1 = \frac{S_1}{S} - 1$$

or $$\frac{r_D - r_F}{1+r_F} = \frac{S_1 - S}{S}$$

or in the limit $1 + r_F \rightarrow 1$ then

$$r_D - r_F = \Delta S \tag{7}$$

i.e. rate of change in exchange rate equals interest rate differential.

Relative Purchasing Power Parities gives us the relationship as:

$$\Delta S = \Delta P_D - \Delta P_F \qquad (8)$$

Combine eq. (7) and (8) we have

$$P_D - PF = \Delta S = r_D - r_F$$

or $r_D - P_D = r_F - \Delta P_F$

Domestic real rate of return = Foreign Market real rate of return

All these theories can be represented by similar diagrams given below:

FIGURE-3

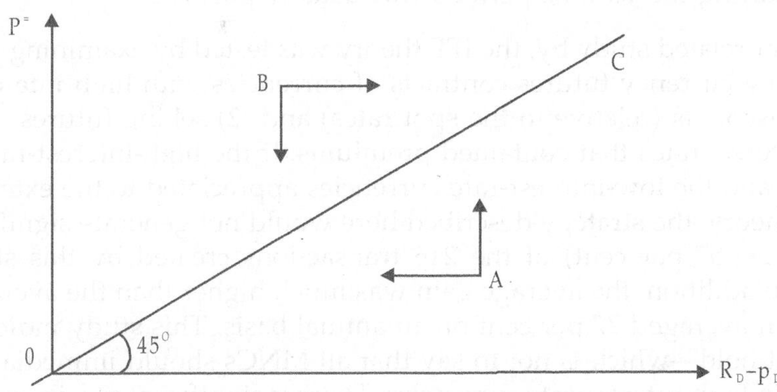

OC in the parity line on which Fisher's equation hold. A and B are the points where Fisher's Equation do not hold. On 'A' domestic real rate of return is greater than foreign rate of return. Therefore, this will initiate inflow of investments from abroad leading to the fall in the rate of return. As there will be an outflow of investment from other economies therefore only an increase in the rate of return would be able to stop the flow. Therefore, two forces are generated on in the domestic economy reducing the domestic rate of return and the other in the foreign economy which increases the rate of return on investment in foreign market. These forces have been represented by arrows at 'A'. Converse holds at 'B'. Because at 'B' the foreign real rate of return is greater than domestic rate of return.

Whether the IFE holds in reality depends on the particular time period examined. From 1974 to 1977, the U.S. interest rates were generally lower than foreign interest rates. As IFE theory would predict, these foreign currencies weakened during this period. In 1978-1979, the U.S. interest rates were generally higher than foreign interest rates, and the foreign currency values strengthened during this period (again supporting IFE theory to an extent). However, during the 1980-1984 period, the foreign currencies consistently weakened far beyond what would have been anticipated according to IFE theory. Furthermore, during the 1985-1987 period, foreign currencies strengthened to a much greater degree than suggested by the interest differential. Whiel the IFE theory may hold during some time frames, there is evidence that it does not consistently hold.

If the IFE holds, then a strategy of borrowing in one country and investing the funds in another country should not provide a positive return on average. The reason is that exchange rates should adjust to offset interest rate differentials on the average. A study simulated a speculative strategy whereby the currency with the lowest quoted interest rate was borrowed by a U.S. speculator and converted and invested it the currency exhibiting the highest interest rate. At the end of the investment period, the funds were withdrawn and loan repayment was made. This strategy was continued periodically over time. If the IFE held for these periods, the *spread* (difference between return on the investment and cost of borrowing) should have been zero on average (in the absence of transaction costs). But the rated trend of spreads during the various periods was usually positive.

In another related study by, the IFE theory was tested by examining the results of (1) purchasing currency futures contracts of currencies with high interest rates that contained discounts (relative to the spot rates) and (2) selling futures on currencies with low interest rates that contained premiums. If the high-interest-rate currencies depreciated and the low-interest-rate currencies appreciated to the extent suggested by the IFE theory, the strategy described here would not generate significant profits. However, 123 (57 per cent) of the 216 transactions created by this strategy were profitable. In addition, the average gain was much higher than the average loss. The rate of return averaged 77 per cent on an annual basis. This study indicates that the IFE does not hold—which is not to say that all MNCs should immediately place all excess cash in high-interest-rate currencies. There is significant risk in such a strategy, as verified by the existence of losses generated in some periods of the study.

As we know that purchasing power has not held over certain periods, and since the international Fisher effect is based on purchasing power parity, it does not consistently hold either. Because there are factors other than inflation that affect exchange rates, the exchange rates do not adjust in accordance with the inflation differential. Assume a nominal interest rate in a foreign country that is 5 per cent above the Indian rate because expected inflation in that country is 5 per cent above expected inflation in India. Even if these nominal rates properly reflect inflationary expectations, the exchange rate of the foreign currency will react to other factors in addition to the inflation differential. If these other factors place upward pressure on the foreign currency's value, they will offset the downward pressure laced by the inflation differential. Consequently, foreign investments will achieve higher returns for the Indian investors than domestic investments will.

COMPARISON OF PPP, IRP AND IFE THEORIES

At this point, it may be helpful to compare three related theories of international finance: (1) interest rate parity (IRP), (2) purchasing power parity (PPP), and (3) the international Fisher effect (IFE). Exhibit 1 summarises the main theme of each theory. Note that all three theories relate to the determination of exchange rates. Yet, they differ in their implications. The theory of IRP focuses on why the forward rate differs

EXHIBIT-1

COMPARISON OF PPP, IRP AND IFE THEORIES

Theory	*Key Variables of Theory*		*Summary of Theory*
Interest rate parity (IRP)	Forward rate premium (or discount)	Interest rate differential	the forward rate of one currency with respect to another will contain a premium (or discount) that is determined by the differential in interest rates between the two countries. As a result, covered interest arbitrage will provide a return that is no higher than a domestic return.
Purchasing power parity (PPP)	Percentage change in spot exchange rate	Inflation rate differential	The spot rate of one currency with respect to another will change in reaction to the differential in inflation rates between the two countries. Consequently, the purchasing power for consumers when purchasing goods in their own country will be similar to their purchasing power when importing goods from the foreign country.
International Fisher effect (IFE)	Percentage change in spot exchange rate	Interest rate differential	The spot rate of one currency with respect to another will change in accordance with the differential in interest rates between the two countries. Consequently, the return on uncovered foreign money market securities will on average be no higher than the return on domestic money market securities from the perspective of investors in the home country.

from the spot rate and on the degree of difference that should exist. This relates to a specific point in time. Conversely, PPP theory and IFE theory focus on how a currency's spot rate will change over time. While PPP theory suggests that the spot rate will change in accordance with inflation differentials, IFE theory suggests that it will change in accordance with interest rate differentials. PPP is nevertheless related to IFE because inflation differentials influence the nominal interest rate differentials between two countries.

As shown in Exhibit-2, there are many potential exchange rate determinants. Economists have traditionally isolated several of these determinants and theorized how they are linked with one another and with spot and forward exchange rates. These linkages are called *parity conditions.* They are sometimes useful in explaining and forecasting the long-run trend in an exchange rate.

EXHIBIT-2

POTENTIAL FOREIGN EXCHANGE RATE DETERMINANTS

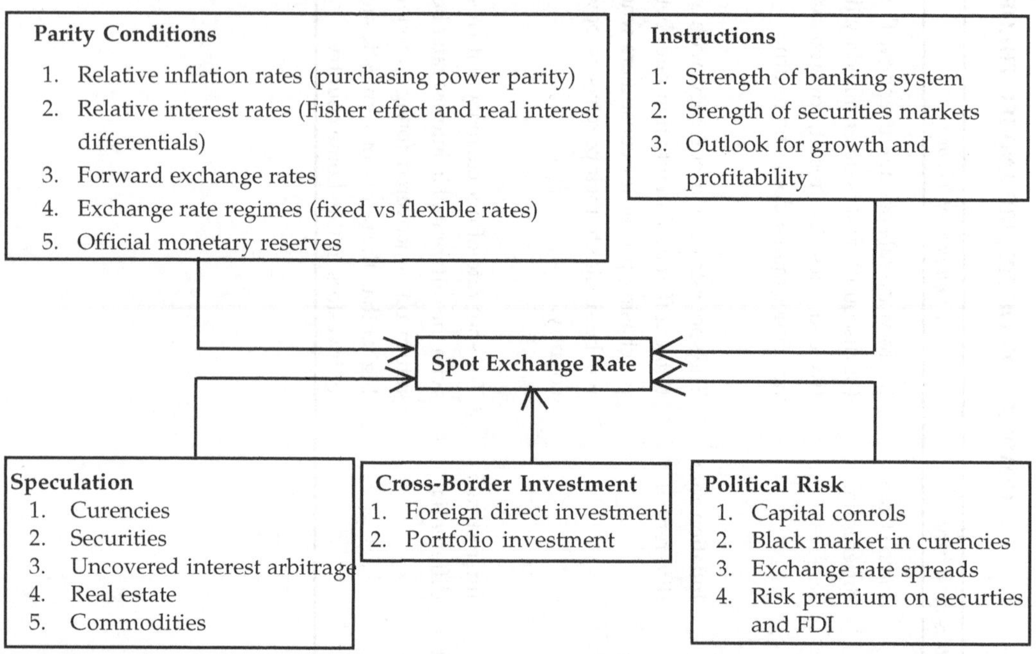

Exhibit-3 illustrates all the fundamental parity relations simultaneously by using the Japanese yen as an example. The yen is expected to strengthen 4% versus the dollar. The spot exchange rate, ¥104/$, is forecasted to change to ¥100/$ one year from now using *purchasing power parity* (PPP, relation A), the international Fisher effect (relation C), and the forward rate (relation E). The forecasted inflation rates for Japan (1.0%) and the United States (5.0%) result in a forecast of ¥100/$. If the difference in nominal interest rates is used (international Fisher effect), the forecasted spot rate is also ¥100/$. Finally, the one-year forward rate on the Japanese yen, ¥100/$, if assumed to be an unbiased predictor of the future spot rate, also forecasts ¥100/$.

EXHIBIT-3

INTERNATIONAL PARITY RELATIONS IN EQUILIBRIUM (APPROMIMATE FORM)

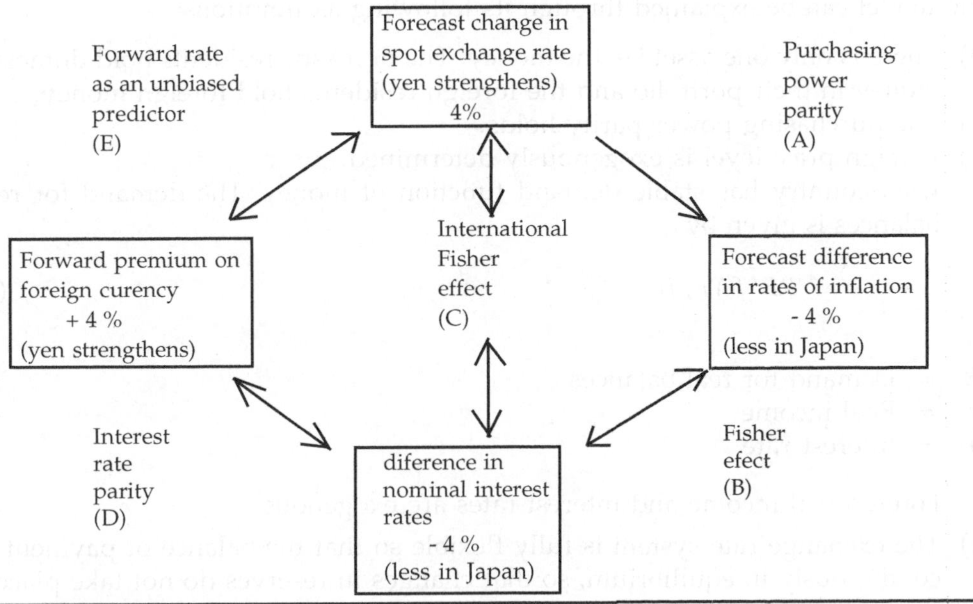

1. ***Exchange rates:***
   (a) Curent Spot Rate $S_1 = ¥\ 104/\$$
   (b) Forward Rate (one year): $F = ¥\ 100/\$$
   (c) Expected Spot rate: $S_2 = ¥\ 100/\$$
   (d) Forward Premium on yen:

$$f^{¥} = \frac{S_1 - F}{F} \times 100 = \frac{104 - 100}{100} \times 100 = +\,4\%$$

   (e) Forecast Change in Spot Rate:

$$\%\,\Delta S = \frac{S_1 - S_2}{S_2} \times 100 = \frac{104 - 100}{100} \times 100 = +\,4\%$$

2. ***Forecast Rate of Inflation:***
   (a) Japan 1%
   (b) United States 5%
   (c) Difference –4%
3. ***Interest on One-Year Government Security:***
   (a) Japan 4%
   (b) United States 8%
   (c) Difference –4%

ASSET MARKET MODELS

These models assert that equilibrium exchange rate is that rate at which the market is willing to hold the given stock of assets denominated in different currencies. This theory assumes that foreign exchange market is highly organised like other financial assets. This theory also assumes the efficiency of financial markets.

There are many forms of asset market approaches. We discuss two important approaches from monetary approach and one from portfolio balance approach.

(A) Current Account Monetary Model

The model can be explained through its following assumptions:

(a) There is only one asset i.e. the money. The domestic residents hold domestic money in their portfolio and the foreign residents hold foreign money.
(b) The purchasing power parity holds.
(c) Foreign price level is exogenously determined.
(d) Each country has stable demand function of money. The demand for real balances is given by

$$RB^d f(Yr\,,i) \quad (7)$$

where

RB^d = Demand for real balances
Yr = Real income
i = Interest rate

Foreign real income and interest rates are exogenous.

(e) The exchange rate system is fully flexible so that the balance of payment is continuously in equilibrium, so that changes in reserves do not take place.

Under the above assumptions nominal money supply in the domestic market is exclusively determined by credit creation and can be controlled by monetary authorities.

In this framework, the model asserts that the domestic residents experiencing a discrepancy between the stock of money they wish to hold and the actual stock of money created by the system i.e. the money created by the monetary authorities, will attempt to correct this disequilibrium by reducing the balance of payment deficits and surpluses. If there is an excess supply they will try to get rid of this excess money by purchasing goods and services from the domestic market and imports. Thus on one side it will put pressure on domestic price level and on the other it will create current account deficits which will lead to the domestic currency depreciation. This in turn may lead to greater exports but if process of monetary expansion continues, the export advantage may not remain for a long time. The final equation that defines current account monetary model and complete treatment and the derivation of the model can be studied from:

$$S = k + (M_D - M_F) - Q(Y_D - Y_F) + \lambda X(r_S - r_F) \quad (8)$$

where S is the exchange rate M_D and M_F are the money supply levels of domestic and foreign economies, Y_D and Y_F are the real incomes and *rd* and *rf* are the interest rates of domestic and foreign economies.

Since S is the spot rate in direct terms, if $M_D > M_F$, the domestic currency will appreciate. If $Y_D > Y_F$, the domestic currency will appreciate, and if $r_D > r_F$, the domestic currency will depreciate.

(B) Capital Account Monetary Model

The assumptions that purchasing power parity (PPP) hold in the short run and the effect of interest rate changes on exchange rate has been recognised as two main weaknesses of current account monetary model. The extension of the above model allows for departure from PPP in the short run and attempts to distinguish between those changes in interest rate which only compensate the inflationary expectations and those which are due to tight monetary policy. The short run stickiness of prices of goods can produce overshooting of exchange rate beyond its equilibrium value. The assumptions of the capital account monetary model are:

(a) PPP holds in the long run.
(b) There are stable demand functions for both the economies.
(c) Expected change in exchange rate in the short run depends on perceived departure from long run equilibrium exchange rate and expected inflation rate differentials.

The final equation to explain the exchange rate movement can be written:

$$S = (M_D - M_F) - Q(Y_D - Y_F) + \alpha(r_D - r_F) + B(\pi^e_D - \pi^e_F) \quad (9)$$

In this equation the additional term containing expected inflation rate (π^e) differentials has been added. The behaviour of other terms is the same as in current account monetary model. The term containing inflation rate differentials explains that if $\pi^e_D e > \pi^e_F$ i.e. expected inflation rate in the domestic market is greater than the expected inflation rate in respect of foreign market, the exchange rate is expected to depreciate.

For example, suppose that the foreign exchange market is in equilibrium or at interest parity (so that the positive interest differential in favour of the foreign nation is equal to the forward discount on its currency). Now suppose that monetary authorities in the home country increases the money supply in the long run, this leads to a proportionate increase in the price level in the home country and depreciation of its currency, as indicated by the PPP theory. For example, if RBI increases the money supply by 10 per cent but nothing changes in the United Kingdom, the general price level in the United Kingdom in terms of Indian currency can be expected to increase by 10 per cent and the exchange rate of the rupee to rise (i.e., the rupee to depreciate) by 10 per cent, say from Rs. 70 pound to Rs. 77 pound. But this occurs only slowly and over time since commodity markets and prices respond sluggishly.

However, the increase in the money supply and resulting decline in the rate of interest in India affect financial markets and exchange rates immediately. Specifically, the decline in the interest rate in India results in increased Indian financial investments flows to the United Kingdom. This leads to an immediate depreciation of the rupee of say, 16 per cent, which exceeds or overshoots (for reasons that we will see in a moment) the 10 per cent depreciation of the Indian currency expected in the long run according to the PPP theory. Subsequently, as prices in India rise relative to the United Kingdom over time, the rupee appreciates by 6 per cent so as to remove the *overshooting* or excessive depreciation that occurred soon after the India increased its money supply and interest rates fell.

The sequence of events in India can be summarised as follows : The money supply increases by 10 per cent, the interest rate falls, capital flows out and this leads to an immediate depreciation of the rupee by say, 16 per cent. Over time (i.e., in the long run), Indian prices rise by 10 per cent and the rupee appreciates by 6 per cent (from the immediate depreciation of 16 per cent to the long-run equilibrium depreciation of 10 per cent) so as to eliminate the overshooting. Why does the rupee depreciate by say, 16 per cent (i.e., overshoot the needed long-run equilibrium depreciation of 10 per cent in the first place)? We can answer this question by the theory of covered interest arbitrage. Starting from interest parity, the decline in the rate of interest in India makes the positive interest differential in favour of the United Kingdom larger than the forward discount on the pound. As a result, more investments flow from India to Britain under covered interest arbitrage. As investors purchase pounds on the spot market (to increase their investment in the United Kingdom in order to take advantage of the higher interest rate there) and at the same time sell pounds forward (to cover their exchange risk), the exchange or spot rate of the rupee rises (i.e. the rupee depreciates) and the forward rate of pound decreases. A declining forward rate on the pound means that the market expects the pound to depreciate and the rupee to appreciate in the future. The only way for the rupee to depreciate immediately and then appreciate over time and still depreciate by the required 10 per cent in the long run is for it to depreciate by more than 10 per cent immediately (i.e., overshoot its long-run equilibrium level) and then appreciate gradually over time to eliminate the overshooting.

PORTFOLIO-BALANCE APPROACH

While the monetary approach is appealing, it has generally failed to explain movements in the exchange rates of major currencies during the floating period since 1973. The monetary approach also overstresses the role of money and downplays the role of trade as an important determinant of exchange rates, especially in the long run. Furthermore, the monetary approach assumes that domestic and foreign financial assets such as bonds are perfect substitutes, when we know this not to be the case. As a result, a related model, the portfolio-balance or asset-markets model, seems now to be generally preferred.

The *portfolio-balance approach* differs from the monetary approach in that domestic and foreign bonds are assumed to be imperfect substitutes, and by postulating that the exchange rate is determined in the process of equilibrating or balancing the stock or total demand and supply of financial assets (of which money is only one) in each country. It also brings trade explicitly into the analysis. Thus, the portfolio balance approach can be regarded as a more realistic and satisfactory version of the monetary approach.

Starting from a position of portfolio or financial and trade balance, the portfolio balance approach postulates that an increase in the home nation's money supply leads to an immediate decline in the interest rate in the nation and to a shift from domestic bonds to the domestic currency and then to foreign bonds. The shift to foreign bonds causes an immediate depreciation of the home currency. Over time, this depreciation stimulates the nation's exports and discourages the nation's imports.

This leads to a trade surplus and appreciation of the domestic currency, which neutralises part of its original depreciation. Thus, the portfolio balance approach also explains overshooting but in contrast to the monetary approach, it does so by explicitly bringing trade into the adjustment process in the long run.

In the monetary models the domestic and foreign bonds are assumed to be perfect substitutes. In portfolio balance approach, the domestic and foreign bonds are assumed to be imperfect substitutes. This provides policy makers another policy instrument to manipulate the exchange rate. Many researches have suggested different portfolio models. A commonly used bilateral portfolio equation is derived from the following set of equations:

$$Z^D = z^F + \Delta s^e + \lambda \tag{10}$$

This equation is risk adjusted interest rate parity. Here λ is risk premium. If bonds are assumed to be perfect substitutes then the risk-premium $\lambda=0$. Then domestic interest rate will be equal to foreign interest rate plus an expected change in interest rate. In the above equation the risk premium λ is defined as:

$$\lambda = v[b^D \ (s + b^F)] \tag{11}$$

i.e. the risk premium is a function of relative outstanding bond stocks. Now if we substitute the value of λ from (10) into (9)

$$z^D = z^F + \Delta s^e + v\ [b^D - s + b^F]$$

or $$[z^D - z^F - \Delta s^e] = v\ [b^D - s + b^F]$$

$$v^{-1}\ [z^D - z^F - \Delta s^e] = b^D - s + b^F \tag{12}$$

Unlike single monetary equations, there is no single interpretation. That can be given to equation (11). In fact the interpretation largely depends on the assumption that a research makes about the asset preference of the economic agents. Uniform preference view of portfolio choice assumes the residents of each country have the same portfolio preferences and therefore the distribution of assets between countries does not have effect on the exchange rate. In this case b^D and b^F turns to net government indebtness of domestic and foreign economies. In preferred habitat models residents of each country are assumed to have preference for domestic assets and therefore hold greater portion of their wealth in domestic currency denominated bonds. In this case preference allows the distribution of assets to imperge on exchange rate. On the basis of alternative assumptions about portfolio choice, different formulations and interpretations are possible.

We can empirically test the portfolio balance equation by assuming that 'λ' is not equal to zero and the reduced form equation is obtained as:

$$S_o = \delta_1(m_o^D - m^F) + \delta_2(y^D - Y^F) + \delta_3(i = i^F) + \delta_4(\pi^{eD} - \pi^{eF}) + \lambda \tag{13}$$

Here π^{eD} and π^{eF} are domestic and foreign inflation rates.

This equation is referred as hybrid-monetary-portfolio balance equation.

USES OF EXCHANGE RATE MODELS TO FORECAST EXCHANGE RATES

All the models discussed above can be used to forecast exchange rates. The basic objective of forecasting is not just to obtain forecasts, but also to obtain accurate forecasts i.e. forecasts should be near to reality. Therefore, one has to choose which model suits a country's foreign exchange data. For this, empirically the models are tested. These models actually are based on certain fundamentals which determine exchange rates in the long run, but some times these models may be used for short run forecasting as well.

In conclusion we can say that because financial markets adjust to disequilibria or clear much faster than commodity markets, exchange rates are much more sensitive from day to day and from week to week to capital market imbalances than to commodity market and trade imbalances. Commodity market imbalances, however, are critical determinants of medium-run and long-run exchange rate trends. While the portfolio balance approach has become the centerpiece for the analysis of exchange rate determination, it still does not provide, in its present form, a complete and unified theory of exchange rate determination that fully and consistently integrates financial and commodity markets in the short run and long run. Furthermore, empirical tests have been hampered by lack of adequate data, and those tests that have been conducted have provided only mixed results. Specifically, while exchange rates are known to be more volatile than commodity prices and to overshoot their long-run equilibrium level, attempts to forecast them over the next month, half a year, and a year have met with little success. Exchange rates have been found to be largely random and unpredictable. Their behaviour in the short run seems to be greatly affected by news and expectations as to their future levels and to be only loosely constrained by purchasing power parity in the long run.

SHORT RUN DETERMINATION OF EXCHANGE RATE

THEORY OF DEMAND AND SUPPLY

The perspective of short run determination of Exchange Rate is Keynesian in the sense that financial markets clear continuously, but unemployment exists because information and transaction costs seriously inhibit rapid reallocation of resources. We assume that real income and price levels are held constant, we are analysing responses that are relatively short compared to the time it takes a multiplier to operate. Our assertion is that the exchange rate is determined by demand and supply of foreign exchange and we examine how exogenous changes in imports and capital flows influence exchange rates. The demand for foreign exchange in an economy is determined by the demand for imports and the demand for foreign assets. Similarly supply of foreign exchange is determined by the demand for exports of the domestic economy and the demand for domestic assets. Thus the demand for exports and assets of a foreign economy represent the supply of domestic currency to the foreign economy and the demand for imports and foreign assets determine the domestic demand for foreign exchange. This can be illustrated by taking an example of two countries. We suppose that we are interested in explaining the exchange rate between

U.K. and India on the basis of demand and supply of foreign exchange. Now as discussed above, the demand for imports in the domestic economy determines the demand for foreign exchange and the demand for imports in the U.K. for exports is the supply of foreign exchange to our economy as shown m the following diagram.

FIGURE-4

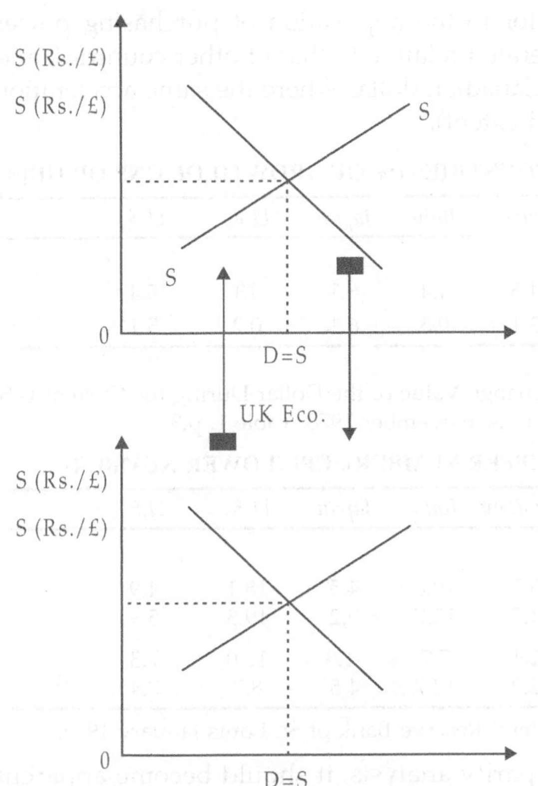

Supply : Demand for imports and Indian Assets in U.K.
Demand: Demand for imports and U.K. Assets
D.S. : Demand and Supply of £

Supply : Demand for imports and U.K. Assets in India
Demand: Demand for imports and Indian Assets in U.K.
D. S. : Demand for Rs. and Supply of Rs.

We see that the import demand in a country determine the supply of foreign exchange to another economy. The equilibrium exchange rate is determined by the equality of demand and supply. These demand and supply functions can be estimated with the help of econometric models.

Exogenous shocks can disturb this equilibrium. The exogenous shock appears in the form of (a) an autonomous increase in imports or exports; (b) an increase in capital inflow or outflow of capital. This disequilibrium is brought into equilibrium by arbitrage (financial or commodity market or both).

Growth Theory of Short-run Exchange Rate Movements in a Free Market

The absence of rapid commodity arbitrage responses to exchange rate changes leaves us with the need to find other factors to explain exchange rate movements. It is often claimed that changes in trade flows in response to differential real growth rates determine exchange rate movements over moderate horizons. If Indian growth exceeds foreign growth, then India is likely to suck in imports faster than foreigners are taking Indian exports, resulting in trade deficits and dollar depreciation.

Unfortunately this viewpoint is hard to reconcile. Some basic facts about the recent past as indicated in the following table indicates that in 1976 through 1977, the United States grew faster than any economy except that of Japan, and yet the dollar appreciated, by about 8% overall on a trade-weithted basis. In the later period, the United States again grew faster than any economy except Japan, but the dollar depreciated by 12½% overall on a trade-weighted basis. As a crude theory of exchange rate determination, this is inferior to the application of purchasing power parity. As can be seen. U.S. inflation accelerated relative to that of other countries, and the dollar depreciated (except against the Canadian dollar where the same acceleration phenomenon took place to a more marked extent).

REAL OUTPUT GROWTH FOR SELECTED COUNTRIES (% OF GROWTH OF GNP OR GDP)

Country	*Belgium*	*Canada*	*France*	*Germany*	*Italy*	*Japan*	*U.K.*	*U.S.*
Period								
1975 I - 1976 IV	3.4	4.1	4.7	4.5	4.4	6.1	13	5.4
19771 - 1978 II	0.4	3.6	2.9	3.1	*0.5*	6.1	0.2	5.1

*Roman numerals denote quarters

Source: D.Mudd. "Movements in the Foreign Exchange Value of the Dollar During the Current U.S. Expansion. Review Federal Reserve Bank of St. Louis. November 1978. Table 1. p.3.

PRICE CHANGE % CHANGE IN WPI (UPPER NUMBER). CPI (LOWER NUMBER)

Country	*Belgium*	*Canada*	*France*	*Germany*	*Italy*	*Japan*	*U.K.*	*U.S.*
Period								
1975 I - 1976 IV	6.1	4.8	5.2	3.5	19.6	4.5	18.1	4.9
	9.1	7.7	9.6	4.7	15.7	9.2	19.3	5.9
1977 I - 1978 II	-2.7	9.2	2.4	1.1	7.7	-1.3	12.0	7.3
	5.0	9.0	9.0	2.9	12.7	4.5	8.7	7.4

Source: "International Economic Conditions" Federal Reserve Bank of St. Louis January 1979.

If we see from the purchasing power parity analysis, it should become apparent that another factor is behind both the exchange rate changes and the inflation (and indeed perhaps behind the short-term growth rate fluctuations as well), namely the relationship between money demand and the growth of the money supply that was extensively discussed in.

Other Theories of Short Run Determination of Exchange Rate and Forecasting

The major deductive hypotheses about expected movements in the spot exchange rate is underpinned by:

- expected inflation differentials
- interest rate differentials (and here we should be looking at free market interest rates such as Euro-rates)
- spot and forward rate differentials

The theoretical relationship between inflation differences, interest rate differences, the forward premium/discount and expected spot movements is important. It must be remembered, however, that the existence of non-traded goods logically gives rise to deviations from the purchasing power parity theory of exchange rates. Also, systematic deviations from purchasing power parity theory are to be expected due to short-term capital flows and current account imbalances.

The purchasing power parity theory of exchange rate movements holds up fairly well in the long term. The fact that short-term deviations abound has stimulated the search for a better model-one of these is the balance of payment approach.

THE BALANCE OF PAYMENTS APPROACH

There are various brands of a balance of payments explanation for exchange rate movements. The emphasis has tended to change through time as the international financial scene has itself undergone change.

In its original form, the explanation tended to ignore capital flows. Prior to the sixties, this was excusable since most major currencies were not convertible, with the consequence that there were minimal private capital flows. The current account theory can best be explained by approaching it under the two distinct systems of exchange rate regime-namely, fixed and floating.

Assume a fixed exchange rate regime first. The national income model suggests that the current account gets worse as national income rises. The basic tendency is then for the domestic currency to weaken (to pay for the increased imports) and the fixed exchange rate system requires that, should it fall beyond certain narrow limits, this should be countered by support from the domestic government. This might take the form of selling reserves of foreign currency in the foreign exchange markets. Usually, it would be accompanied by domestic severity to dempen home demand evidenced by a lower relative money supply growth, with consequent lower relative inflation leading to an improvement in exports and a lowering of imports. According to this formula-which looks fine on paper—the current account deficit is automatically corrected. And so is a surplus. Here, rather than selling foreign exchange reserves, the foreign currency is bought. To pay for this, borrowings are increased- probably by the issue of treasury bills. Being a reserve asset this results in an increase in money supply which in turn leads, *ceteris paribus;* to higher inflation. And in a fixed parity regime, this means that exports become less competitive- hence the surplus reduces-again an automatic corrective mechanism.

Theoretically, the Bretton Woods system should avoid permanent disequilibria — after all, there are automatically correcting means of achieving current account stability at work. But empirically things did not turn out this way as anyone who has examined the evidence of Britain in the fifties and sixties knows. Of course, devaluation or revolution were an available option designed to counter recurrent disequilibria. Predicting changes in exchange rates under these circumstances became a potentially fruitful area of investigation. An interesting study carried out in the seventies by Martin Murenbeeld is worth mentioning. Using discriminant analysis, Murenbeeld studied a series of devaluations and revaluations from the late fifties to early seventies and came up with a discriminating equation. His original hypotheses can be summarised in the format shown below:

Murenbeeld's Devaluation/Revaluation Hypotheses

Devaluation		*Revaluation*
High	Inflation	Low
Up	Trend in unemployment	Down
Low	Ratio of reserves to imports	High
Down	Change in level of reserves	Up

Having obtained data on a number of currency realignments, the researcher arrived at a Z-score predictor of foreign exchange parity change using respective quarterly and monthly data as follows:

$$Z = -0.487 + 0.732RI + 0.058\,\Delta R - 0.123\,\Delta\, WP - 0.145UNEM - 0.250M + 0.167G$$

$$Z = 0.33 + 0.69RI + 0.17\,\Delta R - 2.29\,WP - 0.455UNEM - 0.66M + 15.35G$$

where the quarterly and monthly independent variables are:

RI = ratio of reserves to imports
R = % change in reserves
WP = % change in wholesale price index
UNEM = change in trend of number becoming unemployed as % of total number unemployed
M = change in trend of money supply as % of total money supply
C = change in trend of government budgetary surplus/deficit as % of GNP

According to Murenbeeld, quarterly Z scores in excess of 2.0 are indicators of a revaluation and scores below –1.5 indicators of devaluation. And for monthly data, discriminating scores are respectively 1.0 and - 1.5.

Having deviated slightly from the mainstream let us now return to it by examining the current account theory of the exchange rate under a floating currency regime. Again, in terms of illustrating the mechanism, let us begin with an increase in national income and a worsening of the current account balance. If we leave the capital account out of the equation for the time being, paying for the increased imports results in demand for foreign currency at the expense of the home currency. Buying foreign exchange for domestic current weakens the local currency which then makes exports more competitive and consequently improves the current account. By a reverse route in the argument, current account surpluses lessen with a strengthening exchange rate as the corrective mechanism.

So far, of course, our models have been simplistic to the extent that the capital account and the interest rate have been left out of the equation. Extending the argument now to make good this omission, we came up with the essence of the models. The overall balance of payment is the current account plus the capital account. Using the simple example to illustrate the workings of the model, let us begin by assuming an increase in national income with an accompanying deterioration in the current account balance. If overall balance of payments equilibrium is to maintained at zero as national income increases, the domestic real rate of interest must also rise-this improves capital flows to compensate for the initial deterioration on the current account. This increase in the interest rate dampens domestic demand which, in its turn, has the effect of reducing imports and consequently improves the current account. The mechanism of this version of the balance of payments model involves the interest rate increase as a means of avoiding a weakening in the domestic currency. This is in line with conventional wisdom-but does not accord with the monetary approach.

THE MONETARY APPROACH

In the world of classical economics, trade deficits were associated directly with money supply changes. In its more modern form, the monetary approach predicts that an excess supply of money domestically will be reflected in an outflow across the foreign exchanges.

Beginning with our example of growth in national income, under the monetary approach this will be associated with a growing demand for money for transaction purposes. An excess demand for money can be met in one of two ways-either through domestic credit creation or through a balance of payment surplus. This rationale explains the apparent paradox (remember the Keynesian model predicts that an increase in national income will be associated with a weakening current account balance) of fast-growing countries like Germany which appear to have almost perpetual balance of payments current surpluses. Fast real growth causes a growth in transactions demand for money: the economy induces an inflow of money via the foreign balance to the extent that this money is not created by the central bank.

Assuming that two countries have equal real growth but one increases its money supply (or there is no money supply in either but there are different real growth rates) more than the other, rational expectations would suggest that relative interest rates and expected relative inflation would alter. Either through the purchasing power parity theorem of via the mechanism referred to in the last paragraph, the economy with the high relative money supply growth will have a weakening exchange rate. According to the monetary approach, high interest rates and weakening currencies both flow from high relative money supply growth.

We have looked briefly at a handful of economic means of predicting foreign exchange rates. However, empirical tests indicate that we would not be well advised to risk large amounts to money on the forecasts produced by econometric models. So what about relying on charts? There seem to be plenty of forecasters of exchange rates who produce charts. And how do charts work anyway?

CHARTIST / TECHNICAL ANALYSIS

Applied to share price movements, commodity price movements and currencies, this technique involves the study of past price movements to seek out potential future trends. Implicit in this possibility is the assumption that past price patterns provide a guide to future movements.

Chartists attempt to predict share price movements by assuming that past price patterns will be repeated. There is no real theoretical justification for this. Chartists do not attempt to predict every price change. They are deeply interested in trends and trend reversals (that is, when the price of a share or commodity has been rising for several months but suddenly starts to fall). Features of chartism that are considered important for predicting trend reversals include.

— the observance of resistance levels

— head and shoulders patterns

— double bottom or double top patterns

Consider the following Figure-5. In this, the dotted line represents the lower resistance level on a rising trend. It will be noted that many of the troughs lie on this line, but only at the end it is breached. The chartist would tend to view this breach as an indication that the trend has been reversed.

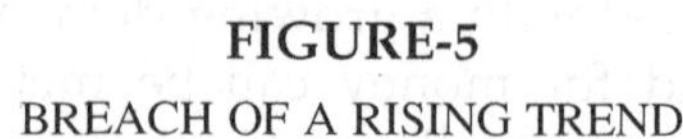

FIGURE-5

BREACH OF A RISING TREND

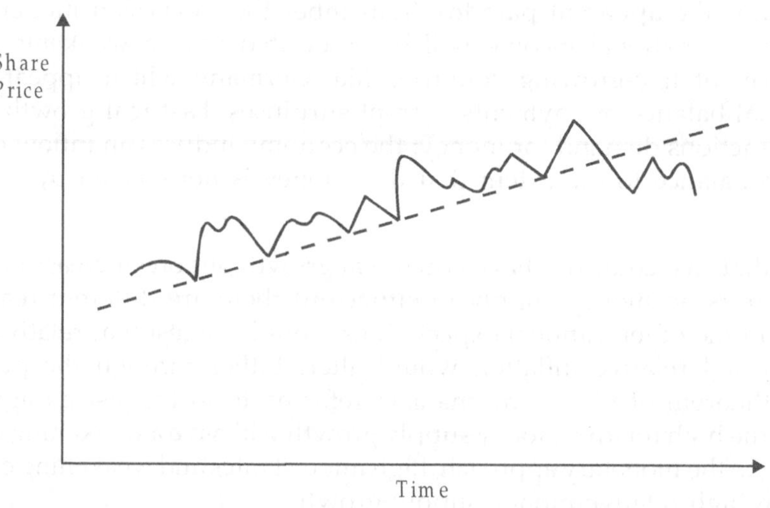

It Figure 5 the basic trend has been flat with oscillations within a channel. There are upper and lower resistance levels which bound this channel and, according to chartists, the breach of either of these will indicate a new trend. This sort of pattern arises from market indecision, as does the triangular pattern in Figure-6. In this exhibit the breach of the resistance lines is said to indicate a change of trend.

Let us now look at a resistance level on a double top. Suppose that the price of a currency has been rising steadily for some time. Recently the price fell as some investors sold to realise profits and it then rose to its maximum level for a second time before starting to fall again. This is known as a double top and, based on experience, the chartist would predict that the trend has reversed. A typical double top might appear as shown in Figure-8. Double bottoms are interpreted in a similar-but reverse-way.

FIGURE-6

MOVEMENT OUT OF A CHANNEL

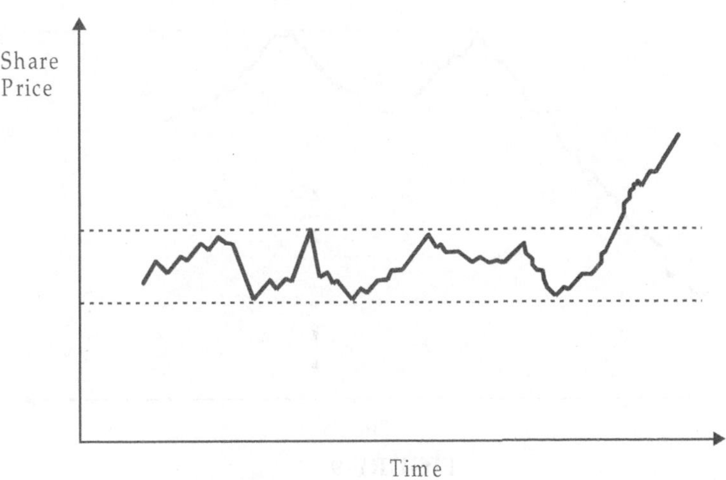

FIGURE-7

BREACH OF A TRIANGULAR PATTERN

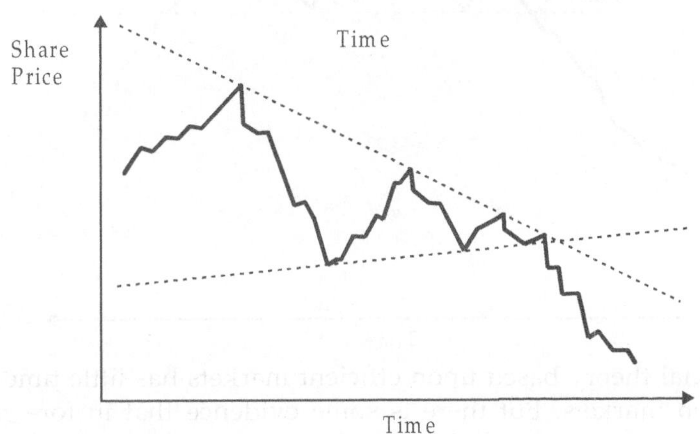

Another indication of a trend reversal is the head and shoulders formation of the type shown in Figure-9. In this kind of situation the chart might be interpreted as follows. The price has been rising for some time. At the peak of the left shoulder, profit taking has caused the price to drop. The price has then risen steeply again to the head before more profit taking causes the price to drop to around the same level as before the neck. Although the price rises again, the gains are not as great as at the head. The level of the right shoulder, together with the frequent dips down to the neck, suggests to the chartist that the upward trend previously observed is over and that a fall is imminent. The breach of the neck line is the indication to sell. An inverse head and shoulders is interpreted using a reverse, but similar argument.

FIGURE-8

DOUBLE TOP FORMATION

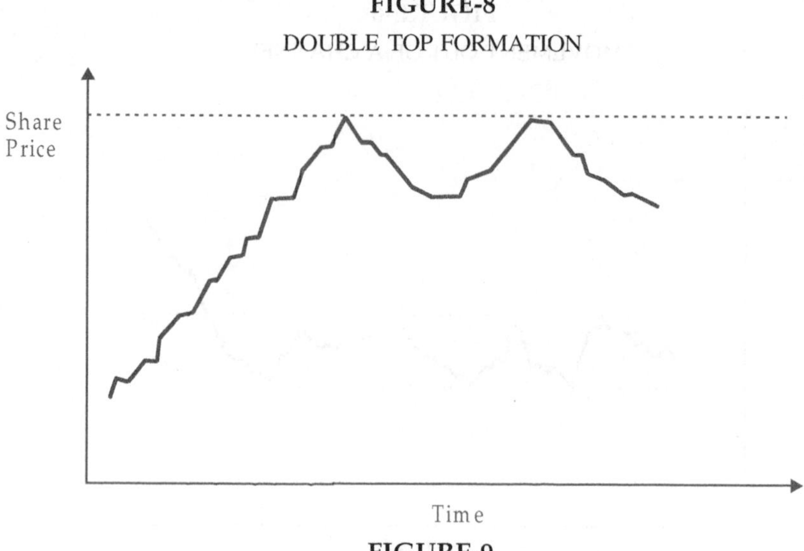

FIGURE-9

HEAD AND SHOULDERS FORMATION

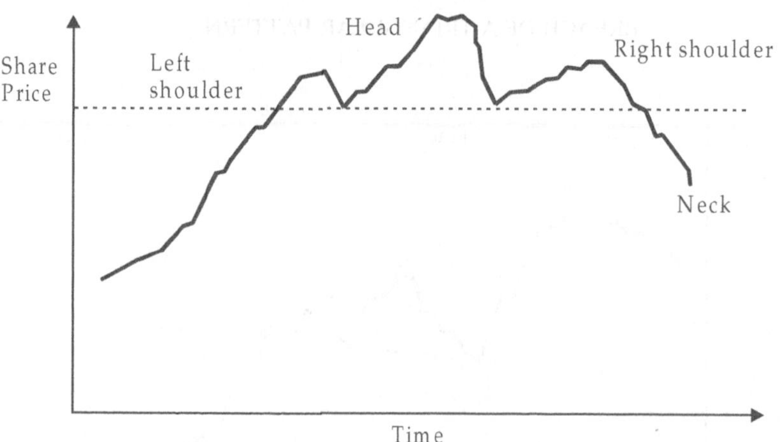

Modern financial theory based upon efficient markets has little time for chartist techniques in deep markets. But there is some evidence that in foreign exchange markets chartism pays greater dividends than does reliance upon econometric models for forecasting exchange rates.

EFFICIENT MARKETS HYPOTHESIS

An initial, and very important, premise of an efficient markets that there are a large number of profit maximising participants concerned with the analysis and valuation of currencies and that they are all operating independently of one another. A second assumption is that new information regarding currencies comes to the market in a random fashion. The third assumption of an efficient market is especially crucial: investors adjust currency prices rapidly to reflect the effect of new information. While the price adjustments made are not always perfect, they are unbiased-sometimes there is an overadjustment; sometimes there is an underadjustment. One does not know which it will be. Adjustment of currency prices takes place rapidly because the market is dominated by profit-maximising investors. The combined effects of new information coming to market participants in a random, independent fashion plus the presence of numerous investors who adjust exchange prices rapidly to reflect this new information means, according to efficient market theorists, that price changes are likely to be independent and random. According to chartism, of course, price changes are not independent-they are to some extent a function of past price movements. It is evident why efficient market proponents utterly reject the claims of chartists.

In the brief overview of efficient markets it should also be mentioned that, because currency prices adjust to all new information and, therefore, supposedly reflect all public information at any point in time, the currency prices that prevail at any point in time should be an unbiased reflection of all currently available information. Based on this brief description, an efficient market is evidently one in which currency prices adjust rapidly to the infusion of new information, and current prices fully reflect all available information including the risk involved. Therefore, the returns implicit in a currency's price reflect merely the risk involved, so that the expected return on a currency is consistent with risk-nothing more. There are three gradations of efficient market-the weak form, the semi-strong and the strong form.

The weak form of the efficient market hypothesis assumes that current currency prices reflect all exchange market information including the historical sequence of prices. Since current prices already reflect all past price changes and any other exchange market information, this implies that there should be no relationship between past price changes and future price changes. That is, price changes are independent of any trading rule-like chartism-that depends upon past price changes. In other words, past market data cannot be of any use in predicting future prices.

The semi-strong efficient market hypothesis asserts that currency prices adjust rapidly to the release of all new public information. In short prices fully reflect all publicly available data. Obviously, the semi-strong hypothesis encompasses the weak form hypothesis because all public information includes all market information such as past currency prices, trends and so on, plus all non-market information such as earnings, economic news, political news. A direct implication of this hypothesis is that investors acting on important new information after it is public cannot derive above- average profits from the transaction, allowing for the cost of trading, because the currency price already reflects the effects of the new public information.

The strong form efficient market hypothesis contends that currency prices fully reflect all information, whether public or otherwise. Hence it implies that no group of investors has a monopolistic access to information relevant to the formation of prices. Therefore, no group of investors should be able consistently to derive above-average profits. The strong form hypothesis encompasses both weak and semi-strong forms. Further, the strong form hypothesis requires not only efficient markets, where prices adjust rapidly to the release of new public information, but also perfect markets in which all information is available to everyone at the same time. This form of the efficient market hypothesis contends that, because all information is immediately available to everyone and is rapidly discounted by everyone, no group has monopolistic access to important new information and, therefore, no individual trader can consistently derive anything more than the average profits for all traders.

The basic premise of an efficient market is that there was a large number of profit-maximising participants. But there are also very large non-profit maximisers- central banks. Their intervention is not designed to make profit but to ease currency price movements designed to achieve a multiplicity of political objectives. The equation is: does this intervention stop currency markets from exhibiting market efficiency? This is entirely an empirical question and it can be loaded separately. To summaries the evidence-it is conflicting. The markets in some currencies exhibit efficiency some of the time, but not all of the time; probably this is because central banks intervene some of the time only. One opinion is that governments' direct intervention in foreign exchange markets and via the levels of interest rates is so great the currency markets cannot, from a deductive standpoint, be expected to exhibit all the characteristics of market efficiency with anything like consistency. The corollary of this is that chartism may well pay off in the foreign exchange markets, some of the time.

CAPITAL MOVEMENTS

According to purchasing power parity, exchange rates are determined by relative price of goods exchanged between countries. Countries with above-average inflation would, until their exchange rate fell, see their exports priced out of world markets and their home markets flooded with imports. The result would be a balance of payments deficit. But this scenario might be reversed by a currency realignment. Exchange rates would therefore move to equalise the prices of traded goods between rival economies and help to stabilise the system.

The international money flows from where it is cheap and plentiful to where it is scarce and expensive. It might be hypothesised that exchange rates move to equalise expected rates of return in rival financial centres. Money moves to where returns are anticipated to be highest. But, as well as interest received, returns include anticipated currency appreciation and depreciation. Hence there is a direct feedback. Currencies attracting funds rise and, in rising, become more attractive. The country perceived to offer the highest true return has the strongest currency. Its strong currency then prices its exports out of world markets and causes its home markets to be flooded with imports. Whereas, traditionally, a trade deficit caused a currency to weaken, it is possible to argue that in the middle eighties the relationship has been reversed. A strong currency causes a trade deficit.

This new order is decidedly unstable. Currencies overshoot due to the effects of positive feedback. Exchange rate movements operate to generate, rather than to correct imbalances in trade and payments, and these imbalances may become both large and unbelievably long-lived by past standards. In this new world it is vital, but extremely difficult to identify whether differing expected rates of return are due to real differences in the returns from capital investment in one economy rather than another. If they are, large imbalances can and do persist for longer than might be thought to be the case in more traditional models.

Is there any single model to rely upon for the purpose of predicting movements in exchange rates? Unfortunately the models that have been developed do not seem to hold in anything like a reliable way; so we do not have the sort of model which can be relied upon with a high degree of certainty in terms of predicting movements in exchange rates. What we do have is a series of competing hypotheses. All compete as tools to predict future exchange rate movements. Our judgement as to which model is to be preferred must wait until we have considered how each stands up empirically in the real world. Suffice it to say, at this stage, that there are many competing explanations designed to be used to predict the dependent variable, the future spot exchange rate.

IMPLICATIONS FOR MANAGERS

Any manager engaging in international business must be familiar with operations of the foreign markets. In most cases, international business requires transactions in the foreign exchange markets when a company converts the foreign exchange it has earned to domestic currency, or when it acquires foreign exchange to pay bills denominated in foreign currency. Even a manager who insists on dealing solely in home currency must be familiar with changes occurring in the foreign exchange markets because those changes affect the buying capacity of its foreign customers and the costs of its suppliers.

Familiarity with the markets and the mechanisms of foreign exchange trading is just one requirement. It is imperative that managers understand the potential effects of inflation on a currency's value in the foreign exchange markets. Empirical estimates of parity conditions are plagued with theoretical and econometric difficulties that make conclusions difficult even In the case of well developed markets. Whether any of the forecasting services are worth their cost depends partly on the motive for forecasting as well as the required accuracy of the forecast. For example, long-run forecasts may be motivated by a multinational firm's desire to initiate a foreign investment in Japan, or perhaps to raise long term funds denominated in Japanese yen. Or a portfolio manager may be considering diversifying for the long term in Japanese securities. The longer the time horizon of the forecast, the more inaccurate but also the less critical the forecast is likely to be. The forecaster will typically use annual data to display long-run trends in such economic fundamentals as Japanese inflation, growth, and the BOP.

Short-term forecasts are typically motivated by a desire to hedge a receivable, payable, or dividend for perhaps a period of three months. In this case the long-run economic fundamentals may not be as important as technical factors in the marketplace, government intervention, news, and passing whims of traders and investors. Accuracy of the forecast is critical, since most of the exchange rate changes are relatively small even though the day-to-day volatility may be high.

Forecasting services normally undertake fundamental economic analysis for long-term forecasts, and some base their short-term forecasts on the same basic model. Others base their short-term forecasts on technical analysis similar to that conducted in security analysis. They attempt to correlate exchange rate changes with various other variables, regardless of whether there is any economic rationale for the correlation. The chances of these forecasts being consistently useful or profitable depend on whether we believe the foreign exchange market is efficient. The more efficient the market is, the more likely it is that exchange rates are "random walks," with past price behavior providing no clues to the future. The less efficient the foreign exchange market is, the better the chance that forecasters may get lucky and find a key relationship that holds, at least for the short run. If the relationship is really consistent, however, others will soon discover it and the market will become efficient again with respect to that piece of information.

Exhibit-4 summarizes the various forecasting periods, regimes, and the authors' opinions of the preferred methodologies. Opinions, however, are subject to change without notice! Differences in estimates arise primarily from the model specifications, choice of techniques and of sample periods over which the models are estimated. Theoretical difficulties arise from existence of trade restrictions, transport and transaction costs, as also from consumption and interest rate smoothing behaviour. In practice, persistent swings in real exchange rate are observed. However, large orders of deviations get corrected over time, whether through market forces or through policy Induced adjustments and therefore, PPP is generally believed to hold in the long-run. The speed of convergence, however, is empirically seen to be slow and generally takes several years. In India, PPP holds in the long run in terms of the presence of a co-integrated relationship between exchange rate and relative prices and the misalignment at any point of time is corrected by 7.7 percent per quarter through nominal exchange rate adjustments. Events in Mexico provide an excellent illustration. Through 1993 and 1994, the Mexican government bought and sold foreign exchange to maintain the peso/dollar exchange rate within a guaranteed band. Among the factors that influence the government's capacity to do this is the effect these actions have on the real value of the peso. These actions, given relative inflation in Mexico and the United States, may increase or decrease the real value of the peso. In the former case, this causes Mexican exports to become less attractive on world markets and to attract large imports to Mexico, producing a current account deficit. Of course, a current account deficit could also arise if investment opportunities in Mexico induce a large inflow of capital. A manager observing a managed exchange rate and a large current account deficit must ask whether the policy is sustainable. Understanding how the real value of the exchange rate has changed over time is crucial in answering that question.

EXHIBIT-4

EXCHANGE RATE FORECASTING IN PRACTICE

Forecast Period	Regime	Recommended Forecast methods
Short-Run	*Fixed-Rate*	1. Assume the fixed rate is maintained
		2. Indications of stress on fixed rate?
		3. Capital conrols; black market rates
		4. Indicators of government's capability to maintain fixed rate?
		5. Changes in oficial foreign curency reserves

	Floating-Rate	1. Technical methods that capture trend
		2. Forward rates as forecasts
		a. < 30 days, assume a random walk
		b. 30-90 days, forward rates
		c. 90-360 days, combine trend with fundamental analysis
		3. Fundamental analysis of inflationary concerns
		4. Government declarations and agreements regarding exchange rate goals
		5. Cooperative agreements with other countries
Long-Run	*Fixed-Rate*	1. Fundamental analysis
		2. BOP management
		3. Ability to conrol domestic inflation
		4. Ability to generate hard curency reserves to use for intervention
		5. Ability to run trade surpluses
	Floating-Rate	1. Focus on inflationary fundamentals and PPP
		2. Indicators of general economic health such as economic growth and stability
		3. Technical analysis of long-term trends; new research indicates possibility of long-term technical "waves"

Interest rate parity explains the premium or discount in the forward markets. There are rarely deviations from IRP in the public markets. Individual firms, however, may confront deviations from IRP in their private dealings with banks and other businesses. The parity relationship creates a benchmark against which to measure other contractual possibilities. Finally, the interrelationships of expected inflation, spot and forward exchange rates, and interest rates create a framework around which a manager can build an understanding of foreign exchange prices, interest rates, and inflation that supports effective decision making.

QUESTIONS

1. Explain the concept of locational arbitrage and the scenario necessary for it to be plausible.
2. Explain the theory of purchasing power parity (PPP). Based on this theory, what is the general forecast of the values of currencies in highly inflated countries?
3. Explain the rationale behind purchasing power parity theory.
4. Explain how you could determine whether purchasing power parity exists.
5. Explain in general terms how various forms of arbitrage can remove any discrepancies in the pricing of currencies.
6. Some countries with high inflation rates tend to have high interest rates. Why?
7. Japan has typically had lower inflation than the United States. How would one expect this to affect the Japanese yen's value? What has this expected relationship not always occurred?
8. Explain the international Fisher effect (IFE). What is the rationale for the existence of the international fisher effect? What are the implications of IFE to firms with excess cash that consistently invest in foreign Treasury bills?

9. Assume Indian interest rates are generally above foreign interest rates. What does this suggest about the future strength or weakness of the rupee based on the International Fisher effect? Explain.
10. Compare and contrast interest rate parity, purchasing power parity (PPP), and the International Fisher Effect (IFE).
11. One assumption made in developing the International Fisher Effect is that all investors in all countries require the same real return. What does this mean?
12. How could you use regression analysis to determine whether the relationship specified by purchasing power parity (PPP) exists on average? Specify the model, and describe how you would assess the regression results to determine if there is a *significant* difference from the relationship suggested by PPP.
13. If the relationship that is specified by interest rate parity does not any period, but does exist on average, then covered interest arbitrage should not be considered by firms. Do you agree or disagree with this statement? Explain.
14. Why do you think currencies of countries with high inflation rates tend to have forward discounts?
15. Assume that the Swiss forward rate presently exhibits a premium of 6 per cent, and that interest rate parity exists. How will this premium change if U.S. interest rates decrease, in order for interest rate parity to be maintained? Why might we expect the premium to change?
16. How is it possible for purchasing power parity to hold, if the international Fisher effect does not?
17. Explain the concept of interest rate parity. Provide a rationale for its possible existence. Describe a method for testing whether interest rate parity exists.
18. Why are transaction costs, currency restrictions, and differential tax laws important when evaluating whether covered interest arbitrage can be beneficial?
19. Why would investors consider covered interest arbitrage in a foreign country where the interest rate is lower than their home interest rate?
20. Shouldn't the international Fisher effect discourage investors from attempting to capitalise on higher foreign interest rates? Why do some investors continue to invest overseas, even when they have no other transactions overseas?

11

CURRENCY FUTURES

INTRODUCTION

In recent years, financial markets have developed many new products whose popularity has become phenomenal. Measured in terms of trading volume, the growth of these products—principally futures and options—has confused traditional investors. Although active markets in futures and options contracts for physical commodities have existed for many years, these markets for foreign currencies have only recently attracted interest.

Multinational companies normally use the spot and forward markets for international transactions. They also use currency futures, currency options, and currency futures options for various corporate functions. While speculators trade currencies in these three markets for profit, multinational companies use them to cover open positions in foreign currencies.

CURRENCY FUTURES

Outside of the interbank forward market, the best-developed market for hedging exchange-rate risk is the currency-futures market. Curency futures are widely used by corporations, banks, and securities firms, sometimes in preference to forward contracts.

FUTURE CONTRACT

The future contract may be defined as a standardised agreement with an organised exchange to buy or sell some item, such as a curency or commodity, at a fixed price at a certain date in the future. Some contracts, notably foreign-currency futures, provide for cash delivery; others, such as Eurodollar futures, are based on some reference price and allow only for cash settlement at maturity. The purpose of futures is not to obtain delivery but to replicate, without credit risk, the gains or losses that would occur from an equivalent forward contact. In principle, currency futures are similar to foreign-exchange forwards in that they are contracts for delivery of a certain amount of a foreign currency at some future date and at *known price*. In practice, most futures contracts are terminated prior to maturity.

FUTURE VS. FORWARD MARKET

Although most investors are unlikely ever to become involved in the forward market, it is important to understand some of the attitudes, particularly as a good deal of the literature, on pricing futures contracts typically refers to those contracts interchangeably. Specifically, it might be inferred form Table-1 that differences resulting form liquidity, credit risk, margin, taxes and commissions could cause futures and forward contracts not to be priced identically. For instance, in dealing with price risk, futures contracts have several transactional advantages relative to spot and forward contracts. Sequential spot contracts, that is spot contracts where the terms of the contract are re-negotiated as events unfold, do not inject any certainty into the transaction. Such a method of contracting is particularly liable to the hazards of opportunism and may deter investment because of the relatively high probability that the contract will be breached. On the other hand, forward and futures contracts inject some certainty into their transaction. Both share the property that the parties agree to perform the terms of the contract at some future date. In fact, time-dated contracts are generally costlier to enforce than spot contracts. This is due to the absence of the self-enforcing, near simultaneous exchange of value characteristic of spot transactions and the greater uncertainty attached both to the eventual outcome and each party's compliance with the term of forward contracts.

Forward and futures contracts differ, however, in their susceptibility to opportunism, especially in their role of reducing price risk. First forward contracts that cover all feasible contingencies are costly to devise. The information and transaction costs will thus preclude a fully specified forward contract and this contractual incompleteness will give rise to enforcement and execution difficulties. Incomplete contracting has a clear economic justification. Given the cost of tailoring the contract to the particular needs of the parties, it will usually be cost-effective to use standard form contracts. In this regard, organised forward and futures contracting have identical properties. Nevertheless, enforcement and execution difficulties can be expected to pose a more serious problem for forward contracts. This is so for several reasons. *First*, in forward contracting, individuals, will have to incur the expense of determining the reliability risk of the opposite party. To the extent that there are scale economies in such specialisation by identity, forward contracting will be more expensive than organised futures contracting where the exchange ensures the integrity of its members and trading practices. Forward contracts also are subject to high enforcement costs where personal market sanctions are weak. The penalty risk of contract law are costly to enforce and may not deal effectively with all types of breaches.

Another disadvantage of forward contract is that they are tied transactions. The forward contract transfers rights relating to quantity, quality and price. The last, however, may best be separated, especially when the parties are risk averse and their access to insurance markets limited. Price changes have an unfortunate zero-sum quality that increases the likelihood of opportunism. Thus, while forward contracts may inject certainty into the quantity and possibly quality dimensions of future transactions, it is not clear that they are the least cost adaptator to price risk. Depending on the transaction costs in alternative markets, and the strength of governance in each, it may be desirable for both risk-spreading and opportunism-

TABLE-1

A COMPARISON OF FUTURES AND FORWARD MARKETS

Futures Market	*Forward Market*
1. Trading is conducted in a competitive arena by" open outcry" of bids, offers, and amount	1. Trading is done by telex or telephone, with participants generally dealing directly with broker-dealers.
2. Contract terms are standardised with all buyers and sellers negotiating only with respect to price.	2. All contract terms are negotiated privately by the parties
3. Non-member participants deal through brokers (exchange members who represent them on the exchange floor.	3. Participants deal typically on a principal-to-principal basis
4. Participants include banks, corporations financial institutions, individual investors, are speculators.	4. Participants are primarily institutions dealing with one other and other interested parties dealing through one or more dealers.
5. The clearinghouse of the exchange becomes the opposite side to each cleared transactions; therefore, the credit risk for a futures market participant is always the same and there is no need to analyse the credit of other market participants	5. A participant must examine the credit risk and establish credit limits for each opposite party.
6. Margins deposits are to be required of all participants.	6. Typically, no money changes hands until delivery, although a small margin deposit might be required of nondealer customers on certain occasions
7. Settlements are made daily through the exchange clearinghouse. Gains on open positions may be withdrawn and losses are collected daily.	7. Settlement occurs on date agreed upon between the parties to each transaction.
8. Long and short positions are usually liquidated easily.	8. Forward positions are not as easily offset or transferred to other participants.
9. Settlements are normally made in cash, with only a small percent age of all contracts resulting actual delivery.	9. Most transactions result in delivery.
10. A single, round trip (in and out of the market) commission is charged. It is negotiated between broker and customer and is relatively small in relation to the value of the contract.	10. No commissions is typically charged if the transaction is made directly with another dealer. A commission is charged to both buyer and seller, however, if transacted through a broker.
	11. Trading is mostly unregulated.
	12. The delivery price is the forward price.

reducing reasons to separate price risk from the other aspects of time-dated transactions. Since spot, forward and futures markets deal in different bundles of rights among different individuals, rights can be divided between those relating to quantity and quality, and those counselling certainty of profits and costs. Forward contracts, especially in personal markets, are best suited to ensuring that contract terms relating to the former are complied with, whereas futures contracts deal with price volatility.

Future contracts permit the price risk to be separated from the reliability risk by removing the former form the set of factors giving rise to opportunism. The governance structure supplied by the exchange authority effectively eliminates reliability risk from futures trading. The seller of a futures contracts incurs a liability not to the buyer, but to the clearing house, and likewise the buyer acquires an asset from the clearing house. The clearing house in effect guarantees all transactions. In addition, the exchange rules, especially regarding its members' contract, severely limit their ability to behave opportunistically. Organised exchanges greatly reduce default and reliability risk from future contracts. This is achieved by transferring transactions over price risks from a personal to an impersonal market through standard form futures contracts traded in a self-regulated market price.

Future contracts are standard form contracts with only one negotiable term: price. The standardisation of future contracts has significant implications for transaction costs. This is so for several reasons. First, contract standardisation eliminates the costs of bargaining over non-price terms and of enforcing contract provisions. Second, it reduces monitoring costs that are generally incurred in principal-agent relationships. The principal only needs to give his broker instructions as to price and quantity which are easily observed. The monitoring costs in the future market are, therefore, significantly lower than those in the spot market, where numerous other matters require attention and provide the broker with opportunities to take advantage of the principal. Third, contract standardisation makes all futures contracts of a particular maturity month perfect substitution. The fungibility of futures contracts is not a property shared by forward contracts.

The liquidity and competitive nature of future trading also reduce the waiting costs of brokers and speculators for acceptable bids and offers. One component of the transaction costs of futures trading is the ask-bid spread which in a competitive situation, is directly correlated with the search costs of finding acceptable bids and offers. We may live in the information age, but much of the information we deal with every day is often perplexing. Perhaps most confusing of all is the world of finance. We are deluged with data, analyses and trends—often couched in jargon that makes ones eyes glaze over. We know in a market with incomplete information, buyers and sellers will have to search each other out. The costs of such search activity will differ and will be greater the more geographically dispersed and heterogeneous are buyers and sellers. In fact, the transaction cost arise because the parties to transactions are different individuals with asymmetric information, divergent motives and mutual suspicions and because expenditure of resources can reduce the gap in information and protect the parties against each other. Search costs will not only raise the cost of activities but may preclude otherwise value maximising transactions from taking place. The importance of market liquidity arise not only because it reduces waiting costs, but also because it ensures that competitive pressures exist to keep waiting costs to a minimum for any volume of trade. Competition among the futures traders will have the effect of weeding out these with excessive search costs and poor forecasting ability. Large speculators make consistent profits whereas small traders make losses since the performance difficulties occasioned by opportunism raise the cost of transacting. Each party is confronted by what can be termed a reliability risk — the risk that the other party will default either on the whole transaction or on individual terms in a way that decreases the expected wealth of the non-defaulting party. Reliability risk is an important source of transaction costs because it will pay individuals to guard against opportunism and contract breach. Acquiring information on the reliability of those with whom one transacts yields benefits in he form of reduced losses due to default and incomplete or inferior performance. Degree of success of futures markets can be explained in terms of a net benefits function. The most actively traded commodities have the most variable prices. Choices can be made among contractual arrangements on the basis of maximum net benefit, taking account of transaction costs.

CURRENCY FUTURES QUOTES

Figure-1 contains a reproduction of the currency-futures quotations that may be found in most business newspapers. These futures are contracts for delivery of a standard amount of a foreign currency in exchange for delivery of a given amount of U.S. dollars at some future date. The funds to be exchanged may be, for example, 125,000 German marks in exchange for the equivalent value in dollars. The figure offers a guideline for interpretation of published futures quotations. As in the forward market, each delivery takes place in the currency of the currency, although as a matter of practice few deliveries actually occur. The futures contract can be used to hedge, speculate or perform arbitrage in much the same way as forwards are used. Many commercial and investment banks are members of the major futures exchanges and are able to buy currencies in the forward market and sell them in the futures markets, and vice versa, ensuring that futures prices stay in line with forward prices for the same delivery date.

HOW TO READ CURRENCY FUTURE QUOTES?

To illustrate, the currency futures quotes are presented in Table-2. These futures exchange rates for the six active currencies were reported in *The Wall Street Journal* on one recent Thursday. Yen prices were the number of U.S. cents per unit of a foreign currency. The other currency prices were the number of U.S. dollars per unit if a foreign currency. Because there is a one-day time lag between the transactions of foreign exchange and the report of these transactions, therefore the Wednesday quotations were secured form the Thursday issue of *The Wall Street Journal*

The top, bold-faced line gives the name of the currency, such as German mark; the exchange on which it is traded according to a key in the table such as the IMM; the size of a single contract, such as 125,000 marks per contract and the way in which prices are quoted, such as dollars per mark.

FIGURE-1

CURRENCY FUTURES DISSECTED

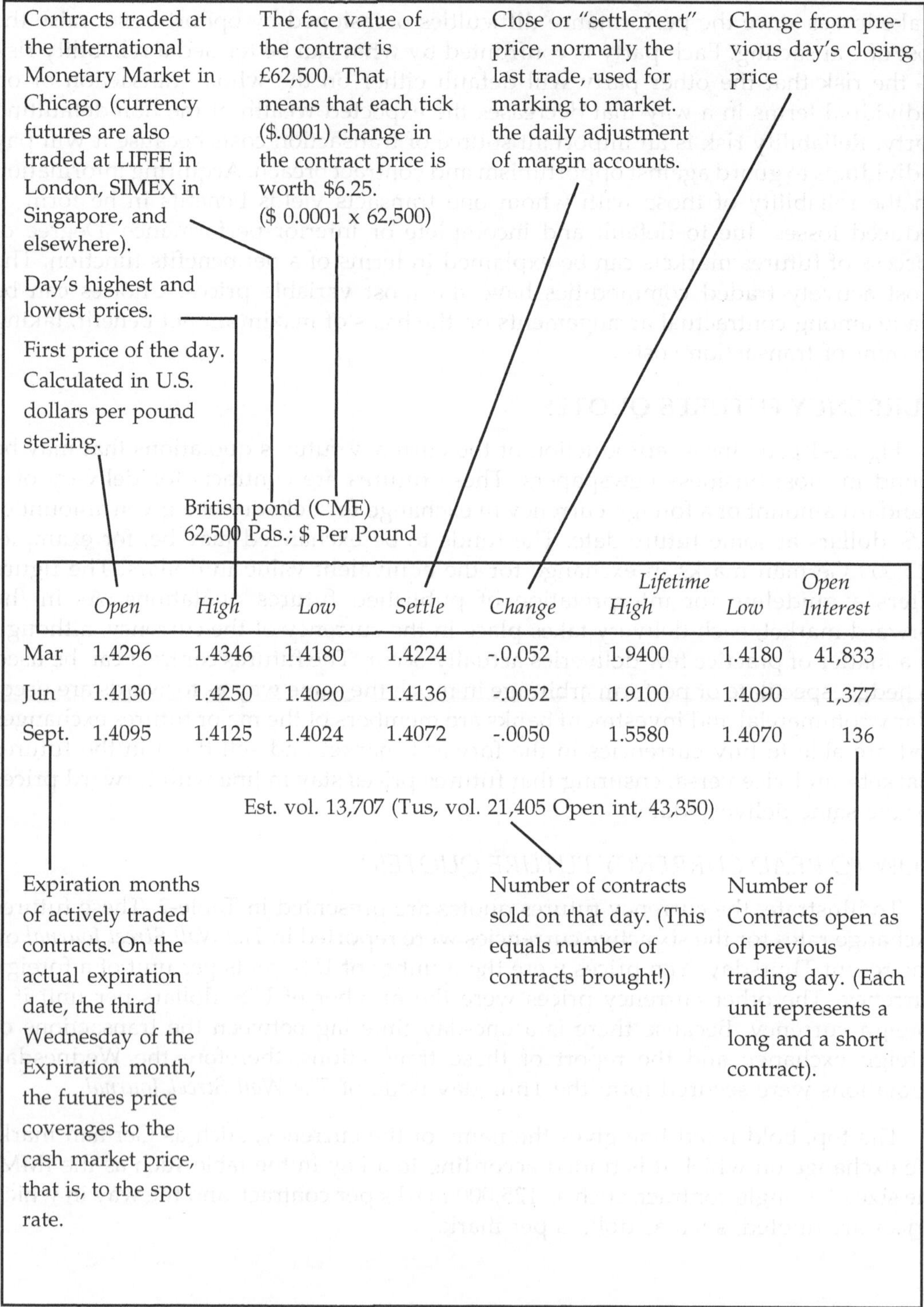

	Open	*High*	*Low*	*Settle*	*Change*	*Lifetime High*	*Low*	*Open Interest*
Mar	1.4296	1.4346	1.4180	1.4224	-.0.052	1.9400	1.4180	41,833
Jun	1.4130	1.4250	1.4090	1.4136	-.0052	1.9100	1.4090	1,377
Sept.	1.4095	1.4125	1.4024	1.4072	-.0050	1.5580	1.4070	136

TABLE - 2
CURRENCY FUTURES

	Open	High	Low	Settle	Change	Life time High	Life time Low	Open Interest
Japanese Yen (IMM) 12.5 — million yen; $ per yen (.00)								
March	.6943	.6953	.6928	+.0030	.8357	.6780	62.846	
June	.6956	.6968	.6949	.6957	+.0030	.7530	.6850	2,981
Est vol 24,926; vol Tues 43,974; open int 65,881, -144.								
German Mark (IMM) — 125,000 Marks; $ per Mark								
March	.5941	,5957	.5921	.5939	+.0059	.6012	.5000	58,276
June	.5938	.5953	.5920	.5938	+.0060	.6007	.5057	4,237
Sept.	.5938	.5940	.5928	.5936	+.0060	.5980	.5410	238
Est vol 46,450; vol Tues 51,925; open int 63,147, -1,062.								
Canadian Dollar (IMM) - 100,000 drs.; $ per Can $								
Mar	.8355	.8397	.8346	.8376	+.0017	.8595	.7890	25,412
June	8283	.8319	.8276	.8304	+.0018	.8522	.8107	3,422
Sept.	.8228	.8260	.8220	.8242	+.0019	.8468	.8100	252
Dec.	.8180	.8215	.8180	.8200	+.0030	.84200	.8120	171
Est vol 5,286; vol Tues 3,478; open int 29,318, +74.								
British Pound (IMM) - 62,500 pds.; $ Per Pound								
March	1.6680	1.6702	1.6620	1.6660	+.0084	1.6668	1.4600	24,107
June	1.6420	1.6444	1.6378	1.6406	+.0082	1.6950	1.4400	2,194
Swiss Franc (IMM) — 125,000 Francs; $ Per Franc								
Mar	.6685	.6700	.6634	.6655	+.0017	.6744	.5740	36,560
June	.6665	.6682	.6615	.6636	+.0018	.6725	.5850	1.315
Est vol 25,917; vol Tues 25,808; open int 38,741,-773.								
Australian Dollar (IMM) — 100,000 Drs.; Per A.$								
Mar	.7606	.7603	.7628	.0063	+.0063	.7854	.7055	3,189
Est vol 323; vol Tues 252; open int 3,248, + 87.								

Source: *The Wall Street Journal.*

The first column gives the months for which delivery of the currency may be obtained. Currency trading takes place in March, June, September, and December. Futures contracts for German marks were only for March, June, and September; December contracts were excluded because they were not active for the day. The second column gives the opening price of the day. For German marks, prices are in terms of dollars per mark; the 0.5941 for March delivery means that German marks opened for sale at $ 0.5941 for March delivery means that German marks opened for sale at $ 0.5941 per mark. The full value of one contract at the open of trading for the day is $74,262.50 (0.5941 X 125,000).

The next three columns tell us the contract's highest, lowest, and closing (settlement) prices for the day. These figures, viewed together, show how volatile the market was during the trading day. After opening at $0.5941 per mark, the mark for March delivery never sold for more than $0.5957 and never for less than $0.5921. Trading finally ended or settled at $ 0.5939 per mark. A broker uses settlement prices to evaluate portfolios or for deciding whether to call for more margin. Currency futures losses must be settled every day, and profits are credited daily to customer accounts.

The sixth column from the left of the quotation, labeled "change," shows the difference between the latest settlement price and the one for the previous day. A plus (+) sign indicates prices ended higher; a minus (–) sign indicates prices ended lower. The +0.0059 in the change column means that the settlement price of the mark for March delivery on the day was $0.0059 higher than the settlement price on the previous trading day.

The next two columns, second and third from the right of the quotation, show the highest and lowest prices at which each contract month has ever traded. We can see that the German mark for March delivery traded as high as $0.6012 per mark and as low as $0.5000 per mark during the lifetime. The difference between the highest and lowest prices of the mark during the lifetime was $0.1012 (0.6012 - 0.5000). This difference is the range. The range represents the volatility of the currency or the dispersion of individual prices for the currency around its average price. The wider the dispersion, the higher the risk. If the highest price and the lowest price are not widely separated from their neighbouring prices, the range may be a good measure of risk. If these two prices are erratic, the range should not be used as a measure of risk because it is unreliable and misleading.

The right-hand column, labeled "open interest," refers to the total number of outstanding contracts; that is, those that have not been cancelled by offsetting trades. This column allows us to see how much interest there is in trading a particular contract. The closest months usually attract the most activity, as we can see from the difference between the March mark (58,276 contracts) and the September mark (238 contracts).

A line at the bottom of each currency quotation gives the estimated number of contracts for the day, the actual trading volume for the preceding day, the total open interest, and the change in the open interest since the preceding day. In other words, Est. vol., vol. Tues., and open interest are total figures for all the months combined for the trading day. For the German mark, the estimated volume for the day (Wednesday) was 46,450; the actual volume on Tuesday (the previous trading day) was 51,925; the total number of the open interests for all of the different contracts maturities was 63,147; and the - 1,062 shows the number of mark contracts that were subtracted from those outstanding at the end of the previous session.

MARKET OPERATIONS

At the heart of futures market procedures is the system of collateral margins that has evolved as a means to reduce default risks. As opposed to margins or stock accounts, a futures margin payment is not a form of down payment on the balance due since a futures transaction is not an investment of initial capital in return for a later payoff, but rather, in its purest form, is an agreement made at no initial investment. *Margin payments are used as a means of gradually settling the losses and gain on the contract and also as collateral against default.* Margin payments are made frequently (usually daily) in small amounts relative to the size of the contract, rather than in one large initial lump sum, so as to preserve the basic character of a futures contract as a forward agreement deferred payments for deferred delivery. Infact, daily cash settlement procedure is an important aspect of the futures markets, integral in maintaining the trading system. Each transaction calls for a good-faith deposit known as initial margin, to be posted with a broker. The minimum amount of *initial margin* required is set by the exchange based on the price volatility of the underlying products. The value of a contract position is assessed, marked to market, daily and these changes are settled in cash on a daily basis. For example, if a contract prices increase, the longs-who have purchased the contract—would receive cash equal to the value of gains, while the shorts—who have sold contracts—would have to pay in funds equal to the value of losses. This procedure, known as *variation margin,* keeps the value of each market participants' position current and constitutes to the credit of the futures market. Initial margin ensures that the participants will pay variation-margin deficit. When the system is tied in with the variation-margin vehicle through which daily *marks to market* occur, an individual gains the ability of offset a position at any time without regard to who was initially on the other side of the transaction. This is a key to ease of trading and confidence in the future markets. This makes the possibility of taking a large market position without committing a large amount of capital. For this reason, futures contracts are considered an extremely highly leveraged instrument relative to most financial securities. Although high leverage is often associated with high financial instability and high default risk, futures markets have a history of financial integrity and low default risk. This unusual combination of high leverage with low default risk is largely a property of the intricate, multi-tiered, continually adjusting margining system.

To illustrate how margin works, consider an investor who contacts his or her broker on July 9, 1998, to buy two December 1998 gold futures contracts on the XYZ commodity Exchange. We suppose that the current futures price is $ 500 per ounce. Since the contract size is 100 ounces, the investor has contracted to buy total of 200 ounces at this price. The broker will require the investor to deposit funds in what is termed a *margin account.* the amount that must be deposited at the time the contract is first entered into is known as the *initial margin.* We assume this is $ 2500 per contract or $ 5,000 in total. At the end of each trading day, the margin account is adjusted to reflect the investor's gain or loss. This is known as *marking to market* the account.

Suppose by the end of July 9, 1998 the futures price has dropped from $ 500 to $ 497. The investor has a loss of 200 X $ 3 or $ 600. This is because the 200 ounces of December 1998 gold, which he or she contracted at $ 500, cannot be sold for $497. The balance in the margin account would, therefore, be reduced by $600 to $4400. Similarly, if the price of December 1998 gold rose to $ 503 by the end of the first day, the balance in the margin account would be increased by $ 600 to $ 5,600. A trade is first marked to market at the close of the day on which it takes place. It is then marked to market at the close of trading on each subsequent day.

Marking to market is not merely an arrangement between broker and client, however, when there is a $ 600 decrease in the future prices so that the margin account of an investor with a long position is reduced by $ 600, the investor's broker has to pay the exchange $ 600 and the exchange passes the money on the broker of an investor with a short position. Similarly, when there is an increase in the futures price, brokers for parties with short positions pay money to the exchange and brokers for parties with long positions receive money from the exchange.

TABLE - 3

OPERATION OF MARGINS FOR A LONG POSITION IN TWO GOLD FUTURES CONTRACTS

Day	*Futures Price*	*Daily Gain/Loss* $	*Cummulative Gain (Loss)*	*Margin Account Balance* $	*Margin Call*
July 9	497.00	-600	-600	4,400	
July 10	496.10	-180	-780	4,220	
July 11	498.20	420	-360	4,640	
July 12	497.10	-220	-580	4,420	
July 13	496.70	-80	-660	4,440	
July 14	495.40	-260	-920	4,080	
July 15	496.70	-80	-660	4,440	
July 16	495.40	-260	-920	4,080	
July 17	**493.30**	**-420**	**-1340**	**3,660**	**1,340**
July 18	493.60	60	-1280	5,060	
July 19	491.80	-360	-1640	4,700	
July 22	492.70	180	-1460	4,880	
July 23	**487.00**	**-1140**	**-2600**	**3,740**	**1,260**
July 24	487.00	0	-2600	5,000	
July 25	488.10	220	-2360	5,220	
July 26	488.70	120	-2260	5,340	
July 29	491.30	460	-1800	5,800	
July 30	492.30	260	-1540	5,060	

The investor is entitled to withdraw any balance in the margin account in excess of the initial margin. To ensure that the balance in the margin account never becomes negative *a maintenance margin,* which is somewhat lower than the initial margin, is set. If the balance in the margin account falls below the maintenance margin, the investor receives a *margin call* and is expected to top up the margin account to the initial margin level the next day. In case the extra funds deposited, known an variation margin, are not provided by the investor, the broker closes out the position by selling the contract. Int he case of the investor considered earlier closing out the position would involve underlying the existing contract by selling 200 ounces of gold for delivery in December 1998. Table-3 illustrates the operation of the margin account for one possible sequence of futures prior in the case of the investor considered earlier. The maintenance margin is assumed for the purpose of the illustration is $ 2,000 per contract or $ 4,000 in total. The contract is entered into on 9 July 1998 at $ 500 and closed out on July 30, 1998 at $ 492.30.

On 17 July 1998 the balance in the margin account falls $ 340 below the maintenance margin level. This triggers a margin call from the broker for additional margin of $ 1,340. Table-3 assumes that the investor does in fact provide this margin by close of trading on July 18, 1998. On July 23, the balance in the margin account again falls below the maintenance margin level and a margin call for $ 1,260 is sent out. The investor provides this margin by close of trading on July 24, 1998. On July 30, 1998 the investor decides to close out the position by shorting two contracts. The future price on that day is $ 492.30 and the investor has a cumulative loss of $ 1,540.

CLEARINGHOUSE AND CLEARING MARGINS

The trade for an outside party must be executed through a broker, and the broker must, in turn, trade through a member of the exchange. Normally, the two parties to a transaction are located far apart and may not even know each other. This raises the issue of trust and the question of whether the traders will perform as they have promised. To resolve this uncertainty about performance in accordance with the contract terms, each futures exchange has a clearing house. The clearing house is a well-capitalised financial institution that guarantees contract performance to both parties. As soon as the trade is commumated, the clearing house interposes itself between the buyer and seller. At this point, the original buyer and seller have obligations to the clearing house and no obligations to each other.

In the calculation of clearing margins, the exchange clearing house calculates the number of contracts on trading on either a gross or a net basis. *Basis is the difference between the current spot price on an asset and corresponding futures prices.* The gross basis simply adds the total of all long positions entered into by clients to the total of all short positions entered into by clients. The *net basis* allows these to be offset against each other. Suppose a clearing house member has two clients, one with a buy position in 50 contracts, the other with a short position in 30 contracts. Gross margining would calculate the clearing margin on the basis of 80 contracts; net margining would calculate the clearing margin on the basis of 20 contracts. The whole purpose of the margining system is to reduce the possibility of market participants sustaining losses because of defaults.

Hedging in the Futures Market

A single forward contract can arrange for the precise amount and maturity that the bank's customer desires. A single futures contract is available only in a predetermined amount for one of the four maturity dates each year. These two features of the futures market may force multinational companies to assume some risks of coverage and of currency fluctuation because they usually need a specified amount of a currency on a specified date. Still, these risks can be minimised in a properly structured hedge. Prices in the spot and futures markets move in the same direction by similar amounts due to arbitrage transactions between these two markets. To illustrate, consider on February 1, an American firm imports 5,000 Swiss watches at a cost of 250,000 francs with payment and delivery due on March 1. The Swiss firm, being a tough negotiator, has demanded that the payment be made in Swiss francs upon the delivery of the watches. The exchange rates are $ 0.6667 per franc in the sport market and $ 0.6655 per franc in the futures market for delivery on March 15.

Given the costs of marketing the watches, the importer decides that the futures exchange rate is low enough of the company to purchase them and make a profit on the transaction. However, the importer must pay for the watches on March 1, though the expiration date of the futures contract is March 15. The importer can hedge most of its exposure by buying March Swiss franc contracts on February 1 with the intention of lifting the hedge on March 1. Because franc contracts are available form the IMM in units of 125,000, the importer would purchase two March contracts, as given in Table-4.

TABLE - 4

BUYING TWO FRANC FUTURES CONTRACTS ON FEBRUARY 1

	Spot Market	*Futures Market for March 15 Delivery*
Exchanges rate	$0.6667/SF	$0.6655/SF
Cost of SF250,000	$166,675	$166,375
Action taken	None	Buy March 15 contract

The importer could trade out of the contracts by selling them before receiving a delivery notice. The importer could buy 250,000 francs in the futures market for $ 166,375 on March 15. The only risk that the company still faces comes from the difference in the value of the contract on March 1 and its value on March 15. Assume that by March 1 the following two things would happen : (1) the spot rate appreciates to $ 0.7658 an (2) the futures rate rises to $ 0.7650. The importer could close out the franc futures contracts by selling them on March 1, as shown in Table-5.

TABLE - 5

REVERSING THE EARLIER FUTURES CONTRACTS

	Spot Market	*Futures Market for March 15 Delivery*
Exchanges rate	$0.7658/SF	$0.7650/SF
Cost of SF250,000	$191,450	$191,250
Action taken	Buy SF250,000	Sell March 15 contract

On March 1, the importer purchases 250,000 francs in the spot market for $ 191,450 and settles its import bill. But, this $ 191,450 is higher ($ 24,775) than its original value on February 1 ($ 166,675) in other words, the exchange loss from the spot transaction is $ 24,775. The futures contract the company sold on March 1 ($ 191,250) is higher ($24,875) than the $166,375 the company anticipated in the futures contract it purchased on February 1; in other words, the exchange gain form the futures transaction is $ 24,875. The $ 24,875 gain form the futures transaction exceeds the $ 24,775 loss from the spot transaction. The risk that the importer assumed on February 1 by purchasing two contracts whose maturity did not coincide with the March 1 usage date of the currency resulted in a windfall exchange gain of $ 100 ($ 25,875-$24,775). This $ 100 gain arose form the difference between the spot rate and the futures rate prevailing on the day the contracts were liquidated. This difference is the basis.

The basis, unlike the spot rate itself, is relatively stable and narrows toward zero as the contract moves toward maturity. For example, the basis on February 1 was $ 0.0012 per franc ($ 0.6667 - $ 0.6655), while by March 1 it had shrunk to $0.0008 ($0.7658 - $0.7650). The degree of uncertainty about the futures price diminishes further as the contract approaches its March 15 expiration date. On March 15, the futures rate, in effect, becomes the spot rate.

The difference of $0.0004/SF in the basis between February 1 and March 1 accounted for the windfall exchange gain of $ 100. This gain might easily have been an exchange loss of a similar amount if the exchange rate of the Swiss franc had depreciated during the same period. The important point is that the importer was protected form any major loss regardless of exchange—rate movements. For example, if the importer had not purchased the futures contract and bought 250,000 francs in the spot market on March 1, the watches would have cost an additional $24,775.

Frequent futures traders may try to coordinate trading between two different markets or two different currencies through a strategy called spread trading. *Spread trading means buying one contract and simultaneously selling another contract.* They will always make money on one contract and lose money on the other contract. Thus, they may make on lose more money on the one contract than they lose or make on the other, but they are protected from major loss regardless of exchange-rate movements.

TRADING SECRETS OF THE PROFESSIONALS

Selected trading secrets of the professionals, based more on their failures than their triumphs, have been identified as a world of wisdom. We know that the same mistakes made 50 and 100 years ago continue to the made every day. Technology may change, but human nature never does. Ultimately, the markets are the best teachers, however. A trader may not use all of these secrets, but if he can absorb just a portion, there is no doubt about success. If he disregards, what's presented below, he may lost in the financial desert.

Secret 1: The Trend is Your Friend

So, don't buck it. The way to make the big money is to determine the major trend and then follow it. If the market will not go in the desired direction, then a trader must go its way. When he is in a bear market, and the major trend is down, the plan should be to wait for rallies and sell short; not try to pick the bottom. In a major bear market, he can miss the bottom several times on the way down and end up losing all his money. The same applies (in reverse) in a major bull market. Always go with the tide, never buck it. It is implement to note that in a major bear market it is safer to sell when the market is down 50 points from the top, than when it is down just 10. The reason is, at down 50, all support is gone, and those who bought the breaks have lost all hope, are demoralised, and in a leveraged market are at the point where they are must try to exit the same small door at the same time. The result at times can be an avalanche. There are many examples of markets that have trended long and far, made some people rich and wiped others out. We may hear about the poor traders who lost their money drawn from provident fund, sale of real estate etc. We can almost guarantee that such traders were bull headed and fought the trend until they run out of money.

So, how does a trader do this, stick with the tend and not fight it? Well, it isn't easy. That's why most people don't make money in futures. They need to have strong willpower. Once they can see the trend of the market, they should not change their mind until the "tape" shows the change. In any major move there will, of course, be corrective moves against the trend at times. Some news will developed which will cause a sharp correction, but it will be followed by a more right back in the direction of the major trend. If they listen to this news they will be tempted to liquidate prematurely. Avoid the temptation and listen to no one but the market. One way to do this is to *never* set a fixed price in mind as a profit objective. The majority of people do this, and there's no good reason for it — it's a bad habit based on hope.

Do not set a fixed time to liquidate either. This is the way the amateurs do it. They buy silver at, because their broker told them it's going to Rs. 8000. Well, it gets to Rs. 7800 turns and head south again, and they're still holding looking for Rs. 7800, watching and waiting as their unrealised profit melt. This is just plain bull-headedness. One can seen the opposite as well. The market closes at Rs. 7700, it looks strong and is fundamentally and technically sound. The amateur has his order sitting to sell at Rs. 8000, because this is his price. The market gaps up on the open the next day at Rs. 8100 and his broker is pleased to report he sold Rs. 100 better at this price. However, this is a form of top picking, and who is smarter than the market? The market probably gapped up above Rs. 8000 cases like this one, where the open was sharply higher, but was the low of the day. The market never looked back until it hit Rs. 10,000. This is all a version of bucking the trend, which is something not to be recommended. Conditions do change, and one must learn to change his mind when they do. A wise man changes his mind, a fool never. Just be sure if a trader change his position it must be based on sound reasoning. There is no way one can possibly know in advance how much profit to expect. The market determines that. The mission is to determine the trend, hope on for the ride, and stay on until the indicators suggest the trend has changed, *and not before.*

Secret 2: When Market is "cheap" or "Expensive" there Probably is Reason

This one goes hand in hand with "don't buck the trend." The intelligent traders always make money selling short low priced markets which are the public's favourite and in which a large long interest had developed. Alternatively, they cash in on expensive markets when "everyone" is bailing out because the public thought the market high enough for a "healthy" reaction. *Always remember, it's not the price that's important, it's the market action.*

Secret 3: The Best Traders are the Hardest to Do

A trader needs, to have guts and be aggressive on entry. He needs to quickly cut losses when the market is not acting right. *The news will always sound the most bullish at the top, and appear to be the most hopeless at the bottom.* This is why the technical tone of the market is so important. If the news is good, but the market has stopped going up, ask why, and then heed the call. Bottoms can be the most confusing. The accumulation phase, where the smart money is accumulating a position, can be marked by reactions, cross-currents, shakeouts, and false reversals. After the bottom is in place, many traders will be looking for the next break to be a buyer. After all, the market has been so weak so long, the odds favour at least one more break, right? But it never comes. The smart money won't let it. The objective after the bottom is in place is to move the market up to the next level, and the best time to buy may actually feel quite uncomfortable.

Secret 4: Have a Plan Before Trade, and then Work it!

If a trader has a plan and follow it, he avoids the emotionalism which is the major enemy of the trader. He must try to stay calm during the heart of the session, and remain focused. To do this, he has to be totally organised prior to the opening bell. His daily mission, should he decide to accept it, is to make money each day or, barring this, at least not lose much. In normal markets, he should take normal profits. In those unusual markets which occur rarely, he needs to go for abnormal profits. This is one of the keys to success. He must *always limit losses on trades which are not going according to plan.*

This takes willpower and is as essential a quality as having plenty of money. In fact, it is more important than having plenty of money. Money is not to hold on with, this is for the sheep and a trader doesn't want to be sheared. *If big risks are required, don't take the trade, wait for opportunities* where he could enter very close to his risk point. In this way his risk per trade is small in relation to the profit potential.

When it's not going right, *when in doubt, get out.* If a trader has a compass in the middle of the desert, and the oasis is north, he shouldn't get fooled into following the mirage to the west. There is nothing better than getting out *quickly* when one is wrong!

Secret 5: Be Aggressive when Taking Profit and/or Cutting Losses *if* there is a Good Reason to do so

A good trader will act without hesitation. When something is not right, he will liquidate early to save cash and worry. Never think too much, Just do it! And, doesn't limit his price—go at the market! Many times a market will give one optimal opportunity to act and that's it—go with it. The way to benefit through tuition is to act immediately!

Secret 6: No Regrets

When an intelligent trader liquidates a trade based on sound reasoning, he never regrets his decision. Go on, and if it was a mistake to get out, just learn from it. We all make them. By taking mistakes seriously, one will lose perspective and become too cautious in the future. Try not to think about the price to be entered. This is irrelevant. If the market isn't acting right, don't try to "get out at break even after commissions." This can get very expensive.

Secret 7: Money Management is the Key

Think about this daily. One need not to have a high win to loss ratio, but average win *must* be higher than average loss if one wants to succeed. To do this, there must be (at least some) "big hits" to offset the inevitable numerous (and hopefully small) losses which are going to happen.

It is noted that trader by being able to just cut losses early, by even a small incremental amount per trade, this can make a major difference to the bottom line. This takes decisiveness, so be decisive if the trade is not acting right. Waiting a "few more ticks" is generally not a recipe for success.

One more point there: it is bad practice to cancel or extend a stop loss order. One should never do this. It's OK to cancel a profit taking order at times, but the sooner a loss is stopped the better. When one gets, out of a bad position quickly, and with a minimum of trauma, not only is his capital base maintained, but his judgment will improve. Without a well-defined risk point, there's no judgment, what it's called is hope.

Secret 8: Success Comes Easier When you Specialise

Every market seems to have its own nature, its own personality. Some markets tend to make tops and bottoms with a fast run up and reverse (called an inverted V top or a V bottom). Some have rounding tops and bottoms, some double tops and bottoms, some tops and bottoms with a long consolidation. A trader can read a market better when he becomes, familiar with it's idiosyncrasies. Familiarity comes from concentration and experience. There are plenty of markets out there to be picked up one for each temperament.

Secret 9: Patience Pays!

Some people are in too big a hurry to get rich and as a result they go broke. Don't try to get rich in a few months. Don't try to catch all the fluctuations. Market movements of importance require weeks and even months to get ready. There's generally plenty of time to buy or ell one or two days, or longer, after a big move gets under way. There are times when a man or woman with nerve, knowledge, and a bit of luck can turn a small amount of money into a fortune. However, this cannot be done continually. The best trades come along only rarely. One needs to have patience to wait for the right trades. When they come, one must have the patience to not be overanxious and get in too soon or overtrade. Remember, every act, either opening or closing a trade, must have a sound basis behind it. Never trade for the thrill of it.

One last point on patience: once one is out of the market with a big profit, shouldn't be in too big a hurry to get back in. The best opportunities may be coming, but they're not there every day. One needs the patience to wait. Big account balances lead to the temptation to lay for less than desirable trades. If one makes a good profit, look at it this way: he can now *afford* to wait a few weeks or months for the signs of the next big mover.

***Secret 10:* Guts are as Important as Patience and More Important the Money!**

Some traders are too bold and as a result overtrade. However, some have trouble pulling the trigger. This is a weakness which must be corrected. One must train oneself to trade so there is no hope, no fear. When one enters or exits a position, one should do it decisively and without emotion. This is particularly important after a tough losing streak. Sometimes the traders who suffer a string of losses, through they still have some money left, and when the best opportunity of the year comes along (one they identified) they did not have the guts to act. In cases like this, guts are more valuable than money. Hence, the traders should have the guts to press hard when they are right. They also need the fortitude to cash in when it is most pleasurable.

***Secret 11:* The "Tape" (The Quote Machine) Will Trick you**

It's impossible for the man who stands over "the ticker" day by day to identify a big move before it starts. The tape will fool him every day while accumulation is taking place (and it takes time to accumulate or distribute a large position). The tape the quote machine) is there to fool traders. *"The tape moves in mysterious ways, the multitude to deceive."* Prices can look the weakest/strongest at the strongest/weakest times. Watching quotes all day will cause trader to constantly change his mind and trade too often, and this increases his percentage of being wrong. If he gets in wrong, the quote machine will tend to keep his in wrong longer than he should be because every tick his way will renew his hopes. If he gets in right, and he watches, the screen too closely, there will come a minor move which, in the long run means nothing, which will get him out. As a result he will lose a good position.

***Secret 12:* Be Skeptical**

In other words, it pays to be a *contrarian.* To be successful, a trader needs to be a student of human nature and do the opposite of the general public. Sell on his first clues of weakness, and doesn't wait until "everyone" is bailing out. The tip giver may be good-intentioned, but tips will invariably influence in the wrong direction. Remember, the market doesn't beat a trader rather a trader beats himself. Following tips and not the market is just another sign of human weakness.

***Secret 13:* Be Time Cognizant**

Know how much time the move has taken to get to the point it's at. This is important, because the longer a market moves in one direction, the greater the velocity of the buying or selling will be as the final stage approaches. In many cases, the significant portion of a major move takes place in the final 48 hours. One should watch the volume closely after a market has made a long-term move. Volume tends to run higher than normal at the end of a move. This is the "distribution zone," where the smart money is unloading their position to a public who is frenzied by news.

Actually, it's important to know what "zone" the market is in. Market phases tend to act in a similar manner. Many times, at the bottom, a market can rally on small volume. This indicates there really isn't much for sale. The bottom can follow a period of panicky conditions, pessimism, and apathy. Even the prior bulls will start to sound more cautions, and hint it could get worse before it gets better. It seems nobody is interested in buying. This is the time to watch moving averages closely. If they flash a buy signal, immediately cover shorts and start to buy. Tops ware the opposite of bottoms. It seems nobody notices the market is saturated, yet the market may top going up. After the first break from the top, many times there will be a low volume "failure test of the high." Once the market fails at a lower high, if the trader is not out already, this could be his last best chance to liquidate.

As a general rule, the big money is made in the last stage of a bull market, when prices are feverishly active. The big profits on the short side are made in the last stage of a bear market, when everyone wants to sell and it seems no one wants to be a buyer. It is always darkest before the dawn, and brightest at noon just before the sun starts to recede.

Secret 14: The Market's Reaction to the News is Crucial

It's not the news, but how the market reacts to the news, that's important. In other worlds, it's the news that sets the public perception. Be alert for divergences between the news and market action. It all has to do with *expectation versus reality.* Look for the divergence between what's happening and what people think is supposed to happen. When the big turn comes, the general public will always be looking the wrong way. There are certain ways to analyse reactions to news (or even a lack of news).

Consider the following:

- If bad news is announced, and the market starts to sell off in large volume, it's a good bet the market's going lower.
- If the market doesn't have much of a reaction to good news, it's probably been discounted.
- Moves of importances invariably tend to begin before there is any news to justify the initial price move. Once the move is under way, the emerging fundamentals will slowly come to light. *A big rally (decline) on NO NEWS is always very bullish (bearish).*
- It is generally not good practice to buy after a lot of very bullish news, or to sell after an extremely bearish report. Both good and bad news are many times already discounted in price. Of course, one should always consider whether the trend is down or up when the news is made known. A well-established trend will generally continue regardless of the news.

1 When unexpected news occurs (news which the market has not had time to prepare for) and the market opens in a wide range or "gaps" lower or higher, sell out longs, or cover shorts and wait. Watch the market for 30 minutes to an hour. If the market opened sharply lower, with heavy selling, and was not able to trade much lower than that, it's into support and can be bought at the market with a tight risk point. Watch the market closely at this point. Note the tone of the rally. If it is small and the market is able to again fall under the levels made when the bad news came out (or above the good) it is safe to assume the market is going lower (higher).

Secret 15: **Never Trade When Sick or Tired**

Good health is essential to success. If a trader is not feeling good, he should closed out positions and start over again when he does. Rest is equally essential to success. It is probably a good idea to periodically close out all trades, get entirely out of the market and go on vacation. The market will still be there at return. Some of the most successful traders trade their best right after a vacation. If one sticks to something too long without rest, judgment will become warped. Traders who are continually in the market day in and day out lose their perspective and will ultimately lose.

Secret 16: **Overtrading is One of Your Greatest Enemies**

Overtrading is the "greatest evil." It is the cause of more losses than anything else. The average novice trader really doesn't have a clue as to how much money is needed to be successful, and he or she invariably buys (or shorts) more than prudence dictates. He may be right in his analysis, or determination of the major trend, but due to too big a position is forced to liquidate at the margin calls. When he's liquidating so are the other novices, and that's when the smart money moves in. The money runs out just at that critical time when it is ripest to enter. The over-trader is exhausted and misses the profit opportunity he had once seen clearly in those more optimistic days.

Be conservative, keep cool, and avoid the temptation to trade more contracts than margin can reasonably support in normal markets. This is especially important at tops and bottoms where the excitement, the rumours, and the news are at fever pitch. Human nature has a tendency towards overconfidence at tops and bottoms. Study charts, and don't let good judgment be influenced by hopes or fears.

Secret 17: **Keep a Cool Head During "Blowoffs"**

Markets nearly always culminate at the top in the same way. When close to the end of a major move, markets can become wild. Volume is huge, activity is feverish and erratic, and the imagination blossoms. If a trader has the vision to ride the trend to this point his pay day has come. However, in extreme markets men and women of reason lose all sense of proportion. They start to believe the propaganda that the world will literally run out of this or that. It never happens. The history of the world shows that there has never been a time when a great demand for any commodity has not led to a supply in excess of demand.

Extreme markets are *not* the time to pyramid. They are the time to become alert for the end. All good things come to an end, and a trader will be to jump before the big bump. There will be a time when the herd will want to all exit out the same door at the same time. Make sure one should have already left the room. When everyone wants to sell, and all buying support disappears, profits can run into losses fast. In the stock market crash of 1987, profits made in the first ten months of the year were wiped out in three days.

How does a trader turn his paper profits into cash in a runaway market? In blowoff markets the corrections are generally short and sweet. The market is feverish and everyone is bullish (the bears have already thrown in the towel). The public is buying madly. Weeks may go by without a major correction. One will hear of fortunes being made, and if someone is fortunate enough to be on the move, his paper profits will grow geometrically. The end may be near, but nobody can see it. In fact, only about 10 per cent of those with big paper profits will ever cash in near the top.

The Golden Rules in this type of market are: first, it does not pay to take a loss amounting to more than two consecutive days' fluctuations. If the market goes against for two days it's likely to go more. *Secondly, be alert for a morning when the market opens off dramatically without any news.* It may weekly rally, but the rally will fail. This is the first sign of the end. The market has reached the saturation point where it's run out of buyers. Supply has finally overwhelmed demand. *Third, watch for a failure test of the high.* Many times after the first break the market will have a secondary rally which will fail *under* the high. If a trader failes to get out on the first break, this is his last good chance.

Secret 18: Never Let a Good Profit Turn into a Loss

There is one of the trading sins which has ruined many hopes. If a trader has a decent profit in any position, and he is sure it is going to grow, the stop won't be hit. Should the market continue to move in favour, keep moving the stop to lock in some profit. The objective is to always protect principal in every way possible, and when he is fortunate enough to start accumulating paper profits, lock 'em in.

Secret 19: When in Doubt, Get Out!

If it's not acting right, according to plan, get out. If the market has not started to move in favour within a reasonable amount of time, get out. A trader's judgment will deteriorate the longer he hangs on to a losing position and at extremes he will do the wrong thing. One of the old timers once said something to the effect: *"I am prudent enough not to stand in the middle of the railroad tracks while I decide if the headlight I see is a freight train or an illusion."*

Secret 20: Diversify

Distribute risk among a variety of trades and markets. Divide capital into tenths and never risk more than a maximum of 10 per cent on any one trade. One good profit will often totally erase four or five small losers. But if a trader takes big losses and small profits he will have no chance of success. He should concentrating on active, liquid markets which will allow him to enter and exit when he wants to with a minimum of slippage.

Secret 21: Pyramid Correctly

The big money can only be made by a pyramiding a good position in a trending market. A trader has an excellent opportunity to use leverage and his unrealised profits to create a larger position than otherwise possible. Pyramiding takes both courage and self-control. The "weak hands" seldom make the big money, primarily because they do not have the guts to pyramid and maximise the opportunities they are correct about (or they do not have the smarts to do it right).

Be advised, there is a right way and a wrong way to pyramid. The traders should never reverse pyramid (that is, add a greater number of contracts than their initial position as the market moves their way). First risk should be greatest risk. It is generally better to decrease the size of position through the journey, not increase it. In this way, a trader has the opportunity to increase his profitability without dramatically increasing his risk. Other useful pyramid rules are:

i) Never try to pyramid after a long advance or decline. The time to begin a pyramid is when the trend first turns up or down after a long move., Technical indicators can help here.

ii) It is always safer to pyramid after a market moves out of accumulation and/ or distribution. In other words, a breakout from consolidation. Remember, the longer the time it takes prior to the breakout, the greater the move one can expect.

Secret 22: **Watch for Those "Breakouts from Consolidation"**

A trader needs to know what kind of market he is in. In a consolidating market money can be made by scalping small moves back and forth. However, one won't make the big money with this kind of market action, and one should never attempt to pyramid. Big profits can be made in the runs between accumulation and distribution. One can make more money by waiting until a commodity plainly declares its trend, than by getting in before the move starts. Too many traders are fixated on picking the top or bottom and as a result miss the big picture. *Get the idea of prices out of head and concentrate on market action. Forget about picking tops and bottoms.*

The longer the consolidation the better. When a market has remained for a long time in a narrow range, a breakout from the range becomes more significant. The market is telling that a major shift in the supply/demand fundamentals is taking place. Because it has taken a long time to form, there is more fuel available for the coming move. This is the best type of market to play to the hilt!

One last point here: remember there is no Holy Grail and at times there will be false breakouts. Watch for them. It's most likely false if the market again trades into the consolidation range. The best ones will never retrace into the breakout range, but it is OK for a market to trade back to the upper or lower edge of the range before resuming new trend action. There is no question it was false once it breaks through to the other side. When this happens, a reversal play is the best course of action.

Secret 23: **Go with the Relative Strength**

It is important to follow the trend of each market and to always buy the strong one and sell the weak one. This is especially important for related markets. Silver and gold are both precious metals and will generally move in the same direction. They will move at different speeds, however. The trader needs to judge a market by its own signs, and always sell the weak one and buy the strong.

Secret 24: **Limit Moves are Important Indicators of Support and Resistance**

When a market moves "bid limit up," or "offered limit down" (for those market which still have limits), this is a level where a trader theoretically is unable to be a buyer or a seller. There is more demand at the limit up price than available supply, and vice versa. The market should continue in the direction of the limit move. On corrections, it should find support above the limit price (or below if a limit down type move). Watch for this. If a market again trades under the limit bid price, or above the limit offered, *go with the flow*. These are reasonably risked trades, since it is an indication the previous support or resistance is now absent. If anyone can now buy a market where it previously was unable to be brought (of sell where he previously couldn't) this is a major sign of weakness or strength.

***Secret 25:* Never Average a Loss**

This is critical. There are some traders who have had great success averaging down. When a stock they liked got cheaper, they bought more. When the long-term trend turned back up, they make out like bandits. A leveraged market is different, however averaging a loss may work four times out of five, but that fifth will wipe the trader out. It is a bad habit to get into.

Look at it this way: if a trader makes a trade, and it starts to go against him, then he is wrong—at least temporarily. Why buy or sell more to average the loss? When it's getting worse day by day, why should he potentially compound the problem? Stop the loss early before it is eternally too large, and don't make it worse. If a trader could avoid three weaknesses—*overtrading, failing to place a stop loss*, and *averaging a loss*—he will be a success.

ILLUSTRATIVE PROBLEMS

1. XYZ Co. buys mark futures contracts to cover possible exchange losses on her import orders denominated in German marks. The company has to put up an initial margin of $ 2,500. The maintenance margin imposed by the exchange is 80 per cent of the initial margin, or $ 2,000. When would XYZ get a margin call from its broker?

Ans.

If the spot rate for marks declines, the value of XYZ company position declines. As long as the decline is less than $ 500, the company does not need to put up any additional margin. Yet, if the cumulative decline in value comes to $ 501, the company margin account would stand at $ 1,999. The company would get a margin call from its brokerage firm and must restore the account to the initial level of $2,500. Otherwise, the exchange will sell out the company position and return any remaining balance in XYZ Co.'s account.

2. R.K. Sen, a speculator, enters into a futures contract for March delivery of 125,000 German marks on February 1. The futures exchange rate of the German mark for March delivery (March 15) is $0.5939 per mark. The margin requirement is 2 per cent. His expectation of the spot rate for marks on March 15 is $0.6117. If his expectation proves correct, what would be his rate of return on investment?

Ans.

Because the margin requirement is 2 per cent, Sen may control this delivery of DM 125,000 for $1,484.75 (DM125,000 x $0.5939 x 0.02). He could buy DM125,000 futures for $74,237.50 at the futures quotation of $0.5939, receive them on March 15, and then sell them at the spot rate of $0.6117 for a gross of $76,462.50. Profit would be $2,225. So, he would earn a net profit of $2,225 or 150 per cent on the original investment of $1,484.75. Here, the exchange rate would rise by only 3 per cent [(0.6117 - 0.5939)/0.5939], but the rate of return on investment is 150 per cent. Yet, the same leverage could lead to equally substantial losses. If the spot rate declines by 3 per cent during this period, Sen would lose about 150 per cent of his investment.

QUESTIONS

1. What are the major differences between forward and futures contracts?
2. What is the most important difference between futures and options contracts?
3. What are the major types of margin with respect to a futures contract? What is the role of margin requirement?
4. How can speculators use currency futures?
5. How can transnational companies use currency futures?
6. Forward contracts entail default risk because either party could walk away from its obligation at the contact's maturity. From a bank's point of view, is this default risk greater or less than a loan of the same face amount?
7. Why are forward contract nontransferable?
8. How can one get out of a forward contract?
9. Why do traders use two transactions instead of just one to hedge a forward-exchange contract?
10. Identify the different ways in which a foreign-exchange dealer can hedge a forward transaction. State briefly how each is done.
11. Why is the long-dated forward market less active than the short-dated market?
12. List the ways in which futures contracts differ form forward contracts.
13. Explain the connection between daily cash compensation of gains and losses in the futures market and the risk of default on these contracts.
14. What are the three ways in which futures contracts reduce credit risk?
15. "Futures contracts are like forward contracts, recontracted daily." Explain.
16. Since a forward market already existed, why was it necessary to establish currency futures and currency options contracts?
17. What are currency future options?
18. Suppose that Timex Instruments (TI) must pay a French supplier FF 10 million in 90 days.
    (a) Explain how TI can use currency futures to hedge its exchange risk. How many futures contracts will TI need to fully protect itself?
    (b) Explain how TI can use currency options to hedge its exchange risk. How many options contracts will TI need to fully protect itself?
    (c) Discuss the advantages and disadvantages of using currency futures versus currency options to hedge TI's exchange risk.

PROBLEMS

1. An American company sells yen futures contracts to cover possible exchange losses on its export orders denominated in Japanese yen. The amount of the initial margin is $20,000, and the maintenance margin is 75 per cent of the initial

margin. The value of the company's position declines by $6,000 because the spot rate for yen has increased.

(a) What is the dollar amount of the maintenance margin?

(b) Should the broker issue margin calls to the company?

(c) What is the amount of additional deposit needed to restore the account to the initial margin level?

2. On April 1, the spot price of the British pound was $ 1.86 and the price of the June futures contract was $ 1.85. During April the pound appreciated, so that by May 1 it was selling for $ 1.91. What do you think happened to the price of the June pound futures contract during April? Explain.

3. A speculator enters a futures contract for September delivery (September 19) of £62,500 on February 2. The futures exchange rate is $ 1.6500 per pound. He believes that the spot rate for pounds on September 19 will be $1.700 per pound. The margin requirement is 2 per cent.

(a) If his expectations are correct, what would be his rate of return on investment?

(b) If the spot rate for pounds on September 19 is 5 per cent lower than the futures exchange rate, how much would he lose on the futures speculation?

(c) If there is a 65 per cent chance that the spot rate for pounds will increase to $ 1.700 by September 19, would you speculate in the futures market?

4. On March 20, a Detroit investor decides to invest $1 million in a British three-month certificate of deposit (CD) with an annual yield of 20 per cent. He expects that this 20 per cent rate of return on the British CD is more than he could have realised by investing in the domestic market. The investor buys British pounds in the spot market and purchases the CD from a British bank. The exchange rates are $ 2.0000 per pound in the spot market and $ 2.0050 per pound in the futures market for June delivery (June 20).

(a) The investor buys enough British pounds in the futures market to cover the principal and accrued interest at the time of maturity. Summarise the transaction.

(b) By June 20, the British pound has depreciated to $ 1.8500 per pound. Remember that the spot rate and the futures rate become the same by the delivery date. On June 20, the investor decides to close the position by selling British pounds in the spot market and reversing the futures contracts. Summarise the transaction.

(c) Compare the exchange gain (loss) from the futures transaction with the exchange loss (gain (loss) from the futures transaction with the exchange loss (gain) from the spot transaction. What is the windfall profit (net exchange gain)?

(d) If the investor had not hedged his investment, how much exchange loss would he have suffered on the transaction? Remember that the British pound depreciated to $ 1.8500 on June 20.

5. Examine the forward and futures prices for the Canadian dollar reproduced in the accompanying tables. Can you identify an arbitrage opportunity between the over-the-counter forward market and the CME futures market? How, specifically, would a bank exploit this opportunity? What are the risks of doing so?

CURRENCY FUTURES ON THE CHICAGO MERCANTILE EXCHANGE. WEDNESDAY, FEB 10, 1998

	Open	High	Low	Settle	Change	Lifetime High	Lifetime Low	Open Interest
Japan Yen (CME)-12.5 million yen; $ per yen (.00)								
Mar	.8258	.8289	.8219	.8261	+ .0008	.8372	.7445	63,699
June	.8284	.8287	.8236	.8264	+ .0008	.8340	.7745	1,361
Sept	—	—	—	.8273	+ .0008	.8260	.7995	1,010
Dec	—	—	—	.8286	+ .0008	.8205	.7970	1,522
Est vol 7851; vol Tues 44,796; open int 67,592, - 12,133.								
Deutschemark (CME)- 125,000 marks; $ per mark								
Mar	.6044	6057	.5988	.5998	- .0025	.7025	.5724	132,596
June	.5965	.5985	.5920	.5927	- .0026	.6920	.5890	16,146
Sept	.5928	.5928	.5870	.5874	- .0026	.6720	.5875	3,095
Est vol 75,749; vol Tues 37,342; open int 151,858, + 942.								
Canadian Dollar (CME) - 100,000 dollors.; $ per Can$								
Mar	.7876	.7894	.7869	.7887	+ .0018	.8712	.7610	19,751
June	.7822	.7833	.7815	.7830	+ .0021	.8360	.7532	2,150
Sept	.7760	.7780	.7760	.7776	+ .0022	.8335	.7515	852
Dec	—	—	—	.7726	+ .0023	.8310	.7470	584
Est vol. 3,023; vol. Tues 6,121; open int 23,366, - 1,239.								

SPOT AND FORWARD INTERBANK FOREIGN EXCHANGE MARKET. WEDNESDAY, FEBRUARY 10, 1998

The New York Foreign-exchange selling rates below apply to trading among banks in amounts of $ 1 million and more, as quoted at 3 p.m. Eastern time by Bankers Trust Co., Telerate, and other sources, Retail transactions provide fewer units of foreign currency per dollar.

	U.S. $ equiv.		*Currency per U.S. $*	
Country	*Wed.*	*Tues.*	*Wed.*	*Tues.*
Argentina (Peso)	1.01	1.01	.99	.99
Australia (Dollar)	.6727	.6705	1.4865	1.4914
Australia (Schilling)	.08564	.08574	11.86	11.66
Bahrain (Dinar)	2.6522	2.6522	.3771	.3771
Belgium (Franc)	.02916	.02923	34.29	34.21
Brazil (Cruzeiro)	.000523	.000523	19110.01	18800.03
Britain (Pound)	1.4260	1.4317	.7013	.6985
30-Day Forward	1.4225	1.4282	.7062	.7035
90-Day Forward	1.4160	1.4215	.7062	.7070
180-Day Forward	1.4090	1.4144	.7097	.7070
Canada (Dollar)	.7913	.7889	1.2637	1.2676
30-Day Forward	.7896	.7871	1.2665	1.2705
90-Day Forward	.7859	.7833	1.2724	1.2767
180-Day Forward	.7803	.7774	1.2815	1.2863

Source: *The Wall Street Journal,* Thursday, February 11, 1998.

6. Jose Ballini is a currency trader and speculator for Abdul Hamid, one of the largest investment banking firms in Middle East. The current spot rate is D1.7800/ $, and the 360-day forward rate is D1.8860/$. Jose believes the dinar will actually appreciate against the U.S. dollar in the coming year.
   (a) What should he do with the D500,000 he has to take a position with?
   (b) If the spot rate at the end of 360 days is D1.4688/$, what was Jose's profit and rate of return on his investment in part (a)?
   (c) If the spot rate at the end of 360 days is D1.9800/$, what was Jose's profit and rate of return on his investment in part (a)?
7. The UK Treasurer of Andy Harris expects to receive a payment for wool exports to a customer in Munich in 3 months time. Her marketing department has sold 1000 '100% wool suits' for a delivered price of 250 euros each. In the *Financial Times* on 10th June she reads the following:

Spot FX rate	0.850 (€/£)
3-month forward FX rate	0.853 (€/£)
£—3-month interest rate (annualised)	r = 5(9/16) (=0.055625)
Euro—3-month interest rate (annualised)	r^* = 7(1/16) (=0.07625)

   (a) Explain, using the above data, how the Treasurer can hedge her receipts in euros by: (i) taking forward cover; (ii) taking money market cover.
   (b) What would be the amount of sterling received if the Treasurer took an uncovered (open) position and the spot rates in 3 months time are as follows: (i) 0.653 (€/£); (ii) 0.658 (€/£); and, (iii) 0.640 (€/£). In each case, compare the hedged outcome with the uncovered outcome.
   (c) Does the set of interest and exchange rates prevailing on 15th June conform with covered interest parity? If not, explain how equilibrium will be established in the relevant markets.
8. Suppose the interest rate in the USA over a 6-month horizon is 10% p.a. (continuously compounded) and in the UK is 5% p.a. The current spot rate S = 2($/£). If covered interest parity holds then is sterling at a forward premium or discount against the dollar, and by how much? Explain. Is the market in 'contango' or 'backwardation'?
9. You are Corporate Treasurer of a US multinational and on 27th June you learn that your British subsidiary will transfer £10m to New York on 28th September. You decided to hedge the position using currency future on IMM (CME). Spot and futures rate on 27th June are:

   S_0 = 1.3630 ($/£) F_0 = 1.3750 ($/£)

   ON 28th September the rates are:

   S_1 = 1.2375 ($/£) F_1 = 1.2380 ($/£)

   (a) What expiry month for the future would you choose (September, October or December)?
   (b) Would you go long or short sterling futures and how many contracts would you purchase/sell? (One sterling futures contract is for deliverity of £62,500).
   (c) What is the unhedged and hedged outcome on September 28th?
   (d) What is the initial 'basis' and the final 'basis'? What do these imply?

12

CURRENCY OPTIONS

INTRODUCTION

In 1902, a team of French archaeologists uncovered an eight-foot high slab of black stone buried in the desert sand near Susa, Iraq. Carved on the stone in ancient Babylonian script was the world's first complete set of written laws—the famous Code of Hammurabi.

Hammurabi, who lived about 3800 years ago, was the king of Babylon and in his Code he claimed his authority from the Gods. The most common punishment for breaking the Code was death. According to legal scholars, the Code was largely a revision of common law existing at the time; in other words Hammurabi was effectively rubber-stamping the individual 'eye-for-an-eye' codes of personal retribution which were then in use.

But one of Hammurabi's laws, paragraph 48, was different. It doesn't mention punishment, but only says that in the event of a crop disaster, those who owe debts need not pay any interest for one year. The Babylonians used clay tablets for writing on, and in Hammurabi's words, debtors could *'wash the debt tablet in water'*, or erase the loan contract, for the year of the crop failure.

At first sight, paragraph 48 resembles insurance. After all, it refers to debts being payable in grain, while the word 'rent' is used instead of 'interest', suggesting that a typical debtor would have been a farmer paying a mortgage on his property. In a year of crop failure, farmers suffer losses, and like a good politician Hammurabi is insuring them against being unable to pay then debts.

However, paragraph 48 is more subtle than that. Firstly, there is that issue of payment in grain, which suggests farmers were involved. But the Babylonian economy was founded on grain, and while loans were made in silver, it made sense to use grain to repay the debts because it was available everywhere.

And if there is one thing we can be sure about with grain, when the harvest fails, the price goes up because demand outstrips supply. In modern finance, we would say that debtors were 'exposed' to the grain price. This brings us to the second point. Insurance is about losses, which have to be proved before claims can be paid. Yet, paragraph 48 doesn't mention losses, and nor does it mention farmers, who after all might even benefit from inflated grain prices. So it can't be insurance.

Then what is paragraph 48 all about? When a crop failure happened, the debtors had the right to pay nothing that year. The lenders, on the other hand, had no choice in the matter: they had to do without the interest. In other words, the debtors had an option to call upon the lenders to cover their interest payments in the event of crop failure, which effectively put a cap on their grain price exposure.

Paragraph 48 is the earliest written example of an option contract, which is often mistakenly attributed to the Greek philosopher Thales, who lived 1200 years later. Hammurabi's option derives its value both from the existence of a loan - it's worthless without one - and also from crop failures which impact the price of grain. What's' missing from paragraph 48 is how crop failure was defined in practice, and one wonders how often Hammurabi himself was asked to settle disputes between lenders and borrowers seeking to 'wash their tablets'.

What does Hammurabi's option tell us about risk? The risk of crop failure hasn't been removed, but only transferred, to lenders. Being wealthy, the lenders might be better suited to take on the risk. Then again, they might not want to, but disobeying Hammurabi tended to result in excruciating death.

However, Hammurabi doesn't say what the interest rate should be on loans. More recent archaeological research has shown that there was a thriving loan market in ancient Babylon where borrowers could search for the best rate, just as homebuyers do today.

Now imagine that we are lenders in the market of Babylon, and we have just heard that Hammurabi is to make us give an option to every borrower. If we are smart, we should increase the interest rate we charge to compensate us for the extra risk. That involves pricing the option—in other words, charging today for what we might have to pay tomorrow. While there is no historical evidence the Babylonian lenders ever actually did this, the problem is similar to that tackled by Black, Merton and Scholes 3800 later.

OPTION: THE CONCEPT

An option is a type of a contract between two parties when one person grants the other person the right to buy a specific asset at a specific price within a specific time period. Alternatively, the contract may grant the other party the right to sell a specific asset at a specific price within a specific time period. The person who has received the right and thus has a decision to make is known as the option buyer since he or she must pay for the right. The person who has sold the right to the buyer and thus must respond to the buyer's decision is known as the *option writer.*

In a forex market with a forward contract, one can lock in an exchange rate for the future. There are a number of circumstances however, in which it may be desirable to have more flexibility than a forward provides. For example, a computer manufacturer in India may have sales priced in U.S. dollars as well as a euro in Europe. Depending on the relative strength of the two currencies, revenues may be realised in either euro or dollars. In such a situation the use of forward or futures would be inappropriate: there's no point in hedging something the company might not have. What is called for is a foreign-exchange option: the right, but not the obligation, to exchange currency at a predetermined rate. A foreign-exchange option is a contract for future delivery of a specific currency in exchange for another, in which the holder of the option has the right to buy (or sell) the currency at an agreed price, the *strike* or exercise price, but is not *required* to do so. The right to buy is a *call;* the right to sell, a *put.* For such a right the buyer pays a price called the **option premium.** The option seller receives the premium and is obliged to make (or take) delivery at the agreed-upon price if the buyer exercises his option. In some options, the instrument being delivered is the currency itself; in others, it is a futures contract on the currency. *American options permit the holder to exercise at any time before the expiration date; European options, only on the expiration date.*

MARKET STRUCTURE

Options are purchased and traded either on an organised exchange (such as the Philadelphia Stock Exchange on in the *over-the counter* (OTC) *market. Exchange-traded options or listed options* are standardised contracts with predetermined exercise prices, standard maturities (one, three, six, nine, and 12 months), and fixed maturities (March, June, September, and December). Options are traded in standard contracts half the size of the IMM futures contracts,. Cross-rate options are also available for the DM/Y, £/DM, and £/Y. By taking the U.S. dollar out of the equation, cross-rate option allow one to hedge directly the currency risk that arises when dealing with nondollar currencies. Contract specifications are shown in Exhibit-1. The PHLX trades both American-style and European-style currency options. It also trades month-end options, which ensure the availability of a short-term (at most, a two- or sometimes three-week) currency option at all times, and long-term options, which extend the available expiration months on PHLX dollar-based and cross-rate contracts—providing for 18-, 24-, 30-, and 36- month European-style options.

In 1994, the PHLX introduced a new option contract, called the *Virtual Currency Option,* which is settled in U.S. dollars rather than in the underlying currency. Virtual Currency Options, also called 3-Ds (dollar-denominated delivery), just formalise the fact that practically no exchange-traded options involve the payment or delivery of the underlying currency. 3-D Deutsche marks were the first Virtual Currency Option to be introduced. They are two-week options, and they settle weekly (meaning that each week a new contract is listed). They expire on Monday mornings, making it easy to hedge currency risk over a weekend.

Other organised options exchanges are located in Amsterdam (European Options Exchange), Chicago (Chicago Mercantile Exchange), and Montreal (Montreal Stock Exchange).

OTC options are contracts whose specifications are generally negotiated as to the amount, exercise price and rights, underlying instrument, and expiration. *OTC Currency Options* are traded by commercial and investment banks in virtually all finance centers. OTC activities is concentrated in London and New York and it centres on the major currencies, most often involving U.S. dollars against pounds sterling, Deutsche marks, Swiss francs, Japanese yen, and Canadian dollars Branches of foreign banks in the major financial centres are generally willing at write options against the currency of their home country. For example, Australian banks in London

EXHIBIT-1

PHILADELPHIA STOCK EXCHANGE SELECTED CURRENCY OPTIONS SPECIFICATIONS

	Australian Dollar	*British Ponds*	*Canadian Dollar*	*Deutschi Mark*	*Currency Unit*	*Swiss Franc*	*French Franc*	*Japanese Yen*
Symbol								
American style	XAD	XBP	XCD	XDM	ECU	XSF	SFF	XJY
European style	CAD	CBP	CCD	DCM	n.a.	CSF	CFF	CJY
Contract size	A$50,000	£31,250	C$50,000	DM 62,500	ECU 62,500	SFr 62,500	FF 250,000	Y6,250,000
Exercise Price Intervals	1¢	2.5¢	1¢[1]	2¢	1¢[1]	0.25c	0.01c	0.01c[1]
Premium Quotations	Cents per unit	Cents per unit	Cents per unit	Cents per unit	Cents per unit	Cents per unit	Tenths of a cent per unit	Hunderedths of a cent per unit
Minimum Price Change	$0.(00)01	$0.(00)01	$0.(00)01	$0.(00)01	$0.(00)01	$0.(00)01	$0.(000)02	$0.(0000)01
Minimum Contract Price Change	$5.00	$3.125	$5.00	$6.25	$6.25	$6.25	$5.00	$6.25
Expiration	**Months**—March, June, September, and December + two near-term months							

Exercise Notice	No automatic exercise of in-the-money options
Expiration Date	Friday before third Wednesday of the month (Friday is also the last trading day)
Expiration Settlement Date	Third Wednesday of month
Daily Price Limits	None
Issuer and Guarantor	Options Clearing Corporation (OCC)
Margin for Uncovered Writer	Option premium plus 4% of the underlying contract value less out-of-the-money amount, if any, to a minimum of the option premium plus 3/4% of the underlying contract value. Contract value equal spots price times unit of currency per contract.
Position and Exercise Limits	100,000 contracts
Trading Hours	3:30 A.M. – 2:30 P.M. Philadelphia time, Monday through Friday[2]

1. Half-point strike prices for DM (0.5c), and Y (0.005c) in the three near-term months only.
2. Trading hours for the Canadian dollar are 7:00 A.M. — 2.30 P.M. Philadelphia Time, Monday through Friday.

Source: Standardised Currency Options Contract Specifications, Philadelphia Stock Exchange, 1995.

write options on the Australian dollar. OTC option are generally traded on round lots, commonly $ 5-$10 million in New York and $2-$3 million in London. The average maturity of OTC options ranges from two to six months, and very few options are written for more than one year American options are most common, but European options are popular in Switzerland and Germany because of familiarity.

The OTC options market consists of two sectors: (1) *retail market* composed of nonbank customers who purchase from banks what amounts to customised insurance against adverse exchange rate movements and (2) a *wholesale market* among commercial banks, investment banks, and specialised trading firms; this market may include interbank OTC trading or trading on the organised exchanges. The interbank market in currency options is analogous to the interbanks markets in spot and forward exchange. Banks use the wholesale market to hedge or "reinsure," the risks undertaken in trading with customers and to take speculative positions in options.

Most retail customers for OTC options are either corporations active in international trade or financial institutions with multicurrency asset portfolios. These customers could purchase foreign exchange puts or calls on organised exchanges, but they generally turn to the banks for options in order to find precisely the terms that match their needs. Contracts are generally tailored with regard to amount, strike price, expiration date, and currency.

CURRENCY OPTION QUOTES

Figure-1 displays a typical newspaper quotation of currency option prices. Currency options, which are now traded worldwide, and regarded as key instruments of the global foreign-exchange market. Daily quotations can be found both in newspapers and on trading screens such as Reuters and Telerate. Exchanges in Philadelphia, Amsterdam, Chicago, and Montreal began to offer options in the early 1980s in several major currencies. Since then, markets for listed options have grown tremendously in size and trading volume. The Amsterdam, Montreal, and Philadelphia stock exchanges offer option on stop currencies, while the Chicago Mercantile Exchange, LIFFE in London, and SIMEX in Singapore trade in options on foreign-currency futures contracts.

Only exchange-traded options are quoted in the press. These "listed" options are standardised. Each option contract is written for the same foreign-currency amount.

The expiration dates are the Saturday preceding the third Wednesday of March, June. September, and December. Listed options are available in maturities of 3, 6, 9, and 12 months only. Today, foreign-exchange options are available in a variety of currencies including Australian dollars, British pounds, Canadian dollars, French francs, Swiss francs, German marks, and Japanese yen. Quotes for these options are listed in *The Financial Times, The Wall Street Journal,* and other financial newspapers daily.

The options in Figure-1 are those traded on the IMM in Chicago, where the contract is for options on futures. From such quotations the investor may see which options are actively traded and perhaps find one that meets his needs. Say, for example, the investor accepts to receive ¥25 million in May and is prepared to pay to be sure of getting at least 68 cents per 100 yen. This implies that the investor wants, to buy *two* Japanese-yen put options at a strike price of 68. According tot he quotations, this could cost the investor 1.39 cents per 1000 yen, or $ 1,737.50 per contract.

FIGURE-1

CURRENCY-OPTIONS QUOTATIONS

OPTIONS ON FUTURES

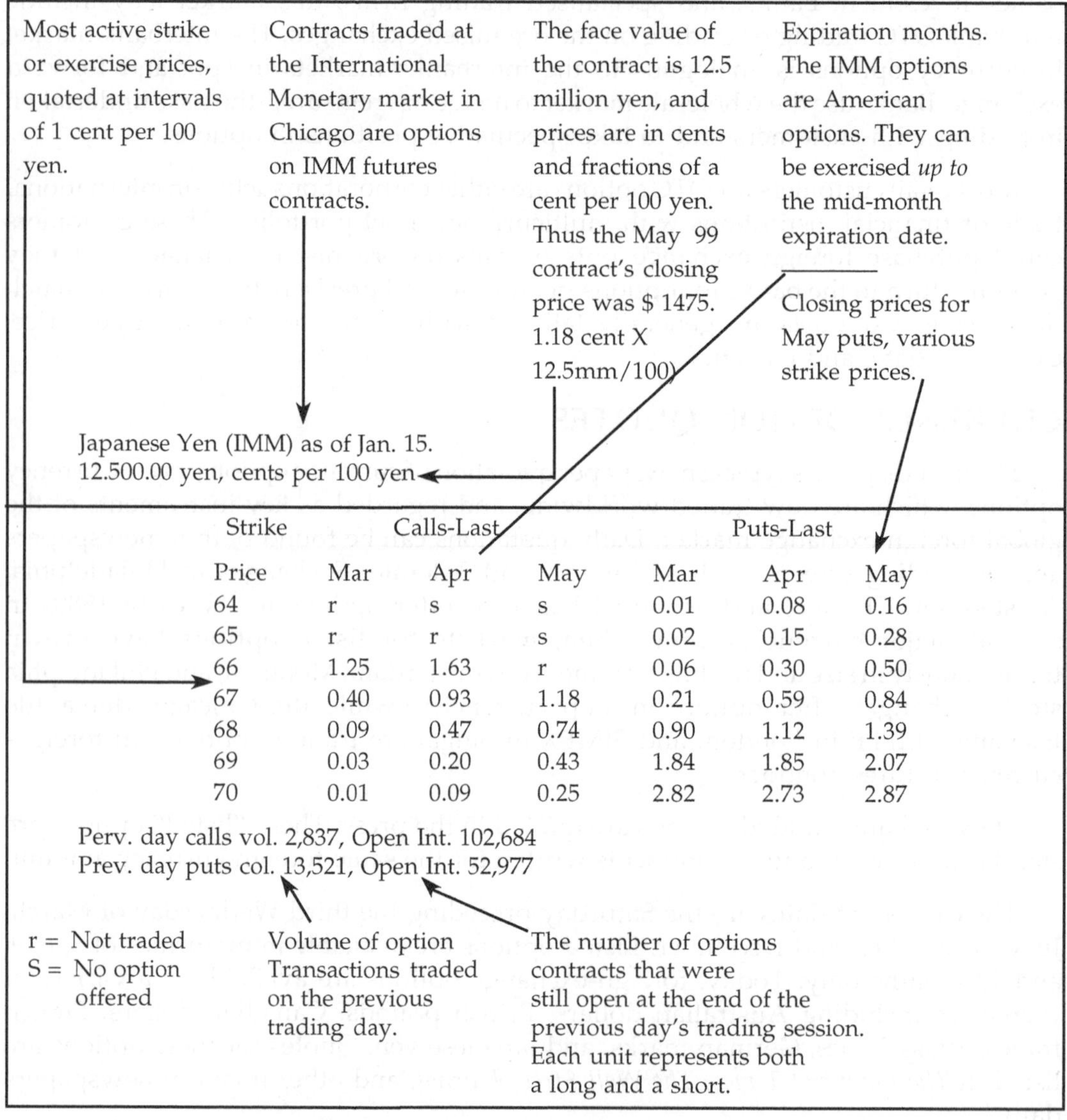

Strike	Calls-Last			Puts-Last		
Price	Mar	Apr	May	Mar	Apr	May
64	r	s	s	0.01	0.08	0.16
65	r	r	s	0.02	0.15	0.28
66	1.25	1.63	r	0.06	0.30	0.50
67	0.40	0.93	1.18	0.21	0.59	0.84
68	0.09	0.47	0.74	0.90	1.12	1.39
69	0.03	0.20	0.43	1.84	1.85	2.07
70	0.01	0.09	0.25	2.82	2.73	2.87

HOW TO READ CURRENCY OPTION QUOTAS?

To illustrate it the closing prices of the options for several currencies as reported in *The Wall Street Journal* on one recent Thursday have been presented in Table-1. The top line gives the size of a single contract, such as 31,250 pounds per contract; the name of the currency, such as British pounds; and the way in which prices are quoted, such as cents per pound. Yen prices and yen option prices are the number of 100ths of a cent per unit of a foreign currency. All other currency prices are the number of U.S. cents per unit of a foreign currency.

The first column shows the name of the currency, such as B Pound (British pound). The 168.17 listed below B Pound is the closing price of the pound on the Philadelphia Exchange that day; that is, the closing price of the British pound during the day was $1.6817 per pound.

TABLE - 1

CURRENCY OPTIONS IN PHILADELPHIA EXCHANGE

Option and Underlying	*Strike Price*	*Calls-Last*			*Puts-Last*		
		Feb	Mar	Jan	Feb	Mar	Jun
31,250 British Pounds-cents per unit.							
B Pound	160	8.10	r	r	r	r	r
168.17	165.5	5.24	r	r	0.25	r	r
168.17	165	r	r	r	r	1.85	r
168.17	167.5	r	2.20	r	1.70	3.00	r
168.17	170	r	1.40	r	r	4.55	r
168.17	171.5	0.30	0.84	r	r	r	r
168.17	175	r	r	1.35	r	r	r
6,250,000 Japanese Yen-100ths of a cent per unit.							
JYen	68	r	r	2.36	0.14	r	0.82
69.29	69	0.75	1.05	1.76	0.34	0.63	1.22
69.29	69.5	0.49	r	s	r	r	s
69.29	70	0.30	0.58	1.37	0.93	1.19	r
69.29	70.5	0.15	r	s		r	s
69.29	71	0.09	0.34	0.92	r	r	r
69.29	72	0.06	0.14	0.64	r	r	r

Total Call Vol. 47,086 Call open int. 369,838
Total Put Vol. 23,701 Put open int. 343,124
r-Not traded. s-No option offered.
Last is premium (purchase price)

Source: *The Wall Street Journal.*

The second column from the left of the quotation shows various strike prices, prices of the underlying currency at which options confer the right to buy or sell. There are seven different strike prices listed for the British pound, which means that there were seven options available for the British pound. These strikes prices ranged from $ 1.60 per pound to $ 1.75 per pound. Then follow two groups of three prices. The first gives closing prices or premiums for call options at a given strike price valid until each of three different months. The second group gives the closing prices or premiums for put options at a given strike price valid until each of the three months. If a given option is not traded, this column shows an "r" footnote. If the option is not offered, it shows a "s" footnote.

The premium for a pound call option with a strike price of $ 1.60 and a February settlement date is 8.10 cents. Because the pound option comes in a standardised volume of 31,250 units, the price of this call option per contract is $2,531.25 (0.081 x 31,250). Thus, one call option on the British pound with a strike price of $ 1.60 and a February settlement date would give the holder the right to buy 31,250 pounds for $ 50,000 ($1.60 x 31,250). The premium for a pound put option with a strike price of $ 1.675 and a February settlement date is 1.70 cents. So, an investor can buy this put option for $531.25 (0.017 x 31,250). One put option with a strike price of $ 1.675 and a February settlement date would give the holder the right to sell 31.250 pounds for $52,343.75 ($1.675 x 31,250).

At the end of the listing is a summary of the trading on the Philadelphia Exchange for the day. Total call volume (47,086) and total put volume (23,701) show the number of options traded that day. Call open interest (369,838) and put open interest (343,124) show the number of options outstanding.

Generally, prices are highest for call options whose strike price is below the spot rate and for put options whose strike price is above the spot rate. The volume of option trading is frequently large relative to trading in the underlying currency. This reflects trading by professionals who make their money on numerous but short-term transactions and by holders of foreign exchange who hedge large blocks with options. Such hedging provides a price protection similar to that offered by currency futures.

CURRENCY-OPTION PRICING

To a large extent, currency options are priced like other kinds of options—stock options, commodity options, interest-rate options, and index options. All options provide the option buyer with downside protection and upside opportunity, and it is the value of this combination that gives the option its value.

Put differently, *the value of any option depends crucially on the probability of the option's being exercised.* Figure-1 illustrates that some of the quoted option contracts are quite likely to be exercised, and others are quite unlikely. It shows that the March futures price was 67.19 cents per 100 yen. A deep-out-of-the-money option, such as the March 70 call, is rather unlikely to be exercised, because there is a pretty trivial probability that the Japanese-yen futures price will rise to 70 by the March 15 exercise date. One shouldn't bet much on that horse; neither, apparently, will the market. Look at Figure-2, a diagram of how theoretical currency-option prices change with different currency-futures prices. The deep-out-of-the-money option, on which the strike price far exceeds the current market-level index, is worth next to nothing.

FIGURE-2

CURRENCY-OPTION PRICING

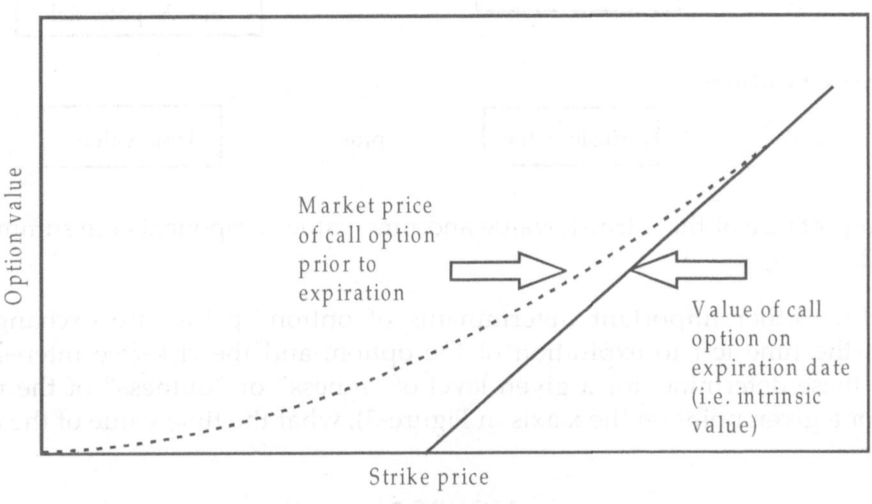

Of course, for out-of-the-money options on which the market price is quite close to the strike price, the upside potential becomes significant and the option becomes more valuable.

Returning now to the option prices in Figure-1, one can easily identify an option whose exercise is a near-certainty. Take the Mar 66 call. Almost sure to win, this option has a price that reflects that fact. Indeed, the investor could exercise it now, locking in the purchase price of 66 cents per 100 yen and sell the futures to receive 67.19. Because it is such a sure thing, it's almost like a futures or forward contract, the ultimate sure thing. But nobody in his right mind pays an up-front premium for a futures contract; any rational mind will come to the conclusion not to pay much more for the option than its intrinsic value—the gain that could be locked in by exercising it now. That gain is 67.19 — 66 = 1.19. The traded price of the call was 1.25. Thus the market paid only 0.06 cent for the negligible downside protection that is the only thing that differentiates a deep-in-the-money option from a futures contract.

Besides these two rather extreme options—a "nothing" option and a "nothing-but-a-futures" option—the investor can move toward the middle ground, toward those options whose downside protection and upside potential are significant. The options are "at-the-money"—those whose strike price is equal or close to the going market price. These are the options worth paying for, and their price reflects that fact. To recap, all option prices consist of two parts:

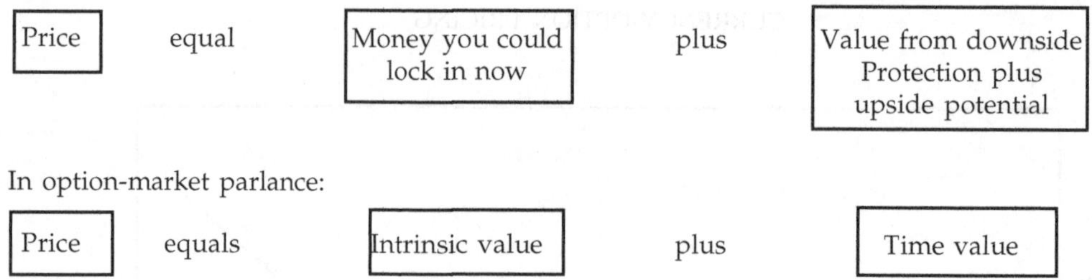

In option-market parlance:

Price	equals	Intrinsic value	plus	Time value

relative importance of the intrinsic-value and time-value components are summarised in Table-2.

The three other important determinants of options prices are exchange-rate volatility, the time left to expiration of the option, and the risk-free interest rate. Together these determine, for a given level of "inness" or "outness" of the money (that is, for a given point on the x axis in Figure-3), what the time value of the option should be.

FIGURE-3

VALUE OF CALL OPTION

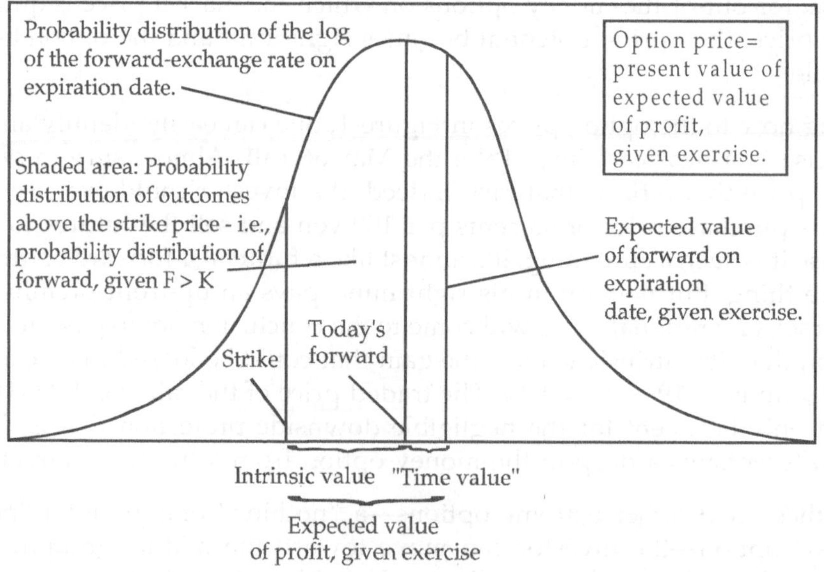

1. The *time value* depends on how much the exchange rate can move between now and expiration. For this reason time value is perhaps better termed *volatility value.* It is a function of the usefulness of the option. How much a downside protection does it provide? How much upside potential does it offer? For a given strike and market price, the answer depends purely on the probability of the market's moving above (or below) the strike between now and the expiration date. That probability depends principally on (1) how much time is left and (2) how volatile exchange rates are. (**Volatility** is defined as the annualised standard deviation of daily price changes).

Obviously, the greater the *time to expiration,* the greater the probability of significant exchange-rate movement and the higher the time value. Other things being equal, the time value drops off sharply as an option approaches maturity, particularly in the last month or so.

2. Time, intrinsic value, and the market interest rate can all be measured quite easily. The hardest thing is *volatility* itself, because what matters is not past but future volatility of exchange rates. Clearly the greater the volatility, the higher is the value of the option, so two traders with a different view of rate volatility will place a different value on the same option. Expected volatility, in short, is the key variable in pricing options. As noted earlier, options prices are not affected by changes in expectations about the level of a currency; only its variability is influenced.

3. The final factor is the *risk-free interest rate.* This is a time-value-of-money factor: the option gain (if any) is reaped at expiration, but the option must be paid for up front. In reality, option prices are normally quite insensitive to the risk-free interest rate.

TABLE - 2

BREAKDOWN OF INTRINSIC VALUE AND TIME VALUE IN OPTION PRICES

Kind of Option (Market price relative to strike price)	*Intrinsic Value*	*Time Value*
Deep-out-of-the-money option	Zero	Negligible, because of trival upside potential
Slightly-out-of-the-money	Zero	Considerable, because of downside protection plus substantial upside potential
At-the-money option	Zero	Maximum, because of greatest downside protection *and* greatest upside potential
Slightly-in-the-money option	Equals difference between strike and futures price	Considerable, because of upside potential plus substantial downside protection
Deep-in-the-money option	Equals difference between strike and futures price; constitutes bulk of option's value	Negligible, because of trivial downside protection relative to futures contract

FISCHER BLACK'S OPTION-PRICING MODEL

Putting the market relative to the strike price, the risk-free interest rate, the time to expiration and the expected volatility together to figure out the theoretical option price requires a model, such as modifications of the famous *Black-Scholes Model.* Even though the mathematics of these quantities can be complex, modern option-pricing theory is derived from building blocks of relatively simple arbitrage strategies—

arbitrage between options and the underlying instrument—that provide the trader with only the risk-free rate of return. Perhaps the most significant feature of these models is that although expectations of *volatility* of prices is a factor, the models do not rely on expectations regarding the *level* of future prices or rates to determine the correct price of an option.

The Black-Scholes model was adapted to non-dividend-paying commodities such as foreign exchange by Fischer Black in 1976. The model has stood the test of time, although it did not find common use in foreign exchange until reinterpreted by German and Kohlhagen.

Let's talks for a moment about how one might derive a model of a currency option's value. Remember that the *intrinsic value* of a call option at expiration is the forward price of the currency (F) minus the strike price (K) i.e., $F - K$, or zero if it's out of the money. Assume we know today what the intrinsic value is going to be at expiration. Then the present value, today's price, of the option would be

$$\text{Max } \{0, PV(F - K)\}$$

This idea is the basis for the Black formula, although the *actual* present value is uncertain, so that the formula represents the present value of the option's *expected* intrinsic value at expiration. Uncertainty implies some probability distribution of the currency's value. We typically assume that the natural logarithm of the exchange rate follows a normal distribution. (Nevertheless, studies have found the distribution of daily exchange returns to be "leptokurtic," which means its shape is more peaked around the mean, and the tails are more massive and longer than in a normal distribution). Figure-4 illustrates how the value is found. First we truncate the probability distribution of the log of the forward rate, because the option expires worthless if the currency ends up below the strike price, K. Then we find the expected value of their probability distribution. The call price is the present value of the difference between the expected forward and the strike. Written in symbols, this idea becomes the famous formula

$$C = PV[F \bullet N(d_1)] - K \bullet N(d_2)]$$

where

$$d_1 = \frac{\ln(F/K)}{\sigma\sqrt{\tau}} + \frac{\sigma\sqrt{\tau}}{2}$$

$$d_2 = d_1 - \sigma\sqrt{\tau}$$

That's it! Note the similarity of this relationship to the known intrinsic-value formula. As for the symbols, F is the forward price of the currency, K is the strike price, σ is the volatility (standard deviation) of the forward rate, τ is the time to expiration (in years) and $N(d)$ is the cumulative normal probability function. Another variable, the risk-free interest rate, also comes into the formula through the present-value function, *PVo*.

The value of the option equals the present value of its expected intrinsic value at expiration, given that the forward is above the strike. The formula makes intuitive sense as well as being useful. First, split it up into two terms: $C = PV[FN(d_2)]$. Keeping in mind that $N(d_1)$ is a probability, the term inside the first square brackets is the expected value of the forward rate, F_τ, at expiration, given that $F_\tau > K$. Similarly, the second term inside the brackets, $KN(d_2)$, is the expected value of the strike price at expiration, again given that $F_\tau > K_j$, *Thus the value of the option is the present value of its expected value of expiration.* Another interesting feature is that $N(d_1)$ is the probability that the call will be exercised, and as such gives the *hedge ratio* for a call, the amount of the underlying instrument needed to hedge an options position. The greater the chance that the writer will have to deliver, the more of the underlying instrument He'd better have purchased to hedge against the likelihood of exercise.

From the Black formula we get the value of a call, and, given the call price, we can easily derive the put price by using the put-call parity equation

$$P = C - PV(F - K)$$

Also, intuitively, when a call is not worth exercising, that is, when $F_\tau < K$, then a put with the same strike *is* worth exercising. Hence the probability of the put's being exercised is one minus the probability of the call's being exercised. So the *put hedge ratio equals 1 minus the call hedge ratio.*

Despite its complexity, the currency-option pricing formula is fairly easy to program on a computer spreadsheet, so that it becomes a useful "black box" in which the user plugs in values for the five parameters (F, K, τ, I, and σ), and the value of the call option, the put option, and their hedge ratios pop out. As such, this model or variations on it are widely used by financial-market practitioners.

No model is perfect. The Black-Scholes option-pricing model and its variants work well for most purposes, but the following should alert the user to some of its limitations:

i) The model's most problematic input variable is volatility. Although it's possible to estimate future volatility from the standard deviation of past data, what's really needed is one's *expectation* of future volatility. Volatility can be just as hard to predict as the exchange rate itself.

ii) The basic model yields the price of a European option; American options are usually worths a little more, by an amount that cannot be found by any straightforward formula.

iii) The formula assumes that the natural logarithm of the forward-exchange rate follows a normal distribution. Evidence suggests that the true distribution of exchange rates has considerably more outliers than is implied by the normal distribution.

iv) The model assumes that rates move continuously. Other models, notably Merton's Jump-diffusion model, have been developed to allow for abrupt changes.

v) The model depends on the forward-exchange rate's being independent of the interest rate. We know this is untrue, although for short-term options it seems not to matter.

vi) To obtain the value of a put from the call price, we assume that put-call parity (PCP) holds, but PCP can break down under some unusual circumstances for American options.

CURRENCY CALL OPTIONS

A currency call option is a contract that gives the buyer the right to buy a foreign currency at a specified price during the prescribed period. People buy currency call options because they anticipate that the spot rate of the underlying currency will appreciate. Currency option trading can take place for hedging or speculation.

Hedging in the Call Options Market

Multinational companies with open positions in foreign currencies can utilise currency call options. Suppose that an American firm orders industrial equipment from a German company, and its payment is to be made in German marks upon delivery. A German mark call option lacks in the rate at which the U.S. company can purchase marks for dollars. Such an exchange between these two currencies at the specified strike price can take place before the settlement date. Thus, the call option specifies the maximum price which the U.S. company must pay to obtain marks. If the spot rate falls below the strike price by the delivery date, the importer can buy marks at the prevailing spot rate to pay for its imports and can simply let its call option expire.

Let's see how call options may be used to cover possible exchange loses on import order denominated in foreign currencies. Assume that on February 1 an American firm has purchased a mainframe computer from a German firm for 625,000 marks; its payment must be made in German marks on June 1. Let us further assume that the premium for a mark call option with a strike price of $0.5000 and a June expiration date is 0.03 cents. Because there are 62,500 units per mark option, the U.S. firm will need 10 call options to buy 625,000 marks. The current spot rate for marks is $0.4900; the U.S. company's bank believes that the spot rate by June 1 will rise to $0.6000.

There are two alternatives available to the U.S. company: do not hedge, or hedge in the options market. If the U.S. company does not want to cover its option position, it would wait for four months, buy marks at the prevailing exchange rate in the spot market, and use these marks to pay for its imports. If the bank 's forecast is accurate, the U.S. company would spend $375,000 to purchase 625,000 marks at the spot rate of $ 0.6000.

The price of 10 mark call option is $187.50 (0.03 cents x 10 options x 62,500 units per contract); on June 1 the U.S. company exercises its right to buy 625,000 marks for $312,500 ($0.500 x 625,000 marks). Consequently, the U.S. firm would spent a total $ 312,687.50 ($187.50 + $312,500) to purchase 625,000 marks. By doing so, the American firm would avoid the risk of a $62,312.50 loss ($375,000 - $312,687.50). Still, if the future spot rate for marks remains below the strike price of $0.5000, the U.S. company can let its option expire and buy German marks at the prevailing spot rate when it must pay for its imports. Here the U.S. firm would lose its option premium of $ 187.50.

Speculating in the Call Options Market

Individual may speculate with currency call options based on their expectations of exchange-rate fluctuations for a particular currency. The purpose of speculation in the call option market is to make a profit form exchange-rate movements by deliberately taking an uncovered position. If a speculator expects that the future spot rate of a currency will increase, he makes the following transactions: the speculator will (1) buy call options of the currency, (2) wait for a few months until the spot rate of the currency appreciates high enough, (3) exercise his option by buying the currency at the strike price, and (4) then sell the currency at the prevailing spot rate. To illustrate, assume that the call premium per British pound on February 1 is 1.10 cents, the expiration date is June, and the strike price is $ 1.60. Kamal Gupta anticipates that the spot rate of the pound will increase to $1.70 by May 1. If Mr. Gupta's expectation proves correct, what would be his dollar profit from speculating one pound call option (31,250 units per contract) in the call options market?

Kamal Gupta could make a profit of $ 2,781.25 by making the following trades:

1. Buy call options on February1	- $ 0.0110 per pound
2. Exercise the option on May 1	- $ 1.6000 per pound
3. Sell the pound on May 1	+ $ 1.7000 per pound
4. Net profit as of May 1	+ $ 0.0890 per pound
5. Net profit per contract	£ 31,250 × $ 0.0890 = $ 2,781.25

Gupta does not need to exercise his call options in order to make a profit. Currency call option premiums rise and fall as exchange rates of their underlying currency rise and fall. If call options become profitable, their premiums will rise. They can be sold on an exchange just like any foreign currency itself. So a call option holder such as Gupta can save the expense and bother of taking possession of the currency and selling it.

Figure-4 shows the typical relationship between the market value of a call option and its intrinsic value. Up to the point where the strike price equals the spot rate, time value increases as the spot rate increases, but the market value exceeds the intrinsic value for all spot rates. Call option have positive values even if they are out-of-the-money because they have time value. It is also important to note that the intrinsic value of a call option become zero whenever the strike price exceeds the spot rate.

CURRENCY PUT OPTIONS

A currency put option is simply a contract that gives the holder the right to sell a foreign currency at a specified price during a prescribed period. People buy currency put options because they anticipate that the spot rate of the underlying currency will depreciate.

Multinational companies with open positions in foreign currencies can employ currency put options to cover such positions. Consider an American company which has sold an airplane to a Japanese firm and has agreed to receive its payment in Japanese yen. The exporter may be concerned about the possibility that the yen will

FIGURE-4

MARKET VALUE OF A CALL OPTION

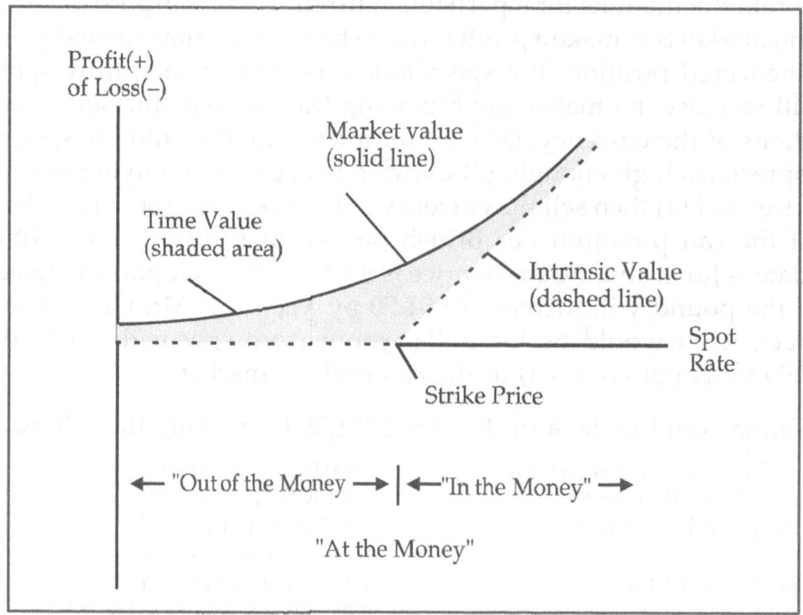

depreciate when it is scheduled to receive its payment from the importer. To protect itself against such a yen depreciation, the exporter could buy yen put options, which would enable it to sell yen at the specified strike price. In fact, the exporter would lock in the minimum exchange rate at which it could sell Japanese yen in exchange for U.S. dollars over a specified period of time. On the other hand, if the yen appreciates over this time period, the exporter could let the put options expire and sell the yen at the prevailing spot rate.

Individuals may speculate with currency put options based on their expectations of exchange rate fluctuations for a particular currency. For example, if speculators believe that the German mark will depreciate in the future, they can buy mark put options, which will entitle them to sell marks at the specified strike price. If the mark's spot rate depreciates as expected, they can buy marks at the spot rate and exercise their put options by selling these marks at the strike price.

Speculators do not need to exercise their put options in order to make a profit. They could make a profit from selling put options because put option premiums fall and rise as exchange rates of the underlying currency rise and fall. The seller of put options has the obligation to purchase the specified currency at the strike price from the owner who exercises the put option. If speculators anticipate that the currency will appreciate, they might sell their put options. But if the currency indeed appreciates over the entire period, the put option will not be exercised. On the other hand, if they expect that the currency will depreciate, they will keep their put options. Then they will sell their put options when the put option premiums go up.

FIGURE-5

PROFIT-LOSS PROFILE FOR AN OPTION TRADER

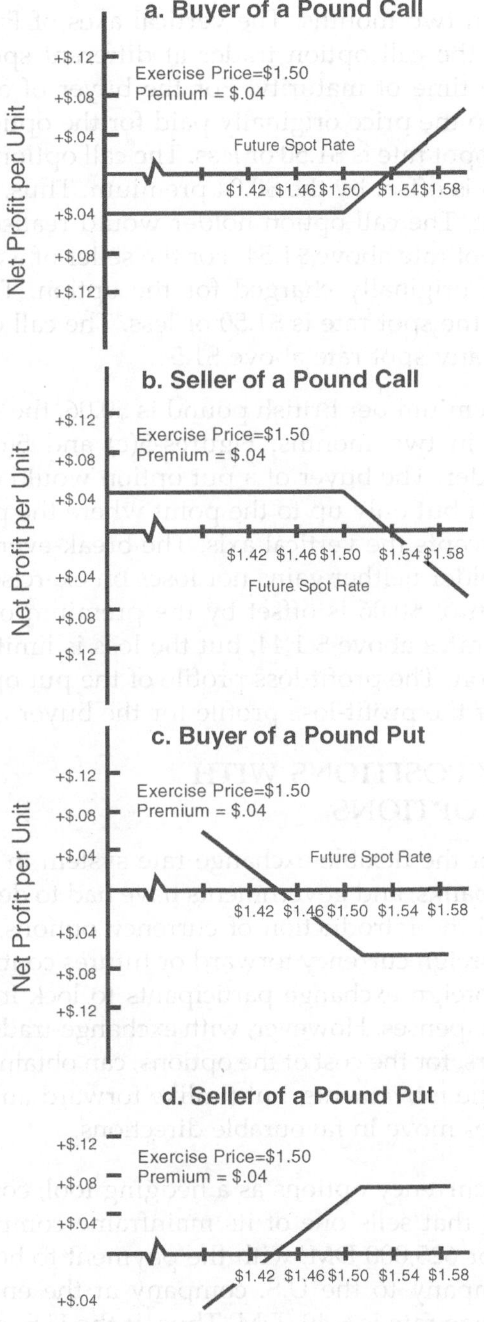

Profit-Loss Profiles of Options. Figure-5 presents "profit-loss profiles" which trace the relationship between the exchange rate at expiration of the contract and the net gain (loss) to the trader.

Assume that the call premium per British pound is $0.04, the strike price is $1.50, and the contract matures in two months. The vertical axes of Figures-5(a) and 5(b) measure profit or loss for the call option trader at different spot rates (horizontal axes) for the pound at the time of maturity. For the buyer of a call option on the pound, the loss is limited to the price originally paid for the option. The entire price ($0.04) would be lost if the spot rate is $1.50 or less. The call option holder would earn $0.04 at $1.54, but this gain is offset by the $0.04 premium. Thus, this point ($1.54) is called the break-even point. The call option holder would realise a one-to-one gain (unlimited profit) at any spot rate above $1.54. For the seller of a call option, the gain is limited to the premium originally charged for the option. The entire premium ($0.04) would be earned if the spot rate is $1.50 or less. The call option seller would suffer a one-to-one loss at any spot rate above $1.54.

Assume that the put premium per British pound is $0.06, the strike price is $1.50, and the contract matures in two months. Figures-5(c) and 5(d) show profit-loss profiles of a put option trader. The buyer of a put option would obtain a one-to-one gain at any rate below $1.44 but only up to the point where the profit-loss profile of the put option holder intercepts the vertical axis. The break-even spot rate of $ 1.44 is the price at which the holder neither gains nor loses on exercise of the option: this is the point where the gain of $0.06 is offset by the premium of $0.06. The holder would lose money at spot rates above $ 1.44, but the loss is limited to the premium originally paid for the option. The profit-loss profile of the put option seller, Figure-6(d), is the mirror image of the profit-loss profile for the buyer of a put option.

HEDGING CURRENCY POSITIONS WITH FOREIGN CURRENCY OPTIONS

Since the reestablishment of the flexible exchange rate system in 1972, multinational corporations, international banks, and governments have had to deal with the problem of exchange rate risk. Until the introduction of currency options, exchange rate risk usually was hedged with foreign currency forward or futures contracts. Hedging with these instruments allows foreign exchange participants to lock in the local currency values of their revenues or expenses. However, with exchange-traded currency options and dealer's options, hedgers, for the cost of the options, can obtain not only protection against adverse exchange rue movements, but (unlike forward and futures positions) benefits if the exchange rates move in favourable directions.

To illustrate the use of currency options as a hedging tool, consider the case of a U.S. computer corporation that sells one of its mainframe computers to a German manufacturing company for 625,000 DM, with the payment to be made in Deutsche marks by the German company to the U.S. company at the end of three months. Suppose the current exchange rate is $.40/DM. Thus, if the U.S. company were paid immediately and the marks were converted, it would receive $250,000. Since payment is not due for three months, the US. company faces both the risk that the $/DM exchange rate could decrease, resulting in fewer dollars, and the possibility of greater dollar returns if the $/DM exchange rate increases. For the costs of DM put options, the U.S. company can protect its dollar revenues from possible exchange rate decreases while still benefiting if the exchange rate increases.

For example, suppose a 40-DM put is available at 1 (X = $0.40/DM and P_0 $0.01/ One unit of foreign currency), with an expiration coinciding with the date the US company is to receive its 625,000 DM. To hedge its future dollar revenue, currently worth ($.40/DM)(625,000 DM) = $250,000, against exchange risk, the US. computer company would need to buy 10-DM put contracts (contract size on a DM option is 62,500) expiring at the end of three months. Table-3 shows the net revenues the U.S. company would receive three months later from converting its receipts of 625,000 DM to dollars at the spot exchange rate (S_T) and closing its 10 put contracts at a price equal to the DM put's intrinsic value. As shown, if the exchange rate is less than $.40/ DM, the company would receive less than $250,000 when it converts the 625,000 DM to dollars; these lower revenues, however, would be offset by the profits from the put position.

For example, at a spot exchange rate of $0.30/DM, the company would receive only $187,500 from converting the 625,000 DM payment, but would earn from the puts a profit of

10 Max[$0.40/DM – $0.30(DM, 0](62,500 DM)
–10($0.0.1/DM)(62,500 DM) = $56,250.

TABLE - 3

HEDGING FUTURE DM RECEIPTS WITH DM PUT OPTIONS

DM revenue at expiration = 625,000 DM
Hedge: long in ten, 40-DM puts
Put contract = 62,500 DM, cost of put = $.01/DM, or $625 per contract

(1)	(2)	(3)	(4)
Spot Exchange Rate at Expiration S_T = *$/DM*	*Put Profit**	*Dollar value of 625,000 DM:* S_T*(525,000 DM)*	*Dollar Receipts* (2) + (3)
$.30/DM	$56,250	$187,500	$243,750
.35/DM	25,000	218,750	243,750
.40/DM	– 6,250	250,000	243,750
.45/DM	– 6,250	281,250	275,000
.50/DM	– 6,250	312,500	306,250

*Put profit = 10 Max[$.40/DM – S_T, 0](62,500 DM) – 10($.01/DM)(62500 DM)

This would result in a combined receipt of $243,750. As shown in the table, if the exchange rate is $0.40/DM or less, the company would receive $243,750. This amount equals the hedged amount ($250,000) minus the costs of the put options. On the other hand, if the exchange rate at expiration exceeds $0.40/DM, the U.S. company would realize a dollar gain when it converts the 625,000 DM at the higher spot, while its losses on the put would be limited to the amount of the premium. Thus, by hedging with currency put options, the company is able to obtain exchange rate risk protection in the event the exchange rate decreases while still retaining the potential for increased dollar revenues if the exchange rate rises.

Suppose that instead of receiving foreign currency, a company had to make a foreign currency payment at some future date. To protect itself against possible increases in the exchange rate while still benefiting if the exchange rate decreases, the company could hedge the position by taking a long position in a currency call option. For example, suppose a U.S. importer bought 10 German automobiles for 62,500 DM each, with the total payment of 625,000 DM to be made at the end of three months. If the current exchange rate again is \$0.40/DM, then the importer's total dollar expenditure would be \$250,000 if the exchange rate did not change. If the exchange rate increased, though, the importer would pay more, and if it decreased, he would pay lest

To benefit from the lower exchange rates and still limit the dollar costs of purchasing 625,000 DM in the event the \$/DM exchange rate rise; the importer could buy DM call options expiring at the end of the three months. Table-4 shows the costs of purchasing 625,000 DM at different exchange rates and the profits and losses from purchasing 10 three-month 40-DM calls at 1 and closing them at expiration at a price equal to the call's intrinsic value. As shown in the table for cases in which the exchange rate is greater than \$.40/DM, the importer has dollar expenditures exceeding \$250,000; the expenditures, though, are offset by the profits from the calls. On the other hand, when the exchange rate is less than \$.40/DM, the dollar costs of purchasing 625,000 DM decreases as the exchange rate decreases, while the losses on the call options are limited to the option premium.

TABLE-4

HEDGING FUTURE DM PURCHASE WITH DM CALL OPTIONS

DM costs at expiration = 625,000 DM
Hedge:long in ten 40-DM calls
Call contract = 62,500 DM, cost of call = \$.0 1/DM, or \$625 per contract

(1)	*(2)*	*(3)*	*(4)*
Spot Exchange Rate at Expiration S_T *= \$/DM*	*Call Profit**	*Dollar value of 625,000 DM:* S_T *(625,000 DM)*	*Dollar Costs (3) – (2)*
\$.30/DM	– \$6,250	\$187,500	*\$193,750*
.35/DM	– 6,250	218,750	225,000
.40/DM	– 6,250	250,000	256,250
.45/DM	25,000	281,250	256,250
.50/DM	56,250	312,500	256,250

*Call profit = 10 Max[S_T – \$.40/DM, 0](62,500 DM) – 10(\$.01/DM)(62,500 DM)

HEDGING WITH CURRENCY FUTURES AND CONTRACTS

Foreign currency positions could be hedged with currency options: By going long in a currency call option, the investor can lock in the maximum dollar costs of a future cash outflow or liability denominated in a foreign currency while still maintaining the chance for lower dollar outlays if the exchange rate decreases. In contrast, by going long in a currency put, the investor can lock in the minimum dollar value of a future inflow or asset denominated in foreign currency while still maintaining the possibility of a greater dollar inflows in case the exchange rate increases. With foreign currency futures and forward contracts, the domestic currency value of future cash flows or the future dollar value of assets and liabilities denominated in another currency can be locked in. Unlike option hedging, however, no exchange rate gains exist when futures or forward contracts are used.

Hedging Future Currency Cash Flows with a Naive Hedge

Large multinational corporations usually hedge their currency positions in the interbank forward market, whereas smaller companies, some portfolio mangers, and individuals often use the futures market. Either way, the currency position usually is hedged with a naive hedging model in which the number of futures or forward contracts is equal to the value of the foreign currency position to be hedged.

To illustrate currency hedging, consider the option hedging example presented above in which a U.S. company expected a receipt of 625,000 DM at the end of three months. Instead of hedging with a DM put, suppose the company decides to hedge its receipt with a DM futures contracts expiring at the end of three months, currently trading at S_f = \$0.40/DM when the spot exchange rate is at S_0 = \$.40/DM. Since the contract size on the DM futures contract is 125,000 DM, the company would need to go short in five DM contracts, if it uses a naive hedging approach:

$$\frac{(\$0.40/\text{DM})(625{,}000\ \text{DM})}{(\$0.40/\text{DM})(125{,}000\ \text{DM})} = 5.$$

Doing this, the company would, in turn, ensure itself of a \$250,000 receipt at expiration when it converts its 625,000 DM to dollars at the spot \$/DM exchange rate and closes its short futures position (see Table-5).

TABLE-5

HEDGING A FUTURE DM RECEIPT WITH DM FUTURES CONTRACTS

Revenue at expiration = 625,000 DM. *Hedge:* short in five DM futures contracts (contract size of 125,000 DM) at S_f = \$0.40/DM

(1)	(2)	(3)	(4)
Spot Exchange Rate Expiration: S_T = *\$/DM*	*Future Cash Flow:* 5[(\$0.40/DM) - S_T]	*Dollar value of 625,000 DM:* (S_T)(625,0000 DM) (125,000 DM)	*Total Revenue* (2) + (3)
\$0.30/DM	\$62,500	\$187,500	\$250,000
0.35/DM	31,250	218,750	250,000
0.40/DM	0	250,000	250,000
0.45/DM	– 31,250	281,250	250,000
0.50/DM	62,500	312,500	250,000

If a multinational company has a future debt obligation that it is required to pay in foreign currency; then it could lock in the dollar cost of the obligation by taking a long futures or forward position. This hedging strategy can be seen in Table-6, where the dollar costs of purchasing 625,000 DM at the end of three months is hedged with five long DM contracts priced at S_f = $0.40/DM In this case, the net costs of purchasing the maria on the spot and closing the futures is $250,000, regardless of the spot exchange rate.

TABLE-6

HEDGING A FUTURE DM COST WITH DM FUTURES CONTRACTS

Debt at expiration = 625,000 DM. Hedge: long in five DM futures contracts (contract size of 125,000 DM) at S_f= $0.40/DM

(1)	(2)	(3)	(4)
Spot Exchange Rate Expiration: S_T = *$/DM*	*Future Cash Flow:* 5[S_T – ($0.40/DM)]	*Dollar value of 625,000 DM:* (S_T)(625,0000 DM) (125,000 DM)	*Total Revenue* (3) – (2)
$0.30/DM	–$62,500	$187,500	$250,000
0.35/DM	– 31,250	218,750	250,000
0.40/DM	0	250,000	250,000
0.45/DM	31,250	281,250	250,000
0.50/DM	62,500	312,500	250,000

Note, in the preceding examples, the hedge involves a foreign currency conversion to or from dollar. However, if the hedge does not involve the dollar and the only currency futures and forward contracts available are those defined in dollars, then the cross-exchange rate relationship needs to be used to set up the appropriate hedge. For example, suppose a German investor wanted to lock in the DM value of his future dividend receipt of 4 FF from XYZ stock using the futures contract available on the IMM. To do this, the investor would need to take positions in the $/DM and $/FF futures contracts, and use the cross-exchange rate relationship to define each futures position. If the futures rates are $0.25/FF and $0.40/DM, then the German investor would need to take a short position in four FF futures at S_f = $0.25/FF, and a long position in 2.5 DM at S_f = $0.40/DM. By doing this, the investor would be able to lock in a receipt of 2.5 DM when he converts the 4 FF to $1 on the short position, then converts the $1 to 2.5 DM on the long position.

HEDGING INTERNATIONAL PORTFOLIOS

Currency futures, forward, and option contracts often are used by portfolio managers to immunize their international portfolios against exchange rate risk. For example, suppose a U.S. investor who owned 1000 shares of a French stock worth 2500 FF per share wanted to hedge the dollar value of his stock. Suppose the $/FF spot and three-month IMM futures exchange rates are both $0. 15/FF (or 6.6667 FF/$), making the current dollar value of the stock worth:

($0.15/FF)(1000)(2500 FF) = $375,000.

If the investor wanted to hedge the dollar value of the stock at the end of three months against exchange rate risk, he would need to go short in ten FF futures contracts expiring in three months (contract size is 250,000 FF):

$$\frac{\$375,000}{(\$0.15/FF)(250,000\ FF)} = 10.$$

If, at the end of three months, no change in the price of the French stock occurred, then the futures-hedged dollar value of the stock would be $375,000, irrespective of the spot $/FF exchange rate. If the $/FF rate decreased by 10% over the period, from $0.15/FF to $0.135/FF, then the dollar value of the stock also would decrease by 10%, from $375,000 to $337,500; this decrease, though, would be offset by a $37,500 profit:

$$10(250,000\ FF)[(\$0.15/FF) - (\$0.135/FF)] = \$37,500.$$

Hedging with currency futures or forward contracts allows international investors to focus on selecting stocks or portfolios without having to worry about short-run changes in the exchange rate. For instance, in our example if the price of the French stock increased by 5% from 2500 FF to 2625 FF at the same time the $/FF exchange rate decreased by 10%, then an unhedged position would lose 5.5% in dollars:

$$\text{Rate} = \frac{[(\$0.135/FF)(1000)(2625\ FF)] - [(\$0.150/FF)(1000)(2500\ FF)]}{(\$0.\ 150/FF)(1000)(2500\ FF)}$$

$$\text{Rate} = \frac{\$354,375 - \$375,000}{\$375,000} = -.055.$$

If the position is hedged with 10-FF futures contracts, however, a $37,500 futures profit would exist, and the rate of return on the exchange-rate hedged investment would be 4.5%:

$$\text{Rate} = \frac{(\$354,375 - \$375,500) + \$37\ 500}{\$375,000} = .045.$$

Thus, the futures hedge allows the investor to profit from good stock selection.

The rate of return in dollars earned from the currency-hedged stock in this example is less than the 5% FF increase in the stock price. This is because a naive hedge protects only the initial value; dividends and stock appreciation are not hedged against exchange rate risk. To hedge stock price changes against exchange rate changes would require knowing the correlation between the exchange rate and the stock price.

USING FORWARD OR FUTURE CONTRACTS VERSUS OPTIONS CONTRACTS

Suppose that on July 1, an American company makes a sale for which it will receive DM 125,000 on September 1. The firm will want to convert those DM into dollars, so it is exposed to the risk that the mark will fall below its current spot rate of $ 0.6922 in the meantime. The firm can protect itself against a declining Deutsche mark by selling its expected DM receipts forward (using a futures contract) or by buying a DM put option.

Table-7 shows possible results for each choice, using options with strike prices just above and just below the spot exchange of July 1 ($0.68 and $0.70). The example assumes a DM decline to $0.6542 and the consequent price adjustments of associated futures and options contracts. The put quotes are the option premiums per DM. Thus, the dollar premium associated with a particular quote equals the quote multiplied by the number of DM covered by the put options. For example, the quote of $0.0059 for a September put option with a strike price of 68 (in cents) represents a premium for covering the exporter's DM 125,000 transaction equal to $ 0.0059 x 125,000 = $ 737.50.

TABLE-7

DECLINING EXCHANGE RATE SENARIO

	July 1	*September 1*
Spot	$0.6922	$0.6542
September futures	0.6956	0.6558
September 68 put	0.0059	0.0265
September 70 put	0.0144	0.0461

In the above example, a decision to remain unhedged would yield a loss of 125,000 x (0.6922 - 0.6542), or $ 4,750. The outcomes of the various hedge possibilities are shown in Table-8.

Table-8 demonstrates the following differences between the futures and options hedging strategies.

TABLE-8

HEDGING ALTERNATIVES: OFFSETTING A $4,750 LOSS DUE TO A DECLINING DM

Result of Selling Futures

(0.6956 - 0.6558) × 125,000 = $ 4,975 profit

Results of Buying Put Options

68 put: (0.0265 - 0.0059) × 125,000 = $2,575.00 profit

70 put: (0.0461 - 0.0144) × 125,000 = $3,962.50 profit

1. The futures hedge offers the closest offset to the loss due to the decline of the Deutsche mark.
2. The purchase of the in-the-money put option (the 70 strike price) offers greater protection (but at a higher premium) than the out-of-the-money put (the 68 strike price).

Note that the September futures price is unequal to the spot rate on September 1 because settlement is not until later in the month. As the DM declines in value, the company would suffer a larger loss on its DM receivables, to be offset by a further increase in the value of the put and futures contracts.

While the company wants to protect against the possibility of a DM depreciation, what would happen if the DM appreciates? To answer this question—so as to fully assess the options and futures hedge strategies—assume the hypothetical conditions in Table-9.

TABLE-9

RISING EXCHANGE RATES SCENARIO

	July 1	*September 1*
Spot	$0.6922	$0.7338
September futures	0.6956	0.4374
September 68 put	0.0059	0.0001
September 70 put	0.0144	0.0001

In this scenario, the rise in the DM would increase the value of the unhedged position by 125,000 *f* (0.7338 – 0.6922), or $5,200. This gain would be offset by losses on the futures or options contracts, as shown in Table-10.

TABLE-10

HEDGING ALTERNATIVES: OFFSETTING A $ 5,200 GAIN DUE TO A RISING DM

Result of Selling Futures

(0.7374 - 0.6956) × 125,000 = $ 5,225 loss

Results of Buying Put Options

68 put : (0.0059 - 0.0001) × 125,000 = $ 725 loss

70 put: (0.0144 - 0.0001) × 125,000 - $ 1,787.50 loss

We can see that the futures hedge again provides the closest offset. Because these hedges generate losses, however, the company would be better served under this scenario by the smallest offset. With rapidly rising exchange rates, the company would benefit most form hedging with a long put position as opposed to a futures contract; conversely, with rapidly falling exchange rates, the company would benefit most from hedging with a futures contract.

COMPARISON OF HEDGING TECHNIQUES

Each of the hedging techniques is briefly summarized in Table-11. When using a futures hedge, forward hedge, or money market hedge, the firm can estimate the funds (denominated in its home currency) that it will need for future payables, or the funds it will receive after converting foreign currency receivables. Thus, it can compare the costs or revenues and determine which of these hedging techniques is appropriate. However, the cash flow associated with the currency option hedge cannot be determined with certainty, because the costs of purchasing payables and the revenues generated from receivables are not known ahead of time. To reinforce an understanding of the hedging techniques, a comprehensive example is provided here.

TABLE-11

TECHNIQUES FOR HEDGING TRANSACTION EXPOSURE

Hedging Technique	*To Hedge Payables*	*To Hedge Receivables*
1. Futures hedge	Purchase a currency futures contract (or contracts) representing the currency and amount related to the payables.	Sell a currency futures contract for contracts) representing the currency and amount related to the receivables.
2. Forward hedge	Purchase a forward contract representing the currency and amount related to the payables.	Sell a forward contract representing the currency and amount related to the receivables.
3. Money market hedge	Borrow local currency and convert to currency denominating payables. Invest these funds until they are needed to cover the payables.	Borrow the currency denominating the receivables, convert it to the local currency, and invest it. Then pay off the loan with cash inflows from the receivables.
4. Currency option hedge	Purchase a currency call option (or options) representing the currency and amount related to the payables.	Purchase a currency put option (or options) representing the currency and amount related to the receivables.

Assume that XYZ Corporation will need £200,000 in 180 days. It consider using (1) a forward hedge, (2) a money market hedge, (3) an option hedge, or (4) no hedge. Its analysts develop the following informations, which can be used to assess the alternative solutions:

* Spot rate of pound as of today = $1.50
* 180-day forward rate of pound as of today = $1.47.
* Interest rates are as follows:

	U.K.	*U.S.*
180-day deposit rate	4.5%	4.5%
180-day borrowing rate	5.0%	5.0%

* A call option on pounds that expires in 180 days has an exercise price of $1.48 and a premium $.03.
* A put option on pounds that expires in 180 days has an exercise price of $1.49 and a premium of $.02.
* XYZ Corporation forecasted the future spot rate in 180 days an follows:

Possible Outcome	*Probability*
$1.43	20%
$1.46	70%
$1.52	10%

Each alternative solution to the existing problem is assessed in Table 12. Now these solutions will be compared to determine the best one.

TABLE-12

COMPARISON OF HEDGING ALTERNATIVES FOR XYZ CORPORATION

Forward Hedge

Purchase pounds 180 days forward

Dollars needed in 180 days =Payables in £ × Forward rate of £
= £200,000 × $1.47
= $294,000

Money Market Hedge

Borrow $, Convert to £, Invest £, Repay $ loan in 180 days

Amount in £ to be invested = $\frac{£200{,}000}{(1+.045)}$
= £191,388

Amount in $ needed to convert into £ for deposit = £191,388 X $1.50
= $287,081

Interest and principal owed on $ loan after 180 days = $287,081 X (1 +.05)
= $301,435

Call Option

Purchase call (the following computations assume that the option is to be exercised on the day pounds are needed, or not at all. Exercise price = $1.48; premium = $.03)

Possible Spot Rate in 180 days	*Premium per Unit Paid for Option*	*Exercise Option?*	*Total Price (Including Option Premium) Paid per Unit*	*Total Price Paid for £200,000*	*Probability*
$1.43	$.03	No	$1.46	$292,000	20%
$1.46	$.03	No	$1.49	$298,000	70%
$1.52	$.03	Yes	$1.51	$302,000	10%

Remain Unhedged

Purchase £200,000 in the spot market 180 days from now

Future Spot Rate Expected in 180 Days	*Dollars Needed to Purchase £200,000*	*Probability*
$1.43	$286,000	20%
$1.46	$292,000	70
$1.52	$304,000	10

Each of the alternative solutions has been analysed to estimate the nominal dollar cost of paying for the payables denominated in pounds. The cost is known with certainty for the forward rate hedge and money market hedge. However, the cost when either using the call option or remaining unhedged is dependent on the spot rate 180 days from now. The costs of the four alternatives are also compared with the use of probability distributions, which shows that the forward hedge is superior to the money market hedge, since the dollar cost is definitely less. A comparison of the forward hedge to the call option hedge shows that there is an 80 percent chance that the call option hedge will be more expensive. Thus, the forward hedge appears to the the optimal hedge.

The probability distribution of outcomes for the no-hedge strategy appears to the more favourable than that for the forward hedge. XYZ Corporation is likely to perform best if it remains unhedged, but it should choose the forward hedge if it prefers to hedge. If XYZ Co. does not hedge, it should periodically reassess the hedging decision. For example, after 60 days it should repeat the analysis shown here, based on the applicable spot rate, forward rate, interest rates, call option information, and forecasts of the spot rate 120 days into the future (when the payables are due).

A similar analysis of transaction exposure could be conducted if a firm desired to hedge receivables. For example, assume that ABC Corporation anticipates no payables in pounds, but will receive £300,000 in 180 days. The same information on the spot, forward, and options prices is used to compare hedging techniques and an unhedged strategy in Table 13.

From the dollar amounts to be received from each of the four alternatives, it appears that the money market hedge is the optimal hedge for this example. The money market hedge would by outperformed by the no-hedge strategy if the spot rate of the pound in 180 days were $1.52. There is only a 10 percent probability of that outcome, though. Therefore, the firm will likely decide to hedge its receivables position.

While this example includes the assessment of the particular currency option, several alternative currency options are normally available with different exercise prices. When hedging payables, a firm could reduce the premium paid by choosing a call option with a higher exercise price. of course, the trade-off is that the maximum amount to be paid for the payables would be higher. Similarly, a firm hedging receivables could reduce the premium paid by choosing a put option with a lower exercise price. In this case, the tradeoff is that the minimum amount to be received for the receivables would be lower. Firms generally compare the available options first to determine which is most appropriate. Then this particular option can be compared to the other hedging techniques in order to determine which technique (if any) should be used.

It should be clear that the optimal hedging technique is dependent on exchange rate projections. If the projections cause the firm to believe that it will definitely be adversely affected by its transaction exposure, a forward hedge or money market hedge is normally appropriate. Conversely, if the firm believes that it may benefit from its exposure, the currency option hedge is more appropriate (if any hedge is used at all).

TABLE-13

COMPARISON OF HEDGING ALTERNATIVES FOR ABC CORPORATION

Forward Hedge

Sell Pounds 180 days forward

Dollars to be received in 180 days = Receivables in £ × Forward rate of £
= £300,000 X $1.47
= $441,000

Money Market Hedge

Borrow £, convert to $, invest $, use receivables to pay off loan in 180 days

Amount in £ Borrowed = $\frac{£300,000}{(1 + .05)}$
= £285,714

$ received from converting £ = £285,714 × $1.50 per £
= $ 428,571

$ accumulated after 180 days = $428,571 × (1 + 0.045)
= $447,857

Put Option Hedge

Purchase put option (assume the options are to be exercised on the day pounds are to be received, or not at all. Exercise price = $1.49; premium = $.02.)

Possible Spot Rate in 180 days	*Premium per Unit Paid for Option*	*Exercise Option?*	*Total Dollars Received per Unit (After Accounting for the Premium)*	*Total Dollars Received from Converting £300,000*	*Probability*
$1.43	$.02	Yes	$1.47	$441,000	20%
1.46	.02	Yes	1.47	441,000	70
1.52	.02	No	1.50	450,000	10

Remain Unhedged

Possible Spot Rate in 180 Days	*Total Dollars Received from Converting £300,000*	*Probability*
$1.43	$429,000	20%
1.46	438,000	70
1.52	456,000	10

The examples provided so far have been simplified to focus on the comparison of hedging techniques. It is implicitly assumed that the amount to be hedged is known with certainty. However, the precise dollar amount in many foreign transactions may not be known until the transaction date. In the receivables example, it is assumed that the £200,000 will be received in 180 days. If the receivables amount could actually be as low as £200,000, should the firm still hedge the expected inflow of £300,000? If the firm overhedges, it will have to make up the difference to fulfill the hedging strategy. For example, if it uses the money market hedge to hedge £100,000, and receivables amount to only £200,000, it will have to purchase £1,00,000 in the spot market to achieve the £100,000. This example shows how overhedging (hedging a larger amount in a currency than the actual transaction amount) can adversely affect a firm.

A solution to avoid overhedging is to hedge only the minimum known amount in the future transaction. In the above example, if the future receivables may be as low as £200,000, the firm could hedge this amount. However, under these conditions the firm may not have completely hedged its position. If the actual transaction amount turns out to be £300,000 as expected, the firm will be only partially hedged and will need to sell the extra £100,000 in the spot market.

This dilemma is very common for firms, since the precise amount in the foreign currency to be received at the end of a period can be uncertain, especially for firms heavily involved in exporting. Based on this example, it should be clear that most MNCs cannot completely hedge all of their transactions. Nevertheless, by hedging a portion of those transactions that affect them, they can reduce the sensitivity of their cash flows to exchange rate movements.

WHO NEEDS CURRENCY OPTIONS?

Currency options are useful for anyone who requires a gain if the exchange rate goes one way, but wants protection against loss if the rate goes the other way. The most the holder of an option can lose is the premium he paid for it. Naturally, the option writer faces the mirror image of the holder's picture: if you sell (or "write") an option (call or put), the most you can get is the premium if the option dies for lack of exercise. The writer of a call option can face a substantial loss if the option is exercised: he is forced to deliver a currency-futures contract at a below-market price. If he wrote a put option and the put is exercised, then he is obliged to buy the currency at an above-market price.

Unlike futures, forwards, and currency swaps, therefore, foreign-exchange options represent an asymmetrical risk profile. This lopsidedness works to the advantage of the holder and to the disadvantage of the writer—but that, after all, is what the holder is paying for. When two parties enter into a symmetrical contract like a forward, both can gain or lose equally and neither party feels obliged to charge the other for the privilege. Forwards, futures, and swaps are mutual obligations; options are one-sided. The holder of a call has a downside risk limited to the premium paid up front; beyond that he gains one-for-one with the price of the underlying security. One who has brought a put option gains one-for-one as the price of the underlying instrument falls below the strike price. Traders who have written or sold options face the upside-down mirror-image profit profile of those who have bought the same options.

From the asymmetrical risk profile of options, it follows that options are ideally suited to offsetting exchange risks that are themselves asymmetrical. The risk of a forward-rate agreement is symmetrical; hence, matching it worth a currency option will not be a perfect hedge, because doing so would leave you with an open, or speculative, position. Forward contracts, futures, or currency swaps are suitable hedges for symmetrical risks. Currency options are suitable hedges for situations in which currency risk is already lopsided, and for those who choose to speculate on the direction *and* volatility of rates.

Options are not only for hedgers, but also for those who wish to take a "view." However, for one who is, say, bearish on the deutschemark, a DM put is not necessarily the best choice. One can easily bet on the *direction* of a currency by suing futures or forwards. A DM bear would simply sell DM futures, limiting his loss, if wants to do so, via a stop-loss order.

For an investor who has a view on direction *and* on volatility, the option is the right choice. If you think the DM is likely to fall below the forward rate, and you believe that the market has underestimated the mark's volatility, then buying a put on German marks is the right strategy.

Who needs an American option? Because if offers an additional right—the privilege of exercise on any date up to the expiration date—it gives the buyer greater flexibility and the writer greater risk. American options will therefore tend to be priced slightly higher than European options. Even so, *the American option is almost always worth more "alive" than "dead," meaning that it pays to sell rather than exercise early.* The reason for this statement lies in the fact that most option trade at a price higher than the gain that would be made from exercising the option.

IMPLICATIONS FOR MANAGERS

International business creates significant opportunities for firms to benefit from changing currency values but also exposes firms to significant risks from changing currency values. The most obvious effect of changing currency values is on the values of individual purchases and sales by firms. Currency changes also affect the value of the assets that firms hold in different countries and the value of liabilities denominated in different currencies. These changing values affect the profitability and values of firms.

It is important for international financial managers to understand both challenges and opportunities associated with currency fluctuations. As part of this understanding, it is important to understand the potential to manage those challenges and opportunities with appropriate financial market transactions. This chapter has described how forward contracts, futures contracts, and options can modify a firm's exposure to currency fluctuations. These derivative securities *allow international financial managers to adjust their exposures to currency fluctuations without having to disrupt their normal business operations. Such flexibility is invaluable in our dynamic international economy.*

To emphasize this reality, we close the chapter by examining a real-life example of a managerial decision that created currency exposure. In mid-1985 Lufthansa German Airlines decided to buy 20 Boeing 737 aircraft. The aircraft cost $500 million and were to be delivered and paid for in mid-1986. This meant that Lufthansa would, if it did nothing, have a $500 million currency exposure for one year. The spot price at the time of the contract was $0.3267 per mark and the one-year forward price was $0.3373. This was an interesting problem for Lufthansa because the mark was at an historic low. If the mark continued to decline in value, the aircraft would cost even more in marks one year hence. If the mark recovered in value, the aircraft would cost less. What should Lufthansa do? One possibility was to avoid this risk by dealing with a German manufacturer. That was not possible, because there was no such manufacturer. There was a European consortium and buying its aircraft would have involved the lower risk of a European currency. Lufthansa must have decided that the Boeing aircraft *were more appropriate on technical grounds or a better economic value. The second approach was to negotiate a price in German marks. The only thing that would have accomplished is shifting the currency risk to Boeing, which might then charge a higher price. If Lufthansa could not avoid this risk, how could it manage it?*

We consider four possibilities: do nothing, hedge 100 percent, hedge 50 percent, and buy calls on the dollar. Calls on the U.S. dollar with an exercise price equal to the forward price cost DM 0.047 per dollar. If we let the price of the mark in mid-1986 be S, we can display these four choices in Table 14. These values are all expressed in terms of marks in mid-1986. That is the reason that the cost of the calls ($500 million)(DM 0.047) is multiplied by the German interest rate of 7 percent. Clearly, once we know the value of the mark in mid-1986, we know which of these choices is best. That is like saying, "Once we know which horse won the race, we know how to bet." Lufthansa had to make its decision without knowing what the outcome would be.

TABLE-14

THE ANTICIPATED COST OF THE AIRCRAFT UNDER EACH ALTERNATIVE

Choice	*Cost*
Do nothing	$500 million/S
Hedge 100%	$500 million/$0.3373
Hedge 50%	($250 million/S) + ($250 million/$0.3373)
Buy $500 million calls	($500 million)(DM 0.047)(1.07) + $500 million/max(S, $0.3373)

In this case, Lufthansa believed that the dollar was likely to depreciate in value. The company was not willing to bet $500 million on that, so it chose to hedge 50 percent of its purchase price and leave 50 percent exposed. Lufthansa was correct. The actual value of the mark in mid-1986 was $0.4548. Table-15 presents the costs of each of the four alternatives. Because the dollar depreciated, doing nothing cost the least. Using options was next cheapest, and hedging 50 percent was third cheapest. Hedging 100 percent was the most expensive. This last sentence is factually accurate, but keep in mind it is equivalent to saying, "Not buying car insurance was a good idea in any year you didn't have an accident."

As a final note to this example, it is worth mentioning the reaction to Lufthansa's decision. The managers could have been praised for having the foresight to hedge only 50 percent and saving DM 91 million compared to hedging 100 percent. Instead, they were criticized for hedging 50 percent and losing DM 92 million as compared to doing nothing.

TABLE-15

ACTUAL COST OF THE AIRCRAFT UNDER EACH ALTERNATIVE

Choice	*Cost*
Do nothing	DM 1.099 billion
Hedge 100%	DM 1.482 billion
Hedge 50%	DM 1.291 billion
Buy $500 million calls	DM 1.125 billion

EIGHT WINNING OPTIONS TRADING RULES

1. Stay away from deep in the money options

The key advantage to buying options are limited risk and high leverage. If an option is too deep in the money, it cuts down on investor's leverage and adds to his risk. He is paying more, and has more to lose, so even the risk is limited it is higher.

The biggest advantage to the option seller is time decay, and with less time the investor has less to gain the easy way (time value decay marches on daily regardless of what the market is doing) and more risk since the intrinsic component is larger.

2. Stay away from deep out of the money options

The illusion is that deep out of the money purchases gives a lot of leverage. In reality they give a lot of hope, promote over-commitment, and offer very little profit opportunity. Yes, they can hit at times, but this is a game of odds, and odds are certainly against an investor if he is buying deep out of the moneys. It may be more realistic to purchase a deep-out of the money option if an investor has a lot of time, but then again he loses some of the leverage because he pays for the time. Surely the odds are in favour when he is to sell deep out of the money options, but the expected reward is minuscule in relation to the risk. The investments could be profitable 99 times out of 100 when selling deep out of the money put options on the stock market, but that crash will come, and when one least expects it. Unless the investor wishes to be "the house", the one who is capitalised enough to cover the powerball lottery, or megabuck jackpot, stay away from deep out of the money.

3. Trade slightly out of the money, at the money, or slightly in the money options

The reasons are the opposite for which one prefers to stay away from the deep options. These have a reasonable chance of providing profitable when buying, one gains from the maximum possible time decay when selling, and they are generally the most liquid of the bunch—which results in a tighter bid/ask spread, which in turn saves on transaction costs. The one variation on this theme has to do with selling options. In this variation it is certainly the fine, or even advantageous, to sell out of the money options with this one caveat—the premium received must warrant the risk. What price might this be? There are no hard and fast rules. One just need to use good judgement.

It is also advisable to use good judgement when cutting losses. This especially involves taking a reasonable or small loss when covering short positions which are not working. However, it also is important to cut losses in long options which are not making money. The fact that most options expire worthless should be strong clue to the buyer to sell out prior to the end in case of non-performance.

4. Know your market

There is a time for all seasons. Option writing can be extremely profitable in dull, flat markets. If the tone changes, cover fast, before that catastrophic loss. If option premiums feel too low to give an adequate cushion of income they probably are. The common wisdom is to "sell flat markets "but this may just be the time to start thinking about buying. Avoid selling in periods of rising volatility, however. Option purchase will start to become more expensive, but then the rising volatility will work in the buyer's favour. Should volatility reach wild proportions, then think about selling. Just make sure that one has adequate margin to take the heat.

5. Covered all writings is a good strategy for what appears to be a bullish environment, and covered put writings is generally good for what looks like a bearish one

This is one of the few strategies where use of future and options together have the ability to profit on both legs. The strategy works well in a modestly bullish or bearish environment as well. It is not risk free, but is less risky than the outright purchase or sale of futures alone.

6. In "normal" markets, write straddles and strangles

Selling puts and calls works in most market environments. It is a good strategy as long as it is managed properly. "Normal" is a term which cannot be defined specifically. In most cases the premiums received when writing straddles and strangles give an adequate cushion to weather most storms. When the typhoon hits, however, and margin is starting to feel impaired, one should run for the exit door.

7. Look for opportunities to backspread

This is a seldom used strategy, but when used consistently has the potential to make one rich. Recall, this involves selling a call or put at one strike price, and buying a greater number of calls at a higher strike price, or buying a greater number of puts at a lower strike price. Look to establish backspreads for a credit to benefit from time decay, and look only at the market from the potential to move big. This strategy always has a predetermined and limited risk and one of the few which can still prove a mildly profitable when one is dead wrong. The profit is unlimited on a major upside or major downside move.

8. Use options to hedge a profitable future position

The trend-following traders are lucky enough to catch a major move which is showing massive unrealised profits, the great dilemma is when to cash in. An investor inevitably will have to give up a large part of the paper gain if he is to wait for confirmation of a trend change. Yet, top and bottom picking are very hard things to do. There is only one top and only one bottom,in major moves of proportion which could unfold over hundreds of trading sessions. Also, many times, the most important leg of major move comes in the last 48 hours. Why not use put options to lock in a bull-move profit, and calls for the bear-move profit? Commercial hedgers use options all the time. Trading is a business and this is the prime tool for an individual trader to hedge profit while still showing for additional profits.

These are wonderful tools, these options. Not a panacea, but to a major extent they can offer the best of both the worlds. Constantly be on the alert for ways to use them to your benefit!

QUESTIONS

1. What are the components of an option premium?
2. Why is the price of an option always greater than its intrinsic value?

3. Discuss the market structure of currency options.
4. Why cannot the intrinsic value of an option be less than zero?
5. Assume that a company wants to use either a currency option or a forward contract to hedge against exchange rate fluctuations. What are the advantages and disadvantages of currency options in this case?
6. When should a company buy a call option for hedging? When should a company buy a put option?
7. When should speculators buy a call option? When should speculators buy a put option?
8. Which contract is likely to be more valuable, an American or a European call option? Explain.
9. Discuss the Fischer Black's Option-Pricidng Model.
10. What are the golden trading risks in winning options ?

PROBLEMS

1. An American company sells yen futures contracts to cover possible exchange losses on its export orders denominated in Japanese yen. The amount of the initial margin is $20,000, and the maintenance margin is 75 per cent of the initial margin. The value of the company's position declines by $6,000 because the spot rate for yen has increased.
   (a) What is the dollar amount of the maintenance margin?
   (b) Should the broker issue margin calls to the company?
   (c) What is the amount of additional deposit needed to restore the account to the initial margin level?
2. The call premium per British pound on March 1 is $0.04, the expiration date is September 19, and the strike price is $ 1.80. A speculator believes that the spot rate for the pound will rise to $ 1.92 by September 19.
   (a) If the speculator's expectations are correct, what would be her dollar profit form speculating two pound call options (£62,500)?
   (b) If the sot rate were $ 1.76 per pound when the option expired, would the speculator exercise the option? What would be her loss from this speculation?
3. Suppose that Bawa Group (BG) wants to hedge a bid on a Japanese construction project. But since the yen exposure is contingent on acceptance of its bid, BG decides to buy a put option for the ¥15 billion bid amount rather than sell it forward. In order to reduce its hedging cost, however, BG simultaneously sells a call option for ¥15 billion with the same strike price. BG reasons that it wants to protect its downside risk on the contract and is wiling to sacrifice the upside potential in order to collect the call premium. Comment on BG's hedging strategy.
4. The put premium per British pound on March 1 is $0.04, the settlement date is September 19, and the strike price is $ 1.80. A speculator anticipates that the spot rate for the pound will fall to $ 1.72 by September 19. If the speculator's expectations are correct, what would be his dollar profit form speculating two put options (62,500 pounds)?
5. A U.S. company has bought 30 personal computers from a British company for 62,500 pounds. Its payment must be made in British pounds 90 days form now.

The premium for a pound call option with a strike price of $ 1.60 and a 90-day expiration date is $0.04 per pound. The current spot rate for pounds is $1.58; the U.S. company expects that the spot rate in 90 days will rise to $1.66. The U.S. company has two alternatives: do not hedge and hedge in the options market. Should the U.S. company choose the call option hedge or no hedge?

6. A U.S. exporter is scheduled to receive 125,000 marks in 60 days. The premium for a mark put option with a strike price of $0.50 and a 90-day settlement date is $0.03 per mark. The company anticipates that the spot rate in 90 days will be $ 0.46. Should the company hedge its accounts receivable in the options market? If the spot rate were $ 0.51 in 90 days, how would it affect the company's decision?

7. The exchange rate for Japanese yen is $0.0069 per yen, and a call option has a strike rice of $0.0065. An investor has two yen call options. If the investor exercises the call options, how much profit would she realise?

8. On October 23, the closing exchange rate of British pounds was $ 1.70. Calls which would mature the following January with a strike price of $ 1.75 were traded at $ 0.10.
   (a) Were the call options in-the-money, at-the-money, or out-of-the-money?
   (b) Compute the intrinsic value of the call.
   (c) If the exchange rate of British pounds rises to $ 1.90 prior to the January option expiration date, what is the percentage return on investment for an investor who purchased a call on October 23?

9. With reference to Problem-8, put options with the same strike price and a January maturity for British pounds were traded at $0.05 on October 23.
   (a) Were the put options in-the-money, at-the-money, or out-of-the-money?
   (b) Compute the intrinsic value of the put.
   (c) If the exchange rate of British pounds falls to $ 1.65 just prior to expiration, what is the percentage return on investment for an investor who purchased a put on October 23?

10. The exchange rate for Japanese yen is $0.0069 per yen, and a put option has a strike price of $0.0070. An investor has two yen put options. If the holder exercises the put option, how much profit would he realise?

11. Bodo Schlegelamich is a currency speculator for a private banking house in Boston. His base currency is therefore the U.S. dollar. He is currently convinced that the euro is overvalued and wishes to take a speculative position to profit from his expectations. He will invest $1 million in his position (spent entirely on option premiums). The current spot rate is $1.0650/€. The current premiums on call and put options (U.S. cents/€) with a strike price of $1.1200/€ are the following:

Strike: $1.12/€ (U.S. cents/€)	*90 days*	*180 days*
Call options on euro: premiums	0.401	1.177
Put options on euro: premiums	6.186	6.143

   (a) What should Bodo do—buy a call, sell a call, buy a put, or sell a put on the euro?
   (b) What would be his profits or losses if he bought a 90-day call at $1.02/€, and the actual spot exchange rate in 90 days, turned out to be $1.08/€?

12. According to Exhibit-1, there are actually a variety of strike prices available on the Swiss franc. Use the strike prices and premiums quoted in the exhibit to answer the following questions.
    (a) If the current spot rate is 58.51 (cents/SF) and the first option strike price listed is a "56," is the August 56 put option *in the money* or *out of the money*?
    (b) As the strike price of the put option rises from 56 upward to 60, how does the August maturity put option premium change? Why?
    (c) What is the break-even exchange rate for the September maturity put option with a strike price of 56½?

EXHIBIT-1

FOREIGN CURRENCY OPTION QUOTATIONS (PHILADELPHIA STOCK EXCHANGE)

Option and Underlying	*Strike Price*	*Calls—Last*			*Put—Last*		
		Aug.	*Sept.*	*Dec.*	*Aug.*	*Sept.*	*Dec.*
62,500 Swiss francs-cents per unit.							
58.51	56	—	—	2.76	0.04	0.22	1.16
58.51	56½	—	—	—	0.06	0.30	—
58.51	57	1.13	—	1.74	0.10	0.38	1.27
58.51	57½	0.75	—	—	0.17	0.55	—
58.51	58	0.71	1.05	1.28	0.27	0.89	1.81
58.51	58½	0.50	—	—	0.50	0.99	—
58.51	59	0.30	0.66	1.21	0.90	1.36	—
58.51	59½	0.15	0.40	—	2.32	—	—
58.51	60	—	0.31	—	2.32	2.62	3.30

13

THE INTERNATIONAL SWAP MARKET

INTRODUCTION

Today's financial swaps markets owe their origin to the exchange rate instability that followed the demise of Bretton Woods system and to the controls on international capital movements that most countries maintained in those days. Swaps are at the centre of the global financial revolution. Fantastic numbers and growth are talked of. All this is true. But what is also certain is that the current heady acceleration of this market cannot continue. Otherwise, there will be no other activity left-only swapping. Already the shakeout has started. In the "plain vanilla" dollar sector, the profits for brokers and market makers, after costs and allocation of risk capital, are measured in fewer than five basis points. This is before the regulators catch up and force disclosure and capital haircuts. At these spreads the more highly paid must move on — to currency swaps, tax-driven deals, tailored structures and Schlock swaps.

What is certain is that, although the excitement may diminish, swaps are here to stay. Already, swaps have had a major macro economic impact forging the linkage between the Euro and domestic markets, flattening the cash yield curves and reducing central bank monopoly influence on markets. We are all swappers now. And, when you are offered sweet deals, remember the Tibetan saying "Beware of honey offered on a sharp knife". The problem in following the chaotic progress of this very important market is quite simply that "he who knows does not speak, he who speaks does not know."

SWAPS—THE CONCEPT

The essence of a swap contract is the binding of two counterparties to exchange two different payment streams over time, the payment being tied, at least in part, to subsequent — and uncertain — market price developments. In most swaps so far, the prices concerned have been exchange rates or interest rates, but they increasingly reach out to equity indices and physical commodities. All such prices have risk characteristics in common, in quality if not in degree. And for all, the allure of swaps may be expected cost saving, yield enhancement, or hedging or speculative opportunity.

Financial swaps, simple in principle and versatile in practice, are revolutionary, especially for portfolio management. A swap coupled with an existing asset or liability can radically modify effective risk and return. Individually and together with futures, options and other financial derivatives, they allow yield curve and currency risks, and liquidity and geographic market considerations, all to be managed separately and also independently of underlying cash market stocks.

GROWTH OF THE SWAP MARKET

Like most other new "products" in international finance, "swap" transactions are not executed in a physical market. Participants in the swap "market" are many and varied in their location character and motives in exciting swaps. However, the sum total of the activity of participants in the swap market have taken on the character of a classical financial market connected to, and integrating the underlying money, capital and foreign exchange market.

Swap in their current form started in 1981 with the well-publicised currency swaps, and in the following year with dollar interest-rate swaps. The initial deals were characterised by three critical features.

1. *Barter*—two counterparties with exactly offsetting exposures were introduced by a third party. If the credit risk were unequal, the third party — if a bank — might interpose itself or arrange for a bank to do so for a small fee.
2. *Arbitrage driven*—the swap was driven by an arbitrage which gave some profit to all three parties. Generally, this was a credit arbitrage or market-access arbitrage.
3. *Liability driven*—almost all swaps were driven by the need to manage a debt issue on both sides.

Activity in FX swaps had grown strongly in recent years, up until the financial crisis. The turnover in traditional global FX markets grew at unprecedented rates over the April 2004 to April 2007 period, with the average daily turnover expanding by 69 percent to $3.2 trillion. More than half the increase was attributable to FX swaps with the average daily turnover rising by 80 percent compared to 45 percent the preceding three-year period. The increasing importance of these instruments was partly attributable to changes in hedging activity.

Overall, the increase in FX swaps transactions between dealers and other financial institutions accounted for about half the growth in the global turnover in this market. Separately, turnover with non-financial customers recorded a strong increase of 10 percent, to account for 45 percent of all FX swap turnovers over the 2004-07 period. During this time, the share of FX swap transactions with a maturity of less than seven days increased to 78 percent from 73 percent.

The FX swap market has also become an increasingly important linkage across countries. Cross-border transactions represented more than 60 percent of the total FX swaps turnover in April 2007. The cross-border turnover in FX swaps had expanded rapidly between April 2004 and April 2007, with the average daily turnover increasing by 78 percent, to $1.1 trillion. About 35 percent of the increase was attributable to interbank transactions, and almost 50 percent to transactions between reporting banks and non-bank financial institutions.

The financial crisis clearly took a toll on activity in the FX swap market. Positions taken in FX derivatives declined sharply in 2008. Among the countries comprising the G-10 and Switzerland, notional amounts outstanding in forwards and FX swaps fell by 33 percent from the first-half of that year, followed by a slight uptick of 9 percent in 2009. However, significant price movements resulted in sharp variations in gross market values, with forwards and FX swaps doubling to $1.6 trillion in the second-half of 2008 trillion, then almost halving again to $870 billion in 2009.

The major dramatic change has been the emergence of the large banks as aggressive market makers in dollar interest-rate swaps. Major US banks are in the business of taking credit risk and interest-rate risk. They, therefore, do not need counterparties to do dollar swaps. The net result is that spreads have collapsed and volume has exploded. This means that institutional investors get a better return on their investments and international borrowers pay lower financing costs. This, in turn, result in more competitively priced goods for consumers and in enhanced returns pensioners. Swap therefore have an effect on almost all of us yet they remains an arcane derivative risk management tool, sometimes suspected of providing the international banking system with tools required to bring about destruction.

Although the swap market is now firmly established, there remains a wide divergence among current and potential users as to how exactly a given swap structure works, what risks are entailed when entering into swap transactions and precisely what "the swap market" is and, for that matter, is not.

THE BASIC SWAP STRUCTURES

The growth and continued success of the swap market has been due small part to the creativity of its participants. As a result, the swap structures currently available and the future potential structures which will in time become just another market "norm" are limited only by the imagination and ingenuity of those participating in the market. Nonetheless, underlying the swap transactions seen in the market today are four basic structures which may now be considered as "fundamental". These structures are:

— the Interest Rate Swap
— the Fixed Rate Currency Swap
— the Currency Coupon Swap
— the Basis Rate Swap

The following is a summary of these fundamental swap structures and some of their primary applications.

The Interest Rate Swap

The basic structure of an interest rate swap consists of the exchange between two counterparties of fixed rate interest for floating rate interest in the same currency calculated by reference to a mutually agreed notional principal amount. This principal amount, which would normally equate to the underlying assets or liabilities being "swapped" by the counterparties, is applicable solely for the calculation of the interest to be exchanged under the swap. At no time it is physically passed between the counterparties. Through this straightforward swap structure, the counterparties are able to convert an underlying fixed rate asset/liability into a floating rate asset/liability and vice versa.

The majority of interest rate swap transactions are driven by the cost savings to be obtained by each of the counterparties. These cost savings, which are often substantial, result from differentials in the credit standing of the counterparties and other structural considerations.

In general, investors in fixed rate instruments are more sensitive to credit quality than floating rate bank lenders. Accordingly, a greater premium is demanded of issuers of lesser credit quality in the fixed rate debt markets than in the floating rate bank lending market. The counterparties to an interest rate swap may therefore obtain an arbitrage advantage by accessing the market in which they have the greatest relative cost advantage and then entering into an interest rate swap to convert the cost of the funds so raised from a fixed-rate to a floating-rate basis or vice versa.

The credit arbitrage available through the use of an interest rate swap may be illustrated by considering two companies, Company A and Company B with the following profiles (see Exhibit-1).

EXHIBIT-1

	Company A	*Company B*	*Comparative Advantage*
	Credit Rating	AAA	BBB
Cost of Raising Direct Fixed Rate Funding	10.80%	12.00%	1.20%
Cost of Raising Direct Floating Rate Funds	6-month LIBOR plus 1/4 %	6-month LIBOR plus 3/4 %	.50%

As expected, Company A with the superior credit quality has a greater relative cost advantage over Company B in the fixed rate debt market Despite the fact that Company A can also raise direct investing rate fluids more cheaply than Company B, a potential arbitrage therefore costs whereby Company A and Company B may both obtain a cost saving by assessing the markets in which they have the greatest relative cost advantage and entering into an interest rate swap. (see Exhibit-2 and 3).

This ability to transfer a fixed rate cost advantage to floating rate liabilities has led to many high quality credits issuing fixed rate Eurobonds purely to "swap" and obtain, in many cases, sub-LIBOR funding. The use of this structure in a fixed rate Eurobond issue enables the issuer to obtain substantial funding at points below LIBOR. This most attractive of rates is made possible by (a) the careful timing of the Eurobond issue to ensure its success at the finest of rates and (b) the use of exact hedging and a deferred swap accrual date to ensure the best possible swap terms for the issuer. The "counterparty" to the swap may be a combination of banks and corporate clients. The banks may want to hedge their fixed rate income into a floating rate return that fully matched their floating rate liabilities in order to alleviate interest rate exposure. The corporate clients may want to hedge their floating rate binding into fixed rate liabilities for a size and maturity unavailable in the direct fixed rate debt market. Acting as principal, the intermending may be able to provide

EXHIBIT-2

	Company A	*Company B*
Direct Funding Cost		
Fixed Rate Funds Raised Directly by Company A	(10.80%)	
Floating Rate Funds Raised Directly by Company B		(6-month LIBOR+3/4 %)
Swap Payments		
Company A pays Company B Floating Rate Interest	(LIBOR)	LIBOR
Company B pays Company A Fixed Rate Interest	10.90%	(10.90%)
All-in Cost of Funding	LIBOR-1/10%	11.65%
Comparable Cost of Equivalent Direct Funding	LIBRO + 1/4%	12.00%
Saving	35 Basis Points	35 Basis Points

EXHIBIT-3

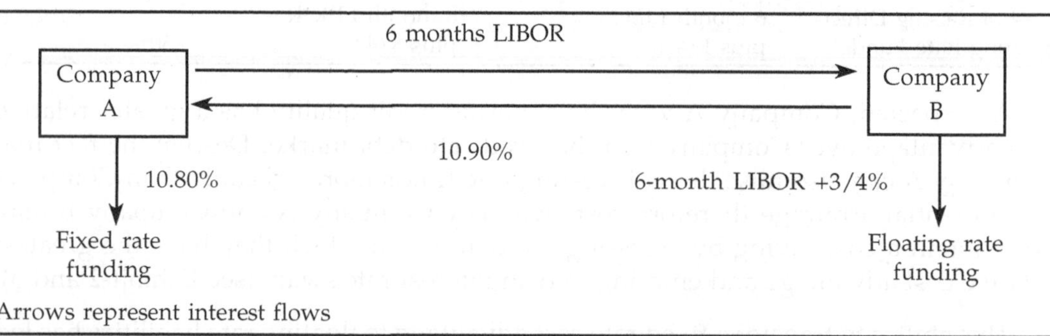

Arrows represent interest flows

both the banks and its corporate clients with swap terms to meet their exact requirementsand then subsequently lock the Eurobond issuer into an opposite swap when the Eurobond market was most receptive to the issue. The resulting structure may be seen in Exhibit-4.

In addition to the cost advantages, interest rate swaps also provide an excellent mechanism for entities to effectively access markets which are otherwise closed to them — whether by reason of credit quality, lack of name familiarity or excessive use. The ability to obtain the benefits of markets without the need to comply with the prospectus disclosures, credit ratings and other formal requirements provides an additional benefit especially for private companies. An excellent example of the swap market's flexibility in providing benefits is the growth of interest rate swaps using commercial paper as the underlying floating rate basis.

EXHIBIT-4

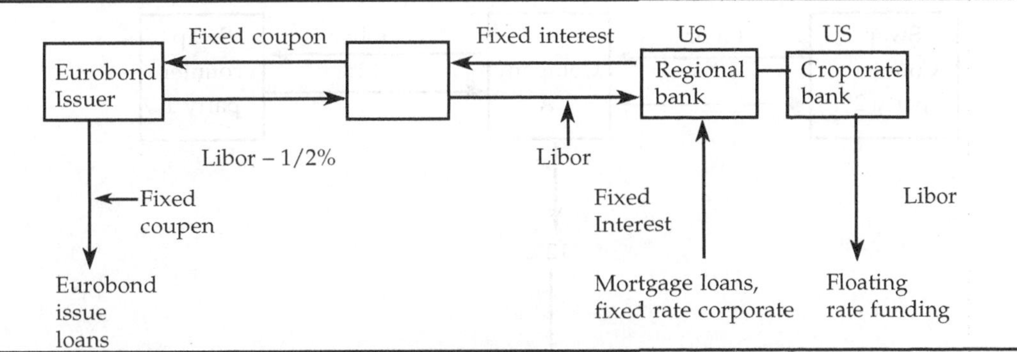

The interest rate swap market also provides finance money with the perfect mechanism for managing interest rate costs and exposure whilst leaving the underlying source of funds unaffected. For example, the cost of fixed rate funding may be reduced in a declining interest rate environment through the use of the interest rate swap technique whilst leaving the underlying funding in place. This may be illustrated by considering the actions of Company A, with underlying fixed rate debt costing 12% per annum, during a period of declining interest rates:

(a) *At the beginning of interest rates declining*— Company A with a fixed rate debt at 12 % would swap to obtain LIBOR handing (see Exhibit-5).

EXHIBIT-5

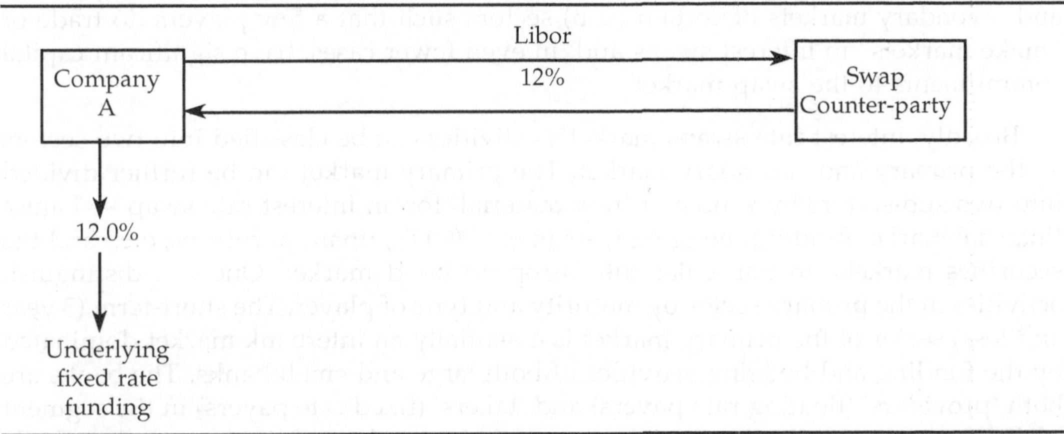

(b) *During the period of interest rate decline:-* Company A would leave the swap in place as interest rates decline.

(c) *At the end of interest rate decline:-* Company A would enter into a second swap to "lock into" the new lower fixed rates of, say, 10% (See Exhibit-6)

The net effect of the above series of transactions is a saving of 2 % for Company A as the net cost of funds is reduced from 12% to 10%.

EXHIBIT-6

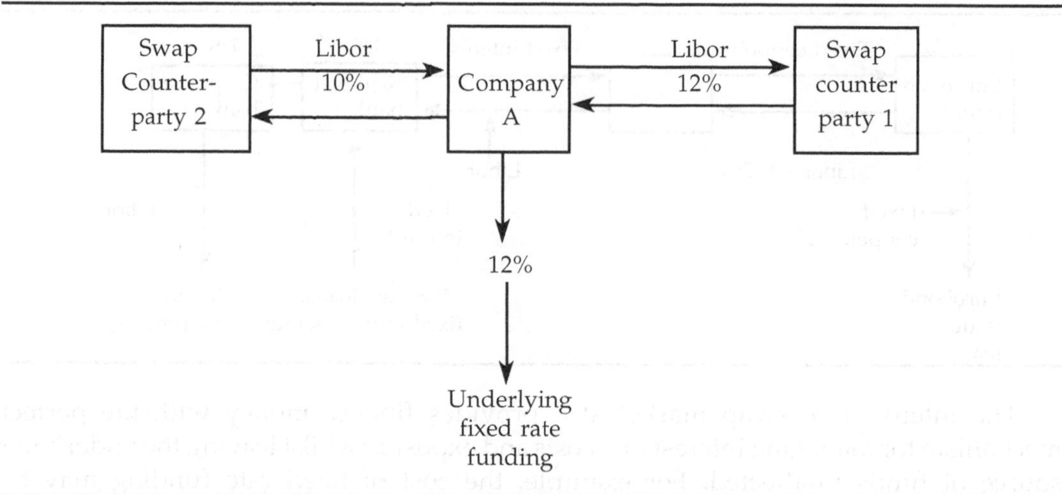

The fact that one can deal in such a range of sizes with numerous counterparties and in a large gross amount amply demonstrates the depth of the secondary market in short-term swaps.

The interest rate swaps market displays certain characteristics of a fairly well-organised financial market. There are a larger number of players with fairly distinct roles in the market; there are several different (or speciality) structures of the market in which certain players specialise; there is both a "primary" and a "secondary" market in interest swaps: and finally, there is sufficient liquidity in both the primary and secondary markets of certain (sub) sectors such that a few players do trade or "make markets" in interest swaps and, in even fewer cases, have significant capital commitments to the swap market.

Broadly, interest rate swaps market's activities can be classified into two sectors — the primary and secondary market. The primary market can be further divided into two sub-sectors by source of 'raw material' for an interest rate swap — bank/ financial market funding/hedging instruments (CD's, financial futures, etc.) and the securities markets, in particular the European bond market. One can distinguish activities in the primary sector by maturity and type of player. The short-term (3 year and less) sector of the primary market is essentially an interbank market dominated by the funding and hedging activities of both large and small banks. The banks are both 'providers' (floating rate payers) and 'takers' (fixed rate payers) in the segment of the market depending on the structure of their asset base. Being extremely volatile in price in terms of spread, the market-making or position taking is, therefore, only for the most experienced dealers. For such dealers, the profit potential is high and the risks in position-taking while similarly high, are manageable due to impressive array of instruments available to manage risks.

The center of this market is New York followed by London and Tokyo. The participants, principally banks, include a number of brokers who have extended their normal money market dealing activities with banks to include interest swap activities. Success as a broker or principal in this segment of primary market is dependent not only on close integration of an institution's treasury and swap operations, but also on distribution and in particular, the ability to move positions quickly due to the price volatility and risks inherent to the market. 'Inventory' (i.e. a booked but not closed position) also quickly becomes stale in the short-term market because most transactions are done on a 'spot' (immediate settlement) basis: holding a position for any period of time may therefore mean one's inventory may not move irrespective of price. However, the growth of the secondary market in the short-term swaps has decreased the risks of position-taking in the short term primary market. Of particular importance to the development of the secondary market has been the use of financial futures market to create 'the other side' of an interest swap. While financial futures-based swaps are highly complex to execute properly, the very quick and sharp movements in this market and hence, the need to "wind and un-wind" these structures to maximise profits has increased the liquidity (or availability of alternative priced swaps) in the secondary market.

As one moves out the yield curve, the primary interest rate swap market becomes dominated by securities transactions and in particular, the Eurodollar bond market. Whether this segment of the swap market is larger than the short-term market is open to debate. However, this market sector is very large: it is estimated that some 75% of all Eurodollar bond issues are swapped and the dollar fixed-rate Eurobond market is currently running at an annual rate of $50 billions plus. The advent of the swap market has also meant that the Eurodollar bond market now never closes due to interest rate levels: issuers who would not come to market because of high interest rates now do so to the extent that a swap is available. Indeed, the Eurodollar bond market owes much of its spectacular growth to the parallel growth of the swap market. The firms that now dominate lead management roles in the Eurodollar bond market all have substantial swap capabilities and this trend will continue.

Pricing in this segment of the market is exclusively related to the U.S. Treasury rates for comparable maturities (on a "spread" versus Treasuries basis) and is marked by the relative stability of these "spreads" by comparison to the short-term market. Given the size of the most Eurobond issues ($ 100 million plus) and the oversupply of entities able and willing to approach the Eurobond market to swap into floating-rate funds, most major houses in the swap market now enter into swap agreements with an issuer without a counterparty (fixed-rate payor) on the other side. This "warehousing" activity is normally hedged in the U.S. Treasury or financial futures market, leaving the warehouse manager with a "spread" risk, or the difference between the spread at which he booked the swap with the issuer and where he manages to find (over a course of time) a matched counterparty. The relative stability of spreads and a positively sloped yield curve (for funding the hedge at a positive carry) have allowed the market to function reasonably well on this basis with only occasional periods of severe oversupply in any particular maturity. The major houses tend to spread their inventory across the yield curve to reduce risk and to ensure ready availability of a given maturity for particular clients' requirements.

Bids for bond-related swaps tend to differ between the major houses by only a few basis points: the swap market is quite efficient in price given the (still relatively) few houses who deal in bond market size and maturities. Hence, a premium is placed on creating bond structures which offer the fixed-rate issuer a lower cost and, therefore, a better spread (below) LIBOR. Apart from creative bond/swap structures, the key to successfully operating in this segment of the market for the bond/swap arranger has been the development of a highly refined sense of timing for the underlying issue. While finding a "window" in the Eurodollar bond market has always been the *sine qua non* for a successful lead manager, with the advent and development of the swap market, the focus of the potential lead manager has shifted from an "investor" window to a "spread" window. Given that the long-term swap market operates on a relatively stable spread level versus U.S. Treasuries and the Eurodollar bond market is notoriously volatile versus Treasuries for different types of issuers, a similar premium to that of creativity applies to the lead manager who can locate a "spread window" for a particular type of issuer. This "creativity" and search for a "spread window" has sometimes led to mispriced and/or virtually incomprehensible bond structures (to the bond investor) but more often than not, the bond/swap structures so created have provided value to both the Eurobond investor and issuer.

However, it is clear that (below) LIBOR spreads available to issuers have declined as the market has become more efficient in pricing the relative value of a given swap: at the outset of the market, a "AAA" issuer could reasonably expect to achieve 75-100 basis points below LIBOR on a bond/swap; under current market conditions. This same issuer might expect only 25-30 basis points below on a "plain vanilla" bond/swap. Indeed many issuers, particularly commercial banks, now find it more cost-effective to approach the floating rate note market than the bond/swap market. The lower spreads available have gone almost entirely to the benefit of the fixed-rate payor; intermediaries (mostly commercial banks) have seen their profit margins reduced to a very substantial degree in the primary market. This reduced profitability and lower spreads available has led, in tum,for most bond/swap arrangers to attempt to put potential counterparties in direct contact with each other and eliminate the intermediation of a commercial bank. This is often a very difficult process due to timing and credit considerations but there is a strong incentive now among all parties concerned to see whether a "direct write" is possible on a new issue.

The secondary market in long-term interest swaps is a highly opportunistic segment of the market. As interest rates fluctuate, a fixed rate provider or taker may find that a substantial profit can be realised by "reversing" (with a "minor" swap) the original swap or cancelling the original swap in return for an up-front cash payment. As dollar interest rates have fluctuated widely since the advent of the swap market, secondary market activity in long-term swaps has grown rapidly but at a substantially slower pace than the primary market. There are several reasons for this slower pace of growth. *First,* banks executing fixed rate bond issues have represented a large portion of the "provider" side of the swap market. Most banks executed a bond/swap to gain long-term floating rate funding for their long-term floating rate loans and, hence, have no reason to reverse. *Second,* the "odd-dates" thrown-off by swap reversals are often difficult to close in the market and, hence, what appears to be an interesting price on a "spot" basis may become substantially less interesting when the "odd dates" are taken, into account. *Third,* many swap intermediaries do not make markets to their clients with whom the original swaps were written and hence, the only option available is to execute a "mirror" swap for which up-fronts cash will be difficult to obtain and entails a doubling of credit/performance risks for the reversor. This latter problem is also prevalent when a swap is written directly with a counterparty without an intermediary bank: in the secondary market, swaps are a "zero-sum" game—one counterparty's gain is another's loss. Most financial managers are willing to take gains but ignore losses — hence, the difficulty in reversing a "direct-write" situation.

Although the market risk may be associated with the fixed flows, there is also risk associated with the LIBOR side. Notably, if a default occurred between two payments, the counterparty would have to borrow money for the remainder of the payment period. This LIBOR rate may differ from the previous 6 month setting rate, which would result in a gain or loss. As a worst case, we assume that a default occurs the day after a LIBOR rate reset on the swap and the market moves 100 basis points against the non-defaulting party. By borrowing a 100 basis points negative spread is effectively "locked in" for 6 months, which results in a 0.5% (50 basis points) additional exposure. Again. this is an extremely conservative estimate given that 100 basis points is a big movement in LIBOR over a matter of days and only an adverse movement in rates is assumed.

An additional potential risk can be assumed depending on the structure of the swap. When a counterparty receives fixed payments semi-annually and pays LIBOR semi-annually, potential risk is minimised. However, if an annual fixed payment is received in return for delivering semi-annual LIBOR payments, and if a default occurs in the second semi-annual period, the counterparty is exposed to an additional potential loss equal to the first LIBOR payment. Assuming a constant 6-month LIBOR at 12.0 percent, this equates to an additional 6.0 percent potential exposure. Since an event of default is assumed to be random and equally likely to occur in the first half of an annual period (when there is no additional potential exposure) as in the second half (when there could be an additional 6.0% potential exposure). It has been assumed that an annual vs semi-annual payment structure adds another 3.0 percent potential exposure. To be conservative, the analysis always assumes an annual versus semi-annual payment structure.

Despite the above problems, the long-term secondary market has shown good growth and several houses have sponsored the growth of this segment through commitment of capital, personnel and systems capabilities to market to making in long term swaps.

The Currency Swap Market

The currency swap market is the oldest and most creative sector of the swap market. We would not distinguish in market terms between what we have called above the "fixed-rate currency swap" and the "currency coupon swap". There should be no distinction in market terms between these two types of currency swaps because the only difference is whether the counter-currency receipt/payment is on a fixed or floating basis — in structure and result, the two types of swaps are identical and it is a matter of taste (or preference) for one or both counterparties to choose a fixed or floating payment. When the dollar is involved on one side of a given transaction, the possibility to convert a fixed rate preference on one side to a floating rate preference on the other side through the interest rate swap market makes any distinction even more irrelevant. However, for those who like fine distinctions, there is a tendency in the market to regard the fixed-rate currency swap market as more akin to the long-date forward foreign exchange market (because when one is executing a fixed currency swap one may often be competing with the long-date FX market) and the currency coupon swap market as more akin to the dollar bond/swap market (because the dollar bond issuer compares the below LIBOR spread available in the dollar market to that available, say, through tapping the Swiss Franc market).

Whatever distinctions one wishes to draw or not to draw between the two basic types of swaps in the currency swap market, there are many reasons why this market is the most creative and therefore, most interesting sector of the swap market. While still smaller than the dollar interest swap market, the currency swap market has great, and perhaps even greater potential for growth than the dollar market, particularly in the light of the growth in local/Euro capital markets in a wide range of currencies

One can classify activity in the currency swap market into the same two basic sectors as the interest swap market—a primary and secondary sector. In the currency swap market, the primary sector is dominant across the yield curve and the key motivating forces underlying this market are "new money" and "hedging" in that order. "New money" or the willingness to execute swap-related public or private financing in one currency to achieve a finer cost or enhanced availability in another currency is the key motivating force behind the currency swap market, particularly for banks and sovereign entities. Such entities have had large capital and refinancing requirements in recent years. The capacity of any one market (e.g. the Eurodollar bond market) to provide all of these requirements at the finest possible cost has been limited. Hence, many banks and sovereign have been willing to approach the private and public debt markets in currencies for which they have no natural requirements (but which the swap market can use) in order to reduce costs and/or gain greater access to a particular currency which is required. Restructuring, or "hedging" current debt portfolios, cash flows or investments, is clearly an influence of second order is comparisons to the influence of "new money". The flexibility of loan repayment clauses and the fact that many corporate and sovereign entities have found their access to a wide range of securities markets greatly expanded in recent years means that even if the fundamental motivation of a currency swap is restructuring/ hedging, this would normally be preceded by an issuer first obtaining a cheaper cost of funds in the base currency through a securities or near securities transactions.

From a market standpoint, the driving force of the currency swap market is creativity. Structures in the currency swap market range from the extremely simple to the complex, multi-faceted, multi-counterpart transactions who economies exist in the dimensions available only to the mathematician. One is limited in the currency swap market only by the problem to be solved, one's imagination, the skills of your personal computer operators and of course, the ability of your colleagues to find suitable counterparts around the world at the right time and price. As opposed to the dollar market, where capital commitment has become increasingly important, the key in the currency swap market is still commitment to creative problem — solving and development of a swap distribution system on a global basis — classic investment banking.

The primary sector of the currency swap market is dominated by "new money" considerations by issuers and on the other side, by greater access to a select few low-interest rate debt markets by often the same type of entities. There is, however, a greater diversity by type of participants in the currency swap market than the interest swap market with financial institutions, particularly banks, playing a smaller role in the currency market and (sovereigns, supranationals and corporate playing a relatively larger role than such entities do in the dollar swap market. Position-taking (capital commitment) is still less important than commitment to creativity and distribution capacity among arrangers. While the currency swap market is highly competitive, there is still the possibility to beat your competitor by being smarter, quicker and developing "niches" of special expertise in a particular currency.

The secondary market is a highly opportunistic subsector of the currency swap market and is relatively larger in comparison to the primary market. Some might suggest that this is due to a given swap counterparty having two chances to "win"—on interest and exchange rates—in a currency swap and that with the enormous volatility of the dollar, a chance to win big on an exchange rate play. Generally, while the best of motivations normally drive an original decision to create a currency swap, the primary motive in the secondary market is to take profit before a currency move places the swap into an unprofitable position. On occasion, the underlying commercial or financial motivation for the swap may be removed, forcing a reversal to avoid an open position. However, for the most part, activity in the secondary market is driven by the profit motive (and/or a change in view that normally results in a profit to the counterparty).

This secondary market phenomenon is therefore part and parcel of the new breed of financial management which aggressively manages their cash flows and debt portfolios because they are judged by results defined as profits. Although spreads tend to be relatively wider in the secondary currency than the secondary interest swap markets, moving quickly when an exchange rate breaks is the key to the level of profitability. The impact of the exchange rate on the profitability of a swap reversal (versus an interest rate impact) is so much greater in the case of the exchange rate that excellent prices and highly attractive rates can be obtained in the secondary market—the reverser needs to move quickly to capitalise on his exchange rate gain. This can lead to virtually wholesale shutdowns of the primary market in currency swaps due to the fact that many counterparties want to reverse at the same time. This in turn leads to substantial discounts in interest rates on the secondary market versus the primary market.

The position-taking and "market-making" are much more common in the secondary market than the primary market, due again to the excellent pricing often times available in the secondary market. Like the dollar market, sophisticated financial managers are aware that the credit risks are greater in currency swap and that when it is time to reverse a position, having an intermediary bank which will make a market on the original swap is as important as the interest rates on the original transactions. Here at Bankers Trust we have made just such a commitment to secondary market making for our clients, in currency swaps.

The Fixed Rate Currency Swap

A fixed rate currency swap consists of the exchange between two counterparties of fixed rate interest in one currency in return for fixed rate interest in another currency. The following three basic steps are common to all currency swaps:-

(a) Initial Exchange of Principal

On the commencement of the swap the counterparties exchange the principal amounts of the swap at an agreed rate of exchange. Although this rate is usually based on the spot exchange rate, a forward rate set in advance of the swap commencement date can also be used. This initial exchange may be on a "notional" basis (i.e. no physical exchange of principal amounts) or alternatively a "physical" exchange.

Whether the initial exchange is on a physical or notional basis its sole importance is to establish the quantum of the respective principal amounts for the purpose of (a) calculating the ongoing payments of interest and (b) the re-exchange of principal amounts under the swap.

(b) Ongoing Exchanges of Interest

Once the principal amounts are established, the counterparties exchange interest payments based on the outstanding principal amounts at the respective fixed interest rates agreed at the outset of the transaction.

(c) Re-exchange of Principal Amounts

On the maturity date the counterparties re-exchange the principal amounts established at the outset. This straightforward, three-step process is standard practice in the swap market and results in the effective transformation of a debt raised in one currency into a fully-hedged fixed-rate liability in another currency.

In principle, the fixed currency swap structure is similar to the conventional long-date forward foreign exchange contract. However, the counterparty nature of the swap market results in a far greater flexibility in respect of both maturity periods and size of the transactions which may be arranged. A currency swap structure also allows for interest rate differentials between the two currencies via periodic payments rather than the lump sum reflected by forward points used in the foreign exchange market. This enables the swap structure to be customised to fit the counterparties exact requirements at attractive rates. For example the cash flows of an underlying bond issue may be matched exactly and invariably.

To illustrate, consider Bankers Trust arranged an "asset swap" with a German corporate on the other side of this transaction. This structure was made possible by Bankers Trust's ability to isolate a fixed-rate US Dollar asset providing a particularly favourable rate of return. Bankers Trust purchased this asset on behalf of the German corporate which was actively managing an investment portfolio. Through the use of a fixed rate currency swap, the paper was then converted into a fully hedged fixed

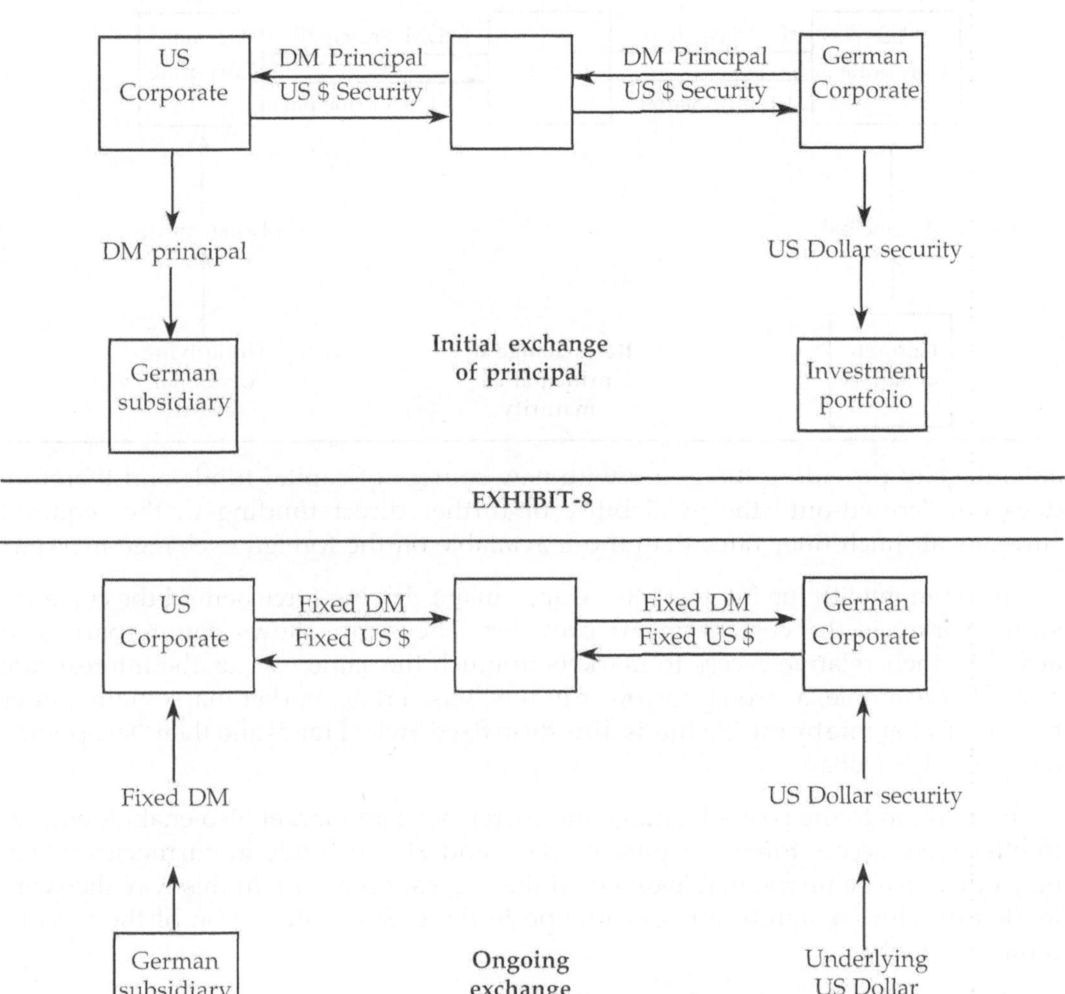

rate Deutsche mark investment providing a higher rate of return than any German securities of a similar credit quality available at the same time (see Exhibit-7, 8 & 9). In this way, the Deutsche mark inter-company loan is effectively converted into a fully headed US Dollar asset.

The currency swap market adds enormous breadth to a borrower's options and possible cross market arbitrage opportunities. A borrower may issue bonds in a currency other than it desired funding base and combine the issue with a currency swap. This structure will achieve a target all—in fixed cost below that available from direct funding in the required currency. This type of structure is essentially opportunistic as it enables issuers to maximise the potential arising from "windows" which open from time to time in specific capital markets. The structure also has the added

EXHIBIT-9

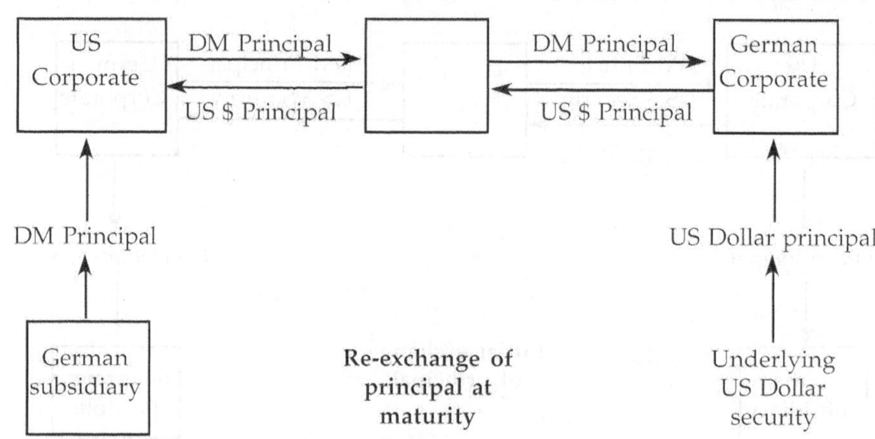

advantage of providing the issuer with new sources of capital funds and therefore does not "crowd-out" the availability of further direct funding in the required currency at much finer rates than those available on the foreign exchange market.

In common with the interest rate swap, a major driving force behind the currency swap market is the cost saving it provides. The swap allows counterparties to arbitrage their relative access to markets in much the same way as the interest rate swap. For example, a strong borrower in the Swiss Franc market may obtain a finer fixed US Dollar rate by raising funds directly in fixed Swiss Francs and then "swapping" them into US Dollars.

In addition to the cost advantage the currency swap market also enables entities to effectively access foreign capital markets and obtain funds in currencies which may otherwise be unobtainable except at the highest premium. In this way the swap market provides a significant contribution to the greater integration of the world's capital markets.

The immense flexibility of the available swap structures together with the longer maturities available, often in excess of those available in the direct funding domestic and Euromarkets, make the currency swap technique an invaluable tool. This is well illustrated by a recent transaction structured by the Bankers. Trust The structure enabled a large US multinational corporate client to discreetly finance its German subsidiary using its US dollar funding pool. The transaction provided for an inter-company loan to be made at a preferential Deutsche mark interest rate. The use of a currency swap ensured that the US parent was able to provide this finance with no foreign currency risk and the minimum of administrative problems. The basic structure of the swap is as follows:

(i) On day one the Bankers Trust exchanges with the US parent company an amount of DM equal to the principal of the intercompany loan in return for an equivalent amount of US$ based on the spot exchange rate. The DM amount is then passed on by the US parent to its German subsidiary by way of an intercompany loan.

(ii) Over the life of the swap the US parent then pays fixed rate DM interest to Bankers Trust to match exactly the payment dates and amounts on the underlying intercompany loan in return for receiving US$ fixed rate interest to match exactly the payment dates and amounts on the underlying intercompany loan.

(iii) At maturity, the German subsidiary repays the DM principal amount which is passed on to the Bankers Trust in exchange for the US$ principal amount.

The Currency Coupon Swap

The currency coupon swap is a combination of the interest rate swap and the fixed-rate currency swap. The transaction follows the three basic steps described for the fixed-rate currency swap with the exception that fixed-rate interest in one currency is exchanged for floating rate interest in another currency.

The benefits to be obtained using the currency coupon swap structure are well illustrated by a transaction structured by Bankers Trust. Consider a US Corporate wished to enter into a major leasing contract for a capital project to be sited in the United Kingdom. The Corporate wanted to obtain the advantage of funding through a UK lease which provided lower lease rentals due to the UK tax advantages available to the UK lessor. However, the Corporate was concerned by both the currency and interest rate exposure which would result form the sterling LIBOR based leasing contract The structure provided by Bankers Trust enabled the Corporate to obtain the cost benefits available from the UK lease and at the same time convert the underlying lease finance into a fully-hedged fixed-rate dollar liability. Under the structure Bankers Trust paid, on a quarterly basis, the exact payments due on the Corporate's sterling LIBOR based UK lease in return for the Corporate paying an annual amount of fixed US Dollars to Bankers Trust. The amount of the fixed US dollars payable reflected the beneficial level of the US sterling lease payments. As principal, Bankers Trust hedged this position by entering into a number of currency coupon swaps for different - maturities and principal amounts to match the amortising structure of the US Corporate's lease (Exhibit-10).

EXHIBIT-10

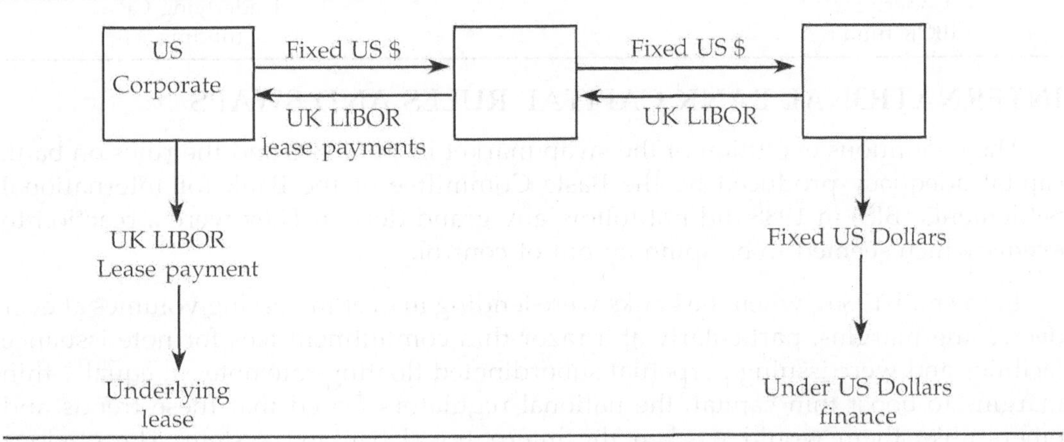

The Basis Rate Swap

A fast developing area in the international swap markets is the basis rate swap. The structure of the basis rate swap is the same as the straight interest rate swap, with the exception that floating interest calculated on one basis is exchanged for floating interest calculated on a different basis. The forerunner of this type of swap was the US Dollar Prime Rate LIBOR swap. However, an even larger market has developed for the exchange of I month US Dollar LIBOR for 6 month US Dollar LIBOR and more recently US Dollar LIBOR for US Dollar commercial paper at much finer rates than those available on the foreign exchange market.

The availability of the basis rate swap market provides an excellent method for entities to arbitrage spreads between different floating rate funding sources. More importantly, it provides a discreet and most efficient method for European entities in particular to simulate the US Commercial Paper funding market without the necessity of meeting the stringent US requirements for a Commercial Paper programme. To illustrate, consider a transaction structured by Bankers Trust which enabled an European Bank to obtain effective 30 day commercial paper funding by converting its 6 month US Dollar funding base into 30 day Commercial Paper via a basis rate swap. The counterparty to the transaction was a second European bank wishing to match its commercial paper funding programme to its LIBOR asset base. (see Exhibit-11).

EXHIBIT-11

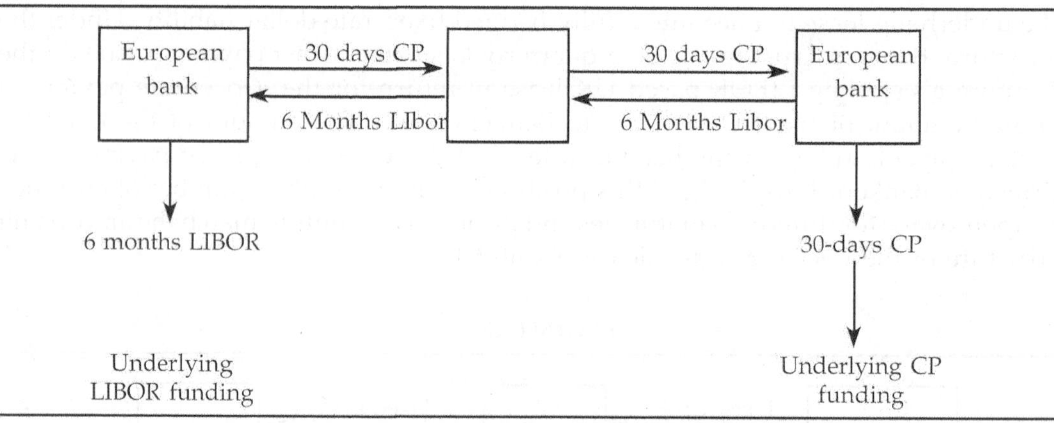

INTERNATIONAL BANK CAPITAL RULES AND SWAPS

The continuous evolution of the swap market in the 1980s and the rules on bank capital adequacy produced by the Basle Committee of the Bank for International Settlements (BIS) in 1988 did not follow any grand design. They were a reaction to events which seemed to be spinning out of control.

In the mid-1980s, when the banks were lending in ever increasing volumes at ever decreasing margins, particularly at a razor-thin commitment fees for note issuance facilities and were issuing perpetual subordinated floating-rate notes at equally thin margins to boost thin capital, the national regulators feared that these trends and others alike them would weaken the international banking system. The obvious forum for their deliberations was the central bankers' central bank, the Bank for International Settlements (BIS) in Basle.

Once agreed, the Basic guidelines addressed the perceived problem areas: capital and assets. They were meant to ensure that banks had enough capital to absorb the losses from assets that turned sour. So capital was divided into tier one' core capital and 'tier two' supplementary capital. Core capital is composed of shareholders' funds—paid-up capital, disclosed revenues and minority interests — including as a concession to the Americans, perpetual non-cumulative preferred shares. Tier two includes perpetual (upper tier equal 8% of risk weighted assets; not more than half of total capital two) and redeemable (lower tier two) subordinated debt. Total capital must be tier two and not more than half of tier two may be lower tier two.

Asset risk weightings range from nil for OECD sovereign debt with no price risk, to 100% for private sector corporate loans. In order to preserve the efficiency, and liquidity of the international inter-bank markets at 20%—requiring only one fifth the capital needed for loans to non-banking companies — except for loans over one year to non-OECD banks, which are weighted at the full 100%; The rationale is that since OECD banks fall under the regulatory responsibility of Basle, they are less risky than banks whose finance is unregulated.

From a prudential standpoint this system looks logical, fair, balanced and coherent. But the failings of Basle arise precisely from its prudential nature and its limited scope. Put into business practice, the Basle guidelines create distortions and these distortions make themselves felt both at the level of individual banks and of the international financial system as a whole.

Distortions in the way banks manage their business occur in both of the main areas: capital and assets. Basle encourages banks to raise a maximum amount of minimum quality capital, making tier—one core capital a scarcer resource and one more highly valued. Banks were no longer to rely on other banks for capital but they were to increase their capital nonetheless. The blunt message to the market was this: Banks are under-capitalised but the regulators will not let the other banks invest in them.

Many banks decided to adopt the 8% minimum as a maximum as well. They would do that they could meet it but they would do what they could not to exceed it. Rather than raising tier one capital — the safest but the dearest—banks began with the least secure but cheapest two dated subordinated debt. Obviously, non-bank investors feel least uncomfortable with this risk: they are repaid within a foreseeable future, they do not share in losses and their coupons need not be suspended if the banks miss a dividend.

Filling lower two tier is easy; filling upper tier two — perpetual subordinated debt —is another matter altogether. Basle permits perpetuals but killed the market because the only buyers of bank perpetuals, in size, were banks themselves, and Basle effectively forbids banks to be buyers themselves. As a result banks have turned to para-perpetuals' which just scrape into that category: variable-rate notes and step-up perpetuals. The chances are that most of these will be redeemed as soon as banks get a fair shot at raising core capital at a competitive cost. For the moment, tier one capital is close to impossible to find for most banks, except by issuing ordinary shares, which are expensive and dilutive both to ownership and to earnings. Under the swaps and the international bank capital rules by December 31, 1992, the banks are to hold qualifying capital of at least 8% of total risk-adjusted assets. The latter including a 50% weighting of credit equivalent exposure on swaps. For Japanese banks; the deadline was end-March 1993. Consistent with other provisions of the BIS rules, the risk weightage on swaps is cut to 20% if the counterparty is a US — or OECD — country-based bank and may be further reduced if cash or qualifying government securities serve as collateral. Accordingly, the commercial banks have become the dominant swap players. For some, in fact, swaps represent a latter-day reincarnation of traditional intermediation — except now with borrower and depositor often one and the same—much conventional corporate lending having been displaced by securitised financings. Commercial banks, however, hold no monopoly. Many face new capital and credit constraints. Meanwhile, some insurers and high rate corporates are going beyond thin narrow financial needs by deploying capital and credit experience to run swap books for trading profit.

Early swap transactions were anything but standardised and typically were arranged between two end-user counterparties with no risk-taking intermediary. Pricing was subject to protected negotiation. And the ultimate terms, which usually included fees for the arranger, were more a matter of mutual acceptance than of precise alignment with those for financing alternatives, if available. Still, it was inevitable with time that moves towards standardisation and increasing competition would render the pricing of swaps keenly sensitive to that of alternatives.

Crucial here was the advent of market makers as principals in most swaps. The term of their dealings with end users are often customised and unpublicised but are nonetheless subject to intense competition. Among the market makers themselves, this same competition —— and the resulting liquidity of the market — allows open quotation of realistic bid and offer swap rates subject always to credit considerations. Swaps quotes are given either outright or, especially in the dollar markets for fixed/ floating interest rate tremendous, as basis-point spreads over Treasuries of the corresponding maturity on the fixed-rate side against 6-month LIBOR on the floating side.

As in many mature financial markets the bid-offer spread provides the market makers' sole compensation, arrangement fees now being a thing of the past. Under the impetus of fierce competition the typical spread has narrowed sharply over the years. Some goes to cover transactions costs — now greatly diminished by progress in standardisation of swap contract language, technological advance, and economies of scale. The remainder remunerates the capital needed to support price and credit risks on swap books.

Is that remuneration adequate? The answer appears broadly affirmative, bearing in mind the continued entry of new participants, the retreat by some of these formerly active, the management and systems sophistication of the presently leading houses, and the heightened priority for rate of return across the industry generally.

To limit their *price risks* market makers normally run swap books that are broadly matched, for example by duration and currency. In the short-run, however, they assume open positions that must be hedged, at least in part, and otherwise managed within prudent bounds until matching positions can be established through new swaps or the runoff of existing ones.

In some cases, mainly in short maturities, market makers can best hedge their open swap position by off-balance-sheet forwards, futures, or options transactions. In other albeit with balance sheet and capital requirement consequences, the cash markets can be tapped. For example, a market maker can hedge the fixed-rate payment side of a fixed/floating interest rate swap by purchasing treasury bonds of the same maturity, financed by a repurchase agreement. In turn, arbitrage ensues that swap rates generally move in sympathy with trends in the derivatives and cash bond markets.

For commercial banks, whatever the rate-of-return, objectives and cost allocation practices of their internal management, the credit risk on swaps is highlighted by the capital requirements now being phased in under the auspices of the BIS. The BIS rules apply to banks with significant international involvement.

The BIS rules conceive the credit risk of a bank's swap book to depend on the sum of two components: "current" plus "potential" exposure. The current exposure of a swap portfolio is the sum of the mark-to-market replacement costs of each and every swap having positive present value of net cash flows to the bank, with no offset for swaps of negative value except in limited circumstances where these quality for netting. Given the relevant market indicators, the summation gives the aggregate amount at risk in the event of immediate default by every counterparty to swaps having positive value to the holder.

More problematic is the measure of potential exposure. The objective is to allow for additional exposure should a counterparty default at some future time when interest and exchange rates may be quite different from current — and the swap's replacement cost correspondingly different. How different depends mainly on a swap's original maturity, the time remaining to its final maturity, and the future volatility of the interest and exchange rate involved.

Assessing this volatility and its implications is a complex matter. Yet for regulatory purposes, the premium goes to simplicity. Table-1 points up how the BIS rules adopted in 1988, though less harsh than initially proposed, make minimal distinction by maturity, and none by portfolio composition let alone differences in currency characteristics. Not surprisingly, the swaps industry has viewed these potential exposure odd-ones as unduly conservative, and consequently too burdensome on profitability in 'relation to capital required. Whatever their virtues for portfolio diversification and risk management—— and these are primary motivations today — the original lure of the swaps markets was the premise of unambiguous cost savings for borrowers and higher yields for investors. The perception has been that, by exploiting price discrepencies within national markets or across international boarders, swap deals deliver gains, even "a free lunch", for all concerned.

Free lunch claims always shall be entertained with caution. Yet they sometimes turn out correct when financial markets are segmented or otherwise interpret. When swaps first were being housed in the late 1970s and early 1980s, segmentation was very much the order of the day. Within national markets, regulatory and tax practices walled off subsectors and often dictated pricing and credit access. Between national markets, most countries enforced capital and foreign exchange controls, which helped preserve regulatory and tax inconsistencies that would have been unviable given market freedom. Often the inconsistencies were egregious, and the rewards of astute application of the swaps concept correspondingly huge.

TABLE-1

Credit Equivalent Exposure (each swap)*	=	Current Exposure + Potential Exposure
Current Exposure of a swap	=	Its mark-to-market replacement value if positive, otherwise zero

Potential exposure of a swap, percent of notional principal**

	Remaining maturity	
	Under one year	Over one year
Interest rate swaps	0.0	*0.5*
Currency swaps	1.0	5.0

* An alternative definition based solely on original notional principal has been authorised, at least on an interim basis, for banking jurisdictions unable or unwilling to implement mark-to-market exposure valuation.

** The assigned percentages may seem low relative to the exposures likely to develop cumulatively during the lives of longer maturity swaps, but should be interpreted in conjunction with the periodic marking-to-market of current exposures required by the International rules.

Governments and regulators eventually noticed the power of derivatives to exploit cross-market distortions created by national laws and regulations. They might have attempted to cripple the emerging instruments. Instead, many were impressed by new technology and communications that made new restrictions problematic, and were mindful too of the checkered record of past interventions. Some also feared to lose financial business to less restrictive rivals. Accordingly, authorities across the industrial world freed up money, capital and exchange markets during the 1980s and have corrected some flagrant fiscal anomalies. By now, the process is far advanced, at least on matters of regulation. In addition, most financial transactions costs have tumbled.

The question then arises at least theoretically, whether swap gains can survive the end of all arbitrage opportunities due to market barriers imperfections, and inconsistencies, as well as the indefinite shrinkage of transactions costs. The answer often has been argued on credit quality ground, yet may be better founded in the economies of business decision incentives and judgements.

Consider a fixed-floating interest rate swap between two borrowers where credit qualities differ. The quality spread favouring the higher-rated party typically is narrower for short-term floating-rate funds than for medium, let alone long-term fixed-rate financing; the two borrowers enjoy differential "comparative advantage". A swap divides the short-term/long-term spread differential such that the higher-related party borrowers fixed and achieves floating rate funding at below direct cost, and so too does the lower-rated party who borrows floating and swaps into fixed.

Some view the resultant "savings" from swaps as compensating increased risk in some form. For example, the fixed-rate payer assumes a funding or liquidity risk avoided by direct bond finance, namely that the firm's access to the underlying short-term finance could be impaired during the life of the swap; difficulties in sitting over the entire principal of the short-term funds could be far more severe than those of making interest payments on a conventional bond. Thus, the swap imposes additional risk on the firm's stockholders (if the floating side of the swap is funded by a *committed* medium-term variable rate facility, the rollover worry diminishes, so too, however, does the achievable cost saving in practice).

Yet swaps (or other hedging strategies) can penetrate savings in perfectly free markets, for example, on the so called agency costs. If funded by long-term, fixed-rate debt, a firm's investments may be skewed towards high-risk activities, on which profits accrue to stockholders but some or all losses are absorbed by bondholders, or the firm may fail to invest in low-risk activities, lest profit safeguard bondholders without benefit to stockholders. To protect their interest, bondholders demand restrictive covenants or exact a risk premium for their long-term fund. The firm can instead borrow short-term—so lenders can swiftly penalise the firm's swap into long-term fixed-rate funding to avoid general interest rate risk.

More generally, swaps can help a firm take advantage of its own information and judgements, when either differ from those of the market place. Thus, contrary to the markets, the firm may expect its credit standing to improve down the road; this would counsel against taking on long-term debt at a high risk premium immediately. Short-term funding plus an interest rate swap would protect against rising interest rates generally but let the firm exploit a lower risk premium later. Likewise, a portfolio may contain a bond that the investor thinks due for positive rerating, pending a realisable capital gain from that event, the investor may wish to benefit against an adverse interest rate trend by swapping the bond's coupons into floating rate income.

Assumptions of perfectly competitive, integrated capital markets with negligible transactions costs obviously are not a realistic description of the world as it is. *First,* differences in name recognition and reputation will continue to provide borrowers compensation advantage in different markets, whether within nations or across borders. *Second,* barriers between markets may be coming down, but it is unlikely that regulatory inconsistencies will be entirely swept away. *Third,* it is still more unlikely that fiscal discrepencies will be eliminated, especially as tax codes contend with ongoing financial innovation. On all these counts, if perhaps less richly than before, opportunities will persist, and new ones spring up. The alert asset/liability manager will want to exploit them, to which end swaps are among the keenest arrows in the quiver. The world turned upside down for dealers in the over-the-counter derivatives. Until more swaps and options teams have been able to beaver away quietly on their financial technology unsupervised by the regulators and, often, uncontrolled by senior management which had only a sketchy grasp of what they do. The regulators' main concern is that some firms, unless they improve their controls, are going to take huge hits from short derivatives. And the regulators are right to be gunning for derivatives. The structure of the derivatives markets is facing a number of tasks. *First,* more and more banks and securities firms are trying to build up or expand derivative operations. This has led to high staff turnover. *Second,* many firms which have grown sizeable derivatives operations in recent years *are* struggling *to* keep technology and management systems developing apace. *Third,* some of the established dealers have written so much business with each other that they are straining credit limits. Too much of the business is characterised by sloppy trading practices—unquantifiable and unhedgeable risks, and computer valuation models that do not work. But the key danger is that the derivatives department in many banks is allowed to run itself, while senior management has little concept of the horrors that lurk inside.

Basle was a response to events. Basle has succeeded in goaling banks towards better capitalisation. But events have moved forward. BIS guidelines should be changed to become broader in scope but much more sharply focussed. Basle should pronounce and police principles hut not their application in practice. The principles ought to be: *prudence, integration, subsidiarity.*

Prudence dictates not only adequate levels of capital and a formal weighting of banking risks. It also requires fine distinctions between the types of capital required and the types of risk undertaken. Liabilities should also be addressed. A bank with all the required capital and asset could fail because of an imprudent liability structure. *What of costs?* Costs are as much a threat to banks' long-term capital building as is insufficient income. Integration means permitting' greater interdependence of banks upon each other and it means not viewing the banking system in isolation from the rest of the world economy. In line with due prudence, banks should be permitted to provide capital to other banks. Once the standard of prudence and a framework of integration has been set up, the last of the work should be delegated to national banking authorities under the principle of subsidiarity. Flexibility and adaptability to local problems and issues must prevail.

In a well-intended and seemingly logical attempt to streamline the international banking system, BIS guidelines have actually made it more difficult for banks to conduct their own business. It places banks at a competitive disadvantage to non-bank provision of funds — securities houses and non-bank consumer and industrial lenders—and encourages macro-economic distortions in the international financial system. The Basle guidelines, if left unchanged, will put the banks out of business at least out of the banking business.

The problem with Basle as it stands today is the problem with many transnational structures: once the structure is in place those who have adhered to it must adapt it; but the structure hardly changes to adapt to them or to changes around it.

Swaps have been a powerful force propelling global capital market integration. Increasingly, they tie together the currency and money markets at all maturities—

not merely at the short end—and erode price discrepencies bred by differences of liquidity and credit standing access markets. All this is a gain for global efficiency, yet at the same time negates policies that relied on the old market segmentation.

Realisation of swaps' practical levels will require resolution by government and judicial authorities of tax and legal issues, plus revamping of management and accounting practices concerning tax exposure. The latter shall include broader use of 'mark-to-market' (fair market value or replacement cost) conventions for positive valuations, in both internal decision making and external regulatory and market reporting.

SWAPTIONS

Options on interest rate swaps are referred as swaptions. The buyer of a swaption has the right to enter an interest rate swap agreement by some specified date in the future. The swaption agreement will specify whether the buyer of the swaption will be a fixed-rate receiver or a fixed-rate payer. The writer of the swaption becomes the counterparty to the swap if the buyer exercises.

If the buyer of the swaption has the right to enter into a swap as a fixed-rate payer, the swap is called a *Call swaption.* The writer therefore becomes the fixed-rate receiver/floating-rate payer. If the buyer of swaption has the right to enter into a swap as a floating-rate payer, the swap is called a *put swaption.* The writer of the swaption therefore becomes the floating-rate receiver/fixed-rate payer.

The strike rate of the swaption indicates the fixed rate that will be swapped versus the floating rate. The swaption will also specify the maturity date of the swap. A swaption may be European or American. Of course, as in all options, the buyer of a swaption pays the writer a premium, although the premium can be structured into the swap terms so that no upfront fee has to be paid.

A swaption can be used to hedge a portfolio strategy that uses an interest rate swap but where the cash flows of the underlying asset or liability are uncertain. The cash flows of the asset will be uncertain if it (*i*) is callable, as in the case of callable bonds, convertible bonds, a loan that can be prepaid etc., and/or (*ii*) exposes the investor/lendor to default risk.

EQUITY CAPS AND FLOORS

An *equity cap* is an agreement in which one party, for an upfront premium, agrees to compensate the other at specific time periods if a designated stock market benchmark is greater than the predetermined level. An *equity* for is an agreement in which one party agrees to pay the other at specific time periods if a specific stock market benchmark is less than a predetermined level. By buying an equity floor and selling an equity cap, a money manager can create an equity collar.

As with equity swaps, these are relatively new derivative contracts. As with interest rate caps and floor, these contracts are nothing more than packages of options and are therefore more transactionally efficient vehicles. They can be customized for any stock market benchmark. However, they are less liquid than exchange-traded options.

MOTIVATIONS FOR SWAP-COVERED FOREIGN CURRENCY BORROWING

There are two commonly cited explanations for the use of swaps: risk management and comparative advantage. Risk management is undeniably an important motivation for the general use of currency swaps. When either the operations or desired financial structure of a firm changes, currency swaps are a cost effective way to transform risk exposures and alter future cash flows. However, changes in operations and financial structures cannot explain swap-covered borrowing; by definition, such borrowing is intended to replicate risks, not transform them. Bond issuers raising funds in one currency with the express intention of swapping the funds for another currency are choosing to replicate cash flows that could be also be achieved by borrowing directly in the desired currency.

Comparative advantage is a more convincing motivation for swap-covered foreign currency borrowing. Indeed, central banks in countries with large volumes of swap-covered borrowing frequently cite comparative advantage as the key motivation for such borrowing. In financial markets, comparative advantage exists when the same risk is priced differently in different markets. If borrowing costs differ across markets, then issuers can reduce their overall financing costs by raising funds in the market in which each has a comparative cost advantage and swapping the proceeds.

Covered Interest Parity

The existence of comparative advantage creates opportunities for arbitrage. As arbitrage takes place, costs should converge consistent with covered interest rate parity. However, the persistence of deviations from covered interest parity does not necessarily prove the availability of arbitrage opportunities. Measured deviations may reflect underlying risks. In other words, estimated differences in borrowing costs across markets may compensate for risks and so, on a risk-adjusted basis, may not indicate a comparative cost advantage. The spread differences for seemingly identical risks reflect compensation for credit risk taken on by the higher quality counterparty in a swap agreement. Counterparty credit risk can be important for currency swaps because they involve an exchange of both principal and interest payments, in contrast to interest rate swaps where only interest payments are exchanged. Similarly, currency basis swap spreads incorporate differences between the credit risk embedded in the money market rates of one currency and that in the other currency. For example, if the non-dollar leg of a currency basis swap is based on a collateralised rate, such as a rate for bankers' acceptances, and the US dollar leg is based on Libor, an unsecured bank lending rate, then the swap spread is fairly priced only when positive.

Nevertheless, several studies find that issuers systematically respond to estimated deviations from interest parity. The choice of currency in international bond issuance is influenced by currency strength and interest rate differentials, suggesting a role for expected, uncovered interest returns. Even if there is no observed deviation from covered interest parity, if market imperfections and frictions give rise to asymmetries between markets that can be arbitraged through swap-covered borrowing large volumes of swap-covered foreign currency borrowing may persist in order to maintain swap-covered interest parity. Imperfections vary significantly among markets. In general, large financial markets, particularly US dollar and euro markets, more closely meet the ideal of a complete market than small markets, such as Philippine peso or Indian rupee markets. Differences among markets potentially give issuers more favourable access to one market than to another, thereby raising the possibility that issuers can gain by exploiting their comparative advantage and engaging in swap-covered borrowing.

There are basically four types of market imperfections that potentially give rise to cross-border arbitrage opportunities: *transactions costs, non-traded assets, agency and information problems,* and *regulations.* The importance of each of these as a motivation for swap-covered foreign currency borrowing is likely to differ across markets and change over time. In liquid, complete markets, prices can adjust to new information without any trading taking place and so arbitrage is unlikely to explain why issuers engage in swap-covered borrowing. In less liquid markets, prices are slower to adjust and thus arbitrage opportunities may exist, but probably only temporarily. In illiquid, incomplete markets, arbitrage opportunities may be substantial and persistent.

Transactions Costs

At the most simple level, the existence of transactions costs would tend to favour borrowing directly rather than through a more complex route involving multiple transactions. Transactions costs, however, differ substantially among markets. In financial markets, some types of transactions costs are a decreasing, non-linear function of volumes. For example, the maintenance of trading systems involves fixed costs and, therefore, total trading costs decline as volumes increase. In addition, the heterogeneity of market participants is often greater in large markets, thereby reducing search costs. The self-reinforcing nature of market liquidity strengthens the link between transactions costs and volumes: the willingness of a market participant to transact in a given market depends on the willingness of other participants to do likewise. As a result, transactions costs can differ significantly for nearly identical instruments. For example, in government securities markets, bid-ask spreads are usually much narrower for recently issued "On the-run"" bonds than for "off-the-run" issues.

In a small market, the volume of transactions in any given instrument will naturally be smaller than in a large market, and transactions costs will be correspondingly higher. If the relationship between volumes and transactions costs is convex, then the cost difference of issuing a large bond in a small market compared to a large market may be less than the difference to issuing a small bond. Owing to differences in *relative* transactions costs, issuers from small markets, especially issuers of small bonds, may be able to lower their borrowing costs by tapping more liquid markets.

Transactions costs can be broadly defined to include enforcement and bankruptcy costs. Enforcement procedures are simpler in certain jurisdictions. In the international bond market, contracts are predominantly governed by English law, regardless of the residency of the issuer or the currency in which the bond is denominated. The probability of a creditor needing to take enforcement action varies according to the credit quality of the borrower and, therefore, low grade borrowers from markets where enforcement costs are high may be able to lower their financing costs by committing to contracts settled in more creditor-friendly jurisdictions, and swapping the proceeds with a nonresident borrower that can signal high credit quality and issues debt in the market with weak enforcement. While this is primarily a motivation for offshore borrowing (the borrower from the weak-enforcement market could issue in the desired currency in the euromarket), if offshore use of a currency is restricted then differences in the legal and information environments can also motivate an exchange of borrowings between low grade and high grade borrowers.

Transactions costs may also help to explain why issuers, rather than investors, appear to be the main arbitrageurs in international bond markets. Investors typically trade in smaller volumes than issuers; one bond issue is typically bought by many investors. If investors are willing to assume credit risk but not currency risk, then it is likely to be cheaper for the issuer to bundle a currency swap together with a foreign currency bond than for multiple investors to buy a foreign currency bond and swap out the currency risk.

Non-traded Assets

The literature on nontraded assets identified a variety of reasons why markets may be segmented and incomplete and, in turn, diversification in international financial markets may be difficult. The range of assets traded differs substantially among markets. The absence of a particular type of asset may arise from either a lack of supply or a lack of demand. The structure of an investor's liabilities may create demand for particular types of assets; conversely the structure of a borrower's assets may create demand for a particular form of funding. This can make it difficult for investors to optimise their portfolios to meet their investment objectives, and make it difficult for borrowers to raise funding without one or the other taking on additional risk. Consequently, investors may end up shunning certain risks altogether. Generally, smaller markets tend to have more non-traded assets than larger markets. The juxtaposition of assets that are traded in one market but not in another can create opportunities for arbitrage.

An important asset missing in some markets is bonds with minimal default risk, i.e. bonds with the highest, AAA credit ratings. National governments are typically the most creditworthy borrowers in their own currency. In countries where the government is not very creditworthy (for example because it has a history of poor macroeconomic management), there are unlikely to be other resident issuers with (international) AAA credit ratings. There is usually a "sovereign ceiling", which caps the perceived creditworthiness of borrowers in a country. Even in countries where the government is very creditworthy, there may be a scarcity of highly rated debt because fiscal prudence restricts the supply of government debt. Swap-covered borrowing involving a highly rated nonresident issuer allows issuers to fill the void, benefiting from the tighter credit spread on top-rated bonds relative to lower rated bonds .

Another important asset missing in some markets is long-term, fixed-rate bonds, i.e. bonds with maturities beyond five years paying a fixed (as opposed to a floating) coupon. In countries with a history of poor macroeconomic management, a high degree of economic uncertainty can cause investors to avoid such investments. Even in countries with a stable policy environment, investors may be constrained (by regulation or by liability structure) from buying long-term, fixed rate bonds, or may prefer not to because of risk preferences. As a result, the cost of issuing a long term, fixed rate bond can vary significantly among markets

Other important assets missing in some markets are foreign exchange, interest rate and credit derivatives. Derivatives facilitate the unbundling of risks. Local currency bonds are typically exposed to exchange rate, interest rate and credit risks, which investors may be willing to bear individually but not in combination, particularly if these risks are correlated (for example, domestic credit risk may be correlated with currency risk). If instruments are available in one market to unbundle risks but not in another, then this can create opportunities for arbitrage. Investors seeking exposure to credit risk may be willing to buy bonds issued by low-grade foreign borrowers, which potentially reduce the idiosyncratic risk in their portfolios, but in the absence of a liquid currency swap market only in a given currency. For investors seeking exposure to exchange rate or interest rate risk, local currency bonds issued by high grade non-residents may be in greater demand than bonds issued by lower grade residents in the absence of a liquid credit derivatives market.

Agency and Information Problems

Agency and information problems are omnipresent in financial markets but are more acute in some markets than others. In particular, the effectiveness of mechanisms to mitigate agency and information problems varies considerably. Some countries have weak disclosure requirements, poor accounting practices, opaque corporate governance rules, and concentrated ownership structures. Such information asymmetries contribute to home bias, whereby investors hold a larger share of local assets in their portfolios than would be optimal in a well diversified portfolio. Moreover, borrowers from countries where mechanisms to mitigate agency and information problems are weak may be able to expand their investor base, thereby lowering their financing costs, by committing to contracts that require them to adhere to higher standards. Foreign bond markets potentially serve this purpose. This is primarily a motivation for offshore borrowing, but if offshore use of a currency is restricted then it may be mutually advantageous for borrowers from markets with weak standards to issue abroad in foreign currency and swap with borrowers that are able to signal higher standards.

Regulations

Regulatory barriers, such as taxes, reporting requirements and exchange controls, can create significant differences in financing costs between markets. Moreover, these differences can persist until there are changes to the regulatory wedge. Regulatory barriers are commonly imposed by governments or government agencies. Market participants themselves may also create regulatory barriers, for example through investment mandates that restrict the range of investible assets.

The list of potential regulatory barriers is long and many create cost differences between onshore and offshore borrowing. Regulatory barriers were pivotal factors in the growth of offshore markets for US dollars. To the extent that regulatory barriers restrict the offshore use of a currency, they may also motivate swap-covered borrowing. Indeed, currency swaps evolved out of instruments structured to circumvent exchange controls. In the 1970s, the United Kingdom restricted capital outflows. Firms planning foreign investments circumvented the restrictions through a parallel loan, in which a UK company made a sterling loan to the UK subsidiary of a foreign company and the foreign company lent the equivalent amount in foreign currency to the foreign subsidiary of the UK firm.

Even in the absence of exchange controls, there are other regulatory barriers that can give different advantages to resident and non-resident borrowers. Restrictions that effectively segment low grade and high grade markets are one potentially important source of comparative advantage. For example, assets eligible for use as collateral in central banks' lending operations often trade at a premium because the available supply is limited. High grade bonds issued by non-residents are sometimes eligible, potentially creating an opportunity for such borrowers to lower their financing costs by engaging in swap-covered borrowing. Furthermore, many institutional investors are restricted by mandate from investing in low grade bonds. These restrictions are less distortionary in markets with heterogeneous investor bases, such as large markets, and so low grade borrowers may gain from issuing in larger markets and swapping the proceeds. Mandates that restrict the range of investible assets or the use of derivatives may also be a factor in explaining why arbitrage opportunities in international bond markets are exploited more actively by issuers rather than investors.

FOREIGN EXCHANG SWAPS: IMPLICATIONS FOR FINANCIAL AND ECONOMIC STABILITY

The rising popularity of foreign exchange ("FX") swaps to obtain FX funding and as a hedging instrument has raised questions about their role in macro-financial stability, in light of developments during the recent global financial crisis. The proliferation of cross-border transactions in FX swaps over time had left this market exposed to the fallout from international liquidity crunch, despite being among the most liquid in the world.

FINANCIAL STABILITY

Policymakers have long recognized the riskiness of banks' FX activities, which tends to heighten during periods of increased volatility in exchange rates. Indeed, the Basel Committee on Banking Supervision (BCBS) had noted that, "*...there are few [activities] in which a bank may so quickly incur large losses as in foreign exchange transactions* ". The BCBS further stated that supervisors needed to be vigilant so that the risks from banks' FX operations never became so large as to threaten their solvency and liquidity, and potentially, the health and stability of the entire banking system.

The promulgation of international standards and regulations attempts to capture the risks posed by the use of FX instruments, and to ensure greater transparency in their disclosure. They include the application of the Basel Accords (Basel I and Basel

II), as well as the International Financial Reporting Standards (IFRS). Participants in the market for OTC FX derivatives, among other derivatives instruments, also enter into standardized International Swaps and Derivatives Association (ISDA) contracts with their counterparties, which include provisions for mitigating credit risk.

CAPITAL CHARGES UNDER THE BASEL ACCORDS

A bank's capital adequacy ratio is derived from regulatory capital and risk-weighted assets. Under the Base! Accords, risk weights are applied to the assets on a bank's balance sheet (risk-weighted assets) in order to calculate the appropriate capital charges, and thus, determine if a bank is adequately capitalized. The use of FX swaps by banks would incur a capital charge for credit risk, but reduce the capital requirements for market risk.

Credit Risk

FX swaps carry a capital charge for credit risk. Under the Basel Accord, a "credit exposure" for derivatives such as swaps, forwards and options on currency, interest rate, equity and commodity products would be calculated as the sum of the current net replacement value (NRV) plus an add-on component that is supposed to capture future exposure, depending on the tenor and type of contract. Counterparty risk weights are then applied to the credit exposure to derive the credit risk charge. Under Basel II, there are three approaches to determining the credit risk weights. They are: (i) the ' Standardized Approach, which is an extension of Basel I, but with finer classification of categories for credit risk, based on external credit ratings; the 50 percent risk weight cap on derivatives is also removed; (ii) the Foundation International Ratings-Based Approach, where banks estimated the probability of default and supervisors supply other inputs; and (iii) the Advanced Internal Ratings-Based Approach, where banks can supply both the estimated probability of default and other inputs as well. Basel II also takes into account credit risk mitigation techniques, such as collateralization, third-party guarantees, credit derivatives, and netting.

Market Risk

FX swaps could be applied to reduce banks' market risk from existing FX positions. In general, FX positions taken by banks could require capital charges for market risk under Basel II. Specifically, there is a capital charge for FX risk, under Pillar I on Minimum Capital Requirements, so that banks which hold overall net open FX positions on their balance sheets will be subject to a capital charge of 8 percent of the overall net open positions. Net open short or long currency positions can lead to sizeable losses when exchange rates are volatile, and capital thus needs to be held to cover such open positions. Thus, banks have significant incentive to close such exposures through hedge transactions, commonly using FX swaps. In other words, banks' use of FX swaps for hedging purposes, despite incurring credit risk, could help to reduce capital charges for market risk.

LIQUIDITY RISK

The use of FX swaps could increase the liquidity risk for banks. A bank that is perfectly hedged in terms of its FX exposure would still be exposed to liquidity movements arising from that hedge. Specifically, marking-to-market under ISDA agreements between counterparties—while decreasing credit risk—may instead create liquidity risk. The practice requires more frequent collateral payments as contracts need to be valued on a regular basis and cash exchanged with the counterparty through the margin call process (Box-1). Thus, variations in the fair value of an FX swap could potentially drain the bank's liquidity in volatile market conditions.

Margin calls by a swap counterparty may be triggered in the event of a sharp depreciation of the domestic currency resulting in a large fair value adjustment (FVA). In a situation where the spot domestic currency exchange rate experiences a persistent weakening trend, which places pressure on the corresponding forward rate, margin calls by the counterparty would continue. Any sustained outflow of liquidity from the bank could get to a point where the bank may no longer be able to meet its short-term cash flow obligations and is ultimately faced with a solvency-problem.

TRANSPARENCY UNDER INTERNATIONAL FINANCIAL REPORTING STANDARDS

In the International Financial Reporting Standards (IFRS), the International Accounting Standard IAS 39 is the main standard for derivatives, and therefore applies to the accounting of FX swaps. The standard prescribes principles for recognizing and measuring financial assets, financial liabilities and contracts for non-financial items, including financial derivatives. Traditionally, financial derivatives were accounted for using historical cost accounting. Given that there is usually no initial cost attached to financial derivatives, their presentation in financial statements would usually be in the form of a note to the accounts, which would not fully reveal a company's real exposures. However, IAS 39 brings derivatives onto financial statements, thus increasing the transparency of exposures.

BOX 1
Margin Calls on an FX Swap Contract

FX swaps are bilateral, or OTC, in nature in that they are contractual arrangements between two counterparties. As such, it creates potentially significant counterparty risks in that if one party defaults under the swap agreement, the other could suffer huge losses. These risks typically have very low probability of realization for instruments that trade in a centrally cleared market, where an adequately capitalized clearinghouse assumes the counterparty risk which is mitigated by the posting of initial collateral by participants with the clearinghouse, and the meeting of maintenance margin requirements. In OTC derivatives markets, counterparties may initially trade up to an agreed threshold of exposure **("margin threshold")**, and then one counterparty may make a **margin call** when the amount of its exposure to the other counterparty exceeds the threshold.

In order to avoid constant margin calls back and forth, FX swap counterparties in most cases establish a mutually agreed upon margin threshold. The margin threshold is determined on a counterparty by counterparty basis, and is typically based on the credit ratings of the individual parties. FX swaps are typically conducted under some form of negotiated master swap agreement, such as that published by ISDA, which contains an exposure threshold mechanism that allows for the collateralization of counterparty exposures beyond a certain level. However, the potential exists for significant future counterparty exposure in the event of a sharp deterioration in the creditworthiness of one or both counterparties from the time the threshold is negotiated.

A margin call is made by a counterparty when its FX swap position is "in the money," i.e., when the position of the other party is "out of the money." The margin is collateral that the holder of the out-of-the-money position in the swap contract has to deposit to cover its credit risk. In other words, the swap counterparty who is out-of-the-money must provide a certain level of margin or collateral in case of default. For the counterparty who is in-the-money, the receipt of the margin or collateral would reduce credit risk. The collateral can be in the form of cash or securities, and it is deposited in a **margin account.** The amount of the collateral is calculated as the difference between the contracted forward exchange rate which must be paid out upon the maturity of the swap contract and the forward exchange rate on the agreed-upon day at which the contract is marked-to-market (e.g., on a fortnightly basis, or on the last day of every month for the duration of the contract), discounted using the market-determined interest rate over that time period to arrive at the net present value, and less the margin threshold.

Swap exposures cannot be netted across counterparties (although it may be netted within the same counterparty), which prevents margin calls from being offset across counterparties. For example, say a bank has a negative swap exposure to one counterparty and a positive swap exposure to another counterparty. If the first counterparty is entitled to make a margin call on the bank, it could not instead choose to make a margin call on the other counterparty to the bank. The outcome may be that the bank's working capital is tied up (if it cannot make a margin call of equivalent amount on the other counterparty) even if its net market exposure turns out to be zero across both counterparties, thus creating a drain on its liquidity.

IAS 39 abolishes the common accounting practice for synthetic instruments which nets hedges in the balance sheet and presents the hedged item and hedge instrument as a single item. Further, all derivatives instruments must be carried at fair value on the balance sheet, for example, through marking-to-market. Any change in the fair value should be recognized in the profit and loss statement (and ultimately, the retained earnings item in the balance sheet), that is, by making an FVA. Gains and losses from a hedging instrument cannot be offset against gains and losses in the value of the hedged item.

FX swaps are carried on the balance sheet at fair value. On the day the FX swap is transacted, its fair value is likely to be zero. On balance sheet date, the value at which the FX swap reported in the balance sheet may be positive (if the swap is in-the-money and an asset), negative (if the swap is out-of-the-money and a liability) or, possibly zero. The main factor that would cause the fair value of the swap to vary from its assumed initial zero value is the movement in the forward rate relative to the contracted forward exchange rate of the transaction. Upon settlement of the swap contract, the item becomes realized—it is closed out at transaction value and, by definition, drops out of mark-to-market.

ECONOMIC STABILITY

A well-functioning FX swap market tends to support macroeconomic and external stabilit by allocating FX liquidity in an efficient manner, and reducing the volatility of the spot exchange rate. However, during periods of stress in financial markets, spillovers to the FX swap market could result in illiquidity and significantly increase transaction costs. Consequently, an external financing gap may arise, creating pressure on a country's currency. In order to mitigate the effects of financial stress and to limit the impact on the real economy, central banks may provide FX swap facilities to market participants.

INCREASED COSTS OF FX FUNDING AND HEDGING

A high reliance on funding through FX swaps could result in severe liquidity shortages during turbulent periods, and consequently, a rise in funding costs. During the recent crisis, for example, U.S. dollar funding became scarce, making it increasingly costly to obtain U.S. dollars through FX swaps with the euro, the pound sterling and the Japanese yen. Prior to August 2007, the U.S. dollar "basis" was close to zero. However, in late-2007, the spread between the two widened, implying a market-based U.S. dollar funding rate that is higher than U.S. dollar LIBOR, i.e., investors had to pay a premium to obtain U.S. dollars in the FX swap market. Furthermore, counterparties who were concerned about liquidity constraints became increasingly reluctant to lend FX over longer periods, leading to a sharp shortening of FX swap maturities and increasingly costly rollover activity.

More costly FX swaps can lead to further FX funding strains for banks, which could then impair macroeconomic stability through several channels. *First,* hedging an existing balance sheet position becomes more expensive for the bank. If the bank cannot hedge an open position, it would incur a regulatory charge on capital. The bank could alternatively decide to shrink its balance sheet position, which could translate into a liquidity squeeze on the domestic economy. *Second,* obtaining FX funding becomes more expensive, potentially increasing the cost of credit to the economy. *Third,* an increase in perceived counterparty risk may require lower margin thresholds, and any subsequent margin calls would directly reduce the liquid assets available to the bank that is out-of-the-money, further reducing its ability to provide credit to the economy.

EXTERNAL FINANCING GAP

A dysfunctional FX swap market could impair the external stability of a country by creating a financing gap in the Balance of Payments ("BoP"). Such a gap could manifest if domestic financial institutions' demand for external financing through FX swaps is higher than the external supply, a situation that could arise during periods of market stress. The increasing degree of cross-border integration of FX swap markets in recent years suggests that the potential impact on a country's external financing needs from disruptions to this market could be significant.

A financing gap in the BoP could materialize in several ways:

i) In a situation where domestic financial institutions transact with foreign counterparties in FX swaps, any shortening of maturities as a result of concerns about rising counterparty risk essentially front-loads rollover requirements. This, combined with higher costs of using FX swaps would increase the institutions' external financing needs. Consequently, those financial institutions may find it difficult to meet their rollover requirements and may be forced to close out their FX swap positions and repay their FX obligations. Financial institutions may need to purchase FX in the spot market, placing pressure on the domestic currency. The outcome would be similar where domestic financial institutions transact with foreign counterparties, who rely on FX swaps themselves to fund carry trade plays.

ii) Alternatively, if foreign counterparties are constrained for liquidity or are concerned about counterparty risk, they may decide to cut their exposures to FX swaps and in doing so, reduce the overall external financing available to the country, and thus increase its external financing gap.

iii) Margin calls could also create an external financing gap. If domestic financial institutions or corporates have to honor the margin calls on their FX swap contracts with foreign counterparties, such payments would result in outflows in the country's financial account. From a macroeconomic perspective, the aggregate outflow could be substantial since margin calls are typically linked to factors such as exchange rate depreciation, which could affect many domestic institutions simultaneously.

The adjustment required to close the external financing gap could have wide-ranging macroeconomic implications. It could create pressure on the exchange rate or the central bank's international reserves, depending on the country's exchange rate regime. It could also squeeze FX liquidity in the domestic economy, affecting trade and other economic activity.

EXCHANGE RATE VOLATILITY

A competitive and liquid FX swap market typically helps to smooth any volatility in the exchange rate, as it enables market participants to manage their FX risks and access short-term FX funding. However, FX swap transactions could potentially act to magnify volatility in illiquid markets or during stressful periods. This can occur as a result of either hedging or speculative transactions (Box 2). Market participants who enter into FX swap transactions for heading purposes typically have open FX positions which they may want to close as part of their risk management strategy; speculators may represent one of the possible counterparties on the other side of these transactions. Such activity in increasingly illiquid markets has the potential to cause volatility in the exchange rate, if they are sufficiently large.

BOX 2

How Would Hedging and Speculation Using FX Swaps Affect the Spot Exchange Rate?

There are several scenarios under which transactions in FX swaps could affect the level and/or the volatility of the exchange rate of a country's currency. In times of market stress, when markets are illiquid or increasingly one-sided, such transactions could exacerbate the volatility in the exchange rate, with potential consequences for risks in the banking system, economic activity and policy.

Scenario 1. Bank Closing a Net Open FX Position

Assume that a local bank has more domestic currency liabilities on its balance sheet than domestic currency assets. The bank would thus have exactly the opposite position with the FX-denominated items—it would have more FX-denominated assets than liabilities, i.e., have a long FX position on its balance sheet.

1. In order to close the net open FX position, the bank converts excess domestic currency liquidity to FX via an FX swap transaction.
2. The bank then sells the FX in the spot market in exchange for domestic currency to close the open FX exposure, *potentially strengthening the* domestic currency.

3. Upon the maturity of the FX swap contract, the bank would sell domestic currency in the spot market in exchange for FX—*potentially weakening the* domestic currency—to repay the FX to, and receive domestic currency from, the counterparty.

Scenario 2. Foreign Investor Holding Local Securities

Assume that a foreign investor holds a portfolio of local securities. The investor thus has an open domestic currency position and wants to hedge the existing exposure against a potential depreciation in the domestic currency:

1. The investor enters into an FX swap to borrow domestic currency and lend FX. In other words, the investor has now taken on a domestic currency-denominated liability (domestic currency is payable in the future) and an FX-denominated asset (FX is receivable in the future).
2. The investor then sells the domestic currency on the spot market for FX, *potentially weakening the* domestic currency.
3. When the investor decides to sell the local securities, the domestic currency from the receipt of the sale is then swapped back for FX.

Scenario 3. Speculator in the FX Market

Assume that a speculator is on the other side of an FX swap transaction with a domestic bank. The speculator has FX but wishes to speculate in domestic currency in anticipation of a sharp depreciation in the latter; the bank has domestic currency but requires FX to fund its operations.

1. The speculator swaps FX for domestic currency (borrows domestic currency and lends FX) with the bank.
2. The speculator then sells down the domestic currency on the spot market for FX, *which could contribute to the weakening of the* domestic currency.
3. When the speculator closes out the position at the maturity of the swap contract, s/he would purchase domestic currency on the spot market at that time—with the anticipation of doing so at a significantly depreciated level— and swap the domestic currency back for FX with the bank.

It should be noted that speculators play an essential role in the market by improving liquidity. While such activity may cause greater volatility at times, it also plays an important part in the necessary process of risk repricing, especially in liquid markets.

Volatile exchange rates could potentially affect various aspects of economic activity. They generally make economic decisions more difficult because of the increase in exchange rate risk. Greater exchange rate volatility could also increase the indirect credit risk for the banking system through unhedged borrowers. For example, in several Central and Eastern European countries, firms and households had taken out foreign currency loans prior to the financial crisis to benefit from lower foreign interest rates, relative to those for domestic currency loans.^If shocks to the economy are accompanied by exchange rate depreciation, the borrowers may have to service rising debts in domestic currency terms. This could lead to a worsening in banks' asset quality arising from a deterioration in borrowers' ability to repay their debt.

CENTRAL BANK MEASURES TO MITIGATE RISKS FROM AND SHOCKS TO FX SWAP MARKETS

FX swap facilities are standard liquidity management instruments that could be utilized by a central bank for various purposes. Their use represents an open market operation—where the central bank acts as a counterparty to domestic financial institutions (or corporations)—to control liquidity in the system, manage the international reserves of the central bank, or to smooth disorderly fluctuations in the exchange rate. In the event of a shock to FX swap markets, a central bank has several tools at its disposal to address FX funding shortages and any resulting pressure on the exchange rate. It may raise interest rates, to try to attract investors; it may intervene by conducting outright sales of foreign reserves to help meet the funding need and alleviate the pressure on the exchange rate; it may also use existing foreign exchange reserves for FX swap operations with market counterparties.

From a balance sheet perspective, the provision of FX liquidity through FX swaps could result in either a temporary or permanent drawdown of the liquid FX assets of a central bank. The reduction in FX assets would typically be offset by an increase in FX assets receivable in the future, through a claim on the counterparty arising at the settlement of the FX swap (Box 3). Given the covered nature of FX swap transactions, the central bank would normally not assume any of the underlying FX risk. However, the drawdown of liquid reserve assets associated with the transaction could be permanent if the swap counterparty defaults. Conversely, FX spot sales would permanently draw down a central bank's reserves.

FX swaps were used as a crisis management tool during the recent crisis. Central banks used FX swap facilities extensively to increase FX liquidity in the system when domestic institutions were faced with FX funding shortages. In situations where domestic financial institutions were unable to roll over their existing FX swaps, central banks' facilities substituted as counterparties to the private sector. Where reserves in the required foreign currencies were insufficient or (liquid) reserves were limited in those currencies, swap lines with the central banks issuing the foreign currencies in shortage were established to backstop losses of liquid reserves.

BOX 3

Impact of Central Bank FX Swap Operations on Its Balance Sheet

FX swaps which are executed for monetary policy purposes affect central banks' balance sheets. Such operations consist of simultaneous spot and forward transactions in the domestic currency ("DC") against foreign currency. If the central bank wants to absorb domestic currency liquidity from the market and provide FX liquidity at the same time, it will borrow domestic currency and lend FX. Conversely, if it wants to provide domestic currency liquidity and absorb foreign currency, it would lend domestic currency and borrow FX. After receiving bids from counterparties (banks), the central bank would decide on the swap points and allotment to each bank. The details of the transactions depend on the type of auction chosen by the central bank e.g. a single rate (Dutch) or multiple rate (American) auction.

Example. Providing FX Liquidity Through FX Swaps

Assume that the central bank decides, in a single rate auction, to provide FX liquidity to the market (and absorb domestic currency liquidity) by executing an FX swap on the domestic currency with FX; it allocates FX100 million, equivalent to DC 105 million at the current spot rate, priced at 5 forward basis points (or 500 *pips*) premium (i.e, the forward rate is 1.05 + 0.05 = DC 1.10 per unit of FX). At the start of the operation, the central bank provides FX100 million to the market, and absorbs DC105 million. On the maturity date of the operation, the central bank removes the FX100 million and injects DC110 million back into the market.

The balance sheet effects of the central bank's FX swaps with the banking system are, in principle, the same as those for outright operations. For the spot leg of the transaction, lending FX has a contractionary effect in that it reduces the central bank's claim on non-residents and banks' reserves. The monetary base falls, but net domestic assets remain unchanged. The forward leg creates, in this case, a forward domestic liability that is matched by a forward foreign asset. These contingent claims and obligations are, in most cases, recorded initially in off-balance sheet accounts and, subsequently, in on-balance sheet accounts for each receipt or payment.

Spot Leg Transaction

Assets		*Liabilities*	
Net foreign assets	-FX1 00 million	Currency in circulation	
Net domestic assets		Bank reserves	— DC105 million
=Monetary base	-FX 100 million	=Monetary base	— DC105 million

Forward Leg Transaction

Assets		*Liabilities*	
Net foreign assets		Currency in circulation	
Net domestic assets	+ FX100 million	Bank reserves	+ DC1 10 million
=Monetary base	+FX100 million	=Monetary base	+ DC110 million

Since FX swaps create assets and liabilities that are contingent, they are, by definition treated as off-balance sheet items. Therefore, central bank's FX swap operations would usually have no permanent impact on their balance sheets. The structure of an FX swap, where the terms of the forward leg are set in advance, ensures that these operations do not carry exchange rate or other market risks, although keeping large notional amounts of short positions of FX swaps vis-a-vis the domestic currency could create FX vulnerabilities for the central bank. Also, default by a counterparty^ would affect the composition of foreign and domestic currency in the balance sheet.

The major central banks coordinated their actions to mitigate the transmission of shocks through the global FX swap market and ensure FX liquidity. The U.S. Federal Reserve and the European Central Bank opened swap lines with each other and with various other countries amid substantial dollar and euro shortages in December 2007, and at various points in 2008. These swap lines augmented the liquid euro and U.S. dollar assets of the receiving central banks, enabling them to credibly commit to providing large amounts of much-needed FX to domestic market participants through their own domestic FX swap facilities.

ILLUSTRATIVE PROBLEMS

1. An American company has an existing swap agreement with a British company. The original exchange rate was \$1.50/£1 (when the swap was agreed) and the current exchange rate is \$2/£1. The fixed interest rates for the swap are 10% for sterling and 5% for the US dollar. Interest payments are annual and such payments have just been exchanged. The swap has a remaining life of 3 years. The American company is the recipient of sterling and the payer of dollars. The original sums were \$15 million and £10. Interest rates are now equal at 5% p.a. What is the value of the swap to the American company?

Ans.

B_F=£1m/(1.05) + £1m/(1.05)^2 + £11m/(1.05)^3 = £11.36m

B_D=\$0.75m/(1.05) + \$0.75m/(1.05)^2 + \$15.75m/(1.05)^3+\$15m

V=\$2 B_F—B_D=\$22.72m—\$15m=\$7.72m

2. Company ABC and XYZ have been offered the following rates per annum on a \$ 200 million five-year loan:

	Fixed Rate	*Floating Rate*
Company ABC	12.0	Libor +0.1%
Company XYZ	13.4	Libor +0.6%

Company ABC requires a floating-rate loan; company XYZ requires a fixed-rate loan. Design a swap that will net a bank acting as intermediary 0.1 percent per annum and be equally attractive the both companies.

Ans.

ABC has a comparative advantage in fixed-rate market but wants to borrow floating. XYZ has a comparative advantage in floating-rate markets but wants to borrow fixed. This provides the basis for the swap. There is a 1.4 percent per annum differential between the fixed rates offered to the two companies and a 0.5% per annum differential between the floating rates offered to the two companies. The total gain to all parties from the swap is, therefore, 1.4 – 0.5=0.9% per annum. Since the bank gets 0.1% per annum of this, the swap should make each of ABC and XYZ 0.4% per annum better off. This means that it should lead to ABC borrowing at LIBOR – 0.3% and to XYZ borrowing at 13%.

3. A \$100 million interest-swap has a remaining life of ten months. Under the terms of the swap, six-month LIBOR is exchanged for 12 percent per annum (compounded semiannually). The average of the bid and ask rate being exchanged for six-month LIBOR in swaps of all maturities is currently 10 percent per annum with continuous compounding. The six-month LIBOR rate was 9.6 percent per annum two months ago. What is the current value of the swap to the party paying floating ? What is its value to the party paying fixed?

Ans.

In four months \$6 million will be received and \$4.8 million will be paid. In ten months \$6 million will be received and the LIBOR rate prevailing in four months' time will be paid. The values of the floating-rate bond underlying the swap is:

$$6e^{-0.3331\times 0.1} + 106e^{-0.8333\times 0.1} = \$\ 103.33 \text{ million}$$

The value of the floating-rate bond underlying the swap is:

$$(100+4.8)\ e^{-0.333\times 0.1} = \$101.36 \text{ million}$$

The value of the swap to the party paying floating is \$ 103.33 – \$ 101.36 = \$ 1.97 million.

The value of the swap to the party paying fixed is 41.97 million. These results can also be derived by decomposing the swap into forward contracts. Consider the party paying floating. The first forward contract involves paying \$ 4.8 million and receiving \$6 million in four months. It has a value of $1.2e^{-0.333 \times 01.}$ = \$1.16 million. To value the second forward contract, we note that the forward interest rate is 10% per annum with continuous compounding or 10.254 per cent per annum with semiannual compounding. The value of the forward contract is:

$$100 \times (0.12 \times 0.5 - 0.10254 \times 0.5)\ e^{-0.83333}$$
$$= \$0.80 \text{ million}$$

The total value of the forward contract is, therefore \$1.16 +\$0.80 = \$1.96 million.

4. XYZ Bank is seeking fixed-rate funding. It is able to finance at a cost of six-month LIBOR +¼% for £100 million for 5 years. The bank is able to swap into a fixed rate at 8.50% versus six-month LIBOR. Treating 6 months as exactly half a year:

(a) Set out the cash flows involved. What will be the all-in cost of funds to XYZ Bank?

(b) Another possibility being considered is the issue of a 'hybrid' instrument which pays 8.50% for the first 3 years and LIBOR —¼% for the remaining 2 years. Given a three-year swap rate of 9% indicate in general terms the method by which the bank would achieve fixed-rate funding.

(c) In principle, without calculating the cash flows involved, does this deal seem attractive?

(d) Briefly outline the risks which would be involved for the bank in such a funding operation.

Ans.

(a) XYZ Bank pays LIBOR +0.25% p.a. for 5 years. The swap involves payment of 8.5% p.a. and receipts of LIBOR.

Interest rates

Inflow	*Outflow*
LIBOR	LIBOR +0.25% + 8.5%

Net interest payment 8.75% p.a.

Cash flows per six-month period

Inflow	*Outflow*
(LIBOR/2) × £100 million	(LIBOR/2)×£100 million + £125,000 + £4,250,000

Net outflow \$4,375,000 (=all-in cost of funds)

(b) Issues hybrid and enter both the five-year and three-year swaps.

First 3 years

Bank pays 8.5% p.a. on hybrid.

Bank pays 8.5% p.a. on five-year swap.

Bank receives 9% p.a. on three-year swap.

Bank receives LIBOR on five-year swap.

Bank pays LIBOR on three-year swap.

Net interest payment 8% p.a.

Final 2 years

Bank pays LIBOR—0.25% on hybrid.

Bank receives LIBOR on five-year swap.

Bank pays 8.5% p.a. on five-year swap.

Net interest payment 8.25% p.a.

(c) The arrangement in (b), compared with that in (a), saves 0.75% p.a. over the first 3 years and 0.5% p.a. over the final 2 years.

(d) The risks would include default risk on the part of the 2 swap counterparties. There may also be liquidity risk in the event that one or both of the swaps may need be adversed. There could also be legal risk, the legality of one or both swaps may be challenged. Taxation risk means that a change in the tax regulation may adversely affect the benefits from the arrangements. There may may be a country risk if a counterparty is based overseas: payments may be inhibited by an overseas government.

5. A currency swap has a remaining life of 15 months. It involves exchanging interest at 14 percent on £20 million for interest at 10 percent on 30 million once a year. The term structure of interest rates in both the U.K and the U.S. is currently flat and if the swap were negotiated today the interest rate exchanged would 8 percent in dollars and 11 percent in sterling. All interest rates are quoted with annual compounding. The current exchange rate is 1.6500. What is the value of the swap to the party paying sterling ? what is the value of the swap to the party paying dollars?

Ans.

The swap involves exchanging the sterling interest of 20 × 0.14= £2.8 million for the dollar interest of 30 × 0.1 = $3 million. The principal amounts are also exchanged at the end of the life of the swap. The value of the sterling bond underlying the swap is:

$$\frac{2.8}{(1.11)^{1/4}} + \frac{22.8}{(1.11)^{5/4}} = \text{£}22.74 \text{ million}$$

The value of the dollar bond underlying the swap is:

$$\frac{3}{(1.08)^{1/4}} + \frac{33}{(1.08)^{5/4}} = \$33.92\,million$$

The value of the swap to the party paying sterling is, therefore, 33.92–22.74 × 1.65 = –$4.60 million.

The value of the swap to the party paying dollars is $4.60 million. The results can also be obtained by viewing the swap as a portfolio of forward contracts. The continuously compounded interest rate in sterling and dollars are 10.43% per annum and 7.70% per annum. The three-month and 15-month forward exchange rates are 1 .65$e^{-0.25 \times 0.0273}$ =1.6388 and 1.65$e^{-1.25 \times 0.0273}$=1.5946. The value of the two forward contracts corresponding to the exchange of interest for the party paying sterling are, therefore,

$$(3 - 2.8 \times 1.6388)\ e^{-0.077 \times 0.25} = -\$\ 1.56 \text{ million}$$
$$(3 - 2.8 \times 15944)\ e^{-0.077 \times 1.25} = -\$1.33 \text{ million}$$

The value of the forward contract corresponding to the exchange of principals is:

$$(30–20 \times 1.5946)\ e^{-0.077 \times 1.25} = -\$1.72 \text{ million}$$

The total value of the swap is:

$$-\$1.56–\$\ 133–\$\ 1.72 = \$4.61 \text{ million}$$

6. For a value date of 1 July 1997 a company entered into a five-year interest rate swap with its bank, under which it has contracted to pay 10% and receive six-month LIBOR, settled semi-annually, on a national principal amount of £10,000,000. It is 1 July 1999 and the swap payments have just settled, so the swap now has exactly 3 years to run. The bank offers to unwind the swap at a rate of 8%. If the company agrees, the transaction will be cancelled by means of a settlement today.

(a) Set out the underlying fixed-rate cash flow that would take place if, instead of cancelling the existing deal, a new deal were made and the 2 deals were to run to maturity. You may assume each interest period has 182.5 days and ignore leap years.

(b) What sum of money would be paid today to cancel the transaction?

(c) To whom?

(d) What assumptions are implicit in the above calculations?

Ans.

(a) £100,000 per six-month period from the company to the bank. This is based on £10,000,000 × (0.05–0.04)), where 0.05 and 0.04 are the old and new unannualised six-month interest rates in decimal form.

(b) The sum of money to be paid to cancel the transaction would be the current equivalent of the future cash flows in (a), i.e. the present value of those cash flows. If the bank offers to unwind the swap at 8% p.a. (i.e. 4% six-month period) then that would appear to be an appropriate discount rate. The sum would thus be:

$$£100,000[1/(1.04) + 1/(1.04)^2 + 1/(1.04)^3 + 1/(1.04)^4 + 1/(1.04)^5 + 1/(1.04)^6]$$
$$= £524,213.69$$

(c) By the company to the bank.

(d) A key assumption in the foregoing calculation is that the yield curve is flat. In other words the same rate of discount (4% per six-month period) is applicable to all 6 future cash flows. If the yield curve were not flat then different discount rates should be applied to each cash flow (although in practice the yield to maturity, 4% per six-month period in this case, is often used to discount all the prospective cash flows).

7. Company A wishes to borrow £10 million at a fixed rate for 5 years and has been offered either 11% fixed or six-month LIBOR + 1%. Company B wishes to borrow £10 million at a floating rate for 5 years and has been offered either six-month LIBOR + 0.5% or 10% fixed.

(a) How may they enter into a swap arrangement in which each benefits equally?

(b) What risks may this arrangement generate?

Ans.

(a) By directly borrowing on the required basis, the total interest paid by A and B is:

£10 million × (11% + LIBOR +0.5%)

By borrowing according to comparative advantage, the total interest paid is:

£10 million × (10% + LIBOR +1%)

Borrowing according to comparative advantage provides a total saving of £10 million X¼% to be shared between A and B. Equal sharing means that both have a¼% reduction in interest charge.

There is a number of alternative swap arrangements that would be consistent with this distribution of the interest rate benefit of borrowing according to comparative advantage. For instance, by synthesising a fixed rate borrowing at 10-3/4% (a saving of ¼% relative to borrowing directly at 11%), then B effectively obtains a floating rate loan at LIBOR +¼% (an improvement of ¼% relative to borrowing directly). It may be noted that, conventionally, swaps are quoted in terms of the fixed rate to be exchanged for LIBOR.

(b) B is at risk from LIBOR rising.

A is at risk from an opportunity loss in the event of a fall in LIBOR.

Both are at risk from default by the other.

8. Company AKR wishes to borrow U.S. dollars at a fixed rate of interest. Company RAK wishes to borrow Japanese yen at a fixed rate of interest. The amounts required by the two companies are roughly the same at current exchange rate. The companies have been quoted the following interest rates:

	Yen	*Dollars*
Company AKR	4.0%	8.6%
Company RAK	5.5%	9.0%

Design a swap that will net a bank, acting as intermediary, 50 basis points per annum. Make the swap equally attractive to the two companies and ensure that all foreign exchange risk is assumed by the bank.

Ans.

AKR has a comparative advantage in yen markets but wants to borrow dollars, RAK has a comparative advantage in dollar markets but wants to borrow yen. This provides the basis for the swap. There is a 1.5% per annum differential between the yen rates and a 0.4 percent per annum differential between the dollar rates. The total gain to all parties from the swap is, therefore, 1.5 – 0.4 = 1.1% per annum. Since the bank requires 0.5% per annum, this leaves 0.3% per annum for each of AKR and RAK. The swap should lead to AKR borrowing dollars at 8.6– 0.3 = 8.3 percent per annum and to RAK borrowing yen at 5.5 – 0.3 = 5.2% per annum.

9. IBM's motivation in entering into its celebrated currency swaps with the World Bank was fueled by its desire to lock in both interest rate gains and currency gains. IBM had borrowed Swiss francs and D-marks, converting the proceeds of its debt to dollars. This created two risks: the first an exposure to interest rates, since it was fixed-rate debt; the second to currency exposure, since dollars would be used to repay the bond issues. Executing the swaps enabled IBM to lock in gains resulting from favorable interest rate and currency movements. IBM could also have realized these gains in the forward foreign exchange market. Liquidity in the forward foreign exchange market would not however have resulted in a price competitive with the cost of the swap. IBM used the swap to create cheap dollar debt.

Here is IBM's outstanding cash flow in D-marks. The cash flows look like those generated by a fixed coupon of 10% on a bullet issue of D-mark 300,000,000. So if IBM is paid 11% in a swap, its interest rate gain is 1% per annum or, in present value terms is 3.696% if the discount rate is also 11%.

	D-marks
Year 1	30,000,000.00
Year 2	30,000,000.00
Year 3	30,000,000.00
Year 4	30,000,000.00
Year 5	330,000,000.00

How much is IBM's currency gain or loss?

Ans.:

In order to calculate this we need to look at the exchange rate movement between the dollar and the D-mark from the time that IBM issued the D-marks bonds to the time when it locked in this gain by executing the currency swaps with the World Bank.

If the US$/D-mark exchange rate was 2.5785 at the time of the swap transaction then the redemption value of the US$ debt would have been US$ 116,346,713.21. So this is effectively the amount of debt which IBM will repay. The foreign currency gain is the difference between this amount and the amount which IBM originally borrowed. If the exchange rate at the time the bond was issued was, for example, US$/D-mark 2.20, then the currency gain would have been US$ 20,016,923.16.

D-mark		US$
300,000,000.00	2.5785	116,346,713.21
300,000,000.00	2.2000	136,363,636.36
		20,016,923.16

Credit arbitrage: IBM's cost of funds

IBM also locked in a gain resulting from credit arbitrage:

All-in cost of bond issue:	D-mark – 10.90%
Swap receipt:	D-mark+ 11.00%
Swap payment:	US$ – 16.80%
Net cost (approximately):	US$ – 16.70%

The total gains, IBM's 10 basis points and the World Bank's 20 basis points are equal to and originate from their funding differentials.

Funding differentials set the boundaries of the swap price between counterparties. There is therefore an implied ceiling and floor for swap prices between which the demand for fixed-rate money and its supply, often in the form of bond issues, fluctuates.

QUESTIONS AND PROBLEMS

1. In a currency swap, counterparties exchange the same sums at the beginning and the end of the swap penod. Explain how this practice relates to the custom of making interest payments during the life of the swap agreement.
2. Why is an interest rate swap simpler to a futures (or forward) contract?
3. Why can a fixed-rate payer in an interest rate swap be viewed as short the bond market and the floating-rate payer be viewed as long the bond market?
4. How can an interest rate collar be created?
5. In a currency swap, both the final principal and the periodic coupons are exchanged. Why is this unnecessary in an interest-rate swap?
6. Discuss the various precautions which can be taken to reduce swap risk.
7. Why in a standard currency swap, is a fixed rate exchanged for a floating rate? Isn't that making things more complicated by comprising an interest-rate risk with a currency risk?
8. A party wants to swap fixed for floating to receive the certificate of deposit (CD) rate for 5 years. The following swap prices are available:

5-year fixed against LIBOR	8% p.a.
5-year fixed against CD rate	7.35% p.a.

Basis swap, pay LIBOR and receive CD rate CD + 50 basis points.

What alternatives does the party have? What are the costs of these alternatives?

9. Discuss the impact of Basle Committee's recommendations on the growth of the swap market.
10. Today is 31 December 2009. We are contemplating an arbitrage between a US$ interest rate swap to 14 December 2010 and the equivalent strip of futures contracts. In the cash deposit market the rate to 16 March 2010 is quoted at 4.25%, and the following Eurodollar deposit futures prices are available:

16 March 2010	95.95
15 June 2010	95.86
14 September 2010	95.64
14 December 2010	95.16

(a) What is the breakeven interest rate swap rate from today to 14 December 2010 implied by the rates given?

(b) If swap rates are quoted 5.05%/5% in an amount of £20 million to 14 December 2010, with LIBOR fixing dates matching the futures dates, construct a trade to take advantage of any arbitrage opportunity which exists.

(c) Ignoring any movements in variation margin, and the reinvestment of interim cashflows, what profit would be earned by such a position?

11. What is a swaption?
12. Explain how you would value a swap that is the exchange of a floating rate in one currency for a fixed rate in another currency.
13. Explain the difference between a plain vanilla interest rate swap and a plain vanilla currency swap.
14. Explain the difference between the credit risk and the market risk in a financial contract. Which of the risks can be hedged?
15. Company ABC and XYZ face the following interest rates:

	ABC	*XYZ*
U.S. dollar (floating rate)	LIBOR + 0.5%	LIBOR + 15%
Japanese Yen (fixed rate)	6.0%	7.5%

Assume that ABC wants to borrow dollars at a floating rate of interest and XYZ wants to borrow Japanese Yen at a fixed rate of interest. A financial institution is planning to arrange a swap and requires a 75 basis point spread. If the swap is equally attractive to ABC and XYZ, what rates of interest ABC and XYZ end up paying.

17. Explain the synthetic futures. Distinguish between the future contracts and option contracts.
18. "Companies with high credit risk are the ones that cannot access fixed rate market directly. They are the companies that are most likely to be paying fixed and receiving floating in an interest rate swap". Do you think it increases or decreases the risk of a financial institution's swap portfolio? Assume that companies are most likely to default when interest rates are high.

14

ROLE OF SWAPS IN MANAGING EXTERNAL DEBT

INTRODUCTION

External debt (or foreign debt) is that part of the total debt in a country that is owed to creditors outside the country. The debtors can be the government, corporations or private households. The debt includes money owed to private commercial banks, other governments, or international financial institutions such as the International Monetary Fund (IMF) and World Bank.

DEFINITION OF EXTERNAL DEBT

Gross external debt, at any given time, is the outstanding amount of those actual current, and not contingent, liabilities that require payment(s) of principal and/or interest by the debtor at some point(s) in the future and that are owed to nonresidents by residents of an economy. IMF defines the key elements of external debt as follows:

i) *Outstanding and Actual Current Liabilities:* For this purpose, the decisive consideration is whether a creditor owns a claim on the debtor. Here debt liabilities include arrears of both principal and interest.

ii) *Principal and Interest:* When this cost is paid periodically, as commonly occurs, it is known as an interest payment. All other payments of economic value by the debtor to the creditor that reduce the principal amount outstanding are known as principal payments. However, the definition of external debt does not distinguish between whether the payments that are required are principal or interest, or both. Also, the definition does not specify that the timing of the future payments of principal and/or interest need be known for a liability to be classified as debt.

iii) *Residence:* To qualify as external debt, the debt liabilities must be owed by a resident to a nonresident. Residence is determined by where the debtor and creditor have their centers of economic interest—typically, where they are ordinarily located—and not by their nationality.

iv) *Current and Not Contingent:* Contingent liabilities are not included in the definition of external debt. These are defined as arrangements under which one or more conditions must be fulfilled before a financial transaction takes place. However, from the viewpoint of understanding vulnerability, there is analytical interest in the potential impact of contingent liabilities on an economy and on particular institutional sectors, such as government.

Generally external debt is classified into four heads: (1) public and publicly guaranteed debt; (2) private non-guaranteed credits; (3) central bank deposits; and (4) loans due to the IMF. However the exact treatment varies from country to country. For example, while Egypt maintains this four head classification. In India, it is classified in seven heads: (a) multilateral, (b) bilateral, (c) IMF loans, (d) Trade Credit, (e) Commercial Borrowings, (f) NRI Deposits, and (g) Rupee Debt, and (h) NPR Debt.

EXTERNAL DEBT SUSTAINABILITY

Sustainable debt is the level of debt which allows a debtor country to meet its current and future debt service obligations in full, without recourse to further debt relief or rescheduling, avoiding accumulation of arrears, while allowing an acceptable level of economic growth.

External-debt-sustainability analysis is generally conducted in the context of medium-term scenarios. These scenarios are numerical evaluations that take account of expectations of the behaviour of economic variables and other factors to determine the conditions under which debt and other indicators would stabilize at reasonable levels, the major risks to the economy, and the need and scope for policy adjustment. In these analysis, macroeconomic uncertainties, such as the outlook for the current account, and policy uncertainties, such as for fiscal policy, tend to dominate the medium-term outlook.

World Bank and IMF hold that "a country can be said to achieve external debt sustainability if it can meet its current and future external debt service obligations in full, without recourse to debt rescheduling or the accumulation of arrears and without compromising growth". According to these two institutions, "bringing the net present value (NPV) of external public debt down to about 150 percent of a country's exports or 250 percent of a country's revenues" would help eliminating this "critical barrier to longer-term debt sustainability". High external debt is believed to have harmful effects on an economy.

INDICATORS OF EXTERNAL DEBT SUSTAINABILITY

There are various indicators for determining a sustainable level of external debt. While each has its own advantage and peculiarity to deal with particular situations, there is no unanimous opinion amongst economists as to one sole indicator. These indicators are primarily in the nature of ratios i.e. comparison between two heads and the relation thereon and thus facilitate the policy makers in their external debt management exercise. These indicators can be thought of as measures of the country's "solvency" in that they consider the stock of debt at certain time in relation to the country's ability to generate resources to repay the outstanding balance.

Examples of debt burden indicators include the (a) debt to GDP ratio, (b) foreign debt to exports ratio, (c) government debt to current fiscal revenue ratio etc. This set of indicators also covers the structure of the outstanding debt including the (d) share of foreign debt, (e) short-term debt, and (f) concessional debt in the total debt stock.

A second set of indicators focuses on the short-term liquidity requirements of the country with respect to its debt service obligations. These indicators are not only useful early-warning signs of debt service problems, but also highlight the impact of the inter-temporal trade-offs arising from past borrowing decisions. Examples of liquidity monitoring indicators include the (a) debt service to GDP ratio, (b) foreign debt service to exports ratio, (c) government debt service to current fiscal revenue ratio etc. The final indicators are more forward looking as they point out how the debt burden will evolve over time, given the current stock of data and average interest rate. The dynamic ratios show how the debt burden ratios would change in the absence of repayments or new disbursements, indicating the stability of the debt burden. An example of a dynamic ratio is the ratio of the average interest rate on outstanding debt to the growth rate of nominal GDP.

SOVEREIGN DEBT DEFAULT

A sovereign debt default is the failure or refusal of the government of a sovereign state to pay back its debt in full. It may be accompanied by a formal declaration of a government not to pay (repudiation) or only partially pay its debts (due receivables), or the de facto cessation of due payments. (Another name is national insolvency if default is not willful, for instance when total debts are more than total assets.) Most authorities will limit the use of "default" to mean failure to abide by the terms of bonds or other debt instruments. Countries have at times escaped the real burden of some of their debt through inflation.

If potential lenders or bond purchasers begin to suspect that a government may fail to pay back its debt, they may demand a high interest rate in compensation for the risk of default. A dramatic rise in the interest rate faced by a government due to fear that it will fail to honour its debt is sometimes called a **sovereign debt crisis**. Governments may be especially vulnerable to a sovereign debt crisis when they rely on financing through short-term bonds, since this creates a situation of maturity mismatch between their short-term bond financing and the long-term asset value of their tax base. They may also be vulnerable to a sovereign debt crisis due to currency mismatch if they are unable to issue bonds in their own currency, as a decrease in the value of their own currency may then make it prohibitively expensive to pay back their foreign-denominated bonds (see original sin).

Since a sovereign government, by definition, controls its own affairs, it cannot be obliged to pay back its debt. Nonetheless, governments may face severe pressure from lending countries. A government may be excluded from further credit and some of its overseas assets may be seized; and it may face political pressure from its own domestic bondholders to pay back its debt. Therefore governments rarely default on the entire value of their debt. Instead, they often enter into negotiations with their bondholders to agree on a delay or partial reduction of their debt payments, which is often called a debt restructuring or 'haircut'.

It can be advisable for regulators and supranational lenders to preemptively engineer the orderly restructuring of a nation's public debt- also called "orderly default" or "controlled default". In the case of Greece, these experts generally believe that a delay in organising an orderly default would hurt the rest of Europe even more. The International Monetary Fund often assists in sovereign debt restructurings. To ensure that funds will be available to pay the remaining part of the sovereign debt, it often makes its loans conditional on austerity measures within the country, such as tax increases or reductions in public sector jobs and services.

Causes of Sovereign Debt Default

According to financial historian Edward Chancellor past instances of sovereign default have tended to occur under some or all of the following circumstances:

i) A reversal of global capital flows
ii) Unwise lending
iii) Fraudulent lending
iv) Excessive foreign debts
v) A poor credit history
vi) Unproductive lending
vii) Rollover risk
viii) Weak revenues
ix) Rising interest rates; and
x) Terminal debt

A significant factor in sovereign default is the presence of significant debts owed to foreign investors who are unable to counter such actions in another nation's political processes or otherwise (e.g., via support from their own government(s) or supranational courts); the enforcement of creditor's rights against sovereign states is frequently difficult. Such willful defaults (the equivalent of strategic bankruptcy by a company or strategic default by a mortgager, except without the possibility of the exercise of normal creditor's rights such as asset seizure and sale) can be considered a variety of sovereign theft; this is similar to expropriation (including inadequate repayment for the exercise of eminent domain).

Insolvency/Over-indebtedness of the State

If a state, for economic reasons, defaults on its treasury obligations, or is no longer able or willing to handle its debt, liabilities, or to pay the interest on this debt, it faces sovereign default. To declare insolvency, it is sufficient if the state is only able (or willing) to pay part of its due interest or to clear off only part of the debt.

Reasons for this include: (i) massive increases in public debt; (ii) declines in employment and therefore tax receipts; (iii) government regulation or perceived threats of regulation of financial markets; and, (iv) popular unrest at austerity measures to repay debt fully. Sovereign default caused by insolvency historically has always appeared at the end of long years or decades of budget emergency (overspending), in which the state has spent more money than it received. This budget balance/margin was covered through new indebtedness with national and foreign citizens, banks and states.

Change of Government

While normally the change of government does not change the responsibility of the state to handle treasury obligations created by earlier governments, nevertheless it can be observed that in revolutionary situations and after a regime change the new government may question the legitimacy of the earlier one, and thus default on those treasury obligations considered odious debt.

Decline of the State

With the decline of the state, its obligations are turned over to one or several successor states. Lost wars significantly accelerate sovereign default. Nevertheless, especially after the Second World War the government debt has increased significantly in many countries even during long lasting times of peace. While in the beginning debt was quite small, due to compound interest and continued overspending it has increased substantially.

Consequences of Sovereign Debt Default

Creditors of the state as well the economy and the citizens of the state are affected by the sovereign default.

Consequences for Creditors

While it is commonly thought sovereign defaults have large costs for the creditor countries, evidence of these costs is hard to find. In this case very often there are international negotiations which end in a partial debt cancellation (London Agreement on German External Debts 1953) or debt restructuring (e.g. Brady Bonds in the 1980s). This kind of agreement assures the partial repayment when a renunciation / surrender of a big part of the debt is accepted by the creditor. In the case of the Argentine economic crisis (1999–2002) the creditors had to accept the renunciation (loss) of up to 75% of the outstanding debts.

For the purpose of debts regulation debts can be distinguished by nationality of creditor (national or international), or by the currency of the debts (own currency or foreign currency) as well as whether the foreign creditors are private or state owned. States are frequently more willing to cancel debts owed to foreign private creditors, unless those creditors have means of retaliation against the state.

Consequences for State

When a state defaults on a debt, the state disposes of (or ignores, depending on the viewpoint) its financial obligations/debts towards certain creditors. The immediate effect for the state is a reduction in its total debt and a reduction in payments on the interest of that debt. On the other hand, a default can damage the reputation of the state among creditors, which can restrict the ability of the state to obtain credit from the capital market. In some cases foreign lenders may attempt to undermine the monetary sovereignty of the debtor state or even declare war.

Consequences for the Citizen

If the individual citizen or corporate citizen is a creditor of the state (e.g. government bonds), then a default by the state can mean a devaluation of their monetary wealth.

In addition, the following scenarios can occur in a debtor state from a sovereign default:

i) a banking crisis, as banks have to make write downs on credits given to the state.

ii) an economic crisis, as the interior demand will fall and investors withdraw their money

iii) a currency crisis as foreign investors avoid this national economy.

Citizens of a debtor state might feel the impact indirectly through high unemployment and the decrease of state services and benefits. However, a monetarily sovereign state can take steps to minimize negative consequences, rebalance the economy and foster social/economic progress (e.g. Plano Real).

EXTERNAL DEBT MANAGEMENT IN INDIA

Cautious and prudent approach towards external debt management pursued in 1990s by the Government of India has helped to place India in comfortable external debt position. India experienced a near balance of payments crisis. One of the causes contributing to the crisis was the rapid growth in external indebtedness and the consequent deterioration in key external debt indicators. India was, however, able to avoid a *debt crisis* and even in times of acute financial crisis never defaulted on her debt obligations. External debt service payments reached a peak in 1995-96 at US $ 13 billion and thereafter maintained a stable payment schedule. Continuous decline in debt service to current receipts ratio and interest payments to current receipts ratio endorse that India's debt service payment capacity has sustainably improved over time. The policy focus has been to concentrate on concessional and less expensive fund sources, preference for longer maturity profiles, an enduring vigil on build-up of short-term debt, premature retirement of high cost external debt and encouragement to non-debt creating capital inflows. Efforts are now on to further consolidate the gains already made. A number of initiatives have been undertaken to meet this objective. This includes, increased coverage and computerisation of external debt data, better co-ordination among agencies reporting debt statistics, prepayment/ refinancing of more expensive external debt and other measures to actively manage sovereign external debt of the country.

Over the years, India's external debt stock has witnessed structural change in terms of composition. The share of concessional in total debt has declined due to shrinking share of official creditors and the Government debt and the surge in non-concessional private debt. The proportion of concessional in total debt declined from 42.9 per cent (average) during the period 1991-2000 to 28.1 per cent in 2001-2010 and further to 13.2 per cent at end-September 2012. The rising share of nongovernment debt is evident from the fact that such debt accounted for 65.6 per cent of total debt during the decade of 2000s, vis-a-vis 45.3 per cent in 1990s. Non-Government debt accounted for over 70 per cent of total debt in the last five years and stood at 77.7 per cent at end-September 2012.

India's external debt has remained within manageable limits as indicated by the external debt to GDP ratio of 19.7 per cent and debt service ratio of 6.0 per cent in 2011-12. The active external debt management policy of the Government of India has helped in containing rise in external debt and maintaining a comfortable external debt position. The policy continues to focus on monitoring long and short-term debt, raising sovereign loans on concessional terms with longer maturities, regulating external commercial borrowings through end-use, all-in-cost and maturity restrictions; and rationalizing interest rates on non-resident Indian deposits.

Corporate borrowers in India and other emerging economies are keen to borrow in foreign currency to benefit from lower interest and longer terms of credit. Such borrowings however, are not always helpful, especially in times of high currency volatility. During good times, domestic borrowers could enjoy triple benefits of (i) lower interest rates, (ii) longer maturity and (iii) capital gains due to domestic currency appreciation. This would happen when the local currency is appreciating due to surge in capital flows and the debt service liability is falling in domestic currency terms. The opposite would happen when the domestic currency is depreciating due to reversal of capital flows during crisis situations, as happened during the 2008 global crisis.

A sharp depreciation in local currency would mean corresponding increase in debt service liability, as more domestic currency would be required to buy the same amount of foreign exchange for debt service payments. This would lead to erosion in profit margin and have mark-to-market implications for the corporate. There would also be 'debt overhang' problem, as the volume of debt would rise in local currency terms. Together, these factors could create corporate distress, especially because the rupee tends to depreciate precisely when the Indian economy is also under stress, and corporate revenues and margins are under pressure.

In this context, it is felt that one of the factors contributing to faster recovery of Indian economy after the 2008 global crisis was the low level of corporate external debt. As a result, the significant decline in the value of rupee did not have major fallout for the corporate balance-sheets. Foreign currency borrowings, therefore, have to be contracted carefully, especially when no 'natural hedge' is available. Such natural hedge would happen when a foreign currency borrower also has an export market for its products. As a result, export receivables would offset, at least to some extent, the currency risk inherent in debt service payments. This happens because fall in the value of the rupee that leads to higher debt service payments is partly compensated by the increase in the value of rupee receivables through exports. When export receivables and the currency of borrowings is different, the prudent approach is for corporations to enter currency swaps to re-denominate asset and liability in the same currency to create natural hedge. Unfortunately, too many Indian corporations with little foreign currency earnings leave foreign currency borrowings unhedged, so as to profit from low international interest rates. This is a dangerous gamble for reasons described above and should be avoided.

THE EXTERNAL DEBT: CURRENT SCENARIO

India's external debt stock at end-March 2012 stood at US$ 345.4 billion (₹ 1,765,333 crore) recording an increase of US$ 39.5 billion (12.9 per cent) over end-

March 2011 level of US$ 305.9 billion (₹ 1,365,929 crore). Component-wise, long-term debt increased by 10.9 per cent to US$ 267.2 billion at end-March 2012 from US$ 240.9 billion at end-March 2011, while short-term showed an increase of 20.3 per cent to US$ 78.2 billion from US$ 65.0 billion at end-March 2011. India's external debt stock increased by about US$ 20.0 billion (5.8 per cent) to US$ 365.3 billion at end-September 2012 over the level at endMarch 2012. The rise in external debt is largely due to higher NRI deposits, short-term debt and commercial borrowings. NRI deposits alone accounted for 42.1 per cent of the rise in total external debt at end-September 2012 over the level of endMarch 2012, while short-term debt and commercial borrowings together accounted for 52.6 per cent of the rise in debt during the period.

The maturity profile of India's external debt indicates the dominance of long-term borrowings. Long-term external debt at US$ 280.8 billion at endSeptember 2012 accounted for 76.9 per cent of the total external debt, while the remaining 23.1 per cent was short-term debt. Long-term debt at endSeptember 2012 increased by US$ 13.6 billion (5.1 per cent) over the level at end-March 2012, while short-term debt increased by US$ 6.3 billion (8.1 per cent). Within long-term, components such as commercial borrowings, NRI deposits and multilateral borrowings taken together, accounted for 62.1 per cent of total external debt at the end of September 2012 while other long-term debt components (viz. bilateral borrowings, export credit, IMF and rupee debt) accounted for 14.8 per cent of total external debt (Table-1).

TABLE-1

COMPOSITION OF EXTERNAL DEBT

(per cent of total external debt)

Sl. No.	*Component*	*March 2011* PR	*March 2012*PR	*June 2012*PR	*September 2012* QE
1	*2*	*3*	*4*	*5*	*6*
1	Multilateral	15.8	14.6	14.3	13.9
2	Bilateral	8.4	7.7	7.8	7.6
3	IMF	2.1	1.8	1.7	1.7
4	Export credit	6.1	5.5	5.5	5.2
5	Commercial borrowings	28.9	30.4	29.9	29.8
6	NRI deposit	16.9	17.0	17.5	18.3
7	Rupee debt	0.5	0.4	0.3	0.4
8	Long-term debt (1 to 7)	78.8	77.4	76.9	76.9
9	Short-term debt	21.2	22.6	23.1	23.1
10	Total external debt (8+9)	100.0	100.0	100.0	100.0

Source : Ministry of Finance and RBI. PR : Partially Revised. QE : Quick Estimates

The currency composition of India's total external debt shows that the share of US dollar denominated debt continued to be the highest in external debt stock at 55.7 per cent at endSeptember 2012, followed by Indian rupee (22.9 per cent), Japanese yen (8.6 per cent), SDR (8.1 per cent) and euro (3.2 per cent). The currency composition of Government (sovereign) debt indicates pre-dominance of SDR denominated debt

(36.6 per cent), which is attributable to borrowing from International Development Association (IDA) i.e., the soft loan window of the World Bank under the multilateral agencies and SDR allocations by the IMF. The share of US dollar denominated debt was 26.2 per cent followed by Japanese yen denominated (19.3 per cent), Indian rupee (14.3) and euro (3.6). At end-September 2012, Government (sovereign) external debt was US$ 81.5 billion. It accounted for 22.3 per cent of India's total external debt. NonGovernment external debt amounted to US$ 283.9 billion which was 77.7 per cent of total external debt at end-September 2012.

The key external debt indicators are presented in Table-2. India's foreign exchange reserves provided a cover of 80.7 per cent to the total external debt stock at end-September 2012 vis-à-vis 85.2 per cent at end-March 2012. The ratio of short-term external debt to foreign exchange reserves was at 28.7 per cent at end-September 2012 as compared to 26.6 per cent at end-March 2012. The ratio of concessional debt to total external debt declined steadily and worked out to 13.2 per cent at end-September 2012 as against 13.9 per cent at end-March 2012.

TABLE 2

INDIA'S KEY EXTERNAL DEBT INDICATORS (PER CENT)

Year	*External debt (US$ billion)*	*Total external debt to GDP*	*Debt-service ratio*	*Foreign exchange reserves to total external debt*	*Concessional debt to total external debt*	*Short-term external debt* to foreign exchange reserves*	*Short-term external debt* to total debt*
1	*2*	*3*	*4*	*5*	*6*	*7*	*8*
1990-91	83.8	28.7	35.3	7.0	45.9	146.5	10.2
1990-91	83.8	28.7	35.3	7.0	45.9	146.5	10.2
1995-96	93.7	27.0	26.2	23.1	44.7	23.2	5.4
2000-01	101.3	22.5	16.6	41.7	35.4	8.6	3.6
2005-06	139.1	16.8	10.1#	109.0	28.4	12.9	14.0
2006-07	172.4	17.5	4.7	115.6	23.0	14.1	16.3
2007-08	224.4	18.0	4.8	138.0	19.7	14.8	20.4
2008-09	224.5	20.3	4.4	112.1	18.7	17.2	19.3
2009-10	260.9	18.2	5.8	106.8	16.8	18.8	20.1
2010-11	305.9	17.5	4.3	99.6	15.5	21.3	21.2
2011-12	345.4	19.7	6.0	85.2	13.9	26.6	22.6
2012-13							
end-June 2012[PR]	348.8	-	5.9	83.1	13.5	27.8	23.1
end-Sept. 2012[QE]	365.3	-	-	80.7	13.2	28.7	23.1

Source : Ministry of Finance and RBI.

Notes : - Not worked out for the broken period. PR : Partially Revised QE-Quick Estimates.

*: Short-term debt is based on original maturity.

#: Works out to 6.3 per cent, with the exclusion of India millennium deposits (IMDs) repayments of US$ 7.1 billion and prepayment of US$ 23.5 million.Debt-service ratio is the proportion of gross debt service payments to external current receipts (net of official transfers).

A cross country comparison of external debt of twenty most indebted developing countries, based on data from the World Bank's 'International Debt Statistics, 2013' which contains the debt numbers for the year 2011 and has a time lag of two years, showed that in 2011 India was in fourth position in terms of absolute external debt stock after China, the Russian Federation and Brazil. The ratio of India's external debt stock to gross national income (GNI) at 18.3 per cent was the third lowest with China's being the lowest at 9.4 per cent (Table-3). In terms of the cover of external debt provided by foreign exchange reserves, India's position was seventh highest at 81.1 per cent.

TABLE-3

INTERNATIONAL COMPARISON OF TOP TWENTY DEVELOPING DEBTOR COUNTRIES, 2011

Sl. No.	*Countries*	*Total external debt stock (US$ million)*	*Total debt to GNI (per cent)*	*Short-term to total external debt (per cent)*	*Foreign exchange reserves to total debt (per cent)*
1	*2*	*3*	*4*	*5*	*6*
1	China	685,418	9.4	69.6	467.3
2	Russian Federation	542,977	31.1	12.9	83.6
3	Brazil	404,317	16.6	10.4	86.7
4	India	334,331	18.3	23.3	81.1
5	Turkey	307,007	40.1	27.3	25.5
6	Mexico	287,037	25.2	17.9	50.2
7	Indonesia	213,541	26.0	17.9	49.9
8	Ukraine	134,481	83.3	24.3	22.6
9	Romania	129,822	72.3	22.9	33.1
10	Kazakhstan	124,437	77.9	7.2	20.2
11	Argentina	114,704	26.3	14.5	37.7
12	South Africa	113,512	28.4	16.6	37.5
13	Chile	96,245	41.0	17.8	43.6
14	Malaysia	94,468	34.8	46.3	139.5
15	Thailand	80,039	24.0	56.2	209.1
16	Colombia	76,918	24.3	14.1	40.8
17	Philippines	76,043	33.6	9.2	88.5
18	Venezuela	67,908	21.8	24.6	14.6
19	Pakistan	60,182	27.3	4.2	24.1
20	Vietnam	57,841	49.1	17.2	23.4

Source : World Bank's International Debt Statistics 2013.
Note : Countries are arranged based on the magnitude of debt presented in Column 3 in the Table.

The widening of the trade deficit to more than 10 per cent of GDP and the CAD crossing 4 per cent of GDP in 2011-12 and the first half of 2012-13 have been matters of concern. In recent years, net invisible balance reduced the need for financing, while capital inflows were sufficient to finance the CAD safely. But the focus has to be on curbing imports, mainly by making oil prices more market determined, and curbing imports of gold. At the same time, further measures to ease the inflow of remittances and steps to diversify software exports could help reduce financing needs. Greater emphasis on FDI including opening up sectors further can help increase the quantum of safe financing. FII flows need to be targeted towards longer term rupee instruments so as to minimize the 'reversal' of capital during risk-off phases. Finally, external commercial borrowing needs to be monitored carefully so that entities without access to foreign exchange revenues do not leave significant exposures unhedged.

MANAGING EXTERNAL DEBT DEFAULT THROUGH SWAPS

CREDIT DEFAULT SWAPS (CDS)

CDS are bilateral agreements to transfer the credit risk of debt obligations of "reference entities"—corporations (financial and nonfinancial), sovereigns, and other legal entities such as securitization special-purpose vehicles. Purchasers of CDS are protected against losses relating to predefined credit events (such as failure to pay) during the term of the contract in return for premium payments to the protection seller. If a credit event occurs, the premium payments terminate and the contract is settled; settlement consists of the protection seller paying an amount equal to the contract notional value minus the value of "deliverable" debt obligations issued by the reference entity ("recovery value").

To illustrate, suppose that CDS protection could be purchased for a spread of 100 basis points per year until contract termination. If it terminates with a credit event, and the recovery value is 20 percent of par, the protection seller would pay 80 percent of the notional value to the protection buyer. The recovery value is based on the value of a reference asset as determined after the credit event; the types and characteristics of the reference assets are contractually specified, with protection buyers effectively determining specifically which of them is used and ultimately the recovery price used to settle the contracts.

USES OF CDS

CDS can be used to take unfunded short (or long positions) in the reference obligations by buying (or selling) protection. Also, traders try to exploit pricing differences between CDS and underlying reference bonds by taking offsetting positions, called "basis trading." For example, suppose that a five-year par bond with a 5 percent coupon could be funded over the full five years at a fixed 4 percent. That would produce expected annual cash inflows of 100 basis points (500 – 400 basis points). For the CDS–bond "basis" to be zero, the CDS referencing that bond must also be trading at 100 basis points. Also, if a credit event occurs, the bond and CDS basis package would suffer identical losses.

When the basis is positive, selling CDS protection and covering it by short selling reference bonds can be profitable. When the basis is negative, it can be arbitraged by buying the bonds and buying CDS protection. These actions should narrow the basis. In practice, the basis is seldom zero due to factors such as transactions costs, funding and counterparty risks, the protection buyer's cheapest-to-deliver option, currency mismatches between the CDS and reference bonds, and nonpar bonds used as reference bonds.

Gross notional values are calculated on a per-trade basis. For example, if Bank A sells $100 of CDS protection to Bank B, the gross notional amounts (the transactions highlighted in the following table) and net notional amounts are reported as $100.

	Gross Sold	*Gross Bought*	*Net Sold*	*Net Bought*
Bank A	–100		–100	
Bank B	100	100		
Total	–100	100	–100	100

If Bank A hedges its position by buying $100 of CDS protection on the same reference entity from Bank C (the transactions highlighted in the following table), the total gross notional amount rises to $200 but the net notional amount remains at $100. The $100 number is a relevant metric of risk transfer, but $200 is relevant as a counterparty risk metric because, although Bank A is "flat" (no exposure), Banks B and C remain exposed to the risk of Bank A defaulting on its contractual obligations.

	Gross Sold	*Gross Bought*	*Net Sold*	*Net Bought*
Bank A	–100	100		
Bank B		100		100
Bank C	–100		–100	
Total	–200	200	–100	100

Gross trade compression and "tear ups" can be used to reduce gross notional amounts by cancelling offsetting redundant contracts. In this case Bank A can transfer ("novate") to Bank B its contractual obligations to Bank C as shown in the table below, bringing gross notional amounts in the system back to $100.

	Gross Sold	*Gross Bought*	*Net Sold*	*Net Bought*
Bank B		100		100
Bank C	–100		–100	
Total	–100	100	–100	100

In reality, a proliferation of these redundant offsetting trades has created large gaps between gross and net notional amounts. That said, compression operations are limited, as some transfers do not work on account of counterparty limits and restrictions, or the offsetting trades are not quite perfect matches (for example, the same reference entity but different contractual terms) and only dealers (and not end users) take part in the operations.

SOVEREIGN CREDIT DEFAULT SWAPS (SCDS)

SCDS are analogous to insurance: in exchange for a fee paid to the seller, they provide protection to buyers from losses that may be incurred on sovereign debt resulting from a "credit event." Credit events include failure to pay interest or principal on, and restructuring of, one or more obligations issued by the sovereign. Many view these swaps as useful market-based risk indicators and valuable hedging instruments. Others consider them to be speculative tools—suggesting their prices do not reflect underlying fundamentals or actual risks and they can therefore unduly raise funding costs for governments, threatening fiscal sustainbility and excebating market tensions. Although CDS that reference sovereign credits are only a small part of the sovereign debt market ($3 trillion notional SCDS outstanding at end-June 2012, compared with $50 trillion of total government debt outstanding at end-2011), their importance has been growing rapidly since 2008, especially in advanced economies.

RISE OF SCDS

SCDS developed in response to the need to use flexible instruments to hedge and trade sovereign credit risks.

Three main purposes are:

(1) *Hedging*. Owners of sovereign debt buy SCDS to protect themselves against losses arising from a default or other credit event affecting the value of the underlying debt. SCDS are also used widely in so-called proxy hedging, that is, to hedge risks of other assets (such as those of domestic banks or utility companies) whose value is correlated with the creditworthiness of the sovereign. For example, an investor can mitigate the market risk of a corporate equity holding if it has a high negative correlation with SCDS spreads referencing the debt of the country in which the firm is domiciled.

(2) *Speculating*. SCDS contracts can be used to buy (or sell) protection on a naked basis—that is, without an offsetting position in the underlying reference assets—to express a negative (or positive) opinion about the credit outlook of the issuer of the underlying bonds. Hence, although SCDS and other CDS are often called "default insurance," they clearly differ from traditional insurance in that the purchasers need not own or have a financial interest in the reference asset. Expressing an opinion about prospective changes in the creditworthiness of a sovereign entity can be executed using other markets (e.g., interest rate futures, cash bond markets, and other derivatives), but they reflect other types of risks in addition to sovereign credit risk.

(3) *Basis trading*. SCDS are used to profit from pricing differences between SCDS and the underlying debt obligations by taking offsetting positions in the two ("basis trading"). This strategy is based on the principle that CDS can be used to replicate the cash flows of underlying obligations. In this regard, when CDS spreads are narrower than the credit spreads of the underlying debt (i.e., the "basis" is negative), arbitragers may be able to profitably buy the obligations and buy CDS protection—and vice versa if the basis is positive. In theory, the basis should always be close to zero as a result of this arbitrage

activity, but in practice there are various costs and frictions that can alter the profitability of these transactions.

SCDS are a small but rapidly growing part of the CDS market, which began in earnest in the early 2000s. Initially, some avenues for hedging or trading the credit risk of sovereigns were provided by Brady bond futures contracts (for three countries—Argentina, Brazil, and Mexico) on the Chicago Mercantile Exchange (CME). Brady bonds were sovereign bonds that had been exchanged for previously defaulted bank loans to those sovereigns and which had partial collateral in the form of set-aside foreign reserves or guarantees. Some argue that the rise of SCDS probably contributed to the demise of these contracts in October 2001 by providing a superior and more flexible hedging alternative. By end-June 2012, the gross notional amount of SCDS outstanding was about $3 trillion, versus $27 trillion in CDS as a whole. However, the size of the SCDS market has increased noticeably since 2008, while other CDS markets have fallen off. The post-2008 surge likely relates to the need to hedge derivative counterparty credit risk exposure that had to be more fully disclosed under new accounting rules that came into effect in 2006.

Before the global financial crisis, the SCDS market consisted largely of contracts on sovereigns of emerging market economies because investors viewed those issuers as having higher and more variable credit risk. However, since end-2009, the deterioration in the perceived safety of the sovereign debt of advanced economies and rising hedging demands have boosted activity in SCDS referencing those economies. Such activity rose first for SCDS referencing the euro area periphery countries, then the core (particularly Germany), and then Japan and the United Kingdom, with some of the countries serving as proxy hedges or as safe haven trades. Nonetheless, as of end-2011, trading in SCDS (gross notional amounts outstanding) tended to be a larger proportion of the underlying government debt for emerging market economies (19 percent) than for advanced economies (3 percent).

Gross notional amounts provide a convenient measure of market size, but net notional amounts (after subtracting the value of the collateral posted) represent the maximum economic transfer if a credit event transpires. The net notional amount represents a counterparty's nominal amount of credit risk exposure to a particular entity at any given time, considering offsetting transactions. Gross notionals far exceed net notionals because of the market practice of reducing or reversing positions by using offsetting transactions rather than by terminating contracts or transferring them to other parties. However, gross notional amounts outstanding are also useful in gauging the risk arising from interconnections among the contract holders ("counterparty risk"), particularly during periods of stress, since the entire value of all the contracts associated with a given counterparty would be at risk if that counterparty failed.

Dealer banks (global systemically important financial institutions or G-SIFIs) dominate the buy and sell sides of the SCDS markets largely because of their market-making activities and risk management of their exposures to sovereigns. A high level of market concentration could potentially lead to market dysfunction when the dominant dealers are under stress. Dealer banks are exposed to sovereigns because of their direct holdings of sovereign debt as well as the counterparty credit risk associated with their derivatives trades with sovereigns, the effective values of which they have been obliged to disclose since 2006. Sovereigns traditionally have not agreed to post collateral to cover the mark-to-market risks of their OTC positions in interest rate and cross currency swaps and other derivatives; therefore, dealer banks have credit exposures on these OTC contracts when sovereigns owe money on them. SCDS can therefore provide dealer banks with a convenient hedge. Non-dealer banks and securities firms are the next most important group of buyers and sellers of SCDS protection, followed by hedge funds, but the SCDS activity of all these is much smaller than that of dealer banks.

A given type of institution has no consistent role as either buyer or seller of SCDS protection. Subtracting notional amounts outstanding sold from notional amounts bought by the dealer banks provides a rough measure of the positions for their counterparties. On this basis, other banks and securities firms have been net sellers of SCDS protection, thereby taking credit risk and earning premiums. Many of these banks also own sovereign debt and are hence "doubling up" on this type of credit exposure. Hedge funds have been prominent net buyers of SCDS protection since 2010, but they were sellers before then. Moreover, hedge fund prominence appears larger in SCDS than in other CDS holdings. The use of SCDS by other investors, including nonfinancial institutions, appears much more limited, although anecdotal evidence suggests that some large asset managers (including some mutual funds) are active participants.

Measures of market liquidity in the SCDS market indicate the following:

i) SCDS transactions volumes vary widely by reference entity and tend to be concentrated in contracts referencing larger emerging market economies and economies experiencing financial stress.
ii) During 2010 and 2012, on average, the number of trades was larger in high-stress periods, when SCDS spreads were relatively elevated.
iii) In general, market liquidity in SCDS (proxied by narrow bid-ask spreads) has been higher for those referencing emerging market economies than for those referencing advanced economies; the difference probably reflects the fact that the SCDS market was largely represented by emerging market sovereigns before the crisis. However, liquidity for SCDS referencing advanced economies began improving after 2008 with higher volumes.

WHAT DRIVES SCDS SPREADS AND HOW DO THEY RELATE TO OTHER MARKETS?

Some view SCDS markets, especially relative to underlying bond markets, as more prone to speculation and opacity and disassociated from economic fundamentals. These views are given plausibility, for instance, by seemingly excessive volatilities of SCDS spreads relative to spreads in government bond markets in some countries.

SCDS spreads and bond spreads represent appropriate measures for comparing SCDS and government bonds. For advanced economies, bond spreads are constructed as bond yields minus the interest swap rate (i.e., fixed rate for floating LIBOR rate);

for individual emerging market economies, they are the EMBI spreads. Use of these measures is motivated by arbitrage trading actually undertaken in markets that identically match the cash flows of the two sides of the trade.

The fundamental economic factors that drive spreads for SCDS and government bonds are generally the same, suggesting that both types of instrument reflect sovereign risk. Government debt, GDP growth, and, to a lesser extent, foreign reserves are significant economic factors for spreads for both instruments, and the magnitudes of the effects for SCDS and government bonds are comparable. There is some evidence that a weaker financial sector (proxied by lower bank returns on assets) adds to sovereign risk in both SCDS and government bond markets, especially during periods of stress. Market microstructure characteristics are also influential in both markets: Larger bid-ask spreads for SCDS and government bonds (i.e., lower liquidity) are associated with higher levels of spreads for both SCDS and government bonds. This could happen if liquidity in the markets for SCDS and government bonds is correlated, or if this measure reflects some elements of underlying sovereign credit risk common to both SCDS and government bonds. Larger SCDS trading volume (relative to government bonds) is associated with higher spreads for SCDS and their reference bonds. This could imply that trading volume surges when the need to hedge or the desire to speculate is higher because of higher credit risks. In most markets, improvements in liquidity with larger volumes are associated with lower CDS spreads. The relationship with variables representing general financial market conditions is also similar across the SCDS and government bond markets. There is evidence that SCDS are more sensitive than government bonds with respect to market risk factors, although the difference between the two is not statistically significant, especially in terms of the VIX and funding costs.

Looking specifically at periods of stress, there is some evidence that the SCDS and government bond markets react to different economic fundamentals and microstructure proxies, but mostly in the same direction as during the nonstress periods.

ARE SCDS MARKETS MORE PRONE TO BE DESTABILIZING THAN OTHER MARKETS?

Concerns about excessive SCDS volatility and contagion across countries partly underpin policies attempting to limit SCDS trading. Hence, it is useful to examine measures that identify spillovers and those that might suggest SCDS move more than warranted using known explanatory factors. Also useful is an examination about whether such overshooting raises the borrowing costs of the underlying sovereign issuer.

Indeed, there is evidence of significant co-movement of SCDS spread volatilities across some countries in the euro area, especially during periods of stress. The effect can be seen by determining the residual volatility of SCDS spreads of selected euro area countries (i.e., the volatility for each country not explained by factors specific to that country) and then decomposing that residual into common market factors (VIX and TED spread) and the spillover effects from the SCDS volatility of other euro area countries. For Germany most of the volatility that is not explained by Germany's own country-specific factors is driven by volatility in the SCDS for Italy and Spain, with other EU periphery countries under stress (Greece, Ireland, and Portugal) having a comparatively small effect. For Spain, almost three-fourths of its residual volatility is driven by Germany's SCDS, while Italy's volatility is also a significant contributor (almost 20 percent), with the other factors having a much smaller impact. Roughly the same results hold for Italy, where Germany and Spain are large contributors and other factors less so.

In general, the question of whether SCDS markets are more likely to be contagious than other markets is difficult to answer because the interconnections across many markets are high. The most critical set of interconnections has probably developed among sovereigns and financial institutions, quite apart from the development of SCDS markets per se. Indeed, risks embedded in SCDS cannot be readily isolated from the risks of the financial system; a more integrated analysis of both sectors is required.

WHAT COULD BE THE IMPACT OF THE DEMISE OF SCDS?

Naked SCDS protection buying is economically equivalent to short selling the underlying bonds. In both cases, trades are usually profitable if the likelihood of a credit event increases. Also, both provide useful functions by increasing the liquidity of the underlying markets. In addition, both CDS protection buying and short selling keep prices from reflecting the activity of only the most optimistic market participants.

In general, SCDS are more efficient than short sales as a means of trading on, or hedging against, negative credit events. Short selling requires a sufficient quantity of bonds that can be borrowed and deep repurchase agreement (repo) markets in which to borrow them. Only a handful of advanced economies have such repo markets (Australia, France, Germany, Japan, the Netherlands, the United Kingdom, and the United States). Particularly for countries experiencing stress, short selling demand can sometimes overwhelm the supply of bonds available to lend. Moreover, such loans may be recalled at any time so, unlike with SCDS, positions cannot be locked in over longer terms. Other alternatives to buying naked SCDSinclude government bond futures contracts and proxies such as the CDS of large financial corporations and utilities. However, government bond futures contracts are available on only a handful of sovereigns, and bond futures embed both credit and interest rate risk, whereas SCDS isolate credit risk. Although the interest rate risk of a futures contract can be mostly offset using interest rate swaps, such transactions will increase operational risks and require the posting of additional safe assets as collateral. The problem with proxy-hedging sovereign risk using the CDS of large financial firms or utilities is that these markets are generally not big enough, plus their usage could involve other unwanted risks. Any meaningful transfer of risk from SCDS to financial CDS markets is likely to further strengthen the connectivity between these two markets—in contrast to the goal of other policies. Also, other, more opaque and customized OTC derivative contracts, such as total return swaps, could serve as alternatives to SCDS.

What would happen to the market for the underlying bonds if SCDS contracts ceased to exist? For advanced economies, especially larger economies and those perceived to be safe, SCDS markets are generally small compared with the underlying government debt outstanding, indicating that the demise of the SCDS market would have little effect on the underlying bond market. However, SCDS gross notional amounts are large relative to underlying government debt for many emerging market economies and some European countries. Generally, prohibiting the purchase of naked SCDS protection could permanently impair SCDS markets, as trading would exclude a set of participants that help provide liquidity and balance to markets—a complete ban on SCDS contracts would be even more dire. However, the effects of a loss of liquidity and pricing influence will likely depend on the type of country. For example, some advanced economies have substitute markets through which negative sovereign credit risk views can be expressed. However, in many emerging market economies, such alternatives are unavailable, so the loss of SCDS as a hedging instrument could have negative consequences for other credit markets, including the underlying bond markets, and could raise issuance costs. In addition, SCDS dealers that hedge their counterparty risk on their other derivative transactions with sovereigns would face higher costs on such hedging activities. In addition, other financial asset markets, not merely those for SCDS, tend to exhibit high and correlated volatility during market. However, sovereigns and their agencies may be exempt from margin posting on bilateral and centrally cleared trades.

Finally, in an effort to remove destabilizing speculation, the likely effects of the ban on naked short selling are a continuing drop in volumes and liquidity, which could harm the hedging role of SCDS markets. Less liquidity is likely to lead to more proxy hedging and higher spillovers to other markets—potentially with the unintended consequence of reducing financial stability. Whether the ban restrains speculation that could be related to overshooting, and hence to unstable market conditions, remains to be seen. The policy of moving OTC derivatives to CCPs appears a concrete method of making the SCDS market safer. Although, in the short term, the cost of posting initial margin would be high, it is expected to have positive stability implications in the medium term, as counterparty risks would be lowered and transparency potentially improved. However, the exemption of sovereign counterparties from posting collateral is problematic, as it continues to leave dealer banks exposed to sovereign default risks that they will likely hedge with the purchase of SCDS protection.

QUESTIONS

1. Define external debt. Discuss the change in profile of India's external debt in recent times.
2. Critically examine the causes and consequences of sovereign default.
3. Discuss the key ratios which are used to assess the sustainability of external debt.
4. Discuss the concept of Credit Default Swaps (CDS) and it use in the financial markets.
5. Are SCDS spreads as good as credit spreads derived from government bonds in reflecting the macroeconomics fundamentals that characterize soveriegn risk.
6. Are SCDS markets as efficient as sovereign cash bond markets in rapidly pricing-in new information ?
7. Are SCDS markets more likely than other financial markets to be destabilizing ?

8. Why is buying naked SCDS protection more economically useful and what are the alternatives ?
9. What would happen to the market for the underlying bonds in SCDS contracts ceased to exist ?
10. Discuss the structural change sin the composition of India's external debt since early nineties.
11. Why has the active management of sovereign external debt portfolio become imperative for India in recent years.
12. Discuss the principal elements of the multi-pronged strategy adopted by the policy-markets in India to bring the external debt situation at a more comfortable level.

15

FINANCIAL DERIVATIVES MARKET: A GLOBAL PERSPECTIVE

INTRODUCTION

The past decade has witnessed an explosive growth in the use of financial derivatives by a wide range of corporate and financial institutions. This growth has run in parallel with the increasing direct reliance of companies on the capital markets as the major source of long-term funding. In this respect, derivatives have a vital role to play in enhancing shareholder value by ensuring access to the cheapest source of funds. Active use of derivative instruments allows the overall business risk profile to be modified, thereby providing the potential to improve earnings quality by offsetting undesired risks. Financial institutions use derivatives primarily as a source of revenue, which is, to say the least, a contentious point. However, derivatives can be also seen as powerful risk-management tools. From the risk-management perspective, the same derivatives allow financial institutions and other participants to identify, isolate, and manage separately the market risks of financial instruments and commodities. Used prudently, they offer managers efficient and effective access to techniques for reducing particular risks through hedging, as well as reducing financing costs and increasing yields on assets. Derivatives may be used in market making, position taking, or risk arbitrage, all of which are sources of potential revenue for a financial institution.

MANAGING DERIVATIVE RISK

Whilst derivative instruments offer countless methods for gaining leveraged exposure to hundreds of markets, it is for this very reason that an independent and formal risk-management and control structure needs to be established. In traditional risk-management terms, *"Even if you have the most sophisticated cash register in the world, who's going to watch the person at the till?"* In order to construct this risk-management and control system, the major types of risk that need to be considered in such a system are discussed below.

TYPES OF DERIVATIVES RISK

The art and science of risk analysis is fundamentally about first identifying potential failures (categorising events into "risk types"), then estimating the frequency of occurrence of these failures, and, finally, determining the magnitude of the consequences ("its value"). The discipline of risk-management takes risk analysis a step further by positively acting on this new found knowledge and thereby, hopefully, reducing the probability of failure. The strategy is that by reducing the probability of failure, the probability of success should increase. In the derivatives business where every instrument is considered "risky," personnel should have a clear grasp of the elementary types of risk which pervade each transaction.

There are many different types of risk which can be considered relevant to any particular derivatives transaction. The following is a list which should be considered by any derivatives risk-management service.

i) *Operational risk:* the risk of loss arising due to procedure errors, omissions or failure of internal control systems.

ii) *Market risk:* the risk of loss arising from adverse market rate movements, e.g. foreign exchange (transaction, translation, or economic), interest rates, commodity and equity prices.

iii) *Interest rate risk:* the change in capital values of an investment resulting from changes in prevailing interest rate levels.

iv) *Systemic risk:* an inherent risk within the inter-bank market, the risk is of a bank finding itself unable to meet its due obligations causing other banks to fail to meet theirs.

v) *Credit risk:* the risk of losses arising from defaults by the counterparty.

vi) *Cashflow risk:* the risk of the institution failing to have sufficient cash resources to meet its obligations, e.g. realised losses being offset by unrealised gains.

vii) *Liquidity risk:* the risk of losses arising from a derivatives market becoming illiquid, or where difficulty or cost issues arise when closing the position.

viii) *Basis risk:* losses arising from the divergence between two prices or rates.

ix) *Aggregation risk (or interconnection risk):* this is the quantification of the problem that some derivatives transactions involve several markets and instruments.

x) *Legal risk: issues* resulting in derivatives contracts becoming unenforceable either by jurisdictional law or by the lack of capacity of the institution.

xi) *Business risk (or specific risk):* the risk, that one transaction or a small group of transactions, causing losses, exposes the firm to risk of failure. This risk can be reduced to the point of insignificance. Diversification is the basic protection strategy. As the number of positions held increases, business risk falls very rapidly. It is very important for institutions to understand that expected rate of return does not fall as a result of diversification. Only the variation around the expected rate of return falls. And, variation is risk!

xii) *Political risk:* this includes tax, trade, regulation, education and social policies. A government's attitude towards capital and business sets the stage for either success or failure of its economy.

xiii) *Audit risk:* the risk of losses arising from failure of the audit function be if internal or external. We hypothesize as a general rule of thumb:

Audit Risk = Inherent risk * Control risk * Non-Sampling detection risk * Sampling detection risk

It is essential that the financial risk review be independent. Equally, the monitoring function should be independent of any front office function to ensure that no conflict of interest or valuation manipulation occurs.

Understanding what types of risks apply where and when is the first task of the risk-management and control function. For example, in an exchange-traded futures contract, the credit and liquidity risk are reduced by the formal exchange mechanism which matches buyers and sellers of futures contracts, and simultaneously guarantees delivery and payment on the contract. However, if there is a weak operational process, comprising inefficient settlement systems, poorly trained and motivated staff, with weak communication lines to the front end of the business, it does not matter what type of derivative is being processed, a high level of operational risk will haunt any transaction. A risk-management policy framework be constructed which takes into account common elements and differences across financial risk-taking activities. This framework must be above all flexible and adaptable to new risks which are discovered or created.

The key requirement, therefore, for any risk-management system is having the infrastructure in place to facilitate the proper identification of not just the size of exposure that exists but also the type of exposure. This reinforces the need for a totally accountable and optimal risk-control system.

AN INTEGRATED APPROACH TO MERGE DERIVATIVE RISKS

The risk issues will be much better served and managed if the elements of risk inherent to the derivatives market are controlled from a centralised source rather than a series of dislocated functions. A close analysis of each risk type also reinforces this by highlighting the existing and potential commonality of risk-control approaches that exist between each area. The following discussion therefore focuses on: i) systemic risk; ii) market risk; iii) credit risk; iv) liquidity risk; v) cashflow management risk; vi) legal risk; and, vii) operational risk.

SYSTEMIC RISK

Systemic risk is the risk that a market disruption causes widespread difficulties to other participants in that market segment or in the financial system as a whole. In other words, it is the risk that a local or organisational problem turns into a global one through a "domino effect." A systemic crisis could start anywhere: from a cascading of asset prices or the demise of a major financial institution. The causal factors are unpredictable and the effects may vary depending on the number and size of firms involved. It would also depend on the general economic environment. Characteristic of a systemic crisis is that market participants start holding back payments, causing gridlock. This can lead to a disruption of payment and settlement systems. As the crisis spreads more broadly it can cause a more general disruption of financial or credit markets.

MARKET RISK

Market risk exposes a company to uncertainty due to movements in factors such as foreign exchange rates, commodity prices, equity prices, and volatilities related to options positions. Evolving from using single-factor models to measure market risk to multiple-factor models such as the Arbitrage Pricing Model and statistical approaches based on parameters involving correlations and standard deviations, market risk quantification is at the core of all activities relating to market risk.

Both regulators and practitioners consider the following activities to be prerequisites for effective market risk management.

i) *Marking to market:* Measuring the fair value of the organisation's portfolio should be done at least on an intra-day basis with an evolution towards real-time mark to market data.

ii) *Stress testing/simulation:* Analysis should be performed which tests the valuation effect of the derivatives portfolio under stressful market conditions. Market shifts beyond the parameters of conventional probability-based risk models have occurred in recent years

iii) *Management reporting:* There is a definite split between the tactical information requirements of the trading room and the strategic level information required by senior management. For example, management may wish to allocate capital in a manner which diversifies the total portfolio but the trader may wish to focus on concentrating capital on particular plays.

iv) *Risk limit structures:* Risk limit structures using effective risk measurements must be formally introduced and rigorously applied. They must be balanced, however, against business requirements and appetite for risk among senior management and shareholders.

v) *Risk capital and aggregation:* Establishing a common risk and performance measurement framework across product and functional groups is increasingly recognised as being essential for the comprehensive management of risk.

One of the prominent features of market risk management is how the techniques used there can be transferred to other risk types, thereby facilitating the integration of risk control at an organisational level. Thus, the concept of risk capital is not concerned solely with market risk considerations but can be designed to encompass credit, liquidity, and operational risk elements as well.

CREDIT RISK

It is important to remember that risk-control areas need to manage risk not only on a product basis but also on a counterparty basis. Like other forms of risk inherent in a derivatives portfolio the amount of credit risk that exists in a portfolio depends largely on the size and nature of the products. An exchange-traded futures contract, for example, is likely to have significantly less counterparty exposure than an interest rate swap.

It is also important to differentiate between counterparty risk and credit risk *per se.* A number of factors need to be examined in order to determine the quality of the counterparty's ability to make good its financial obligations. This is part of a bank's normal operations. However, the credit risk *per se* of a portfolio may be traded in the form of credit derivatives. In this case, the main concern would be not so much about the counterparty risk but about issues of liquidity and the widening or thinning of spreads between the buying and selling price of the instruments.

For risk-control purposes there are a variety of methods that an organisation can use to control credit risk, but most techniques can be categorised as either counterparty enhancement tools or part of an ongoing process of credit analysis. Credit enhancement techniques include: *Collateral agreements:* provision for security in case of default; *Netting agreements:* provision setting off total amounts of reciprocal obligations; *Credit guarantees:* third party usually with superior credit rating guarantees principal balance, *Credit triggers:* where outstanding contracts can be terminated if the counterparty's credit rating goes below a certain predetermined level; and, the *Mutual termination options:* which permit either counterparty to terminate unconditionally on a specified date before maturity.

Credit analysis comprises the techniques that are used to measure the ongoing credit risk that the institution is taking, as implied by its portfolio customer mix. It is within the area of credit analysis that there lie significant opportunities for integration with other risk categories, most notably market risk. Conventional credit risk-management procedures include: establishing credit limits; maintaining a database with counterparty ratings information; seeking to avoid excessive concentration among counterparty types; and, the maintaining a list of preferable counterparties.

The most significant aspect of new approaches to credit risk analysis is how they are converging with market risk methodologies. Full-scale integration of market and credit risk is far from a common practice and this is due to tradition as opposed to any practical reason against integration. The advantages of integrating credit risk and market risk analysis range from cost and efficiency issues to improved capital adequacy provision.

A combined area would:

1. ensure a consistent approach between credit and market risk by centralising responsibility for measurement and control policy across the organisation;
2. achieve scale efficiencies by pulling together what are normally two independent and disparate areas;
3. improve risk assessment by aggregating market and credit risk at the product rather than group level.

In derivatives markets the size of the exposure in the event of a counterparty default depends on how the value of the contract has moved, which in turn depends on how the underlying market rates have moved since the trade was executed. However, whilst there is a clear transactional based relationship between credit risk and market risk the two risk elements are not additive. For example, when a derivatives position increases in value there is an increase in credit risk but normally a corresponding reduction in market risk. The situation would be reversed if the position reduced in value.

There are currently a host of quantitative frameworks for credit risk analysis that resemble market risk approaches. Over time, these techniques and their progeny should replace the relatively unsophisticated "gut feet" techniques of traditional credit analysis. These techniques include: using risk adjusted return calculations (similar to value at risk) to measure individual and portfolio level default risk based on expected exposure; applying options theory to credit default analysis; using efficient portfolio theory based on the incremental impact of a deal on the overall level of risk in a portfolio; and, the aggregating risks into a single measurement by the statistical correlation between individual credit risks.

For credit risk control, an approach is required which measures the expected risk-adjusted return on the portfolio before and after the addition of a new deal. In the context of market price risk the common risk denominator is the volatility of price movements, whereas for credit risk the appropriate common denominator is the standard deviation of the distribution of possible credit losses. However, techniques based upon probability distributions of credit default and market price movement can use the same standing data for both market and credit risk.

In short, as the importance of sound credit risk analysis for derivatives has grown, so has the scope for integrating credit and market risk control techniques using a common data platform. A fully integrated market risk and credit risk system is now both feasible and desirable.

LIQUIDITY RISK

Liquidity risk relates to the fluctuation of derivatives instruments according to a number of factors: the size and maturity of the market; the number of participants in the market; market turnover rates; level of market information; split between over-the-counter (OTC) and exchange-traded.

As shown in Table-1, the liquidity of the market governs many of the risk-control approaches relating to the other types of risk. It is therefore difficult to examine liquidity risk in isolation from the other risk types.

TABLE-1

THE RISK CONTINUUM

Market conditions	*Highly illiquid*	*Illiquid*	*Liquid but variable*	*Liquid*
Basis for valuation	Reserve adjusted Book value Supplemented by mark to model	Mark to market Supplemented by mark to market	Mark to market Checked with mark to model Benchmark data	Mark to market
Basis for market, credit and liquidity risk calculations	Loss modelling Scenario analysis based on credit defaults and market shocks	Loss modelling Value at Risk adjusted liquidity	Value at Risk Supplemented by stress testing	Value at Risk Supplemented by stress testing
Ex-ante risk control mechanisms				
Credit	Pricing and underwriting approval by senior management	Limit approval	Limits Credit enhancements	Limits Credit enhancements
Operational	Documentation of transaction Appraisal of	Documentation of transaction Appraisal of	Efficiency measures based on exception	Efficiency measures based on exception

	settlement systems for exposure monitoring	settlement systems for exposure monitoring	reporting	reporting
Legal	Consider Ultra Vires* Suitability**	Consider Ultra Vires Suitability	Conform to industry standards)	Conform to Industry standards
Ex-post mechanisms	Risk detection models Testing of mark to model parameters	Risk detection models Testing of mark to model parameters	P&L level and volatility	P&L level and volatility

* *Ultra vires* (Latin for "beyond the power") is the legal doctrine that the contract in question was entered into without the authority of the corporate entity.

** The question of "suitability" is hotly debated. Derivative marketers should be legally responsible for determining the suitability of customers for derivatives transactions, including the commercial question of whether the product was appropriate for the risk in question. Whatever the legal responsibilities are, it would seem prudent and good business sense that the bank itself ask whether the products sold are suitable to the customers' purposes.

Two elements of liquidity risk that arise come from the relative ability of an organisation to transfer its assets into cash and the mismatch between a bank's cash inflows and outflows arising out of derivatives activity. Both these areas can be managed in tandem with credit and market risk requirements and, for most aspects of liquidity risk, using the techniques similar to both areas. One of the major issues related to liquidity is the ability of the bank to transfer the instrument into cash.

Transfer Ability

The ability to transfer derivatives into cash at fair value depends largely on the existence of a secondary market. Clearly, the mix in the derivatives portfolio between OTC and exchange-traded instruments is crucial. OTC instruments such as interest rate swaps do have a secondary market which is growing but as yet is not wholly liquid.

Methods that are used in market risk analysis can also be used to determine the potential cost incurred from closing down a position. Using a VaR methodology, for example, the calculation of liquidity risk would be based on three factors:

1. the transaction costs incurred in liquidation, determined largely by the bid-ask spread and the mean average size of trade for a particular instrument;
2. the cost of exposure of the position while it is being maintained;
3. the cost of hedging the exposure, where possible.

The trade-off between the three components would determine the rate of liquidation that minimises the sum of the overall costs and also pinpoints the liquidity adjusted value at risk of the derivatives portfolio at any one point in time.

In the case of more exotic instruments the effect of liquidity risk on a conventional value at risk calculation can be significant. The cost of close-out of exotic or non-standard derivatives positions must also factor in the cost of liquidity-as it would for emerging market debt instruments. This could significantly magnify the value of risk on these positions. The effect of liquidity on currency positions increased conventional VaR by hundreds of per cent during well-known crises.

Liquidity risk, in the context of *transfer ability*, therefore, must be accounted for as an integral part of the market risk analysis process especially when illiquid transactions form part of the derivatives portfolio.

CASHFLOW MANAGEMENT RISK

Large derivatives portfolios can be subject to sudden cash demands from their ongoing derivatives positions making liquidity management for off-balance sheet products crucial. The method by which banks monitor their derivatives cashflow risk is similar to that used for other banking products, where cash requirements arising from potential price and volatility changes at each point are calculated and then compared to funding availability. Sudden liquidity changes can arise out of either credit risk, through the threat of a counterparty default, or by market risk factors such as a run on a currency. Therefore, the risk manager can use information relating to credit risk analysis and market risk analysis to adjust future cashflow requirements.

LEGAL RISK

The external risk management (ERM) risk area takes into account information supplied by the global database and the legal and compliance teams. It is important to note that senior management will need to be informed of their legal duties and therefore there is a direct communication link from the legal and compliance teams to senior management. The legal and compliance teams will also supply any new legislation and changes to old legislation ("new data") to the global database. The ERM risk area may also wish to interrogate the legal and compliance teams to check whether they have understood the new data from the global data-base and to ensure that their advice to senior management is legally suitable and appropriate.

OPERATIONAL RISK

Operational risk is the most difficult risk area to define and integrate into an enterprise-wide risk-management system. The main reason for this is that operational risk is everywhere within an organisation.

Table-2 shows various types of error and failure that may occur within their respective functions.

TABLE 2

ERRORS AND FAILURES CAUSING RISK

Risk category	*Functional responsibilities*	*Examples*
PEOPLE	Business line Human resources Security	Human error Internal fraud Staff shortage
TECHNOLOGY	Business line technologies Central infrastructure Data center maintenance	Technology failure Outmoded systems Poor data integrity
REGULATORY	Compliance Finance and accounting Legal	Regulator disputes Misstating accounts

The potential exposures commonly associated with operations are diverse and may relate to: technology choices: batch versus real-time processing; intra-day settlement exposure: no quantification or intra-day or overnight risk; cross-border payment issues; reliance on manual controls; multilateral versus bilateral payment systems; and, timing of payment and delivery. Many of these issues go beyond the organisational level to focus on the effectiveness of settlements and payments organisations such as: bilateral netting and settlement services: FXNET, SWIFT, and VALUENET; multilateral netting and settlement services such as ECHO; and, private sector clearing and payments services such as Euroclear.

Operational risk is relevant to the entire "value chain" of an organisation and cannot be managed simply through a centralised risk-control process. Technology, people, and manual and automated controls throughout the organisation all have a part to play in creating a secure operational environment. However, such is the scale of the potential exposure created by these activities in today's financial system that an operational risk-management function is increasingly seen as an essential to the overall risk-management process.

The question is, then, how can operational concerns be integrated into the integrated risk framework but avoid duplicating the functions of the existing operational controls as well as those of external payments and clearing systems; plus the internal audit function, which is normally concerned with the operational control environment? A solution to this problem may be approached by breaking down aspects of operational risk into their constituent risk elements in an attempt to: qualify the costs involved in specific operational breakdowns; establish the common elements, if any, that are in existence when each breakdown occurs; and, develop a probability-based model for attributing capital to operational risk.

The prerequisites of this type of attributional operational risk system are similar to those utilised in an insurance organisation, namely: gathering information on operational events; seeking expert opinion to estimate loss amounts that are most difficult to quantify; and, sorting each loss type into a relevant category so that correlation analysis can be performed.

In the context of risk management, quantified risk exposures relating to operational events can then be integrated into the overall risk process through: (i) techniques for measuring credit risk and liquidity risk being utilised to calculate the probability of specific operational failures; (ii) responsibility for establishing settlement exposure calculations being given to credit control staff with the information required for this being generated through the centralised data depository or data warehouse; (iii) providing an early warning system for payments, settlements, and other operational risks and so facilitating actionable risk-management designed to mitigate the exposure.

Thus, the operational risk can be mitigated internally through proper controls and procedures and a detailed understanding of all the stages of the operational process. However, in order to be able to quantify the risk there also needs to be a framework for operational risk control. It is this last element that should be controlled and provided by an integrated risk area.

VALUE AT RISK (VaR) ANALYSIS: RISK AGGREGATION

The notion of risk capital is one of the most important developments in risk management in recent years and has become the standard of choice among regulators and sophisticated bankers alike. Essentially risk capital is encapsulated in a class of risk measures, often called value at risk techniques, which are designed to aggregate diverse product and currency positions into a common risk measure. The various risks may be aggregated into a single measure. Value at risk, or VaR, has become a standard in the derivatives industry assisting senior management in both financial institutions and industrial corporations and regulators to under stand the risk exposure of particular derivative instruments. It is important to realise the power and limitations of VaR as well as how the underlying principles of the method can be applied to other forms of risk analysis.

The tendency towards risk aggregation has largely been encapsulated in the increasing use and acceptance of value at risk concepts, which calculate "the expected loss from an adverse market movement within a specific probability over a particular period of time." From this formal definition comes a more intuitive definition of VaR "as the amount of economic or equity capital which must be held to support that particular level of risky business activity".

VALUE AT RISK (VAR): A BIRD'S-EYE VIEW

Value at risk is a probability-weighted aggregation of current results in gains and losses embedded in a trading portfolio, under various market scenarios. VaR typically assumes that no trading occurs during the pricing exercise. In other terms, at least on an instantaneous basis there is zero liquidity in the market.

The daily estimate of value at risk can take the form of a revenues-and-exposures graph as well as of a holding period over 10 days with no risk-reducing trades. The computation should be made at the 99 percent confidence level to be consistent with the 1998 Market Risk Amendment by the Basle Committee.

As seen in Figure-1 the calculation of value at risk assumes a normal distribution of exposures, which is evidently an approximation, whether we talk of individual instruments or of the contents of the whole trading book. A positive aftermath of this approximation is that we can use the concept underpinning the operating characteristics curve (lower part of Figure 1) to estimate the 99 per cent probability that the worst case will not exceed the value derived from computation. This 99 percent level of confidence corresponds to a *Type 1* error, on the OC curve, of 1 percent. This is known as α. In the long run, in 1 percent of cases the VaR estimate will not cover the worst case.

In the computation of VaR there may be other errors too that are not statistical in nature, but depend on assumptions and on the correlations. Empirically derived correlations are used for aggregation within each of three basic risk classes: currency exchange, interest rates, and equities. Other classes, too, can be distinguished depending on the business of the bank. Across risk classes, cumulative exposure is computed assuming zero correlation among highly defined risk classes. This is, of course, another approximation reflecting the diversification that might or might not exist in business areas. Hence, depending on the institution and its trading habits, this hypothesis may be weak or outright false.

FIGURE 1 :

VALUE AT RISK ASSUME A NORMAL DISTRIBUTION OF EXPOSURE, WHICH IS AN APPROXIMATION

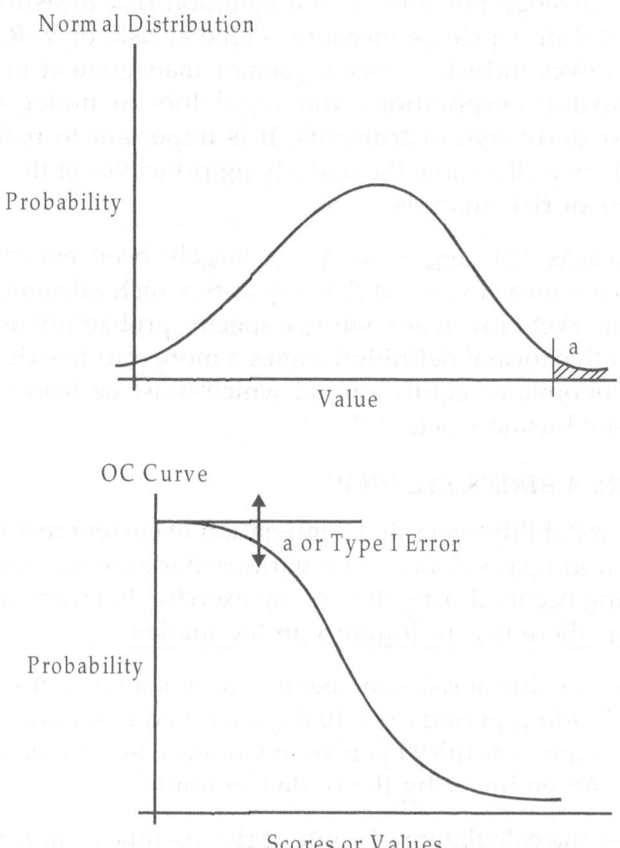

From a statistical viewpoint, VaR is a scalar *estimate* of an unknown parameter of the loss distribution. Sampling errors can affect the accuracy of point estimates so institutions using VaR must be careful with the hypotheses that they make and the way these hypotheses influence the outcome.

Confidence intervals for the VaR can be derived through a parametric or nonparametric approach taken in connection with a portfolio structure and its distributed returns. Some analysts prefer to compute VaR through interval estimates and choose the use of asymptotic confidence intervals, but the basic methods for VaR calculation are two:

i) Parametric (VaR/P) based on the assumption of a normal distribution of asset and liability prices.
ii) Nonparametric or simulation (VaR/S), which uses Monte Carlo[1] and can lead to stress analysis.

Practical applications of VaR include the measurement of and report on exposure, which is demanded by regulators, as well as the management of market risk. VaR extensions now target credit risk. Senior management can benefit from VaR if it has taken care to appropriately define capital at risk. This has two aspects: i) What's the level of capitalisation-essentially the entrepreneurial capital-that is required by the market? ii) What is the capital at risk-i.e.,the economic capital-*our*bank can afford to put on the block?

Because VaR provides a basis for experimentation, the visibility senior management is after will be achieved iteratively between these two poles of reference. Sophisticated experimental approaches, however, require handling nonlinear distributions for daily changes in market variables; using Monte Carlo simulation; and employing Taylor Series expansion to calculate VaR when distributions are non-normal.

Senior management finds these issues awfully technical. Yet, they are crucial in defining and measuring market risk in an accurate way. Just as important is that the board and senior management understand the role of *backtesting* for tuning the parameters of VaR calculations, as well as the importance of using *stress scenarios* for measurement of catastrophic market risk.

VaR itself is a generic term covering a number of methodologies that are used for a variety of purposes by organisations, all relating to risk management and risk-adjusted performance measurement. Value at risk has become a key component of the analysis of market risk, because it measures what is ultimately of interest from a risk manager's perspective: *the most that can be lost with a given degree of confidence.* However, it is crucial for a risk manager to recognise the inherent limitations in using VaR: something which does not always seem to be the case.

VaR should be seen as a *catalyst* for change towards a more structured risk-analysis approach rather than a "failsafe" measure of risk control. The primary value of VaR as a risk-control tool is that many of the theoretical elements that underpin it can be used to analyse not just market risk exposures but also credit, liquidity, and even operational risk exposure.

The three underlying methodologies commonly used for calculating VaR - historical, parametric, and simulation - each have relative strengths and weaknesses. To counter the inherent weaknesses of the approaches, variations of these standard methodologies have been adopted by different users and in some cases the basic models have been extended to include recognition of more complex characteristics of non-linear risk such as convexity and gamma risk.

Characteristics of VaR Models

The uses of VaR fall broadly into three categories: determination of capital adequacy; performance measurement; and, supporting risk takers and business managers.

Determination of Capital Adequacy

In the regulatory and the supervisory context, the notion that risk capital is the relevant measure for determining capital requirements has become increasingly adopted.

Performance Measurement and Risk Control

For the risk manager, VaR facilitates analyses across time and business areas thereby allowing conclusions to be drawn over the performance of one business over another. However, the risk manager does need to consider the relative strengths and weaknesses of the methodology being used.

VaR is not a Black Box

More than one approach to calculating value at risk should be pursued, using both Monte Carlo simulation techniques in conjunction with a parametric-based approach. The outputs from both systems should then be adjusted to account for the inherent weaknesses in each approach.

The organisational implications of each approach should be taken into account as the accuracy of any risk methodology is heavily dependent on the internal controls and procedures that are in place in each organisation. Central to this is an understanding by senior management of how to use the results generated by these models to enhance the market risk control within the organisation. One final note, as one global head of risk management aptly sums up the proper attitude towards all these various forms of risk measures: *I would prefer a C-rated model with weaknesses and have people with experience and intuition to run our risk management than an A-rated model with a C-rated team of people who don't understand the model and are therefore unable to question the numbers that the system churns out.*

Satisfying Regulatory and Managerial Requirements

The 1966 Market Risk Amendment outlines regulatory specifications for VaR. These are the 99 percent confidence interval a 10-day holding period; a historical observation period of at least one year; a minimum three-month frequency for the update of data sets; and the recognition of correlations across broad risk factors categories, interest rate, currency exchange, equities, and commodities. Another regulatory requirement is a scaling factor for VaR results.

For internal management accounting reasons the bank may also follow another list of "musts". Many institutions have started to internally differentiate between value at risk and capital at risk. Also, for internal management control purposes VaR has started to be endowed with delta/gamma hedging to calculate risk based on a one-day holding period, exponential moving average volatilities, and correlations within risk factors.

This enlarges the implementation horizon of value at risk, and the use of estimates of potential losses in the bank's portfolio for a predetermined probability and holding period. Attention must be paid to the methodology employed to capture all significant risks and meet or exceed industry standards in terms of accuracy and timeliness.

There are number of weaknesses connected to VaR. In real life risk and returns are not normally distributed-as it is assumed. When markets are calm the bell shaped distribution may be acceptable, but in nervous markets it leads to implementation flaws: *Firstly,* VaR models are particularly weak at the edges, because of extreme movements, *Secondly,* outliers occur much more frequently than suggested by the normal distribution. *Thirdly*, VaR fails to account for fat fails. Yet, leptokyrtotic distributions very commonly appear with financial time series. The discarding of extreme or repetitive values weakens the benefits obtained from the model. *Fourthly*, VaR incorporates a significant probability of financial disaster-particularly if the 95 per cent level of confidence is used instead of the regulatory 99 percent. Neither the parametric VaR nor the simulation VaR say anything about extreme values: precisely what might happen in the "other" 1 percent, beyond the 99 percent confidence limit. It was found out that in the case of LTCM's near-bankruptcy this other 1 per cent showed a loss of $1.36 billion. Banks should be very careful with extreme events. *Finally*, One major weakness with the *method* (but not necessarily with the model) is the use of meager databases, which leads to meaningless if not outright misleading results.

Challenges with the Test of Hypothesis Used in the Model

Analysts with experience in modeling, and in the computation of credit risk and market risk, have evidence that mapping the market into the computer and doing a rigorous experimentation allows divesification. This brings up a number of other issues relating to management culture, skills requirements, the hypotheses being made, and technological leadership.

A basic but not always appreciated policy is that, in principle, the more diversified is the trading book, the lower the corresponding capital requirements will be. There are regulatory measures, however, that do not permit this flexibility; neither are the available eigenmodels able to serve reliably all sorts of diversification moves.

Beyond the pricing models and the risk models for derivatives, an institution also needs optimisation models that address the contents of the trading book for diversification reasons. Since the algorithms being used most often rest on the normal distribution and its confidence intervals, one of the concerns is the existence of correlations, outliers, and spike volatilities.

Usually spike patterns see to it that data are not normally distributed. Therefore the hypotheses are not substantiated by market facts. Furthermore, because the way to bet is that every distribution has outliers, one of the critical questions is how well model will cope with them. Is it really sensitive to extreme events? Will such events upset its behaviour?

As Dr.Paul Embrechts suggests, we want to have methods for estimating conditional probabilities that account for fat tails. An institution may incur a loss beyond VaR; but how far can it expect it to go? The study of extreme events can be done through extreme value theory. Because extreme events matter, in all likelihood this theory will become an important part of methodology.

The best way to judge models is by what they deliver. Sometime down the line the current linear models based on the normal distribution will become inaccurate. Then they will become unacceptable, if we have not been careful enough to test for outliers in a dual sense; as predictors and as deviators of model behaviour. A similar point can be made about correlations. Usually the algorithms we develop are based on a hypothesis of independent events. This rarely happens in real life, and if we have not been careful about the existence of correlations or their neutralisation, the model will give inadequate results.

The opposite is also true. Fairly frequently the assumption of th existence of correlation is made without the appropriate study and associated tests. It is, for instance, often assumed that the G-10 stock markets move in synergy and that they highly correlate because of globalisation. Yet, a recent study by the Bank of England documents that from 1988 onward the market behaviors of the London Stock Exchange and of the Tokyo Stock Exchange don't positively correlate in any significant manner. Indeed, it intraday statistics are considered, then sometimes the correlation is negative. Such findings invalidate the hypotheses we sometimes make. They also impact model behaviour, and for this reason they should be kept in perspective. Other issues, too, influence the choice of value at-risk algorithms to be used.

RECENT DEVELOPMENTS IN GLOBAL FINANCIAL DERIVATIVE MARKETS

The factors identified as a major driving force behind the explosive growth of financial derivatives are: (i) increased volatility in asset prices in financial markets; the increased integration of national financial markets with the international markets; the marked improvement in communication facilities and sharp decline in their costs; the development of more sophisticated risk management strategies; and the innovations in the derivatives markets, which optimally combine the risk and returns over a large number of financial assets, leading to higher returns, reduced risk as well as transaction costs as compared to individual financial assets. It is estimated that the gross noted outstanding amount of the OTC derivative contracts had reached a peak level of US$ 684 trillion in June 2008; post-Lehman, contracted to US$ 548 trillion. The decline in trading activity reflects a combination of significantly reduced risk appetite expectations of stable low interest rates in major markets and lower hedge fund activity.

Major central banks lowered policy rates to historical lows and interbank money markets became more stable after havinq frozen in September and early October, 2008. Reflecting these developments, after reaching record highs during the crisis, interest rate derivatives turnover decreased to $345 trillion from $458 trillion in the previous quarter. In contrast to the overall picture, a few Asia-Pacific currencies including the New Zealand dollar and the Malaysian ringgit saw an increase in the turnover for interest rate derivatives. This may be partly due to portfolio rebalancing as these currencies weakened vis-a-vis the US dollar.

Notional amounts of all over-the-counter (OTC) derivatives increased modestly (2%) in the second half of 2009, reaching $615 trillion by the end of December. The increase was evenly spread among risk categories, with the exception of commodity derivatives and credit default swaps (CDS), where amounts outstanding fell by 21% and 9%, respectively. The decline in reporting banks' gross credit exposures, which provide a measure of counterparty risk, slowed to 6%, after an 18% fall in the first half of 2009. Gross market values also decreased, by 15% to $22 trillion. Notional amounts outstanding of interest rate derivatives rose by 3%, with limited variation between currencies.

Sharp movements in asset prices and ongoing efforts to mitigate counterparty risk both had a strong influence on over-the-counter (OTC) derivatives markets in the first half of 2010. The notional amount of outstanding OTC derivatives fell by 3% in dollar terms during this period. However, substantial movements in asset prices, partly related to growing concerns about sovereign risks, drove up the gross market value of these contracts by 15% and the gross credit exposures associated with them by 2%. The smaller rise in gross credit exposures than in gross market values reflects increased netting, which is consistent with greater use of central counterparties (CCPs) in some segments of the market. The ratio of gross credit exposures to gross market values consequently fell to 14.5% at the end of the first half of 2010, down from 16.3% at the end of 2009 and 24.0% at the end of the first half of 2007. There was considerable variation in changes in notional amounts and market values across segments of the OTC derivatives market. Outstanding notional amounts increased for foreign exchange (8%) and equity (5%) derivatives, declined for credit (7%) and commodity (3%) derivatives and were broadly unchanged for interest rate contracts. Gross market values increased for foreign exchange (22%) and interest rate (25%) derivatives, declined for credit (7%) and commodity (16%) contracts and remained stable for equity derivatives.

Notional amounts outstanding of over-the-counter (OTC) derivatives rose by 3% in the second half of 2010, reaching $601 trillion at end-December. Much of the increase was a direct consequence of the appreciation of major currencies against the US dollar, the currency in which the data are reported. Gross market values of all OTC contracts fell by 14%, driven mainly by the 17% decline in the market value of interest rate contracts. Finally, gross credit exposures dropped by 7% to $3.3 trillion, compared with a 2% increase in the first half of the year.

In the interest rate segment, the largest risk category in the OTC derivatives market by any measure, notional amounts outstanding went up by 3% to $465 trillion, largely owing to exchange rate effects. Contracts on dollar rates dropped by 8%. Positions increased in the euro (10%), yen (7%), Swiss franc (10%) and Swedish krona (14%), but this probably reflected the appreciation of those currencies against the US dollar rather than any genuine increase in activity. Among the major currencies, only the Canadian dollar segment showed a decline. Amounts outstanding of contracts denominated in that currency fell by 4%, despite its 6% appreciation against the US dollar.

For the first time since the financial crisis, positions in over-the-counter (OTC) derivatives went up significantly in the first half of 2011. Notional amounts outstanding of contracts in all risk categories rose by 18% to $708 trillion at the end of June, well above the $673 trillion peak in mid-2008. By contrast, gross market values of these contracts fell by 8%, owing mainly to a 10% reduction in the market value of interest rate contracts. Since interest rates remained roughly unchanged over the period since the previous survey, this suggests that a significant number of contracts with large mark to market values have either expired or been terminated. Gross credit exposure dropped by 15% to $3.0 trillion, the lowest since the end of 2007.

The notional amount of outstanding over-the-counter (OTC) derivatives fell by 8%, to $648 trillion, in the second half of 2011. But with an increase in price volatility, their market value rose by 40%. Gross credit exposures also increased significantly, by 32%. The bulk of these changes were in the interest rate market segment. Here, notional amounts outstanding declined by 9%, to $504 trillion. This corresponded closely to cuts to positions in dollar, euro and sterling contracts and to positions with residual maturities of one year or less. Market participants may have perceived little near-term risk of changes in short-term interest rates in these currencies and therefore elected not to replace maturing short-dated contracts. Such a perception would be consistent with the declines in probabilities of near-term increases in policy rates implied by market prices and the proximity of these rates to zero, which limited the scope for cuts. The increase in the market value of outstanding interest rate derivatives was also concentrated in dollar, euro and sterling contracts, for which replacement values increased by 39%, 67% and 71%, respectively. For each of these currencies, swap rates of all maturities fell to low levels by historical standards. This suggests that swap rates moved further away from those prevailing when many outstanding contracts were signed, thus raising their cost of replacement.

Positions in the OTC derivatives market continued to decline in the first half of 2012. Notional amounts outstanding of the face value of all contracts fell to $639 trillion at the end of June 2012, 10% lower than the high recorded 12 months previously and 1% lower than at end-2011. Gross market values, which measure the cost of replacing existing contracts, dropped by 7% to $25 trillion. Gross credit exposures, which measure reporting dealers' exposure after taking account of legally enforceable netting agreements and thus provide a measure of counterparty risk in the OTC derivatives market; declined to $3.7 trillion.

Smaller positions in the interest rate and credit default swap (CDS) segments more than offset slight increases in foreign exchange and equity-linked contracts. Notional amounts outstanding of interest rate contracts and CDS fell by 2% and 6%, respectively, to $494 trillion and $27 trillion. In contrast, the volume of foreign exchange contracts outstanding rose by 5% to $67 trillion, and that of equity-linked contracts by 6% to $6.3 trillion. Positions in commodity contracts declined slightly (3%) to $3 trillion.

Within the interest rate segment, the trend away from inter-dealer positions towards positions with other finaricial institutions - a category that includes banks and securities firms which are not reporting dealers as well as central counterparties, hedge funds, special purpose vehicles, insurance companies, mutual funds and other financial companies - continued. Notional amounts of inter-dealer positions fell by $18 trillion (12%) to 28% of the total while those with other financial institutions rose by $6 trillion (2%) to 64%. In the mid-2000s, before the financial crisis, inter-dealer positions and positions with other financial institutions were of similar size, each accounting for 40-45% of the market total, Positions with non- financial customers accounted for the remaining 10-15% of the market, but this share has since fallen, to just 8% in mid-2012. This is partly related to the increased use of central counterparties. Interest rate contracts have become increasingly short-term in recent years. Notional amounts of contracts with maturities of more than five years fell by 9% in the first half of 2012 to $117 trillion, or 24% of total interest rate contracts. By contrast, the volume of contracts with a maturity of up to one year went up by 4% to $207 trillion, or 42% of the total. In the mid- and late 2000s, longer-term contracts accounted for up to 35% of all interest rate contracts.

Notional amounts outstanding of CDS continued the decline that started in early 2008. In the first half of 2012, they fell another 6% to $27 trillion, less than half the amount at the end of 2007. Gross market values fell by 25% to $1.2 trillion, The decline in open positions in the CDS market mainty affected contracts referencing non-financial firms. Notional amounts of such contracts fell by 10% to $10 billion. CDS referencing sovereign debt or debt issued by financial institutions remained relatively stable at $3 trillion and $7 trillion, respectively.

OTC MARKET DEVELOPMENTS IN THE SECOND HALF OF 2012

OTC derivatives notional amounts outstanding totalled $633 trillion at end-December 2012, down from $639 trillion at end-June 2012. Exchange rate movements masked a somewhat larger underlying decline because the depreciation of the US dollar against the euro and Swiss franc between end-June and end-December 2012 increased the dollar value of contracts denominated in those currencies. Over the same period, the appreciation of the US dollar against the yen tended to lower the dollar value of yen-denominated contracts.

The gross market value of all contracts, ie the cost of replacing the contracts at current market prices, equalled $24.7 trillion at end-2012. Gross credit exposure, which deducts from the gross market values the amounts that reflect legally enforceable bilateral netting agreements, equalled $3.6 trillion. This was equivalent to 14.7% of market values, about the same percentage as at end-June 2012.

Interest Rate Derivatives

Notional amounts for interest rate derivatives, the largest segment of the market, stood at $490 trillion at end-2012. While the overall figure was more or less unchanged from end-June 2012, breakdowns showed offsetting movements (Table 3). For swaps, notional amounts dropped in the second half of 2012 by about 2% to $370 trillion, owing in part to the compression of trades through central counterparties (CCPs). This was offset by an increase in forward rate agreements (FRAs) to $71 trillion.3 Contracts between reporting dealers fell 16% to $117 trillion, while those with other financial institutions increased to $338 trillion. Maturities shifted to the intermediate part of the spectrum, with contracts maturing in one to five years rising to 36.8% of notional amounts at end-2012 from 34.4% at end-June 2012.

Gross market values as a share of notional amounts outstanding were almost unchanged in aggregate at 3.8%. In the US dollar segment, the value of outstanding interest rate contracts dropped from 4.5% to 4.0% of amounts outstanding. This contrasted with an increase from 4.4% to 4.8% in the market value of contracts on euro interest rates relative to notional amounts outstanding.

Foreign Exchange Derivatives

Notional amounts of FX derivatives rose slightly in the second half of 2012 (+1%), to $67 trillion at end-December 2012. This reflected increases in medium-term maturities (+7%) and deals with other financial institutions (+5%). Contracts with the reporting dealer sector declined. The currency composition of contracts remained broadly stable, with the US dollar on one side of 85.5% of all contracts, followed by the euro at 35.3%.

TABLE 3

GLOBAL OTC DERIVATIVES MARKET[1]
AMOUNTS OUTSTANDING, IN BILLIONS OF US DOLLARS

	Notional amounts outstanding				*Gross market value*			
	H1 2011	*H2 2011*	*H1 2012*	*H2 2012*	*H1 2011*	*H2 2011*	*H1 2012*	*H2 2012*
Amounts outstanding, in billions of US dollars								
GRAND TOTAL	**706,884**	**647,777**	**639,366**	**632,579**	**19,518**	**27,278**	**25,392**	**24,740**
A. Foreign exchange contracts	**64,698**	**63,349**	**66,645**	**67,358**	**2,336**	**2,555**	**2,217**	**2,304**
Outright forwards and forex swaps	31,113	30,526	31,395	31,718	777	919	771	803
Currency swaps	22,228	22,791	24,156	25,420	1,227	1,318	1,184	1,247
Options	11,358	10,032	11,094	10,220	332	318	262	254
Memo: Exchange-traded contracts[2]	389	308	325	337	...	...	...	...
B. Interest rate contracts[3]	**553,240**	**504,117**	**494,427**	**489,703**	**13,244**	**20,001**	**19,113**	**18,833**
FRAs	55,747	50,596	64,711	71,353	59	67	51	47
Swaps	441,201	402,611	379,401	369,999	11,861	18,046	17,214	17,080
Options	56,291	50,911	50,314	48,351	1,324	1,888	1,848	1,706
Memo: Exchange-traded contracts[2]	76,039	53,298	55,635	48,630	...	...	...	...
C. Equity-linked contracts	**6,841**	**5,982**	**6,313**	**6,251**	**708**	**679**	**645**	**605**
Forwards and swaps	2,029	1,738	1,880	2,045	176	156	147	157
Options	4,813	4,244	4,434	4,207	532	523	497	448
Memo: Exchange-traded contracts[2]	6,416	2,956	3,561	3,583	...	...	...	...
D. Commodity contracts[4]	**3,197**	**3,091**	**2,994**	**2,587**	471	481	390	358
Gold	468	521	523	486	50	75	62	53
Other	2,729	2,570	2,471	2,101	421	405	328	306
Forwards and swaps	1,846	1,745	1,659	1,363	...	...	...	...
Options	883	824	812	739	...	...	...	...
E. Credit default swaps5	32,409	28,626	26,931	25,069	1,345	1,586	1,187	848
Single-name instruments	18,105	16,865	15,566	14,309	854	958	715	527
Multi-name instruments	14,305	11,761	11,364	10,760	490	628	472	321
Index products	...	10,514	9,731	9,663	...	...	...	...
F. Unallocated[6]	46,498	42,610	42,057	41,611	1,414	1,976	1,840	1,792
GROSS CREDIT EXPOSURE[7]	...	...	...	...	**2,971**	**3,912**	**3,668**	**3,626**
Memo: Exchange-traded contracts[2]	882,844	56,563	59,522	52,550	...	...	...	...

1 Based on the data reported by 11 countries up to H1 2011. Includes data reported by Australia and Spain from H2 2011 onwards. Data on total notional amounts outstanding, gross market value and gross credit exposure are shown on a net basis, ie transactions between reporting dealers are counted only once. The definitions of notional amounts outstanding, gross market value and gross credit exposure are available under Section 2 of the statistical notes.
2 Sources: FOW TRADEdata; Futures Industry Association; various futures and options exchanges.
3 Single e currency contracts only.
4 Adjustments for double-counting partly estimated.
5 See Tables 4 to 8.
6 Includes foreign exchange, interest rate, equity, commodity and credit derivatives of non-reporting institutions, based on the latest Triennial Central Bank Survey of Foreign Exchange and Derivatives Market Activity, in 2010.
7 Before 2011, excludes CDS contracts for all countries except the United States.
8 Excludes commodity contracts.

Gross market values of FX derivatives remained almost unchanged as a share of notional amounts outstanding, at 3.4% at end-2012. For euro contracts, the ratio decreased from 3.6% to 3.2%, but this move was largely offset by a jump in the ratio of yen contract market values to notional amounts outstanding, from 3.7% to 5.9%. The increase in the gross market value of FX contracts referencing the yen was driven by renewed volatility in the yen exchange rate.

The market value of contracts referencing the Swiss franc continued to decline, to $154 billion outstanding at end-December 2012. This brought to $167 billion the cumulative decline in notional amounts outstanding from the $321 billion peak reported in June 2011, prior to the announcement by the Swiss National Bank of a ceiling on the EURCHF exchange rate. Contracts referencing the Swiss franc were broadly stable in terms of the ratio of market value to amounts outstanding, at 4.0%.

Equity-linked and Commodity Derivatives

For equity-linked derivatives, notional amounts outstanding were almost unchanged at $6.3 trillion at the end of 2012, after a 6% expansion in the first half of 2012. An increase in forwards and swaps almost offset the 5% decline in outstanding options. Market values of equity-linked contracts slipped another 6% in the second half of 2012, to $605 billion; this was more than accounted for by the drop registered for options (–10%).

Amounts outstanding of commodity derivatives fell 14% from $3 trillion to $2.6 trillion, although market values contracted by substantially less (–8%), implying that the remaining contracts increased in average value. Notional amounts outstanding on gold declined to $486 billion. While gross market values on gold and other commodity contracts had both fallen by almost 20% in the first half of the year, in the second half the slide in the value of gold contracts was relatively bigger (–15%) than that in other commodity contracts (–7%).

Credit Default Swaps (CDS)

CDS notional amounts outstanding continued to decline during the second half of 2012, to $25 trillion at end-2012. This brought the cumulative reduction since June 2011 to $7 trillion, partly due to ongoing contract compression. During the half-year to end-2012, the reduction was concentrated among reporting dealers (–10%) and in maturities over five years (–37%). Contracts with special purpose vehicle (SPVs), however, moved in the opposite direction, growing 28% to $0.6 trillion. The sectoral share of CDS counterparties was divided mainly between reporting dealers (56%) and other financial institutions (43%), while non-financial customers continued to be almost entirely absent (1%). The notional amounts outstanding referencing sovereigns declined by only 2% to $2.9 trillion.

The decline in gross market values was more pronounced than that in notional amounts outstanding. Market values fell to $0.8 trillion at end-2012, equivalent to 3.4% of notional amounts. This was down from 4.4% of notional amounts at end-June 2012 and 5.5% at end-2011. Although all segments declined, there was some differentiation by counterparty. The ratio of market value to outstanding amounts slid the most with SPV counterparties (from 10% to 4.6%) and the least with other financial customers (largely unchanged at 4.7%).

The share of total CDS notional amounts that was centrally cleared remained about 20%. This means that approximately 11% of all original trades were cleared centrally, since a single contract initially agreed between two CCP members is replaced by two separate contracts, between the CCP and each of the counterparties. Non-rated CDS cleared with CCPs were down 28%, which more than negated the 27% increase in the previous half-year. The compression of contracts contributed to these changes. In contrast notional amounts of non-investment grade CDS cleared with CCPs increased 24%, offsetting the 20% decline in the half-year up to June 2012.

The geographical division of CDS counterparties on an ultimate risk basis indicates that activity concentrated on counterparties in the dealers' home country. Notional amounts of CDS vis-à- vis foreign counterparties dropped to $19 trillion, whereas those vis-à-vis counterparties headquartered in the reporters' home country increased to $6 trillion. At end-2012, counterparties in the home country accounted for 24.4% of notional amounts outstanding, up from 19.4% a year earlier.

Concentration Indices

Herfindahl indices calculated on the basis of responses from individual dealers provide a measure of size concentration for dealers in OTC derivatives markets. In the interest rate swap segment, which is the single largest segment in OTC derivatives markets, concentration is highest for Swiss franc swaps and lowest for euro and yen swaps. Concentration in Canadian dollar interest rate options continued to rise and reached the highest level among all OTC interest rate derivatives contracts at end-2012, driven by developments in inter-dealer business. In contrast, concentration in yen FRAs declined from the high levels that had been building up since end-2010.

For FX derivatives, Herfindahl indices showed increased concentration for options in particular, which increased to a new high. Increased concentration was evident for contracts with other reporting dealers as well as non-reporting counterparties.

DERIVATIVES MARKET IN INDIA

The presence and role of derivatives in India, both over-the-counter (OTC) and exchange-traded, has been increasing steadily over the years. These instruments are an important component of the overall financial sector strategy and the broad regulatory objective is to ensure that they are used to their potential in ways that are consistent with both financial development and the contribution of financial markets to economic growth. As instruments for transfer and dispersal of risk, derivatives facilitate socially useful but risky projects, which would not be undertaken in the absence of such risk management framework. Derivatives may either be standard or customized according to the needs of the participants. While the standardized products mostly trade on exchanges, the customized products are traded over the counter.

Interest Rate Derivatives in India

In the Indian markets, four OTC interest rate products are traded, viz., Overnight Index Swap (OIS) based on overnight MIBOR, a polled rate derived from the overnight unsecured inter-bank market, contracts based on Mumbai Inter-Bank Offered Rate (MIFOR), contracts based on Indian Government Securities Benchmark Rate (INBMK), and contracts based on MIOIS. A typical characteristic of the Indian interest rate market is that unlike in the overseas inter-bank funds markets, there is very little activity in tenors beyond overnight and as such there is no credible interest rate in segments other than overnight. Absence of a liquid 3-month or 6-month funds market has been a hindrance for trading in FRAs as also in swaps based on these benchmarks. Recent emergence of a deep and liquid CD market with significant secondary market trading may perhaps address some of these issues.

In terms of gross notional outstanding, the OIS based on overnight Mumbai Inter-Bank Offered Rate (MIBOR) is the most dominant product traded, accounting for about 90per cent of the outstanding followed by MIFOR which accounts for nearly 10per cent and the remaining two products almost insignificant.

As far as the regulatory regime is concerned, all scheduled commercial banks (SCBs) excluding Regional Rural Banks, primary dealers (PDs) and all-India financial institutions have been allowed to use IRS and FRA for their own balance sheet management as also for the purpose of market making. The non-financial corporations have been allowed to use IRS and FRA to hedge their balance sheet exposures, with a caveat that at least one of the parties in any IRS/FRA transaction should be a RBI regulated entity.

Interest Rate Swap (IRS) Market

The Report of the Committee on Financial Sector Assessment noted that the notional principal amount of outstanding Interest Rate Swaps (IRS) of all commercial banks increased from ₹ 10 trillion+ as on 31st March 2005 to ₹ 80 trillion+ as of 31st March 2008. However, due to trade compression, involving multilateral early termination, by the Clearing Corporation of India Ltd. (CCIL), the notional principal amount of outstanding IRS of commercial banks declined to ₹ 50 trillion+ as of 30th June 2012. A granular analysis reveals that of all the commercial banks engaging in IRS, public sector banks with about 74% of total bank assets accounted for less than 2% of notional principal amount of outstanding IRS and private sector and foreign banks, with about 19%, and 7%, of total bank assets, accounted for 18%, and 80%, of total notional principal amount of outstanding IRS, respectively. In other words, with combined assets of just ₹ 6 trillion or so, foreign banks accounted for notional principal amount of outstanding IRS of ₹ 40 trillion.

Significantly, it is disturbing to note that, day in, and day out, the IRS yields trade way below yields of comparable maturity Government securities. Specifically, currently the 5 year IRS yield is trading at a negative spread of 120 basis points to 5 year G-Sec. Besides, while the G-Sec yield curve is almost flat, the IRS yield is steeply inverted to the extent of 120 basis points defying term, credit risk and liquidity risk premia which typically characterize a normal yield curve of risk assets. A typical, but fallacious, and vacuous, rationalization offered of this counter-intuitive, warped, wierd and preposterous feature is that while IRS yields are influenced by expected path of future interest rates, those of G-Secs are influenced by their supply. Nothing could be farther from the truth for this rationalization turns the very logic and reason on their head. For, being pure time value of money, G-Secs are influenced by, and immediately price in, inflationary expectations arising from higher fiscal deficit which, in turn, is the cause of additional supply of G-Secs and not the other way round. Thus, here IRS market is completely up side down and running on its head. This is completely anti-thetical to the law of one price, or the no-arbitrage argument. For, if this law held, given hugely negative spreads to Govts., fixed rate receivers, who far exceed, and overwhelmingly outnumber, fixed rate payers, would have engaged in a very simple arbitrage, involving buying corresponding maturity G-Sec in the cash market by financing it in the overnight repo market, and paying fixed, and receiving overnight, in the IRS market. This very normal, and logical, arbitrage would have had the effect of benefiting all the three stake-holders, viz., (a) fixed rate receivers receiving much higher yield than they are currently, (b) Government of India borrowing at much lower cost, and (c) business and industry in general, and infrastructure sector, in particular, getting long-term-fixed-rate-low-cost financing solutions. In other words, this would have been a win-win for all key stake- holders but, the fact of the matter is that, if anything, this is just not happening. As to the explanation of this almost a permanent, structural, though quirky and weird, counter-intuitive, perverse, and preposterous feature of the Indian IRS market, the stock, but specious, refrain is that arbitrage, involving receiving fixed on G-Secs and paying fixed in IRS, is not possible because of the so-called 'basis risk'. But this is totally untenable for the simple reason that 'basis risk' applies just as much to 'hedging' as indeed it does to 'arbitrage'. In other words, 'basis risk' is "arbitrage-hedging" agnostic and, therefore, it inevitably, and incontrovertibly, follows that the IRS market is also not being used even for 'hedging'. If that be so, as indeed it is, the question, especially, but significantly, when one also considers the fact that only 2% of the notional principal amount of the outstanding IRS is accounted for by the real sector i.e. business customers, it begs is what then is 98% of this ₹ 50 trillion+ IRS market being used for. In other words, in the case of the Indian IRS market, what holds instead is the "law-of-two-prices-and-no-arbitrage-argument". In this background, it would be no exaggeration to say that these hugely negative spreads of IRS to G-Secs are as counter-intuitive, quirky, anomalous, warped and preposterous as a father's negative age spread to his son's is. Indeed, in the analytical framework of my Singapore Speech for identifying systemic financial risks, this situation can be reasonably interpreted, in a disturbing and sit-up-and-take-notice manner of speaking, as a veritable IRS 'Super-Bubble', signifying 'huge huge' under-pricing of interest rate/ credit risks. Because a 'bubble', signifying 'huge' under-pricing of risks, is typically diagnosed with spreads of riskier assets to risk-free G-Secs being unusually low, but still positive, whereas, here in the IRS segment, spreads to G-Secs have persistently, and consistently, been negative to the extent of 100 to 150 basis points for 5 year maturity. It thus follows that where the IRS market, instead of being a means to an end of sub serving the real sector is, to all intents and purposes, existing, almost entirely for its own sake to almost complete exclusion of the needs of the real sector, creating a massive "financial sector-real sector imbalance". On this touch-stone, and hallmark, the IRS market in India is then a non-derivative, nay, a financial innovation that never was.

Credit Default Swap (CDS)

Like Interest Rate Swap, or for that matter any other derivative, Credit Default Swap is no exception to cash market replication principle of derivatives pricing. Without going into mathematical gymnastic proper, price of a CDS, in spread terms, is reasonably approximated by the difference between the spread of a reference bond to corresponding maturity G-Sec yield and the spread of IRS to the same maturity G-Sec yield. Thus, if Sc be corporate bond spread and Ss be IRS spread to risk-free G-Sec yield of corresponding maturity, then the fair/theoretical/model value/price of a CDS is approximately equal to Sc minus Ss. Tautologically, since G-Sec yield is common to both spreads, another way to approximate CDS price is simply to take the difference between the yield of the reference bond and the same maturity IRS yield. As this learned audience is aware, finally when the product was launched on 7th December, 2011, it was a stillborn. In fact, its epitaph was written in the warped, anomalous, quirky and preposterous feature of hugely negative IRS yield spreads to corresponding maturity G-Sec yields itself. For, as this discerning audience will readily see from the above formula, because of hugely negative IRS spread, fair price of a CDS would be so high as to make it both pointless, and useless, to buy a reference bond and also hedge it with a CDS. In other words, one is much better off straightaway buying a corresponding maturity risk-free G-Sec itself. Significantly, if actual CDS premium/price/spread is higher than the above theoretical/model price, then an arbitrageur will sell a CDS (which is equivalent to going long the reference corporate bond) and receive this actual spread and short the reference bond and invest the proceeds of short sale at the going corporate bond repo rate and receive fixed, and pay overnight, in an IRS, and do the opposite arbitrage if the actual CDS spread is lower than the theoretical/model spread/price until the arbitrage opportunity disappears and theoretical/model and actual market prices align again. But this arbitrage is just not possible simply because of its complete absence, in the IRS market and, therefore, a desired happening in corporate bond market cannot happen, *inter alia*, to supplement huge infrastructure funding needs of the Indian economy.

Interest Rate Futures (IRFs)

If the CDS was a stillborn, IRF too suffered mortality in its infancy the second time round after its 2003 version which itself was almost a stillborn. For, after their second launch in August 2009, Interest Rate Futures on 10-year notional government bond had seen two settlements, viz. the December 2009 contract and March 2010 contract. Significantly, both traded volumes and Open Interest (OI), witnessed decline over the two settlements, eventually decaying very quickly to zero permanently. In particular, the December 2009 contract, which had a peak Open Interest of ₹ 980 million declined to a pre-settlement Open Interest of ₹ 610 million and settled "entirely" by physical delivery, representing physical settlement of 62% of the peak Open Interest. In contrast, the March 2010 contract, which witnessed a peak Open Interest of ₹ 570 million declined to a pre-settlement Open Interest of ₹ 420 million and also settled entirely by physical delivery, representing physical settlement of 72%. Both these settlements were a far cry from the hall-mark and touch-stone of an efficient, frictionless, seamlessly coupled, and organically connected, physically-settled futures market even where physical delivery typically does not exceed 1% to 3% of the peak Open Interest. This happened because of the inefficient 'disconnect' and 'friction' in the IRF market due to only one way arbitrage viz. buying the cheapest-to-deliver (CTD), with the highest implied repo rate (IRR), by financing the same at the actual repo rate and simultaneously selling futures. In fact, as ascertained from one market participant, who accounted for almost the entire ₹ 600 million worth of physical delivery into the December 2009 contract, the implied repo rate of the CTD was 6.75% as against the actual repo rate of 3.4%, representing a risk-free arbitrage profit of 3.35%. Unlike this, on the other side, for the so-called benchmark, and most expensive-to-deliver, Government security, the IRR was almost zero to negative, suggesting an arbitrage opportunity of short-selling this bond and investing the proceeds of short sale at much higher actual repo rate and buying the futures contract. But this arbitrage could not be engaged in for want of short selling for a period coterminus with that of the futures contract. It is the possibility of this two-way arbitrage, working in the opposite directions, that, like a "good conductor" of 'heat' and 'electricity' in physics, will seamlessly conduct/transmit liquidity from the relatively more liquid (the most-expensive-to-deliver) benchmark government bonds to the so-called illiquid (the cheapest-to-deliver) bonds in the deliverable basket. Here, caution must be observed on this totally misplaced temptation, and impatience, to introduce/launch "cash-settled" IRF, any how, some how, and at any cost, must be firmly, and decisively, resisted for such medicine will be worse than the disease. The reason is that unlike assets such as equity, foreign currencies, commodities which are "homogeneous", government bonds, except , of course, for their same credit risk, are, given their differing coupons and maturities, "heterogeneous" and, therefore, for the cogent arguments adduced above, "physically-settled" contracts will make for seamless transmission/conduction of liquidity from the most liquid benchmark bonds to the relatively less liquid bonds in the deliverable basked and thus impart, and permeate, "much-needed" homogeneity in the entire deliverable basket of government bonds. But that it is perfectly legitimate to have "cash-settled" derivatives contracts in the case of 'homogeneous' assets like equity, currencies and commodities. For any 'cash-settled' derivative, where physical settlement is possible, tends to become a "non-derivative", violating the cardinal principle of arbitrage-free pricing/valuation and, therefore, comes to exist almost entirely for its own sake and to almost complete exclusion of the larger public policy purpose of sub-serving the hedging needs of the real sector, creating a massive "financial sector-real sector imbalance" and, thus, in turn, become the very antithesis of responsible financial innovation.

Market Segmentation

Continuing market segmentation in India is the biggest undoing of an efficient, deep, liquid, organically connected, and seamlessly integrated financial market which is also a 'sine qua non' for effective, efficient and instantaneous monetary transmission. Market fragmentation/segmentation contributes to price distortion and inefficiency. The most tangible and manifest evidence of market segmentation in India is the 'disconnect' between IRS, IRF and government securities markets as reflected in the IRS (bank credit risk) yields being 100 to 125 basis points below G-Sec yields and IRF yields (when last traded) being about 70 basis points higher than their fair value, signifying almost complete absence of arbitrage and thus a pernicious violation of the 'no-arbitrage', or what is the something as, the 'law-of-one-price, argument' which, as the discerning audience is by now well aware, is the most fundamental basis of 'fair value derivatives pricing'. Such manifest 'disconnect' militates against the development of a seamlessly integrated financial market with coupling and organic connect between all the three. However, this market segmentation can be credibly, effectively and decisively addressed if the nuts-and-bolts reforms propositioned below, which are equally also the necessary, and sufficient, conditions, are synchronously orchestrated in all-at-the-same-time-no-piecemeal- and-no-half-way-house manner :

i) For the cogent reasons the totally misplaced temptation, and impatience, to introduce/launch cash settled IRF must be firmly, and decisively, resisted. For else, this will tantamount to "doing the 'easy' and not the 'right' thing" and, in the process, replicating an IRS genie in the IRF/CDS markets which then grows so fast so much that it becomes difficult to put it back into the regulatory bottle.

ii) What must certainly not be done is even to contemplate, much less permit, the most-liquid-single-bond IRF for the very simple reason that this benchmark security represents less than 10% of the current 10-year IRF deliverable basket and would, therefore, at a time, when we are talking about 'inclusion', this will amount to veritable 'exclusion' of 90% of the 10-year Government securities from the benefit of hedging which arguably runs counter to the public policy purpose of IRF providing hedging to as wide a universe of government securities as possible.

iii) What also must certainly not be done is even to contemplate, much less allow, selling/repoing of securities acquired under market repo, another name for 'rehypothecation', if the IMF finding in the wake of the 2007-Global Financial Crisis is anything to go by. The IMF noted that pre-2007, thanks to re-hypothecation, the shadow-banking system in the USA generated funding/liquidity of US $ 4 trillion with the underlying "original collateral" of just US $ 1 trillion, implying astronomical and whopping margins/haircuts of "minus" US $ 3 trillion.

iv) What also must certainly not be done is allocate specific government securities to different Primary Dealers for market making as this will be a "triple whammy" in that this will straight away fragment/segment market, lead to concentration of risk and militate against portfolio diversification.

v) Symmetrical and uniform accounting treatment of both cash and derivatives (IRF/IRS/CDS) markets.

vi) Removal of the 'hedge effectiveness' criterion of 80% to 125% which militates against use of derivatives for hedging purposes for it is better to have 'ineffective' hedge than to have no hedge at all.

vii) Roll-back of the Held to Maturity (HTM) protection i.e. substituting the current "accounting hedge" with "derivative hedge". This is because with HTM, there is no incentive/compulsion whatsoever for use of market-based solutions like IRS/IRF which also require constant monitoring, infrastructure, transaction costs like brokerage and margins etc. Indeed, fears that such roll-back may be disruptive, and disorderly, are totally unfounded if one considers the fact that there is "overwhelming net fixed rate receiving" appetite/interest in the ₹ 50 trillion+ IRS market which will be even more so with the introduction of IRF, what with the total outstanding amount of dated Government securities at ₹ 30 trillion being much less than the outstanding amount of IRS of ₹ 50 trillion.

viii) Delivery-based short-selling in the cash market for a term co-terminus with that of the futures contract and introduction of term repo, and reverse repo, markets, co-terminus again with the tenure of futures contract for borrowing and lending of cash and G-Secs.

ix) Both for IRS and IRF, actual notional/nominal amount of IRS/IRF must be allowed on duration-weighted basis unlike the current regulation which restricts the maximum notional/nominal amount of hedging instrument to no more than the notional/principal amount of the exposure being hedged resulting in under-hedging of risk.

Foreign Currency Derivatives

Over the last decade or so, the foreign exchange market has acquired depth, liquidity and has witnessed increase in turnover. In the USD-INR segment, the daily average turnover increased from USD 7.83 billion in 2005-06 to USD 18.97 billion in 2009-10. The OTC derivative segment of the forex market includes forwards, forex swaps and forex options. During 2009-10, of the total turnover in the forex market of USD 6.92 trillion, the OTC derivative turnover was USD 3.53 trillion. Of the forex derivatives, the forex swaps are dominant accounting for over 60 per cent of the total turnover during 2009-10. Rupee-forex options, which were allowed in July 2003, have not seen as much trading as the other products.

The foreign exchange market in India has been subject to by a regulatory framework, salient features of which are as under.

a) Need to carry out a foreign exchange transaction, cash or derivative, with an authorized dealer who, in turn, is subject to regulatory covenant,

b) Derivative transactions to be supported by underlying exposures, either specific or based on historical exposures

c) Restriction on dynamic hedging of currency risk

d) Restriction of net open positions that banks/authorized dealers can carry

Broadly three classes of derivatives trade in the foreign exchange market, viz., (outright) forwards, swaps, and options.

Foreign Exchange (Outright) Forwards

A foreign exchange forward contract is an agreement to buy a certain amount of a foreign currency against another currency (in our context, Rupee, the domestic currency) at a rate fixed at the time of entering into the contract. It is used to hedge against the exchange risk arising out of an future exposure, eg., export proceeds, import payments, debt servicing or repayment, etc. The intensity of activity in the forward segment expresses a view of the different class of market participants as to the future path of the exchange rate. A person resident in India may enter into a forward contract with an Authorized Dealer Category-I bank (AD Category I bank) in India to hedge an exposure to exchange risk in respect of a transaction for which sale and/or purchase of foreign exchange is permitted under the Foreign Exchange Management Act, 1999. Outright forward contracts are essentially between banks and their merchant clients and these are much less frequent in the interbank markets, globally as well as in Indian markets. After approval by RBI, CCIL is guaranteeing

(December 2009 onwards) the forex forward trades from the trade day to the settlement day acting as a central counterparty. The netting done at CCIL virtually eliminates the credit risk, reduces counterparty exposures and frees the capital which otherwise would have been locked till the settlement of trade.

Swaps

A foreign exchange swap is usually a combination of a spot and a forward transaction, entered into simultaneously. Swaps are mostly inter-bank contracts and are neutral with respect to position as well as impact on the volatility of the exchange rate. Swaps do not have a separate regulatory framework and are covered by the foreign exchange regulations applicable to forward / spot contracts.

A Foreign currency swap is an agreement between two parties to exchange cash flows (viz., the principal and/or interest payments) of a loan in one currency for equivalent cash flows of an equal (in net present value) loan in another. Globally, foreign currency swaps constitute a large segment of foreign currency derivatives. Resident Indians may enter into foreign currency-rupee swap within regulatory limits.

Currency Options

Forex option is a financial derivative under which the buyer of the option has the right but not the obligation to exchange one currency against another at a given point in time at a predetermined exchange rate. Though introduced in the 1990's, the OTC forex options market is not yet very liquid in India. As regards information on the forex options available in the public domain, the Foreign Exchange Dealers' Association of India (FEDAI) publishes foreign currency option volatility rates including ATM volatility, 25-delta risk reversal and 25-delta strangles.

Most of the data of foreign currency derivative is collected by the Foreign Exchange Department (FED) of the RBI. It is important to note that most of the data collection by RBI on foreign exchange markets, for historical reasons, has been motivated by the potential impact of foreign exchange transactions on the volatility of the exchange rate. Each of the AD Category-I banks has to submit daily statements of Foreign Exchange Turnover in Form FTD and Gaps, Position and Cash Balances in Form GPB through the Online Returns Filing System (ORFS). AD Category-I banks have to consolidate the data on cross currency derivative transactions undertaken by residents and submit half-yearly reports (June and December). AD Category-I banks are required to submit a monthly report (as on the last Friday of every month) on the limits granted and utilized by their constituents under the facility of booking forward contracts on past performance basis. AD Category – I banks are required to submit a quarterly report on the forward contracts booked & cancelled by SMEs and Resident Individuals. Apart from the data collected at Foreign Exchange Department (FED), forex forwards data is available at CCIL also, but the data set is not complete as all of the banks are not settling their forex forward deals through CCIL.

a) ***Currency Forward:*** This data is collected at FED on a daily basis. The FTD report that is submitted online contains both inter-bank and merchant data on transactions in spot, swaps and forwards (including cancellation). CCIL also has a subset of this data as they are undertaking clearing and guaranteed settlement of forex forward and swaps transaction for banks. The data available at CCIL include date of contract, exchange rate, value date, details of buyers and sellers accounts and details of intermediary. Under risk based supervision, DBS collects data on forex forwards including notional principal, credit equivalent, MTM value, PV01 and daily VaR.

b) ***Currency swaps:*** FED is receiving weekly return on the rupee-foreign currency swaps, where banks are providing data on number of transactions and notional principal amount in USD.

c) ***Currency Options:*** AD Category-I banks are permitted to offer foreign currency – Rupee options. AD Category-I banks can offer only plain vanilla European options and the transactions undertaken have to be reported to RBI on a weekly basis. The data sent to FED includes trade date, client name, notional amount, option type, strike, maturity, premium and purpose. Further, option position report (weekly) with FED contains net portfolio gamma and net portfolio vega. Strike concentration report includes strike price and bucket-wise (1-week, 2-week, 1-month, 2-months, 3-months and more than 3-months) concentration for a range of 150 paise around the current spot level.

THE ROADMAP FOR THE DEVELOPMENT OF DERIVATIVES

The roadmap for the development of derivatives, or for that matter, any new financial product or service, will strive to maintain a balance between the following four objectives:

Efficiency: We can look at the notion of efficiency from two perspectives. For the provider of products and services, it means the ability to do this at the lowest possible cost, with the full benefit of technology and market infrastructure. For the user, efficiency relates to the availability of products and services which address his/her requirements at the lowest possible price.

Stability: From the viewpoint of the financial system, stability requires that aggregate risk is bounded in some way. This requires, in turn, that individual participants be required to mitigate and manage their own risks. However, in situations in which systemic risk goes beyond the aggregate individual risk, additional measures may be warranted.

Transparency: The basic premise is: 'what cannot be measured cannot be managed'. The more market participants know about overall activities and outcomes, the better able they are to make their cost- benefit calculations and act on them, contributing to the overall effectiveness of the market.

Inclusion: Financial development is not an end in itself. It serves the broader purpose of facilitating economic activity, through resource mobilisation and risk management. The more accessible the financial system is to individuals in pursuit of these two objectives, the better.

From this perspective, the approach should be neutral to the form and nature of the product or service; it should be concerned only with whether it is helping to meet the objectives, or at least not detracting from any of them. The emphasise on the objective of inclusion, which, in this context, looks at the desirability of a product in terms of how effectively it might meet the requirements of a very heterogeneous group of producers of various goods and services.

Taking the specific example of OTC fore x products, it is apparent that they remain attractive to a majority of people with forex exposures because they can be customised to the specific characteristics of each transaction. However, the parallel development of the futures market suggests that there may be some complementarities between the two. A hub-and-spoke analogy comes to mind, with OTC products serving as the spokes and the counter-parties to these transactions then aggregating their exposures and managing them with exchange-traded products. Although this phenomenon is not quite prevalent in India at present but this provides a useful way to think about the overall roadmap, with each component playing a legitimate role.

QUESTIONS

1. Discuss the major factors influencing the risk management in a globalised financial derivatives markets.
2. Can all the risks relating to financial derivatives activity be identified, and are they being managed and controlled?
3. Can the market risk methodology be adjusted to measure credit and liquidity to the risk solution being reviewed capable of attributing capital to cover operational and legal risk exposure?
4. To deal with financial derivatives risk, what types of formal structures need to be in place in order to implant a risk culture throughout the whole organisation?
5. Most of the losses from derivatives transactions have come from unclear implementation of risk visions and cultures in approach to risk-management." In the light of the this statement discuss the policies and procedures which can serve as an example of the major types of issue which should be made explicit and implemented by a company.
6. What is the strategic importance of derivatives risk control?
7. Discuss the different types of risk which can be considered relevant to any particular derivatives transaction.
8. How can the integrated risk framework build into its role of activity all the complexity of legal risk?
9. Discuss the growth of financial derivatives in the global financial markets.
10. "The changing nature of financial industry, especially as reflected in developments in the financial derivatives market, provides a considerable opportunities for risk sharing or inter-temporal smothering." What actions can be taken to control or plan for these risks? Can value be produced through risk management strategies? Explain.
11. Discuss the various financial derivatives instruments traded on organised exchanges in world financial markets.
12. "Global networking is no longer a mere metaphor for worldwide activities but now describes in very literal terms the advances in information and communication technology which have been a major driving force behind internationalisation in many areas of life, but especially in the economy. Within the economic sector, in turn, it is in the financial markets that globalisation has been particularly dynamic." Comment.
13. Critically examine the Value-at-Risk (VaR) approach.
14. "Derivatives are sometimes deliberately mispriced in order to conceal losses or to make profits by fraud"" Comment.

PART III

This Page has been intentionally left blank

16

FOREIGN EXCHANGE RISK EXPOSURE

INTRODUCTION

Corporate exposure management is a very complex problem. It is complex largely because of (a) the increasing size and variety of exposures which companies encounter as they develop internationally and (b) the increasing volatility of the exchange rates. Given this complexity, a logical and structured approach is needed to formulate company's foreign exchange risk management programme. The starting point in such a programme must be to decide exactly what is exposed to international environment and what is at risk.

FOREIGN EXCHANGE RISK EXPOSURE: THE CONCEPT

The general concept of exposure refers to the degree to which a company is affected by exchange rate changes. Quite simply, an asset, liability or income is said to be exposed to exchange risk when a currency movement will change, for better or for worse, its parent or home currency (HC) value. Exposure is thus a neutral concept signifying that a company has assets, liabilities or income streams denominated in currency other than its own. The "risk" element is that the currency movements may produce variability, in the value of assets, liabilities and incomes.

ALTERNATIVE DEFINITIONS OF FOREIGN EXCHANGE RISK EXPOSURE

All foreign currency denominated assets, liabilities and income streams are, therefore, exposed to exchange risk. Basically, this exposure is of two types. *First,* there is the exposure inherent in foreign currency transactions, known as 'transaction exposure'. This consists of lot of trading items (foreign currency-invoiced trade receivables and payables) and capital items (foreign-currency dividend and loan payments). *Second,* there is the exposure associated with the ownership of foreign currency denominated assets and liabilities. Transactions' exposure is clear and easy to understand. For example, if an Indian company invoices an export customer, for, say, French Franc 1 million, then for the period between the contract date and the date of receivables, the exporter has an exposure of FF 1 million. If the French Franc were to appreciate by 10% against Indian rupee during this period, then a realised gain of 10% of the exposure will occur. Thus, a change in the value of French Franc may lead to cash gain or loss to a company. It may also affect the company's tax position. This kind of exposure is now fully recognised by all participants in international business. But the confusion arises from the ongoing foreign operations since the accounting practice and economic logic give two very different scenario of the way in which currency fluctuation affect the value of foreign operations. Briefly, the accounting approach is concerned essentially about translation adjustments in a company's consolidated accounts whereas economic or cash flow exposure is concerned with the effect of currency movements in the future cash flows produced by foreign operations. The first type of effect gives rise to neutralised adjustments, while the latter leads to gains or losses which will actually be realised.

ACCOUNTING EXPOSURE

Accounting (translation) exposure arises on the consolidation of foreign subsidiaries' accounts into the parent-currency - denominated group financial statements. If exchange rates have changed since the previous accounting period, this translation or restatement, of those assets, liabilities, revenues, expenses, gains and losses that are denominated in foreign currency will result in foreign exchange gain or losses. The possible extent of these gains or losses is measured by the translation exposure figures.

Translation Methods

Assets and liabilities that are translated at the current (post change) exchange rate are considered to be exposed; those translated at a historical (pre change) exchange rate will maintain their historical (HC) values and hence are regarded as not exposed. Since only those items translated at current rates are (in the accounting sense) exposed to exchange risk, then the question of which items should be tranaslated at which rate is a vital one in determining a company's accounting exposure. Unfortunately, there is worldwide disagreement on the question. Four principal translation methods are the monetary/non- monetary method, the temporal method, the current/non-current method and the all current rate method. Each method in use has its own assumptions as to the applicability of historical or current rates to various balance sheet items. Table-1 summarises the tranaslation rules of each of these four methods.

(a) Monetary/Non-Monetary Method

This method is based on the distinction between monetary assets and liabilities - those items that represent a claim to receive or an objective to pay a fixed amount of foreign currency units - and non-monetary or physical assets and liabilities. Monetary items (e.g. cash, accounts payable and receiveable, and long-term debt) are translated at the current rate, non-monetary items (e.g. inventory, fixed assets, and long-term investments) are translated at historical rates.

Income statement items are translated at the average exchange rate during the period , except for revenue and expense items related to non-monetary assets and liabilities. The latter items, primarily depreciation expense and cost of goods sold, are translated at the same rate as the corresponding balance sheet hems. As a result, the cost of goods sold may be translated at a rate different from that used to translate sales.

TABLE-1

TRANSLATION RULES USE

	Monetary/ Non-monetary		*Temporal*		*Current/ Non-current*		*Current rate for all assets*	
	*CR**	*HR***	*CR**	*HR***	*CR**	*HR***	*CR**	*HR***
ASSETS								
Current Assets								
Cash/marketable securities	x		x		x		x	
Receivables#	x		x		x		x	
Inventory (at cost)		+	x		x		x	
Prepaid expenses		+		+	x		x	
Fixed Assets less Accumulated Depreciation		+		+		+	x	
Goodwill		+		+		+	x	
LIABILITIES								
Current Liabilities	x		x		x		x	
Long-term debt	x		x			+	x	
Deferred Income taxes	x		x			+	x	
Equity***		Res.		Res.		Res.		Res.

*CR = Current rate; ** HR = Historical rate;

***Adjusted for the translation gain/loss.

#Any long-term receivables (settlement date beyond one year) will be translated at the historical rate, under the current/non-current method.

(b) Temporal Method

Modified version of the monetary/non-monetary method is the temporal method. The only difference is that under monetary/non- monetary method, inventory is always translated at the historical rate whereas under the temporal method, the inventory is normally translated at the historical rate but it can also be translated at the current rate if the inventory is shown on the balance sheet at market values. Despite the similarities, however, the traditional basis of each method is different. The choice of an exchange rate for translation is based on the type of asset or liability in the monetary/non-monetary method; in the temporal method, it is based on the underlying approach to evaluating cost (historical versus market).

Income statement items are normally translated at an average rate for the reporting period. However, cost of goods sold and depreciation and amortisation charges related to balance sheet items carried at past prices are translated at historical rates.

(c) Current/Non-current Method

Current/non-current method differentiate between assets and liabilities on the basis of maturity With this method, all the foreign subsidiaries' current assets and liabilities are translated into home currency at the current exchange rate. Each non-current asset or liability is translated at the historical rate. On the other hand, items in the income statement are translated at the average exchange rate of the period, except for those revenue and expense items associated with non-current assets or liabilities. The latter items, such as depreciation expense, are translated at the same rate as the corresponding balance sheet items. Thus, it is possible to see different revenue and expense items with similar maturities being translated at different rates.

(d)Current Rate Method

Under current rate method, all balance sheet and income statement items are translated at the current rate. If a firm's foreign currency-denominated assets exceed its foreign currency-liabilities, a devaluation/depreciation will result in a loss and a revaluation/appreciation in a gain.

Given this diversity of translation methods in the consolidation of financial statements the choice of translation method can have a significant effect on home-currency accounting results. Indeed, identical firms could share different translation gains or losses merely because they used different methods of translating their foreign subsidiaries accounts. This can be clearly demonstrated by the use of a simple example of an Australian company which has set up a subsidiary in India on 1st January 2003. The underlying transactions were booked at the prevailing exchange rate, say ₹ 20/$A. The opening balance sheet and its rupee equivalent are shown in columns (1) and (2) of Exhibit-1.

The Indian subsidiary could not begin operations in the first quarter of 2003, so that at fiscal year end (31 March 2003) the rupee balance sheet was exactly the same as on 1st January 2003. However, during this quarter, rupee depreciated by 25 percent against the $A so that the closing rate of exchange was Rs.25/$A. This rate was applied in the consolidation of some or all of the subsidiary's items, depending on which translation method was used. The results, as measured by each of the four methods, are shown in Column (3) - (6). If the rupee had appreciated or $A depreciated and the new exchange rate is Rs.12.50/$A, the impact of use of each translation method on the consolidation of the balance sheet is shown through column (7)-(10) of Exhibit-1. This demonstrates the significance of the use of different methods with results ranging from a loss of $A600,000 to a gain of $ 3,550,000 when currency fluctuates. Since these various methods are recognised by the accounting professions in most parts of the world, then the identification of accounting exposure and the concomitant balance sheet translation gains and losses is surely an arbitrary process. The fundamental point is that none of the outcomes shown in Exhibit-1 have very much to do with the economic or cash flow effects of currency movements on a company's foreign operations.

ECONOMIC (CASH FLOW) EXPOSURE

Economic (cash flow) exposure is concerned with the effects of an exchange rate change on the home currency value of the future cash flows generated by a company's foreign operations. Economic exposure to exchange risk can be separated into two components: Transaction exposure and Real operating exposure.

Transaction exposure is defined as *change in the value of monetary (contractual)*

EXHIBIT-1

FINANCIAL STATEMENT IMPACT OF TRANSLATION ALTERNATIVES

($A thousands)

	Local Currency (LC)	$A Prior to exchange rate changes (LC20=$A)	After Devaluation of Local Currency (LC25 = $A)				After Revaluation of Local Currency (LC12.5 =$A)			
			Monetary/ Non-monetary	Temporal	Current/ Non-current	Current rate for all assets and liabilities	Monetary/ Non-monetary	Temporal	Current/ Non-current	Current rate for all assets
	1	2	3	4	5	6	7	8	9	10
ASSETS										
Current Assets										
Cash, marketable securities, and receivables	60,000	3,000	2,400	2,400	2,400	2,400	4,000	4,000	4 000	4,000
Inventory (at cost)	82,500	4,125	4,125	3,300	3,300	3,300	4,125	5,500	5,500	5,500
Prepaid expenses	3,000	150	150	150	120	120	120	150	200	200
Total current assets	145,500	7,275	6,675	5,850	5,820	5,820	8,275	9,650	9,700	9,700
Fixed Assets less Accumulated Depreciation	75,000	3,750	3,750	3,750	3,750	3,000	3,750	3,750	3,750	5,000
Goodwill	52,500	2,625	2,625	2,625	2,625	2,100	2,625	2,625	2,625	3,500
Total Assets	273,000	13,650	13,050	12,225	12,195	10,920	14,650	16,025	16,075	17,200

	Local Currency (LC)	$A Prior to exchange rate changes (LC20=$A)	After Devaluation of Local Currency (LC25 = $A) Monetary/ Non-monetary	Temporal	Current/ Non-current	Current rate for all assets and liabilities	After Revaluation of Local Currency (LC12.5 =$A) Monetary/ Non-monetary	Temporal	Current/ Non-current	Current rate for all assets
	1	2	3	4	5	6	7	8	9	10
LIABILITIES										
Current Liabilities	67,500	3,375	2,700	2,700	2,700	2,700	4,500	4,500	4,500	4,500
Long-term debt	97,500	4,875	3,900	3,900	4,875	3,900	6,500	6,500	4,875	6,500
Deferred Income taxes	3,000	150	120	120	150	120	200	200	150	200
Total Liabilities	168,000	8,400	6,720	6,720	7,725	6,720	11,200	11,200	9,425	11,200
Capital Stock	42,000	2,100	2,100	2,100	2,100	2,100	2,100	2,100	2,100	2,100
Retained Earnings	63,000	3,150	4,230	3,405	2,370	2,100	1,350	2,725	5,550	3,900
Total Equity	105,000	5,250	6,330	5,505	4,470	4,200	3,450	4,825	7,650	6,000
Total Liabilities plus equity	273,000	13,650	13,050	12,225	12,195	10,920	14,650	16,025	16,075	17,200
TRANSLATION GAIN/LOSS	—	—	(600)	(1,425)	(1,455)	2,730	1,000	2,375	2,425	3,550

cash flows due to unexpected change in exchange rates. Every foreign currency transaction—whether an infolw or an outflow—is exposed to this risk. Since transaction exposure is the most visible exposure to currency risk, it commands the most attention from multinational financial managers. Less visible, but no less important, is the firm's operating exposure to currency risk. **Operating exposure**, also called competitive exposure or strategic exposure, to currency risk is defined *as change in the value of non-monetary cash flows (i.e., the noncontractual cash flows of the firm's real assets) due to unexpected changes in the foreign currency values.* Although operating exposure is more difficult to measure and manage than transaction exposure, it is usually the more important long-term exposure because it involves the firm's core business activities.

In *transaction exposure,* there is the possibility of incurring exchange gains or losses upon settlement at a future date on transactions already entered into and denominated in a foreign currency. Some of these unsettled transactions, including foreign-currency-denominated debt and accounts receivable, are already listed on the firm's balance sheet. The other obligation, such as contracts for future sales or purchase, are not. Although transaction exposure is often included under accounting exposure, it is more properly a cash flow exposure and hence part of economic exposure. On the other hand, since *real operating exposure* arises because of currency fluctuations, together with price changes, it can alter a company's future revenues and costs (i.e. its operating cash, it flows). Consequently, measuring a firm's operating exposure requires detailed knowledge concerning its operations and their sensitivity to exchange rate changes. Such a measurement also requires a long-term perspective viewing the firm as an ongoing concern with operations whose cost and price competitiveness can be effected by exchange rate changes. Thus, the firm faces operating exposure the moment it invests in servicing a market subject to foreign competition or in sourcing goods or inputs abroad. This investment includes new product development, a distribution network, foreign supply contracts, or production facilities. Transaction exposure arises later on, and only if the company's commitments lead it to engage in foreign-currency- denominated sales or purchases.

The management of economic exposure is made especially difficult because it is impossible to assess the effects of an exchange rate change without simultaneously considering the impact on cash flows of the underlying relative rates of inflation associated with each currency. A generally accepted method of valuing an asset is to discount the future net cash flows (after tax) which the asset is expected to produce. This is known as the net present value (NPV) of future cash flows. In the valuation of foreign assets, the additional step required is that the NPV of cash flows (including indirect cash flows generated by the subsidiary but arising elsewhere in the corporate group, such as trading profits, management fees, and royalties) must then be translated into the home currency at same rate of exchange. The NPV of a foreign subsidiary should therefore be described as follows

$$\text{NPV}_o = \sum_{t=0}^{n} \frac{(CIF_t - COF_t)ER_t}{(1+d)^t}$$

where: NPV — Net present value (home currency equivalent); CIF — Cash inflows (denominated in foreign subsidiary's local currency); COF — Cash outflows (denominated in foreign subsidiary's local currency), including tax payments; ER —

Exchange rate (home currency value of one unit of foreign currency; d — Discount rate (the rate of return required by the parent company for its investment in the foreign subsidiary); t — Period t; and finally, n — The last period in which cash flows are expected.

Thus, the impact of currency movement occurs in the economic or cash flow valuation of the foreign subsidiary. The economic evaluation of exchange risk should therefore be defined as the possibility that the parent-company-denominated NPV of the foreign subsidiary's future cash flows will be adversely affected by exchange rate movements. In other words, exposure is that component of a firm's value (future cash flows) which is related to the future exchange rate scenario. A change in the foreign subsidiary's exchange rate will not only have the automatic effect of altering the 'price' at which future local currency (LC) cash flows are transformed into the home currency (ER in the above equation), but it may also change the quantity (CIF-COF) and timing (t) of these cash flows. Hence the economic analysis of exchange risk is concerned with estimating the effects of currency movements on foreign operations' future LC cash inflows and cash outflows.

Cash Inflows

A change in the subsidiary's host country exchange rate (irrespective of whether it moves in relation to the home currency) can have two types of effects or the subsidiary's sales revenue. It can alter the size of the market in which the subsidiary operates ('market size' effect) and/or it may also alter the share of this market which the subsidiary holds ('market share' effect). The dilution and incidence of these effects will vary according to the market characteristics of the subsidiary. These market characteristics can be categorised into three market types: the export sector; the import competing sector of the domestic market; and, the 'pure' domestic market.

Export Sector

When a depreciation will have little or no effect on the total size of the export market; it will have a favourable market share effect. Hence the LC revenues produced by the foreign subsidiary's exports shall be increased. The export oriented subsidiary may reduce its foreign (i.e. foreign to the subsidiary's host country) currency setting price by the depreciation percentage (maintaining the LC equivalent), which will presumably lead to a higher sales volume. Alternatively, it can maintain its foreign currency prices (raising the LC equivalent), thereby increasing by the depreciation percentage the LC revenue per unit of an unchanged volume. In other words, depreciation should produce increased sales and/or higher profit margins — either way, LC export revenues should benefit from the depreciation. They may not benefit by the full depreciation percentage, however, since foreign markets may be the subject of increased competition from other exporters.

Domestic Market Import Competing Factor

As in the export sector, the market share will be favourable because it will increase the competitiveness of local vis-a-vis foreign goods. Hence subsidiaries selling goods which compete with imports in the domestic market should also produce increased revenues, unless overseas exporters are willing and able to suffer a fall in revenue denominated in their own currencies. Typically, then, depreciation will lead to an increase in the LC price of imported goods, in the short term at least. The long- term outcome may be that foreign suppliers move their production facilities to depreciation-prone markets. Foreign subsidiaries located in the depreciation country and operating in the import- competing sector of the domestic market will therefore benefit, again in the form of increased sales volume and/or higher profit margins. Depreciation will also have a positive effect on nominal domestic income because of the foreign trade multiplier. However, the rising price of inputs and import competing goods in the depreciating country may reduce real income. More importantly, domestic demand is likely to be dampened by the government deflationary measures which usually accompany depreciation. The favourable market share effects of a depreciation may therefore be partly offset by adverse effects on the total size of the domestic market.

Pure Domestic Market

Foreign subsidiaries operating in this market category are most likely to lose from a depreciation, since there will be no favourable market share effects to offset the probable adverse domestic income effect.

Cash Outflows

For analytical purpose, it is useful to make the distinction between 'physical' inputs (labour, raw material and plant) costs and 'financing' (working capital and producing) costs.

Physical Sector

Depreciation will increase the LC cost of physical inputs for most firms operating in the depreciating country. The extent of input price increases will depend on such macro-economic factors as the pre-depreciation employment situation, the effectiveness of the government deflationary programme and the speed with which inputs can be shifted between different sectors of the economy. Within this general framework, a three fold classification of the depreciation factors could be made into imported, traded domestic, and non-traded domestic inputs. Those companies which import a large proportion of their inputs will be hardest hit by a depreciation under this general framework of classification. Their costs may not rise by the full depreciation percentage, however, if competition from domestic producer forces overseas suppliers to absorb part of the cost increase. Even firms using mainly domestic inputs will be subject to rising costs, since expansion in the export and import competing sectors will force up factor prices. This will, of course, affect traded rather than non-traded input costs, which will be least affected by the depreciation.

Financial Sector

Depreciation will have a two-fold impact on financing costs, since it will alter companies' working capital requirements as well as the cost of borrowing. In terms of working capital requirements, it has been argued that a depreciation may lead to increased sales revenues and rising cost inputs. If this is the case then larger cash and inventory balance will be required and customers' credit needs will be larger, resulting in additional working capital requirements.

The effect on borrowing costs will depend on the currency denomination of the company's liability structure. The obvious impact on the cost of foreign (i.e. foreign to subsidiary's host currency) currency - denominated loans, as most companies are now fully aware, is that the effective interest rate will be increased. Not so obvious, however, is the effect on domestic interest rates. These usually rise when a currency comes under pressure and a devaluation is expected. Also, interest rates will remain high after a devaluation if continuing inflationary pressures are expected. Hence, the interest cost of almost all loans is likely to rise as a result of devaluation - the only exception is a company's existing fixed-rate domestic debt.

After adjusting expected future LC cash inflows and outflows for the 'quantity' effect of a devaluation, the cash flow analysis must finally take account of the 'price' effect. The adjusted net LC cash flow which the subsidiary is now expected to produce is therefore translated into the present currency at the new rate of exchange, giving the home currency denominated net cash flow. If the loss on translation at the new rate (the 'price' effect) is more than offset by an improvement in LC cash flows (the 'quantity' effect), then the parent company will benefit from the depreciation since the value of its foreign subsidiary is increased. If the reverse is true then the parent company should consider neutralising the exposure by, for instance, changing the financing, servicing and marketing structure of its subsidiary.

CURRENCY RISK-SHARING METHODS

An analysis of future cash flows is a very difficult and complex task since it requires the estimation of such variables as the devaluation reactions of competitors (for elasticity of supply), consumers (price elasticity of demand) and the local government (will price controls be introduced?). Nevertheless, it is essential that each firm tries to measure its currency exposure. To overcome the exchange rate gyratious, the currency risk-sharing methods are adopted by companies involved in long- term export import contracts since they reduce both the frequency of contract revisions and the impact of currency fluctuations on profits. To illustrate assume company ABC, a German based company, has entered into a 5-year contract with company XYZ, an Indian company, to import software developed by Indian company in accordance to company ABC's specifications. The prospective parties to the currency risk-sharing agreement may consider following points while negotiating the contract.

Base price of the product

The price is typically set in the exporter's currency. If the unit price is set equal to ₹ 10,00,000, all future adjustments are made relative to this base price.

Base Exchange Rate

The base exchange rate can be set equal to the rate prevailing at the time the contract is negotiated or when the first delivery actually takes place. Company ABC and Company XYZ decide to use the actual exchange rate at the time of negotiation, which was ₹ 20/DM. Thus, the base DM price is DM 50,000 (₹ 10,00,000/20).

Frequency of revision

The firm may choose for price revision to adjust the variations. However, too frequent revisions will become an administrative hassle while less frequent revisions might lead to prices that could seriously be out of range.

Method of determining actual revised exchange rates

The exchange rate selected might be the average of closing prices on all business days during the quarter. It could have been the final closing price for the quarter, the average of the previous quarter's exchange rate and the final closing price, or some other variation. It is also necessary to specify whether the bid, ask, or mid-point price is to be used.

Method of adjustment

In this case, the companies decide that actual exchange rate changes in any quarter would be reflected in the rate used in the next quarter. Alternatively, the parties could have decided to retroactively adjust prices for the past quarter, based on actual exchange rates during the quarter.

Selection of a neutral zone

The neutral zone can be specified in absolute or percentage terms. Moreover, the exchange rate may be expressed as the currency A price of currency B, or vice versa. For example, the parties may agree to specify the neutral zone in absolute terms; a band ranging from ₹ 19-21 : DM 1, with a base rate of ₹ 20/DM. If the neutral band is zero, the currency risk sharing agreement boils down to the importer buying a forward contract for a portion of the transactions amount at the spot rate from the exporter. The larger the fraction of risk borne by the exporter, the greater the portion of the transaction amongst covered by the forward contract; similarly, if the neutral band is very wide, the risk-sharing agreement means that the customer has effectively brought a forward contract for the entire transactions amongst from the supplier at the current sport rate.

Fraction of risk shared by each party

The parties must also agree on how to share the risk of currency movements beyond the neutral zone. The sharing can be equal or unequal. If company ABC and company XYZ decide to share the risk equally and the exchange rates depreciates from ₹ 20/DM to ₹ 24/DM, the actual rate have moved beyond ₹ 4—the upper band of the neutral zone (₹ 21/DM). This amount is shared equally, resulting in an exchange rate for the subsequent quarters of ₹ 21.50/DM [₹ 20 + ₹ 3/2] and a new DM price of DM 46,511.6 (₹ 10,00,000/21.50).

Price reopener

This provision gives either party the option to reopen the contract if the exchange rate moves beyond a much broader band, say Rs.5-25 DM.

Invoice currency

The parties could use either the exporter's or importer's currency to actually settle the contract each period.

Adjustment of other contract terms

The contract may contain other related provisions such as adjustment of the base rupee price to reflect Indian inflation and productivity.

The above listed currency risk-sharing methods would avoid two pricing extremes : (I) adjusting prices continuously as exchange rate move or (2) holding the price constant so that one party has a price fixed in its home currency while the other party either has windfall profits or suffers a drastic loss in profit margin or market share. How can this be done in practice?

Even if cash flow adjustment may be less significant currency risk can still reduce an MNC's present value by increasing the required discount rate on the firm's foreign-source-earnings. Many international financial managers, for example, presume that fluctuations in currency values increase the variability (riskiness) of corporate earnings. The fear of management is that the volatile profits pattern could affect the firm's perceived riskiness and, in turn, its ability to raise capital at a reasonable cost. But this fear may not be justified. First of all, earnings and changes in net worth must be distinguished from cash flows. There are many instances in which a reduction in earnings or net worth marks an increase in cash flow. More importantly, a firm's actual exchange risk can be determined only by examining the impact of variations in nominal exchange rates or variations in the firm's worldwide consolidated cash flows.

DOES FOREIGN EXCHANGE RISK MATTER?

There are several reasons to believe that the real impact of this nominal currency changes will be less severe than is generally supposed. First, of course, are the offsetting effects of inflation. Currency depreciation is almost always associated with a relatively high rate of inflation, especially in a floating rate system. For example, inflation will have an adverse market share effect on sales revenues in the export and import competing sectors, whilst it will have a favourable (nominal) income effect on domestic demand. It will drive up the cost of physical inputs in domestically sourced production functions, whilst not affecting imported inputs. Indeed, it is only in the financial sector that the impact of a fall in the value of a currency and inflation will be similar : both can be expected to increase working capital and borrowing costs.

In sum, then, a fall in the value of a currency will tend to favour companies in the exports and import-competing sectors and those which are domestically sourced and financed. Inflation will tend to have the opposite effects. It should also be added, of course, that inflation and currency depreciation are experienced simultaneously. Indeed, this interaction between the opposing process of inflation and currency depreciation poses the question of whether exchange risk really exists at all. *If the adverse (beneficial) effects of LC depreciation are simultaneously and exactly offset by beneficial (adverse) effects of LC inflation, then does exchange risk exist?*

The rationale of this view is based on two economic theorems : the purchasing power parity (PPP) theory and the interest rate theory of exchange rate expectations (the Fisher effect). The rationale of both theorems is based on arbitrage : commodity arbitrage in the first case and covered interest arbitrage in the second. The PPP theory states that the difference between the inflation rates of two countries tends over time to equal the rate of change of the exchange rate between their two currencies. The implication is that if gains and losses from exchange rate changes tend over time to offset by differences in relative inflation rates, it matters little in which currency the firm buys its inputs or sells its products since any devaluation (revaluation) of a foreign currency will sooner or later be offset by a correspondingly higher (lower) rate of inflation in that currency. According to the Fisher effect, the difference between interest rates of two currencies should equal the expected rate of change of the exchange rate during the appropriate maturity period. Hence, it would not matter in which currency the firm borrowed or loaned funds, given a sufficiently long time horizon, since any exchange loss (gain) would eventually be offset by an interest rate advantage (disadvantage).

The question 'does foreign exchange risk matter?' becomes an empirical one. If these two theories hold then it will not matter in which currency a firm buys/sells or borrows/lends since the effects of currency movements will be offset by counterveiling changes in inflation and interest rates. There is a lot of evidence which suggests that these theories do hold in the long run. In the long run, then, the rate of return on the asset side and the cost of capital on the liability side both adjust to offset the effects of currency movements. In the long run, exchange risk does not exist. Unfortunately, however, both the PPP theorem and the Fisher effect fail a crucial real-life test — they do not hold in the short run. When the theorems are tested on an annual basis there are significant deviations from the projected exchange rate path and the correlations are much worse for quarterly tests. In other words, whilst the long-term trend is accurately reflected in the PPP and Fisher paths, in the short run actual exchange rates will deviate around these paths. Hence, exchange risk stems from deviations from the expected rate (indicated by the forward rate or interest rate differential). These unexpected exchange rate changes cause a variability in cash flow, and it is this which constitutes the firm's exchange risk.

WHICH TRANSLATION METHOD IS THE MOST REALISTIC?

Which translation method is the most realistic from the perspective of the financial theory? The current/noncurrent method is clearly the least realistic, because it values long-term debt (a monetary liability) at historical cost. The other translation accounting methods correctly value monetary assets and liabilities at the current exchange rate.

The key issue is whether the real assets of a foreign subsidiary should be translated at historical exchange rates or at the current exchange rate. The answer depends on the nature of the firm and its operating exposure to currency risk. The temporal method assumes that the real assets of a foreign subsidiary are unaffected by currency risk. The current rate method assumes that real assets are exposed one for one to exchange rate changes. For most firms, the truth is somewhere between these two positions.

The most obvious effect of a foreign currency depreciation is to decrease the domestic currency value of foreign assets. However, a foreign currency depreciation also tends to increase the competitiveness of foreign assets and to increase their value in the foreign currency. This increase in the foreign currency value of foreign assets may or may not be enough to offset the decrease in the value of the foreign currency. Consequently, each of these translation accounting method is a simplified view of the true operating exposure of the foreign subsidiary's real assets. No simple accounting convention can hope to accommodate the variety of operating exposures observed in practice. Indeed, importers and exporters often have operating exposures that are of opposite signs.

A number of empirical studies have compared the *temporal method* to the current rate method. These studies typically measure an earnings response coefficient - the relation of stock returns to earnings surprises (actual minus expected earnings) around the time of corporates earnings announcements. If earnings provide value-relevant information to investors, then earnings that are above expectations (positive earnings surprises) will be associated with positive stock returns. Conversely, earnings that are below expectations (negative surprises) will be associated with negative returns. By examining the strength of this relation, the information content of earnings announcements and the quality of reported earnings can be appraised. Contrary to these studies, it has also been found that the earnings response coefficients of U.S. multinational corporations with foreign operations improved when *current rate method* was adopted. The source of improvement in the quality of reported earnings may not have been in the switch from the temporal to the current rate method, but in the isolation of reported earnings from changes in translated balance sheet accounts through the cumulative translation adjustment account. Regardless of source of improvement, the current rate method seems to have improved the information quality or valuation relevance of accounting earnings for multinational corporations.

CORPORATE HEDGING OF TRANSLATION EXPOSURE

Finance theory states that the firm should only consider hedging risk exposures that are related to firm value. Hedging has value when it can reduce the variability of firm value and thereby reduce expected taxes, costs of financial distress, or agency costs. There is no value in hedging noncash transactions that do not cost or risk cash.

In a perfect and efficient financial market, the firm's borrowing capacity and required return on investment are determined in the marketplace by rational, informed investors. Managing translation exposures that do not involve cash flows will not add to the value of the firm.

In the real world of imperfect and less-than-efficient markets, there are situations in which translation exposure to currency risk can have valuation-relevant consequences above and beyond the firm's economic (transaction and operating) exposure. Management of translation exposure is justifiable in these circumstances. In particular, hedging can improve the informativeness of corporate earnings by reducing extraneous noise. Better-quality accounting earnings allow investors to more accurately assess the ability of management and the quality of the corporation's investments.

Here are three practical reasons for hedging exposure to currency risk. Each justification relies on costly or restricted access to information on the part of investors or information providers.

i) **Satisfying Loan Covenants.** Loan covenants require that a firm maintain certain levels of performance, such as in operating profit or interest coverage. Violation of a loan covenant can lead to a reduction in borrowing capacity. In these circumstances, a hedge of translation exposure can ensure that the corporation retains its access to funds. The efficient markets view is that the firm's borrowing capacity is determined in the marketplace and not through artifices such as loan covenants. Nevertheless, accounting constraints can have an indirect effect on borrowing capacity and hence on cash flow and the value of the firm.

ii) **Meeting Profit Forecasts.** The efficient markets view is that investors see through accounting profits to the cash flows and intrinsic value of the firm. In a less-than-efficient market, a firm that has announced a profit forecast might wish to retain its credibility with analysts and investors by hedging against a translation loss from its currency exposure. Management's credibility might be worth protecting, even if it means hedging a noncash translation exposure with a financial market hedge that costs and risks cash.

iii) **Retaining a Credit Rating.** Managers have an incentive to hedge translation exposure if the firm's credit rating depends on accounting profits and not just on its underlying cash flows. Although an efficient market would see through to the firm's underlying cash flows and intrinsic value, information is imperfect and costly to acquire in the real world. To the extent that hedging translation exposure can avoid a downgrade in a credit rating, hedging can preserve value by maintaining the firm's access to funds.

Aligning Managerial Incentives with Shareholder Objectives

Managerial performance evaluations should be tied to financial performance — to underlying cash flows and values — and not merely to accounting profits. Nevertheless, managers are often evaluated based on accounting performance simply because it is easier to measure accounting flows than economic or financial performance. If risk-averse managers are not allowed to hedge, they may forgo value-creating investments that would expose them to too much currency risk. Allowing managers to hedge against translation exposure can reduce **agency costs** (i.e., the costs of ensuring that managers act in the best interests of shareholders) by aligning managerial incentives with shareholder objectives.

The multinational treasury can facilitate this process by providing internal hedges to managers of individual operating units. For example, if a division manager wants to hedge divisional accounting performance against a drop in the local currency, treasury can quote prices on currency forward or option contracts that allow the manager to lock in an accounting profit for performance evaluation purposes. The internal cost of this hedge to the operating division should be based on market prices, such as forward rates or option premiums. Even though it has provided a hedge to an internal operating division of firm, treasury does not have to actually execute this hedge in the external financial markets. Instead, treasury should make its own assessment of the desirability of hedging based on cash flow (rather than accounting profit) considerations after netting exposures across the individual operating divisions.

Value-based incentive plans based on economic value added are another way to align managerial incentives with shareholder objectives. **Economic value added (EVA)** is a method of financial performance evaluation that adjust accounting performance for a charge reflecting investors' required return on investment. Alternatively, divisional performance can be benchmarked to the performance of other divisions or to firms with similar exposures to currency risk. Each of these methods of performance evaluation is an attempt to align managerial incentives with shareholder objectives.

The decision of whether to hedge translation exposure to currency risk depends on the company, its owners and managers, and the markets in which it is trade. It must therefore be made on a case-by-case basis. Nevertheless, here are some general recommendations:

1. Do not hedge translation exposures in the financial markets unless the purpose of the hedge is to reduce economic (transaction or operating) exposure to currency risk.
2. Foreign affiliates should use local sources of debt or equity capital to the extent permitted by the corporation's overall financial goals. This will minimise the translation and, more importantly, the economic exposure of foreign affiliates.
3. Managerial performance evaluation and compensation should be structured in a way that insulates managers from unexpected changes in exchange rates. This can be done by benchmarking divisional performance to the performance of other divisions or firms with similar exposures to currency risk.
4. If hedging of an individual unit's translation exposure is deemed necessary to align managerial incentives with shareholder objectives, the corporate treasury should quote market prices to the individual units. If individual units have noncash exposures, the treasury should hedge internally. External financial market hedges should be used only for hedging the firm's net transaction or operating exposures to currency risk.

It should be noted that accounting performance can impact real costs in the real world of imperfect and less-than-efficient financial markets. Providing a way for managers to reduce this source of uncertainty will ultimately benefit shareholders and other corporate stakeholders.

TAX TREATMENT OF GAINS AND LOSSES FROM FOREIGN EXCHANGE RISK EXPOSURE

Foreign exchange transactions can result in a profit or loss if the relative value of the two currencies changes between contract date and the date of payment of the contract. There can be a gain or loss in one currency expressed in terms of the other. A similar situation can arise when accounts expressed in one currency are translated into another currency. In either case the profit or loss on foreign exchange may affect the taxation charge imposed on the company at home or abroad. However, the complication start when the tax rates differ between countries, hence an exchange gain may suffer a different tax charge depending on where the revenue authorities deem it to be sourced. Some countries differentiate between foreign exchange deals covering revenue and those covering capital transactions. Foreign exchange gains on capital transactions often suffer a lower rate of tax or may avoid tax altogether. Conversely, foreign exchange losses on appreciation of a foreign loan may not be accepted by the revenue authorities as an allowable charge against tax.

Some tax authorities ignore foreign exchange gains or losses unless they are actually realised, while others consider unrealised gains and losses to be fully taxable. Profits stored in a foreign bank account which is blocked by exchange control regulations are not usually taxed until released, and so on. The tax effects of foreign exchange are complex and so provide considerable scope for the company treasure to use his ingenuity to minimise the tax bill of his company. The overall policy of the tax adviser is to arrange matters in such a way that gains on exchange rate adjustments are made to arise in a form which are not taxable and losses in a form which are allowable against other income.

BASIC PHILOSOPHIES

Two basic approaches are discernible in the tax treatment of foreign exchange gains and lowers. The first approach is to treat the foreign exchange bought or sold as an asset which is quite distinct from the transaction it finances. This is sometimes called the *separate transactions* approach. The gain or loss on foreign exchange is thus separated from any gain or loss on the underlying transaction. The tax effect will arise when the transaction is closed by payment, not when the contract is signed.

In contrast to the above approach, the *integrated approach* ties the foreign exchange gain or loss into the contract it finances. In effect this approach implies that the foreign currency is simply a medium of exchange and not an independent asset. Any profit or loss on foreign exchange would be added to or subtracted from the profit on the underlying transaction, and the tax treatment of this profit or loss might be affected by the nature of the underlying transaction, i.e. whether it is of a capital or revenue nature.

Terminology

For tax purposes we define *ordinary income* as income earned in the normal course of trade and differentiate this type of income from a *capital gain* arising from the sale of a fixed asset, etc. Many countries apply different tax rates to these two types of income.

The tax law on foreign exchange gains and losses often needs to distinguish between an *open* and *closed* transaction. A transaction remains open until the final payment is acknowledged by the seller, when it is closed.

The profit on a foreign exchange transaction is *realised* when the deal is closed by final payment. Many countries do not tax a foreign exchange gain until it is realised.

The sourcing of income can have important tax implications. If the foreign exchange gain is treated as being sourced abroad, i.e. arising in a foreign tax regime, the tax charge may be eliminated or reduced by an imputed foreign tax credit.

We will now examine the tax treatment of four types of foreign exchange transactions:

1. Import—export transactions
2. Foreign currency loans
3. Forward exchange transactions
4. Balance sheet translations

Import—Export Transactions

In most countries foreign exchange gains/losses arising from a contract denominated in a foreign currency are treated as if they were ordinary income. The gain is taxable and the loss is allowable against other trading income. In a few countries, the gain is taxable as ordinary income but the loss may not be allowable. The short-term gains and losses on normal trading transactions are treated as ordinary income for tax purposes. However, debts between companies in the same group may be treated as loans if the debt is held outstanding for more than six months. The tax authorities may ignore unrealised gains or losses on foreign exchange if the company have always ignored them in the past or if generally accepted accounting principles would exclude them from the account until realised.

Exchange rate gains or losses on transactions which are not of a normal trading nature are treated as being capital gains or losses. The gain or loss has a tax effect only when the gain or loss is realised. If fixed assets held abroad and denominated in a foreign currency are sold, the foreign exchange gain or loss is amalgamated with the gain or loss on the underlying transaction for tax purposes.

In many countries the separate transactions theory is applied. The gain or loss on the exchange of currency is treated separately from the gain or loss on the underlying transaction. This applies to both exports and imports. The gain on the debt denominated in a foreign currency is not recognised for tax purposes until the transaction is closed by payment. If the debt is unpaid at the accounting year and the profit or loss has no tax effect until payment takes place in the following period. The separate transactions theory also applies to payment for fixed assets, even if payment is by instalment. If the foreign currency is devalued, the foreign exchange gain is taxed on each future instalment.

Generally tax legislation states that foreign exchange gains or losses on trading transactions, whether current or fixed, have a tax effect only when the transaction is closed by payment. A problem will only arise when a credit transaction in one period is paid up in the following period and the exchange rate changes between these points in time. The gain or loss will have a tax effect in the latter period. There may be an exception to this rule in the case of royalties.

Foreign Currency Loans

Many countries treat a gain or loss on exchange on repayment of a loan in a foreign currency as taxable or allowable against tax. If a loan is denominated in a foreign currency the repayment value of the loan in the home currency is affected by an adjustment in exchange rates between the two currencies. The exchange value of the interest payment is also affected.

The tax treatment of these exchange rate gains and losses varies a great deal between countries. In some countries the gain or loss on both capital and interest is treated as ordinary income for tax purposes. Gains are taxed, losses are allowable against tax. However, in many countries the gain or loss has no tax effect until the payment is made, i.e. the loss on revaluation of foreign currency is not allowed until the loan is repayed or interest payment is transferred. In other countries gains are not taxed until realised but losses are allowed on the revalued foreign loan.

Forward Exchange Transactions

When a corporation enters into a forward foreign exchange contract, using the separate transactions approach, it usually happens that the forward rate differs from the future spot rate at the time the contract matures. This results in a loss or gain on the contract. In most countries this loss or gain is treated as ordinary income for tax purposes. Gains are taxable, losses deductible. But a number of variations occur. These are:

1. The tax effect may not occur unless the gain loss is actually realised. No effect will occur if it is carried forward.
2. Occasionally the use to which the funds are put affects the tax position. A gain or loss on a forward contact covering a capital transaction may have no tax effect.
3. The length of the forward contract may affect the position. A long-term contract gain or loss may have no tax effect or may be taxed at a capital gains rate.

Balance Sheet Translation

When a multinational company consolidates its accounts into the single currency of the parent country a gain or loss on translation will arise. This gain or loss on currency translation may have a tax effect. Some countries tax an unrealised translation gain and allow an unrealised loss to be set off against profits from other sources. The key questions here appear to be:

1. Does the unrealised translation gain or loss have a tax effect?
2. Can this tax effect be avoided if the gain or loss it omitted from the consolidated accounts?

The most common treatment seems to be that unrealised losses *must* be deducted for tax purposes but unrealised gains may be deferred.

THE MULTICURRENCY MANAGEMENT CENTER

Some multinational companies have set up currency handling centers to centralise the control of the many currencies used by a multinational company. It is likely that the cost of such a center will outweigh the benefits unless the value of currency handled is substantial. There may also be problems in persuading the various tax authorities to accept the center as a legitimate business venture and not simply a vehicle for tax avoidance. However, once a multicurrency management center (MMC) has been set up, it can provide possibilities for minimising a corporation's tax bill, although this is unlikely to be the prime objective for setting up the center.

Since the MMC is likely to be used to centralise the processing of invoices in various currencies, it can be arranged that the MMC carries the foreign exchange risk for the entire corporation. However, the tax implications of such a move need to be studied carefully. The problem is that an offshore tax haven may eliminate or reduce the tax charge on foreign exchange gains, but not provide any relief for foreign exchange losses or the cost of administering the MMC itself. The MMC should also be set up in a location which has tax treaties with other countries which are beneficial to the multinational involved. For example, tax on interest or dividend withheld at source should be amenable to reduction and foreign tax credits should be capable of being offset against local taxes. The location will be chosen after a careful assessment of the worldwide tax burden of the company in the context of the tax legislation in each operating location.

If a multinational wishes to charge the foreign exchange losses and the administration cost of the MMC between its various subsidiaries it will require to prove the need for the MMC other than as a tax avoidance device. This is best effected by charging a fee for the use of the MMC to subsidiaries, perhaps 0.5% of the value of each deal. This charge would be in line with a fee charged by an independent agency. Tax authorities tend to view fees paid to offshore MMCs with great suspicion, particularly where the local corporation rate is very low. A scheme for pooling foreign exchange gains or losses plus MMC costs is likely to meet a more favourable response from the tax authorities.

DEVISING A FOREIGN EXCHANGE TAX STRATEGY

The multiplicity of rules imposed on foreign exchange gains and losses by the tax authorities makes it difficult to see the wood for the trees. The treasurer, or his tax adviser, tends to be overwhelmed by the sheer volume of rules, controls, and exceptions. The problem is compounded by the frequent changes in the rules of the game. Infact, tax effect of foreign exchange profits and losses is, unfortunately, one of the most volatile and obscure aspects of international taxation.

The *first step* in devising a tax strategy must be to decide on an objective. This is to maximise profit net of tax, not, be it noted, to minimise the tax bill. This objective, however, must be placed in a proper perspective. Tax planning is a subsidiary activity within the general business strategy. The tax strategy is subject to more important business goals. For example, if a multinational decides to maximise the autonomy of its foreign subsidiaries it is not likely to allow a tax tactic of repaying loans to obtain tax credits to compromise this key policy objective. Low profits in certain foreign subsidiaries, manipulated for tax reasons, could demoralise the key staff of the foreign subsidiary and damage the image of the corporation.

Tax planning must be integrated into the corporation's overall business policy. This said, the variation of the tax treatment of exchange gains and losses provides considerable scope for the ingenuity of the corporation treasurer. Particular attention should be paid to the lack of symmetry in the tax laws.

The *second step* in devising tax strategy is to set out a table of the tax rules, exchange controls and tax rates in each country where the multinational operates. This is the frame within which the tax strategy is built. The *third step* is to set down the expected cash flows in each currency and the assets and liabilities held in each currency. This table should already have been prepared as one of the stages in conventional exposure management. The *fourth step* is to examine the possible tax effects of future transactions, in particular loans in foreign currencies, forward cover and translation gains or losses. The possible benefits and costs of channeling transactions through an offshore tax haven should also be considered at this stage. The treatment of individual transactions will depend upon the tax laws and exchange control extant at that particular time. The flavour of what is possible can perhaps be gauged from the various tax strategies which are directed to maximise income *net of tax*. To illustrate, the financial assets can be shifted between subsidiaries so that translation gains will occur in countries where the tax on such gains is low or non-existant. Intercompany debt repayment can be accelerated to avoid expected exchange gains on a loan if the tax on this gain is significant. One subsidiary can borrow from another in a weak foreign currency if the exchange gain on the loan devaluation is not taxed, and borrow in a strong currency if the loss on the loan revaluation is allowable. In both cases the tax effect may be the key factor in the decision as to which currency one should borrow. If the unrealised loss on a foreign loan is not allowed against tax until the loan is repaid, repay it and refinance funding. Ensure that allowable exchange losses occur in those countries where tax rates are highest. Exchange rate gains may be concealed by off-balance sheet financing such as leasing in a weak currency country. A subsidiary in a weak currency country can be funded by a foreign loan. The exchange loss can be set off against local profits. If additional depreciation is not allowed on the assets held in a devaluing country, sell the assets and re-equip the corporation, perhaps with second-hand assets from abroad. Finance a venture with a series of short-term roll-over loans which are exchange loss allowable against tax rather than with a long-term loan which is only allowable on termination of the loan. Make all currency contracts assignable, i.e. saleable. A gain may be taxed at the lower capital gains rate or be free of tax. All of these schemes must conform to the local exchange control regulations, but within the framework of the regulations much can be done to alleviate the tax burden.

ILLUSTRATIVE PROBLEMS

1. Which of the following transactions of affiliate A of a U.S. parent company results in transaction exposure to the parent company? Explain in each case the reasoning behind your answer.

(a) Affiliate ABC enters into a long-term lease agreement denominated a country ABC's currency.

(b) Affiliate ABC acquires new equipment payable in cash in country ABC's currency.

(c) Affiliate ABC sells good son credit terms to residents of country ABC.

(d) Affiliate ABC buys equipment from the parent company denominated in U.S. dollars.

(e) Affiliate ABC enters a contract to provide raw materials to affiliate XYZ over a period of time (transaction denominated in currency ABC).

(f) Affiliate ABC enters a contract to provide components to affiliate XYZ over a period of time (transaction denominated in currency XYZ).

(g) Affiliate ABC expedites collection of its local accounts receivables.

(h) Affiliate ABC executes a forward contract to sell currency ABC forward against U.S. dollars.

(i) Affiliate ABC executes a forward contract to sell currency ABC forward against Japanese yens.

(j) Affiliate ABC leases equipment to another company operating in country ABC specifying that lease rates are payable in U.S. dollars.

(k) Affiliate ABC declares a dividend to the parent company payable immediately.

(l) Affiliate ABC declares a dividend to the parent company payable in three months.

Ans.:

(a) Yes, Although Affiliate ABC cannot have transaction exposure in its own currency, the commitment creates an exposure for the parent company.

(b) No.

(c) Yes, See (a).

(d) No. The U.S. parent cannot have transaction exposure in U.S. dollars.

(e) Yes.

(f) Yes.

(g) No.

(h) No. Transaction creates exposure for Affiliate ABC, not the U.S. parent.

(i) Yes. Transaction creates exposure for both the affiliate and the parent.

(j) No.

(k) No.

(l) Yes. Transaction creates a receivable for the parent denominated in ABC's currency.

2. Translate the following balance sheets of the two subsidiaries of ABC, Inc. (a U.S. MNC) into U.S. dollars, using: (a) monetary-nonmonetary method, and (b) the current method of translation.

	U.K. Subsidiary (Millions of Pounds Sterling)		*French Subsidiary (Millions of French Francs)*	
	12/31/2011	12/31/2012	12/31/2011	12/31/2012
Cash and marketable securities	120	143	2,143	1,915
Accounts receivable	315	407	4,020	3,775

Inventories	612	750	3,950	3,850
Fixed assets (net)	1,350	1,300	7,010	6,850
Total assets	2,397	2,600	17,123	16,390
Bank loans	500	450	3,000	2,800
Accounts payable	490	553	4,873	4,658
Long-term debt	650	700	4,250	4,000
Net worth	757	897	5,000	4,932
Total liabilities and net worth	2,397	2,600	17,123	16,390

Assume the following exchange rates

12/31/2012 £1.00 = U.S. $1.40 U.S. $1.00 = FF7.25
12/31/2011 £1.00 = U.S. $1.05 U.S. $1.00 = FF9.00

Show also how the parent company will reflect the exchange gains (losses) in its consolidated statements, using the monetary-nonmonetary method as against the current method.

Ans.:

U.K. SUBSIDIARY
(MILLION OF U.S. DOLLARS)

		£ 1.00=$1.40	
	£1.00=$1.05 12/31/2012	*Current 12/31/2012*	*Temporal 12/31/2012*
Cash and marketable securities	150	200	200
Accounts receivable	427	570	570
Inventories	788	1,050	788
Fixed assets (net)	1,365	1,820	1,365
Total assets	2,730	3,640	2,923
Bank loans	472	630	630
Accounts payable	581	774	774
Long-term debt	735	980	980
Net worth	942	942	539
Adjustment to stockholders' equity		314	
Total liabilities and net worth	2,730	3,640	2,923
Translation gain (loss)			(404)

Exchange gain (loss) under the current method:

(Exposed assets—exposed liabilities) (change in exchange rate)
= (2,600–1,703) ($0.35) = $314 million

Exchange gain (loss) under the monetary – nonmonetary method =

(Exposed assets – exposed liabilities) (change in exchange rate)

= (550–1,703) ($0.35) = –$404 million

FRENCH SUBSIDIARY
(MILLIONS OF U.S. DOLLARS)

		$1.00=FF7.25	
	$1.00=FF9.00 12/31/2012	*Current 12/31/2012*	*Temporal 12/31/2012*
Cash and marketable securities	212.8	264.1	264.1
Accounts receivable	419.4	520.7	520.7
Inventories	427.8	531.0	427.8
Fixed assets (net)	761.1	944.8	761.1
Total assets	1,821.1	2,260.7	1,973.7
Bank loans	311.1	386.2	386.2
Accounts payable	517.6	642.5	642.5
Long-term debt	444.4	551.7	551.7
Net worth	548.0	548.0	393.3
Adjustment to stock-holders' equity		132.2	
Total liabilities and net worth	1,821.1	2,260.7	1,973.7
Translation gain (loss)			(154.7)

Exchange gain (loss) under the current method:

= (16,390–11,458) ($0.1379–0.1111) = (4.932) (+$0.0268)

= –$132.2 million

Exchange gain (loss) under the monetary—nonmonetary method (temporal) method:

$(5,690–11,458) ($0.1379–$0.1111) = (–5,768) (+$0.0268)

= –$154.6 million

3. Show the impact on the cash flow of ABC, Inc., and U.S. MNC in years 1-3, arising from the appreciation of the French franc from U.S. 1.00 = FF9.00 to U.S. 1.00 = FF7.25, given the following data:

Base Cash Scenario			
Sales	*Units*	*Unit Price (FF)*	*Total (FF million)*
Domestic	5,000,000	3.50	
Export	1,500,000	4.50	
Total sales revenue			

Production Costs				
Local labour	500,000	man-hours	12.00	
Local inputs	6,500,000	units	0.75	
Imported inputs (from parent co.)	4,500,000	units	1.25	
Total production cost				
Net operating income				
Overhead costs				1.25
Depreciation				1.00
Net profit before tax				
Income tax at 40%				
Profit after tax				
Add back depreciation				
Cash flow in French francs				
Cash flow in U.S. dollars				

OTHER ASSUMPTIONS

Scenario 1

All variables remain unchanged. Sale price in export markets remain fixed in foreign currencies, which depreciated vis-a-vis the French franc by an average of 10 per cent.

Scenario 2

Unit price for domestic sales decreases by 5 per cent in year 1 and by another 5 per cent in year 3.

- Foreign sales decline by 10 per cent and unit price (in French franc equivalent) decreases by 5 per cent to offset in part the appreciation of the franc against currencies of export markets.
- Labour cost increases by 5 per cent annually. Unit price of imported inputs reflects the full impact of the depreciation of the U.S. dollar vis-a-vis the

Scenario 3

No change in domestic sales and unit price.

- Foreign sales remain unchanged both in volume and unit price (the consumers in those markets absorb the full price increase in terms of their local currencies).
- Due to lower cost of inputs imported from the parent company, 1,000,000 units of imported inputs are substituted in each of year 2 and 3 for 1,500,000 units of local inputs.
- ABC, Inc., uses a cost of capital of 15 per cent to evaluate capital investments abroad.
- No changes in working capital requirements are assumed in this problem.

Ans.:

BASE CASE SCENARIO

Sales	*Units*	*Unit Price (FF)*	*Total (FF million)*
Domestic	5,000,000	3.50	17.50
Exports	1,500,000	4.50	6.75
Total sales revenue		24.25	
Production Costs			
Local labour	500,000 man-hours	12.00	6.00
Local inputs	6,500,000 units	0.75	4.88
Imported inputs (from parent co.)	4,500,000 units	1.25	5.63
Total production costs			16.51
Net operating income			7.74
Overhead costs			1.25
Depreciation			1.00
Net profit before tax			5.49
Income tax at 40%			2.20
Profit after tax			3.29
Add back depreciation			1.00
Cash flow in French francs			4.29
Cash flow in U.S. dollars	(4.29/9.00)=$476,667		

SCENARIO 1

Sales	*Units*	*Unit Price (FF)*	*Total (FF million)*
Domestic	5,000,000	3.50	17.50
Export	1,500,000	4.05	6.08
Total sales revenue			23.58
Production Costs			
Local labour	500,000 man-hours	12.00	6.00
Local inputs	6,500,000 units	0.75	4.88
Imported inputs (from parent co.)	4,500,000 units	1.25	5.63
Total production cost			16.51
Net operating income			7.07
Overhead costs			1.25
Depreciation			1.00
Net profit before tax			4.82
Income tax at 40%			1.93
Profit after tax			2.89
Add back depreciation			1.00
Cash flow in French francs			3.89
Cash flow in U.S. dollars	(3.89/7.25)=$536,552		

SCENARIO 2 (YEAR 1)

Sales	*Units*		*Unit Price (FF)*	*Total (FF million)*
Domestic	5,000,000		3.325	16.63
Export	1,350,000		4.275	5.77
Total sales				22.40
Production Costs				
Local labour	500,000	man-hours	12.60	6.30
Local inputs	6,500,000	units	0.75	4.88
Imported inputs (from parent co.)	4,500,000	units	1.01	4.55
Total production cost				15.73
Net operating income				6.67
Overhead costs				1.25
Depreciation				1.00
Net profit before tax				4.42
Income tax at 40%				1.77
Profit after tax				2.65
Add back depreciation				1.00
Cash flow in French francs				3.65
Cash flow in U.S. dollars	(3.65/7.25)=$503,449			

SCENARIO 2 (YEAR 2)

Sales	*Units*		*Unit Price (FF)*	*Total (FF million)*
Domestic	5,000,000		3.325	16.63
Export	1,350,000		4.275	5.77
Total sales revenue				22.40
Production Costs				
Local labour	500,000	man-hours	12.60	6.30
Local inputs	6,500,000	units	0.75	4.88
Imported inputs (from parent co.)	4,500,000	units	1.01	4.55
Total production costs				16.05
Net operating income				6.35
Overhead costs				2.25
Depreciation				1.00
Net profit before tax				4.10
Income tax at 40%				1.64
Profit after tax				2.46
Add back depreciation				1.00
Cash flow in French francs				3.46
Cash flow in U.S. dollars	(3.46/7.25)=$477,241			

SCENARIO 2 (YEAR 3)

Sales	*Units*		*Unit Price (FF)*	*Total (FF million)*
Domestic	5,000,000		3.159	15.79
Export	1,350,000		4.275	5.77
Total sales revenue				21.56
Production Costs				
Local labour	500,000	man-hours	12.60	6.30
Local inputs	6,500,000	units	0.75	4.88
Imported inputs (from parent co.)	4,500,000	units	1.01	4.55
Total production costs				16.05
Net operating income				5.51
Overhead costs				2.25
Depreciation				1.00
Net profit before tax				3.26
Income tax at 40%				1.30
Profit after tax				1.96
Add back depreciation				1.00
Cash flow in French francs				2.96
Cash flow in U.S. dollars	(2.96/7.25)=$408,276			

SCENARIO 3 (YEAR 1)

Sales	Units		Unit Price (FF)	Total (FF million)
Domestic	5,000,000		3.50	17.50
Export	1,500,000		4.50	6.75
Total sales revenue				24.25
Production Costs				
Local labour	500,000	man-hours	12.00	6.00
Local inputs	6,500,000	units	0.75	4.88
Imported inputs (from parent co.)	4,500,000	units	1.25	5.63
Total production costs				16.51
Net operating income				7.74
Overhead costs				1.25
Depreciation				1.00
Net profit before tax				5.49
Income tax at 40%				2.20
Profit after tax				3.29
Add back depreciation				1.00
Cash flow in French francs				4.29
Cash flow in U.S. dollars	(4.29/9.00)=$476,667			

SCENARIO 3 (YEAR 2 AND 3)

Sales	*Units*	*Unit Price (FF)*	*Total (FF million)*
Domestic	5,000,000	3.50	17.50
Export	1,500,000	4.50	6.75
Total sales revenue			24.25
Production Costs			
Local labour	500,000 man-hours	12.00	6.00
Local inputs	5,000,000 units	0.75	3.75
Imported inputs (from parent co.)	5,500,000 units	1.01	5.56
Total production costs			15.31
Net operating income			8.94
Overhead costs			1.25
Depreciation			1.00
Net profit before tax			6.69
Income tax at 40%			2.68
Profit after tax			4.01
Add back depreciation			1.00
Cash flow in French francs			5.01
Cash flow in U.S. dollars	(5.01/7.25)=$691,034		

Aggregate PV of Changes in Cash Flow from Base Case (U.S. dollars)

Year	*PV factor at 15%*	*Scenario 1*	*Scenario 2*	*Scenario 3*
1	.8696	+ 59,885	+ 26,783	—
	PV	+ 52,076	+ 23,290	—
2	.7561	+ 59,885	+ 574	+ 214,367
	PV	+ 45,279	+ 434	+ 162,083
3	.6575	+ 59,885	− 68,391	+ 214,367
	PV	+ 39,374	− 44,967	+ 140,946
Aggregate PV at 15%		+$136,723	—$17,752	+$303,029

The overall change in the value of the firm reflecting the 3-year impact of the appreciation of the currency of the affiliate (French francs), ranges from an increase of $303,029 in Scenario 3 to a decrease of $17,751 in Scenario 2.

QUESTIONS AND PROBLEMS

1. Explain why economic exposure cannot arise from expected changes in the exchange rates. Does this hold true even if exchange markets are not efficient?
2. Show how each of the following factors may impact the economic exposure of a

U.S. parent company resulting from the operations of its affiliate in country. ABC whose currency has depreciated against the U.S. dollar.

a. The cost structure of affiliate ABC.
b. The elasticity of demand ABC's products in country ABC.
c. Competition to affiliate ABC's products in third-country markets.
d. Ability of affiliate ABC to substitute local inputs for components sourced from the parent company.
e. The time value of money.

3. Why is economic exposure difficult to measure? Suggest a scenario where an expected decline in the present value of a firm (due to negative economic exposure) may actually turn out to be beneficial to the firm.
4. What are the basic translation methods? How do they differ?
5. Define exposure, differtiating between accounting and economic exposure. What role does inflation play?
6. Does foreign exchange risk matter? Discuss what multinational companies used to manage their exposure. Examine both the economic fundamentals and the behavioural consideration of the corporate treasurer.
7. Calculate the balance sheet translation gain/loss using the all-current, current/non-current monetary/non-monetary and temporal methods, for the following:

   US parent company
   Indian subsidiary
   Indian rupee depreciates from ₹ 53.50 to ₹ 57.50 against dollar
   Indian balance sheet is as follows:

	₹ crore
Cash	20
Marketable securities (valued at cost)	40
Inventory (written down to current market value)	100
Fixed assets	140
Total assets	300
Short-term payables	80
Long-term debt	120
Total Liabilities	200
Net worth	100

8. Why are even cash flows of a purely domestic firm exposed to exchange rate fluctuation?
9. What factors affect the firm's degree of translation exposure? Explain how each factor influences translation exposure.
10. Compare and contrast transaction exposure and economic exposure. Why would an MNC consider examining only its "net" cash flows in each currency when assessing its transaction exposure?
11. According to finance theory, what determines whether an exposure to currency risk should be hedged.

12. List three information-based reasons for hedging a translation exposure to currency risk.
13. How can corporate hedging of translation exposure reduce the agency conflict between managers and other stakeholders? In what other ways can agency conflicts be reduced?
14. Identify several cross-border differences in corporate hedging of translation exposure. What might account for these differences?
15. Recommend some general policies for deciding whether to hedge a translation exposure to currency risk.
16. What factors affect a firm's degree of transaction exposure in a particular currency? For each factor, explain the desirable characteristics that would reduce transaction exposure.
17. What options are open to reduce exposure in a devaluation/depreciation-prone subsidiary? How might each of these options affects the business and the management incentives of the subsdiary?
18. You are a financial manager of a multinational manufacturing company and your finance director has asked you to prepare a paper on exposure definition. Outline the accounting and cash flow approaches and make your recommendations.
19. Finlandiva, a furniture manufacturer based in Finland, is owned by Couch Potato, Inc. of the United States. Finlandiva's balance sheet at the current exchange rate of $1.00/e is shown in the following table:

	Value in euros	*Value at $1.00/e*	*Value at $0.80/e*	*Translation gains or losses*
Assets				
Cash & marketable securities	e50,000	$50,000		
Accounts receivable	e30,000	$30,000		
Inventory	e20,000	$20,000		
Plant & equipment	e900,000	$900,000		
Total assets	e1,000,000	$1,00,000		
Liabilities				
Accounts payable	e125,000	$125,000		
Short-term debt	e75,000	$75,000		
Long-term debt	e750,000	$750,000		
Net worth	e50,000	$50,000		
Total liabilities & net worth	e1,00,000	$1,000,000		

Answer each of the following questions under the current/noncurrent rate method, the temporal method, and the current rate method. (Use current exchange rates for inventory in the temporal method.)

(a) Identify Couch Potato's exposed assets, exposed liabilities, and net exposed assets under each accounting translation method.

(b) Identify the impact of a 20 percent depreciation of the euro on Couch Potato's consolidated balance sheets under each accounting translation method.

20. **Vincent**'s Folly, a yo-yo manufacturer based in Canada, is owned by YoBeta, Inc. of the United States. Vincent's balance sheet at the current exchange rate of C$1.60/$ is shown as follows

	Value in C$	Value at C$1.60/$	Value at C$1.50/$	Translation gains or losses
Assets				
Cash & marketable securities	C$320,000	$200,000		
Accounts receivable	C$160,000	$100,000		
Inventory	C$640,000	$400,000		
Plant & equipment	C$480,000	$300,000		
Total assets	C$1,600,000	$1,000,000		
Liabilities				
Accounts payable	C$320,000	$200,000		
Wages payable	C$160,000	$100,000		
Net worth	C$1,120,000	$700,000		
Total liabilities & net worth	C$1,600,000	$1,000,000		

Answer each of the following questions under the current/noncurrent rate method, the temporal method, and the current rate method. (Use current exchange rates for inventory in the temporal method.)

a. Identify YoBeta's exposed assets, exposed liabilities, and net exposed assets under each accounting translation method,

b. Identify the impact of a depreciation of the U.S. dollar from C$1.60/$ to C$1.50/$ on YoBeta's consolidated balance sheets under each accounting translation method.

21. Silver Saddle Motel of Sante Fe, New Mexico, has the following balance sheet.

Assets		*Liabilities and Owners' Equity*	
Current assets		Current liabilities	
Cash & marketable securities	$15,000	Accounts payable	$30,000
Accounts receivable	$10,000	Wages payable	$10,000
Fixed assets		Short-term debt	$50,000
Supplies (towels, etc.)	$25,000	Long-term liabilities	
Property and buildings	$950,000	Long-term debt	$500,000
		Owners' equity	$410,000
Total assets	$1,000,000	Liabilities & owners' equity	$1,000,000

Silver Saddle's accounts payable balance is a Peso300,000 purchase of authentic Mexican rugs and blankets for use in the motel. The purchase was placed on the books at an exchange rate of $0.10/peso. The balance is due in six months and is payable in Mexican pesos. To hedge this peso exposure, Silver Saddle buys Peso300,000 six months forward at a forward rate of $0.10/peso.

(a) What will Silver Saddle's accounts look like if this forward transaction is capitalized on the balance sheet?

(b) Calculate Silver Saddle's debt ratio (total debt to total assets) and current ratio (current assets to current liabilities) before and after the forward contract is capitalized.on the balance sheet. Is Silver Saddle's financial risk higher or lower after Mexican peso liability is hedged? How do you reconcile this conclusion with the apparent deterioration in Silver Saddle's debt and current ratios? Explain.

22. Why do you think foreign exchange gains on capital transactions are often exempt from tax, or suffer a lower rate of tax compared to profits on revenue transactions?
23. 'Two basic approaches are discernible in the tax treatment of foreign exchange gains and losses.' Describe these two basic approaches.
24. Provide an example of the profit on foreign exchange arising from the sale of 10,000 widgets from a Nanda Enterprises to a British company. Assume a rise in sterling against the Indian rupee.
25. Sterling & Company is a world renowned manufacturer of silverware. Their factory is in Sevenoaks in the United Kingdom. Although Sterling exports to companies around the world, its biggest customers are in the United States. Accounts that are denominated in dollars are indicated in the following balance sheet The exchange rate is currently \$1.50/£.

	Value in local currency	*Value in pounds*		*Value in local currency*	*Value in pounds*
Cash (\$)	\$30,000	£20,000	Payable (\$)	\$45,000	£30,000
Cash(£)		£20,000	Payables (£)		£10,000
Receivable(£)		£30,000			
Inventory)£)		£10,000			
Currency assets		£80,000	Current liabilities		£40,000
			Long-term debt (\$)	\$90,000	£60,000
			Long-term debt (£)		£20,000
Real assets		£80,000	Net worth		£40,000
Total assets		£160,000	Total liabilities	£160,000	

(a) What is the value of monetary assets and of monetary liabilities that are exposed to the dollar? What is the value of net monetary assets with a dollar exposure?

(b) If the dollar appreciates by 10 percent, by how much will monetary assets change in value? By how much will monetary liabilities change in value? What are the r-squares of these relations?

(c) Suppose inventory is not exposed to the dollar and that the exposure of real assets to the value of the dollar is $b^{\$} = r_{R,s}$ (sR/ss), where $r_{R,s} = 0.10$, $s_R = 0.20$, and $s_s = 0.10$. If the dollar rises in value by 10 percent, by how much are Sterling & Company's real assets likely to change in value? Do you have much confidence in this estimate of the change in value? Why or why not

(d) Given your results in parts b and c, by how much is Sterling & Company's equity likely to change in value with a 10 percent appreciation of the dollar?

(e) Sterling has a relatively large amount of debt denominated in dollars. Is this amount of dollar debt reasonable given their operating exposure from part c? Relate your answer to the r-square of the exposure coefficient in part c.

(f) Sterling is considering opening a manufacturing plant in the United States to hedge their exposure to the dollar. Discuss the advantages and disadvantages of this operating hedge of Sterling's dollar exposure.

26. Why is operating exposure to currency risk more difficult to manage than transaction exposure?

27. Studies have found that corporations based in the United States typically have low exposures to other currencies. In contrast, studies have found that a much higher percentage of firms in other countries (including Canada, Germany, and Japan) are exposed to the dollar. Why might this be? What does it suggest about currency risk management in these countries relative to currency risk management in the United States?

28. Do you consider it fair to tax unrealised foreign exchange gains?

29. Describe the possible tax advantages of setting up an MNC.

17

THE EXPOSURE INFORMATION SYSTEM

INTRODUCTION

Just as with other areas of corporate exposure management, no single exposure information system will be right for all companies. The appropriate system must be firm-specific. It must take account of the size of the company and its constituent units, the exposure objectives and strategy of the company, its operating and organizational characteristics, personnel strengths, and so on.

GENERAL REPORTING PRINCIPLES

There are, five basic elements which should be present in all exposure information systems:

1. *The information should be anticipatory.* Since the objective is to make decisions about how to handle future events then the focus should be on forecast data. Historical information per se is of limited value
2. *Reporting frequency must be adequate.* In practice, quarterly reporting from major operating units is usually too infrequent for treasury management purposes, given that significant operational and exchange rate changes can take place in the interim. Hence infrequent reporting can mean that exposure decision making is overtaken by actual events.
3. *The information flow should be direct to the treasury.* The channeling of treasury information flows via controller/accounting departments causes delays and weakens the link between operating and group treasury management. This can also impede exposure identification if such information is aggregated by division or into a single currency.
4. *The rationale of the information requirement must be understandable.* For motivational purposes it is essential that the data gathers (operating units) understand how their information is to be used, and its importance. The onus of communication here lies with corporate and/or regional treasury.
5. The degree of information required should be subsidiary-specific. While the typical problem is that exposure reports are insufficiently detailed it is also a mistake to ask all operating units, big and small alike, to adhere to the same reporting requirements. A 20-line monthly balance sheet exposure report from a subsidiary with Rs. 250 crores annual sales may be worthwhile; if the same report is requested from the Rs. 5 crores units then management time and motivation are needlessly wasted.

These are the general reporting principles which should be the basis of all exposure information systems. For analytical purposes these systems can be categorized into two functional components: the **exposure identification** system, which supplies information on the accounting and/or cash flow *exposures generated by* group companies; and the **exposure management information system**, which provides details of the decision parameters and constraints to be considered in deciding what exposure management action is required. These 2 components are analyzed separately below.

THE EXPOSURE IDENTIFICATION SYSTEM

The structure of the exposure identification system requires a set of exposure reports is required for each of balance sheet translation, income statement translation, and cash flow exposures. The scope and frequency of these reports should be a function of the size and exposure characteristics of each operating unit - the larger and more unstable are the exposures, the more frequent should be the exposure reporting system. An outline of a comprehensive exposure information system in given in Table-1.

TABLE-1

Outline of Exposure Identification System

Reporting Unit / *Reporting Frequency*	*Major units*	*Minor Units*
ANNUAL	Pro-forma balance sheet Pro-forma income statement. Pro-forma flow of funds Review of credit facilities and investment opportunities	Pro-forma balance sheet Pro-forma income statement. Pro-forma flow of funds Review of credit facilities and investment opportunities
QUARTERLY	Balance sheet exposure forecast long form Income statement exposure forecast	Balance sheet exposure forecast long form Income statement exposure forecast
MONTHLY	Balance sheet exposure forecast short-form Transactional exposure forecast	
INTRA-MONTHLY	Adhoc notification of material changes in exposures	Adhoc notification of material changes in exposures

The annual reports simply consists of financial statement projections and an outline of available credit facilities and investment opportunities. Most of these reports should already be prepared for general planning purposes. Hence their inclusion in the exposure identification system does not represent a significant additional reporting identification system, does not represent a significant additional reporting burden for either major or minor units. The objective here is to give the treasury department a broad picture of the future activities of each of the units.

Quaterly reporting should be oriented much more towards exposure measurement and management. The basic accounting exposure information is provided in the balance sheet exposure report (long form for major units, short form for minor units) and income statement exposure forecast (major units only). Specimen copies are provided in Table 2, 3 and 4 respectively. A key characteristic of these reports is that

TABLE-2
Balance Sheet Exposure Forecase—Long Form

Unit	Prepared By__________
Unit Code No.	Date Prepared__________
Location	Balance Sheet Reporting Date__________
Local Currency	

All amounts in $1000 equivalent, using budget exchange rates issued by Corporate Treasury

Balance sheet - line	*Balance sheet account*	*Items translated at current exchange rates*			*Items translated at historical exchange rates*	TOTAL
		Parent currency (US$)	*Local currency*	*Foreign* currency*		
	ASSETS					
1	Cash					
2	Short term investment					
	Trade receivables:					
3	intercompany					
4	third party					
5	Short term intercompany loans					
6	Inventory					
7	Prepaid expenses					
8	Other current assets					
9	TOTAL CURRENT ASSETS					
	Long term receivables					
10	intercompany					
11	third party					
	Long term investment:					
12	intercompany					
13	third party					
14	Net fixed assets					
15	Other long term assets					
16	TOTAL LONG TERM ASSETS					
17	TOTAL ASSETS					
	LIABILITIES					
	Short term debt.					
18	intercompany					
19	third party					
	Trade payables					
20	intercompany					
21	third company					
22	Current tax payable					
23	Deferred income					
24	Other current liabilities					
25	TOTAL CURRENT LIABILITIES					
	Long term payable:					
26	intercompany					
27	third party					
28	Long term debt					
29	Other long term liabilities					
30	TOTAL LONG TERM LIABILITIES					
31	TOTAL LIABILITIES					
32	Minority interest					
33	Capital					
34	Retained earnings					
35	TOTAL EQUITY					
36	TOTAL LIABILITIES AND EQUITY					
37	Net Exposed Assets/(Liabilities) Pre-tax					
38	Forward currency Sales(Purchases)					
39	Uncovered Net Exposed Assets (Liabilities), Pre-Tax					
40	MARGINAL TAX RATE = %					

*Specify foreign currencies.

TABLE-3

Balance Sheet Exposure Forecast — Short Form

UNIT ______ UNIT LOCATION ______ PREPARED BY ______ FORECAST DATE ______

UNIT CODE NO. ______ LOCAL CURRENCY ______ DATE PREPARED ______ REPORTING DATE ______

(All amounts in $'000 equivalents, using budget exchange rates issued by corporate treasury)

Balance sheet accounr / Currency	1	2	3	4	5	6	7	8	9	10	11	12	13	14
			Receivables					Payables				PRE-TAX SUMMARY		
	Current exchange rate per $	Cash and securities	Inter company	Third party	Other assets carried at current rates	Inventory	Short-term debt	Inter company	Third Party	term debt	Long-liabilities carried at currer rate	Other Net expos-assets (liabi-lities)	Forwar currenc purchas s (sales)	Uncover-ed assets (liability) exposure
Parent currency (US $)														
Local Currency														
£														
DM														
FFr														
etc.														
Total														

Marginal Tax Rate = %

they should be broken out by currency and by unit and country of operation-otherwise tax effects are hidden, since each unit may have a different marginal tax rate. Group balance sheet and income statement exposures can then be calculated by tax adjusting each exposed line item and summarising the after-tax exposures by currency.

TABLE-4

Quarterly Income Statement Exposure Forecast

Unit ______________________ Prepared By______________________

Unit Code No. ______________________ Date Prepared______________________

Location______________________ Forecast Date: Quarter Ending__________

Local Currency ______________________

All amount in $'000 equivalents using budget exchange rates issued by corporate treasury

Income statement line	*Income statement item*	*Items translated at current exchange rates*			*Items translated at historical exchange rates*	TOTAL
		Parent currency (US$)	*Local currency*	*Foreign* currency*		
	Revenues:					
1	Domestic					
2	Intercompany					
3	Third party export					
4	Total sales					
	Less Cost of sales:					
5	Domestic					
6	Intercompany import					
7	Third party import					
8	Total cost of sales					
9	Gross profit					
	less Expenses:					
10	Selling, general, administrative					
11	Depreciation					
12	Other					
13	EBIT					
14	Interest expenses					
15	EBT					
16	Tax expenses					
17	NET INCOME					

*Specify foreign currencies
EBIT - Earning Before Interest and Tax
EBT - Earning Before Tax

The minimum reporting frequency for transactional exposures information should be monthly for major units and quarterly for minor units. This report is simply a foreign currency cash flow forecast broken out by currency and by maturity. It should differentiate between the following : (a) intercompany versus third party flows - relevant for the exposure management (e.g. lead/lag) decision; (b) capital (e.g. loan amortization, dividends, royalties) versus trading flows - relevant for the exposure management decision because of exchange controls (e.g. restrictions on the netting of financial with commercial flows and on the forward purchase or sale of foreign currency); (c) planned versus firm contractual flows - again relevant for exposures management purposes because of exchange controls on, for instance, forward cover and foreign currency borrowing; and (d) the transactional exposure report should also include details of forward contracts. Apart from identifying the net uncovered position, this also enables corporate and/or regional treasury to monitor the forward cover activities of local operating units.

In addition to periodic exposure reports, all units should submit ad hoc telex reports of material changes in exposures (accounting or cash flow) immediately the changes are anticipated or take place. Materiality should be set at a specific threshold level, defined in terms of significance to the corporate group rather than to each entity - hence it would be very unlikely that such reports would emanate from minor units. This ad hoc reporting ensures a quick management response to significant exposure developments.

The final component of the exposure identification system is a report summarizing group exposures by currency and by exposure type. This should be prepared periodically (monthly or quarterly) by corporate treasury. A sample of such a report is given in Table-5. Two important points to note are, firstly, the currencies are categorized according to the availability of forward cover. This distinction is useful since, if forward cover is not available, the pricing flexibility of the local operation becomes critical. Secondly, long and short positions in the various currencies should not be netted since the summary number would be meaningless. A net zero position across a number of currencies can hide significant exposures - for example, a company is 'long' in Brazilian cruzeiros and simultaneously is equally 'short' in Deutsche Marks, it is certainly not in a neutral exposure position.

THE EXPOSURE MANAGEMENT INFORMATION SYSTEM

Once a company has calculated its exposures on a group basis there remains the problem of deciding what management action should be taken. For most companies the first and fundamental step in the decision process is to form a view of how exchange rates are likely to change over the exposure period. This involves the collection and summation of both internal information (from international treasury, the corporate economies department, local unit personnel) and external information (major banks or currency forecasting groups).

Two common weaknesses here are that the summation process is done informally and the resulting forecast takes the form of a single point estimate. The histogramming technique is a useful means of correcting these two weaknesses. The approach is a simple one. Each forecasting rates, rather than a single point estimate. These ranges

TABLE-5

Group Exposure Projection - Summary (Rs. Crore)

PREPARED BY__________ DATE PREPARED__________

Exposure type / Currency	Balance sheet exposures as at:______	Income statement exposure period:______	Cash flow exposure period:______	Forward purchases (sales) period:______
FORWARD MARKETS				
Belgian frac				
Canadian dollar				
Dutch guilder				
French franc				
German mark				
Italian lira				
Sweden krona				
Swiss franc				
UK pound				
etc.				
TOTAL COVERABLE				
NO FORWARD MARKET				
Argentinian peso				
Brazilian cruzeiro				
Colombian peso				
Greek drachma				
Venezuelan bolivar				
etc.				
TOTAL NON-COVERABLE				

are then summarized, using weights assigned to each participant weighted probability range, expressed in histogram form, can then be compared with the appropriate forward rate for decision- making purposes. Hence subjective and implicit 'gut feeling' are systematically quantified and made explicit. Histogramming formats for the individual and summary exchange rate forecasts are shown in Table 6 and 7.

The local input into the group currency forecast, which is often neglected, is particularly important. To the extent that local management are making decisions which implicitly or explicitly are based on judgement about future exchange rates then there should be a regular two-way flow of information between local treasury, purchasing and sales personnel and corporate treasury. Local units currency reports can also be used to update corporate and/or regional treasury's records on local exchange control and tax constraints on such exposure management technique as leading and lagging, forward cover and foreign currency borrowing/investing.

TABLE-6

Exchange Rate Histogramming — Individual Forecast

INDIVIDUAL HISTOGRAM—£/$

Forecaster Assistant Treasurer International

Currency £ against US $

Forecast period THREE months

Current spot rate $2.2000 = £1

Appropriate forward rate $2.1800 = £1 (£ discount)

Date 13 December 1979

Forecast

A Expected Values	B Confidence level probability of expected values occurring *	C Forecast weighting	D Weighted probability (B × C)
2.1200 - 2.1499 (mid point) (2.1350)	0.05	0.25	0.0125
2.1500 - 2.1799 (2.1650)	0.2	0.25	0.05
2.1800 - 2.2099 (2.1950)	0.3	0.25	*0.075*
2.2100 - 2.2399 (2.2250)	0.35	0.25	0.0875
2.2400 - 2.2699 (2.2550)	0.1	0.25	0.025
	1.00		0.25

Once the currency probability ranges have been formed, these can then be applied to group exposures to produce range estimates of expected foreign exchange gains and losses. Table 8 provides a sample format for the kind of gain/loss projection which should be made for each exposure type. This format on the expected case and the projected best and worst cases, which may then be compared with the costs of eliminating the exposures. This is sensitivity analysis at its simplest but it does serve to indicate the fallibility of single point estimates. A broader range of possible outcomes can be analyzed if required.

Exposure management actions can then be taken based on a comparison of projected costs and benefits. It is important that the effectiveness of these decisions and actions are monitored. The simplest case is the analysis of the forward cover decision. Opportunity gains/losses can be estimated by comparing the forward currency receipts (payments) with those which would have been received (paid) by

TABLE-7

Exchange Rate Histogramming - Summary Forecast

Tabulated Summary Forecast

Participant weighted international* \ Expected values	2.1200-2.1499 (2.1350)	2.1500-2.1799 (2.1650)	2.1800-2.2099 (2.1950)	2.2100-2.2399 (2.2250)	2.2400-2.2699 (2.2550)
Assistant Treasurer International	0.0125	0.05	0.075	0.0875	0.025
International Economist	0.0225	0.06	0.0525	0.0150	0
International Purchasing Manager	0	0	0.06	0.09	0
Regional Treasurer	0.015	0.045	0.045	0.0375	0.0075
UK Financial Manager	0.003	0.015	0.045	0.06	0.027
Banker/consultant	0.0075	0.0525	0.0525	0.03	0.0075
Total	.0605	0.2225	0.33	0.32	0.067

*Column D of Histogramming - exercises 1 for each participant Graphical summary forecast

Graphical summary forecast

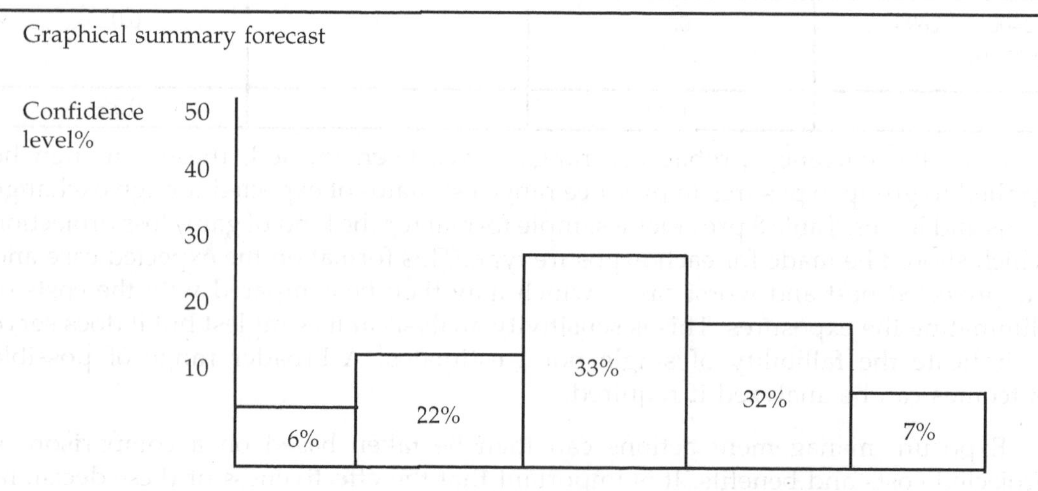

TABLE 8
FOREIGN EXCHANGE GAIN/LOSS PROJECTION

PREPARED BY________________ EXPOSURE TYPE________________

DATE PREPARED________________ EXPOSURE TIME HORIZON________________

A	B	C	D	E	F	G	H	I	J		
Currency	Exposure $'000	Expected Rate Change %	Expected Gain (Loss) $'000	Best Rate Change %	Best Case Gain (Loss) %	Worst Rate Change %	Worst Case Change %	Forward Premium (Discount) %	Net Benefit (Cost of Forward		
									Expected Case	Best Case	Worst Case
TOTAL	X	X		X		X		X			

taking the settlement date spot rate. The selective hedging strategy should also be evaluated against a 'hedge everything' as well as a 'do nothing' approach. This kind of 'post- modern' analysis is useful both for performance evaluation purposes and as an input into subsequent forward cover decision making. Similar audits can be applied to other exposure management actions.

We have outlined the kind of exposure identification and management reports which, in general terms, should be a useful element multinational company's exposures management system. It should be re-emphasized, however, that the precise form of each company's exposure information system must be tailored to its specific operating and organizational characteristics and its exposure management objectives. No single system can possibly be right for all companies.

The probabilities assigned to the expected values must add up to 1.00 (i.e. 100%) for each forecaster

Each forecaster is assigned an accuracy weighting. The weighting for all the forecaster participants must add up to 1.00 (i.e. 100%) should be supplemented (not supplanted) by a radically new approach to the evaluation of portfolio risk based on modern capital market theory. This approach enables us to assess, on a statistical basis, the riskiness of loans to projects of various types, to a number of projects in one country, and even, to some extent, of loans to governments.

QUESTIONS

1. Discuss the general principles of supporting in exposure information system.
2. Explain the structure of exposure identification system for major and minor companies.
3. Discuss the functional components of exposure information system
4. "For most companies the first and fundamental step in decision process is to form a view of how exchange rates are likely to change over the exposure period." Comment.
5. Give an outline of a comprehensive exposure information system.
6. Form group of five or six and carry out a histogramming exercise for the dollar/ sterling rate one month out. Then decide whether to cover a £1 million receivable due in one month. Finally, after one month, carry out a 'post-mortem' on your forward cover decision.
7. Devise a six-month transactional exposure forecast for the Italian subsidiary of a French company. Plug in some numbers for the Italian subsidiary's imports (on three months terms), dividend remittances and forward exchange contracts. Note that Italy and France have extensive exchange controls.
8. Construct a simple numerical example which shows that exposure reports (either balance sheet, income statement or cash flow) should be broken out by entity and country of operation if exposures are to be identified on an after-tax basis.

18

STRATEGIES FOR EXPOSURE MANAGEMENT AND TECHNIQUES FOR FOREIGN EXCHANGE RATE PROJECTIONS

INTORUDCTION

All corporate exposure management strategies must address two questions. Firstly, which definition(s) of exposure is our company concerned with? If the answer embodies more than one definition then priorities and the trade-off between the alternatives should be clearly defined—for example, how much cash are we willing to spend to protect against a given unrealised translation loss? Secondly, given our definition of exposure, what is our corporate attitude towards risk? Are we trying to maximise foreign exchange gains or minimise exchange losses? Also, what time frame are we considering—do we want to smooth short-term results at the expense of longer-term fundamentals, or vice-versa? (The time frame consideration is also relevant to the first strategy question, since short-term profit priorities will tend to induce companies to emphasise accounting rather than cash flow exposures).

STRATEGY FOR MANAGING EXPOSURE

To develop a strategy for managing the exposures, a company can take either an aggressive or a defensive approach, depending on its willingness to try to out-predict the forward rates. A key factor here is corporate's risk / return attitudes and senior management's weighting of opportunity foreign exchange losses. These do not appear in financial statements but nevertheless represent a reduction in the accounting or economic returns that the company could have made. For instance, if the treasury management decide to cover a foreign currency receivable in the forward markets and the eventual settlement date spot rate is more favourable than the forward rate previously taken, has the treasury made a bad decision? The answer will depend on how aggressive are the risk guidelines given on the treasury department by the top management.

AGGRESSIVE AND DEFENSIVE STRATEGIES

Analytically, at least, two fundamental exchange risk management strategies can be distinguished which we will call 'aggressive' and 'defensive.' (In practice, of course, these fundamental strategies rarely exist—rather, companies will tend to lie somewhere on a spectrum of risk/return trade-offs between the two polar types). The difference between these two approaches can be most easily demonstrated by reference to the case of a single and one-off export sale. The aggressive exporter would try to invoice the sale in what he expected to be a hard currency (relative to his own currency), and he would only cover the currency receivable when the forward rate of exchange was more favourable than the spot rate which he expected would prevail at the settlement date. Exchange forecasts therefore play a key role in the invoicing and forward-cover decisions. In contrast, the defensive firm would try to invoice the export sale in its home currency. Where this is not possible the exposed receivable would be automatically covered, irrespective of the view of future currency movements. Indeed, such firms would not be concerned with exchange rate forecasts since their cover policy is automatic.

These two strategies can also be applied to decisions of a more fundamental and long-term nature. As regards currency of financing, for instance, the aggressive firm would choose that currency-denomination of debt which would minimise expected effective interest costs (i.e. interest cost plus expected exchange gain/loss). In contrast, the defensive firm would match either the currency-denomination of assets with liabilities (minimising translation exposure) or the currency-denomination of cash inflows with outflows (minimising cash flow exposure), depending on how the firm defined exchange risk. Either way, a lower level of 'risk' is traded off against higher expected effective interest costs.

Now, which of these two ideal types should international companies lean towards as the basis for their exposure management strategies? A key factor here will clearly be the company's ability to forecast exchange rates and, in particular, its ability to 'beat' the forward rate.

NEED FOR FOREIGN EXCHANGE RATE PROJECTIONS

The decision of MNCs are influenced by exchange rate projection. The exchange rate forecasts are necessary in corporate decision-making to perform in global markets.

1.Hedging decision

MNCs are constantly confronted with the decision of whether to hedge future payables and receivables in foreign currencies. Whether a firm hedges may be determined by its forecasts of foreign currency values. As a simple example, consider a firm in the United States that plans to pay for Gems imported from India in 90 days. If the forecasted value of the Indian rupee in 90 days in sufficiently below the 90-day forward rate, the MNC may decide not to hedge.

2. Short-term financing decision

When large corporations borrow, they have access to several different currencies. The currency they borrow will ideally (1) exhibit a low interest rate and (2) weaken in value over the financing period. If, for example, an Indian firm borrowed Indian rupee, and the French franc depreciated against the French franc dollar over the financing period, the firm could pay back the loan with fewer rupees (when converting those rupees in exchange for the amount owed in francs). This financing decision should therefore be influenced by exchange rate forecasts of any currencies available for financing.

3. Short-term investment decision

Corporations sometimes have a substantial amount of excess cash available for a short term. Large deposits can be established in several currencies. The ideal currency for deposits would (1) exhibit a high interest rate and (2) strengthen in value over the investment period. Exchange rate forecasts of the currencies denominating available deposit accounts should therefore be considered when determining where to invest the short-term cash.

4.Capital budgeting decision

When an MNC attempts to determine whether to establish a subsidiary in a given country, a capital budgeting analysis is conducted. Forecasts of the future cash flows used within the capital budgeting process will be dependent on future currency values. This dependency can be due to (1) future inflows or outflows denomination in foreign currencies that will require conversion to the home currency, and/or (2) the influence of future exchange rates on demand for the corporation's products. There are several additional ways by which exchange rates can affect the estimated cash flows, but the main point here is that accurate forecasts of currency values will improve the estimates of the cash flows, and therefore enhance the MNC's decision-making abilities.

5. Long-term financing decision

Corporations that issue bonds to secure long-term funds may consider denominating the bonds in foreign currencies. As with short-term financing, corporations would prefer the currency borrowed (denominating the debt) to depreciate over time against the currency they are receiving from sales. To estimate the cost of issuing bonds denominated in a foreign currency, forecasts of exchange rates are required.

6. Earnings assessment

When earnings of an MNC are reported, subsidiary earnings are consolidated and translated into the currency representing the parent firm's home country. For example, consider an MNC with its home office in the United States and subsidiary in India. The Indian subsidiary's earnings francs must be measured by translation to U.S. dollars. "Translation" does not suggest that the earnings are physically converted to U.S. dollars. It is simply a recording process to periodically report consolidated earnings in a single currency. Using the scenario just described, appreciation of the rupee will boost the India subsidiary's earnings when repoted in (translated to) U.S. dollars. Forecasts of exchange rates thus play an important role in the overall forecast of an MNC's consolidated earnings.

FORECASTING TECHNIQUES

The numerous methods available for forecasting exchange rates can be categorised into four general groups: (1) technical, (2) fundamental, (3) market-based, and (4) mixed.

TECHNICAL FORECASTING

Technical forecasting of exchange rates is similar to technical forecasting of stock prices. If the pattern of currency values over time appears random, then technical forecasting is not appropriate. Unless historical trends in exchange rate movements can be identified, examination of past movements will not be useful for indicating future movements.

Technical forecasting models have helped some speculators in the foreign exchange market at various times. However, a model that has worked well in one particular period will not necessarily work well in another. With the abundance of technical models existing today, some are bound to generate speculative profits in any given period.

Many foreign exchange participants argue that even if a particular technical forecasting model is shown to lead consistently to speculative profits, it will no longer be useful once other participants begin to use it. The trading based on its recommendation would push the currency value to a new position immediately. Speculators using technical exchange rate forecasting often incur large transaction costs due to frequent trading. In addition, it can be time-consuming to monitor currency movements in the search for any systematic patter. Furthermore, speculators need sufficient capital to absorb losses that may occur.

From the corporate point of view, use of technical forecasting may be limited in that it typically focuses on the near future, which is not that helpful for developing corporate policies. Also, it rarely provides point estimates or a range of possible future values. Because technical analysis will not typically estimate future exchange rates in precise terms, it is not, by itself, an adequate forecasting tool for for corporate treasurers of MNCs.

FUNDAMENTAL FORECASTING

Fundamental Forecasting is based on fundamental relationships between economic variables and exchange rates. Given current values of these variables along with their historical impact on a currency's value, corporations can develop exchange rate projections. For example, high inflation in a given country can lead to depreciation in the currency representing that country. Of course, all other factors that may influence exchange rates should also be considered.

A forecast may arise simply from a subjective assessment of the degree to which general movements in economic variables in one country are expected to affect exchange rates. From a statistical perspective, a forecast would be based on quantitatively measured impacts of factors on exchange rates. To illustrate the application of fundamental forcasting technique, we may consider that the corporate objective is to forecast the percentage change (rate of appreciation or depreciation) in the Indian rupee with respect to the U.S. dollar during the next quarter. For simplicity, assume the firm's forecast for the Indian rupee is dependent on only two factors that affect the rupee value:

1. Inflation in the U.S. relative to inflation in India.
2. Income growth in the U.S. relative to income growth in India (measured as a percentage change).

The first step is to determine how these variables have affected the percentage change in the rupee value based on historical data. This is commonly achieved with regression analysis. First, quarterly data can be compiled for the inflation and income growth levels of both India and the U.S. The dependent variable is the quarterly percentage change in the Indian rupee value (called IR). The independent (influential) variables may be set up as follows:

1. Previous quarterly percentage change in the inflation differential (U.S. inflation rate minus Indian inflation rate), referred to as *INF*.
2. Previous quarterly percentage change in the income growth differential (U.S. income growth minus Indian income growth), referred to as *INC*.

The regression equation can be defined as

$$\text{IR} = b_o + b_1\text{INF} + b_2\text{INC} + \mu,$$

where b_o is a constant, b_1 measures the sensitivity of IR to change in *INF*, b_2 measures the sensitivity of IR to changes in *INC*, and μ represents an error term. A set of historical data would be needed to obtain previous values of *IR*, *INF*,, and *INC*. Using this data set, regression analysis will generate the values of the regression coefficients (b_o, b_1, and b_2). That is, regression analysis determined the direction and degree to which IR is affected by each independent variable The coefficient b_1 will exhibit a positive sign if, when *INF* changes, *IR* changes in the same direction (other things held constant). A negative sign indicates that *IR* and *INF* move in opposite directions. In the equation given, b_1 is expected to exhibit a positive sign, because when inflation in the U.S. relative to India increases, this exerts upward pressure on the rupee value.

The regression coefficient b_2 (which measures the impact of *INC* on IR) is expected to be positive, since when income growth exceeds Indian income growth, there is upward pressure on the rupee value.

Once regression analysis is employed to generate values of the coefficients, these coefficients can be used to forecast. To illustrate, assume the following values: b_o = .002, b_1 = .8, and b_2 = 1.0. The coefficients can be interpreted as follows. For a one-unit percentage change in the inflation differential, the rupee is expected to change by .8 percent in the same direction, other things held constant. For a one-unit percentage change in the income differential, the Indian rupee is expected to change by 1.0 per cent in the same direction, other things held constant. To develop forecasts, assume that the most recent quarterly percentage change in *INF* (the inflation differential) is 4 per cent, and that in *INC* (the income growth differential) it is 2 per cent. Using this information along with our estimated regression coefficients, the forecast for IR is

$$\begin{aligned} IR &= b_o + b_1\ \text{INF} + b_2\ \text{INC} \\ &= .002 + .8(4\%) + 1(2\%) \\ &= .2\% + 3.2\% + 2\% \\ &= 5.4\%. \end{aligned}$$

Thus, given the current figures for inflation rates and income growth, the rupee should appreciate by 5.4 per cent during the next quarter.

This example is simplified to illustrate how fundamental analysis can be implemented for forecasting. A full-blown model may include many more than two factors. Yet, the application would still be somewhat similar.

Use of Sensitivity Analysis for Fundamental Forecasting

When a regression model is used for forecasting, and the values of the influential factors have a lagged impact on exchange rates, the actual value of those factors can be used as input for the forecast. For example, if the inflation differential has a lagged impact on exchange rates, the inflation differential in the previous period may be used to forecast the percentage change in the exchange rate over the future period. However, some factors may have an instantaneous influence on exchange rates. Since these factors are not known, forecasts must be used. Firms recognise that poor forecasts of these factors can cause poor forecasts of the exchange rate movements, so they may attempt to account for the uncertainty by using *sensitivity analysis,* in which more than one possible outcome is considered for the factors exhibiting uncertainty.

Use of PPP for Fundamental Forecasting

The theory of purchasing power parity (PPP) specifies the fundamental relationship between the inflation differential and the exchange rate. In simple terms, PPP states that the currency of the relatively inflated country will depreciate by an amount that reflects that country's inflation differential. If this theory were accurate in reality, there would not be a need to even consider alternative forecasting techniques. However, using the inflation differential of two countries to forecast their exchange rate is not always accurate. Problems arise because (1) the timing of the impact of inflation fluctuations on changing trade patterns, and therefore on exchange rates, is not known with certainty, (2) data used to measure relative prices of two countries may be somewhat inaccurate, (3) barriers to trade can disrupt the trade patterns that should emerge in accordance with PPP theory, and (4) other factors, such as the interest rate differential between countries, can also affect exchange rates. For these reasons, the inflation differential by itself is not sufficient to most accurately forecast exchange rate movements. Yet, it should be included in any fundamental forecasting model.

Limitations of Fundamental Forecasting

While fundamental forecasting accounts for the expected fundamental relationships between factors and currency values, the following limitations exist:

i) Uncertain timing of impact
ii) Forecasts needed for factors with instantaneous impact
iii) Omission of other relevant factors from model
iv) Change in sensitivity of currency movements to each factor over time.

First, the precise timing of the impact of some factors on a currency's value is not known. It is possible that the impact of inflation on exchange rates will not completely occur until two, three, or four quarters later. The regression model would need to be adjusted accordingly.

A second limitation is related to those factors that exhibit an immediate impact on exchange rates. Their inclusion in a fundamental forecasting model would be useful only if forecasts could be obtained for them. Forecasts of these factors should be developed for a period that corresponds to the period in which a forecast exchange rates for is necessary. In this case, the accuracy of the exchange rate forecasts will be somewhat dependent on the forecasting accuracy of these factors. Even if firms knew exactly how movements in these factors affect exchange rates, their exchange rate projections could be inaccurate if they could not predict the values of the factors.

A third limitation is that there may be factors that deserve consideration in the fundamental forecasting process that cannot be easily quantified. For example, what if large Indian exporting firms experienced an unanticipated labour strike, causing shortages? This would reduce the availability of Indian goods for consumers, and therefore reduce demands. Such an event, which would place downward pressure on the value, is not-normally incorporated into the forecasting model.

A fourth limitation of the fundamental model is that coefficients derived from the regression analysis will not necessarily remain constant over time. Yet, if a country imposed new trade barriers, or eliminated existing barriers, the impact of the inflation differential on trade (and therefore on the exchange rate) could be affected.

Evaluation of Forecast Performance

An MNC that forecasts exchange rates must monitor its performance over time to determine whether the forecasting procedure is satisfactory. For this purpose, a measurement of the forecast error is required. There are various ways to compute forecast errors. One of the possible measurement is defined as follows:

$$\text{Absolute forecast error as a percentage of the realised value} = \frac{\text{Forecasted value} - \text{Realised value}}{\text{Realised value}}$$

The error is computed using an absolute value, since this avoids a possible offsetting effect when determining the mean forecast error. For example, consider a simplified example, in which the forecast error is .05 in the first period and -.05 in the second period (if the absolute value is not taken). The mean error here over the two periods is zero. Yet, that is misleading, since the forecast was not perfectly accurate in either period. The absolute value avoids such a distortion.

When measuring forecast performance of different currencies, it is often useful to adjust for their relative sizes, so forecasting ability can be compared among currencies. As an example, consider the following forecasted and realised values by a U.S. firm during one period:

	Forecasted Value	*Realised Value*
British pound	$ 1.35	$ 1.50
French franc	$ .12	$ .10

In this case, the difference between the forecasted value and the realised value is $ .15 for the pound, compared to $ .02 for the franc. This does not necessarily imply that the forecast of the franc is more accurate. When considering the size of what is forecast (dividing the difference by the realised value), one can see that the British pound has been predicted with more accuracy on a percentage basis. With the data given, the forecasting error of the British pound is

$$\frac{|1.35-\$1.50|}{\$1.50}=\frac{\$.15}{\$1.50}=.10, \text{ or } 10\%$$

In comparison, the forecast error of the French franc is

$$\frac{|.12-.10|}{.10}=\frac{.02}{.10}=.20, \text{ or } 20\%$$

Thus, the French franc has been predicted with less accuracy.

MARKET-BASED FORCASTING

The process of developing forecasts from market indicators, know as *market-based forecasting,* is usually based on either (1) the spot rate or (2) the forward rate.

Use of the Spot Rate

To clarify why the spot rate can serve as a market-based forecast, assume the British pound is expected to appreciate against the rupee in the very near future. This will encourage speculators to buy the pound with rupee today in anticipation of its appreciation, and these purchases could force the pound's value up immediately. Conversely, if the pound is expected to depreciate against the rupee, speculators will sell off pounds now, hoping to purchase them back at a lower price after they decline in value. Such action could force the pound to depreciate immediately. Thus, the current value of the pound should reflect the expectation of the pound's value in the very near future. Corporations can use the spot rate to forecast, since it represents the market's expectation of the spot rate in the near future.

Use of the Forward Rate

To understand why the forward rate can serve as a forecast of the future spot rate, consider the following example. Assume the 30-day forward rate of the British pound is Rs. 70 and the general expectation of speculators is that the future spot rate of the pound will be Rs. 72.50 in 30 days. If speculators expect the future spot rate to be Rs. 72.50 and the prevailing forward rate is Rs. 70, they might buy pounds 30 days forward at Rs. 70 and then sell them when received (in 30 days) at the spot rate existing then. If their forecast is correct, they will earn Rs. 2.50 per pound. If a large number of speculators implement this strategy, the substantial forward purchases of pounds will cause the forward rate to increase until this speculative demand stops. Perhaps this speculative demand will terminate when the forward rate reaches Rs. 72.50, since at this rate, no profits will be expected by implementing the strategy described. This example shows that the forward rate should move toward the market's general expectation of the future spot rate. In this sense, the forward rate serves as a market-based forecast, since it reflects the market's expectation of the spot rate at the end of the forward horizon (30 days from now in the example above).

MIXED FORECASTING

Because no single forecasting techniques has been found to be consistently superior to the others, some MNCs may prefer to use a combination of forecasting techniques. This method is referred to as **mixed forecasting.** Various forecasts for a particular currency value could be developed using several forecasting techniques. Each o the techniques used could be assigned weights in such a way that the weights totalled 100 percent, with the techniques thought to be more reliable being assigned higher weights. The actual forecast of the currency by the MNC would be a weighted average of the various forecasts developed. At present, there are three situations within present flexible exchange rate systems which have an important bearing here.

Situation 1: *Foreign Exchange Market Biases.* These occur because such market imperfections as government control and intervention cause the forward rate to deviate in systematic way from the market's actual expectation of future spot rates. This is the kind of bias which is illustrated in the *ex post,* analysis which show that the forward buying rate of US dollars and Deutsche Marks consistently under-estimated actual future dollar/sterling and Deutsche Mark/sterling rates in 1975 and 1976. When treasury management is aware of such situations then a selective forward-cover policy, for example, is worthwhile. Hence in 1975—76 a company selling dollars or Deutsche Marks for sterling would have done consistently better by taking the spot rate of settlement date rather than the forward rate; conversely, the *buyer* of dollars or Deutsche Marks for sterling should have taken the forward rate.

Situation 2: *Special Forecasting Abilities.* This is similar to the first situation in that once again there are profitable opportunities to be gained from aggressive currency management, but this time the opportunities arise because the firm has an unusual forecasting ability. It should be stressed, however, that such forecasts are unlikely to be obtained from reading the financial newspapers/journals. This kinds of information will already be embodied in the market's expected or forward rate (unless Situation 1 holds). The firm must have access to information not available to most other market participants, or access to some special expertise in interpreting generally available information, if it is to consistently 'beat' the forward rate.

Apart from the fact that both give rise to profit opportunities, these two situations have one other thing in common—they are much less likely to prevail in present flexible rate system than in the Bretton Woods era. Under the Bretton Woods system, even in its deteriorating stages in the late sixties, the forecasting game consisted of the following three-step procedure:

1. from balance of payments trends one derived the pressures on a currency.

2. the level of central bank foreign exchange reserves (including borrowing facilities) gave an indication of when the situation became critical;
3. then came the crucial step of predicting which one of the rather limited policy options the nation's economic decision makers would resort to in a crisis: internal deflation, interventionism and exchange controls, or devaluation.

Clearly, the success or failure of forecasting depended largely on step (3) and there was no doubt that some participants did very well. Some US corporations, for example, spent considerable resources on analysing both the power structure and the economic ideology of key decision makers in various countries. Moreover, since the downside risks of actions taken on the basis of these forecasts were quite limited, and also as more people caught on to this game, forecasting became more and more self-fulfilling.

Yet this situation has changed considerably. The actions of monetary authorities have become much less predictable under 'dirty' or managed floating. Short-term pressures on currencies have both increased and are no longer uni-directional—sterling, for instance, has weakened in one day by as much as 5% only to strengthen in the next few days by about 3%. Clearly, foreign exchange risks are now much greater. Essentially these developments mean that currency forecasting has become much more difficult, both in terms of the likelihood of making the right decision and the costs associated with getting the forecast wrong. This brings us to the third and most likely situation which may now prevail.

Situation 3: *Efficient Foreign Exchange Markets.* Here, the foreign exchange markets are reasonably efficient and normally financial management knows of no systematic biases or constraints on market rates. Management's currency expectations are synonymous with those of the market, as generally embodied in forward rates. Unlike the first two situations, profit opportunities are rare, occurring only when there is discernable bias in the forward rate because of government intervention and exchange controls. In this situation the aim of the international financial management should be to arrange the affairs of a company so that, whatever the exchange rate change may be, its detrimental effects on expected returns are minimised.

Before applying this general risk-minimising principle to some practical situations we must first comment, albeit briefly, on the kind of 'detrimental' effects which can arise from currency fluctuations. The kind of exposure we are concerned with here is the potential effect of currency movements on the future cash flows produced by foreign operations. In the long run the effects of an exchange the change on cash flows tend to be offset by countervailing movements in inflation and interest rates. The detrimental effects of currency movements — foreign exchange risk—therefore arises form the short-run deviations of the exchange rate around its long-run path.

DEFENSIVE STRATEGIES FOR THREE PROTOTYPE FIRMS

Rather than use an abstract microeconomic model of the firm we will introduce three prototypes, each of which exemplifies a particular kind of international operation. The aim here is to develop the sort of financial policies, appropriate for each of these three types, which will minimise the effects of a given exchange rate change. The types of operation we will discuss can be identified as follows: the capital equipment producer who *occasionally exports* one of his products; the producer of consumer goods who has developed a *significant export market*, and the *multinational company* with interrelated operations in many countries.

The Occasional Exporter

The occasional exporter is a paradoxical animal. This type of company hardly exists in reality, yet it seems that conventional exchange risk analysis is concerned exclusively with the problems faced by such a firm. The company usually produces for the domestic market but occasionally it obtains an order from abroad, and here it runs into a problem. If the export sale is invoiced in foreign currency then its receivable is subject to exchange risk. (The exporter could denominate the contract in his own currency, of course, but this simply throws the risk on the overseas company).

Conventional wisdom suggests that the solution to this kind of exchange risk problem lies in using the forward exchange markets. During the negotiations the exporter should check the forward rates quoted for the time the payment is to be received. This exchange rate is then used to decide whether or not the receipt in terms of the exporter's home currency is attractive enough to go through with the export sale.

Simultaneously with the agreement of an export sale, the exporter enters into an offsetting forward exchange transaction. This takes the form of a promise by the export company to deliver at some date in the future a certain amount of foreign currency (the export receivable). In return its contracting party, usually a bank, would promise to pay the exporter at the time a fixed amount of domestic currency. This amount is, of course, determined by the forward exchange rate prevailing at the time when all commitments are made.

Should the spot rate at settlement date—or, indeed, any appropriate forward rate available during the credit period—be more favourable than the contracted (forward) rate, then the exporter will have incurred an opportunity loss. However, this is not really relevant. He has made the decision to sell on the basis of a certain receipt (abstracting from the credit risk) at which he found the export transaction to be profitable and worthwhile. Of course, with the covering transaction he has avoided the loss resulting from a possible depreciation of the foreign currency over the credit period; in doing so he has also forgone the possibility of a gain if the foreign currency appreciates. The rationalisation for this is that the exporter is in the business of making and selling a product, and not in the foreign exchange business.

The important point to emphasise, however, is that this 'classical' covering operation will only work for a particular type of business. Should the amount that the exporter receives through the forward market be below his minimum selling price, he will simply sell his equipment in the domestic market—and this is precisely the problem. How many firms really do have this ready alternative? A far more frequent situation is the one represented by the second prototype.

The Significant Exporter

The distinguishing feature of the significant exporter is that he has permanently committed substantial resources to servicing the foreign market(s). A depreciation of the foreign currency will shrink not only the value of foreign receivables already booked, a one-time loss, but it will also affect future cash flows. The real problem, then, is the effect on the future stream of home currency revenues. What action can management take to alleviate this problem? One obvious option for exporter is to raise foreign currency prices. The long run validity of the purchasing power parity (PPP) theorem suggests that the cash flow effects of a currency movement will be offset by countervailing inflation rate changes. In the long run, then, foreign currency selling prices can be increased sufficiently to re-establish the home currency value of the export revenues to their former level. This assumes that the exporter can adjust his selling prices quickly in response to the relatively high inflation/currency depreciation rate in his exporter market. However, lengthy price adjustment lags are often an important source of exchange risk to the individual firm. (Hence a company may take forward cover against the foreign currency receipts which it expects to collect during the price adjustment period).

This 'long-run' argument also assumes that the exchange rate is located on its long-run equilibrium path. In the short run, however, exchange rates deviate significantly from their expected long-run paths—hence the definition of foreign exchange risk in terms of *unexpected* exchange rate movements. Moreover, these deviations are sufficiently large to concern management: a 'temporary' adverse deviation of an exchange rate from its expected path for a few months could have a drastic effect on exporter's cash position, rate of return on assets, and management performance reviews. For example, if the currency depreciation in the export market exceeds the compensating foreign currency price increases, the rate of return on export operations will obviously fall. It will be little comfort to the outgoing management that the exchange-rate/inflation-rate relationship will correct itself in the long—run management may not be able to afford to wait that long.

How could the classical hedging policy outline above for the 'occasional exporter' help in such a situation? Let us assume the significant exporter makes regular (monthly) shipments and bills accordingly on 90-day terms. How would the situation look if he sold his expected foreign currency receipts forward at each shipment date, instead of waiting of the currency to be remitted and then exchanging these funds through the spot market? There are two possible conditions which might have a bearing on such action: the relative transaction costs and the relative stability of the spot and forward markets.

Foreign exchange transaction costs consist of two elements: foreign exchange commissions and the spread between buying and selling rates. If transaction costs are higher in one market than the other then this might influence the choice between spot and forward markets. This issue can be settled quickly: foreign exchange commissions on forward contracts are either the same or higher than those on spot deals, and spreads tend to be larger in the forward market. Hence transaction costs in the spot market tend to be smaller. More important for our analysis is the stability of spot versus forward rates, which can be measured by the expected deviation from the current rate (spot or forward) for a given future time period. If this deviation should be less in the forward market than in the spot market then it can be argued that exchange risk will be reduced by taking the forward rate.

To illustrate, assume that the exporter receives a regular (monthly) amount of foreign currency. This he must convert into his own currency, either through the spot market as he receives the foreign exchange or by selling the expected amount receivable on a 90-days forward basis (or whatever period is appropriate to his billing procedures). Assuming that we are now operating in the Situation 3 forecasting environment (Efficient Foreign Exchange Markets), where the firm is unable consistently to outpredict forward rates, his exchange rate expectations will not influence the 'spot versus forward' choice. Yet if he were to expect greater variability from one period (month) to the next in one market versus the other, he may prefer going through the market which has less variability since he would expect its scope for unpleasant surprises to be smaller.

During the Bretton Woods era, the spot rate was expected to fluctuate less than the forward rate because central banks (with a very few, albeit notable, exceptions) concentrated their stabilising interventions in the spot market. This left forward rates free to fluctuate around the spot rates, as interest rate differentials and expectations about the future spot rates fluctuated. In the post-Bretton Woods era, however, the volume of official intervention in spot markets seems to have been considerably reduced for most currencies. A corollary of this is that the volatility of spot rates relative to forward rates of major currencies has increased.

Can our second type of exporter now use the forward market to protect profits from its export sales? We have seen that the major advantage of going through the forward market for occasional exporter was that he was able to avoid an unprofitable transaction by taking account of the forward rates. Yet what about the exporter who has developed a significant export market and whose very existence depends on this market? If he does not like the promised rate received through the forward market he has very little choice, besides shutting down his operation. Therefore he must continue to sell in the export market, his only hope being that either the 'temporary' exchange-rate/inflation-rate imbalance will reverse itself in the not-too-distant future or that he may be able to take some policy action.

Only prayer might help our firm as regards the first possibility. The second option is of more interest. Our exporter can, of course, seek out opportunities for further raising his selling prices and lowering his costs. Yet we are assuming here that our exporter is already selling at the maximum price which his markets will bear. Similarly, the question must be asked whether the firm really needs a depreciation of the currency in its export market in order to look for opportunities for cost reduction. The only type of cost reduction we are concerned with here is that which is caused directly by the currency movement. Clearly, insofar as inputs denominated in the depreciating currency are being used or can be used in the production process, some relief will be obtained. Whether this is possible or not is largely a matter of the specific production process. Little can be said here except that treasury and operating management must routinely explore this opportunity after a change in the exchange-rate/inflation-rate relationship. The result of this exploration is a significant determinant of a firm's exchange risk.

The focus of attention here, however, is on the scope for financial management action, and specifically on the exposure implications of the currency-of-financing decision. Currency-of-financing policy is potentially a very powerful exposure management tool. If a company's operations generate exposed assets or cash inflows, these exposures can be neutralised by creating financial liabilities or cash outflows in the same currencies. The net asset or cash flow variability resulting from the deviations of an exchange rate from its expected path can thus be neutralised. In concrete terms this principle suggests that a company which has built a significant export market in foreign currencies should hold a portion of its liabilities in the currency(ies) of its export markets, so that it gets relief from the very event that degenerates its operating margins.

The Multinational Company

The term 'multinational company's is used here to refer to companies which have interrelated operations in many countries. Since the shift from a discussion of the case of the exporter to that of the multinational enterprise appears to be a mental giant-step we will deal here with the simplest case possible, viz. a company that has *one* foreign manufacturing subsidiary.

Again, the important question is how the currency movement will affect the benefits (future cash flows) derived by the parent from its foreign venture. Remember that the long-run validity of the PPP and fisher theorems means that the cash flow effects of currency movements are offset, *in the long run,* by countervailing changes in relative inflation and interest rates. So what we are concerned with here is the impact of unexpected deviations of an exchange rate (either short-term oscillations or structural changes caused by, for instance, the discovery of new source of energy) from its long-run path. This impact will consist of two kinds of effects, analagous to the price and quantity effects of basic economic theory.

The first and obvious result is that foreign currency revenues will be repatriated to the parent company at a different rate of exchange. What ultimately counts, of course, is the effect on profits in terms of the currency which the parent company uses as a base currency and, more importantly, in which the company's shareholders hold their wealth.

The second type of impact is that an exchange rate change will affect the quantity of future local currency (LC) cash flows generated by foreign operations. This is the focus of financial analysis: how will the LC cash flows produced by the subsidiary be affected by, say, a depreciation of the LC? The macroeconomic adjustment process provides us with the relevant variables for such an analysis. As far as operating profit is concerned, three relevant market sectors can be distinguished in which the subsidiary buys its inputs and sells its output: the export market, the import competing sector of the domestic market, and the 'pure' domestic market (zero or negligible import penetration).

The analysis of the 'extreme case' is relatively simple. For instance, a subsidiary that sells its output in the export market and buys its inputs in the 'pure' domestic sector will undoubtedly experience a rise in LC operating profits, if the LC devaluation is greater than the compensating price-level change. This should be sufficient to convert into an increased flow of home currency (HC) units for the parent—the beneficial 'quantity' effect more than outweighs the adverse 'price' effect.

At the other extreme is the case of a subsidiary which sells its output in the 'pure' domestic market (where it faces strong competition from other local producers) while it obtains the bulk of its inputs from, say, its foreign parent. If the devaluation again overcompensates for higher LC inflation then in this case LC profitability will suffer, and the situation will look even worse in terms of the HC (i.e. 'quantity' as well as 'price' effects are adverse).

Many permutations lying between these two extremes are possible. Yet the essential point has been made: the effect of an unexpected exchange rate change on the profitability of foreign operations for the parent company depends entirely on the specific operating pattern of that subsidiary, and any management policy that does not take account of such differences is suboptimal. More particularly, the effects of a currency movement are determined by four factors: the origin of the subsidiary's inputs; the destination of its output; the degree of competition in input and output markets; and the degree of flexibility of the operation. Given the unpredictability of currency markets, the last factor is a key determinant of the susceptibility of a subsidiary to changes in exchange rates. To the extent that it can or cannot switch its sourcing and selling patterns between foreign and domestic markets and/or raise its prices, the exchange risk situation will be more or less serious.

This case flow analysis now leads us to the question of changes in stock values. The starting point here is that the economic values of assets are determined by future cash flows: as expectations about such future flows change, so do assets values. For example, the plant and equipment of the subsidiary whose export revenues are favourably affected by a currency depreciation in relation to its cost stream will be worth more, regardless of whether or not this increased value is reported in our accounting methods. Yet what about current assets and liabilities?

Inventories are relatively easy to evaluate. If the currency movement has caused the unit LC price of our final product to increase, the LC value of inventories should rise proportionately. The resulting economic value for the parent should be computed by translating the increased LC value at the new exchange rate into HC units.

The analysis becomes more controversial as we proceed to LC-denominated monetary assets, especially cash, receivables and payables. Let us again consider the exporting subsidiary whose profits increased because of the depreciation. A certain level of LC cash is required to conduct operations. What will happen to the value of this LC cash as the LC depreciates *vis-a-vis* the HC? As regards its economic value the answer will depend on the function that this monetary asset performs for the subsidiary and, most importantly, whether this function changes because of the exchange rate change.

In the case where the subsidiary's export sales volume is unchanged but it is able to raise its LC selling price by the depreciation percentage (thus leaving the foreign currency price of its output unchanged), then the normal level of LC cash balance required to continue operations will very probably stay unchanged. Since it still performs the same service for the subsidiary, it seems to us that its economic value to both subsidiary and parent company is unchanged. In other words, its HC value is unchanged.

Alternatively, should the subsidiary increase its volume of operations because of the currency movement and therefore increase the necessary level of liquid funds, a loss would be incurred. The difference between the old and the new (higher) cash balance must come from funds that otherwise would have bene transferred to the parent as profit. Instead, these funds are now tied 'forever' and become art of the investment base—in an ongoing firm they are committed forever. This change in the required cash balance should be included with the change in operating cash flows for that period in order to calculate the overall impact of a currency movement on the firm.

The same kind of analysis also holds for the subsidiary's receivables and payables. For example, an *increase* in LC payables would free LC funds and provide the parent company with additional HC cash. The analysis of payables is important, for all borrowings can be viewed as such after allowances are made for maturity.

All this will be anathema to those who tend to think about these matters in accounting terms. Just the thought of LC cash not decreasing in value in terms of the HC by the same percentage as the LC depreciation will cause considerable consternation. It may help to emphasise that the cash balance that concerns us here must be regarded as an integrated element of that bundle of assets and liabilities that make up an ongoing foreign subsidiary. It cannot be compared with a discretionary cash balance left in another country, which is obviously subject to exchange risk.

To sum up, then, the general rule governing economic loss or gain on current assets and liabilities is as follows: to the extent the exchange rate causes additional (or fewer) net current assets to be required, a one-time loss (or gain) is incurred. This loss (or gain) for the parent is equal to the additional HC funds forgone.

THE MULTINATIONAL'S RISK-MINIMISING FINANCING POLICY

Now that we have analysed the economic effects of currency movements on a firm's profitability we can turn to the problem of an appropriate currency-of-financing pattern. The rules we developed earlier for the *Significant Exporter's* can again be applied. If exposure neutralisation is the company's objective, then its liability portfolio should be structured in such a way that the outflow on liabilities (effective interest costs) offsets as much as possible the change in the inflow on assets (operating profits).

The rationale of this approach is straightforward. Manufacturing companies expect to make a profit because of their ability to exploit certain specialised market opportunities—to make cars, chemicals or computers. The role of financial management is to protect this expected profit from unexpected changes in financial market (interest and exchange rate) conditions. Protection can be achieved by manipulating operating and/or financial variables. The operating response consists of structural or business opportunities to create matched currency cash flow patterns. Operating actions, such as altering sourcing, product, plant location, market selection, credit, pricing and currency-of-invoicing policies, need to be examined. However, the currency-domination of operating variables is determined largely by intrinsic business conditions (production and marketing factors). such constraints are far less important as regards financial variables, although even here credit availability is a problem in certain environments. Generally, then, adjustments to offset exchange risk will occur on the liability rather than the asset side.

How can this general principle be implemented? The basic step is to estimate how deviations around the expected exchange rate will affect the operating cash flows of the firm as a whole. This may not be an easy task. As indicated above, operating cash flows can be affected positively, negatively or not at all by a currency movement depending on where the firm buys its inputs and sells its output and on the pricing an locational flexibility of these markets. Having established how net operating cash flows will be affected, it is then a straightforward task to choose the risk-minimising liability structure. A unit should be financed in the currency(ies) against whose value its operating cash flows are positively correlated. Take the case of a French subsidiary, exporting to Japan. Here the operating returns of the subsidiary are positively correlated with movements in the Yen and so the subsidiary should be financed in Yen. A depreciation of the Yen would then reduce not only cash inflows (operating returns) but also cash outflows (effective interest costs). In this way the change in the net cash flow on the asset side can, to some extent at least, be offset by a change on the liability side. The firm's cash flow (economic) exposure to exchange risk is thereby reduced.

QUESTIONS

1. Explain corporate objectives for forecasting exchange rates, what is the rationale forming market-based forecasts?
2. Discuss the mixed technique and the market-based technique for forecasting exchange rates.
3. Discuss the use of fundamental and technical technique for forecasting exchange rates. What are the limitation of these using forecasting techniques to predict exchange rates.
4. You are the treasurer of a multinational company and your finance director has asked you to prepare a paper on exposure management strategy. Outline the aggressive and defensive approaches and make your recommendations.
5. For a major exchange rate tabulate and graph the three-month forward (mid) rate, against the spot (mid) rate at maturity, by month over a two-year period (i.e. 24 comparisons). Does this shows the forward rate to be an inaccurate but unbiased predictor of future spot rates?
6. For the same exchange rate and period, calculate the buy-sell spreads and the stability (month-to month percentage deviations) of spot versus forward rates. Discuss the exposure management implications.
7. Why should the *occasional* exporter's exposure management strategy differ form that of the *significant* exporter or *multinational company*?

19

EXPOSURE MANAGEMENT

INTRODUCTION

There is a large and perhaps confusing variety of techniques which can be used in corporate exchange risk management. To understand the rationale underlying their use it is helpful to classify them according to their basic origin. The distinction can be made between those techniques which are *internal* to the company (mainly used as part of a company's regulatory financial management aimed at minimising its continuing exposure to exchange risk); and those which are *external* to the company, (consisting basically of contractual measures to insure against an exchange loss—realised or unrealised—which may arise from an existing transaction or exposed position).

EXPOSURE MANAGEMENT TECHNIQUES

The major internal and external techniques are listed in Table-1. The policies adopted under the internal exposure management techniques are generally aimed at *reducing* or *preventing* an exposed position from arising; the external management techniques are used to *insure* against the possibility that exchange losses will result form the exposed position which the internal measures have not been able to eliminate. The distinction is not quite as clear-cut as this, as will become evident in the following analysis, but it is nevertheless a useful way of summarising the overall range of choices available.

TABLE-1

Internal and External Exposure Management Techniques

Internal	—	Netting
	—	Matching
	—	Leading and lagging
	—	pricing policies
	—	Asset and liability management
External	—	Forward contracts
	—	Short-term borrowing
	—	Discounting
	—	Factoring
	—	Government exchange risk guarantees

This distinction is also useful because it pinpoints a common weakness of corporate exposure management—an overemphasis on external (market-related) techniques.

In all too many companies the exposure manager simply receives exposure reports from operating units and then, based on a currency forecast, decides whether or not to cover on the money markets. With this kind of approach little or no consideration be given to internal (business-related) tactics, such as matching the currency denomination of cash inflows and outflows by changing sourcing and currency of invoicing patterns. The emphasis should be placed on business-related exposure management tactics. The role of market-related techniques, which can be very costly and may even disappear when exposure are of greatest concern, should not be the sole focus.

It should also be emphasised that the various exposure management techniques described here are not available in all circumstances. This is mainly because of limitations imposed by the market-place (no forward market exists in many of the 'exotic' currencies of the less-developed nations) and by regulatory authorities (the hedging of translation exposures on the forward market is not allowed in many countries).

EXPOSURE MANAGEMENT: *INTERNAL TECHNIQUES*

The availability of internal techniques is largely a function of the international involvement of each company. The international business literature abounds with definitions of what a 'multinational' company really is, but for our present purpose a twofold classification of international penetration will suffice. *International* companies, which are simply defined here as importers or exporters, have a fairly limited range of internal exposure management options available. By contrast, *multinational* companies, defined as those which have overseas operating subsidiaries, will probably have a much more complicated network of foreign operations and hence currency exposures. Consequently, the multinational company will have access to a much broader range of exposure management techniques, both internal as well as external.

1. Netting

Netting simply means that affiliated companies which trade with each other receive or pay, at regular intervals, only the *net* amount of the intergroup debt. Gross intergroup trade receivables and payables are netted out. In the simplest kind of scheme, known as *bilateral netting,* each pair of subsidiaries nets out their own positions with each other. Flows are reduced by the lower of each company's purchases from or sales to its netting partner. There is no attempt to introduce the net positions of other group companies.

Bilateral netting is easily demonstrated by the use of a simple example. If XYZ Corporation (India) owes XYZ Corporation (UK) the sterling-equivalent of $1 million, and if XYZ Corporation (UK owes Rupees the equivalent of $3 million, then the actual cash remittance is netted out so that XYZ Corporation (UK) pays XYZ Corporation (India) the rupees (or some other currency) equivalent of only $2 million. The two companies have saved between them the exchange and transfer costs associated with $1 million of eliminated flows. Hence netting is not so much an exposure management technique but more a way of reducing the amount of intercompany receipts and payments which go through the foreign exchanges. In their more developed forms, however, netting schemes do have important organisational implications for exposure management.

Bilateral schemes are fairly straightforward to operate. The two main practical problems are that participants must decide on the currency denomination of the net remittance and on a reconciliation and settlement schedule. A centralised control system is not necessary.

Whereas bilateral netting is possible only when there are reciprocal flows between two companies, *multilateral netting* can take place whenever affiliates both import from and export to companies within the same corporate group. Flows are reduced by the lower of each company's *total* purchases from/sales to affiliates. We can illustrate multilateral netting (figure-1) by the following example. XYZ Corporation's intergroup trading is as follows: XYZ Corporation (UK)'s monthly purchases from XYZ Corporation (India) are $3 million and monthly sales to XYZ Corporation (Singapore) are $1 million; XYZ Corporation (India) monthly purchases from XYZ Corporation (Singapore) are $1 million. The netting potential in this trading pattern XYZ Corporation is demonstrated in Figure-1. The netting matrix shows that multilateral netting could eliminate 1 million in transfer from each applicate's monthly payments, even though in this example there is no scope for bilateral netting. After multilateral netting, intercompany payments consist solely of 2 million monthly form UK to India.

FIGURE-1

NETTING MATRIX ($ MILLION)

Paying unit / *Receiving unit*	*India*	*UK*	*Singapore*	*Total receipts*	*Net receipts*	*Eliminated receipts*
India	**	3	0	3	2	1
UK	0	**	1	1	—	1
Singapore	1	0	**	1	—	1
Total paymnets	1	3	1	5	**	**
Net payments	—	2	—	**	2	**
Eliminated payments	1	1	1	**	**	3

Netting potential Gross flows = $5 million
Net flows = $2 million
Eliminated flows =$3 million

The focal point in a multilateral netting scheme is the central information point (see Figure-2). Participating units must report all intercompany positions at the end of a given period, and the center then advises the units of the net amount which they are to pay or receive at a certain date. Multilateral netting, therefore, requires a centralised communications system and a lot of discipline on the part of participating units. In this process of multilateral netting, the three most common constraints are: (a) prior approval for netting may be required; (b) trading (rather than financial) transactions only may be netted; and (c) intercompany (rather than third party) transactions only may be netted.

FIGURE-2

MULTILATERAL NETTING

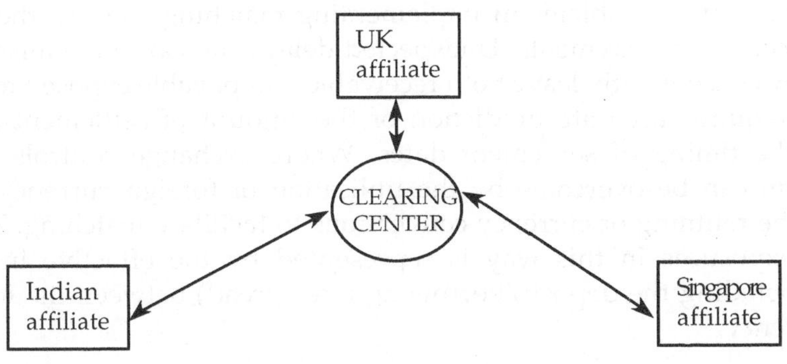

Key ⟷ = netting arrangement

The major benefits of netting are reduced banking costs and increased control of inter-company settlements. The reduced number and total amount of payment produces savings in the form of lower flow and lower exchange costs (i.e. the buy/sell spread in the spot and forward markets plus the elimination of bank charges, if any). No simple savings percentage can be universally applied to the amount netted since savings will be determined by prevailing buy/sell spreads and the structure of the payment flows eliminated. In addition, the introduction of a netting system does create opportunities for exposure and liquidity management and tax planning. A quick and easy decision format can be evolved to produce an intercompany settlement patterns which will help to achieve the company's liquidity and exposure management objectives.

2. Matching

The terms 'netting' and 'matching' are often used interchangeably. But the netting is typically used only for inter company flows to the netting out of groups receipts and payments. As such it is applicable only to the operations of a multinational company rather than the exporter or importer. In contrast, matching can be applied to both third party as well as inter-company cash flows, and it can be used by the exporter/importer as well as the multinational company. It is a process whereby a company matches its currency inflows with its currency outflows with respect to amount and (to an appropriate degree) timing. Receipts in a particular currency may then be used to make payments in that currency so that the need to go through the exchanges (spot and forward) is limited to the unmatched portion of foreign currency cash flows. The aggressive company may decide to take forward cover on its currency payables and leave the currency receivables exposed to exchange risk, if it takes the view that the forward rate looks cheaper than the expected spot rate.

The basic requirement for a matching operation, then, is a two- way cash flow in the same foreign currency. This kind of operation is sometimes called *'natural'* matching. There is a further possibility, however, which we will call 'parallel' matching. Here the match involves two currencies whose movements are expected to run closely *''parallel'*. In a parallel matching situation, gains in one foreign currency are expected to be offset by losses in another. Needless to say, with parallel matching there is always the risk that the exchange rates will move contrary to expectations, so that both sides of the parallel match lead to exchange losses (or gains).

The major practical problems in implementing matching concern the timing of third party receipts and payments. Unexpected delays can cause the mistiming of a match and may consequently leave both receivable and payable exposed to exchange risk. Success requires accurate prediction of the amount of settlement and, more particularly, the timing of settlement dates. Where exchange controls allow, the timing problem can be overcome by the utilisation of foreign currency accounts, which allow the retiming of currency conversions to facilitate matching. The cost of neutralising exposures in this way is represented by the effective interest rate differential (including the deposit/borrowing rate spread) between the foreign and domestic currency.

3. Leading and Lagging

This simply refers to the adjustment of intercompany credit terms, 'leading' meaning a prepayment of a trade obligation and 'lagging' a delayed payment. This is primarily an intercompany technique because in third party trade there is a clear conflict of interest between buyer and seller. Whilst netting and matching are purely defensive measures, intercompany leading and lagging can be used as part of either a risk-minimising strategy (to facilitate matching) or an aggressive strategy (to maximize expected exchange gains). In either case a central information and decision point is usually required, to ensure that the timing of intercompany settlement is effective from a group point of view rather than purely a local one.

As with other schemes involving central decision making, leading and lagging requires a lot of discipline on the part of participating subsidiaries. Apart from the exposure impacts, such operations can seriously affect the liquidity—and hence profitability—of each subsidiary. To overcome the consequent evaluation problem, multinational companies which make extensive use of leading and lagging may either evaluate subsidiary performance on a pre-interest basis or impute interest charges and credits where appropriate.

One very important complicating factor, however, is the existence of local minority interests. If there are powerful local shareholders in the 'losing' subsidiary there will be strong objections because of the added interest cost/lower profitability resulting from the consequent local borrowing. In such cases of leading and lagging the interests of the minority shareholders are subordinated to those of the majority shareholder (the parent company). Host governments, via credit and exchange controls, may well restrict such operations.

4. Pricing Policy

For exposure management purposes, there are two kinds of pricing tactics: *price variation* and *currency-of invoicing policy*. In effect, the latter tactic is a subtle variant of the former. For each of these it is necessary to distinguish between external and intercompany trading, since each kind of trading gives rise to a different set of problems and opportunities.

(a.1) Price Variation: External Trade

One obvious way for a company to protect itself against exchange risk is to raise selling prices to offset the adverse effects of exchange rate fluctuations. But the question which always arises with the pricing option, of course, is that if the company is able to raise prices then why has it not done so already, irrespective of exposure considerations? Given an adverse exchange rate change (or trend), how quickly can local selling prices be increased to bring the parent currency equivalent of the foreign operation's cash flows back to the pre-depreciation level? The determination of this lag requires an analysis of the following questions:

— *Competitive situation:* what sector of the market are the firms in? A firm selling in the import or import-competing sectors is likely to have greater pricing flexibility than one in the purely domestic sector. The question of timing is also important: is there any scope for anticipatory price increases, given an expectation of an adverse currency movement?

— *Customer credibility:* when did the company last increase its prices and will there be customer resistance to another price rise?

— *Price controls:* are these in existence or likely to be introduced in the near future? Given the existence of such controls, to what extent do they allow the adverse impact of an exchange rate change to be recouped by subsequent price increases, and how quickly?

— Internal delays: what are the administrative lags involved in raising prices? Foreign currency price lists can be the source of significant delays, depending on how regularly they are reviewed and how lengthy is the review process. For a price list involving thousands of items such delays can be serious.

— *Trading/financing pattern:* if a firm does not have pricing flexibility for any of the above reasons, does it have a trading pattern or can one be created in which adverse currency impacts in one area of the business will be offset by positive effects elsewhere? For example, a foreign subsidiary which imports raw materials and sells locally is exposed to a local currency depreciation. To the extent that it can shift its sourcing (to domestic suppliers) or its selling (to foreign customers), this economic exposure may be reduced.

(a.2) Price Variation: Intercompany Trade

Intercompany (or transfer) price variation refers to the arbitrary pricing of intercompany transfers of goods and services at a higher or lower figure than the 'fair' or 'arm's length' price (the market price if there is an established market or the price which would be charged to a third party customer if there is not). However, multinational companies must always not set intercompany prices on an arm's length basis, as generally required by tax and exchange control authorities. In establishing international transfer prices, they try to satisfy a number of objectives not relevant to domestic transfer pricing. For example, the firm wants to minimise taxes and at the same time win approval from the government of the host country. Yet the basic objectives of profit maximisation and performance evaluation also are important. Often it is not possible to satisfy all these objectives simultaneously, so a company must decide which objectives are the most important. As a result, a particular transfer price, rather than evolving from a transfer pricing technique, may be established arbitrarily to fulfil an objective involving international considerations.

(b.1) Currency-of-invoicing : External Trade

Currency-of-Invoicing tactics can be either aggressive or defensive. An aggressive strategy would be to try to invoice exports in relatively strong currencies—relative to the exporter's home currency (HC)—and imports in relatively weak currencies. Here the company is increasing its exposure to exchange risk in the expectation that this exposure will produce exchange gains rather than losses.

For the strong currency exporter the defensive approach is the only one available for export invoicing since the HC is probably also the strongest currency acceptable to the customer. For the weak currency exporter, however, there may be significant opportunity gains from an aggressive currency-of-invoicing policy. In such circumstances foreign currency invoicing may be attractive to the exporter, in the expectation that the HC equivalent sales proceeds would be increased by a foreign currency appreciation over the credit period. It should be added, however, that there are risks involved in switching from a weak currency to a supposedly stronger one. The relative strengths of the two currencies could reverse themselves in the future and, once having changed to foreign currency billing, companies will find it difficult to switch back to HC-involving if the currency situation alters. In any case, currency-of-invoicing cannot be changed regularly—quite apart from customer objections and the loss of customer credibility, there is the problem of price list adjustment lags.

Currency-of-invoicing changes will also have to be 'sold' to subsidiary management as well as to customers. Indeed, resistance at operating unit level may present major problems to a corporate treasury trying to make the initial switch to foreign currency invoicing. Subsidiaries may be reluctant to give up the perceived marketing advantages of weak currency invoicing, particularly since—if corporate exposure management is to be centralised (often a corollary of the switch to foreign currency invoicing)—the benefits of foreign Currency billing may accrue at corporate treasury.

(b.2) Currency-of-Invoicing : Intercompany Trade

On a pre-tax basis, the distinction between aggressive and defensive approaches to currency-of-invoicing disappears in the context of intercompany trade, since what is one subsidiary's benefit (higher profit or lower risk) is another subsidiary's loss. On an after-tax basis, however, there is scope for an aggressive intercompany currency-of-invoicing policy. As an extreme example, if subsidiaries A and B trade with each other and A pays a higher tax rate, then A might be directed to invoice B in a weak currency and B to invoice A in a strong currency. After-tax group income may be increased, although such an approach can also create internal (motivation and evaluation) and external (tax) problems.

5. Asset and Liability Management

Asset and liability management techniques can be used to manage balance sheet, income statement and/or cash flow exposures. They can also be used aggressively or defensively. The aggressive approach is to increase exposed assets, revenues, and cash inflows denominated in strong currencies and to increase exposed liabilities, expenses, and cash outflows in weak currencies. In contrast, the defensive firm will seek to minimize foreign exchange gains and losses by matching the currency denomination of assets/liabilities, revenues/expenses, and cash inflows/outflows, irrespective of the distinction between strong and weak currencies.

In analysing how these objectives can be achieved, it is useful to make the distinction between *operating variables* (trade receivables and payables, inventory, fixed assets) and *financial variables* (cash, short-term investments and debt).

The currency denomination of operating variables is largely determined by intrinsic business conditions, such as production and marketing factors. Nevertheless, some fine tuning of existing exposures is often possible. Consider the case of a foreign subsidiary located in a weak currency country. If the 'all-current' method of translation is used then operating variables will tend to generate positive balance sheet exposures. Hence, the aim of asset/liability management here might be to reduce the subsidiary's local currency (LC) asset exposures and increase LC liabilities. LC receivables could be reduced by shortening the length of credit terms, offering special discounts and discounting or factoring-all of which involve costs (lower sales, high cash discounts or factoring charges) which may well outweigh the potential benefits. Similarly, local inventories could be run down to lower levels. The reverse process is applied on the liability side. Trade payables can be increased by deferring payment, which may mean missing trade discounts and a loss of goodwill if applied to third party suppliers. Such costs must be compared with the perceived benefits of reducing the net asset exposure in a given currency.

The next step is to consider how financial variables can be manipulated for exposure management purposes, and it is here that corporate financial management has most discretion over currency denomination. Let us revert to the case of the positive balance sheet exposure of a foreign subsidiary located in a weak currency country. The treasury management objective here would normally be to reduce net exposed financial assets, which means reducing local currency (LC) cash/near cash balance and increasing LC denominated debt. The scarcity of weak currency finance is often a major constraint here but, subject to availability, the parent company would typically borrow the weak currency long term, whilst the subsidiary is usually restricted to local bank (short term) borrowing. This is because (a) most subsidiaries are not individually listed on a stock exchange, so that the public issue of debt instruments is very difficult (hence the bulk of long- term loans taken out by foreign subsidiaries are private placements), (b) many foreign subsidiaries are relatively small and not well known to the local financial community, and (c) host governments may be reluctant to allow long-term borrowing by expatriate subsidiaries, arguing that-for balance of payments reasons—long-term funds should be supplied by the parent company.

In the context of cash flow exposure management, the distinction between aggressive and defensive currency-of-financing policies is an important one. With an aggressive financial management strategy the aim of currency-of-financing policy is simply to borrow in those currencies which have the cheapest effective interest cost, after tax. For the defensive firm the aim of international financial management should be to arrange the financing pattern of the company so that the detrimental effects of currency movements are minimised, whatever the exchange rate scenario. This can be done by structuring the group's liabilities in such a way that any change in cash inflows (operating revenues) induced by a currency movement is offset as much as possible by a countervailing change in cash outflows (effective interest costs).

EXPOSURE MANAGEMENT: EXTERNAL TECHNIQUES

In contrast to internal exposure management methods, the complete range of external techniques can be used by both exporters and importers as well as by multinational companies. Further, the costs of the external exposure management methods are fixed and predetermined. The main external exposure management techniques are examined below:

1. Forward Exchange Contracts

By covering forward the currency commitment, exporter/importer need no longer worry about the exchange risk element in the foreign transactions. What price has been paid for this protectionism is clearly an important question. Since, in deciding between various covering techniques it is the least-cost alternative which should be chosen. There is, however, some disagreement on how to calculate the cost of forward cover, mainly because there are two kinds of 'cost' involved: an *ex-ante* cost and an *ex-post* (opportunity) cost.

The ex ante cost of a forward contract is simply the difference between the *booked* receivable or payable (the foreign currency amount converted into the home currency (HC) at the spot rate prevailing on the invoice date) and the amount actually received or paid (the foreign currency amount converted into HC at the forward rate).

The *ex ante* cost is often interpreted as representing the cost of forward cover. This view is incorrect it as in normal, 'cost' is used as a decision making criterion. The *ex-ante* cost is simply the annualised percentage discount (or premium) of the foreign currency vis-a-vis the HC. A discount/premium in the forward market does not represent a cost, but rather it reflects (a) the difference between the free (euro)—market interest rate of the exporter's currency and that of the foreign currency. (Any difference between forward and euro currency; interest rates would very quickly disappear since this represents a profitable Opportunity for covered interest arbitrage. The only exception to this rule is in those countries where exchange controls restrict the access of residents to the euro-markets. In such countries, the domestic 'forward' rate is determined by the differential between the domestic interest rate available to residents and the euro-interest rate of the foreign currency. This 'domestic' forward rate will generally be different from the 'euro' forward rate available to non-residents, and (b) the combined judgement of all market participants in the future spot rate—otherwise participants could enter into forward contracts and expect to make a profit on settlement date. Unfortunately, it is usually impossible to distinguish between these two elements because of the feedback effects which changing forward premiums and discounts have on interest rates.

The most useful definition of the cost of forward cover is the *ex post* or opportunity cost approach. This defines the cost of forward cover as the HC amount which would have been received (paid) if the exposed receivable (payable) had been left uncovered, less the HC amount which the forward contract yields. In other words, it represents the difference between the foreign currency amount converted into HC at the settlement date spot rate and the foreign currency converted at the forward rate.

The forward rate versus settlement spot rate approach is, of course, a rather limited definition of the opportunity cost concept. The difference between the forward rate and the settlement spot rate represents just one possible opportunity foregone, of which there are many incurred daily. Strictly speaking, the 'real' opportunity cost of a forward contract is the difference between the forward rate taken and the most favourable rate available (between the contract date and the maturity date) for that maturity date. In other words, the forward rate taken should be compared not only with the settlement date spot rate but also with all the possible forward rates available over the exposure term.

Clearly, such a definition of opportunity cost is very strict measure of the efficacy of a firm's forward covered policy-inevitably, almost every forward cover decision would result in such an 'opportunity loss'. Very few companies try to measure the 'true opportunity' cost of their forward cover actions, and even then only one or two forward rates per day are used in the calculations. For practical purposes, then, the forward rate versus settlement spot rate' approach provides a reasonable estimate of opportunity cost.

The opportunity cost of forward cover cannot be known until settlement date. It is only with the aid of hindsight the finance manager can judge whether the forward deal is in fact the cheapest exchange risk management option. Hence, the opportunity cost approach does not explicitly provide this decision making criterion that will help determine when a company should cover forward. This is the basis of some practitioners' criticisms of the opportunity cost definition. Yet a decision rule can be easily distilled from the *ex post* approach; a company should compare the forward rate with its *forecast* of the future spot rate. If the forward rate underestimates the expected rate of appreciation, the firm might be willing to sell the currency forward and buy at future spot rates. If the forward rate overestimates the expected depreciation or underestimates the expected appreciation, the firm might prefer to sell at future spot rates and buy at present forward rates. The inherent assumption in these decision rules is, of course, that the firm believes its currency forecasts can out predict the forward rate. However, cash flows are not so discrete or predictable for vast majority of companies. Analytically, at least, two kinds of practical difficulties can be distinguished. The *first* problem is that of settlement date cannot be predicted exactly. (This is especially relevant to the case of the exporter, but even for the importer shipping delays can produce uncertainty of settlement dates). The *second* difficulty is that cash flows (receipts and payments) occur on a continuing basis and are not normally composed of large and discrete transactions-hence they do not readily lend themselves to large and discrete forward deals.

The two basic ways of covering a foreign currency receivable (or payable) with an impartial settlement date by using the forward market are forward option and forward swap deals. The first alternative, forward option, whilst the simplest method of dealing with an uncertain payment date, it can also be costly because of the uncertainty regarding the option exercise. The second technique for handling an unspecified settlement date is by the use of a swap deal, which simply means the simultaneous buying and setting of a currency for different maturities.

Swap deals can be of two types: a forward/forward swap and a spot/forward swap. A forward/forward or forward swap is simply a pair of forward exchange deals involving a forward purchase and a forward sale of a currency, simultaneously entered into but of different maturities. The first leg is for the delivery date of the original and arbitrarily dated forward contract, but in the opposite direction so that the original contract can be met. The second leg is for the desired new delivery date (not known exactly), in the same directions as the original contract so that the underlying transactions' exposure remains covered. A spot/forward swap is again a simultaneous pair of foreign exchange deals, except here the first leg is a forward sale (purchase). The technique works in much the same way as the forward/forward swap, except that the exporter may meet the original, fixed-date forward sale by a spot-purchase at the contract maturity date (the first leg of the swap). At the same time, the exporter may enter into a new forward sale contract, thereby extending the cover. Eventually, when the receivable is settled the receipts would liquidate the forward sale.

The main shortcoming of swap (forward/forward swap and spot forward) deals is that they do not give complete protection against exchange risk. The residual risk is of two types. The most obvious problem is that there may be an adverse change in the premium/discount between the date of the original contract and the date of adjustment. The second risk is that a breakdown of the forward market might prevent the company making the adjusting swap. The longer the period and the more exotic the currency, the fewer are the market makers and the fewer the possibilities (higher the cost) of adjusting an unwanted forward position. It may be added, however, that unless there are heavy speculative pressures or significant interest rate changes between the two currencies involved, swaps are generally cheaper than forward option contracts.

When a firm's foreign business is composed of a large number of low-value foreign currency transactions, it will obviously be expensive, both in terms of administration as well as transaction costs, to cover each exposed transaction individually. One way of handling this continuing exposure problem is to take out a simple, large forward contract to cover a number of different receivable (or payable) expenses. Since the receivable exposures to be covered would normally be of different settlement dates, forward option contracts are preferable to fixed-date contracts for this kind of operation. Also, the value of the forward contract would usually be rounded oft to reduce the higher transaction costs associated with 'odd-values'. For this reason, and also because some of the receivables may not be settled in the option period as expected, such 'bulk' forward contracts are often closed-out by a spot purchase or sale.

Upto now, we have been looking at various ways of covering the exchange risk inherent in a foreign currency transaction. Forward contracts are also used to have transaction exposures and, for exchange control and tax purposes. It is necessary to distinguish between these two types of operation.

The point about exchange controls is simply that, in most countries resident firms are not allowed to enter into forward contracts unless these relate to firm underlying commercial transactions. In other words, forward contracts designed to cover unrealisable transaction exposures are forbidden. The basis of the tax distinction is that, whilst translation gains/losses (not realisable) are usually not taxable/tax-allowable, gains/losses on forward exchange contracts (which are realisable) are, generally subject to tax. In this context, the two important tax qualifications which need to be examined. First, whilst the gains and losses on transactions-oriented forward deals (forward covering) are added to or subtracted from taxable profits, the tax treatment of translation-oriented forward contract (forward hedging) may be asymmetrical. In particular, forward hedging losses may not be tax-allowable. The second tax qualification is that, even when forward hedging gains/losses are taxed/tax-allowable, the group treasures must obviously ensure that the company which enters into the forward hedge has earned sufficient taxable profits to absorb any loss on the contract. Otherwise, of course, the tax treatment becomes in effect assymetrical because of poor tax planning. In real world, however, the generally valid assumption is that both gains and losses from forward hedging enter into corporate tax computations whilst translation gains and losses do not. What is the significance of this for a company which takes out a forward contract to hedge a projected translation loss? The company would be offsetting a taxable projected gain on the forward contract against a non-tax allowable projected loss on translation. Hence the size of forward contracts aimed at hedging translation exposures might be grossed up to take account of the differential tax treatment.

If the forward rate is assumed to be at par with the initial balance sheet spot rate, the parent company can calculate the exact amount of forward cover necessary to offset the translation loss, and this amount can be fixed irrespective of the future balance sheet spot rate. However, when the forward rate delivery at the future reporting date is not equal to be prior reporting date spot rate, then the extent of both realised and unrealised exchange gains and losses will depend on the initial forward discount (or premium) and on the eventual spot rate at the subsequent reporting date. Clearly, whilst today's forward rate is known with certainty, the future balance sheet date spot rate will not be known until the reporting date. Therefore, the actual size of the translation loss (gain) and gain (loss) to be made by the forward hedge, and hence the size of forward contract required to offset the translation loss cannot be known in advance. In most circumstances, then, companies must use exchange rate forecasts to decide the extent of forward sale required to exactly nullify a prospective translation loss. If this forecast is inaccurate then the company will report either a net exchange loss (foreign currency depreciation more than forecast) or a net exchange gain (foreign currency depreciation less than forecast).

2. Short-term Borrowing

An alternative to covering or hedging on the forward market is the short-term borrowing technique. A company can borrow either dollar (or some other foreign currency) or the local currency. Through short-term borrowing techniques, the settlement dates and the continuing stream of foreign currency exposure, two main practical transactions' exposure management difficulties, can be handled quite easily. Indeed, short-term borrowing has some advantages here over forward cover. The *ex post* cost of short-term borrowing cover is the HC amount which would have been received if the exposed receivable had been left measured (i.e. the foreign currency converted into HC at the settlement date spot rate), less the HC amount which the short-term borrowing technique yielded. Again, a company may cover a continuing stream of foreign currency exposures by arranging a borrowing facility, as an alternative to entering into 'bulk' forward option contracts, either in the currency of invoicing (in the case of exporter) or the home currency (for the importer). This technique can be used to simultaneously handle the problems of continuing foreign currency exposures and uncertain settlement dates.

Government controls and differential tax effects are relevant to the distinction between handling and covering of translation exposures, since (a) the borrowing of a foreign currency and its conversion into a stronger currency for the purposes of protecting a translation exposure will often be restricted by government credit and exchange controls; (b) translation gains and losses are unrealised and hence do not enter into corporate tax computations. Further, the interest receipts and payments are realised and are taxes or tax allowable. When an interest rate differential exists the size of both the usually market gain (or loss) and the translation loss (gain) will depend on interest rate differential and the closing spot rate. In these circumstances a forecast of the closing rate must be used in order to decide the amount of borrowing required to offset the projected translation loss.

3. Discounting

Unlike the first two techniques, discounting can be used to cover only export receivables. It cannot be used to cover foreign currency payables or to hedge a translation exposure. Where an exports receivable is to be settled by bill of exchange the exporter can discount the bill and thereby receive payment before the receivable settlement date. The bill may be discounted either with a foreign bank in the customer's country, in which case the foreign currency proceeds can be reptriated immediately, at the current spot rate; or it can be discounted with a bank in the exporter's country so that the exporter may receive settlement direct in home currency (HC). Either way the exporter is covered against exchange risk, the explicit cost being the discount rate charged by the bank.

The discounting technique for covering receivables exposures is very similar to the alternative of short-term borrowing except here the *ex-ante* cost is the effective discount rate less the HC deposit rate, rather than the foreign currency borrowing rate less the HC deposit rate. With both techniques, of course, the basic aim is to convert the proceeds from the foreign currency receivable into the HC as soon as possible. As with straight borrowing operations, discounting is a non-sequitur in many exchange-controlled countries since foreign currency borrowing of any sort is permitted only under certain conditions.

4. Factoring

Like discounting, factoring can only be used as a means of covering export receivables. When the export receivable is to be settled on open account, rather than by bill of exchange, the receivables can be assigned as collateral for selected bank financing. Under which circumstances such a service will give protection against exchange rate changes, though during unsettled periods in the foreign exchange markets appropriate variations may be made in the factoring agreement.

For the exporter the technique is very straight forward. He simply sells his export receivables to the factor and receives HC in return. The costs involved include both credit risks (the customer may default) and the cost of financing (if the exporter wants to receive payment before the receivable maturity date), as well as the cost of covering the exchange risk (the forward discount/premium). Factoring therefore tends to be a high-priced means of covering exposure, although there may be offsetting benefits such as obtaining export finance and reducing sales accounting and credit collection costs (the exporter may simply hand over the invoices against payment, the book-keeping and credit collection being done by the factor).

5. Government Exchange Risk Guarantees

To encourage exports, government agencies in many countries offer their exporters insurance against export credit risk and special export financing schemes. In recent years a few of these agencies have begun to offer exchange risk insurance to their exporters, as well as the usual export credit guarantees. Typically, the exporter will pay a small premium on his export sales and, for this premium, the government agency will absorb all exchange losses (and gains) beyond a certain threshold level.

Initially, such exchange risk guarantee schemes were introduced to aid capital goods' exporters, where receivable exposure-terms can be of a very long-term nature. More recently, however, some schemes have been extended to cover the exchange risk arising on consumer as well as capital goods' export. Government exchange risk guarantees are also given to cover foreign currency borrowing by public bodies.

To conclude, it may be noted that the various exposure management techniques described above are not available in all circumstances. This is mainly because of limitations imposed by the market-place (as forward market exists in many of the 'exotic' currencies of the developing countries) and by regulatory (the hedging of translation exposures on the forward markets is not allowed in many countries). Similarly, the availability of internal techniques is largely a function of the international involvement of each company.

ILLUSTRATIVE PROBLEMS

1. A French firm has contracted to buy parts form Japan worth ¥15 billion payable in three months. The firm has receivables for goods sold to a Japanese firm valued at ¥5 billion, also due in three months. It is the policy of the firm to hedge all residual currency positions. Given the following exchange and interest rates data:

Exchange rates: Spot	**3-month forward rate**
¥/FF FF1.00 = ¥27.00	¥/FF FF.100 = 26.65

Interest rates (% per annum)

France	13.2%
Japan	8.0%

(a) Show how the firm can execute the desired hedge in the forward market.

(b) If, instead, the hedge is executed in the money market, what steps need to be taken? (*Hint:* The amount borrowed in French francs should be such that when it is invested in Japan for three months, it will result in sufficient proceeds to pay off the obligation in Japanese yens).

(c) Calculate the foreign exchange gains (losses) of an unhedged position (compared to a hedged position) if the spot rate in three months is FF 1.00 = ¥26.50.

Show all calculations in a, b, and c, disregarding all transaction costs.

Ans.

¥10 billion need to be hedged

(a) $\frac{10}{26.65}$ = FF 375,230,000 (costs of forward hedge)

(b) $\frac{10}{1.02}$ = ¥9.804 billion

$\frac{9.804}{27}$ = FF 363,111,111

(363,111,111) (1,033) = FF 375,093,760 (cost of money market hedge)

Hedging in the forward market and in the money market would involve approximately the same cost because a condition of virtual interest rate parity exists in the markets.

(c) $\frac{10}{26.50}$ = FF 377,350,000

An unhedged position would involve a loss of Ff 377,350,000—FF 375,230,000, or FF 2,120,000 compared with hedging the yen obligation in the forward market.

2. Your affiliate in the Philippines declared a dividend of 50,000,000 pesos which is transferable in six months to the parent company in the United States. You are worried about adverse economic and political developments in the Philippines that could trigger a sharp depreciation of the peso during the next six months. Your attempts to hedge in the forward market were unsuccessful, as your bankers were not able to quote you a forward rate for the peso. Your are looking at two options:

(a) Invest the peso funds in Philippine government securities yielding 10 per cent per annum, and take the risk of the exchange rate that will prevail six months form now.

(b) You were approached by a U.S. firm operating in the Philippines which needed local funds. They expressed their wilingness to borrow ₱50,000,000 from your affiliate against a payment in U.S. dollars of $ 2,250,000 to your bank in the United States in six months.

You asked your staff to research the prospects of the peso/dollar exchange rate in the next six months. They compiled the following data:

EXCHANGE RATE-PESOS PER U.S. DOLLAR

	Spot Rate in Six Months		
Current Spot Rate	*No Change*	*Best case scenario*	*Worst case scenario*
18.5	18.5	20.0	24.0

The no-change case assumes that the Central Bank of the Philippines will support the rate at the current level during the next months.

(a) Which course of action will you take in each of the three scenarios? (Show all calculations).

(b) Which course of action will you take, assuming that you assign the following probabilities to the future spot rate scenarios?

No Change	10%
₱/ $ 20.0	25%
₱/ $ 24.0	65%

Ans.

(a) Option (1) Invest pesos in the Philippines

No change

$$\frac{52.5}{18.5} = \$\ 2,837,838$$

Best case scenario

$$\frac{52.5}{20.0} = \$2,625,000$$

Worst case scenario

$$\frac{52.5}{24.0}\ \$ = 2,187,500$$

Option (2) accept a payment of $ 2,250,000 from another U.S. firm in return for 50 million pesos.

Investing the funds available for dividends in the Philippines for six months, and then transferring them at the spot rate prevailing at the time of transfer would generate more dollars than option (2) except under the worst case scenario.

(b) S* (P/$) Expected future spot rate

S* (P/$) (.10)(18.5) + (.25)(20.0) + (.65)(24.0)

= 22.45

$$\frac{52.5}{22.45} = \$2,338,530$$

You are better off investing the proceeds in the Philippines, then converting them into U.S. dollars after six months.

3. If you were the financial manager of a multinational corporation in charge of foreign exchange operations, explain how you would minimise the risk to your firm in each of the following situations.

(a) Your firm has modest amounts of receivables and payments in currencies A, B, C, D, E, F, and G not coincident in timing.
(b) Your firm has a fairly large 3-month receivables in currency A, but it also has a subsidiary in country A to which you intend to make a transfer in four months equivalent to one-half of your receivables.
(c) Your firm has a receivable in currency Y maturing in six months and an equivalent payable in currency X for payment about the same time. Currencies Y and X are positively correlated against the dollar.
(e) Your firm has to meet a tax payment in country Z three months from now.

Ans.

(a) Firm's exposure is diversified among a number of currencies some of which move in tandem with the parent's currency, while others move opposite to the parents' currency. A situation of natural hedge seems to prevail. No hedging action may be necessary.
(b) Lead the transfer to your subsidiary one month, and sell the other half of the amount receivable in currency A in the forward market.
(c) No hedging action is necessary since currency X and currency Y move together in the same direction, the risk in the receivable would offset the risk in the payable.
(d) Sell currency Y forward and buy currency X forward.
(e) Buy currency Z three months forward.

QUESTIONS

1. Select one U.S. MNC that has a highly centralised exchange exposure management strategy and another which has a highly decentralised approach. Contrast the two approaches and indicate why multinational financial managers may pursue one or the other.
2. Among the three types of exposure: translation, transaction, and economic, which is the easiest to manage? Which is the most difficult? Explain your reasoning.
3. Contrast an aggressive vs. a defensive strategy in hedging transaction exposure. Can the latter strategy achieve a perfect hedge?

4. Explain how a flexible policy of leading and lagging accounts receivable from or payable to other entities might work to reduce the transaction exposure of an affiliate. Why do some countries, particularly developing countries, impose limits on leading and lagging for import payments, for export receipts, and other types of transfers?
5. Contrast the forward market hedge and the money market hedge as to (a) cost, (b) convenience, and (c) effectiveness. Under what conditions would the second hedge become the only viable option?
6. Your affiliate is located in a developing country that has a soft currency with no forward exchange market, and where there is no organised money market. Assume additionally that parallel loans and credit swap opportunities are not available. Suggest an optimum strategy to minimise transaction exposure.
7. How would your answer differ if the Japanese firm conducts operations involving the manufacture and distribution of a number of items (such as motorcycles, snowmobiles, and the like) in addition to cars, in a number of countries in addition to the German market?
8. A South Korean firm is exporting subcompacts to the Indian market, relying on low production cost in South Korea to penetrate the India market primarily on the basis of price appeal. Faced with a combination of stiffening competition from Japanese cars in the same category and a sharp depreciation of the Indian rupee against its own currency, what production and marketing adjustments are advisable to protect its market in the India.

8. A South Korean firm is exporting subcompacts to the Indian market, relying on low production cost in South Korea to penetrate the India market primarily on the basis of price appeal. Faced with a combination of stiffening competition from Japanese cars in the same category and a sharp depreciation of the Indian rupee against its own currency, what production and marketing adjustments are advisable to protect its market in the India.

20

ORGANISATION OF THE EXPOSURE MANAGEMENT FUNCTION

Each Company must organise the exposure management function. Today, to perform effectively in the globalised world, all managers operating in the international markets, not just international financial managers, need to understand (a) the mechanism of exchange fluctuation, (b) how to measure foreign exchange exposure and (c) how to hedge against exposure risk.

Keeping in view that each company has its own organisational peculiarities and so no single exposure management system is right in all situations, the focus of the chapter is to examine the organisation of the exposure management functions. We are looking at only one of a number of functions carried out by financial manager though the organisational requirements of exposure and liquidity management, the two basic problem areas of international financial management, are very similar. Nevertheless, the following analysis is a partial one.

ORGANISATIONAL OBJECTIVES

No single exposure management system is right in all situations. Each corporation has its own peculiarities in terms of operating characteristics, business environment, management philosophy, legal structure, personnel strengths, and so on. Companies differ, and their exposure management systems should reflect these differences. A treasury structure which is right for IBM is unlikely to be appropriate for Unilever. Nevertheless, there are two organisational objectives which we believe all international companies should try to attain in the treasury area. *Firstly,* treasury (exposure) management must be *integrated* with the operating side of the business. This means that treasury must get involved with production, purchasing, and marketing decisions. Treasury influence should not be limited to traditional, purely financial functions. *Secondly,* treasury (exposure) management, must be *coordinated* if it is to be fully effective. Coordination requires a centralised (corporate and/or regional) information system — in both exposure and liquidity management a group-wide focus is essential. However, coordination does not require that all decisions or actions be taken centrally. The operating and other characteristics of each company will often provide constraints here and so the costs of centralisation (such as demotivation at the local level) should be weighed against the costs of decentralisation (reduced control, unnecessary transactions' costs). More specifically, the organisational objectives of an exposure management system can be: (i) it should enable group-wide exposure identification, decision making and control; (ii) it should facilitate the integration of treasury within the company, preferably involving direct liaison between central treasury and operating units; (iii) It should not cause motivational problems. In particular, it should be clear that individuals/units are held responsible only for those decisions which they control; (iv) it should not involve unnecessary management effort and administrative costs; and finally, (v) it should facilitate the achievement of other business objectives, both non-financial (helping the marketing effort) as well as financial (improving cash and liquidity management, reducing financing costs). The method of attaining these two objectives and the extent to which they can be achieved will clearly vary from company to company. However, these objectives are almost inviolate, so let us examine the advantages of integration and coordination.

INTEGRATED EXPOSURE MANAGEMENT

A common failing of exposure management systems is that the management process begins after the exposure has been generated. This is too late. Exposure management decision making must begin *before* exposures are generated, otherwise (a) fundamental operating decisions are being taken on the basis of unnecessarily incomplete information, which may mean that incorrect decisions are made; and (b) from the very beginning, exposure management choice is limited to a narrow range of tactics. To avoid these weaknesses senior management must recognise that exposure management should be a fundamental business consideration. Everything that a company does internationally has some impact on its foreign exchange exposure. Each major function contributes to the generation of exposures or has the opportunity to reduce or increase them:

Capital budgeting: the choice of product and the location of manufacturing operations;

Purchasing: the selection of country of sourcing or the choice between bids denominated in different currencies;

Selling: the selection of country and currency denomination of sales;

Marketing: the trade-off between advertising effort, easier credit terms, and lower sales prices;

Controllership: the manipulation of working capital by enforcing changes in credit terms;

Budgeting: the behavioral impact of performance evaluation systems;

Finance: the currency of financing decision.

Since exposures arise primarily from operating decisions, exposure management cannot and must not be separated from the operating activities of the company. This objective can only be met if the treasury function is fully integrated into the firm. Operating personnel (purchasing, manufacturing, sales and marketing) and financial management (taxation, treasury and controller) should meet routinely to review the fundamental strategic and tactical decisions which create currency exposures. A two-way flow of information and advice is necessary. The exposure manager must educate operating personnel on the foreign exchange implications of fundamental operating decisions, and operating personnel must ensure that the exposure manager understands how the business operates and how it generates exposures.

A fundamental characteristic of an integrated exposure management system is that it enables the utilisation of a wide range of exposure management techniques. Initial emphasis is on internal (business related) responses such as utilising better local cash management techniques, changing sourcing patterns, raising prices or changing the currency of intercompany sales. It is only after the application of internal techniques that treasury need go to the markets, to apply such external techniques as forward exchange contracts or eurocurrency borrowing.

In contrast, if the treasury function is isolated from operating decisions then exposure management becomes a much narrower and more straightforward process. In this kind of set-up the foreign exchange manager receives exposure numbers from operating units and, based on a currency forecast, decides whether or not to cover on the forward markets. Too much emphasis is placed on external tactics; internal responses are almost entirely pre-empted. In a centralised system there may be some netting or matching, but it is too late to consider changing the price levels or the currency of invoicing, far less to consider whether the manufacturing unit might have been better located elsewhere.

In this kind of system the focus of exposure management is on curing the symptoms rather than the causes of the problem. The exposure manager is more concerned with where the foreign exchange markets seem to be going rather than with where the company's business is taking group exposure. This preoccupation with the foreign exchange markets means that the company (and the exposure manager) will often get hurt when currencies move abruptly.

COORDINATED EXPOSURE MANAGEMENT

Treasury (exposure and liquidity) management must be coordinated if it is to be fully effective. For a company with real concerns about exposure (and liquidity) management, the organisational question is not so much whether the treasury function should be coordinated or not. Rather, the relevant question is what degree of coordination is possible given the firm's specific characteristics. For efficiency reasons, a centralised treasury bias will exist in all companies, regardless of the degree of (de)centralisation in other functional areas. A coordinated viewpoint is essential if exposure identification and exposure management decisions are to be effective on a group basis.

No matter which exposure definition is chosen as the primary focus, the identification of a company's exposures will only be completely meaningful on a consolidated, group-wide basis. Similarly, rational exposure management decision making is possible only if a coordinated group viewpoint is taken. Otherwise two separate operating units could each have offsetting positions and each could independently be taking offsetting actions. Moreover, the exposure definitions applied by these units could be contrary to the concerns of senior corporate management. Other typical weaknesses of a decentralised exposure management system include unnecessary foreign exchange costs, overemphasis on external tactics and inadequate control over foreign exchange trading.

The concept of treasury coordination is easy to justify; its implementation can be much more difficult. In practice, the efficiency bias towards coordination is constrained by decentralising biases in other parts of a company. Examples of such constraints are:

Operating characteristics: a divisional organisation based on heterogeneous product groups

Corporate development: growth by acquisition (and rationalisation by divestiture); foreign subsidiaries which are mature, financially strong and powerful; a historically small and uninfluential corporate treasury

Profitability: the more profitable the company, the less pressing will be the need for strict financial controls; this is often related to the product life cycle, since the need for coordinated treasury management strengthens as the company and its product mature

Legal structure: the existence of minority interests places severe limits on the ability of a company to defer local interests to the good of the group as a whole;

Personnel and personality strengths: these can also create very real barriers to coordination.

Nevertheless, the potential exposure (and liquidity) management benefits of a treasury system will often outweigh its costs. Let us now examine how this centralisation can be achieved.

METHODS OF CENTRALISATION

Conceptually, there are two methods of centralising exposure management: (a) reporting-based approaches which shift some decision making authority from the operating units where exposures arise to a central exposure management body; and (b) structural approaches which shift the actual incidence of exposures from operating units to a central location. These two methods are not mutually exclusive. Indeed, they are often complementary since some kind of reporting/communication system is always necessary if internal business-related exposure management tactics are to be identified. Nevertheless, for the purpose of understanding how centralisation can be achieved the distinction is a useful one.

Reporting-based Centralisation

The essence of this approach is that central treasury (corporate or regional) receives exposure information from operating units, makes certain exposure, management decisions and then communicates these decisions back down to operating units. Exposure information systems have been discussed in Chapter 12, so our focus here is on exposure decision making and action. Three levels of centralisation of exposure management are identified in Table 1.

TABLE 1

LEVELS OF REPORTING-BASED CENTRALISATION

Exposure management role	*Level of centralisation*		
	General guidelines	*Specific directives*	*Centralised action*
Sets overall exposure management guidelines	C	L	L
Makes specific decisions on each operating unit's exposures	C	C	L
Takes exposure management action	C	C	C

C = Central treasury (corporate or regional)
L = Local unit (division, subsidiary)

General Guidelines

At the very lowest level of centralisation, corporate treasury sets overall guidelines on how exposures are to be managed. These guidelines can take various forms depending on the nature of the company's exposures. However, they are often too rigid and simplistic or else so vague as to be meaningless, as the following examples indicate: cover all net transactional exposures; cover all weak currency receivables and strong currency payables (currencies specified); do not use forward cover; minimize foreign exchange losses, and, finally, minimize foreign exchange losses/ maximize foreign exchange gains.

With this approach, exposure management action (e.g. forward cover) is taken at operating unit level. So also are specific exposure decisions (e.g. should next month's payables be covered forward), although local responsibilities can be heavily constrained if corporate guidelines are inflexible. The information requirements of such a system can be minimal. Indeed, corporate treasury may not even monitor exposures except for a review of the foreign exchange gain/loss calculation in the periodic reporting package.

Specific Directives

At the next level of centralisation, treasury makes specific currency exposure decisions which operating units are then directed or recommended to act upon. This can take two basic forms. In the first case the central foreign exchange manager or committee makes regular (weekly, monthly) forecasts on each currency in which the company operates. These forecasts are then transmitted to operating units together with the related currency-specific advice (cover US dollar receivables, French franc payables). As with general directives, the exposure information requirements of this approach are minimal. Alternatively, the foreign exchange manager or committee discusses future currency movements in the context of the company's existing and anticipated exposures. Hence operating units must now submit exposure information to the center. This approach allows a much wider range of exposure management techniques to be applied, such as matching, leading and lagging, and pricing policies. With either of these approaches, operating units get regular and specific exposure management advice from treasury.

Centralised Action

At the highest level of centralisation the treasury not only makes specific exposure management decisions but it also takes the appropriate action on behalf of operating units, where this is cost-effective. Benefits arise from the greater treasury expertise which can be brought to bear on exposure management and the more favourable terms which can often be obtained on the broader range of available techniques.

Whilst the second and third levels of centralisation produce a more coordinated approach they can also create important evaluation and motivational problems. In terms of evaluation the basic concept to be applied is that management should be responsible only for the decisions which it controls. Clearly, irrespective of who takes the exposure management action, it is the unit/individual who made the underlying decision who should be evaluated on the effectiveness of that decision. (The same principle can be applied to the liquidity implications of exposure management. For instance, if treasury directs subsidiaries to lead or lag intercompany payments then subsidiary profitability should be evaluated on a pre-interest basis.) This means that *if treasury only advises operating units, then responsibility lies at operating level; if treasury directs, then responsibility rests with treasury.*

Even with such an evaluation system, however, the centralised approach is not necessarily free of motivational and management problems. With a compulsory system, for example, operating units may not fully accept that they are not held responsible for exposure management actions taken under the direction of treasury. After all, it is their cash balances which are affected by such decisions. Alternatively, with an advisory system the problem is that, if operating units reject treasury advice, should subsidiaries be allowed to take actions which treasury believe will harm the group?

One simple way to avoid such problems is the implementation of an *internal forward cover (hedging) system.* This can be either optional or compulsory. The basic idea of the optional approach is that operating units make their own forward cover decision but, if they decide to cover, it must be done with central treasury. Treasury then issues an internal ('paper') forward contract, and this 'paper' rate (based on the current forward rate) is used for subsidiary evaluation purposes. Treasury is left with the decision of whether the company as a whole should actually take the forward rate or stay uncovered — and the foreign exchange manager is evaluated on this decision. Table 2 illustrates the allocation of responsibilities within an optional system for each combination of treasury/operating unit forward cover decisions. In practice, however, most internal hedging systems are compulsory: operating units *must* take the internal forward rate and treasury is left with the company's *spot versus forward* decision.

Structural Centralisation

This approach seeks to redirect exposures to a central location within the company, where both exposure management decisions and action can be carried out. The two basic ways of achieving this are (a) the manipulation of intercompany currency-of-invoicing policy, and (b) utilisation of an exposure management-oriented intermediary company, typically either a factoring or a re-invoicing vehicle. Whilst the following

TABLE 2

INTERNAL FORWARD COVER SCHEME — RESPONSIBILITY ALLOCATION

Cover/no cover decision			
Operating unit	*Treasury*	*External action*	*Internal responsibility allocation*
Cover	Cover	Treasury takes cover	Costs/benefits for account of operating unit
		Or operating unit takes over	Automatic
	No cover	None	Internal forward contract between treasury and operating unit. Costs/benefits for account of operating unit
No cover	Cover	Treasury takes cover	Costs/benefits for account of treasury
		Treasury directs take cover	Memorandum adjustment to operating unit to unit accounts. Costs/benefits for account of treasury
	No cover	None	None

analysis focuses on the exposure management role of such policies or vehicles, it should be emphasised that these also have very important liquidity management and tax-planning functions. Vehicle companies have also been set up for non-financial reasons, to control the purchasing, marketing or accounting functions of a corporation. Clearly, these other functions are integral elements in the choice of an exposure management system.

(a) Intercompany Currency-of-Invoicing Policy

For companies with extensive intercompany trade, transactional exposures can be easily redirected to one or more locations by the restructuring of intercompany currency-of-invoicing policy. The simplest case is where foreign operations consist merely of sales companies which sell locally and are sourced from parent country manufacturing affiliates. If intercompany exports are invoiced in exporters' currencies, as is often the case, then transactional exposures are dispersed throughout the group. This makes it more difficult to manage group exposures on a coordinated basis. Also, overseas sales companies are typically thinly staffed and hence unlikely to have the expertise to manage these exposures effectively. A policy of invoicing such exports in the buyers' currencies will automatically redirect the transactional exposures back to parent country operating units, where corporate treasury influence is likely to be much stronger. Centralisation can then be completed by a reporting-based system or an intermediary vehicle involving parent-country manufacturing units only.

The same principle can be applied to more extensive intercompany trading patterns. For the company which sources its sales companies from manufacturing affiliates located in a number of countries, transactional exposures can be concentrated at the major manufacturing locations (parent country and overseas) by invoicing sales' affiliates in their local currencies. This again facilitates a group exposure management viewpoint, since an exposure reporting system or vehicle company need only involve the principal manufacturing subsidiaries.

(b) Intermediary Companies

The basic intermediary concept is that payment for goods provided by one entity to another is channeled through an agent or 'intermediary'. The intermediary acts as a conduit for the transfer of funds between the parent company, its subsidiaries (as exporters/importers), and/or third parties. Hence the intermediary is ideally placed to manage exposures (and liquidity) on a global or regional basis.

The intermediary's function is often limited to a designated geographic area of the firm's foreign operations. The location of the intermediary within that area is dependent on such factors as exchange controls, customs regulations, fiscal treatment, the sophistication of the capital and labour markets, and the presence of existing group entities. Specific regional examples of countries with the appropriate environmental background are the UK, Netherlands and Switzerland in Europe, Panama and Puerto Rico in the Americas, and Hong Kong and Singapore in Asia.

The two most common types of intermediary company are the export (import) finance vehicle and the re-invoicing vehicle. These carry out essentially the same exposure management function, the main practical difference being the broader scope of the intermediary function of the re-invoicing vehicle.

(i) Export Finance Vehicle

This operates as an export factor, buying the export receivables of affiliate companies for settlement in the affiliate's local currency. If intercompany exports are then invoiced on to the foreign affiliate in the importer's currency, transactional exposures are shifted from operating units to the vehicle company. This creates opportunities for internal exposure management (matching, leading and lagging) and low-cost export financing (taking advantage of interest differentials between domestic and Eurocurrency rates).

The export factoring function can be applied automatically to all export sales or on a 'best efforts' basis. With a best efforts scheme the finance vehicle offers external sources of financing to the exporter, who then compares this with the domestic interest rate. Subsidiary treasurers thereby remain autonomous.

A simple (pre-tax) example of how a single export financing deal works is depicted in Figure-1. The Belgian company exports to its Italian affiliate on one-year terms. Due to limited local credit availability and high cost (Belgium 12%, Italy 18%)

the two subsidiaries were unwilling or unable to finance the transaction domestically. Nor did either party want to carry a foreign currency exposure for one year. Instead, the export finance company borrows Euro-French francs for one year at 10% and immediately converts to Belgian francs to settle the Belgian receivable, thereby eliminating the Belgian company's receivables exposure. Export Finance Ltd's receivable from the Italian affiliate is denominated in lira, which again removes exchange risk from the operating unit. Export Finance Ltd now has an unmatched book (lira receivables, French franc payables, both for settlement in one year) which is neutralised by a forward contract at a cost of 6%. (Alternatively, the finance vehicle might have matched these positions with opposite flows from other parts of the group, or left them uncovered.) The pre-tax cost of funding is 16% and all exposures are fully covered.

FIGURE 1

EXPORT FINANCING DEAL

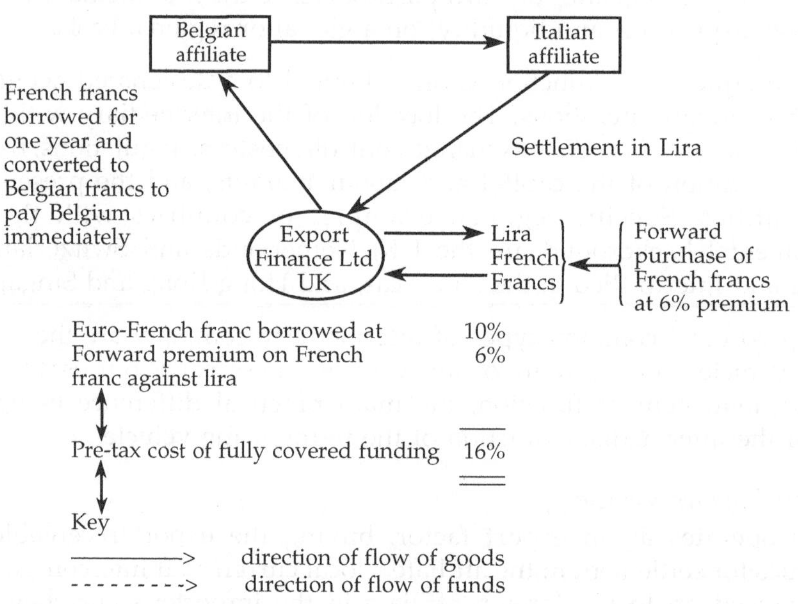

This example has described the export financing of intercompany trade. The same approach can be applied to third-party exporting and importing.

(ii) Re-invoicing Vehicle

The mechanics of re-invoicing are illustrated in Figure 2. Goods exported from an affiliate company are shipped direct to either third party or affiliate customer, but the invoice (and hence payment) is channeled through the re-invoicing vehicle. Transactional exposures can be centralised at the vehicle company by invoicing affiliates (exporters and importers) in their local currencies. This centralisation facilitates internal exposure management by the application of such techniques as leading and lagging, multilateral netting, and matching.

FIGURE 2

EXPOSURE CENTRALISATION WITH A RE-INVOICING VEHICLE

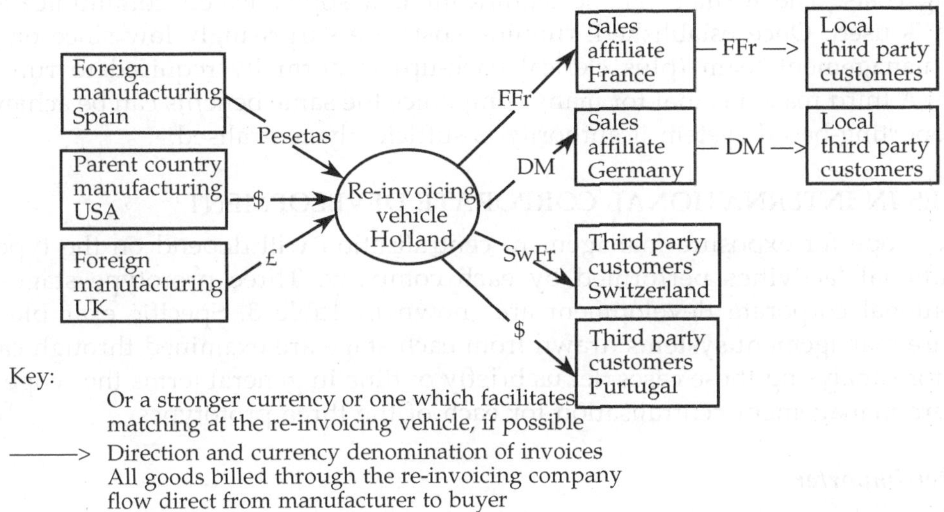

For the purpose of analysing the costs and benefits of an intermediary company, export finance and re-invoicing vehicles can be analysed jointly since they function in much the same way. Benefits go beyond purely exposure management considerations — the rationale for an intermediary could equally be based on liquidity or operating (purchasing, marketing) considerations. Major benefits are:

Exposure management: centralizes exposures at one location where information and expertise is developed.

Exposure (and liquidity) management: the doubling of trade flows maximizes the flexibility to lead and lag. The central decision point also allows leading/lagging decisions to be made on a group basis, involving the after-tax trade-off between expected translation gains/losses, transactional gains/losses, forward cover gains/losses and interest income/expense.

Liquidity management: creates a central liquidity pool, to be funded or invested in supranational markets. In particular, profitable opportunities arising from after-tax interest rate differentials between domestic and Euro-money markets can be utilised. Liquidity management creates a channel for reallocating funds between previously unconnected units by leading and lagging.

Banking costs: reduces foreign exchange transactions, producing savings of around one-sixth of one per cent of the amount netted. Also, finer rates, commissions and value compensation charges may become available to the central unit.

Operating management: improves bargaining power with external markets (purchasing and sales) without placing negotiating burden on operating units.

This list of benefits seems very impressive, so why are intermediary vehicles still relatively uncommon? One reason is simply management inertia and opposition from the operating unit level of decentralised companies. Another is start-up and running costs. The former can be significant if a sophisticated communications system is used. Once established, running costs are surprisingly low since only a small management team (plus clerical back-up) is normally required to run the system. A third reason is that for many companies the same benefits can be achieved by a reporting-based system if authority is sufficiently centralised.

STAGES IN INTERNATIONAL CORPORATE DEVELOPMENT

The scope for exposure management centralisation will depend on the type of international 'activities performed by each company. Three prototype stages of international corporate development are shown in Table 3. Specific examples of exposure management systems drawn from each stage are examined through cases but before analysing these cases, let us briefly outline in general terms the scope for exposure management centralisation for each of the three prototypes.

Exporter/Importer

All subsidiaries are located in a single country and international business consists solely of sales to or purchases from third parties overseas. Operations generate transactions' exposures only; this type of company has no foreign subsidiaries. The only kinds of exposure management centralisation available here are the application of reporting-based or structural centralisation to export/import exposures.

Parent-Country-Oriented Multinational Operations

Principal manufacturing operations still remain in the parent country. Instead of exporting direct to third parties, this type of company exports to foreign sales subsidiaries, which then sell in their local markets. Exposures are still heavily transactions-oriented.

With the predominance of intercompany cross-border trade, intercompany currency-of-invoicing policy becomes a very useful means of bringing foreign subsidiaries' potential transactional exposures back to the parent country. To the extent that the overseas sales companies' cross-border trade consists of imports from parent country manufacturing operations, transactional exposures can be switched to the parent country simply by invoicing this trade in subsidiaries' local currencies. As in the case of the exporter/importer, group transactional exposure management can then be centralised by the introduction of an appropriate reporting system or vehicle company.

'Pure' Multinational Operations

Manufacturing operations are now located overseas as well as at home. Intercompany cross-border trade is extensive, existing between foreign subsidiaries as well as emanating from the parent country. Third-party transactional exposures also arise in a number of countries. Cross-border financial flows (dividends, intercompany loans, and third party financings) become extensive. Translation exposures increase significantly. In short, group exposures tend to be very large, various and dispersed. The organisational opportunities for centralising the management of such a complex pattern of exposures are extensive. These include both reporting-based systems and structural manipulation of the exposures themselves, and can be applied on a regional or group-wide basis.

TABLE 3

INTERNATIONAL LIFE CYCLE — TREASURY ORGANISATION AND EXPOSURE CHARACTERISTICS

Stage of international life cycle	*Treasury organisational trend:* *Decentralised*	*Centralised*	*Exposure characteristics* *Transactional*	*Translation*
Exporter/ importer	A ⟶	B	Third party export/import trade from/to parent country	Foreign currency loans No foreign assets
Multinational: foreign sales companies only	C ⟶	D	Intercompany export trade from parent country Limited intercompany financial (dividend) flows back to parent country	Foreign currency loans Limited foreign assets
Multinational: foreign manufacturing and sales operations	E ⟶	F	Intercompany export trade from worldwide manufacturing centers Third-party import trade into worldwide manufacturing centers Intercompany financial (dividend and loan) flows	Extensive foreign currency loans Extensive foreign assets

CENTRALISATION *VERSUS* DECENTRALISATION: *SOME CASE STUDIES*

Six case studies are presented below: a decentralised and a centralised example for each of the three stages of international corporate development. The objective is to show that, wherever firm-specific characteristics permit, coordination of exposure management from corporate or regional treasury should be adopted.

Case A: Decentralised Exporter

Background. Company A is a Indian consumer products company. Annual sales exceed Rs. 300 crore. Reflecting a multi-product base, operations are organised along independent subsidiary lines. Parent company influence over the operations of these subsidiaries is minimal. Basically, if profitability is adequate then subsidiaries are left alone.

Exposure Characteristics. Exposures are purely transactional, arising from third party import and export trade. The company has no foreign subsidiaries and no foreign currency loans. On a group basis the gross transactional exposures consist (in rupee-equivalent terms) of approximately Rs. 40 crore of currency payables and Rs. 100 crore of currency receivables. A simplified picture of these exposures is depicted in Figure 3.

FIGURE 3

COMPANY A — EXPOSURE CHARACTERISTICS

PARENT

SUBSIDIARY 1	SUBSIDIARY 2	SUBSIDIARY 3
Import payments:	Export receipts:	Export receipts:
Germany = 20	Germany = 10	Germany = 30
Holland = 10	Holland = 20	Holland = 10
Other = 10	Other = 15	Other = 15

Third party funds flows (Rs. crore equivalent)

Exposure Management System. This is highly decentralised, reflecting the company's operating characteristics and the way it has developed. There is no corporate treasurer. This function, insofar as it exists, is one of a number of tasks carried out at head office by the group chief accountant. Subsidiaries do not report their exposures to head office.

In effect, the corporate exposure management role consists of a general directive from the board of directors that all foreign exchange exposures should be covered immediately. Subsidiaries do not always adhere to this policy, however, and the group chief accountant cannot detect this from the existing uni-currency information system. Head office does review an exchange gain/loss item in subsidiaries' monthly accounts. However, this number simply represents the difference between monthly booking rates and the aggregate of all exchange rates actually taken by each subsidiary — its exposure management implications are unclear. The approach taken by the group chief accountant is that, as long as this number is not significantly negative, then exposure management is satisfactory. In effect, then, subsidiaries manage their exposures independently of each other and of the parent company.

Strengths and Weaknesses. The principal advantage of this system is that, from a head office viewpoint at least, the administrative costs are low. Also the system is easily accommodated within the existing organisational structure of Company A. However, the opportunity costs of this exposure management system are significant.

i) The subsidiary focus restricts an overall identification of exposures and exposure management opportunities, and this has led to a number of inefficiencies. Most obvious is the fact that existing matching opportunities (two-way Deutsche Mark and guilder flows) are not being realised. More generally, there is inadequate awareness of exposure management techniques and an overemphasis on external tactics.
ii) Subsidiary responsibilities are unclear: if they adhere to the always cover directive this can affect their profitability (including foreign exchange gains/losses) upon which they are evaluated.
iii) Control over subsidiaries' exposure management action is weak.

Case B. Centralised Exporter

Background. Company B is a UK textile manufacturer. Annual sales exceed $500 million. The company is highly divisionalised, primarily the result of a long history of growth by acquisition and merger. Operating decision making is highly decentralised but in recent years the company has made an effort to centralise the finance function.

Exposure Characteristics. Exposures are purely transactional. Annual exports and imports, all third party, equal $70 million and $50 million respectively. Exposures are spread across the company's six operating divisions. The international textile markets are very competitive and so pricing flexibility is limited.

Exposure Management System. Exposures are handled by a vehicle company which performs import paying agent and export factoring functions.

The export factoring function works as follows. When a division receives an export order a confirmation note is sent to the vehicle, Company B Export Ltd. Internally, the division receives the current forward rate for the appropriate maturity (i.e. the order date to settlement date period). Externally, the foreign exchange manager must then decide, within guidelines set by senior management, whether to sell the currency receivable forward immediately or carry the receivables exposure on his books. This decision will depend on the exchange rate outlook and the existing portfolio of currency positions.

Irrespective of this decision, Export Ltd will settle its debt (at the in-house forward rate) with the division on the 20th day of the following month. In this particular case no factoring charge is made. Export Ltd is a cost center and divisions pay only an annual management fee.

Import exposures are picked up at the purchase order stage. Unlike the export factoring business, where Export Ltd actually takes title of the goods, on the import side the vehicle acts only as paying agent. However, the exposure management function is exactly the same: divisions automatically receive an internal forward rate and exposure management responsibilities rest firmly with the foreign exchange manager of Export Ltd. The operation of the vehicle is depicted in Figure 4.

FIGURE 4

COMPANY B — EXPORT FACTORING/IMPORT PAYMENT VEHICLE

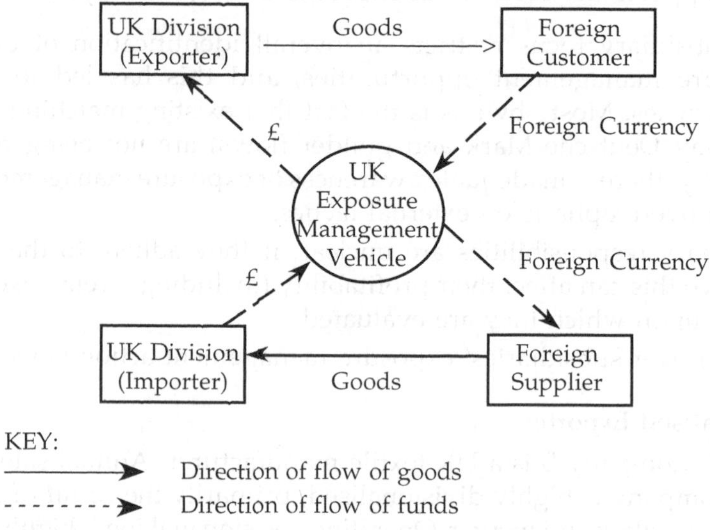

KEY:

——→ Direction of flow of goods

- - - - → Direction of flow of funds

Costs and Benefits For Company B. Set-up costs primarily involve the treasury management time and effort required to 'sell' the idea to divisional management — often a very difficult hurdle to be overcome. Running costs are surprisingly small, consisting of the following three elements: (a) labour —a single professional and a clerical assistant; (b) Reuters foreign exchange rate service, plus equipment rental and the cost of a telephone line to the nearest computer installation; and (c) the subscription fee for a currency forecasting service.

Benefits go beyond purely exposure management considerations and are predominantly intangible, which makes the justification for such vehicles difficult to quantify. The major quantifiable benefit is that foreign exchange commissions and costs are reduced because of the matching of currency receivables and payables of different operating units. The intangible benefits of the export vehicle are potentially far more significant:

1. It enables a coordinated group currency-of-invoicing policy. This can be used to facilitate matching and netting and to implement a policy of foreign currency invoicing — none of which would typically occur if currency-of-invoicing is left entirely to divisional management.
2. It aids export marketing in two ways. First, Export Ltd will hold open a forward quotation for one week, which is a great help to a division in the final and critical stages of contract negotiations. Second, Export Ltd also provides expert advice on exchange rates to be used in foreign currency price lists, which are reviewed every six months. This 'long-term rate' is also used for small (less than $20,000) internal forward contracts.

3. A central dealing situation offers economies of scale: concentration of management expertise, sophisticated equipment and information system, better quality banking advice and better rates.
4. Financing benefits primarily include the possibility of cheaper interest charges by selective use of Euro-currency financing.
5. There are cash management improvements: reduced administrative burden and better forecasting at operating unit level; centralised credit control and collection allows better identification of credit risk.
6. In Company B's case, the distribution function is also handled by Export Ltd (involving significant non-treasury manpower), producing higher transport capacity utilisation and better rates.
7. Responsibility allocation is clearly defined: divisions manage the operating side of the business and the foreign exchange management at Export Ltd are evaluated on their forward cover policy by comparing the actual (spot or forward) rate obtained with the internal forward rate. So long as the internal forward rate is an objective and consistently calculated market rate, this comparison effectively evaluates the selective forward cover policy against the 'all cover' alternative.

It should be emphasised that many of these benefits could be realised without a vehicle company. This approach has, however, been successful at Company B.

Case C. Decentralised Parent-Country-Oriented Multinational

Background. Company C is a US manufacturer of equipment and components for the engineering, electrical, and automotive industries. Total third party sales are $1,500 million, split between US domestic ($1,100 million), US export ($100 million) and overseas companies' sales ($300 million). The company is organised along divisional lines and a decentralised management philosophy prevails. Divisions operate as autonomous profit centers and corporate treasury does not have the staff or, in practice, the authority to intervene except in a very general way.

Exposure Characteristics. These are mainly transactional. US based companies have both third party export ($100 million) and import ($300 million) exposures and also export in US dollars to assembly and sales affiliates overseas ($100 million). Overseas subsidiaries also have limited third party imports but sell almost entirely in local markets (more than 30 countries). Overseas companies rely largely on local financing; net translation exposures are not significant.

Exposure Management System. The corporate role is minimal and the exposure management function is devolved to the divisions. For US-based subsidiaries this function is highly centralised at divisional head office. Subsidiaries report export and import exposures as they arise. The divisional treasury manager then decides if forward cover should be taken and, if so, takes out the contract on behalf of operating units. Exposure management at overseas' subsidiaries is subject to much less divisional control, due to the wide spread of locations and the existence of minority interests in some of the manufacturing operations. Overseas companies tend to be left alone, unless divisional management has a very strong currency recommendation or the company books significant foreign exchange losses.

Strengths and Weaknesses. The strength of this system is that it fits into the existing management philosophy, organisation and legal structure of Company C. Also, the administrative costs of running the system are relatively cheap — or rather, are hidden (dispersed) in the company. So long as this general policy of decentralisation produces adequate profits it is unlikely to be changed. However, this approach does involve substantial opportunity costs:

1. The divisional focus means that interdivisional opportunities for matching or netting are not recognised. This generates unnecessary foreign exchange costs, since two divisions with offsetting currency flows will be entering into spot and/or forward exchanges in different directions. (The divisional focus will also very probably mean wasted opportunities for inter-divisional liquidity reallocation.)
2. Similar wasted opportunities arise at overseas subsidiary level, again because of the lack of a global exposure information system and decision point.
3. Lack of corporate guidelines on and control over exposure management.
4. Dispersion of decision making to divisional and, more particularly, to overseas subsidiary level means opportunities for economies of scale (expertise, dealing) are unrealised. Overseas exposures could be largely centralised by a policy of invoicing US intercompany exports in buyers' currencies.
5. Overemphasis on market-related techniques, to the exclusion of internal tactics (matching, leading and lagging, pricing flexibility). A global viewpoint might also lead to a better understanding of the interaction of operating and exposure decisions and a more integrated treasury.
6. Unclear responsibility allocation: US subsidiaries are evaluated on operating performance, which automatically includes the effects of the forward-cover decision made by divisions. Hence subsidiaries are held responsible for a decision over which they have no control.

Case D. Centralised Parent-Country-Oriented Multinational

Background. Company D is a US manufacturer of consumer and industrial products. Annual sales exceed $2 billion, around two-thirds of which is on the domestic market. Organisationally the company is dispersed: it has over 10 operating divisions with subsidiaries (sales and manufacturing) in over 30 countries.

Exposure Characteristics. Exchange risk arises from translation as well as transactional exposures. US-based companies have both third party export and import exposures. Overseas manufacturing and sales companies are sourced domestically and from US affiliates, and sell only in local markets. Most of the overseas operations are located in Europe.

Exposure Management System. This has been centralised at corporate treasury by the manipulation of intercompany currency-of-invoicing policy and a comprehensive exposure reporting system for US companies. A dual intercompany currency-of-invoicing policy is adopted. All European companies are invoiced in their local currencies from the US, thereby eliminating their payables' exposures. Non-European affiliates are invoiced in US dollars, and so have dollar payables exposures. The rationale here is that the amounts are not significant, many of the local currencies do not have forward markets, and the management time and administrative costs of doing otherwise would be excessive. The intercompany currency-of-invoicing policy is thus a mixture of two themes: centralize exchange risk but do not create an excessive managerial and administrative burden.

This policy has achieved the objective of redirecting the vast bulk of transactional exposures back to the USA. The exposure reporting and management system can then focus on US operations. Each month all US divisions submit to corporate treasury an exposure forecast, by month for six months out, consisting of both invoiced and forecast transactions. The report gives a currency breakdown of intercompany and third party receipts and third party payments. Within policy guidelines set by senior management, the assistant treasurer-international then takes the exposure management decisions and action (e.g. leading and lagging, matching, forward cover) on behalf of the subsidiaries. Irrespective of this action, for evaluation purposes subsidiaries receive the in-house forward rate. Hence responsibility allocation is clear.

Strengths and Weaknesses. The major weakness of this approach is that, with over 10 divisions, the aim of an integrated treasury function is unavoidably difficult. This constrains treasury liaison on sourcing, marketing, and other operating decisions. Given these organisational complexities, however, Company D's system represents a sensible trade-off between the advantages of centralisation and the administrative and organisational costs of taking the centralisation concept to an unnecessary extreme. The key benefits are:

1. The vast majority of exposures are identified and managed on a group basis. This enables natural matched positions to be identified and also 'artificial' ones to be 'manufactured' (by changing billing currencies). Centralised management also enables a wider range of techniques to be used and produces more favourable rate quotations on the larger deals.

2. The in-house forward rate system is a clear and fair means of allocating responsibilities between treasury and operating units. Performance evaluation and motivation are not adversely affected.

3. Management effectiveness is increased. The central exposure management operation is run by a single, expert professional (plus back-up staff). This leaves operating management free to concentrate on its major tasks.

Case E. Decentralised 'Pure' Multinational

Background. Company E is a German engineering company and this stage of its development occurred around 1970. Annual third party sales exceeded $2 billion. Operations were centered on manufacturing units in four countries: Germany, UK, Holland, and Italy. Each of these companies produced the same products and operated independently, selling to third parties and sales affiliates (at arm's length) both domestically and internationally. Head office's role consisted basically of acting as banker to the group and monitoring the profit performance of subsidiaries.

Exposure Characteristics. Both transactional and translation exposures were significant. The latter were not a major concern because of flexible accounting regulations (German companies are not required to consolidate foreign subsidiaries in their published financial statements).

Exposure Management System. This was highly decentralised: subsidiary companies managed their own transactional exposures and accordingly were evaluated on their overall profit performance. Given the existence at that time of a relatively fixed exchange rate system, foreign exchange risk was not seen as a major concern. The only element of cooperation between subsidiaries was the operation of bilateral netting arrangements between the four manufacturing companies. Its scope was limited, however, because of the limited nature of trade flows between these entities.

Strengths and Weaknesses. Judged in its historical context this organisation was reasonable and typical of many European multinational companies. In the context of the floating exchange rate era, however, its weaknesses are fundamental:

1. Exposures are not clearly defined or identified on a group basis. Hence global exposure management is impossible and control over local exposure management actions is inadequate.
2. The organisation does not facilitate the application of treasury expertise to operating decisions.
3. Evaluation of exposure management performance is inadequate.

As the next example shows, the advent of floating exchange rates and changes in the company's operating pattern have led to a rethink of how its exposure management function should be organised.

Case F. Centralised 'Pure' Multinational

Background. Company F is Company E ten years on. Annual third party sales have doubled to around $4 billion. Operations are still centered on the four manufacturing units in Germany, UK, Holland, and Italy. However, significant integration of the manufacturing process has taken place, mainly for production reasons. Rather than manufacture complete items, each unit now specializes in the production of certain components which are then traded with the other manufacturing units for final assembly. This massive increase in intercompany trade, together with fluctuating exchange rates, has created a bias towards greater treasury centralisation in Company F.

Exposure Characteristics. The same basic exposure pattern exists as before, but it is now significantly larger and more complex because of extensive intercompany trading.

Exposure Management System. Company F decided to centralize exposure management by the establishment of a re-invoicing vehicle, International SA (Switzerland). The rationale for a re-invoicing vehicle was also based on other financial considerations: to minimize the banking costs relating to foreign exchange transactions and intercompany flows and to assist operating companies with cash forecasting and short-term financing. But from an exposure management viewpoint the basic aim is clear: arrange the currency-of-invoicing policy so that transactional exposures arise at International SA and not at subsidiary level. This is achieved by invoicing all exports to the vehicle company in the exporter's currency. The vehicle company then re-invoices affiliate customers in their local currencies and third party customers in either local or a more appropriate currency. The only transactional exposures remaining at subsidiary level are third party payables, which are generally not significant. These, together with translation exposures, are currently monitored by detailed currency reporting to International SA.

Strengths and Weaknesses. The costs of this system are essentially the development and running costs. The vehicle company is run by three professionals plus clerical staff. For this outlay Company F obtains the following benefits:

1. Exposures are identified and managed on a group basis, with all the attendant economies of scale: realisation of potential matching opportunities, concentration of management expertise, access to a wider range of exposure management options, greater focus on internal tactics, better currency advice and finer rates from banks.
2. The re-invoicing vehicle facilitates leading and lagging and automatically acts as a clearing center for multilateral netting.
3. Treasury and operating responsibilities are clearly and rationally allocated.
4. Cash and liquidity management improvements are facilitated: better cash forecasting at subsidiary level, liquidity reallocation is easily effected through adjustment of intercompany credit terms, cheaper financing costs at the center.

REVIEW QUESTIONS

1. Select three dissimilar companies, such as a manufacturing (e.g. consumer products) company, a service (e.g. airline) company and a trading (e.g. oil) company. Discuss how the operating and organisational characteristics of each has affected the exposure management function.
2. Devise a practical internal hedging system (optional or compulsory) for a US company whose operating divisions make hundreds of foreign currency export sales each year. Your proposal should include the following details: (a) how should the 'paper' rate be set?; (b) if the market forward rate is used, for what maturity?; (c) when should treasury settle with the operating unit and what happens if the customer pays late?; (d) who is responsible for credit collection?; and (e) exactly how should treasury performance be evaluated? Note that, given the number of export sales, it is impractical to monitor foreign currency receipts on a transaction-by-transaction basis.
3. Discuss alternative methods of centralising group transactional exposures for (a) a US company exporting to domestically oriented sales companies, and (b) a Japanese company with manufacturing operations in the UK and Germany, and with domestically oriented sales companies in the rest of Europe (sourced intercompany from Japan, the UK and Germany) and the Far East (sourced intercompany from Japan).
4. Discuss how an export finance company can be used in group exposure/liquidity management. To illustrate, construct an export financing deal using current interest rates (domestic and Euro-) and exchange rates.
5. Suggest how the exposure management systems of companies A and C might be improved.
6. If operating units rejects treasury advice, should subsidiaries be allowed to take action which treasury believe will harm the group?

PART IV

This Page has been intentionally left blank

21

FINANCING OF INTERNATIONAL TRADE

INTRODUCTION

Financing international trade is a complex process, involving many variables, ranging from corporate policy and marketing strategy to exchange risk and general borrowing conditions. The reason behind this complexity is that trade involves two countries with *different currencies* and *jurisdictions.* In addition, payments must be made *at a distance* and *across time,* so the exporter, the importer, or both need credit during part or all of the period from the initial manufacture of goods by the exporting firm to the time of the final sale and collection by the importer. The main objective of a good corporate export financing policy should be financing the greatest possible amount of sales with the greatest possible management simplicity and with minimal risk.

International trade financing, one of the oldest functions of international business, is also one of the least glamorous. Nevertheless, for the majority of firms engaged in international business, export financing forms the core of international finance. While the techniques are standardised, the range of applications is as varied as the content and destinations of a nation's exports, and things can easily go wrong. Among the potential problems are that of *exchange risk,* the problem of *inadequate information* regarding financial strength of foreign customers. And the problem of *special financing sources,* and costs. In addition, many of the less-developed nations have strict and sometimes unpredictable *exchange controls* on remittance and convertibility of hard currencies. The export financing manager must develop experience in handling all of these details in addition to the extensive, often tedious, documentation needed for the transfer of goods and payments internationally.

These obstacles aside, the exporter can count on readily available support and expertise from major commercial banks. Moreover, it is almost every government's policy to promote exports in order to improve the balance of payments and increase employment. Various countries have programme to assist the exporter, whether in the financing of trade or in managing the different risks involved. The Indian government is no exception. There are several government programmes available to promote exports, whether directly or indirectly through supporting the private sector by extending the much needed credits. The purpose of this chapter is to analyze the *international trade phase* for a domestic firm that begins to import goods and services from foreign suppliers and to export to foreign buyers.

TRADE FINANCING: THE FLOW OF GOODS AND THE FLOW OF FUNDS

Trade financing shares a number of common characteristics with the traditional value chain activities conducted by all firms. All companies must search out suppliers for the many goods and services required as inputs to their own goods production or service provision processes. A global firm's purchasing and procurement department must determine whether each potential supplier is capable of producing the product to required quality specifications, producing and delivering in a timely and reliable manner, and continuing to work with the firm in the ongoing process of product and process improvement for continued competitiveness. All must be at an acceptable price and payment terms. As illustrated in Exhibit 1, this same series of issues applies to potential customers, because their continued business is equally critical to firm's operations and success.

EXHIBIT 1

FINANCING TRADE: THE FLOW CHART

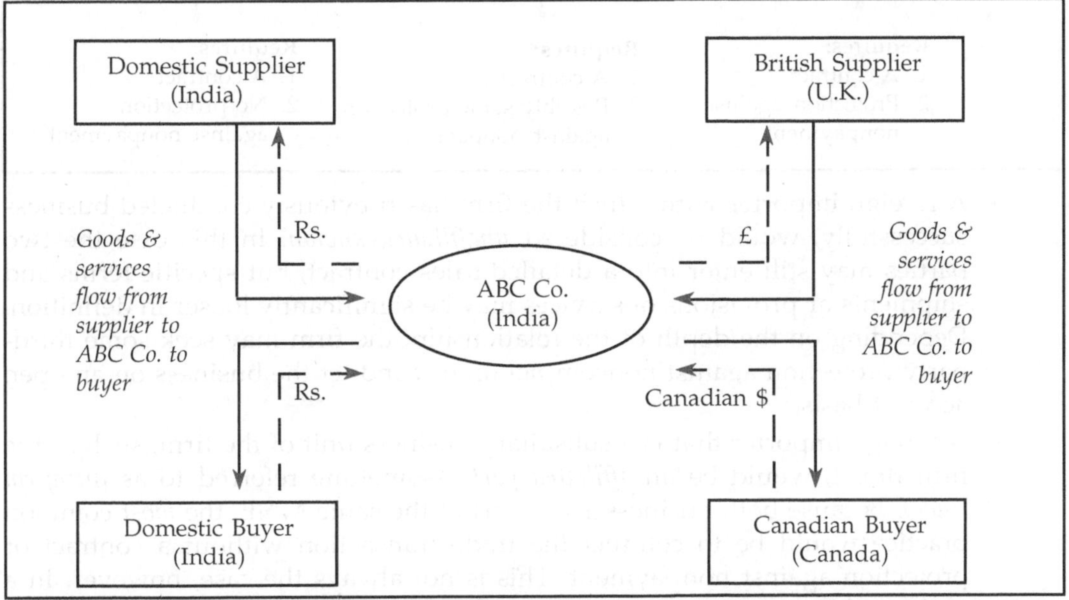

The nature of the relationship between the exporter and the importer is critical to understanding the methods for import-export financing utilized in industry. Exhibit-2 provides an overview of the three categories of relationships: *unaffiliated unknown, unaffiliated known,* and *affiliated.*

- A foreign importer with which the firm has not previously conducted business would be considered *unaffiliated unknown.* In this case the two parties would need to enter into a detailed sales contract, outlining the specific responsibilities and expectations of the business agreement. The firm would also need to seek out protection against the possibility that the importer would not make payment in full in a timely fashion.

EXHIBIT-2

ALTERNATIVE INTERNATIONAL TRADE RELATIONSHIPS

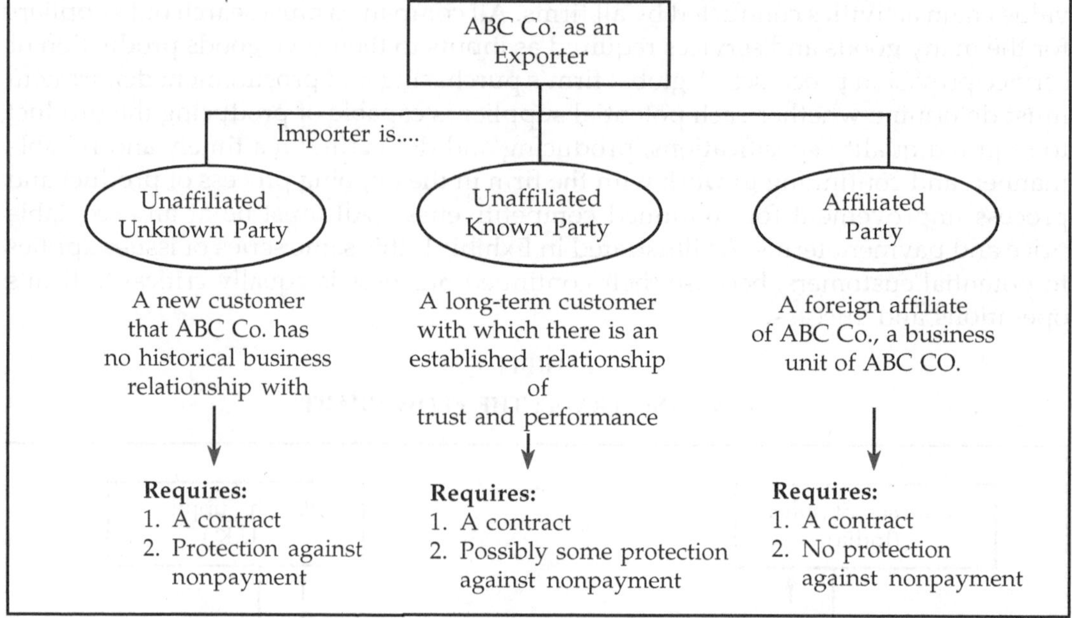

- A foreign importer with which the firm has previously conducted business successfully, would be considered *unaffiliated known.* In this case the two parties may still enter into a detailed sales contract, but specific terms and shipments or provisions of services may be significantly looser in definition. Depending on the depth of the relationship, the firm may seek some third-party protection against noncompletion or conduct the business on an open account basis.
- A foreign importer that is a subsidiary business unit of the firm, such as the firm Brazil, would be an *affiliated party* (sometime referred to as *intrafirm trade).* Because both businesses are part of the same MNE, the *most* common practice would be to conduct the trade transaction without a contract or protection against nonpayment. This is not always the case, however. In a variety of international business situations it may still be in the firm's best interest to detail the conditions for the business transaction and possibly to protect against any political or country-based interruption to the completion of the trade transaction.

The composition of global trade has changed dramatically over the past few decades. Whereas for centuries international trade was dominated by interfirm trade (transactions between unaffiliated parties), affiliated party trade has become increasingly dominant during the past 40 years. Although this may make management of these transactions simpler in terms of contracts and trade risks, it increases the complexity of the management of the total value and performance of the MNE.

ELEMENTS OF AN IMPORT/EXPORT TRANSACTION

Each individual trade transaction will need to cover three basic elements: description of goods, prices, and documents regarding shipping and delivery instructions.

Contracts

An import or export transaction is by definition a contractual exchange between parties in two countries that may have different legal systems, monies, languages, religions, or units of measure. Religious practices in countries may have significant impacts on international commercial transactions. In many Islamic countries, for example, interest payments are not allowed and therefore contracts must be constructed carefully to avoid putting parties in conflict with national regulations and religious practices. It is therefore critical to define all terms used in export contracts carefully and fully within the contracts themselves.

All contracts should include definitions and specifications for the quality, grade, quantity, and price of the goods in question. Definitions should be complete and should not use abbreviations. Whenever possible, terms such as "ton" should be defined further to include quantities if possible (2,000 or 2,200 pounds, for example). References in the contract to published prices or catalogs with associated descriptions are often helpful, as are product, blueprints or diagrams that include any engineering or other technical details related to expected product qualities and characteristics.

Prices

Price quotations can be a major source of confusion. Price terms in the contract should conform to published catalogs, specify whether quantity discounts or early payment discounts are in effect (and how they are calculated), and state whether finance charges are relevant in the case of deferred payment, transportation charges, insurance fees, or specific surcharges or fees relative to the countries in question.

Documents

Documentation covers a variety of issues of particular importance from a financial management perspective. An importer wishing to take possession of goods at a dock, airport, or any other point of delivery and clear them through customs, must possess certain customs and shipping documents. These typically include *bills of lading, commercial invoices, insurance policies, consular invoices,* and *packing lists.*

i) A *bill of lading*, or *B/L*, is issued to the exporter by a common carrier transporting the merchandise. It will be described more fully later in this chapter.
ii) A signed *commercial invoice* is issued by the exporter and contains a precise description of the merchandise. Unit prices, financial terms of sale, and amount due from the importer are indicated, as are shipping conditions related to charges, such as "FOB" (free-On board), "FAS" (free alongside), "CFR" (cost and freight), or "CIF" (cost, insurance, freight).
iii) *Insurance documents* must be as specified in the contract of sale and must be issued by insurance companies or their agents. The insurance may be issued to the exporter, who must then endorse the policy to "the importer, or it may be issued in the name of the importer. Insurance must be of types and for risks specified in the letter of credit.

iv) *Consular invoices* are issued in the exporting country by the consulate of the importing country to provide customs information and statistics for that country and to help prevent false declarations of value. The consular invoice may be combined with a certificate of origin of the goods.

v) *Packing lists* may be required so that the contents of containers can be identified, either for customs purposes or for importer identification of the contents of separate containers. In addition, an *export declaration* prepared by the exporter to assist the government in the preparation of export statistics may be required.

Shipping Deadline

Most importers insist on a specified deadline or time interval by which the shipment will be made. If the goods in question are particularly time-sensitive (such as products for seasonal sale), remedies will be included in the sales contract for failure to meet time commitments.

Payment Instructions

Which of the parties—the exporter or the importer—is to pay such charges as freight, insurance, import duties, handling fees, taxes, etc., must be specified carefully in the sales contract. The currency in which all payments are to be made between importer and exporter must also be specified clearly. The payment terms state whether cash is to be paid in advance, whether letters of credit are required, and what documents need- to be presented against payment, consignments, or payment on open account. These terms must be detailed in the sales contract.

Packaging and Marking

Depending on the nature of the goods, proper packaging may be critical to preserving and protecting items being shipped. Proper markings on the inner and outer boxes and containers are needed to conform with customs regulations in countries. These markings typically include clear and conforming invoices of the value of all items for import duty calculation and payment purposes.

Warranties, Guarantees, and Inspections

Assurances regarding the performance or qualities demonstrated by the goods from the exporter may also be included in the sales contract. This may include not only protection against product defects and proper performance, but protection against any consequential damages from defective parts or performance. In some cases the importer may wish to have the right to inspect the goods before paying (and even the right to inspect the goods while being manufactured before shipping). These stipulations should of course be delineated in the sales contract.

Included in documents may be *certificates of analysis,* required to ascertain that certain specifications such as weight, purity, or sanitation have been met. These conditions may be required by health or other officials of the importing country—especially in the case of foods and drugs—or they may be insisted on by the importer as assurance that it is receiving what it ordered. The certificates may be issued by government or private organizations, as specified in the letter of credit.

INTERNATIONAL TRADE RISKS

In order to understand the risks associated with international trade transactions, it is helpful to understand the sequence of events in any such transaction. Exhibit-3 illustrates, in principle, the series of events associated with a single export transaction.

From a financial management perspective, the two primary risks associated with an international trade transaction are *currency risk* (currency of denomination of payment) and *risk of noncompletion* (timely and complete payment). Exhibit-3 illustrates the traditional business problem of credit management: The exporter quotes a price, finalizes a contract, and ships the goods, losing physical control over the goods based on trust of the buyer or the promise of a bank to pay based on documents presented. The risk of default on the part of the importer is present as soon as the financing period begins, as depicted in Exhibit-3.

In many cases the initial task of analyzing the creditworth of foreign customers is similar to procedures for analyzing domestic customers. If a firm has had no experience with a foreign customer but that customer is a large, well-known firm in its home country, the firm may simply ask for a bank credit report on that firm. The firm may also talk to other firms that have had dealings with the foreign customer. If these investigations show the foreign customer (and country) to be completely trustworthy, the firm would likely ship to them on open account, with a credit limit, just as they would for a domestic customer. This is the least costly method of handling exports because there are no heavy documentation or bank charges. However, before a regular trading relationship has been established with a new or unknown firm, the firm must face the possibility of nonpayment for its exports or noncompletion of its imports. The risk of nonpayment can be eliminated through the use of a letter of credit issued by a creditworthy bank.

EXHIBIT-3

THE TRADE TRANSACTION TIME LINE AND STRUCTURE

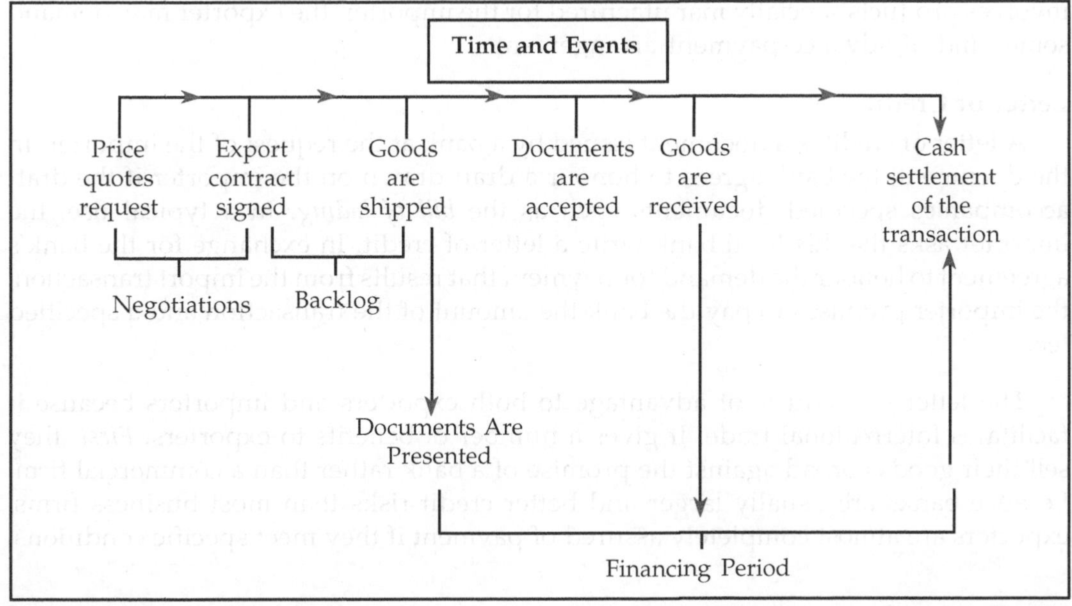

PAYMENT METHODS FOR INTERNATIONAL TRADE

In any international trade transaction, credit is provided by either the supplier (exporter), the buyer (importer), one or more financial institutions, or any combination of these. Supplier may have sufficient cash flow to fund the entire trade cycle, beginning with the production of the product until payment is eventually made by the buyer. This form of credit is known as *supplier credit.* In some cases, the exporter may require bank financing to augment its cash flow. On the other hand, the supplier may not desire to provide financing, in which case the buyer will have to finance the transaction itself, either internally or externally, through its bank. Banks on both sides of the transaction can thus play an integral part in trade financing.

Cash Terms

Cash terms may be either COD or CBD. COD terms mean cash on delivery of the goods and CBD terms mean cash before delivery of the goods. Under either COD or CBD terms, the exporter does not extend credit. Although credit risk does not exist under either terms, COD terms are accompanied by the risk that the importer may refuse the shipment while CBD terms avoid all risk. Under CBD terms, the exporter may insist on cash at the time of order or he may specify the time of cash payment prior to shipment. Another possible arrangement is that a part of the payment is made at the time of order, that progress payments are made between the time of order and the time of shipment, and that the final payment is made just before the release of the goods to a common carrier.

Cash terms are exceptional in these days of serve international competition. While cash-type transactions are ideal from the exporter's point of view, the importer does not like such transactions. This is because the importer is forced to accept all risks in transit, in exchange fluctuations, and in the quality of the goods received. Consequently, the exporter will insist on cash terms only in instances of the importer's poor credit standing or extreme political risks in the importing country. If the sale involves products specially manufactured for the importer, the exporter may demand some kind of advance-payment arrangement.

Letter of Credit

A letter of credit is a document issued by a bank at the request of the importer. In the document, the bank agrees to honour a draft drawn on the importer if the draft accompanies specified documents such as the *bill of lading*. In a typical use, the importer asks that his local bank write a letter of credit. In exchange for the bank's agreement to honour the demand for payment that results from the import transaction, the importer promises to pay the bank the amount of the transaction and a specified fee.

The letter of credit is of advantage to both exporters and importers because it facilitates International trade. It gives a number of benefits to exporters. *First,* they sell their goods abroad against the promise of a bank rather than a commercial firm. Because banks are usually larger and better credit risks than most business firms, exporters are almost completely assured of payment if they meet specific conditions.

Second, they can obtain funds as soon as they have such necessary documents as the letter of credit and the bill of lading. When shipment is made, the exporter prepares a draft on the importer in accordance with the letter of credit and presents it to his local bank. If the bank finds that all papers are in order, it advances the funds, the face value of the draft less fees and interest.

Although its major beneficiaries are exporters, the letter of credit also gives a number of benefits to importers. First, it assures them that the exporter will be paid only if he provides certain documents, all of which are carefully examined by a bank. If the exporter is unable or unwilling to make proper shipment, recovery of the deposit is much easier from the bank than from the exporter. Second, the letter of credit enables the importer to remove the commercial risk for the exporter in exchange for other considerations. Thus, the importer can bargain for better terms such as a lower price. Moreover, it is comparatively cheaper to finance the goods under a letter of credit than by borrowing. Letter of credit will be described in greater detail later in this chapter.

Drafts

A draft or a bill of exchange is an order written by an exporter that requires an importer to pay a specified amount of money at a specified time. Through the use of drafts, the exporter may use its bank as the collection agent on accounts that the exporter finances. The bank forwards the exporter's drafts to the importer directly or indirectly (through a branch or a correspondent bank) and then remits the proceeds of the collection back to the exporter.

A draft involves three parties: the drawer or maker, the drawee, and the payee. The drawer is the person or business who issues the draft. This person is ordinarily the exporter who sells and ships the merchandise. The drawee is the person or business against whom the draft is drawn. This person is usually the importer who must pay the draft at maturity. The payee is the person or business to whom the drawee will eventually pay the funds. If the draft is not a negotiable instrument, it designates a person or bank to whom payment is to be made. Such a person, known as the payee, may be the drawer himself or a third party such as the drawer's bank. However, this is generally not the case because most drafts are a bearer instrument. Drafts are negotiable if they meet a number of conditions. (I) They must be in writing and signed by the drawer-exporter. (2) They must contain an unconditional promise or order to pay an exact amount of money. (3) They must be payable on sight or at a specified time. (4) They must be made out to order or to bearer. If a draft is made out to order, the funds involved should be paid to the person specified. If it is made out to bearer, the funds should be paid to the person who presents it for payment.

There are two types of drafts: *sight drafts* and *time drafts*[1]. A sight draft is payable

1. Drafts are also classified as clean or documentary. Unlike a documentary draft, a clean draft does not require any other document. When a clean draft is used in trade, the exporter usually sends the shipping documents directly to the buyer. Clean drafts are sometimes used when multinational companies ship the goods to their own subsidiaries, because matters of trust and credit are not important. However, most international trade transactions involve documentary drafts which require various shipping documents.

on demand to the drawee-importer. A time draft is payable a specified number of days after presentation to the drawee. When a time draft is presented to the drawee, the drawee or his bank accepts it. This acceptance acknowledges in writing the drawee's obligation to pay the sum indicated on the face of the draft. When drafts are accepted by the importer, they become trade acceptances. When drafts are accepted by the bank, they become bankers' acceptances.

Because bankers' acceptances are highly marketable, the exporter can sell them in the market or discount them at his bank. Whenever they are sold or discounted, the seller adds his endorsement on the back of the draft. In the event of the importer's failure to pay at maturity, the holder of the draft will have recourse for the full amount of the draft from the last endorser.

There are a number of reasons why drafts are used in foreign trade. (1) They provide written evidence of obligations in a comprehensive form. (2) They allow both the exporter and the importer to reduce the cost of financing and to divide the remaining costs equitably. (3) They are negotiable and unconditional. That is, drafts are not subiect to disputes which may occur between the parties involved.

Consignments

Goods for export may be consigned to the exporter's own agent (subsidiary), an independent agent, or an import house. Assume that an exporter in India ships to an importer in London, 100 cases of quart bottles on a consignment basis. Because the exporter pays all the expenses connected with the shipment, the importer incurs no expenses at the time this shipment is delivered to this warehouse. Actually, the 100 cases of bottles are still the exporter's inventory. Thus, if the importer should fail, the exporter can demand that all the unsold bottles be returned to him.

Let us further assume that this consignment arrangement involves a ten per cent commission on all bottles sold. If the importer sold all the 100 cases at ₹ 2000 per case, he would deduct his commission of ₹ 20,000 (100 × ₹ 2000 × .10) and remit to the exporter a dollar draft for ₹ 1,80,000.

Consignment to the independent agent or the import house raises most of the same problems encountered in open account transactions. Under a *consignment* arrangement, the exporter ships the goods to the importer while still retaining actual title to the merchandise. The importer has access to the inventory, but does not have to pay for the goods until they have been sold to a third party. The exporter is trusting the importer to remit payment for the goods sold at that time. If the importer fails to pay, the exporter has limited recourse, since there is no draft involved and the goods have already been sold. As a result of the high risk, the consignment method is seldom used except by affiliated and subsidiary companies trading with the parent company. Hence, this type of operation is usually confined to companies working very closely together and between companies that completely trust each other.

Credit Terms

Most importers are not required to pay for goods before or on delivery but are allowed a short deferment period before payment is made. During this period, the exporter extends credit to the importer. There are three types of trade credit: *open account*, *notes payable*, and *bankers' acceptances/ trade acceptances.*

Open account credit does not require the importer to sign a formal debt instrument to evidence the amount that he owes the exporter. The importer simply charges his purchases, much in the same fashion that domestic retail stores extend credit to their customers. Then the importer's account is carried on the books of the exporter like any other receivables. This arrangement places the entire financial burden upon the exporter. Because banks usually refuse to advance against accounts receivable, it ties up large amounts of the exporter's capital. In addition, with this arrangement the exporter assumes the risks of foreign exchange blockage and buyer default. Therefore, open account terms are extended only to trusted customers in countries that have no foreign exchange or political problems.

In some export transactions, promissory notes are employed instead of open account credit. In this case, the importer is requested to sign a note that evidences his debt to the exporter. Thus, this arrangement makes the importer recognise his debt formally. The note calls for the payment of the obligation at some future date.

Bankers' acceptances are time drafts or bills of exchange drawn on, and accepted by the importer's bank (drawee bank). By accepting the draft the drawee bank assumes an unconditional obligation to pay a specified (face) amount at the draft's maturity to a bona fide holder. In effect, bankers' acceptances at the draft's maturity are guarantees of the debt by the importer's bank. Bankers' acceptances are negotiable instruments and, since the bank's name backs the instrument, they are discountable. These features allow the exporter who receives a bankers' acceptance in lieu of immediate payment to realise cash on the sale immediately by selling the acceptance, at a discount, to either the drawee or any other bank. Or, if the exporter does not need cash immediately, the acceptance can be held until the maturity date and then presented to the drawee bank for payment.

Banker's acceptances can be created under a letter of credit, in which case a number of shipping documents must be submitted by the exporter to the drawee bank. There are also so-called clean acceptances, which do not require a presentation of the shipping documents to the accepting bank: in this instance the importer must have an acceptance agreement with the bank, which entitles the importer to request the issuance of bankers' acceptances.

Trade acceptances are similar to bankers' acceptances but instead of being drawn on and accepted by the importer's bank they are drawn on and accepted by the importer, who, by this acceptance, promises to pay to the holder in due course the face amount of the acceptance at the specified maturity date. Trade acceptance and bankers' acceptances are negotiable. They cannot, however, be discountable if the importer on whom it is drawn is not well known and regarded in the market.

A trade acceptance is a form of short-term financing common in almost all foreign trade activities. In fact, it is the largest source of short-term funds for importers. Under this method of financing, the exporter draws a draft on the importer ordering him to pay the draft at some specified future date. The exporter will not release the goods until the importer accepts the draft. When the importer accepts the draft, it becomes a trade acceptance.

An exporter can specify the credit terms under which he is willing to extend with a foreign export sale. The degree of competition has a strong impact on the actual terms. The exporter may be compelled to grant 60 or 90 day credit even if he would like to be paid immediately after shipment. The shortest credit term is extended when the exporter draws a sight draft on a correspondent bank of the importer's bank. Payment is made to the exporter on demand when the draft arrives at the importer or his bank. Longer credit terms are achieved when the exporter draws a time draft, which specifies the time period after presentation when the funds must be paid.

When a time draft is employed in foreign trade, the exporter may carry the credit for his own account or refinance it through a local bank. Under the latter arrangement, the letter of credit ordinarily specific who will pay the expenses of financing. Although these expenses may be paid by the exporter or the importer, the ultimate choice depends largely upon the conditions of competition at the time of the transaction.

TRADE FINANCING METHODS

Most international trade involves a time lag between the date of shipment and when payment is made. Although some international transactions are of course paid for in cash up front, such advance payment is as rare internationally as it is domestically. For transactions between unrelated parties, however, financing is usually needed. Many other international trade transactions are between different units of the same multinational enterprises.

A bank can finance goods in transit, as well as goods held for sale, based on the three key documents, without exposing itself to questions about the quality of the merchandise or other physical aspects of the shipment. The bank in effect promises to pay the exporter on behalf of the importer, and receives reimbursement from the importer at some agreed-upon date. The bank thus acts like a trusted intermediary between the two parties.

Letter of Credit (L/C)

Introducted earlier, the *letter of credit, (L/C)*, is a bank's conditional promise to pay issued by a bank at the request of an importer (the applicant/buyer), in which the bank promises to pay an exporter (the beneficiary of the letter) upon presentation of documents specified in the L/C. An L/C reduces the risk of noncompletion, because the bank agrees to pay against documents rather than actual merchandise. The relationship between the three parties can be seen in Exhibit-4.

An importer (buyer) and exporter (seller) agree on a transaction and the importer then applies to its local bank for the issuance of an L/C. The importer's bank issues an L/C and cuts a sales contract based on its assessment of the importer's creditworthiness. The bank might require a cash deposit or other collateral from the importer in advance. The importer's bank will want to know the type of transaction,

EXHIBIT-4

PARTIES TO A LETTER OF CREDIT (L/C)

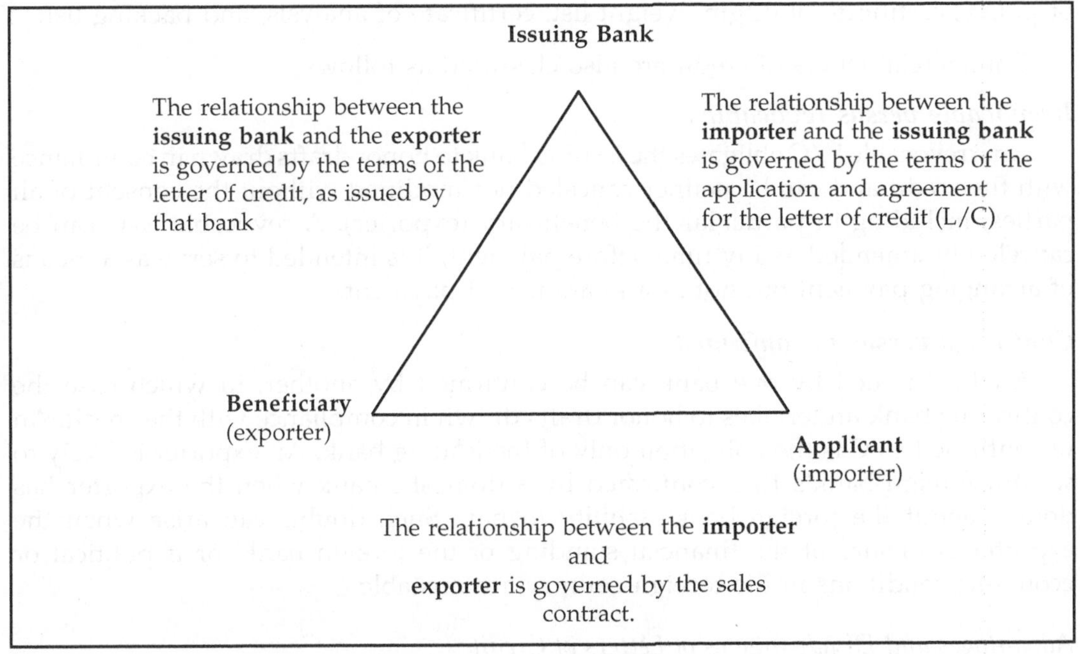

the amount of money involved, and what documents must accompany the draft that will be drawn against the L/C.

If the importer's bank is satisfied with the credit standing of the applicant, it will issue an L/C guaranteeing to pay for the merchandise if shipped in accordance with the instructions and conditions contained in the L/C.

The essence of a L/C is the promise of the issuing bank to pay *against specified documents*, which must accompany any draft drawn against the credit. The L/C is not a guarantee of the underlying commercial transaction. Indeed, the L/C is a separate transaction from any sales or other contracts on which it might be based. To constitute a true L/C transaction, all of the following five elements must be present with respect to the issuing bank:

1. The issuing bank must receive a fee or other valid business consideration for issuing the L/C.
2. The bank's L/C must contain a specified expiration date or a definite maturity.
3. The bank's commitment must have a stated maximum amount of money.
4. The bank's obligation to pay must arise only on the presentation of specific documents, and the bank must not be called on to determine disputed questions of fact or law.
5. The bank's customer must have an unqualified obligation to reimburse the bank on the same condition as the bank has paid.

Most commercial letters of credit are *documentary*, meaning that certain documents must be included with any drafts drawn under their terms. Required documents usually include an order bill of lading (discussed in more detail later in the chapter), a commercial invoice, and any of the following: consular invoice, insurance certificate or policy, certificate of origin, weight list, certificate of analysis, and packing list.

Commercial letters of credit are also classified as follows.

Irrevocable versus revocable

An irrevocable L/C obligates the issuing bank to honor drafts drawn in compliance with the credit and can be neither canceled nor modified without the consent of all parties, including in particular the beneficiary (exporter). A revocable L/C can be canceled or amended at any time before payment; it is intended to serve as a means of arranging payment but not as a guarantee of payment.

Confirmed versus unconfirmed

An L/C issued by one bank can be confirmed by another, in which case the confirming bank undertakes to honor drafts drawn in compliance with the credit. An unconfirmed L/C is the obligation only of the issuing bank. An exporter is likely to want a foreign bank's L/C confirmed by a domestic bank when the exporter has doubts about the foreign bank's ability to pay. Such doubts can arise when the exporter is unsure of the financial standing of the foreign bank, or if political or economic conditions in the foreign country are unstable.

Advantages and Disadvantages of Letters of Credit

The primary advantage of an L/C is that it reduces risk—the exporter can sell against a bank's promise to pay rather than against the promise of a commercial firm. The exporter is also in a more secure position as to the availability of foreign exchange to pay for the sale, since banks are more likely to be aware of foreign exchange conditions and rules than is the importing firm itself. If the importing country should change its foreign exchange rules during the course of a transaction, the government is likely to allow already outstanding bank letters of credit to be honored for fear of throwing its own domestic banks into international disrepute. Of course, if the L/C is confirmed by a bank in the exporter's country, the exporter avoids any problem of blocked foreign exchange.

An exporter may find that an order backed by an irrevocable L/C will facilitate obtaining preexport financing in the home country. If the exporter's reputation for delivery is good, a local bank may lend funds to process and prepare the merchandise for shipment. Once the merchandise is shipped in compliance with the terms and conditions of the credit, payment for the business transaction is made and funds will be generated to repay the preexport loan.

The major advantage of an L/C to the importer is that the importer need not pay out funds until the documents have arrived at the bank that issued the L/C and after all conditions stated in the credit have been fulfilled. The main disadvantages are the fee charged by the importer's bank for issuing its L/C, and the possibility that the L/C reduces the importer's borrowing line of credit with its bank. It may, in fact, be a competitive disadvantage for the exporter to demand automatically an L/C from an importer, especially if the importer has a good credit record and there is no concern regarding the economic or political conditions of the importer's country.[2]

Bankers' Acceptances

When a draft is accepted by a bank, it becomes a bankers' acceptance. As such it is the unconditional promise of that bank to make payment on the draft when it matures. In quality the bankers' acceptance is practically identical to a marketable bank certificate of deposit (CD). The holder of a bankers' acceptance need not wait until maturity to liquidate the investment, but may sell the acceptance in the money market, where constant trading in such instruments occurs.

The first owner of the bankers' acceptance created from an international trade transaction will be the exporter, who receives the accepted draft back after the bank has stamped it "accepted." The exporter may hold the acceptance until maturity and then collect. On an acceptance of, say, ₹ 10,00,000 for six months the exporter would receive the face amount less the bank's acceptance commission of 1.5% per annum:

Face amount of the acceptance	₹ 10,00,000	
Less 1.5% per annum commission for 6 months	-7,500	(.015 x 6/12 x ₹ 10,00,000)
Amount received by exporter in 6 months	₹ 9,92,500	

Alternatively, the exporter may "discount"—that is, sell at a reduced price—the acceptance to its bank in order to receive funds at once. The exporter will then receive the face amount of the acceptance less both the acceptance fee and the going market rate of discount for bankers' acceptances. If the discount rate were 10% per annum, the exporter would receive the following:

2. The landscape of trade finance in Asia is changing. Given the proliferation of electronic and online facilities, traditional trade finance resources such as the letter of credit (L/C) stand to be replaced, perhaps totally, in a very short time frame. More important, banks and companies need to change their business mind set in order to accomodate the different type of financing arrangements required by the e-commerce business model. Tai Kah Chye, vice president and Asia Head of e-commerce trade and supply chain at JP Morgan, sums up the shift of balance: "The emergence of e-commerce technologies continues to capture the headlines in trade financing. Whilst it is true that e-commerce is not a substitute for financing, it is nonetheless fundamentally changing the way that trade financing has been conducted in the past."

Although the L/C is the most conventional trade finance tool, and one that still has a function in the region, its level of usage has declined in some Asian countries. Notes Wenyir Lu, senior vice president and general manager at bank SinoPac in Taiwan: "In Taiwan, the use of L/C has declined from 50%-60% of total trade transactions three years ago to below 30% today." The main reason for the drop in L/C usage in countries like Taiwan, Hong Kong, and Singapore is the long processing time: negotiating an L/C (from the time of shipment to the time of presentation by the issuing bank) can take over 20 days.

It's easy to pick electronic and online application service providers in the market. One is Bolero, a service launched in late 1999 and jointly owned by SWIFT and the Through Transport Club. By standardizing the architecture through which electronic documents are exchange, Bolero acts as a third-party authenticator of messages, allowing trading parties and banks to excahnge documents with confidence. This means the entire L/C cycle can be processed electronically, with greater speed and with less fraud. See "The LC Goes On-Line," *Asimoney*, February 2001, pp. 72-76.

Face amount of the acceptance	₹ 10,00,000	
Less 1.5% per annum commission for 6 months	-7,500	(.015 x 6/12 x ₹ 10,00,000)
Less 10% per annum discount rate for 6 months	50,000	(.10 x 6/12 x ₹ 10,00,000)
Amount received by exporter at once	₹ 9,42,500	

The discounting bank may hold the acceptance in its own portfolio, earning for itself the 10% per annum discount rate, or the acceptance may be resold in the acceptance market to portfolio investors. Investors buying bankers' acceptances provide the funds that finance the transaction.

The *securitization* of export receivables for financing trade is an attractive supplement to bankers' acceptance financing. A firm can *securitize* its export receivables by selling them to a legal entity established to create marketable securities based on a package of individual export receivables. An advantage of this technique is to remove the export receivables from the exporter's balance sheet because they have been sold without recourse.

The receivables are normally sold at a discount. The size of the discount depends on four factors:

1. The historic collection risk of the exporter
2. The cost of credit insurance
3. The cost of securing the desirable cash flow stream to the investors
4. The size of the financing and services fees

Securitization is more cost effective if there is a large value of transactions with a known credit history and default profitability. A large exporter could establish its own securitization entity. While the initial setup cost is high, the entity can be used on an ongoing basis. As an alternative, smaller exporters could use a common securitization entity provided by a financial institution, thereby saving the expensive setup costs.

Bill of Lading (B/L)

The third key document for financing international trade is the *bill of lading,* or *B/L.* The bill of lading is issued to the exporter by a common carrier transporting the merchandise. It serves three purposes: a receipt, a contract, and a document of title.

As a receipt, the bill of lading indicates that the carrier has received the merchandise described on the face of the document. The carrier is not responsible for ascertaining that the containers hold what is alleged to be their contents, so descriptions of merchandise on bills of lading are usually short and simple. If shipping charges are paid in advance, the bill of lading will usually be stamped "freight paid" or "freight prepaid." If merchandise is shipped collect—a less common procedure internationally than domestically—the carrier maintains a lien on the goods until freight is paid.

As a contract, the bill of lading indicates the obligation of the carrier to provide certain transportation in return for certain charges. Common carriers cannot disclaim responsibility for their negligence through inserting special clauses in a bill of lading. The bill of lading may specify alternative ports in the event that delivery cannot be made to the designated port, or it may specify that the goods will be returned to the exporter at the exporter's expense.

As a document of title, the bill of lading is used to obtain payment or a written promise of payment before the merchandise is released to the importer. The bill of lading can also function as collateral against which funds may be advanced to the exporter by its local bank .prior to or during shipment and before final payment by the importer.

Characteristics of the Bill of Lading

Bills of lading are either *straight* or *to order. A straight bill of lading* provides that the carrier deliver the merchandise to the designated consignee only. A straight bill of lading is not title to the goods and is not required for the consignee to obtain possession. Because a straight bill of lading is *not* title, it is not good collateral for loans. Therefore, a straight bill of lading is used when the merchandise has been paid for in advance, when the transaction is being financed by the exporter, or when the shipment is to a subsidiary.

An *order bill of lading* directs the carrier to deliver the goods to the order of a designated party, usually the shipper. An additional inscription may request the carrier to notify someone else of the arrival. The order bill of lading grants title to the merchandise only to the person to whom the document is addressed, and surrender of the order bill of lading is required to obtain the shipment.

The order bill of lading is typically made payable to the order of the exporter, who thus retains title to the goods after they have been handed to the carrier. Title to the merchandise remains with the exporter until payment is received, at which time the exporter endorses the order bill of lading (which is negotiable) in blank or to the party making the payment, usually a bank. The most common procedure would be for payment to be advanced against a documentary draft accompanied by the endorsed order bill of lading. After paying the draft, the exporter's bank forwards the documents through bank clearing channels to the bank of the importer. The importer's bank, in turn, releases the documents to the importer after payment (sight drafts), after acceptance (time drafts addressed to the importer and marked D/A), or after payment terms have been agreed upon (drafts drawn on the importer's bank under provisions of a L/C).

Factoring

When an exporter ships goods before receiving payment, the accounts receivable balance increases. Unless the exporter has received a loan from a bank, it is initially financing the transaction, and it must monitor the collections of receivables. Since there is a danger that the buyer will never pay at all, the exporting firm may consider selling the accounts receivable to a third party, known as a *factor.* In this type of financing, the exporter sells the accounts receivable without recourse. The factor then assumes all administrative responsibilities involved in collecting from the buyer and the associated credit exposure. As one would expect, the factor performs its own credit approval process on the foreign buyer before purchasing the receivable. For providing this service, the factor usually purchases the receivable at a discount and also receives a flat processing fee.

Factoring provides several benefits to the exporter. *First,* by selling the accounts receivable, the exporter does not have to worry about the administrative duties involved in maintaining and monitoring an accounts receivable accounting ledger. *Second,* the factor assumes the credit exposure to the buyer, so the exporter does not have to maintain personnel to assess the creditworthiness of foreign buyers. *Finally,* the sale of the receivable to the factor provides immediate payment and improves the exporter's cash flow.

Since it is the importer who must be creditworthy from a factor's point of view, *cross-border factoring* is often used. This involves a network of factors in various countries who assess credit risk. The exporter's factor contacts a correspondent factor in the buyer's country to assess the importer's creditworthiness and handle the collections of the receivable. Factoring services are usually provided by the factoring subsidiaries of commercial banks, commercial finance companies, and other specialised finance houses.

Forfaiting

Because capital goods are often quite expensive, an importer may not be able to make payment on the goods within a short time period. Thus, longer-term financing may be required here. The exporter could be able to provide financing for the importer but may not desire to do so, since the financing may extend over several years. In this case, a type of trade finance known as forfaiting could be used. Forfaiting refers to the purchase of financial obligations, such as bills of exchange or promissory notes, without recourse to the original holder, usually the exporter. In a forfait transaction, the importer would issue a promissory note in favour of the exporter to pay for the imported capital goods. The term generally ranges from three to seven years. The exporter would then sell the notes, without recourse, to the forfaiting bank. In some respects, this is similar to factoring, in that the forfaiter (or factor) assumes responsibility for the collection of payment from the buyer and the underlying credit risk and country risk. Since the forfaiting bank assumes the risk of nonpayment, it should asses the creditworthiness of the importer as if it were extending a medium-term loan. Forfait transactions are normally collateralised by a bank guarantee or letter of credit issued by the importer's bank for the term of the transaction. Since financial information is usually difficult to obtain on the importer, the forfaiting bank places a great deal of reliance on the bank guarantee as the collateral in the event the buyer fails to pay as agreed. It is this guarantee backing up the transaction that has fostered the growth of the forfait market, particularly in Europe, as a practical means of trade finance.

Forfaiting transactions can be denominated in most currencies. For some larger transactions, more than one bank may be involved. In this case, a syndicate is formed wherein each participant assumes a proportionate share of the underlying risk and profit. A forfaiting firm may decide to sell the promissory notes of the importer to other financial institutions willing to purchase them. However, the forfaiting firm is still responsible for payment on the notes in the event the importer is unable to pay

Countertrade

The term countertrade denotes all types of foreign trade transactions in which the sale of goods to one country is linked to the purchase or exchange of goods from that same country. Some types of countertrade, such as barter, have been in existence for thousands of years. However, only recently has countertrade gained popularity and importance. The growth in various types of countertrade has been fueled by large balance of payments disequilibriums, foreign currency shortages, and developint countries' debt problems, and stagnant worldwide demand. As a result, many multinationals have been confronted with countertrade opportunities, particularly in Asia, Latin America, and Eastern Europe. The most common types of countertrade include barter, compensation, and counterpurchase.

Barter represents the exchange of goods between two parties without the use of any currency as a medium of exchange. Most barter arrangements are one-time transactions governed by one contract.

In a *compensation* or clearing-account arrangement, the delivery of goods to one party is compensated for by the seller's buying back a certain amount of product from that same party. The transaction is governed by one contract, and the value of the goods is expressed in monetary terms. The buy-back arrangement could be for a fraction of the original sale *(partial compensation)* or more than 100 per cent of the original sale *(full compensation)*. An example of compensation would be the sale of phosphate from Morocco to France in exchange for purchasing a certain percentage of fertiliser. In some countries, this is also referred to as an industrial cooperation arrangement. Such arrangements often involve the construction of large projects, such as power plants, in exchange for the purchase of the project's output over an extended period of time. For example, a hydroelectric plant was sold by Brazil to Argentina in exchange for Brazil's purchase of a percentage of the plant's output over a long-term contract.

The term *counterpurchase* denotes the exchange of goods between two parties under two distinct contracts expressed in monetary terms. Delivery and payment of both goods are technically separate transactions.

The countertrade market is still developing. The primary participants are governments and multinationals, with assistance provided by specialists in the field, such as attorneys, financial institutions, and trading companies. The transactions are usually very complex and large. Many variations of countertrade exist, and the terminology used by the various market participants is still forming. Nonetheless, despite the economic inefficiencies of countertrade, it has grown in significance and is used by the experienced traders and governments.

EXPORT FINANCE IN INDIA

As the process of internationalisation of national economies gathers momentum, promotion of external trade assumes added importance. External trade opens up vast opportunities in terms of access to the global supply market and having the world as the potential market for exports, with the trade barriers being progressively brought down. Countries that can attune their policies to the demands of global forces can alone benefit from the new trends. Many countries that had, hitherto, instituted import-substitution regimes, obviously, need to reform their trade policies quite substantially. Although the export promotion drive in India had begun in early 70s, the import-substitution policy continued due to the scarcity of funds for the required imports. The Economic Reforms Process initiated in mid 1991 focussed initially on liberalising the Export Import Policy regime with equal importance being given to the simplification and rationalisation of the procedural system. Since finance being the back-bone of trade, whether domestic or international, Reserve Bank of India has taken various steps to ensure free flow of financial assistance to export sector at lower rates of interest.

Banks, being the main source of finance, are encouraged in several ways to extend export finance, to achieve the objectives of the foreign trade policy. Though export credit is not formally categorised as a priority sector credit by RBI, banks have to achieve a minimum floor level of export credit at 10% of each bank's net bank credit. Further it is of greater significance to banks since the credit is being extended to one of the vital sectors of the economy and serves the process of economic development, which is a national objective. In order to compensate the banks for extending export finance at lower rates of interest and encourage them to extend more liberal finance, various measures are taken. These include liberal export refinance by Reserve Bank of India (RBI) and Export/Import Bank of India (Exim Bank) and credit guarantee coverage facilities by Export Credit Guarantee Corporation of India Ltd. (ECGC).

Reducing export finance to be a critical area of reforms, commercial banks and other financial institutions in India have been constantly coming up with new schemes for financing different stages of export activity. Under the Post Shipment Credit Denominated in Foreign Currency (PSCFC) scheme introduced with effect from January 1, 1992, exporters can avail of post-shipment credit denominated in foreign currency and pay interest at internationally competitive rates. The rates, however, continued to be administered by the RBI. The LIBOR (London Inter Bank Offered Rate) linked Export Bills Discounting/Rediscounting (EBD/R) scheme introduced subsequently in October '93 effectively deregulated interest rates at the post-shipment stage. This was a landmark step. It was soon followed by the effective deregulation of interest rates at the pre-shipment stage as well with the launching of Pre-shipment Credit in Foreign Currency (PCFC) scheme in November '91. The scheme enables exporters to finance both domestic and imported inputs of exportable goods at interest rates linked to LIBOR. Normally, the credit period in the export financing schemes run by commercial banks is restricted upto 180 days. Thus, the cost of short-term export finance in India now compares favourably with that in other competing countries, provided the finance is taken in foreign currency. However, this facility is generally available only at designated offices of banks. Most of the small exporters at upcountry centres still have to manage with relatively expensive rupee finance. Letting interest rates being determined by market forces rather than artificially by any direct or indirect subsidy may enable all exporters to benefit from lowering of interest rates. It is also seen that export credit on deferred payment terms is more expensive in India because of the weak government support to export credit agencies like the ECGC and the EXIM Bank. It appears that ECGC is constrained from effectively discharging its intended role in the development of exports due to inadequate budgetary support. (On the other hand, a number of foreign insurance companies are waiting to enter the huge Indian insurance sector). It may be worthwhile to explore the possibility of allowing the foreign insurance companies to enter India on condition of undertaking certain level of export insurance commitments as part of their overall insurance exposures in India.

The Exim Bank offers credit mainly on deferred term basis. Exim Bank has designated special lending programmes for export oriented units and units in export processing zones. Forfaiting, which enables exporters to convert credit sales to cash sales without recourse, is the latest addition in its lending programmes. However, a policy push is required to make it a big success.

As far as adequacy of credit is concerned, the RBI has given very clear directives to banks to ensure that they must meet the needs of exporters fully. However, this would become possible only if banks start taking decisions based on the past track records rather than on the exporters' capacity to offer security. Modern techniques like factoring and forfaiting should be developed to facilitate financing the export ventures of small and new exporters who find it difficult to secure L/C backed contracts. Likewise, in the area of project exports too, forfaiting would prove helpful in making adequate credit available.

Procedural bottlenecks and obstacles is another vital area of concern. There are considerable delays in appraising and sanctioning of finance and other facilities. Top priority must, therefore, be accorded to upgradation of technology. The increasing complexities arising from the availability of export credit in foreign currencies, multi-currency accounting and managing floating interest rate exposures make it imperative for banks to switch over completely to computerised book-keeping and accounting. Simultaneously, the communication channels need to be strengthened to ensure speedy realisations and credit of export proceeds as also for advising export letters of credit, dissemination of other relevant information, etc. Further, it may be necessary to create a credit rating agency exclusively for exporters if banks have to successfully implement the lending guidelines that require a new proposal for export finance to be cleared within 45 days, a request for review/renewal of credit facilities within 30 days and a request for adhoc facility within 15 days.

It may also be necessary to increase the range of services for exporters such as increasing the period of suppliers' credit from 180 days to one year, permitting exporters to tie up lines of credit with branches of Indian and foreign banks abroad with provisions to repay the borrowings within one year, extending finance for market development and business travel to small and medium size exporters to help them in their marketing efforts, increasing the number of branches offering special services to exporters, financing against duty drawback receivables, allowing overseas buyers to maintain interest bearing deposit accounts in India, permitting exporters to book forward cover for exports based on their average exports rather than on the basis of firm orders in hand, permitting exporters direct access to forex markets rather than through authorised dealers as at present, making the Exchange Earners' Foreign Currency (EEFC) account fully convertible, etc. A review of some financing schemes is also called for. For example, there does not seem adequate logic for continuing with the Post-shipment Credit Denominated in Foreign Currency (PSCFC) scheme after the introduction of the Export Bill Discounting/Rediscounting (EBD/R) scheme. Similarly, the- Foreign Currency Account (FCA) scheme for exporters has become almost completely redundant especially, after the expansion of the size of Exchange Earners' Foreign Currency (EEFC) account scheme with which exporter can now release foreign exchange currency by them even beyond 1 year provided they justify its wealth.

Export finance is broadly classified into two categories, depending upon at what stage of export activity the finance is extended namely:

Financial assistance extended to the exporters, prior to shipment of export, goods, falls within the scope of pre-shipment finance. Financial assistance extended after the shipment of export goods falls within the scope of post-shipment finance.

Export finance (both at pre-shipment and post-shipment stages) in India is governed by and large by RBI directives and FEDAI rules. Since export finance is related to foreign trade, knowledge of the trade policy, procedures and directives of Export Trade Control authorities, international trade practices, particularly those of International Chamber of Commerce (ICC) Paris and the pulse of local as well as international markets is very much essential. Government of India has set up a vast network of institutional infrastructure to strengthen and subserve the objective of export promotion. Information regarding functional areas of these institutions will also help bankers very much.

Export finance is made available at concessional and liberal terms, as it is specifically aimed at serving a vital national cause. A banker extending such finance is expected to be prudent and judicious. Further, the exports being a part of external sector of the economy, is subject to several rules and regulations directly and indirectly. Thus, it casts an additional responsibility on the lending banker, who has to keep in view all such rules and regulations, in addition to usual principles of lending, while financing exports.

Some of the general lending guidelines to banks relating to export finance are:

1. Export Finance proposals should be expeditiously disposed off so that timely and adequate credit is made available to exporters. The applications for credit limits for export sector are to be disposed off, within the time frame given below:

(a) Sanction of fresh/enhanced credit limits 45 days

(b) Renewal of existing limits30 days

(c) Sanction of adhoc limits 15 days

2. Banks should adopt a flexible approach to export lending and norms of lending. At the same time, it is their responsibility to see that exporters do not misuse this concessional and liberal finance. It should be strictly "PURPOSE ORIENTED & NEED BASED".
3. Whenever a bank is considering export finance facilities, it should view the entire gamut of export activity transaction and sanction adequate facilities required, at both pre & post-shipment stages. Provisions of any pre- shipment facilities in isolation, without relating them to post-shipment operations and requirements (should not be restored to). Preferably, all requisite facilities should be considered at the same time as a package deal. This is in view of the interwoven links and regulations.
4. Banks must keep in view the past performance of exporters and future potential, while assessing the credit proposals. In the case of new exporters, their experience in domestic market in dealing with the relative commodities and other background factors must be taken into consideration.
5. Banks must keep a close watch on the end-use of finance and timely fulfillment of export orders.
6. RBI has allowed several relaxations in respect of export lending, including relaxations of credit norms. Some of them are listed below:

(a) While computing the overall working capital gap/maximum permissible bank finance (MPBF), banks can exclude export receivables out of such computation process and export sales finance limits can be assessed and sanctioned separately, over and above the permissible bank finance.

(b) Wherever exporters are unable to bring in additional contribution (margin) in respect of additional credit facilities required for specific export transactions, banks can waive such additional contribution required from exporters.

(c) If borrowing units have substantial export activity and the bank has identified excess finance as per applicable methods of lending in respect of such units and decides to convert such excess finance into WORKING CAPITAL TERM LOAN (WCTL), any excess finance in respect of pre-shipment finance limits should be carved out separately on notional basis, so that, on such WCTL concessional rates of interest as applicable to export finance can be levied.

(d) Banks are free to decide the levels of holding of individual items of inventory and receivables which should be supported by bank finance, after taking into account the production/processing cycle of the industry in question, as also other relevant factors. (This will apply to all categories of borrowers).

(e) Additional credit needs of exporters arising out of firm orders/confirmed letters of credit (and which are not taken into account while fixing the regular credit limits) should be met in full, even if sanction of such additional credit limits exceed MPBF.

TRADE FINANCE : INTERNATIONAL DEVELOPMENTS AND IMPACT ON INDIA

Trade financing has been used in more than 90 per cent of trade transactions (mostly short-term credit) in the world. The global financial crisis, which has resulted in slowdown in economic growth, has also impaired the access to trade finance. Developing and emerging economies are most vulnerable to the shortages in trade finance.

During the period of economic boom, trade (particularly when it takes place between associated companies in developed countries) was not financed by banks through letters of credit, but by general credit extended by the companies, usually secured on other types of collateral. This type of credit has been badly affected by the financial crisis, due to the general pessimism about the prospects of the companies, and the prices of their assets. International banks, which used to extend credit to local banks (by way of letters of credit confirmations, bill of exchange endorsements or interbank loans, swaps, hedges and other treasury activities, which enable the local banks to offer trade finance denominated in foreign currencies), started adopting a cautious approach, in the wake of financial market turmoil, and reduced the "bank limits" or "country limits." As a result, the cost of trade finance in developing countries went up by 3 to 4 per cent.

Exporters in general started seeking confirmed letters of credit, where they had exported on the basis of open account or cash against delivery (CAD). The banks' perception of risk was leading to tightening of liquidity, and therefore greater difficulty in getting confirmed letters of credit. According to Bankers' Association for Finance and Trade (BAFT), USA, in addition to cost escalation due to financial turmoil and low level of risk appetite, increased capital costs under Basel- II, is also expected to increase the cost of trade finance for developing country exporters. There are also reports that even developed country buyers/banks, in the guise of intense scrutiny, were rejecting/delaying the processing of trade documents on the basis of minor discrepancies. In such a situation, the acceptability of letters of credit from least developed markets, as also from some of the developing markets, was scrutinized by the banks critically, restricting the wheels of trade finance.

Scarcity in trade finance was a result of pressures from both demand-side and supply-side. In the initial months of crisis, Indian credit market faced credit squeeze, which was led by net capital outflows, as international investors withdrew capital from India to compensate their losses incurred in exotic derivatives trading. This eventually affected the Indian firms as there was lending restraint shown by the banks. Further, there was contraction in trade credit extended by supplier firms, as also increase in demand for trade credit by the end-user firms, affecting the working capital liquidity of exporters. To combat the working capital liquidity, Indian companies turned to trade financing.

The shortage of availability of trade credit, following the financial crisis, could be viewed from the decline in short-term trade credit inflows into India, as reflected in India's overall balance of payment statistics. During the period April- December 2008, net capital inflows under the head "short-term trade credit" have shrunk to US$ 0.5 billion, as compared to US$ 10.7 billion received during the corresponding period of the previous year. Short-term trade credit to India witnessed a net outflow of US$ 3.1 billion in the third quarter of 2008-09 (as against inflows of US$ 4.1 billion during the same period of 2007-08), mainly due to lower disbursements reflecting tightness in the overseas market and increased repayments as roll over was difficult. Exporters were also reporting challenges of liquidity in foreign currency, and high cost of foreign currency, especially for pre-shipment credit, where they need to source raw materials to service an export order.

The drying up of global liquidity combined with a general reassessment of risks by commercial banks led in the second half of 2008 to a rise in the cost of trade finance instruments such as letters of credit, and in some cases, to serious gaps between demand and supply with spreads above LIBOR increasing by some 25 to 300 basis points per annum and in some cases as much as 600 basis points. Trade finance experts who met in WTO in March 2009 have pointed out to a market gap in developing countries that is imminent demand for trade financing of between US$ 100 billion and US$ 300 billion on an annual and roll-over basis. Various measures have been taken by the multilateral institutions to enhance trade financing. World Bank/International Finance Corporation (IFC) has announced tripling of the ceiling of the trade finance guarantees available under the IFC's Global Trade Finance Programme (GTFP), a trade facilitation measure introduced to support trade from developing countries, from US$ 1 billion to US$ 3 billion.

IFC is also developing a programme to provide funded support to major financial institutions with wide trade finance networks in emerging markets, and to increase engagement with export credit agencies. IFC has also proposed to create a Global Trade Liquidity Pool (GTLP), in association with multilateral/regional institutions that are active in trade finance, to fund trade transactions for up to 270 days, which is expected to be self-liquidating once the conditions of trade finance improve. The Asian Development Bank (ADB) has announced expansion of its Trade Finance Facilitation Programme (TFFP) from the existing US$ 150 million to US$ 1 billion. The African Development Bank (AfDB) intends to support trade finance through a US$ 1 billion trade finance initiative (TFI). The European Bank for Reconstruction and Development, which expects the demand for trade finance from the member countries, proposes to hike the budget for its trade facilitation programme, from the present euro 800 million to euro 1.5 billion for the year 2009, to boost trade with and within eastern Europe, Central Asia, Russia and Ukraine. The Inter-American Bank for Development (IADB) has also announced increased limit for its Trade Finance Facilitation Programme (TFFP) from US$ 400 million to US$ 1 billion. G-20 has announced a US$ 250 billion trade finance package to be available over a period of two years.

The core of this package is a pool of money in which international institutions and national governments contribute 40 per cent, and commercial banks, the remaining 60 per cent. Berne Union proposes to strengthen its network and various means of coordination among members, to share the experiences in tackling the previous financial crisis in Asia and Russia, and real-time knowledge exchange, to enhance export credit, credit insurance and reinsurance.

The national governments have been supporting trade finance activities, some of them through the respective export credit agencies or developmental institutions. For example, the United States through U.S.-Exim Bank is making additional resources available to increase access to affordable trade finance. U.S.-Exim Bank, has already announced a programme to provide US$ 4 billion in new short-term trade finance facilities and US$ 8 billion in medium- and longterm trade finance facilities to support export of U.S. goods to emerging markets. Other countries like China, Japan, South Korea have also been providing similar facilities

The national governments have also been extending guarantees stimulating the financing system in a crisis period. For example, U.S.-Exim Bank has announced US$ 2.9 billion insurance cover to help meet the growing demand to insure U.S. lenders' confirmation of letters of credit issued by 11 Korean financial institutions. The U.K. Government has announced plans to guarantee as much as £ 20 billion of bank loans to small and medium companies ensuring flow of credit. Other countries like Germany, France, Hong Kong, Japan have been providing similar guarantees.

Various measures have been taken by the RBI/Government of India to address the liquidity challenges faced by the exporters, as also to enhance the availability of trade finance which include interest subvention of 2 per cent as a temporary measure for the period December 1, 2008 to September 30, 2009 to many labour-oriented sectors, increase in the period of pre-shipment and post-shipment credit, extension of period of realization of export proceeds from six months to 12 months, raising the ceiling on export credit in foreign currency, enhancing the eligible limit of export credit refinance (ECR) facility, expanding the lendable resources available to EXIM Bank of India and extension of back-up guarantee to Export Credit Guarantee Corporation (ECGC).

ILLUSTRATIVE PROBLEMS

1. A Canadian distributor purchases perfume from France in the amount of French francs 22,850 (approximately $5,000). Payment is due in three months in French francs.

		Day 90		
	Day 1	*Case A*	*Case B*	*Case C*
Exchange rates.				
Spot	$0.218850	$0.218550	$0.240735	$0.196965
3-month forward	$0.218140			
Interest rates:				
Canada	6.00%	6.00%	6.00%	6.00%
France	7.30%	7.30%	6.80%	7.80%

(a) On day 1 what is the premium or discount on the forward French franc? What is the interest differential between the Canada and France? Is there an incentive for interest arbitrage?

(b) If the importer wants to cover its transaction against foreign exchange risks, what alternatives are open?

(c) What is the cost of each alternative? (i) if a three-month treasury bill is bought; (ii) if a one-year bill is bought (do not make specific calculation in the latter case).

(d) Would you advise the importer to cover the foreign exchange transaction? Why?

Ans.:

(a) $$\text{Premium or discount} = \frac{(\text{Forward rate} - \text{spot rate})}{\text{spot rate}} \times \frac{12}{3}$$

$$= \frac{(.218140 - .218850)}{.218850} \times 4$$

Discount = –1.30%

Interest differential = 7.30 - 6.00 = 1.30% in favour of France

Since forward discount on French francs is of the same magnitude as the interest differential in favour of France, there is no incentive for covered interest arbitrage.

(b) There are two alternatives to cover the foreign exchange risk:

1. *In the forward market:* Buy French francs 22,850 for delivery in 90 days. (This insures the exchange rate at \$.218140/FF.) Pay the import bill with the French francs obtained in the forward transaction.
2. *In the money market:* Borrow \$5000.00 at 6%. Convert the proceeds into French francs and buy a 3-month French Treasury bill. Pay import bill with the funds derived from the sale of the treasury bill.

(c) Cost of covering in the forward market:

By buying future French francs, the U.S. importer is able to fix the exchange rate at \$.218140/FF. The final cost of the transaction depends on the spot rate at the end of the period, i.e., the rate at which the exporter would have to purchase the French francs in the absence of the forward contract.

	Case A	*Case B*	*Case C*
Spot rate - Day 90	\$ .218850	\$ .240735	\$ .196965
Less forward rate	.218140	.218140	.218140
Gain or loss (-) per FF in covering transaction	\$ .000710	\$ .022595	-\$ .021175
FF in transaction	FF22,850	FF22,850	FF22,850
Total gain or loss (-) in transaction	\$16.22	\$516.30	\$483.85
Exchange gain or loss (-) as % of transaction (\$5000) on a quarterly basis	.32%	10.33%	-9.68%

That is, by locking in the $0.218140 price the importer took advantage of a little discount in the forward market, in case of no change in the spot market; and he insured against a risk of appreciation in the FF that could have cost him $500.07 [(0.240735 - 0.218850) x 22,850. However, it is true that he also deprived himself of the opportunity of making $483.85 if a devaluation of the French franc vis-a-vis the U.S. dollar had taken place.

Cost of Covering in the Money Market:

If a perfect match of maturities among the trade cash flow, the loan, and the investment can be found, then the cost of covering in the money market is only the interest differential. In this case, the interest differential favours moving funds into Francs; therefore, if the above conditions are met the foreign exchange coverage in this case will produce a gain of 1.30% plus the foreign exchange loss or gain on the interest earned in French franc.

Cost of Covering in the Money Market - 3-month bill

	Case A	*Case B*	*Case C*
1) Spot rate: Day 90	$0.218850	0.240735	$0.19
2) Day 1	0.218850	0.218850	0.21
3) Appreciation (–) or depreciation of the French franc	—	$-0.021885	$0.2
4) Gain or loss (–) on payment FF22,850 × (line 3)	—	$ -500.07	$ 500
5) Proceeds from investment in FF (22,850) + 22,850 × .0730 × 3/12 = FF 23,267 (pay interest at end)			
6) Foreign exchange gain or loss (-) on conversion of bill proceeds (line 5) × (line 3)	—	$ 509.20	$ -509
7) Gain on interest differential 0.130 × $5,000 × 3/12	$ 16.25	$ 16.25	$ 16.25
	$ 16.25	$ 25.38	$ 7.12

Cost of Covering in the money Market - 1-year bill:

In this case, the previous calculations will have to be adjusted to reflect the capital gains and losses incurred in the sale of the Treasury bill.

Case A - no capital gain or loss

Case B - a capital gain

Case C - capital loss

QUESTIONS

1. Show how export-import transactions are closely related to receivables and inventory management for the multinational firm. In particular, explain the link between the choice of an invoicing currency and the credit decision.
2. Are the L/C and banker's acceptance instruments that are exclusively used in financing foreign trade? Why are these two instruments especially adapted to foreign trade? State the advantages that each instrument provides for the exporter and importer in a typical foreign trade transaction.
3. Why have major capital goods exporting countries found it necessary to establish government export financing programmes, instead of relying on banking and other private financing facilities? Does EX-IM Bank subsidise India exports?
4. Distinguish between factoring and forfaiting as techniques for managing receivables arising from exports. Which particular situations lend themselves best to forfaiting?
5. Distinguish between marine and export credit insurance: Which particular risk or risks are covered under each type?
6. How does the management of receivables generated by affiliate sales differ from the management of intracompany receivables? For example, what measure are appropriate if the currency of the affiliate is expected to depreciate?
7. Why is international factoring of accounts receivable relatively more costly than factoring domestic receivables? Would you advise a highly diversified MNC which regularly generates substantial receivables in a large number of countries to resort to factoring?
8. What is stockpiling? Under what circumstances is stockpiling strategy recommended for affiliates' operations?
9. The inventory management solution for the MNC does not differ from that of a typical domestic firm and can be determined by the same techniques. Comment on the statement, pointing out differences, if any, between the two situations.
10. Explain the differences in the risk to the exporter between accounts receivable financing and factoring.
11. Explain why so many international transactions require international trade credit faciliated by commercial banks.
12. An English exporter scheduled to receive payment in Italian liras sells the liras on a forward contract, so that she knows the US $ value of the receivable. How will she know the cost of this cover? When will she know the cost?
13. "As long as the forward rate for the currency is below the spot rate, I should cover my transactions if I have receivables in that currency; the forward discount shows that the currency is likely to devalue." Do you agree with this statement? Why?
14. If there is no change in the spot rate of a currency in a given period, does it make any difference whether one covers a transaction in the forward market or the money market? Give an example to support your answer.
15. What is the purpose of a letter of credit? What are the major types of L/C's?
16. Why might different documentation be used for an export to a non-affiliated

foreign buyer who is a new customer as compared to an export to a nonaffiliated foreign buyer to whom the exporter has been selling for many years?

17. For what reason might an exporter use standard international trade documentation (letter of credit, draft, order bill of lading) on an intrafirm export to its parent or sister subsidiary?

18. What reasons can you give for the observation that intrafirm trade is now greater than trade between nonaffiliated exporters and importers?

19. Explain the difference between a letter of credit (L/C) and a draft. How are they linked?

20. Explain the difference between a straight bill of lading and an order bill of lading.

21. What is the major difference between currency risk and risk of noncompletion? How are these risks handled in a typical international trade transaction.

22. Identify each party to a letter of credit (L/C) and indicate its responsibility.

23. Most letters of credit are irrevocable. The bank must honor drafts drawn in accordance with the L/C. However same letter of credit are revocable. Why would a recovable letter of credit be used?

24. Why would an exporter insist on a confirmed letter of credit?

25. How may an exporter use a letter of credit to extend credit to an importer?

26. Can a banker's acceptance be sold to another party? Since it does not pay interest, why would a person buy it? Who guarantees payment?

27. Disucss the steps taken by the RBI to extend export finance to achieve the objective of the foreign trade policy.

28. Edward M. Graham, a United States wholesaler of specialty clothes for men and women, hopes to expand his operations considerably by emphasising a new line of leisure wear to be marked through various clothing boutiques. As part of this plan, he has contacted three exporters with a view toward supplying his needs. He considers the products and offerings of each comparable in terms of his business, although each reflects certain national styles and trends.

Assume the three potential suppliers have offered him various terms. Mary freed Ltd. of London has suggested that an appropriate financial arrangement would involve a revocable letter of credit since she knows his general reputation. They agree that, if Mr. Graham can arrange the letter of credit through a bank, Mr. Freed will draw a time draft payable 60 days after sight, in sterling.

Venkat Sundram from India has an interest in supplying Mr. Graham, but indicates that he would expect a confirmed irrevocable negotiable letter of credit, with drafts drawn under the 1/c payable at sight. Credit would be available, he suggests, at a rate of 2% per month, but should not exceed 90 days after shipment.

Finally, Heinz Riehl of Geneva manufactures in Austrian style of apre-ski lounging clothes, has indicated that he has long wished to have an American distributor. He suggests that an appropriate method of operation would be for Mr. Graham to deposit funds to the Riehl account in Basel 30 days prior to a shipment, with the deposit equal to 50% of the invoiced value of the goods. After shipment, the balance would be due within 10 days of receipt by Mr. Graham. Mr. Riehl noted that his general impressions of Mr. Graham's business were sufficient to commend the Graham firm as a customer, and he has no need for a letter of credit arrangement.

If you were to help Mr. Graham with this decision, what data would you need? How would you analyse the decision. In addition to any factors you believe are particularly important, consider the following elements, and how they would alter the decision. Give an example of how Mr. Graham might favour one supplier over the others depending on the facts surrounding each item noted below:

(a) The currency prospects of each of the exporters vis-a-vis Mr. Graham's currency, the U.S. dollar.

(b) The cost of funds for payable financing by Mr. Graham.

(c) The option to accept or reject the Spanish credit terms as each order is due.

(d) The cost of different letters of credit from the banks involved.

29. Critically examine the impact of global financial turmoil and international developments on world trade financing with particular references to India's export-import financing.

22

INSTRUMENTS OF THE INTERNATIONAL MONEY MARKET

INTRODUCTION

The *international money market* can be regarded as the market for short-term financing and investment instruments that are issued or traded internationally. Such instruments include short-term bank loans, Treasury bills, bank certificates of deposit, commercial paper, bankers' acceptances and repurchase agreements, and other short-term asset-backed claims. The core of this market is the Eurocurrency market, where bank deposits are issued and traded outside the country that issued the currency. However, each of the instrument is a substitute to a degree for each of the other instrument, and the yield and price of each is sensitive to many of the same influences, so we may feel justified in lumping them together in something called a market. The fact that many of the other instruments of the international money market are priced off LIBOR, the interest rate on Eurodollar deposits, suggests that market participants themselves regard the different instruments as having a common frame of reference.

THE ROLE OF THE INTERNATIONAL MONEY MARKET

As a key element of the financial system of a country, the money market plays a crucial economic role: that of reconciling the cash needs of so-called deficit units with the investment needs of surplus units. Holding or borrowing liquid claims is more productive than holding cash balances. A smoothly functioning money market can perform these functions very efficiently if borrowing-lending spreads (or bid-offer spreads for traded instruments) are small *(operational efficiency)*, and if funds are lent to those who can make the most productive use of them *(allocational efficiency)*. Both borrowers and lenders prefer to meet their short-term needs without bearing the liquidity risk or interest-rate risk that characterises longer-term instruments, and money-market instruments allow this. In addition, money-market investors tend not to want to spend much time analysing credit risk, so money-market instruments are generally characterised by a high degree of safety of principal. Thus the money markets sets a market interest rate that balances cash-management needs, and sets different rates for different uses that balance their risks and potential for productive use. Unlike stock or futures markets, the money markets of the major industrial countries have no central location.

SELECTED INSTRUMENTS OF THE INTERNATIONAL MONEY MARKET

Eurocurrency Time Deposits and Certificates of Deposit

The overwhelming majority of bank deposits in the Eurocurrency market takes the form of non-negotiable time deposits. To illustrate, consider an investor who puts money in London branch, today; he gets it back, plus interest, in three months' time. Canceling a time deposit is awkward and expensive, so the investor sacrifices liquidity. Those who want greater liquidity invest in shorter maturities. A very high proportion of Eurodollar time deposits, especially in the interbank market, mature in one week or less.

Alternatively, the investor can buy a negotiable Euro certificate of deposit (Euro CD), which is simply a time deposit that is transferable and thus has the elements of a security. Some banks are a little reluctant to issue CDs, because they would prefer not to have their paper traded in a secondary market, especially at times when the bank might be seeking additional short-term funding. The secondary paper might compete with the primary paper being offered. Others will issue CDs readily if investors prefer them, perhaps paying 1/8 per cent or more below their equivalent time-deposit rate to reflect the additional liquidity and the somewhat greater documentary inconvenience of CDs.

Other banks (particularly if they wish to have their names better known in the market) might deliberately undertake a funding a programme using Euro CDs. In this circumstance, the CDs are to be distributed like securities, so as to increase awareness of the issuer's name and raise a longer volume of funds for longer maturities than might be possible in the conventional Eurodeposit market.

Banker's Acceptances and Letters of Credit

Banker's acceptances are money market instruments arising, typically, from international trade transactions that are financed by banks. The banker's acceptance (BA) itself represents an obligation by a specific bank to pay a certain amount on a certain date in the future. To simplify a bit, it is a claim on the bank that differs little from other short-term claims such as CDs. Indeed BAs, when they are traded in a secondary market, trade at a return that seldom deviates much from comparable CDs issued by the same bank. *Letters of credit* (L/C) are documents issued by banks in which the bank promises to pay a certain amount on a certain date, if and only if documents are presented to the bank as specified in the terms of the credit. A letter of credit is generally regarded as a very strong legal commitment on the part of a bank to pay if the conditions of trade documents are fulfilled.

In a typical export transaction, the exporter will want to be paid once the goods arrive (and are what they are supposed to be) in the foreign port. So the exporter asks for *acceptance* by the importer's bank of a *time draft* (essentially an invoice that requests a money-market instrument. Banker's acceptances are sold at discount from face value, like Treasury bills and commercial paper, and yields are quoted as discount yields. Why should the bank pay the exporter? The reason is that it has promised the exporter that it will do so upon presentation of documents conveying title to the goods. That promise is called the letter of credit.

Standby letters of credit are related instruments entailing a commitment to pay on the part of a bank, but they normally do not involve the direct purchase of merchandise or the presentation of title documents. The standby letter of credit says unconditionally that "I'll pay you X dollars on *Y* date if you show me Z document." That's all you have to do: show him Z document and you receive the money. Standby letters of credit are used to support bid and performance bonds, advance-payment guarantees, and other financial commitments. Nowadays, they are also widely used as a sort of guarantee, or more precisely a substitute for someone else's obligation. For example, a relatively unknown Japanese bank, Hokkaido Trust, might wish to issue a CD in the U.S. market. In exchange for a fee and perhaps the pledging of collateral, a prominent Japanese bank such as Sanwa Bank might support the CD with a letter of credit. Sanwa has, in effect, substituted its own liability for that of Hokkaido Trust. Investors prefer in L/C to a guarantee, which obligates the guarantor to pay only if the original obligor fails to do so. The letter of credit, in contrast, is unconditional: it is payable by the issuer of the L/C simply against a draft.

Euronotes and Eurocommercial Paper

Both Euronotes and Eurocommercial papers are short-term instruments, unsecured promissory notes issued by corporations and banks. *Euronotes,* the more general term, encompasses note-issuance facilities, those that are underwritten, as well as those that are not underwritten. The term *Eurocommercial paper* is generally taken to mean notes that are issued without being backed by an underwriting facility—that is, without the support of a medium-term commitment by a group of banks to provide funds in the event that the borrower is unable to roll over its Euronotes on acceptable terms. Most actual issuance in the Euronote market takes the form of nonunderwritten Eurocommercial paper (ECP), so the actual paper that an investor will find available for investment is likely to be ECP.

Like U.S. commercial paper, Euronotes and ECP are traded by convention on a *discount basis,* and interest is calculated as "actual/360," meaning that the price is set as 100 minus the discount interest rate multiplied by the actual number of days to maturity, over 360.

Medium-Term Notes and Deposit Notes

The role of international banks in arranging and managing Eurocommercial-paper facilities in the international credit market has evolved from one of providing loans, to include the underwriting of syndicated facilities and perhaps trading the participations, and finally to being the auctioneer in the distribution of corporate paper. The latter role has carried over into an offshoot of the commercial-paper market, the *medium-term note (MTN)* market. *Deposit notes* are simply MTNs issued by international banks. International institutions such as the World Bank are prominent issues.

Medium-term notes are in many respects simply fixed-rate corporate bonds but of a generally shorter maturity than Eurobonds or domestic bonds. As an investment vehicle, the MTN is often regarded by institutional investors as a temporary investment that can be designed to suit the particular investor's requirements. The reason is that MTNs, unlike conventional bonds, are offered on a continuous basis in smaller amounts—as little as $2 to $5 million at a time—rather than in single large issues. An investor such as a pension fund might have $7 million to invest for 11 months in a good corporate name. He will call several MTN dealers to see what companies are borrowing, and when he makes his choice the note will be issued *specifically for the investor*. This specificity explains why MTN financing programmes are often described as "investor driven." In effect, the distribution process in the MTN market resembles a commercial-paper-issuance programme, although without the backstop lines of credit that commercial paper programmes typically have. Under a comprehensive MTN issuance programme, an issuer can raise funds by issuing fixed-rate, floating-rate, or deep-discount paper in any of a number of currencies. Liquidity is provided by either one or a number of "committed" dealers.

The MTN and its offshoots have turned-out to be one of the most important developments in longer-term funding in the 1980s and 1990s.[1] The MTN is a commercial-paper-like instrument that has a maturity rivaling that of a corporate bond. Indeed medium-term notes are issued today with maturities ranging from 9 months to as much as 30 years—a lot longer than is available in the Eurobond market. The notes are typically unsecured but need not be. They pay interest on a 30/360—day basis, unlike deposits that pay on actual/360 terms. Some have floating rates based on an index such as LIBOR, just like floating-rate notes. Unlike corporate bonds, few are callable. Like commercial paper, most domestic MTNs are rated, whereas most Euro-MTNs are unrated.[2] Their most significant distinguishing feature is a subtle one—the fact that their issuance and even maturity is largely investor determined, not issuer determined. Corporate bonds are issued infrequently and often entail relatively heavy issuance costs, so the borrower wants to do the issue in large amounts as a known cost and get it distributed as widely as possible. This means that there must be an underwriting syndicate. Not so with MTNs or deposit notes; paper is issued through dealers at the time, in the amount, and for the maturity that the investor wants. MTNs and deposit notes issued by Top-name banks have achieved the status of a commodity; very few Eurobonds have.

In the primary market, MTNs by their nature lack the magnitude of placing power of identical bonds issued in a big corporate bond issue, but they have borrowed so many of the successful features of the commercial paper market—such as broker-sponsored programmes, continuous offerings of primary paper, and good market-maker support—that they have replaced underwritten Eurobonds and domestic bonds as the preferred source of longer-term funds for major international banks.

1. Deposit notes are issued by commercial banks and have the status of deposits; medium-term notes are issued by corporations, including bank holding companies, and are treated like corporate bonds from a legal point of view. In the United States, bank-deposit notes are exempt from SEC registration, as are all MTNs placed privately.
2. Like the commercial-paper market, the medium-term market had its origins in the United States. Euro-MTNs are very much like domestic MTNs, with many of the same issuers and the same cast of broker-dealers, although a somewhat different investor base. And of course, there's no Euro-SEC, so some issuers prefer the MTN from a disclosure point of view. As with the commercial-paper market most MTN programmes are now global: they offer the issuer access to either market, to spread its sources and tap the cheapest market.

In the secondary market, one potential problem with MTNs from the investor's point of view is that if each note is tailored to a specific investor's needs, then it is somewhat unique and hence is likely to lack liquidity. To be able to price a security and to buy or sell it without difficulty, there should be a reasonable amount of the same or closely comparable securities outstanding in the market. Two approaches have been taken to help improve liquidity, at the expense of some flexibility:

1. *Use multitranche tap notes.* Under this structure, the borrower must issue a minimum amount of paper, such as $50 million, in each tranche. Beyond the minimum the issue can be expanded to satisfy demand; but the minimum ensures that there is always a reasonable quantity of paper outstanding with identical characteristics.

2. *Insist upon standard annual or semiannual coupon dates,* irrespective of the note's issuance and maturity dates. Normally a bond issued on April 1 would have its first annual coupon paid a year later, on March 31.

The yield on an MTN is calculated in the same way as a bond yield. That is, it is the internal rate of return that gives the cash flows a present value equal to the total price of the instrument.

Floating-Rate Notes

The floating-rate note is, as the name implies, an instrument whose interest rate floats with prevailing market rates. Like Eurodollar deposits, it pays a three—or six-months interest rate set above, at, or below LIBOR. Like international loans, this interest rate is reset every three or six months to a new level based on the prevailing LIBOR level at the reset date. More precisely, floating-rate notes issued outside of the country of the currency of denomination are issued in the form of *Eurobonds,* which makes them in some respects as much a capital-market instrument as a money-market instrument. But the framework we use places *pricing* at the center of what defines an instrument, and FRNs are priced in part like money-market instruments and in part like conventional fixed-rate bonds.

The floating-rate note has grown up with the Euromarket as a whole. The instrument was introduced in the early 1970s after many investors had gotten their fingers burned by dabbling in the fixed-rate Eurobond market, in which prices fell as inflation drove interest rates up to historically high levels. Investment bankers thought that they would have a ready demand for floating-rate notes among those investors who wanted longer-maturity instruments than bank deposits, ones that would maintain their value in the face of higher interest rates. It turned out that the biggest buyers of floating-rate notes were not banks' customers, but banks themselves. Some saw them as another trading instrument: *buy today, sell later at a profit.* Most, however, bought them as medium-term substitutes for loans. Some, with a low cost of funds but a dearth of prime borrower customers, were looking for a way to earn a spread with little risk or effort. Other banks preferred them to bank loans because they were treated by the regulators as securities, a treatment that improved the liquidity of the banks' asset portfolios. Whatever the reason, the bulk of FRNs are today held by financial institutions whose cost of funds varies with short-term rates, because an FRN pays a rate that is tied to changes in short-term interest rates.

Features of FRNs

All floating-rate notes have a coupon that is reset at fixed intervals in accordance with some preset formula, but there are many variations on this theme. Most FRNs can be characterised by the following features:

i) *The reference rate.* The reference rate is the interest rate to which the coupon payment is linked. This is normally a short-term rate, so that some see FRNs as a substitute for money-market instruments. In the Euromarkets, the reference rate is usually LIBOR, although a few FRNs have used other reference rates (such as LIBID, LIMEAN, or the U.S.-Treasury-bill rate). The rate is normally reset at the beginning of each coupon period, and interest is paid in arrears.

ii) *The margin.* The margin is the spread between the coupon payment and LIBOR. Coupon payments on FRNs are generally LIBOR plus (or minus) some fixed amount. This spread reflects the differential risk at the time of issue between investing in the FRN and investing in a bank deposit paying LIBOR. LIBOR itself is usually about 1/8 per cent higher than prime banks' bid rate in the interbank market, reflecting the risk of the bank with which funds would be deposited, and perhaps a discount for illiquidity. An FRN carries the default risk of the issuer over the life of the note and the liquidity risk of a tradable, but not necessarily traded, security.

iii) *The reference-rate period.* The reference-rate period is the maturity of the security to which the FRN's coupon is linked, such as three—or six-month Eurodollar deposits. An FRN coupon is quoted as the LIBOR—period rate and the margin—for example, six-month LIBOR plus 3/16 per cent.

iv) *Frequency of reset.* Reset frequency is the period between coupon-reset dates and normally coincides with the reference-rate period.

v) *Coupon-payment frequency.* This is the interval between coupon payments, and normally coincides with the coupon-reset periods.

vi) *Maturity.* The date on which the principal on an FRN will be redeemed is the maturity date. Many FRNs have *call* features—that is, the issuer may, at its option, redeem the FRN at certain prespecified dates prior to maturity.

A "plan vanilla" FRN is a fixed-maturity bond whose reference-rate period, frequency to reset, and coupon-payment period are all of the same length. A *mismatch* FRN is one in which reference-rate period, the frequency of reset, and/or the coupon-payment period are of different lengths. The rate is reset monthly but paid semiannually. The coupon is the arithmetic mean of the six one-month interest periods within the six-month coupon period.

Each FRN has a specific method for calculating the LIBOR rate to be used as a reference rate to reset coupons. The method is usually as follows:

> *On the second business day prior to the beginning of each coupon period, the agent bank collects the offered quotations prevailing at 11 A.M. on that day for interbank deposits with the London branches of leading banks from a series of reference banks (listed in the prospectus). The arithmetic mean of these rates, rounded up to the nearest sixteenth, is then taken as LIBOR. Using this rate, the coupon is then calculated on an actual/360-day basis, rounded upwards or downwards to the nearest cent on each note. An agent bank calculates and publishes the coupon rate for each period.*

Pricing FRNs

In some respects, an FRN is like a short-term money-market instrument. The rate on the FRN at issue is set high enough that the note is worth 100. At each reset period, the rate is raised or lowered to match the prevailing market rate. So, credit-risk changes aside, its price should return to 100. That means you could buy it today (a reset date) and sell it six months later at par, collecting your six-month coupon—just like a Eurodollar CD. Even if the investor made some other assumption about the rollover price (the price at the next reset date), he could use this approach to calculate the money-market return.

This is somewhat naive approach the *money-market method.* It is helpful to those who wish to compare the yield on an FRN held as a short-term investment in lieu of another money-market instrument, and the fact that the rate is reset to market offers some comfort to such investors, but not much: FRN's are medium—or long-term bonds, and their prices at reset dates can deviate, and have deviated, far from par, for reasons associated with general FRN market conditions as well as the creditworthiness of the specific issue. Thus we can identify three distinct influences on the price of an FRN:

1. *Credit condition of the issuer.* The price at the reset date will fall below par if the promised margin relative to LIBOR is perceived as insufficient reward for an issuer's deteriorated credit condition. The most direct measure is the issue's *credit rating.* A note issued as a AA may be downgraded to A or worse for reasons specific to the issuer.
2. *Market perceptions of FRNs in general.* Changes in investors' perceptions of the FRN market as a whole or of a particular segment of the market may cause a particular issuer's FRN to trade above or below par on reset dates. In the early days of the market, many issues were seen as generously priced and trade above 100. Then in the late 1980s, the opposite happened. Subordinated bank debt was priced in much the same way as unsubordinated debt until the Bank of England changed its rules concerning the investment by one bank in the debt of another bank. After the change, the market reassessed the relative risk of subordinated to unsubordinated FRNs. This reassessment resulted in a sharp widening of required margins and a fall in bid prices on subordinated debt relative to unsubordinated debt of the same issuers. The most visible and devastating effect was on the price of perpetual FRNs.
3. *Money-market rates.* The FRN price will be affected by changes in short-term rates—specifically, the level of LIBOR between now and the next coupon reset date. A change in this rate will change the FRN's value as if it were a money-market instrument maturing on the reset date.

The method used for pricing and comparing FRNs reflects the fact that they are, in some respects, bond instruments and, in some respects, money-market instruments. When comparing two straight bonds, the standard approach is to consider the yield to maturity of each bond and the liquidity and credit risk of the bonds. The yield is sometimes expressed as a spread over "benchmark" U.S. Treasury yields, But because the FRN's coupon rate fluctuates, the standard yield measures are useless. For this reason, and because so many FRNs are held by those seeking a spread over their short-term cost of funds, the market has developed a measure of an FRNs effective spread over LIBOR: To get the effective spread over the instrument's remaining life. We adjust the quoted margin by amortising the premium or discount at which the FRN is trading. The *discount-margin approach* is the industry standard for comparing FRN spreads.

The Discount Margin and the Neutral Price

The *discount margin* is a measure of the effective spread, relative to LIBOR, that an investor would earn if he bought the FRN at some price today and held it to maturity.

It is the margin relative to LIBOR that is necessary to discount the cash flows from an FRN so that the sum of the present value of the flows is equal to the gross price of the note. It is calculated in a manner similar to the yield to maturity of a fixed-rate bond. Because the coupon stream is uncertain, it is necessary to make some assumption about average LIBOR from the next coupon date until maturity, although fortunately, the discount margin is not very sensitive to the assumption made.[3] Naturally, nobody can be sure what rates will prevail over the life of the FRN, but one acceptable method is to use the implied forward rate for the remaining life from the yield curve for equivalent fixed-rate instruments. Better still, use the swap yield curve: this is preferable because, an FRN can be converted into the equivalent of a fixed-rate bond using an interest-rate swap.

FRN prices are conventionally quoted *clean*—that is, not including accrued interest. Accrued interest is calculated on a money market actual/360-day basis by using the formula A = (LIBOR + Quoted margin)(Days/360). The variable Days is the actual number of days from, and including, the date of the last coupon up to, but excluding, the settlement date. The gross price is the clean price plus accrued interest—that is, the total price paid.

The *discount margin (DM)* is found by solving, by iteration, the following equation for *DM:*

$$P+A=\frac{(L+QM)/m}{1+\frac{L_s+DM}{100}\cdot\frac{D_s}{360}}$$

$$+\left[\frac{1}{1+\frac{L_s+DM}{100}\cdot\frac{D_s}{360}}\right]\left[\sum_{t=1}^{n}\frac{(L_a+QM)/m}{1+\frac{(L_a+DM)/m}{100}}\right.$$

$$\left.+\frac{100}{1+\frac{(L_a+DM)/m}{100}}\right]$$

3. That's because it appears in both the numerator and the denominator of the valuation formula.

where

P	=	today's price
A	=	Accrued interest, (LIBOR + Quoted margin) (Days since last coupon/360)
QM	=	Quoted margin
DM	=	Discount margin
L	=	Current LIBOR in effect, so that $L + QM$ is the current coupon
L_s	=	LIBOR for time between settlement and next coupon date
L_a	=	Assumed average LIBOR rate over remaining life of FRN (using the swap rate)
D_s	=	Days from settlement to next coupon date
m	=	Number of coupon periods per year[4]
n	=	Number of coupon periods to maturity

This formula looks complicated but it's really not. It simply discounts the note's cash flows as in a fixed-rate bond. The equation is having three parts:

Total price paid equals *present value of next coupon* plus *sum of present values of all subsequent coupons* plus *present value of final principal repayment.*

For some investors it is useful to abstract from the money-market aspect of a FRN to gauge the extent to which changes in *risk*, rather than in short-term rates, have affected the note's price. This analysis can be done by waiting until a coupon date to see whether the FRN trades at a discount or a premium when the coupon is reset to a market level. Alternatively, we can determine the price that the FRN would have to trade at on a coupon date to ensure that the investor receives the discounted margin. This price is known as the *neutral price;* it may be considered the price at which a new issue with the same quoted margin as the FRN would be set in order to give a return equal to the discounted margin.

The discounted margin neutral price is the price of the floating-rate note on the next coupon date that gives a return over the period from the settlement to the next coupon equal to the rate plus the discounted margin:

$$\text{Neutral Price} = (P + A)\left[\frac{1}{\frac{L_s + DM}{100} \cdot \frac{D_s}{360}}\right] - \text{coupon}$$

where

P	=	Today's price
A	=	Accrued interest
DM	=	Discounted margin
L_s	=	LIBOR for the time from settlement to the first coupon
D_s	=	Days from settlement to first coupon date.

The neutral price will move toward par as the time to maturity decreases.

Caps, Floors, Calls, and Puts in FRNs

Many floating-rate notes have option features. Most, in fact, have a minimum coupon level; this is called a *floor.* Some have a maximum coupon level, called a *cap.* An FRN that has both a floor and a cap is said to be *collared.*

From the investor's viewpoint, buying a floored FRN may be regarded as purchasing a plain FRN plus a strip of European call options on LIBOR with strike prices equal to the floor level minus the margin. On each coupon date, the investor receives LIBOR plus the margin, plus the intrinsic value of the option, if any. In the early 1990s, many FRNs were issued with both caps and floors. In effect, the investor sold a cap with sufficient value to pay for the floor.

A "cap floater" may be considered as an uncapped FRN, plus a strip of European puts on LIBOR that the investor has sold, with a strike price equal to the cap level minus the margin. The number of puts equals the number of reset periods in the note's remaining life. The investor is paid in the form of a higher stated margin or a lower price than plain-vanilla FRNs—in other words, with a higher discounted margin.

Credit considerations aside, the neutral price of a capped or floored FRN will depend on the volatility of interest rates, the level of interest rates, and the shape of the yield curve. How a cap or a floor affects an FRN's price depends on the value of the embedded options: for a floor, the strip of long calls; for a cap, the strip of short puts. The value of both caps and floors depends on the forward rates implied in today's LIBOR yield curve. With an upward-sloping yield curve and steeply rising implied forward rates, the strip of calls embedded in a floor may be much further out-of-the-money than one would guess by simply comparing the floor level with today's LIBOR rate. The reverse is true for a cap; with an upward-sloping yield curve, the high forward rates place the cap further into-the-money (or closer to being in-the-money). As the yield curve moves upward and steepens, caps become relatively expensive, hurting the investor and lowering the capped FRN's neutral price.

This and other effects of caps and floors on FRN's prices of changing interest rates are summarised below.

		Effect on Neutral Price of Capped FRN	*Effect on Neutral Price of Floored FRN*
Interest-Rate Volatility	Falling	Increases	Decreases
	Rising	Decreases	Increases
Interest-Rate Level	Falling	Increases	Increases
	Rising	Decreases	Decreases
Shape of Yield Curve	Flattening	Increases	Increases
	Steepening	Decreases	Decreases

Many floating-rate notes are *callable* by the issuer, others are *puttable* by the investor, and some are both. *In all cases the call or put provisions are exercisable only on coupon reset dates. As a result the call or put decision is influenced only by credit-risk considerations and not by interest rates.* This is in sharp contrast to similar provisions in fixed-rate bonds. FRNs tend to be called when the issuer can refinance at a cheaper spread (as indicated by the discount margin) and put when the investor can get a better spread for the same credit risk, irrespective of the level of rates. Investors find that how callable FRNs trade depends on the note's neutral price compared to the call price (which is normally the issue price). Callable FRNs with a neutral price significantly above the call price will tend to trade as if the call date were the redemption date. If a call date is approaching, the discount margin, measured to the call date, will be similar to the spread the borrower pays on its commercial paper. From the borrower's point of view, the call provision in a floating-rate note is similar to that in a note-issuance facility: it is the *right*, but not the *obligation*, to borrow at a preset spread.

RETURNS ON MONEY-MARKET INSTRUMENTS

The finance manager considers the alternative money-market instruments by comparing their returns, risks, and other characteristics. In principle, the range includes all the instruments in two dozen or so domestic money-markets open to international investors. Realistically, though, one would normally limit one's attention to a few major currencies and to the more liquid instruments.

The basic idea of a return is that investor who invests a sum of money today expects more to get back at a later date. The increase, expressed as an annualised percentage of the original investment, is typically how we measure return. Thus if you invest Rs. 100 today and you receive Rs. 114 in one year the return is 14 per cent. In practice this idea takes three different forms: (1) the bank discount rate, (2) the add-on yield, and (3) the yield to maturity, known in the Euromarkets as the bond-equivalent yield.

1. The *bank-discount-rate method* is a formula devised to make calculations easy to do by hand, but its use persists in these days of financial calculators and computers, for money-market instruments such as Treasury bills, banker's acceptances, and commercial paper. These carry no coupon but are sold on a discount basis from a face-principal value of 100. The yield quoted on such instruments is calculated as follows:

$$\text{Bank discount rate} = \frac{\text{Discount}}{100} \times \frac{360}{\text{Days}}$$

where Discount is the dollar amount of discount from the face value of \$100 and Days is the actual number of days to maturity.

For example if the discount on \$100 of commercial paper were \$1.50 and it had 92 days to maturity, its yield on a discount rate basis would be

$$\frac{1.50}{100} \times \frac{360}{92} = 5.87 \text{ per cent}$$

Not only is the percentage return based on the maturity value rather than the amount invested, but also the formula assumes 360 rather than 365 days in the year. This convention may be summarised as *discount basis, actual/360.*

2. The *add-on yield* is used in Eurodollar—and Eurocurrency-deposit calculations, because these are typically issued at a price of 100 and the coupon added on at the end. The formula changes to:

$$\text{Add-on yield} = \frac{\text{Interest payment}}{100} \times \frac{360}{\text{Days}}$$

where

Interest payment is the dollar amount of payment made at maturity on an investment of $100
Days is the number of days to maturity

For example, if the interest payment on a 90-day Eurodollar deposit is $2.50, then the add-on yield is 10 per cent.

The trouble with the add-on yield is that it ignores compounding, which can be important because a one-year Eurodeposit that pays interest semiannually is more desirable than one that pays annually. To take compounding into account we need the yield to maturity or the bond-equivalent yield.

3. The *bond-equivalent yield* or yield to maturity is the rate that equates the present value of all future interest and principal payments with the market price of the instrument. If as in the Eurobond market, interest is paid annually, we can solve the following equation for r, the yield to maturity.

$$P = \frac{I}{1+r} + \frac{I}{(1+r)^2} + \ldots + \frac{I}{(1+r)^n} + \frac{FV}{(1+r)^n}$$

where

PV = the present market price of the instrument
I = the annual coupon payment
n is the number of years to maturity
FV is the face value of the instrument (usually 100)

For a portion of a year we use the *30/360 convention,* which assumes that each month has 30 days and each year 360 days.

To find the yield to maturity when interest is paid m times per year, we find r such that:

$$PV = \frac{I/m}{1+r/m} + \frac{I/m}{(1+r/m)^2} + \ldots + \frac{I/m}{(1+r/m)^{mn}} + \frac{FV}{(1+r/m)^{mn}}$$

The first mn terms form a geometric progression, so PV can be simplified to

$$PV = \frac{I/m[1 - (1+r/m)^{-mn}]}{r/m} + \frac{FV}{(1+r/m)^{mn}}$$

which is a more convenient formula because it can be calculated in one cell of a spreadsheet.

The frequency of payment will make a difference to the effective yield to maturity. The more frequent the payment, the greater the effective yield, because it is always nicer to get money sooner. A common way of comparing apples with apples in the Euromarket is to convert everything to its annual-pay equivalent. The formula for interest conversions of this kind is $(1 + i/m)^m - 1$, where m is the frequency of payments per year. For example, converting a 9 per cent rate paid semiannually to its annual equivalent would yield $(1 + .09/2)^2 - 1 = 9.20$ per cent.

Some instruments have interest calculated on the basis of the *actual* number of days to maturity—that is, from settlement (delivery) date to maturity date—the number of days, counting the settlement date but not counting the maturity date—while others make the simplifying assumption that there are only 30 days in every month. And in some cases, the year is assumed to have 360 days, in others 365. In the U.S. and Japanese markets, coupons are paid semiannually, and in the Eurodeposit and floating-rate-note markets, interest may be paid semiannually or quarterly.

ILLUSTRATIVE PROBLEMS

1. Boldman sells you Erikssen ECP maturing on December 17 at an agreed rate of 8 per cent. If the value date for delivery is October 12, how much do you pay Boldman?

Ans.

ECP is priced at a discount from par, and the rate quoted is a discount rate. To get the price as a percentage of the face value, we use the calculation

ECP price = 100 — Discount rate Actual days/360

The actual number of days to maturity is 61, so the price is 100 — 8.61/360 = 98.64.

2. What is the yield to Maturity on an 18-month Euro-Canadian-dollar CD sold at 99 with a 9 per cent annual interest rate paid quarterly?

To answer this we have to find by iteration the value of the r that satisfies the following equation:

$$PV = \frac{9/4[1 - (1 + r/4)^{-4 \cdot 1.5}]}{1 + r/4} + \frac{100}{(1 + r/4)^{4 \cdot 1.5}}$$

Ans.

After using a spreadsheet programme, the answer turns out to be 9.72 per cent.

3. Convert the 9 per cent rate paid semiannual to its annual equivalent.

Ans.

Converting a 9% rate paid semiannually to its annual equivalent would yield:

$(1 + .09/2)^2 - 1$

$= 9.20$ per cent

4. On June 18, 1999, a Banque Nationale Belgique floating-rate note maturing on July 29, 2015, is priced at 99.26. The stated margin is 12.5 basis points over 6-month LIBOR. The discount-margin approach amortises the discount of 0.74 over the remaining 12-year life of the note to approximate the effective margin over LIBOR, so the effective margin should be greater than 12.5 basis points. Using the discount-margin formula, what is the discount margin on the BNB floater?

Ans.

To answer this we need some more information: The current coupon is 7.5 per cent. A purchase of the note would settle a week later, on June 25, and the next coupon date is July 29, 1999. The LIBOR rate for this remaining 34 days is 7.0042. The current 12-year rate for interest-rate swaps against 6-month LIBOR is 7.5625, which we shall assume to be the average rate for the remaining life.

Based on this information, a spreadsheet version of the formula gives a discount margin of 21.7 basis points.

5. On January 15, 2011, a secondary-market dealer has approached you about buying an Air Zenda 6 per cent deutschermark MTN that matures on October 31, 2013. The MTN has a June 30 coupon date. In the view of your boss, the note should yield at least 6.5 per cent to be worth buying. What is the maximum price, including accrued interest, that you should be willing to offer for the note?

Ans.

The 6 per cent coupon is paid annually on June 30. To find the price of the bond that will give a yield of 6.5 per cent, we use the conventional present-value formula used in fixed-income securities pricing: the sum of the present values of each of the cash flows. The interest that has accrued since the last coupon date is part of the total payment to be made.

TABLE-1

CASH FLOWS FOR EXAMPLE

Cash flow	*Date*	*No. of days (using 30/360 basis)*	*No. of years*	*Amount*	*Present value*
1st coupon	30 Jun 2011	165	0.46	6	5.83
2nd coupon	30 Jun 2012	525	1.46	6	5.47
3rd coupon	30 Jun 2013	885	2.46	6	5.14
Final coupon and principal	31 Oct 2013	1005	2.79	102	85.56
Present value of cash flows @ 6.5%					102.00
Accrued interest	15 Jan 97	195	0.54	6	3.25
Present value minus accrued interest					98.75

The computations for medium-term notes are done using the convention of the Eurobond market, namely that interest accrues on a 30-day month, 360-day year basis.

Thus the maximum you should be willing to pay for the MTN is a *clean price* of 98.75, or a total price of 102.00, including accrued interest. Conventionally, in the international market, the clean price is the one quoted; it is understood that accrued interest will be paid as well.

6. Repeat the problem-5, consider you had the opportunity to sell a three-year Eurobond at a yield of 7.20 per cent and replace it with the Air Zenda MTN at a clean price of 96.50, how much "yield pickup" could you gain?

Answer

Using the same cash flows as in Table-1, the internal rate of return that results in the January 15, 2011, value of 99.75 (96.50 plus accrued interest of 3.25) turns out to be 7.43 per cent, so the yield pickup is 23 basis points.

QUESTIONS

1. In what respect can the different instruments described in this chapter be regarded as belonging to a single money market?
2. Why would an international bank fund itself by the issue of Eurodollar CDs rather than by non-negotiable time deposits?
3. What is the connection between a letter of credit and a banker's acceptance?
4. How does Eurocommercial paper differ from other forms of Euronotes?
5. Under what circumstances might an industrial company like Hoechst prefer to issue a Eurobond rather than a MTN?
6. Why are medium-term notes likely to prove illiquid? What measures have banks taken to remedy this?
7. What market variables influence the price of an FRN? Which of these render the FRN more like a bond-market instrument than a money-market instrument?
8. Why is a flattening of the yield curve likely to increase the neutral price of FRNs with floors *as well as* of those with caps?

PROBLEMS

1. The price of a $1 million Euronote sold on July 4 for settlement on July 10 is $782,000. If the note matures on October 15, what is its yield on a discount-rate basis?
2. Assume you buy in the secondary market a 180-day Eurosterling CD paying an interest rate of 12%. If the £5 million CD has 45 days to run, how many pounds will you receive at matured.
3. What is the yield to maturity on an eighteen-month Euro-Canadian dollar CD sold at 99 with a 10% annual interest rate paid semiannually?
4. Would you be better off with a CD paying 9% quarterly or one that pays semiannually? Quantify your answer.
5. You are a medium-term note trader at XYZ Company. A client has an interest in the 12.5% ABC Ltd.that matures on November 10, 1999, as long as it yields 12%

or better. All ABC Ltd. pay coupons on April 1 and October 1. If the note is to be sold for settlement on December 19, 1998, what price would make your customer happy?

6. You are the manager of Bank Bumiputra's London investment portfolio. On June 18, 2008, you are offered a Bavaria Bank floating-rate note maturing on July 29, 2013, at a price of 110.50. The FRN pays a margin of 12.5 basis points over 6-month LIBOR.

   The LIBOR rate currently in effect is 6.90%, and you also find the prevailing LIBOR rates are: one month, 7.25%; three months, 7.4%; and six months. 7.72%. Assuming LIBOR stays at its current level for the remaining life of the FRN, what is the effective spread Bumiputra could earn over LIBOR by investing in the Bavaria Bank floater?

23

WORKING CAPITAL MANAGEMENT

INTRODUCTION

Managing short-term internationational financial transactions (working capital management) is the process of planning and controlling the level and mix of current assets of the firm as well as financing of these assets. It involves the use of certain prescribed aids such as the risk-return tradeoff, credit standards, and inventory models. From an international perspective, the working capital management is very complex because of different laws among countries that pertain to cross-border transactions. The chapter focuses on the MNC's management of short-term assets and liabilities.

OBJECTIVES AND CONSTRAINTS

The management of working capital can be viewed as either a static (stock) responsibility or a dynamic (flow) process. The static approach focuses on individual processes such as management of cash, accounts receivable, and inventories. The important aspect of this approach is how to determine appropriate levels of cash balances, accounts receivable, and inventories. On the other hand, the dynamic approach focuses on transfers of liquid funds from one geographic locations or currency to another. These transfers involve many constraints and uncertainties.

The objective of working capital management is to determine the optimal amount of investment in various current asset accounts. The optimal amount of investment in current assets is the level of current asset holdings that maximises return on investment. The basic objectives of working capital are to provide various current assets and short term credit necessary to support the anticipated sales by minimising the investment in current assets.

Because multinational companies operate across national borders, they face political, tax, foreign exchange, and other economic constraints. To achieve the predetermined objective of working capital management, the financial manager must give special consideration to these constraints.

Political constraints can block dividend repatriation or other forms of fund remittances. This blockage occurs because of restrictions on the international movement of funds and other exchange controls. Tax constraints limit the free flow of affiliate funds to the parent or to sister affiliates. These may occur because higher taxes on all corporate earnings or extra taxes on dividends may be imposed to curb inflation.

Foreign exchange constraints are a third limiting factor on fund flows from one country to another. International fund flows involve foreign exchange transaction costs and exchange rate fluctuations. Other economic factors such as inflation and interest rates also have an important impact on the international mobility of corporate funds.

INTERNATIONAL CASH MANAGEMENT

The word "cash" may mean different things to different people. A retailer may accept cash only, thus no cheques or credit cards; a corporation may show cash on its balance sheet and include coins, bills, bank demand deposits, and uncollected cheques. When the word "management" is added, corporate financial officers may also think of short-term investments, and with the word international, foreign exchange exposure comes to mind. In the domestic market cash management may be defined in a rather narrow sense as the art of managing the movement of money into, through, and out of a company with the objective of maximising cash availability under control of the company, international cash management, then, is defined as cross-border movement of funds, from and to other companies as well as within the company. Since foreign exchange exposure management has been treated in previous chapters that will not he discussed here despite its importance to cash management. It is not possible to manage something without appropriate information; therefore, cash management is divided into two parts: the movement of money and the movement of information relating to the movement of money. Money and information, however, do not always travel along the same track; in fact, it can be argued that disregarding payments in bills and coins, money never moves at all.

Money movements generally arise as a result of a company's operational activities. Cash comes in from customers, is invested, and is used to pay for goods and services bought. This rather elementary cash grows when the company borrows and repays money, when collections and disbursements happen in different locations, and when transactions are effected in different currencies. The number of cash movements to support the company's increasingly complex operations escalates into a mass of internal and external flows that require close supervision for proper payment execution and avoidance of the costs associated with excess cash on bank accounts. This shows why cash management, although an autonomous function in many corporate treasuries, should be an integral part of the overall treasury management of the company. It can have a dramatic impact on the amount of cash available for the company's operations. The cash manager achieves phenomenal results on the basis of careful analyses of their companies' domestic operations, with particular emphasis on sales purchasing, and investments. By instituting collection systems that accelerate the receipt of incoming funds and disbursement arrangements that eliminate the need *to* keep funds in a bank account to cover outstanding cheques, they have sharply reduced their needs for working funds. Even more important, their better knowledge of the company's business has enabled them to prepare more reliable cash forecast, in the process increasing the amounts that could be profitably invested rather than kept on demand accounts.

As with every other corporate-activity, cash management begins with planning.

The corporate long-term strategic plan and the annual business plan result in the preparation of budgets for each department. One of these, the capital budget, covering the planned capital expenditures for various time horizons, will generally not have an immediate impact on the cash manager. Rather, it underlies the company's long-term financial requirements. But the annual sales forecast and the operating budgets, broken down by month or by quarter, do provide the basis for the statement of anticipated sources and applications of funds to be reduced by the treasury department to the cash budget. Thus, since the entire business of the company ultimately finds expression in cash movements, there is no way a treasurer can do any thorough cash forecasting without corporate plans and budgets as a foundation.

While the operating divisions thus provide the basis for the treasurer's cash forecasts, he or she can, in turn, with a knowledge of the financial systems in various countries, provide valuable input to the divisions. With the treasurer's assistance, foreign exchange exposure on international transactions can be better controlled, special arrangements can be made for collections on large sales, or an unusual financing can facilitate the receipt of a specific contract. Such items all have their influence on the resulting payments. The treasurer can help to avoid problems with local banking practices and regulatory requirements with which an operating division is not necessarily familiar.

BASIC PRINCIPLES OF INTERNATIONAL CASH MANAGEMENT

Well-designed cash management programmes follow a few simple ground rules:

1. There is a cash management center that receives and distributes timely information relating to cash movements on a number of bank accounts strategically placed to serve the needs of the company's operating divisions,
2. Information is distributed on the basis of a need to know, which is different from cash requirements.
3. Short payment channels, involving a minimum number of banks, allow for maximum control.
4. Modern communications systems are used.
5. Efficient banks with high standards of customer service are employed.
6. There is a minimal impact on the internal corporate organisation, decision making pattern, and accounting system.

With these ground rules in mind, cash management is divided into four areas: *collection, disbursement, intercompany payments, and control.*

COLLECTION

The cash manager's motto is: "as soon as the customer has initiated payment to us, the money is our." The cash manager is entitled to use every means in his or her power to gain control over incoming funds as quickly as possible after the payment process is started. The typical method used to achieve this is the establishment of collection accounts close to the customers. These collection points are called "**lock boxes**." The company directs its customers to send their cheques to certain post office boxes placed around the country for this purpose, which are opened and emptied each day by local banks on the company's behalf. These banks deposit the cheques to collection accounts and collect them from the drawee banks, after which the company concentrates the funds into its main bank, using depository transfer cheques or wire transfers. Payment information is sent by the lock-box banks to the company's credit department, while the treasury is advised of the total funds credited. Lock boxes are a simple and effective method to cut the float on incoming funds.

Internationally, the objectives of collection are the same, but the technique differs international payment is made in a domestic banking system, namely, in the country of the currency in which the payment is denominated, International collection systems therefore, require collection accounts in the countries of the currencies of the payments, not necessarily in the countries of the customers. A German company with a dollar receivable on a British buyer should receive the funds on a U.S. collection account rather than channeling the dollars to its local bank. This shortens the chain of banks handling the payment and, through the use of the U.S. bank's automated reporting system, makes the relative information available sooner. Through a variety of arrangements such a collection account can be connected to interest-paying short-term investment media. Similarly, lire should be collected in Italy, pesetas in Spain. When a company thus ends up with a variety of collection accounts in different countries it may benefit from the services of a bank to manage the flows through these accounts, to concentrate the funds efficiently, and to manage the foreign exchange exposure. A few banks provide expert specialised services in this field.

INTERNATIONAL TRANSFER PRICING MECHANISM

To further optimise cash flows, the MNC must consider the tax consequence of altering its cash flow through necessary adjustments in the transfer pricing policy. In establishing international transfer prices, a firm must try to satisfy a number of objectives not relevant to domestic transfer pricing. For example, the firm wants to minimise taxes and at the same time win approval from the government of the host country, Yet the basic objectives of profit maximisation and performance evaluation also are important. Often it is not possible to satisfy all these objectives. Simultaneously, so a company must decide which objectives are the most important. As a result, a particular transfer price, rather than evolving from a transfer pricing technique, may be established arbitrarily to fulfill an objective involving international considerations, The discussion that follows examines some of these objectives.

Income Tax Minimisation

By far the most persuasive objective in international transfer pricing is tax minimisation. The economic advantages are obvious and immediate if a transfer price shifts profit from a country with a high tax rate to a country with a low tax rate. For example, if a product is being manufactured in a country with a favorable tax structure, a high transfer price will result in more of the profit from the sale of the product being taxed at the favorable rate. An example of using transfer pricing to minimise income taxes is shown in Exhibit-1. It may be noted that the transfer price of $100 per unit results in $30,000 of the ultimate profit of $96,000 remaining in the country with the 20 percent tax rate. Clearly, it is to the economic benefit of the company to raise the transfer price as high as the government in Country B will allow. In so doing, more of the profit is shifted into Country A and taxed at a lower rate. For example, if the government of Country B will allow a transfer price of $150 per unit, $50,000 of the $70,000 contribution margin in Country B will be shifted back to Country A, giving Country A a total contribution margin of $90,000 with tax of $16,000. The tax in Country B will decline from $26,400 to $6,400. Thus, a transfer price of $150 per unit gives the same before-tax profit of $96,000 but increases the after-tax profit from $63,600 to $73,600 because of the $10,000 reduction in total tax.

As the example in Exhibit-1 has shown, tax minimisation via transfer pricing is a simple process, When a firm minimises taxes by shifting profit between countries, however, other objectives of transfer pricing, such as performance evaluation and profit maximisation, may become harder, if not Impossible, to attain.

On the surface it would appear that tax minimisation would meet the objective of profit maximisation, but whether it does or not depends upon the specific circumstances, It is unlikely, however, that a transfer price which minimises taxes also will guide a company toward profit-maximising decisions such as whether to sell a product internally or externally or whether to invest in additional productive facilities. Furthermore, a program of tax minimisation may result in different transfer prices for same product transferred to different countries, so foreign affiliates in different countries will have different transfer prices with which to make other profit maximising, decisions.

EXHIBIT-1
TAX MINIMISATION

	Manufacture in Country A	→	*Sell in Country B*	=	*Company View*
	↓		↓		↓
Sales Price			$ 200		$ 200
Transfer Price	$ 100	→	($ 100)		
Variable Costs	(60)	+	(30)	=	(90)
Contribution Margin Per Unit	$ 40	+	$ 70	=	$ 110
Number of Units	× 1,000		× 1,000		× 1,000
Total Contribution Margin	$40,000	+	$70,000	=	$110,000
Fixed Costs	(10,000)	+	(4,000)	=	(14,000)
Profit	$30,000	+	$66,000	=	$96,000
Tax Rate	× .2		× .4		
Tax Payable	$ 6,000	+	$26,400	=	(32,400)
Company Profit					$63,600

The other objective, performance evaluation, is even more difficult to attain when the objective of tax minimisation is pursued. The profit in one country will be greater than the profit in another country, not because of better management but because of the transferring system for control purposes so performance evaluation is price. One way around this problem is to establish a separate reporting on more realistic reports.

The tax rate is not the only factor to consider in tax minimisation because countries have different requirements for calculating taxable income. Even though Country A has a tax rate of 20 percent on all taxable income and Country B has a 40 percent rate, total taxes may be lower in Country B if, for example, Country A severely restricts deductions for depreciation while Country B does not.

Although income taxation is the most persuasive objective to influence transfer prices, other objectives will from time to time assume a position of importance or perhaps dominance. Among these factors are import duties, avoidance of financial problems, and currency fluctuations.

Import Duties

Import duties, as well as income taxes, can be minimised. For example, a company benefits economically if it transfers products at low prices to a country with high import duties. All other things being equal, the company can reduce the total cost for import duties through transfer pricing.

Although import duty minimisation sounds easy, frequently it is complicated because "all other things" are rarely equal. For example, a country with low import duties may have high income taxes, or a country with high import duties may have low income taxes. Another factor is the tax rate of the country from which the product is shipped. Thus, the company must consider import duties along with income taxes in both the shipping and receiving countries. However, adjusting transfer prices for the effects of import and income taxes a delicate balancing act. For example, the higher the import tax assessed to the importer, the lower the profit remaining as a basis for income taxes. Since there is virtually no coordination of the two revenue-collecting departments in [most countries], the income-tax collecting branch may be unduly exercised. An added difficulty results from the attempt of the parent to balance the extra cost of duty resulting from a high import price paid by its affiliate against as the lower income taxes that the affiliate will be charged with, as well as the potent ally higher income taxes that the exporting affiliate may be required to remit.

Balancing import duties and income taxes is more complicated than simply minimising taxes. The different prices may draw the attention of customs officials and income-tax authorities. The result is a comprehensive review of pricing practices used by the company, which may lead to required changes in pricing practices and higher total income taxes. In addition, the investigation had a ripple effect. The other countries, learned of the investigation may start comprehensive reviews of the company's pricing practices in their countries. In the process, in addition to all-around higher income taxes, the company suffers a great deal of bad publicity.

Minimisation of income taxes and import duties is an important goal. Recently, however, taxing authorities in many countries have begun to pay closer attention to attempts by companies to transfer profit to countries with lower taxes. As one unfortunate company discovered, overzealous efforts to minimise import duties and taxes may result in short-run gains but long-run losses.

Avoiding Financial Problems

Transfer pricing often can be used to circumvent economic restrictions placed on multinational companies by host countries. For example, Israel places severe restrictions on the amount of profit that can leave the country. A way around this is to charge high prices for imports. Of course, a country that imposes such a restriction probably will watch import and export prices closely.

A second economic restriction by some countries is disallowing certain expenses against taxable income. For example, some general administrative expenses or research and development expenses may be disallowed if they are performed elsewhere. Another example is royalty fees charged by management against subsidiary income. To the extent these are disallowed by the host country, the amount can be recaptured by increasing the price of goods shipped into the country.

Transfer pricing also can be used to improve the financial condition of an affiliate, thereby presenting a favourable profit picture to satisfy earnings criteria by foreign lenders. In this manner the parent company can avoid committing capital to a foreign affiliate, even though the affiliate may be required to secure the loan. Furthermore, besides improving the affiliate's financial picture, low transfer prices provide the affiliate a competitive edge that can be very useful during the startup period of a new venture.

Currency Fluctuations

During periods of currency instability, the performance reports of foreign affiliates can be affected dramatically by exchange rate fluctuations. Many United States-based multinational companies find it convenient to evaluate the performance of foreign affiliate with reports stated in U.S. dollars. If currency exchange rates fluctuate during the performance period, however, it may be difficult to evaluate the performance of the affiliate. At the same time, management of the affiliate often finds it more convenient to evaluate its performance with reports stated in local currency rather than U.S. dollars.

This performance evaluation problem is compounded by transfer pricing unless the transfer price changes with changes in currency values. The difficulties that arise when the transfer prices are not adjusted for currency exchange fluctuations and a proposed solution have been illustrated in Exhibits-2 and 3, respectively.

As a simple solution to the difficulties illustrated in Exhibit-2, an *indexing formula* may be applied. The indexing formula, is shown below:

$$\text{NTP} = \text{OTP} \times \frac{\text{CER}}{\text{PER}}$$

where NTP = new transfer price, OTP = old transfer price, CER = current exchange rate, and PER = planned exchange rate. This formula is applied in Exhibit-3.

The indexing formula is both simple and effective. The formula is similar to formula used for price-level adjustments in inflation accounting. Furthermore, just as inflation accounting can isolate price-level gains and losses, the indexing formula can isolate operational results and exchange fluctuation results. It also should be noted that the indexing formula shifts the burden of foreign currency fluctuation to Subsidiary A who is in the best position to make decisions that are affected by the fluctuations.

EXHIBIT-2

TRANSFER PRICES *NOT* ADJUSTED FOR CURRENEY EXCHANGE FLUCTUATIONS

Under fixed United States dollar transfer pricing, performance measurement is distorted whenever the actual exchange rates for the producing or purchasing country deviate from the planned exchange rate. For example, suppose Subsidiary A (a manufacturing location) plans to produce and sell 1,000 devices to its affiliated subsidiaries at $10 per unit, the approved transfer price, Suppose also that Subsidiary A's total local currency cost to produce these devices is LCA 18,000 and that the planned exchange rate is $1.00 = LCA2. Thus, the planned P&L's for Subsidiary A, measured in United States dollars and in local currency, will be:

Subsidiary A—Plan

	United States dollars	*Exchange rate*	*Local currency*
Sales (intercompany)	$10,000	$1.00 = LCA2	LCA 20,000
Costs	9,000	LCA1 = $.50	18,000
Profit	$ 1,000		LCA 2,000
Percent of sales	10		10

Now suppose that the year actually progresses exactly as planned, except that the United States dollar devalues so that $1.00 = LCA1. Thus, the actual P&L results for Subsidiary A measured in United States dollars and in local currency will be:

Subsidiary A—Results

	United States dollars	*Exchange rate*	*Local currency*
Sales (intercompany)	$10,000	$1.00 = LCA1	LCA 10,000
Costs	18,000	LCA1 = $1.00	18,000
Profit	$ (8,000)		LCA (8,000)
Percent of sales	(80)		(80)

As you can see, even though Subsidiary A actually achieved planned device volume and contolled its local currency manufacturing costs precisely as planned, its profit performance completely obliterated by the exchange rate change, This "distortion" occurred in both the United States dollar P&L and in the local cunency P&L.

EXHIBIT-3

TRANSFER PRICES ADJUSTED FOR CURRENCY EXCHANGE FLUCTUATION

Consider what would happen if all suppositions were the same as in Exhibit-2), except that dollar indexing was in effect. Since Subsidiary A's planned exchange rate was LCA1 = $.50, but the actual exchange rate was LCA1 = $1.00, its dollar transfer would be increased through the use of the formula:

$$NTP = OTP \times \frac{CER}{PER}$$

$$= \$10 \times \frac{\$1.00}{\$.50}$$

$$= \$20.00 \text{ per device}$$

Assuming that actual volumes were achieved, at planned local currency costs, Subsidiary A's actual P&L results would be:

Subsidiary A—Results

	United States dollars	*Exchange rate*	*Local currency*
Sales (intercompany)	$20,000	$1.00 = LCA1	LCA 20,000
Costs	18,000	LCA1 =$1.00	18,000
Profit	$ 2,000		LCA 2,000
Percent of sales	10		10

As you can see, Subsidiary A actually achieves its planned profit rate, measured in dollars and local currency. Thus, under dollar indexing, factory performance is not distored due to exchange rate fluctuations.

A number of international objectives have been discussed-income tax minimisation, import duty minimisation, adjusting for currency fluctuations, avoiding economic restrictions, and presenting a favourable financial picture of a foreign affiliate in order to enhance borrowing opportunities or provide a temporary competitive edge. These objectives are not always compatible with the objectives of the management control process, goal congruence (profit maximisation) and performance evaluation, so a firm sometimes must maintain one set of books for foreign authorities and another set for parent company performance evaluation purposes.

Sometimes the practice of maintaining two sets of books causes problems. The books used for foreign authorities are likely to be the best known set both inside and outside the company. Managers of foreign affiliates that are profitable by virtue of favourable transfer prices may assume an unjustified aura of superiority over managers of affiliates that are subject to less favourable transfer prices. The parent company management also may overlook, at least temporarily, the source of a profit of a foreign affiliate that enjoys favorable transfer prices. If these situations occur, and they are likely to at least to a small degree, they can cause hard feelings between foreign affiliates or between the parent and foreign affiliates.

In addition, a company must be at least prudent and probably cautious in establishing and changing transfer prices. Authorities in other countries are becoming increasingly sophisticated, and even among third world countries, blatant efforts to shift profit to the obvious detriment of a country will be detected quickly and dealt with swiftly. A considerable amount of goodwill may be lost. On the other hand, a company that consistently pursues policies designed to satisfy to the greatest extent possible the taxing authorities of all host countries, even at some economic sacrifice, can build up goodwill. Even if a company, in order to be as even-handed as possible, establish all transfer prices so that the profit on transferred products is split 50-50 between the sending country and the receiving country. This policy may also end with many difficulties that the company can have with taxing authorities.

In spite of the varied international objectives that can be accomplished by transfer pricing, income tax and import duty minimisation seem to dominate international transfer pricing decisions. *What factors affect an MNC's transfer pricing decision?* It may be said that the overall profit to the company is the most important factor affecting the transfer pricing decision. Other factors that had a strong influence in the transfer pricing decision are (1) the competitive position of subsidiaries in foreign countries, (2) the performance evaluation of subsidiaries, (3) restrictions imposed by host governments on remitted earnings, (4) the need for cash by foreign subsidiaries, (5) the interests of local partners in foreign subsidiaries, and (6) rules and requirements of financial reporting for foreign subsidiaries. Some other, less influential factors are (1) rates of inflation in foreign countries, (2) the volume of interdivisional transfer, (3) the risk of expropriation in foreign countries, and (4) domestic government requirements on direct foreign investments.

DISBURSEMENT

In addition to the use of cheques, companies make international payments by giving payment instructions to their banks on paper, by telephone, the banks will accept instructions on tape to store payment orders for a few days, match the orders to foreign exchange transactions done separately, and execute them on the dates indicated by the customer. The data on the tapes often come directly out of the customer's accounts payable system. In some countries, automation has taken place more on the output side of the banks, supplying account information via electronic means. However, banks use the same electronic networks to accept payment instructions, the processing of which is more and more automated, with the exception of foreign currency payment orders. These are still usually handled in the traditional ways. Companies that have foreign currency collection accounts abroad or foreign currency accounts at their own banks can, of course, make payments directly from those accounts. This will save considerable expense and reduce foreign exchange exposure. All that is required is a test-key arrangement with each bank involved.

Intercompany Payments

Payments among companies belonging to the same group should be considered separately because the cash manager can exercise a much greater degree of control over them than over third-party items, provided he or she has the authority and the information to do so. When subsidiary A sends a cheque to subsidiary B in another country, there is a float benefit to subsidiary A but the corporation as a whole suffers. For many days, the item is out of control for cash and foreign exchange management purposes. Similarity, when a transfer from subsidiary A to subsidiary B takes a week to wind its way through the banking system interest is lost by both companies for those days and the item is also out of control. These problems lead companies to institute arrangements to influence these intercompany funds flows from their headquarters in any of a large variety of ways. Perhaps all that takes place is some consultation on ways to improve the payment methods used. Setting a fixed intercompany payment day for each month improves the possibilities for control. It may be desirable to combine all the foreign exchange conversions in one bank, which then also takes responsibility for the prompt execution of the transfers. Or the company may benefit from a *multilateral netting* system to eliminate payments that go back and forth among its various units. The particular system used depends on the structure of the company's cash flows, its form of organisation, and the savings generated. Several international banks are able to assist companies with the necessary evaluations underlying these systems; only a few banks have the specialised know-how to implement and run them.

Another problem international cash managers face is the control and management of the foreign exchange exposure generated by these intercompany transactions. If foreign exchange exposures are numerous and complex, a captive finance company or a reinvoicing company might be established to take over the intercompany receivables from all units of the group. Besides a foreign exchange exposure management center such a company also becomes the central collection agent for all group members with its own international collection system. It can centrally finance the entire intercompany receivable portfolio of the group, presumably at better rates than the individual members, and serve in many other capacities in the financial markets on behalf of the group. Offsetting these considerable advantages may be many internal and external arguments involving the company's organisational structure, its management incentive systems, its accounting policy, or legal, tax, and foreign exchange regulatory problems. Finance and reinvoicing companies can certainly be important cash and financial management tools, but they require very careful and detailed feasibility studies.

Finally, the international cash manager should try to maximise the use of excess cash in the foreign subsidiaries of the company. Often one subsidiary will have excess cash in its currency, while another subsidiary is borrowing another currency. Depending on the cash forecasting abilities of both, it might be desirable to arrange an intercompany loan at a rate that benefits both parties. When there are several such situations an international cash pool—perhaps as part of a finance company—can serve as the vehicle to distribute excess liquidity. Companies with excess cash deposit this to the pool; companies with shortages borrow from the pool. Because of their effect on the group foreign exchange exposure these operations should always be centrally managed and a comprehensive information system is an absolute prerequisite. Here also the various laws can create serious complications and not all companies' organisational structures will tolerate such cash pools.

CONTROL

Control problems have received a great deal of attention. Perhaps control of money movements in some countries is more difficult than in other countries because of the highly fragmented banking systems. Also, the banks may have traditionally maintained separate international and domestic operating divisions that could pass work between each other only in paper form. Only very recently did the most advanced money center banks succeed in electronically integrating these two groups. Finally, the banks routinely provide monthly statements of account; daily statements are usually obtainable but they are always a few days late and may not be free of charge.

Treasurers, therefore, once they had solved their most obvious float problems, started to put pressure on the banks to provide more timely account information. Above all, they wanted balance information but, more and more, they became interested in activity data with full details of each posted item. The banks' answer has been an electronic system with an automated link to the accounting system to deliver the information to the customer via a bank-operated or external time-sharing network. A variety of reports can thus be made available, such as plain account balances, balances plus activity in several levels of detail, averages over a specified period of time, listings of cheques paid, securities received and delivered on custody account, and others. Most banks constantly improve systems and several have the ability to report transactions immediately after they are processed, without waiting for end-of-day posting.

In many countries, the control problem is different. The banks issue daily statements that, because of their geographic proximity, reach the customers reasonably promptly. Also, large amounts are routinely advised by telephone and value-dating conventions tend to postpone the use of the money by the customer. Foreign currency conversions, of course, always delay the availability of the local currency equivalent by two days. Finally, the customs of overdraft banking and interest on credit balances mean that prompt information on incoming funds is not critical; the money is immediately productive. Therefore, companies do not have the same problem keeping track of their accounts. They have, however, a different control problem: in many countries the banks are accustomed to executing payment orders at their leisure, enjoying the float for a few days. These practices vary widely between countries and also between individual banks. All a company can do is to follow its transactions as closely as possible and to work with banks that will provide the best service. Float, however, is an important source of income for banks and as long as the payment is in their systems it is out of control for the companies.

Thus automated control systems have arisen in response to specific requirements. The companies' effort are directed to controlling the float the banks create for themselves, at the companies' expanse.

The points made above can be illustrated by reviewing a complex export collection problem and showing how the solution addresses both the cash movement aspects and the distribution of information for control purposes. As an example, ABC Company has subsidiaries in every country in Europe, five of which have plants that export directly to third-party buyers all over Europe. Many of these customers regularly place orders with more than one of the five ABC plants. While the accounts receivable are maintained on the books of the exporting plants, the ABC company located in the buyer's country has direct credit and collection responsibility. Headquarters monitors consolidated credit and foreign exchange exposure. Most invoices are denominated in the currencies of the buyers.

A bank was asked to design a system that would (1) maximise the availability of the export proceeds in the currencies designated by the exporting plants; and (2) provide prompt advice of payment to all ABC parties concerned-the exporter, the company responsible for credit and collection, and headquarters. The following collection and concentration system was developed. (See Exhibit-4).

EXHIBIT-4

EXPORT CONCENTRATION SYSTEM FOR ABC COMPANY

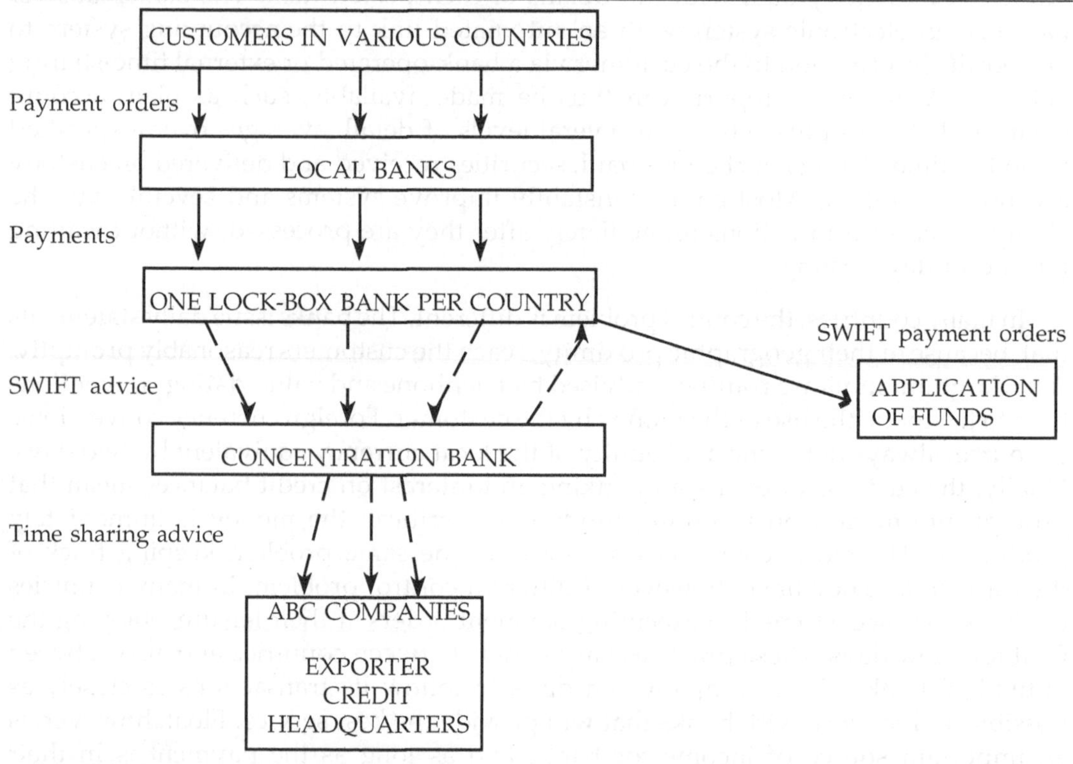

1. ABC designated a concentration bank and opened accounts a this bank in all currencies received.
2. The concentration bank opened one lock-box account in each country from which ABC receives the currency. Lock-box banks were chosen for their known internal efficiency and their SWIFT membership.
3. ABC requested its customers to make their local currency payments to the designated lock-box banks via their own local banks.
4. The lock-box banks advised the concentration bank via SWIFT of incoming amounts.

5. The concentration bank sold the incoming amounts to a sate in the foreign exchange market, credited them to a currency account in its hooks, or deposited them at interest. Processing at the concentration bank is highly automated, requiring minimal intervention by staff.
6. The concentration bank reported the amounts received and their application to the three ABC units concerned via a time-sharing system to which all ABC companies have easy access and which has an automated link to the bank's processing system.

The result was a system with the following advantages.

1. Optimal availability of usable funds through application of the lock-box collection concept coupled with fast communication (SWIFT)
2. Concentration of funds with one bank, which facilitates final application of the money in ABC's cash pool or wire transfers to other banks
3. One central source of payment information that is made available simultaneously to all parties.
4. Efficiencies in operations, communications, and auditing because of the use of one concentration bank for all money flows.

BEYOND CASH MANAGEMENT

Companies that practice cash management as a discipline and familiarise themselves with the different environments in which they have to work generally succeed in obtaining important improvements in funds availability without too many problems. They bring money flows under more effective control, make use of modern transfer systems, and influence their customers to do the same. They also realise that some float is unavoidable and that there are limits to the demands they can set on their banks, limits that differ from country to country.

At this point, a change takes place in the challenge of the job. The increased control the cash manager has obtained over funds flows brings with it the flow of a large amount of information to his or her desk, ranging from plans, budgets, and forecasts to data from internal systems that monitor accounts payable and receivable, capital expenditures, and short-term investments. From the outside, the banks supply a constant stream of transaction data and information on economic conditions: foreign exchange market and interest rate information comes in from a variety of sources. Somehow, all of this has to be sorted, analysed, distributed, and acted upon in the treasury department-truly, a formidable challenge that goes well beyond cash management into the problems of managing information to maximise the opportunities for cash management.

The large companies that have solved their cash management problems in a technical sense are now faced with the problem of integrating the data they receive from these many sources into a coordinated information system that (1) facilitates decision making and (2) makes the appropriate information available to other relevant parties. Many of the data originate in computer systems of one kind or another, both, internal and external, but are then coordinated manually in the treasury department.

Balance and activity figures are used in several reports and forms are filled out by hand for different purposes, often to be reentered into other computer systems. This kind of work, and many tasks like it, can be more efficiently and accurately done if the treasury department collects the data relevant to its function into a data bank maintained on a minicomputer in its department. The necessary reports can then be programmed and much manual work saved.

Today, the leading companies look for ways to gain access data via electronic means, to employ this in models used as decision-making aids, and to communicate electronically with both their other corporate systems and banks. This requires a new approach to data processing, entirely different from the construction of the typical large-volume processing systems in companies and banks. A treasury information system works with a large variety of different inputs, each in its own format, and has to produce usable output in a highly time-critical environment. The financial markets operate with rigid deadlines for payment orders and investments. Therefore, the system has to be highly flexible and extremely responsive while also allowing for simulations and comparisons of different solutions to a problem.

Most important, however, a treasury information system has to respond to the company's precise, specific requirements as to priorities, organisational and financial structure, methods of doing business, and cash management techniques. Every company is different in these respects. For that reason, treasury information systems must be custom-designed for each company. They are never an off-the-shelf product. A company's needs can grow beyond the standard cash management services of banks to highly individual information requirements. Bank's main line cash management products can, of course, continue to be used but now in the framework of a larger, coordinated system that can be designed only with a thorough understanding of the total function of the treasury department in the company.

What impact will this have on international cash management? To even begin to answer the question one first has to make an inventory of the kinds of information the international cash manager needs and one has to explore techniques for organising this information. Internal corporate information comes into the treasury from accounting, controllers, international divisions, overseas units, exporting and importing units. These data concern transactions, balances, investments, borrowings, foreign exchange exposure and transactions, credit terms, and so forth. Banks supply transactions and balance data, information on markets, and advice of various kinds. Other sources bring in economic and financial information. The media used by these many sources include mail, wire services, telex, and computer networks accessible via terminal. Few treasurers believe that all of this information is put to optimal use.

A system is needed that receives information into a central file, a library with separate "volumes" containing different kinds of data that are accessible not only individually but in a coordinated way. For instance, in order to monitor cash balances of overseas subsidiaries and to suggest better uses of funds, information on the balances can be combined with cash forecasts, foreign exchange forecasts, interest rates, regulations, and foreign exchange exposure into an optimisation model. Such a model can make mathematically based recommendations, within parameters that reflect policy and other subjective considerations. In the absence of a model, the cash manager can either refrain from any action because there are too many data to consider or use his or her intuition adjusted by opinions of trusted advisers and of colleagues in the company. With a model to convert a multitude of data into logical recommendations the treasurer has a better decision-making tool. bne to be used jointly with personal knowledge and personal contacts.

In this way, many treasury functions that are presently very difficult to systematise can be better performed. In some cases, information management is a question of consolidating data; sometimes, decision making is the objective. Always the problem revolves around the need to integrate data from a variety of sources in a variety of formats into a form that is presented as useful information rather than a collection of data. This is the new challenge to the cash manager. When the cash manager has solved immediate cash flow problems he or she has to improve the sources and uses of information, without which one cannot go beyond technical cash management. This development underlines the interrelationships between the different functions in the international treasury department, including foreign exchange exposure, cash movements, investments, bank relations, and current borrowing. For many aspects of these functions the same information is needed and it is the cash manager whose needs will be most urgent on a day-to-day basis.

INTERNATIONAL RECEIVABLE MANAGEMENT

The level of receivable depends upon the volume of credit sales and the average collection period. These two variables in turn depend upon credit standards, credit terms, and collection policy. As management moves from customers who are more likely to pay their bills to customers who are less likely to pay their bills, sales tend to increase. However, the lenient credit policy is also likely to increase bad debt losses and investments in accounts receivable. In theory, the company should liberalise its credit standards to the point where the marginal profit on its increased sales equals the marginal cost of credit.

Because money has a time value, accounts receivable have a cost in terms of foregone interest. Nevertheless, many multinational companies frequently decide to sell for credit in order to expand sales volume and profits. If sales are made on the basis of drafts on importers, trade acceptances or bankers' acceptances are created and these may be discounted at banks or sold in the money market. In addition, in many countries, government agencies extend export credit at preferential interest rates which make the accumulation of accounts receivable even more desirable.

Multinational accounts receivable are created by two separate types of transaction: *sales to outside the corporate group* and *intra-company sales*. These two types of transactions must be considered separately because their economic consequences are different. One truly unique problem area of multinational accounts receivable management has to do with the risk of currency value changes. The accounts receivable manager should understand this risk and take all necessary actions to minimise such a risk.

Sales to Independent Customers and Intracompany Sales

Management of accounts receivable from independent buyers involves two types of decision: the denomination of currency to be used for payments and the terms of payment. Domestic sales are always denominated in the local currency. In contrast, export sales can be denominated in the currency of the exporter, the currency of the importer, or a third country currency. The exporter would prefer to price and to invoice in the strongest currency, while the importer would prefer to pay in the weakest currency. Competition or custom will frequently resolve the problem, but the usual result is a tradeoff between the term of payment and the denomination of currency. For example, the exporter may grant a longer credit period in exchange for the importer's promise to pay its purchase in a hard currency.

Many factors affect the terms of payment, but perhaps one of the most important is the strength of the currency denominated in the - transaction. If payments are to be made in a soft currency, accounts receivable should be collected as quickly as possible in order to minimise the possibility of exchange losses between the sale date and the collection date. Sales made in a hard currency may be permitted to remain outstanding Somewhat longer. If the devaluation of its home currency is imminent, the exporter might want to encourage slow payment of its hard currency receivables.

Intracompany sales differ from sales to independent customers in that little concern is given to credit standing and that the timing of the payments may depend upon the company's desire to allocate resources rather than normal payment schedules. Such sales are necessary for many reasons. Subsidiaries produce different products and often sell to each other. Like the location of cash balances, the location of intracompany receivables and their amount are a policy problem of the multinational company in the allocation of its resources on a global basis. If the parent company desires to transfer funds to its affiliate, it may do so by having the affiliate delay the payment of intracompany purchases.

Because intracompany sales usually cross national boundaries, governments are concerned about such sales. If subsidiaries are located in countries whose currencies are likely to devalue or to float downward, the parent company may instruct its subsidiaries to pay their purchases more quickly. In contrast, if subsidiaries are located in countries whose currencies are expected to upvalue or to float upward, the parent company may instruct its subsidiaries to delay payments. It is important to note that early payments and later payments in conjunction with intracompany sales are feasible only when the parent company owns 100 percent of its various affiliates.

Currency Value Problems

Accounts receivable risks result from changes in exchange rates between the sales date and the collection date. There are several ways that the accounts receivable manager may be able to reduce these risks. The seller may require that all payments are to be made in hard currencies. This requirement would assure the seller that payments are to be made in currencies likely to face little or no devaluation on the foreign exchange market. In certain instances, the multinational company refuses credit sales denominated in foreign currencies altogether. It is often possible for multinational companies to buy currency credit insurance.

The use of *factors* is another way to minimise accounts receivable risks from changes in exchange rates between the sale date and the collection date. Factoring is a process whereby a company sells its accounts receivable on a nonrecourse basis. Nonrecourse means that the factor takes the loss if the customers of its client do not pay their accounts. In addition to risk bearing, the factor performs a number of additional services such as credit checking, bookkeeping, and the collection of accounts. .

INTERNATIONAL INVENTORY MANAGEMENT

The overall efficiency of inventory management is extremely important for two reasons. (1) Inventories represent a significant segment of total assets for most business firms. (2) They are the least liquid of current assets and thus errors in inventory management are not quickly remedied. Hence, it is not surprising to note that for the last few decades the greatest improvements within the area of current asset management have been made in the area of inventory control and investment. With the application of computers and mathematical models, the size of inventories in relation to sales has been greatly reduced.

The level of sales, the length of the production cycle, and the durability of the product are the major determinants of investment in inventory. In domestic or one-country operations, companies attempt to balance their inventory level in such a way that both carrying costs and stockout costs are minimised. However, differentials in the costs of production and storage in different countries allow the multinational company to maintain more flexible inventory policies. For instance, multinational companies can take advantage of the cheaper costs that may exist in a particular country by shifting its production or storage function to that country. These advantages are offset by such disadvantages as tariff levels and other forms of import restrictions used by governments.

Given the fact that many foreign affiliates operate under inflationary economic conditions, it is important for a multinational company to determine whether to buy inventory in advance or to delay purchase until the inventory is actually needed. Advance purchase involves such carrying costs as interest on funds tied up in inventory, insurance premiums, storage costs, and taxes. Later purchase increases the possibility of higher costs either through inflation or devaluation. Inflation increases the costs of locally purchased items and devaluation increases the costs of imported items.

Despite the desire for optimisation of inventory levels, many companies that rely on imported inventories maintain over-stocked inventory accounts. The fears of continued inflation, raw materials shortages, and a number of other environmental constraints are inducing companies to maintain high overseas inventory levels rather than risk curtailment of their overseas operations. The additional environmental constraints include anticipated import bans in foreign countries, anticipated delivery delays caused by dock strikes and slowdowns, the lack of sophisticated production and inventory control systems, and increased difficulty in obtaining foreign exchange for inventory purchases.

Protective Measures Against Inflation

Many foreign affiliates operate under inflationary economic conditions. Thus, it is important for multinational companies to determine the effects of an increasing local price level or devaluation on their inventory management policies. The type of inventory normally stocked by subsidiaries is of importance to this decision. Some subsidiaries rely heavily on imported inventories, while other subsidiaries depend heavily upon locally acquired inventories. Some other subsidiaries may rely almost equally on imported and locally acquired inventories.

If a subsidiary relies heavily on imported goods, it should seek to build up its inventory of supplies, equipment, and components in advance of an expected devaluation. This is because devaluation at a later date effectively increases the costs of imported goods. For example, if the host country should declare a ten percent devaluation of its currency in relation to the dollar, the subsidiary should pay ten percent more local currency for the same amount of imported goods from the United States.

On the other hand, if a subsidiary depends heavily upon locally purchased goods, it should seek to minimise its inventory of supplies, equipment, and components. This is because devaluation at a later date effectively reduces the dollar value of inventories acquired locally. If inventories are translated at current rather than historical exchange rates, a ten percent devaluation of the local currency against the dollar would reduce the dollar value of its inventory by ten percent.

Finally, if a subsidiary relies almost equally on imported inventories and locally purchased inventories, it should seek to reduce its locally acquired inventories and to increase its imported inventories in advance of an expected devaluation. However, if accurate forecasts of devaluation are not possible, the company should maintain the same amount of imported goods and locally purchased goods to avoid foreign exchange risks. This is because a devaluation would affect both types of inventories equally and thus the subsidiary would experience neither a gain nor a loss.

Pricing

Along with the preventive measures that multinational companies may take to reduce the risks associated with devaluation, additional action can be taken in the area of pricing to reduce these risks. To illustrate, assume that 10 American-made radios have been imported into Korea which subsequently devalues its wons by 100 percent. The original exchange rate was KW50 per $1, the original cost was KW1,000 per radio, and the original selling price was KW1,500 per radio.

The Korean subsidiary has two basic policies with respect to price: (1) it can maintain the original price of its inventory in an effort to undercut competition and (2) it can increase the price of its inventory in order to earn all or part of the original dollar profit expected. Table-1 shows the effects of both policies to the Korean subsidiary. Maintenance of the old price will result in a dollar loss of $50 on the sale of the 10 radios even if local figures indicate a profit of KW5,000. If the subsidiary increases its selling price to the dollar equivalent of the original selling price, it will earn a profit of $100. However, it is important to note that this assumes the Korean government does not maintain price controls. Although there are no price controls imposed by the Korean government, a price increase of the magnitude indicated in Policy (2) would perhaps discourage some sales. If the price elasticity of demand for the merchandise is extremely high, the local market may not bear the higher price. Nevertheless, a certain level of price rise is required to prevent a deterioration of converted earnings.

TABLE-1

EFFECT OF PRICING ON PROFITS

			(1) Maintain old price		*(2) Adjust price*	
Exchange Rate			*Korean Currency*	*Dollars (current value)*	*Korean Currency*	*Dollars (current value)*
KW100	(now)	Sold for	KW15,000	$150	KW30,000	$300
KW50	(old)	Cost	KW10,000	$200	KW10,000	$200
		Profit	KW 5,000	($50)	KW20,000	$100

Another important question is whether the subsidiary should continue to import that type of merchandise. If local sales prices can be raised to cover the now higher dollar import prices, imports should continue. If not, imports should cease. Although the decision not to import the merchandise does not cause any translation loss, it may result in idle production capacity and an eventual operating loss due to the surrender of that particular foreign market. If possible, multinational companies should price their inventory goods in such a way that sales revenues include the sum of the increase in replacement cost of the inventory sold, plus the loss in real value of the monetary profit expected, plus the increased income taxes.

Reducing Vulnerability to Inflation and Devaluation

When it becomes clear that inflation will continue and devaluation is imminent, it is advisable that managers consider the following adaptations. Cash balances should be minimised and foreign debts denominated in convertible currencies should be liquidated. When the host government appears likely to impose foreign exchange controls, remittances should be accelerated. If controls are already in effect, any excess funds should be reinvested in assets which are not so vulnerable as cash. At the same time, the subsidiary must be careful at a sensitive time. Remittances through the black market may result in serious economic reprisals.

It is worthwhile to take all the normal procedures of speeding up the collection process and delaying payments. If the subsidiary needs funds on a short-term basis, it should obtain them from local banks. However, under conditions of an imminent devaluation and/or a rapid increase in price levels, bank loans are usually not obtainable. It then becomes necessary to obtain local currency loans by factoring receivables or by pledging inventories. If the subsidiary has preestablished overdraft facilities with local banks, it is desirable to exhaust them before it secures its assets for loans. This is because overdraft facilities are normally the cheapest local credit available.

Unless local buyers will ignore higher prices and respond to credit offerings positively, accounts receivable should be reduced to the extent that local operating circumstances permit. Investments in locally purchased goods should be minimised and investments in imported goods should be maximised under inflationary conditions. Such prepaid expenses as deposits on materials and insurance premiums should be kept as small as possible. Forward contracts may be necessary to protect the convertible currency value of funds between accumulation and transfer.

Thus, the international working capital management techniques are essentially similar to those employed domestically, but additional variables are involved. In domestic operations all transactions are subject to the same rules of movement, accumulation, and reinvestment, but these rules vary when these transactions occur across national boundaries. These additional variables include political tax, foreign exchange, and other economic constraints.

To manage working capital from a global perspective, the multinational company must carefully evaluate various constraints such as foreign exchange rate fluctuations and base ultimate decisions about the transfer of funds on this evaluation. The company then must establish clear lines of accountability for asset deterioration and exchange losses. Finally, a workable system of controls must be developed to help measure the performance of working capital management.

Cash management can be centralised or decentralised on a company level. Although decentralisation is popular among subsidiary managers, it does not permit the multinational company to use its most liquid asset on a widespread basis. Effective cash management requires the establishment of cash centers. This system calls for each local subsidiary to hold at the local level the minimum cash balance for transaction purposes. All funds not needed for transaction purposes are channeled to a central cash center. This cash center has responsibility for placing the central pool of funds in such currencies and money market instruments which will best serve the needs of the multinational company on a worldwide basis.

Multinational accounts receivable are created by two separate types of transaction: sales to independent customers and intracompany sales. Management of accounts receivable from independent customers involves the denomination of currency to be used for payments and the terms of payment. Intracompany sales differ from sales to independent customers in that little concern is given to credit standing and that the timing of the payments may depend upon the company's desire to allocate resources rather than normal payment schedules. One truly unique area of multinational accounts receivables management has to do with the risk of currency value changes. The accounts receivable manager should understand this risk and take all necessary actions to minimise such a risk.

The overall efficiency of inventory management is extremely important for two reasons: (1) Inventories represent a significant segment of total assets for most business firms. (2) They are the least liquid of current assets and thus errors in inventory management are not quickly remedied.

When foreign subsidiaries operate under inflationary conditions, it is important to determine whether to purchase inventory in advance or to delay purchase until the inventory is actually needed. Advance purchase involves such carrying costs as interest on funds tied up in inventory, insurance premiums, and storage costs. Later purchase involves the possibility of higher costs either through inflation or devaluation. Thus, the inventory manager should compute the optimal tradeoff between higher carrying costs and higher purchase costs for inventory.

ILLUSTRATIVE PROBLEMS

1. Given the following data about the cash requirements of an MNC and its affiliates:

Location	*Mean Expected Cash Needs ($ million)*	*Standard Deviation ($ million)*
Parent	350	50
Affiliate X	75	15
Affiliate Y	120	34
Affiliate Z	95	25

Assuming that the MNC wishes to insure that all cash needs of the parent and affiliates can be met on time:

a. How much cash would be needed by each entity under a decentralised cash management system?

b. How much savings would accrue from a centralised system? Show how these savings are possible.

Ans.

If it is desired to reduce the probability of not being able to meet cash needs on time, then cash balances maintained should be equal to the mean expected requirement plus three standard deviations.

Decentralised System

Parent	$350 + 3 \times 50$	= $500 million
Affiliate X	$75 + 3 \times 15$	= $120 million
Affiliate Y	$120 + 3 \times 34$	= $222 million
Affiliate Z	$95 + 3 \times 25$	= $170 million
Total requirements		=$1012 million

Centralised System

$\sqrt{(50)^2 + (15)^2 + (34)^2 + (25)^2} =$

\$67.1 million

Total requirements = 640 + 3 × 67 = \$841 million

The centralised system entails savings of about \$171 million. The savings are possible since the variance of the whole is less than the sum of the variance of the parts. Since the probability distributions of the four units are independent, the variance of the aggregate probability distribution is the sum of the individual variances.

2. A U.S. multinational firm maintains a multilateral interaffiliate netting system, with netting operations conducted by a currency center, which is also in charge of investing the excess cash resources of all affiliates. The affiliates report their payables to other affiliates on the fifteenth each month. The currency center issues instructions to net paying affiliates on the twentieth of each month, using market exchange rates on that date. Given the data in Table-1.

Affiliate	*Amounts Due To Other Affiliates*	*Funds Available*	*Funds Required For Operations May 15-31, 2013*
	Position as of May 15, 2013		
Affiliate A (£)	FF2,000,000 to B DM3,500,000 to C	£100,000,000	£5,000,000
Affiliate B (FF)	£1,500,000 to A DM2,000,000 to C	FF27,000,000	FF45,000,000
Affiliate C (DM)	£3,000,000 to A FF10,000,000 to B	DM45,000,000	DM15,000,000

(a) Devise a netting system for the firm showing and currencies of actual transfers made on May 20, 2013.

(b) The firm's cash management policy requires that all cash surplus affiliates transfer their surpluses to the center (on the 15th and the last day of each month). The center handles all money market investments. Deficit affiliates are asked to cover their temporary needs by drawing on their overdraft facilities with local banks. What will be the total resources (in U.S. dollars) available for investment during the second half of May? Which affiliate (or affiliates) will be using local credit lines and in what amounts?

(c) Outline the advantages (and disadvantages if any) which the firm derives from the netting plan developed in (a), and from the centralised investment feature covered in (b). Spot exchange rates on May 20, 2013 were

£1.00 = \$1.45

\$1.00 = FF6.50.

\$1.00 = DM2.35

Ans.

(a) When positions are reported to the currency center, the center will convert these positions to U.S. dollars using the spot exchange rate on May 20, 2013. The following matrix shows the amounts due to and from cash affiliate to the other affiliates in U.S. dollars.

	A	*B*	*C*	*Total Payable*
A	—	307,692	1,489,368	1,797,060
B	2,175,000	—	851,060	3,026,060
C	4,350,000	1,538,460	—	5,888,450
Total Receivable	6,525,000	1,846,152	2,340,428	10,711,580

The center issues instructions to affiliates B and C to make the following payments to affiliate A in pounds sterling as follows:

B to A, the equivalent of $1,179,908, or £ 813,730.

C to A, the equivalent of $3,548,032, or £ 2,446,912.

(b) The affiliates have the following resources available for the second half of May 2013 showing excess funds, which are transferred to the center for investment, or deficits, which have to be covered by drawing on local overdraft bank facilities:

Affiliate	*Currency*	*Total resources available*	*Funds required*	*Surplus or (deficit)*
A	£	£10,000,000+3,260,289	£5,000,000	£8,260,289
B	FF	FF27,000,000–7,669,402	FF45,000,000	(FF25,669,402)
C	DM	DM45,000,000–8,337,875	DM15,000,000	DM21,662,125

(c) By using multilateral netting, the firm is able to reduce the number of transfers from six to two, and the amount of total transfers from the equivalent of $10,711,580 to the equivalent of $4,727,940. Moreover, the center is able to place the excess funds of affiliates A and C (the equivalent of $21,195,345) to generate the highest available rate of return during the second half of May, while affiliate B draws on the local banking overdraft facility to meet its requirements during the same period.

3. Assume that in India one-year interest rate is 14%. Also assume the Indian rupee is expected to appreciate by 8% over the next year against the U.S. dollar. What is the expected effective yield on a one-year deposit in India by a. U.S. firm?

Ans.

$$\begin{aligned} E\,(cf) &= (1 + if)\,[1 + E\,(ef)] - 1 \\ &= (1 + .14)\,(1 + .08) - 1 \\ &= .2312 \\ &= 23.12\% \end{aligned}$$

4. Assume that the one-year forward rate is used as the forecast of the future spot rate. The French franc's spot rate is $.20, while its one-year forward rate is $.19. The

French one-year interest rate is 11%. What is the expected effective yield on a one-year deposit in France by a U.S. firm?

Ans.

E (ef) = (Forward Rate—Spot Rate)/Spot Rate
= (\$.19–\$.20)/\$.20 = –5%

E (ef) = (1 + if) [1 + E (ef)] –1
= [1 + .11] [1 + (–.05)]–1
= 5.45%

5. Assume the Venezuela one-year interest rate is 90%, while the U.S. one-year interest rate is 6%. Determine the break-even value for the percentage change in Venezuela's currency (the bolivar) that would cause the effective yield to be the same for a one-year deposit in Venezuela as for a one-year deposit in the U.S.

Ans.

$$\text{ef} = \frac{(1+l)}{(1+if)} - 1$$

$$\frac{(1+.06)}{(1+.90)} - 1$$

$$= -44.21\%$$

If the bolivar depreciates by less then 44.2% against the \$ over one-year period, a one-year deposit in Venezuela will generate a higher effective yield than a one-year U.S. deposit.

6. A subsidiary of a U.S. MNC in India is considering relaxation of its credit policy in an attempt to increase sales and to use unutilised capacity. The new policy calls for extending credit to lower credit class groups, and extending the credit period from 90 days to 120 days to all accounts with no cash discount allowed.

Current Situation		*New Policy*
Sales ₹ 1,000,000		₹ 2,000,000
Contribution margin to profits		10% 15% (all sales)
Bad debt experience	4%	5% (on all accounts)
Cost of financing receivables	12% per annum	12% per annum
Credit period	90 days	120 days

(a) Should the new credit policy be instituted if it is assumed that the Indian rupee is not expected to depreciate against the U.S. dollar in the next four months?

(b) Should the new credit policy be instituted if the Indian rupee is expected to depreciate by one per cent per month against the U.S. dollar?

(c) Calculate the monthly rate of depreciation of the Indian rupee against the U.S. dollar that would leave the management of the U.S. firm indifferent as to whether or not to adopt the new credit policy.

(d) Would the subsidiary be better off by expanding sales up to ₹ 1,500,000 given the following changes?

Contribution margin	15%	(on additional sales only)
Bad debt experience	5%	(on additional sales only)
Financing cost	6%	per annum (on additional sales only through subsidised local financing)
Depreciation of the Indian rupee	1%	per month
Credit period	90	days (unchanged)

Ans.

(a) ₹ 1,000,000 (.10) > ₹ 1,000,000 (.04) + 1,000,000 (.03)

100,000 > 40,000 + 20,000

100,000 > 70,000 = ₹ 30,000

₹ 2,000,000 (.15) > ₹ 2,000,000 (.05) + 2,000,000 (.04)

300,000 > 100,000 + 80,000

300,000 > 180,000 = ₹ 120,000

The new credit policy should be put into affect since contribution to profits considerably exceed contribution to profits under the current situation.

(b) The new credit policy should still be instituted even if the rupee is expected to depreciate by one per cent per month against the U.S. dollar.

₹ 30,000–1,000,000 (0.96) (.03) = ₹ 1,200

₹ 120,000–2,000,000 (0.95) (.04) = ₹ 44,000

(c) Assuming that the depreciation of the pound impacts contribution to profits of the Indian subsidiary in U.S. dollar terms under the current situation as well as under the new policy, then the new policy is superior irrespective of the depreciation rate of the Indian subsidiary. However, the new policy ceases to make contribution to profits when the depreciation rate of the Indian rupee is about 1.6 per cent monthly.

₹ 120,000-2,000,000 (.95) (.064) $\geq$ 0

(d) ₹ 500,000 (.15) > 500,000 (.05) + 500,000 (0.015) + (500,000) (0.95) (.03)

₹ 75,000 > 25,000 + 7,500 + 14,250

₹ 75,000 > 46,750 = ₹ 28,250

The Indian subsidiary would be better off by expanding sales to ₹ 1,500,000 compared with the current situation. There is a positive incremental contribution to profit after allowing for the depreciation of the Indian rupee. However, a depreciation of the rupee against the dollar of 3 per cent monthly would render this credit relaxation unprofitable (see below).

₹ 75,000 $\leq$ 25,000 + 7,500 + (500,000) (0.95) (.09)
$\leq$ 25,000 + 7,500 + 42,750
$\leq$ 75,250

7. A U.S. firm is attempting to determine the optimal amount of stockpiling of components which are shipped from the parent company (in terms of months' requirements) for its affiliate in India. The relevant data are given below:

* Price of components is $15.00 per unit, rising at 1.5 per cent per month.
* Holding costs are two per cent per month.
* Excess ₹ balances held in the India and invested in marketable securities earn 24 per cent per annum.
* The ₹/U.S. dollar exchange rate is expected to remain unchanged in the first two months, and to depreciate thereafter by three per cent per month.

(a) Calculate the optimal stockpiling requirement for the Indian affiliate.

(b) Rework the optimal solution if the rupee is projected to depreciate against the U.S. dollar by three per cent in each of the next two months, two per cent in the third month, and one per cent in each of the subsequent months.

(c) Would you answer to (a) or (b) be different if the parent company expects imminent controls imposed by the Indian government on imports of raw materials and components?

Ans.

(a)

Month	*Opportunity[1] Cost of Local Funds (%)*	*Holding Cost (%)*	*Total[2] Monthly Carrying Cost (%)*	*Cumulative Carrying Cost (%)*	*Cumulative Price Increase (%)*
1	2	2	4	4	—
2	2	2	4	8	1.5
3	–1	2	1	9	3.0
4	–1	2	1	10	4.5
5	–1	2	1	11	6.0
6	–1	2	1	12	7.5
7	–1	2	1	13	9.0
8	–1	2	1	14	10.5
9	–1	2	1	15	12.0
10	–1	2	1	16	13.5
11	–1	2	1	17	15.0
12	–1	2	1	18	16.5
13	–1	2	1	19	18.0
14	–1	2	1	20	19.5
15	–1	2	1	21	21.0
16	–1	2	1	22	22.5

The table shows that the cumulative price increase does not start to exceed the cumulative carrying cost until after the 15th month. Stockpiling during the first 14 months is counterproductive as in doing so the Indian affiliate will be incurring a higher carrying cost on the stockpiled components than the expected rise in the price of components. Beginning with the 15th month, the cumulative price increase will progressively exceed the cumulative carrying cost by one half of one per cent per month. A stockpiling policy limited only by the financial resources of the affiliates is recommended then.

(b)

Month	*Opportunity*[3] *Cost of Local Funds (%)*	*Holding Cost (%)*	*Total*[4] *Monthly Carrying Cost (%)*	*Cumulative Carrying Cost (%)*	*Cumulative Price Increase (%)*
1	–1	2	1	1	—
2	–1	2	1	2	1.5
3	0	2	2	4	3.0
4	1	2	3	7	4.5
5	1	2	3	10	6.0
6	1	2	3	13	7.5

No stockpiling is recommended under the assumptions given as at no time does the cumulative price increase exceed the cumulative carrying cost. Moreover, the gap between the two will be widening with the passage of each month.

(c) If controls on the importation of raw materials and components which are essential for the manufacturing process are imminent, the affiliate should immediately begin to stockpile, irrespective of the variables involved in the above tabulations.

QUESTIONS

1. Some managers believe that multinational working capital management is just an extension of domestic management policies. Do you agree? Should MNC develop a set of working capital policies for its international operations that is different from its guidelines for domestic operations?
2. If multinational working capital management calls for new policy guidelines, which variables or factors should the manager consider in formulating these guidelines?
3. Why are multinational financial managers keen on *unbundling* payments made by affiliates to the parent company? Is unbundling a panacea for all transfer restrictions and blockage problems?
4. If you are negotiating an agreement with the government of a developing country regulating the operations of the affiliate that you are about to set up in that country, what particular provisions would you like to include in that agreement?

Would you insist that the same type of agreement should apply to your affiliates in other countries?

5. Why is the transfer of dividends from affiliates to parent companies the most restricted type of transfers by host governments? Should a financial manager of an MNC endeavour to conceal such transfers by negotiating artificially inflated royalty or service payments?
6. "Transfer pricing is a potent and flexible tool which managements of MNCs can use freely to circumvent transfer restrictions imposed by host governments." Comment on this statement, highlighting particularly the mechanisms used by such governments (as well as the parent country's government) to blunt the effectiveness of this tool.
7. Transfer pricing, in the opinion of some managers, is not as effective a tool as it may seem in managing intracorporate transfers. What are the reasons behind this position? How do you reconcile it with the reluctance of most MNCs to reveal the full extent of transfer pricing operations?
9. Outline a strategy to deal with the problem of an imminent blockage of transfers by the host government in a country where your affiliate is operating. Would your strategy be different if the expected blockage is deemed to be of a temporary nature? Explain.
10. Is the technique of "fronting loans" effective in discouraging governments of developing countries from blocking loan service payments by affiliates located within their boundaries? (Consider in your answer high-debt LDCs experiencing problems in servicing their obligations to international banks.)
11. What are the major prerequisites of an effective cash management system? Could such a system be developed without incorporating the firm's exchange exposure and financing policies?
12. What strategy should the international financial manager follow with respect to positioning of funds if his objectives were:
    a. to minimise transaction costs?
    b. to minimise foreign exchange risk?
    c. to minimise the political risk?
    d. to insure that payments due from affiliates are effected on time?
    e. to maximise the rate of return on investment of liquid assets?
13. What is meant by "cash mobilisation"? Why is centralisation of cash management a necessary prerequisite to effective cash mobilisation?
14. Show how an intracorporate multilateral netting is a necessary component of an effective cash mobilisation system. Identify the savings that would accrue from multilateral netting conducted by a central depository.
15. How does value dating fit in an MNC's cash management system? What measures can be taken by the firm to overcome the limitations imposed by the practices of the banking community in the countries where it operates?
16. Explain why a parent may prefer to charge some subsidiaries higher prices for the supplies it provides them than it charges other subsidiaries.
17. Discuss the general functions involved in international cash management.

18. What is netting, and how can it improve an MNC's performance?
19. How can an MNC implement leading and lagging techniques to help subsidiaries in need of funds?
20. Explain how the MNC's optimisation of cash flow can distort the profits of each subsidiary.
21. How can a centralised cash management system be beneficial to the MNC?
22. Why would a firm consider investing short-term funds overseas?

PROBLEMS

1. Assume a U.S.-based MNC has $2,000,000 in cash available for 90 days. It is considering the use of covered interest arbitrage, since the British 90-day interest rate is higher than the U.S. interest rate. What will determine whether this strategy is feasible?
2. Assume a U.S.-based MNC has $1,000,000 in cash available for 30 days. It can earn 1 per cent on a 30-day investment in the U.S. Alternatively, if it converts the dollars to French francs, it can earn 1½ per cent on a French deposit. The spot rate of the French franc is $.12. The spot rate 30 days from now is expected to be $.10. Should this firm invest its cash in the U.S. or in France? Substantiate your answer.
3. Assume a U.S.-based MNC has $3,000,000 in cash available for 180 days. It can earn 7 per cent on a U.S. Treasury bill or 9 per cent on a British Treasury bill. The British investment does require conversion of dollars to British pounds. Assume that interest rate parity holds and that the MNC believes the 180-day forward rate is a reliable predictor of the spot rate to be realised 180 days from now. Would the British investment provide an effective yield that is below, above, or equal to the yield on the U.S. investment? Explain your answer.
4. Repeat Question 3, but this time assume that the firm expects the 180-day forward rate of the pound to substantially overestimate the spot rate to be realised in 180 days.
5. Repeat Question 3, but this time assume that the firm expects the 180-day forward rate of the pound to substantially underestimate the spot rate to be realised in 180 days.
6. Assume the one-year U.S. interest rate is 10 per cent, and the one-year Canadian interest rate is 13 per cent. If a U.S. firm invests its funds in Canada, what percentage will the Canadian dollar have to depreciate to make its effective yield the same as the U.S. interest rate, from the U.S. firm's perspective?
7. Corpus Company has a subsidiary in Country X that produces computer components and sells them to another subsidiary in Country Y, where the production process is completed. The tax rate in Country X is 50 per cent, while the tax rate in Country Y is 20 per cent. The pro forma income statements of the Corpus subsidiaries are shown in Table-1. Assume that Corpus headquarters adjusts its transfer pricing policy so that sales by Subsidiary X are reduced from $400,000 to $320,000 (this also affects the cost of goods sold at Subsidiary Y by the same amount). Determine the change in total tax payments of the consolidated subsidiaries as a result of this revised transfer pricing policy.

TABLE-1
CORPUS COMPANY PRO FORMA INCOME STATEMENTS

	Subsidiary X	*Subsidiary Y*	*Consolidated Subsidiaries*
Sales	$400,000	$700,000	$1,100,000
Less: cost of goods sold	220,000	400,000	620,000
Gross profit	180,000	300,000	480,000
Less: operating expenses	80,000	100,000	180,000
Earnings before interest and taxes	100,000	200,000	300,000
Interest expense	10,000	30,000	40,000
Earnings before taxes	90,000	170,000	260,000
Taxes (50% for Sub X and 20% for Sub Y)	45,000	34,000	79,000
Earnings after taxes	45,000	136,000	181,000

8. A. U.S.-based MNC plans to invest its excess cash in France for one year. The one-year French interest rate is 19 per cent. The probability of the French franc's percentage change in value during the next year is as follows:

Possible Rate of Change in the French Franc Over the Life of the Investment	*Probability of Occurrence*
–3%	20%
4	50
10	30

What is the expected value of the effective yield based on this information? Given that the U.S. interest rate for one year is 17 per cent, what is the probability that a one-year investment in francs will generate a lower effective yield than could be generate if the U.S. firm simply invested domestically?

9. If a U.S. firm believes that the international Fisher effect holds, what are the implications regarding a strategy of continually attempting to generate high returns by investing in currencies with high interest rates?

10. A. U.S. firm considers placing 30 per cent of its excess funds in a one-year French franc deposit and the remaining 70 per cent of its funds in a one-year Canadian dollar deposit. The French one-year interest rate is 15 per cent, while the Canadian one-year interest rate is 13 per cent. The possible percentage changes in the two currencies for the next year are forecasted as follows:

Currency	*Possible Percentage Change in the Spot Rate over the Investment Horizon*	*Probability of that Percentage Change in the Spot Rate Occurring*
French franc	–2%	20%
French franc	1	60
French franc	3	20

Canadian dollar	1	50
Canadian dollar	4	40
Canadian dollar	6	10

Given this information, determine possible effective yields of the portfolio and the probability associated with each possible portfolio yield.

Given a one-year U.s. interest rate of 16 per cent, what is the probability that the portfolio's effective yield will be lower than the yield achieved from investing in the United States?

11. Why would a firm consider investing in a portfolio of foreign currencies instead of just a single foreign currency?

12. ABC Company has $2 million in excess cash that it has invested in Mexico at an annual interest rate of 60 per cent. The U.S. interest rate is 9 per cent. By how much would the Mexican peso have to depreciate to cause such a strategy to backfire?

13. Galant Corporation has several subsidiaries in less developed countries that trade goods and supplies with each other. Explain how transfer pricing could be used by Galant Corporation to reduce its overall tax payments.

14. XYZ Company has determined that the French interest rate is 16 per cent, while the U.S. interest rate is 11 per cent for one-year Treasury bills. The one-year forward rate of the French franc has a discount of 7 per cent. Does interest rate parity exist? Can XYZ Company achieve a higher effective yield by using covered interest arbitrage than by investing in U.S. Treasury yield by using covered interest arbitrage than by investing in U.S. Treasury bills? Explain.

24

EUROCURRENCY MARKET

INTRODUCTION

The Eurocurrency markets constitute the short-to-medium term debt part of the international capital flow structure. The market is made by banks and other financial institutions that accept time deposits and make loans in a currency or currencies other than that of the country in which they are located. The latter characteristic defines the Eurocurrency market - it is a non-domestic financial intermediary. In the light of the rapid growth of similar institutions in Hong Kong and Singapore (and to a lesser extent in the Middle East) the market is new worldwide and is more appropriately called the "offshore" or "external" money market. Growth of this new work of intermediaries has been spectacular. The Eurocurrency market is extremely large and has grown rapidly in a short interval. It has received a bad press from central banks, which continue to call it a major cause of inflation and an obstacle to their control of domestic monetary systems. A number of basic questions and issues crop up soon as one looks at the offshore capital markets. First, what separates them from domestic markets? Second, why were they needed and how could they grow so fast when sophisticated domestic capital markets already existed? Third, is there a process of offshore money creation analogous to money creation in a domestic banking system and what effect does this have on world inflation?

THE CREATION OF EUROMONEY

There are no offshore currencies, only national currencies of different countries. A national currency deposit becomes part of the offshore currency market when it is transferred to a bank outside the controlled national monetary system. This usually means transferred to a bank outside the nation in question. Offshore deposits can be created in two ways:

1. One can take the physical currency of a country and deposit it in a bank in another country. Banks do hold currency of other countries but mainly for the convenience of travellers. And large quantities of currency have been smuggled out from time to time in recent years. However this is usually done with the expectations of a depreciation of the currency being smuggled, and the receiving banks quickly convert these balances into some hard currency. So this method is in general of trivial importance as a creator of deposits.
2. One can transfer deposits from within the country whose currency is in

question to an offshore bank. This may well be an overseas subsidiary of the very same bank with which the original deposit was held.

If we confine our attention to domestic money supplies, the offshore currency markets could only cause inflationary pressure if they could lower statutory reserves against deposits by allowing transformation of deposits from one category to another (and if there were different reserve requirements against the different categories of deposits). This actually happened briefly in the United States in the late 1960s. While there were reserve requirements against ordinary deposits, there were none against banks' borrowings from foreign branches. When domestic rates came to exceed the Certificate of Deposits (CD) ceilings, then in effect, funds from domestic U.S. CDs were transferred to London branches of American banks (which faced no interest rate ceilings) and were then loaned to the parent banks. Since there were no reserve requirements, the same volume of CDs supported more loans than before.

Of course, once offshore banking systems exist in tandem with domestic banking systems it is no longer particularly meaningful to measure money supplies according to the domestic banking system exclusively. What are you interested in when you measure the money supply? What purpose do these measurements serve? If our interest is inflation, we are concerned with the demand for and the supply of money balances for transactions purposes. To the extent that they are negotiable, Euromarket CDs are probably used as transactions balances. Analysis of problems involving the money supply should, therefore, embrace a money supply consisting of the domestic monetary aggregates plus the negotiable part of offshore deposits in the currency concerned. If the relevant domestic monetary aggregate includes time deposits, then one should include also Eurotime deposits of the same maturity.

The offshore banking system is outside the control of the central banks whose currencies it uses. We should consider briefly whether this is good or bad, or even, for some purposes, true. Let us consider first the question of whether the central banks have now lost control of the money supply and therefore of inflation. Since every Eurocurrency unit has its origin in a domestic currency deposit or cash unit, this cannot be true. Just as in a system of purely domestic banking, the central bank controls the monetary base and so controls the money supply, up to the vagaries of the money multiplier. The monetary based multiplied to create the money supply, because deposits are relent except for the portion held as reserves plus the portion held as cash by the public. The offshore currency markets might make the multiplier different in size, or they might make it more variable. A multiplier different in size from that in a purely domestic banking system does not affect the monetary control of the central bank. The latter body must simply know that it is working with a multiplier of size x rather than size y. Hence problems in monetary control arise from variability of the size of the multiplier.

For practical purposes we have one short-term CD cum time deposit market, and whatever practical problems there are in the conception and implementation of monetary policy cannot be sensibly described as more severe in one part of this whole than in another part.

If this is so, we must explain the hostility central bankers often voice towards the offshore markets. A number of factors are important here. *First,* while the central banks have as much control as they ever had on creation of money, they have no control over allocation of credit in the offshore capital market. *Second,* as the Euromarkets are still viewed by the press and the public as mysterious and omnipotent, they make convenient scapegoats for failures of nerves in the handling of domestic monetary policy. *Finally,* the European central banks made fools of themselves in the 1960s in their Euromarket dealings in a way which they would rather forget, but which is instructive for us to examine.

In the 1960s the European central banks were pegging exchange rates, and absorbing growing dollar deficits. In the early 1960s these dollar deficits, which became dollar reserves of the absorbing central banks, were matched by growth of U.S. official obligations to foreign central banks in the U.S. balance of payments accounts. However, in the late 1960s the European central banks were surprised to observe a growing discrepancy between the change in U.S. official obligations to foreign central banks and their own record of dollar reserves held. The central bankers kept getting more and more dollars than the United States seemed to be losing on the official settlements definition of the balance of payments. The well-known economist Fritz Machulp said of them, "Most magicians who pull rabbits out of their hats know full well that they put them there before the beginning of the show. The magicians in .... (this) story, however, are more naive, they are just as surprised as the audience by the emergence of the rabbits from their hats."

What happened? Commonly when central banks undervalued their countries' currencies against the dollar they would take the dollars they received in pegging the price and buy U.S. Treasury Bills with them. From an accounting viewpoint, the U.S. deficit with Germany, say, equaled in dollar value the German surplus with the United States. A U.S. deficit with Germany meant that more dollar cheques were written to purchase DM and DM cheques were written to purchase dollars. The Bundesbank became the owner of the excess U.S. demand deposits, which it used to purchase Treasury-bills. Thus the U.S. deficit was represented by these excess demand deposits but entered the official settlements balance only when the demand deposits were converted to bills.

Now suppose a foreign central bank decided to earn higher interest on its reserves by converting its acquired U.S. demand deposits to Eurodollar CDs rather than Treasury bills. As we have seen, such an action transfers the ownership of the U.S. demand deposits representing the new foreign reserves to some private, offshore bank. Originally, these U.S. deposits were turned into foreign exchange to create the capital outflow that the European central bank absorbed. Subsequently they became the property of the private foreign bank. This was not recorded on the official settlements part of the balance of payments accounts though it certainly constituted foreign reserves created by the deficit, just as before. This explains part of the mystery, but the best part is yet to come.

Consider what might have happened to the Eurodollar deposits owned by the foreign central banks. Under the fixed exchange rate system there were periodic exchange crises, during which people would try to switch other currencies into DM or Swiss francs in anticipation of appreciation. Frequently the offshore banks would lend the dollar deposits of the Swiss and German central banks to speculators who convened them into DM or Swiss francs. Under their exchange pegging policies, these tendered dollars had to be absorbed by the central banks, who re-deposited in the offshore markets, so that they could be lent again ! This is the rabbit in the hat trick of which Machlup was speaking. The central banks came to own very large Eurodollar claims by this circular process, but these large claims were not on the United States but rather (indirectly) on the speculators.

EXPLANATION FOR THE GROWTH OF THE EUROMARKETS

The Euromarkets are not a bogeyman but an unregulated financial intermediary. They bring together borrowers and lenders, frequently from the same country. They deal only in the currencies of individual countries and are thus a substitute for the domestic banking system. The incredibly rapid growth of the Euromarkets show that they were a strongly preferred substitute. But why? The question has an obvious answer. An offshore credit market will not exist unless:

— depositors receive better terms than they can receive onshore, and

— borrowers can borrow more, possibly at lower rates, than they can onshore.

That is, banks in the offshore market must operate with a lower spread between the interest rates they charge to borrowers and the ones they pay to lenders.

The rapid emergence in the 1960s of a world-wide Eurocurrency market that co-exists and competes with traditional foreign exchange banking resulted from the peculiarly stringent and detailed official regulations governing residents operating with their own national currencies. These regulations contrast sharply with the relatively great freedom of non-residents to make deposits or borrow foreign currencies from these same constrained national banking systems. On an international scale, offshore unregulated financial markets compete with onshore regulated ones. The differences in national regulatory regimes and the internationalisation of finance brought the birth of the Eurodollar markets.

EURODOLLAR MARKETS

Eurodollars are bank deposit liabilities denominated in U.S. dollars but not subject to U.S. banking regulations. For the most part, banks offering Eurodollar deposits are located outside the United States. However since late 1981 non-U.S. residents have been able to conduct business free of U.S. banking regulations at International Banking Facilities (IBFs) in the United States. Eurodollar deposits may be owned by individuals, corporations, or governments from anywhere in the world, with the exception that only non-U.S. residents can hold deposits at IBFs.

Originally, dollar-denominated deposits not subject to U.S. banking regulations were held almost exclusively in Europe; hence, the name Eurodollars. Most such deposits are still held in Europe, but they also are held at U.S. IBFs and in such places as the Bahamas, Bahrain, Canada, and Cayman Islands, Hong Kong, Japan the

Netherlands Antilles, Panama, and Singapore. Regardless of where they are held, such deposits are referred to as Eurodollars.

Bank in the Eurodollar market, including U.S. IBFs, compete with banks in the United States to attract dollar-denominated funds. Since the Eurodollar market is relatively free of regulation, banks in the Eurodollar market can operate on narrower margins or spreads between dollar borrowing and lending rates than can banks in the United States. This gives Eurodollar deposits an advantage relative to deposits issued by banks operating under U.S. regulations. In short, the Eurodollar market has grown up largely as a means of avoiding the regulatory costs involved in dollar-denominated financial intermediation that contributed to the rise of the Eurodollar markets. Some of the basic factors are: (i) U.S. financial regulation played a very large role in the creation of the Eurodollar markets, especially Regulation Q. (Restriction on currency convertibility prevented the commercial exploitation of U.S. dollar held in Europe, while low interest rates in the U.S. enforced by Regulation Q depressed the returns. This was reinforced by Interest Equalisation Tax in 1963. These conditions were in part responsible for the Eurodollar market centered in London). (ii) The U.S. balance of payments deficits and to the accumulation of dollars stride the U.S. (iii) The U.S. dollar was the key international currency for trading and for reserve purposes, (iv) No reserve ratios were required in many of the countries, therefore, off-balance sheet funding outside the regulatory controls was possible enabling the establishment of Eurodollar markets.

Within the turbulent environment the inter-bank (Eurodollar) market soon became the central mechanism to channel international flows of funds amongst banks. This truly international market linked the various components of the international financial system to the corresponding domestic market.

The internationalisation of finance placed international and national regulatory systems era under further stress to liberalise financial markets and remove the long standing barriers to trade in financial services. This trend enveloped several related developments, most notably: some countries allowed foreign institutions a larger role in domestic financial markets; the erosion of domestic restrictions on capital markets; and the increasing integration of domestic and international markets.

These changes initiated national policies of liberalisation and deregulation which were designed to attract capital to its financial markets. Furthermore, they have been characterised by a trend toward a breakdown in the segmentation of financial markets. Distinctions among services offered by different financial institutions are blurring in many countries, and national markets are becoming increasingly integrated internationally. The nature and extent of these changes differ across countries, but almost everywhere competition in financial markets has intensified.

The Size of the Eurodollar Market

Eurodollar volume is measured as the dollar-denominated deposit liabilities of banks located outside the United States. For example, the Bank for International Settlements (BIS) defines and measures Eurodollars as dollars that have "been acquired by a bank outside the United States and used directly or after conversion into another currency for lending to a nonbank customer, perhaps after one or more redeposits from one bank to another."

The sum of all dollar-denominated liabilities of banks outside the United States measures the gross size of the Eurodollar market. For some purposes, it is useful to net some interbank deposits out of the gross to arrive at an estimate of Eurodollar deposits held by original suppliers to the Eurodollar market. Roughly speaking, to construct the net size measure, deposits owned by banks in the Eurodollar market are netted out. But deposits owned by banks located outside of the Eurodollar market area are not netted out because these banks are considered to be original suppliers of funds to the Eurodollar market. For still other purposes, such as comparing the volume of deposits created in the Eurodollar market with the U.S. monetary aggregates, it is useful to further net out all bank- owned Eurodollar deposits. Doing so leaves only the nonbank portion of the net size measure, or what might be called the net-net size of the Eurodollar market.

Instruments of the Eurodollar Market

The overwhelming majority of money in the Eurodollar market is held in fixed-rate time deposits (TDs). The maturities range from overnight to several years, although most are from one week to six months. Eurodollar time deposits are intrinsically different from dollar deposits held at banks in the United States only in that the former are liabilities of IBFs or of banks located outside the United States. The bulk of Eurodollar TDs are interbank liabilities. They pay a fixed, competitively determined rate of return.

Another important Eurodollar instrument is the Eurodollar certificate of deposit (CD). Essentially, a Eurodollar CD is a negotiable receipt for a dollar deposit at a bank located outside the United States or in a U.S. London Interbank offered Rate (LIBOR) *is the rate at which major international banks are willing to offer term Eurodollar deposits to each other.* An active secondary market allows investors to sell Eurodollar CDs before the deposits mature. Secondary market makers' spreads for short-term fixed-rate CDs have been 1 to 3 basis points for European bank dollar CDs and around 5 basis points for Japanese bank dollar CDs. Eurodollar CDs are issued by banks to tap the market for funds and are commonly issued in denominations of from $250,000 to $5 million. Some Eurodollar CDs, called Tranche CDs, are issued in very large denominations but marketed in several portions in order to satisfy investors with preferences for smaller instruments. The latter are issued in aggregate amounts of $10 million to $30 million and are offered by banks to individual investors in $10,000 certificates, with each certificate having the same interest rate, issue date, interest payment dates, and maturity

In the late 1970s Eurodollar floating-rate CDs (FRCDs) and Eurodollar floating-rate notes (FRNs) came into use as means of protecting both borrower and lender against interest rate risk. By making their coupon payments float with market interest rates, these "floaters" stabilize the principal value of the paper. The market for FRCDs is no longer active.

Eurodollar FRNs have been issued in maturities from 4 to 20 years, with the majority of issues concentrated in the five- to seven-year range. Eurodollar FRNs tend to be seen as an alternative to straight fixed-interest bonds, but they can in principle be used like FRCDs. Eurodollar FRNs have been issued primarily by banks and sovereign governments. FRNs issued by governments are not Eurodollars proper since they are not bank liabilities. Strictly speaking, they should be referred to as Eurodollar instruments together with the NIFs and Euro commercial paper.

Eurodollar FRCDs and FRNs are both negotiable bearer paper. The coupon or interest rate on these instruments is reset relative to the corresponding LIBOR every three or six months. The rate is set below LIBOR for sovereign borrowers and above for U.S. banks. Yields on Eurodollar FRNs range from 1/8 percent under the London Interbank Bid Rate (LIBID) up to LIBOR. To determine LIBOR for Eurodollar FRNs, "the issuer chooses an agent bank who in turn polls three or four Reference Banks—generally the London offices of major international banks. Rates are those prevailing at 11:00 a.m. London time two business days prior to the commencement of the next coupon period."

A secondary market exists in FRNs. The spread quoted on FRNs in the secondary market is generally 10 cents per $100 face value for the liquid sovereign issues. Other spreads are quoted on an indicative basis and are somewhat higher.

Note Issuance Facilities (NIFs) became a significant Eurodollar instrument in the mid-1980s. A NIF is a medium-term, usually five- to seven-year arrangement between a borrower and an underwriting bank under which the borrower can issue short-term, usually three- to six-month, paper known as Euro-notes in its own name. Under such an arrangement, the underwriting bank is committed either to purchase any notes the borrower cannot sell or to provide standby credit at a predetermined spread relative to some reference rate such as LIBOR. Underwriting fees are paid on the full amount of the line of credit, regardless of the amount currently drawn.

For most U.S. corporations, the U.S. commercial paper market probably remains a cheaper source of funds than Euro commercial paper. For some non- U.S. corporations, however, Euro commercial paper may be as cheap as U.S. commercial paper because of the premium that foreign issuers pay in the U.S. commercial paper market. Like the U.S. commercial paper market, the secondary market for Euro commercial paper is relatively underdeveloped. If a client needs to sell paper before maturity he will almost always sell it to the dealer who sold him the paper initially. Any trading usually occurs in the first few days after the paper is issued. Trading is most frequent in the sovereign sector, which accounts for about 20 percent of Euro commercial paper outstanding.

Creation of Eurodollars

Eurodollar markets are well organised, very efficient, and very large. They serve a number of valuable purposes for multinational business operations. Eurodollars are a convenient money market device for multinational firms to hold their excess liquidity. Eurodollars are a major source of short-term loans to finance corporate working capital needs and foreign trade. Many multinational companies and governments have learned to employ the Eurodollar market as readily as they do the domestic or banking system. The major sources of Eurodollars are (1) the growing dollar reserves of oil-exporting countries, (2) foreign governments or businessmen who prefer to hold dollars outside the United States, (3) foreign banks with dollars in excess of current needs, and (4) multinational companies with excess cash balances. Once Eurodollars come into existence, they can create themselves through the lending and investing activities of commercial banks. T-accounts may be used to illustrate such Eurodollar creation.

Example-1

Assume that the International Trading Company holds $1,000 on deposit in a New York bank. If the reserve requirement is 20 percent, the $1 ,000 deposit will be reflected in the books of the New York bank, the International Trading Company, and the Federal Reserve Bank of New York as follows:

New York Bank

		Deposit of International Trading Company	$1,000

International Trading Company

Deposit held with New York Bank	$1,000		

Federal Reserve Bank of New York

		Deposit of New York bank held as part of its reserve requirement	$ 200

Cash flows in a commercial bank involve four major elements of information: (1) currency, (2) institution and location, (3) maturity date, and (4) interest rate. To better understand how bank transfers take place and how Eurodollars come into existence, let us examine a few transactions.

Step 1. Assume that the International Trading Company decides to transfer its $1,000 deposit from the New York bank to a London bank. Let us further assume that the International Trading Company decides to maintain its dollars in a dollar-denominated 90-day deposit account at the going rate with the London bank. This situation will be reflected in the books of the New York bank, the London bank, and the International Trading Company as follows:

New York Bank

		Deposit of International Trading Company	-$1,000
		Deposit of London bank	+$1,000

London Bank

Deposit in New York bank	+$1,000	Deposit of International Trading Company	+$1,000

International Trading Company

Deposit in New York bank	-$1,000		
Deposit in London bank	+$1,000		

By this step, a Eurodollar deposit has been created. The London bank has now obtained the power to deal in dollars outside the United however, that total deposit levels in the United States have not changed; the $1,000 liability of the London bank is matched deposit in the New York bank. The only change at the New York bank was in the name of the depositor from the International Trading Company to the London bank.

Step 2. Because the London bank has to pay interest on its 90-day deposit liability to the International Trading Company, it decides to extend a Eurodollar loan of $1,000 to a Paris firm. This loan transaction will be reflected in the books of the London bank and the Paris firm as follows:

London Bank

Dollar loan to Paris firm	+$1,000	Dollar deposit of Paris firm	+$1,000

Paris Firm

Dollar deposit in London bank	+$1,000	Dollar loan repayable to London bank	+$1,000

Because the New York bank still has $1 ,000 deposit liability to the London bank, its balance sheet has not changed. But the London bank has increased its deposits and loans by $1,000. This expands the total Eurodollar deposit liabilities of non-U.S. banks to $2,000. The International Trading Company now holds $1,000 of Eurodollars with the London bank and the Paris firm has an additional $1,000 of Eurodollars in the London bank.

The London bank exhausted its dollar lending capacity. Thus, if the Paris firm had held its dollar deposit with the London bank, the multiple creation of Eurodollars would have stopped. However, if the Paris firm withdraws its dollar deposits from the London bank and deposits it with a Paris bank, the Eurodollar creation process could continue.

Step 3. Assume that the Paris firm withdraws its deposit from the London bank and deposits it in a Paris bank. The following set of T-accounts record the event.

New York Bank

		Deposit of London bank	-$1,000
		Deposit of Paris bank	+$1,000

London Bank

Deposit in New York bank	-$1,000	Dollar deposit of Paris firm	-$1,000

Paris Bank

Deposit in New York bank	+$1,000	Dollar deposit of Paris firm	+$1,000

Paris Firm

Dollar deposit in London bank	-$1,000		
Dollar deposit in Paris bank	+$1,000		

After Step 3 the amount of Eurodollars is still $2,000, but the Paris bank has obtained Eurodollar deposits that it can lend out. The potential expansion of Eurodollars is infinite in the case where banks do not maintain any reserves a against their Eurodollar deposits.

DEFAULT RISK OF EUROCURRENCY BANKS

The offshore monetary system is an unregulated banking system with no lender of last resort. Except in a very informal way there are no bank inspections by any central bank to evaluate the soundness of the loan portfolio. Parent banks obviously have a very large stake in the credit-worth mesa of their subsidiaries but ultimately do not give unconditional guarantees. This contrasts sharply with domestic banking systems, whose very comprehensive regulation has been in large part justified by the need to protect depositors. Yet there have been very few defaults of unregulated offshore banks, despite the immense pressures they have experienced in the 1970s, starting with the oil embargo and the recycling of the petro-dollars. We must explain this remarkable record of solvency. The key to any such explanation is the principle that in an unregulated banking system the riskiness of a bank's loan portfolio will be policed by depositors. They have no choice. In a regulated system, depositors have little or no incentive to care how or to whom their bank lends. The bank inspectors are a necessary corollary of regulation and deposit insurance.

The two principle sources of risk for banks are:

1. bad loans, and
2. default due to dependence on maturity transformation and the occurence of an unfavourable term structure.

The bad loan problem is the same for domestic as for foreign banks for the most part. The striking thing about the Eurobanking system is its restraint in the matter of maturity transformation. Perhaps 90% or more of Eurocredit its are on a floating rate basis. Regardless of maturity, the usual adjustment being at six-month intervals. Thus the borrower is obliged to compensate the lender for the cost of six-month money and the only effective maturity transformation is from liabilities of less than six months maturity to these six-month assets.

There are a number of differences between dealing in Euromarket and dealing in domestic money markets. Two important features characterise the Eurocurrency market : the absence of reserve requirement and the international character of the competitive advantage in dealing with reservable transactions - that is, those involving lending to corporations or other non-banks - in comparison to its domestic counterparts. It was, of course, from this competitive advantage that the rapid growth of the Euromarket originally sprang. A corollary of the absence of reserve requirements is the absence of direct control by central banks. This means that there is - at least in theory - no direct lender of last resort for the Euromarkets. Central bankers are gradually feeling their way toward some partial solutions of this problem, but the situation is certainly not as clear-cut as in each country's domestic markets.

The international character of the Eurocurrency market means that, like the foreign exchange market, the Euromarket does not exist in any particular location. It consists of participants all around the world linked together by telephones, telexes, and increasingly by computerized information systems, such as those provided by Reuters and Telerate. It is therefore a continuous market, starting in the Far East and running throughout the Middle East and Europe until it comes around to San Francisco, which over laps again with the Far East. The international nature of the market raises a number of problems, not the least of which are language and telecommunications problems. More important, though, there are a number of gray legal areas, such as jurisdiction, the acceptability of a freeze on deposits in one country by another country whose currency is being traded in the first country, the question of whether booking a loan in one centre rather than another is merely legitimate tax planning, or tax evasion, and many other questions that have not been fully resolved. Because the Euromarket is a fluid and evolving market, certainly the most dynamic deposit dealing market in the world, many of these questions probably will never be finally settled; in some respects this is probably for the best since the innovative capacity of the market has depended greatly on its relative freedom from bureaucratic regulations.

Another important feature of the market in which it differs from domestic markets is that it is a purely wholesale market. Although some banks in the United States allow some individual customers to place funds through them into the Euromarket with a view to obtaining a better return, trading in the Euromarket proper is typically done in blocks of$ 1 million and upward. The major advantage, again, is the relative freedom from regulation in a wholesale market compared with the retain banking market, which is typically heavily regulated in many countries.

Finally, another significant difference between the Euromarket and many domestic deposit markets is that the Euromarket is almost exclusively concerned with matched deposit dealing. That is, each deposit (liability) of an international bank will tend to be matched by an asset (usually a deposit in another bank) of the same currency and of similar maturity. Deliberate mismatches might be incurred with a view to making a profit, but the book of each bank as a whole will be matched within certain periods. Hence loans are typically made for a specified period and funded by a deposit of a similar period. This is very different from a domestic market where typically large amounts of lending are done on the basis of a prime (or base) rate, with these loans being funded day to day in the domestic overnight or short-date money market, or from normal customer deposits.

OPERATION OF THE EUROMARKETS

There are two levels of offshore currency transactions.

1. A highly competitive wholesale market centered in London which determines the basic deposit rates on placements by large non-bank firms and by commercial banks. These banks sell their funds to each other as need arises, at a basic interest rate called LIBOR (London Interbank Offered Rate). All transactions are undertaken by telephone or telegraph, telex, dealing screen via brokers, so the bank cannot be sure which other banks they are negotiating with until after a deal is consummated. The use of such quick means of communications means that a person's word must validate transactions in huge sums of money. Thus only the best "name" banks can transact on this wholesale market. Certain very large and well known nonbank borrowers have access to the wholesale market, but most do not.

2. A retail business on loans: Smaller banks, nonbank borrowers, governments of developing countries can acquire loans only after credit investigation. The first to borrow Eurodollars were corporations whose name, size and good standing enabled banks to make loans to them with a little more than a cursory analysis of credit standing. In recent years, the range of corporate and governmental borrowers has spread considerably. Even domestic firms with no international activities are relying on Euroloans when local credit conditions become tight.

In order to explore the lending practices of the Eurocurrency system, it is useful to refer to the hypothetical balance sheet of a Eurobank, presented in Table-1.

TABLE-1
TYPICAL EUROBANK BALANCE SHEET COMPONENTS

Liabilities	*Assets*
1. Interbank deposits	1. Reserve balances
2. Nonbank time deposits	2. Liquid assets
3. London dollar and other currencies CDs	3. Interbank loans
4. Notes and bonds	4. Other loans
5. Loans from other branches	
6. Loans from parent bank	
7. Equity capital held by parent bank.	

An important financial obligation now shown on financial statements of a Eurobank is the loan commitments held with the bank by other financial or nonbank institutions. These involve a commitment by the bank to lend funds at some future date, and therefore can involve a substantial financial liability at a time of tight credit. Conversely, the asset side of the balance sheet does not show the lines of credit that the Eurobank might have contracted for some future date with other Eurobank and domestic banks. Interbank deposits, nonbank time deposits, and London dollar CDs represent the bulk of the liabilities of a Eurobank. Interbank transactions bulk particularly large and we will shortly see why. The final depositor in the Eurocurrency market can choose among two major financial instruments. Most funds are raised by fixed time deposits (TDs), the other source being certificates of deposit (CDs). The maturities of time deposits range from one day to several years but most of them are in the one week to six months range. Negotiable certificates of two different forms : the top CDs issued in single amounts by a bank, which remain an interbank financial instrument; and the tranche CDs, which are managed issues by several banks and denominated in smaller amounts, so that they can be attractive to corporations and individual investors.

While borrowers often want to borrow for longer than five years, CDs are not currently issued for any longer maturities. Thus there have developed forward CDs, whereby a bank will issue and other banks will agree to contract CDs at a fixed or floating interest rate at some given future date. This device allows banks to make medium term loans to corporations or governments which extend beyond five years and be certain of available resources.

Loans in a specific currency are priced according to a "LIBOR plus" principle. Three parameters usually determine the cost: a *commitment fee*, which is per annum fee expressed as a per cent on the undrawn, uncancelled portion of the loan; *a front end fee* which is a one-time payment, expressed as a percentage of the amount of the loan, usually paid shortly after the signing of the loan; and *a spread* which is the per cent per annum margin added to the bank's cost of funds, which is LIBOR. The sum of these pricing elements allows us to determine a total spread, which is annualised and represents the total margin of the loan expressed as an annualised percentage over LIBOR. Under this pricing procedure, the most common in the Eurocurrency market, Euroloans are floating rate loans which depend on the value of LIBOR. The total spread over LIBOR varies with market conditions. Historically it has varied between ½% to 3%. If one compares the pricing of Euroloans with domestic loans, the principle difference are as follows: Euroloans do not involve compensating balances but rather involve commitment fees on the unused part of credit lines, and the front-end fee has become of substantial importance in the Euromarkets. Since credit standing is measured by markup over LIBOR, there has arisen a willingness of weaker borrowers to trade larger front-end fees for lower markups. On a present-value basis the outcome is equivalent, but a lower markup is supposed to have cosmetic advantages.

FUNCTIONS OF THE EUROMARKETS

We can distinguish three distinct functions served by the offshore financial system:

1. Foreign Exchange Hedging

In the Eurocurrency markets, commercial banks can take positions that cover the forward commitments they have made vis-a-vis their customers. Let us suppose, for example, that the London branch of Citibank has agreed to loan French francs to a French corporation. It has then acquired a foreign currency asset which it can turn immediately to a dollar asset by engaging in the forward sale of French francs with the BNP in London, with the maturity of the forward sale corresponding to the maturity of the loan. Conversely, a dollar loan can be converted immediately into any foreign currency asset by a forward purchase of the foreign currency in which the bank wants to have the asset. Also, forward currency commitments can be hedged by offsetting depositing or borrowing transactions. It is only a short step from such activities to covered interest arbitrage, which is an important interbank activity.

2. Domestic Intermediation

The offshore markets can at times partially supplant normal channels of domestic financial intermediation when the government imposed a severe credit policy on the banking system and at the same time encouraged corporations to seek the necessary financing they needed in the Eurocurrency system.

3. International Intermediation

The offshore markets channel liquid resources from countries with a loanable surplus to those with a desire to borrow. The most striking example of this is the so-called "recycling of petrodollars". When OPEC countries started rolling in cash in 1973, almost everyone predicted a collapse of the world financial system because all those dollars were going to the Arab countries, and everybody wondered how all the importing countries would pay their bills. The dollars were in fact deposited by the OPEC countries in the Eurocurrency system and relent to the importing countries as one might have expected. The real impact of OPEC oil price rise has been a transfer of income it has brought about, not the financial flows that have resulted.

WHY ARE THERE SO MANY INTERBANK TRANSACTIONS?

As was mentioned earlier when we presented the theoretical balance sheet of a Eurobank, interbank transactions represent a large part of the activity of a Eurobank. The actual figure for the size of the Eurocurrency markets vary depending on the source and method of calculation. The most agreed-upon figures are those given by the Bank for International Settlements (BIS) annual reports. Other sources include Morgan Guaranty Trust and Bankers Trust. More than a third of the volume of transactions is interbank trade rather than transactions with non-bank depositors or non-bank borrowers. The BIS figures for the size of the Eurocurrency system net out all the interbank transactions. The BIS figures, which are the most commonly reported ones, treat the system only as a financial intermediary. If the covered interest arbitrage and foreign exchange hedging aspects of the market are considered, a good part of the inter-bank transactions represent legitimate economic transactions and not just reshuffling of funds within the network of intermediaries.

ILLUSTRATIVE PROBLEMS

1. XYZ Trading Co. of the United Kingdom receives \$1,000,000 in payment for exports to ABC Electronics Philadelphia, Pa. (XYZ Co. banks with Barclays-London, and ABC banks with Philadelphia Security Bank. S_0 \$/£ = 1.35.)

(a) XYZ Trading Co. keeps amount in deposit in Philadelphia Security Bank.

(b) XYZ Trading Co. asks its bank to transfer export proceeds to its account in pounds sterling.

(c) Instead of (b), XYZ Trading Co. transfers dollar proceeds from Philadelphia Security Bank, and places it with its own bank as a time deposit denominated in dollars.

Show the above transactions in T-accounts of Barclays and Philadelphia Security Bank.

Ans.

(a) Philadelphia Security Bank

	Deposits of ABC Electronics –\$1,000,000 Deposits of XYZ Trading Co. +\$1,000,000

No records are needed in Barclays Bank's books.

(b) Philadelphia Security Bank

	Deposits of XYZ Trading Co.	–\$1,000,000
	a/c of Barclays Bank	+\$1,000,000

Barclays Bank (London)

a/c with Philadelphia Security Bank + £ 800,000	Deposits of XYZ Trading Co.	+ £ 800,000

(c) Transaction will appear in Philadelphia Security Bank as in (b)

Barclays Bank (London)

a/c with Philadelphia Security Bank + \$1,000,000	Time deposits of XYZ Trading Co. + \$1,000,000

Hence, a Eurodollar deposit of \$1,000,000 was created in (c).

2. (a) Show the following transactions in T-accounts of the banks involved in the transactions.

(b) Indicate the total amount of Eurodollar deposits created by these transactions.

(c) What is the value of the Eurodollar deposit multiplier? Identify the factors that determine the value of the multiplier.

Transaction (1)

XYZ Co. (Netherlands) exported to ABC, Inc. (U.S.) goods valued at $1,000,000. The importer paid by a cheque drawn on Citibank (N.Y.). XYZ Co. asked its bank (Algemene Bank of the Netherlands) to credit its account in Dutch guilders with the proceeds of the transaction. (The exchange rate on the value date of the transaction S_0F1/$ is 2.7715.)

Transaction (2)

Algemene Bank places the $1,000,000 it has in Citibank (N.Y.) as a time deposit in Shanghai-Hong Kong Bank (Hong Kong).

Transaction (3)

Shanghai-Hong Kong Bank makes a loan of $900,000 to Nestle Co. (Netherlands). Nestle Co. deposits the cheque in its account with the National Bank of the Netherlands and asks its bank to credit its account with the equivalent in Dutch guilders. (The exchange rate on the value date of the transaction is S_0F1/$ = 2.7750.)

Transaction (4)

The National Bank of the Netherlands makes a loan of $750,000 to Nova Industries (Denmark). Nova Industries uses the loan to settle an import transaction from Bristol Myers (N.Y.). Bristol Myers maintains its accounts with Chase Manhattan Bank (N.Y.).

Ans.

(a) *Transaction (1)*

Citibank (NY)		*Algemene Bank (Netherlands)*	
	(1) Deposits of ABC, Inc.—$1,000,000	(1) Account with Citibank (NY) + F12,771,500	(1) Deposits of XYZ Co. + F12,771,500
	(1) Deposits of Algemene Bank + + $1,000,000	(Equivalent to $1,000,000)	

Transaction (2)

Citibank (NY)		Algemene Bank (Netherlands)	
	(2) Deposits of Algemene Bank —$1,000,000	(2) Account with Citibank with –$1,000,000	
	(2) Deposits of Shanghai-Hong Kong Bank + $1,000,000	(2) TD with Shanghai, H.K. Bank + $1,000,000	

Shanghai—Hong Kong Bank

(2) Account with Citibank (NY) + $1,000,000	(2) TD of Algemene Bank + $1,000,000

Transaction (3)

Citibank (NY)

	(3) Deposits of Shanghai-Hong Kong Bank—$900,000
	(3) Deposits of National Bank of Netherlands + $900,000

Shanghai-Hong Kong Bank

(3) Account with Citibank (NY) —$900,000	
(3) Loan to Nestle Co. + $900,000	

National Bank of Netherlands

(3) Account with Citibank (NY) + $900,000	(3) Deposit of Nestle Co. + F1 $2,497,500 (Equivalent to $900,000)

Transaction (4)

Citibank (NY)

	(4) Deposits of Natl. Bank of Netherlands —$750,000
	(4) Deposits of Chase Manhattan Bank (NY) + $750,000

National Bank of Netherlands

(4) Account with Citibank (NY) —$750,000	
(3) Loan to Nova Industries + $750,000	

Chase Manhattan Bank (NY)

(4) Account with Citibank (NY) + $750,000	(4) Deposits of Bristol Myers + $750,000

(b) Total amount of Eurodollar deposits created is $1,000,000 (time deposit of Algemene Bank with Shanghai-Hong Kong Bank denominated in U.S. dollars).

(c) The value of the Eurodollar deposit multiplier here is unity. The value of the multiplier depends on:

(1) successive stages of time deposits denominated in U.S. dollars placed at financial institutions outside the continental United States, prior to leakages in the form of deposits in local currency or payment to U.S. residents, and

(2) The ratio of reserves observed on a voluntary basis by lending institutions outside the United States.

2. The following transactions are designed to follow the path of some of the flows that take place in the Euro-dollar market.

Assume: 1. All foreigners keep their balances in the United States with the Chase Manhattan Bank.

2. All banks keep 10% of their deposits in reserves.

At the end of each transaction determine what is the impact on:

1. Each of the parties involved.
2. The U.S. money supply.
3. The U.S. balance of payments on the liquidity basis and on the official transactions basis.
4. The money supply of each foreign country involved.
5. The balance of payments of each foreign country involved.

Transaction No. 1. The German Central Bank, which maintains part of its foreign exchange reserve in the form of treasury bills, decides to sell $100 worth of treasury bills to Mr. Smith, an American resident. Mr. Smith pays with a check drawn on his account with Chase Manhattan.

Transaction No. 2. The German Central Bank transfers its deposits to a German commercial bank. (Sometimes this is done as part of domestic monetary policy in which case the Central Bank exchanges dollar deposits for deutsche marks with the commercial banks. The objective is to reduce credit in the domestic market and give incentives for capital outflows.)

Transaction No. 3. A french importer asks for a Euro-loan from the German commercial bank. Assuming that the commercial bank keeps a precautionary reserve of 10%, it can make a loan in the amount of $90.

Transaction No. 4. The French importer uses the Euro-loan to pay a debt owed to a German exporter.

Transaction No. 5. The German exporter deposits its dollar balances with the German commercial bank.

Transaction No. 6. Citibank wishes to borrow Euro-dollars from the German commercial bank to take care of anticipated loan demand.

Transaction No. 7. Citibank wishes to make a loan. In order to convert the deposit at Chase into lendable funds it asks Chase to provide cash or deposits with the Federal Reserve Bank. Since Chase was fully loaned-up, it has to sell some loans in order to collect the required amount of cash.

Show these transactions in T-accounts of the banks involved in the transactions.

Ans.:

The transactions described below are represented by "T accounts" at end.

Transaction No. 1

Chase: There is only a change in deposit ownership from Mr. Smith to the German central bank.

German Central Bank: There is an exchange of assets from securities to deposits.

Money supply in U.S. and Germany remains constant.

Balance of payments of each country has offsetting entries.

Transaction No. 2

Chase: There is only a change in deposit ownership from the German central bank to the German commercial bank.

German Central Bank: An exchange of assets from claims on Chase to claims on the German commercial banks.

German Commercial Banks: Euro-dollar deposits have been created. The assets associated with these deposits can now be used to make loans.

Money supply in U.S. remains constant.

Money supply in Germany has increased by the size of the Euro-dollar deposit except if it was in exchange for DM's in which case the money supply remains constant.

Balance of payments of the U.S. on the liability basis has cancelling entries. On the official basis there is an improvement as claims of official institutions on the U.S. are reduced.

Balance of payments of Germany deteriorates on an official transaction basis as official institutions' claims on foreigners decrease.

Transaction No. 3

Chase: There is only a transfer of deposit ownership from the German commercial bank to the French importer.

German Commercial Bank: Claims on Chase decrease by $90 while Euro-loans increase by the same amount.

French Importer: He has acquired an asset and a liability denominated in dollars.

Money supply in the U.S. remains constant.

Money supply in Germany remains constant.

Balance of payments of the U.S. is unaffected.

Balance of payments of Germany has a capital outflow in the form of loans to foreigners (French) and an inflow as a deposits at Chase decrease - no net effect.

The French balance of payments has a capital inflow as resident has increased its debts and an outflow as the foreign assets have increased - no net effect.

Transaction No. 4

Chase: There is only a transfer in ownership of deposits from the French importer to the German exporter.

Importer and exporter: Have their debt cancelled by the acquisition of the German exporter of dollar balances.

Money supply in U.S. and Germany remain constant.

Balance of payments of U.S. is unaffected.

Balance of payments of France and Germany have similar effects to the ones described in Transaction 3.

Transaction No. 5

Chase: There is only a transfer in ownership of deposits.

German exporter: A change in type of assets.

German Commercial Bank: Another Euro-dollar deposit has been created.

Money supply in U.S. remains unaffected.

Money supply in Germany has increased by the size of the new Euro-dollar deposit.

Balance of payments of U.S. is unaffected.

Balance of payments of Germany is unaffected.

Transaction No. 6

Chase: There is only a transfer of ownership in the deposits.

German Commercial Bank: Decreases its claims on Chase, but increases its claims on Citibank by a fraction of their Euro-dollar balances.

Citibank: It has acquired a claim on Chase, and a Euro-dollar debt.

Money supply of U.S. and Germany remain constant.

Balance of payments of both countries have offsetting entries.

Transaction No. 7

Chase: It has $81 of excess reserves which can now be lent.

Money supply in U.S. remains constant as the deposits created by Citibank are really at the expense of the deposits and loans that Chase gave up.

Balance of payments remain unaffected.

3. XYZ Trading Co. of the United Kingdom receives $1,000,000 in payment for exports to ABC Electronic of Philadelphia, Pa. (XYZ Co. banks with Barclays-London, and ABC banks with Philadelphia Security Bank S_0 \$/£ = 1.25.)

a. XYZ Trading Co. keeps amount in deposit in Philadelphia Security Bank.

b. XYZ Trading Co. asks its bank to transfer export proceeds to its account in pounds sterling.

c. Instead of (b), XYZ Trading Co. transfers dollar proceeds from Philadelphia Security Bank, and places it with its own bank as a time deposit denominated in dollars.

Show the above transactions in T accounts of Barclays and Philadelphia Security Bank.

Ans.:

(a) Philadelphia Security Bank

	Deposits of ABC Electronics -$1,000,000
	Deposits of XYZ Trading Co. +$1,000,000

No records are needed in Barclays Bank's books.

(b) Philadelphia Security Bank

	Deposits or XYZ Trading Co. -$1,000,000
	a/c of Barclays Bank +$1,000,000

QUESTIONS

1. Outline the major factors that have been responsible for the growth in the Eurocurrency markets, particularly the Eurodollar component of these markets. Which of these factors are still significant in fostering the use of these markets by investors and borrowers?
2. Under what circumstances would a financial manager of an MNC consider using Eurocurrency markets? What advantages or special features can these markets offer compared to borrowing from domestic markets? Are there drawbacks? Explain.
3. Is there a multiplier process in the placement of Eurocurrency deposits and subsequent Eurocurrency loans granted by financial institutions which receive these deposits? What are the major factors determining the size of the multiplier coefficient?
4. There are several methods of measuring the size of the Eurocurrency market. Comment on this statement and list the reasons for these different measurements.
5. Why are Eurocurrency deposit rates closely related to rates obtainable on instruments

of corresponding maturity in home money markets? For example, why is the overnight Eurodollar rate closely aligned to the federal funds rate in the U.S. money market? Why is the former deposit rate usually (but not always) higher by some 25 to 50 basis points than the latter?

6. What is LIBOR? What determines the spread over LIBOR charged borrowers for Eurocurrency credits and loans?
7. Discuss the major advantages which the syndicated Eurocurrency loan market offers to lenders and borrowers, compared to domestic lending operations. Why is the quoted rate (spread over LIBOR) not an accurate indicator of the cost of a typical syndicated Eurocurrency loan?
8. List the major factors that are responsible for the growth of the international bond market. Indicate which of these factors (or other considerations) explain the large number of innovations in this market.
9. Distinguish between a Eurobond and a foreign bond. List the major participants in this market. Why does the share of developing countries in this market remain fairly modest?
10. Define (a) a multiple-currency Eurobond, (b) a dual-currency convertible bond, and (c) a floating-rate Eurocurrency note. Explain in each case the distribution of risk (the exchange rate risk or the interest rate risk) between the lender (investor) and the borrower (issuer).
11. How do you explain the yield differentials among Eurobonds denominated in different currencies? Does interest parity operate in the capital market (as it does in the international money market) to eliminate these differentials on a covered basis? Do you expect an alignment between the yield on a Eurodollar bond and a dollar bond of the same risk grade and maturity?

25

THE GLOBALISATION OF MONETARY POLICY

INTRODUCTION

In the past two decades, the world has moved closer. This has been brought about not only by the dismantling of various regulatory barriers but also, and in particular, by financial innovations. The central banks observe and analyse these developments since they are closely affected by these changes. Monetary policy—beginning with "archaic" forms of direct monetary contract by mean of credit ceilings and administratively set interest rates, moving on to the increasing use of indirect control mechanisms in still largely segmented markets and finally to global financial system—has been drifting ever closer toward ultimate impotence. Diametrically opposed to this view is the observation that now the financial markets are responding more sensitively than ever before to possible changes in the stance of central bank policy; the research departments of the institutional investors are incessantly trying to figure out, at a huge expense of time and money, what the future course of the central bank be. If it really were ineffective, monetary policy would hardly be the focus of so much attention.

FACTORS DRIVING THE GLOBALISATION OF MONETARY POLICY

The period since the 1990s has witnessed some convergence in the conduct of monetary policy, worldwide. Currently, there are striking similarities in the tools that monetary authorities employ to assess macroeconomic developments and the formation of expectations. In the choice of instruments as well as in the operating procedures, there are common features. The institutional architectures have begun to display several commonalities. The communication strategies and, thereby, the public accountability are in the forefront in all central banks with progressively increasing globalisation of financial markets and emphasis on central bank autonomy. There is greater universal recognition of the trade-offs confronting monetary policy decisions.

While individual country experiences vary in tune with country-specific diversities, the cross-country evidence highlights the fact that there are several common features driving this phenomenon. *First*, cycles of economic activity have become increasingly synchronized across countries, irrespective of the level/stage of development. *Second*, there is now widespread recognition of the adverse implications of high fiscal deficits on the conduct of monetary policy. *Third*, there have been significant shifts in instrument mix. Drastic reductions in statutory pre-emptions, greater reliance on indirect instruments, emphasis on flexibility and timing of policy response and, in general, a greater market orientation are all major elements of this shift. *Fourth*, there is a greater activism in liquidity management and a focus on the short-end of the market spectrum; this has also been engendered by the growing integration of financial markets domestically and internationally. *Fifth*, at an operational level, there is greater transparency amongst the monetary authorities as a strategic objective. This, in turn, has brought in emphasis on information management - the quality and quantity of data dissemination represented by release of adequate, timely and reliable information in a standardised form, and dissemination of information on the dynamics of policy decisions. *Sixth*, there is greater coordination between central banks, fiscal authorities and regulatory bodies governing financial markets. *Seventh*, there is a greater focus on appropriate institutional structures that promote efficiency in the conduct of monetary policy. *Eighth*, in an environment of synchronized economic activity, international policy coordination has become extremely important. *Finally*, there is a greater recognition that amidst the generalised uncertainty, monetary marksmanship is better adjudged in terms of ranges rather than in precise estimates.

These developments have been globally associated with a distinct lowering of inflation. In conjunction with more effective communication policies, this has earned for the monetary authorities what has been described as a "credibility bonus," which has helped in building a reputation for them in achieving the objectives of monetary policy. There is also a greater sophistication in the conduct of monetary policy today, and central bankers are constantly engaged in refining their technical and managerial skills to deal with the complexities of financial markets.

On the downside, the challenges facing monetary authorities have become sharper. The heightened uncertainty surrounding the conduct of monetary policy has made interpretation of macroeconomic and financial data difficult. Uncertainty is more easily transmitted across the world than before through the 'confidence' channel, forcing the monetary authorities to contend with the contagion from shocks. Since the 1990s, considerations of financial stability have assumed an increasing importance in monetary policy across the globe.

It is useful to recognise some of the forces at work that indicate the pace of such globalisation of monetary policy. First, the increasing flow of goods and services across national borders brings about networking of production systems, even standardisation of products, tastes and preferences. Second, financial integration powered by mobile capital flows leads to the merging of financial markets across national borders. Third, the explosion of communication technology makes this integration even closer and faster. Fourth, since the late 1980s, a factor driving the globalisation of financial sector is the setting of common standards in terms of prudential regulations, supervisory practices and disclosures. Under these conditions, monetary policy responses in various countries have tended to exhibit common characteristics. Undoubtedly, complete congruence of national monetary policies is not feasible because of country-specific factors but there are growing elements of globalisation in the sense that there are considerable similarities in the overall setting and conduct of monetary policy.

MONETARY POLICY COORDINATION BY THE CENTRAL BANKS DURING THE CRISIS

During the central financial crisis the central banks have been coordinating actions to an unprecedented extent. It was a preferred options the middle of 2008, when central banks faced the twin problems of slowing output growth and persistently high inflation. The extent and timing of the slowdown differed across countries. Economic growth in the major advanced economies had been relatively strong in early 2008, but turned negative towards mid-year. Emerging market economies continued to experience solid growth, but the export-oriented economies of East Asia and central Europe showed signs of slowing before the crisis of confidence in September and October 2008. Inflation rates were well above (implicit or explicit) targets almost everywhere, owing to sharp rises in food and energy prices during the first half of 2008.

Finding the appropriate monetary policy response in this environment proved challenging. With the benefit of hindsight, one can see that policymakers underappreciated the extent of the slowdown in mid-2008 and the strength of the associated disinflationary forces. Although slowing growth would at some point create the slack necessary to stabilise prices, few central banks expected inflation to fall before late 2009. In the meantime, there was a real danger that persistently high inflation might feed into permanently higher inflation expectations, which in turn could result in a higher pass-through from commodity prices to other prices and wages. As a consequence, central banks in both advanced and emerging market economies either held rates constant or raised them.

The September 2008 bankruptcy of Lehman Brothers, followed by weeks of extreme pressure in the credit markets, escalating threats to the stability of major financial institutions and an accelerating pullback in economic activity, marked a turning point for the world economy and for monetary policy. On October 2008, when they simultaneously announced cuts in their policy rates, six major central banks undertook the first ever round of coordinated rate action. Other central banks around the world also began rapidly cutting rates.

As policy rates in many countries reached historically low levels, the zero lower bound became a binding constraint, making it impossible to follow policy rules that called for negative nominal interest rates in many advanced economies in view of widening output gaps and falling inflation rates. Moreover, a number of considerations led central banks to stop easing once policy rates reached a level slightly above zero. Given that bank deposit rates are generally below money market rates, the former may reach zero even if the latter are still positive. When that happens, any further reduction in market rates may not be passed on to households and firms, as banks need to maintain a margin between deposit and lending rates to remain profitable. Similarly, money market mutual funds may become unprofitable once rates fall to a certain level.

The central bank responses to the crisis so far. In particular, the responses can be divided into three broad categories according to how the associated operations are related to their proximate objectives. The *first* category consists of measures to ensure that the market rate is consistent with the policy rate. The *second* involves initiatives to alleviate strains in wholesale interbank markets. The *third* consists of responses aimed at supporting specific credit markets – particularly the non-bank segments – and easing financial conditions more broadly. The last two categories, insofar as they involve operations directed at particular segments of the transmission mechanism over and above the traditional interest rate target, fall under the umbrella of balance sheet policy.

With respect to the first category, the implementation of interest rate targets largely involved accommodating the greater instability in the demand for reserves through a more flexible supply, in terms of both size and frequency. To help anchor short-term rates to the policy target, the Bank of England and the Federal Reserve also reduced the width of the effective corridor on overnight rates by changing the rates applied on end-of-day standing facilities. At the same time, central banks had to expand their capacity to reabsorb excess reserves to neutralise the impact on overnight interest rates of the much expanded operations. As reflected in the composition of central bank liabilities, this was implemented in a number of ways. The Bank of England and the Swiss National Bank began to issue central bank bills; the ECB and the Reserve Bank of Australia relied increasingly on accepting interest bearing deposits; and the Federal Reserve took in greater amounts of deposits from the Treasury and started to pay interest on reserves.

The second group of measures, prominent during the first two crisis stages, centred on reducing term interbank market spreads, seen as an indicator of tensions in that key market segment. This was tackled both directly, by providing more term funding so as to offset some of the shortfall in market supply, and indirectly, by addressing impediments to the smooth distribution of reserves in the system and ensuring access to funding from the central bank. To this end, conditions for the provision of reserves were eased by relaxing eligible collateral and counterparty coverage, lengthening the maturity of refinancing operations, and establishing inter-central bank swap lines to alleviate mostly dollar funding pressures in offshore markets. The use of the swap lines was a significant driver of balance sheet expansions for major central banks during this period. In addition, many central banks introduced or eased conditions for lending out highly liquid securities – typically sovereign bonds – against less liquid market securities in order to improve funding conditions in the money market.

The third category of policy responses, which received more emphasis as the turmoil in financial markets deepened, focused on directly alleviating tightening credit conditions in the non-bank sector and easing broader financial conditions. Prominent measures included the provision of funds to non-banks to improve liquidity and reduce risk spreads in specific markets – such as commercial paper, asset-backed securities and corporate bonds – as well as the direct purchase of public sector securities to influence benchmark yields more generally. In a notable step, the Swiss National Bank intervened in the foreign exchange market to contain upward pressure on the Swiss franc as part of its efforts to reduce deflationary risks and loosen monetary conditions more generally.

As a by-product of these actions, central bank balance sheets expanded substantially and their composition changed significantly. An important difference across countries is the relative emphasis given to private versus public sector securities and bank versus non-bank markets. The Federal Reserve focused heavily on non-bank credit markets as well as on operations involving private sector securities, as exemplified by measures such as the Commercial Paper Funding Facility and the Term Asset-Backed Securities Loan Facility. The Bank of England, on the other hand, initially concentrated its Asset Purchase Facility primarily on purchases of government bonds while the ECB emphasised banking system liquidity by conducting fixed rate full-allotment refinancing operations with maturities of up to 12 months and by purchasing covered bonds. In the case of the Bank of Japan, substantial efforts were directed at improving funding conditions for firms through various measures pertaining to commercial paper and corporate bonds. The varying emphasis reflects, in part, differences in financial structures. More direct intervention in non-bank credit markets in the United States, for example, is consistent with that country's predominantly market-based system, while the greater focus accorded in the euro area to supporting banks reflects a larger reliance on bank-based intermediation in the region.

Greater reliance on balance sheet policy has entailed an increasingly pervasive role for central banks in the intermediation process and a more significant influence on the relative supplies of claims on the public sector. This heightens the need for close cooperation with the fiscal authority for two key reasons. First, large purchases of government securities and the accompanying rapid expansion of central bank liabilities affect the overall profile of public sector debt. Their effect could potentially be undermined by debt management operations, not least given their typically larger size, unless the objectives of the two types of operations are consistent. Second, central banks are taking on greater credit and market risk, as evidenced by the higher proportion of private sector securities in the collateral accepted in monetary operations. As a result, close coordination between the central bank and the government is necessary to put in place mechanisms to ensure that potential losses do not impair the operational independence of central banks.

LESSONS FROM THE FINANCIAL CRISIS FOR MONETARY POLICY IN EMERGING MARKETS

Origins of the Crisis

The crisis was precipitated by monetary excesses. These excesses took the form of interest rates that were held too low for too long by the Federal Reserve and some other central banks. The low interest rates led to a housing boom which eventually ended in a bust and was a significant factor in the crisis. The low interest rates also were a probable factor in excessive risk-taking as people searched for higher yields.

It is important to note that the excessive risk taking and the low interest rate monetary policy decisions are connected. Delinquency rates and foreclosure rates are inversely related to housing price inflation during this period. During the years of the rapidly rising housing prices, delinquency and foreclosure rates declined rapidly. The benefits of holding onto a house are higher when the price of the house is rising rapidly. When prices are falling, the incentives to do so are much less and turn negative if the price of the house falls below the value of the mortgage. Hence, delinquencies and foreclosures rose.

Since mortgage underwriting programs take account of the actual realisations of foreclosure rates and delinquency rates in cross section data, the programs would have been overly optimistic during the period when prices were rising unless they took account of the time series correlation. Thus, there is an interaction between the monetary excesses and the risk-taking excesses. The rapidly rising housing prices and the resulting low delinquency rates likely threw the underwriting programs off track and misled many people.Contrary to this view,it is argued that mortgages are based on long-term interest rates, while the Fed sets the short rate. However, over 30 percent of mortgages at that point were adjustable rate mortgages. In fact, there was a huge move into adjustable rate mortgages. That enabled the so called "teaser rates" which made the adjustable rate mortgages attractive to people.

Some have put forth alternative explanations for the origins of the crisis. One explanation is a global savings glut. This does not seem to be a plausible explanation. Long-term interest rates are globally determined. No matter how you think about it, there was no global savings glut. Savings rates were high in some countries and low in other countries, but globally, savings rates were low. In order to argue that a savings glut occurred, one must show that desired saving was high relative to desired investment, but these "desired" concepts cannot be measured very well.

The Year before the Panic

Why did the crisis last so long? The crisis was evident in the summer of 2007, when the money markets started behaving strangely. In particular interest rate spreads between three month LIBOR and the overnight federal funds rate jumped to unprecedented levels in August 2007 and remained high for over a year.

In addition to being a measure of financial stress, these interest rate spreads affect the transmission mechanism of monetary policy to the economy because trillions of dollars of loans and securities are indexed to LIBOR. An increase in the spread, holding the overnight interest rate constant, will increase the cost of such loans and have a negative effect on the economy. Bringing this spread down therefore became a major objective of policy, as well as a measure of its success in dealing with the market turmoil. From the interbank loan market, it can be observed whether the flare-up was caused by a liquidity shortage or counterparty risk in the banking system due to defaults and expected defaults of securities on the bank's balance sheets. In other words, was the Fed providing inadequate liquidity or were banks unwilling to lend to each other? Counterparty risk did not seem plausible to many at the time, but that was the culprit. Today it seems obvious. The policy makers misdiagnosed the problem, treating it as a shortage of liquidity rather than an increase in risk. As a result their policy interventions–and there were many – either delayed treatment or were harmful. For example, the Fed introduced a new term auction facility (TAF) in December 2007. With this facility banks could avoid going to the discount window if they needed to borrow. The aim of the TAF was to reduce the spreads in the money markets and thereby increase the flow of credit and lower interest rates. But Fed's TAF could not affect the interest rate spreads in the money markets.There were other actions. The Fed cut rates sharply in the winter of 2007-

2008. The result was some rapid dollar depreciation, and oil prices went up sharply, helping bring on the recession. Thus, the government's initial reaction exacerbated the problem. Fiscal policy was also tried. The Economic Stimulus Act of 2008 was passed in February,2008. This package sent cash totaling over $100 billion to individuals and families in the United States; the hope was that they would have more to spend and thus jump-start consumption and the economy. Most of the cheques were sent in May, June, and July 2008. As predicted by the permanent income theory of consumption, people spent little of the temporary infusion of cash, and consumption was not jump- started. Personal disposable income jumped at the time the cheques were sent, but personal consumption expenditures did not increase. The effect was not significantly different from zero.

The Panic

Why did the crisis get so much worse in the fall of 2008? Understanding the events surrounding the Lehman bankruptcy is particularly important for assessing what went wrong. During the six months between the collapse of Bear Stearns and Lehman Brothers, regulators made little effort to articulate a strategy. It became increasingly obvious that things were ad hoc. Severe damage came with the realisation that there was really no policy at all. The rollout of the Troubled Asset Relief Program (TARP) scared people with the claims that they were confronting another Great Depression. Many in government now argued that the cause of the panic in the fall of 2008 was the failure of the government to intervene and prevent the bankruptcy of Lehman. This view gives a rationale for continued extensive government intervention–starting the very next day with AIG–and to proposals for a more expansive resolution process, perhaps in the hands of a new systemic risk regulator. However, the problem was not the failure to bail out Lehman Brothers but rather the failure of the government to articulate a clear predictable strategy for lending and intervening into a financial sector. This strategy could have been put forth in the weeks after the Bear Stearns rescue, but was not. Instead market participants were led to guess what the government would do in other similar situations.

However, it does not mean that all the government's actions were inappropriate, because there were many things that had to be done by the time the panic was underway. Nevertheless, if government policy had been explained and had not scared everybody, then the panic would not have occurred, or certainly would not have been as bad.

Resiliency in Emerging Markets

The panic turned the ongoing recession in the United States into a great recession and spread quickly around the world. The big surprise, however, was the amazing resiliency of the emerging market countries in the face of these shocks. The contrast with the 1990s, when emerging markets were suffering their own crises, was stark. For countries such as Brazil and Turkey which were in crisis as late as 2003, the difference was especially stark. Why were emerging markets so resilient? The most important reason is that they had moved toward better macroeconomic policies in the 1990s and they stuck to those policies during the crisis. They were careful not to borrow in foreign countries, and Indian regulatory policy followed a policy to discourage such borrowing by Indian banks. They built up their foreign reserves so they could intervene in the case of a big shock like they received. They kept inflation relatively low and were more careful with public sector deficits.

How important were the special actions taken after the crisis, such as the Keynesian stimulus packages, in many countries? There is evidence that the impacts of the panic were bottoming out before the packages were implemented. Investment orders stopped falling in December 2008 and January 2009, when people realised this was not a repeat of the Great Depression. Stock markets started moving up around the world in early March 2009. The impact of the 2009 stimulus package in the United States shows that it was similar to that of the stimulus package of 2008. It had little impact.

What about Mistakes in the Private Sector?

Of course, throughout this period there were market problems of various sorts. Mortgages were originated without sufficient documentation or with overly optimistic underwriting assumptions, and then sold off in complex derivative securities which credit rating agencies rated too highly, certainly in retrospect. Individuals and institutions took highly risky positions either through a lack of diversification or excessive leverage ratios.

But mistakes occur in all markets and they do not normally become systemic. In each of these cases there was a tendency for government actions to convert non-systemic risks into systemic risks. The low interest rates led to rapidly rising housing prices with very low delinquency and foreclosure rates, which likely confused both underwriters and the rating agencies. The failure to regulate adequately entities that were supposed to be, and thought to be, regulated certainly encouraged the excesses. Risky off balance sheet operations connected to regulated banks were allowed by regulators. The U.S. Securities and Exchange Commission was to regulate broker-dealers, but its skill base was in investor protection rather than prudential regulation. Similarly, the U.S. Office of Thrift Supervision was not up to the job of regulating the complex financial products division of AIG. These regulatory gaps and overlapping responsibilities added to the problem.

Implications for Economics

Some economists are calling for a complete reformulation of economics – or for a return to a version of the subject popular thirty years ago. They say that economics failed to prevent the crisis or even led to it. Many of these economists have argued for a more interventionist government policy, saying that John Maynard Keynes was right and Milton Friedman was wrong. Paul Samuelson observed "today we see how utterly mistaken was the Milton Friedman notion that a market system can regulate itself… This prevailing ideology of the last few decades has now been reversed…I wish Friedman were still alive so he could witness how his extremism led to the defeat of his own ideas". Then Paul Krugman wrote an article faulting modern economics (especially modern macroeconomics and "rational expectations") for bringing on the crisis. He says it focused too much on beauty over practicality and did not recognise the need for more government intervention to prevent and cure the crisis. His fix is to add more psychology to economics or to build better models of credit.

However, the financial crisis provides no evidence of a failure of modern economics. Rather the crisis vindicates the theory. The crisis was caused by a deviation of policy from the type of policy recommended by modern economics. In the case of monetary policy it was an interventionist deviation from the type of systematic policy that was responsible for the remarkably good economic performance in the two decades before the crisis. Economists call this earlier period the Great Moderation because of the remarkably long expansions and short shallow recessions. In other words, the financial crisis gives more evidence that interventionist government policies have done harm. The financial crisis did not occur because economic theory went wrong. It occurred because policy went wrong, because policy makers stopped paying attention to the economics.

Implications for Policy

This explanation of the crisis suggests that the emphasis should be on proposals to reduce the likelihood of government interventions and actions that led to the crisis. Going forward this means dealing with the very large budget deficits and rising government debt; scaling back or at least not adding more Keynesian stimulus packages; exiting as fast as possible from the extraordinary monetary policy actions which have questioned central bank credibility and threatened their independence; and ending the bailout mentality that will take governments further into the operations of private businesses.

Some have suggested the creation of a new systemic risk regulator, either at the national or international level. However, it is doubtful that such a systemic risk regulator would have prevented the current crisis. It would not have prevented the very low interest rates or the other government actions. Moreover, the experience during the panic of fall 2008 raises doubts that such an agency could resolve failing private institutions without causing more systemic risk. It would be helpful if it could warn about the major existing systemic risks, including the exploding debt, central banks' balance sheet, and the bailout mentality. But groups such as the Financial Stability Board, working along with the IMF and G20, are better suited to that role.

Another suggestion is that central banks, including emerging market central banks – take actions to burst market bubbles in financial or other markets. I do not think that is a good idea. First, the lags in the effect of monetary policy will likely mean that the impact of policy will be its greatest when the bubble is bursting only adding to the damage. Second, the problem in the current crisis was not that central banks failed to burst bubbles but rather that they created them. If interest rates had not been held so low and we still had bubbles then such a proposal might have merit. But that is not what happened.

Yet another reform, recently suggested by the IMF research department is that central banks should raise their inflation targets. The reason is that with the two percent target in policy rules such as the Taylor rule the interest rate would have to go negative in a severe crisis, and this is not possible. But in the current crisis, the Taylor rule has interest rates going close to zero and not remaining there for long. Moreover, raising inflation targets – especially when government debts are rising and central banks' balance sheets are expanded – could easily reduce credibility about an inflation target at all, further damaging central bank credibility. This would be especially inappropriate for central banks in emerging market countries.

For the most part, the policy implications of the crisis are that those central banks that deviated from good policy should get back to what they were doing before the crisis. They need to earn back credibility and preserve their independence. Systematic monetary policies focusing on a credible goal for inflation worked well in the past and they will work well in the future. For central banks that were following sounder policies – and here credit should be given to the progress made in India and other emerging market central banks – they should continue to do so. There is no reason to change.

But the crisis does reveal some potential new fault lines, largely related to the increased globalisation and international connection between financial markets, which was so evident during the panic. These interconnections raise questions about the impact of central banks on each other. In the period leading up to the crisis there is evidence that the European Central Bank and other central banks held interest rates lower than they would otherwise be because the Federal Reserve set its interest rate so low. The reason, of course, is the exchange rate. A large gap between interest rates would cause the exchange rate to appreciate with adverse consequences on exports. And during the panic the shock from the developed world on the developing world was severe and central banks had to cope with this.

Is there a better way? Making the movements in the interest rates less erratic in the developed countries would help the emerging market countries. Deviations from policy rules have increased interest rate volatility, so keeping interest rates more on track will have the added advantage of reducing their erratic nature. Another possibility is to think about a global target for the inflation rate, or at least a multi-country target, a G20 target perhaps. If there was a multi-country target and this was at least considered in the deliberations of each central bank then there would be a smaller tendency to swing individual interest rates around by large amounts.

Getting the narrative about the financial crisis right is very important. A view frequently heard now is that "the markets did it." The crisis was due to forces emanating from the market economy which the government did not control, either because it did not have the power to do so, or because it chose not to because of the influence of economic theories which emphasised the advantages of free markets. This view sees the crisis as a market failure that can and must be dealt with by government actions and interventions. The economic theories and the policies implied by them must change.

Another view put forth is that largely the opposite is true. The crisis was due more to forces emanating from government. According to this view government interventions caused, prolonged, and worsened the financial crisis and did relatively little to pull us out of it. This view sees government as the more serious systemic risk in the financial system.

A policy of "Keynes at home and Adam Smith aboard" eventually led to the poor macroeconomic performance in the 1970s. When most countries moved to "Adam Smith both at home and abroad," the twenty year wave of progress and stability was unprecedented. Leading up to this recent crisis and during it we let "Keynesian policies" creep back in and ironically we seem to be going down the path now of "Keynes both at home and abroad." If we learn the lessons from this crisis, we should get back to "Adam Smith at home and abroad" as soon as possible. Of course we cannot go completely back home again. The world is different. Policy, including monetary policy, needs to adapt this approach to deal with increased globalisation.

RECENT MONETARY POLICY RESPONSES: AN ASSESSMENT

Highly accommodative and unconventional monetary policies in advanced economies are providing essential support to aggregate demand, but there is growing tension between these policies and future risks to financial stability. Monetary policy easing has pushed beyond conventional means in the effort to counter a weak recovery. In several advanced economies, asset purchases and commitments to a long duration of low interest-rate policies have supplemented traditional policy easing. This approach has been essential to support the recovery.

As intended, these policies are generating a substantial rebalancing of private investor portfolios toward riskier assets. This trend is dominated by corporate credit markets and amplified by constrained net supply of fixed income instruments, after accounting for central bank purchases.

Ultra-low short-term interest rates have reduced the cost of debt for corporate borrowers, enabling firms to lengthen their debt maturity profiles and rendering debt servicing ratios more favorable, even at higher debt loads. This comes at a time when traditional valuations of corporate credit show little signs of excess. These developments are healthy, desirable elements of the monetary transmission mechanism.

But other elements of the current credit cycle do not fit a healthy stylized situation. Capital spending remains depressed relative to cash flows. Corporate bond issuance is more elevated than usual at this point of the cycle and is increasingly geared toward less-productive uses, such as funding equity buybacks. Balance sheet leverage is steadily rising on the back of higher debt levels and slowing earnings. Yield-enhancement through financial leverage and weaker underwriting standards are also increasingly prevalent, and in some cases are back to prior cycle peaks.

These trends are most relevant to the United States, where unconventional monetary policy has been forceful; the credit cycle is more advanced; capital markets are deeper and play a larger role in credit intermediation; the spillover effects to emerging markets may be significant; and potential upside economic risks could lead to a faster normalization in monetary policy. In other advanced economies with accommodative monetary policies, firms are either using a more typical blend of equity and bond financing at this early stage of the cycle or are squarely focused on balance sheet repair and leverage reduction. By contrast, in emerging market economies, the decline in corporate borrowing costs has, as in the United States, led to a surge in bond financing, which is also a departure from previous cycles in those economies.

These elements may not pose imminent systemic risk, but they bear close monitoring. A prolonged period of low interest rates may create incentives to increase leverage beyond manageable levels, extend the decay in underwriting standards, and reinforce the search for yield.

Four channels of instability are emerging from the protracted period of low interest rates and suppressed market volatility:

1. Growing medium-term vulnerabilities: Despite the strong starting point for credit fundamentals, corporate credit risk has the potential to be mispriced. Nonfinancial corporate balance sheet leverage is rising, and investor demand for yield-enhancement is increasingly evident in the decline of underwriting standards and growing demand for financial leverage. A sharp rise in risk tolerance among various asset managers could add to these vulnerabilities.
2. Rise in risk-free rates: There is little to derail current trends, and the rise in leverage appears manageable in an environment of low debt service and sustained earnings. However, the risk is skewed toward future higher government bond yields. Unconventional monetary easing has lowered short-term interest-rate expectations and term premiums to rock-bottom levels. A sharp rise in risk-free rates could expose credit vulnerabilities.
3. Illiquidity could act as an amplifier: The impact on credit markets has the potential to be amplified by market illiquidity. The shift in broker-dealer business models to reduce credit inventories means that a tightening of credit conditions could have a larger-than-usual market impact.
4. Spillovers to emerging market economies: In emerging markets, corporate borrowers who have recently more heavily focused on U.S. dollar issuance may be vulnerable to a reversal in favorable credit trends.

Credit fundamentals are at a good starting point, but recent trends point to future risks. The decline in corporate borrowing costs and the rise in demand for credit are consistent with broader, strong fundamentals. Corporate liquidity—cash holdings relative to debt—is high, interest expenses are near cycle lows relative to earnings, and the debt maturity profile has been extended to reduce near-term refinancing risk.

But there are reasons for,being vigilant. Higher borrowing in an environment of slower earnings growth is boosting corporate leverage, reversing the post-crisis trend of maintaining conservative balance sheets. Other evidence that points to a weakening of corporate credit conditions includes: an easing in financing terms (e.g., covenant-light loans are back to prior cycle high levels and payment-in-kind, perpetual, and hybrid bond issuance has also risen), a rising share of issuance proceeds being used to pay special dividends and fund share buybacks (rather than to finance corporate investment), growth in weaker quality and lower-rated credit issuance, and a loosening in bank lending conditions. The strong starting point in corporate balance sheets helps to mitigate the effects of the more recent trend toward weaker underwriting standards. As a result, default rates in the current cycle are expected to be relatively modest. However, a further extension or intensification of these recent developments could set the stage for future credit deterioration, in turn extending and exacerbating the default cycle, particularly if it is accompanied by a rising rate scenario with less benign macro conditions.

The search for yield may eventually increase the demand for financial leverage and push risks to the nonbank sector. The low-yield environment may also encourage the use of financial leverage—borrowing against assets that are generating current income—to enhance yield. Leverage can be provided either directly through financial intermediaries, such as via financing of repos (repurchase agreements), or indirectly through embedded leverage in financial instruments. Over-exuberant financial engineering and the use of embedded leverage was an important trigger for the global financial crisis of 2007–09. Financial leverage has been less prominent in the search for yield at least at this stage. One reason is that tighter regulations increase the constraints on the balance sheets of banks and broker-dealers, thus making them less willing to provide loans. Another reason is the residual effects of the massive underperformance of mortgage structured products during the financial crisis.

Nonetheless, the potential shift in the way that leverage is provided deserves more attentive monitoring. In their search for higher returns, investors have selectively returned to certain types of structural leverage, via leveraged loans, collateralized loan obligations, and structured notes, which fared well during the crisis. Leveraged loans are taken out by highly indebted companies that are either unrated or rated no higher than BB+ and that may have difficulty directly tapping the high-yield corporate bond market. Mortgage real estate investment trusts (REITs) have also emerged as an important alternative intermediary in the secondary mortgage market. Residential mortgage REITs get short-term funding in the repo market to purchase mortgage-backed securities in the secondary market. Leverage is usually around 10 times. A further potential concern is the opportunistic provision of leverage by nonbank intermediaries operating outside of the regulatory perimeter as they seek to fill the void left entities that are more balance sheet-constrained. For instance, nonbank financial intermediaries with large amounts of high-quality assets may seek to engage in liquidity or maturity transformation (e.g., though securities lending or repos).

Gamble for resurrection: pension funds and insurers could add to vulnerabilities. Slow-moving risks are also emerging for some types of asset managers amid an extended period of low interest rates. This is apparent for U.S. public defined-benefit pension plans, which have suffered from weak asset returns. Funding of those programs has deteriorated substantially in the past decade, from being fully funded in 2001 to an estimated shortfall of 28 percent as of end-2012. Risks are slow to build, as the issue for pension plans is solvency rather than liquidity (in contrast to most banking crises).

Life insurance companies face a similar dilemma, as low interest rates create asset-liability mismatches and diminish net interest margins. Low interest rates mean that insurers face the prospects of investing in lower yielding assets as bonds mature. On the liability side, long-term fixed-rate legacy products are costly because minimum guarantee rates cannot be easily reduced.

The effect is a compression in net interest margins, that is, a reduction in the difference between returns on underlying investments and rates that insurance companies pay to policyholders. To counter the effects of lower rates, life insurers have engaged in liability management operations. For instance, they have lowered rates on legacy products where possible, curtailed interest-sensitive products, sought to renegotiate terms, and sold blocks of business to private equity funds. But because the limits to most of these measures have already been reached, insurance companies have migrated into higher-risk, less-liquid assets.

Capital shortfalls do not appear to be an immediate risk, as the industry has built excess liquidity and capital buffers since the crisis. But a protracted period of low rates could depress interest margins further and erode capital buffers, potentially driving insurance companies to further increase their credit and liquidity risk. At the same time, life insurers operate with significant balance sheet leverage and are thus exposed to credit shocks.

The "gamble for resurrection" in response to solvency risk, asset-liability mismatches, or diminishing net margins applies more broadly to insurance companies and pension funds operating in a low interest rate environment. A re-risking via changes in business models or asset allocation needs to be closely monitored.

A shock to the risk-free rate could potentially expose vulnerabilities and destabilize credit markets. A sharp, unanticipated rise in risk-free rates could expose vulnerabilities that are currently masked by low interest rates and ample liquidity. Despite the reduction in tail risks and improvement in economic conditions, markets are currently not pricing in any meaningful rise in interest rates. But a more rapid economic recovery that results in a faster-than expected rise in interest rates would likely have less destabilizing effects, and policy officials would aim to manage a more gradual rise. Systemic stability risks would likely be greater if, instead, interest rates remain low for a more protracted period. This would allow for a further decay in credit conditions and increasing vulnerability to a faster-than-expected rise in yields, coupled with rising sovereign risk premiums or weaker potential growth. Where historical experience does provide guidance is on the speed of the rise in bond yields being a key consideration for stability risks. A faster increase would have important direct and indirect consequences, including, for instance, greater risk of a sudden stop or reversal of capital flows to emerging market economies; destabilizing losses in large, leveraged nonbank credit channels sensitive to interest rate risk, such as mortgage REITs; and asset-liability mismatches in the banking system and elsewhere.

Credit ris can be amplified by poor liquidity. The decline in U.S. corporate bond market liquidity could amplify the vulnerabilities in credit markets in the event of a sharp rise in government bond yields. Illiquidity is currently being masked by low rates, strong asset performance, and the one-way nature of inflows to corporate bond markets. The effects of the decline in liquidity could become evident once those dynamics reverse, potentially raising volatility, increasing funding costs for issuers, straining other credit channels, and discouraging longer-term investment plans. This is especially relevant for the high-yield sector, where liquidity and volatility are important determinants of spreads.

It is also relevant for asset managers who have increased their corporate bond exposure significantly since 2008. Increased exposure does not in itself pose a stability risk. On the contrary, increased holdings of corporate bonds by traditionally long-term investors with greater capacity to absorb liquidity risk (owing to less liquid liabilities) may enhance stability. But in an environment of rising rates and with greater volatility, rising balance sheet leverage combined with large recent purchases at very low yields and growing margin pressures could prove to be a toxic mix. The result could be forced asset sales (or unforced sales due to valuation losses) that further compound margin pressures and erode capital buffers.

Against this backdrop, policy-makers need to monitor developments closely and stand ready to counter excesses early on. Tension is building between the ongoing need for extraordinary monetary policy accommodation and credit markets that are maturing more quickly than in typical cycles. High unemployment and low inflation may justify an accommodative monetary policy stance. But other tools need to be employed to counteract undesirable excesses in credit. Increased surveillance and macroprudential tools, such as countercyclical buffers to lean against rising leverage, are essential to manage undesired credit expansion.

The most immediate risk for nonbank financial intermediaries is complacency toward the slowmoving nature of liability loss recognition. Pension funds need to engage in active liability management operations without delay, which can most likely be achieved by restructuring benefits, extending working years, and gradually increasing contributions to close funding gaps. Insurance companies need to proceed with the disposal of legacy products to reduce margin pressure and limit duration mismatches on new products.

An undesired buildup of excesses in broader asset markets is a potential risk over the medium term. Asset reallocations of institutional investors to alternative asset managers, excess cash holdings by those asset managers, the decline in underwriting standards, and the sharp rise in bond valuations are all intertwined. Constraining those potential excesses is a financial stability imperative.

RELATIONSHIP BETWEEN CORPORATE FINANCE, FINANCIAL STRUCTURE AND MONETARY POLICY

The relationship between corporate finance, financial structure and monetary policy is of considerable importance to the development of financial markets and economic growth, and has received much attention from both academics and policy-makers. Problems caused by asymmetric information that exist on financial markets between borrowers and lenders may force certain borrowers to seek specific forms of finance and thus influence their capital structure and the cost of capital. In practice, these information problems combined with a large number of institutional, legal and historical characteristics determine the use of specific sources of corporate finance and the development of the financial structure of an economy. It is important to stress that a bank-oriented financial structure is neither more nor less efficient than a securities-based structure. Rather, it is the complementarity of financing options that contributes to economic efficiency.

There are signs that non-financial corporations are increasingly resorting to securities-based finance, such as debt securities issuance and shares listed on both the mainstream and "high-growth" exchanges. In this development, the move towards and the introduction of the euro have acted as an important catalyst, especially with regard to the issuance of debt securities, improving the efficiency of the euro area capital markets and reducing existing information asymmetries to some extent. At the same time, loans continue to be an important source of net external financing for non-financial corporations in the euro area, in particular those extended by MFIs.

The analysis of corporate finance is of relevance to monetary policy and also has implications for financial stability. If the financing of non-financial corporations through the issuance of securities continues to grow, this may imply a larger exposure of firms to developments in financial markets, may lead to more competitive pricing of loans by banks, and could render the economy more sensitive to wealth effects. The process of monetary transmission could be affected through all these channels. The dynamics of the evolution in the external financing flows of non-financial corporations in the euro area suggest that debt securities are playing a growing role in financing, even though they started from a low base by comparison with the United States. As regards equity, quoted shares gained importance. If developments towards increased reliance on securities were to influence policy decisions in the economy, then it seems appropriate to reflect on their implications for monetary policy. These include: 1) a larger exposure of firms to swings in financial markets; 2) more competitive pricing of loans by banks; and 3) a greater importance of wealth effects.

Larger Exposure of Firms to Swings in Financial Markets

The prices of financial instruments, such as corporate bonds and equities, are determined in a forward-looking manner, and, *inter alia*, incorporate the expectations of economic agents regarding future economic developments and premia for various risks. An increase in the exposure of corporations as a result of a higher share of debt securities and quoted shares would imply that companies' financing conditions might be affected more quickly by developments in financial markets than before.

More Competitive Pricing of Loans by Banks

If there are no major competitive pressures, the pricing of bank loans may not reflect market conditions. This behaviour tends to make the interest rate channel of the transmission mechanism of monetary policy weaker than in an economy where securities predominate. If a liquid market for corporate securities develops, then corporations may go directly to the market and bypass banks. This should lead to more competitive pricing by banks. In the case of the euro area, some large firms with direct access to credit have been able to obtain finance from banks at rates similar to money market races. In this context, a financial structure in which securities play a more important role in debt financing implies that changes in Bank Rates are likely to affect bank lending interest rates more quickly.

Greater Importance of Wealth Effects

Changes in interest rates may affect the prices of assets, be they financial instruments or real assets such as property, and thus the wealth of households and non-financial corporations. The importance of wealth effects depends on the absolute value and the composition of wealth, on the impact of monetary policy and on how changes in wealth affect consumption and investment decisions. If there is a move towards a greater importance of securities, companies and households are likely to increase the share of financial assets in the form of securities in their portfolios. Thus, changes in the financial structure towards greater recourse to securities markets are likely to reinforce the importance of wealth effects, as households and non-financial corporations will probably hold a larger share of their wealth in the form of financial market instruments such as corporate bonds or equity.

GLOBALISATION AND MONETARY POLICY: THE INDIAN EXPERIENCE

In reality, while there are growing tendencies towards globalisation, the conduct of monetary policy depends on a number of factors that are unique to a country and the context. Given policy goals, the contours of the monetary policy are shaped by the macroeconomic structure of the economy and its institutional setting. Other important factors that have a decisive role are the degree of openness of the economy, the stage of development of financial markets, payment and settlement systems and the technological infrastructure. Against this backdrop, let us examine the specific features of the monetary policy in India.

First, although there is no explicit mandate for price stability, the conduct of monetary policy has evolved around the objectives of maintaining price stability and ensuring adequate flow of credit to the productive sectors of the economy for sustaining overall economic growth. The relative emphasis between price stability and growth depends on underlying macroeconomic conditions. In essence, monetary policy in India strives for a judicious balance between price stability and growth. The democratic processes in India work in favour of price stability which, in some ways, amounts to an informal mandate to the central bank for maintaining an acceptable level of inflation.

Second, the monetary policy framework in India is guided by a 'multiple indicator' approach wherein besides monetary aggregates, information pertaining to a range of rates of return in different financial market segments along with the movements in currency, credit, the fiscal position, merchandise trade, capital flows, the inflation rate, the exchange rate, refinancing and transactions in foreign exchange - which are available on a high frequency basis - is juxtaposed with data on output and the real sector activity for drawing policy perspectives. The transition to a multiple indicator approach has been a logical outcome of monetary policy reforms. It has provided necessary flexibility to the RBI to respond more effectively to the changes in domestic and international economic and financial market conditions. In a medium-to long-term perspective, the impact of money supply on inflation, however, cannot be ignored and for the purposes of policy, the Reserve Bank still continues to announce projections of money supply compatible with the outlook on GDP growth and expected inflatin.

Third, liquidity management is carried out through open market operations (OMO) in the form of outright purchases/sales of government securities and reserve repo/repo operations, supplemented by the newly introduced Market Stabilisation Scheme (MSS). The Liquidity Adjustment Facility (LAF), introduced in June 2000, enables the Reserve Bank to modulate short-term liquidity, of a temporary nature, under varied financial market conditions in order to ensure stable conditions in the overnight (call) money market. The LAF operates through reverse repo and repo auctions, thereby setting a corridor for the short-term interest rate consistent with the policy objectives. The LAF operations, combined with strategic OMO consistent with market liquidity conditions, have evolved as the principal operating procedure of the monetary policy of the Reserve Bank.

Fourth, notwithstanding concerted reforms undertaken since the 1990s, e.g. freeing monetary policy from the burden of automatic monetisation and a significant marketisation of the government's borrowing programme, monetary policy in India continues to be constrained by the fiscal dominance. Debt management considerations of ensuring a smooth passage of the borrowing programme of the government, at minimum costs and roll over risks, make the overall monetary management difficult when large and growing borrowing year after year puts pressure on the absorptive capacity of the market and on liquidity management. In this context, the Fiscal Responsibility and Budget Management Act of 2003 which envisages a vacation of primary financing of the fiscal deficit by the Reserve Bank from 2006-07 would enhance the flexibility for monetary management.

Fifth, the predominance of publicly-owned financial intermediaries has its implications for monetary policy. Cross holdings and inter-relationships in the financial sector emphasised in planned development were to achieve the social goals of the "joint family" headed by the Government. These are being gradually revamped consistent with the needs of a market economy.

Sixth, a factor that further complicates the transmission mechanism of monetary policy is the limited size of the Indian financial system. Although India is essentially a bank-based economy, commercial credit penetration in the Indian economy is still relatively low. Concerns about credit to agriculture and small- and medium-enterprises usually relate to inadequacy, constraints on timely availability, high cost, neglect of small and marginal farmers, low credit-deposit ratios in several States and continued presence of informal credit markets with high interest rates. It is in this context that the monetary policy in India continues to take cognisance of the need for ensuring financial inclusion of all segments of population, interests of depositors and for promoting a conducive credit culture.

Seventh, the Indian financial system still shows some signs of stickiness in interest rates. Consequently, apart from the efforts to ensure reduction in existing high levels of revenue and fiscal deficits, rationalising administered interest rates on contractual savings to impart efficiency and operational flexibility to the financial sector is amongst the priorities in policy.

Eighth, monetary management in India is somewhat constrained by the lack of comprehensive and timely information in some areas relative to the demands of a fast growing and increasingly globalising economy. One lacuna is the absence of credible data on the labour market. Employment data essentially pertain to the organised sector which constitutes less than 10 per cent of the total labour force. There is also considerable ambiguity about the very definition of 'employment' given the prevalence of underemployment and disguised unemployment. In the absence of data on the natural rate of unemployment, it is difficult to assess with reasonable level of confidence the underlying conditions. Similarly, an assessment of the inflationary conditions in the economy is constrained by the lack of a comprehensive measure of consumer price inflation. The multiple consumer price indices, on the basis of occupational classification and residence (rural/urban), compound the problem, especially when differences in weighting diagrams of the commodity baskets lead to differences in inflation numbers.

Ninth , the financial system in India, however, has a relatively low vulnerability to asset bubbles. There is limited exposure of bank lending to the sensitive sectors, including real estate. While the demand for housing is strong, overall exposure is moderated by assigning higher risk weights to housing loans than required under the Basel norm. The share of housing loans in the overall loan portfolio stood at about 10 per cent in March 2004 and net non-performing assets were 1.4 per cent of the net outstanding loans as compared with 2.8 per cent of the aggregate portfolio.

An assessment of expectations *vis-a-vis* outcomes suggests that monetary policy in India has performed reasonably well in terms of its objectives. First, compared to many developing countries, India has been able to maintain a moderate level of inflation. Historically, inflation rates in India have rarely touched double digits and when they did, it was the result of supply shocks from agricultural commodity prices or international oil prices. Second, monetary policy has been reasonably successful in dampening the volatility of output and imparting to the economy a growing resilience. The trend rate of GDP growth has risen steadily to around 6.0 per cent for about 25 years, and India has emerged as one of the fastest growing economies in the world. Third, monetary policy has been successful in ensuring financial stability in India through a decade and a half when frequent visits of financial crises led to debilitating losses in growth and welfare in large parts of the developing world. This period was also marked by pressures from within such as geo- political tensions, drought and international sanctions. While we might have enjoyed an element of luck, we believe that we also benefited from exercise of sound judgment and enhancement of skills at all levels. It is useful to note that the Reserve Bank has been engaged in the development of sound and efficient financial intermediaries and markets so as to provide solid foundations for effective transmission of monetary policy. Fourth, success has been achieved in turning around and strengthening the external sector. Restrictions on imports have been virtually abolished and current account convertibility has been instituted since 1994. The capital account is virtually open for non- residents. An exchange rate policy of focusing on managing volatility with no fixed rate target, while allowing the underlying demand and supply conditions to determine the exchange rate movements over a period in an orderly way, has stood the test of time. India's external sector management has been endorsed by the growing international investor confidence in the face of sub-investment grade sovereign ratings. Today, India holds the sixth largest stock of reserves in the world, sufficient to cover its entire external debt. Since 2002, India has turned creditor to the IMF and is engaged in pre- paying bilateral and multilateral debt.

The conduct of monetary policy is getting increasingly sophisticated and forward looking, warranting a continuous upgradation of monitoring scan and technical skills. Flexibility and timeliness in policy response coupled with transparency and accountability hold the key to further enhance credibility. Above all, the monetary authority has to address dilemmas, which exert conflicting pulls at every stage, and blend the desirable with the feasible.

QUESTIONS

1. Critically examine the implications of globalisation for monetary policy.
2. "On an increasing globalisation of financial markets, the conduct of monetary policy depends on a number of factors that are unique to the country and the context." Do you agree?
3. Critically examine the specific features of monetary policy in India in that context of globalisation of monetry policy.
4. Does globalisation introduce new objectives for monetary policy? How should monetary policy account for globalisation?
5. What are the factors driving the globalisation of monetary policy?
6. Discuss the relationship between corporate finance, financial structure and monetary policy.
7. Critically examine the recent monetary policy responses. ARe highly recommendative and unconventional monetary policies of advanced economics leading to future risk of financial stability.

26

INTERNATIONAL BANKING

INTRODUCTION

International banking has expanded markedly over the last 30 years. Its form and geographical coverage reflect two important aspects of the role international banks play in the global economy.*First,* international banking has been an important component of a broader process of financial globalisation and integration. Historically, it has expanded in concert with international trade and has performed key functions for the business of international firms. In addition, the local operations of foreign banks have spurred the development of financial systems in emerging markets and helped to alleviate information problems via close and sustained customer relationships.The demand for financial services from multinational corporations and rapidly growing emerging markets promises to shape international banking and its contribution to economic progress in the future. A shift of trade flows and multinational production towards emerging market economies may accelerate financial integration. This could result in both increased participation in these economies by foreign banks and greater international activity by locally headquartered banks. Thus, banks from emerging market countries may well play an increasingly prominent part in future cross-border consolidation in the financial sector.*Second,* the role of international banks in the global economy is closely related to that of international financial markets. As they perform complementary functions, both forms of financial intermediation are indispensable, together with a resilient market infrastructure, for the healthy functioning of the financial system. Deep international capital markets often ease the funding strains of large corporations when bank credit contracts. By contrast, banks are the main source of external financing for households, as well as for small and medium-sized companies, whose access to credit markets tends to be restricted by asymmetric information issues.

International banking is likely to continue growing in line with further economic integration, but questions have been raised as to the limits of such growth. Underpricing of financial risks before the recent crisis led to high leverage, as well as opaque and illiquid exposures, in both the foreign and domestic components of many bank balance sheets. These exposures proved hard to manage at a time of stress. More generally, growth in cross-border lending over the last decade has outpaced that of international trade, suggesting that the relationship between international banking and real economic activity may have changed.

The cross-border structure of the funding and management of international banks may also be subject to change. Deeper, more sophisticated financial markets led banks to rely increasingly on wholesale funding and to accept cross-currency funding risks. These trends exposed banks, as well as their creditors and borrowers, to the risk of sudden reversals in funding flows. They also made host jurisdictions vulnerable to financial problems originating in third countries.

The role of financial sector consolidation may also change, particularly a trend towards globally active universal financial service providers and greater functional specialisation among financial firms. This trend and its international dimension may now stop or even reverse as market participants and authorities change their perceptions of the risk/benefit trade-off embedded in some financial business models.

Finally, recent experience has underscored the joint role that banks and markets need to play in stabilising the financial system at a time of distress. Over the years, banks and markets have become increasingly integrated. Performing largely complementary functions, the two forms of intermediation have helped to diversify financial services and the financial system. By extension, the simultaneous healthy functioning of both markets and banks is crucial for the future resilience of international intermediation.

As the recent crisis unfolded, the complementarity of markets and banks became hard to miss. International securities markets did pick up some of the demand for credit that deleveraging banks could not accommodate. This was only a partial solution, however, as companies that could provide detailed financial information benefited more than borrowers with asymmetric information issues. When they are healthy, banks can deal with such issues better than markets do, thanks to their close customer relationships and long-term local representation. The resilience of banks – underpinned by a resilient market infrastructure – is particularly valuable at times of stress, as they can alleviate the problem that "some information is not easily transferable or 'marketable' (being) hard to codify, often tacit in nature" .

DEFINITION OF INTERNATIONAL BANKING ACTIVITIES

International banking can be defined as intermediation activity that falls into one of the following categories. The extension of credit by a bank headquartered in a particular country to residents of another country can occur via: (i) cross-border lending; (ii) local lending by affiliates established in the foreign country; or (iii) lending booked by an affiliate established in a third country (e.g. an international financial centre). In addition, the BIS international banking statistics on a residency basis include the extension of credit by a bank headquartered in a particular country to residents of the same country but in a foreign currency. The underlying financial instruments could be loans, deposits or securities as well as derivatives contracts and contingent facilities.

In order to illustrate different forms of international banking, we consider the case of a bank that is headquartered in United States and lends to a borrower located in the India. Table 1 provides a non-exhaustive list of six examples of how the lending could be extended. In examples 1 and 2, the funds are raised in United States by taking deposits from United States residents, and then lent to the an Indian borrower, either cross-border or through a local affiliate. In example 3, a depositor in India places funds in a United States bank in United States that then lends cross-border to an entity in India. Such round-tripping also qualifies as international banking.

TABLE 1

HOW A US BANK COULD FUND A LOAN TO AN INDIAN BORROWER

Example	*Residents of USA*				*Cross-border*	*Residents of the India*	
1.	Saver	Deposit →	Head office	Loan→		→	Borrower
2.	Saver	Deposit →	Head office	Deposit→	Bank affiliate	Loan**	Borrower
3.			Head office	←Deposit Loan→		← →	Saver Borrower
4.					Bank affiliate	←Deposit Loan→	Saver Borrower
5.	Saver	→		Deposit→	Bank affiliate	Loan→	Borrower
Germany	*Residents of border Kingdom*		*Cross- the United*	*Resident of*	*Cross-border United States*	*Residents of the*	
6.	Saver	→	Deposit →	Bank affiliate→	Deposit→	→	Borrower

The last three examples illustrate forms of international banking that have gained in importance over the years. Example 4 illustrates what is sometimes referred to as global banking: funds are raised in India by the Indian affiliate of a US bank and lent by the same affiliate locally to borrowers in India. Example 5 illustrates another variant of global banking, where the funds are raised in the country where the bank is headquartered but the depositor rather than the bank bears the transfer risk. Finally, example 6 illustrates the use of an international banking centre in order to raise funds and then extend a loan in two different countries, neither of which is the country in which the bank is headquartered. Most international banking transactions are variations on these examples and often also involve routing through an offshore centre in the Caribbean or Asia.

ORGANISATIONAL FEATURES OF INTERNATIONAL BANKING

The growth and importance of doing banking business across the border through different forms of foreign bank organisations is described below:

Correspondent Banking

An informal linkage between banks and different countries is set up when banks maintain correspondent accounts with each other. The purpose of maintaining foreign correspondents is to facilitate international payments and collections for customers. The term 'correspondent' comes from the mail or cable communications that the banks maintain when setting customer accounts. For example, if any Indian company wishes to pay a Canadian supplier, it would ask its bank, which would then communicate with its Canadian counterpart bank by mail or cable or through SWIFT Network. The Canadian bank would credit the account of the Canadian firm, while the company's bank would debit the company's account and then settle with the Canadian bank.

Correspondent banking allows banks to help their customers who are doing business abroad, without having to maintain any persons or officers overseas. The relationship between the banks is primarily for settling customer payments, but it can extend to providing limited credit for each other's customers and to setting up contacts between local business people and the clients of the correspondent banks.

Resident Representatives

In order to provide their customers help from their own personnel on the spot in foreign countries, banks open overseas business offices. These are not banking offices in the sense of accepting local deposits or providing loans. The primary purpose of these offices is to provide information about local business practices and conditions, including the credit worthiness of potential customers and the bank's clients. The resident representatives will keep in contact with local correspondent banks and provide help when needed. Representative offices are generally small; they have the appearance of an ordinary commercial office rather than a bank.

Bank Agencies

An agency is like a full-fledged bank in every respect except that it does not handle ordinary deposits. The agencies deal in the local money markets and in the foreign exchange markets, arrange loans, clear bank drafts and cheques and channel foreign funds into financial markets. Agencies also often arrange long-term loans for customers, but they deal primarily on behalf of the home office to keep it directly involved in the important foreign financial markets.

Foreign Branches

Foreign branches are operating banks like local banks, except that the directors and owners tend to reside elsewhere. Generally, foreign branches are subject to both local banking rules and the rules at home, but because they can benefit from loopholes, the extra tier of regulations is not necessarily onerous. The books of a foreign branch are incorporated with those of the parent bank, although the foreign branch will also maintain separate books for revealing separate performance, for tax purposes, and so on. The existence of foreign branches can mean very rapid cheque clearing for customers in different countries, because the debit and credit operations are internal and can be initiated by a telephone call or through SWIFT. This can offer a great advantage over the lengthy clearing that can occur via correspondents. The foreign branch also offers bank customers in small countries all the services and safety advantages of a large bank that the local market might not itself be able to support.

Foreign Subsidiaries and Affiliates

A foreign branch is a part of a parent organisation that is incorporated elsewhere. A foreign subsidiary is a locally incorporated bank that happens to be owned either completely or partially by a foreign parent. Foreign subsidiaries do all types of banking, and it may be very difficult to distinguish them from an ordinary locally owned bank except perhaps by the name.

Foreign subsidiaries are controlled by foreign owners, even if the foreign ownership is partial. Foreign affiliates are similar to subsidiaries in being locally incorporated, and so on, but they are joint ventures, and no individual foreign owner has control (even though a group of foreign owners might have control).

Consortium Banks

Consortium banks are joint ventures of the larger commercial banks. They can involve half a dozen or more partners from numerous countries. They are primarily concerned with investment, and they arrange large loans and underwrite stocks and bonds. Consortium banks are not concerned with taking deposits, and they deal only with large corporations or perhaps governments. They will take equity positions - part ownership of an investment—as well as make loans, and they are frequently busy arranging takeovers and mergers.

Underlying the philosophy of free-market economics and financial liberalisation there have been a number of international accords between the central banks of the major economic powers. These agreements have been made in an attempt to restore equilibrium and stability to the international financial system and to reconcile differences in national regulatory framework exposed by the collapse of Brettonwood.

The first international accord was the Basle Concondrat in 1975, which was agreed under the auspices of the BIS (Bank for International Settlement). This accord, which was revised in 1983, provided the correct framework for international monetary co-operation. During the 1980's agreements, such as the Plaza and the Louvre exchange control accords in 1985 and 1988 respectively, have attempted to create a "level-playing field" by co-ordinating central bank intervention in the international financial system. The most important development in this process was the Cooke Report (BIS, 1986). This report established capital adequacy ratios for all banks and was ratified under the Bank Agreement 1988. Furthermore, the BIS Annual Report (1993) concludes that financial deregulation has led to extreme volatility in share, property and asset prices and that these dynamics raise the prospect of wider systematic instability - arguably, these developments signify a move towards supranational regulation, not unlike the disbanded Bretton Woods, but centered around the new economic trading levels of NAFTA North American Free Trade Area), the Pacific Rim and the EU (European Union).

INTERNATIONAL BANK LOAN FINANCING

Definition and Classification

International bank loans are classified into two categories: foreign loans and Euroloans. Foreign loans are raised by borrowers who are foreign to the country where the loans are raised. International loans, however, mostly take the form of Euroloans or Eurocredits, which are denominated in a currency other than the currency of the country where the loans are raised. Euroloans and foreign loans are also distinguished as follows. While Euroloans are financed wholly out of Eurocurrency funds, irrespective of whether the borrower is a resident or a nonresident of the country in question, foreign loans are domestic currency credits extended to non-resident borrowers.

Syndicated loans (Euro or foreign) are characterised by being so large in size that it becomes necessary to form a syndicate or a group of lending banks to finance the loan. The advantage of syndication is that it enables banks to spread the risk of very large loans amongst themselves. This is important because a large multinational firm may need credit in excess of what a single bank can offer. A syndicated loan is arranged by a lead bank on behalf of a client such as a multinational firm. The lead bank seeks the participation of a group (syndicate) of banks, each providing a portion of the loan. One or more banks are designated as reference banks, which is necessary to establish the reference interest rate.

Pricing international loans

Pricing an international loan, which amounts to the determination of the interest charged to the borrower, depends on a number of factors. It is also influenced by a combination of risk evaluation, market conditions, and shifts in the demand for and supply of loans. The following factors are important for determining the interest rate charged to the borrower.

The Spread and the Reference Rate

The interest paid on syndicated loans is usually computed by adding a spread to the London interbank offer rate (LIBOR) or another reference rate such as the US prime rate or the Singapore interbank offer rate (SIBOR). The following factors determine the spread:

1. The availability of liquidity or loanable funds relative to demand. Spreads are likely to be higher in a market that is characterised by a shortage of liquidity and excess demand for loanable funds.
2. The creditworthiness of the borrower, as high-quality borrowers are charged lower spreads than low-quality borrowers.
3. The maturity of the loan, with higher spreads charged on long-maturity loans.

In domestic bank lending, interest rates allow for the narrowest loan spread when the central government is the borrower because there is no credit risk (the government can print money or tax people to meet its debt obligations). When non-government borrowers are involved the spreads increase as a function of credit risk. In international lending, central government borrowers pay varying interest rates because of differences in perceived country risk. Other borrowers pay higher interest rates because of (i) differences in country risk, (ii) differences in credit risk, and (iii) differences in the currency of loan denomination.

The Fees Charged

In addition to interest payments, the borrower is expected to pay management fees, participation fees, commitment fees and taxes. Management fees are charged by managing banks for their services. These are one-time charges levied when the loan agreement is signed. Participation fees are divided among all banks in relation to their share of the loan. Commitment fees are charged to the borrower as a percentage of the undrawn portion of the loan. There is normally a trade-off between fees and the spread over the reference rate. Banks prefer a combination of high fees and low spreads because they can advertise a low spread (which is good for business) without losing revenue.

Currency of Denomination

The currency of denomination affects loan pricing in two ways: (i) interest rates vary from one currency to another; and (ii) the potential gain/loss on a currency must be considered when the currency of denomination is different from the base currency of the borrower.

Loan Documentation

Loan agreements specify the rights and obligations of the borrower and lender, they specify the timing, calculation and the method of paying interest, principal, and fees. Several clauses have been developed for international lending, including the following:

1. *Changes in circumstances:* If any law or regulation changes such that the loan becomes illegal, the borrower must repay the loan. A second part of the clause protects against changes in reserve requirements or changes that may lead to an increase in the bank's cost of funding the loan.
2. *Sovereign immunity:* Under most laws, a sovereign state is immune from the seizure of assets.
3. *Governing law and jurisdiction:* This clause specifies the law that governs the contract.
4. *Cross default:* A default by the borrower under any loan agreement constitutes an automatic default under the bank's agreement.
5. *Negative pledge:* This clause forbids any secured borrowing unless the bank is secured equally. It prevents a bank's position from deteriorating relative to other lenders.

Risk Sharing and Reduction

International banks use the following techniques to reduce and shift risks involved in international lending:

1. *Loan selection and structuring:* This process includes an analysis of credits to screen out inferior loans, application of loan limits, emphasis on booking higher quality credits and adherence to country, customer and currency limits.
2. *Participation in loans:* Many banks participate in large loans, each taking a small portion of the amount.
3. *Use of guarantees and insurance:* Central government agencies, central banks, and commercial banks provide loan guarantees.
4. *Floating rate loans:* These loans provide protection for the lender bank against interest rate risk (risk is shifted to the borrower).

GLOBAL BANKING CRISES AND ITS IMPACT ON BANK FUNDING

Banks fund themselves through a wide range of financial instruments, from both retail and wholesale sources. Accounting for most of the former sources are customer deposits, predominantly from households. The latter consists broadly of funding from private markets, used to supplement customer deposits in financing bank operations. On the short end, wholesale funding includes interbank loans, with a prominent role for short-term US dollar funding and other short-term debt, most notably repurchase agreements (repos) and commercial paper (CP), as well as certificates of deposit. At longer maturities, banks issue medium-term notes (MTNs) and bonds. In addition to deposit and wholesale funding, banks can access central bank liquidity and raise capital, much of which consists of equity.

During the past few decades, the composition of bank funding has changed significantly owing to various structural developments. First, financial markets and banks became strongly interconnected. Banks improved their risk-hedging abilities through financial markets and opened new avenues of funding, such as the "originate-to-distribute" securitisation model. Second, the rapid growth of investment banking activity, both by pure investment banks and universal banks, led to a growing reliance on wholesale funding, especially at short maturities. Third, financial globalisation let banks tap funding markets beyond national borders, promoting the rapid growth of international interbank US dollar markets on which banks from various countries became heavily dependent. In all of this, changes to supervisory and regulatory frameworks often played a crucial role.

The funding pattern that emerged from these structural changes underwent unprecedented dislocations during the 2007–09 global financial crisis. This acted as a catalyst for major adjustments in banks' business and funding models – adjustments that, in many cases, were reinforced by the subsequent euro area crisis. While the 2007–09 episode was predominantly a banking crisis, the euro area's problems have centred on strongly interconnected sovereign and banking crises.

HOW CRISES AND FUNDING ARE INTERCONNECTED

Financial crises and developments in bank funding are strongly intertwined, as weaknesses on the asset side of banks' balance sheets tend to trigger funding problems. Ultimately, these strains expose growing problems in the quality of the underlying assets, leading to fire sales of assets which accelerate declines in asset prices, resulting in further balance sheet pressures. Throughout this process, funding liquidity crises can exacerbate solvency concerns. These tensions feed on imbalances in bank funding structures, such as excessive recourse to debt financing that is reflected in historically high degrees of leverage. As the increase in debt often finances expansion into riskier business areas, this spills over into a deterioration of the quality of bank assets. If it goes unchecked, the process may lay the foundation for future financial crises and severe dislocations in bank funding markets.

Many financial crises have been characterised by major currency and maturity mismatches between banks' assets and liabilities, while in others a prominent role has also been played by large off-balance sheet exposures in the banking sector. In numerous cases, these mismatches were of systemic proportions and helped to propagate shocks across countries, exposing shortcomings in existing measures of system-wide funding risk.

A CLASSIFICATION OF FINANCIAL CRISES

Financial crises may be categorised into *banking, currency* and *sovereign debt* crises. For a large sample of both mature and emerging market economies during the 1970–2011 period, currency crises occurred most frequently, followed by banking crises and sovereign debt crises.

The links between financial crises and bank funding may be strongest during banking crises. Such crises tend to arise primarily from deteriorating economic fundamentals, notably declines in asset quality. Banking crises often originate in credit-induced asset price boom-bust cycles, during which banks build up large exposures to specific asset classes such as real estate or equity. During the bust, plummeting asset prices lead to a sharp rise in non-performing loans, thus eroding the banking sector's financial strength. Examples of important banking crises – which are all related to shocks originating from the real estate sector – are the Nordic and Japanese crises of the 1990s and the 2007–09 global crisis.

Banking crises have been amplified by banks' overreliance on specific sources of financing. With the growing diversification and complexity of funding instruments, the variety of channels through which these imbalances may develop into systemic banking crises has greatly increased. These vulnerabilities relate to the composition of funding in terms of type of instrument, maturity and currency. The 2007–09 global banking crisis showed the shortcomings of business models that depended disproportionately on short-term wholesale funding, such as those adopted by Northern Rock in the United Kingdom and Bear Stearns and Lehman Brothers in the United States. The crisis revealed particularly serious problems with funding instruments in the realm of structured finance and the quality of the underlying assets, which included asset-backed commercial paper (ABCP) and mortgage-backed securities. It also helped to trigger a shift towards more stable sources of bank funding.

The overreliance of banks on specific funding sources has also been implicated in *currency crises* – as characterised by large declines in exchange rates and foreign reserves. A case in point is the 1997–98 East Asian crisis. This episode was precipitated partly by domestic banks' sudden loss of access to largescale, short-term borrowing in foreign currency that had been insufficiently hedged in terms of both maturity transformation and currency risk. The resulting banking and currency crises exposed major problems in the banking systems of countries hit by exchange rate depreciations.

The *sovereign debt* crisis the third main category of financial crisis. Since the first quarter of 2010, sovereign debt tensions and their spillovers into banks and funding markets have dominated financial and economic developments in the euro area. Events have thrown into stark relief the strong two-way interaction between government finances and banks. Sovereign risk may affect bank funding through several channels. First, many banks hold significant amounts of predominantly domestic sovereign bonds on their balance sheets and these large exposures may easily lead to valuation losses and solvency concerns when sovereign yields rise sharply. Second, sovereign debt serves as collateral for various financial transactions, including private repos. Sovereign tensions may result in lower collateral values, due to larger haircuts or margin requirements, which effectively reduce the ability of banks to obtain funding. Third, sovereign downgrades may spill over to banks, affecting both their access to funding and its cost, while reducing the funding benefits they derive from implicit and explicit government guarantees.

The 2007–09 Global Banking Crisis and Its Impact on Funding

During the global banking crisis, banks experienced unprecedented shocks to their funding models, in terms of both market access and cost. Large internationally active banks had built up considerable maturity and currency mismatches between assets and liabilities, exposing them to major vulnerabilities. In particular, investment banking-oriented institutions had significantly leveraged up their funding structures mainly through short-term wholesale funding from repo and commercial paper (CP) markets. Hence, strong growth in total assets was supported by relatively low levels of equity. Banks had also resorted to other volatile funding sources on the "originate-to distribute" model, such as direct loans sales and securitisation.

In the summer of 2007, tensions from the US subprime mortgage markets spilled over to banks' short-term wholesale funding markets, causing liquidity conditions to deteriorate rapidly, particularly for highly leveraged banks. Contagion through the interconnectedness of major global banks and their funding models led to sharp and unprecedented increases in interbank spreads. European banks experienced severe difficulties in obtaining US dollar liquidity. Moreover, highly leveraged US investment banks were hit by severe dislocations in their predominantly short-term debt funding markets. The failures of Bear Stearns and Lehman Brothers in March and September 2008 were precipitated when investors lost confidence in their business models and the firms were shut out of these markets. These problems were not limited to US investment banks, as exemplified by the demise of Northern Rock in the United Kingdom with its dependence on short-term wholesale financing. With solvency concerns on the rise, bank share prices tumbled across the globe.

The disruptions in short-term funding markets prompted central banks worldwide to provide unprecedented amounts of funds. Indeed, central bank liquidity became a major source of wholesale funding. At the same time, governments across the globe provided support through a range of measures, including capital injections, guaranteed issuance programmes for bank bonds and higher deposit insurance ceilings. The crisis led many banks to adjust their funding models towards more stable sources, with an increasing reliance on customer deposits, while reducing their recourse to short-term debt. International banks also gradually started to increase funding through local sources of financing in the foreign markets where they operate.

Banks that relied more heavily on deposit funding fared better in the global financial crisis 2007-09 than those more dependent on other sources. Deposit-funded banks continued to lend during the crisis relative to other banks, showed better overall performance and were less risky. Providers of short-term wholesale funding may have little incentive to monitor banks and instead may simply withdraw their funds at the first negative market signal regarding the client bank's financial health, thus triggering immediate funding tensions. This funding behaviour seems to be the most relevant systemic factor across a set of large international banks in general and those from the euro area in particular. In the same vein, the degree of dependence on sources of funding other than deposits and equity has significant predictive power for various types of financial crises.

In addition, innovations in bank funding instruments contributed to the 2007–09 crisis. For example, securitisation undercut the credit standards of both bank and non-bank lenders, reduced the incentives of lenders to carefully screen borrowers and increased loan delinquency rates, while at the same time hiding increases in defacto leverage. More broadly, financial innovation interacting with financial market imperfections was a central contributory factor to the credit and real estate booms in the United States that led up to the financial crisis.

That said, there were positive aspects of wholesale funding and financial innovations as well as their negative externalities. It may be a rational strategy for banks to resort to wholesale funding in the face of economic uncertainty and volatile demand for bank loans. But the advantages of such funding flexibility during normal times are overshadowed in a crisis by the prohibitively high adjustment costs of short-term wholesale funding in particular. Regarding financial innovation, both empirical and theoretical research has emphasised its positive contribution to economic growth. For example, various financial innovations may have helped to stabilise economic activity in the mid-1980s (the "Great Moderation"). Moreover, financial and technological innovations can interact to support economic growth. Hence, impediments to financial innovation in the form of certain institutions, policies and regulations may slow technological change and economic growth.

BANKING CHALLENGES: DELEVERAGING, BUSINESS MODELS AND SOUNDNESS

Banking systems are at different stages of the balance sheet repair process. While European and U.S. banks have substantially increased their regulatory capital ratios, leverage and reliance on wholesale funding remain relatively high in the core euro area banks.

Many periphery euro area banking systems remain relatively weak as buffers are low relative to reported impaired loans, asset quality continues to deteriorate, and profitability is poor. Some of these issues are being tackled through programmes supported by the ECB, the European Commission, and the IMF (Greece, Ireland, and Portugal), through system-wide reforms supported by the European Stability Mechanism (Spain), or through targeted financial sector action aimed at increasing provisions, improving bank efficiency, and strengthening capital and funding plans, where needed (Italy). These banking systems are likely to see further pressure on asset quality amid poor economic growth. However, contingency buffers to cover additional stress have been included under the programmes: some banking systems have been recapitalized (Portugal, Spain), while others are expected to receive further capital injections (Greece).

In other banking systems—including in Sweden, the United Kingdom, and a number of core euro area countries—asset quality is stable, but certain balance sheet weaknesses remain. In some of these banking systems, buffers against impaired loans are not as strong as in their peers (Austria, the United Kingdom); in others (core euro area, Sweden), leverage and reliance on wholesale funding are still relatively high. While major U.K. and core euro area banks have been actively de-risking and deleveraging, more needs to be done to complete the repair of their balance sheets. Moreover, some segments in the core euro area banking system (e.g., Landesbanks) are still in need of restructuring and consolidation.

Banking systems of Japan, Switzerland, and the United States are in a relatively better position. The loss absorption capacity is higher, asset quality is more stable, and reliance on wholesale funding is lower. Nonetheless, these banking systems still face a number of challenges related to future profitability and business models.

Profitability and asset quality will be further pressured by the weak economic environment. While funding conditions have improved, concerns about asset quality and profitability have moved to the forefront. A prolonged period of low interest rates will likely put pressure on banks' pre-provision profits. Net interest margins (NIMs) of many advanced economy banks have been on a declining path for a number of years, with pressures from low policy rates becoming more acute for banks that offer fixed-rate savings products to customers. NIMs of the periphery banks have been relatively stable throughout 2012, having been supported by the interest income from their LTRO-funded holdings of sovereign bonds. Although some U.S. banks have been able to offset NIM pressures by writing back some of their loan loss reserves (as asset quality continued to improve), there will be less scope for this strategy in the future.

The weak economic environment is likely to lead to further worsening in asset quality, and the resulting larger provisions may absorb an increasingly large share of already weak operating earnings. Banks that are more exposed to economies with poor growth prospects are more vulnerable to a further deterioration in asset quality. Some banks (mainly from the euro area periphery) have both low levels of buffers and exposures to weak economies, making them most vulnerable to a downturn. In some cases, the asset quality concerns are exacerbated by the fact that banks are holding hard-to-value assets (for example, commercial real estate exposures). Some of these assets have been moved to asset management companies (for example, in the case of Spain).

Furthermore, litigation risks continue to be a headwind to earnings for major banks in Europe and the United States. The LIBOR scandal and several other high profile fines and lawsuits related to compliance failures and misselling allegations continue to weigh on banks' profits. In the United States, banks continue to work through legacy mortgage issues that have resulted in litigation and mortgage repurchase liabilities.

Uncertainty over asset valuations and risk weights is reinforcing investor concerns. Bank asset quality and capital adequacy tend to be scrutinized by investors, especially when the economy is weak. If these are hard to ascertain from reported data, for example, due to differences in disclosure in financial statements, investors demand higher risk premiums, which further raises bank funding costs. Two major issues are of concern: *First,* regulators and market participants are concerned that some banks may be engaging in lender forbearance. In some cases, this is done to smooth the recognition of impaired loans, especially if banks have low profits and thin capital buffers, or where legal frameworks make it difficult to resolve problem loans. Even if it ultimately benefits both the lender and the borrower, lender forbearance can make it difficult to assess the quality of assets and to estimate the full scale of potential losses and required provisions and capital. *Second,* there are significant uncertainties around the calculation of risk-weighted assets. The dispersion of risk weights across banks is too wide to be fully explained by accounting, regulatory, and business model differences.

Cyclical and structural pressures force banks to change their funding models. Although large institutions continue to play a dominant role in the global banking system, markets and regulators are putting pressure on banks to become smaller, simpler, and more focused on servicing their home markets. Banks are altering the liabilities side of their balance sheet to reduce their use of wholesale, short-term, and cross-border funding. This is in response to: (1) the wholesale funding runs during the crisis; (2) the higher cost of wholesale funding, particularly where there is the prospect of bailing-in senior debt holders; (3) Basel III liquidity requirements (which favour more stable funding sources); and (4) the increased incidence of regulatory ring-fencing of bank liquidity and capital along national lines (in part because of the slow progress in establishing robust cross-border resolution frameworks). For U.S. banks, strong deposit growth and weak loan demand have helped to reduce their reliance on wholesale funding. For some European banks, where reliance on wholesale funding is much higher, these structural pressures are more acute.

Some internationally active banks are increasingly aiming to match their assets and liabilities on a country-by-country basis in a move to make their subsidiaries self-funded over time, which in a number of cases is encouraged by regulators. This trend has been playing out at a faster pace in the euro area, in part because of concerns about redenomination risk, but it is also happening in other advanced economies, and the trend is viewed as hard to reverse, which can potentially increase and entrench financial fragmentation. Furthermore, the transition to this new cross-border banking model may add to deleveraging pressures. For many banks, matching assets and liabilities on a country-by-country basis means that they would have to close larger deposit funding gaps. One way of closing the gaps is by raising deposits or other funding locally; another way is by reducing lending. Encouragingly, recent trends suggest that foreign subsidiaries of large EU banks (notably those operating in eastern Europe) have been fairly successful in raising local deposits.

In addition to greater regulatory scrutiny over intragroup cross-border transfers, new regulations are being put in place that require affiliates of foreign banks to hold more capital and liquidity locally. For example, the Federal Reserve has recently released proposals to require operations of foreign banks to establish a holding company structure over all bank and nonbank subsidiaries operating in the United States. These holding companies will be subject to the same capital and liquidity requirements as U.S. bank holding companies. These measures may cause some European banks to rethink the scale of their operations in the United States.

Regulatory changes as well as market pressures, are forcing banks to focus on fewer and less capital-intensive business lines. Pressures to raise the return on equity, which remains below the average cost of equity, and raise market valuations, which are still well below historical averages, are forcing banks to concentrate on cutting costs, exiting business lines where they do not have critical mass, and enhancing fee and commission income. Recent examples suggest that such a strategy is rewarded by shareholders. For instance, UBS's stock price rose 18 percent in two days following the announcement that it was cutting 10,000 jobs and exiting the fixed income business; Citigroup and Barclays made similar moves.

Operational restructuring by banks to increase efficiency, while a welcome development, could still have negative consequences as banks pull out of certain activities. Fewer players in any given market entails higher concentration risk. It also means that market liquidity could decline, or would at least be dependent on a smaller number of banks, potentially exacerbating asset volatility particularly in a crisis.

As a result, European banks continue to de-risk and deleverage their balance sheets. Large EU banks have continued to reshape their balance sheets via capital raising, liability management and asset reduction, with cutbacks in total assets broadly on track with the baseline scenario. This has helped to strengthen banks' financial positions, and also confirms that the worst-case outcome has been avoided thanks to swift policy responses.

However, banks have reduced their balance sheets in very different ways. Some have focused on asset disposals. For example, German banks created noncore units to gradually wind down legacy assets (trading, commercial real estate, shipping and public finance exposures); French banks completed their 2011 adaptation plans to reduce U.S. dollar funding needs and commercial and investment banking exposures, and also sold their Greek subsidiaries; U.K. banks have largely reduced noncore assets (trading portfolios and loans in Ireland, the United Kingdom, and the United States), and large Italian and Spanish banks reduced domestic lending, while expanding foreign loans (mainly in emerging market economies where deposit levels have grown) and domestic government bond holdings. In addition, Italian banks have reduced other assets.

As banks continue to reduce their balance sheets, in addition to cutting back non-core assets, banks may need to restructure or shrink their loan books, which may be more challenging. As the credit quality of loan books continues to deteriorate, especially in the euro area periphery, banks with relatively low capital buffers will be less able to crystallize losses, and therefore, less able to reduce the drag from impaired assets on new lending. Furthermore, the lack of a well-functioning market for distressed bank assets may force banks to reduce their loan books by rolling off rather than selling loans, and in some cases forbear by amending the terms of nonperforming loans, which could consume capital and put a drag on banks' ability to extend new loans to productive sectors.

As European banks have reduced foreign lending, other banks with stronger balance sheets have stepped in to fill in the gap. Asian and North American banks' foreign claims continued to grow. For example, Japanese banks' foreign credit recovered steadily in 2010; the growth was concentrated in syndicated lending in Asia, where they were well positioned to capture market share as European banks reduced their exposures. As a result, foreign exposures of the top three Japanese banks rose to almost 20 percent of their loan book.

The foreign expansion of Japanese banks has increased their reliance on external funding, which involves foreign currency liquidity risk that has to be managed. Foreign credit provided by Japanese banks is denominated largely in dollars. And although Japanese banks have raised additional foreign currency funding in the form of retail or corporate deposits, they also had to raise this funding in wholesale markets or rely on the swap market to swap yen deposits into dollars. The Japanese banking system's external funding position—the difference between its foreign assets and liabilities—has thus increased to $1.6 trillion. In contrast, the Australian, U.K., and U.S. systems all have substantial net surplus positions, while other European banks have cut their funding position from $1.5 trillion to below zero by reducing their U.S. dollar lending. Japanese banks' relatively large external funding position exposes them to shocks to the availability, maturity, and cost of foreign currency funding. That said, Japanese banks have shown resilience to such shocks in the past and are limiting the liquidity risks by matching the maturities of external assets and liabilities and by holding highly liquid foreign government securities.

The risks of European bank deleveraging are being either too large, too fast, or too concentrated in a few sectors or economies. European banks have made progress in de-risking and deleveraging their balance sheets; but the process is not complete. Policymakers need to encourage financial institutions to continue deleveraging in a "healthy" and growth-friendly manner, that is, by raising equity levels as well as by cutting business lines that are no longer viable.

Moreover, given the risk of a prolonged economic slowdown, the necessary adjustment may be delayed. Banks with weak capital buffers may be more reluctant to recognize losses, causing them to restrain lending to viable firms, which would reinforce weakness in the corporate sector and lead to further deterioration of credit quality of bank loans. Hence, a comprehensive set of policies is needed to address both weak banks and weak nonfinancial firms.

Outside Europe, banks are also under pressure to change their business models to improve profitability. New financial stability risks (related to rapid cross-border expansions, increased concentration in certain markets, and shift of certain financial intermediation activities from banking sector to nonbank sector) may emerge as a result of these changes and require monitoring.

THE EURO AREA CRISES: ACUTE RISKS HAVE DECLINED, MUCH LIES AHEAD

Acute short-term stability risks have declined in the euro area on the back of strong policy action. Prices and liquidity conditions in sovereign, bank, and corporate debt markets have improved dramatically, and insurance has soared. However, medium-term risk reamin, reflecting a weak economic outlook, persistent fragmentation, and structural challenges. Some banks in the euro area periphery, consisting of Cyprus, Greece, Holand, Italy, Portugal, and Spain, remain challenged by deleveraging pressures, still-elevated funding costs, deteriorating asset quality, and weak profits. Corporation in the predatory are directly affected by bank deliberating, cyclical headwinds, and their own debt overchanges. More work need to be done with short-term to improve bank and capital market functioning while moving steadily toward a full-fledged banking union.

Policy action have urgently reduced near-term perception of total risk. The ECB's announcement of the Outright Monetary Transactions (OMT) programme—together with the decision to support additional debt relief for Greece and agreement on the Single Supervisory Mechanism (SSM)—has greatly reduced redenomination tail risks. In response, external investors have moved from short to long positions on the periphery. During 2012:Q3, the foreign investor share in total government debt in Italy and Spain stabilized at about 35 percent and 30 percent, respectively. Although foreign banks continued to reduce exposures to Italian and Spanish government debt, the process slowed down considerably in 2012:Q3. At the same time, foreign nonbanks started to increase their holdings of Italian and Spanish bonds. Even so, the foreign share is still estimated to be far below the levels seen in mid-2011, before market pressures emerged.

Though market liquidity conditions are not yet back to normal, they have improved. Correspondingly, the spread of short-term (two-year) periphery sovereign bonds over German bunds has fallen back toward January 2011 levels. The relief for short-term debt markets provided by the OMT pledge has been partly transmitted further along the curve. Still, markets continue to reflect medium-term challenges: the longterm (10-year) spread has reversed only about half of its previous widening, while Target imbalances are declining at a slower pace, with about one-fifth of the previous widening reversed so far.

Private funding markets have reopened for periphery borrowers. The reduction in perceived risks was felt in credit markets more broadly, benefiting even some lower-tier periphery companies. The demand for bank debt has strengthened, compressing spreads and prompting a surge in issuance. More than 32.7 billion (gross) was issued by banks and other firms in January 2013 alone. Excluding bank self-funded issues, that was the strongest month since the run in February 2012 in the wake of the ECB's longer-term refinancing operations (LTROs). Of this amount, lower-tier bank and corporate issuers accounted for about one-fourth. This includes all issuers from Cyprus, Greece, Ireland, and Portugal, and high-yield issuers from Italy and Spain. Some larger Italian and Spanish companies have used the surge in bond issuance to replace bank loans, while some banks have started to repay LTRO funds early.

However, the "virtuous dynamic" prompted by the OMT programme has slowed, while adverse events could still revive market stress. Although investors and officials appear comfortable that the ECB's OMT remains a virtual programme, this dynamic could change. In particular, political developments could complicate implementation, as underscored by the uncertainty surrounding the election outcome in Italy. And while prospects for sovereign financing in 2013 have brightened, net financing needs remain challenging for some countries. Assuming that domestic investors keep exposures to their own sovereigns constant (as some of them indicated), foreign investors will need to continue to increase their allocations to sovereign bonds to facilitate government financing at more moderate yields.

Furthermore, there are concerns that if growth and fiscal outturns in the periphery do not improve, or if progress on euro area architecture reform stalls, recent improvements in market conditions could be reversed. A lasting improvement in growth and fiscal trajectories across the periphery hinges on the successful implementation of structural reforms. Some market participants are concerned that progress on this front could fall short if political support for reform wanes.

The potential for contagion from developments in Cyprus is an important reminder of the fragility of market confidence. Although the adverse reaction to increased risk has not been intense in all markets, there was a renewed flight to safe assets and a selloff in some euro area assets. The clearest impact has been on those markets with direct links to Cyprus—notably Greek government bonds and Greek and Russian bank stocks. Slovenian government bonds were also affected. Other effects have included higher funding costs for euro area periphery banks and a selloff in euro area bank equities. The impact of recent events on periphery euro area sovereign spreads was limited, likely reflecting the existence of backstops (including the ECB's OMT).

Despite substantial improvements in funding conditions, fragmentation between the core and the periphery persists. Although the divergence between wholesale funding costs for core and periphery borrowers has partially reversed, the gap has not fully closed. This partly reflects investor concerns about the quality of bank assets and increased asset encumbrance: issuance of covered bonds and other asset-backed securities declined in the past year, while some banks in the periphery have seen a marked rise in the cost of collateral-backed debt issuance. While the previous declines in foreign investors' claims on periphery sovereigns have begun to reverse, the cross-border banking market in the euro area remains deeply fragmented. Some of the retrenchment in cross-border bank claims may be encouraged by regulatory ring-fencing.

Fragmentation, in turn, impairs credit transmission to the real economy. Recent market improvements are only just beginning to feed through to the cost and availability of credit for productive sectors of the periphery economies. The differences between periphery and core in terms of bank lending rates and corporate borrowing costs continue to persist, as bank repair is still incomplete and funding costs are higher for banks and sovereigns in the periphery. Credit to the real economy remains restrained (especially in the periphery and to SMEs), reinforcing divergence in economic outcomes.

Private nonfinancial sector deleveraging could impede the recovery and raise financial strains, as corporations face high debt burdens in an environment of lower growth and higher interest rates.

The transmission mechanism is still impaired and credit conditions remain weak in the periphery. This weakness in periphery lending is arguably due to credit supply constraints—as banks face balance sheet pressures—combined with low demand from potential borrowers (given the anemic economic environment and, in many cases, with balance sheets burdened by high debt levels). Disentangling the demand-side from the supply-side drivers of credit developments is not straightforward. The relationship between credit demand and supply is complex. For example, cutbacks in credit supply raise the cost of borrowing and lead to lower demand. Furthermore, both supply constraints and falling demand can adversely affect the real economy, which in turn can lower demand and tighten supply further. A weaker economic outlook can also worsen the quality of bank and borrower balance sheets, further affecting the supply and demand for credit.

But even if demand were seen as driving the weakness in credit, barriers to supply would need to be removed so that banks do not hold back the economic recovery once it takes hold.

In any case, there is some evidence to suggest that credit supply is tight in the periphery.

i) Interest rates on new bank lending are significantly higher in the periphery than in core countries. This divergence reflects, in part, the increased margin that banks require to compensate them for the greater risk of lending in the periphery. But it also reflects the increased cost of new funding as institutions have made less use of official funding and have competed both among themselves and with retail sovereign debt holders for term deposits. The increase in term deposits comes at a price, as interest rates on them are higher than those on sight deposits.

ii) Lending trends also provide evidence. The recent euro area bank lending trends show a continued tightening in bank lending conditions, as well as a further weakening in demand for loans. There has been an increase through 2011–12 in the proportion of Italian and Spanish SMEs that wanted a bank loan but did not obtain most or all of the credit for which they had applied.

For the euro area core, "macro risk" is the main driver of recent credit conditions, as ECB policies have substantially reduced banks' balance sheet constraints and their cost of funding.

The high cost and restricted supply of credit to small and medium enterprises (SMEs) impede recovery. The combination of high bank funding costs and increased risk premiums on lending has impaired the credit transmission mechanism. For example, interest rates on new periphery SME loans are now priced at spreads over the ECB policy rate that are significantly higher than in the past. Loan originations for SMEs have also been falling more sharply than for large firms, suggesting that

SMEs are bearing the brunt of the reduction in bank credit. This is particularly worrisome given that SMEs typically lack access to capital markets.

The debt overhang poses challenges for the corporate sector. Firms in the euro area periphery have built a sizable debt overhang during the credit boom, on the back of high profit expectations and easy credit conditions. The debt overhang is defined a debt burden that generates such large interest payments that it prevents firms from undertaking profitable investment projects that would enable them to organically reduce debt over time. The size of the debt overhang is estimated as the required debt reduction such that interest expense declines and net free cash flows become positive. While the construction sectors in Ireland and Spain were at the epicenter of the crisis, the increase in leverage was broad-based across the periphery. Firms in these countries now face the challenge of reducing the debt overhang in an environment of lower growth and higher interest rates, in part related to financial fragmentation in the euro area.

The size of the debt overhang is particularly large in Italy, Portugal, and Spain. To achieve nonnegative net free cash flows in the medium-term, corporate leverage in these countries would have to be reduced by 6–10 percent of assets under the baseline and to converge to the levels in the core under the downside scenario with continued fragmentation and lower growth.

There is urgent need for restructuring and consolidation in the periphery corporate sector, where a range of measures will be needed to smooth deleveraging. While large diversified companies may sell assets—including foreign units—to reduce leverage, potential profitable sales are likely to negatively affect their revenues and earnings going forward. Furthermore, additional cuts in operating costs, dividends, and capital expenditures may also be required, posing additional risks to growth and market confidence. Thus, a move to the upside scenario with reduced fragmentation and productivity gains from restructuring will be critical to lower funding costs and support orderly deleveraging. In special cases, where the debt overhang issue is systemic, a mandatory suspension of dividends can be considered as a policy option, as well as principal reduction workouts.

QUESTIONS

1. Discuss the motives that led to the growth of international banking.
2. What is syndicate lending? Why do banks sometimes prefer this form of lending?
3. Describe the possible differences in risk between a purely domestic bank and an international bank.
4. Offer your own opinion on why banks are unable to recognise the potential financial problems of developing countries when they extend loans to these countries.
5. Why were large commercial banks among the first institutions to develop strong interest in assessing and quantifying country risks?
6. Explain the organisational factors of international banking.

7. Discuss the various settlement system used in the payment mechanism among developed financial systems.
8. Discuss the factors behind the globalisation of international banking and changing role of financial instruments.
9. Discuss the main issues of concern in international banking.
10. Critically examine the recent trends in international banking growth.
11. Identify the factors that would likely to be used by banks to assess the creditworthiness of a government and of a corporation. Why are these assessments by banks not always accurate?
12. Disucss the global banking crises' impact on international bank funding.
13. Disucss the concept of deleveraging in the context of banking.

27

REFORMING THE INTERNATIONAL BANKING

INTRODUCTION

The financial crisis severely tested banking systems. The dominant role of the choices and decisions of financial institutions and other economic agents in determining global liquidity has important implications for the design of policy frameworks aimed at ensuring financial stability. *First,* policies need to take into account the full liquidity cycle – liquidity surges and their associated contributions to systemic risk as well as liquidity shortages or disruptions in the provision of private liquidity. *Second,* policy frameworks need to be sufficiently robust to uncertainty about the exact sources and impact of global liquidity surges and sufficiently flexible to address sudden shortages in liquidity conditions at the global level.

FROM BASEL II TO BASEL III

Policy responses to surges in global liquidity are closely associated with the financial reform agenda. Post-crisis, the global initiatives to strengthen the financial regulatory system are driven by the political leadership of the G20 under the auspices of the Financial Stability Board (FSB) and the Basel Committee on Banking Supervision (BCBS). Immediately after the crisis, the Basel Committee, in July 2009, came out with certain measures, also called enhancement to Basel II or Basel II.5, to plug the loopholes in its capital rules, which were exploited to arbitrage capital by parking certain banking book positions in the trading book which required less capital.

These measures, under Pillar 1, include introduction of an incremental risk charge (IRC) for specific risk or credit risk in trading book under the internal models approach (IMA). Capital charge for securitisation of commercial real estate was increased and that for re-securitisation introduced. The Value-at- Risk (VaR)-based measure for capital charge for market risk under IMA has been substantially enhanced by including a stressed-VaR element. The overall capital requirement for the trading book is expected to rise by about 3 times. Pillar 2 has been strengthened by issuing guidance on firm-wide risk management; managing reputation risk and liquidity risk; improving valuation practices; and implementing sound stress testing practices. Appropriate additional disclosures complementing enhancements in Pillar 1 and 2 have also been introduced.

The Basel Committee and the FSB introduced a series of strong international measures, capped by the Basel III framework issued in December 2010 (see Box-1).

Box-1

Banking Supervision Reform – Basel III

(Strenthens microprudential regulation and supervision, and adds a macroprodential overlay that includes capital buffers)

	Capital Pillar 1		Pillar 2	Pillar 3	
	Capital	*Risk coverage*	*Containing leverage*	*Risk management & supervision*	*Market discipline*
All Banks	**Quality and level of capital** Greater focus on concern equity. The minimum will be raised to 4.5% of risk-weighted assets, after deductions **"Gone concern" contingent capital** "Gone concern" capital proposal would requires contractual terms of capital instruments to include a allowing at the direction of the relevant authority write off the conversion to common shares if the bank is judged to be non-viable "Gone concern" contingent capital increases the contribution of the private sector to revolving future ban-king crises and thereby reduces moral hazard. **Capital conservation buffer** Comprising common equity 2.5% of risk- weighed assets, bringing the total common equity standard to 7% constraint on a bank's discretionary distributions will be imposed when banks fall into the buffer range. **Countercyclical buffer** Imposed within a range of 0-2.5% comprising common equity, when authorities judge credit growth is resulting in an unacceptable build up of systematic risk.	**Securitisations** Strengthens the capital treatment for certain complex securitisations requires banks to conduct more rigo rous credit analyses of externally rated securitiza tion exposures. **Trading book** Significantly higher capital for treading and derivatives activities, as well as comp lex securitization of a stressed value-at-risk framework to help mitigate procyclicality. **Counterparty credit risk** Substantial strengthening of the counterparty credit risk framework. Includes more stringent requirements for measuring for banks to use central counterparties for derivatives, and higher capital for inter-financial sector exposures.	**Leverage ratio** A Non-risk-based leverage ratio that includes off-balance sheet exposures will serve as a backstop to the risk-based capital requirement Also helps contain system wide build up of leverage.	Address firm-wide governance and risk management capturing the risk of off-balance sheet exposures and securitization activities, managing risk concentrations; providing incentives for banks to better manage risk and returns over the long term sound compensation practices, stress testing, accounting standard for financial instruments corporate governance, and supervisory colleges.	**Revised Pillar 3 Disclosures requirements** The requirements introduced relate to securitization expoures & sponsorship of off-balance sheet vehicles Enhanced disclosures on the detail of the components of regulatory capital and their reconciliation to the reported accounts will be required, including a comprehensive explanation of how a bank calculates its regulatory capital ratios.
SIFIs	In addition to meeting the Basel III requirements, global systemically important financial institutions (SIFIS) must have higher loss absorbency capacity to reflect the greater risks that they pose to the financial system. The Committee has developed a methodology that includes both quantitative indicators and qualitative elements to identify global SIFIs. The additional loss absorbency requirements are to be met a progressive Common Equity Tier 1 (CETI) capital requirement ranging from 1% to 2.5% depending on a bank's systemic importance.				

"Basel III" is a comprehensive set of reform measures, developed by the Basel Committee on Banking Supervision, to strengthen the regulation, supervision and risk management of the banking sector. These measures aim to:

i) improve the banking sector's ability to absorb shocks arising from financial and economic stress, whatever the source
ii) improve risk management and governance
iii) strengthen banks' transparency and disclosures.

The reforms target:

i) bank-level, or microprudential regulation, which will help raise the resilience of individual banking institutions to periods of stress.
ii) Macroprudential, system wide risks that can build up across the banking sector as well as the procyclical amplification of these risks over time. These two approaches to supervision are complementary as greater resilience at the individual bank level reduces the risk of system wide shocks.

BASEL III AND FINANCIAL STABILITY

The key elements of Base-III framework are summarized in Table-1 to provide an overview of the various measures taken by the Committee.

As the source of credit intermediation between lenders and borrowers, banks provide essential domestic and international financial services to consumers, businesses and government. A strong and resilient banking system is thus the foundation for sustainable economic growth. Throughout history, however, financial crises have occurred at one time or another in every region of the world and for a wide range of reasons. The most recent crisis, in 2007–09, revealed fundamental shortcomings in the operation and regulation of the banking system in many countries.

The crisis had its roots in the United States and spread primarily to other advanced economies, having originated in the imprudent use and inadequate regulation of complex securitisations by large banks. However, in a broader sense, the causes and evolution of the crisis reflect deficiencies that are typical of financial crises in general: investors chasing yield, too much credit, weak underwriting standards, an underpricing of risk, excessive leverage, and contagion.

TABLE-1

Key Objectives and Features of the Basel III Framework

Capital Standards

I. Raising Capital Base

Objective – Ensuring *quality, consistency* in definition across jurisdictions and *transparency* in disclosure of capital base.

Measures – I.1 Tier 1 capital predominantly held as common shares and retained earnings. I.2 Remainder of Tier 1 capital comprising of subordinate instruments with fully discretionary non-cumulative dividends and with no maturity date or incentive to redeem; I.3 Innovative hybrid instruments with an incentive to redeem would be phased out.

II. Enhancing Risk Coverage

Objective – Strengthening risk coverage of capital framework especially for on – and off – balance sheet items and derivative exposures.

Measures II.1. Introduction of stressed Value-at-Risk (VAR) capital requirement based on a continuous 12 - month period of significant financial stress; II.2. Higher capital requirements for re-securitisation in banking and trading book; I. Raising Capital Base

Objective – Ensuring *quality, consistency* in definition across jurisdictions and *transparency* in disclosure of capital base.

Measures – I.1 Tier 1 capital predominantly held as common shares and retained earnings. I.2 Remainder of Tier 1 capital comprising of subordinate instruments with fully discretionary non-cumulative dividends and with no maturity date or incentive to redeem; I.3 Innovative hybrid instruments with an incentive to redeem would be phased out.

II. Enhancing Risk Coverage

Objective – Strengthening risk coverage of capital framework especially for on – and off – balance sheet items and derivative exposures.

Measures II.1. Introduction of stressed Value-at-Risk (VAR) capital requirement based on a continuous 12 - month period of significant financial stress; II.3. Introduction of capital charge for potential mark-to-market losses related to credit valuation adjustment risks associated with deterioration in creditworthiness of counterparty; II.4. Strengthening standards for collateral management. Banks with large illiquid derivative position to a counterparty would have to apply longer margining periods for determining regulatory capital requirements.

III. Supplement Risk-based Capital Requirements with Leverage Measure

Objective – Containing leverage in the banking sector thereby mitigating risk related to deleveraging.

Measures – III.1. Introduction of a simple transparent and independent measure of leverage, comparable across jurisdictions by adjusting for differences in accounting standards.

IV. Reduce Pro-cyclicality Through Counter-cyclical Buffers

Objective – Dempening pro-cyclical movements within the banking system by making it a "shock absorber" rather than a transmitter of risk to the real economy.

Measures – IV.1. Movement to a relatively less pro-cyclical Expected Loss (EL) approach as against existing Incurred Loss (IL) and updation of supervisory guidance consistent with the EL approach; IV.2. Creation of capital conservation buffers above the minimum capital and adjust the buffer range during periods of excess credit growth.

Liquidity Standards

I. Minimum Liquidity Standards

Objective – Introducing internationally harmonized and robust liquidity standards since stronger capital requirements may be necessary but not a sufficient condition for banking sector stability.

Measures – I.1. Introduction of liquidity coverage ratio to ensure sufficient high quality liquid resources to cope with an acute stress scenario lasting one month; 1.2 introduction of net stable finding ratio, which has a longer time horizon of one year to provide sustainable maturity structure of assets and liabilities.

II. Quantitative Liquidity Metrics

Objective – Imparting consistency in quantitative metrics used by supervisors to capture liquidity risks.

Measures – II. 1. Introduction of metrics, which include among others, contractual maturity mismatch, concentration of funding, available unencumbered assets and liquidity coverage ratio by currency.

Reference:

"Basel III: A Global Regulatory Framework for More Resilient Banks and Banking System," Bank for International Settlements, June 2011.

Given the speed at which crises can arise and be transmitted around the globe, and given ever more rapid financial innovation, banks in all countries need to hold higher capital and liquidity buffers to protect the global banking system and economy from unforeseen risks. Unfortunately, memories tend to be short, and significant risks to the banking sector generally emerge after a period of complacency bred of apparent calm. Thus, the work to strengthen banking systems must be carried through now, when the crisis is still fresh in people's minds and policymakers and the wider public understand the urgency of an effective response.

With its release of the Basel III rules on 16 December 2010, the Basel Committee on Banking Supervision set out new global regulatory standards on bank capital adequacy and liquidity to correct the deficiencies revealed by the crisis. Some of the new rules represent a significant overhaul of existing global standards, others introduce rules where none previously existed. Taken together, they strengthen capital and liquidity regulation to promote more resilience in global banking. Thus fortified by Basel III, the international regulatory framework will better shield the financial sector from the next crisis, whatever its origin, and reduce the risk of spillover from the financial sector to the real economy. As risk-taking in the financial sector resumes, banks have started to accumulate capital and to adapt their funding strategies and broader business models to the new regulatory framework, which will call on them to target lower, more stable returns on equity.

HOW THE FINANCIAL CRISIS IS SHAPING REGULATORY REFORM

The severity of the crisis owed much to the fact that the banking sector in many countries had taken on too much risk without a commensurate increase in capital. Furthermore, this inadequate *level* of capital was of insufficient *quality*, as the latter had gradually eroded. Basel III tightens capital requirements, encompasses a broader array of risks, and explicitly addresses macroprudential aspects of banking system stability.

Bank Capital

The leverage ratio will provide a backstop to the risk-basedmeasures and help curb the build-up of excessive leverage. Basel III substantially raises the quality as well as the quantity of capital, with a much greater emphasis on common equity (Box-2). During the crisis, losses reduced banks' common equity. However, some banks maintained deceptively high ratios of Tier 1 capital to risk-weighted assets through the inclusion of other forms of financial instruments in the capital base. Moreover, non-common Tier 1 capital instruments often did not share in banks' losses through reduced coupon or principal payments and so did not contribute to maintaining the institutions as going concerns in any meaningful way. The artificially high Tier 1 risk-based ratios also meant that banks were building up high levels of leverage. Basel III therefore also introduces a simple leverage ratio that provides a backstop to the risk-based regime. The supplementary ratio, which is a measure of

BOX -2

Capital Instruments

The global banking system entered the crisis with an insufficient level of high-quality capital. The crisis revealed an inconsistency in how regulatory capital is defined across jurisdictions and the lack of disclosure that would have enabled the market to fully assess and compare the quality of banks' capital. In response, Basel III introduces a harmonised definition of capital that comprises the following components:

- **Common Equity Tier 1** – consists of the bank's common shares and retained earnings less regulatory adjustments (eg the deduction of goodwill). This component of capital fully absorbs losses while the bank remains a going concern. It is therefore the highest-quality component of a bank's capital. A key element of the new definition of capital is the greater focus on Common Equity Tier 1.
- **Additional Tier 1 capital** – consists of preferred shares and other capital instruments that comply with a set of criteria to ensure they can absorb losses while the issuing bank remains a going concern. These criteria include requirements that the instruments be subordinated, have fully discretionary non-cumulative dividends or coupons and have neither a maturity date nor an incentive to redeem.
- **Tier 2 capital** – consists of debt instruments that comply with a set of criteria to ensure they are able to absorb losses when a bank fails (ie when it has become a "gone concern"). These criteria include requirements that the instruments be subordinated, have a minimum original maturity of at least five years and contain no step-ups or other incentives to redeem. Regulatory recognition of these instruments is amortised over the five years before maturity.

During the crisis, a number of distressed banks were rescued by the injection of public sector funds in the form of common equity and other forms of Tier 1 capital. While this had the effect of supporting depositors, it also meant that certain capital instruments did not absorb losses. Therefore, in addition to the characteristics noted above, instruments in Additional Tier 1 and in Tier 2 must have a feature ensuring that they can be written off or converted to common equity when the issuing bank reaches the point of non-viability (ie the point at which the bank is unable to support itself in the private market) as determined by the relevant authority.

The Basel III definition of capital phases out innovative hybrid capital instruments, which provided an incentive to redeem through features such as step-up clauses. It also eliminates Tier 3 capital, which was short-term subordinated debt that was previously permitted to cover market risk.

In addition to the Basel III elements of capital, certain other instruments are being considered in the context of systemically important banks:

- **Contingent capital** (also called cocos) – debt instruments that convert to Common Equity Tier 1 capital through a write-off or conversion to common shares before a bank reaches the point of non-viability.
- **Bail-in-able debt** – debt instruments that convert to Common Equity Tier 1 capital through a write- off or conversion to common shares when a bank reaches the point of non-viability.

a bank's Tier 1 capital as a percentage of its assets plus off-balance sheet exposures and derivatives, will serve as an additional safeguard against attempts to "game" the risk-based requirements, and will mitigate model risk (Table-2). By helping contain the build-up of excessive leverage, the leverage ratio will also complement other macroprudential measures, discussed below, to reduce systemic risk.

Turning to the minimum capital requirements, the higher minimums for common equity and tier 1 capital will be phased in beginning in 2013, and will become effective at the beginning of 2015. The schedule will be as follows:

- The minimum common equity and Tier 1 requirements will increase from the current 2% and 4% levels to 3.5% and 4.5%, respectively, at the beginning of 2013.
- The minimum common equity and Tier 1 requirements will be 4% and 5.5%, respectively, starting in 2014.
- The final requirements for common equity and Tier 1 capital will be 4.5% and 6%, respectively, beginning in 2015.

The 2.5% capital conservation buffer, which will be comprised of common equity and is in addition to the 4.5% minimum requirement, will be phased in progressively starting on 1 January 2016, and will become fully effective by 1 January 2019.

Finally, the leverage ratio will also be phased in. The test (the so-called "parallel run period") will begin in 2013 and run until 2017, with a view to migrating to a Pillar 1 treatment on 1 January 2018 based on review and appropriate calibration.

TABLE 2

STRENGTHENED CAPITAL FRAMEWORK: FROM BASEL II TO BASEL III

In percentage of risk-weighted assets	*Capital requirement*								*Additional macroprudential overlay*
	Common Equity			*Tier 1 capital*		*Total capital*		*Counter-cyclical buffer*	*Additional loss absorbing capacity for SIFI*
	Minimum	*Conservation buffer*	*Required*	*Minimum*	*Required*	*Minimum*	*Required*	*Range*	
Basel II	2			4		8			
Memo	*Equivalent to around 1% for an average international bank under the new definition*			*Evuivalent to around 2% for an average international bank under the new definition*					
Basel III New definition and calibration	4.5	2.5	7.0	6	8.5	8	10.5	0-2.5	Capital surcharge for SIFLs?

*Modalities to be defined.

Risk Coverage

The Basel Committee has also improved the risk coverage of the regulatory capital framework for capital market activities – a salient feature of the recent crisis, where trading exposures accounted for much of the build-up of leverage and were an important source of losses. (Trading exposures include positions in financial instruments and commodities held either with the intent to trade them or to hedge other trading activities. For purposes of calculating regulatory capital, such positions are subject to the Basel Committee's market risk rules and are said to be held in the "trading book"). Weak capital, excessive leverage and inadequate risk coverage prevented the banking system from fully absorbing systemic trading and credit losses. Nor could it cope with the reintermediation of large off-balance sheet exposures that had built up in the shadow banking system. Under Basel III, banks will have to hold more capital against their less liquid, credit-sensitive assets whose holding periods are much longer than traditional trading positions. Trading activities will also be subject to a stressed value-at-risk requirement. In addition, securitisation exposures in the trading book will be subject to capital charges more consistent with those for the banking book. Basel III also imposes higher capital requirements for counterparty credit risk, that is, for the amount that would be lost in the event of default by a counterparty to a financial contract. Moreover, Basel III creates incentives for banks to increase the use of central counterparties (CCPs) – financial institutions that act as intermediaries between market participants (see Box -3) – while ensuring that the risk arising from banks' exposures to CCPs is adequately capitalised.

BOX-3

The Role of Financial Market Infrastructures

Transactions in financial markets are conducted either on organised exchanges or over the counter (OTC). After the transaction is concluded, it is passed on to what is commonly known as the post-trade infrastructure. This process starts with the matching of the transaction and ends with its settlement. Settlement typically involves the transfer of money against the delivery of an asset or a financial instrument such as a derivative. In modern financial systems, settlement takes place in financial market infrastructures like large-value payment systems, securities settlement systems and central counterparties (CCPs).

The way these post-trade infrastructures are designed and how they function has important implications for financial stability because they can act as a channel through which disruptions can spread among financial market participants. Put differently, these infrastructures can serve as an important means to mitigate the risks arising from the "interconnectedness" of market participants and can reduce the risk of contagion.

The financial crisis revealed a striking weakness in the way important OTC derivatives, in particular credit default swaps, were processed in the post-trade phase. Many of these transactions were inadequately reported, and the bilateral exposures between counterparties were insufficiently collateralised.

Against this background, authorities from around the world are pushing for two significant changes in the post-trade infrastructure for OTC derivatives. Both should be implemented by the end of 2012.• First, OTC derivatives will need to be reported to a trade repository (TR). A TR is an electronic registry that keeps a record of all relevant details of an OTC derivative transaction over its lifetime. This information can be used in various ways by the reporting institutions, authorities and the public. If all trades are reported to a TR, and the information is made available to the relevant supervisory authorities, then these authorities will be able to attain an overall view of the OTC derivatives markets, including the most important (gross and net) positions taken by the major dealers in these markets. If TRs had existed before the crisis, the build-up of huge derivative positions, such as those at American International Group (AIG), would have been observed much earlier.

Second, clearing OTC derivatives through a CCP instead of bilaterally can bring about several benefits from a financial stability perspective. A CCP interposes itself between the two original counterparties of a financial transaction, becoming the buyer to the seller and the seller to the buyer. In other words, the CCP isolates the original counterparties from each other should one of them default. Thus, it makes financial institutions less interconnected. However, since risks become concentrated in the CCP, the CCP itself needs to be highly robust: it must protect itself against the default of one or more of its members. To that end, the CCP requires its members to adjust their collateral at the CCP at least daily in accordance with the price movements of their positions.

Liquidity

During the build-up to the crisis, many banks had operated with increasingly thin liquidity margins, placing undue reliance on easy access to market liquidity. At the height of the crisis, counterparties lost confidence in the liquidity of many banking institutions, severely straining their access to funding. Basel III addresses the liquidity deficiencies that the crisis laid bare. The internationally harmonised liquidity framework consists of two minimum regulatory standards: the liquidity coverage ratio (LCR) and the net stable funding ratio (NSFR). They have complementary objectives.

The LCR is designed to bolster the short-term resilience of a bank's liquidity risk profile by ensuring that it has high-quality liquid assets in sufficient quantity to survive a plausibly severe stress scenario lasting for 30 calendar days. The stress scenario, designed by the Basel Committee, incorporates many of the shocks experienced during the crisis. It includes a partial run-off of retail deposits, a partial or complete drying-up of wholesale funding sources, a need to post additional collateral due to a credit rating downgrade, and unscheduled draws on unused credit and liquidity facilities.

The NSFR is designed to promote resilience over a longer time horizon by creating additional incentives for banks to use more stable sources of funding on an ongoing basis. These standards complement the Committee's 2008 *Principles for sound liquidity risk management and supervision*, the implementation of which will be assessed in the near term.

Macroprudential Aspects

Basel III was designed to enhance both bank-specific soundness and wider banking sector stability. Thus, besides its firm-specific approaches, it incorporates macroprudential measures to explicitly address systemic risk.

During the crisis, mounting losses and the resulting strain on capital impaired banks' ability to lend – precisely at the time when economies were most in need of credit. This tendency for the financial system to amplify cyclical effects in the real economy, or procyclicality, combined with the interconnectedness of financial institutions that were considered too big to fail, exacerbated the crisis.

To help mitigate procyclicality in banking and the broader financial system, the new regulatory capital framework provides for building up capital in good times to levels above the minimum requirement. The resulting *capital conservation buffer* will help banks absorb losses during periods of financial and economic stress. As a bank's capital level moves closer to the minimum requirement, the conservation buffer imposes a progressively tightened constraint on the bank's discretionary distributions, such as dividends. Retaining a bigger proportion of earnings during a downturn will help ensure that capital remains available to support banks' ongoing business operations during the period of stress.

Basel III also introduces a *countercyclical buffer*. It is based on the observation that private sector credit growth that is out of line with historical experience often ultimately imposes losses on the lenders. The ratio of aggregate credit to GDP will serve as the reference for the build-up of the buffer, which will be implemented through restrictions on capital distributions identical to those that apply to the conservation buffer. Within countries, the authorities will impose this buffer only when they judge that credit growth is resulting in an unacceptable build-up of system-wide risk. Conversely, the buffer will be released when, in the judgment of the authorities, the capital can help absorb banking system losses that pose a risk to financial stability. The ability to run down the buffer without penalties will help reduce the risk of constraining the availability of credit.

The macroprudential elements of Basel III contribute significantly to the development of the broader macroprudential policy framework. The BIS has advocated such a framework for some time and is encouraged to see the growth of national and international efforts to develop and implement it (see Box-4). However, while much has been accomplished, more needs to be done, especially on practical implementation of the broad consensus now evident around the framework's core concepts.

BOX -4

National and International Progress on Implementing Macroprudential Policy Frameworks

One of the key lessons of the recent financial crisis is that regulatory policy must have an enhanced macroprudential orientation to comprehensively address systemic financial risks. The national and international work to develop such a macroprudential policy has intensified and continues to grow, building on conceptual efforts by the BIS since the apparent coining of the term "macroprudential" by the Cooke Committee, the forerunner of the Basel Committee, in 1979.

Recent initiatives in a number of international forums, have aided the formation of a clear consensus regarding the key features of an effective macroprudential framework. These include:

- effective integration of supervisory information, market intelligence and aggregate indicator data;
- recognition of the importance of domestic and cross-border interlinkages across financial institutions and markets;
- macroprudential instruments matched to the particular risks or imbalances diagnosed;
- macroprudential policy responsibility assigned to an independent central agency or formal committee, either within the central bank or involving the central bank in a key role;
- clarity of mandate, adequacy of powers and strong accountability; and
- clear macroprudential policy communications that link financial stability assessments to policy decisions and that manage public expectations about the capabilities of macroprudential policy. Formal macroprudential policy arrangements that will enable these principles to be realised have

been established or are well in train in many jurisdictions, including the United States, the

United Kingdom and the European Union. In many cases, operations under new arrangements have begun. The emerging frameworks feature advancements in the structured, regular diagnosis of systemic risk. For example, these diagnoses are conducted at the international level by the Committee on the Global Financial System (CGFS), the Financial Stability Board (FSB) Standing Committee on the Assessment of Vulnerabilities, and the IMF-FSB Early Warning Exercise; and national financial stability reports are progressively strengthening their support of macroprudential policy. Basel III incorporates macroprudential capital elements, and many jurisdictions continue to accumulate practical experience with macroprudential instruments such as loan-to-value ratio caps and reserve requirements.

The powers, tools and accountability requirements for macroprudential policy are either well defined or in an advanced stage of development. The imperative now is to get actual policy operations up and running. To do so, key operational issues must be resolved, including the selection, design and calibration of instruments, the translation of risk indicators to instrument settings, and arranging for efficient decision-making by committees encompassing diverse policy interests and knowledge. In short, the development of macroprudential policy is moving from conceptual issues of design to practical questions of implementation.

The more technical phase of macroprudential policy development is being facilitated by increasingly useful data generated by the growing number of actual macroprudential interventions and improvements to statistical coverage. Nonetheless, a substantial amount of trial and error is likely to be needed for the time being, given the still-limited history of macroprudential policy usage. Sharing of practical experiences among macroprudential policymakers, including through the BIS and FSB processes, will promote the development of the international dimension of macroprudential policy and the refinement of national frameworks.

IMPACT OF THE NEW REQUIREMENTS

A stronger, safer banking system allocates credit more efficiently, reduces the risk of a costly financial crisis and stabilises the environment for long-term business decisions. These benefits will begin to be reaped when the reforms are implemented. But the process of implementing the new framework will also impose some costs on banks and their customers as banks adjust their balance sheets and business models.

How much adjustment will be needed? The answer varies substantially across institutions and jurisdictions. In some economies, particularly those affected by the financial crisis, banks are still rebuilding capital and running off certain assets. In others, capital and liquidity levels already meet the new requirements. Regardless of their starting point, all economies will see some adjustment, given the significant qualitative and quantitative changes in supervisory definitions and approaches in Basel III.

OUTSTANDING ISSUES AND FUTURE WORK

The reform agenda now encompasses implementation of regulations complemented by more intensive and intrusive supervision; more extensive regulation and supervision of systemically important financial institutions (SIFIs) and development of effective cross-border resolution regimes; and broader consideration of non-bank financial firms and the shadow banking system. The Basel Committee is also reviewing the distinction between the regulatory banking book and the trading book.

Implementation

The Basel III rules need to be implemented in a timely and globally consistent manner. All member countries of the Basel Committee must now translate the Basel III texts into national regulations and legislation in time to meet the 2013 deadline.

The Committee and its oversight body of Governors and Heads of Supervision have consistently stated that the new standards will be introduced in a manner that does not impede the economic recovery. Thus, they have chosen a staggered timeline for implementation . For example, the July 2009 enhancements that strengthen regulatory capital and disclosure requirements are due to take effect no later than the end of 2011. The Basel III requirements themselves begin to take effect from the beginning of 2013 and will be phased in by 2019. This time frame includes an observation period to review the implications of the liquidity standards for individual banks, the banking sector and financial markets, with a view to addressing any unintended consequences. Similarly, the Committee will assess the impact of the leverage ratio on business models during the transition period in order to ensure that it achieves its objectives.

Like all Basel Committee standards, Basel III sets out *minimum* requirements, and the transitional arrangements are the deadlines for adopting the new standards. Countries should move faster if their banks are profitable and are able to apply the standards without having to restrict credit. Banks should not be permitted to increase their capital distributions simply because the deadline for achieving the minimum standards is still some way off, particularly if there are signs of growing macroeconomic risks and imbalances. Therefore, banks, for their part, must also begin to plan and to prepare.

Basel III is the core regulatory response to problems revealed by the financial crisis. Delay or weakening of the agreements would jeopardise financial stability and the robustness of the recovery over the long term. The full, timely and consistent implementation of *all* relevant standards by banks, along with rigorous enforcement by supervisors, is critical. Ultimately, both the official and the private sector will reap the benefits of a more stable financial system.

More Intensive and More Intrusive Supervision

Implementation efforts need to be supplemented by strong and enhanced supervision of individual banks. Strong supervision is needed to ensure that banks operate with capital levels, liquidity buffers and risk management practices that are commensurate with the risks taken. It must also address the consequences of financial innovation or risks of regulatory arbitrage that regulation cannot fully capture and, more generally, address the firm-level consequences of emerging risks and economic developments. National authorities must supervise in a more intensive and more intrusive fashion, especially for the largest and most complex banks. It will also be important to reinforce both the firm-specific and macroprudential dimensions of supervision and the way they interact.

In particular, as it carries forward its work on the implementation of the supervisory review process under Basel II (ie Pillar 2), the Basel Committee will foster the adoption of better supervisory practices.

Systemically Important Financial Institutions

Reducing the risks posed by financial institutions that are systemic in a global context (global systemically important financial institutions, or G-SIFIs) is a high priority for the international regulatory community. Basel III will enhance the quality and quantity of capital for all banks, but it does not fully address the externalities or spillover effects that G-SIFIs generate. Additional policy tools are necessary.

In November 2010, the FSB introduced a policy framework for these institutions. It recommends that G-SIFIs have higher loss-absorbing capacity to reflect the greater risks that they pose to the global financial system and that these institutions be subject to more intensive and coordinated resolution planning to reduce the probability and impact of their failure. This will help ensure that G-SIFIs can be closed or wound up quickly without destabilising the financial system or exposing the taxpayer to the risk of loss. In addition, the FSB calls for enhanced supervision of SIFIs that will be more intensive and effective than in the past.

The Basel Committee has developed quantitative indicators and qualitative elements to identify G-SIFIs. Work is also continuing on calibrating the additional loss absorbency that G-SIFIs should have, which could be met through some combination of common equity and contingent capital. The Committee will pursue this work in close cooperation with the FSB in the coming months.

More Effective Cross-border Bank Resolution

Higher loss-absorbing capacity for G-SIFIs and their effective resolution complement each other, but neither by itself is sufficient. The financial crisis also illustrated the importance of effective cross-border crisis management. The scope, scale and complexity of international financial transactions expanded at an unprecedented pace in the years preceding the crisis, while the tools and techniques for handling cross-border bank resolution have hardly evolved. Some of the events during the crisis revealed gaps in intervention techniques and, in many countries, a lack of appropriate resolution tools. Actions taken to resolve cross-border institutions during the crisis tended to be ad hoc, severely constrained by time, and dependent on a significant amount of official support.

In March 2010, the Basel Committee issued recommendations to strengthen national resolution powers and their cross-border implementation. The recommendations also covered firm-specific contingency planning for banks and home and host country authorities. Contagion can be reduced through risk mitigation mechanisms such as netting arrangements, collateralisation practices and the use of regulated central counterparties. These and other measures would help limit the market impact of a bank failure. The recommendations should lead to practical and credible plans to promote resilience in periods of severe financial distress and to facilitate a rapid resolution if necessary.

Building on the recommendations, the Basel Committee and the FSB are assessing progress in national and multinational efforts to enhance authorities' ability to manage and resolve distressed banking institutions in a manner that minimises disruptions to the financial system. The two bodies are evaluating legal and policy changes that would assist authorities in addressing future needs for crisis management and bank resolution.

Other Financial Sectors and Firms

Work to strengthen the regulation of SIFIs also needs to take account of differences across financial sectors. The FSB will review how the different regulatory measures fit together and whether there are inconsistencies or contradictions among the standards. For instance, deeper consideration is needed to assess the systemic importance of insurance companies and their role in financial stability. Insurance companies tend to have very different risk characteristics from those of banks, particularly regarding liquidity. Insurance company balance sheets also differ considerably across countries, for example in terms of the exposure to equity markets . Except for unusual cases such as American International Group (AIG) and the monoline insurers, these institutions proved broadly resilient during the financial crisis .

Hedge funds are another set of firms for which regulatory instruments and objectives differ sharply from those appropriate to banks. Despite major investment losses and outflows during the crisis, assets and leverage in the hedge fund sector have been broadly stable in the post-crisis period.

Shadow Banking

Shadow banking refers to credit intermediation that takes place outside the traditional banking system and involves maturity or liquidity transformation. Examples include the activities of money market funds, lending by unregulated finance companies, the issuance by specialised conduits and investment vehicles of commercial paper backed by longer-term assets, and the funding of securitisation activities through repo markets. The shadow banking system is, however, closely intertwined with the regulated system. Large banks typically draw substantial income from shadow banking activities and retain both direct and indirect credit and operational exposures to them through business lines such as loan origination, credit enhancements, backup liquidity lines, brokerage services, warehousing and credit insurance.

Shadow banking can perform valuable functions, including facilitating credit extension to certain sectors and providing banks and investors with a range of vehicles for managing credit, liquidity and maturity risks. However, the financial crisis demonstrated that shadow banking can also give rise to a number of risks in the broader financial sector. Some of these risks (such as those related to bank exposures through contingent credit lines) are being addressed through the improvements in bank regulation as well as through initiatives such as stronger regulation of credit rating agencies and money market funds. Other aspects are more difficult to deal with, especially those that call for a high degree of coordination across regulatory agencies, both within and across national boundaries. For example, judging the extent of liquidity mismatch in a bank-sponsored investment vehicle may require input from banking and market regulators in several jurisdictions.

Another lesson of the crisis was that activities in the shadow banking system need to be monitored in order to improve the ability of authorities and market participants to understand and anticipate the build-up of systemic risks. For example, in the years leading up to the crisis, US money market funds were important providers of funding to European banks. As a result, the disruption to the US money market fund sector in the aftermath of the Lehman Brothers bankruptcy in September 2008 had knock-on implications for European bank funding as well as for foreign exchange swap markets because the banks had used these instruments to swap their funding from dollars into local currencies. Existing statistical frameworks do not provide adequate information for assessing these risks .

Shadow banking's potential threats to financial stability must be reduced. First, firm-level disclosure and system-wide statistical frameworks need to be improved to ensure that the build-up of risks can be monitored properly. Improved data need to be accompanied by regular monitoring of those indicators that can be informative about the nature and locus of potential systemic risks. Second, gaps in regulation need to be identified and addressed, with the goal of reducing risky build-ups of leverage and maturity and liquidity mismatches, wherever these occur in the financial system. Rules that mitigate these risks in a consistent way across different entities and activities would reduce the scope for regulatory arbitrage. Given the global nature of many shadow banking activities, these efforts need to be coordinated at the international level.

Other Regulatory and Supervisory Initiatives

The financial crisis exposed significant flaws in the existing regulatory capital approach to market risk and trading activities. The most immediate shortcomings were remedied in the July 2009 enhancements to the regulatory capital framework. The Basel Committee is now also carrying out a fundamental review of the trading book framework and expects to conduct a public consultation on its findings around end-2011.

There are a number of key questions: how to remove opportunities for arbitrage across the banking book and trading book, how to define trading activities, and how to capture risks in trading books (and possibly market risk more generally). Under the current regime, banking book exposures are subject to capital charges against credit risk (through the Basel II credit risk framework) and also against foreign exchange risk and commodities risk (through the market risk framework). Positions in the trading book are subject to capital charges against interest rate risk, foreign exchange risk, equity position risk and commodities risk (through the market risk framework).

INTERACTION BETWEEN BANK- AND MARKET-BASED INTERNATIONAL INTERMEDIATION

It is widely recognised that bank-based and market-based activities perform complementary functions. Both are often inseparable aspects of financial intermediation that depend heavily on the resilience of market infrastructure. The same is true in the international dimension. For instance, banks invest retail deposits in foreign securities, lengthening the intermediation chain by involving markets. Or they issue debt in international markets to fund corporate loans and other assets. International banks' reliance on market-based funding increased at the beginning of the crisis as many of them had to fund the assets of off-balance sheet vehicles that they had taken onto their balance sheets. Conversely, markets rely on banks to alleviate issues arising from limited public information about financial counterparties, especially when these issues stem from international transactions. In addition, banks provide liquidity by engaging in market-making activities, providing credit lines or custodial services.

Financial frictions help underscore the functional differences between markets and banks and hence the circumstances under which each channel for intermediation may have a comparative advantage. Bank-based intermediation may offer risk-smoothing services – by maintaining, for example, a close link between prices and fundamentals – that financial markets cannot provide. Furthermore, long-term bank-client relationships may underpin the only source of credit when asymmetric information, moral hazard or financial frictions are particularly acute .That said, bank-based intermediation could also be suboptimal if it is associated with excessive rent-seeking by banks, to the detriment of economic growth .

Market-based intermediation has a comparative advantage when diversity of opinion is important. An example in this respect is the venture capital market, often promoted as a way to finance and develop high-tech industries. Diversity of opinion also helps to distil information and embed it in prices, facilitating efficient resource allocation, particularly in high-technology R&D-type industries . In addition, markets may enhance the overall degree of corporate governance prevailing in a particular economy and facilitate risk management . At the same time, more developed financial markets may disproportionately promote the growth of industrial sectors that are relatively more in need of external finance . In addition, the market-based system is only accessible to larger companies and tends to be more volatile.

The complementarity of banks and markets goes hand in hand with a deepening and widening of the network of bank-market relations. This is likely to improve risk-sharing. At the same time, however, the strong interconnectedness of institutions and markets may also enhance the propagation of shocks across borders. This raises the question of which institutions and markets should be included in the regulatory perimeter and highlights the need for international cooperation . International cooperation should seek to restrain regulatory arbitrage by ensuring that banks and markets that perform similar functions receive similar regulatory treatment.

Long-term Developments

Functional differences between banks and markets help to illuminate how the balance between bank- and market-based intermediation evolves in individual countries (or regions). When a country is at an early stage of its economic and financial development, it typically relies heavily on international sources of intermediation.(Financial systems that are at an early stage of development are typically dominated by bank-based financial intermediation). Since it is exactly in such\ circumstances that financial frictions – associated with transactions in different currencies, across jurisdictions and time zones – are most acute, banks are virtually the only source of financing. Banks have also proven more apt at dealing with such frictions by establishing local operations in foreign countries. As the country develops, it more easily gains access to international financial markets. Typically, the initial access is effected by issuing securities in a major (foreign) currency, which helps alleviate frictions. Then, later stages are associated with foreign direct investment and with the transfer of international know-how for the development of domestic markets.

Market-based intermediation and bank-based intermediation have generally expanded in parallel, although the pace of expansion has differed across countries. How this expansion has evolved depends on historical factors, technological innovations, monetary and fiscal policies, and specific legal and accounting systems. For instance, the banking systems in Japan and Germany still account for the majority of financial system assets. Roughly 80% of euro zone non-financial credit instruments are loans, while this share is close to 50% in the United States.

In the run-up to the recent crisis, the integration of bank and market financing was taken to a new level by the development of securitisation, structured finance and the enhanced use of risk transfer instruments. These innovations reduced market incompleteness, thereby facilitating the diversification of risk by banks and the efficient allocation of capital. However, they also increased banks' vulnerability. The opaqueness and illiquidity of many securitised products have contributed to banks' credit- and funding-related stress. For instance, substantial, albeit temporary, investor demand for securitised retail exposures allowed Swedish banks to rapidly expand their lending in the Baltic region without properly evaluating the associated credit risks. Similarly, as German banks financed investments in US securities with German retail deposits, they exposed themselves to large cross-currency funding risks.

Better regulation is critical but not enough. It is just one piece of the puzzle. The promotion of financial stability requires a broad policy framework, of which prudential policy is only one element. The BIS has been a consistent and long-standing advocate of the essential role played by macroeconomic policies, both monetary and fiscal as an important element in fostering financial stability.

At the same time, the Basel Committee, its governing body and the G20 Leaders have consistently stated that the reforms will be introduced in a way that does not impede the recovery of the real economy. In addition, time is needed to translate the new internationally agreed standards into national legislation. National authorities can, and in fact should, impose higher standards if deemed appropriate in the local circumstances and prevailing economic conditions; similarly, they can impose shorter transition periods where appropriate.

The new, strengthened definition of capital will be phased in over five years: the requirements will be introduced in 2013 and fully implemented by the end of 2017. In addition, existing public sector capital injections will be grandfathered until the end of 2017. Capital instruments that no longer qualify as non-common equity Tier 1 capital or Tier 2 capital will be phased out over 10 years beginning 1 January 2013.

Basel III thus provides a combination of capital and liquidity standards that will help increase the resilience of the financial sector in the face of stress. In this context, four key points must be noted:

First, the new Basel III package affords the financial industry **more clarity** on the regulatory front. In today's still challenging economic and financial conditions, uncertainty is the enemy. Removing regulatory uncertainty can contribute importantly to the ongoing recovery.

Second, the new Basel III package combines enhancements at both the micro- and the macroprudential level. The new standards improve on the Basel II framework at the micro level of individual financial institutions, especially by strengthening the level and quality of capital. But Basel III also has **a macroprudential overlay** to promote the greater stability of the financial system as a whole. The aim is to establish appropriate capital schemes to address the procyclicality of the financial system and to deal with systemic risk. The countercyclical capital buffer will be activated by national authorities within the general guidance provided by an international agreement, depending on circumstances in specific jurisdictions. Tools will be available to limit systemic risk, and this will surely put a premium on effective supervision within jurisdictions, as well as on international peer reviews of local arrangements to ensure their international consistency. Last but certainly not least, the foundation of a sound macroprudential framework has now been laid.

Third there will be an appropriately **long transition period**. The new definition of capital, higher risk weights and increased minimum requirements will entail a significant amount of additional capital. The agreed transitional arrangements will help ensure that the banking sector can meet the higher capital standards through reasonable earnings retention and capital-raising, while still supporting the flow of new lending to the economy.

Fourth, **complacency must be avoided**. True, the financial industry will have time to adapt so as to both maintain an adequate supply of credit for the economy and repair balance sheets. Banks and supervisors alike will have to redouble their efforts to foster behavioural changes to ensure a sustained global recovery from the deep financial crisis. From this perspective, it goes without saying that those banks that already meet the minimum standards but do not meet the conservation buffer should apply the conservation principle. In other words, they should do their best to satisfy the conservation buffer requirement as soon as reasonably possible. Supervisors, for their part, must remain vigilant and actively promote a transition to the new standards as bank-specific and broader economic conditions warrant. Market discipline also plays an important role in guarding against complacency.

IMPLICATIONS OF BASEL III ON INDIAN BANKS

In general, higher capital and tighter liquidity requirements under Basel III will increase the capital requirements in Indian banks, as in other countries. However, the actual impact would vary in different countries depending upon the amount of exposures impacted under Basel III, existing capital structure of banks, i.e., extent of reliance on non-common equity capital elements, existing rules relating to regulatory adjustments, credit growth experienced by the economies and existing credit to GDP ratio. The impact of these requirements on the profitability of banks would depend upon sensitivity of lending rates to capital structure of banks and sensitivity of the credit growth to the lending rates.

Capital: Under Basel III, the trading book exposures, especially those having credit risk and resecuritisations exposures in both banking and trading book, attract enhanced capital charges. The credit valuation adjustment (CVA) for OTC derivatives will also attract additional capital. Since the trading book and OTC derivative portfolios of Indian banks are very small and they do not have any exposures to re-securitised instruments, impact of these changes in capital regulation on their balance sheets is insignificant.

The average Tier 1 capital ratio of Indian banks is around 10 per cent with more than 85 per cent of it comprising common equity. The regulatory adjustments will reduce the available equity capital only marginally for various reasons. First, items such as goodwill, deferred tax assets (DTAs) etc. are already deducted from Tier 1 capital for Indian banks. Secondly, some other items which are subject to deduction such as mortgage servicing rights, treasury stocks, gains on account of fair valuation of liabilities which exist in other developed economies, do not exist in India. Thirdly, reciprocal cross-holdings of capital and other investments in the capital of banking, financial and insurance entities are insignificant because the investments are restricted due to existing regulatory limits. Thus, Indian banks will have high common equity capital ratio even under Basel III which will stand them in good stead. It is worth noting that more than 50 per cent of Indian banks have common equity ratio of higher than 8 per cent at present and can implement Basel III even today without any phase-in.

Bank credit to GDP ratio of India is around 55 per cent which is relatively lower as compared with that in many other countries. However, the past trend shows that it is likely to increase in future as the credit penetration in the economy has been steadily increasing. The Indian economy is also expected to grow at an annual growth rate of 8-9 per cent for next 10 years or so. This would undoubtedly necessitate a considerable growth in bank capital. However, at present many Indian banks have actually been operating with equity capital ratio of 7-8 per cent for last 5 years when the economy continued to grow at an average rate of about 8 per cent. This provides comfort in terms of both the ability of banks to operate at higher equity capital levels required under Basel III and also the capacity of the Indian capital market to provide the required equity capital to banks.

Government of India has progressively reduced its shareholding in public sector banks and in the case of many of these banks, the Government's shareholding is close to 51 per cent. This means that in the future, the Government of India would provide the matching contribution to meet the additional equity requirements of banks, in contrast to the past when it had allowed a large part of additional equity requirements to be met from the market by letting its shareholding fall from 100 per cent to 51 per cent. Thus, the demand for equity from the capital market would be less to that extent but public sector banks' dependence on the Government for capital support will increase.

Liquidity – Issues relating to SLR and LCR: In India, banks are statutorily required to hold minimum reserves of high-quality liquid assets. Currently, such reserves (statutory liquidity ratio – SLR) are required to be maintained at a minimum of 24 per cent of net demand and time liabilities. Since these reserves are part of the minimum statutory requirement, the Reserve Bank faces a dilemma whether and how much of these reserves can be allowed to be reckoned towards the liquidity coverage ratio (LCR). If these reserves are not reckoned towards the LCR and banks are to meet the entire LCR with additional liquid assets, the proportion of liquid assets in total assets of banks will increase substantially, thereby lowering their income significantly. The Reserve Bank is examining to what extent the SLR requirements could be reckoned towards the liquidity requirement under Basel III.

Profitability: Studies have suggested that internationally, Basel III requirements will have a substantial impact on profitability. One such study conducted by McKinsey & Company suggests that all other things being equal, Basel III would reduce return on equity (RoE) for the average bank by about 4 percentage points in Europe and about 3 percentage points in the United States. The retail, corporate, and investment banking segments will be affected in different ways. Retail banks will be affected least, though institutions with very low capital ratios may find themselves under significant pressure. Corporate banks will be affected primarily in specialised lending and trade finance. Investment banks will find several core businesses profoundly affected, particularly trading and securitisation businesses. Banks are already seeking to manage RoE in the new environment by balance-sheet restructuring and business model adjustments. The study suggests that the balance sheet restructuring and businessmodel adjustments could potentially mitigate up to 40 per cent of Basel III's RoE impact, on an average.

A sense of likely impact on the lending rates of banks can be gauged by taking on example of a typical Indian bank which has RoE of 15 per cent and interest paid on nonequity elements of capital is 10 per cent. Further, suppose that the equity to RWAs ratio of the bank is 6 per cent. Now if the bank is required to maintain an additional 1 per cent equity, the weighted average cost of funds would rise by 5 basis points only. If the equity capital required rises by 2 per cent, the increase in lending rate to pass on the full increase in cost of capital to borrowers would be 10 basis points. There is likely to be some increase in cost of non-equity capital as well. But, all this is unlikely to push the cost of lending significantly. And, Indian banks should keep in mind that their net interest margins (NIMs) are very high as compared with their counterparts in many other countries. This only indicates the need for improving efficiency and considerable scope for bringing down the cost of intermediation. It should also be noted that while many large international banks are required to increase their equity capital by more than 100 per cent over the existing levels, many Indian banks would certainly not be required to increase their equity levels by that order. Therefore, the impact on their RoE is likely to be much less than 3 to 4 percentage points as observed in the case of US and European banks.

BENEFITS OF EFFECTIVE IMPLEMENTATION OF BASEL III

Effective implementation of Basel III will demonstrate to regulators, customers, and shareholders that the banking system is recovering well from the global financial crisis of 2008 and has been developing resilience to future shocks. A smooth implementation will also contribute to a bank's competitiveness by delivering better management insight into the business, allowing it to take advantage of future opportunities. At the same time, the challenges in implementation of Basel III should not be underestimated. For every bank, working out the most cost-effective model for implementing Basel III will be a critical issue. The comfortable capital adequacy levels at present for the Indian banking system do provide some comfort. However, as the economy grows, so will the credit demand requiring banks to expand their balance sheets, and in order to be able to do so, they will have to augment their capital; more specifically the equity capital.

While implementation of Basel III would undoubtedly imply some costs, this should not be the criterion to determine whether Basel III would add value to the financial system. The correct measure should be whether or not Basel III would deliver a much safer financial system with reduced probability of banking crises at affordable costs. Moreover, the impact of costs is minimised through long phase-in.

At times a question is asked whether it is appropriate for the countries which neither contributed to the crisis nor have exposure to the toxic assets need to implement Basel III. The answer is a clear 'Yes'. The reason is that in the present-day globalised world it is difficult for any local financial and economic system to completely insulate itself from the global economic shocks. The indirect effects of events happening in any part of the world can very well be transmitted throughout the world through various channels. In addition, many provisions of Basel III address the weaknesses in the measurement of risk under Basel II framework revealed during the crisis. Thus, Basel III would strengthen the financial system of both developing and developed countries. It needs to be appreciated that if the implementation of Basel III is not consistent across jurisdictions there would be a race to the bottom to make use of arbitrage opportunities, which nobody wins!

Indian banks should minimise costs by retaining maximum amount of earnings in the initial years of implementation, even though they might meet the capital requirements at that point in time with smaller retentions. This would avoid costs involved in fresh issuances. Indian banks are also comfortably placed in terms of liquidity requirements as they have a large reservoir of liquid Government securities to meet the SLR stipulation. The Reserve Bank is considering how much of it can be allowed to be reckoned towards compliance with the LCR. It is also expected that as the proportion of equity in the capital structure of banks rises, it would reduce the incremental costs of raising further equity as well as non-common equity capital.

Banks will have to issue fresh capital particularly to replace the ineligible non-equity capital towards later years of implementation. Successful issuance of fresh capital would demand greater transparency and greater market discipline.

The Reserve Bank of India has issued the draft guidelines on capital and liquidity rules of Basel III on December 30, 2011 and February 21, 2012, respectively. The Reserve Bank's approach has been to adopt Basel III capital and liquidity guidelines with more conservatism and at a quicker pace. Finally, the Basel III is just a part of the financial sector reforms agenda being pursued by G20. While the immediate challenge is to ensure consistent implementation of Basel II and Basel III across banks and jurisdictions. Other important issues such as strengthening the corporate governance, compensation practices, and resolution regimes; enhancing the regulatory and supervisory framework for global and domestic Systemic Important Banks

(SIBs); improving the OTC derivatives markets; and regulation of shadow banking system have also been addressed.

QUESTIONS

1. Should the banking system be more closely regulated to prevent another international debt crisis or any other banking crisis?
2. Discuss the key elements of Basel III framework, and its implications on Indian Banks.
3. Critically examine the role of financial crisis in shaping the current regulatory reform.
4. What steps have been recently initiated to promote broader financial stability?
5. Discuss the steps taken to strengthen the capital framework from Basel II to Basel III.
6. Discuss the interaction between bank- and market-based international intermediation.

PART V

This Page has been intentionally left blank

28

GLOBALISATION AND FOREIGN INVESTMENT

INTRODUCTION

Economic development remains an urgent global need. Globalisation - which links countries closer than ever before with each other - reinforces this need. Although many countries have achieved impressive increases in income, over a billion people in more than a hundred countries still live in poverty. Economic inequalities within countries remain large, and there is little sign of convergence in incomes across countries. In fact, a number of developing countries face increasing marginalisation.

Globalisation accentuates the increasing importance of the international economy for developing countries. Flows of finance, information, skills, technology, goods and services between countries are increasing rapidly. In a world of intensifying competition and accelerating technological change, this complementary and catalytic role of these flows can be very valuable. Since globalisation has its dangers, countries need to prepare their own capabilities to harness its potential, including through foreign investment. Foreign investment on its own cannot counteract the marginalisation of developing countries. This chapter examines the role of foreign capital movement, channels of capital flows, cross-country experience on capital flows and, in particular, the role of capital controls in stabilising the growth process. Box-1 covers the theoretical underpinnings on foreign investment flows.

BOX 1

FOREIGN INVESTMENT FLOWS - THEORETICAL UNDERPINNINGS

The research on this subject has so far been largely devoted to factors determining the FDI and policy formulations in response to those factors. Until 1960s, FDI was modelled as a part of neoclassical capital theory and the basic motive behind the movement of this capital into a host country was search for higher rate of returns. Over the period, with growing realisation the motives for capital movement have been far more diverse than mere search for higher returns, there has been a plethora of theoretical and empirical research directed towards identifying factors determining different types of capital flows. It was the Insight of Hymer (1960) who by differentiating direct investment from portfolio investment created basis for studies on factors determining the FDI flows, Hymer highlighted certain facts and evidences* on the basis of which he concluded that the nature of the direct and portfolio investment differs and therefore same theories cannot be applied to both types of investment. The key feature that Hymer identified for motivation of FDI was the level of control which a firm of home country gets through direct investment in host country. He also stressed upon market imperfections such as the ownership of knowledge not known to rivals, existence of differentiated products giving profit advantage to a firm investing abroad, problems related to licensing the product, *etc.*, for supporting FDI decisions. However, the literature argues that his theory over-emphasised the role of structural market failure and ignored the transaction cost side of market failure (Dunning 1981, Rugman. 1980). Moreover, his theory did not explain the locational and dynamic aspect of FDI.

Kindleberger held that an investor must possess some advantage that would allow a direct investment to earn sufficient return to justify competing with firms in the host country. Under conditions of perfect markets and factors, no one can possess an advantage that would justify direct investment. He then cites a number of imperfections that cause direct investment in an imperfect world. For example, market imperfections may arise from the limited amounts of natural resources such as mineral deposits. Other imperfections may arise from the creation of competitive advantages from product differentiation practiced by oligopolistic firms. Governments may create market imperfections by imposing tariffs or nontariff trade barriers on imports.

Later, Caves (1971) expanded upon Hymer's theory of direct investment and embedded it in the industrial organisation literature. By differentiating horizontal and vertical FDI, he identified factors such as possession of superior knowledge or information, motives to avoid uncertainty in a market characterized by a few suppliers and objective of creating entry barriers, ere, as being responsible for rising FDI flows. With the rising presence of multinational enterprises in the global economy, the view on FDI was expanded with the internationalisation theories of FDI that stressed on transaction costs. The internationalisation theory of FDI identified accumulation and internalisation of knowledge as the motivation for FDI, which bypasses intermediate product markets in knowledge. Thus, Caves indicated that FDI tended to occur only in a few of many possible institutional forms and only within a few industries in developed countries. Caves agreed with Hymer and Kindleberger that, for FDI to occur, the firm investing abroad must have an advantage in information about its special asset to offset the information disadvantage of its alien status. In addition, it must also find production abroad preferable to any other means of obtaining income from the foreign market, such as exporting, licensing, or the establishment of a native producer. The MNC has the power to differentiate its products and can produce a stream of them at lower cost.

The theorists such as Horst (1972), who stressed upon locational determinants of FDI, identified prevalence of natural resources as an important factor for FDI inflow. Wheeler and Mody (1992) identified ergodic and non-ergodic systems that determine the location of FDI. The ergodic system focussed on classical variables such as geographical features, labor costs, transport costs and market size as factors determining the FDI flows. Various empirical studies still rely on these variables to determine potential for FDI flows. The non-ergodic system focussed on externalities that emerge from investment in firms experiencing agglomeration economies, in other words, indicating the clustering effects of FDI.

In 1981, a number of hypotheses were formulated by Louis Calvet that were intended to explain foreign direct investment. Calvet identified these hypotheses as (1) market equilibrium, (2) government imposed distortions, (3) market structure imperfections, and (4) market failure imperfection. *Market equilibrium hypothesis:* This hypothesis focuses on the short-term nature of disequilibria. Profit seeking firms and arbitrageurs cause FDI to flow abroad until a new equilibrium emerges. In other words, FDI flows from high labour cost countries to low labour cost countries in order to minimize cost. The result is a finite life for FDL; *Government-Imposed Distortions:* This hypothesis holds that governments distort markets and create profit opportunities when they impose tariffs, import quotas, or legislate national tax systems that are different from those in other countries. A classic case can be found in the European Community where, first, U.S. firms moved large amounts of

FDI to EC member countries and, second, where Japan has now become a large direct investor in order to get around the EC's trade barriers; *Market structure imperfections:* Under this hypothesis, firms have oligopoly power to interfere with market pricing mechanisms. These firms then set up barriers to entry with the creation of unique products in the marketplace. In addition, such firms may display their interdependence by predicting and then emulating the actions of their competitors. Such actions have been explained by Vernon's product life cycle theory of FDI, by Knickerbocker's follow Sleader behaviour and by Caves; *Market failure imperfections:* Finally, Calvet hypothesized that markets fail because they depart from perfect market assumptions about production techniques and commodity properties. Existing knowledge—technology—should be available to other firms as a free good because of social efficiency. This creates a dilemma about how firms can be motivated to produce new knowledge if no property rights will be granted. Calvet held that the natural characteristics of knowledge favour its transfer within a single firm and, hence, FDI is justified over other alternatives of exploiting foreign markets when firms transfer their technology within the firm and across borders to their foreign affiliates.

Buckley and Casson developed a broader theory for the rationale of the MNC; they referred to this theory as internalization. The MNC consists of many interconnected activities such as marketing, research and development, finance, training, as well as production. Buckley and Casson held that these connections create a series of flows of intermediate products such as knowledge, expertise—the technology to which Calvet referred—as well as semiprocessed materials and tangible goods. The markets for these incomplete or intangible products are difficult to organize and such a problem is compounded when one deals with an intangible such as knowledge. An incentive is created for the firm that has produced this technology to bypass regular markets and *internalize* such transaction within the firm and, in the case of FDI, across national borders.

Buckley and Casson and, then, Buckley, have attempted to further refine their internalization theory. In 1985, they noted several advantages of internalization including: (1) the increased ability to control and plan production and, in particular, to coordinate flows of crucial inputs, (2) the exploitation of market power by discriminatory pricing, (3) the avoidance of bilateral market power, (4) the avoidance of uncertainties in the transfer of knowledge between parties, and (5) the avoidance of potential government intervention. Buckley then explored the problems of empirically testing the internalization theory. Different types of costs and demand conditions that arise in the internal and external markets have to be specified properly. The measurement of key variables and proxies presents a problem as does the introduction of dynamic elements into the theory.

Buckley then attempted to differentiate between internalization and market structure and internalization and competitive advantage. He observed that some industries were relatively fixed and concentrated in structure and this characteristic encouraged these firms to diversify. Other industries were more open and their market structure was not so well developed; these industries encouraged internalization in order to overcome these imperfections in their market structure.

The research work of Dunning (1977, 1981) provided a comprehensive analysis of FDI based on ownership, location and the internationalisation (OLI) paradigm. His eclectic theory of FDI highlighted various benefits emerging from FDI: the ownership-specific advantages which comprise access to spare capacity, economies of joint supply, greater access to markets and knowledge, diversification of risk, technology and trademarks, firm size; the location-specific advantages consisting of distribution of inputs and markets, costs of labor, materials and transport costs, government intervention and policies, commercial and legal infrastructure, ete.; internalisation-specific advantages covering reduction in search, negotiation and monitoring costs, tariff avoidance, *etc.* The critics of eclectic theory of FDI have regarded it as a taxomony rather than a theory of FDI as it covered a range of theories and employs a large number of variables. It has also been criticised for reformulation over time to incorporate new ideas and to reflect contemporary trends in FDI. The prior version of his theory ignored the role of strategy in determining the FDI flows. The role of strategic motivations, which was first analysed by Knickerbocker (1973). were extended by Acocella (1991). As per these strategic theories, the reasons behind strategic alliances included economies of scale, the reduction of risk and access to knowledge and expertise. The strategic alliances highlight the motivation for mergers and acquisitions taking place in the current era of M&A boom.

Dunning's eclectic theory has been critically examined by Itaki (1991). Itaki examinee the theoretical redundancy of the "ownership advantage," the inseparability of the "ownership advantage" from the "location advantage," the conceptual ambiguity of the "location advantage," and the possible methodological dangers of a multifactor analysis under the three headings of the eclectic theory. His major conclusion was that further analysis should be conducted. He suggested that FDI theory should not be separated from international trade theory and that comparative advantage should be considered in any analysis of FDI theory.

Another explanation for FDI has been labelled the "Japanese School" approach. Kojima and Qzawa (1984) suggested that the market cannot efficiently handle industrial adjustment in a global marketplace. They argued that government intervention be used to ensure a successful adjustment by encouraging trade and FDI, including acting as trade intermediaries and participating in new forms of FDI such as joint ventures, direct overseas loans, and plant exports and management.

All these theories mainly explain the supply side of FDI that creates a push to FDI for flowing out of the home economy. Broadly, these factors and motives comprise profit expansion through knowledge advantage, lower cost advantage, greater market access, gains from scale economies, strategic motives such as acquiring input supplies or creating worldwide near to monopoly powers, locational advantages, reduction in risk and agglomeration gains.

A vast literature on demand side factors that pull FDI into a host economy is also available. The studies such as World Bank (1995), Blomstrom and Kokko (2001). highlight gains from FDI in the form of competition and efficiency effects, spillover effects, effects of backward and forward linkages, technological effects, accumulation of knowledge capital, stable flow of funds with no .debt-servicing obligation attached, greater external market discipline on macroeconomic policy, broadening and deepening of national capital markets, *etc.* for the host country. These theoretical studies have given a lot of space for empirical research on factors determining the inflow and outflow of FDI and the role played by policy initiatives undertaken on the part of host countries to attract FDI, The country specific studies have analysed the role of regulatory regime of the host country in attracting FDI, These studies have focussed on timing, activities of supervisory authorities and content of external and internal regulatory measures.

A lot of literature highlighting the role played by policy environment discusses the issues of creating investor friendly environment for FDI. As per Qxelheim (1993). in attracting inward investment during the period of transition from a national market to an integrated part of the global market, governments can influence the relative cost of capital by using an adequate mix of interventions. Policymakers may affect die corporate decision about where to locate a production facility by managing a set of international relative prices: exchange rates, relative inflation and interest rates. In general, they can create investment incentives or business opportunities by creating deviations from the international purchasing power parity and the international Fisher effect. Additional business incentives controlled by policymakers are relative taxes and relative political risk. This study has argued that appropriate policies appear to be a necessary precondition for attracting FDI.

The United Nations Centre for Transnational Corporation has provided seven policy instruments used to attract FDI: ownership policies, tax and subsidy measures, policies concerning convertibility of foreign exchange and remittance of earnings, price control measures, performance requirements, sector-specific limitations and incentives and miscellaneous entry and procedural rules that are assumed to impose a considerable cost on a potential FDI. A World Bank report on indicators of FDI regulation (2010) has found that restrictive and obsolete laws and regulations impede FDI, red tape and poor implementation of laws creates further barriers to FDI, good regulations and efficient processes matter for FDI and effective institutions help in fostering FDI. Thus, the report highlights the importance of regulatory framework.

* Hymer highlighted the evidences such as the case of US as a net exporter of FDI but a net Importer of portfolio investment, the predominance of direct Investment in manufacturing and of portfolio investment in financial organisations and investment into a single country despite the opportunity available to mitigate risk by diversifying investment across different countries.

THE ROLE OF FOREIGN CAPITAL

Foreign capital in the growth process generally yields conflicting results. Conventionally, the standard analysis of growth accounting in an open economy encounters an apparent contradiction between "export-led growth" on the one hand, and "capital-flow induced growth" on the other, even though in reality both strategies could be operationalised simultaneously to strengthen the growth process. The apparent contradiction arises from the macro-economic identity which suggests that while a surplus in the external goods and services account—reflecting the result of an export-led growth strategy—could increase GDP, that would tantamount to no role for net external financing as the country must neessarily save more than it can invest, leading to net capital outfolws. The underlying assumption behind this assessment is that an export-led growth stretegy can stimulate growth only by generating a surplus in the external goods and services account. The actual external resource transfer process and the stages over which the importance of each form of transfer changes can explain how a developing country could simultaneously benefit from both export-led and capital-flow-induced growth strategies. This two-gap approach justifies the role of foreign capital for relaxing the two major constraints to growth. In the neo-classical framework, however, capital neither explains differences in the levels and rates of growth across countries nor can large capital flows make any significant difference to the growth rate that a country could achieve. In the subsequent resurrection of the two-gap approach, the emphasis was generally laid on the preconditions that could make foreign capital more productive in developing countries. The important preconditions comprised presence of surplus labour and excess productive demand for foreign exchange. With the growing influence of the new growth theories in the second half of the 1980s that recognised the effects of positive externalities associated with capital accumulation on growth, the role of foreign capital in the growth process assumed renewed importance. In the endogenous growth framework, the sources of growth attributed to capital flows comprise the spillovers associated with foreign capital in the form of technology, skills, and introduction of new products as well as the positive externalities in terms of higher efficiency of domestic financial markets, improved resource allocation and efficient financial intermediation by domestic financial institutions. Since the spillovers and externalities associated with different forms of foreign capital could vary, a pecking order approach to the composition of capital flows is often pursued which helps in prioritising the capital flows based on the growth enhancing role of each form of capital.

The dominant view on what drives cross-border capital flows is that marginal productivity of capital is higher in a country where capital is scarce. If marginal productivity of capital widely differed across countries, then in the presence of capital flows shortfalls in domestic saving should not constrain investment. The seminal finding that domestic saving and investment rates are highly correlated, however, indicated that the degree of capital mobility across countries may not be high. The marginal productivity of capital in India was 58 times that of the United States as obtained through the standard estimation of Cobb-Douglas production functions. India, however, could never attract enough foreign capital to take advantage of the productivity differentials. Unlike the wide differences in estimated productivity of capital, however, real interest rates - a measure of real return received by the investors - turned out to be much less divergent across countries in reality. Capital markets could be imperfect, preventing capital flows from being driven by productivity differentials. Incremental investment would be more productive in countries with skilled workforce and well developed physical infrastructure. Thus, the presence of internal growth supportive factors appear important, not only for attracting higher private foreign capital but also for enhancing the growth inducing effects of such foreign capital. The importance of internal growth supportive factors is amply demonstrated by the extremely lopsided pattern of private capital flows to the emerging markets. About 12 emerging markets account for more than 80 per cent of the total private flows to all emerging markets.

The role of relative prices and profitability of investment has been offered as an alternative explanation to the Feldstein and Horioka puzzle. The presence of factors such as technology and human capital can induce growth and attract capital flows to strengthen a virtuous cycle and show deviations from the Feldstein and Horioka findings. Corrected for relative prices (*i.e.*, at domestic price of capital instead of at international price), the dispersion of the marginal product of capital across countries could be small. Disincentives to capital formation in the form of high prices of capital goods could also lower growth. Cross-country experience shows that high-income countries are generally more open to capital flows and more open economies benefit from capital flows if the internal sources of growth are strong and their past growth record is satisfactory.

FOREIGN INVESTMENT DECISION PROCESS

The foreign investment decision process is composed essentially of five steps. They are the initial decision to look abroad, the investigation process, the decision to invest abroad, project reviews and negotiations with home or host government agencies, and changes to the project through modifications. Box-2 shows the foreign investment decision process.

BOX 2

THE FOREIGN INVESTMENT DECISION PROCESS

I. The Decision to Look Abroad
   - A. Initiating forces
      1. drive of high-ranking executives
      2. outside proposals
      3. fear of losing a market
      4. the bandwagon effect
      5. strong competition from abroad
   - B. Auxiliary forces
      1. markets for components and other products
      2. utilization of old machinery
      3. capitalization of know-how and spreading fixed costs
      4. indirect return to lost markets

II. The Investigation Process
   - A. Risk and uncertainty
   - B. Changes in perceived risk through investigation
   - C. Size of market

III. The Decision to Invest
   - A. Concept of commitment
   - B. Creation of commitments during investigation
   - C. Evolving set of constraints

IV. Reviews and Negotiations
   - A. Bargaining with reviewing bodies
   - B. Modifications and negotiations
      1. reduction of company's own capital investment
      2. search for local partners
      3. flexibility
      4. foreign government concessions, etc.

V. Changes through Repetition: The International Division
   - A. The time element
   - B. Organizational evolution
   - C. Institutional forces
      1. changes in strategy
      2. roles
      3. information
   - D. Attitudes toward risk and uncertainty
   - E. Top management involvement

THE DECISION TO LOOK ABROAD

The company's management makes the decision to look abroad for a foreign investment project by initiating forces—those forces that are imposed directly upon the firm—and auxiliary forces—forces that stem indirectly from some rather remotely related reason. Initiating forces include the drive of high-ranking executives toward international business, the fear by a firm of losing a market, the bandwagon effect—everyone is doing it, so we had better do it—and strong competition from abroad.

Auxiliary forces that result in using capital equipment or funds for foreign projects may stem from some unrelated reason for doing the foreign project. The foreign project may create a market for components and other products made by the parent firm. Old machinery may be obsolete in the home country but may be useable in some developing countries. Capitalization of know-how and spreading fixed costs can be accomplished by the FDI project. And the FDI project might lead to an indirect return to lost markets.

THE INVESTIGATION PROCESS

Once the decision is made to analyze potential foreign projects, the process then turns to an investigation of the proposal. Initially, some level of risk and uncertainty is generated by the project among top management. As the project is further analyzed, the firm will make changes in its perceived risk; usually, the more top management knows about the project and the host country, the less risk that management will perceive. The size of the market will be estimated during this marketing feasibility stage.

THE DECISION TO INVEST

The firm then decides to make the foreign investment. At this stage, the firm's management will conceive some commitment toward the project. During the investigation further commitments will still be created, including how much to invest, the size of the plant and its employment, and whether home office personnel will be sent to the overseas project. A set of constraints evolve including currency convertibility, profitability, and other operating characteristics.

REVIEWS AND NEGOTIATIONS

At this time, the firm has decided to commit some finite amount of resources to the project. It may then find it necessary to review the project with home and host country officials. Modifications in and negotiations about the project may be required. These may include a reduction in the company's own capital investment, the search for local partners, and foreign government concessions, e.g., tax holidays or abatements, and low-interest government loans, etc.

CHANGES THROUGH REPETITION

Finally, as the project progresses and the firm makes more and more foreign investments, changes will be made in its FDI analysis process. The firm may become more interested in the time element, i.e., how long a project will take to mature. An organizational structure that is more and more internationally oriented may evolve. Institutional forces may be formulated that will facilitate further foreign investment. These include changes in strategy, assignment of roles to top management so that their expertise can be utilized in FDI questions, and the development of an intelligence inventory to assist in FDI analysis. Further repetitions in FDI will cause management's attitudes toward risk and uncertainty to be modified, enhancing the firm's ability to make better FDI decisions in the future. Finally, the firm's top management will become more involved in international business as more and more FDI is made.

CHANNELS OF CAPITAL FLOWS

Capital flows have followed a boom-bust patterns, notwithstanding the large regional and compositional variations. The main channels through which capital flows take place are discussed below:

FOREIGN DIRECT INVESTMENT (FDI)

Capital flows in the form of FDI flows have been widely believed to be an important source of growth in recent year. FDI is the process whereby residents of one country (the source country) acquire ownership of assets for the purpose of controlling the production, distribution and other activities of a firm in another country (the host country). The International Monetary Fund's *Balance of Payments Manual* defines FDI as "an investment that is made to acquire a lasting interest in an enterprise operating in an economy other than that of the investor, the investor's purpose being to have an effective voice in the management of the enterprise". The United Nation's 1999 *World Investment Report* (UNCTAD, 1999) defines FDI as "an investment involving a long-term relationship and reflecting a lasting interest and control of a resident entity in one economy (foreign direct investor or parent' enterprise) in an enterprise resident in an economy other than that of the foreign direct investor (FDI enterprise, affiliate enterprise or foreign affiliate)". The term "long-term" is used in the last definition in order to distinguish FDI from portfolio investment, FDI does not have the portfolio investment characteristic of being short term in nature, involving a high turnover of securities.*

Classification of FDI

FDI can be classified from the perspective of the investing firm and from the perspective of the host country (the recipient of FDI). *From the perspective of the investor*, it is possible to distinguish among *horizontal FDI*, *vertical FDI* and *conglomerate FDI*. Horizontal FDI is undertaken for the purpose of horizontal expansion to produce the same or similar kinds of goods abroad (in the host country) as in the home country. Hence product differentiation is the critical element of market structure for horizontal FDI. More generally, horizontal FDI is undertaken to exploit more fully certain monopolistic or oligopolistic advantages such as patents or differentiated products, particularly if expansion at home were to violate anti-trust laws. Vertical

---

* The common feature of these definitions lies in words like "control" and "controlling interest", which represent the most important feature that distinguishes FDI from portfolio investment, since a portfolio investor does not seek control or lasting interest. There is no agreement, however, on what constitutes a controlling interest, but most commonly a minimum of 10% shareholding is regarded as allowing the foreign firm to exert significant influence, either potentially or actually exercised, over the key policies of the underlying project. Many firms are unwilling to carry out foreign investment unless they have 100% equity ownership and control. Others refuse to make such investments unless they have at least majority control (that is, a 51% stake). In recent years, however, there has been a tendency for indulging in FDI cooperative arrangements where several firms participate and no single party holds majority control (for example, joint ventures).

FDI, on the other hand, is undertaken for the purpose of exploiting raw materials (backward vertical FDI) or to be nearer to consumers through the acquisition of distribution outlets (forward vertical FDI).

From the perspective of the host country, FDI can be classified into (i) *import-substituting* FDI, (ii) *export-increasing FDI and* (iii) *government-initiated FDI*. Import-substituting FDI involves the production of goods previously imported by the host country, necessarily implying that imports by the host country and exports by the investing firm will decline. This type of FDI is likely to be determined by the size of the host country's market, transportation costs and trade barriers. Export-increasing FDI, on the other hand, is motivated by the desire to seek new sources of input, such as raw materials and intermediate goods. This kind of FDI is export-increasing in the sense that the host country will increase its exports of raw materials and intermediate products to other countries, where the investing firm and its subsidiaries are located. Government-initiated FDI may be triggered, for example, when a government offers incentives to foreign investors in an attempt to eliminate a balance of payments deficit.

FDI may also be classified into expansionary and defensive types. *Expansionary FDI* seeks to exploit firm-specific advantages in the host country. This type of FDI has the additional benefit of contributing to sales growth of the investing firm at home and abroad. On the other hand, *defensive FDI* seeks cheap labour in the host country with the objective of reducing the cost of production.

FDI may take one of *three forms: greenfield investment, cross-border mergers and acquisitions (M&As)*, and *joint ventures*. Greenfield investment occurs when the investing firm establishes new production, distribution or other facilities in the host country. Typically, host countries prefer greenfield investment because of the job-creating potential and value-added output. FDI may occur via an acquisition of, or a merger with, an established firm in the host country (the vast majority of M&As are indeed acquisitions rather than mergers). This mode of FDI has two advantages over greenfield investment: (i) it is cheaper, particularly if the acquired project is a loss-making operation that can be bought at a low price; and (ii) it allows the investor to get quick access to the market. Firms may be motivated to engage in cross-border acquisitions to bolster their competitive positions in the world market by acquiring special assets from other firms or by using their own assets on a larger scale. A large number of M&As fail in the sense that the firms engaging in this activity do not produce better results in terms of share prices and profitability than those firms that do not indulge in this activity.

FDI can also take the form of joint ventures either with a host country firm or with a government institution, as well as with another company that is foreign to the host country. One side normally provides the technical expertise and its ability to raise finance while the other side provides valuable input through its local knowledge of the bureaucracy as well as local laws and regulations.

Determinants of Foreign Direct Investment

A number of theories have been put forward to explain FDI. Series of hypotheses on which various theoretical models built to explain FDI have been critically examined below:

FDI Depends on the Rate of Return on the Underlying Project

The differential rates of return hypothesis represents one of the first attempts to explain FDI flows. This hypothesis postulates that capital flows from countries with low rates of return to countries with high rates of return move in a process that eventually leads to the equality of *ex ante* real rates of return. The hypothesis obviously assumes risk neutrality, making the rate of return the only variable upon which the investment decision depends. Risk neutrality in this sense implies that the investor considers domestic and foreign direct investments to be perfect substitutes, or in general that direct investment in any country, including the home country, is a perfect substitute for direct investment in any other country.

One problem with the differential rates of return hypothesis is that it is not consistent with the observation that countries simultaneously experience inflows and outflows of FDI. This is because a rate of return differential implies capital flows in one direction only, from the low-rate country to the high-rate country, and not vice versa. There is, obviously, something missing in this hypothesis. Furthermore, the validity of the differential rates of return hypothesis can be questioned on theoretical grounds. First of all, multinational firms may indulge in FDI for reasons other than profit, particularly in the short run and medium run. For example, the objective may be to maximise sales revenue in accordance with the market penetration objective. Or the objective may not be purely financial, but rather logistical and operational, such as the desire to circumvent trade barriers. In general, multinational firms are faced with a multiplicity of objectives for their international operations, and these objectives are likely to change with the passage of time. More importantly, however, risk aversion implies that the FDI decision does not only depend on return but also on risk. Finally, the differential rates of return hypothesis does not explain why a firm indulges in FDI rather than portfolio investment.

FDI Depends on Return and Risk

When the assumption of risk neutrality is relaxed, risk becomes another variable upon which the FDI decision is made. If this proposition is accepted, then the differential rates of return hypothesis becomes inadequate, in which case we resort to the diversification (or portfolio) hypothesis to explain FDI. The choice among various projects is therefore guided not only by the expected rate of return, but also by risk. The same idea of reducing risk via diversification that is relevant to portfolio investment is used here. Because of risk aversion, a rate of return differential will not induce capital flows in one direction until the differential disappears via arbitrage. Rather, capital mobility will be constrained by the desire to minimise or reduce risk, which is achieved via diversification.

FDI Depends on Market Size

The volume of FDI in a host country depends on its market size. This hypothesis is particularly valid for the case of import-substituting FDI. As soon as the size of the market of a particular country has grown to a level warranting the exploitation of economies of scale, this country becomes a potential target for FDI inflows. The rationale for the hypothesis that firms increase their investment in response to their sales is based on neoclassical domestic investment theories.

One way to test the market size hypothesis is to find out whether or not the share of FDI of a given country going to a group of host countries is correlated with the individual income level of the host country. The empirical studies using this testing approach seem to support the hypothesis that higher levels of sales and the host country's income are positively related to FDI.

Size does matter, according to a survey by A.T. Kearney, the results of which were summarised in the 17 February 2000 issue of *The Economist*. This survey is based on the views of 135 executives of the world's 1000 largest companies who gave marks on a scale of 0-3 for the likelihood of investing in a particular country. The top three countries favoured for investment turned out to be the USA, China and Brazil. Mexico was ranked sixth, whereas India was ranked seventh. Needless to say, the ranking of countries from the top to the bottom of the list did not exactly match the ranking of countries in terms of size, because of the influence of other determinants of FDI. For example, Japan was twentieth, whereas the UK was fourth.

FDI Can be Explained in Terms of Firm-specific Advantages

When a firm establishes a subsidiary in another country it faces several disadvantages emanating from differences in language, culture and the legal system as well as other inter-country differences. If, in spite of these disadvantages, a firm engages in FDI, it must have some advantages arising from intangible assets such as a well-known brand name, patent-protected technology, managerial skills and other firm-specific factors. It is, therefore, firm-specific advantages that explain why a firm can compete successfully in a foreign market. This hypothesis, however, does not explain why a firm chooses to invest in country A rather than country B.

FDI is Triggered by the Need for Internalisation

According to the internalisation hypothesis, FDI arises from efforts by firms to replace market transactions with internal transactions. For example, if there are problems associated with buying oil products on the market, a firm may decide to buy a foreign refinery. These problems arise from imperfections and failure of markets for intermediate goods, including human capital, knowledge, marketing and management expertise. The advantages of internalisation are the avoidance of time lags, bargaining and buyer uncertainty. The internalisation hypothesis explains why firms use FDI in preference to exporting and importing from foreign countries. It also explains why they may shy away from licensing. Because of the significant time lags and transaction costs associated with market purchases and sales, firms replace some of the market functions with internal processes (that is, with intra-firm transactions).

FDI Exists because of the International Immobility of Factors of Production

According to the location hypothesis, FDI exists because of the international immobility of some factors of production such as labour and natural resources. This immobility leads to location-related differences in the costs of factors of production. One form of location-related differences in the costs of factors of production is the locational advantage of low wages. Thus, the level of wages in the host country relative to wages in the home country is an important determinant of FDI. This is why countries like India attract labour-intensive production (such as footwear and textiles) from high-wage countries. It is also why multinational firms wanting to establish production facilities in North America choose Mexico in preference to Canada.

Locational advantages do not only take the form of low wages, as they are also applicable to other factors of production. For example, a firm may indulge in FDI by building a factory in a country where it is cheap to generate hydroelectric power. Similarly, a factory could be located near a copper mine in the host country if copper is an important input in the production process. This is a locational advantage because significant savings can be made on the cost of shipping copper from where it is produced to where it is used. Apart from these savings, the firm can avoid delays in the delivery of copper shipments arising from the time it takes to ship the metal and the red tape that may be involved in this operation. In general, the location hypothesis emphasises the importance of unavoidable government constraints such as trade barriers. Capital may also be the underlying factor of production, particularly if capital markets are segmented. The idea here is that FDI flows to countries where the cost of capital is low.

The Eclectic Theory

The eclectic theory results from the integration of the industrial organisation hypothesis, the internalisation hypothesis and the location hypothesis without being too precise about how they interrelate. The eclectic theory aims at answering the following two questions. First, if there is demand for a particular commodity in a particular country why is it not met by a local firm producing in the same country or by a foreign firm exporting from another country? Second, suppose that a firm wants to expand its operations, why does it not do so via other means, which include (i) producing in the home country and exporting to the foreign country; (ii) expanding into a new line of business within the home country; (iii) indulging in portfolio investment in the foreign country; and (iv) licensing its technology to foreign firms that can carry out the production.

Suppose that there is demand for a particular product in which a particular domestic firm has an ownership advantage. What happens depends on the internalisation and locational advantages. If there are no internalisation gains, the firm will license its ownership advantage to another firm, particularly if locational factors favour expansion abroad. If there are internalisation gains and if locational factors favour home expansion, the firm expands at home and exports. And, if there are internalisation gains and if locational factors favour foreign expansion, FDI will take place.

The Role of the Product Life Cycle

According to the product life cycle hypothesis, products go through a cycle of initiation, exponential growth, slowdown and decline. The hypothesis postulates that firms indulge in FDI at a particular stage in the life cycle of the products that they initially produce as innovations.

FDI takes place as the cost of production becomes an important consideration, which is the case when the product reaches maturity and standardisation. FDI is thus a defensive move to maintain the firm's competitive position against its domestic and foreign rivals. The product life cycle hypothesis predicts that the home country where the innovative product first appears switches over time from an exporting to an importing country.

The Role of Oligopolistic Reaction

The oligopolistic reaction hypothesis postulates that FDI by one firm triggers a similar action by other leading firms in the industry in an attempt to maintain their market shares. An implication of the oligopolistic reaction hypothesis, which is incompatible with some stylised facts, is that the process of FDI is self-limiting, since the invasion of each other's home market leads to an increase in competition and a decline in the intensity of oligopolistic reaction. Moreover, this hypothesis also fails to identify the factors that trigger the initial investment.

The Role of Internal Financing

Internal financing refers to the utilisation of profit generated by a subsidiary to finance the expansion of FDI by a multinational firm in the same country where the subsidiary operates. The internal financing hypothesis postulates that multinational firms commit a modest amount of their resources to their initial direct investment, whereas subsequent expansions are financed by reinvesting the profits obtained from operations in the host country. It therefore implies the existence of a positive relationship between internal cash flows and investment outlays, which is plausible because the cost of internal financing is lower. The hypothesis seems to be more appropriate for explaining FDI in developing countries for at least two reasons: (i) the presence of restrictions on the movement of funds, and (ii) the rudimentary state and inefficiency of financial markets.

The Effect of Exchange Rates

The currency areas hypothesis postulates that firms belonging to a country with a strong currency tend to invest abroad, whereas firms belonging to a country with a weak currency do not have such a tendency. In other words, countries with strong currencies tend to be sources of FDI, whereas countries with weak currencies tend to be host countries or recipients of FDI. This hypothesis is based on capital market relationships, foreign exchange risk and the market's preference for holding assets denominated in strong currencies. It is arguable that a multinational firm in a hard currency area is able, based on reputation, to borrow at lower rates than local firms in a country that has a soft currency. In essence, the crucial assumption is that there is bias in capital markets, which arises because an income stream located in a country with a weak currency is associated with foreign exchange risk. Hence the view arises that a strong currency firm may be more efficient in hedging foreign exchange risk. In this context, market imperfections may further explain the effect of exchange rates since a weak currency is likely to be associated with FDI inflows owing to informational imperfections in the capital market and that these imperfections make the cost of external financing higher than the cost of internal financing.

Changes in exchange rates are theoretically bound to have an effect on FDI. *First* of all, depreciation of the domestic currency makes domestic assets more attractive for foreigners while foreign assets become more expensive for residents in the home country. Thus FDI inflows will increase. This explains the increase in FDI in the US as a result of the depreciation of the US dollar that started in March 1985. But this argument can be dismissed as follows. In a world with mobile capital, risk-adjusted expected returns on all international assets will be equalised. For this equality to hold, depreciation of the domestic currency will result in a rise in the prices of domestic assets. The question that arises here is that if foreigners can buy domestic assets with an appreciating currency, why can't domestic residents with access to global capital markets borrow the foreign currency and take advantage of the situation just like the foreign investors? Still, it may be argued that "the view that exchange rates are irrelevant to FDI is at odds with more than just casual empiricism.

The effect of exchange rates on FDI may be ambiguous because the latter is affected by both the level and variability of exchange rates. Moreover, the effect of the level of the exchange rate depends on the destination of the goods produced. If the investor aims at serving the local market then FDI and trade are substitutes, in which case appreciation of the currency of the host country attracts FDI inflows. Alternatively, if FDI is aimed at re-exports then FDI and trade are complements. In this case appreciation of the currency of the host country reduces FDI inflows through lower competitiveness. The effect of exchange rate variability also depends on the objective of FDI. If the investor aims at serving the local market then exchange rate variability encourages FDI. If, however, the objective is to re-export then this benefit vanishes.

Diversification with Barriers to International Capital Flows

For international diversification to be carried out through firms, two conditions must hold: (i) there must exist barriers or costs to portfolio flows that are greater than those associated with direct investment, and (ii) investors must recognise that multinational firms provide diversification opportunities that are unavailable otherwise. It has been found that there is a systematic relationship between the extent of international involvement and excess market value. This relationship gets stronger in periods characterised by the presence of barriers to capital flows.

The Role of Political Risk and Country Risk

Lack of political stability discourages inflows of FDI. Political risk arises because unexpected modifications of the legal and fiscal frameworks in the host country may change the economic outcome of a given investment in a drastic manner. For example, a decision by the host government to impose restrictions on capital repatriation to the investor's home country will adversely affect the cash flows received by the parent company.

The Role of Tax Policies

Domestic and foreign tax policies affect the incentive to engage in FDI and the means by which it is financed. Tax policies affect the decisions taken by multinational firms via three channels. *First,* the tax treatment of income generated abroad has a direct effect on the net return on FDI. *Second,* the tax treatment of income generated at home affects the net profitability of domestic investment and the relative profitability of domestic and foreign investment. *Third*, tax policies affect the relative cost of capital of domestic and foreign investment.

While simple intuition might suggest that higher taxes should discourage both foreign and domestic investments but in reality at has been found that increased taxes boost inward FDI. The general equilibrium effects on asset returns combined with a careful consideration of foreign tax systems reveals reasons for foreign investors to increase their investments in response to high taxes in the host country.

The Effect of Trade Barriers

FDI may be undertaken to circumvent trade barriers, such as tariffs, because FDI can be viewed as an alternative to trade. This means that open economies without many restrictions on international trade should receive less FDI flow. The surge in FDI in countries like Mexico and Spain is partly attributed to the desire of multinational firms to circumvent the trade barriers imposed by NAFTA and the EU. Sometimes, the threat of protectionism by the host government triggers FDI.

The Effect of Government Regulations

Most governments adopt policies aimed at both encouraging and discouraging inward FDI by offering incentives on the one hand and disincentives (taking the form of restrictions on the activities of multinational firms) on the other. Typically, they offer incentives (such as financial and tax incentives as well as market preferences) while simultaneously placing restrictions on the activities of multinational firms.

One particular case of using incentives to offset disincentives is when the host government uses a package that includes trade-related investment performance (TRIP) requirements, which are seen by some as a significant obstacle to FDI. TRIP requirements include two components: (i) local content and (ii) export minima. These requirements should be viewed as disincentives to FDI because the local content requirements may lead to increased cost and decreased earnings, which makes the underlying project less competitive. Likewise, export minima may lead to lower earnings, adversely affecting the attractiveness of FDI. Normally, TRIP requirements are combined with incentives such as preferential tax status, access to foreign exchange and import protection.

The Role of Strategic and Long-term Factors

Some strategic and long-term factors have been put forward to explain FDI. These factors include the following:

1. The desire on the part of the investor to defend existing foreign markets and foreign investments against competitors.
2. The desire to gain and maintain a foothold in a protected market or to gain and maintain a source of supply that may prove useful in the long run.
3. The need to develop and sustain a parent-subsidiary relationship.
4. The desire to induce the host country into a long commitment to a particular type of technology.
5. The advantage of complementing another type of investment.

6. The economies of new product development.
7. Competition for market shares among oligopolists and the concern for strengthening bargaining positions.

FOREIGN PORTFOLIO INVESTMENT (FPI)

Portfolio capital has emerged as the key channel for integrating capital markets worldwide. Investment in equity provides returns in two firms: dividends and capital appreciation. Foreign equity investment is preferred even if it offers lower dividend yield and rate of capital appreciation than domestic equity investment if the foreign currency appreciates by more than the sum of dividend yield differential and the capital appreciation rate differential. Notice, however, that at the time when the decision concerning the choice is made, the value of these variables are unknown, so the decision should be made on their expected or *ex ante* values.

There are five alternative investment vehicles for foreign equity investment, which will be described in turn.

Direct Purchase of Securities in Overseas Markets

The firm carrying out the purchase or sale of foreign securities must have a branch or correspondent securities firm authorised to deal on the foreign stock exchange. When a firm buys individual foreign stocks, it would be exposed to four different kinds of risk: (i) country risk, which relates to economic and political events that have adverse effects on price or the liquidity of the market; (ii) foreign exchange risk, which results from fluctuations in exchange rates; (iii) systematic risk, or market risk, which is the risk that cannot be eliminated via diversification; and (iv) unsystematic risk, which refers to the variability of the return on a single security.

The Use of American Depository Receipts (ADRs)

An ADR is a receipt issued by a US bank certifying that the bank holds an equivalent number of shares issued by a foreign company. Securities brokers provide the market-making function in ADRs. The market price of an ADR (in US dollar terms) is the price of the underlying security in foreign currency terms multiplied by the exchange rate adjusted for the number of shares included in one ADR (say, ten). ADRs have two advantages over the direct purchase of equities: (i) avoidance of foreign exchange transaction costs; and (ii) ability to trade the foreign securities during regular stock market trading hours of the investor's stock market.

Single Country Funds

Single country funds trade the shares of companies of a single country. The majority of country funds have a closed end status. A closed end fund issues a given number of shares that are traded on the stock exchange as if the fund were an individual stock by itself. Unlike the shares of an open-end fund, shares of a closed-end country fund cannot be redeemed, and the underlying net asset value is set at the home market of the fund. The share value of a fund may very well diverge from the underlying net asset value in the fund's home market. The difference is known as the premium/discount.

International Funds

International funds trade the shares of foreign companies belonging to several countries. The risk related to international funds is called "modified systematic risk" (international diversification reduces risk below the level of risk experienced in most or all national markets).

Global Funds

Unlike international funds, global funds also trade domestic shares. In the USA, international funds are defined to include no more than 24% in US securities, whereas global funds have 50% These funds are issued by large organisations. They tend to be cost-effective in that they sell and redeem shares at net asset value.

International long-term portfolio investment is investment in long-term securities (bonds and equity) denominated in various currencies. The secondary equity markets of the world (also called stock markets or share markets) serve two purposes by providing marketability and equity valuation. Investors or traders who buy shares from the issuing firm in the primary market may not want to hold them indefinitely: the secondary market allows share owners to reduce their holdings of unwanted shares and purchasers to get the shares. Firms will have a difficult time attracting buyers in the primary market without the marketability provided through the secondary market. Competitive trading in the secondary market establishes fair market prices for existing issues.

Foreign portfolio investment has, since the 1980s, been going through spectacular growth, which can be attributed to the following reasons: 1. Deregulation of financial markets. 2. The desire of international investors to improve performance, which can be accomplished via international diversification that enables them to obtain a better risk-return combination. 3. The advent of floating exchange rates. While floating rates produce more risk, they also provide an opportunity for a better risk-return combination. The exchange rate factor can contribute significantly to the overall base currency rate of return. 4. The incorporation of the academic literature on international portfolio diversification in the strategies of portfolio managers. Most of the academic research has become more concerned with practical issues, as academics strive to win consultancy work from financial institutions. 5. Modernisation and increased competitiveness of stock exchanges. For example, the New York Stock Exchange switched from fixed to flexible commissions in 1975. In London there was the Big Bang in the 1980s that made the London Stock Exchange truly international. In general, there has been competition between stock exchanges to attract listings. 6. The development of technology and online trading has made it easier to buy and sell foreign securities. 7. The trend towards more disclosure and provision of information. 8. Expanded pool of liquidity. The growth of the Eurocurrency market and national money markets has led to an expanded international pool of liquidity that is available for international investors, enhancing their ability to finance portfolios.

Foreign portfolio investment is different from domestic portfolio investment in many respects. Some of these differences arise because of: i) The differences in risk and perceptions of risk, including business risk, economic risk and liquidity risk. Furthermore, international investment is subject to foreign exchange risk; ii) the differences in market mechanisms, which can be an obstacle to investment. For example, some markets are illiquid, whereas others are characterised by a concentration of activity. Furthermore, some stock exchanges do not have a trading monopoly, and there are invariably differences in the settlement and how long it takes. Typically, there are some differences in transaction costs and government regulation; iii) the differences in the availability and quality of available information, including disclosure; and finally iv) the (a) differences in accounting standards, which arise from lack of agreement on the objectives of financial standards; (b) different requirements under the company laws of individual countries; (c) differences in tax laws; and (d) differences in the development of the local professional bodies. Specific differences in accounting standards pertain to consolidation practices, disclosure, foreign exchange accounting, auditing and accounting for inflation.

International portfolio management may be conducted by following one of three approaches. The first is passive indexation, whereby international fund managers concentrate on a large number of large capitalisation share issues belonging to leading market indices. The second is the tactical asset management strategy which is based on a broad economic analysis of the leading market indices. The third is the global approach, which is based on measuring risk, return and correlation in terms of the investor's base currency.

Passive management has its theoretical support in the efficient market hypothesis. If the market has priced securities according to all available information, and if the market responds to newly arriving information in a rational manner, then it may be difficult, if not impossible, to outperform the market. Active management, on the other hand, requires considerable analysis and forecasting. The forecaster must provide detailed forecasts of the (i) national economic trends and their influence on each national market in terms of risk and return; and (ii) industrial trends on a worldwide basis, together with their implications for risk and return of specific company shares on a worldwide basis.

There is also modified active management, which requires a basic amount of forecasting for risk return and correlation of the securities or the national indices. Based on this information set, an efficient frontier can be estimated and used as a basis for portfolio selection and construction.

EXTERNAL AID

At the G-8 meeting in Gleneagles, Scotland, in 2005, world leaders pledged a large increase in official development assistance to low-income countries. The objective was to help poor countries achieve the Millennium Development Goals agreed upon at the Millennium Summit of the United Nations in 2000. The promised surge in aid flows is a unique opportunity to fight poverty on a large scale; however, it raises some macroeconomic challenges that need to be addressed to ensure that aid flows have the most beneficial impact.

The problem of managing large aid inflows has several dimensions. *First*, the volatility and unpredictability of aid can complicate public expenditure management. It would be highly damaging if spending on recurrent expenditures (such as in the health and education sectors) had to be adjusted upward and downward on an annual basis because of aid fluctuations. Moreover, sustained periods of large aid inflows could weaken efforts in mobilising domestic revenues, resulting in significant public financing gaps when aid is phased out. *Finally,* institutional constraints (such as weak capacity to manage and monitor public expenditure, or even corruption) may limit the capacity to quickly absorb large amounts of aid effectively.

Another key macroeconomic concern arises when large aid flows are spent on goods and services produced in the domestic economy, which can push up the price of nontraded goods relative to the price of traded goods (the real exchange rate), resulting in a loss of competitiveness in export-oriented, high-value-added sectors. This phenomenon is often called *Dutch disease*. As an example, consider the case in which aid is spent on hiring skilled workers, such as nurses, doctors, and teachers. Because skilled workers are in short supply, their wages quickly go up. As a result, wages of educated people in manufacturing industries and other sectors also increase, hurting exporters who can-not pass on their higher costs to customers.

Generally aid-recipient countries are often reluctant to let the real exchange rate appreciate as aid flowed in. In some countries, the fiscal authority simply did not spend the aid in the year it was received, while the central bank accumulated foreign exchange reserves (Ethiopia and Ghana). In other countries, the fiscal authority increased spending in line with the surge in aid, while the monetary authority tried to prevent real exchange rate appreciation by sterilizing the monetary expansion associated with the increase in public spending (Mozambique, Tanzania, and Uganda).

Gradually phasing in a spending buildup so as to limit the strain on domestic capacity and sterilizing the monetary expansion associated with aid spending both amount to temporarily saving part of the aid in the form of international reserves and can mitigate Dutch disease problems and other side effects of aid. Indeed, these policy responses eased the aggregate demand and real appreciation pressures associated with aid inflows. However, policies aimed at redistributing aid resources over time for the purpose of managing the macroeconomic consequences of large aid flows pose specific challenges. In poor countries, shallow financial markets may make it difficult to execute sterilization operations in the bond markets and result in a burden on banks, for example, through higher reserve requirements. Sterilization policies could also lead to an undesired increase in interest rates and crowding out of private investment.

As a general principle, countries receiving aid should aim at spending it over time as part of their poverty reduction strategy. However, in the short term, saving part of volatile and unpredictable aid flows in the form of international reserves can be justified from both a public finance and a macroeconomic management perspective. *First,* from a public finance perspective, if a temporary spurt of aid is all spent when it arrives (as was often the case in the past), a subsequent sharp drop in aid receipts could prompt the need for either a costly retrenchment of spending or recourse to higher domestic financing of expenditures, which could lead to loss of monetary control and inflation In contrast, saving part of temporary aid surges would help avoid excessive reliance on on domestic financing and prevent an unsustainable buildup of expenditure. On the whole, effective medium-term budgeting requires that: aid-recipient countries smooth recurrent expenditures, so that all programmes undertaken are funded while providing for key lumpy expenditures. *Finally*, to prevent aid dependency, periods of sustained large flows should not diminish efforts to mobilize domestic revenues.

From a macroeconomic management perspective, saving part of temporary increases in aid flows reflects the need to smooth aggregate consumption and to balance demand against supply. Building reserve buffers to self-insure against future negative shocks is particularly important in countries that have low reserve coverage of imports and are subject to frequent exogenous shocks (such as terms-of-trade shocks and droughts). Saving part of aid to smooth spending paths may also be necessary when a country's absorptive capacity is weak and when there are risks of loss of competitiveness from Dutch disease.

In choosing aid spending and absorption paths, policymakers in recipient countries should take into account country specifics such as macroeconomic stability, current and projected improvements in absorptive capacity, the risks of Dutch disease, and debt sustainability. Given the challenges associated with achieving optimal aid spending paths through macroeconomic policy adjustments, donors would contribute to a more effective use of aid by committing to coordinated multi year aid disbursements tailored to country-specific circumstances.

COMMERCIAL DEBT CAPITAL

Commercial debt capital includes a whole range of soources of foreign capital where the overriding consideration is commercial, *i.e.* risk adjusted rate of return. External commercial lonas could include bank loans, buyer's credit, supplier's credit, securitised instruments such as Floating Rate Notes and Fixed Rate Bonds, and commercial borrowings from the private sector window of multilaterial financial institutions.

FOREIGN INVESTMENT: *RECENT TRENDS*

Markets have rallied and near-term stability risks have eased in response to accommodative monetary policies and precautionary policy measures. In the euro area, the authorities have clearly signaled their dedication to achieving "more and stronger Europe." Commitments by the European Central Bank (ECB) have reduced sovereign liquidity risk, and together with the ongoing advance toward a banking union and additional debt relief for Greece, have greatly reduced redenomination risk. These broad improvements in risks and conditions have helped boost the resilience of markets to political uncertainty in Italy and the events in Cyprus. The United States avoided a year-end fall from the "fiscal cliff." However, the postponement of decisions on the debt ceiling, automatic spending cuts, and budget appropriations continue to weigh on sentiment. The Federal Reserve's move from time specific to indicator-specific forward guidance has provided assurance that the policy stance will remain accommodative until meaningful increases in activity and inflation are realized. The Bank of Japan has also undertaken further easing steps by adopting a 2 percent inflation target and a commitment to open-ended purchases of assets.

Improved financial market conditions are benefiting the broader economy, but the transmission is slow and incomplete. Overall macroeconomic risks have declined. In the United States, prospects have brightened; a recovery in the housing market and progress in household deleveraging are bolstering consumption, while banks are poised to increase lending. Emerging market risks have also declined, as growth has stabilized and external funding conditions for emerging market economies are very favorable. However, near-term economic prospects in the euro area remain weak, as public and private balance sheet repair and bank deleveraging continue. However, the reduced likelihood of an acute European crisis, and increased global liquidity contributed to a recovery in global equity markets. After losing about 10 percent of their value between mid-March 2012 and mid-May 2012, global stock markets have recovered with a full year gain of 13.9 percent in developing countries and 12.7 percent in developed countries. Despite these improvements, investors remain concerned over the US fiscal challenges, global economic growth and implementation of the Euro area rescue plan.

Improved sentiment was accompanied by a recovery in gross capital flows to developing countries. Gross capital flows (international bond issuance, cross-border syndicated bank loans and equity placements) to developing countries have fluctuated widely with investor sentiment over the past few years. After rebounding during the first quarter of 2012, flows fell by about 30 and 40 percent in May-June, 2012 following the heightened uncertainty related with the Euro-area debt crisis. Nevertheless, flows have rebounded since July, 2012— the easing of flows in August, 2012 reflecting a normal seasonal lull—as the ECB measures reduced the perceived probability of an acute Euro-area crisis and monetary-easing by Federal Reserve and Japan Central Bank increased global liquidity. With the highest monthly flows since 2007 in September and robust flows since then, gross flows totaled $530 billion, recording a 17 percent increase compared to 2011.

Bond issuance by developing countries reached a historic high in 2012 at $257 billion, almost 50 percent higher than last year's strong flows. Issuances in September ($32.2 billion) was the highest monthly issuances by developing countries on record followed by around $30 billion issuances both in October and November 2012. While corporate issuers from Brazil, Russia, Mexico, and China in financial and oil& gas sectors continued to dominate the market, there were also several sovereigns and developing country corporate borrowers that came to the market for the first time—attracted by low borrowing costs due to unprecedented global liquidity and investors' intense search for yield. Bond emissions have also been boosted by the relative weakness of bank-lending and volatility in equity markets, both symptoms of the financial turmoil of the past few years.

Equity issuance by developing countries was also weak in most part of 2012 as companies stayed away from initial public offerings (IPO) due to volatility in equity markets. Nevertheless the issuance has picked slightly since September. The over-subscribed equity placement by Russia's Sberbank for $5.2 billion in September was followed by few large deals by companies from China, Russia and Turkey in November and December. As a result, total equity issuance totaled $103.4 billion in 2012, 17 percent higher than 2011.

In contrast to bond and equity issuance, syndicated bank lending to developing countries remained subdued this year at $169.5 billion recording a 12.4 percent decline compared to last year. While it is difficult to disentangle effects, deleveraging by high-income country banks and the low cost of bonds are among the factors behind these low flows. However, bank-lending has also shown some tentative signs of recovery in recent months perhaps reflecting less intense Euro Area deleveraging. Syndicated bank lending to developing countries between September and December was the higher than like periods in 2010 and 2011.

Foreign direct investment inflows to developing countries declined by 5% (year-overyear) during the first half of the year following the increased uncertainty in the global financial markets due to Euro-zone problems in late 2011. The decline in actual flows was much less acute than the 20 percent suggested by high-frequency cross-border mergers and acquisitions and green-field investment data. The relative resilience of overall FDI, likely reflects more stable re-invested earnings and intracompany loans.

FDI performance during the first half of the year varied across regions. Flows were very weak for most Eastern European countries including Russia, Latvia, Lithuania, and Serbia as these countries continued to be affected by the economic weakness in high-income Europe. With the exception of Thailand and Philippines, FDI inflows to most East Asian economies also declined. In contrast, FDI inflows increased in almost all Latin American countries supported by high commodity prices and increased investment from the United States, especially to Argentina and Colombia.

Mixed FDI performance is expected to have continued in the second half of the year. The favorable financial conditions since July have encouraged cross-border acquisitions in some developing countries. Flows to Latin America are expected to be strong in the second half as the Belgian beer company AB InBEv's mega buy-out of Mexico's Mexican beer maker Grupo Modelo for $20.1 billion is fully reflected in the data. At the same time, several countries in emerging Europe including Russia, and Turkey have announced plans to accelerate privatization efforts. That said, there have already been few postponements and less successful sales in Russia's banking sector since Russia's successful sale of a stake in Sberbank—one of its largest banks—in September 2012, suggesting that investor appetite might be still limited for these assets. In addition, inflows to large middle income countries such as China and India are expected to decline this year. China is experiencing structural adjustments in their FDI flows, including the relocation of labor-intensive and low-end market-oriented FDI to neighboring countries. Slow growth and some regulatory uncertainties held back the investment flows to India. As result, FDI inflows for the whole year are expected to fall around 6 percent to $600 billion.

Net private capital inflows to developing countries are estimated to have declined to $0.99 trillion (4.1 percent of GDP) in 2012 from $1.1 trillion (4.7 percent of GDP) in 2011. Despite the volatility in market sentiment throughout the year, significant progress in Euro Area crisis response followed by monetary easing by the high-income economies ceased the downward trend in capital inflows to developing countries toward the middle of the year. Nevertheless with exception of net bond and portfolio equity inflows, all other flows marked a decline. The largest drop was in net bank lending (disbursement minus repayments). Net bank lending with both types of maturities (short- and medium & long term) declined by 33 percent. The fall in short-term flows partly reflects slower trade growth and reduced demand for trade finance.

Deleveraging by international banks cut into acquisition and trade finance. The 2008/9 financial crisis has put significant deleveraging pressures on global banking system. Banks have been forced to cut their loan portfolios to offset balance sheets losses from loan and capital losses. The pressures have been particularly strong among high-income European banks as faltering growth prospects and debt problems undermined the value of their sovereign and other assets. Funding conditions were exacerbated toward the end of 2011, when new regulations tightened capital ratio requirements and increased dollar liquidity constraints. Deleveraging was achieved through a combination of reduced lending, sales of nonstrategic assets, and exit from riskier businesses subject to tighter capital buffer requirements. High-income bank deleveraging and tightened credit standards cut directly into capital flows to developing countries—most notably those countries and regions with close ties to European banks.

Since 2008 spreads on all types of loans widened sharply from a range of 100 to 150 bps to a range 250 to 350 bps. Despite the sharp increase in spreads, borrowing cost actually declined because of the sharp compression in the underlying pricing benchmark six-month Libor rate. Most of the reduction in syndicated bank lending to developing countries concerned loans for acquisitions purposes. Acquisition loans are usually given to a company to buy specific assets and are typically used of short-term tenor. Some of the 70 percent fall likely reflects a decline in demand for loans due to weak economic activity and the cancelation or postponement of expansion plans given increased economic uncertainty. Such loans fell most sharply in Europe and Central Asia (93 percent)—the developing region hardest hit by the crisis, and Latin America (73 percent) a region with close ties to the European banking system. Loans to South Asia were broadly stable.

Syndicated lending for trade finance purposes was also considerably affected with a 35 percent fall compared to its pre-crisis levels. The decline mostly reflects retrenchment by the European banks that played a pivotal role in global trade finance provision. In addition to their need to rebuild their capital stock, dollar funding challenges of European banks constrained their ability to fund trade activity. Most of the trade transaction settlements are made in US dollars, and European banks suffered from limited access to dollar funding during the second half of 2011 after US money market funds withdrew some of their investment as the European debt crisis. Trade related funding shortfalls were sharpest for Sub-Saharan Africa (70 percent) and European countries (50 percent), followed by Latin America and Middle East and North Africa (25 percent). Anecdotal evidence suggests that other international lenders (mainly Asian financial institutions such as Japanese banks) and domestic banks (mostly in Latin America) filled the funding gap in their corresponding regions. The world bank group WBG has increased its support to trade finance in low income countries, through the IFC's Global Trade Finance Program, and a program to support commodity traders from low income countries.

Despite the decline in total loans, average maturity for all types of syndicated bank loans remained at their pre-crisis levels, around five to six years. Even for project finance which tends to be funded by longer-term loans—maturities have remained more or less stable at around 9 years since 2005.

One cautionary factor, however, is the increased concentration of bank loans since 2009. Investment grade borrowers accounted for 80 percent of bank loans since 2009, up sharply from 72 percent during 2005-2008. Increased bias toward investment grade borrowers might partly reflect preparation for the upcoming regulatory changes. For example, some banks soon will start operating under Basel III with a range of

TABLE 1

NET CAPITAL FLOWS TO DEVELOPING COUNTRIES ($BILLIONS)

	2008	*2009*	*2010*	*2011*	*2012e*	*2013f*	*2014f*	*2015f*
Current account balance	412.9	240.5	187.5	152.1	12.6	-8.0	-65.4	-80.4
Capital inflows	812.6	701.7	1,219.1	1,112.4	1,007.2	1,134.1	1,250.9	1351.5
Private inflows, net	782.2	620.7	1,145.9	1,082.4	993.1	1,123.4	1,244.2	1348.4
Equity inflows, net	583.3	542.0	710.8	647.8	644.5	761.2	856.1	902.9
Net FDI inflows	636.9	427.9	582.7	638.8	600.1	693.2	756.5	782.96
Net portfolio equity inflows	-53.6	114.2	128.2	8.9	44.4	68.0	99.6	119.90
Private creditors, net	198.8	78.7	435.1	434.6	348.6	362.2	388.1	445.50
Bonds	-8.6	61.0	129.7	123.8	143.3	126.1	108.4	110.50
Banks	223.3	-11.9	37.2	108.2	71.5	80.6	88.9	105.10
Short-term debt flows	-17.1	17.8	257.6	189.3	126.7	146.3	180.4	220.10
Other private	1.3	11.7	10.7	13.3	7.1	9.2	10.4	9.80
Official inflows, net	30.4	81.0	73.2	30.0	14.1	10.7	6.7	3.10
World Bank	7.2	18.3	22.4	6.6	4.6			
IMF	10.8	26.8	13.8	0.5	-3.9			
Other official	12.4	35.9	36.9	22.8	13.4			
Capital outflows	-321.4	-174.5	-310.0	-320.0	-370.6	-373.4	-414.3	-463.6
FDI outflows	-211.8	-144.3	-213.9	-213.1	-238.0	-275.0	-325.0	-370.0
Portfolio equity outflows	-32.3	-75.2	-46.5	-15.9	-17.6	-19.4	-22.3	-28.6
Private debt outflows	-78.3	50.7	-57.3	-81.0	-103.0	-72.0	-61.0	-56.0
Other outflows	1.0	-5.7	7.7	-10.0	-12.0	-7.0	-6.0	-9.0
Net capital flows (inflows + outflows)	491.2	527.2	909.1	792.4	636.6	760.7	836.6	887.9
Net unidentified flows/a	-78.3	-286.7	-721.6	-640.3	-624.0	-768.7	-902.0	-9

Note: e = estimate, f = forecast.

/a Combination of errors and omissions, unidentified capital inflows to and outflows from developing countries.

Source: World Bank

provisions and tightening of conditions. These banks may have been adjusting their balance sheets in response to the enhanced recognition of counterparty risk and an increase in risk-weight of certain lines of business. There are concerns that some of the provisions under Basel III may exacerbate further deleveraging and increase the borrowing costs for trade finance and project finance.

Even without the burden of additional regulatory measures, the cost of borrowing for both bond and bank financing will increase in the medium term when developed countries start monetary tightening as low benchmark rates have kept the costs down especially after the crisis.

Medium-term prospects for capital flows to developing countries are for continued modest increases (as a share of recipient GDP). With more upgrades than downgrades market assessment of the credit quality this year, the risk profile of developing countries continued to improve compared with high-income countries which experienced further deterioration in 2012—suggesting that they will continue to attract a growing share of international capital flows. Despite the weak growth environment, developing countries are expected to grow between five to six percent in coming years more than twice as fast as high-income countries. Flows are also likely to be attracted by these higher growth prospects and risk-adjusted interest rates (despite the recent easing of monetary policy in many developing economies, interest rates in these economies are expected to remain higher than in rich countries).

Under the baseline scenario that there will not be a major set-back in the resolution of Euro-area crisis and US fiscal challenges, and that there will be no major loss of confidence in the global financial markets, net private capital flows are projected to increase to $1.12 trillion (4.15 percent of developing-country GDP) in 2013 and gradually reach $1.35 trillion (4.1 percent) by 2015. Increased global liquidity and monetary accommodation in major high-income countries (the US Federal Reserve indicates its policy rate will remain low till 2014) are expected to keep high-income country interest rates low, prompting search for yield and supporting capital flows to developing countries in coming years. Bank lending is expected to rise gradually as intense deleveraging pressures have now eased. Nevertheless the growth in private debt flows to developing countries in the medium term will be hindered by a tightening of regulatory and a gradual policy tightening after 2014 in developed countries.

FDI inflows to developing countries are expected to increase throughout the forecast period reaching $783 billion (2.4 percent of GDP) by 2015. Despite the considerable realside uncertainties in the short-term, multinationals continue to be attracted to developing countries' medium-term growth prospects, large and growing consumer base, natural resources and still low labor costs. In addition, many developing countries are bringing down barriers on foreign investment. For example, following its recent WTO accession Russia has committed to reducing restrictions on foreign investors in number of services industries. Several countries in Eastern Europe have been pursuing privatization in their services sector. Similarly, India might attract influx of investment in coming years as the cap on foreign ownership in multi-brand retail and aviation businesses has been raised comes in the backdrop of a worrisome decline this year. While China continues to be experiencing rising wages and productions costs, multinationals are investing in China to serve its rising middle income. FDI inflows to developing countries will be supported by increasing South-South flows as the capital outflows increase over the years.

FDI inflows are expected to increase also in low-income countries supported by rising South South FDI and resource-related investments. This is particularly important as FDI is an important source of external financing for these economies with limited or no access to other types of capital flows. In addition, the outlook for net overseas development assistance (ODA), which has been a stable source of development financing for the poor economies, looks gloomy. As many high-income countries continue to struggle with fiscal sustainability, it is unlikely that they will be able to meet their Monterrey targets of providing 0.7 per cent of their national income in ODA— except in a few instances.

The outlook for private capital flows is still subject to serious downside risks. First despite the recent progress towards a resolution for Euro -area debt crisis, considerable uncertainties remain related to the implementation of the ECB's announced but not-tested OMT plan; its ability to resolve the debt issues of high-spread economies; the speed of economic adjustment in high-spread countries; and the establishment of a single bank supervision mechanism. Any major set-back could lead to a renewed crisis of confidence and potentially a freezing up of financial markets. A lack of progress in dealing with the fiscal challenges in the US and Japan have similar potential to generate confidence issues. These uncertainties are likely to generate volatility on the way even if they do not get to a level to reverse the upward trend in capital flows.

QUESTIONS

1. Discuss the role of foreign capital in growth process. Why has it generally yielded conflicting results?
2. Critically examine the recent measures taken by the countries worldwide to improve their investment climate.
3. "Foreign direct investment has different implications for the host and recipient countries as compared to other capital flows." Discuss.
4. Discuss the economic rationale to attract foreign investment. What is the effect of these incentives on investment decisions?
5. "Liberalisation of national policy frameworks is one of the key driving force of globalisation." Comment.
6. Critically examine the main determinants of foreign direct investment (FDI).
7. "Foreign Direct Investment (FDI) exists because of the international immobility of the factors of production." Do you agree?
8. Discuss the role of strategic and long-term factors in the foreign capital movement.
9. Discuss the foreign capital flows in the context of improved risk dimensions of global financial stability.
10. Explain the foreign investment decision process.

29

FOREIGN INVESTMENT AND INTERNATIONAL INVESTMENT AGREEMENTS

INTRODUCTION

Current investment policies at the national and international levels are being shaped by a number of important developments, which are likely to also define future policy directions: There are simultaneous moves to (i) further liberalise investment regimes and pro-investment (FDI) on the one hand, and (ii) regulate and harness FDI in pursuit of broader policy objectives on the other. This dichotomy in investment policy trends contrasts with the clearer trends of the 1950s-1980s (that focused on regulation) and the 1990s-early 2000 (that focussed on liberalisation); At the national level, there is an increasing emphasis on the rights of the State and the obligations of the investors, including through new entry and operational measures. Economic stimulus packages and State aids have impacted on foreign investment while instances of investment protectionism have so far not been observed; Rebalancing is also emerging within the rapidly growing multifaceted and multilatered network of international investment agreements (IIAs), in addition, the systemic evolution of the IIA regime in content and structure points towards achieving greater coherence; Other international investment initiatives—including those addressing broader economic, social and environmental issues—also point towards a greater emphasis on the role of regulation.

NATIONAL POLICY DEVELOPMENTS

The trend towards investment liberalisation, facilitation and promotion is remarkable in light of the ongoing financial crisis. Governments did not revert to open investment protectionism, as was feared. Liberalisation measures extended to many industries and a broad range of issues. Policies included, inter alia, the opening up of previously closed sectors, the liberalisation of land acquisition, the dismantling of monopolies and the privatisation of state-owned companies.

In addition to continuous liberalisation efforts, numerous countries also took steps to further promote and facilitate foreign investment. Typical examples have been sector-specific policies and regulations, such as fiscal and financial incentives to encourage foreign investment in particular industries or regions, including special economic zones. Facilitation measures involved easing screening requirements, streamlining approval procedures, enhancing cooperation among national investment authorities in approval procedures or accelerating licensing processes for investment projects. Some of the measures also sought to promote outward FDI by simplifying approval and administrative procedures applicable to these investments, or granting preferential tax treatment.

In 2010, at least 74 countries around the globe adopted upwards of 149 policy measures affecting foreign investment (table 1). Of these measures, 101 related to investment liberalisation, promotion and facilitation, while 48 introduced new restrictions or regulations relevant to FDI. Compared to 2009, the percentage of more restrictive policy measures increased only slightly, from approximately 30 per cent to 32 per cent.

TABLE 1

NATIONAL REGULATORY CHANGES, 2000–2010
(NUMBER OF MEASURES)

Item	*2000*	*2001*	*2002*	*2003*	*2004*	*2005*	*2006*	*2007*	*2008*	*2009*	*2010*
Number of countries that introduced changes	70	71	72	82	103	92	91	58	54	50	74
Number of regulatory changes	150	207	246	242	270	203	177	98	106	102	149
Liberalisation/promotion	147	193	234	218	234	162	142	74	83	71	101
Regulations/restrictions	3	14	12	24	36	41	35	24	23	31	48

Source: UNCTAD. Investment Policy Monitor database.

This maintains the long-term trend of investment policy becoming increasingly restrictive, rather than liberalising. Overall, the percentage of investment liberalisation and promotion measures was slightly higher in developing countries and transition economies than in developed countries.

A closer look at the type of policy measures adopted reveals that most related to operational conditions for TNCs, followed by measures affecting the entry and establishment phase, and promotion and facilitation measures (table 2). Overall, measures aimed at improving investment conditions continued to outnumber measures introducing new restrictions or regulations, but the margin is diminishing. The numerical difference was particularly large with regard to the entry and establishment category.

As regards the geographical distribution, developing countries were especially active in revising investment policy. Asian countries (including West Asia) were the most active (56 measures), followed by Africa (29) and Latin America (25). Asia stands out, with a total of 46 out of 56 measures being more favourable to FDI. Measures from West Asia, for instance, were mainly in the area of liberalisation of entry conditions, whereas for South, East and South-East Asia, promotion and facilitation also played an important role. In Africa, governments focused particularly on new promotion and facilitation measures to foster a more favourable investment climate. Due principally to developments in a small number of Latin American countries, this region stands out for the number of policy measures that were less favourable to FDI. These measures involved the strengthening of State control (up to and including nationalisation) over natural resources based industries, including both agribusiness and extractive industries. For developed countries the number of more favourable and less favourable entry measures was equal, while in transition economies these measures mainly related to the introduction of new privatisation schemes.

TABLE 2

NATIONAL REGULATORY CHANGES IN 2010, BY TYPE OF MEASURE AND REGION[A]

(NUMBER OF MEASURES)

	Entry and establishment[b]		*Operation[c]*		*Promotion and facilitation[d]*
	More favourable to FDI	*Less favourable to FDI*	*More favourable to FDI*	*Less favourable*	
Total	40	16	34	33	35
Developed countries	6	6	10	6	4
Developing economies	30	10	19	24	27
Africa	4	2	8	4	11
South, East and South-East Asia	12	5	5	5	12
West Asia	10	0	4	0	3
Latin America and the Caribbean	4	3	2	15	1
South-East Europe and the CIS	4	0	5	3	4

Source: UNCTAD, Investment Policy Monitor database.

a Since some of the measures can be classified under more than one type, overall totals differ from table III.1.

b Entry measures and establishment: measures related to ownership and control or approval and admission conditions for (both inward and outward) FDI and other measures affecting the entry or establishment of TNCs.

c Operation: measures related to non-discrimination, nationalisation or expropriation, capital transfer, dispute settlement, performance requirements, corporate tax rates and other measures affecting the operating conditions for TNCs.

d Promotion and facilitation: measures related to fiscal and financial incentives, procedural measures related to approval and admission, or investment facilitation and other institutional support.

Approximately half of the investment policy measures taken in 2010 related to one or more specific industries. Many different industries were involved, some more than others (in particular, extractive industries and financial services). For most industries, measures in the area of liberalisation or promotion of FDI dominated those of a restrictive nature (table 3). The main exceptions to this were the extractive industries and to a lesser extent agribusiness. These industries were responsible for a large share of the restrictive measures in 2010, including measures such as the introduction of performance requirements and new tax regimes, and the renegotiation of contracts.

TABLE 3

NATIONAL REGULATORY CHANGES IN 2010, BY INDUSTRY

(Per cent)

	Liberalisation/ promotion	*Regulations/ restrictions*
Total	67	33
No specific industry	84	16
Agribusiness	38	62
Extractive industries	7	93
Manufacturing	50	50
Electricity, gas and water	75	25
Financial services	59	41
Other services	61	39

Source: UNCTAD, Investment Policy Monitor database.

Investment Liberalisation and Promotion

At least 56 countries adopted new investment liberalisation or promotion measures in various industries. The number of these measures increased from 71 in 2009 to 101 in 2010. Of the 40 new investment liberalisation measures implemented in 2010, 25 were specifically taken to liberalise foreign investment, and 15 were of a more general nature improving the overall policy framework for FDI. These measures were most pronounced in Asia and related to a broad range of industries. Of the 34 measures improving operational conditions for TNCs, most relate to the lowering of corporate tax rates.

Most of the measures to promote or facilitate foreign investment were taken by countries in Africa and Asia. A few categories of facilitation and promotion measures stand out as having been frequently used. These include the streamlining of admission procedures and the opening of new – or the expansion of existing – special economic zones.

From a practical point of view, facilitation measures can often be more important for investors than a formal easing of investment restrictions. Informal barriers are regularly cited as major investment hurdles in developing countries. Removing such bottlenecks is also politically less sensitive than investment liberalisation. Moreover, the smaller the differences between countries in their formal openness to FDI, the greater the importance of "soft" investment conditions, like a welcoming, competent and efficient administration.

Investment promotion measures have also been taken in the context of industrial policy. Several countries have taken steps to encourage FDI in specific economic activities, such as hitech industries or car manufacturing. Promotion measures included fiscal and financial incentives, and the establishment of special economic zones.

INVESTMENT REGULATIONS AND RESTRICTIONS

The regulatory framework for foreign investment tightened in numerous countries and across several regions, either through new measures concerning entry and operations, the stricter application of existing rules and regulations, or expropriation and nationalisationing and electricity. Less severe measures affecting the operation of foreign investors included the introduction of local-content and other performance requirements. In addition, numerous States increased their shares in companies as part of financial bailout measures, sometimes leading to the nationalisation of the companies in question.

Regarding FDI entry, new limitations on foreign participation were introduced in some industries, or the approval and screening procedures for inward FDI were tightened, sometimes on national security grounds.

Greater State intervention in the economy was most obvious in expropriations, some of which affected foreign investors. Expropriations occurred in a few Latin American affecting industries such as banking and electricity. Less severe measures affecting the operation of foreign investors included the introduction of local-content and other performance requirements. In addition, numerous States increased their shares in companies as part of financial bailout measures, sometimes leading to the nationalisation of the companies in question.

A number of reasons may explain the move towards stronger State intervention in the economy. *First,* the protection of strategic industries and national security interests has gained momentum in recent years. *Second,* concerns over the crowding out of domestic companies by foreign ones, the perception that foreign investment failed to generate sufficient links with the domestic economy or the wish to achieve a "fairer" redistribution of wealth may have further accentuated this development. *Third,* the financial and other crises (such as the food crisis) have translated into a desire to regulate specific industries more strictly. *Fourth,* after a period of unrestricted growth, emerging economies are giving more weight to environmental and social protection. Likewise, least developed countries are filling gaps in their regulatory framework.

The rebalancing of investor rights and obligations continued, with a particular focus on the financial sector. Notwithstanding the continuing predominance of investment liberalisation and promotion, numerous countries have adopted measures to strengthen the regulatory framework for investment, both domestic and foreign. The number of measures restricting or regulating FDI increased from 31 in 2009 to 48 in 2010. This has been the case particularly in the financial sector, where several countries tightened existing rules in order to prevent future financial crises. Most of these measures have been taken by G-20 countries, and other members of the Basel Accord. In general, these new financial regulations focus on an increase in bank capital and liquidity requirements, reducing the existing risks in connection with financial institutions that are "too big to fail", and reinforcing oversight. Different opinions exist as to the impact of the new regulations on FDI in the financial sector. Concerns have been expressed about the potential negative impact of the new regulations on existing investments, but regulators argue that the beneficial impact on the macro economy should more than offset the transitional adjustment costs.

More State intervention also became apparent in the natural resources based industry. A number of countries, in particular in Latin America, pursued nationalisation policies, with foreign investors being one target. Some nationalisations occurred also in other industries, including financial services. Likewise, a move towards stricter regulations manifested itself in new operational conditions for foreign investors, such as local content requirements. Once again, the extractive industry was particularly affected.

Compared to the quantity of nationalisations and new operating conditions for investment, new FDI entry and establishment restrictions have been less common. In large part, these measures have related to screening and approval regulations (Box 1). No clear pattern emerged according to which certain industries would be specifically liable to new entry restrictions. The latter vary between countries due to individual political sensitivities. A few foreign investments have been rejected on national interest grounds. The nationalisations and sector-specific entry restrictions are part of broader developments in industrial policy, characterised by an extension of protective measures to national champions and strategic industries and by the intrusion of national security concepts into industrial policy considerations. Together, this raises important questions on how to safeguard adequate policy space for countries to adopt FDI restrictions that they consider necessary, while at the same time avoiding such policies degenerating into investment protectionism.

Although still a minority, overall the number of restrictive investment regulations and administrative practices has accumulated to a significant degree over the past few years. Together with their continued upward trend, as well as stricter review procedures for FDI entry, this poses the risk of potential investment protectionism.

BOX 1

EXAMPLES OF ENTRY RESTRICTIONS FOR FOREIGN INVESTORS IN 2010-2011

- Australia rejected Singapore Exchange's US$88.3 billion offer to take over Australian Securities Exchange, which it concluded was not in Australia's national interest.[a]
- Brazil reinstated restrictions on rural land-ownership for foreigners by modifying the way a law dating back to 1971 is to be interpreted. The reinterpreted law establishes that, on rural land-oownership, Brazilian companies which are majority owned by foreigners are subject to the legal regime applicable to foreign companies.[b]
- The Minister of Industry of Canada announced the blocking of the Australian mining company BHP Billiton's US$339 billion takeover of Potash Corp. (a Canadian fertilizer and mining company).[c]

Source : UNCTAD.

a Australian Treasury, Foreign Investment Decision, 8 April 2011.

b New Interpretation of Law No. 5 609/71. Papecen CGU/AGU No. 01/2008, 23 August 2010.

c Ministry y of Industry Press Releease 3 November 2010.Catas dolor sint facia niatur rerendi dit intur sinventedas val

ECONOMIC STIMULUS PACKAGES AND STATE AID

Managing the impact of crisis-response measures on investment flows, including public exits from bailed-out firms, constitutes a great challenge for governments. The great majority of new policy measures potentially affecting FDI relate to the financial crisis. They include firm-specific, sector-specific and cross-sectoral measures intended to help improve economic conditions in host countries, which in turn can improve the investment climate and affect the economic determinants of foreign investments. Some countries' rescue packages also involved the temporary nationalisation of distressed domestic companies, in full or in part.

As a result of these sizable interventions, State control over distressed industries – in particular the financial services industry – continues to be high. For instance, the total amount of public commitments of the G20 countries – equity, loans and guarantees – on 20 May 2010 exceeded $1 trillion. In the financial sector, only about a tenth of the financial firms that had benefited from such support had reimbursed loans, repurchased equity or relinquished public guarantees at that time. Several hundred financial firms thus continued to benefit from public support, and in non-financial sectors, at least 20,000 individual firms continued to benefit from emergency support programmes.

Allegations have been made that the State control over these companies has affected their investment behaviour, in particular with regard to their investments abroad. A nontransparent application of State aids leaves ample room for discriminatory interventions in companies' economic decision-making – both from the point of view of curtailing new investment plans or dealing with ongoing foreign operations and their role on a company's value chains.

Managing the investment impacts of emergency measures taken in response to the crisis still constitutes a great challenge for governments. This is a particular concern for developing countries whose industries might be negatively affected by unfair competition resulting from State aid, and who do not have the financial means to offer comparable aid to their companies. Developed countries should therefore ensure that such programmes are wound down at an appropriate pace without unduly affecting economic recovery and that the crisis is not used as a pretext to discriminate directly or indirectly against certain investors, including foreign investors.

More than two and a half years after the outbreak of the financial crisis, some countries continue to hold considerable assets following bail-out operations, have substantial outstanding loans to individual firms, or continue emergency support schemes for the financial and non-financial sectors. However, in the financial sector, many countries have ceased to accept applications from financial firms to public assistance schemes. With the closure of support schemes to new entrants, the main outstanding issue relates to the unwinding of assets and liabilities that remain on government books as a legacy of the emergency measures. So far, this process has advanced relatively slowly, and less than a fifth of the financial firms that received crisis-related support have repaid loans fully, repurchased equity or relinquished public guarantees. In the non-financial sectors, legacy assets and liabilities are much lower, but the number of companies that benefited from crisis-related government support is much greater. The unwinding of emergency aid to the non-financial sector has also started. For instance, in the automotive industry – one of the main industries at which aid was targeted – companies in Canada, France and the United States have partly repaid loans, and some of the government equity holdings in the companies have been acquired by private investors.

In all, in April 2011, governments were estimated to hold legacy assets and liabilities in financial and non-financial firms valued at over $2 trillion. By far the largest share relates to several hundred firms in the financial sector. This indicates a potential wave of privatisations in years to come.

THE INTERNATIONAL INVESTMENT AGREEMENTS (IIAs)

As the IIA universe continues to expand, the policy discourse about how to enhance IIAs' contribution to sustainable development is intensifying, at both the national and international levels. In 2010, a total of 178 new IIAs were concluded (54 bilateral investment treaties (BITs), 113 double taxation treaties (DTTs) and 11 IIAs other than BITs and DTTs ("other IIAs"). As a result, at the end of 2010 the IIA universe contained 6,092 agreements, including 2,807 BITs, 2,976 DTTs and 309 "other IIAs". The trend seen in 2010 of rapid treaty expansion – with more than three treaties concluded every week – is expected to continue in 2011, the first five months of which saw the conclusion of 48 new IIAs (23 BITs, 20 DTTs and five "other IIAs") and more than 100 free trade agreements (FTAs) and other economic agreements with investment provisions currently under negotiation. At the same time, the shift of responsibility for FDI from EU member States to the European level in likely to affect the IIA regime (with EU member States being parties to more than 1,300 BITs with third countries) (Box 2).

In terms of total numbers of IIAs, as of May 2011, the United Kingdom is party to 320 IIAs, followed by Germany (304) and France (297). Amongst the developing countries, China tops the list, with 249 IIAs, followed by the Republic of Korea (190) and Turkey (183). The Russian Federation (141) and Croatia (118) rank first among the transition economies.

Twenty of the 54 BITs signed in 2010 were between developing countries and/or transition economies, as were four of the 11 other IIAs, a trend possibly related to developing countries' growing role as outward investors. With respect to "other IIAs", treaties concluded in 2010 continue to fall into the three categories: IIAs including obligations commonly found in BITs (three treaties in 2010); agreements with limited investment-related provisions (five treaties); and IIAs focusing on investment cooperation (three treaties).

Countries continue to conclude IIAs, sometimes with novel provisions aimed at rebalancing the rights and obligations between States and investors and ensuring coherence between IIAs and other public policies. At the same time, the policy discourse about international investment policymaking intensifies at both domestic and international levels, amounting to a period of reflection on the future orientation of the IIA regime to make it work better for sustainable development. Nationally, different investment stakeholders have started to voice their concerns about the costs and benefits and the future orientation of IIAs, including civil society, business and parliamentarians. While IIAs have traditionally been negotiated by the relevant government ministry, there is now an emerging trend of inter-ministerial or inter-agency coordination. This process is particularly prominent at the European level, but is also evident in EU member States and other countries around the globe. To the extent that countries are reviewing their model BITs, or that IIAs need to undergo domestic ratification processes, the call for increasing transparency and inclusiveness of IIA-related decision-making is gaining additional traction.

BOX 2

EU FDI POLICYMAKING

The entry into force in December 2009 of the Lisbon Treaty shifted responsibility in the field of FDI from the member States to the EU.While European member States continue concluding BITs a the shift of responsibility has given rise to a number of substantive and procedural questions about future EU investment policymaking at the international level. In that context, the relevant European institutions and non-governmental investment stakeholders have expressed their views.

While there seems to be agreement among EU institutions on the general orientation of future EU IIAs (i.e. that they should contribute to sustainable and inclusive growth and be guided by the principles and objectives of the Union's external action, notably human rights and sustainable development), differences of opinion have emerged regarding the details (e.g. provisions on scope and definition, the content and formulation of key substantive and procedural protection provisions, and the extent to which IIAs should refer to corporate social responsibility (CSR)).

Opinions differ even more when considering non-governmental investment stakeholders. A number of civil society groups consider IIAs a threat to the public interest, and suggest that it is time for a radically new approach to foreign investment. In contrast, some European industry groups highlight the positive role BITs play in increasing the competitiveness of European industry.

The disagreement is compounded by questions about future development of the EU IIA regime, including how to deal with the selection of future negotiating partners, with ongoing negotiations and with existing EU BITs (both intra- and extra-EU BITs). The outcome of this debate is likely to have a major impact on the global IIA regime. EU member States are among the countries with the largest numbers of BITs. Moreover, over the last three years, Europe as a whole accounted for approximately 30 per cent of global FDI flows.

The EU debate offers great potential in so far as it allows the putting into practice of lessons learned regarding the design and substance of IIAs and their impact on sustainable development. However, open questions, attendant uncertainties, lack of predictability and stability will all serve to complicate the situation for EU negotiating partners and the IIA regime generally.

Source: UNCTAD.

a. Thirty of the 54 BITs concluded in 2010 involved an EU member State. Seventeen of the 30 European BITs were renegotiated ones.

IIA COVERAGE OF INVESTMENT

The intended purpose of IIAs is to protect and to promote foreign investment. Today, about two-thirds of global FDI stock benefits from post establishment protection with comprehensive sectoral coverage granted by BITs or "other IIAs". However, this represents only one-fifth of possible bilateral relationships. To provide full coverage another 14,100 bilateral investment treaties would be required.

These 14,100 treaties would include, on the one hand, many bilateral relationships with little propensity to invest (i.e. where FDI flows are negligible) or with little propensity to protect (e.g.between OECD member countries). On the other hand, they would also include a few bilateral relationships where substantial FDI stocks exist that are not covered by any existing investment protection agreement (e.g. China and the United States, Brazil and China).

These findings beg a number of questions with regard to the effectiveness of IIAs in terms of generating investment flows and promoting development gains. For example, the existence of considerable FDI stocks in the absence of post establishment treaty coverage suggests that for some investment relationships, IIAs fall short of being a determining factor for investment.

Furthermore, some of the FDI stock is subject to protection offered by two or more IIAs. In fact, 570 BITs at least partially duplicate the post-establishment protection offered by other agreements. The extent of overlap and risk of contradictory provisions depends on the precise formulation used in BITs and/or "other IIAs" in terms of protection granted and flexibilities offered.

A further 630 BITs overlap with "other IIAs" that contain investment liberalisation provisions only (e.g. EU partnership, association and cooperation agreements), resulting in a situation where post-establishment protection (offered by BITs) complements pre-establishment protection/liberalisation (offered by "other IIAs"). Whether such comprehensive coverage is desirable is an important question, the answer to which is highly context- and situation-specific, and needs to be assessed against the overall objective of ensuring that IIAs promote investment for sustainable development. Furthermore, investment relationships have to be seen from a dynamic perspective, as the propensities to invest, and hence to protect through IIAs, may change over time (as witnessed by the growing interest of some emerging outward investing countries in IIAs).

OTHER INVESTMENT-RELATED POLICY DEVELOPMENTS

The agricultural sector in low-income countries has been suffering from serious underinvestment for decades. Private investment can contribute to long-term solutions to food security and development, provided that such investment is socially responsible and environmentally sustainable.

At the Seoul Summit, the G-20 leaders considered the disproportionate effect of the financial crisis on the most vulnerable in the poorest countries, and the slow progress toward achieving the Millennium Development Goals (MDGs). The G-20 leaders committed to work in partnership with other developing countries, low-income countries (LICs) in particular, to help build the capacity to achieve and maintain their economic growth potential.

The Seoul Consensus consists of a set of principles and guidelines to achieve the MDGs. The six core principles focus on economic growth, global development partnership, global or regional systemic issues, private sector participation, complementarity, and outcome orientation. In addition, the G-20 leaders identified nine areas, or "key pillars", where action is necessary to resolve the most significant bottlenecks to inclusive, sustainable and resilient growth in developing countries. These areas are: infrastructure, private investment and job creation, human resource development, trade, financial inclusion, growth with resilience, food security, domestic resource mobilisation, and knowledge-sharing.

The G-20 leaders also endorsed the Multi-Year Action Plan on Development, with deadlines running from 2012 to late 2014. This Plan includes 16 specific and detailed actions on the nine key pillars identified in the Seoul Consensus. Three pillars in the Multi-Year Action Plan on Development are closely related to investment. Under the "Private Investment and Job Creation" pillar, the G-20 leaders emphasised the importance of domestic and foreign private investment as a key source of employment, wealth creation and innovation, which in turn contributes to sustainable development and poverty reduction in developing countries. The leaders committed to support and assist investors, developing countries and key development partners in their work to maximize the economic value-added of private investment.

In the past few years, the investment community has been mainly concerned with the financial crisis and its impacts on FDI and the global economy. However, political risk considerations are expected to return to the fore of investors concerns, both in the developed and in the developing world. So far, however, these concern have not yet resulted in greater reliance on political risk insurance. As a consequence of the global economic crisis, the volume of liability underwritten by Berne Union (BU) investment insurers fell by 6 per cent to $137.1 billion from 2008 to 2009. Reflecting the recovery in new business, the volume of liability totalled over $142 billion as of June 2010, an increase of 7.7per cent in 12 months. The slight pick-up in 2010 results from the modest recovery in FDI during the year.

Political risk insurance evolved in 2010. For example, the Non-Concessional Borrowing Policy (NCBP) was updated to avoid the re-accumulation of external debt in low-income countries that have benefited from the "multilateral" debt relief initiative of 2006. Since April 2010, the NCBP has been successful in attracting an increased number of creditors to adhere to NCBP for promotion of financing of low-income countries. Finally, political risk insurance has linkages with other areas of investment policymaking. For example, some entities condition the granting of political risk insurance on the existence of an IIA with the host country in question.

Over a period,IIA obligations have become increasingly sophisticated and refined. This partly reflects treaty makers' response to arbitral awards that had revealed difficulties arising from the traditionally broad language of older IIAs and which, on a number of occasions, had led to unintended and contradictory outcomes.

Many recent treaties – both new and renegotiated IIAs as well as revised model BITs– suggest that governments seek to formulate agreements more precisely, paying greater attention to ensuring that the treaty language reflects their domestic policy objectives, reaffirming and strengthening States' right to regulate in the public interest, and trying to enhance the legitimacy of ISDS processes. The following broad developments emerge from a review of selected recent IIAs:

Clarifying the scope of the treaty

(i) Excluding from the scope of the treaty certain areas of regulation: taxation, government procurement, grants and subsidies or financial services; (ii) excluding specific assets (such as public debt securities, claims arising from purely commercial contracts, trade finance operations, shortterm loans) from the definition of investment; (iii) including objective criteria as to what constitutes an investment; and/or (iv) requiring that an investment be specifically approved in writing by the competent authority of a member State (e.g. the ACIA).

Introducing general exceptions that allow more room for regulation by host economies

(i) general exceptions that exempt measures necessary to protect human, animal or plant life or health, or for the conservation of exhaustible natural resources, public morals, etc.; (ii) national security exceptions, at times of a self-judging nature – that is, as considered necessary by the contracting party and not amenable to an arbitral review; (iii) prudential carve-outs that typically cover measures aimed at the protection of financial market participants, the maintenance of the safety, soundness and integrity of financial institutions and ensuring the integrity and stability of a financial system and, finally, (iv) traditional balance-of payment exceptions.

Clarifying the scope and meaning of specific obligations

(i) FET: specifying that the concept of FET does not require treatment in addition to, or beyond that, which is required under customary international law (Mexico-Singapore BIT (2009)) or even limiting FET to denial of justice only; (ii) full protection and security: clarifying that the standard relates to police protection and thus concerns only physical security, rather than other types of security (legal, economic, etc.); (iii) MFN: clarifying whether the MFN obligation encompasses ISDS provisions and thus allows an investor to invoke more favourable ISDS provisions from IIAs with a third country or not; (iv) indirect expropriation: introducing language that draws a line between a compensable indirect expropriation and the adverse effects endured by a foreign investor as a result of bona fide regulation in the public interest; (v) expropriation: specifying that the issuance of compulsory licenses; (vi) umbrella clauses: omitting such clauses from the treaty altogether.

Environmental clauses

Adding specific language to ensure the protection of the environment is not compromised – but instead enhanced – by IIAs. To this end, some countries have (i) included examples such as environmental protection measures in the general exceptions clauses; (ii) confirmed that each party has a right to establish its own level of environmental protection; (iii) committed to refrain from relaxing domestic environmental legislation to encourage investment; (iv) carved out environment-related disputes from ISDS; and/or (v) included language aimed at enhancing coherence between IIAs and multilateral environmental agreements.

Some have proposed including provisions that commit investors to transparency, which include publishing information on payments made by foreign investors to public authorities in host countries. While IIA references to issues related to corporate social responsibility (CSR) are usually of a non-binding nature, obligations for investors are starting to emerge in the CSR framework (in relation to reporting).

Modernising treaty content raises the question whether arbitral tribunals, when interpreting older IIAs, would take guidance from clarifications found in the same country's newer IIAs concluded with other countries.

The ISDS system is also undergoing changes, including new language in IIA provisions dealing with ISDS, revisions to international arbitration rules, and domestic efforts to strengthen ADR and dispute prevention policies (DPPs).

Ensuring appropriate corporate behaviour, including with respect to environmental and social practices

While absent in traditional BITs, provisions aimed at rebalancing rights and obligations of foreign investors and host countries can be found in a number of recent FTAs and regional integration agreements. Such provisions vary considerably, ranging from a simple reiteration that foreign investors shall comply with the laws and regulations of the host countries, to more elaborate provisions on anti-corruption requirements, respect of environmental and labour standards and the establishment of local community liaison processes (Caribbean Countries have been further refining ISDS provisions in their IIAs, particularly in areas where ISDS cases could touch upon noninvestment public policy concerns.

Examples include new clauses which seek to reduce host countries' exposure to investor claims, by (i) carving out certain areas from ISDS provisions or limiting claims in certain industries to selected IIA obligations or (ii) introducing a limitation period for IIA claims of usually three years and sometimes five years. Other examples focus on increasing the legitimacy and efficiency of ISDS processes, for instance by: (i) addressing frivolous claims on a timeand cost-effective basis through the introduction of a procedure leading to an early decision that a claim is manifestly without legal merit; (ii) allowing the consolidation of claims, when two or more claims have a question of law or fact in common and arise of the same facts or circumstances; (iii) improving the transparency of arbitral proceedings, which can include making available to the public all relevant documents, starting with the notice of intent and finishing with the arbitral award, and opening hearings to the public; and (iv) allowing amicus curiae briefs.

With respect to international arbitration rules, several revisions are underway, with two being completed. These revision processes address issues such as transparency, openness, independence of arbitrators, tribunal's costs and efficiency. ICSID, whose rules have undergone continued revision since their drafting in 1965, focused its most recent revision on substantive issues, in response to public concerns over lack of transparency, jurisdictional efficiency and tribunals' costs. The Stockholm Chamber of Commerce, which revised its 1999 rules in 2006, focused on remedying textual ambiguities and improving the effectiveness of the proceedings. In 2008, the International Chamber of Commerce (ICC) created a task force on the revision of the 1998 ICC Rules of Arbitration. The task force was mandated to make proposals for enhancing the existing rules with special regard to procedural considerations. A second task force was created in 2009 to look into specific requirements for ICC arbitrations involving States or State entities. UNCITRAL started the first-ever revision of its

1976 procedures in 2006, with a view towards modernising its rules (for instance by filing documents electronically).

POSSIBLE FUTURE DIRECTION OF THE IIA REGIME

Overall, there are indications that the IIA regime, which has been characterised by a multitude of overlapping and sometimes contradictory rules, is moving towards a such as those dealing with social, broader economic and environmental concerns. Additional elements that are central in this context include, the identification of a suitable forum for consensus-building; sharing of experiences and best practices, including through multilateral cooperation, as well as novel – and operational – initiatives for fully harnessing the development enhancing potential of IIAs and attendant FDI flows. Capacity and institution-building is central for developing countries to effectively participate in – and benefit from – international efforts to reform the international policy framework for foreign investment and to deal with an increasingly complex policy agenda. Novel initiatives, in turn, would combine the benefits of investment liberalisation and protection with tangible contributions, allowing developing countries to effectively benefit from FDI in terms of strengthening their productive and supply capacities, maximising business linkages and ensuring that potential FDI-related benefits will spill over to the local economy and attendant stakeholders, including the poor and marginalised. All of this would go a long way in ensuring that the international investment regime will function in a way that is more efficient and conducive to growth and development. However, making IIAs effectively work for development remains a challenge.

INVESTMENT AND FINANCIAL SYSTEM REFORMS

The global financial crisis highlighted serious gaps and weaknesses in the regulation of financial markets. As a result, governments – particularly those in the developed world – as well as intergovernmental bodies have introduced various initiatives to strengthen financial regulation and reform financial regulatory frameworks. These initiatives may have significant implications for foreign investment. They are committed to act together to raise capital standards, implement strong international compensation standards, improve the derivatives market and create more powerful tools to hold large global firms to account for the risks they take. At the operational level, national and international regulatory bodies (such as the Basel Committee of Central Banks) are formulating stricter principles for regulation and supervision. Attention needs to be given to the coherence between these efforts at reforming the international financial system and the international investment system, as both govern shortand long-term cross-border capital flows.

BOX 3

THE UNCTAD–OECD–WTO REPORTS ON G20 TRADE AND INVESTMENT MEASURES

In response to the request of the G20, UNCTAD, OECD and WTO have since September 2009 monitored adherence to the G20 undertakings to refrain from protectionism and to promote global trade and investment. The quarterly reports published so far have covered the period of sharp economic contraction that began in 2008 and accelerated in the first quarter of 2009, and the fragile recovery observed in the last quarter of 2009 and beginning of 2010.

With no indication of widespread trade or investment restrictions in reaction to the crisis, the first report of September 2009 concluded that G20 members and other governments have succeeded in keeping domestic protectionist pressures under control. In the area of investment, the thrust of G20 policy changes has been, for the most part, towards greater openness and clarity, with a substantial number of the policy changes meant to facilitate international investment and financial flows. G20 members have also continued to conclude international investment agreements. Some G20 governments, however, have established support schemes that could discriminate against foreign-controlled companies or obstruct outward investment flows.

In the wake of the fragile recovery, the second report of March 2010 also found that most investment and investment-related measures still point towards greater openness and clarity for investors. Yet the potential for non-transparent and discriminatory application of emergency measures remains a serious challenge. The report recommends paying close attention to the design, application and winding-up of policy measures taken in response to the crisis, and ensuring well-timed, credible and transparent withdrawals from emergency programmes.

The third report of June 2010 also considered that some G20 countries have moved into a new phase of the administration of their emergency measures and programmes. This includes the dismantling of some emergency schemes and the unwinding of advantages provided to individual companies under emergency schemes, but also the continuation and expansion of programmes and the introduction of schemes for new sectors. G20 leaders should ensure that such programmes are wound down at an appropriate pace and that the crisis is not used as a pretext to discriminate directly or indirectly against certain investors, including foreign investors. International monitoring by UNCTAD, OECD and WTO can help ensure that current efforts to avoid investment protectionism do not remain one-off initiatives. In the same vein, UNCTAD continues to monitor global investment trends and policy developments on a quarterly basis.a

Source: UNCTAD, based on UNCTAD, OECD and WTO, 2009; 2010; UNCTAD and OECD, 2010.
a UNCTAD, 2009g; 2010d; 2010e.

Strengthened financial regulation across the world may have significant implications for global FDI flows. A healthier financial system at national and international levels, better monitored and controlled financial risks and improved macroeconomic stability will help the long-term growth of global FDI flows. Companies operating in a predictable financial and economic environment will be more willing to invest both at home and abroad, and banks more likely to lend.

In the short and medium term, however, the impact of financial regulatory changes on FDI flows is likely to be mixed. On the one hand, the propensity and ability of TNCs to invest abroad will improve, thanks to safer credit and regained confidence in the financial system. On the other hand, to the extent that restrictive measures make international investment and the operation of financial institutions more difficult, these measures may have a negative impact on FDI flows, especially in financial industries. For instance, private equity funds' foreign investment, one of the key drivers of global FDI growth during the past few years, is likely to slow down due to both de-leveraging and strengthened regulation. In addition, restrictive policy measures may hamper FDI financing by affecting national and international lending. Finally, investment could be diverted to countries where regulatory standards remain comparatively low, unless international action is well coordinated.

QUESTIONS

1. Discuss the systemic evolution of the international investment agreements (IIA) regime.
2. Critically examine the liberalisation of world foreign direct investment (FDI) policies in the new millennium.
3. Discuss the recent trends towards increased investment regulations and restricitons.

30

FOREIGN CAPITAL FLOWS AND INDIA

INTRODUCTION

Capital flows have played a major role in the process of globalisation. It is a natural extension of globalisation process that often begins with exports. In the process of globalisation countries try to access markets or resources and gradually reduce the cost of production and transaction by expanding overseas manufacturing operations in countries where certain ownwership-specific advantages can help them to compete globally. Adoption of such strategies helps them to catch up with competing economies. While these flows bring several benefits, they pose certain risks. The current chapter focus is on to and fro foreign capital flows and the measures taken by the RBI and Government of India to promote market-oreinted polices to integrate Indian economy with global economy.

HISTORY OF PRIVATE CAPITAL FLOWS

Capital flows pose a puzzle both in theory and practice. On the one hand, they are credited with a key role in the development of the modern day economies by alleviating resource constraints and facilitating technology transfer. On the other hand, they are also blamed for several external debt and financial crises. Understanding the various facets of capital flows has been intellectually challenging as the reality runs counter to theory. For example, the neoclassical economic theory suggests that capital should flow from advanced countries that have relatively high capital-to-labour ratios (capital abundant countries) to developing countries that have relatively low capital-to-labour ratios (labour abundant countries). Paradoxically, capital often flows uphill from developing to advanced countries as was seen in the recent years.

In the pre-First World War period spanning the 19th century and the early 20th century, London was the pre-eminent financial centre, and many of today's developed countries were developing then. This period saw a great expansion of private investment in developing countries, notably in the United States (US), Canada and Australia. It also stretched to Argentina, Brazil, Mexico and India. The capital flows to developing countries took two main forms: bond issues by various levels of public administration and foreign direct investment (FDI).

In the interwar period, in the 1920s the US emerged as a major lender. Consequently, New York emerged as a key center for international lending up until the Great Depression of 1929. The interwar period was also marked by extensive defaults.

Latin America was affected by the abrupt halt in foreign lending. In the immediate post-Second World War period there was virtually no borrowing by developing countries in the world capital market. Private portfolio investment and bank lending resumed only in the 1960s. By the 1980s, private capital flows had picked up substantially. This is the period when the Latin American debt crisis erupted reflecting macroeconomic imbalances arising out of high budget deficits and overvalued exchange rates. Later, the East Asian Economies were faced with a currency crisis in 1997 even though they had good macroeconomic fundamentals. The infirmity emanated primarily from huge short-term external borrowings by banks and corporates.

Another strength has been the increase in foreign exchange reserves in the overall external assets of EDEs. This has provided a counterweight to risk taking by the private sector. Of course, it is another issues as to how much of reserve is adequate and at what level benefits outweigh costs. But there is no disagreement that reserves provide inherent strength and stability to an economy, particularly EDEs.

FOREIGN CAPITAL FLOWS MANAGEMENT IN INDIA

India's capital account liberalisation began in a substantive sense in 1991 following a severe balance of payments (BoP) crisis. The analytical foundations for reforms were provided by three reports: Report of the High Level Committee on Balance of Payments (Chairman: C. Rangarajan, 1991) and the two reports on Capital Account Convertibility (Chairman: S.S. Tarapore, 1997 and 2006). These reports, inter alia, suggested: (i) encouragement to private capital inflows; (ii) shift from debt creating to non-debt creating flows, (iii) a shift within the debt inflows from short-term to long-term debt, (iv) emphasised on monitoring of external commercial borrowings, and (v) gradual liberalisation of outflows.

The capital account liberalisation in India was considered as a process rather than an event. The sequencing of the process was conditional on underlying domestic macroeconomic fundamentals and sustainability of the balance of payments (BoP). Considerable progress has since been made as reflected in the volume and variety of capital flows without undermining the stability of external account.

India's status with regard to capital account liberalisation could be seen in terms of its policy stance towards capital transactions by residents and non-residents on the one hand and by the underlying instruments of cross border flows on the other. Nonresidents have been provided considerable extent of convertibility whereas permission to residents to undertake capital account transactions across borders is relatively restrained. Moreover, distinction is made not only between residents and non-residents but also between different categories of residents.

Residents

If residents are classified into corporates, financial institutions and individuals, the regime is most liberal in the case of corporates followed by financial intermediaries and individuals. Corporates and financial intermediaries are permitted to raise equity resources through American Depository Receipts (ADRs)/Global Depository Receipts (GDRs) and are allowed to borrow through debt instruments from abroad. External Commercial Borrowings (ECBs) could be raised under both automatic and approval routes subject to quantity as well as price restrictions. Under automatic route, eligible borrowers in industry, infrastructure sector and NBFCs (excluding micro finance companies) can now borrow upto US$ 750 million in a year. For borrowing above this stipulation prior approval is required. There is an all-in-cost ceiling currently ranging between 350 basis points and 500 basis points over 6 month LIBOR for loans with minimum maturity of 3 years to more than 5 years. Banks can borrow upto 50 per cent of their unimpaired Tier I capital. Apart from inflows, corporates are allowed to invest abroad in overseas joint or wholly owned subsidiaries up to 400 per cent of their net worth. Banks can invest overseas up to 25 per cent out of their demand and time liabilities in India. Indian mutual funds can invest abroad within overall aggregate limit of US$ 7 billion. Individuals can remit an amount equivalent to US dollar 200,000 in a year under liberalised remittance scheme.

Non-residents

Non-resident corporates and financial intermediaries can invest in domestic companies and instruments across sectors subject to some instrument-wise and sector-wise conditions. For portfolio investment, they need to register themselves with the SEBI. Recently, Qualified Foreign Investors (QFI) including individuals and groups or associations have also been permitted to invest directly in the equity market in India after meeting the stipulated norms including Know Your Customer (KYC).

INSTRUMENTS

In terms of instruments, inflows to India are subject to a hierarchy of preferences with direct investment preferred over portfolio flows, rupee denominated debt preferred over foreign currency debt and medium and long-term debt preferred over short-term debt.

As regards, non-debt flows, the overall approach has been to substantially liberalise FDI flows so as to meet domestic investment requirements and raise growth potential of the economy. However, keeping in view socio-economic implications, FDI is prohibited in certain sectors, viz., lottery business, chit funds, nidhi companies, tobacco products, agriculture and plantation, and activities/sectors not open to private sector investment, e.g., atomic energy and railway transport other than mass rapid transport systems.

Apart from direct investment, non-residents can acquire equity stakes through portfolio investment as well. Portfolio investment could be made by the entities which are registered with the SEBI as Foreign Institutional Investors (FIIs). FIIs do not need prior approval as long as they are within the sectoral and individual limits. There are no restrictions on repatriation of equity investments.

With regard to debt flows, policy levers comprise both quantity and price based prudential prescriptions. There is a ceiling on the extent of FII investment in sovereign debt (US$ 15 billion) and corporate debt (US$ 45 billion) and there is also a withholding tax. ECBs flows under both the automatic and approval routes are moderated by interest rate ceilings and those under the automatic route through an additional quantity ceiling. In addition, there are end use and minimum maturity restrictions of

3 years for ECB. However, trade credit is available for short-term with quantity and price restrictions.

Foreign Currency denominated Non-Resident Indian (NRI) deposits are regulated through an interest rate ceiling linked to LIBOR/SWAP rate of the corresponding currency. However, rupee denominated NRI deposits have recently been deregulated with the condition that interest rate on those should not be more than the rate offered on domestic deposits of comparable maturities. There is no restriction on repatriation of NRI deposits.

TRENDS IN CAPITAL FLOWS TO INDIA

In the period leading up to the crisis, the capital account was dominated by debt creating flows. For example, in 1990-91, debt creating flows constituted about 97 per cent of capital inflows. In the debt creating flows, there was a large component of external assistance. However, this scenario changed substantially following the BoP crisis that triggered wide ranging reforms.

The period since 1991-92 can be seen in three phases on the basis of our economic performance based on economic growth: Phase I (1992-93 to 2002-03) when India's economic growth recovered from a low of 1.4 per cent in 1991-92 to an annual average of 5.8 per cent; Phase II (2003-04 to 2007-08) when India registered its highest average annual growth rate of 8.7 per cent; and Phase III (2008-09 to 2011-12), the most recent period following the global financial crisis which dented both India's economic growth and volume of capital inflows (Table 1).

TABLE 1
CAPITAL FLOWS

(US$ billon)

Component	2011-12				2012-13		
	Q1	Q2	Q3	04	Q1	Q2	Q3
	Avarage of montnly flows						
1	2	3	4	5	6	7	8
FDI in India	2 4.1	33.1	4 2.3	51.5	62.0	7 3.4	81.9*
FDI by India	1.0	1.0	0.6	1.0	0.7	0.5	0.9*
FIIs	0.8	-0.5	0.6	4.7	-0.6	2.6	3.3
ADRs/GDRs	0.1	0.1	0.03	0.01	0.03	0.03	0.0
ECB	1.0	1.6	-0.3	0.8	0.1	0.5	1.3
NRI	0.4	0.9	1.1	1.6	2.2	0.9	0.9*

*: October— November

During the 11-year period 1992-2003, capital inflows to India resumed to an annual average of US$ 8.6 billion. There was a significant shift in favour of equity which accounted for over 54 per cent of capital inflows. Within equity, the FDI component was dominant. In the debt component, NRI deposits were dominant.

During the 5-year period 2003-08, there was a sharp increase in capital inflows to an annual average of US$ 45 billion. The composition of inflows continued to be towards equity, though its share moderated slightly to 53 per cent. However, within equity there was a shift towards portfolio investment. The debt flows were dominated by trade credit and external commercial borrowings.

During the recent 4-year period of 2008-12, net capital inflows moderated to an annual average of US$ 39 billion. Initially, the adverse impact of the global financial market turmoil and liquidity problems on India's BoP was felt in terms of reversal of FIIs inflows and decline in long-term and short-term debt flows. A positive development was, however, turnaround in NRI flows and resilience of FDI inflows in the face of reversal of capital flows, reflecting the attractiveness of India as a long-term investment destination. The capital account balance moderated during April-December 2008 mainly due to higher gross capital outflows coupled with lower gross capital inflows.

The deteriorating external financing conditions also rendered Indian firms' access to external commercial borrowings and trade credits somewhat difficult. The resilience shown by FDI inflows, however, reflects the continued confidence in the Indian economy as a long-term investment destination. There was massive decline in net capital flows from US$ 106.6 billion in 2007-08 (8.8 per cent of GDP) to US$7.2 billion (0.6 per cent of GDP) in 2008-09. The decline was mainly due to net outflows under portfolio investment including foreign institutional investments (FIIs), American depository receipts (ADRs)/ global depository receipts (GDRs) (US$ 14.0 billion), banking capital including NRI deposits (US$ 3.2 billion) and short-term trade credit (US$ 1.9 billion). However, notwithstanding these adverse developments, the resilience of FDI inflows (US$ 17.5 billion in 2008-09) reflected the growing perception of India as one of the favourite long-term investment destinations.

All the components under net capital flows, except loans and banking capital, showed improvement during April-September 2009 from their levels in the corresponding period of the previous year. In banking capital, net inflows under non-resident deposits remained higher during April-September 2009 as compared to their previous year's level. Net inward FDI into India remained buoyant at US$ 21.0 billion during April-September 2009 (as against US$ 20.7 billion in April-September 2008) reflecting the continuing liberalization and better growth performance of the Indian economy. During this period, FDI was channeled mainly into manufacturing (21.4 per cent) followed by communication services (12.8 per cent) and the real estate sector (12.6 per cent). Net outward FDI of India at US$ 6.8 billion in April-September 2009 remained at almost the same level as that of the corresponding period of 2008-09. Due to the large inward FDI, the net FDI (inward minus outward) was marginally higher at US$ 14.1 billion in April-September 2009.

The net external commercial borrowings (ECBs) inflow remained lower at US$ 0.7 billion in April-September 2009 than the US $ 3.2 billion in April-September 2008. Banking capital (net) amounted to US$ 1.1 billion in April-September 2009 as compared to US$ 5.0 billion in April-September 2008. Among the components of banking capital, NRI deposits witnessed higher net inflows of US$ 2.9 billion in April-September 2009 as compared to US$ 1.1 billion in April-September 2008. Short-term trade credit recorded a net outflow of US$ 0.6 billion (inclusive of suppliers' credit up to 180 days) during April-September 2009 as against a net inflow of US$ 4.9 billion during the same period of the previous year. Other capital includes leads and lags in exports, special drawing rights (SDR) allocation, funds held abroad, advances received pending issue of shares under FDI and other capital not included elsewhere (n.i.e). Other capital recorded a lower net outflow of US$ 4.3 billion in April-September 2009 as compared to US$ 10.3 billion in April-September 2008.

Stronger recovery in India, ahead of the global recovery along with positive sentiments of global investors about India's growth prospects, encouraged a revival in capital flows during 2009-10. The turnaround was mainly driven by large inflows under the FIIs and short-term trade credits. The gross capital inflows at US$ 345.7 billion during 2009-10 were 10.2 per cent higher than the US$ 313.6 billion in 2008-09, while gross capital outflows at US$ 292.3 billion were lower by 4.8 per cent from US$ 306.9 billion in 2008-09. As a result, net capital flows at US$ 53.4 billion (3.8 per cent of GDP) were much higher during 2009-10 as compared to US$ 6.8 billion (0.5 per cent of GPD in 2008-09.

Both inward as well as outward FDI showed declining trend in 2009-10 vis-a-vis 2008-09. The inward FDI declined by 12.4 per cent to US$ 33.1 billion in 2009-10 from US$ 37.8 billion in 2008-09. Similarly outward FDI declined by 19.6 per cent from US$ 17.9 billion in 2008-09 to US$ 14.4 billion 2009-10. Consequently, the net FDI (inward FDI minus outward FDI) was marginally lower at US$ 18.8 billion in 2009-10, as compared with US$ 19.8 billion in 2008-09. The FDI was channelled mainly into manufacturing followed by constructional financial services and the real estate sector.

Portfolio investment witnessed net inflow of US$ 32.4 billion in 2009-10 as against a net outflow of US$ 14.0 billion in 2008-09. The attractive domestic market conditions facilitated net FII inflows of US$ 29.0 billion in 2009-10 (as against net outflows of US$ 15.0 billion in 2008-09). At US$ 3.3 billion, the ADRs/GDRs remained at the same level in 2009-10 as in 2008-09. Net ECBs slowed down to US$ 2.8 billion (US$ 7.9 billion in 2008-09) mainly due to increased repayments.

The net short-term trade credit to India increased significantly to US$ 7.6 billion in 2009-10 from net outflows of US$ 2.0 billion a year earlier, reflecting international confidence in domestic importers. After recording net inflows under non-resident deposits during the first three quarters, there were outflows during the last quarter of the 2009-10. Overall net non-resident deposits inflows stood lower at US$ 2.9 billion during 2009-10 as compared to US$ 2.9 billion during 2009-10 as compared to US$ 4.3 billion during 2008-09.

Net capital inflows increased significantly during 2010-11, mainly due to FII inflows, short-term trade credits and ECBs. The net surplus in the capital account in the first quarter of 2010-11 exceeded the levels of the previous two quarters, as well as the financing need in the current account. There was a compositional shift across different components of capital flows. Foreign investment, which used to be a major constituent of the capital account, showed some moderation, mainly due to the slowdown in Foreign Direct Investment (FDI) inflows. Net inflows by FIIs were also lower during the April-June, 2010-11. FIIs, which were traditionally investing in equity market, started diversifying towards debt markets. The attraction of the debt market could be attributed to the rising interest rate environment in India and the near zero interest rate conditions in advanced countries over an extended period. Strong domestic demand along with the rising interest rate differentials also led to higher net inflows of External Commercial Borrowings (ECBs) during the quarter. Short-term trade credit to India recorded a large net inflow of US$ 5.6 billion in the first quarter of 2010-11 (as against a net outflow of US$ 1.5 billion during the corresponding quarter of 2009-10) in line with the increase in imports associated with strong domestic economic activity and improved conditions in the global financial markets. Banking capital recorded inflows of US$ 4.0 billion during the quarter, mainly due to overseas foreign currency borrowings of banks and net inflows under NRI deposits. Debt flows during the quarter at about US$12 billion accounted for almost 64 per cent of total net capital flows.

In 2010-11 both gross inflows of US$ 499.4 billion outflows of US$ 437.4 billion under the capital account were higher than gross inflows of US$ 345.8 billion and outflows of US$ 294.1 billion in the preceding year. In net terms, capital inflows increased by 20.2 per cent to US$ 62.0 billion (3.7 per cent of GDP) in 2010-11 vis-a-vis US$ 51.6 billion (3.8 per cent of GDP) in 2009-10 mainly on account of trade credit and loans (ECBs and banking capital). The Non-debt flows or foreign investment comprising FDI and portfolio investment (ADRs/GDRs and FIIs) on net basis decreased by 21.4 per cent from US$ 50.4 billion in 2009-10 to US$ 39.7 billion in 2010-11. Decline in foreign investment was offset: by the debt flows component of loans and banking capital which increased by 130.3 per cent from US$ 14.5 billion in 2009-10 to US$ 33.4 billion in 2010-11.

Inward FDI showed a declining trend while outward FDI showed an increasing trend in 2010-11 vis-a-vis 2009-10. Inward FDI declined from US$ 33.1 billion in 2009-10 to US$ 25.9 billion in 2010-11. Sector-wise, deceleration during 2010-11 was mainly on account of lower FDI inflows under manufacturing, financial services, electricity, and construction. Country-wise, investment routed through Mauritius remained the largest component of FDI inflows to India in 2010-11 followed by Singapore and the Netherlands. Outward FDI increased from US$ 15.1 billion in 2009-10 to US$ 16.5 billion in 2010-11. With lower inward FDI and rise in outward FDI, net FDI (inward minus outward) to India stood considerably lower at US$ 9.4 billion during 2010-11 (US$ 18.0 billion a year earlier).

Net portfolio investment flow witnessed marginal decline to US$ 30.3 billion during 2010-11 as against US$ 32.4 billion in 2009-10. This was due to decline in ADRs/GDRs to US$ 2.0 billion in 2010-11 from US$ 3.3 billion in 2009-10, even though FII inflows showed marginal increase to US$ 29.4 billion in 2010-11 from US$ 29.0 billion in 2009-10. Other categories of capital flows, namely debt flows of ECBs, banking capital, and short-H1 of 2010-11 as compared to USS 9.5 billion during H1 of 2009-10.

Risk aversion in the global financial markets has slackened the pace of capital flows to India. FDI inflows remained robust averaging US$ 4.9 billion per month during April-August 2011 but moderated to US$ 3.2 billion per month during September-November 2011. Pick up in FII flows has been mainly on account of investment in debt instruments. Several measures have been undertaken to improve inflows of external commercial borrowings (ECBs) and NRI deposits. While inflows on account of NR(E)RA and NRO accounts were higher during April-December 2011, the same on account of FCNR (B) accounts were negative. ECBs and FCCBs by Indian companies due for redemption in Q4 of 2011-12 are estimated to be less than US$ 4 billion. Recognising the global macro-economic and financial market conditions, the Reserve Bank raised all-in-cost ceiling on ECBs. The increase in the all-in-cost ceiling, and emphasis on bringing immediately the proceeds of the ECBs meant for rupee expenditure in India, augur well for raising overseas borrowings and financing the CAD. Also, greater flexibility has been given to banks in mobilising nonresident deposits by further deregulating interest rates on NRE and NRO accounts.

Although recent measures by the European Central Bank and other central banks may have eased financing conditions for banks in the euro area, deleveraging by some European banks has begun to affect cross-border lending to the emerging markets. Therefore, actual ECB inflows in the coming quarters would largely depend on risk perception of European banks. If risk aversion persists in the global financial markets, there might be some implications for cost of obtaining external funding.

The exacerbation in CAD during 2011-12 led to depletion of reserves notwithstanding improved capital flows. Since Q1 of 2012-13, concerns about the growth and financial health of euro area countries have further intensified. In addition, signs of weakness in the US and China have also made investors more cautious and driven up global financial market volatility. These factors, combined with weakening domestic macroeconomic conditions, led to a net FII outfiow of US$ 1.7 billion in Q1 of 2012-13. Concerns about the domestic business environment appear to be weighing on FDI inflows as well. NRI deposits, however, have picked up. Since concerns about the growth outlook for AEs seem to have prompted investors to reconsider the resilience of emerging market growth as well, the outlook for capital flows to EDEs including India remains subdued. The second quarter of 2012-13 witnessed a turnaround in FII flows. While in Q1 of 2012-13, FIIs disinvested in the equity segment that were partially offset by their net investments in the debt segment, FII investments in Q2 improved distinctly in both segments. There was a surge in portfolio inflows after the reform measures were initiated in mid-September 2012, with net FII investment of over US$ 5.5 billion in a month and a half. FDI flows to India moderated to US$ 10.7 billion during April-August 2012 compared with US$ 19.6 billion during April-August 2011.

While net inflows under FDl moderated somewhat during April-November 2012, net inflows by foreign institutional investors (FII) have shown a significant uptrend. Net FII inflows during 2012-13 (up to January 18} at US$ 18.8 billion were significantly higher than during the corresponding period of the previous year (US$ 7.6 billion), thus providing temporary comfort for financing of CAD (Table 1). Besides improved global liquidity and sentiment, robust FII inflows were largely the outcome of improved perception about the domestic economy, driven by recent reforms announced by the government since September 2012. These reforms include, inter alia, liberalised FDl norms for the retail, insurance and pension sectors, a roadmap for fiscal consolidation and an increase in FII limits in the corporate and government debt markets. The FII Investment limits in government Securities and corporate bonds were raised by US$ 5 billion each, taking the total investment limit in domestic debt (including corporate debt for infrastructure) to US$ 75 billion, while the increased limit may enhance debt inflows, they do not provide a solution to CAD financing on a sustainable basis.

Much of the recent FII Investment under the G-sec limits has flown into short term T-bills, enhancing the refinancing risks to external debt. On the other hand, a range-bound currency after a bout of depreciation has made the Indian equity market attractive for FIIs. Going forward, the implementation and acceleration in domestic reforms would be critical for sustained equity flows to the economy. Though the risk aversion in global markets declined during the previous quarter, the flows could be volatile given the euro area risks.

Benefitting from higher interest rates and a weakening rupee, non-resident Indians (NRIs) nearly doubled their deposits with banks in India during April-November 2012 compared with the corresponding period of 2011-12. Net flow through external Commercial borrowings (ECBs) was higher during Q3 of 2012-13 compared to previous quarter, despite high principal repayments made by the Indian corporate sector. ECBs were mainly raised for the import of capital goods, new projects and the redemption of FCCBs.

India's outward FDI peaked from US$ 2.2 billion in 2004-05 to US$ 19.4 billion in 2008-09 before moderating somewhat to US$ 16.5 billion in 2010-11. This underscores maturing of India's capital account liberalisation process which has encouraged two-way flows. *How did this rising trend and shift in composition of capital flows impact the BoP?* Table-2 presents the relative share of debt and equity flows since 1990-91.

TABLE 2

RELATIVE SHARE OF DEBT AND EQUITY IN CAPITAL FLOWS

(in per cent)

	Crisis Year		*Period Average*		
	1990-91	*1991-92*	*1992-93 to 2002-03*	*2003-04 to 2007-08*	*2008-09 to 2010-11*
1. Equity	1.5	3.0	54.0	52.8	62.6
1.1 Net FDI	1.4	2.9	28.0	17.2	31.2
1.2 Portfolio Investment	0.1	0.1	26.0	35.6	31.4
2. Debt	98.5	97.0	46.0	47.2	37.4
2.1 External Assistance	30.7	68.9	8.8	2.5	6.4
2.2 External Commercial Borrowings	31.4	33.2	16.5	22.9	14.0
2.3 NRI Deposits, net	21.4	6.6	21.0	5.2	6.6
2.4 Short Term Trade Credits	15.0	-11.7	-0.3	16.6	10.4

Note: Equity Debt composition of Capital Accounts excludes other capital.

What key conclusions can we draw from a review of international financial flows and our BoP developments in India over the past two decades since the crisis of 1991?

First, global capital flows now increasingly show a two-way movement between EDEs and advanced economies. However, EDEs remain vulnerable to volatility and sudden stops in capital flows. This is because EDEs have limitation in borrowing in their own currencies in international capital markets, a phenomenon known as '*original sin*'. This is evident from the recent crisis. The epicenter of 2008 crisis was the US but capital flows to EDEs, including India, was severely affected. Now the epicenter has shifted to Europe but capital flows to EDEs continues to be impaired.

Second, considerable lessons seem to have been learnt by EDEs from their past experience debt and currency crises, particularly from the Latin American debt crisis of the 1980s and the East Asian currency crisis of 1997. This has reinforced the hierarchy of capital flows with a preference by EDEs for equity flows. This is also reflected in a discernible shift in the composition of capital flows to EDEs in favour of equity, particularly FDI.

Third, capital flows to EDEs depend on push factors emanating from low interest rate and lack of investment opportunity in advanced economies as well as by pull factors emanating from strong economic fundaments and growth prospects in the recipient country. Particularly, stable flows like FDI are guided more by pull factors.

Fourth, availability of foreign capital is not an unmixed blessing. While it alleviates domestic resource constraints, it could also destabilise the economy in two ways: one, excess capital inflows could result in asset price inflation and loss of competitiveness through over valuation of exchange rate; two, sudden outflow on risk aversion could trigger a currency crisis.

Fifth, the earlier dominant view was tilted towards unfettered capital movement. But, following the recent global financial crisis of 2008, there is explicit recognition – even by multilateral bodies such as the IMF, World Bank and the G20 – that capital controls may be desirable under certain circumstances.

Sixth, India's external sector policy had always believed in some form of management of capital account with a preference for equity inflows, though there is now international recognition of this policy. This policy of cautious opening of the capital account has served India well as reflected in the stability of its BoP since the 1991 crisis. The composition of its capital account has shifted from almost entirely debt to predominantly equity.

Seventh, notwithstanding relative stability of our BoP, some stress has developed post-2008 global financial crisis as capital inflows have moderated in the face of expanding current account deficit. This is reflected in worsening of some of the vulnerability indicators of the external sector. India's dependence on private capital inflows to finance current account deficit has increased. Moreover, India has to factor in uncertainties in the global financial markets. These developments call for vigorous domestic policy reforms with a greater emphasis on trade competitiveness and energy security so as to enhance the pull factor for FDI.

MAJOR POLICY INITIATIVES TO INCREASE ACCESS TO INDIAN CAPITAL MARKET

Direct Investment by QFIs in Indian Equity Markets: QFIs were allowed to directly invest in the Indian equity market in January 2012. This was done to widen the class of investors, attract more foreign funds, reduce market volatility, and deepen the Indian capital market. The QFIs shall include individuals, groups, or associations, resident in a foreign country that is compliant with the Financial Action Task Force (FATF) and that is a signatory to International Organisation of Secruities Commissions (IOSCO's) multilateral memorandum of understanding (MoU). QFIs do not include FIIs/ sub-accounts. Earlier, only FIIs/sub-accounts and non-resident Indians (NRIs) were allowed to directly invest in the Indian equity market. Under this arrangement, a large number of QFIs, in particular a large set of diversified individual foreign nationals who were desirous of investing in the Indian equity market, did not have direct access to it. The RBI and SEBI have issued the relevant circulars on 13 January 2012 to operationalize this scheme.

In order to further liberalize the portfolio investment route, the Budget for 2011-12 permitted SEBI-registered MFs to accept subscriptions for equity schemes from foreign investors who meet the KYC requirements. The scope of the Budget announcement has now been expanded to allow SEBI-registered MFs to accept subscriptions from QFIs for debt schemes in the infrastructure sector. The QFI scheme has been operationalized on 9 August 2011.

FII investments in Government Securities and Corporate Bonds: In November 2011, the government reviewed the policy in the context of India's evolving macroeconomic situation and the need for enhancing capital flows and making available additional financial resources for the corporate sector and decided to (i) increase the current limit of FII investment in government securities by US $ 5 billion, raising the cap to US $ 15 billion (the incremental limit of US $ 5 billion can be invested in securities without any residual maturity criterion); and (ii) increase the current limit of FII investment in corporate bonds by US $ 5 billion, raising the cap to US $ 20 billion (the incremental limit of US $ 5 billion can be invested in listed corporate bonds). The investment limit in long-term infrastructure corporate bonds, however, has been kept unchanged at US$ 25 billion. With this, overall limit for FII investment in corporate bonds and government securities now stands at US$ 60 billion.

External Commercial Borrowings (ECB) Policy: A prospective borrower can access ECBs under two routes, namely the automatic route and approval route. ECBs not covered under the automatic route are considered on case-by-case basis by the RBI under the approval route. The High Level Committee on ECB took a number of decisions on 15 September 2011 to expand the scope of ECBs. These include:

(i) High networth individuals (HNIs) who fulfil the criteria prescribed by SEBI can invest in IDFs.

(ii) IFCs have been included as eligible issuers for FII investment in the corporate bonds long-term infra category.

(iii) ECB would be permitted for refinancing of rupee loans of infrastructure projects on the condition that at least 25 per cent of such ECBs shall be used for repayment of the said rupee loan and 75 per cent invested in new projects in the infrastructure sector. This would be permitted only under the approval route.

(iv) Refinancing of buyer's/supplier's credit through ECBs for the purchase of capital goods by companies in the infrastructure sector was approved. This would also be permitted only under the approval route.

(v) ECBs for interest during construction (IDC) that accumulates on a loan during the project execution phase for companies in the infrastructure sector would be permitted. This would be subject to the condition that the IDC is capitalized and is part of the project cost.

(vi) Renminbi (RMB) was approved as an acceptable currency for raising ECBs subject to a limit of US$ 1 billion within the existing ECB ceiling. Such borrowings shall be allowed only through the approval route.

(vii) The existing ECB limits under the automatic route were enhanced from US$ 500 million to US$ 750 million for eligible corporates as per the extant ECB guidelines. For borrowers in the services sector, the limit has been enhanced from US$ 100 million to US$ 200 million and for NGOs engaged in micro-finance activities from the existing US$ 5 million to US$ 10 million. All other conditions apply as per the extant ECB guidelines.

(viii) INR denominated ECBs would be permitted from foreign equity holders to 'all eligible borrowers' except in the case of ECBs availed of by NGOs as per extant ECB guidelines under the automatic route.

In November 2011, ECB policy was modified keeping in view the developments in global financial markets and macro-economic conditions. The all-in- cost ceiling was enhanced and the proceeds of ECBs raised abroad for Rupee expenditure in India should be brought immediately. The change in the all-in-cost ceiling came into force on November 23, 2011 and is applicable up to 31 March 2012, subject to review thereafter.

FOREIGN CAPITAL FLOWS FROM INDIA

In recent years, emerging market economies (EMEs) are increasingly becoming a source of foreign investment for rest of the world. It is not only a sign of their increasing participation in the global economy but also of their increasing competence. More importantly, a growing impetus for change today is coming from developing countries and economies in transition, where a number of private as well as state-owned enterprises are increasingly undertaking outward expansion through foreign direct investments (FDI). Companies are expanding their business operations by investing overseas with a view to acquiring a regional and global reach. The overseas investment of domestic corporate sector through foreign investment has provided them better access to global networks and markets, transfer of technology and skills and also enables them to share research and development efforts and outcomes. It can also be seen as a corporate strategy to promote the brand image and utilisation of raw materials available in the host country. In the Indian context, overseas investments have been primarily driven by either resource-seeking or market-seeking or technology-seeking motives. Of late, there has been a surge in resource-seeking overseas investments by Indian companies, especially to acquire energy resources in Australia, Indonesia and Africa.

EVOLUTION OF OUTWARD FOREIGN INVESTMENT POLICY IN INDIA

Change in policy environment across the economies has greatly influenced the outward investment pattern in the global economy. Nonetheless, recognising the concerns of capital outflows, governments in different countries, particularly emerging and developing economies, have been relatively more circumspect on undertaking policy liberalisation of outward investment. Therefore, it is important to highlight how the Indian policy in this regard has evolved over time.

In the Indian context, overseas investments in joint ventures (JV) and wholly-owned subsidiaries (WOS) have been recognised as important channels for promoting global business by the Indian entrepreneurs. The broad approach has been to facilitate outward foreign direct investment through joint ventures and wholly-owned subsidiaries and provision of financial support to promote exports including project exports from India. With a steady rise in capital inflows, particularly in the second half of 2000s, the overall foreign exchange reserve position provided comfort to progressive relaxation of the capital controls and simplification of the procedures for outbound investments from India. Three distinct overlapping phases as under can be discerned in the evolution of the Indian outward FDI policies.

Phase I (1992 to 1995): Period of Liberalisation of Indian economy

Guidelines on outward FDI were in place before the process of liberalisation and globalisation of Indian economy in 1991-92. Policy changes since 1992 were undertaken keeping in view the changing needs of a growing economy. Understandably, the rules were quite restrictive and subject to conditions of no cash remittance and mandatory repatriation of dividend from the profits from the overseas projects. In 1992, the 'automatic route' for overseas investments was introduced and cash remittances were allowed for the first time. Nonetheless, the total value was restricted to US$ 2 million with a cash component not exceeding US$ 0.5 million in a block of 3 years.

Phase II (1995 to 2000): Creation of a Fast Track Route

In 1995, a comprehensive policy framework was laid down and the work relating to approvals for overseas investment was transferred from Ministry of Commerce to the Reserve Bank of India to provide a single window clearance mechanism. The policy framework articulated a cohesive approach that was flexible enough to respond to likely future trends. It reflected the need for transparency, recognition of global developments, capturing of Indian realities and learning of lessons from the past. The basic objectives of the policy, inter alia, was to ensure that such outflows, were determined by commercial interests and were also consistent with the macroeconomic and balance of payment compulsions of the country, particularly in terms of the magnitude of the capital flows. In terms of the overseas investment policy, a fast track route was adopted where the limits were raised from US$ 2 million to US$ 4 million and linked to average export earnings of the preceding three years. Cash remittance continued to be restricted to US$ 0.5 million. Beyond US$ 4 million, approvals were considered under the 'Normal Route' approved by a Special Committee comprising the senior representatives of the Reserve Bank of India (Chairman) and the Ministries of Finance, External Affairs and Commerce (members). Investment proposals in excess of US$ 15 million were considered by the Ministry of Finance with the recommendations of the Special Committee and were generally approved if the required resources were raised through the global depository receipts (GDR) route.

In March 1997, exchange earners, other than exporters, were also brought under the fast track route. Indian promoters were allowed to set up second and subsequent generation companies, provided the first generation company was set up under the fast track route. A series of measures to encourage the software industry in India to expand capacity, reduce costs, improve quality and also invest abroad were put in place. As part of the reforms process preceding the introduction of FEMA, the neutrality condition attached to the Overseas Direct Investment was done away with in 1999. The scope for outward FDI, however, expanded significantly after the introduction of the Foreign Exchange Management Act (FEMA) in June 2000.

Phase III (2000 till date): Liberalised Framework under Fema

In 2002, the per annum upper limit for automatic approval was raised to US$100 million. Such upper limit was, however, discontinued when the automatic route for outward FDI was further liberalised in March 2003 to enable Indian parties to invest to the extent of 100 per cent of their net worth. Since then the limit of outward FDI has been gradually increased to 400 per cent. The ceiling of 400 per cent of net worth, however, is not applicable for

a. investments made out of balances held in the Exchange Earners' Foreign Currency (EEFC) account of the Indian party or out of funds raised abroad through ADRs/GDRs.
b. Indian companies engaged in the energy and natural resources sectors, such as, oil, gas, coal and mineral ores, though they would require prior approval of the Reserve Bank of India.

Overseas investments in unincorporated entities in oil sector (e.g., by way of taking up participation interest) by Navaratna Public Sector Undertakings were allowed under the automatic route and subsequently the facility was extended to other Indian entities as well. Further, in 2004, the External Commercial Borrowing policy was modified and funding of JVs/ WOS abroad was included as a permissible end-use of the funds raised.

At present, any Indian party can make overseas direct investment in any bona-fide activity except certain real estate activities {i.e., buying and selling of real estate or trading in Transferable Development Rights (TDRs)} and banking business (which are considered by an inter-Ministerial group) that are specifically prohibited. For undertaking activities in the financial services sector, certain conditions as specified by the Reserve Bank, however, need to be adhered to. Access to international financial markets was also progressively liberalised for the Indian corporate sector and they were allowed to use special purpose vehicles (SPVs) in international capital markets to finance their cross-border acquisitions. The impact of policy liberalisation is now reflected in cross-border acquisitions by Indian corporate growing at an accelerated pace.

TREND ANALYSIS OF OUTWARD FDI

Even though policy changes undertaken in respect of overseas investment have facilitated the growing cross-border acquisitions by the Indian corporate sector, other structural reforms undertaken since 1992, such as, industrial deregulation, trade liberalisation and relaxation of regulations governing inward FDI, led to major restructuring in the Indian industry. In fact, many of the leading companies owe their competitiveness to the reform process. Greater exposure to internal as well external competition proved to be instrumental in building confidence among the Indian companies to compete with foreign competitors in world market. Apart from liberalised policy environment for overseas investment, India has gained ground as an important investor on the back of (a) rapid economic growth, (b) easy access to financial resources and (c) strong motivations to acquire resources and strategic assets abroad.

One should not assume that overseas investment by Indian companies is a phenomenon of 1990s. In fact, Indian firms began to invest overseas in the 1960s, but India's restrictive policies for overseas investment limited them to small, minority joint ventures in developing economies. First major overseas Indian venture was a textile mill set up in Ethiopia in 1959 by the Birla Group of companies. Overseas investment operations were, however, geographically concentrated in West and East Africa, Middle East, and South and East Asia with which India shared a colonial heritage and historical linkages. Sustained growth in Indian overseas investment could be seen starting during 1970s when the industrial licensing system was more stringent.

Trend of Outward Investments during the Past One Decade

A trend analysis shows that the level of outward FDI from India has increased manifold since 1999- 2000. The level of net outward FDI flows (on BoP basis), however, recorded a sharp uptrend at US$ 74.3 billion during the second half of 2000s (2005-06 to 2009-10) as compared to US$ 8.2 billion in the first half of 2000s (2000-01 to 2004-05). Even though trend in India's outward FDI was moderately affected during the crisis year of 2009-10, a sharp rebound was seen in 2010-11 (Table-3).

TABLE 3

YEAR–WISE POSITION OF ACTUAL OUTFLOWS IN RESPECT OF OUTWARD FDI & GUARANTEES ISSUED

Period	*Equity*	*Loan*	*Guarantee Invoked*	*Total*	*Guarantee Issued*
2000-2001	602.12	70.58	4.97	677.67	112.55
2001-2002	878.83	120.82	0.42	1,000.07	155.86

2002-2003	1,746.28	102.10	0.00	1,848.38	139.63
2003-2004	1,250.01	316.57	0.00	1,566.58	440.53
2004-2005	1,481.97	513.19	0.00	1,995.16	315.96
2005-2006	6,657.82	1,195.33	3.34	7,856.49	546.78
2006-2007	12,062.92	1,246.98	0.00	13,309.90	2,260.96
2007-2008	15,431.51	3,074.97	0.00	18,506.48	6,553.47
2008-2009	12,477.14	6,101.56	0.00	18,578.70	3,322.45
2009-2010	9,392.98	4,296.91	24.18	13,714.07	7,603.04
2010-2011	9,234.58	7,556.30	52.49	16,843.37	27,059.02
2011-12	4,031.45	4,830.01	0.00	8,861.46	14,993.80
*Total	75,247.61	29,425.32	85.40	10,4758.30	63,504.05

* April 2011 to February 22, 2012

In recent years, outward FDI continued to be mainly financed through equity and loans. Although guarantees issued have been rising, their invocation has been negligible during 2009-10 and 2010-11. It has been observed that the number of outward FDI proposals under the Automatic Route during 2000s has also been on the rise (Table-4) indicating the growing appetite of the Indian corporates to establish their foot prints abroad and the liberal regulatory regime.

TABLE 4

NUMBER OF PROPOSALS UNDER APPROVAL AND AUTOMATIC ROUTE

Period	*Approval Route*	*Automatic Route*	*Total*
2008-09	6	974	980
2009-10	4	690	694
2010-11	19	1,187	1,206
2011-12*	10	1,123	1,133

* April 2011 to February 22, 2012

Position of India in the Global Context

Outward FDI from India has mainly been by way of equities and loans. Based on the magnitude of FDI outflows, India is placed 21st in the world. In terms of value of net purchases (i.e., cross-border acquisition deals) by Indian companies in 2010, India was placed fifth in the World after the US, Canada, Japan and China.

Investment Trends of Indian Transnational Companies

Importantly, scale of overseas investment by domestic companies has also expanded as India was placed second in 2010 only after China in terms of average size of net purchase deals (US$190 million in India as compared to US$ 197 million in China). Similarly, India also figures among the top five emerging and developing economies whose state-owned enterprises are increasingly becoming transnational corporations. It is not surprising as in recent years, India's Public Sector Units (PSUs), viz., NTPC,

GAIL, ONGC and NALCO have undertaken significant overseas green-field investments.

Sectoral Investment Trends

Sectoral pattern of outward FDI during 2006-07 to 2010-11 shows that it has been mainly invested in services and manufacturing sector. In 2010-11, within manufacturing, major sub-sectors which attracted outward FDI from India included agriculture machineries and equipments, basic organic chemicals, drugs, medicines & allied products, refined petroleum products, indigenous sugar, etc. Similarly, within services sector, a majority of outward FDI had gone into business services, data processing, financial services, architectural and engineering, engine architectural and other technical consultancy activities (Table-5).

TABLE 5

MAJOR SECTOR-WISE OVERSEAS INVESTMENTS BY INDIAN COMPANIES

(Amounts in Billion US Dollar)

Period	*2008-09*	*2009-10*	*2010-11*	*2011-12**	*Total*
Manufacturing	10.18	5.35	5.4	2.74	23.31
Financial Insurance, Real Estate Business & Business Services	3.55	4.41	6.53	2.53	17.03
Wholesale & Retail Trade, Restaurants & Hotels	1.17	1.13	1.89	1.00	5.19
Agriculture & allied activities	2.38	0.95	1.21	0.41	4.49
Transport, Communication & Storage Services	0.31	0.38	0.82	1.34	2.85
Construction	0.35	0.36	0.38	0.37	1.46
Community, Social & Personal Services	0.39	0.18	0.70	0.18	1.45
Electricity, Gas & Water	0.14	0.84	0.10	0.04	1.19
Miscellaneous	0.12	0.11	0.18	0.10	0.51
Total	18.58	13.71	16.84	8.73	57.86

* April 2011 to February 22, 2012

Since late 1990s, Indian outward FDI began to be in more high-tech and trade supporting sectors. Many Indian IT firms like Tata Consultancy Services, Infosys, WIPRO, and Satyam acquired global contracts and established overseas offices in developed economies to be close to their key clients. In addition, other sectors which have attracted significant share of outward FDI from India in the recent years included extraction of crude petroleum, oil and gas field services and services incidental to mining.

Investments Trends for Acquisition of Natural & Strategic Resources

Sectoral pattern suggests that greater outward investment by the Indian corporate sector seems to have been motivated by long-term strategic considerations rather than by short-term profitability. For instance, ONGC Videsh Ltd., a fully-owned subsidiary of ONGC, presently has overseas assets in 33 projects in 14 countries of Middle East, Africa, CIS & Far East and Latin America. Oil India Limited has presence in eight countries mainly in terms of exploration blocks in Libya, Gabon, Iran, Nigeria and Sudan. Similarly, Coal India Limited has formed a subsidiary Coal Videsh Ltd. to acquire coal assets abroad and also set up a joint venture company

International Coal Ventures Ltd with other companies to acquire metallurgical and thermal coal assets outside India. Overseas investment by Indian companies in extractive industries assumes importance as it is required to support rapid economic growth, industrialisation and urbanisation in the domestic sector and guarantee a long-term, stable supply of natural resources to the country against a background of rising commodity prices.

Such trend has also been observed in the case of other major emerging market economies, especially other members of BRIC group. In fact, number of companies investing abroad from the BRIC group in the FT 500 list has increased from 20 in 2006 to 62 in 2008, reflecting their growing overseas business operations. A common feature is that domestic companies in BRIC economies have been seeking to enhance their access to supplies of raw materials and moving into new segments of strategic commodities and move up the value chain. Nonetheless, oil and gas and other natural resource-based industries are relatively less prominent in Indian outward FDI compared to that by Brazil and China.

Other major overseas acquisitions in recent years by Tata Steel, Hindalco, Bharti Airtel, etc. have also been a part of their inorganic growth strategies. In these cases, acquisitions were specifically undertaken to attain global size and status, and to build new competitive advantages by combining the best international technology with low-cost Indian labour.

Destinational Investment Trends

Direction of outward FDI shows that it is getting more diversified across countries. Diverting from the past trend (i.e., pre-1990s) when Indian companies were investing in countries where there was little technological competition, the more recent trend shows that Indian overseas investment is increasingly flowing to developed economies (Table-6), partly reflecting growing confidence of the Indian corporates and availability of overseas assets at competitive rates.

TABLE 6

TOP TEN COUNTRY-WISE OVERSEAS INVESTMENTS BY INDIAN COMPANIES

(amount in billion US Dollar)

Country	*2008-09*	*2009-10*	*2010-11*	*2011-12**	*Total*
Singapore	4.06	4.20	3.99	1.86	14.11
Mauritius	2.08	2.15	5.08	2.27	11.57
Netherlands	2.79	1.53	1.52	0.70	6.54
United States of America	1.02	0.87	1.21	0.87	3.97
United Arab Emirates	0.63	0.64	0.86	0.38	2.51
British Virgin Islands	0.00	0.75	0.28	0.52	1.55
United Kingdom	0.35	0.34	0.40	0.44	1.53
Cayman Islands	0.00	0.04	0.44	0.14	0.62
Hong Kong	0.00	0.00	0.16	0.31	0.46
Switzerland	0.00	0.00	0.25	0.16	0.41
Other countries	7.65	3.19	2.65	1.23	14.71
Total	18.58	13.71	16.84	8.86	

*April 2011 to February 28, 2012

Trend of Using SPV or M&A Route for Investments Abroad

Indian companies going for overseas investments have largely used either their overseas locally- incorporated subsidiaries or have set up holding companies and/or special purpose vehicles (SPVs) in offshore financial centres or other regional financial centres. In 2005, Indian companies were allowed to float SPVs in international capital markets to finance acquisitions abroad facilitating the use of leveraged buy-outs. Since then, SPVs set up in off-shore financial centres, such as, Mauritius, Singapore and the Netherlands, have been mainly used as conduits to mobilise funds and invest in third countries mainly keeping in view the business and legal consideration, taxation advantages and easier access to financial resources in the countries.

While overseas investment in developed economies is going mainly through M&As, mode of entry into developing economies is observed to be mainly through green-field investments. One of the reasons for Indian companies to adopt M&As route for foreign investment in developed countries is that markets in these economies tend to be mature and saturated and, therefore, companies prefer to gain market share through acquisitions rather than green- field investments. Big acquisitions by companies like Tata were a way of reaching the required scale quickly. Today, Tata Group companies are reportedly the biggest manufacturer and employment provider in the UK.

Today, India has enabling regulatory environment for encouraging overseas investments by individuals. However, there is a need to examine the existing caps and link it to the monetary ceilings applicable under the Liberalised Remittance Scheme (LRS) (remittance of US$ 200,000 for permitted current and capital account transactions). Some of the ceilings which may require rationalisation include ceiling to acquire qualification shares and shares of a foreign entity in part/full consideration of professional services rendered to the foreign company or in lieu of Director's remuneration, to acquire shares offered through an ESOP scheme globally, on uniform basis, in a foreign company which has an equity stake, directly or indirectly, in the Indian company. The Reserve Bank of India in consultation with the Ministries concerned has since decided to

a. remove the existing cap of one per cent on the ceiling for resident individuals to acquire qualification shares and to link the same to the monetary ceiling under the LRS;
b. to grant general permission to resident individuals to acquire shares of a foreign entity in part/full consideration of professional services rendered to the foreign company or in lieu of Director's remuneration with monetary ceiling as per the limit prescribed under LRS; and
c. to grant general permission to Indian resident employees or Directors to acquire shares through an ESOP scheme globally on uniform basis in a foreign company which has an equity stake, directly or indirectly, in the Indian company.

Issues relating to allowing individuals to set-up JVs/WOS abroad under a transparent policy framework within the LRS ceiling are also being examined. Further, the extant regulations allow registered partnership firms to invest abroad.

With the passing of the LLP Act, there is a need to review the regulation and examine if LLPs can also be permitted to invest in JV/WOS abroad. Finally, in the context of multi-layered structures, taxation remains a contentious issue and a subject of debate. This issue, euphemistically, referred to as 'Treaty Shopping' or 'Tax planning' or 'Tax Avoidance', has implications for outbound FDI. We need to have clearer policy prescriptions on the issue after considering the legal/business requirements of the various jurisdictions before embarking on any policy that may either facilitate or restrict such investment motives. The Reserve Bank, in consultation with the government and all the stakeholders, would like to examine the issues involved in a holistic manner.

Success of outward investment projects would also depend on the business cycles in the global economy. An outward FDI project undertaken during upswing phase of business cycle may not remain viable during downward phase. For instance, MNCs operating in sectors, viz., automotives, metals and chemicals proved to be quite sensitive to adverse shocks of recent global crisis. Hence, even though direct investment is generally undertaken with lasting interest in the host economy, companies need to recognise the degree of sensitivity of their business activity to the global business cycle as well.

As the Indian corporate becomes increasingly competitive, they may aggressively explore globalisation opportunities as part of their future growth plans. Outward FDI related to acquisition of strategic resources, expansion of market base, leveraging new technologies for local markets, etc. would facilitate long-term growth in India and absorption of technology by Indian corporates along with improvements in the managerial skills. At the same time, through such overseas investments, Indian companies would play a critical role in the developed as well as developing countries by rejuvenating the economies and providing employment.

QUESTIONS

1. "New Economic Policy has encouraged the India has encouraged the India companies to explore the euro-market." Comment.
2. Discuss the importants of the NRI investments and Deposits in capital inflows.
3. Comment on the recent steps taken by the Government of India to attrack foreign portfolio investment.
4. Discuss the emerging trends and policy developments on foreign portfolio investments.
5. Critically examine the external commercial borrowings (ECBs) as an additional source of funding for corporate finance.
6. Discuss the special deposit schemes designed to attract the funds from non-residents.
7. Discuss the role of foreign capital in growth process. Why has it generally yielded conflicting results?
8. Critically examine the recent measures taken by the countries worldwide to improve their investment climate.
9. "Foreign direct investment has different implications for the host and recipient countries as compared to other capital flows." Discuss.

10. Discuss the economic rationale to attract foreign investment. What is the effect of these incentives on investment decisions?
11. "Liberalisation of national policy frameworks is one of the key driving force of globalisation." Comment.
12. Critically examine the main determinants of foreign direct investment (FDI).
13. "Foreign Direct Investment (FDI) exists because of the international immobility of the factors of production." Do you agree?
14. Discuss the role of strategic and long-term factors in the foreign capital movement.
15. Discuss the alternative vehicles for foreign equity investment.
16. Critically examine the factors which led to the spectacular growth in foreign portfolio investment since 1990s.
17. Critically examine the macroeconomic consequence of large and volatile aid flows. How should these challenges be addressed to ensure that aid flows have a beneficial impact?

31

MULTINATIONAL CORPORATIONS

INTRODUCTION

Multinational corporations have existed since the beginning of overseas trade. They have remained a part of the business scene throughout history, entering their modern form in the 17th and 18th centuries with the creation of large, European-based monopolistic concerns such as the British East India Company during the age of colonization. Multinational concerns were viewed at that time as agents of civilization and played a pivotal role in the commercial and industrial development of Asia, South America, and Africa. By the end of the 19th century, advances in communications had more closely linked world markets, and multinational corporations retained their favorable image as instruments of improved global relations through commercial ties. The existence of close international trading relations did not prevent the outbreak of two world wars in the first half of the twentieth century, but an even more closely bound world economy emerged in the aftermath of the period of conflict.

In more recent times, multinational corporations have grown in power and visibility, but have come to be viewed more ambivalently by both governments and consumers worldwide. Indeed, multinationals today are viewed with increased suspicion given their perceived lack of concern for the economic well-being of particular geographic regions and the public impression that multinationals are gaining power in relation to national government agencies, international trade federations and organizations, and local, national, and international labor organizations. Top management of MNC is to distinguish between planning for domestic operations and planning for international operations before deciding on a financial strategy for operating in a foreign environment. An understanding of what to expect in global operations is imperative to successful international financial management. The focus of the chapter is on the conceptualisation of the finance function by a MNC while taking into consideration the cultural, economic, legal, political and social differences encountered in global operations.

WHAT IS MULTINATIONAL CORPORATION?

The term 'multinational' is widely used today, the phrase is still subject to varying interpretations practitioners and researchers use the terms 'international', 'supranational', 'global', 'transnational', and 'multinational' interchangeably. While some writers have a clear idea of what constitutes a MNC, others have vague notions. To some multinational corporations are *business entities* that operate in more than one country. The typical multinational *corporation* or MNC normally functions with a headquarters that is based in one country, while other facilities are based in locations in other countries. In some circles, a multinational corporation is referred to as a multinational enterprise (MBE) or a multinational corporation (MNC).

The exact model for an MNC may vary slightly. One common model is for the multinational corporation is the positioning of the executive headquarters in one nation, while production facilities are located in one or more other countries. This model often allows the company to take advantage of benefits of incorporating in a given locality, while also being able to produce goods and services in areas where the cost of production is lower. Another structural model for a multinational organization (MNO) is to base the *parent company* in one nation and operate subsidiaries in other countries around the world. With this model, just about all the functions of the parent are based in the country of origin. The subsidiaries more or less function independently, outside of a few basic ties to the parent. A third approach to the setup of an MNC involves the establishment of a headquarters in one country that oversees a diverse conglomeration that stretches to many different countries and industries. With this model, the MNC includes affiliates, subsidiaries and possibly even some facilities that report directly to the headquarters.

The economic definition emphasizes the ability of owners and their managerial agents in one country to control the operations in foreign countries. There is a frequent confusion that equates the ability to control with the flow of capital across national borders. It is recognized widely that capital flow is not the distinguishing characteristic of a multinational corporation. Capital can flow from one country to another in expectation of higher rates of return. However, this flow may be invested in the form of bonds, or in equity amounts too insignificant to grant control to foreign owners. In this case, this type of investment is treated as a 'portfolio' investment. The central aspect of 'direct investment' is the ownership claim by a party located in one country on the operations of a foreign firm or subsidiary in another. The multinational corporation is, thus, the product of foreign direct investment that is defined as the effective control of operations in a country by foreign owners.

The economic definition, however, does not capture the importance of the multinational corporation as the organizational mechanism by which different social and economic systems confront each other. The multinational corporation, because usually it develops in the cultural and social context of one nation, exports its organizational baggage from one institutional setting to another. In this regard, it plays a powerful role as a mechanism by which to transfer organizational knowledge across borders. However, while being foreign implies that it might serve the valuable role of importing new practices, its foreign status also implies that its practices are likely to conflict with existing institutions and cultural norms. Moreover, since multinational corporations are often large, they pose unusual challenges to national and regional governments who seek to maintain political autonomy and yet are often anxious to seek the investment, technology, and managerial skills of foreign firms.

There are, thus, economic and sociological definitions of the multinational corporation that differ, and yet complement, each other. In the economic definition, the multinational corporation is the control of foreign activities through the auspices of the firm. In the sociological definition, the multinational corporation is the mechanism by which organizational practices are transferred and replicated from one country to another.

HISTORY OF MNCs

The multinational corporation is defined in some sense arbitrarily by where frontiers are drawn. In ancient Greece, these frontiers were the borders among city-states. In imperial Rome, the new administrative units of an expanding empire and its external boundaries defined the borders. Political borders correspond only approximately to the distribution of cultural and ethnic dispositions. The history of the multinational corporation is tied closely to the origins of trade in and between cultural communities, and these communities remain important in many sectors in the modern economy.

Early trade was often characterized by the difficulty of transacting across borders. Trading has always instigated from the unequal and varied distribution of resources across geographies. The trading of salt was an important factor in most continents and still can be found in rather ancient forms in east Africa. Towns, such as Salzburg, owed their origins to their fortuitous access to salt mines.

This unequal distribution incited traders to travel long distances and undergo unusual risks for the hope of gain. The dilemma is quite apparent. How can markets for trade develop between distant cultures? Indeed, there is good evidence that early trading was quite precarious. Brown notes that Hermes was not only the god of messengers but also of theft and trade. He was often worshipped at borders, marking the place of trade. Herodotus describes the practice of the 'silent trade' of goods at boundary markings in which one party would deposit their goods at the border, the second party would later deposit a corresponding offer. The original party might accept this bid, take the goods, and leave their initial offer. Clearly, only a strong demand for unusual foreign goods could sustain such a treacherous institution of transaction.

Not surprisingly, Curtin doubts the accuracy of this account. Instead, he stresses the importance of ethnic groups, such as the Gujarati or overseas Chinese, or the force of imperialism and military power as ways in which 'cross-cultural trading' was permitted to develop. But such solutions remained fragile, with foreign enclaves and ethnic groups subject to local hatred and military rule often confronting competition from other powers.

Yet, trade persisted through the centuries. Indeed, the demand for foreign goods was so strong that incredible profits could be realized by international trade. Since transportation was poor, and technology to hold inventories rudimentary, an agent in the right spot at the right time could earn fortunes. And in this laid the great problem. For in times of great demand, prices could rise astronomically, as Braudel documents in his history of material life. With such distances between the agent and the principal in the exporting country, an agent could easily, and often did, disappear with the profits.

The early solutions were many and provide insight into one of the great properties of the multinational corporation: its ability to organize transactions within its own organizational boundaries. Great fairs were one solution, where principals met their customers in one place. But fairs were intermittent and often distant from final markets. The further development of Roman commercial law during the medieval and Renaissance periods strengthened the liability of the principal and also legal recourse in principal-agent conflict. However, the application of law between two parties in different legal jurisdictions has always been a difficult form of dispute resolution. In his study of the Jewish Magrebi traders of the twelfth century, Greif places considerable emphasis upon the value of membership in ethnic 'trading communities.' Since ethnic enclaves in foreign sites could monitor the activities of agents, principals could be informed of malfeasance. Agents could then be excluded from future contracts within the community, thus deterring dishonest behavior. Partnerships were also another way in which agents were also bonded to the firm.

However, another solution was the company, a word whose roots come from the Latin meaning 'with bread' which implies the familial origins of this business organization. The company permitted in time the investing of capital in its ownership by outsiders in promise of future dividends. The capital might be raised for a single voyage or, eventually, could be maintained in the company in the form of stock ownership. With the evolution of limited liability law in the nineteenth century, and the diminished role of the state in restricting the growth of the joint stock company, this organizational form expanded rapidly in many European countries as well as in the United States. Along with the growth of equity markets, the financial resources to invest overseas became more available due to advances in the banking system and also in bond markets. Indeed, the great capital needs of the railway industry created an international market for the sale and purchase of railroad bonds. However, international loans and bonds were risky and it was not uncommon for sovereign governments to default, including state governments within the United States.

The increasing wealth of western countries, along with constraints on the speed by which national industries could absorb new loans, encouraged massive foreign investments by the end of the nineteenth century and early twentieth century. This was a period of globalization in terms of the percentages of capital outflows to total capital accumulation. Great Britain is estimated to have exported some 25 percent of its capital prior to World War I and French capital exports were often greater. This capital went to countries hungry to finance their industrial expansion, including the newly industrializing countries of Russia and especially America.

The British were unusual in directing a considerable amount of their outward capital flows in the form of direct investments. A great deal of this investment went into their colonies. Prior to the mid-1800s, companies operating overseas engaged largely in wholesale operations; they did not run factories, operate mines, or own agriculture. The British direct investments were, thus, different than before, as British came to own and run local operations. Moreover, the British invested in South and North America.

The 'free-standing' company, as labeled by Wilkins, was a peculiar form of investment that was quite prominent in many British colonies. This firm raised capital in the domestic financial market where its administrative office was located, but it operated no domestic activities. All operations were overseas. This form of company represents the advantage of western countries in being able to raise capital from efficient financial markets. However, it posed the same problem as facing the medieval agent relationship, namely, how could foreign investors be confident that they would recover profitably their investments if the assets were located overseas, often in countries with very poor legal infrastructures? Wilkins found that oversight occurred through the executive boards of the companies, where prominent people located in the home market faced the loss of reputation if the company should prove to be dishonest.

The United States offers an unusual case. A rapidly growing country, it imported more capital than it exported up to World War I. However, whereas it imported largely portfolio investments, its outward flows were dominated by foreign direct investments. In other words, American companies showed an early penchant for expanding overseas. The Singer Company built within two decades of its founding a large factory employing thousands of workers in Scotland. Oil companies, Kodak, Westinghouse, Ford, and mining and agricultural companies all invested overseas. Companies in oil, mining, and agriculture often invested in poorer markets where there were resources to be found. These early investors were often involved inextricably in the politics of the foreign governments, and the American military itself intervened aggressively numerous times in the Caribbean, Mexico and Central America, and South America. As in the British case, the history of American direct investment occurred in the context of an expanding military presence of the home government. Moreover, since many of these countries were poor, the multinational corporations responded to the demands of the host nation, especially in the form of concessionary contracts, to provide public services, e.g., hospitals, roads, and power. This complicated legacy of the early history of the multinational corporation created hostility on the part of the local population that persisted throughout most of the twentieth century.

It is important to underscore that the multinational corporation usually evolved in the context of specific national institutions. As many others have pointed out, the multinational corporation is a growing firm whose organizational borders have spilled across borders. Moreover, since this large firm is usually tied to a larger domestic network of suppliers and customers, its expansion overseas is accompanied by the co-investments of these other members. This is a pattern seen in American investments in the United Kingdom in the 1950s and repeated by Japanese multinational corporations investing in the United Kingdom in the 1980s and 1990s.

Chandler noted that these multinational corporations reflected the national characteristics of management. In comparing the cases of the largest firms in the United Kingdom, Germany, and the United States, Chandler found that differences in managerial capabilities, reflecting national institutions, explain their success and failure patterns. He particularly criticized the managerial capabilities of British firms, a point not shared by some British historians (Hannah). But more importantly, Chandler's thesis assumed that size itself constituted the realization of scale and scope economies instead of the outcome of success and growth. This observation is especially important for understanding the lack of large multinational corporations in Italy or in Taiwan, both of which have very successful small firm economies but do not have multinational corporations comparable to other countries of similar levels of economic wealth. Yet, both countries are relatively wealthy and successful, and their many small companies have achieved high rates of exporting. Even in the case of the United States, the evidence implies that American firms, large and small, came to Europe, riding on the back of the national organizing principles of standardization in work methods (Kogut). Chandler's larger point of the effect of national systems on firm capabilities is largely accepted; his belief that large firms reflect better management because they achieve scale is disputed far more.

ORGANIZATION OF MULTINATIONAL CORPORATIONS

The national origins of the multinational corporation influence their subsequent organizational evolution. In the United States, the great post-World War II expansion of multinational corporations coincided with the diffusion of their adoption of the multi-divisional structure. Indeed, the refinement of 'organizational technologies' permitted American firms to manage their rapidly growing operations on a worldwide basis.

The young American multinational corporation began with little knowledge and experience of the foreign market. Initial foreign sales are exports executed within the existing organizational structure. These structures could be functional (e.g., organized by production and sales) or divisional (e.g., organized by geographic area or product division). As foreign sales increased, an international division was created to make the sale and to provide customer support. In consequence, the domestic organizational unit would sell to the international division its products at an internal 'transfer price.' As this price was set by the domestic market, it was unlikely to reflect the competitive conditions in the foreign country. Moreover, the products were often not designed to the tastes of foreign demand. Because of this internal conflict, the American multinational corporation would replace the international division by transferring responsibilities to area divisions (e.g., Europe, Asia-South America) or to product divisions. While these structures diminished the internal conflict, they ran the hazard that the divisional managers across areas did not cooperate or that managers across product divisions tended to fall back upon focusing on the home market.

European firms grew up in a different environment. Europe was a highly unstable continent during the twentieth century, with significant political and economic conflicts. Borders sometimes changed, and they also marked the necessity to pay commercial duties. The gradual creation of the European Union in the last third of the twentieth century eliminated tariffs and lessened national differences. This history marked their firms. The organizational technologies in most of these countries were quite different to those found in the United States. Holding company structures were common, banks or other financial institutions played powerful roles in ownership and cross holdings, and firms were tied together in complex financial webs. These structures, often called 'mother-daughter' organizations, reflect the linguistic terms used in northern Europe to describe headquarters and subsidiary. These mother-daughter structures consisted often of a headquarters that held a portfolio consisting of ownership control over dozens of companies, many of them in the same sector but located in different countries. Reporting relationships among these companies and headquarters was less formal than found in American companies, and control was often exercised through the movement of managers who were lifetime employees. These structures were often seen as inefficient, especially compared to the size and organization of American multinationals that were investing rapidly in Europe at this time. European critics called for the restructuring of European firms and industry along American lines.

The structure of Japanese companies reflected also their historical origins. In Japan, the trading company performed an extraordinary role in the exports during the first two-thirds of the twentieth century. These companies started primarily as wholesalers, but over time developed their own industrial companies located in Japan and eventually overseas. Though the forced imposition of American antitrust law after World War II disrupted these patterns, trading companies and other affiliated company networks, called *keiretsu*, reconstituted the earlier pattern of constellations of domestic companies competing in home and, through their trading companies, in foreign markets. As in the American and European cases, Japanese firms varied in their internal structures, with functional and even factory-based organization being the predominant structures. Still, a dominant trend emerged over time as the role of trading companies declined, especially for the exportation of industrial and high technology goods. This trend consisted of the appendage of an international division to the existing structure.

These different national structures confronted an increasingly more globally integrated environment in the course of the twentieth century. This environment posed the classic organizational problem of balancing integration and differentiation. For the multinational corporation, this problem posed itself as meeting the demands to achieve global scale against the needs of national markets and governments. Given different national principles of organizing the activities of multinational corporations, there was not a rapid convergence to a global structure. The growth of multinational corporations, especially in Europe, was stymied by these traditions. Continuing national differences and the failure to develop harmonized European corporate law deterred the emergence of pan-European multinational corporations. Many of the most important cross-European mergers failed initially within a decade lnstead. American multinational corporations, less bound by these separate national traditions, were able to create integrated European strategies.

Nevertheless, it was in Europe where new organizational structures developed to resolve the conflict between integration and differentiation. Multinational corporations from smaller countries offered the laboratory experiments that influenced the evolution of multinational corporations from larger nations. Because of the small size of many European countries, large firms in Sweden, Switzerland, and the Netherlands quickly became multinational corporations, and these corporations had far more assets and employees outside their home countries than within. Over the course of the last two decades of the twentieth century, organizational structures developed, labeled as transnational corporations, that distributed global responsibilities to national subsidiaries, created global teams and projects, and encouraged the transfer of 'best practices' across borders.

MNCs FROM EMERGING MARKETS

Multinational companies from the emerging world are a relatively new phenomenon. Emerging Markets Multinationals (EM-MNCs) have become important in almost every industry. India's Infosys and TCS have become two of the world's leading information technology companies. China's Haier is the fourth-largest maker of home appliances in the world, and its ZTE is on its way to becoming one of the world's top five manufacturers of telecommunications equipment and systems.

According to the United Nations Conference on Trade and Development (UNCTAD), multinationals in emerging economies accounted for only 0.4 percent of world outward foreign direct investment (FDI) in 1970. That share grew to 15.8 percent by 2008.Alone, emerging nations in Asia and Oceania accounted for 11.9 percent of world outward FDI in 2008; among these nations, China has seen the most dramatic and continuous growth.

Recent trend of multinationals from emerging countries shows that firms from emerging countries are very heterogeneous in terms of their origin, maturity, position in the value chain and strategy. This suggests a variety of drivers for internationalization. Such huge heterogeneity makes it difficult to generalize about how EM-MNCs are similar or dissimilar to more traditional multinationals. EM-MNCs do not usually possess strong global brands or cutting-edge technologies that place them close to the technology frontier. Rather, they often acquire established brands to become well-known—such as the Tata Group of India, which acquired the automobile manufacturers Jaguar and Land Rover—or acquire firms that already developed proprietary technology. However, this does not mean that they do not possess ownership advantages. One view is that EM-MNCs expand to other countries in order to obtain new advantages to serve as a further springboard for internationalization. One of these advantages is the ability to adapt products developed elsewhere to domestic markets, gaining greater production efficiency by using inputs more efficiently or by using more labor and less capital, or by reducing overhead costs. Some EM-MNCs have advantageous access to resources and markets, and also have "adversity advantages," that is, the ability to survive poor infrastructure, corrupt bureaucracies, regulatory uncertainties and weak educational institutions all of which hamper multinational from advanced economies that operate within emerging economics.

HOW MULTINATIONALS CAN GAIN TRACTION IN EMERGING MARKETS

The growth of the world's emerging markets may no longer be a surprise, but the sheer scale of their transformation still has the ability to shock. Recent McKinsey Global Institute research demonstrates the size of the opportunity presented by emerging markets: annual consumption of $30 trillion by 2025. That is not a typo. China and India, the two biggest emerging markets, are experiencing economic acceleration 10 times that of Europe's industrial revolution—on 100 times the scale. It represents the biggest opportunity in the history of capitalism.

And yet, multinational companies are failing to compete successfully in these energetic emerging markets. In 2010, annual consumption in emerging markets was $12 trillion, or about 32% of the world's total. (And by 2025, about 50% of the world's economic growth will be driven by cities such as Ahmedabad, Calcutta, Manila and Wuhan.) But among 100 of the world's largest companies headquartered in developed economies, just 17% of total revenue comes from emerging markets—about half the "natural share" these global organizations could be expected to hold.

Even though such internationals work from small bases as they build operations in emerging markets, their average annual revenue growth remains barely half that achieved by incumbent emerging-market players. There is a fundamental disconnect between the way companies from developed economies should operate in emerging markets and the way they actually do.

So what can be done? There is no easy answer, of course; these emerging markets are complex and present a range of challenges. But there are three broad fronts across which companies must develop their capabilities to succeed in emerging markets.

First, they must carefully choose their opportunities and focus on cities. Existing size and strength offers no guarantees, and companies should take advantage of the wealth of data now at their disposal to target specific consumers in specific geographies and cities in very specific ways. For example, two of China's biggest cities — Guangzhou and Shenzhen — are in the same province and just two hours apart. Yet Guangzhou residents are mostly born locally, speak Cantonese, and spend their leisure time at home with family and friends. More than 80% of Shenzhen residents are migrants, most speak Mandarin and spend their leisure time away from home. A provincewide approach — let alone a countrywide one, will not work.

Second, once companies commit to expand, they must do so aggressively. In general, companies from emerging markets invest more, and more often, than their counterparts in the developed world: between 1999 and 2008, emerging-market companies paid out half as much in dividends, but invested much more in fixed assets. Companies in emerging economies choose to generate wealth for shareholders not by paying dividends, but by aggressively reinvesting capital to spur growth. Newcomers will have to adjust their definitions of success accordingly.

Finally, companies must be persistent. Capturing the emerging-market opportunity is a long-term effort: management processes and structures may need to be changed, and new models adopted. Be prepared to compete on your own turf as well, and soon: companies from emerging markets also are increasingly succeeding within developed economies. Actually, the companies from emerging markets achieve superior revenue growth pretty much everywhere, leaving established multinationals struggling to both capture emerging-market growth and defend against new competitors in traditional markets. They do this by getting exactly these basics right: they carefully identify opportunities, invest appropriately and stick with it.

For established multinationals, this should hardly be radical. Today, however, too few of them appear to be heeding these lessons. However, even a tiny slice of the biggest opportunity in the history of capitalism is something worth grasping.

AN INTEGRATED STRATEGY OF MNCs

The multinational corporation (MNC) is the first institution in human history to plan on a global scale. Its purpose is to organise and integrate economic activity around the world in order to maximise profit. In fact, the revenues of these transnational corporations exceed the gross national product of many of the countries in which they operate. Its failures and successes are measured through growth in global profit and market share. International trade usually benefits all parties involved. The basic assumption in such trade is that the growth of the whole strengthens the welfare of all. The overall focus is increased efficiency. International companies now have significant influence on world productivity and technological advancement. Their influence has grown so vast that it affects all aspects of society. Furthermore, the average rate of growth of the most successful MNCs is two to three times higher than that of most advanced countries.

Manufacturing firms usually follow a four-step process to enter the international environment: (1) A corporation exports goods requested by foreign customers. (2) A firm initiates marketing activities abroad. (3) A firm establishes other functional activities overseas, such as manufacturing. Firms in this stage are called **multinationals**. (4) A firm is characterised by widespread operation and is no longer identified with just one particular country. Firms in this stage are called **transnationals**.

Going International

Modern corporations are trying to grain and advantage over their competitors. Most are finding that a good way to do so is through the complex process of going international. By going international, corporations can extend their product lines to other cultures. They can also save money on labour costs by taking advantage of the lower standard of living in some countries. One big advantages of doing business in foreign countries, particularly developing countries, is that high unemployment rates provide inexpensive and vast labour pools. This helps companies to generate more capital and, therefore, bring in more revenue. These countries are ideal for industrial companies in labour-intensive industries. Many U.S. manufacturing firms have found that they incur lower input costs by locating their manufacturing facilities outside the United States and thus can export their products at lower prices than if those same products were manufactured at home. The *maquiladora* in Mexico is a case in point; by sending parts to Mexican plants for assembly, manufacturers can save on labour costs. By going international, a company can make and save money simultaneously, depending on the geographic area.

Several factors both influence the decision to go international and make the move feasible. The ever-pressing need to get ahead of the competition may be a good reason to go abroad. In underdeveloped nations, labour is inexpensive, which means that a company pays less to get the same job done. Another reason for going abroad is rapid expansion, in an effort to keep up with product demand. A home-based company may be expanding rapidly, but not rapidly enough to keep up with market demand. An overseas facility can satisfy such demand. A final reason for going international is the absence of trade barriers vital to many economies throughout the world. This trend is reflected in the increased efforts of many countries to promote international trade.

Strategy Formulation

Objectives and strategies are formulated by considering mission, strategic policy, and information. When a firm operates outside its home country, its strategic objectives and overall strategy change. To adjust its strategy to its various environments, a firm can implement a number of options. Depending on the type of change required, it can choose either expansion or expansion and diversification. However, a firm that chooses expansion as its strategy to achieve corporate development and efficient use of existing resources for higher profits will soon find that it needs to diversify to maintain systematic growth. In the diversification strategy, a firm has two alternatives for expansion:

1. **Geography** (the international route): A strategy is prepared to weight the pros and cons of developing foreign markets and the implications of the decision.
2. **Product**: A firm can choose a move into a new business as an alternative to going international or as a way to enter foreign markets. A company can also purchase another business that operates in a foreign environment.

The stages of strategy formulation can be categorised as follows: (1) decision preparation stage (also called long-term planning), (2) matching stage (also called intermediate-term planning), and (3) implementation stage (also called short-term planning). In the preparation stage, strategists gather questions and ideas and develop ways to measure and determine feasibility. Other activities include establishing a more objective view of the company's future and setting policies to aid in achieving corporate objectives. It also involves the preparation of a timetable for supplementary decisions. The strategists at this stage plan for the efficient use of corporate resources to the greatest possible advantage and design a system to manage the constant flow of information. When the basic decisions about strategy have been made, a corporation is ready to undertake the next step. The matching stage involves the development of systematic guidelines to forecast opportunities and threats, along with setting deadlines to measure progress and establishing mechanisms to cope with possible problems. The strategists develop a structure for international logistics to purchase raw materials and distribute products. Then the strategists select methods to integrate and compromise between the company's resources and the design of the decision system. In the third stage, tasks and available machinery are assigned to each operating unit for implementation. Other activities in this stage include developing efficient inventory procedures, financial practices, and the flexibility to accommodate delays when a part of the program runs late.

MNCs are highly dependent on a strategic advantage, as are most organisations. Many multinational firms key in on the superiority of some resource, such as capital, labour, or technology. Capitalising on an advantage can compensate for a weakness. Strategy formulation gives a company a competitive advantage in that it improves quality and reduces costs. It also facilitates innovation through open lines of communication among team members.

A key factor for success in going multinational is a strong integrated strategy. *An integrated strategy should always include costs and margins*. A corporation that wants to be strong in the international arena must consider competitive advantage. In a long-range strategic plan, it would be senseless to operate an international subsidiary whose costs exceed its profits. The same is true in integrated strategy.

Two assumptions are connected with a successful multinational integration strategy: (1) integration provides a MNC with an advantage over its competitors and (2) an organisation can trade off some proceeds of its competitive advantage with host governments. Once these assumptions have been implemented, a company must pay close attention to economies of scale and the economic situation in the countries to which it expands.

Another function of integration is supplier partnership, which facilitates better communication with suppliers and can prove to be valuable in product design.

Implementing an integrated strategy usually requires several compromises with the host country. These usually involve sharing the economic benefits of the new subsidiary or branch of the MNC. Laws and regulations, whether domestic or international, also need to be considered, because they differ from country to country.

An integrated strategy should also consider customer needs and tastes, which vary from culture to culture. An integrated strategy allows a company that is going international to adjust its product line to suit a variety of customers and cultures. It also allows room for improvements, such as new distribution channels, for optimal international commercial practices.

A strong integrated strategy includes logistic management, which is the central operational task. Logistic strategy analysis must start with economic factors, because the production-marketing system exists to implement the resource transmission capabilities rooted in these factors. The major factors are economic differentials and the efficiencies available through a unified global system. However, analysis based on economic factors must be modified by other influences, including government actions and corporate characteristics. Logistics strategy for a MNC has three main goals:

1. To efficiently transmit resources so as to maximise their flow in a natural direction as determined by economic differentials and government actions.
2. To utilise the potential and make maximum use of the special advantages of a MNC as a global organisation
3. To effectively implement resource transmission, with special regard to communication as a critical factor.

MNCs use logistics systems to keep production balanced and to check inconsistencies in the schedules of integrated plants. At monthly meetings, key managers and company experts schedule production, lines and corporate goals for the upcoming month. A key topic is generally inventory control.

Unfortunately, many companies fail due to inconsistencies. Decisions in the expansion of an integrated system are more complicated than the daily operations of a domestic corporation. Efficiency of operation and flexibility of supply must be carefully monitored on a daily basis. The number of integrated plants should be kept at a limited or optimal level in order to avoid unnecessary complexities. For example, when Volkswagen invested in the United States, it did not realise the magnitude of the risk involved. First, the cost of labour was extremely high. Then, when the dollar rose dramatically, the cost of operation was affected by the exchange rate, which made the integration obsolete. Integration strategies and logistic play an important role in the expansion process, not only for U.S.-based companies but for growing companies throughout the world.

HOST COUNTRY CONTROLS AND REGULATIONS

Companies must adhere to different rules in international marketing, and, therefore, strategies must also be altered. Indeed, the governments of different countries impose different regulations on MNCs, in varying degrees. Host countries often restrict the following:

i) **Ownership:** Host countries typically require that a local firm own a majority or controlling interest;
ii) **Employment:** Almost all host countries demand that certain managerial and technological positions he held by host country nationals;
iii) **Profits and fees:** Profits and fees are typically set at some maximum level;
iv) **Internal debt capital:** Internal debt capital is often set according to a preestablished formula;
v) **Training and development:** Insistence on training and development for host country nationals is common;
vi) **Host country markets:** Most host countries demand development of their exports;
vii) **Technological bases:** Most host countries seek technology-based industries rather than extractive industries.

Setting objectives is also significantly affected by a multinational environment because: growth may he legislatively limited; efficiency may be held to an undesirably low level by extra costs as dictated by governments; use of resources may be set at specified levels; contribution to owners (profits) is usually set at arbitrary levels; contribution to customers may be modified to meet government-established levels; contribution to employees focuses on technical training and often includes guaranteed employment as opposed to true development; contribution to society is stressed by the government's involvement in all areas.

A basic strategy of Japanese companies is to diversify early in their history. U.S. firms do not diversify quite as early, and European firms tend to diversify later still. Japanese companies pay closer attention than any other country to quality in production. Japanese management philosophy is oriented toward the group or team. In virtually all countries, negotiation with the government is becoming increasingly more critical than it has in the United States and Canada. While objectives and strategies will vary, *the basics of strategy are the same.* The differences in the basic strategies of MNCs can be traced to cultural/historical factors.

DESIGNING STRATEGY

Whether to globalise, and how to globalise, have become two of the most burning strategy issues for managers around the world. Many forces are driving companies around the world to globalise by expanding their participation in foreign markets. Almost every product market in the major world economies has foreign competitors. Trade barriers are also falling. Maturity in domestic market is also driving companies to seek international expansion.

Companies are also seeking to globalise by integrating their worldwide strategy. Such global integration contrasts with the multinational approach whereby companies set up country subsidiaries that design, produce, and market products or services tailored to local needs. This multinational model (also described as a "multidomestic strategy") is now in question. Several changes seem to increase the likelihood that, in some industries, a global strategy will be more successful than a multidomestic one. One of these changes is the growing similarity of what citizens of different countries want to buy. Other changes include the reduction of tariff and nontariff barriers, technology investments that are becoming too expensive to amortise in one market only, and competitors that are globalising the rules of the game.

Companies want to know how to globalise - in other words, expand market participation - and how to develop an integrated worldwide strategy. As depicted in Figure-1, three steps are essential in developing a total worldwide strategy:

FIGURE-1

TOTAL GLOBAL STRATEGY

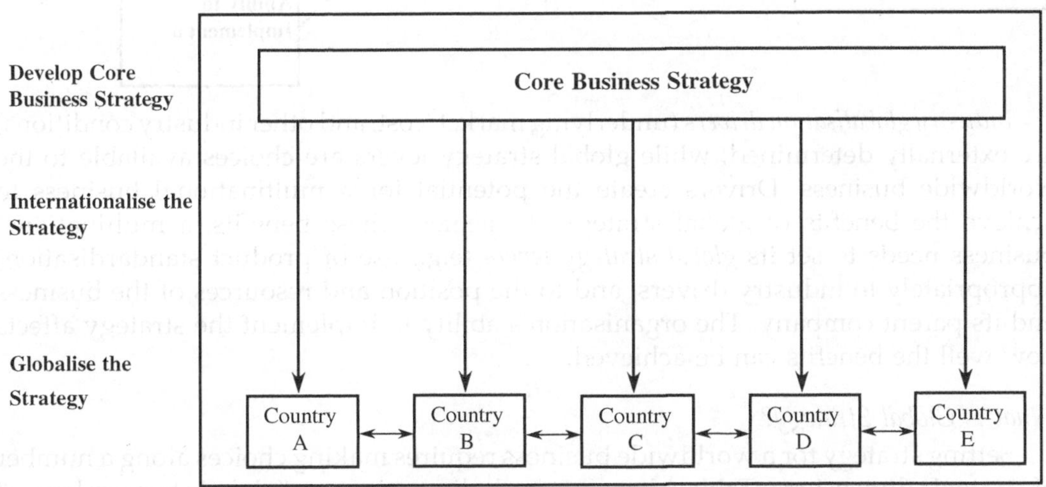

i) Developing the core strategy - the basis of sustainable competitive advantage. It is usually developed for the home country first.

ii) Internationalising the core strategy through international expansion of activities and through adaptation.

iii) Globalising the international strategy by integrating the strategy across countries.

Multinational companies know the first two steps well. They know the third step less well since globalisation runs counter to the accepted wisdom of tailoring for national markets. *How might a global strategy work and directs manager toward opportunities to exploit globalisation. What are the drawbacks and costs of globalisation?* Figure-2 lays out a framework for thinking through globalisation issues.

FIGURE-2

FRAMEWORK OF GLOBAL STRATEGY FORCES

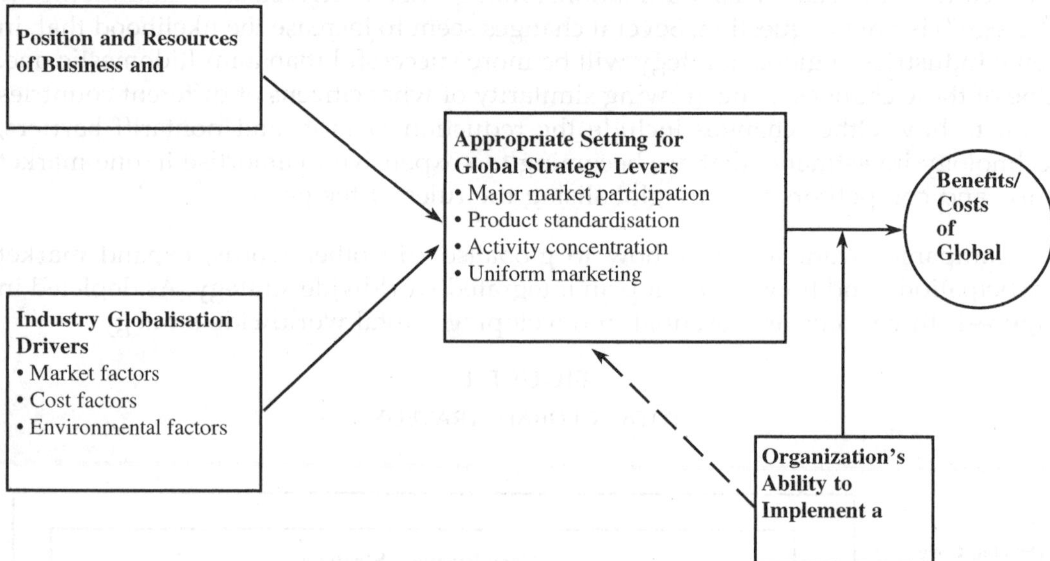

Industry globalisation drivers (underlying market, cost, and other industry conditions) are externally determined, while global strategy levers are choices available to the worldwide business. Drivers create the potential for a multinational business to achieve the benefits of global strategy. To achieve these benefits, a multinational business needs to set its *global strategy levers* (e.g., use of product standardisation) appropriately to industry drivers, and to the position and resources of the business and its parent company. The organisation's ability to implement the strategy affects how well the benefits can be achieved.

What is Global Strategy?

Setting strategy for a worldwide business requires making choices along a number of strategic dimensions. Table-1 lists five such dimensions or "global strategy levers" and their respective positions under a pure multidomestic strategy and a pure global strategy. Intermediate positions are, of course, feasible. For each dimension, a multidomestic strategy seeks to maximise worldwide performance by maximising local competitive advantage, revenues, or profits; a global strategy seeks to maximise worldwide performance through sharing and integration.

TABLE-1

GLOBALISATION DIMENSIONS/GLOBAL STRATEGY LEVERS

Dimension	*Setting for pure multidomestic strategy*	*Setting for pure global strategy*
Market Participation	No particular pattern	Significant share in major markets
Product Offering	Fully customised in each country	Fully standardised worldwide
Location of Value-Added Activities	All activities in each country	Concentrated—one activity in each (different) country
Market Approach	Local	Uniform worldwide
Competitive Moves	Stand-alone by country	Integrated across countries

Market Participation

In a multidomestic strategy, countries are selected on the basis of their standalone potential for revenues and profits. In a global strategy, countries need to be selected for their potential contribution to globalisation benefits. This may mean entering a market that is unattractive in its own right, but has global strategic significance, such as the home market of a global competitor. Or it may mean building share in a limited number of key markets rather than undertaking more widespread coverage. A pattern of major share in major markets is advocated in Ohmae's USA-Europe-Japan "triad" concepts. In contrast, under a multidomestic strategy, no particular pattern of participation is required - rather, the pattern accrues from the pursuit of local advantage.

Product Offering

In a multidomestic strategy, the products offered in each country are tailored to local needs. In a global strategy, the ideal is a standardised core product that requires minimal local adaptation. Cost reduction is usually the most important benefit of product standardisation. Levitt has made the most extreme case for product standardisation. Others stress the need for flexibility, or the need for a broad product portfolio, with many product varieties in order to share technologies and distribution channels. In practice, some multinationals have pursued product standardisation to a greater or lesser extent. Differing worldwide needs can be met by adapting a standardised core product.

Location of Value-added Activities

In a multidomestic strategy, all or most of the value chain is reproduced in every country. In another type of international strategy - exporting - most of the value chain is kept in one country. In a global strategy, costs are reduced by breaking up the value chain so each activity may be conducted in a different country. One value chain strategy is partial concentration and partial duplication. The key feature of a global position on this dimension is the strategic placement of the value chain around the globe.

Marketing Approach

In a multidomestic strategy, marketing is fully tailored for each country, being developed locally. In a global strategy, a uniform marketing approach is applied around the world, although not all elements of the marketing mix need be uniform. Similarly, a product that serves a common need can be geographically expanded with a uniform marketing programme, despite differences in marketing environments.

Competitive Moves

In a multidomestic strategy, the managers in each country make competitive moves without regard for what happens in other countries. In a global strategy, competitive moves are integrated across countries. The same type of move is made in different countries at the same time or in a systematic sequence: a competitor is attacked in one country in order to drain its resources for another country, or a competitive attack in one country is countered in a different country. Perhaps the best example is the counterattack in a competitor's home market as a parry to an attack on one's own home market. Integration of competitive strategy is rarely practised, except perhaps by some Japanese companies. For instance, Bridgestone Corporation, the Japanese tire manufacturer, tried to integrate its competitive moves in response to global consolidation by its major competitors - Continental AG's acquisition of Gencorp's General Tire and Rubber Company, General Tire's joint venture with two Japanese tire makers, and Sumitomo's acquisition of an interest in Dunlop Tire. These competitive actions forced Bridgestone to establish a presence in the major U.S. market in order to maintain its position in the world tire market. To this end, Bridgestone formed a joint venture to own and manage Firestone Corporation's worldwide tire business. This joint venture also allowed Bridgestone to gain access to Firestone's European plants.

BENEFITS OF A GLOBAL STRATEGY

Companies that use global strategy levers can achieve one or more of these benefits: *cost reductions; improved quality of products and programmes; enhanced customer preference; and increased competitive leverage.* (see Table-2)

Cost reduction: An integrated global strategy can reduce worldwide costs in several ways. A company can increase the benefits from economies of scale by *pooling production or other activities* for two or more countries. Understanding the potential benefit of these economies of scale, Sony Corporation has concentrated its compact disc production in Terre Haute, Indiana, and Salzburg, Austria. A *second* way to cut costs is by *exploiting lower factor costs* by moving manufacturing or other activities to low-cost countries. This approach has, of course, motivated the recent surge of offshore manufacturing, particularly by U.S. firms. *Thirdly,* the global strategy can also cut costs by *exploiting flexibility.* A company with manufacturing locations in several countries can move production from location to location on short notice to take advantage of the lowest costs at a given time. Dow Chemical takes this approach to minimise the cost of producing chemicals. Dow uses a linear programming model that takes account of international differences in exchange rates, tax rates, and transportation and labor costs. Finally, an integrated global strategy can also reduce costs by *enhancing bargaining power.* A company whose strategy allows for switching

TABEL 2

GLOBAL STRATEGY LEVERS AND GLOBALISATION BENEFITS.

Global Strategy Levers	*Benefits* *Cost Reduction*	*Improved Quality of Products and Programs*	*Enhanced Customer Preference*	*Increased Competitive Leverage*	*Major Drawbacks* *All Levers Incur Coordination Costs, Plus*
Major Market	Increases volume for economies of scale		Via global availability, global servicetability and global recognition	Advantage of earlier entry Provides more sites for attack and counter-attack, hostage for good behaviour	Earlier or greater commitment to a market than warranted on own merit
Product Standardisation	Reduce duplication of development efforts Allows concentration of production to exploit economies of scale	Focuses development and management resources	Allows consumers to use familiar product while abroad Allow organisations to use some product across country units.	Basis for low-cost invations of markets	Less responsibe to local needs
Activity Concentration	Reduces duplication of activities Helps exploit economies Exploits differences in country factor costs Partial concentration allows flexibility vs. currency changes, and vs. bargaining parties	Focuses effort Allows more consistent quality control		Allow maintenance of cost advantage independent of local conditions	Distance activities from the customer Increases currency risk
Uniform Marketing	Reduce design and production costs of marketing programmes	Focuses talent and resources Leverages scares, good ideas	Reinforces marketing messages by exposing customer to same mix in different countries	and marketing	Reduces adaptation to local customer behaviour environment
Integrated competitive Moves				Provides more options and leverage in attack and defense.	Local competitiveness may be sacrificed

production among different countries greatly increases its bargaining power with suppliers, workers, and host governments.

Improved quality of products and programmes: Under a global strategy, companies focus on a smaller number of products and programmes than under a multidomestic strategy. This concentration can improve both product and programme quality. Global focus is one reason for Japanese success in automobiles. Toyota markets a far smaller number of models around the world than does General Motors, even allowing for its unit sales being half that of General Motors's. Toyota has concentrated on improving its few models while General Motors has fragmented its development funds.

Enhanced customer preference: Global availability, serviceability, and recognition can enhance customer preference through reinforcement. Soft drink and fast food companies are, of course, leading exponents of this strategy. Many suppliers of financial services, such as credit cards, must have a global presence because their service is travel-related. Manufacturers of industrial products can also exploit this benefit. A supplier that can provide a multinational customer with a standard product around the world gains from worldwide familiarity. Computer manufacturers have long pursued this strategy.

Increased competitive leverage: A global strategy provides more points from which to attack and counterattack competitors. In an effort to prevent the Japanese from becoming a competitive nuisance in disposable syringes, Becton Dickinson, a major U.S. medical products company, decided to enter three markets in Japan's backyard. Becton entered the Hong Kong, Singapore, and Philippine markets to prevent further Japanese expansion.

DRAWBACKS OF GLOBAL STRATEGY

Globalisation can incur significant management costs through increased coordination, reporting requirements, and even added staff. It can also reduce the firm's effectiveness in individual countries if overcentralisation hurts local motivation and morale. In addition, each global strategy lever has particular drawbacks. For instance, a global strategy approach to *market participation* can incur an earlier or greater commitment to a market than is warranted on its own merits. Many American companies are struggling to penetrate Japnese markets, more in order to enhance their global competitive position than to make money in Japan for its own sake. Again, a *product standardisation* can result in a product that does not entirely satisfy *any* customers. When companies first internationalise, they often offer their standard domestic product without adapting it for other countries, and suffer the consequences. For example, Procter & Gamble stumbled when it introduced Cheer laundry detergent in Japan without changing the U.S. product or marketing message (that the detergent was effective in all temperatures). After experiencing serious losses, P&G discovered two instances of insufficient adaptation. *First,* the detergent did not suds up as it should because the Japanese use a great deal of fabric softener. *Second,* the Japanese usually wash clothes in either cold tap water or bath water, so the claim of working in all temperatures was irrelevant.

Uniform marketing can reduce adaptation to local customer behaviour. A globally standardised product is designed for the global market but can seldom satisfy all needs in all countries. For instance, Canon, a Japanese company, sacrificed the ability to copy certain Japanese paper sizes when it first designed a photocopier for the global market. Further, the *activity concentration* distances customers and can result in lower responsiveness and flexibility. It also increases currency risk by incurring costs and revenues in different countries. Recently volatile exchange rates have required companies that concentrate their production to hedge their currency exposure. Moreover, *integrated competitive moves* can mean sacrificing revenues, profits, or competitive position in individual countries, particularly when the subsidiary in one country is asked to attack a global competitor in order to send a signal or to divert that competitor's resources from another country.

Finding the Balance

The most successful worldwide strategies find a balance between overglo balizing and underglobalising. The ideal strategy matches the level of strategy globalisation to the globalisation potential of the industry. In Figure both Business *A* and Business *C* achieve balanced global and national strategic advantage. Business *A* does so with a low level of strategy globalisation to match the low globalisation potential of its industry (e.g., food products). Business *C* uses a high level of strategy globalisation to match the high globalisation potential of its industry (e.g., computer equipment). Business *B* is at a global disadvantage because it uses a strategy that is less globalised than the potential offered by its industry. The business is failing to exploit potential global benefits such as cost savings via product standardisation. Business *D* is at a national disadvantage because it is too globalised relative to the potential offered by its industry. The business is not tailoring its products and programmes as much as it should. While there is no systematic evidence, it seems that far more businesses suffer from insufficient globalisation than from excessive globalisation. Figure-3 is oversimplified in that it shows only one overall dimension for both strategy and industry potential. A global strategy has major dimensions and many subdimensions. Similarly, the potential of industry globalisation is multidimensional.

IMPLEMENTING GLOBAL STRATEGY

The *zeitgeist* of the new millennium will be the spirit of free economic competition and co-evolution between nations. Nations peopled by highly educated, open-minded, driven entrepreneurs who create productive enterprises through constant innovation and fast imitation will flourish. Such nations must also be led by progressive politicians who understand that central to their economic policy is the fostering of progressive knowledge about design and manufacturing processes.

Global Enterprise is awaiting a new day, anticipating the encounter with its international competitors. *Global Enterprise* is visualised as being capable of outmaneuvering its predecessor, the international corporation, by reading to market demands more efficiently and effectively. Multinational corporations identify themselves in terms of such barriers as national borders and sociocultural differences; their customers are domestic markets, and they allocate products according to the preferred tastes of each country. The reward and control structures of multinational

FIGURE-3

GLOBALISATION POTENTIAL OF INDUSTRY *Vs.* GLOBALISATION STRATEGY

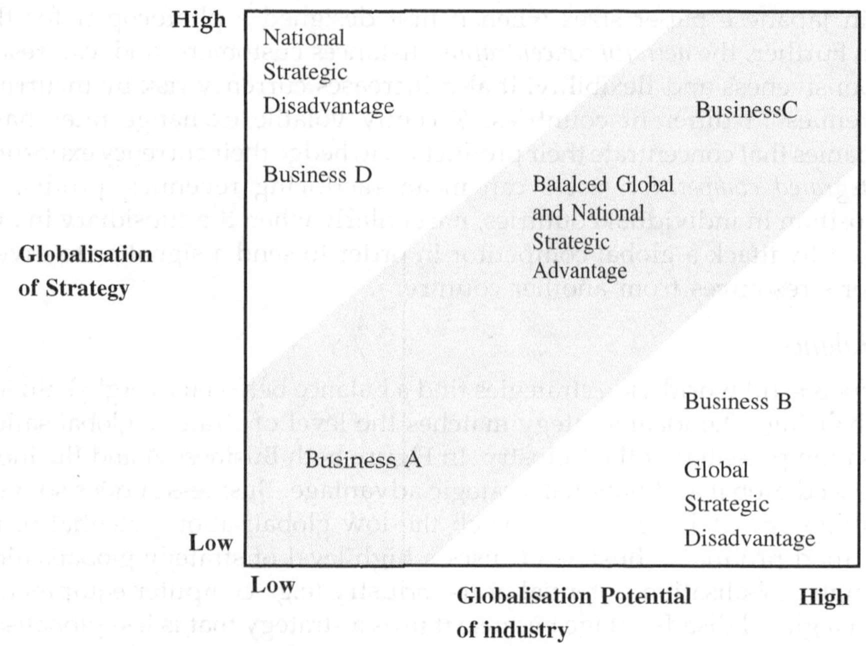

corporations are oriented more toward the growth of domestic markets than the growth of the world as a market.

Unlike the multinational corporation, the global enterprise does not limit itself to the boundaries imposed by national markets and views the whole world as its market. Instead of running subsidiaries under the control of a centralised management structure, the global enterprise is a decentralised system, composed of various management, manufacturing, marketing, resource, and financial nodes. The nodes are structured to operate with full efficiency and effectiveness. The manager of each node is given the latitude and authority to adapt the operation to local conditions and, occasionally, to contact counterpart nodes to resolve problems directly. At the name implies, a multinational corporation should be well positioned to become a global enterprise. A small but growing number of companies that are not multinationals may, however, be better positioned to become a global enterprise because they already have the flexible, efficient structure that many multinationals lack.

For a company that would aspire to become a global enterprise, the time to make the transition is now. Those that wait will not be prepared to face new forms of competition on a truly global scale. How long will it take for the leadership of a country to change its geopolitical diplomacy and trade policy to the new reality? These organisations of the future will be knowledge based, evolving through a painful trial-and-error process. Strategy-structure research indicates that numerous firms have failed by clinging to the old ways, looking to their formal structures to provide the necessary organisational capacity to compete in a complex global business environment. This same research is beginning to provide hints of the practices that organisations are finding successful in this environment. These practices emphasise the information processing capability necessary for the knowledge transfer that permits optimisation of responsiveness and efficiency. They also look to self-direction and self-control by task-oriented individuals and teams.

The effective implementation of global decisions is a challenge that top-level managers face. Top management must understand the concept of due process and make a serious attempt to implement it in the decision-making process. There are additional problems to contend with. The collapse of appraisal and control capability, the eroding power of the head office, and the decline in common values and expectations are among the serious issues confronting managers. Managers also have to go beyond their normal duties and be creative in their decision making.

Managers of multinational concerns must have a broad understanding of the cultural and political environments in which they are doing business. Careful business management is critical in international markets, where the possibility of both loss and gain is high and many complex factors can affect the outcome. All management functions should be followed along with an integrated strategy. Despite the complexities, the promise for multinationals is high, not only in monetary terms, but also in the accumulation of knowledge and new business ideas.

It is in the context of informal work groups that we can best understand the motivation and behavior of both individuals and teams. Behavior is shaped by the norms of a group which, in turn, are shaped by the values and beliefs of its members. It is obvious that if the behavior of these informal work groups is to be consistent with the strategies and goals of a firm, the values and beliefs of Its members must also reflect that congruity.

Managers can directly control the shape of the formal organisation and can do many things to influence both the shape of the informal organisation and its culture. A few of these things have been outlined here, and the subject is abundantly covered in the literature on motivation and group behavior. The difficult task for managers is to forfeit direct control of parts of the organisation in order to achieve enhanced organisational capability. Through the use of authority, managers can substitute for direct control the indirect control that can be derived only from managing the culture.

So how might a country become number one? The primary responsibility for determining how a nation competes with other nations rests with the managers and owners of industry. They decide whether to implement new production strategies and training policies, to invest in new equipment, to launch research projects, or introduce new products. Their decisions, which cannot be dictated by government, will shape the competitiveness of industry— and, ultimately, the standard of living of workers. The government cannot dictate corporate policy, but it can influence and support research and training to help owners, managers and engineers learn to make ever better decisions about whether to implement new production strategies and training policies, to invest in new equipment, to launch research projects, or introduce new products. If the primary responsibility rests with managers to make excellent decisions, then the primary responsibility of government should be to do everything it can to help firms help themselves improve the quality of their managerial decision making and develop the nation's "powers of production."

The most effective way of increasing the global competitiveness of firms is to improve the management of innovation in products and processes. The best way of improving such skills is for the governments to energise the market for production and management process skills in four ways: i) making the *market* for process skill learning more efficient through higher quality market information; ii) encouraging a better supply of process management skills through very focused public-private sector education and research initiatives; iii) encouraging more demand among firms for higher process skills through tax incentives; and iv) encouraging innovations in learning and training by designing processes and technology to match the skills of workers, rather than vice versa.

ECONOMICS AND POLITICS OF MULTINATIONAL CORPORATIONS

Since the multinational corporation is definitionally equivalent to foreign direct investment, theories of foreign direct investment must account for why one country invests in another and why this investment is carried out within organizational boundaries of a firm. In distinguishing between portfolio and direct investment, Hymer noted that firms operate at a disadvantage in foreign markets and hence they must have an offsetting competitive advantage to compete overseas. These advantages for overseas investments are the same ones that allow a firm to compete and grow in the home market. These observations have important implications. The first is that direct investment is the growth of the firm across borders and hence the firm expands internationally on what it has learned at home. This observation is the basis for the evolutionary theory of the firm. The second observation that Hymer made is that firms that expand overseas, because they have competitive resources, are also likely to be large and to belong to oligopolistic industries.

In these observations, we can understand the ambivalence expressed in popular and policy debates regarding the multinational corporation. Competition among multinational corporations often is the extension of their home domestic and oligopolistic rivalry that spills across national borders. In many global industries, the same company names dominate each country's list of the largest firms inside their national frontiers. No matter if it is China or India, Singapore or Mexico, the same multinational corporations will be found in the local oligopolistic industries (e.g., consumer goods or automobiles). Because they are large even in their home markets, investments by multinational corporations can have a large impact on a host country.

As a consequence, the multinational corporation has often been the subject of debates concerning national sovereignty and welfare. In recent decades, acquisitions have generally been the primary way by which multinationals invest in wealthy foreign countries, where the vast proportion of direct investment is concentrated. Given the size of a multinational corporation and occasional national importance of the targeted acquisition, even wealthy countries frequently evidence discomfort, if not out-right public hostility, to multinational investments. Moreover, multinational corporations are sometimes the vehicles for foreign policies of their home or host country.

Multinational corporations are especially problematic in developing countries. By definition, developing countries are relatively poor, thus both in need of capital and yet concerned over their loss of independence. As discussed above, the history of multinational corporations in developing countries is marked by its origins in policies of imperialism and colonialism. Especially in Latin America, where a school of thought labeled *Dependencia* has been influential, the concern over dependence on the United States resulted in efforts to curb the power of the multinational corporations by restricting the amount of equity ownership a foreign firm could hold in a domestic company or by prohibiting investment in certain sectors.

The other side of the coin is that multinational corporations bring investment and technology to the foreign country. Vernon hypothesized that innovations start in wealthy countries. As the market is saturated and as oligopolistic rivalry increases, multinational corporations are pushed out from their home markets to expand abroad in new markets and to locate less expensive places. Thus, Vernon seized both sides of the debate, recognizing the value of the transfer of technology but also emphasizing the oligopolistic nature of multinational investment.

It is, in fact, difficult to draw simple conclusions regarding the relationship of foreign investment and national growth. Countries such as Singapore, Malaysia, and Thailand have encouraged foreign direct investment actively. The growth in China's coastal sector is indisputably linked to the massive investments by multinational corporations. However, historically Japan and Korea have pursued more cautious policies regarding investments by multinational corporations. In these countries, the state has often negotiated the terms for entry by multinational corporations, sometimes requiring licensing to domestic competitors as a price. The efficacy of such policies for these countries is much disputed. However, for many other countries, the intervention of the government in demanding licenses unquestionably leads to internal corruption and to insufficient domestic competition.

There are many channels by which a country can absorb foreign technology and managerial techniques. Most of the evidence shows, however, that prohibitions on the in-flows of direct investment can be very costly for many countries. With their domestic industries still to be developed, a developing country requires substantial investment. Some countries, primarily in Asia, have been able to achieve very high savings rates to finance their industries without direct investment. Moreover, high savings rates, plus political stability, create growth, and growth attracts foreign portfolio capital. A poor country that prohibits foreign direct investment but does not have high rates of saving is entirely dependent upon portfolio capital. The history of debt and currency crises convinced many poor countries that foreign direct investment was a preferable means of attracting capital, because it could not be easily pulled out of a country on short-notice in response to a financial crisis.

However, multinational corporations also respond to the volatility in the global market. This volatility derives from changes in exchange rates, politics, and productivity. Once having achieved sufficient experience and having established subsidiaries around the world, the multinational corporation might choose to close a plant in one location and open plants in new locations. Of course, such actions might provoke a response by labor, but historically, labor has been organized by national, not by international, organizations. Yet, there is also the possibility that locations lose some kinds of plants but gain more sophisticated investments. Some regions and countries pull multinational investments. It has long been noticed that foreign direct investment among developed countries flows to high cost locations. Regions such as Silicon Valley, Baden-Wuertemberg, and Singapore attract multinational investments not because wages are low, but because productivity levels are high and workers are well trained. In many cases, developing countries have given rise to their own multinational corporations acting in the region and sometimes globally. In this sense, the multinational corporation acts as a training center in the developmental strategies of emerging economies.

The peculiar conflict in the world economy is the growing trend toward economic integration without a concomitant growth in global political and social institutions to regulate and arbitrate this trend. Multinational corporations are rapidly adopting advanced information technologies to increase the efficiency and capabilities of their operations. Valuable information, such as software or financial services, is transmitted digitally. Governments are often unable to tax the value of these services or control their content. Moreover, information technologies, often supported by private telecommunication networks, permit for example, a unit in US to control the manufacturing operations located in India. Digital technologies permit a high degree of integration and, in the short run, aggravate the gap between countries that are rich and those that are poor and do not have the infrastructural capabilities. However, these technologies are beginning to have profound effects on some regional economies. In parts of China, India, Israel, and elsewhere, advanced satellite transmission transmits digitally encoded work between their sites and other organizational units of multinational corporations located elsewhere. Whereas before the Indian engineer from Bangalore might have tried to migrate to the US to bring his human capital to a more attractive labor market, the increasing wages and job prospects in India are encouraging many to stay at home and participate digitally in the world economy.

These trends have unclear effects on multinational corporations. They permit more easily the development of projects that are in continual development, as work passes from one unit to the next as the day advances. They also allow more easily the coupling of less expensive labor in one country with more expensive skilled labor in another.

At the same time, the origins of the multinational corporation laid in its ability to organize labor on a worldwide basis on principles other than ethnic and cultural identities. This organization has never been without cost and risk. The growth of a world digital economy permits alternative ways by which labor can cooperate and be coordinated on a world basis. The intriguing question at this point in history is whether the multinational corporation, though still a vital presence in the world economy, nevertheless will recede relatively in importance as information technologies reduces the meaning of geographic distance.

QUESTIONS

1. Define multinational corporations (MNCs) and also critically examine the economics and politics of MNCs.
2. Discuss the evolution of multinational corporations (MNCs). What are the challenges posed by emerging market multinational corporations (EM-MNCs) in recent times to the MNCs from developed countries ?
3. Discuss the organisational evolution of MNCs and also explain the contradiction in their evolution.
4. How can multinational companies (MNCs) gain traction in emerging markets ?
5. Discuss an integrated strategy of MNCs to enter the international market. What are the strategic issues by faced mangers around the world to be considered while designing global strategy.
6. What is global strategy ? Discuss the main global strategy levers. Explain the benefits and costs of global strategy.

32

MULTINATIONAL CAPITAL BUDGETING

INTRODUCTION

In evaluating projects that cut across national boundaries, firms must deal with a variety of issues seldom encountered within a single country that affect the distribution of net operating cash flows available to the parent, as well as the valuation of these cash flows. Factors influencing the statistical distribution of net operating cash flows, in addition to differences in fundamental economic and political conditions in various countries, include differing rates of inflation and volatile exchange rates that may or may not cancel each other, differences in tax rules and tax rates, and restrictions or taxes on cross- border financial transactions. Factors that may influence the valuation of operating cash flows with a given statistical distribution include incomplete and often segmented capital markets that result from controls on financial transactions both within and among countries; the dependence of net of tax cash flows available to the parent on the firm's over all tax and cash-flow position in various countries; the availability of project-specific concessional finance-loans, guarantees, or insurance against commercial or political risks; and, on occasion, requirements to issue securities-especially equity- within markets partially or totally isolated by barriers to internal or cross-border financial transactions. Further, the available cash flows and their value to the firm often depend on the specific financing of the project, not only because of concessional financing opportunities, but also because the costs or limits on cross-border transfers often depend on the nature of the financial transaction involved, e.g., interest on principal, fees, dividends, or payment for goods.

As a result of these various factors, it is often necessary to distinguish project and parent cash flows, to recognise interactions between the financing and valuation of a project, to take into account dependencies between project valuation and the corporation's overall tax and cash-flow situation, and to incorporate in the valuation criterion the perspectives of multiple investors not sharing a common capital market. Thus, traditional weighted-average cost of capital rules that implicity separate investment and financing decisions often are inapplicable or misleading, as well as exceedingly complex. A variety of alternative approaches have been put forward, some involving multiple investment criteria, others requiring the consideration of the "full-system" effects of the project in question, and others providing relatively complex criteria reflecting the existence of multiple investors based in less than fully integrated capital markets.

INTERNATIONAL CAPITAL BUDGETING: THE BASIC FRAMEWORK

In the international capital budgeting decision-making process, the finance manager is to analyse the variables by using standard discounted cash flow (DCF) techniques (used by firms to weed out unviable projects and rank profitable ones in the order of their contribution to the profitability of the firms) along with additional variables unique to the international capital budgeting and apply the alternative methods of treating them. A checklist of the variables that are unique to multinational capital budgeting includes:

1. Cash flows from foreign projects must be converted into the currency of the parent firm.
2. Cash flows from foreign projects may be subject to various restrictions that are imposed by the host country.
3. Initial investment in the host country may benefit from a partial or total release of blocked funds.
4. Profits generated from projects undertaken in other countries are subject to two taxing jurisdictions: the host country and the parent country.
5. Cash flows generated from foreign projects may replace revenue-producing exports to the host country.
6. Profitability of foreign projects may be enhanced from concessionary financing arrangements and other benefits provided by the host country.
7. Foreign investment may produce diversification benefits to shareholders of the parent firm.
8. Foreign investment may contribute to the corporate overall strategy of growth and gaining foothold in markets to preempt competitors.
9. Terminal value is more difficult to estimate than in the case of domestic projects. Such value to the parent company may differ from the valuation put on the facilities by potential buyers in the host country or from third countries.

The adjusted present value (APV) approach provides a divide and conquer approach to capital budgeting. Financial contribution to a project's value are recognised separately and explicitly, the total present value is the sum of the present value of the basic project cash flows, and the treatment of the various financial effects can be generalised to incorporate the special situations encountered in evaluating foreign projects. In particular, the cash flows can be separated into operating and contractual components, as well as into those components that can be estimated independently for the project and those that depend on system-wide cash flow and tax interactions.

ISSUES IN FOREIGN INVESTMENT ANALYSIS

Multinational corporations (MNCs) evaluating foreign investments find their analyses complicated by a variety of issues rarely if ever encountered by domestic firms. In examining number of such issues including differences between project and parent company cash flows, foreign tax regulations, expropriation, blocked funds, exchange rate changes, inflation and segmented capital markets, the major focus is on to maximise the use of available information while reducing arbitrary cash flows and cost of capital adjustments. For this, the approach is to adjust project's cash flows rather than its cost of capital. This is because there is normally more and better information on the specific impact of a given risk on a project's cash flows than on its cost of capital. Furthermore, adjusting a project's cost of capital to reflect incremental risk does not usually allow for adequate consideration of the time pattern and magnitude of the risk being evaluated. Moreover the use of a uniformly higher discount rate to reflect additional risk involves to penalise future cash flows relatively more heavily than present ones.

Parent Vs. Project Cash Flows

Substantial differences can exist between project cash flows and cash flows back to the parent firm because of tax regulations and exchange controls, for example. Furthermore, many project expenses such as management fees and royalties are returns to the parent company. In addition, the incremental revenue contributed to the parent MNC by a project can differ from total project revenues if, for example, the project involves substituting local production for parent company exports. In general, incremental cash flows to the parent can be found by subtracting world-wide parent company cash flows. Given such differences, the question arises as to the relevant cash flows in project evaluation.

One suggested position is that "to the extent that the corporation views itself as a true multinational, the effect of restrictions on repatriation may not be severe". Thus the parent MNC should value only those cash flows which are or can be repatriated, since only accessible funds can be used to pay dividends and interest, amortise the firm's debt, and be reinvested. This principle also holds true for a domestic firm.

Exchange Rate Change and Inflation

Inflation and exchange risk are opposite side of the same coin. It is worthwhile, however, to analyse each effect separately since there is normally a lag between a given rate of inflation and the necessary exchange rate change. This is particularly true when government intervention occurs, such as in a fixed rate system or a managed float. Furthermore, local price controls may not permit or may retard the effect of internal price adjustments.

Exchange Risk

As with political risk, many companies account for exchange risk by raising their discount rates. However, to the extent that exchange risk is unsystematic, the discount risk should not be adjusted. Rather, the expected value or cash flows should reflect the impact of exchange rate changes. The recommended approach here is to isolate the different sources of a project's cash flows and to analyse each stream separately. This would involve identifying the impact of an exchange rate change on the project's revenues (what percentage of its sales is local as opposed to exports), its costs (what percentage of its inputs is domestic) and on depreciation. It is also necessary to isolate those revenues and costs that are contractually fixed in either local or foreign currency from those inputs and sales whose prices can adjust to a changed exchange rate. For example, while local currency devaluation can increase present profits, present cash flows from depreciation will unambiguously decline by the devaluation percentage unless indexation of fixed assets is permitted. However, indexation, where it exists, is generally tied to an inflation index related to the exchange rate only to the extent that a devaluation will increase local currency prices. Furthermore, working capital requirements will probably change because of the changed competitive situation the firm faces. These changes would have to be incorporated in the analysis.

Inflation

Exchange rate changes are normally preceded by relatively high or lower local rates of inflation than in the home country. As with exchange rate changes, a given inflation rate will not lead to a similar increase in profits or cash flows. Cash flows should be separated into their component parts to analyse each part on its own. The competitive as well as the cost effects of inflation can vary from firm to firm depending (as with exchange rate changes) on the location of a firm's markets as well as on the sources of its inputs. For example, a firm selling locally at inflated prices will find profits rapidly increasing if a large percentage of its costs is fixed in terms of either the local or a foreign currency. Items such as rent, power, labour and imported inputs will exhibit either fixed prices or prices whose increases may lag increases in the firm's product prices.

One danger faced by firms in many countries is a price freeze imposed either during rapid inflation or following devaluation of the local currency. Generally these price freezes are more effective in controlling a firm's output prices than in controlling its input costs, thus leading to a profit squeeze. Furthermore, a foreign firm is less likely or able to flout local price control measures since it is under certain subtle pressures to be a "good corporate citizen". In such a situation, a firm could raise its prices in advance of an anticipated price freeze and take on the burden of competing with inflated prices. When the price freeze occurs, however, and costs inevitably rise afterwards, the firm would be in a better position to continue operating profitably. This is especially true if imported materials are being used and a devaluation has occured. Local companies that are unable to raise their prices when production costs rise will probably start producing inferior merchandise and cut back on service, sustain considerable losses, and/or go out of business. All these factors would have to be reflected through an adjustment of future cash flows.

Inflation will normally influence a firm's cash flows by causing a rise in working capital requirements. This is due to higher costs, increases in its required cash balances, and an easing of credit terms leading to high accounts receivable.

When indexation is permitted, cash flows from depreciation should increase in times of inflation. As noted above, however, this benefit will disappear or at least be reduced following a devaluation.

Tax Treatment of Foreign Source Income

Since only after-tax cash flows are relevant, it is necessary to determine when and what taxes must be paid on foreign-source profits. While the tax treatment of foreign-source earnings is quite complex, there are several stages in the taxation of all income from foreign investments. First the local government involved taxes profits. If tax concessions are granted, however, the tax rate can be zero. Ordinarily, the company then pays a withholding tax to the local government on that portion of profits which is repatriated in the form of dividends, interest fees and royalties. These withholding taxes can sometimes be avoided, however, if the company remits profits in the form of loan repayments, for example, rather than as dividends. Furthermore, the dividend withholding rate can actually be negative.

Political and Economic Risk Analysis

There are several methods by which multinational corporations can account for the added political and economic risks of overseas operations. One is to use a higher discount rate for foreign operations, another to require a shorter payback period. Neither approach, however, lends itself to a careful evaluation of a particular risk's actual impact on investment returns. Though risk analysis requires assessment of the magnitude of the risk's effects on cash flows as well as an estimate of the time pattern of the risk. For example, an expropriation five years from now is likely to be much less threatening than the one expected next year. Thus, using a uniformly higher discount rate just distorts the meaning of a project's present value without obviating the necessity for a careful risk evaluation. Furthermore, the choice of a risk premium (or risk premia if the discount rate is allowed to vary over time) is an arbitrary one, whether it is 2% or 10%. Instead, adjusting cash flows makes it possible to fully incorporate all available information about a specific risk's impact on an investment's future returns.

The capital risk may be justified as long as the systematic risk of a proposed investment remains unchanged. To the extent that the risks dealt are unsystematic, there is no theoretical reason to adjust a project's cost of capital to reflect them. In fact, though, foreign investments appear to reduce a firm's systematic risk by supplying international diversification. If anything, therefore, this approach underestimates rather than overestimates a project's present value.

It is unlikely, however, that management will be concerned solely with the systematic component of total risk. Furthermore,the parent and subsidiary company are likely to have differing attitudes towards these risks. It is likely that ignorance of the former and bias of the latter may cause conflicts in recognition of these risks. An alternative approach is to use certainty-equivalent method where risk-adjusted cash flows are discounted at the risk-free rate. However, this method requires generating certainty-equivalent cash flows, for which no satisfactory procedure has yet been developed. Furthermore, it involves losing some information on the valuation of future cash flows that is provided by shareholders in the form of their required yield on a typical firm investment.

Expropriation

The extreme form of political risk is expropriation. This is of course an obvious case where project and parent company cash flows diverge. A sophisticated cash flow adjustment technique is to charge each year's flows a premium for political risk insurance whether or not such insurance is actually purchased. This solution, however, does not really measure the effect of a given political risk on a project's present value.

In the case of expropriation, political risk insurance normally covers only the book value, not the economic value, of expropriated assets. The relationship between the book value of a project's assets and the project's economic value as measured by its future cash flows is tenuous at best. It is worthwhile, of course, to compare the cost of political risk insurance with its expected benefits. Insurance though is no substitute for a careful evaluation of the impact of political risk on a given project.

Blocked Funds

If funds are blocked or otherwise restricted can be utilised in a foreign investment, the capital cost to the investor may be below the local project construction costs. From the investor's perspective, there is a gain from activated funds equal to the difference between the face value of those funds and the present value of funds if the next best thing is done with them. This gain should be deducted from the capital cost of the project to find the cost from the investor's perspective. For example, if the best thing that can be done is to leave blocked funds idle abroad, the full value of the activated funds should be deducted from the capital cost. Alternatively, if half of the funds can be returned to the investor after the investor pays taxes or uses an internal funds transfer system, the half of the value of the blocked funds should be subtracted from the cost of the project. From the investor's point of view, the appropriate discount rate is the marginal cost of unrestricted funds, because this figure more accurately reflects the firm's opportunity cost of funds. To maximise the present value of shareholder wealth, project costs flows should be discounted at the yield foregone on the most profitable investment opportunity rejected, or the required rate of return, whichever is higher. This opportunity cost of funds will actually equal the firm's marginal cost of capital. When capital market segments exist, however the firm's opportunity cost of funds may well differ from the project's marginal cost of capital.

Amenities and Concessions Granted by Host Countries

While governments do offer special financial aid or other kinds of help for certain domestic projects, it is very common for foreign investments to carry some sort of assistance. This may come in the form of low-cost land, income-tax holidays for a stated number of years, exemption from or reduction in custom duties on imported parts or raw materials (permanent or temporary), exemption from, or preferential treatment of, tax withheld on net income, concessionary loans (for initial investment and/or working capital purposes), subsidised utility rates, and so on. Most of these benefits require no special interest in the capital budgeting exercise, because they are, or should be, already reflected in capital costs. But concessionary lending is problematic since such financing will replace financing by the parent or from other higher interest sources. However, with the APV technique, we can add a separate term to include the subsidy. This is particularly important, since the special concessionary loan will be available to the corporation but not directly to the shareholders. This will make the appropriate cost of capital for foreign investment projects differ from that for the domestic projects, which is what happens in segmented capital markets.

PROJECT EVALUATION CRITERIA

MNCs involved in evaluating foreign projects face a number of variables, many of which are encountered in the domestic capital budgeting decision-making process. Broadly, the criteria used in project evaluation classified as non-discounted cash flow criteria and discounted cash for criteria, as discussed below[1]:

NON-DISCOUNTED CASH FLOW CRITERIA FOR PROJECT EVALUATION

PAYBACK PERIOD (PP)

Payback is a measure of the rapidity with which the project will return the original capital outlay. The payback period is the number of years it takes the firm to recover the original outlay from the cash inflows of the project. *Projects offering a payback period less than some firm determined number of years (N) are accepted and those projects with a payback period (PP) greater than that acceptable number of years are rejected. In symbols:*

$PP \leq N$ accept

$PP > N$ reject

The payback period method for choosing among alternative proposals is very popular among corporate managers. However, its popularity has also brought with it serious scrutiny, and criticism of its shortcomings. To wit payback has been both defended and attacked vehemently, while serious efforts have also been made to reconcile it, through some approximation, with other, more refined methods of project selection. Let us first start with its *advantages.*

1. It is easy to understand, compute, and communicate to others. Its quick computation makes it a favourite among finance managers who prefer snap answers. This is an interesting defence but also hard to comprehend in view of the educational requirements expected of managerial personnel.
2. It is only used as a quick method of approximation for screening proposals. To the extent that it is used only lightly, the harm may not always be great; although as we shall see, it can result in bypassing profitable investment opportunities.
3. It is an adequate measure for firms with very profitable internal investment opportunities, whose sources of funds are limited by internal low availability and external high costs. Thus it is said that if shortage of funds limits the company to the acceptance of projects with a small payback, say two years, the use of more refined methods of selection might not change the composition of selected projects.
4. It is useful for approximating the value of risky investments where the income from the investment is highly uncertain and its life expectancy more. Under such circumstances, payback may become important, not so much as a measure of profitability but as a means of establishing an upper hand on the acceptable degree of risk. When one can appraise the near future with some confidence, but is completely in the dark about longer term prospects, a short payout period may be an adequate guarantee against loss, investment being

undertaken as a sporting proposition in the hope that some of the projects will last long enough to make the whole operation profitable. It examplifies the importance of liquidity and control as goals of business behaviour, while also pointing to *satisficing* rather than *maximising* objectives.

5. When the payback period is set at a large number of years, and income streams are uniform for each year, the payback criterion is a good approximation to the reciprocal of the internal rate of return. However, since the payback period is purposely set at a low values, this conditional advantage lacks generality.

For every advantage claimed by the advocates of payback, there is a disadvantage claimed by its opponents, often based on same information. Let us explore some of its *disadvantage:*

1. Even if the utilisation of the method is justified at times for certain firms under special conditions, these firms are in the minority. Hence the generality of the technique is severely constrained.
2. It overlaps the importance of liquidity as a goal of the capital expenditure decision. While no firm can ignore its liquidity requirements with impunity, there are more direct and less costly means of safeguarding liquidity levels. This disadvantage, of course, overlooks the possibility that liquidity or satisficing, or even survival, may indeed be the primary managerial goal in capital budgeting decisions.
3. It ignores capital wastage and economic life by restricting consideration to the project's gross earnings (before depreciation).
4. It fails to consider the earnings from an investment *after* the pay back period, thus treating them as a windfall.
5. Another weakness in the use of the payback method for ranking investment proposals lies in its *failure* to take into account the *time value of money.*

To summarises, under conditions of certainty, payback is a poor method of ordering the attractiveness of projects. Under conditions of uncertainty, however, the measure may have some value as one of the constraints that limit a firm's range of options. More important, it can be a rough guide to reduce the degree of uncertainty associated with a project, since if a project has a quick payback, the decision-maker is left only with the problem of whether the useful life of the project beyond the payback period is long enough to make it attractive. If a project has a long payback period, the firm may not even recover its costs let alone a return on its investment.

ACCOUNTING RATE OF RETURN (AROR)

Some corporations measure project profitability as an annual percentage of capital employed. These expost measures are derived from financial statements and are intended to present a so-called *true rate of returns.*

The first most elaborate version, and the most thoroughly consistent one, take average income, as measured by a series of proforma income statements, as a percentage of average investment, *i.e.,* average book value after deducting depreciation.

The second version uses original cost rather than average book value as the denominator. This is a little less consistent, in that income is averaged but investment is not. As an approximation to the internal rate of return, this usually gives better results than using average investment.

A second type of accounting measure is the single year rate of return. This, as the name implies, is a measure of profit in a single year, which may be the first year, the "first full year" or some other equally elusive standard. It may be applied either against average investment over the life of the project, against average investment in the year selected for study, or simply against initial cost.

Now, this may seem very confusing, and indeed it is. The widely varying results point to the desirability of ensuring uniformity of practice if an accounting measure is to be employed. These versions ignore all years other than the one studied. Their dangers when applied to projects having anything except a stable income are too obvious to require elaboration. Moreover, the diverse concepts of earnings, whether before or after taxes, as well as whether original or average investment is selected, provide varying rates of return under the accounting or financial statement method. In addition, the initial determination of what part of the project will be expensed currently and what part will be capitalised also affects the rate of return. For example, had more of the cost of the project above been expensed and less capitalised, the rate of return could have changed considerably owing merely to a variation of accounting technique.

The chief limitation of this financial statement method is that it does not allow for the time element in the return of funds. It gives the same weight to future money as it gives to current. New and distant earnings are assumed to have the same value, and this is, of course, contrary to fact. The time value of money is ignored and the same value is given to receipt of the last as to the first year.

Inspite of the foregoing criticism, the accounting rate of return has been a very popular tool for capital budgeting analysis, primarily because accounting measures are very useful for purposes of performance measurement and management control. How much did we earn last year? Were last year's earnings above or below the prior year's earnings? Were they above or below profit plan? What has been the trend in earnings? What has been the trend in AROI? Are investments be more profitable or less in terms of profit per rupee of outlay? Accounting measures such as profit after tax, earnings per share, and return on investment are very useful for answering such questions.

One flaw that eliminated from consideration each of the measures reviewed has been the inability of the measures to take proper account of the timing of cash proceeds from the investments. The payback period represents one extreme in this regard, because all the proceeds received before the payback period are counted and treated as equals, and all the proceeds received after the payback period are ignored completely. With the return on investment, the proceeds were related by simple averaging techniques to such things as the original cost of the investment on its book value. Neither of these methods succeeds in bringing the timing of cash proceeds into the analysis.

DISCOUNTED CASH FLOW CRITERIA FOR PROJECT EVALUATION

NET PRESENT VALUE (NPV)

The net present value of a project is defined as the difference between the present value of all cash outflows and the present values of the expected cash inflows when discounted at a rate of return, which may be firm's cost of capital or another rate developed using capital asset pricing model. The net present value of an investment proposal is

$$\text{NPV} = \sum_{t=1}^{n} \frac{A_t}{(1+k)^t} - 10$$

where,

A_t = the cash inflow for period

k = the appropriate discount rate, that is required rate of return or the cost of capital.

IO = the initial cash outlay.

n = the project's expected life.

An investment with a net present value equal to or greater than zero is acceptable using this single criterion. In the word, the firm will accept those proposals whose net present values are positive, and will reject those projects whose net present values are negative.

PROFITABILITY INDEX (BENEFIT/COST RATIO)

The profitability index or, benefit/cost ratio, is the ratio of the present value of the future net cashflows to the initial outlay. The profitability index (PI) can be expressed as follows:

$$\text{PI} = \frac{\sum_{t=1}^{n} \frac{A_t}{(1+k)^t}}{\text{IO}}$$

The decision criterion with respect to the profitability index is to accept the project if the PI is greater than 1.00, and to reject the project if the PI is less than 1.00. However, if the PI exactly equals 1.00, we are indifferent between acceptance and rejection of the project. The accept reject criterion is illustrated below :

PI>1.0 Accept

PI≤1.0 Reject

Looking closely at this criterion, we see that it will always gives the same accept-reject decision as does the net present value criterion. Whenever the present value of the project's net cash flow is greater than its initial cash outlay, the project's net present value will be positive, signalling an accept decision. While this is true, then the project's profitability index will also be greater than one, as the present value of the net cash flows (the PI's numerator) is greater than initial outlay (the PI's denominator).

These relationships may be summarised as :

If NPV>0 then PI>l

If NPV=0 then PI=l
lf NPV<0 then PI<1

However, it should be noted that while these two decision criteria will always yield the same accept-reject decision, they will not necessarily rank acceptable projects in the same order.

INTERNAL RATE OF RETURN (IRR)

The internal rate of return is that rate of discount which equates the present value of the expected after tax cash inflows with the present value of the after-tax outflows. In other words, the internal rate of return is the rate of discount that sets the net present value equal to zero. The net present value has to be zero if the present value of the project's income streams is equal to the present value of the project's cash outlay. Mathematically, the internal rate of return is defined as the value in the following equation :

$$\sum_{t=1}^{n}\frac{A_t}{(1+r)^t}-10=O$$

Notice that the internal rate of return formula is simply the NPV formula solved for that particular value of r that causes the NPV to equal zero. In other words, the same basic equation is used for both methods, but in the NPV method the discount rate *(k)* is specified and the NPV is found, while in the IRR method, the NPV is specified to equal zero and the value of r that forces the NPV to equal zero is found.

Notice too that r is the internal to the project itself, in contrast to the external nature of the given cost of capital, k, used in the NPV analysis. The project are accepted or rejected by comparing the internal rate of return (r) to the required rate of return (k) under the following decision rule.

IRR (r) > RRR (k)	Accept
IRR (r) < RRR (k)	Reject
IRR (r) = RRR (k)	Indifferent

Thus projects earnings as internal rate of return in excess of the cost of capital are accepted while those earnings less than the cost are rejected. If the internal rate of return is equal to the cost of capital, accepting the project should not result in any change in the firm's share price. This is because the firm is earning exactly the rate that its shareholders are requiring. On the other hand, if the project yields or internal rate of return are greater than the investor's required rate of return, its acceptance should increase the firm's share price. Similarly, the acceptance of a project with an internal rate of return below the investor's required rate of return will decrease the firm's share price.

The IRR criterion appeals to many firms because r is expressed as a percentage and is readily comparable to the firm's computed cost of capital, *k*, which is also expressed as a percentage. Further, a few feel that the seperation of the IRR calculation from the cost of capital presents a better position from which to judge the proposed project on its own operating merits, independently of the cost of capital, which appears to the few to fluctuate widely, frequently, and beyond their control.

ADJUSTED PRESENT VALUE METHOD

The adjusted present value (APV) method offers a slightly different approach to risk adjustment. It is based on adjusting the discount rate, but it customizes the adjustment to match the different risk characteristics of the individual components of the cash flows. This approach has been applied to both domestic and international project evaluation.

The APV method begins with the premise that the project's cash flows can be decomposed into their constituent parts. Each is discounted at a different rate, thus providing the needed flexibility to allow the various variables and other features of the project to impact the outcome. The APV approach also makes possible the use of different discount rates for different segments of the total cash flow, depending on the degree of certainty of the eventual materialisation of each segment. Moreover, the APV framework enables the capital budgeting analyst to test the profitability of the foreign project prior to accounting for all the complexities. If the project proves acceptable, no further evaluation based on accounting for other cash flows will be necessary. If it fails to meet the acceptance criteria, then an additional segment is added, and the evaluation in process is repeated. For example, the analysis may be conducted on the basis of the contractual cash flows which are remittable to the parent company under existing foreign exchange regulations of the host country. If the project does not pass the hurdle rate, another cash flow component, such as the cash flow the MNC can unblock through the transfer pricing mechanism, will be added to ascertain whether or not it could nudge the project toward profitability.

Components of Adjusted Present Value

The main components of APV framework are discussed below:

Initial Capital Outlay

The elements of this term are unambiguous for items purchased by the firm, but are more complex for capital items sourced internally. The major obstacle in the latter case is calculating the true incremental cost to the system, which may differ substantially from the registered book value of the item in question. Contractual capital costs should be distinguished from non-contractual costs and discounted at nominal rates. In addition, capital expenditures are paid out of accumulated funds from existing operations whose use is restricted by exchange controls or because special tax advantages will be forfeited in addition parent country's taxes imposed if the funds are remitted rather than reinvested. The APV framework lends itself readily to incorporating the incremental value of a project resulting from its ability to employ such funds. The use of restricted funds reduces the investment outlays by the difference between their face value and the present value of these funds if remitted via the best alternative mechanism. Thus, the initial investment consists of the cost of the project (denominated in dollars) representing cash, equipment, and other asses contributed by the parent U.S. company plus local loans (if any) for working capital purposes. The latter part is to be converted into U.S. dollars at the spot exchange rate. In the event that the foreign project will release blocked funds the parent owns in the host country, the face value of the blocked funds which are activated by the project (if it is assumed that such funds have a zero opportunity cost) will be treated as a reduction in initial investment. This component may be expressed as follows:

$$-[I_0(\text{U.S.}) + I_0(\text{local}) \times S_0(\text{H/L}) - \text{UF} \times S_0(\text{H/L})$$

where

I_0(U.S.) = initial investment of parent company in U.S. dollars
I_0(local) = initial local investment expressed in local currency
S_0(H/L) = spot exchange rate at period zero (year of initial investment) expressed in home currency per unit of local currency
UF = unblocked funds expressed in local currency

Remittable After-tax Operating Cash flows

In the domestic case, there is little difficulty in defining after-tax operating cash flows. They are the total project cash flows less taxes, whether they are reinvested in the project or not makes no difference, since all flows are deemed available to the corporate cash pool. With foreign project, there are two major issues in defining operating cash flows: (1) whether to use project cash flows or only those flows remitted to the parent, and (2) what taxes to assume, since there will be a function of financing and remittance decisions. The first distinction arises because of foreign exchange restrictions and ceilings on profit remittances; the second because of the interactions of various national tax systems.

Clearly, the only cash flows of value to the parent are those available for remittance in one form or another, not necessarily those actually remitted. Furthermore, after-tax flows must take into account the incremental taxes to the entire corporation. However, the specific choice of ways to deal with the two issues is a question of managerial art. There are two basic approaches. One is to begin with the most favourable set of assumptions regarding taxation and remittability and, in later terms of the APV equation, to subtract two present values of reductions due to specific restrictions or international tax transactions. The other is to start with conservative assumptions regarding remittability and taxation, later adding the present value of gains resulting from various mechanisms for circumventing restrictions or deferring taxes. The second alternative is more appropriate with the far more complex set of calculations regarding tax and remittance adjustments that require consideration of the total corporate cash flow and tax situation.

A further and perhaps more serious issue in the computation of operating cash flows is the difficult of measuring the true incremental cash flows of a project in an interdependent mathematical system. For example, the establishment of a manufacturing plant in a country previously served by exports will result in an erosion of profits elsewhere in the system, but it may also create new profit opportunities for other parts of the system that provide intermediate or complimentary products. This difficulty is exacerbated by departure from arm's length transfer policy among units, some of which may result from conscious manipulation of tax and exchange control systems, but most of which result from the war impossibility of allocating the joint cost and benefits associated with "soft" factors of production, such as technology and managerial expertise used by more than one unit of the corporation. Clearly, an attempt should be made to measure incremental cash flows to the total system.

Thus, the projects cash flows consist of several components. The major component is the cash flows generated by sales in the host country, adjusted downward by the lost income on sales previously realised on exports made by the parent to the host country market. It also includes cash flows generated by sales from the new project to third country markets, also reduced by profits on lost exports to these markets (if any). In addition, remittable cash flow includes royalties and fees agreed upon by the parent and the affiliate for the use of patents and services, respectively, provided by the parent. Contractual payments to the parent also include interest on loans advanced to the affiliate by the parent. It should be emphasised that this component of the APV formula includes only those cash flows which are legally remittable to the parent. It may be expressed as follows:

$$\sum_{t=1}^{N}\left[\frac{(CF_t^*)(S_t^*(\text{H/L})\text{-}(L_t)[1\text{-}T]}{(1+\text{DR}_1)^N}\right]+\frac{CF_{t_2}^*S_t^*(\text{H/L})}{(1+\text{DR}_2)^N}$$

$$+\left[\frac{(CF_{t_3}^*(S_t^*(\text{H/O})-L_{t_3})}{(1+\text{DR}_1)^N}\right][1-T]$$

where

CF_t^* = cash flows generated by expected sales in the host country in time period t.

$S_t^*(\text{H/L})$ = expected exchange rate in period t (home currency per one unit of local currency).

L_t = loss profits on exports to host country in time period t expressed in home currency.

T = applicable tax rate in host country or home country, whichever is higher.

CF_{t2}^* = expected cash flows from royalties and fees and other contractually remittable transfers in time period t.

CF_{t3}^* = expected cash flows generated by expected sales in third country markets in time period t.

$S_t^*(\text{H/0})$ = expected exchange rate in time period t — home country currency in terms of one unit of third country currency.

L_{t3} = lost profits on exports to third countries in time period t expressed in home currency units.

DR_1 = discount rate applicable to project's cash flows from sales in host and third country markets. This rate reflects discount rates applied to projects of similar risk in host country or home country.

DR_2 = discount rate applicable to transfer of contractual payments. DR_2 is lower than DR_1, because both the materialisation and transfer of such flows are subject to less uncertainty than the cash flows generated by sales.

N = life expectancy of the project, i.e., number of years over which cash flows are expected to materialise.

Contribution of Concessionary Arrangements to Project

The value of subsidies in the form of concessionary credit or penalties resulting from local financing requirements can be computed by comparing the present value of the total pretax payments on the debt, including interest and principal, discounted at the rate that would apply if the same debt were issued to competitive capital markets with the face value of the debt. For example, if a project is eligible for a concessionary loan at 9 per cent instead of a market rate of, say, 12 per cent, financial subsidies would be the difference between the present value of the total pre-payments on the 9 per cent debt discount at 12 per cent, and the face value of the debt.

The special concessions and other benefits granted by the host country will automatically impact cash flows. These may include provision of free land for the site of the project (to be treated as a reduction in the initial investment), tax holidays, lower tariffs on imports, and lower utility rates. As such, there is no need to assign a separate term of the APV formula to incorporate these benefits in the evaluation process.

A concessionary arrangement that would require a separate treatment in the APV format is when the project can obtain a loan at a low interest rate from a local financial institution. Such a loan, which is usually provided to meet all or part of the working capital requirements of the foreign project, represents a one-time contribution to the APV of the project. This contribution is measured by the difference in home currency terms between the face value of the loan and the amount of repayments, discounted to the present at the rate of interest (probably home country borrowing rate) that would have been incurred had the concessionary loan not been available.

This may be expressed as follows:

$$S_0(\mathrm{H/L})\ CL - \sum_{t=1}^{n} \frac{R_t}{(1+\mathrm{DR}_3)^N}$$

where

CL = face value of concessionary loan in local currency.
R_t = loan repayments on concessionary loan in local currency.
DR_3 = applicable discount rate; an appropriate rate is the borrowing rate in the home country or Eurocurrency market.

For a variety of reasons, including the availability of concessionary credit, the existence of tax or exchange considerations that favour remittances in the form of interest payments, and the desire to hedge currency or political risks, foreign projects are often financed with a different and typically higher proportion of debt than the corporation as a whole. Further, the debt issued to finance the project often exceeds the increment to overall debt capacity provided by a project. Thus approaches that directly utilise the project capital structure in computing a weighted-average cost of capital are likely to overstate the worth of the project, but a weighted average based on the total firm's capitalisation also is likely to be misleading. APV equation, in contrast, captures the tax shields associated with a project's incremental contribution to corporation debt capacity. Further, some elements of operating costs or revenues, as well as capital costs, may be set contractually. Typically, this will be true only for a relatively short period, and the distinction is thus immaterial for capital budgeting. However, when long-term sourcing or sales contracts are involved, explicit recognition of the contractual cash flows is called for. As far as depreciation tax shields—contractual cash flow—is concerned, it is deterministic, subject to the corporation's ability to use or to sell the tax shield, given investment outlays. The relevant tax rate and set of tax rules that should be used are those binding at the margin.

The critical element in discounting contractual operating flows is determining the appropriate nominal interest rate for (near) riskless debt. Undoubtedly there is some risk of default associated with the various contractual flows, and hence a risk premium may be required. Nevertheless, as a first approximation, the corporation's borrowing rates in unregulated markets can be used. Technically, the depreciation tax shields are subject only to the risk that the firm cannot make use of them. This may be serious in certain cases, but in general if the firm cannot take the deductions directly, it can carry them forward or backward in time, or, in the ultimate case, transfer them to another firm through mergers. Thus, it will have only a small risk premium and can be approximated by the interest rate on the firm's debt in the currency in question. Similar arguments apply to interest tax shields and financial subsidies.

Transfer Pricing Mechanism to Reduce/Defer Taxes

This term of the APV formula is somewhat conjectural and is not normally added unless the project proves unacceptable on the basis of remittable cash flows and the contribution of the concessionary arrangements. The transfer of restricted flows through inter-affiliate pricing, management fees, special export programmes, or other mechanisms enables an MNC to effect transfers over and above the legally remittable contractual cash flows. MNCs, through the transfer pricing mechanism, are often able to move funds from high-tax locations to low-tax locations, as well as to defer tax payments by transferring funds to tax havens. Tax savings realised from these operations contribute to the viability of the project by lowering the effective tax rate for the determination of net cash flows. The transfer pricing mechanism also enables an MNC to effect transfers over and above the legally remittable cash flows. It can also serve as a tool for overcoming to some extent future obstruction of transfers of legally remittable contractual cash flows. In principle, the present value of these changes can be readily incorporated in an APV term by discounting the potential contribution of tax savings and extra remittable income at a substantially higher rate than contractually remittable income—in recognition of the higher degree of risk involved, although computing them may require a complex corporate tax model.

This term may be expressed as follows:

$$\sum_{t=1}^{n} \frac{S_t^*(\mathrm{H/L})(\mathrm{ATTS}_t^*)}{(1+\mathrm{DR}_4)^N}$$

where

$ATTS_t^*$ = additional expected transfers and tax savings in period t.

DR_4 = appropriate discount rate for such transfers.

Terminal Value

The terminal value is to be calculated to ascertain whether the projected market values are likely to attain or exceed that figure. In discounting the estimated terminal value, the same discount rate which is applicable to project's cash flows from sales in host country is applied since it reflects the similar risk in host country or parent country.

Estimation of terminal value is perhaps the most subjective part of the multinational capital budgeting process, unless there exists a prior arrangement with the host country's government or local private investors. In some cases, the host government stipulates that the projects will revert to it after a stated number of years for a nominal sum. If such is the case, or where the management of the parent company deems the terminal value to be insignificant, no adjustment is needed in the evaluation process.

In practice, MNCs view foreign affiliates as a continuing venture just like their operating facilities at home. Nevertheless, accounting for the terminal value may prove to be as crucial a step in determining the financial viability of foreign projects as in the evaluation of domestic projects. The problem lies in arriving at a reasonable estimate of the terminal value, based on the most realistic assumptions possible. The range of possible values may be very wide, depending on whether the estimate is based on the project's potential value if retained as a going concern or if liquidated and sold to local investors.

The importance of estimating a realistic terminal value is especially crucial when the capital budgeting process is based on a relatively short project life span and in capital-intensive undertakings. MNCs have used several techniques to arrive at an acceptance estimate for the terminal value. One approach is to assume that net cash flows generated at the terminal year are to continue at the same level for a stated number of years. The terminal value will thus be the present value of this annuity at the terminal year discounted at an appropriate rate, probably reflecting local interest rates. Alternatively, a *break-even terminal* value may be computed. This value is defined as the value which would result in an APV of zero; that is, the project is just barely acceptable. Thus, calculated, the terminal value is examined by the management to ascertain whether the projected market values are likely to attain or exceed that figure. In any event, if the project can achieve a positive APV without allowance for the terminal value, this adjustment would not be necessary.

The estimated terminal value is the last term of the APV equation and will be discounted at DR_1, the same rate applied to discounting cash flows generated by sales in the host country, thus:

$$\frac{S_t^*(\mathrm{H/L})(\mathrm{TV}_t^*)}{(1+\mathrm{DR}_1)^N}$$

where TV* denotes the expected terminal value.

The various terms of the APV formula are now aggregated as follows:

APV = -Initial capital outlay reduced by the value of unblocked funds + present value of project's remitted after-tax cash flows + project value of concessionary arrangements to project + present value of additional transfer and tax savings achieved by the transfer pricing mechanism + present value of cash flow from estimated terminal value

$$\text{APV} = -[\text{I}_0(\text{U.S.}) + I_0\,(\text{local})\,S_0\,(\text{H/L}) - (\text{UF})\,(S_0(\text{H/L})] +$$

$$\sum_{t=1}^{N}\frac{[S_t^*(\text{H}/\text{L})CF_t^* - L_t][1-T]}{(1+\text{DR}_1)^N} + \frac{CFt_2^*S_t^*(\text{H}/\text{L})}{(1+\text{DR}_2)^N}$$

$$+\frac{(CF_{3t}^*S_t^*(\text{H}/\text{L}) - L_{t3})(1-T)}{(1+\text{DR}_1)^N} + S_0(\text{H}/\text{L})\left[CL - \sum_{t=1}^{N}\frac{R_t}{(1+\text{DR}_3)^N}\right] +$$

$$\sum_{t=1}^{N}\frac{S_t^*(\text{H}/\text{L})(\text{ATTS}_t^*)}{(1+\text{DR}_4)^N} + \frac{S_t^*(\text{H}/\text{L})(\text{TV}_t^*)}{(1+\text{DR}_1)^N}$$

The APV approach provides a generalised framework capable of incorporating most of the special considerations that arise in evaluating foreign projects. Its attractiveness vis-a-vis traditional approaches, which attempt to force all these factors into a single term, rests only in part on its conceptual superiority. Much of its *attention lies in its transparency and simplicity* of use in certain situations.

When a parent firm uses either the NPV or the APV method to evaluate foreign investment projects, a problem is typically encountered as to the accuracy of the cash flows that are expected to materialise in the future as a result of operating the project. Risk means that cash flows generated by the project may fluctuate far away from the expected value that would normally be used to calculate the NPV and the APV. If it is felt that this is the case then some adjustment may be made to account for risk. There are three methods to deal with risk in situations like these.

RISK DISCOUNTED RATE

The greater the risk associated with future cash flows the greater should be the discount rate used to calculate the present value of the future cash flows". This is why the discount rate may differ from the cost of capital. This is also the reason why different discount rates are used in the APV as more risky cash flows are discounted at higher rates. For example, cash flows associated with tax saving from depreciation and interest payments to creditors are less risky than operating cash flows, and this is why the latter are discounted at a higher rate.

This approach to the adjustment for risk is easy to implement, but it is criticised as being somewhat arbitrary. Furthermore, it does not take into account changes in the riskiness of cash flows from one time period to another, since the discount rate is assumed to be constant across time for a class of cash flows with a particular degree of risk. An example of changes in the riskiness of cash flows over time is changes in blocked funds and tax laws in a country 'with a high degree of political risk. Despite these shortcomings, the method of adjusting the discount rate is used because of its simplicity. It is also arguable that this technique is more appropriate to deal with country risk than with market risk.

RISK-ADJUSTED CASH FLOWS (CERTAINTY EQUIVALENT APPROACH)

Some economists argue that adjusting the cash flows is more appropriate than adjusting the discount rate, particularly if the project involves market risk. This approach, it is arguable, allows the parent firm to reflect more specially the impact of the risk during the investment since better information is available on the effect of risk on cash flows than on the discount rate.

This approach is normally known as the certainty equivalent approach, as it is based on a reduction of risky future cash flows to a lower level that is accepted by the market. This adjustment is made separately for each period of the project's life. The adjusted risk-free cash flows are then discounted at the risk-free discount rate to estimate the NPV of the project. The difference between this method and the adjusted discount rate method is that this method considers time and risk separately, whereas the previous method treats them jointly. Although this method is theoretically more appealing, it is not widely used because there are practical problems in identifying the equivalent risk-free cash flows.

SENSITIVITY ANALYSIS

Sensitivity analysis entails the use of "what if" scenarios, which are implemented by changing the input variables, including the exchange rate. If the NPV or APV remains positive for several scenarios, then the parent firm should become more comfortable with the project. Sensitivity analysis can be applied to the discount rate or rates as well.

SIMULATION

Simulation can be used to generate a probability distribution for the NPV or the APV based on various combinations of the values of input variables. Consider, for example, a situation in which the exchange rate is forecast to be within a certain range such that any value within this range can materialise with equal probability. A large number of iterations are performed: in each iteration the value assumed by the exchange rate is picked randomly. This value is then used to calculate the cash flows and subsequently the NPV or APV. Each iteration produces a value for the NPV or APV, and after a large number of iterations we end up with a probability distribution for the APV or the NPV. From the probability distribution it is possible to estimate the probability with which the NPV or APV will be positive.

BREAK-EVEN ANALYSIS

In break-even analysis, the focus is placed on the point at which the NPV or the APV switches from positive to negative. The initial cash flow, does not depend on sales revenue, whereas the present value of subsequent cash flows is a positive function of sales revenue. The equality of the initial cash flow and the present value of subsequent cash flows defines the level of sales that generates a zero NPV, the break-even level of sales. Below this level, the NPV is negative, and above this level the NPV is positive.

INCORPORATING COUNTRY RISK ANALYSIS IN CAPITAL BUDGETING

Country risk analysis can also be incorporated in capital budgeting analysis. One way to do this is by adjusting the discount rate or the cash flows. The higher the country risk is, the higher the discount rate applied to the project's cash flows. If, for example, blocked funds are anticipated then the discount rate may be raised from 10 to 13%. The problem with this procedure is that there is no precise formula for adjusting the discount rate for country risk, which makes adjustment rather arbitrary. The use of a shorter payback period may be resorted to for the same purpose. However, neither of these two methods provides a detailed examination of the risk involved or a true reflection of the investor's fear. This is why it may be preferable to incorporate country risk analysis by adjusting the cash flows

Suppose that a project is analysed under three scenarios derived from country risk analysis: (i) that nothing will happen, (ii) that the host country will block a certain percentage of the funds to be transferred to the parent firm, and (iii) that the project will be confiscated after few years. Suppose also that these scenarios produce three net present values (NPV_1, NPV_2 and NPV_3) with probabilities of p_1, p_2 and p_3 respectively. The NPV of the project in this case should be calculated as the expected NPV, which is the weighted average of NPV_1, NPV_2 and NPV_3, where the weights are the probabilities. Hence

$$NPV = \sum_{i=1}^{3} p_i NPV_i$$

To illustrate, the formalisation process of incorporating the country risk in capital budgeting, let X_t be the cash flow expected to arise from a project in the absence of country risk. Further assume that country risk is present such that the project would cease to exist (for example, because of a takeover by the host government) at year t with a probability p. Hence the probability that a cash flow arises in each individual year is $1 - p$. This means that the probability that cash flows arise for t years is $(1 - p)^t$. The expected value of the cash flow in year t is $X_t(1 - p)^t$. If X_t is constant such that $X_t = \overline{X}$, then the present value of the cash flow is given by

$$PV = \sum_{t=1}^{n} \frac{(1-p)^t X_t}{(1+k)^t} = \overline{X} \sum_{t=1}^{n} \frac{(1-p)^t}{(1+k)^t}$$

As $n \to \infty$, we obtain

$$\sum_{t=1}^{n} \frac{(1-p)^t}{(1+k)^t} = \frac{1-p}{k+p}$$

Hence

$$PV = \frac{\overline{X}(1-k)}{k+p}$$

In the absence of country risk, we have

$$PV = \frac{\overline{X}}{k}$$

It is obvious that the present value of the cash flows in the absence of country risk is greater than what is obtained when country risk is present.

Agmon has suggested a workable and comprehensive way to integrate country risk into capital budgeting. Agmon's method is based on the proposition that the potential dependence of a project on the external environment is divided into two components: vulnerability and cost. Vulnerability is expressed in terms of the probability that an event that is likely to affect the project (such as tax changes) will occur. Vulnerability is also defined in terms of a probability distribution, and for simplicity it is assumed that the distribution can be fully described by its first and second moments. Cost, on the other hand, is measured as the actual impact on the cash flows of the project if a given event occurs. The distinction between vulnerability and cost is crucial because firms do not need to be concerned with all possible events. Only the non-trivial effects on cash flows have to be weighted by the probabilities that they will take place.

DIVERSIFICATION BENEFITS OF MULTIPLE PROJECTS

Like any investor, an MNC with projects positioned around the world is concerned with the risk and return characteristics of the projects. The portfolio of all projects reflects the MNC in aggregate. International projects can possibly allow MNCs to achieve lower risk than what is possible from only domestic projects, without reducing their expected returns. International diversification tends to be more capable of risk reduction when the direct foreign investment is targeted for countries whose economies are somewhat unrelated to an MNC's home country economy.

By extending the previous example to multiple projects, one can gain further insight on the benefits from international diversification. Consider a set of 60 possible U.S. projects, each of which has expected returns to a firm over the next five years. Assume that the variance of each project's expected returns has been estimated, and that the average variance of these 40 projects also has been determined. Now consider all possible sets of two projects combined (and equally weighted). If the returns on these projects are not all perfectly positively correlated, the average variance of a typical two-project portfolio will be less than the average variance of individual projects. Similar, the variance of all possible three-project portfolios (equally weighted) should be even lower. As more projects are added, the portfolio variance should decrease on average. Initially, the average reduction in variance of returns (a measure of risk) associated with the addition of one more project is substantial. However, after some point, the average reduction in variance becomes negligible, meaning that the remaining risk cannot be diversified away by adding more U.S. projects.

Now consider another set of 40 projects, of which some are in the United States and the rest are in various foreign countries. If the procedure just described is applied to this set, the degree of risk reduction resulting from adding an additional project is greater for the global set than for the U.S. set. For any given number of projects, the global portfolio has less risk. The advantage to the global set is attributed to the lower correlations between returns of projects implemented in different economies.

A COMPREHENSIVE EXAMPLE

Consider a an Indian firm that plans to invest in a new project that will be located either in India or in Great Britain. Once the project is complemented, it will constitute 30 per cent of the firm's total funds invested in itself. Assume the firm's current investment in its business (the remaining 70 per cent) is exclusively in the India. Characteristics of the proposed project are forecasted for a five-year period for both a India and a British location, as shown in Exhibit-1.

EXHIBIT-1

EVALUATION OF PROPOSED PROJECTS IN ALTERNATIVE LOCATIONS

	Characteristics of Proposed Project if Located in India	*Characteristics of Proposed Project if Located in Great Britain*
Mean expected annual return on investment (after taxes)	25%	25%
Standard deviation of expected annual after-tax returns on investment	.09	.11
Correlation of expected annual after-tax returns on investment with after-tax returns of prevailing Indian business	.80	.02

Assume the firm plans to assess the feasibility of each proposed project based on expected return and on risk, using a five-year time horizon. Also assume the firm's expected annual after-tax return on investment on its prevailing business is 20 per cent, and its variability of returns (as measured by standard deviation) is expected to be .10. The firm can assess its expected overall performance based on developing the project in India. Then it can repeat the analysis based on developing the business in Great Britain. It is essentially comparing two portfolios. The first portfolio is 70 per cent of its total funds invested in its prevailing India business, plus the remaining 30 per cent of funds invested in a new project located in the India. The second portfolio again represents 70 per cent of the firm's total funds invested in its prevailing business, but the remaining 30 per cent of funds in a new project located in Great Britain. Therefore, 70 per cent of each portfolio's investment is identical. The difference is reflected in the remaining 30 per cent of funds invested.

If the new project is located in India, the overall firm's expected after-tax return (r_p) is

r_p = (70%)	(20%)	+ (30%)	(25%)	=	21.5%
% of funds invested in prevailing business	Expected return on prevailing business	% of funds invested in new project in India	Expected return on new project in India		Firm's overall expected return

This computation is based on weighting the returns according to the percentage of total funds invested in each investment.

If the firm calculates its overall expected return when locating the new project in Great Britain instead of India, the results would remain unchanged. This is because the new project's expected return is the same regardless of the country of location. Therefore, in terms of return, neither new project has an advantage.

With regard to risk, the new project is expected to exhibit slightly less variability in returns during the five-year period if located in India (see Exhibit-2). Since firms typically prefer more stable returns on their investments, this is an advantage. However, estimating the risk of the individual project without consideration of the overall firm would be a mistake. The expected correlation of the new project's returns with those of the prevailing business must also be considered. The portfolio variance is determined by the individual variability of each component as well as their pairwise correlations. The variance of a portfolio (σ_p^2) composed of only two investments (A and B) is computed as

$$\sigma_p^2 = w_A^2\,\sigma_A^2 + w_B^2\,\sigma_B^2 + 2w_A w_B \sigma_A \sigma_B r_{AB}$$

where w_A and w_B represent the percentage of total funds allocated to Investments A and B, respectively; σ_A and σ_B are the standard deviations of returns on Investments A and B, respectively, and r_{AB} is the correlation coefficient of returns between Investments A and B. This equation for portfolio variance can be applied to the problem at hand. The portfolio reflects the overall firm. First, compute the overall firm's variance in returns assuming it locates the new project in the India (based on the information provided in Exhibit-2). This variance (σ_p^2) is

$$\begin{aligned}\sigma_p^2 &= (.70)^2\,(.10)^2 + (.30)^2\,(.09)^2 + 2\,(.70)\,(.30)\,(.10)\,(.09)\,(.80)\\ &= (.49)(.01) + (.09)(.0081) + .003024\\ &= .0049 + .000729 + .003024\\ &= .008653\end{aligned}$$

EXHIBIT-2

SUMMARY OF BENEFITS RESULTING FROM FOREIGN DIRECT INVESTMENT

Possible Benefit	Means of Using FDI to Achieve This Benefit
1. Attract new sources of demand.	Establish a subsidiary or acquire a competitor in a new market.
2. Enter markets in which superior profits are possible.	Acquire a competitor that has controlled its local market.

3. Fully benefit from economies of scale.	Establish a subsidiary in a new market that can sell produced elsewhere; this allows for increased production and possibly greater production efficiency.
4. Use foreign factors of production.	Establish a subsidiary in a market that has relatively low costs of labour or land; sell the finished product to countries where the cost of production is higher.
5. Use foreign raw materials.	Establish a subsidiary in a market in which raw materials are cheap and accessible; sell the finished product to countries in which the raw materials are more expensive.
6. Use foreign technology.	Participate in a joint venture in order to learn about a production process or other operations.
7. Exploit monopolistic advantages.	Establish a subsidiary in a market in which competitors are unable to produce the identical product; sell products in that country.
8. React to exchange rate movements.	Establish a subsidiary in a new market in which the local currency is weak but expected to strengthen over time.
9. React to trade restrictions.	Establish a subsidiary in a market in which tougher trade restrictions will adversely affect the firm's export volume.
10. Diversify internationally.	Establish subsidiaries in markets whose business cycles differ from those where existing subsidiaries are based.

If the firm decides to locate the new project in Great Britain instead of in India, its overall variability in returns will be different, because that project differs from the new project in India in terms of individual variability in returns and correlation with the prevailing business. The overall variability of the firm's returns based on locating the new project in Great Britain is estimated by variance in the portfolio returns (σ_p^2):

$$\begin{aligned}\sigma_p^2 &= (.70)^2\,(.10)^2 + (.30)^2\,(.11)^2 + 2(.70)\,(.30)\,(.10)\,(.11)\,(.02)\\ &= (.49)\,).01) + (.09)\,(.0121) + .0000924\\ &= 0.0049 + .001089 + .0000924\\ &= .0060814\end{aligned}$$

Most MNCs pursue FDI based on their expectations of capitalising on one or more of the potential benefits summarised in Exhibit-2. While most attempts to increase international business are motivated by one or more of the benefits listed here, there are some corresponding disadvantages as well. For example, the potential cost savings associated with establishing a subsidiary in a less developed country are obvious. However, the expense of establishing the subsidiary, the uncertainty of inflation and exchange rate movements, and the political risk should not be ignored. Decisions to invest in a foreign country must weigh the potential benefits against such costs or additional risks.

Thus, the firm will generate more stable returns if the new project is located in Great Britain. The firm's overall variability in returns in almost 29.7 per cent less if the new project is located in Great Britain rather than in India.

The reason for the reduced variability when locating in the foreign country is based on the correlation of the new project's expected returns of the prevailing business. If the new project is located in the firm's home country (India), its returns are expected to be more highly correlated with those of the prevailing business than they would be if the project were located in Great Britain. When economic conditions of two countries (such as India and Great Britain) are not highly correlated, then a firm may reduce its risk by diversifying its business in both countries rather than concentrating in just one.

The optimal method for a firm to penetrate a foreign market is partially dependent on the characteristics of the market. Exhibit-2 summarises the possible benefits of FDI, and explains the means by which MNCs could use FDI to achieve those benefits.

GROWTH OPTIONS

The present value of growth options may be significant in many international investment decisions and are too important to ignore. Estimating their magnitude using a Black and Scholes (1973) routine is appropriate where all of the conditions of the model are met — — but, where they are breached, a decision tree approach may provide a thoroughly acceptable route towards putting a value upon them. Most international investment decisions promise a non-normal distribution of potential outturns and, because of this feature in particular, it is argued that a decision tree methodology promises both a relevant and valuable appendage in cross-border capital budgeting. In the example that follows, an attempt is made to summarise the problem and its solution.

Imagine an Indian firm, United Chemicals and Colloids (UCC), confronted with a foreign investment which is likely to absorb ₹ 70 crore and promises a best estimate of remittable future net cash flows, in real terms, amounting to

years 1 and 2	₹ 11 crore per annum
years 3 to 12 inclusive	₹ 14.5 crore per annum

The firm forecasts remittable cash flow for 12 years only and uses a 10% discount rate to evaluate the project. As shown in Table-1, the investment promises a best estimate net present value of ₹ 22.7 crore

TABLE 1

UCC CASE: BEST ESTIMATE NET PRESENT VALUE (₹ CRORE)

Year	*0*	*1-2*	*3-12*
Investment	-70.0		
Remittable net cash flow		+11.0 p.a.	+ 14.5 p.a.
Discount at 10%	-70.0	+19.1	+73.6
Net present value	₹ 22.7 crore		

However, note the probability distribution of potential remittable cash flows. This is summarised in Table-2 and it shows that there is a 5% chance (based on subjective probability estimates) of the project yielding annual remittable cash generation equal to ₹ 40 crore per annum from year 3 through to year 12. However, if this level of outturn is achieved, the firm would, most likely, scale up and invest the equivalent of a further ₹ 300 crore in year 4 and would, according to best estimates, achieve very creditable returns reflecting the potential buoyancy which would translate into remittable cash flows of foreign currency giving ₹ 160 crore per annum from year 5 to year 12 inclusive.

TABLE 2

UCC CASE: EXPECTED REMITTABLE CASH FLOWS (AND THEIR PROBABILITIES) (₹ CRORE)

Year	*0*	*1-2*		*3-12*	
		Probability	*Amount*	*Probability*	*Amount*
Investment	-70				
Remittable cash flow		0.4	+ 20	0.05	+ 40
		0.4	+10	0.50	+ 20
		0.1	0	0.30	+ 10
		0.1	-10	0.10	0
				0.05	- 10

* At this level of outturn, UCC would invest a further ₹ 30 crore in year 4 with best estimate remittable cash generation for years 5 to 12 inclusive of ₹ 160 crore per annum.

What should be apparent is that with the scale-up decision incorporated into the analysis, the net present value of the project would only by coincidence remain at ₹ 22.7 crore. As shown by Table 3, the new net present value of the project comes out at ₹ 34.4 crore. In other words, the value of the call option embedded in the project may be said to approximate ₹ 11.7 crore.

Clearly the project referred to is simplistic. This is deliberately so to illustrate the routine required, and, in any case, the company concerned would have gone ahead with the project since its base case best estimate net present value was positive. Of course, it would have been no problem to concoct a slightly different set of numbers where this would not be so. For example, had the initial outlay in year 0 been ₹ 100 crore, best estimate cash flows would have thrown up a negative net present value base case which would, with the inclusion of the scale-up option, have yielded an overall positive net present value.

TABLE 3

UCC CASE: CALCULATION OF NET PRESENT VALUE WITH SCALE-UP OPTION (₹ CRORE)

Year	*0*	*1 and 2*		*3 and*		*4 4*		*5-12*	
		Probability	*Amount*	*Probability*	*Amount*	*Probability*	*Amount*	*Probability*	*Amount*
Investment	-70					0.05	-30		
Remittable cash flow		0.4	+ 20	0.05	+ 4			0.05	+ 160
		0.4	+ 10	0.50	+ 2			0.50	+ 20
		0.1	0	0.30	+ 1			0.30	+ 10
		0.1	- 10	0.10	0			0.10	0
				0.05	- 1			0.05	- 10
Expected PV at 10% discount rate	-70	+19.1		+ 20.8		-10.2		+ 74.7	
Expected NPV ₹ 34.4 crore									

Furthermore, there is also the question of how complex the process of valuing real operating options should be. In the example cited, maybe the firm would expand further if outturns were even more successful than to throw off ₹ 160 crore in annual remittable cash flows. After all, the ₹ 160 crore per annum shown in Table-3 is a best estimate figure — it would be arrived at via a probability spread which would yield an expected value of ₹ 160 crore per annum if flows were as high as ₹ 200 crore, perhaps further expansion would follow. So we might have an option on an option.

ILLUSTRATIVE PROBLEMS

1. Agricultural Equipment (AE), a leading Indian manufacturer of small engines and related equipment, was recently approached by the Minister of Economic Development of Zeroland to set up a plant to manufacture small irrigation pumps in that country. AE is not currently exporting its products to Zeroland, and the establishing of a manufacturing facility in that country is not expected to cut into current AE exports to other countries in the region.

Zeroland is a small republic in Africa with a fairly stable and democratic system. The favourable political climate has been fostered by an open and constructive economic policy which favours foreign investment. The inflation rate has averaged 20 per cent in recent years, a very reasonable rate by developing countries' standards.

The facility in Zeroland is to be a wholly owned affiliate of AE which will provide all funds needed to build the manufacturing facility, as well as equipment. Total initial investment is estimated at Zeroland dollars (Zd) 50,000,000. Working capital requirements, estimated at Zd 20,000,000, would be provided by a local financial institution at 6 per cent per annum, repayable in five equal installments beginning on December 31 of the first year of operation. In the absence of this concessional facility, AE would have financed these requirements by a loan from its bankers in India at 15 per cent per annum.

The cost of the entire manufacturing facility is to be depreciated over five years on a straight-line basis. At the end of the fifth year of operation, all remaining assets would be taken over by a public corporation to be designated by the government of Zeroland with no compensation.

Sales, price, and exchange rate projections are presented in Table-1.

TABLE-1

Year	*Sales in Units*	*Unit Price*	*Exchange Rate SH/$*
0			Spot rate Zd4.50 / Rupee
1	100,000	Zd1,000	5.50
2	125,000	1,200	6.50
3	150,000	1,440	7.50
4	175,000	1,728	8.50
5	200,000	2,074	9.50

i) Variable costs are Zd 500 per unit in year 1 and are expected to rise by 20 per cent each year.
ii) Fixed costs (other than depreciation) are Zd 25 million in year 1 and are expected to rise by 10 per cent per year.
iii) Sale price per unit already reflects the annual inflation rate of 20 per cent.
iv) All initial investment is to be made at the spot rate.

All profits after tax realised by the affiliate are transferable to the parent at the end of each year. Depreciation funds are to be blocked until the end of year 5. These funds may be invested in local money market instruments, yielding a tax-free 10 per cent per annum. When the operating assets are turned over to a local corporation, the balance of these funds including interest, may be repatriated. Zeroland taxes corporate income at the rate of 35 per cent, but has no withholding tax on transfer of dividends. Dividends received by AE in India would be subject to a 45 per cent tax with credit allowed for taxes paid on affiliate's income abroad. AE uses a 20 per cent weighted average cost of capital for evaluating domestic projects similar to the ones planned in Zeroland. For foreign projects in developing countries a 5 per cent political risk premium is added.

a. Perform DCF analysis on the data to compute both the APV and the IRR for the project from the standpoint of the parent company. What are your recommendations for the proposal?
b. Test the sensitivity of the project to the political and exchange risks by reperforming the analysis on the assumptions that all dividends are blocked until the end of year 5. Blocked funds (like depreciation funds) are investable locally in money market instruments, yielding a tax-free rate of 10 per cent per annum.
c. Briefly evaluate the political risk in this project and indicate the extent to which it has been allowed for in the planning phase (as reflected in the assumptions or data given in the question). What other measures are available to the management of AE to reduce the political risk?

The present value of the concessional loan facility may be viewed as a reduction in initial investment in year 0.

Ans.

AGRICULTURAL EQUIPMENT (AE)

	Cash Flow Zd. (in millions of Zd.)				
(a)	*Year 1*	*Year 2*	*Year 3*	*Year 4*	*Year 5*
Sales (units)	100,000	125,000	150,000	175,000	200,000
Unit price (Zd.)	1,500	1,200	1,440	1,728	2,074
Sales revenue	100.00	150.00	216.00	302.40	414.80
Cost					
Variable cost (per unit)	500	600	720	864	1036.80
Units sold	100,000	125,000	150,000	175,000	200,000
TVC	50.00	75.00	108.00	151.20	207.36

FC (excluding dep.)	25.00	27.50	30.25	33.28	36.60
Depreciation	10.00	10.00	10.00	10.00	10.00
Total cost	85.00	112.50	148.25	194.48	253.96
Profit before tax	15.00	37.50	67.75	107.92	160.84
Local tax (35%)	5.25	13.13	23.71	37.77	56.29
Profit after tax	9.75	24.37	44.04	70.15	104.55

CASH FLOW ('000 RS.)

Spot	*Year 1*		*Year 2*	*Year 3*	*Year 4*	*Year 5*
Exchange rate (Zd./Rs.)	4.50	5.50	6.50	7.50	8.50	9.50
Profit after tax		1,772	3,749	5,872	8,253	11,005
Depreciation		—	—	—	—	6,426[1]
Total inflows		1,772	3,749	5,872	8,253	17,431
Total outflows[2]	(10, 231)	272[3]	576[3]	904[3]	1,270[3]	1,694[3]
Net cash flows	(10,231)	1,500	3,173	4,968	6,983	15,737
Discount factor at 25%	1.000	.8000	.6400	.5120	.4096	.3277
PV of CF	(10,231)	1,200	2,031	2,544	2,860	5,157
Cumulative PV	(10,231)	(9,031)	(7,000)	(4,456)	(1,596)	3,561

NPV = ₹ 3,561,000 IRR = approximately 33.8%

1. Depreciation is blocked until the end of the 5th year. Blocked amounts are invested at 10% in Zeroland. Transferable amount in ₹ is calculated as follows:
   (10,000,000) (FVIFA, 10%, years) =
   (10,000,000) (6.1051) = Zd. 61.05 million
   Zd. 61.05 million/9.50 = ₹ 6.426 million
2. Initial investment = Zd. 50,000,000—the PV of the concessional loan facility

CALCULATION OF PV OF CONCESSIONAL LOAN FACILITY (ZD. MILLION)

Year	*Loan Outstanding*	*Applied to Interest*	*Applied to Principal*	*Total Payment*	*PV of Payment*[1]
1	20.00	1.20	4.00	5.20	4.52
2	16.00	0.96	4.00	4.96	3.75
3	12.00	0.72	4.00	4.72	3.10
4	8.00	0.48	4.00	4.48	2.56
5	4.00	0.24	4.00	4.24	2.11
					16.04

1. Discounted at 15%, the cost of funds if borrowed in India (in the absence of the concessional arrangement).

Contribution of concession loan to project =

20.00–16.04 = Zd. 3.96 million

Initial investment in ₹ = 50.00—3.96/4.5 = ₹ 10.231 million

3. Taxes paid in India calculated on a "grossing up" basis as follows:

	Year 1	*Year 2*	*Year 3*	*Year 4*	*Year 5*
Dividends received	1,772	3,794	5,872	8,253	11,005
Plus tax paid in Zd.	955	2,020	3,161	4,444	5,925
Taxable income	2,727	5,769	9,033	12,697	16,930
Tax in India (45%)	1,277	2,596	4,065	5,714	7,619
Less credit for tax paid in Zd.	955	2,020	3,161	4,444	5,925
Tax due in India	272	576	904	1,270	1,694

The project passes the parent firms' criteria for feasibility. It has an APV of ₹ 3.56 million and IRR of 33.8 per cent, well above the hurdle rate of 25 per cent.

(b) Assumes that all flows (dividends and depreciation) are blocked until the end of the 5th year, and that amounts blocked are invested in Zeroland at 10% per annum.

Year	*Cash flow (millions of Zd.)*	*Reinvested at 10%*	*Future value (millions of Zd.)*
1	10.00 + 9.75 = 19.75	4 yrs at 10%	28.92
2	10.00 + 24.37 = 34.37	3 yrs at 10%	45.75
3	10.00 + 44.04 = 54.04	2 yrs at 10%	65.39
4	10.00 + 70.15 = 80.15	1 yr at 10%	88.17
5	10.00 + 104.55 = 114.55	— —	114.55
	Total		342.78
	342.78/9.5 = ₹ 36.082 million		

CALCULATION OF TAX DUE IN INDIA USING "GROSSING UP" METHOD

	millions of ₹
Dividends received at end of year 5 (₹ 36.082 – ₹ 6,426)	₹ 29.565
Plus taxes paid in Zd. over five years	5,925
	₹ 35.581
In India tax at 45%	16.011
Less credit for taxes paid in Zd	5.925
Tax due in India	10.086
Cash inflows	₹ 36.082

Cash outflows	(10.086)
FV of net cash flow	₹ 25.986
PV (initial investment)	₹ 10.231
Net terminal value	₹ 15.755

$$\frac{FV}{PV} = \frac{25.986}{10.231} = 2.5399$$

Terminal rate of return (TROR) = 20.5% approximately

The blockage assumption seems to hurt the viability of the project significantly. The terminal rate of return (based on a reinvestment rate of 10% for intermediate cash flows) is below the hurdle rate of 25% established by AE.

(c) Political risk involved in this project appears to have been well thought out at the planning stage and incorporated in the capital budgeting evaluation process. In the first place, a political risk premium of 5% was added to the firm's weighted average cost of capital of 20%. Second, the financing of working capital was localised by the concessional loan arrangement.

There were at least two other avenues for reducing or managing the political risk which AE, Inc. did not pursue. Part of the initial fixed investment of Zd. 50 million could also have been raised in Zeroland, from financial institutions and/or local joint venture partners. AE could have purchased political risk insurance. The cost of such insurance could then be treated as a deduction from the annual cash flows.

2. Benzy Food Industries (BFI) is a producer and exporter of a diversified line of packaged food products, sweets, and soft drinks, based in Dreamland (D). The company is organised in three divisions: (1) Packaged Foods Division (2) Sweets and Confectionery Division, and (3) Soft Drinks Division. Sales in India and exports for 2007-2012 were as shown in Table-1.

TABLE-1

(In million of Ringy)

	Sales in D	*Exports*	*Total Sales*	*Percentage of Exports to Total Sales*
2007	127.4	258.4	385.8	67.0
2008	125.3	256.3	381.6	67.2
2009	121.2	260.7	381.9	68.3
2010	130.3	300.9	431.2	69.8
2011	145.9	350.2	496.1	70.6
2012	142.0	410.0	552.0	74.3

BFI has an arrangement with Bon Bon Swisse, S.A., a Swiss confectionery company, to manufacture and sell a selected line of its products in Western Europe and in the Middle East under a Licensing agreement. It also has a 49 per cent interest in BFI

(Kenya), a joint venture with private local investors to produce and market a limited line of its products in Kenya and other East African countries. Sales of Bon Bon Swisse S.A., and BFI (Kenya) for 2007-2012, which are not included in BFI exports listed above, are as shown in Table-2. BFI (Dreamland)'s overall net profits for the indicated period are calculated in Table-3.

TABLE-2

(In million of Ringy)

	Bon Bon Swisse (S.A.)		*BFI (Kenya)*	
	Sales	*Royalties Paid to BFI (D)*	*Sales*	*Dividends Transferred to BFI (D)*
2007	34.2	3.4	20.0	1.7
2008	38.5	3.9	23.9	1.9
2009	29.6	3.0	34.5	2.8
2010	37.2	3.7	36.8	4.2
2011	45.9	4.6	40.2	3.8
2012	50.0	5.0	36.7	4.0

TABLE-3

(In millions of Ringy)

	2007	*2008*	*2009*	*2010*	*2011*	*1995*
1. Net income from sales in D	10.8	10.0	9.5	11.3	13.5	12.9
2. Net income from exports	20.0	19.2	21.5	27.5	30.8	35.2
3. Total net income from BFI (D) (1+2)	30.8	29.2	31.0	38.8	44.3	48.1
4. Royalties from Bon Bon Swisse	3.7	3.9	3.0	3.7	4.6	5.0
5. Dividends from BFI (Kenya)	1.7	1.9	2.8	4.2	3.8	4.0
6. Total net income from operations (3+4+5)	35.9	35.0	36.8	46.7	52.7	57.1
7. Income tax at 40%	14.4	14.0	14.7	18.7	21.1	22.8
Net Profit	21.5	21.0	22.1	28.0	31.6	34.3

The management has been considering for some time terminating its licensing agreement with Bon Bon Swisse (S.A.) and the joint venture in Kenya and setting up a wholly owned affiliate in Milan, Italy. A committee headed by Andy Simon has concluded that the company's profits from sales in these markets can be tripled or even quadrupled within a few years, given aggressive marketing and direct control on activities. These have been lacking under the present arrangements. The committee, which was entrusted with investigating the project, is impressed by the favourable investment climate in Italy, but is concerned over the prospects of the exchange rate of the Italian lira against the ringy.

The committee analysed the degree of volatility in the Ringy/Italian lira exchange rate in recent months. The period under review, end of 2010 to mid-2012, shows a pattern of relatively and volatility. When both the Italian lira and the ringy (Ry) were depreciating against the U.S. dollar, Ringy was depreciating was faster rate. When both currencies began appreciating vis-a-vis the dollar (beginning March 2012), the Ry. was appreciating at a faster rate than the lira. During the 18-month period covered, the Ry. swung from a depreciation of 8.3 per cent against the lira at the end of January 2012 to an appreciation of 4.8 per cent at the end of June 2012, a swing of over 13 per cent in five months.

TABLE-4

EXCHANGE RATES

Date	*Italian Lira per U.S. Dollar*	*U.S. Cents per (Ringy)*	*Italian Lira Per Ringy*	*Percentage Changes*
Year end 2010	1655	145.25	2404	
4/30/11	1679	139.80	2347	–2.4
5/31/11	1688	138.65	2340	–2.7
6/30/11	1709	135.70	2319	–3.5
7/31/11	1774	130.70	2319	–3.5
8/31/11	1788	130.85	2334	–2.9
9/28/11	1897	123.45	2342	–2.6
10/31/11	1882	122.00	2296	–4.5
11/30/11	1915	119.80	2294	–4.6
12/31/11	1933	115.92	2241	–6.8
1/31/11	1950	113.10	2205	–8.3
2/28/11	2075	108.25	2246	–6.6
3/31/11	1965	124.00	2437	+1.4
4/30/11	1981	124.40	2464	+2.5
6/30/11	1932	130.41	2520	+4.8

* Percentage change from year end 2010. A negative change denotes depreciation of ringy against Italian lira, and vice versa.

In its recommendations on the exchange rate risk, the committee indicated that the lira-Ry. exchange rate would remain volatile over the intermediate term. However, the committee felt that, barring a sharp acceleration in Italy's inflation rate not accompanied by a similar resurgence of the inflation rate in Dreamland, the exchange risk would be manageable, and would probably be primarily influenced by long-term factors such as purchasing power parity over the time horizon of the contemplated project. Along with the exchange rate gyrations, the committee considered Italy in recent years as an European country with the highest political risk, with the probable exception of Greece, following the assumption of political power by the Socialists in the latter country. This assessment has been due more to the control of labour unions by the communists and the size and influence of the communist party, than to the restrictive nature of the economy and the financial process. The increasing violence caused by extremist groups, such as the Red Brigade, further added to the fluidity of the political situation.

A task face was constituted to collect data for APV evaluation of BFI (Italy). It compiled data on projected sales exports, profit margins, taxable income, transferable dividends and other payments to BFI (D), concessionary arrangements made available by the city of Milan, and terminal value estimates.

Sales and profit margin projections covering the period from 2014, the year the project will commence operations, to 2020 and projected exports by BFI to Europe, Africa, and the Middle East during the same period are given in Table-5. Export projections are denominated in U.S. dollars, since all exports to these areas will be billed in U.S. dollars, and are payable in the same currencies.

TABLE-5

	Italy (in billions of Italian lira)		*Europe, Africa and the Middle East (in millions of U.S. dollars)*	
	Sales	*Profit Margin*	*Exports*	*Profit* Margin
2014	17.8	.13	180.5	.11
2015	20.2	.14	200.3	.12
2016	24.7	.14	225.8	.13
2017	30.3	.15	275.7	.13
2018	35.9	.16	320.5	.14
2019	40.0	.16	380.5	.14
2020	47.5	.17	420.7	.15

Sales and exports by BFI (Italy) will replace, to some extent, sales and exports currently undertaken as follows:

1. Sales currently made to Europe by Bon Bon Swisse (S.A.) under a licensing agreement. These sales were projected to grow at the average growth rate realised during 2007-12, at a profit margin equaling the average margin realised during this period.
2. Sales currently made by BFI (Kenya). These sales were projected to increase at the average growth rate of 2007-2012, and to realise profit margin equivalent to the average margin during the same period.
3. Ten per cent of exports made by BFI (D) worldwide (except Europe, Africa, and the Middle East). These exports were projected to increase at the average growth rate attained during 2007-2012, at a profit margin equivalent to the average margin realised during the same period.

The operations of BFI (Italy) will be subject to the following provisions:

1. Profits originating from domestic sales will be subject to thereafter 15 per cent income tax rate during the first five years, rising to 20 per cent thereafter.
2. Up to 90 per cent of net profits of BFI (Italy) will be transferable to BFI(D) during the first five years of operation, falling to 75 per cent of net profits thereafter. Depreciation charges are to be used for replacement of fixed

assets and are, therefore, not transferable. There is no withholding tax on dividends transferred to the parent company.

3. All royalties and management fees are freely transferable to the parent. It is planned that the agreement between BFI(D) and BFI (Italy) will stipulate a royalty of 10 per cent and a management fee of 5 per cent on all combined domestic sales and exports.
4. BFI (Italy) can borrow up to Lit 25 billion from local financial institutions with a guarantee from the Italian government. It is anticipated that Lit 10 billion will be drawn in 2013 to finance part of the fixed investment, and Lit 15 billion will be drawn in 2014 to finance working capital requirements. Borrowed funds are repayable in seven equal annual installments with interest at five percentage points below a reference money market rate. It is projected that the reference rate will be 19 per cent in January 2013 and 18 per cent in January 2014. In the absence of the concessionary financing arrangement, BFI (Italy) would have had to borrow at two percentage points above the reference rate.

Estimates for the initial investment on the project broken down by currency and by year are as shown in Table-6. All funds, with the exception of the local concessionary loan of Lit 25 billion, are to be provided by the parent company as an equity investment in BFI (Italy). The terminal value in 2020 is estimated at five times the after-tax profits generated by the affiliate from domestic sales and exports in that year.

TABLE-6

Year	*Currency*	*Amount*	*Purpose*
2013	Italian lira	30 billion	Construction of plant
2013	U.S. dollar	35 million	Equipment shipped from the U.S.
2014	Italian lira	18 billion	Equipment purchased locally
2014	Italian lira	15 billion	Working capital

V.D. John, manager of the Capital Budgeting Division and chairman of the task force entrusted with evaluating BFI (Italy), is hoping to finalise his report on the project, supported by APV calculations and appropriate recommendations. John is planning to present in his report a brief description of the project, followed by a synopsis of the investigating committee's report on the exchange rate and political risks. This will be followed by the APV calculations under the most likely conditions. He is also planning to perform at least two sensitivity tests, one dealing with adverse exchange risk and the second with adverse political risk assumptions. An overall assessment and recommendations of the task force will conclude the report.

Ans.

The proposed affiliate in Milan, which is scheduled to start operations in 2014, will produce BFI's full line of products for sale in Italy, the rest of Europe, and African and Middle Eastern countries. It will replace sales currently made by the Swiss and Kenyan facilities, as well as some exports from the parent company to these markets. The project benefits from a number of concessions granted by the local government in Milan, as well as other advantages accruing from its location and proximity to the major markets.

As the evaluation year is 2013 the outlay in 2014, consisting of equipment purchased in Italy and working capital, will have to be discounted one year at 18%, so:

$$\begin{aligned} I_o &= \text{Lit 30 billion}/2250 + \$35 \text{ million}/1.42 \\ &\quad + (\text{Lit 18 billion}/2272)\ (0.8475) \\ &\quad + (\text{Lit 15 billion}/2272)\ (0.8475) \\ &= \text{Ry. } 13{,}333{,}333 + 24{,}674{,}880 + 6{,}714{,}349 + 5{,}595{,}290 \\ &= \text{Ry. } 50{,}317{,}852 \end{aligned}$$

According to the facts, sales and exports by BFI (Italy) will replace exports or sales currently made by the facilities in Switzerland and Kenya, and a certain proportion of exports made by the parent company. The replaced sales and exports are projected to increase at the average growth rate realised during 2007-2012, at a profit margin equaling the average margin realised during this period. The growth rates and the average margin are calculated below:

TABLE-7

	Average Growth Rage 2007-2012	*Average Profit Margin 2007-2012*
Bon Bon Swisse (S.A.)	8.0%	10.0% of sales
BFI (Kenya)	12.9%	9.6% sales
BFI (D)		
Total exports	9.7%	8.4% of sales

TABLE-8

CALCULATION OF PROFITS ON LOST EXPORTS

(In million of Ry.)

	Bon Bon Swisse		*BFI (Kenya)*		*BFI (D)*[1]		*Total*	
	Exports	*Profit*	*Exports*	*Profit*	*Exports*	*Profits*	*Exports*	*Profit*
2014	58.3	5.83	46.8	4.49	49.3	4.14	154.4	14.46
2015	63.0	6.30	52.8	5.07	54.1	4.54	169.9	15.91
2016	68.0	6.80	59.6	5.72	59.4	4.99	187.0	17.51
2017	73.5	7.35	67.3	6.46	65.1	5.47	205.9	19.28
2018	79.3	7.93	76.0	7.30	71.5	6.01	226.8	21.24
2019	85.7	8.57	85.8	8.24	78.4	6.59	249.9	23.40
2020	92.5	9.25	96.9	9.30	86.0	7.22	275.4	25.77

1. Based on replacement of 10% of total exports of BFI (D) worldwide, except exports to Europe, Africa, and the Middle East, which are served by Bon Swiss and BFI (Kenya).

TABLE-9

CALCULATION OF PRESENT VALUE OF CONCESSIONARY LOAN FACILITY (LIT $10 BILLION)
(IN MILLIONS OF ITALIAN LIRAS)

	Amount Outstanding	*Repayment of Principle*	*Interest*[1]	*Total Repayments*	*PV Factor*[2]	*PV of Repayment*
2013	10,000.00	1,428.57	1,400.00	2,828.57	0.8266	2,338.10
2014	8.571.43	1,428.57	1,200.00	2,628.57	0.6834	1,796.36
2015	7,142.86	1,428.57	1,000.00	2.428.57	0.5651	1,372.38
2016	5,714.29	1,428.57	800.00	2,228.57	0.4675	1,041.86
2017	4,285.72	1,428.57	600.00	2.028.57	0.3867	784.45
2018	2,857.15	1,428.57	400.00	1,828.57	0.3199	584.96
2019	1,428.57	1,428.57	200.00	1,628.57	0.2648	431.25
2020	—	—	—	—		
						8,349,36

1.14% or 5% below the reference rate of 19%.

2. Discounted at 21%, 2 percentage points above the reference rate of 19%.

PV of concessionary loan on Lit 10 billion

10,000.00 – 8,349.36 = Lit 1,650.64 million
Lit 1,650.64 million/2250 = Ry. 0.73 million

TABLE-10

CALCULATION OF PRESENT VALUE OF LOAN FACILITY (LIT 15 BILLION)

(In millions of Italian Liras)

	Amount Outstanding	*Repayment of Principle*	*Interest*[1]	*Total Repayments*	*PV Factor*[2]	*PV of Repayments*
2014	15,000.00	2,142.86	1,950.00	4,092.86	0.8333	3,410.58
2015	12,857.14	2,142.86	1,671.43	3,814.29	0.6944	2,649.07
2016	10,714.28	2,142.86	1,392.86	3,535.72	0.5787	2,046.12
2017	8,471.42	2,142.86	1,114.28	3,257.14	0.4823	1,570.92
2018	6,428.56	2,142.86	835.71	2,978.57	0.4019	1,197.09
2019	4,285.70	2,142.86	557.14	2,700.00	0.3349	904.23
2020	2,142.84	2,142.86	278.57	2,421.43	0.2791	675.82
						12,453.83

1.13% or 5% below the reference rate of 18%.
2. Discounted at 20%, 2 percentage points above the reference rate of 18%.

PV of concessionary loan of Lit 15 billion =
15,000.00 – 12,453.83 = Lit 2, 546.17 million
Lit 2,546.17 million/2250 = Ry. 1.13 million

TABLE-11

BFI (ITALY) PROJECT'S CASH FLOW

(millions of Italian Liras)

	2014	2015	2016	2017	2018	2019	2020
(1) Sales in Italy	17,800	20,200	24,700	30,300	35,900	40,000	47,500
(2) Profit on sales in Italy	2,314	2,828	3,458	4,545	5,744	6,400	8,075
(3) Exports	294,694	337,064	391,623	492,757	590,263	722,342	823,175
(4) Profit on exports	32,416	40,448	50,911	64,058	82,637	101,128	123,476
(5) Royalties on sales in Italy[1]	2,670	3,030	3,705	4,545	5,385	6,000	7,125
(6) Royalties on exports[1]	44,204	50,560	58,743	73,913	80,593	108,351	123,476
(7) Taxable income from sales in Italy (2)-(5)	(356)	(202)	(207)	0	359	400	950
(8) Taxable income from exports (4)–(6)	(11,788)	(10,112)	(7,832)	(9,856)	(2,044)	(7,233)	0
(9) Tax on income from sales in Italy[2]	—				90	120	285
(10) Tax on income from exports[3]	—				307		
(11) Total net income (7 + 8) –(9 + 10)	(12,144)	(10,314)	(8,079)	(9,856)	2,006	(6,953)	665
(12) Transferable dividends[4]	—	—	—	—	1,805	—	499

1. 15 per cent of sales in Italy and exports
2. 25 per cent for first 5 years, 30 per cent thereafter.
3. 15 per cent for first 5 years, 20 per cent thereafter.
4. 90 per cent of net profit first 5 years, 75 per cent thereafter. There is no withholding tax.

TABLE-12

BFI (ITALY) CASH FLOWS ACCRUING TO PARENT COMPANY

(millions of Italian Liras)

	2014	2015	2016	2017	2018	2019	2020
Royalties and fees	46,874	53,590	62,448	78,459	85,978	114,351	130,601
Dividends	—	—	—	—	1,805	—	499
Total transfers	46,874	53,590	62,448	78,459	87,783	114,351	131,100
Exchange rate	2,272	2,295	2,318	2,341	2,364	2,388	2,412

(In crore of Rs.)

	2013	2014	2015	2016	2017	2018	2019	2020
Initial investment	(50.32)							

Total transfers		20.63	23.35	26.94	33.55	37.13	47.89	54.35
Adjustment for lost exports		(14.46)	(15.91)	(17.51)	(19.28)	(21.24)	(23.40)	(25.77)
Adjustment for concessionary loan[1]	1.86							
Terminal value[2]								.59
Total cash flow	(48.46)	6.17	7.44	9.43	14.27	15.89	24.49	29.17
PV factor at 18%	1.000	.8475	.7182	.6085	.5158	.4371	.3704	.3139
PV of cahs flows	(48.46)	5.23	5.34	5.74	7.36	6.95	9.07	9.16
Cumulative PV	(48.40)	(43.17)	(37.83)	(32.09)	(24.73)	(17.78)	(8.71)	.45
IRR just over 18%								

1. Ry. 0.73 million (the present value of the Lit 10 billion loan) + Ry. 1.13 million (the present value of the Lit 15 billion loan).
2. Five times the after tax profits generated by BFI (Italy) from domestic sales and exports in 2020.

The project barely passes the APV test and must, therefore, be considered marginal at best. Table-11 reveals that the proposed project in Italy, will be incurring substantial losses in five out of the seven years of the evaluation period, after accounting for payment of royalties and management fees to the parent. The viability of the project was particularly impaired by the assumptions of lost exports given in the case.

No useful purpose can be served by performing the sensitivity tests assuming adverse exchange and political risks. The project will obviously fail these tests. The fate of BFI (Italy) in the final analysis hinges on how highly the management of the parent company values direct control over their foreign operations. Despite the marginal outcome of the capital budgeting test, they may decide to go ahead for strategic reasons, and due to their concern about the continued viability of the current arrangements in Switzerland and Kenya. It would seem, however, that the expectation of tripling or quadrupling profits from the markets now being served by Bon Bon Swisse and BFI (Kenya), within a few years is largely unfounded.

3. Washmate International, a U.S. MNC, is considering setting up a washing machine plant in India. The plant will require initial capital outlay of $ 100 million and will have a salvage value of $ 40 million at the end of 10 years (the expected life cycle of the project). The company sales are projected at 5,00,000 units annually at a net price ofn ₹ 9,500 and a net cost of ₹ 7,500, including allocation for overhead. Both sales price and unit cost are expected to rise in line with the rate of inflation in India which is 15 per cent per annum in India as against 8 per cent per annum in U.S. Current $/₹ exchange rate is $ 0.03175/₹ which will adjust to the differential rate of inflation between the two countries in accordance with purchasing power parity (PPP) principle. Corporation tax rate in India is 30 per cent on net in core, which Washmate International is subject to a 40 per cent tax in U.S. with full credit allowed for tax paid in India.

The Government of India does not grant concessionary loans to foreign projects, but allots free land to such projects. Land will revert back to the government at the end of the life cycle of the project. The government stipulates that the foreign projects be sold to domestic investors at the indicated salvage value. Further, the foreign exchange regulations in India permit transfer of net profits in their entirety, but not the depreciation allowances. However, Washmate International will have no problem in using intersubsidiary transfer pricing to get the depreciation proceeds out of India at exchange rates roughly equivalent to those prevailing in the market.

Washmate International has been exporting washing machines to meet most of the requirements of India. However, unless it takes immediate to establish a plant in that country, all exports will be lost to competitors exporting low-priced washing machines soon to be manufactured in Japan. The project will add $ 40 million to the borrowing capacity of Washmate International. Borrowing rate at home is 12 per cent per annum. The risk-free rate in the U.S. is 8 per cent per annum. Washmate International employs an all equity discount rate of 25 per cent for foreign projects, which includes a premium for the political risk.

Using the APV approach, evaluate the project from the standpoint of the parent company.

Ans.

In the form of APV equation, the main data in the problem is listed below:

I_o = $ 100 million

BC_o = $ 40 million

LS = 0

CL_o = 0

S_o ($/₹) = $ 0.03175

S_x ($/₹) = (0.03175) $(1—0.06087)^t$

Rupee depreciates annually by the differential inflation rate according to PPP

$$S^* = \frac{.08 - .15}{1.15} = .06087$$

CF^*_t = (5,00,000) (2000) $(1.15)^t$ +

Terminal Value = $ 40 million at the end of year 10

Depreciation = $ 6 million for each year.

T = 40%

DR_1 = 25%

DR_2 = 12%

TABLE-1
CASH FLOW WORK SHEET

Year	*Exchange Rate $/Rupee* S_t	*Expected operational cash flow in Rupees CF* (00,000 Rs.)*	*CF* (00,000$)*	*CF* (1-T) (00,000$)*	*Present value Factor at 25%*	*PVCF* (00,000$)*
0	$0.03175	0	0	0	1.0000	0
1	0.02982	11,500	342.93	205.76	.8000	164.61
2	0.02800	13,225	370.30	222.18	.6400	142.19
3	0.02629	15,209	399.84	239.91	.5120	122.83
4	0.02469	17,490	431.83	259.09	.4096	106.61
5	0.02319	20,114	466.44	279.87	.3277	91.71
6	0.02178	23,131	503.79	302.28	.2621	79.23
7	0.02045	26,600	543.97	326.38	.2097	68.44
8	0.01921	30,590	587.63	352.58	.1678	59.16
9	0.01804	35,179	634.63	380.78	.1342	51.21
10	0.01694	40,456	685.32	411.19	.1074	44.16

PVCF* = 930.15

TV $ 40,000,000 (.10737) 42.95

$\frac{D_t}{(1+DR_1)^t}$ =(60,00,000) (3.5705) 21.42

$\frac{rBC_o \times T}{(1+DR_2)^t}$ (4,00,00,000) (.12) (4) (5.6502) 10.85

1005.37

I_o $ 100 million 1000.00

APV 5.37

The project meets the Washmate International's acceptance criteria.

QUESTIONS

1. Describe some potential benefits to the MNC as a result of direct foreign investment (DFI). Elaborate on each type of benefit.
2. Offer your opinion on why economies of some less developed countries with strict restrictions on international trade and direct foreign investment are somewhat independent from economies of other countries. Why would MNCs desire to

enter such countries? If these countries relaxed their restrictions, would their economies continue to be independent of other economies? Explain.

3. Once an MNC establishes a subsidiary, DFI remains an ongoing decision. What does this statement mean?
4. Why would foreign governments provide MNCs with incentives to undertake DFI there?
5. What are some risks of international business that may not exist for local business?
6. What is the relationship between degree of international business and risk of MNCs?
7. Country X typically has a high interest rate, and its currency is expected to strengthen against the dollar over time. Country Y typically has a low interest rate, and its currency is expected to weaken against the dollar over time. Both countries have imposed a "blocked funds" restriction over the next four years on the two subsidiaries owned by a U.S. firm. Which subsidiary will be more adversely affected by the blocked funds, assuming that there are limited opportunities for corporate expansion in both countries?
8. Can investment in the stock of a well-diversified multinational firm afford the investor the same benefits of diversification obtainable from a portfolio of stocks selected from different countries? If that is the case, why do portfolio managers incur the cost, and perhaps the inconvenience, of buying shares of foreign firms to diversify their portfolios?
9. What are the factors which make the cash flow from a project create different values for the parent and for the subsidiary which undertakes the project?
10. How does the terminal rate of return differ from the rate of return? How would you use it in a project which has revaluations (appreciation or depreciation) likely for the local currency against the parent's currency? Does it make a difference if the funds are blocked or remitted?
11. How does the adjusted present value technique (APV) differ from other techniques of discounted cash flow analysis?
12. Why is the APV format more suitable for evaluating foreign projects than the conventional NPV format?
13. Discuss the pros and cons of reflecting the exchange rate and political risks in the discount rate. Would the expected life cycle of the project affect the choice of the appropriate vehicle for incorporating these risks in the quantitative exercise of the project evaluation process? Are there variables other than the project's life cycle which could influence the choice of the appropriate technique?
14. Under what circumstances would an assumption of blockage of transfers of dividends from an affiliate to the parent company hurt the project's viability most? Incorporate the following concepts in your answer?
    a. Timing of assumed blockage or restrictions on transfers.
    b. The expected or projected behaviour of the exchange rate (the host country's currency against the parent's currency).
    c. The reinvestment assumption, that is, the rate at which intermediate cash flows can be reinvested locally, if they are not expected to be used in financing the activities of the project.

d. The expected cash flows pattern of the project.
e. The expected life cycle of the project on the basis of which the foreign project is being evaluated.
f. The estimated terminal value (if any) of the project, and the size of the terminal value in relation to the initial investment and annual cash flows.

15. Show how facilities for financing on concessional terms offered by the host government improve the likelihood of a foreign project's acceptability. Is there an alternative procedure to measure the contribution of such financing to the project to the one used in the APV formula? Does this procedure reflect the full contribution of such a facility to the project's present value? (How would you deal with the political risk reduction aspect of local financing?)
16. Evaluate the treatment of profits on exports lost or foregone in the local and third-country markets suggested in the APV format. How realistic is the assumption that lost exports in physical terms (based on exports prior to the coming into operation of the foreign project) remain unchanged irrespective of changes in exchange rates over the life cycle of the project? Should we invoke the concept of the price elasticity of demand for imports?
17. Discuss the two-step approach in the process of evaluating foreign projects using the APV technique. Which components of the cash flow are likely to be considered last in the overall evaluation process?
18. Suggest at least four discount rates used in the APV technique and discuss the rationale for using these different rates in discounting the several components of the cash flow.
19. "I don't worry about anticipating currency changes; all I care about it for absolute level of inflation. I just reduce the value of the funds by that amount is to the equivalent in German marks."—German corporate executive. Do you agree with this analysis?
20. How would you attempt to cope with the political risks in a country when you plan to locate a project when the government has a record of rapid changes to personnel?
21. "If the parent's cost of capital is 15%, its equity investment in a subsidiary only needs to be charged to the subsidiary at 15%." Why or why not?
22. "Regardless of the interest rate, we always borrow in a cheap currency with a likely devaluation, since that minimises our financing costs." Give an example where this strategy would fail. Do you think it is a good rule of thumb?
23. What data would you desire in order to evaluate the risk of a project in a particular country? Why would one corporation find the same level of risk acceptable while another one might reject it? Does this indicate the irrationality of corporate management?
24. With worldwide operations, IBM has about 300 American nationals working for it outside the United States. Do you think this policy is a good one? What firms could use it more profitably than other firms, or do you believe it makes sense for all firms?
25. What are the arguments for the existence of a corporation's ability to be an efficient diversifier? Do you believe the arguments?
26. Why does a joint simulation produce the covariances between projects?

27. Under what conditions is variance a bad measure of risk?
28. How can a firm obtain a reasonable estimate of the local cost of capital for a project? Why might a multinational corporation have an advantage over a local firm in terms of the cost of capital?
29. Why should capital budgeting for subsidiary projects be assessed from the parent's perspective?
30. What additional factors deserve consideration in multinational capital budgeting that are not normally relevant for a purely domestic project?
31. What is the limitation of using point estimates of exchange rates within the capital budgeting analysis?
32. Explain how simulation can be used in multinational capital budgeting.
33. Why is simulation applicable to multinational capital budgeting? What can it do that other risk adjustment techniques cannot?
34. List the various techniques for adjusting risk in multinational capital budgeting. Describe any advantages or disadvantages of each technique.
35. Project X has an NPV estimated by your employees to be $1.2 million. Your employees state in their report that they have not accounted for risk, but that with such a large NPV, the project should be accepted, since even a risk-adjusted NPV would likely to be positive. You have the final decision as to whether to accept or reject the project. What is your decision?
36. How does international diversification help explain in part direct foreign investment? Can the benefits of diversification (such as reducing the systematic risk and stabilising the overall cash flow pattern of the firm) be achieved by other forms of market penetration?

PROBLEMS

1. Grahm Baker Motors (GBM) a German multinational firm, is evaluating a project to build and market a modified version of its subcompact "the Hozi" in India. If the project proves viable, an agreement is to be signed with a Indian government. So far, the German share of the car market in India has been declining steadily in recent years due to stiff competition from imported cars from countries such as Japan, the United Kingdom, France, and Italy. The management is of the viewpoint that unless they establish a wholly owned affiliate in India, they will have to abandon this market altogether.

If approved, GBM (India) is projected to produce and market 10,000 cars in the first year of operation (2013). Local sales in units are projected to rise by 10 per cent annually over the next four years. The increase in output and sales is to be accommodated by the initial capacity built into the project. The project has a fairly long life extending up to 20 years. However, the Indian government corporation, with which GBM will be negotiating the concession agreement, has indicated that the agreement will be subject to renegotiation at the end of 2025. At that time, GBM may be asked to turn over the affiliate either to the corporation, or to a joint venture involving the corporation, GBM, and local private sector interests. In that eventuality, the project will be given a terminal value equal to five times the after-tax net profit actually realised in 2025.

The initial investment in plants and equipment, to be entirely provided by the parent company in 2013, was estimated at ₹ 1400 crore. Because GBM will be building the plant in a depressed and high unemployment state of Bihar, the concession agreement will include three concessional features:

a. Financing for working capital requirements (estimated at ₹ 500 crore needed at the outset of operations) may be provided by a local financial institution at 12 per cent per annum. In the absence of this facility, GBM will have had to raise the funds from Eurocurrency markets at an estimated rate of 14 per cent. The concessional loan facility is to be repaid in five equal annual installments plus accrued interest. The first installment is due at the end of 2020.
b. During the first five years of operations, GBM (India) applicable corporate income tax and withholding tax rates will be 25 per cent and 15 per cent, respectively.
c. A rent-free plot of land will be assigned to house the operating facilities and the administrative offices of the project.

To insure its competitiveness with comparable subcompact GBM is planning to price the "Hozi" at ₹ 800,000 to be adjusted upward by 5 per cent annually. Production costs are as follows:

Variable Cost Per Unit	
Materials and Components	
Domestic component	₹ 1,25,000
Imported component (from the parent)	₹ 1,20,000
Labour	₹ 80,000
Fixed Costs (Annually)	
Royalties and fees to the parent	₹ 25 crore
General, selling, and administrative expenses	₹ 30 Crore
Depreciation (plant and equipment to be depreciated over a ten-year period to ₹ 400 Crore salvage value)	₹ 100 Crore

The domestic component of raw materials and components as well as labour are subject to an upward adjustment by the average projected rate of inflation in India. General, selling and administrative costs are estimated to rise by 5 per cent annually, while the other two components of fixed costs (royalties and fees to the parent company and depreciation) will remain unchanged. The parent company provides the affiliate with components priced on a cost basis.

The volatility of exchange rates which characterised exchange markets in early '90s presents perhaps the greatest risk facing the project. This period witnessed a sharp decline in the value of ₹ vis-a-vis the German mark and currencies of major industrial countries. The evaluating team compiled the inflation and exchange rate data in Table-1, which are projected to prevail during the life cycle of the project.

German tax laws distinguish between distributed and undistributed income of domestic corporations, which apply also to branches of foreign corporations doing business in Germany. Corporations with capitalisation of DM 500 million and over are subject to 33.3 per cent on distributed income and 43.3 per cent on undistributed income. This distinction is intended primarily to lessen somewhat the incidence of double taxation in the case of distributed profits.

TABLE-1

	Exchange Rates		*Inflation Rates*	
	Rs./DM		*India*	*Germany*
Spot Rate 12/31/12	24.65	Actual 2012	7.5	2.5
Average 2012	24.50	2013	9.0	2.0
Average 2013	24.75	2014	8.0	3.5
Average 2014	24.90	2015	10.0	4.0
Average 2015	25.20	2016	12.0	5.0
Average 2016	25.35	2017	13.5	5.5
Average 2017	25.50	2018	15.0	6.0

For the purpose of this case problem, GBM follows a policy of distributing one-half of realised profits. Consequently, the effective tax rate is 38.3 per cent. German corporations operating overseas can claim full credit for corporate income tax and withholding tax paid to foreign tax jurisdictions.

As a member of the project's evaluation team you have been asked to prepare and analyse the cash flow data, and to test the acceptability of the project, using standard DCF techniques (NPV and IRR). GBM requires a 20 per cent return on car manufacturing and assembly plants established in foreign countries. Similar projects in India employ a hurdle rate of 18 per cent.

The project is to be evaluated from the standpoint of the Indian affiliate (in Rs.) as well as from the standpoint of the parent firm (in DM).

You are also given the following additional information:

a. All profits after tax realised by the Indian affiliate are freely transferable to Germany. Royalties and management fees are also freely transferable.
b. Only one-half of depreciation charges is transferable. The other half is to be maintained in a local noninterest-earning escrow account, pending renegotiation of the status of the affiliate in 2020.
c. The terminal value, which is estimated to equal five times the projected after-tax net profit of the affiliate in the fifth year of operation, is also transferable to Germany. However, capital gains on the transaction are taxable in Germany at the rate of 25 per cent. Because of the uncertainty of the amount, the terminal value is to be discounted at five percentage points above the discount rate applicable to regular cash flows.

It is the policy of GBM to subject foreign-project proposals to a series of tests to ascertain the sensitivity of those projects to adverse developments, particularly those relating to sales projections, the exchange risk, and the political risk. You have, therefore, been also asked to perform the following tests on the project's cash flow in yen separately:

a. Projected sales are 8000 units annually (instead of 10,000 units), rising by 15 per cent annually.
b. Exchange rates adjust to the projected average inflation rates in India and Germany

during the 2013-2018 period in accordance with the PPP principle (instead of using the projected rates given in the text of the problem).

c. Blockage of transfers from India affects 50 per cent of profits after tax and the 50 per cent of depreciation charges that is transferable. Blocked amounts can be invested in India at 10 per cent and are to be transferred to Germany at the end of 2020.

You may also want to consider subjecting the project to both (b) and (c) simultaneously. (Blockage hurts the project's viability more if the currency of the host country's is expected to depreciate against the parent's currency.)

2. Indu Enterprises presently has no existing business in Germany but is considering the establishment of a subsidiary there. The following information has been gathered to assess this project:

i) The initial investment required is DM50 million. Given the existing spot rate of ₹ 25 per mark, the initial investment ₹ 1250 million million. In addition to the DM50 million initial investment on plant and equipment, DM20 million is needed for working capital and will be borrowed by the subsidiary from a German bank. The German subsidiary of Indu will pay interest only on the loan each year, at an interest rate of 14 per cent. The loan principal is to be paid in 10 years.

ii) The project will be terminated at the end of Year 3, when the subsidiary will be sold.

iii) The price, demand, and variable cost of the product in Germany are as follows:

Year	*Price*	*Demand*	*Variable cost*
1	DM500	40,000 units	DM30
2	DM511	50,000 units	DM35
3	DM530	60,000 units	DM40

iv) The fixed costs, such as overhead expenses, are estimated to be DM6 million per year.

v) The exchange rate of the mark is expected to be ₹ 26 at the end of Year 1, ₹ 27 at the end of Year 2, and ₹ 28 at the end of Year 3.

vi) The German government will impose an income tax of 30 per cent on income. In addition, it will impose a withholding tax of 10 per cent on earnings remitted by the subsidiary. The Indian government will allow a tax credit on remitted earnings and will not impose any additional taxes.

vii) All cash flows received by the subsidiary are to be sent to the parent at the end of each year. The subsidiary will use its working capital to support ongoing operations.

viii) The plant and equipment are depreciated over 10 years, using the straight-line depreciation method. Since the plant and equipment are initially valued at DM50 million, the annual depreciation expense is DM5 million.

ix) In three years, the subsidiary is to be sold. Indu plans to let the acquiring firm assume the existing German loan. The working capital will not be liquidated, but will be used by the acquiring firm. Indu expects to receive DM52 million after subtracting capital gains taxes when it sells the subsidiary. Assume that this amount is not subject to a withholding tax.

x) Indu requires a 20 per cent rate of return on this project.

(a) Determine the net present value of this project. Should Indu accept this project?

(b) Assume that Indu also considers an alternate financing arrangement, in which the parent invests an additional ₹ 500 million to cover the working capital requirements, so that the subsidiary avoids the German loan. If this arrangement is used, the selling price of the subsidiary (after subtracting any capital gains taxes) is expected to be DM18 million higher. Is this alternative financing arrangement more feasible for the parent than the originally proposed arrangement? Explain.

(c) Would the NPV of this project from the parent's perspective be more sensitive to exchange rate movements if the subsidiary used German financing to cover the working capital or if the parent invested more of its own funds to cover the working capital? Explain.

(d) Assume Indu uses the original proposed financing arrangement and that funds are blocked until the subsidiary is sold. The funds to be remitted are reinvested at a rate of 6 per cent (after taxes) until the end of Year 3. How is the project's NPV affected?

(e) What is the break-even salvage value of this project, if Indu Enterprises uses the original proposed financing arrangement and funds are not blocked?

(f) Assume that Indu decides to implement the project, using the original proposed financing arrangement. Also assume that after one year, a German firm offers Indu a price of ₹ 1350 million after taxes for the subsidiary, and that Indu's original forecasts for Years 2 and 3 have not changed. Should Indu divest the subsidiary? Explain.

DRIVE POWER MOTORS: *A CASE*

Drive Power Motors plc (DPM) is a British-based multinational engaged in the manufacture, distribution and export of advanced electrical motors around the world. Its headquarters staff are currently considering replacing export sales to the Arthurian continent by building a manufacturing plant in Avalonia, one of the largest, most progressive and dynamic countries in Arthuria. Key financial data relating to the new project are summarised below:

- Existing export sales from the UK to Arthuria total 5000 motors. It is estimated that, if the new overseas plant is not built, the company's volume sales will grow by 10% per annum compound. These sales would utilise marginal capacity at DPM's Birmingham plant and they are estimated to earn a contribution to sales ratio of 30%. Executives at DPM consider that sales to Arthuria can be vastly increased should a local manufacturing and distribution facility be sited on the continent.
- The local currency of Avalonia is the Sword and the year 0 exchange rate is likely to be 4 Swords = £1. Estimates are for future movements in currency values to follow purchasing power parity. UK and Avalonian inflation are forecast to be constant at 6% p.a. and 9% p.a. respectively. DPM's investment is to be via a local 100% owned company, DPM (Avalonia).
- The capital cost of buildings, plant and machinery for the Avalonian facility is realistically put at Swd120mn. Avalonian tax rules allow such cost to be written off over a five-year period using the straight-line method. The practice is for accounting treatment to mirror tax rules exactly. Investment is to be made at the end of year 0.
- Of the Swd120mn capital cost, one-third is likely to come from local commercial banks at market rates of interest, one-third is expected to come from a parent injection of equity and one-third is likely to come from subsidised finance sources, such as buyer credits on capital equipment and government loans from Avalonia. The net effect will be that DPM Avalonia will have access to Swd40mn at 12% p.a. interest rate repayable over a five-year period in equal loan amortisations. This compares with market rates for a similar maturity and repayment schedule of 15% p.a.
- DPM plans to charge its wholly owned Avalonian subsidiary a royalty of 5% on sales and a management fee of 2½% on sales. This is perfectly acceptable in terms of local law and regulations. DPM (UK), the Birmingham-based operating company, will sell components to DPM (Avalonia) at a contribution to sales ratio of 20%. Such components will amount to 40% of variable costs of the Avalonian project.
- In terms of evaluating overseas projects, DPM uses the adjusted present value criterion and opinion is that a k^* of 14% in nominal sterling terms would be appropriate for this project. It is estimated that, because of the relative political stability of Avalonia, a debt to capital employed ratio as high as 30% would be right for this investment. The company's procedures for overseas project appraisal

involve a seven-year cash flow horizon with a terminal value based solely on recapture of working capital input.

- There is general agreement that a ratio of 20% for working capital to sales would be the likely order of magnitude for the Avalonian project.
- DPM (UK) will be selling to DPM (Avalonia) capital equipment for use in this project. The capital equipment will be sold for its market value, £5mn. The book value of this equipment is £2mn and its tax-written-down value is £1mn. Any capital gain is chargeable to UK tax at 33%.
- Respective corporate tax rates for the UK and Avalonia are 33% and 20%. Avalonia levies a 5% withholding tax on dividends, royalties and management fees. Avalonia and Britain have tax treaties which give rise to credits for foreign taxes paid in each other's countries.
- Given the proximity of the Avalonian facility to the Arthurian continent, sales volumes from the new plant are estimated as follows:

Year 1	20 000 motors @ Swd3,080 each
Year 2	24 000 motors @ Swd3,320 each
Year 3	30 000 motors @ Swd3,590 each
Year 4	32 000 motors @ Swd3,910 each
Year 5	36 000 motors @ Swd4,230 each
Year 6	40 000 motors @ Swd4,560 each
Year 7	40 000 motors @ Swd4,930 each

- It is estimated that, in respect of sales of components from DPM (UK) to DPM (Avalonia), transfer prices will be £168 per motor for year 1 and then will rise in line with UK inflation.
- Avalonian fixed overheads for the new project, put at Swd 2mn for year 1 of operations, are expected to rise in line with Avalonian estimates of local inflation.
- Avalonia has no exchange control regulations.
- Assume that all cash flows occur at the end of the year concerned.
- The project under consideration will be DPM's first direct investment in Avalonia.
- Assume that Avalonia operates the classical tax system and that the UK uses the imputation system. In the UK, assume a basic rate of personal tax at 25%.

Calculate the Potential of the Avalonian Project from both Project and Parent Standpoints.

Solution

To arrive at the relevant adjusted present value take the following steps:

i) calculation of Avalonian sales revenues;
ii) estimation of foreign exchange rates in the future;
iii) calculation of Avalonian costs;
iv) calculation of Avalonian profit;
v) calculation of working capital input and terminal value;
vi) estimation of Avalonian k^*;
vii) calculation of present value of cash flows arising to project only;
viii) calculation of present value of subsidised interest in Swords;
ix) calculation of present value of tax shield in Swords;

x) specification of APV from a project standpoint alone;
xi) calculation of parent cash flows and the present value of cash flows available to the parent;
xii) calculation of present value of subsidised interest in pounds sterling;
xii) calculation of present value of tax shield in pounds sterling; and, finally
xiii) specification of APV from a parent viewpoint.

These are 14 steps to be taken then, and the necessary figuring relating to the path towards the parent adjusted present value is shown in Tables 1 to 14 A number of points are likely to emerge from carefully working through the tables. Some of them are listed below:

TABLE 1

DPM Case: Avalonian Project Sales Revenues

Year	*1*	*2*	*3*	*4*	*5*	*6*	*7*
Motors sold - estimate (units)	20,000	24,000	30,000	32,000	36,000	40,000	40,000
Price per unit (Swd)	3,080	3,320	3,590	3,910	4,230	4,560	4,930
Sales revenue (Swd mn)	61.6	79.7	107.7	125.1	152.3	182.4	197.2

TABLE 2

DPM CASE: PURCHASING POWER PARITY ESTIMATE OF EXCHANGE RATE

Year		*FX rate (Swd per £)*
0	Exchange rate given as	4.00
1	Using PPP formula, we get: $\dfrac{0.09 - 0.06}{1.06}$ = 4.1132	4.11
2	Given constant inflations of 9% for Avalonia and 6% for the UK, the Sword will depreciate at a constant rate. So it can be calculated on the basis of: $er = \dfrac{4.1132}{4.00} \times er - 1$	4.23
3	Using the same approach for year 3 and following years	4.35
4		4.47
5		4.60
6		4.73
7		4.86

Where there are no exchange controls in place it is just as easy to employ an NPV approach - although, of course, this will not involve calculating the tax shield on debt as a separate item. However, when in a situation where exchange controls are in place, we are confronted with a problem. This arises because the multinational firm frequently uses various devices to circumvent some of the impediments created by such regulations. One of these involves financing overseas projects with parent company debt because the servicing of such debt may provide a means of getting otherwise blocked funds out of a host country. Because such flows are debt related, a conceptual problem is created under the NPV criterion. At what rate should we discount such flows back to the parent? Should we use the risk-adjusted weighted average cost of capital, the usual routine with the NPV approach, or should we use the cost of debt given such flows are clearly a function of financing with debt? Also, what about debt capital repayments to the parent. The normal routine is to exclude this last item from an NPV calculation. However the reality of the matter is that by creative financing of the overseas project remittable cash flows are being enhanced via debt repayment.

TABLE 3

DPM CASE: AVALONIAN PROJECT - COST ESTIMATE

Year	1	2	3	4	5	6	7
Volume sold (units)	20000	24000	30000	32000	36000	40000	40000
Components ex UK (£ per unit)	168	178.1	188.8	200.0	212.1	224.8	238.3
Local cost of components ex UK (Swd per unit)	690.5	753.4	821.3	894.0	975.7	1,063.3	1,158.1
Other variable costs (Swd per unit)*	1,035.7	1,130.1	1,231.9	1,341.0	1,463.6	1,594.9	1,737.1
Total variable costs (Swd mn)**	34.5	45.2	61.6	71.5	87.8	106.3	115.8
Royalties and management fee (Swd mn)	4.6	6.0	8.1	9.4	11.4	13.7	14.8
Overheads (Swd mn)	2.0	2.2	2.4	2.6	2.8	3.1	3.4
Depreciation (Swd mn)	24.0	24.0	24.0	24.0	24.0	—	—
	65.1	77.4	96.1	107.5	126.0	123.1	134.0

* Based on UK components, previous line, being 40% of total variable costs.

** Volume sold multiplied by the sum of components ex UK and other variable costs per unit.

TABLE 4

DPM CASE: AVALONIAN PROJECT - PROFIT FORECAST (SWD MN)

Year	1	2	3	4	5	6	7
Sales revenue	61.6	79.7	107.7	125.1	152.3	182.4	197.2
Estimated costs	65.1	77.4	96.1	107.5	126.0	123.1	134.0
Profit before tax and interest	(3.5)	2.3	11.6	17.6	26.3	59.3	63.2
Avalonian tax (20%)	—	—	(2.1)	(3.5)	(5.3)	(11.9)	(12.6)
Profit after tax but before interest	(3.5)	2.3	9.5	14.1	21.0	47.4	50.6

TABLE 5

DPM CASE: AVALONIAN PROJECT-WORKING CAPITAL REQUIREMENT

Year	*Sales (Swd mn)*	*Working capital @20%*	*Working capital input*
0			12.3
1	61.6	12.3	3.6
2	79.7	15.9	5.6
3	107.7	21.5	3.5
4	125.1	25.0	5.5
5	152.3	30.5	6.0
6	182.4	36.5	2.9
7	197.2	39.4	

Terminal value = Swd 39.4mn

TABLE 6

DPM CASE: ESTIMATE OF AVALONIAN K^*

In the absence of any beta estimates based on Avalonian markets and any indication of returns from Avalonian investment, we use the UK k^* for this project adjusted for inflations in the two countries:

UK k^*	0.14
UK inflation estimate	0.06
Real k*	$\frac{1.14}{1.06} - 1$
	= 0.075
Avalonian inflation estimate	0.09
Avalonian k^*	(1.075)(1.09)-1
	= 0.172
	say 0.17

Such problems are avoided by employing the APV approach. We home in on all remittable cash flows, including those that accrue from creative financing, and apply a discount rate of k , the all-equity cost of capital, to these and then add in the value of the tax shield on debt as a separate routine. This provides a far more practical, but nonetheless theoretically sound, solution to the problem of valuation of overseas projects. The approach accords with that advocated by Lessard (1981), who observes that much of the APV method's attractiveness 'lies in its transparency and simplicity of use in certain situations'.

TABLE 7

DPM CASE: CASH FLOWS ARISING FROM AVALONIAN PROJECT - PROJECT VIEW POINT EXCLUDING SUBSIDISED INTEREST AND TAX SHIELD (SWD MN)

Year	*0*	*1*	*2*	*3*	*4*	*5*	*6*	*7*
Fixed capital investment	(120.0)							
Working capital	(12.3)	(3.6)	(5.6)	(3.5)	(5.5)	(6.0)	(2.9)	39.4
Profit after tax but before interest		(3.5)	2.3	9.5	14.1	21.0	47.4	50.6
Depreciation		24 .0	24.0	24.0	24.0	24.0	—	—
	(132.3)	16.9	20.7	30.0	32.6	39.0	44.5	90.0
Discount factor at k^* of 17%	1.00	0.85	0.73	0.62	0.53	0.46	0.39	0.33
	(132.3)	14.4	15.1	18.6	17.3	17.9	17.4	29.7
Σ = (1.9)								

TABLE 8

DPM CASE: CALCULATION OF PRESENT VALUE OF SUBSIDISED INTEREST (SWD MN)

Year	*0*	*1*	*2*	*3*	*4*	*5*
Capital flows in terms of borrowing and repayments	40.0	(8.0)	(8.0)	(8.0)	(8.0)	(8.0)

Interest (gross)		(4.8)	(3.8)	(2.9)	(1.9)	(1.0)
Tax allowance*				2.3	0.4	0.2
	40.0	(12.8)	(11.8)	(8.6)	(9.5)	(8.8)
Discount at Avalonian market cost of debt less tax, i.e. 15% less 3% = 12%	40.0	(11.4)	(9.4)	(6.1)	(6.1)	(5.0)
Σ = 2.0						

* Tax allowance on year I and 2 interest payments deferred to year 3 when profits are available within DPM Avalonian.

In short, we use the APV approach whether exchange controls are operative or not, although the NPV routine might be equally applicable where exchange controls are absent - but rather less so where they are present.

TABLE 9

DPM CASE: CALCULATION OF PRESENT VALUE OF TAX SHIELD DUE TO DEBT IN SWORDS

Capital cost in year 0	=	Swd 132.3mn
Estimated debt to capital employed ratio of project		30%
Debt sustainable by project	=	Swd39.7mn
Present value of tax shield (Swd mn) = [39.7 x 0.15 x 0.2] annuity factor for		
Debt interest Tax rate 7 years @ 15%		
= [1.19] 4.16		
= Swd4.95mn		
We now calculate the multiplier tax shield effect:		
Present value created by project	=	Swd 5.05 mn
This gives rise to further debt at 30% of		Swd 1.52 mn
Multiplier tax shield value (Swd mn)		
= (1.52 x 0.15 x 0.2) 4.16		
= Swd 0.19mn		
Total tax shield	=	Swd 5.14mn

TABLE 10

DPM CASE: ADJUSTED PRESENT VALUE - PROJECT STANDPOINT ALONE (SWD MN)

Present value of project excluding subsidised interest and tax shield (see Table 7)	–1.9
Present value of subsidised interest (see Table 8)	2.0
Present value of tax shield (see Table 9)	5.1
Adjusted present value - project standpoint	5.2

TABLE 11

DPM CASE: AVALONIAN PROJECT - PARENT CASH FLOWS AND PRESENT VALUE CALCULATION (£MN)

Year	*0*	*1*	*2*	*3*	*4*	*5*	*6*	*7*
Project cash flows, per Table 7, converted to sterling	(33.1)	4.1	4.9	6.9	7.3	8.5	9.4	18.5
Additional tax on profit (from 20% to 33%)*				(0.3)	(0.5)	(0.7)	(1.6)	(1.7)
Royalties and management fee before tax, per Table 3 converted to sterling		1.1	1.4	1.9	2.1	2.5	2.9	3.0
Tax on royalties and management fee		(0.4)	(0.5)	(0.6)	(0.7)	(0.8)	(1.0)	(1.0)
Equipment sale tax on £4mn of capital gain for tax purposes**	1.3							
Contribution on export of components to Avalonia ***		0.7	0.9	1.1	1.3	1.5	1.8	1.9
Tax on contribution immediately above		(0.2)	(0.3)	(0.4)	(0.4)	(0.5)	(0.6)	(0.6)
Loss export sales - contribution thereon §		(1.2)	(1.4)	(1.6)	(1.9)	(2.2)	(2.6)	(3.0)
Tax on contribution on lost exports		0.4	0.5	0.5	0.6	0.7	0.9	1.0
	(31.8)	4.5	5.5	7.5	7.8	9.0	9.2	18.1
Discount at 14% — factor	1.00	0.88	0.77	0.67	0.59	0.52	0.46	0.40
	(31.8)	4.0	4.2	5.0	4.6	4.7	4.2	7.2
	$\Sigma = 2.1$							

* In this example, UK tax has not been lagged twelve months - this sophistication could be added to all tax lines. The additional tax takes the Avalonian rate from 20% to 33 % and includes withholding tax and UK tax on assumed remittance of profit. The figures shown are based on the tax amount in Table 4 uplifted to 33% and converted to £.

** Remember that the initial capital cost - £33. 1 mn - includes £5mn for equipment transferred from the UK to Avalonia. By using this equipment in the Avalonian project DPM forgoes £5mn (market value) less capital gains tax thereon. The asset transferred has a tax written-down value of £1mn.

*** The contribution on exports of components to Avalonia can be computed by reference to Table 3. It shows volumes sold and component prices. By multiplying these two and allowing for a contribution to sales ratio of 20%, the figures shown are obtained.

§ The contribution on lost exports is found thus:

Year	*Motors exported*	*Price (Swd)*	*FX rate*	*Sales lost (£mn)*	*Contribution @ 30%*
0	5000				
1	5500	3080	4.1 1	4.12	1.2
2	6050	3320	4.23	4.75	1.4
3	6655	3590	4.35	5.49	1.6
4	7321	3910	4.47	6.40	1.9
5	8053	4230	4.60	7.41	2.2
6	8858	4560	4.73	8.54	2.6
7	9744	4930	4.86	9.88	3.0

The focus is on parent cash flows, subject to profit remittances on withholding taxes and UK taxes. The effect is to debit this project with the harshest tax treatment possible. If the project stands up on this severe set of assumptions, it can only be enhanced should moneys be parked in a tax haven - for example, for onward remission to meet capital needs elsewhere in the group. In this connection, it is perfectly acceptable for financial analysts at head office to perform a sensitivity analysis to assess what returns would look like if cash were transferred to a tax haven as opposed to being remitted to the head office. The results of such an analysis might be useful in enabling board members to exercise judgement in reaching decisions on investment propositions.

In the DPM example, PPP is used to estimate future exchange rates. Again, the international project appraisal might be greatly enhanced if a sensitivity analysis accompanies submissions showing the effect of different scenarios, perhaps a catching up in exchange rates to make good an existing disequilibrium or the like. Such analysis should facilitate decision making.

TABLE 12

DPM CASE: CALCULATION OF PRESENT VALUE OF SUBSIDISED INTEREST IN STERLING

Present value of subsidised interest, per Table 8 (Swd mn)	Swd2.0mn
Convert to £ at existing exchange rate to give present value of subsidised interest (£mn)	£0.5mn

TABLE 13

DPM CASE: CALCULATION OF PRESENT VALUE OF TAX SHIELD DUE TO DEBT IN STERLING

Capital cost in year 0	=	£31.8mn
Estimated debt to capital employed ratio of project		30%
Debt sustainable by project	=	£9.5mn
Gross interest thereon (£mn)		
= 9.5 × 0.12	=	£1.14mn
Annual amount of the tax shield (£mn)	=	£ 1. 14(0.33 – 0.25)
	=	£0.091
Present value of tax shield (£mn)		
= £0.091mn × annuity factor for 7 yrs @ [12% (I -0.25)]		
= £0.09lmn × 6.51523		
= £0.594mn		
We now calculate the multiplier tax shield effect -		
Present value created by project	=	£3.2mn
This gives rise to further debt at 30% of		£1.0mn
Gross interest thereon (£mn)		
= 1.0 x 0.12	=	£0.12mn
Annual amount of tax shield (£mn)	=	£0.12(0.33 – 0.25)
	=	£0.01

Present value of multiplier tax shield (£mn)

= £0.01 × 6.51523

= £0.07

Total tax shield	=	£0.66mn

TABLE 14

DPM CASE: ADJUSTED PRESENT VALUE — PARENT STANDPOINT (£MN)

Present value of parent flows excluding subsidised interest and tax shield (see Table 11)	2.1
Present value of subsidised interest (see Table 12)	0.5
Present value of tax shield (see Table 13)	0.7
Adjusted present value - parent standpoint	3.3

It should be noted that, if there is an export credit available in a third currency which gives rise to a subsidised interest rate - for example, in the Avalonian case, had there been soft yen finance available linked to purchase of equipment from a Japanese supplier - it may be necessary to take foreign exchange protection via forward cover or a swap if the subsidy is not to be eroded by exchange rate movements.

Note also that Table 12 merely takes the amount of the present value of the subsidised finance in Swords and converts it to sterling at the current exchange rate. One may convert all flows into home currency, apply home tax and work out the present value by applying a discount rate which reflects home country market interest rates less home country tax. Usually differences between these two approaches are small. The approach adopted in the DPM figuring is conservative.

Finally, on the DPM case, note that the approach adopted involves calculation using an APV methodology. It would have been equally acceptable to use a net present value route to the solution of the problem. This would have involved the application of a weighted average cost of capital to the parent incremental cash flows in Table 11 rather than an all-equity discount rate.

METRO ALLIED FOODS (MAF): *A CASE*
(SCENARIO - I)

Metro Allied Foods (MAF) is a multinational food manufacturing and distributing company headquartered London. There is a proposition before the head office staff to replace export sales to the Camelot continent with a new manufacturing facility located in Excalibur, one of the largest countries in that part of the world. Most countries on the Camelot continent have exchange controls and Excalibur is no exception. However, its economic and political environment and attitude to business in general make it one of the most reliable locations for international investment. Key financial data relating to the new project are summarised below.

i) MAF uses the adjusted present value method to appraise international capital investment projects. In terms of UK parent cash flows, the firm would use a cost of capital, k^*, of 12% for this project.

ii) Its evaluation procedure involves a horizon for operating cash flows of seven years, at the end of which MAF staff put a conservative terminal value on a project's equity based on a P/E ratio of five times the most recent year's profit after tax.

iii) MAF's investment is required to be via a local company. This will be a 100% owned subsidiary, MAF (Excalibur).

iv) Excalibur's exchange control regulations permit the transfer of only 75% of a foreign firm's profit after tax. Capital, as opposed to operating earnings, may be repatriated without penalty. The exception to this is that parent debt can only be repatriated after a minimum of five years by way of a bullet repayment. The host country has strict rules about capital ratios for a foreign company operating in Excalibur. It may not have a debt/equity ratio in excess of 3 to 1. If at any year-end its debt/equity ratio exceeds this level, it must input more equity from overseas.

v) In connection with the project under consideration, 50% of the required capital will come from a subsidised local currency loan carrying a 10% p.a. coupon against a market rate of 15% p.a. Parent equity input will account for 25% of the capital input and the remaining 25% will be sourced from parent debt. The maximum interest rate chargeable on parent debt amounts to 12% p.a.

vi) Excalibur's local currency is the Harris (Hs) and the initial capital input (that is, debt plus equity) will amount to Hs 62mn. The local subsidised debt is repayable in equal annual instalments over five years. If necessary, it will be replaced by local debt at market rates of interest.

vii) Excalibur's estimated inflation rate over the seven years of the project's cash flow horizon life is 7% p.a. compared with 6% p.a. for the UK.

viii) Excalibur's corporate tax rate is 25% and the UK rate is 33%. Excalibur imposes no withholding taxes.

ix) Excalibur allows a royalty payment of 5% on sales but does not sanction management fees of any other sort.

x) Estimates are that the project will bear a debt to capital employed ratio of 20%.

xi) The capital cost of the project is put at Hs 35.8mn for fixed assets and Hs26.2mn for initial working capital requirements.

xii) The existing exchange rate is Hs2.57 to £1.

xiii) MAF (UK) will lose profit as set out below, as a result of the new Excalibur project.

Year	*Profit before tax (£mn)*
1	7.2
2	8.0
3	8.7
4	9.6
5	10.6
6	11.7
7	12.9

xiv) The levels of sales and profits (after depreciation) expected to be achieved in respect of the new project are set out below. No intergroup sales are expected.

Year	*Sales (HS mn)*	*Profit before royalties (Hs mn)*
1	131	23.6
2	154	29.2
3	181	36.2
4	216	45.2
5	274	57.7
6	331	69.5
7	400	84.1

xv) Accounting and tax regulations converge in Excalibur in connection with allowable write-offs for depreciation. Fixed assets are written off over ten years using the straight-line method.

xvi) In the UK, the interest rate that MAF would have to pay on seven-year debt is estimated at 13% p.a.

xvii) There is no capital gains tax in Excalibur but there is in the UK, where a rate of 33% on realised sterling gains is levied.

xviii) Assume that Excalibur operates the classical tax system and that the UK uses the imputation system. In the UK, assume a basic rate of personal tax at 25%.

Estimate the worth to MAF of the Excalibur project.

Solution:

The steps towards a parent adjusted present value for the Excalibur proposition involve the following:

i) calculation of royalties and loan interest to lead towards a profit-before-tax figure for the Excalibur project (remember that profit before royalties is already given);

ii) calculation of the project net cash flows in local currency terms;
iii) forecast of MAF (Excalibur) dividends and the financing side of the balance sheet to ensure that no further equity input is necessary (remember the 3 to 1 maximum debt/equity ratio);
iv) forecast of exchange rates;
v) forecast of parent cash flows and present value;
vi) calculation of tax shield on debt in sterling terms;
vii) specification of APV from a parent view point.

The steps involved in this process are set out in numerical terms with appropriate footnote explanations where necessary in Tables 1-7.

TABLE 1

MAF EXCALIBUR PROJECT: SCENARIO I - CALCULATION OF PROFIT BEFORE TAX (HS MN)

Year	*Sales*	*Profit before royalty*	*Royalty (5% of sales)*	*Interest payable on*			
				Subsidised debt (10%)	*Parent debt* (12%)*	*New debt** (15%)*	*Profit before tax*
1	131	23.6	6.5	3.1	1.9	—	12.1
2	154	29.2	7.7	2.5	1.9	0.7	16.4
3	181	36.2	9.0	1.9	1.9	1.5	21.9
4	216	45.2	10.8	1.2	1.9	2.3	29.0
5	274	57.7	13.7	0.6	2.0	3.6	37.8
6	331	69.5	16.5			6.9	46.1
7	400	84.1	20.0			7.0	57.1

* The amount of parent debt is £6,031,000 at the exchange rate for year 0. This gives Hs15.5 mn. Interest at 12% on the £ debt gives an interest charge of £724,000 per annum.

** New debt is necessary to balance cash projections in Table 3.

TABLE 2

MAF (EXCALIBUR): SCENARIO I — PROJECT CASH FLOWS (HS MN)

Year	*0*	*1*	*2*	*3*	*4*	*5*	*6*	
Profit before tax		12.1	16.4	21.9	29.0	37.8	46.1	57.1
Tax @ 25%		3.0	4.1	5.5	7.2	9.5	11.5	14.3
Profit after tax		9.1	12.3	16.4	21.8	28.3	34.6	42.8
Depreciation		3.6	3.6	3.6	3.6	3.6	3.6	3.6
Fixed asset expenditure	(35.8)							
Working capital*	(26.2)	(4.6)	(5.4)	(7.0)	(11.6)	(11.4)	(13.8)	
Terminal value								
Equity								214.0
Debt**								33.7
	(62.0)	8.1	10.5	13.0	13.8	20.5	24.4	294.1

* Based on 20% of turnover.

** Based on debt as shown in Table 3.

At a 13% value of k, the above flows clearly produce a substantially positive present value and this is before adding back interest. After all, the 7-year discount factor at 13% is 0.43.

The host country flows are shown in the local currency concerned. They are converted to sterling when appropriate — that is, when remittance is available and flows are logically being calculated in terms of British pounds. The operating flows all remain in the host currency.

TABLE 3

MAF (EXCALIBUR): SCENARIO 1 - FINANCING FORECAST (HS MN)

Year	*0*	*1*	*2*	*3*	*4*	*5*	*6*	*7*
Operating cash flows (see Table 2)	(62.0)	8.1	10.5	13.0	13.8	20.5	24.4	46.4
Dividend - 75% of profit after tax (see Table 2)		(6.8)	(9.2)	(12.3)	(16.3)	(21.3)	(25.9)	(31.1)
Subsidised loan repaid		(6.2)	(6.2)	(6.2)	(6.2)	(6.2)		
Parent loan repaid						(16.4)		
New debt drawn (repaid) to balance figures		4.9	4.9	5.5	8.7	23.4	1.5	(14.3)
Split of financing								
Debt	46.5	45.2	43.9	43.2	45.7	46.5	48.0	33.7
Equity*	15.5	17.8	20.9	25.0	30.5	37.5	46.2	56.9

*Equity increases each year by profit after tax (Table 2) less dividend paid.

In the parent evaluation (see Table 5) we take account of remittable cash flows from Excalibur, rather than the bottom line of cash generation in the host country. This is consistent with the fact that the net cash generation in the host country is not accessible in terms of flows back to the parent.

Table 5 is one of the routes by which the parent obtains remittance from Excalibur. This is via debt interest received from the loan to MAF (Excalibur) and its subsequent repayment. This represents a considerable departure from the rules of domestic capital budgeting. However, it is a genuine technique by which multinationals hasten the transfer of moneys out of blocking host territories and it needs to be reflected in international capital-budgeting analysis. Clearly, it reinforces the idea that financing does affect parent cash flows in capital appraisal when exchange controls create constraints on remittances. An obvious question follows. Why not finance all overseas projects by parent loans? First of all, host countries rarely allow it - part of their exchange controls frequently requires a substantial equity input from the foreign parent. Note the thin capitalisation rules in the MAF case. Secondly, excessive use of parent debt closes a route by which political risk is minimised - namely, the use of local funding.

TABLE 4

MAF CASE: EXCHANGE RATE FORECAST BASED ON PPP

Inflation UK	*6% p.a*	*Inflation UK*	*6% p.a*
Excalibur	*7% p.a.*	*Excalibur*	*7% p.a.*
Initial exchange rate	*2.57*	*Initial exchange rate*	*2.57*
Year	*Hs per £*	*Year*	*Hs per £*
0	2.57	4	2.69
1	2.60	5	2.72
2	2.63	6	2.75
3	2.66	7	2.78

Methodology follows that used in Table 8

There is a difference in the approach to subsidised interest and its present value in the DPM case and in the MAF exercise. Remember that the big difference in environment was that Avalonia had no exchange controls but Excalibur has. In terms of calculating parent cash flows in the DPM case, the path involved specifying remittable flows - before interest - converting these to home currency and calculating a present value. However, because, in this case, flows are looked at before interest, this process fails to identify the effect of subsidised interest - hence the separate routine of calculating it. This was the route followed in the DPM case, but where remittance of cash flows back to the parent is constrained by local regulations (as is the case with MAF) which specify that only a percentage of profits may be remitted as dividend, then the situation is different — and difficult. We are forced to calculate remittable profit by first of all finding profit after tax for MAF (Excalibur), and profit after tax is necessarily after charging interest, including subsidised interest. Thus, doing our calculations on a profit-after-tax basis necessarily takes account of subsidised interest. To calculate it again as a discrete element would be double counting. This always needs to be borne in mind when exchange controls restrict dividends payable.

As in the DPM case, the MAF exercise could also have been solved by using a weighted average approach to the cost of capital. In Table 4 there is a further illustration of the calculation of the tax shield due to debt based on the imputation system.

In this table, the tax shield has been conservatively estimated since it has only been computed using a seven year time horizon. In reality, the project is reckoned to go on beyond year 7 and this is borne out by the terminal value applied. We have calculated a terminal value of the foreign investment based upon a P/E ratio of 5 - see Table 2 — and the UK holding company's sterling value of this derives from translating the foreign currency value at the expected exchange ratio and allowing for a capital gains tax impact. The rationale for the use of a 5 times multiple of earnings is not scientific — it was merely felt that it was a conservative figure. Incidentally, the application of a 13% discount rate (since we are looking at flows in Excalibur, this represents a k^* of 12% as in the UK plus a further 1% for inflation differentials) for a ten year period would give a multiple of 5.43 — and this would be on the assumption of zero growth.

The effect of subsidised interest has already been effectively taken into account because it is chargeable before arriving at Excalibur profits and remittances are constrained to a proportion of post-tax profits in the home country. To take it again as a separate item would be double counting.

Table 5 shows charge against the project full capital cost irrespective of whether it involves funding from the UK or whether local funds are used. Remember that 50% of the project's initial cost comes from local funds and 50% from parent funds. Local financing should not deducted from the initial capital cost as one of the big differences between domestic investment and international capital budgeting — especially when the host restricts remittance - is that the financing can affect remittable cash flows. However, not to count overseas funds used in a project seems excessively liberal. After all, the debt used to fund an overseas subsidiary's project will appear as a liability on the consolidated group accounts. As such, it could realistically be argued that the use of local debt in a project of this kind would tend to crowd out debt-raising possibilities on some other, later project. To give the existing project a free ride seems naive.

TABLE 5

PARENT CASH FLOWS TO MAF (UK) - SCENARIO 1 (£MN)

Year	0	1	2	3	4	5	6	7
Fixed assets	(13.9)							
Working capital initial input	(10.2)							
Royalty receipts before tax		2.5	2.9	3.4	4.0	5.0	6.0	7.2
Tax on royalty at 33%*		(0.8)	(1.0)	(1.1)	(1.3)	(1.7)	(2.0)	(2.4)
Interest (net of tax) and repayment		0.5	0.5	0.5	0.5	0.5		
of parent loan						6.0		
Dividends net of all tax**		2.3	3.1	4.1	5.4	7.0	8.4	10.3
Export profit forgone net of tax***		(4.8)	(5.4)	(5.8)	(6.4)	(7.1)	(7.8)	(8.6)
Terminal value of								
Equity at 5 P/E								
net of capital gains tax §								54.6
Royalties at 5 P/E								24.0
Loss exports at 5 P/E								(43.0)
	(24.1)	(0.3)	0.1	1.1	2.2	9.7	4.6	42.1
Discount at k' of 12%	1.00	0.89	0.80	0.71	0.64	0.57	0.51	0.45
$\Sigma = 4.8$	(24.1)	(0.3)	0.1	0.8	1.4	5..5	2.3	18.9

* Tax payments are not lagged for twelve months in this example. A better simulation of UK tax would involve this sophistication.

** Dividends are based on foreign currency amount as shown in Table 3 converted to UK currency and then subject to UK taxation to bring the effective rate from 25% to 33%.

*** Export profit lost is as given in the question, but it is shown here net of tax.

§ Terminal value of equity is based on local currency figures shown in Table 2 less UK capital gains tax thereon. UK base capital gains value is £24.1mn times 25%. Remember that equity-only funded a quarter is the capital interest. Indexed for inflation, this £6mn becomes £9mn as at year 7. The terminal value before capital gains tax is Hs214mn/2.78 = £77.0mn. Capital gains tax is 33%(77-9) = £22.4mn.

A P/E of 5 has been applied to royalties and lost exports. This seems fair since choice of year 7 as a terminating date seems arbitrary - flows could be expected to go on beyond that date.

TABLE 6

MAF CASE: CALCULATION OF PRESENT VALUE OF TAX SHIELD DUE TO DEBT IN STERLING

Capital cost in year 0	=	£24.1 mn
Estimated debt to capital employed ratio of project		20%
Debt sustainable by project	=	£4.8mn
Gross interest thereon (£mn)		
= 4.8x0.13 = £0.62mn		
Annual amount of the tax shield (£m)	=	£0.62mn (0.33-0.25)
	=	£0.050mn

Present value of the tax shield (£mn)

= £0.050mn x annuity factor for 7 years @ [13%(1 -0.25])

= £0.050mn x 4.91

= £0.25mn

We now calculate the multiplier tax shield effect

Present value created by project	=	£5.1mn
This gives rise to further debt at 20% of		£l.0mn
Gross interest thereon (£mn)		
= 1.0 x 0.13	=	£0.13mn
Annual amount of tax shield (£mn)	=	£0.13mn (0.33 - 0.25)
	=	£0.01
Present value of multiplier tax shield (£mn)		
= £0.01 X 4.91		
= £0.05		
Total tax shield	=	£0.30mn

The calculation as undertaken through Tables 1-7 has been on the grounds that the project, net of dividend payment, is anything but cash positive through the early years of its life. This is borne out by the figuring in Table 3. It will be seen there that the local debt of Hs 31mn has been repaid, but this has been achieved by replacing it with other local debt. Note that the level of debt - see the penultimate line in the table - actually increases over the first six years. This has been made feasible against their capitalisation rules because the equity base has increased - but only in terms of blocked retained earnings. Overall, given the essence of scenario 1 of the MAF case, this is the correct analysis

TABLE 7

MAF CASE: SCENARIO I - ADJUSTED PRESENT VALUE - PARENT STANDPOINT (£MN)

Present value of parent flows excluding tax shield on debt effects (see Table 5)	4.8
Present value of tax shield on debt (see Table 6)	0.3
Adjusted present value - parent standpoint	5.1

To see how project appraisal from a parent viewpoint works when there is potential for local debt repayment from operating flows, the assumptions in MAF (scenario 1) are changed.

METRO ALLIED FOODS (MAF): *A CASE*

(SCENARIO - II)

Under scenario 2, there are two changes to the data in the original MAF case. First of all, the permitted dividend distribution is now equal to 40% of profits after tax. Reflecting this lower distribution level, the parent applies a P/E of 4 in order to obtain a rough approximation of the UK terminal value of overseas operations. Note that the terminal value of royalties and lost exports continues to be evaluated on a P/E of 5. The terminal value to be applied to local operations from an Excalibur standpoint, rather than from a parent viewpoint, is also 5. This means that in the project cash flow evaluation - see Table 9 — the terminal value P/E is 5 but in the parent cash flow evaluation (see Table 12) we use a P/E of 4 - hence 80% of the project cash flow terminal value referred to in footnote 4 of Table 12.

These very minor changes will have the effect of leaving more cash and profit in Excalibur rather than distributing it to the UK. This means that the need to draw down debt to fund sales expansion, which was so much a feature of the MAF case under scenario 1, is not so significant. Indeed, as can be seen from the tables relating to scenario 2, there is progressive repayment of debt during the project's life.

The analysis follows very much the same path as under scenario 1 but with two major differences. The first of these relates to the lower level of distribution to the UK. The second concerns debt repayment. Since local borrowing may be repaid from cash left in Excalibur during the project's life, the present value of this can legitimately be set against parent capital cost. The tables which are designed to achieve the adjusted present value for the MAF project under scenario 2 are now set out. Their route towards this goal takes the following steps.

i) Project profit before tax and royalties is calculated (Table 8). This table is very similar to Table 1 for scenario 1.
ii) The project net cash flows in local currency terms are calculated (Table 9). This table is very similar to Table 2 for scenario 1.

TABLE 8

MAF EXCALIBUR PROJECT: SCENARIO 2 — CALCULATION OF PROFIT BEFORE TAX (HS MN)

Year	*Sales*	*Profit before royalty but after depreciation*	*Royalty (5% of sales) Subsidised debt*	*Interest payable on*			
				Parent debt (10%)	*New debt* (12%)*	*(15%)*	
1	131	23.6	6.5	3.1	1.9	—	12.1
2	154	29.2	7.7	2.5	1.9	0.3	16.8
3	181	36.2	9.0	1.9	1.9	0.4	23.0
4	216	45.2	10.8	1.2	1.9	0.2	31.1
5	274	57.7	13.7	0.6	2.0	0.3	41.1

6	331	69.5	16.5		2.0	51.0
7	400	84.1	20.0			64.1

* New debt is necessary to balance cash projections shown in Table 10

TABLE 9

MAF (EXCALIBUR): SCENARIO 2 - PROJECT CASH FLOWS (HS M)

Year	0	1	2	3	4	5	6	7
Profit before tax		12.1	16.8	23.0	31.1	41.1	51.0	64.1
Tax @ 25%		3.0	4.2	5.7	7.8	10.3	12.7	16.0
Profit after tax		9.1	12.6	17.3	23.3	30.8	38.3	48.1
Depreciation		3.6	3.6	3.6	3.6	3.6	3.6	3.6
Fixed asset expenditure	(35.8)							
Working capital*	(26.2)	(4.6)	(5.4)	(7.0)	(11.6)	(11.4)	(13.8)	
Terminal value								
Equity								240.5
Debt**								—
	(62.0)	8.1	10.8	13.9	15.3	23.0	28.1	292.2

* Based on 20% of turnover,

** Based on debt as shown in Table 10.

At a 13% value of k^*, the above flows clearly produce a substantially positive present value and this is before adding back interest. After all the 7-year discount factor at 13% is 0.43.

iii) MAF (Excalibur) dividends and financing side of the balance sheet are forecast to ensure that the debt to equity ratio remains within the 3 to 1 constraint and to identify local debt repayment (Table 10). This table is similar to Table 3 for scenario 1.

TABLE 10

MAF (EXCALIBUR): SCENARIO 2 - FINANCING FORECAST (HS MN)

Year	*0*	*1*	2	3	4	5	6	7
Operating cash flows (see Table 9)	(62.0)	8.1	10.8	13.9	15.3	23.0	28.1	51.7
Dividend - 40% of profit after tax (see Table 9)		(3.6)	(5.0)	(6.9)	(9.3)	(12.4)	(15.3)	(19.2)
Subsidised loan repaid		(6.2)	(6.2)	(6.2)	(6.2)	(6.2)		
Parent loan repaid						(16.4)		
New debt drawn (repaid) to balance figures		1.7	0.4	(0.8)	0.2	11.8	(12.4)	—
Cash deposited	—	—	—	—	—	—	0.4	32.5
Split of financing								
Debt	46.5	42.0	36.2	29.2	23.2	12.4	—	—
Equity*	15.5	21.0	28.6	39.0	53.0	71.4	104.4	133.3

* Equity increases each year by profit after tax (Table 9) less dividend paid.

iv) Local debt repayment that can be achieved from local cash generation is forecast (Table 11). This table needs careful study. It culminates in specification of the present value, in sterling terms, of local loan repayments. For reasons stated earlier, it is contended that this is logically part of MAF (Excalibur)'s present value seen from the parent's point of view. Note that net-of-tax debt service is discounted at a net-of-tax discount rate.

TABLE 11

MAF (EXCALIBUR): SCENARIO 2 - PRESENT VALUE OF LOCAL DEBT REPAYMENT

(a) Debt service according to loan agreement (Hs mn)

Year	*Capital*	*Interest gross of tax*	*Interest net of tax at 25%*	*Total debt service (net of tax)*
1	6.2	3.1	2.3	8.5
2	6.2	2.5	1.9	8.1
3	6.2	1.9	1.4	7.6
4	6.2	1.2	0.9	7.1
5	6.2	0.6	0.4	6.6
	31.0	9.3	6.9	37.9

(b) Actual cash generated and available for loan repayment (Hs mn). Data available from Table 10.

Year	*Operating Cash flows*	*Dividend*	*Parent loan repaid*	*Available*
1	6.2	3.1	2.3	8.5
1	8.1	3.6	—	4.5
2	10.8	5.0	—	5.8
3	13.9	6.9	—	7.0
4	15.3	9.3	—	6.0
5	23.0	12.4	16.3	(5.7)
6	28.1	15.3	—	12.8
7	51.7	19.2	—	32.5

(c) Debt service costs amount to Hs37.9mn net of tax in respect of local borrowings - see (a) above. The first Hs37.9mn generated under (b) above are available, subject to their not exceeding cumulatively on a per annum basis the figures in the right-hand column of (a). Therefore repayment out of cash generation is possible as below.

Year	*Debt service from cash flow (Hs mn)*	*Discount at local market rate of (net of tax) 11¼ (15% less 25% thereof)*	
		Factor	*Present value (Hs mn)*
1	4.5	0.90	3.9
2	5.8	0.81	4.7

3	7.0	0.73	5.1
4	6.0	0.65	3.9
5	(5.7)	0.58	(3.3)
6	12.8	0.53	6.8
7	7.4	0.47	3.5
	37.8		24.6

(d) Present value of loan repayments out of cash flow is seen to be Hs24.6mn. In sterling terms this may be converted at the year 0 exchange rate of 2.57, thus:

$$\text{Sterling present value of loan service} = \frac{24.6}{2.57} = £9.6\text{mn}$$

v) The forecast of the exchange rate remains as per Table 4 for scenario 1.

vi) Table 12 shows the forecast of parent cash flows incorporating the present value of local currency loan repayments. With this exception, plus the terminal value being based on a 4 P/E, this table compares with Table 5 for scenario 1.

vii) Calculation of the sterling present value of the tax shield due to debt which is supportable by the project remains as for Table 6. This assumes that a project with a lower dividend remittance level can support the same level as one with a higher remittance level.

viii) The APV is specified from a parent view point (see Table 13). This table compares with Table 7 for scenario 1.

TABLE 12

PARENT CASH FLOWS TO MAF (UK) - SCENARIO 2 (£MN)

Year	*0*	*1*	*2*	*3*	*4*	*5*	*6*	*7*
Fixed assets	(13.9)							
Working capital initial input	(10.2)							
Royalty receipts before tax		2.5	2.9	3.4	4.0	5.0	6.0	7.2
Tax on royalty at 33%*		(0.8)	(1.0)	(1.1)	(1.3)	(1.7)	(2.0)	(2.4)
Interest (net of tax) and repayment of parent loan		0.5	0.5	0.5	0.5	0.5 6.0		
Dividends net of all tax**		1.2	1.7	2.2	2.9	3.7	4.5	5.5
Export profit forgone net of tax***		(4.8)	(5.4)	(5.8)	(6.4)	(7.1)	(7.8)	(8.6)
Present value of local debt repaid (see Table 11)	9.6							
Terminal value of								
Equity at 4 P/E net of capital gains tax§								49.3
Royalties at 5 P/E								24.0
Loss exports at 5 P/E								(43.0)
	(14.5)	(1.4)	(1.3)	(0.8)	(0.3)	6.4	0.7	32.0
Discount at k* of 12%	1.00	0.89	0.80	0.71	0.64	0.57	0.51	0.45
	(14.5)	(1.2)	(1.0)	(0.6)	(0.2)	3.6	0.4	14.4

$\Sigma = 0.9$

* Tax payments are not lagged for twelve months in this example. A better simulation of UK tax would involve this sophistication.

** Dividends are based on foreign currency amount as shown in Table 10 converted to UK currency and then subject to UK taxation to bring the effective rate from 25 to 33%.

*** Export profit lost is as given in the question, but it is shown here net of tax.

§ Terminal value of equity is based on 80% of local currency figures shown in Table 9 less UK capital gains tax thereon. UK base capital gains value is £24.1mn times 25%. Remember that equity only funded a quarter is the capital interest. Indexed for inflation, this £6mn becomes £9mn as at year 7. The terminal value before capital gains tax Hs 192 mn/2.78 = £69.1 mn. Capital gains tax is 33%(69.1 - 9) = £ 19.8mn.

A P/E of 5 has been applied to royalties and lost exports. This seems fair since choice of year 7 as a terminating date seems arbitrary - flows could be expected to on beyond that date.

In connection with scenario 2 of the MAF project, there are a number of points worth considering. The first five tables are plain sailing. The choppy waters begin with Table 11, the calculation of the parent value of debt. Note that the project fails to generate sufficient cash to cover local debt service in each year of operations. Therefore what has been done is to specify net cash thrown off. Debt service totals Hs37.8mn net of taxes. The first Hs37.8mn remaining out of cash thrown off is available for debt service (without having to draw down more debt to achieve this). We have to go out to year 7 to service debt out of uncommitted cash flow. The present value of this stream is calculated and then converted to sterling. This present value is penalised because a debt repayable over five years has to be stretched to seven in terms of its coverage out of net cash thrown off by the project. On the other hand, it is bolstered because of its subsidised nature. Remember that it carries a 10% interest rate versus a 15% market rate - it is this latter rate, after allowing for tax, that has been used to calculate the present value of the loan. After all, net-of-tax debt service should be discounted at the net-of-tax interest rate.

TABLE 13

MAF CASE: SCENARIO 2—ADJUSTED PRESENT VALUE - PARENT STANDPOINT (£MN)

Present value of parent flows excluding tax shield on debt effects (see Table 12)	0.9
Present value of tax shield on debt (see Table 6)	0.3
Adjusted present value - parent standpoint	1.2

The effect of subsidised interest has already been taken into account because it is chargeable before arriving at Excalibur profits. Remittances are constrained to a proportion of post-tax profits in the home country, on the one hand, and on the other the calculations in Table 11 charge interest at 10%, the rate actually paid, but the present value has been computed using a market discount rate of 15%.

Table 11 should present few problems because of its similarity to Table 5 in scenario 1, and Table 13 merely summarises the financial analysis for scenario 2 showing the adjusted present value as £1.2mn.

33

INTERNATIONAL MERGERS, ACQUISITIONS AND DIVESTURES

INTRODUCTION

Cross-border M&As are playing an increasingly important role in the growth of international production. Not only do they dominate FDI flows in developed countries, they have also begun to take hold as a mode of entry into developing countries and economies in transition. The reasons for, and the full extent of, the world-wide growth of cross-border M&As have not yet been fully explored, nor have the implications of this shift in the preference of TNCs regarding the choice of entry mode for expanding internationally been considered in a systematic fashion.

DEFINITIONS AND CLASSIFICATIONS

A firm can undertake FDI in a host country in either of two ways: greenfield investment in a new facility, or acquiring or merging with an existing local firm The local firm may be privately or state owned: privatisations involving foreign investors count as cross-border M&As, which entail a change in the control of the merged or acquired firm. In a cross-border merger, the assets and operations of two firms belonging to two different countries are combined to establish a new legal entity. In a cross-border acquisition, the control of assets and operations is transferred from a local to a foreign company, the former becoming an affiliate of the latter. Figure-1 presents the structure of cross border M&As.

To the extent that both greenfield investment and cross-border M&As place host country assets under the governance of TNCs — and, hence, contribute to the growth of an international production system — there is no reason to distinguish between them. Both involve management control of a resident entity in one country by an enterprise resident in another. To the extent, however, that the assets placed under TNC control are newly created in the case of greenfield FDI, and existing assets are transferred from one owner to another in the case of cross-border M&As, then there is reason to consider them separately. The normal definitions of FDI apply to entry through M&As as well. The country of the acquirer or purchaser is the "home country" and the country of the target or acquired firm is the "host country or in one". In mergers, the headquarters of the new firm can be in both countries. Acquisitions can be minority (foreign interest of 10 to 49 per cent of a firm's voting shares), majority (foreign interest of 50-99 per cent), or full or outright acquisitions (foreign interest of 100 per cent). Acquisitions involving less than 10 per cent constitute portfolio investment. Portfolio investment is usually associated with purely financial investment. However, the distinction between portfolio and direct investments is not always obvious. While FDI involves a long-term relationship reflecting an investor's lasting interest in a foreign company, portfolio acquisitions can also involve management control, e.g. if there are accompanying nonequity arrangements, especially where non-institutional investors are involved.

Cross-border M&As can be **functionally** classified as:

i) *Horizontal* M&As (between competing firms in the same industry). They have grown rapidly recently because of the global restructuring of many industries in response to technological change and liberalisation. By consolidating their resources, the merging firms aim to achieve synergies (the value of their combined assets exceeds the sum of their assets taken separately) and often greater market power. Typical industries in which such M&As occur are pharmaceuticals, automobiles, petroleum and, increasingly, several services industries.

ii) *Vertical* M&As (between firms in client-supplier or buyer-seller relationships). Typically they seek to reduce uncertainty and transaction costs as regards forward and backward linkages in the production chain, and to benefit from economies of scope. M&As between parts and components makers and their clients (such as final electronics or automobile manufacturers) are good examples.

iii) *Conglomerate* M&As (between companies in unrelated activities). They seek to diversify risk and deepen economies of scope.

Cross-border M&As may also be classified differently:

- M&As can be driven primarily by short-term financial gains, rather than strategic or economic motivations such as the search for efficiency. Typical examples include deals where buy out firms and venture capital companies acquire other firms.
- Friendly M&As can be distinguished from those that are hostile. In friendly M&As, the board of a target firm agrees to the transaction. (This does not exclude the possibility that, initially, the management of the target firm was against the transaction.) Hostile M&As are undertaken against the wishes of the target firms, i.e. the boards of the latter reject takeover/merger offers. Regardless of whether hostile M&As involve bidding by several prospective acquirers, the price premium tends to be higher than in friendly transactions. The overwhelming number of M&As, both domestic and international, are friendly. In case of hostile acquisitions, generally the target companies develop various defence mechanisms, including *"poison pills"*, selling off *"crown jewels"* and calling in *"white knights"* to avoid becoming a target (see Box-1).

BOX-1

POISON PILLS AND OTHER DEFENCE MECHANISMS

Companies adopt various measures to avoid takeovers. Poison pills are used by companies that fear hostile takeovers to ensure that a bid, if successful, will trigger events that will significantly reduce the value of the firm. For instance, *flip-in* poison pills allow all existing holders of target company shares to buy additional shares at a bargain price. *Flip-over* poison pills allow holders of common stock to buy (or holders of preferred stock to convert into) the acquirer's shares at a bargain price. This defence measure has been installed in many companies, in particular United States companies. Although it is not certain how much poison pills alone have contributed to the low number of hostile takeovers, they have forced raiders to negotiate with the board of target firms to agree to a fair market price for the acquired firms's shares.

Another type of defense mechanism is when a target company warns an acquirer that, in the event of a successful takeover, the entire management team will resign at once, leaving the company without experienced leadership.

Other measures include selling off "crown jewels" (dilute the intention of the acquirer by selling the assets of a target frim to a third party); and calling in "white knights" (find a more preferable firm and ask it to acquire the target firm).

WHY DO FIRMS ENGAGE IN CROSS-BORDER M&As?

Why are firms increasingly engaging in cross-border M&As when undertaking FDI? Although cross-border M&As represent one mode of FDI entry into foreign locations, the received literature on international production can only partly explain this phenomenon. Indeed, the "OLI paradigm" — the most prominent explanation of FDI — does not distinguish between different modes of entry and was formulated primarily in reference to greenfield FDI (box 2). Thus, it is useful to consider first the basis reasons for M&As in general, and for cross-border M&As in particular.

1. MOTIVATIONS FOR CONDUCTING M&As

To explain why firms may prefer to grow via M&As rather than through organic growth, two factors stand out as being particularly important: *speed* and *access* to proprietary assets.

Speed is crucial. M&As often represent the fastest means of reaching the desired goals when expanding domestically or internationally. For example, when time to market is vital, the takeover of an existing firm in a new market with an established distribution system is far more preferable to developing a new local distribution and marketing organisation. For a latecomer to a market or a new field of technology, M&As can provide a way to catch up rapidly. Enhanced competition and shorter product life cycles accentuate the necessity for firms to respond quickly to opportunities in the economic environment, preferably before competitors move. The pressure of time and the feeling of urgency are highlighted in the observations often made in the business slogan that *Speed is our friend— time is our enemy*. While erstwhile planning may have taken place in five-year intervals, the watchword today is *"plaction"*— plan and act at once.

The second main motivation for firms to merge with or acquire an existing company, rather than to grow organically, is the *quest for strategic assets*, such as R&D

or technical know-how, patents, brand names, the possession of local permits and licences, and supplier or distribution networks. Ready made access to proprietary assets can be important because, by definition, they are not available elsewhere in the market and they take time to develop.

BOX–2

THE OLI PARADIGM AND CROSS-BORDER M&AS

The OLI paradigm (Dunning, 1993). addresses *three questions* related to FDI:

Which firms undertake FDI? Firms investing abroad must possess specific proprietary or ownership ("O") advantages to overcome the extra costs of operating in a different, less familiar environment. These advantages are generally costly to create, but can be transferred to new locations at relatively low cost. The analysis of "O" advantages draws on industrial organisation, resource based, evolutionary and management theories, with advantages residing mainly in firm-specific technology, brand names, privileged access to factor or product markets or superior technological or management skills. Initial "O" advantages allow firms to grow and invest abroad, but size and international spread can, in turn, feed back and provide new advantages (accessing capital markets and information, spreading risks and so on). In some cases, firms may go overseas to supplement or enhance their existing "O" assets ("asset-seeking" FDI) seeking synergies between their own strengths and those of foreign firms or institutions.

Where do firms choose to exploit their advantages, in the home country (by exports) or abroad, and in which foreign locations? They select sites with location ("L") advantages that best match the deployment of their "0" assets. The analysis of "L" advantages draws on trade and location theory, the main factors determining comparative costs being factor and transport costs, market size and characteristics, and government policies (e.g. stability, predictability, tariffs, taxes and FDI regulations). Asset-seeking FDI is drawn to locations with strong technological, educational or information creation activities.

Why do firms choose to internalize their advantages by direct investment in preference to selling them to other firms? The analysis of internalisation ("I") draws on transaction-cost theories of the firm, and centres on the feasibility of and returns to contracting the sale of intangible advantages to other firms. The most valuable and new advantages tend to be internalized, since these are the most difficult to price and contract over time. The more mature ones are easier to price, less" subject to uncertainty and less valuable to the owner: these are licensed more readily. Internalisation can also explain vertical FDI, where a particular process or function is located abroad by TNCs to serve its production system (rather than subcontracted to independent suppliers). Transaction-cost analysis can also help explain why it is difficult or costly to contract independent firms for such arrangements, particularly in technology-intensive or strategic activities.

While the paradigm does not explicitly distinguish between different modes of FDI entry, the origins of the paradigm were more in greenfield investments than M&As. On the "ownership" side, the original thesis on which it draws explained the growth of United States companies in terms of an industrial organisation analysis of barriers to entry in setting up new facilities (Hymer, 1960). The extension made to multi-plant operations again was conceived in terms of firms setting up new plants. The "internalisation" analysis was based upon work explaining how firm boundaries were drawn in terms of the costs of hierarchical control (internalisation) versus market control (externalisation) of their assets. The implicit setting was the expansion of firms by the building of new facilities rather than the joint internalisation of assets by different firms involved in M&As. With regard to international investment in developing host countries, the analysis was entirely conducted in terms of greenfield FDI. Until recently, cross-border M&As in these countries were rare.

It is therefore useful to consider OLI factors specifically for M&As, and to distinguish mergers from acquisitions (table: A-1). Mergers are taken to involve firms of roughly similar size and capacity that jointly internalize their "ownership" advantages to gain economies of synergy, size and scope. Acquisitions are taken to involve larger, more powerful or better capitalized firms taking over smaller or weaker ones, and using this to gain speedy access to the latter's "ownership" and "locational" assets. The OLI factors can be considered separately for the three main types of M&As (horizontal, vertical and conglomerate), bearing in mind that horizontal transactions account for nearly two-thirds of cross-border M&A activity.

TABLE A-1

THE OLI PARADIGM AND CROSS-BORDER M&AS

Type	*Horizontal*	*Vertical*	*Conglomerate*
Mergers	*O:* Both firms have O advantages complementing each other in scale, synergy, finance or market power. *L:* Standard location factors are not relevant where two TNCs merge their global production systems. *I:* Both firms seek to gain economies of scale by internalizing joint advantages. Joint internalisation differs from "internalisation" in usual OLI terms, but determinants (transaction costs in some sense) are similar. Mergers provide a much faster way of exploiting each other's advantages.	*O:* Both firms have O advantages that complement each other in different processes of the production chain. *L:* As with greenfield FDI, but also see horizontal mergers. *I:* Merging firms both seek to gain security, information, finance or market power, and to reduce transaction costs.	*O:* Both firms have O advantages in unrelated activities that may have economies of scope, but not technological complementarity. A merger is thus not based on O advantages in the usual sense; it may just involve access to finance. *L:* Mainly market size/growth or prospects of capital appreciation, not location advantages in the OLI sense. *I:* Merging firms seek a larger capital base or economies of scope, but are not internalizing their O assets to save on transaction costs.
Acquisitions	*O:* Acquiring firms tend to have greater O advantages than acquired firms, or seek specific new O advantages (technology, contacts, etc.). *L:* As with greenfield FDI, except that many L advantages are "embodied" in the acquired firm. *I:* As with greenfield FDI, acquiring firms strengthen their competitive positions by internalisation.	*O:* Acquiring firms have a stronger financial or managerial base that allows them to acquire vertically linked firms abroad. *L:* As with horizontal acquisitions. *I:* As with greenfield FDI, acquiring firms strengthen their competitive positions by internalisation.	*O:* Acquiring firms have greater financial and/or managerial resources, but no O advantages in the usual sense. *L:* Mainly market size and growth and prospects of capital appreciation, not location advantages. *I:* Acquiring firms seek diversification or economies of scope, but are not internalizing in an OLI sense.

Cross-border M&As and their characteristics call for an adaptation of the conventional analysis. The fact that M&As allow investors much faster access to, or offer new, ownership advantages accounts partly for their growing use in the current international competitive environment. The internalisation factors are also different in that there is *joint* internalisation, particularly in M&As between similar firms. In addition, the traditional OLI paradigm does not take into account non-economic, explanations, such as personal motivations of managers or corporate responses under strategic interdependence. The traditional OLI analysis of locational factors is thus not particularly relevant in explaining mega mergers between TNCs, pooling not only their ownership-specific advantages, but also the global locational advantages of their worldwide production networks. The framework can still be applied to acquisitions by more advanced firms of less advanced ones — and so to FDI flows from developed to developing countries or economies in transition.

Such assets may be crucial to advance a firm's *static* advantages, i.e. its income-generating resources and capabilities at a given moment in time, or to strengthen its *dynamic* advantages, i.e. its ability to sustain and increase the income-generating assets over time. To take just one example of where the need for speed — the alternative between "build" or "buy" — and the search for proprietary assets came together: the main reason for the Indian company Tata Tea to acquire Tetley Ltd. in the United Kingdom was to obtain access to a global brand name and a global distribution network; reaching the same objective through organic growth would have been more or less impossible. To quote Tata Tea's Vice-Chairman who engineered the acquisition: *For us to develop a global market in the time frame we had in mind, the acquisition of Tetley, with its brand name and distribution system, was the only option.*

These two main advantages of M&As interact with a number of other driving forces, which play out differently in different industries and markets, and which often simultaneously affect the decision to undertake M&As. Many of the driving forces listed below can also motivate FDI in general, but, when speed enters the picture, they tend to favour M&As, as the objectives sought for can be realized more quickly:

i) The ***search for new markets and market power*** is a constant concern for firms. Where domestic markets are saturated, in particular, foreign ones beckon. High transaction costs associated with arm's-length transactions involving intangible assets may explain why firms possessing ownership specific capabilities often prefer to exert direct control (instead of exporting or licensing) when exploiting them in new geographical locations or industry segments. Through M&As, firms can quickly access new market opportunities and develop critical mass without adding additional capacity to an industry. By taking over an existing company, immediate access to a local network of suppliers, clients and skills can be obtained. This motivation is of particular importance for cross-border M&As as the need for knowledge about local conditions increases when leaving the home market. Beyond this, and especially in markets characterized by oligopoly, M&As can also be motivated by the pursuit for market power and *market dominance.* Especially in the case of horizontal M&As, the motivation can well be the search for oligopolistic positions; in addition, consolidated market control may provide opportunities for anti-competitive practices and increased barriers to entry.

ii) Anticipated ***efficiency gains*** *through synergies* are probably the most cited justification for M&As. Synergies can be static (cost reduction or revenue enhancement at a given point in time) or dynamic (e.g. innovation-enhancing) in character. Examples of the former kind of synergies include the pooling of management resources (one head office instead of two), revenue enhancement by using each others' marketing and distribution networks, purchasing synergies (greater bargaining power), economies of scale in production leading to cost reductions, and the avoidance of duplication of production, R&D or other activities. Dynamic synergies may involve the matching of complementary resources and skills to enhance a firm's innovatory capabilities with long-term positive effects on sales, market shares and profits. The search for static synergies may be particularly important in industries characterized by increased competitive pressure, falling prices and excess capacity, such as in the automotive and defence industries. Meanwhile, dynamic synergies may be crucial in industries experiencing fast technological change and that are innovation-driven, such as in information technology and pharmaceuticals. The efficiency-through-synergy motive is present for both domestic and cross-border M&As. However, the scope for rationalisation and improving company performance by achieving an international specialisation of the value chain can be particularly high in the case of cross-border investments that allow firms to locate different activities in places with appropriate mixes of locational advantages.

iii) In a globalizing economy, ***greater size*** can be a crucial parameter, particularly in operations requiring economies of scale, large expenditures for R&D and the expansion of distribution networks for example. Size in itself can also make it more difficult to be taken over and, therefore, can have a protective' function. Large size can furthermore create financial, managerial and operational synergies that reduce the operational vulnerability of firms. Sheer size normally means lower-cost access to investible funds as there are economies of scale in capital raising. Information asymmetries between corporate insiders and investors can make internal financing more favourable. A company can use its internal capital market by letting cash rich divisions with few profitable projects finance capital expenditures in cash poor divisions with better growth opportunities. Another advantage of size is that larger firms with multiple operations across geographical locations and segments can have an advantage in the collection and adoption of new information and innovation. The size motive can apply to both domestic and cross-border M&As.

iv) A fourth driver behind M&As is the desire for risk reduction (operational risks, foreign exchange risks, etc.) through product or geographical market ***diversification***. Firms may make cross-border M&As on the basis that industry returns across countries may be less correlated than within an economy. By acquiring foreign companies, a firm may be able to circumvent tariff and non-tariff barriers and thereby lower the level of uncertainty. As intensified global competition and rapid technology development have led firms to focus on their core activities, however, the product diversification motive has become less important although geographical diversification plays a role.

v) There can be important ***financial motives*** behind M&As. Stock prices do not always reflect the true value of a firm. A potential acquirer can, for example, value a company's anticipated earnings stream higher than current shareholders do. Bad management of a firm, imperfections in the capital market and major exchange rate realignments may provide short-term capital gains to be made by acquiring an undervalued firm, or affect the timing of planned M&As. Such motivations are particularly important in the case of portfolio-type M&As and in economies with poorly developed capital markets or in financial crisis. In addition, some M&As are undertaken partly for tax considerations, e.g. to exploit unused tax shields.

The ***personal gains (or behavioural)*** explanation argues that corporate managers pursue their own self-interest, especially where corporate governance is weak (a manifestation of what economists have denoted the principal-agent problem). They may seek expansion or empire building to enhance executives' power, prestige, job-security or remuneration, even when this is not technically efficient or in the interest of shareholders. They can also be under the pressure of financial markets — especially where double-digit growth rates are considered the norm — to show high growth and profit rates; M&As can provide the easiest route in this respect, compared to organic greenfield investment growth. Individual managers may also overestimate their ability to manage acquisitions and think that they are especially well equipped to make a merger-deal work.

The factors discussed so far basically apply to both domestic and cross-border M&As. While all factors are important to consider when explaining why firms undertake cross-border M&As, it is seldom only one factor that is decisive. In fact, mergers occur for a myriad of reasons, and in any given case, several different motives may simultaneously influence the merging parties' behavior.

2. CHANGES IN THE ECONOMIC ENVIRONMENT

The acquisition behaviour of firms is also greatly affected by changes in the economic and regulatory environment and, when it comes to cross-border M&As, by the international economic and regulatory environment. Some of the major changes — as regards technology, the regulatory framework and capital markets — that have taken place in the past decade and that have facilitated cross-border M&As and, indeed, encouraged firms to pursue them are discussed below:

Technology

The rapid pace of technological change has intensified competitive pressures on the world's technology leaders. Consequently, the costs and risks of innovation have risen in most industries, as has the need to incorporate continuously new technologies and management practices. Firms thus need more efforts to maintain innovative leads, to find new areas of technological leadership, and to keep up with new knowledge and shorter product-life cycles. In an environment characterized by rapid technological change and rising expenditures for risky R&D projects, many firms feel compelled to enter into cross-border M&As as a way of sharing the costs of innovation and accessing new technological assets to enhance their innovatory capabilities. M&As allow firms to do this quickly. Such asset-seeking FDI by TNCs from developed (and increasingly from developing) countries is a rising form of FDI. It is likely to become more common as intangible, knowledge-based assets and access to a pool of skilled people and work teams become more important in the world economy.

But technological developments also have other implications. Some of the most important changes relate to the new information and communication technologies. They enable a better management of operations distributed worldwide, and provide new ways of organizing contacts within and between firms as well as with consumers. The use of electronic commerce, for example, makes it possible to restructure the supply chain and reduces the costs of reaching large consumer markets. By lowering transport, information-access and communication costs, technical progress has dramatically shrunk economic space. One result is more intense competition, as foreign competitors may be able to deliver goods and services more cheaply, technologies are diffused more rapidly and information is more broadly available. Another, however, is that TNCs can compete more effectively. They can communicate better across their international production systems, transfer goods and personnel across borders more cheaply and break up production and management processes to locate sub-processes in different countries to minimize cost. Even between different headquarters operations — finance, strategy, R&D, design, marketing — locational links are being loosened, as some TNCs place some of these operations in dispersed sites.

Technological change thus has an impact on the size of firms, reduces costs and facilitates better management of far-flung transnational operations. It allows new management systems to be applied more effectively across the globe, and makes globally integrated production systems more feasible and cost-effective. Cross-border M&As play a critical role in allowing TNCs to set up and expand these systems to develop a portfolio of locational assets. As a result, too, TNCs gain more experience in "digesting" acquired enterprises into existing corporate systems which, in turn, makes the M&A route more enticing than before.

Changes in the Policy and Regulatory Environment

If the crucial role of technology makes asset-seeking FDI "more important and technological changes have facilitated the operation of international production systems, changes in the policy and regulatory environment during the past decade have provided more space for these systems to expand, including through M&As. Key here are the liberalisation of FDI and trade regimes, regional economic integration, privatisation and the deregulation of various industries.

(i) Policies on FDI and Cross-border M&As

The liberalisation of FDI regimes has continued apace, typically on a unilateral basis. Most countries are now trying to attract direct investment, not just by removing restrictions, but also through active promotion and by providing high standards of treatment, legal protection and guarantees. Examples of such changes relevant to M&As include the removal of compulsory joint venture requirements, restrictions on majority ownership and authorisation requirements. The international regulatory framework has also been strengthened, especially through the conclusion of bilateral investment protection and double taxation treaties. Multilateral agreements support these trends. For instance, WTO agreements limit the use of certain investment-related measures that affect trade, like local content requirements on TNCs, and certain types of export requirements. World Bank and IMF programmes encourage countries to adopt more open, transparent and welcoming regimes towards foreign investors.

As FDI regimes typically apply to both greenfield investment and cross-border M&As, the latter have also been facilitated by FDI policy liberalisation in developed and developing countries. Generally, most laws dealing with FDI do not explicitly make a distinction between greenfield investment and M&As. When industries are removed from closed lists, both forms of FDI are typically permitted; and when restrictions on foreign ownership are removed, majority acquisitions of domestic firms are also allowed. Within this overall trend, however, a number of host countries have various policy instruments to deal with cross-border M&As, including special authorisation requirements for cross-border M&As under their FDI laws. Some countries also have instruments to screen cross-border M&As for particular purposes, e.g. national security considerations. Moreover, governments may reserve the right to approve some proposed investment projects and reject or modify others to preserve important public interests. Furthermore, when governments screen FDI projects, it may well be that more greenfield proposals have been approved than M&As; but as the relevant bodies do not normally publish their results and reasoning, no precise conclusions are possible. Finally, governments have sometimes kept "golden shares" in privatized companies in order to be able to preserve essential strategic interests; golden shares have been used to veto undesirable further changes in ownership and control of the privatized company.

(ii) Other Changes in the Regulatory Environment

Trade liberalisation gathered pace in the 1990s with the conclusion of the Uruguay Round. The cumulative effect has been a radical change in the signals and competitive setting for international investors. Firms now face more intense competition at home as well as abroad.

The formation of regional free trade areas has facilitated both greenfield investment and cross-border M&As in several ways. Regional trade agreements enlarge the size of the immediately accessible market for firms, and so attract foreign investors to serve them by setting up new facilities. They can enhance market transparency and, if they link national currencies, lower the costs of cross-border transactions. If they incorporate investment agreements, they make M&As more feasible. From a TNC perspective, the need to establish a local presence is particularly strong if an integrating area sets up high common external tariffs; but even low external barriers to trade can be a powerful magnet in rich or expansive regional markets. The formation of the European Community, for instance, provided a major stimulus to inward FDI and promoted restructuring by national, regional (intra-EU) and cross-border (non-EU) M&As. The initial impetus was greatly strengthened by the creation of a single market and, more recently, the launch of the Euro, which adds to competitive pressures and to the restructuring of previously segmented markets. Increased competition underlines the role of rapid responses by companies, thus favouring cross-border M&As in particular. Regional trade agreements in the developing world, like ASEAN in South-East Asia and MERCOSUR in Latin America, are stimulating similar restructuring, even if the markets involved are not as large and the integration processes less intense.

In parallel with trade liberalisation and regional integration processes, there has been widespread *privatisation* and *deregulation* of activities, most notably in such service industries as telecommunications, transportation, power generation and financial services. These changes have provided another stimulus to M&As in general and cross-border ones in particular. Privatisation programmes in many developing countries and economies in transition have increased the availability of domestic companies for sale. In fact, the combination of privatisation and deregulation has created a number of new TNCs. Previously state-owned utility companies, for example, facing new competitive pressures at home, have responded by becoming dynamic international investors. In Europe, activities that have long been strongly homebound, like water supply, power generation, rail transports, telecommunications, and airport construction, are now populated by transnational operators. The first wave of expansion (with foreign participation in privatisation) is being followed by further consolidation and restructuring, with M&As again set to play a vital role.

(iii) Changes in Capital Markets

Cross-border M&As have been facilitated by changes in world capital markets. The liberalisation of capital movements, new information technology providing instant information across the globe, more active market intermediaries, and new financial instruments have had a profound impact on M&A activity worldwide.

The increased use of cross-border M&As mirrors changes in the market for corporate ownership. The number of available targets, both among publicly listed and non-listed firms, is rising. Financial advisors have been expanding their operations and are more widely presenting potential "deal opportunities" to prospective clients. Corporate executives are also under increased pressure from the stock market to participate actively in the global restructuring process to seize potential opportunities. This combines with new ways of financing major transactions. The liberalisation of foreign equity ownership has facilitated M&As based on stock swaps rather than cash deals. Major M&As have also been facilitated by the rise of stock markets and ample liquidity in capital markets, which has allowed firms to raise large amounts of money through banks and bond issues. This was accentuated by the introduction of the Euro, which has created a liquid market in European corporate bonds. Companies are increasingly issuing Euro-denominated bonds to refinance debt and to raise money for takeovers.

A Secular Trend

M&As are part of a process of regional and global restructuring, in which actions by national and international policy-makers trigger responses by firms and vice versa. While this process is far from complete and its incidence is highly uneven, its direction is quite clear. The major changes that have simultaneously taken place in the international business environment have profoundly affected the setting in which firms are operating and have provided new and expanded business opportunities, as well as risks.

The advent of the internet has added to this as it stimulates M&A activity between "old economy" and "new economy" firms in search of opportunities and as it may lead firms to try to find new solutions to some of the problems to which M&As have traditionally represented the solution. An example is the business-to-business exchanges, which may be akin to functional mergers.

In this new and continuously evolving environment, the key strategic issue for firms becomes how to survive and prosper, knowing that there is a market for firms and that sanctions await them if they fail to deliver growth and profits. One such sanction is to be taken over. All the basic motivations for firms to undertake cross-border M&As then combine to become key elements in the overarching strategic goal to defend and develop competitive positions. Cross-border M&As are growing so rapidly in importance precisely because they provide firms with the fastest way of acquiring tangible and intangible assets in different countries, and because they allow firms to restructure existing operations nationally or globally to exploit synergies and obtain strategic advantages. In brief, cross-border M&As allow firms rapidly to acquire a portfolio of locational assets, which has become a key source of competitive strength in a globalizing economy.

FIGURE-2

THE DRIVING FORCES OF CROSS-BORDER M&AS

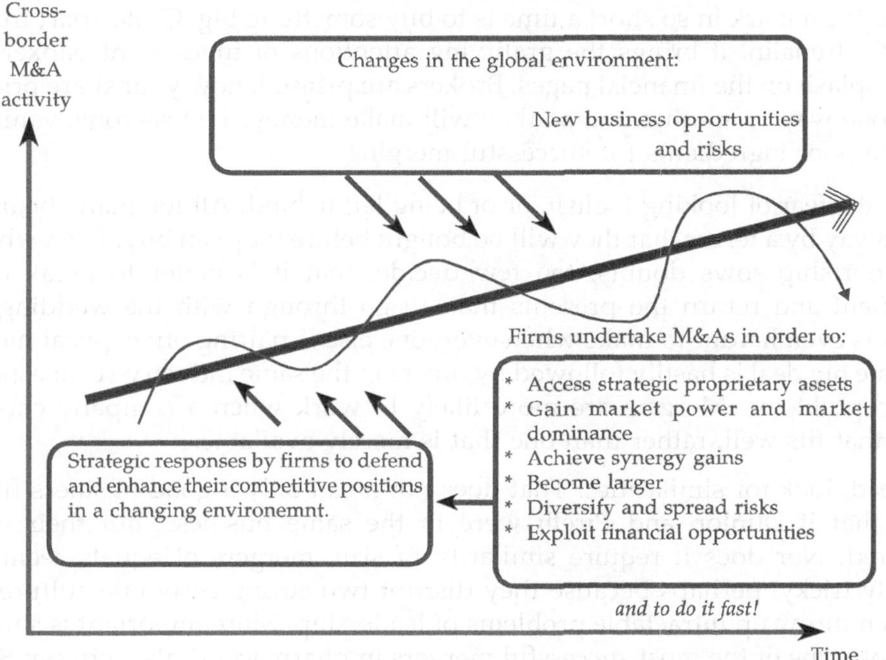

The fact that a considerable part of the current expansion of M&A activity consists of major deals in industries in which a limited number of companies dominate the market, leading to a consolidation at the regional or global level, suggests that strategic interactions among the leading firms also play an important role. Indeed, under conditions of strategic interdependence and uncertainty, once the established equilibrium is disturbed by the move of a major player (say, to acquire a foreign company) it can be expected to have a strong impact on key competitors and to trigger a chain reaction of countermoves at both domestic and international levels by rivals anxious to protect their positions. By pursuing a merger or acquisition, management minimizes the largest possible regret, which occurs when *ex post* successful moves by other players have not been imitated, or when they themselves become a target for a takeover. Thus, even firms reluctant to pursue this course may be forced into it for fear of becoming an acquisition target themselves. Such pre-emptive actions can be intended to create "strategic comfort" rather than shareholder value or economic wealth. Moreover, if they do not move quickly enough, there may be fewer desirable partners left. By moving, however, they will help amplify a merger wave that has just started.

SO HOW TO SUCCEED?

The most basic principle is to be crystal clear about the logic of the deal. However wrapped up in sonorous stuff about synergy, plenty of mergers begin with sheer executive boredom. For the executives at the top, running a company can be dull. Organic growth, in a mature market, is grindingly slow. Doing deals is easier—hire ire a bunch of investment bankers and set them to work-and much more exhilarating. A chief executive spends perhaps five years in the top job: the surest way to make a mark in so short a time is to buy something big. Quite apart from the surge of adrenalin, it brings the gratifying attentions of investment bankers, and makes a splash on the financial pages. Brokers are pleased: now your share price will move—one way or another-and so they will make money. Testosterone, vanity and greed are poor ingredients for successful merging.

So is the fear of looking foolish, or of being left behind. All too many boards are carried away by a terror that they will be bought before they can buy. Even when the initial courtship sows doubts, too few decide, that it is better to break off the engagement and return the presents than to go through with the wedding. That decision is even harder to make when everyone else is pairing off: copycat mergers-where one big deal is hastily followed by others in the same industry-seem especially prone to problems. Mergers are more likely to work when a company chooses a partner that fits well, rather than one that is merely available.

Instead, look for similarities. That does not mean only a good business fit, vital though that it Dunlop and Pirelli were in the same business, but their merger floundered. Nor does it require similarity of size: mergers of equals seem to be especially tricky, perhaps because they disrupt two strong corporate cultures, and they often throw up intractable problems of leadership. More important is similarity of outlook. One of the most successful mergers in pharmaceuticals, between Sandoz and Ciba Geigy to form Novartis, was between two firms whose closeness of approach was the greater for being based in the same Swiss town (and doubtless run by executives who had done national service together).

Even more crucial, concentrate on the marriage, not the wedding. Doing a deal involves delicate compromises. And once a merger is agreed, put a managerial heavy-weight in charge, full-time, of making it work. This is more essential than ever when a merger is the product of weakness rather than strength, as so many of today's art. Such deals will succeed mainly by cutting capacity, which may mean product lines or branches, but almost always means jobs. To push through these cuts quickly, explaining them to bewildered and resentful employees, is often the hardest part of making a merger succeed, when the investment bankers have taken their cheques and moved on, that is the job the managers are left with. In fact, the whole consulting industry thrives by advising companies on post- merger integration, a salvage operation to recover something from the wreckage of impossible promises and ill-considered goals. Companies that agree on a clear strategy and management structure before they tie the knot stand a better chance of living happily ever after.

RECENT TRENDS AND CHARACTERISTICS OF CROSS-BORDER M&AS

Firms may enter host economies through greenfield investments or M&As. The choice of mode is influenced by industry-specific factors. For example, greenfield investment is more likely to be used as a mode of entry in industries in which technological skills and production technology are key. The choice may also be influenced by institutional, cultural and transaction cost factors, in particular, the attitude towards takeovers, conditions in capital markets, liberalization policies, privatization, regional integration, currency risks and the role played by intermediaries (e.g. investment bankers) actively seeking acquisition opportunities and taking initiatives in making deals.

The value of private equity-sponsored cross-border M&As increased by 14 per cent to $122 billion in 2010, compared to $107 billion in 2009 after two years of consecutive decline (table 1).5 At the same time, the corresponding number of cross-border M&As reached a record high, with 2,050 deals completed.

The factors behind the increase in FDI by private equity funds are largely related to the stabilization of macroeconomic conditions. Also, investors were looking for yields, in a declining interest rate environment. Positive trends were supported by stronger private equity activity in emerging markets. Thus 31 per cent of FDI by private equity firms, amounting to $38 billion, was directed to developing and transition economies in 2010, up from 26 per cent in 2009. This rise reflects the increasing interest of private equity firms in developing country firms and venture capital business, which provide better business opportunities than before.

Despite stronger private equity-sponsored cross-border M&As in 2010, their value is still more than 70 per cent lower than the peak level in 2007. The volume share of private equity in total cross-border M&As fell from 19 per cent in 2009 to 17 per cent in 2010. The relative contribution of private equity funds to total FDI contracted by nearly 40 per cent from 2004, its peak year, to 2010.

A more benign global economic environment should see fundraising and investment picking up in 2011, also bolstering a more positive outlook for private equity-sponsored FDI. Private equity investors were estimated to have held nearly a trillion dollars of uninvested capital at the beginning of 2010, including reserves for future use, that could result in a surge in volume of cross-border M&As in 2011.

On the supply side, there are now more opportunities. There are two factors. First, companies owned by private equity firms are becoming targets for other private equity firms. The relative performance of these secondary buyouts (i.e. buyouts of private equity invested firms) is only slightly lower than that of primary buyouts: this is because the former can be executed faster than the latter in issuing IPOs (initial public offerings), and because secondary buyouts entail a lower risk profile. Second, private equity firms are now seeking smaller firms, and are engaged in smaller-scale buyouts. This is an area to which private equity firms have not paid much attention in the past, yet one where many attractive firms are to be found.

TABLE 1

CROSS-BORDER M&AS BY PRIVATE EQUITY FIRMS, 1996–MAY 2011 (NUMBER OF DEALS AND VALUE)

	Number of deals		*Value*	
Year	*Number*	*Share in total (%)*	*$ billion*	*Share in total (%)*
1996	932	16	42	16
1997	925	14	54	15
1998	1 089	14	79	11
1999	1 285	14	89	10
2000	1 340	13	92	7
2001	1 248	15	88	12
2002	1 248	19	85	18
2003	1 488	22	109	27
2004	1 622	22	157	28
2005	1 736	20	207	22
2006	1 698	18	271	24
2007	1 917	18	457	27
2008	1 785	18	322	25
2009	1 993	25	107	19
2010	2 050	22	122	17
2011	591	17	91	20

Source: UNCTAD, cross-border M&A database (www.unctad. org/fdistatistics).

Note: Value is on a gross basis, which is different from other M&A tables based on a net value. The table includes M&As by hedge funds. Private equity firms and hedge funds refer to acquirers as "investors not elsewhere classified". This classification is based on the Thomson Finance database on M&As.

M&As IN INDIA

Indian companies—owing to health performance, strong management capabilities and access to competitive financing—have seen a spurt in the cross-border merge and acquisition (M&A) activity. As they go beyond borders to acquire foreign assets to serve global markets, the total value of M&A deals in India has grown at a compounded annual growth rate of around 28 per cent during 2002-06. Most of this growth has come over the last 2 years, with the value of M&A deals increasing from US$7.5bn in 2004 to US $2.14bn in 2006. The number of cross-border deals from India in 2006 grew much faster than domestic deals. Last years the M&A deals in India stood at 480 with a total value of about $20.3bn. Of these, more than half, or 266, were cross-border deals (value $15.3bn). Of the 480 M&A deals, only 40 head a deal value of over US $100 mn. The domestic, inbound and outbounds deals increased in the range from 26%-42%. The share of domestic, inbound and outbound deals were more or less stable, with domestic deals having a share of 44% inbound deals 16% and outbound deals 40%.

From 1995 to August 2006, the largest proportion of outbound acquisition has been in North America, accounting for 32% of total outbound deals. This was followed by Europe that accounted for 29% of total deals. Europe is now emerging as the prime destination for Indian companies making acquisitions abroad.

Tata Steel's acquisition of the Anglo Dutch steel maker Corus at a price of US $12.1bn has already set the trend. Hindalco's announcement of acquisition of Novelis for $ 6 bn has further fuelled this trend. Vodafone's deal of US $11.1bn for Hutchison's stake in telecom operator Hutchison-Essar spells the trend for inbound investment. However, outbound deals from India have had a sectoral trend with Pharma companies being particularly aggressive in scouting for opportunities abroad, going to the top of M&A league with total deal of a little over $2.2bn. The other sector that has take the leads is the IT Sector. In the energy sector, ONGC's acquisition of equity stakes in a couple of oil blocks in Columbia and Brazil as also Suzlon Energy's acquisition of Hansen led the M&As deals. Overall M&As were on the rise in 2007 . Both the inbound and outbound M&As increased dramatically and the deals crossed $100 billion. But the constant growth in M&As activities witnessed a fall by a third in 2008 due to bearish capital markets and credit lockup .The average valuation of Indian deals declined by 9%,while the BSE increased by 4.6%. The share of Indian National deals in the total number slightly increased by 2%. The increase in national deals was relatively modest in the context of global downturn. The share of Indian cross-border deals also declined ,but was still high with 66%. With respect to industry number, it was noted that most deals had taken place in the consumers, industrials, materials and high technology sectors. By value most important sectors have been energy& power, healthcare, industrials and materials. With respect to the number of transactions, almost all sectors have experienced a decline with the notable exceptions of real estate, healthcare, energy & power, high technology, and consumer products, services and staples have increased. Cross-border deals dominated the list of top deals in 2008. Only one out of the 15 deals a share buyback, taking advantage of lower valuations.

M&As activities, which were in vogue in the pre-economic crisis meltdown period, hit rock-bottom after the collapse of Lehman Brothers in September 2008. During January-March 2009, the inbound M&As deals,which had the maximum share in total M&As deal during October-December 2008, contracted by a whopping 85.28%. The outbound M&As deals shrunk 48.62 % as the number of deals declined from 28 in October-December 2008 to 16 in January-March, 2009. The aggregate M&As deals size plunged more than 70%in the first quarter of 2009. The number of deals also declined from 58 to 45 during the period. The total number of deals announced during the first half of 2009 stands at 123, with total value of $4.93 billion.Though recovery talk is doing the rounds but companies are still apprehensive about using their reserves to acquire other businesses and assets. Second half of 2009-10 is expected to kickstart inbound M&As activities in view of the strong financial position of domestic companies and robust demand in sectors like telecom, pharma and capital goods.

DIVESTURE ANALYSIS

Even after MNC's accept/reject decisions are made, they should be reassessed at various times. Some foreign projects that have been rejected may become acceptable as a result of a reduction in the MNC's cost of capital, increased host government incentives, improved economic conditions in the host country, or more favourable projections of exchange rates. Foreign projects that have been implemented must be assessed to determine whether they should be continued or divested.

Indian government unveiled a road map for the *big bang* disinvestments programme in major Central Public Sector Undertakings (CPSUs) for 2009-10, indicating that nearly 60 CPSUs, including SAIL, BSNL, COAL INDIA,for selling government stake. The government also announced that NTPC and Rural Electrification will make their follow-on public offer (FPO) within the fiscal along the Satluj Vidyut Nigam,which is expected to come out with an initial offer (IPO) to offload 10% stake.

A COMPREHENSIVE EXAMPLE

Zinco, a Greenland-based manufacturer of high-quality tennis rackets, has recently considered exporting rackets to Zeroland. However, it anticipates that the Zeroland government will prohibit these exports in retaliation for recent trade restrictions placed by the Greenland government on some Zeroland exports. Consequently, Zinco considering the development of a subsidiary in Greenland that could manufacture and sell the tennis rackets locally. Various departments of Zinco were asked to supply relevant information for a capital budgeting analysis. In addition, some executives of Zinco met with government officials of Greenland regarding the proposed subsidiary. All relevant information follows.

A. 1. *initial investment.* An estimated 20 million Green francs (GF), which includes funds to support working capital, would be needed for the project. Given the existing spot rate of $.50 per Green franc, the dollar amount of the parent's initial investment is $10 million.

2. *Project life.* The project is expected to end in four years. The host government of Zeroland has promised to make a payment to the parent in order to purchase the plant after four years.

3. *Price and demand.* The estimated price and demand schedules during each of the next four years are shown here:

Year	*Price per Racket*	*Demand in Zeroland*
1	GF350	60,000 units
2	GF350	60,000 units
3	GF360	100,000 units
4	GF380	100,000 units

4. *Costs.* The variable costs (for materials, labour, etc.) per unit were estimated and consolidated as shown here:

Year	Variable costs (VC) per Racket
1	GF200
2	GF200
3	GF250
4	GF260

The expense of leasing extra office space is GF1 million per year. Other annual overhead expenses are expected to be GF1 million per year.

5. *Exchange rates.* The spot exchange rate of the Green franc is $.50. The spot rate is used by Zinco as its best forecast of the exchange rate that will exist in the future periods. Thus, the forecasted exchange rate for all future periods is $.50.
6. *Host country taxes on income earned by subsidiary.* The Zeroland government will allow Zinco to establish the subsidiary and will impose a 20 per cent tax rate on income. In addition, it will impose a 10 per cent withholding tax on any funds remitted by the subsidiary to the parent.
7. *Greenland government taxes on income earned by Zinco subsidiary.* The Zeroland government will allow a tax credit on taxes paid in Greenland, so that earnings remitted by the parent will not be taxed by the Greenland government.
8. *Cash flows from Zinco subsidiary to parent.* The *Zinco* subsidiary plans to send all net cash flow received back to the parent firm at the end of each year. The Zeroland government promises no restrictions on the cash flows to be sent back to the parent firm, but does impose a 10 per cent withholding tax on any funds sent to the parent, as mentioned above.
9. *Depreciation.* The Zeroland government will allow the subsidiary of Zinco to depreciate the cost of the plant and equipment at a maximum rate of GF2 million per year, which is the rate to be used by the subsidiary.
10. *Salvage value.* The Zeroland government will send a payment of GF12 million to the parent to assume ownership of the subsidiary at the end of four years. Assume there is no capital gain or loss on the sale of the subsidiary.
11. *Required rate of return.* Zinco requires a 15 per cent return on this project.

B. Present the optimistic and perimistic using different exchange rates as follows:

	Year 1	Year 2	Year 3	Year 4
Strong-franc Scenario				
Exchange rate of GF	$.54	$.57	$.61	$.65
Weak-franc Scenario				
Exchange rate of GF	$.47	$.45	$.41	$.37

C. If the project is partially financed by the foreign subsidiary, can there by any influence on the feasibility of the project. Consider that the subsidiary borrows GF10 million to purchase the offices that are leased initially. Assume that interest payments on this loan (of GF1 million) are to be paid by the subsidiary annually, and the principal (GF10 million) will be paid at the end of year 4, when the project is terminated.

D. Consider one more alternative arrangement, in which the parent uses its own funds to purchase the offices. That is, its initial investment is $15 million, composed of the original $10 million investment plus an additional $5 million to obtain an extra GF10 million to purchase the offices.

E. Consider all the funds are blocked minimum for three years until the subsidiary is sold but these funds can be used to purchase marketable securities that are expected to yield 5% annually, after taxes.

F. Without a subsidiary, Zinco's export business to Zeroland is expected to generate net cash flows of $1 million over the next four years. With a subsidiary, these cash flows would be foregone. How much should it effect the viability of the project?

G. Assume that the project is implemented, and after two years, the spot rate of the GF is $.46. In addition, forecasts have been revised for the remaining two years of the project, indicating that the Green should be worth $.44 in Year 3 and $.40 in the project's final year. Because these forecasts have an adverse effect on the project, Zinco considers divesting the subsidiary. For simplicity, assume that the original forecasts of the other variables remain unchanged, and that a potential acquirer has offered GF13,000,000 (after adjusting for any capital gains taxes) for the subsidiary if the acquirer can assume the existing local and retain the existing working capital.

H. Incorporate following two countries risk characteristics in the Zinco analysis, to determine how the NPV is affected by:

First, assume that there is a 30% chance that the withholding tax imposed by the Zeroland government will be at a 20% rate rather than a 10% rate.

Second, assuming that there is a 40% chance that the Zerolandgovernment will provide Zinco a payment (salvage value) of GF7 million rather then GF 12 million.

Assume that these scenarios of country risk are the two possible unrelated situations of country risk.

EXAMPLE ANALYSIS

The capital budgeting analysis will be conducted from the parent's perspective, based on the assumption that the subsidiary is intended to generate cash flows that will ultimately be passed on to the parent. Thus, the net present value from the parent's perspective is based on a comparison of the present value of the cash flows received by the parent to the initial outlay by the parent. An international project's NPV is dependent on whether a parent or subsidiary perspective is used. Since the Greenland parent's perspective is used, the cash flows of concern are the dollars ultimately received by the parent as a result of the project. The initial outlay of concern is the investment by the parent. The required rate of return is based on the cost of capital used by the parent to make its investment, with an adjustment for the risk of the project. If the establishment of the subsidiary is beneficial to Zinco's parent,

TABLE-1.1

CAPITAL BUDGETING ANALYSIS: ZINCO

	Year 0	Year 1	Year 2	Year 3	Year 4
1. Demand		60,000	60,000	100,000	100,000
2. Price per unit		GF350	GF350	GF360	GF380
3. Total revenue = (1) x (2)		GF21,000,000	GF21,000,000	GF36,000,000	GF38,000,000
4. Variable cost per unit		GF200	GF200	GF250	GF260
5. Total variable cost = (1) x (4)		GF12,000,000	GF12,000,000	GF25,000,000	GF26,000,000
6. Annual lease expense		GF1,000,000	GF1,000,000	GF1,000,000	GF1,000,000
7. Other fixed annual expenses		GF1,000,000	GF1,000,000	GF1,000,000	GF1,000,000
8. Noncash expense (depreciation)		GF2,000,000	GF2,000,000	GF2,000,000	GF2,000,000
9. Total expenses = (5) + (6) + (7) + (8)		GF16,000,000	GF16,000,000	GF29,000,000	GF30,000,000
10. Before-tax earnings of subsidiary = (3)– (9)		GF5,000,000	GF5,000,000	GF7,000,000	GF8,000,000
11. Host government tax (20%)		GF1,000,000	GF1,000,000	GF1,400,000	GF1,600,000
12. After-tax earnings of subsidiary		GF4,000,000	GF4,000,000	GF5,600,000	GF6,400,000
13. Net cash flow to subsidiary = (12) + (8)		GF6,000,000	GF6,000,000	GF7,600,000	GF8,400,000
14. GF remitted by subsidiary (100% of CF)		GF6,000,000	GF6,000,000	GF7,600,000	GF8,400,000
15. Withholding tax on remitted funds (10%)		GF600,000	GF600,000	GF760,000	GF840,000
16. GF remitted after withholding taxes		GF5,400,000	GF5,400,000	GF6,840,000	GF7,560,000
17. Salvage value					GF12,000,000
18. Exchange rate of GF		\$.50	\$.50	\$.50	\$.50
19. Cash flows to parent		\$2,700,000	\$2,700,000	\$3,420,000	\$9,780,000
20. PV of parent cash flows (15% discount rate)		\$2,347,826	\$2,041,588	\$2,248,706	\$5,591,747
21. Initial investment by parent	\$10,000,000				
22. Cumulative NPV		–\$7,652,174	–\$5,610,586	–\$3,361,880	\$2,229,867

the present value of future cash flows (including the salvage value) ultimately received by the parent should exceed the parent's initial outlay.

The capital budgeting analysis to determine whether Zinco should establish the subsidiary is provided in Exhibit 1. The first step is to incorporate demand and price estimates in order to forecast total revenue (see Lines 1 through 3). Then, the expenses are summed to forecast total expenses (see Lines 4 through 9). Next, before-tax earnings are computed (in line 10) by deducting total expenses from total revenue. Host governemnt taxes (Line 11) are then deducted from before-tax earnings to determine after-tax earnings for the subsidiary (Line 12).

The depreciation expense is added to the after-tax subsidiary earnings to compute the net cash flow to the subsidiary (Line 13). All of these funds are to be remitted by the subsidiary, so Line 14 is the same as Line 13. The subsidiary can afford to send all net cash flow to the parent, since its loan from the local bank is providing the working capital to support corporate operations. The funds remitted to the parent are subject to a 10 per cent withholding tax (Line 15), so the actual amount of funds to be sent after these taxes is shown in Line 16. The salvage value of the project is shown in Line 17. The funds to be remitted must first be converted into dollars at the exchange rate (Line 18) existing at that time. The parent's cash flow from the subsidiary is shown in Line 19. The periodic funds received from the subsidiary are not subject to Greenland corporate taxes, since it was assumed the taxes paid in Zeroland would represent a credit offsetting taxes owed to the Greenland government.

Although several capital budgeting techniques are available, a commonly used technique is to estimate the cash flows and salvage value to be received by the parent and compute the net present value (NPV) of the project, as shown here:

$$NPV = -IO + \sum_{t=1}^{n} \frac{CF_t}{(1+k)^t} + \frac{TV_n}{(1+k)^n}$$

where IO = initial outlay (investment)

CF_t = cash flow in period t

TV_n = terminal value

k = required rate of return on the project

n = lifetime of the project (number of periods).

The *present value (PV)* of each period's net cash flow is computed using a 15 per cent discount rate (Line 20). The discount rate should reflect the parent's cost of capital with an adjustment for the project's risk. Finally, the cumulative NPV (Line 22) is determined by consolidating the discounted cash flows for each period, and subtracting the initial outlay (in Line 21). For example, as of the end of Year 2, the cumulative NPV was —$5,610,586. This was determined by consolidating the $2,347,826 in Year 1, the $2,041,588 in Year 2, and subtracting the initial investment of $10,000,000. The critical value in Line 22 is in the last period, since this reflects the NPV of the project.

The cumulative NPV as of the end of the last period is $2,229,867. Because the NPV is positive, the MNC may accept this project, if the discount rate of 15 per cent has fully accounted for the project's risk. However, if the analysis has not yet accounted for risk, the decision may be to reject the project.

B. Weak-franc and strong-franc scenarios are illustrated in Table-1.2. At the top of the table, the anticipated after-tax franc cash flows (including salvage value), are shown for the subsidiary, from Lines 16 and 17 in Table-1.1. The amount in dollars that these francs convert to depends on the exchange rates existing in the various periods in which they are converted. The number of francs multiplied by the forecasted exchange rate will determine the estimated number of dollars received by the parent.

Notice from Table-1.2 the differences in cash flow received by the parent in the strong-franc scenario from those received in the weak-franc scenario. A strong franc is clearly beneficial, as verified by the increased dollar value of cash flows received. The large differences in cash flow received by the parent in the different scenarios illustrate the impact of exchange rate expectations on the feasibility of an international project.

TABLE-1.2

ANALYSIS USING DIFFERENT EXCHANGE RATE SCENARIOS

	Year 0	*Year 1*	*Year 2*	*Year 3*	*Year 4*
GF remitted after withholding taxes (including salvage value)		GF5,400,000	GF5,400,000	GF6,840,000	GF19,560,000
Strong-Franc Scenario					
Exchange rate of GF		$.54	$.57	$.61	$.65
Cash flows to parent		$2,916,000	$3,078,000	$4,172,400	$12,714,000
PV of cash flows (15% discount rate)		$2,535,652	$2,327,410	$2,743,421	$7,269,271
Initial investment by parent	$10,000,000				
Cumulative NPV		–$7,464,348	–$5,136,938	–2,393,517	$4,875,754
Weak-Franc Scenario					
Exchange rate of GF		$.47	$.45	$.40	$.37
Cash flows to parent		$2,538,000	$2,430,000	$2,736,000	$7,237,200
PV of cash flows (15% discount rate)		$2,206,957	$1,837,429	$1,798,964	$4,137,893
Initial investment by parent	$10,000,000				
Cumulative NPV		—$7,793,043	—$5,955,614	—$4,156,650	—$18,575

The estimated NPV is highest if the franc is expected to strengthen and lowest if it is expected to weaken. The estimated NPV is negative for the weak-franc scenario but positive for the stable-franc and strong-franc scenarios. This project's true feasibility would depend on the probability distribution of these three scenarios for the franc during the project's lifetime. If there is a high probability that the weak-franc scenario will occur, this project should not be accepted.

C. Since the Zeroland government permits a maximum of GF2 million per year in depreciation for this project, the subsidiary's depreciation rate will remain unchanged.

The offices are expected to have a market value of GF10 million at the end of Year 4, at which time they will be sold. Given the revised assumptions, the following revisions must be made to the capital budgeting analysis:

1. Since the subsidiary is borrowing funds to purchase the offices, the lease payments of GF1 million per year will not be necessary. However, the subsidiary will pay interest payments of GF1 million per year as a result of the loan. Thus, the annual cash outflows for the subsidiary are still the same.
2. The subsidiary must pay the GF10 million in loan principal at the end of four years. However, since the subsidiary expects to receive GF10 million (in 4 years) from the sale of the offices it purchases with the funds provided by the loan, it can use the proceeds of the sale to pay the loan principal.

Since the subsidiary's maximum depreciation expense allowed by the Zeroland government already has been taken even before the subsidiary owned the offices, it cannot increase its annual depreciation expenses. The cash flows ultimately received by the parent when the subsidiary obtains financing to purchase offices are similar to the cash flows determined in the original example (when the offices are to be leased).

Given the revised assumption that the parent rather than the subsidiary will purchase the offices, the following revisions must be made to the capital budgeting analysis:

1. The subsidiary will not have any loan payments (since it will not need to borrow funds), as the offices are to be purchased by the parent. Since the offices are to be purchased, there will be no lease payments either.
2. The initial investment by the parent is $15 million instead of $10 million.
3. The salvage value to be received by the parent is GF22 million instead of GF12 million, because the offices are assumed to have a market value of GF10 million at the end of Year 4. The GF10 million to be received from selling the offices can be added to the GF12 million to be received from selling the rest of the subsidiary.

The capital budgeting analysis for Zinco under this revised financing strategy in which the parent finances the entire $15 million investment is shown in Table-1.3. This analysis uses our original exchange rate projections of $.50 per Green franc for each period. The numbers that are directly affected by the revised financing arrangement are bracketed. Other numbers are also affected indirectly as a result. For example, the subsidiary's after-tax earnings increase as a result of avoiding interest or lease payments on its offices. The NPV of the project under this alternative financing arrangement is positive, but less than in the original arrangement. Given the higher initial outlay of the parent and the lower NPV, this arrangement in which the parent finances the $15 million investment is not as feasible as the arrangement in which the offices are either leased or purchased with funds borrowed by the subsidiary.

TABLE-1.3

ANALYSIS WITH AN ALTERNATIVE FINANCING ARRANGEMENT: ZINCO

	Year 0	*Year 1*	*Year 2*	*Year 3*	*Year 4*
1. Demand		60,000	60,000	100,000	100,000
2. Price per unit		GF350	GF350	GF360	GF380
3. Total revenue = (1) x (2)		**GF21,000,000**	**GF21,000,000**	**GF36,000,000**	**GF38,000,000**
4. Variable cost per unit		GF200	GF200	GF250	GF260
5. Total variable cost = (1) x (4)		GF12,000,000	GF12,000,000	GF25,000,000	GF26,000,000
6. Annual lease expense		[GF 0]	[GF 0]	[GF 0]	[GF 0]
7. Other fixed annual expenses		GF1,000,000	GF1,000,000	GF1,000,000	GF1,000,000
8. Noncash expense (deprec.)		GF2,000,000	GF2,000,000	GF2,000,000	GF2,000,000
9. Total expenses = (5) + (6) +(7) + (8)		**GF15,000,000**	**GF15,000,000**	**GF28,000,000**	**GF29,000,000**
10. Before-tax earnings of subsidiary = (3)– (9)		GF6,000,000	GF6,000,000	GF8,000,000	GF9,000,000
11. Host government tax (20%)		GF1,200,000	GF1,200,000	GF1,600,000	GF1,800,000
12. After-tax earnings of subsidiary		GF4,800,000	GF4,800,000	GF6,400,000	GF7,200,000
13. Net cash flow to subsidiary = (12) + (8)		**GF6,800,000**	**GF6,800,000**	**GF8,400,000**	**GF9,200,000**
14. GF remitted by subsidiary (100% of CF)		GF6,800,000	GF6,800,000	GF8,400,000	GF9,200,000
15. Withholding tax on remitted funds (10%)		GF680,000	GF680,000	GF840,000	GF920,000
16. GF remitted after withholding taxes		**GF6,120,000**	**GF6,120,000**	**GF7,560,000**	**GF8,280,000**
17 Salvage value					[GF22,000,000]
18. Exchange rate of GF		$.50	$.50	$.50	$.50
19. Cash flows to parent		$3,060,000	$3,060,000	$3,780,000	$15,140,000
20. PV of parent cash flows (15% discount rate)		**$2,660,870**	**$2,313,780**	**$2,485,411**	**$8,656,344**
21. Initial investment by parent	[$15,000,000]				
22. Cumulative NPV		–$12,339,130	–$10,025,350	–$7,539,939	$1,116,405

E. A reevaluation of Zinco's cash Table-1.1 to incorporate the blocked-funds restriction is shown in Table-1.4. The withholding tax is not applied until the funds are remitted to the parent, which is in Year 4. The original exchange rate projections are used here. In addition, the risk of the project is greater, because the parent does not recover any funds until the project is terminated. Thus, all parent cash flows depend on the exchange rate four years from now.

If the foreign subsidiary has a loan outstanding, it may be able to better utilise blocked funds by repaying the local loan. For example, the GF6 million at the end of Year 1 could be used to reduce the outstanding loan balance rather than invested in marketable securities, assuming that the lending bank allows early repayment. The local loan could be paid off early, if this is permitted by the lending institution.

F. The effects of these assumptions are shown in Table-1.4. The previously estimated cash flows to the parent from the subsidiary (drawn from Table-1.1) are restated in Table-1.5. These estimates do not account for forgone cash flows, since the export business was assumed to be prohibited in the future. However, if the export business were allowed to exist, the forgone cash flows attributable to this business would have to be considered, as shown in Table-1.5. The adjusted cash flows to the parent account for the project's impact on prevailing cash flows.

TABLE-1.4

CAPITAL BUDGETING WITH BLOCKED FUNDS: ZINCO

	Year 0	*Year 1*	*Year 2*	*Year 3*	*Year 4*
GF to be remitted by subsidiary		GF 6,000,000	GF 6,000,000	GF 7,600,000	GF8,400,000
					GF7,980,000
GF accumulated by reinvesting					GF6,615,000
funds to be remitted					GF6,945,750
					GF29,940,750
Withholding tax (10%)					GF2,994,075
GF remitted after withholding tax					GF26,946,675
Salvage value					GF12,000,000
Exchange rate					$.50
Cash flows to parent					$19,473,338
PV of parent cash flows (15% discount rate)					$11,133,944
Initial investment by parent	$10,000,000				
Cumulative NPV		–$10,000,000	–$10,000,000	–$10,000,000	$1,133,944

G. The present value of adjusted cash flows and cumulative NPV are also shown in Table-1.5. The project's NPV is now negative, as a result of the adverse effect on prevailing cash flows. Thus, the project would not be feasible if the exporting business to Greenland could be continued.

TABLE-1.5

CAPITAL BUDGETING WHEN PREVAILING CASH FLOWS ARE AFFECTED

	Year 0	*Year 1*	*Year 2*	*Year 3*	*Year 4*
Cash flows to parent, ignoring impact on prevailing cash flows		$2,700,00	2,700,000	$3,420,000	$9,780,000
Impact of project on prevailing cash flows		–$1,000,000	–$1,000,000	–$1,000,000	–$1,000,000
Cash flows to parent, incorporating impact on prevailing cash flows		$1,700,000	$1,700,000	$2,420,000	$8,780,000
PV of cash flows to parent (15%) discount rate)		$1,478,261	$1,285,444	$1,591,189	$5,019,994
Initial investment	$10,000,000				
Cumulative NPV		–$8,521,739	–$7,236,106	–$5,645,106	–$625,112

Zinco can conduct a divestiture analysis by comparing the after-tax proceeds from the possible sale of the project (in terms of dollars) to the present value of expected dollar inflows that the project will generate if it is not sold. This comparison will determine the net present value of the divestiture (NPV_d), as illustrated in Table-1.6. Since the present value of forgone cash flows exceeds the price at which the project could be sold, NPV_d is negative. Thus, the project should not be divested.

H. To determine now the NPV is affected by each of these scenarios, a capital budgeting analysis similar to that shown in Table-1.1 could be used. The NPV could be easily estimated by adjustment of line items no. 15 (withholding tax imposed on remitted funds) and no. 17 (salvage value). The capital budgeting analysis measures the effect of a 20% withholding tax rate in Table-1.7. Since none of the items before line no. 14 are affected, these items are not shown here. If the 20% withholding tax rate is imposed, the NPV of the four-year project is $1,252,160.

TABLE-1.6

DIVESTITURE ANALYSIS

	End of Year 2 (Today)	*End of Year 3 (One Year from Today)*	*Edn of Year 4 (Two Years from Today*
GF remitted after withholding taxes		GF6,840,000	GF19,560,000
Selling price	GF13,000,000		
Exchange rate	$.46	$.44	$.40
Cash flow received from divestiture	$5,980,000		
Cash flows forgone due to diverstiture		$3,009,600	$7,824,000
PV of forgone cash flows (15% discount rate)		$2,617,044	$5,916,068

NPV_d = $5,980,000 - ($2,617,044 + $5,916,068)
= $5,980,000 - $8,533,112
= –$2,553,112

TABLE-1.7

ANALYSIS OF PROJECT BASED ON A 20% WITHHOLDING TAX

	Year 0	Year 1	Year 2	Year 3	Year 4
14. GF remitted by subsidiary		GF6,000,000	GF6,000,000	GF7,600,000	GF8,400,000
15. Withholding tax imposed on remitted funds (20%)		GF1,200,000	GF1,200,000	GF1,520,000	GF1,680,000
16. GF remitted after withholding taxes		GF4,800,000	GF4,800,000	GF6,080,000	GF6,720,000
17. Salvage value					GF12,000,000
18. Exchange rate of GF		$.50	$.50	$.50	$.50
19. Cash flows to parent		$2,400,000	$2,400,000	$3,040,000	$9,360,000
20. PV of parent cash flows (15% discount rate)		$2,086,956	$1,814,745	$1,998,849	$5,351,610
21. Initial investment by parent		$10,000,000			
22. Cumulative NPV		-$7,913,044	-$6,098,299	—$4,099,450	$1,252,160

Now consider the possibility of the lower salvage value, while using the initial assumption of a 10% withholding tax rate. The capital budgeting analysis accounts for the lower salvage value in Table-1.8. The estimated NPV is $800,484, based on this scenario.

TABLE-1.8

ANALYSIS OF PROJECT BASED ON A REDUCED TERMINAL VALUE

	Year 0	Year 1	Year 2	Year 3	Year 4
14. GF remitted by subsidiary		GF6,000,000	GF6,000,000	GF7,600,000	GF8,400,000
15. Withholding tax imposed on remitted funds (20%)		GF600,000	GF600,000	GF760,000	GF840,000
16. GF remitted after withholding taxes		GF5,400,000	GF5,400,000	GF6,840,000	GF7,560,000
17. Salvage value				GF7,000,000	
18. Exchange rate of GF		$.50	$.50	$.50	$.50
19. Cash flows to parent		$2,700,000	$2,700,000	4,420,000	$7,280,000
20. PV of parent cash flows (15% discount rate)		$2,347,826	$2,041,588	$2,248,706	$4,162,364
21. Initial investment by parent		$10,000,000			
22. Cumulative NPV		–$7,652,174	–$5,610,586	–$3,361,880	$800,484

Finally, consider the possibility that the higher withholding tax and the lower salvage value occur. The capital budgeting analysis in Table-1.9 accounts for both of these situations. The NPV is estimated to be –$177,223.

TABLE-1.9

ANALYSIS OF PROJECT BASED ON A 20% WITHHOLDING TAX AND A REDUCED TERMINAL VALUE

	Year 0	*Year 1*	*Year 2*	*Year 3*	*Year 4*
14. GF remitted by subsidiary		GF6,000,000	GF6,000,000	GF7,600,000	GF8,400,000
15. Withholding tax imposed on remitted funds (20%)		GF1,200,000	GF1,200,000	GF1,520,000	GF1,680,000
16. GF remitted after withholding date		GF4,800,000	GF4,800,000	GF6,080,000	GF6,720,000
17. Salvage value					GF7,000,000
18. Exchange rate of GF		$.50	$.50	$.50	$.50
19. Cash flows to parent		$2,400,000	$2,400,000	$3,040,000	$6,860,000
20. PV of parent cash flows (15% discount rate)		$2,086,956	$1,814,745	$1,998,849	$3,922,227
21. Initial investment by parent		$10,000,000			
22. Cumulative NPV		–$7,913,044	–6,098,044	–$4,099,450	–$177,223

Once estimates for the NPV are derived for each scenario, the firm can attempt to determine whether the project is feasible. In our example, there are two country risk variables that are uncertain, and there are four possible NPV outcomes, as illustrated in Table-1.5. Given the probability of each possible situation, and the assumption that the withholding tax outcome is independent from the salvage value outcome, joint probabilities can be determined for each pair of outcomes by multiplying the probabilities of the two outcomes of concern. Since the probability of a 20% withholding tax is 30 per cent, the probability of a 10% withholding tax is 70 per cent. Given that the probability of a lower salvage value is 40 per cent, the probability of the initial estimate for the salvage value is 60 per cent. Thus, scenario no. 1 (10% withholding tax and GF12 million salvage value) created in has a joint probability (probability that both outcomes will occur) of (70%) x (60%) = 42%.

TABLE-1.10

SUMMARY OF ESTIMATED NPVS ACROSS THE POSSIBLE SCENARIOS

Scenario	*Withholding Tax Imposed by Green Government*	*Terminal Value of Project*	*NPV*	*Probability*
1	10%	GF12,000,000	$2,229,867	(70%)(60%) = 42%
2	20%	GF12,000,000	$1,252,160	(30%)(60%) = 18%
3	10%	GF7,000,000	$800,484	(70%)(40%) = 28%
4	20%	GF7,000,000	-$177,223	(30%)(40%) = 12%

E(NPV) = $2,229,867 (42%)
+ $1,252,160 (18%)
+ $800,484 (28%)
- $177,223 (12%)
= $1,264,801

From Table-1.10, scenario no. 4 is the only scenario in which there is a negative NPV. Since this scenario has a 12% chance of occurring there is a 12% chance that the project proposed will adversely affect the value of the firm. Put another way, there is an 88% chance that the project will enhance the firm's value. The expected value of the project's NPV could be measured as the sum of each scenario's estimated NPV multiplied by its respective probability across all four scenarios, as shown in the bottom of Table-1.10. Most MNCs would accept the proposed project, given the likelihood that the project will have a positive NPV, and the limited loss that would occur even under the worst case scenario.

M&As AND GREENFIELD INVESTMENT: A COMPARISON

The corporate motivations for M&A deals vary and so do the effects of cross-border M&As for countries. The private and public costs and benefits of cross-border M&As can also diverge significantly. Viewed from a host country's standpoint, cross-border M&As are one form of FDI inflows, along with greenfield investments. These two types of inward FDI are often compared in their desirability for host countries. It is argued that, other things being equal, greenfield FDI is more desirable than M&A FDI, since the former immediately and directly adds to the existing industrial capacity in host countries, whereas the latter merely transfers ownership of local assets from domestic to foreign interests. This may be true as far as the immediate impact is concerned, and greenfield FDI is normally preferred by host countries for this reason. In addition to this short-term capital stock effect, however, there are a host of possible long-term effects that also need to be taken into account in evaluating the relative merits of these two kinds of FDI.

Capital Formation

Greenfield FDI is, by definition, investment in new productive facilities. Hence, assuming that no viable domestic investment will take place in the absence of such FDI, it immediately adds to the stock of capital in the host country. Furthermore, it is necessarily accompanied by the transfer of foreign TNCs' intangible assets such as technology and managerial skills, which are internalised / embodied in their greenfield projects, assets that enable foreign TNCs to stay competitive relative to host country firms in the latter's own backyard. Greenfield projects are thus likely to result in new capital formation, both physical and human.

In contrast, M&As may not lead to capital formation in the short run. The immediate effect is merely an asset transfer from a host country owner to a foreign TNC. But the acquirer may carry out modernisation and capacity expansion (perhaps as a condition of the deal, as is usually the case with privatised state properties in developing countries and Central and Eastern Europe) or induce other related investments (perhaps other related FDI undertaken by suppliers). New incremental or supplementary capital formation may then eventually occur in the form of both sequential and associated FDI which is larger than the original purchase. Furthermore, if the acquired firm would otherwise have gone bankrupt, thereby decreasing the capital stock involved, the M&A may have been instrumental in maintaining or revitalising a host country's capital formation There is, of course, the danger that the acquisition may have been undertaken for the sole purpose of eliminating competition by eventually closing down the acquired firm.

Employment and the Tax Base

Just as with capital accumulation, greenfield FDI immediately creates new jobs (assuming again the absence of credible domestic investment). M&As would have no such positive employment effect in the short run. In fact, job reduction may ensue if an acquisition involves a troubled high- cost firm that needs to be restructured and slimmed down. In the long run, however, if a TNC turns an acquired firm into a successful unit as part of its corporate network, employment may rise.

In general, the tax base is likely to expand more favourably under greenfield FDI than through M&As for the very reason that new business units are created by the former as additional taxable entities. For this reason, in their eagerness to create employment opportunities and expand the tax base, host governments are generally more interested in attracting greenfield FDI than in seeing existing local firms sold off to foreign TNCs It is thus no surprise that special incentives are often given to greenfield FDI.

Nonetheless, it is conceivable that an acquired firm will end up contributing as much or more to the local tax base, depending on whether it might have gone bankrupt in the absence of the acquisition or on the effectiveness with which it handles new infusions of capital and technology under foreign ownership.

Structural Diversification

From a host country's point of view, FDI is desirable in part because it may bring new assets (e.g. industrial knowledge) in new fields, thereby contributing to industrial diversification in the local economy. Since M&As mostly involve transfers of existing productive assets, they are not likely to help a host economy diversify into new industrial activities, unless the acquired firm itself later diversifies. If the acquired units become integrated with the foreign TNCs' corporate systems, however, they may have an opportunity to move into new fields. Besides, there is no guarantee that greenfield FDI necessarily opens up new industrial sectors, although the chances of structural diversification are probably greater in greenfield FDI than in M&As.

Competition

Market competition is desirable because it stimulates and improves efficiency, resulting in lower prices for consumers. Greenfield FDI can enhance local competition if its superior assets/market power are harnessed in such a way as to prevent predatory practices and to attract competitors. In contrast, while M&As will not generate new competition in the short run, they can maintain the level of competition that prevailed before, if the acquired firms might have gone out of business in the absence of a deal. In addition, if a new owner revitalises a moribund local firm, local competition will be revitalised as well. On the other hand, if the acquiring firm were pan of a small number of firms at the global level, the takeover might reduce global competition as well as competition in the host country.

Political and Cultural Considerations

Since M&As involve the transfer of ownership of a local productive activity and assets, a national security issue arises when local assets (e.g. technology) have military applications and can thus damage national security if they fall into foreign hands. Greenfield FDI does not directly pose this problem but some greenfield ventures may be aimed at monitoring local technological progress. Similar considerations apply with respect to national sentiment and culture. For example, some countries may consider the broadcasting or film-making industry a cultural industry critical to the preservation of national traditions. It all depends upon the nature of the industry involved, the market power of the new entrant, and the characteristics of the host countries themselves.

Liquidity

FDI is often welcomed because it brings liquidity, whether in the form of foreign exchange at the national level or in the form of needed funds at the company level. Liquidity is usually a priority for any country that experiences a balance-of-payments crisis and is in dire need of foreign exchange. In terms of national liquidity considerations, greenfield FDI and M&As are equally desirable alternatives.

In developed countries with flexible exchange rates, however, this 'foreign reserves" rationale hardly exists. Only a company-level need for liquidity may arise. For example, founders may want to sell because they wish to retire or some young start-up ventures may reach a point where they need additional capital. Here, obviously, greenfield FDI is not an alternative to M&As from the point of view of the individual enterprise.

In some developing countries, on the other hand, the sales of local businesses to foreign firms can become important, precisely because both the governments and the local firms are desperately in need of liquidity. Partial M&A deals may also occur to secure a minimum level of liquidity.

Supplementary Resources

Both M&As and greenfield FDI can bring in some critical supplementary resources such as new managerial, production and marketing techniques that are lacking in host countries. The new owners of local firms may apply new techniques to make their acquired businesses profitable. M&As are also often motivated by the desire to capture synergies by combining sets of corporate assets between the deal-making parties; the intra-corporate supplementing of local assets with foreign assets is a possibility unique to cross-border M&As. The Daimler-Chrysler merger and the VW-Rolls Royce merger are examples. Synergy-creating M&As certainly add to both the host and home countries' stock of resources and may bring both public and private benefits.

Similarly, greenfield FDI is likely to transplant supplementary resources at the national level, since the ownership-specific advantages they internalise are supposed to be superior to their local counterparts if such FDI is to succeed. Hence, the upshot is an augmentation of the host country's resource base. A prime example of such greenfield FDI is NUMMI (New United Motor Manufacturing Incorporated), a joint venture between GM and Toyota, in the United States, which has served as a learning conduit for GM in flexible manufacturing.

In contrast, an M&A may not involve any transfer of new resources from the acquiring foreign firm. It may even cause a reverse transfer, particularly if the new owner's intention is to siphon off knowledge from the acquired firm to the new owners, as is the case with some asset-seeking FDI. In such a case, an M&A results in the draining of resources (e.g. technology) from host countries.

So which is better from a host country's point of view? "It all depends" is the appropriate answer. Depending upon specific circumstances and the policy priorities of host countries, one or the other may be preferable. At the individual firm level, M&As can enable local firms directly to become parts of transnational corporate systems with a number of competitiveness-enhancing advantages. This source of gain is important, especially when dealing with distressed, non-performing local businesses. They require immediate and direct transfusions of new capital and supplementary resources at the firm level In fact, when it comes to distressed local business units, whether privately or publicly owned, the requirement is simply a buyer, whether foreign or domestic. These units need to be sold off, if not entirely then at least partially, for they have to be acquired by or merged into other firms if they are to avoid their ever-accumulating losses or debts and eventual demise. They need transfusions of both new capital and new managerial resources to survive and prosper. In many cases, these existing businesses cannot be purchased and upgraded by domestic firms, simply because they may themselves be short of capital and deficient in technological resources. In these cases, foreign firms may be the only possible suitors.

QUESTIONS

1. What are the important considerations in evaluating the long-run impact of a merger or the combined firm on earnings per share? Why may a long-run view change a merger decision?
2. Often in merger-especially in conglomerate merger-tax considerations are a key motive for a business combination. Why and in what situations may the acquisition of a firm with a tax-loss carryforward be quite acceptable?
3. Can a merger with a large, stable company serves as an effective way to raise capital for a growth oriented smaller company?
4. Is the public interest served by an increase in merger activity? Give arguments both pro and con.
5. Are the negotiations for merger agreements more difficult if the firms are in different industries or in the same industry? If they are about the same size or quite different in size? If the ages of the firms are about the same or if they are very different? Why?

34

FOREIGN PORTFOLIO INVESTMENT

INTRODUCTION

Foreign Portfolio Investment (FPI) has traditionally been concentrated in developed markets, new interest has been sparked by the co-called "emerging" capital markets. The emerging markets have at least three attractive qualities, two of which are their high average returns and their low correlations with developed markets. Diversification into these markets in expected to give higher expected returns and lower overall volatility.

Many individual investors, as well as portfolio and pension fund managers, are reexamining their basic investment strategies. The 1990s, fund managers realised that significant performance gains could be obtained by diversifying into high-quality global equity markets. These gains are limited, however, by the fairly high cross-correlations returns in these markets. The resulting investment strategy reflects current information. In terms of portfolio theory, adding low-correlation portfolios to an optimisation enhances the reward-to-risk profile by shifting the mean-variance frontier to the left.

The portfolio optimisation problem requires important inputs—the expected returns and the variance-covariance matrix. In principal, all of these measures should be forward-looking. That is, the returns, volatilities, and correlations should be forecasted.

THEORETICAL EFFECTS OF FOREIGN PORTFOLIO INVESTMENT

Portfolio theory indicates that as we diversify internationally, as long as all of the economies of the world are not perfectly positively correlated with each other we should expect gains from diversification. It is a fact that, given any particular group of assets, various optimal weightings of those assets exist that create portfolios with the maximum possible return for a given level of risk. These are the so-called efficient-frontier portfolios.

The efficient frontier for an internationally diversified portfolio lies above the efficient frontier for portfolios limited to their own domestic market, because the range of potential returns is wider internationally and because the correlations of return are typically lower. As a result, the internationally diversified investor has the potential to achieve a higher level of return than the domestic investor for any given level of risk, or, viewed from a different perspective, to expect a lower variability of return than a domestic investor for any given level of return. These relationships are shown in Figure-1.

FIGURE -1

INTERNATIONAL VERSUS DOMESTIC EFFICIENT FRONTIERS

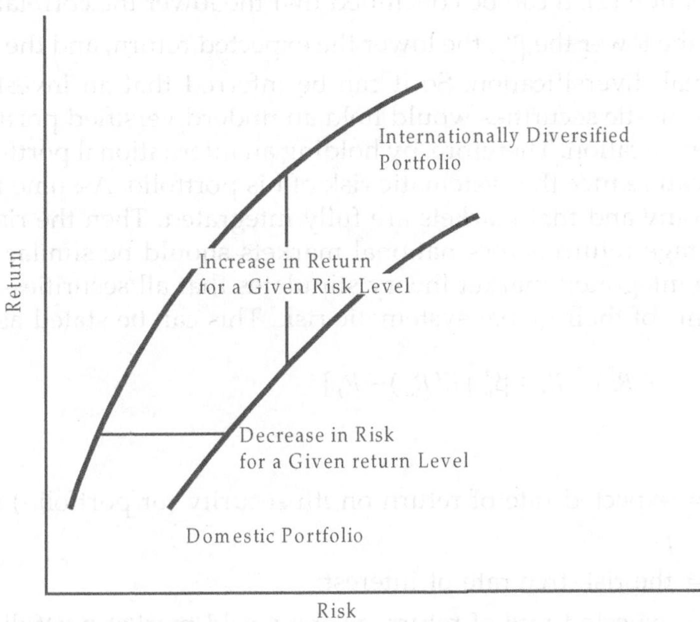

Segmented verus Integrated World Financial Market

The question of whether the international market is integrated or segmented appears particularly elusive. The segmented market theory states that capital assets are priced in terms of their "domestic systematic risk." The capital asset pricing model (CAPM) can be extended to account for the correlation between national securities markets in determination of securities on a given international market:

$$E(R_i^j) = R_f + \beta_{di}^j [E(R_m) - R_f] \tag{1}$$

where:

$E(R_i^j)$ = expected rate of return on *i*th security (or portfolio) in *j*th country;

$E(R_m)$ = expected market rates of return in *j*'th country;

β_{di}^j = the beta coefficient for *j*th country in terms of domestic country's market rate of return; and

R_f = the risk-free rate in the domestic country.

Equation (1) is a nationalistic model that postulates that security rates of return on each marketplace have in common a national factor, R_m. This national factor R_m is in turn dependent on a single common world factor, R_w^j (return for the world market portfolio), defined:

$$E(R_m) = R_f + \beta^j_w \; (E(R_w) - R_f] \tag{2}$$

where β^J_w is the international systematic risk of country *j*.

From Equation (2), it can be concluded that the lower the correlation between the two markets the lower the β^i_w, the lower the expected return, and the higher the value of international diversification. So it can be inferred that an investor who holds a portfoio of domestic securities would hold an underdiversified portfoio with respect to world diversification. Therefore, by holding an international portfolio (or security), the investor can reduce the systematic risk of his portfolio. Assume that the world is one big economy and that markets are fully integrated. Then the risk- (world beta-) adjusted average return across national markets should be similar to those of U.S. markets. The integrated-market theory stipulates that all securities in the world are priced in terms of their global systematic risk. This can be stated as:

$$E(R_i^j) = R_f + \beta^J_{wi}[E(R_w) - R_f] \tag{3}$$

where:

$E(R_i^j)$ = expected rate of return on *i*th security (or portfolio) in country *j*;

R_f = the risk-free rate of interest;

$E(R_W)$ = expected rate of return on the world market portfolio;

β^j_{wi} = $(\rho_{i,w}\sigma_i\sigma_w)/\sigma^2_w$ (correlation coefficient between the rate of return on security *i* in country *j* and the world market, times the standard deviation of security *i*, times the standard deviation of the world market, divided by the variance of the world market portfolio.

The relationship between β^j_d, β^j_w , and β^j_{wi} can be defined:

$$\beta^j_{wi} = \beta^j_w \beta^j_{di} \tag{4}$$

Equation (4) indicates that the international systematic risk of a security *i* in country *j* (β^j_{wi}) is equal to the product of the national systematic risk of that security (β^j_{di}) and the international systematic risk (β^j_w).

From the formula it can be inferred that the riskiness of a portfolio results from the covariance of a portfolio rate of return with a national stock-market index. Nevertheless, that index is not the only way to determine the price of a portfolio since the national market now has a relationship with the world market and has a certain influence on the world portfolio. That influence depends on the weight that the nation's financial market index has on the world market index.

The following conclusions can be drawn from the available knowledge on the subject of world market integration:

1. The world market lies in an area of being "mildly segmented"—that is, the economy of each country is its own world, to a significant degree of integration (the economy of each country has a substantial impact on the world economy, depending on the role that the particular country plays in the world markets as a whole).
2. International diversification can substantially reduce the risk and increase the wealth of the portfolio holders of any country, provided that the portfolio is properly constructed to accommodate the utility function of the portfolio holder.

   The argument for segmented markets relies on the existence of barriers that prevent the free flow of capital around the world. These barriers include (1) legal restrictions, (2) transaction costs, (3) lack of information, and (4) discrimination against foreign investors either by taxation or outright exclusion. Whether the world markets are segmented or integrated seems to ebb and flow as world conditions change. Presently the trend appears to be toward a greater degree of integration as the barriers mentioned are reduced or eliminated.

The CAPM and the APT Applied Internationally

The capital asset pricing model (CAPM) assumes that each investor faces the same efficient frontier of potential portfolios. In general, the efficient frontier will differ among investors because of differences in expectations. In a portfolio context, the concern of the investor with the characteristics of individual securities is justified in terms of the effect that each security has on the distribution of the rate of return of the portfolio. Specifically, the CAPM states that the relevant risk of a single security is the nondiversifiable risk, beta, the covariance of the security with the market divided by the variance of the market. The issue in an international context, therefore, is how international diversification affects the riskiness of the portfolio and its rate of return. Asset-pricing models similar in form to the CAPM have been derived for international financial assets in a manner parallel to the CAPM. Solnik (1974) developed an *international asset pricing model* (IAPM) and tested it.[1] In his empirical tests Solnik used daily data on stocks of eight European countries and the United States. The results were weakly consistent with his IAPM. However, Solnik generated some empirical estimates for the risk of an internationally diversified portfolio compared to a purely domestic portfolio. Using weekly data on stocks in eight major European countries and the United States, Solnik found that an internationally diversified portfolio would be one tenth as risky as a typical security and one half as risky as a well diversified U.S. portfolio.

A new development in the field of IAPM parallels an advance in the *domestic asset pricing theory*. Breeden (1979) developed an asset-pricing model which explicitly noted that individuals derive their utility from consumption. Maximizing lifetime utility from consumption. Breeden developed a more complete model for asset

1. Solnik, B., "The International Pricing of Risk: An Compirical Investigation of the World Capital Market Structure." *Journal of Finance,* v. 29, May, 1974

pricing, wherein pricing of an asset depended on covariances with aggregate consumption rather than any market index or portfolio. Application of the Breeden model to various economies of the world may give some insight into how financial assets are priced.[2]

The *arbitrage pricing theory (APT)*, formulated by Ross in 1976, offers a feasible alternative to the CAPM.[3]

The APT assumes that the rate of return on any security is a linear function of k factors, or:

$$\tilde{R}_i = E(\tilde{R}_i) + b_{i1}\tilde{F}_1 + \ldots + b_{ik}\tilde{F}_k + \tilde{e}_i$$

where:

$\tilde{R}_i$ = the random rate of return on the ith asset;

$E(\tilde{R}_i)$ = the expected rate of return on the ith asset;

b_{ik} = the sensitivity of the ith assets returns to the kth factor;

$\tilde{F}_k$ = the kth factor common to all assets; and

$\tilde{e}_i$ = a random mean noise term for the ith asset.

The most important feature of the APT is that in equilibrium all portfolios that can be selected from among the set of assets under consideration and that satisfy the two conditions of (1) using no wealth and (2) having no risk must earn no return on average.

Solnik extended the APT to the international capital markets, leading to the *international arbitrage pricing theory (IAPT)*. Solnik shows that IAPT overcomes the problem of aggregation when asset demands are summed in the universe of investors who use different numeration to measure returns. This is because the portfolios in the IAPT context represent weighted averages of individual assets. Further, Solnik shows that even in foreign terms the domestic arbitrage portfolio bears no risk and hence should earn zero return in equilibrium.

Cho, Eun, and Senbet (1987) empirically tested the IAPT and rejected the first hypothesis, that the international capital market is integrated and that the APT is valid internationally.[4] However, their study used international common factors. Abbeyekra and Mahojocar (1985) utilized domestic common factors and directly tested Solnik's claim on the IAPT. The results of their study "strongly support the hypothesis that the IAPT accurately predicts the risk-free rate."[5]

---

2. Breeden, D.T., An Intertemporal Asset Pricing Model with Stochastic Consumption and Investment Opportunities." *Journal of Financial Economics*, v. 7, Sept. 1979.
3. Ross, R., "A Critique of Asset Pricing Theories Tests: *Journal of Financial Economics*, v. 4, March, 1976.
4. Cho, D.C., C.S. Eun, and L.W. Senbet. "International Arbitrage Pricing Theory: An Empirical Investigation." *Journal of Finance*, v. 41, June, 1987.
5. Abbeyekra, S.P. and Mahojecer, "The International Arbitrage Pricing Theory: An Empirical Investigation." Working Paper presented in Western Finance Association Annual Meeting, June, 1985.

Are World Markets Efficient?

A final issue of importance in the theoretical discussion of international diversification is whether the world market is efficient. Domestic theoretical models such as the CAPM and the APT are dependent to a considerable extent on the assumption of market efficiency. The validity of extending these models to world markets will be seriously threatened if the international market is not as efficient as the U.S. market.

An efficient market, again, is a market where any new information would be immediately and fully reflected in prices, and the adjustment in price would be very rapid. Therefore, investors using publicly available information will not be able to earn above-average returns.

The issue of *world market efficiency* has been tested by Roll. He set the expected return on international speculation conditional on information at the beginning of the period equal to zero, using *purchasing-power parity (PPP),* which means that people will value currencies for what they will buy. He concludes that the deviations from PPP attributable to relative price fluctuations are dominated by the effects of inflation on the exchange rate. Hence relative inflation is an important determinant of exchange rates.

One requirement of market efficiency is that arbitrage profits are zero. Frankel and Levich (1975) tested whether deviations of interest-rate parity outside of the countries of transactions can exist.[6] They concluded that if arbitrage assets are comparable, arbitrage opportunities do not exist.

Simple tests of market efficiency have implied that the forward exchange rate should be an unbiased predictor of the spot rate. However, Stockman's (1980) theoretical development states that a bias should exist, since a premium is associated with the risk investors face in forward exchange markets.[7] Nevertheless, he found evidence of a bias for only a few countries and then only when the risk premium changes erratically.

There have been many studies on the efficiency of national stock markets around the world. Hawawini (1984),[8] Kato and Schallheim (1985),[9] Jaffe and Westerfield (1985),[10] and Ang and Pohlman (1978), to name a few, all conclude that the national stock markets they studied are at least semi-strong-form efficient. Given the increasing interest in financial analysis and portfolio management in these markets, these findings are not too supristng.

6. Frankel, J., and R. Levich. "Covered Interest Arbitrage: Unexploited Profits?" *Journal of Political Economy,* v. 83, April, 1975.
7. Stockman, A., "A Theory of Exchange Rate Determination." *Journal of Political Economy,* v. 88, August, 1980.
8. Hawawini, G., *European Equity Markets: Price Behaviour and Efficiency,* NY University, 1984.
9. Kato K., and J.C. Schallheim. "Seasonal and Size Anomalies in the Japanese Stock Market." *Journal of Financial and Quantitative Analysis,* v. 20, June, 198.
10. Jaffe, J. and R. Westerfied, "Patterns in Japanese Common Stock Returns: Day of the Week and Turn of the Year Effects," *Journal of Financial and Quantitative Analysis,* v. 20, June, 1985.

One issue remains unresolved at present: the efficiency of the world market. In other words, is it possible for portfolio managers to allocate funds to certain national markets and thereby generate performance that is better than a world market index? To date there is little empirical evidence to resolve this issue. What is required is a simultaneous evaluation of financial markets, currency markets, and real markets to ascertain whether they are efficient from a world perspective.

Empirical Evidence Supporting International Diversification

As early as 1968 evidence was being accumulated in empirical studies regarding the potential advantages of international diversification. Grubel (1968) found that international diversification can pay off, if portfolios are properly selected.[12] More recently, Stehle (1977) showed that low-beta securities of internationally diversified portfolios outperformed high-beta securities of domestically diversified portfolios, on a beta-adjusted basis.[13] Adler and Dumas (1983) stated in their study that "the potential of international diversification to reduce the risk seems unquestionable."[14]

The growth of international financial markets coincided with the increasing integration of national financial institutions through international firms. Integration of financial institutions as well as portfolio investment was a major phenomenon of the 1970s and 1980s. The effect of market integration has important implications in many sectors of the economy. It is important, therefore, when studying effects of international financial integration, to realize the benefits that could be used as a reference for policy making.

Studies by Senchack and Beedle (1980)[15] and Jacquillat and Solnick (1978)[16] suggest that U.S. investors who hold portfolios of U.S. multinational firms do not receive the same risk reduction as investors who hold portfolios of U.S. and foreign securities This probably results from the restrictions imposed on the multinational management by the various governments of the countries in which they operate.

ISSUES POSED BY FOREIGN PORTFOLIO INVESTMENT

The revival of capital inflows is sometimes treated as though it were a measure of success and an end in itself. The sad history of Latin American involvement in the international capital market should suffice to demonstrate the error of equating borrowing with success. Time and again since Latin American countries achieved independence in the early nineteenth century, they have borrowed and then encountered debt-servicing problems that dragged down their growth rate: the debt crisis was

11. Ang, J. and R. Pohlam. "A Note on the Price Behaviour of far Eastern Stocks," *Journal of International Business Studies*, v. 9, Spring, 1978.
12. Grubel, H.G. "International Diversified Portfolios." *American Economic Review*, v. 58, Dec., 1968.
13. Stehle, R. "An Compirical Test of the Alternate Hypothesis of National and International Pricing of Risky Assets." *Journal of Finance*, v. 32, May, 1977.
14. Adler, M. and D. Dumas. "International Portfolio Choice and Corporate Finance: A Syntehsis" *Journal of Finance*, v. 38, June, 1983.
15. Senchach, A. and W. Beedles. "Is Indirect International Diversification Desirable?" Journal of Portfolio Management, v. 6, Winter, 1980.
16. Jacquillat, B. and B. Solnik, "Multinational Are Poor Tools for Diversification." *Journal of Portfolio Management*, v. 4, Winter, 1978.

only the latest episode in a pattern that has been repeated as many as four times. Despite the undoubted potential for capital mobility to increase economic welfare by permitting investment to be reallocated internationally to the area with the highest potential rate of return, it is arguable that the region would have done better had it never borrowed anything. Hence, it is wrong to assume simply that more is better. Rather, the danger of over-borrowing is one of five issues posed by the emergence of portfolio flows. These five issues, are:

Potential Size

Are the potential flows of portfolio capital large enough, and can they be sustained long enough, for this source to play a significant role in channeling funds of developing countries?

In an ideal world, one could anticipate very large capital flows from industrial countries to developing countries over the next half century, while the developing countries completes the demographic transition. During this period the working population of the industrial countries will be fairly stagnant, implying limited investment needs but comparatively high savings, especially in the coming decades as a relatively large proportion of the population is in the pre-retirement high-savings phase of the life-cycle. Hence one would expect these countries to wish to run current account surpluses, so as to accumulate foreign assets whose income could help them pay the pensions of their increasing population of retirees. In contrast, the developing counties will have growing populations and the opportunity of benefiting from catchup growth, implying high investment needs relative to savings capabilities and the ability to pay high rates of return. An important additional benefit of such capital flows is that they would reduce the pressure for mass migration. Thus there would seem to be clear mutual benefits from large capital flows.

How large is "large"? The conjecture is: as large as is consistent with reasonable certainty that credit worthiness can be maintained. And how *large is that*? The best answer we are able to give at the moment is based on various ad hoc rules of thumb about a maximum prudent level of debt or debt service relative to variables that influence the ability to service debt, such as exports, GNP, or the capital stock. The most famous of such rules of thumb state that the debt/export ratio should not exceed 200 percent, that the debt service ratio (that is, the ratio of debt service to exports) should not exceed 25 per cent, and that the debt/GNP ratio should not exceed 40 per cent. Such rules of thumb doubtless ought to be combined in some way, but they do at least provide a starting point for analysis.

What do these rules of thumb imply about sustainable (desirable) current account deficits? A little algebra can show us Let D = foreign debt and Y = nominal income (expressed in dollars, like the debt mostly is), and use a hat over a variable to signify its rate of change so that D/D is the proportionate rate of change of debt. Consider a typical country, which may expect a long-term growth rate of nominal income of 8 per cent, consisting of 3 per cent inflation and 5 per cent real growth. In steady state the rate of growth of debt must be the same as the rate of growth of nominal income. Then the prudent steady-state current account deficit according to the debt/GNP rule of thumb would be D/Y = (D/D). (D/Y) = 0.08 x 0.4 = 0.032, that is, the steady-state deficit should not exceed 3.2 per cent of GNP. Of course, a country that starts out with a lower debt/GNP ratio than 40 per cent can run a greater deficit for a transitory period, but it is well-advised to prevent the deficit getting too much larger because of the difficulty of adjusting back as the debt limit approaches. (It is appropriate to focus on the debt/GNP ratio for a country with an export/GNP ratio in excess of 20 per cent, and on the debt/export ratio or a country with an export/GNP ratio below 20 per cent, to ensure that both constraints are satisfied).

The total GNP of developing countries, measured at market exchange rates (as is appropriate here since GNP is providing a measure of the size of the domestic economy relative to its foreign obligations), is $ 4.1 trillion (17.7 percent of a gross world product of $ 23 billion). If one accepts five per cent as an estimate of the medium-term potential growth rate of developing countries in general, then a rough estimate of how much capital inflow would be desirable is $ 130 billion per year. That can be compared with the annual flow of portfolio capital that had built up to $ 37 billion by last year, out of a total flow of $ 118 billion (excluding grants).

Portfolio flows are therefore a substantial part of a total flows that now seems close to a best guess estimate of what might be considered optimal. (Admittedly this calculation assume that all developing countries are capable of borrowing all that it would be prudent for them to accept, whereas most of the lower-income countries still have little access to the international capital market). Without portfolio flows, it is difficult to envisage the total flow being as large as desirable. The question therefore arises as to how dependable these flows are. It can be argued, for example, that portfolio lows provide the channel for repatriation of flight capital, which is an inherently transitory phenomenon. While true, the pool from which the flight capital is being drawn is extremely large: the World Bank made an estimate that it amounted to an average of 32 per cent of GDP for 58 developing countries at the end of 1990, which would suggest a total stock of around a trillion dollars for all developing countries.

Furthermore, the other pools from which portfolio flows are drawn (the funds invested in world bond and equity markets) are vast and growing rapidly. Holdings in emerging markets are still marginal: So far less than 0.25 percent of the total assets of institutional investors in industrial countries were laced in emerging markets. The owners of these funds are becoming increasingly predisposed to consider investments in the emerging markets on their merits. Hence there is ample scope for portfolio flows not just to be sustained, but to grow further in coming years.

One other argument for questioning the permanence of recent levels of inflow of portfolio capital is that much of the equity investment has been attracted by the opportunities for buying newly privatised assets, and that the process of privatisation is inherently transitory because in due course there will be nothing left to privatise. This is surely true, although the process of privatisation still has a long way to go in most countries. Moreover, if future growth remains healthy, it will produce a string of new flotations that will offer similar opportunities to investors.

Therefore the potential size issue must be analysed from a wider perspective and the portfolio flows must be potentially large enough to be and remain an important source of external finance to developing countries.

The Terms of Lending

This has two main dimensions, maturity and yield. Borrowers have an interest in borrowing long-term (unless they anticipate a forthcoming decline in interest rates), primarily to minimise the danger of a withdrawal of funds precipitating debt difficulties, and in paying little. How well do the various forms of portfolio capital do in meeting these interest? Consider bonds. The terms still evokes in many people's minds the image of long-term fixed-interest bonds that prevailed before the First World War. The present-day reality is different. Most "bonds" nowadays have a maturity of eight years or less, and some of them carry floating interest rates. This means that a large part of the stock of outstanding debt can be withdrawn rather rapidly. It also means that the cost of servicing the bonds does not vary with the borrower's ability to pay (where the interest rate floats, debt service may indeed rise at a time when ability to pay is squeezed, as happened at the beginning of the debt crisis when high world interest rates caused a recession that cut debtors' ability to pay).

In one respect bonds tend to be even more inflexible than bank credits: they lack any mechanism for achieving an agreed rescheduling. Ironically it was precisely this difficulty that made bonds popular with lenders during the 1980s. While it was possible for distressed debtors to maintain debt service on bonds when these were a minute fraction of their total obligations, it will be impossible to do the same if debt difficulties arise in a country with a large proportion of its debt in the form of bonds. Thus creditors are living in something of a fool's paradise.

Money market instruments are short term. An advantage of both money market instruments and bonds is that they are relatively cheap. It is that unless and until it again becomes possible to borrow in the form of long-term (30 years or more) bonds, developing countries would be well-advised to restrain their borrowing in the form of both bonds and money market instruments to rather modest levels. In other words, it is worth paying a premium on the cost of funds in order to get repayment obligations that are better matched to ability to pay and less likely to precipitate debt difficulties.

Equity investment has very different characteristics. It has the advantage of a degree of cyclical sensitivity of the dividends paid, thus helping match debt-service payments to ability to pay. Nor is there as much danger of a disruptive capital outflow. It is true that foreigners may decide at any time that they wish to sell their shares, and that such a desire is quite likely to prove general as the herd instinct takes over. But, unless a sudden desire of foreigners to sell is matched by an increased desire of nationals to buy, the effect will be to depress the stock market rather than to lead to a demand for foreign exchange. One then has to ask whether a decline of the stock market is worse than a loss of foreign exchange reserves: it can be argued that the stock market is a natural place to absorb risk and that the costs of a decline in stock prices are usually modest, with the exception of instances where high stock prices have come to underpin other parts of the financial system.

The cost of equity finance is typically quite high. However, a large part of it usually takes the form of capital gains rather than being a drain on foreign exchange earnings in the short or medium run. Hence equity provides an attractive way in which to borrow.

Macroeconomic Destabilisation

The principal reason for preferring borrowing on long maturity is to limit the danger of a withdrawal of funds leading to debt-servicing difficulties. But there is also a danger of an excessive inflow of funds destabilising macro-economic management. An inflow is excessive when it is so large as to threaten the maintenance of a competitive exchange rate (because of nominal appreciation under a flexible exchange-rate regime or inflation under a fixed exchange-rate regime), and therefore jeopardises the prospects of maintaining export-led growth.

There are various possible reactions to a capital inflow:

i) To allow a nominal appreciation of the currency that will result in the transfer being accomplished, thus in effect accepting market forces rather than the judgment of the authorities as the factor determining the level of transfer.

ii) To engage in unsterilised intervention, which will also result in the transfer being accomplished, though with a delay and with inflation rather than nominal appreciation producing the real appreciation.

iii) To pursue a contractionary fiscal policy, so as to reduce internal absorption and permit a reduction in interest rates that will reduce the incentive for an inflow of capital.

iv) To maintain some controls on capital inflows, such as variable deposit requirements against foreign borrowings, that can be raised when inflows become excessive.

v) To engage in sterilised intervention, thus attempting to resist the transfer, though there is a danger that the market will ultimately overwhelm this attempt.

vi) To manipulate the flow of domestic liquidity into the banking system using excess government savings, which may be regarded as a generalised form of sterilised intervention.

vii) To widen the band of permissible exchange rate fluctuations, so as to allow a temporary appreciation without undermining the confidence of exporters that the exchange rate will remain competitive in the medium term.

viii) To eliminate any remaining subsidies to inward investment, such as free deposit insurance.

One school of thought argues that either the first or second reaction is appropriate, the first corresponding to the flexible and the second to a fixed exchange-rate regime. The implicit judgment is that the authorities should not challenge the presumption that the market knows best, but should rely on the market to limit borrowing/ lending to what is prudent. The historical record, including that of the last 20 years, suggests rather strongly that this is not a case where a policy of neglect can be relied on to be benign. Capital markets are precisely those where contagion effects are strongest. Both lenders and borrowers seem to find it easy to convince themselves that times have changed and that past rules of prudence no longer apply, until such time as some event triggers a loss of confidence and causes lenders to decide simultaneously that the debtor is no longer creditworthy. Thus, although many neoclassical economists argue against any governmental concern with the size of capital inflows or the associated current account deficits, their position seems to be unwise.

If one takes the view that government has a duty to try and prevent excessive capital inflows, then it has to select form the remaining six reactions on the above list. The evidence to date suggests that none of them taken individually is likely to be very effective, but that jointly they can constitute a viable programme. Chile provides a great examples which shows that a judicious combination of policies can prevent even strong inflows wreaking havoc with macro management. The maintenance of some capital inflow controls as one of the admissible options, and complete liberalisation should not be introduced prior to (a) evidence that such controls have become completely ineffective (or hopelessly corrupting), or (b) assurance that inflows will not be excessive.

The Recipients of Capital Inflows

In retrospect, it is clear that one of the disadvantages of syndicated bank credits is that they channelled funds principally to the public sector, because that was where governments were prepared to provide the sovereign guarantees that most banks demanded. This contributed to the excessive growth in the size of the public sector in many developing countries, and it excluded the private sector, which is now widely regarded as providing the best investment opportunities.

Portfolio capital is very different in this regard. While there is nothing to prevent parastatals from issuing bonds or money market instruments, they can also be issued by the private sector. Equity is issued exclusively by the private sector. Hence, if one regards it as desirable to see a flow of external capital to the private sector, one should welcome the replacement of syndicated bank credits by portfolio flows.

But does it follow that equity investment will necessarily lead to an increase in real investment in the private sector? After all, most stock purchases are on the secondary market rather than involving the purchase of newly issued shares. The first impact is to increase the price of shares rather than the flow of funds to companies that wish to increase investment. Increased wealth of local investors can be expected to lead them to increase their consumption, so that the counterpart to a part of the capital inflow must be expected to be an increase in consumption. However, one expects the same to be true of other forms of capital inflow: a government that is able to borrow abroad will be able to reduce taxes (if nothing else, it will be able to reduce its reliance on the inflation tax) and a part of the counterpart will be increased consumption, expect in a world with full Ricardian equivalence. The other impacts of a foreign equity purchase will tend to increase investment. This might come abut as a result of a lower cost of capital encouraging new equity issues, or it might happen because the sellers of stock decide to increase investment in unquoted assets (such as small business). Thus there remains a presumption that a substantial part of foreign investment in equities will feed through into increased investment in the private sector.

Foreign equity investment (except through the medium of American Depository Receipts (ADRs), which are traded offshore) has the virtue of stimulating the development of the domestic equity market, which until recently was one of the most underdeveloped parts of the financial system of most developing countries. Bonds and money market instruments, on the other hand, are placed offshore, and hence—like syndicated credits—reduce the incentive for the development of the local financial market.

Financial Innovation

The forms in which capital should and would flow to developing countries as the international capital market revived after the debt crisis is argued that it is neither desirable nor probable that syndicated bank credits would regain the central role that they had in the late 1970s. It is undesirable since they threw too many of the risks on the borrowers and they channeled funds almost exclusively to the public sector. Moreover it is unlikely because the banks had been badly burned and new lenders would demand the chance of upside gains to compensate them for the downside risks that the debt crisis had shown to exist.

What sources might replace the bank? It is suggested that the possibility of both increased flows form traditional private sources, form the public sector, and from innovative private sources. For example, both foreign direct investment and equity (portfolio) investment might increase along with the multilateral development banks (MDBs) (at least the regional development banks) may expand their lending.

However, so far not much action on the more innovative following proposals for private lending has been taken.

i) Investment by multinationals in projects with a return determined by a "quasi-equity" contract, such as production sharing, revenue sharing, or profit sharing.

ii) Lending by banks or other financial institutions on a stand-alone basis for export-oriented projects whose earnings could be escrowed to provide debt service provided that the project prospered.

iii) Long-germ, index-linked bonds issued by a consortium of developing countries [perhaps organised by one of the regional development banks] with a partial guarantee by donors endowing a modest guarantee fund.

iv) Commodity-linked bonds with a yield tied by formula to the prices of major commodities, which would be issued by the exporters of those commodities.

All these proposals still seem to make as much microeconomic sense as they did at the time of debt crisis. On the other hand, the fact that other sources, notably FDI and equity investment (as well as money market instruments and bonds), have grown far more means that there is no longer the same macroeconomic need to foster alternatives. Thus a proper policy stance would seem to be to draw attention once again to these possibilities, to encourage consideration of whether they do not offer microeconomic advantages compared with the current set of instruments, but to avoid any pressure to adopt these proposals.

On the whole, the development of flows of portfolio capital, or more specifically its equity component, seems to be a thoroughly benign event. Equity portfolio capital does not bring with it the access to foreign technology, techniques, and markets that FDI does, but it is capable of channelling funds to the private sector and it has much better risk-sharing properties than do syndicated loans. Moreover, its relatively high cost is at least partly offset by the indefinite postponement of any cash drain because much of the return takes the form of capital gains. Since virtues of bonds and money market insturments are less overwhelming, given that most bonds are still of much shorter maturity than those that prevailed before World War I, The countries should limit their borrowings from these sources, so as to minimise the danger that new debt difficulties will arise. This is very pertinent since the sums available in the form of portfolio investment are (in conjunction with likely flows from other sources) large enough to satisfy the prospective borrowing levels that can be undertaken with prudence.

The principal source of concern about portfolio flows is that they may be too much of a good thing. The development of alternative sources of finance, while perhaps still desirable on micro grounds, is less urgent than it seemed during the debt crisis. The market may not automatically regulate capital inflows to a level consistent with macroeconomic prudence, and hence the bubbles will develop. A major challenge for macroeconomic policy in developing countries is to prevent excessive capital inflows which lead to real appreciations that will undermine the prospects for increasing exports, and therefore for sustainable medium-term growth. Success in restraining capital inflows to prudent levels will also help to minimise the danger that a new debt crisis will develop.

PORTFOLIO CAPITAL FLOWS: HOT OR COLD?

Much of the literature implicitly presumes that it is possible to distinguish hot from cold capital flows simply by knowing the nature of the financial instrument being traded or the identity of the transactor. Perhaps the most salient example of this is the presumption that short-term flows are hotter than long-term flows. The basic idea in the literature is that a hot money inflow is likely to disappear or even reverse itself in the near future, whereas a cold money inflow is more likely to persist. Short-term capital inflows are like cars sitting in the parking lot with the engine running.

The notion that one can make inferences about the characteristics of financial flows by just observing their label is not new in economic. There is much conventional wisdom that show capital flows reflect speculative, unstable behaviour while other flows reflect evaluations of long run profitability and are based on fundamental economic condition. The flows of funds approach used by many central banks and others for an analysis of the domestic economy developments is based on labels which are deemed meaningful.

This view has also been an important part of the traditional analysis of international finance for many years. In fact, the structure of balance of payments accounts reflects an implicit theory that different types of capital flows have different economic implications. For example, the distinction between short-term "hot money" and long-term capital flows undoubtedly reflects the view that short-term capital movements are speculative and reversible while long-term capital flows are based on fundamentals and are reversed only when the fundamentals change. The fact that capital control programmes in many countries distinguish between short-and long-term positions also points to the importance attached to this distinction.

Another important distinction found in balance of payments accounts is between official capital flows, including changes in international reserves, and private capital flows. A common view in the context of current capital inflows into developing countries—which is based on labels—is that such flows are fundamentally different form inflows to these same countries in the 1970s because the current inflows are private-to-private transactions not guaranteed by the government of any country.

Finally, it is often argued that direct investment has different implications for the host and recipient countries as compared to other capital flows. For example, direct investment capital flows are often associated with technology transfers and a range of costs and benefits for both countries. An implicit assumption behind these ideas is that the transactions reported in the balance accounts are closely related to the behaviour of interest in the real economy.

This reasoning—based on the label of the flow—at times underlies substantive policy measures. Once a flow is identified as "hot money," it is then seen as requiring some policy response. At various times countries (especially developing countries) have responded with exchange rate management, (sterilised) intervention, fiscal contraction, borrowing taxes, absolute foreign borrowing constraints, and reserve requirements.

There are a number of good reasons to doubt, however, that the micro nature of international capital flows reveals much about the economic importance of such flows. Since many assets are (increasingly becoming) tradable, a distinction between flows based on their terms (for example, short versus long) is (increasingly becoming) less meaningful. A treasury bond with a 30-year maturity can easily be more liquid, and thus lead to a higher volatility of short-term flows than a 30-day time deposit at a commercial bank. And, a short-term asset which is rolled over can in many ways be identical to a long-term asset.

Furthermore, the explicit label given to a flow may not cover its implicit nature. For instance the inflows to developing countries in the 1970s were private capital flows in name, the universal government guarantees of both lenders and borrowers considerably subdued the discipline of the market. In effect the capital flows that helped generate the debt crisis of 1982 should have been considered official capital flows since the private parties undertaking the transactions relied on a government guarantee (and ex post, private claims indeed became the liability of the government).

This presumably made private investors less careful than they would have been in the absence of guarantees.

This experience should act as a warning against evaluating capital flows according to their label (for example, the instrument traded or the transactor recorded in the balance of payments statistics). In the past few years inflows to developing countries have taken the form of non-guaranteed portfolio investments and direct investments. If the behaviour behind such investments is different in some important way, it follows that we may not be inviting another debt crisis even if conditions change as they did in 1982. But if the flows are to a significant extent guaranteed by the government, their label "private" may be meaningless. Clearly, in thinking about stability, an important attribute is thus the contingent liability of the government.

The starting point should then also be a clear methodology on how the hypothetical economic implications of different types of capital flows can be identified empirically. If credit markets were perfect and complete, the form of capital flows would not be important. A useful analog here is the Miller-Modigliani theorem from corporate finance. Under a set of strong assumptions, the structure of assets and liabilities among various types of debt and equity have no effect on the value of the firm because investors can offset the structure chosen by the firm in credit markets. If we think of the balance of payments accounts as records of how a country finances its international capital position, it follows that under the Miller-Modigliani assumptions, the structure of capital flows and the structure of the gross international asset and liability positions would be unrelated to the country's net indebtedness.

It might be useful here to look at an analogous issue that has recently been carefully explored in a closed economy context. That issue is whether a "credit crunch" contributed to a downturn in economic activity. This is an interesting hypothesis because it explicitly rests on the view that one type of financial transaction, in this case loans by domestic banks to domestic nonfinancial firms, had important economic effects.

This view is an important part of the (new literature on business cycles, which links financial structures and real activity. This literature provides a useful analytical framework that can be adapted to a discussion of international financial flows. It points out that the importance of changes in bank credit for economic activity, as opposed to bank liabilities or money, is an empirical issue. If good substitutes for bank credit exist in an economy, it follows that a decline in bank credit that is not matched by a decline in money will have no effect on economic activity. Firms would easily substitute other forms of credit, for example commercial paper, to offset the reduction in bank credit. In contrast, if banks have special information about their customers that is not easily transferred to other lenders, a reduction of bank credit will not be easily offset by borrowing from other institutions or markets. In this case an interruption in bank credit could have a depressing effect on expenditures and output.

There are two important lessons from this,. First, meaningful tests of the importance of capital account transactions require a specification of the economic behaviour of interest. Second, a financial transaction is likely to have measurable effects on the specified economic behaviour in cases where the institutional environment, information structures, or other departures from complete markets limit the ability of investors to substitute one type of transaction for another in response to changing incentives.

The view that labels matter can take comfort from the fact that international financial markets are not complete and transactions are subject to a large number of distortions. Many of these are imposed by governments in the form of controls on types of transactions that are considered undesirable. Moreover, subsidies often take the form of a government guarantee of private liabilities, favourable tax treatment on earnings (direct investment), or access to special government facilities (debt equity swaps). Each of these distortions is designed to encourage or discourage a given type of capital transaction.

Furthermore, governments also intervene directly in international capital markets. Developing country governments borrow for long-term objectives and, increasingly, in middle-income countries, to offset short-run pressures on exchange rates and domestic interest rates. A difficulty thus arises in interpreting private capital flows that are sterilised by intervention transactions by the central bank as, to some extent, the composition of private capital flows is conditioned by governments' capital transactions. Clearly a country trying to maintain interest rates above its trading partners in some sense generates the private capital inflow by standing ready to match private inflows with official outflows in the form of increases in reserve assets. Such private inflows are "sustainable" as long as the official capital outflows are "sustainable."

In general, if international capital transactions are effectively distorted by taxes, subsidies and direct intervention, the structure of private capital flows might follow predictable patterns as long as the structure of distortions itself is stable. Over a period the financial transactions are motivated by a variety of economic forces. Over time the institutional framework changes, the behaviour of the official sector probably changes, the exchange rate regime changes, capital control programmes come and go, and banking markets (both on and offshore) develop, fail, and are recapitalised.

The final economic behaviour that seems to provide the most appropriate test for the importance of various capital flows is the net intertemporal trade among countries, conventionally measured by the current account. While there are other interesting candidates, for example, the exchange rate, questions about the sustainability of certain type of capital flows are motivated by concern about the sustainability of a path for changes in net indebtedness to the rest of the world, that is, the mirror image of the cumulative current account balance. Policymakers wish to assess the likelihood of sudden and destabilising changes in the total capital account—not just its components.

On a macro level, national accounts identities state that the sum of all capital flows is equal to the difference between savings and investment. For a given savings investment imbalance, capital flows have to satisfy an adding-up constraint. Unless flows influence domestic investment or domestic savings (or a combination of the two), some substitution between the various flows has to occur, for a given current account, the volatility of one flow will on aggregate be canceled out. The extent of interaction between the various components and the possibility of systematic interactions between components thus needs to be addressed before making inferences from the parts to the whole.

A fundamental difficulty this is that the linkage between current account and any of the capital flows data series might be very weak. For one thing we know that gross capital inflows and outflows are several times larger than net capital flows. Yet it is the net flow that we are interested in when considering sustainability of current account position. It seems clear that the motivation for two-way flows of international capital are very different from the general view that developing countries should be net capital importers and that each type of transaction should show a net inflow.

For example, residents of a small open economy might hold most of their financial wealth in the form of foreign clams since this allows them to diversify their income streams and protect themselves from domestic taxation and income shocks. Offsetting this preference would be the tendency for foreign investors to purchase claims on the country again in order to diversify their risk. This diversification motive for international capital movements might account for much of the recorded flows in balance of payments data.

Moreover, it might be the case that residents of wealthy countries prefer long-term investments such as bonds or loans while residents of developing countries prefer short-term investments such as bank deposits. In this case, we would expect to see short-term capital outflow from developing countries matched by long-term loans to residents of developing countries. These preferences imply nothing about the desired imbalance in the capital or current account.

In fact, the short-term positions of residents might be quite stable if there are relatively few alternative investments. In contrast, the long-term capital inflow to the developing country might take several alternative forms. In one year foreign investors might prefer equities, in another bank loans, and in another bonds. These preferences might in turn reflect subtle changes in tax rules (in the industrial countries) that the analyst would find difficult to identify. The point is that the pattern of financial intermediation might be quite stable for a while but that small differences in the institutional framework, due to either regulation or innovation in credit markets, might alter the form that the intermediation taken in balance of payments statistics.

In general, direct investment is a difficult capital flow to interpret. Balance of payments data on direct investment include short-and long-term capital transactions of a loosely defined set of reporters who own more than a given percent of the equity in a domestic or foreign chartered firm. Because direct investors hold factories and other assets that are impossible to move, it is sometimes assumed that a direct investment inflow is more stable than other forms of capital flows.

This need not be the case. While a direct investor usually has some immovable assets, there is no reason in principle why these cannot be fully offset by domestic liabilities. Clearly, a direct investor can borrow in order to export capital, and thereby generate rapid capital outflows. In most developing countries, there are laws against this, so it would be surprising to see negative flows for foreign domestic investment in a developing country. There could, however, be offsetting movements in other balance of payments accounts or in errors and omissions.

On a micro level, there is also much (anecdotal) evidence that, from the point of view of foreign direct investors, flows with very different classifications are actually close substitutes. Multinationals often substitute between and among the various forms of intercompany transfers (retained earnings, provision of and repatriation of capital, and intercompany loans) and loans from local or foreign banks—for example, to achieve higher profits net of overall taxes. In other cases, flows may be complementary, that is foreign investment may take place through a combination of FDI and portfolio equity investment.

QUESTIONS

1. What is the potential size of portfolio capital flows? Could they be sufficiently large and sustained to make a serious contribution to the financing needs of developing countries in the coming decades?
2. Are the portfolio terms well-suited to the needs of developing countries? Is there a serious danger that the withdrawal of such funds will lead to the emergence of new debt difficulties?
3. "Country Fund are the most efficient, if not the only, vehical for foreign investors to invest in emerging stock markets." Do you agree?
4. Are foreign capital flows hot or cold? Based on the label of the flow, explain the policy measures taken in the emerging stock markets.
5. Discuss the issues posed by the emergence of portfolio flows in emerging stock markets.
6. What are the motivations for investors in emerging stock markets? Discuss the major institutional constraints in the sustained inflow of foreign portfolio investment in developing countries.
7. Is there a danger that excessive inflows of portfolio funds will destabilise macroeconomic management? What can be done to counter such a danger?
8. "Short-term capital flows are like cars sitting in the parking lot with the engine running." Comment.

9. Does portfolio capital channel funds to the agents that are best placed to use them to increase productive investment? Will their entry stimulate to retard the development of domestic financial markets?
10. Why would world capital markets be segmented?
11. Are world capital markets efficient? What factors need to be considered in answering this quesions?

35

SOVEREIGN WEALTH FUNDS AND CAPITAL FLOWS

INTRODUCTION

Sovereign Wealth Funds (SWFs), also refered as Govrnment-owned Investment Vehicles (GIVs), existed for long but they have acquired significance very recently due to their proliferation, growth in size and, above all, active participation in capital infusion in the aftermath of the recently observed financial turbulance. This growth of SWF-type institutional arrangements can be seen as a policy response to the strong accumulation of foreign assets by the offi cial sector. However, SWFs are not new, especially in countries rich in natural resources (e.g., oil). SWFs have recently gained prominence in several (non- oil) emerging markets and commodity-based developing countries, refl ecting large balance of payments surpluses.

Despite the global turmoil that has seen the assets of other institutional investors drop over the course of 2008/2009, the formation of a number of significant new sovereign wealth funds has seen the aggregate capital controlled by these giant Investment vehicles grow by 6% from 2008 figures. These funds currently control an aggregate $3.22tn in assets under management, up from $3.05tn In 2008. They remain a vitally important source of capital, and have been making important investments across all the different asset classes over the past year.

CHARACTERISTICS OF SWFs

Various governments have created special investment funds to hold foreign assets for long-term purposes. In recent years, a number of these SWFs have emerged as direct investors. There is no universally agreed-upon definition of such funds, but their original objective was wealth preservation. Their objectives vary, but their investment strategies tend to be quite different from those of traditional TNCs and private equity funds.

What are SWFs?

SWFs are government investment vehicles that are funded by the accumulation of foreign exchange assets and managed separately from the official reserves of the monetary authorities. They usually have a higher risk tolerance and higher expected returns than traditional official reserves managed by the monetary authorities. They aim at systematic professional portfolio management to generate a sustainable future income stream. Their portfolio investment includes bonds, equities and alternative asset classes.

Although there is no universally agreed-upon definition, SWFs can generally be defined as special investment funds created or owned by governments to hold foreign assets for long-term purposes. SWFs can be classified according to at least two criteria:

(1) the sources of sovereign wealth, and

(2) their policy objectives.

Sources of Sovereign Wealth Funds

The funding of SWFs comes from different sources, which can be combined. Some funds are byproducts of fi scal budget surpluses accumulated due to a combination of revenues from exports and spending restraint. Fiscal surpluses and public savings generated domestically, such as privatization receipts, can also be sources for SWFs, as can large balance of payment surpluses, with or without a corresponding budget surplus.

They have existed since the 1950s, especially in countries that were rich in natural resources (particularly oil), but had largely gone unnoticed until the middle of the present decade. Two of the largest of these funds, Kuwait Investment Authority and Temasek Holdings of Singapore, were founded in 1953 and 1974 respectively. In recent years, the assets of SWFs have grown considerably, reflecting the rapidly growing current account surpluses of many developing countries and the accompanying accumulation of foreign exchange reserves.

Sovereign funds (SWFs) from public savings and privatization are more akin to nonrenewable resource funds, as they represent an increase in net financial wealth.The reporting of sovereign financial assets has focused thus far on the appropriate methodological treatment of reserve assets. In 1990, sovereign funds probably held, at most, $500 billion; the current total is an estimated $2-3 trillion and, thereby exceeding assets managed by hedge funds (US$ 1.9 trillion). In fact, such Funds today account for between 1/4 -1/3 of all foreign assets held by sovereigns. SWF assets are projected to surpass the stock of global foreign exchange reserves in the not so distant future and to top US$ 7-11 trillion by 2013.

Is $3 trillion a lot of money? It depends on the comparison. U.S. GDP is $12 trillion, the total value of traded securities (debt and equity) denominated in U.S. dollars is estimated to be more than $50 trillion, and the global value of traded securities is about $165 trillion. In that context, $3 trillion is significant but not huge.

It is, however, large relative to the size of some emerging markets. The total value of traded securities in Africa, the Middle East, and emerging Europe combined is about $4 trillion; this is also roughly the size of these markets in all of Latin America. And total assets under management by private hedge funds — a broad category of private investment funds that seek high returns and, as a consequence, often take on considerable risks — are estimated to be around $2 trillion.

Home Country Policy Goals

While SWFs share the goal of efficiently and effectively managing their country's official financial wealth, they have specific economic policy roles.

(i) For example, for countries exporting nonrenewable resources, the principal challenge is to transform such resources into sustainable and stable future income, compensating for the reality of volatile commodity prices and finite supplies. Placing commodity revenue in a Sovereign Wealth Fund is a means to avoid boom/ bust cycles, such as those experienced during the 1970s, by accumulating adequate international assets. Moreover, a well- managed and effective SWF can help protect the economy's non-commodity sectors from destabilizing currency fluctuations while helping to spread the country's wealth more equitably across generations.

(ii) Indeed, 30 of the 38 existing SWFs have been established by commodity-exporting countries for stabilization and/or saving purposes. The Fund for Social and Economic Stabilization (FESS) that the government of Chile established long ago is now being managed as just such a Sovereign Wealth Fund. The purpose of this Fund is to smooth government spending by putting aside fiscal surpluses that are in excess of a structural target, so as to be used in periods of weak terms of trade.

(iii) Some Sovereign Wealth Funds also aim explicitly at developing a broader base for economic growth. Developing an efficient and diversified economy reduces the impact of commodity price volatility and helps to prepare the economy for a post-commodity era. This has been one of the stated purposes of 5 recently established SWFs.

(iv) Ageing populations create a need to fund future social obligations.

(v) Finally, reserve accumulation is putting pressure on some central bank balance sheets in terms of carry cost and currency mismatches, driving the need for higher risk-adjusted asset returns. Some countries are seeking prudent and effective management of such type of foreign currency accumulation via Sovereign Wealth Funds.

NECESSARY CONDITIONS FOR SUCCESS OF SWFs

While Sovereign Wealth Funds can help generate long-term economic benefits, several important conditions must be fulfilled in order to produce the intended results.

First, appropriate budget and monetary policies represent the most important of these preconditions. Thus, the operations of the SWF must be well integrated in the overall policy framework. Failing this, an SWF could produce potential policy pitfalls, such as creating parallel budgets, or—through ill-timed withdrawals—undermining the operations of the central bank.

Second, for the Fund's operations to be properly integrated into the home country economic policy framework, it is critical that adequate information is reported to the relevant agencies, and that accurate data are included in national accounts, as well as monetary, government finance, and external sector statistics.

Third, recent cross-country evidence suggests that SWFs are successful in achieving efficient resource management when they have well-designed funding and withdrawal rules that are consistent with their stated goals. Most recently, following such rules, the government of Chile has established its two existing SWFs as an integral part of Chile's macroeconomic framework. The fiscal framework adopted in 2006 apportioned fiscal surpluses between the SWFs within a fiscal rule designed to smooth government expenditures across the business cycle.

Fourth, an SWF should be underpinned by well-framed corporate governance arrangements. These include the government as its owner setting the Fund's objectives, its governance structure, and an effective accountability framework. Governance structures typically articulate clear roles, responsibilities, and interrelationships between the different bodies involved in the SWF's administration and management with the goal of facilitating operational independence in making investment decisions.

Fifth, clear accountability procedures among the different levels of SWF governance, and to the public, are important in order to prevent misuse of public resources and to gain public support for the Fund and its objectives. These arrangements can generate public support for saving resources rather than spending them, inform the public about the accumulated revenue, and provide the economic rationale for the buildup of SWF resources. Transparency arrangements, in this regard, entail regular public disclosure of the investment objectives of the SWF, its funding, the withdrawals and spending on behalf of the government, the governance framework, and the Fund's asset size and its allocation, and return.

Finally, the success of a Sovereign Wealth Fund is contingent upon responsible investment policies that are consistent with its policy purpose. These include care, skill, and prudence in investment practices, and a robust framework to identify, assess, and manage the risks of its operation. For instance, stabilization funds—that are the most common form of SWF and have shorter investment horizons—are more likely to invest conservatively and may hold relatively large stocks of liquid assets. In contrast, savings funds seek to earn higher returns over a longer horizon, and may invest across all major asset classes, including alternative investments. Pension reserve funds may even determine their investment policies in an asset and liability context to match entitlement payments, thereby choosing portfolios similar to those of funds with direct pension liabilities.

A TAXONOMY BASED ON POLICY OBJECTIVES

The following types of funds can be distinguished, based on their dominant objectives:

i) *Stabilization funds* are set up by countries rich in natural resources to insulate the budget and economy from volatile commodity prices (usually oil). The funds build up assets during the years of ample fiscal revenues to prepare for leaner years.

ii) *Savings funds* are intended to share wealth across generations. For countries rich in natural resources, savings funds transfer nonrenewable assets into a diversified portfolio of international financial assets to provide for future generations, or other long-term objectives .

iii) *Reserve investment corporations* are funds established as a separate entity either to reduce the negative cost-of-carry of holding reserves or to pursue investment policies with higher returns. Often, the assets in such arrangements are still counted as reserves.

iv) *Development funds* allocate resources for funding priority socioeconomic projects, such as infrastructure.

v) *Pension reserve funds* have identified pension and/or contingent-type liabilities on the government's balance sheet. To some extent, development funds and even pension reserve funds can be considered as subsets of SWFs that are (explicitly or implicitly) linked to long-term fi scal commitments.

Additional objectives include enhancing transparency in the management of revenues from (commodity) exports and fiscal policy. In practice, SWFs typically have multiple or gradually changing objectives. For example, some countries set up funds for both stabilization and savings objectives. As circumstances change, the objectives of the funds may also change. This is especially true for countries that export natural resources. Initially, a stabilization fund is established to smooth fiscal revenue or sterilize foreign currency inflows. As the assets in the fund continue to grow beyond the level needed for the purpose of stabilization, country authorities may revisit the objectives and redesign the structure of the fund to broaden the objective. This often leads to assets being split into several branches for different objectives, or to the creation of separate funds with different objectives.

The institutional arrangements for managing these different types of arrangements are broadly of three categories. The first two pertain to those managed by the central bank and/or an independent agency. A third category of SWFs consist of those funds already established that acquire the modality of "tiers of accounts," that is, separate funds for different purposes. In some instances, the central bank transfers funds to the SWF, while in other cases funds are transferred to the central bank for management purposes.

SOVEREIGN WEALTH FUNDS AND STRATEGIC ASSET MANAGEMENT

Two major considerations usually guide the allocation and distribution of SWF assets. The first is the accumulation and withdrawal rules regarding the fund's future cash flows where applicable. The second is the fund's objectives. Together, these considerations drive the strategic asset allocation (SAA), which reflects the return objective, risk tolerance, and identified constraints (such as liquidity and financing needs, investment horizon, and legal and regulatory requirements).

SWFs may hold assets with negative correlation to the country's major exports (e.g., oil) or offset the price risk of future imports (depending on the country's risk profile) via its SAA decisions. Funds without identified liabilities allow for a more exclusive focus on a return objective and acceptable level of risk. However, for some SWFs, sterilization instruments used to mop up excess liquidity may need to be considered as liabilities, especially from an integrated asset and liability management perspective. Returns on the SWFs are therefore net of interest payments to the holders of the sterilization instruments. At the same time, the currency mismatch, often resulting from issuing domestic currency liabilities, would need to be taken into consideration when setting the SWFs investment strategy

The objectives of SWFs could be undermined by the accumulation of liabilities elsewhere in the public sector. Accumulating assets in an SWF may not affect the net wealth of the public sector if, for instance, the fund is being financed by issuance of public debt. Some funds, such as pension reserve funds, may have identified liabilities to be matched within the SAA framework to allow for a clear operational framework and transparent objectives.

SWFs' allocations of sovereign reserve assets to domestic investments have macroeconomic implications, especially for developing and emerging market economies. To invest domestically, SWFs would typically need to convert part of their accumulated assets back into domestic currency, possibly reversing the economic policies that led to reserve accumulation. Investing domestically could stimulate domestic demand with inflationary consequences. Issues of fiscal accounting, transparency, and risk could also emerge if those investments are actually government spending operations that should take place within the budget. Therefore, domestic investments are generally seen to be ruled out in SWFs.

Different types of SWFs could have markedly different SAAs reflective of their different objectives and constraints. Stabilization funds, for instance, are generally conservative in their SAA, using shorter investment horizons and low risk return profiles, or other instruments (perhaps longer-term) that vary inversely with the risk the fund is meant to cover. Typically, such funds are designed to insulate the budget from terms-oftrade shocks and to meet contingent financing requirements. In this regard, they are akin to reserves, which are managed for safety and liquidity, and it is only after such considerations are satisfied that higher risk/return objectives are set.

SWFs with long-term objectives, such as savings funds, may be better able to accommodate short-term volatility in asset returns. Nonetheless, savings funds and pension reserve funds also aim to preserve a minimum amount of capital, in real terms, so that the purchasing power of the funds is guaranteed. Pension reserve funds with explicit liabilities typically design SAA benchmarks that preserve their solvency..

HOW ARE SWFs DIFFERENT FROM PRIVATE EQUITY FUNDS?

Both SWFs and private equity firms have become increasingly important players in global investment activities. However, since SWFs hold more financial resources than private equity or hedge funds, they could have a significant influence on financial markets worldwide.

They have diversified the investor base and contributed to a better environment for managing risks and absorbing shocks during crises. They can play a complementary role to TNCs as important sources of much-needed investment in the developing world. Potentially, this could have a positive impact in helping to reduce disparities in the global economy. Taken as a whole, the activities of SWFs are also increasing the stake of developing countries in the global economy.

Both SWFs and private equity funds have generated significant benefits through their investments, but they have also given rise to some important concerns. Significant challenges at both the systemic and national levels relate largely to regulatory issues and the need to strengthen transparency and oversight without undermining the benefits that these institutions generate. This requires policy development at both national and multilateral levels.

There are some major differences between SWFs and private equity funds:

(i) Unlike private equity funds, SWFs are controlled directly by the home country government.
(ii) SWFs can hold stakes for a longer period than private equity funds.
(iii) Non-economic rationale sometimes combines with economic motivations in investment decisions by SWFs.

These differences manifest themselves in the investment strategies of SWFs.

SOVEREIGN WEALTH FUNDS ON THE RISE DESPITE THE CRISIS

SWFs, which are relatively new investors, registered a record $20 billion in FDI in 2008, a rise of 16% over the previous year. Their assets under management at the end of the year totalled $3.9 trillion, despite the fall in oil prices. Since 2005, SWFs have embarked on a conspicuous quest to participate in FDI or cross-border M&As. Indeed, fuelled by higher export surpluses in merchandise trade, and rising incomes from the export of oil and other natural resources, they have generated rapidly growing foreign-exchange reserves for their home countries. Several SWFs have also started to diversify their asset portfolios by investing in equity capital abroad, including FDI. This increase bucked the downward trend in global FDI as a whole. However, during the course of the calendar year 2008, the sharp economic downturn in developed countries and the worldwide slump in stock prices led to large losses in SWFs' investments and depressed the pace of growth of their crossborder M&A investments.

SWF-sponsored FDI declined substantially because of severely reduced investment from the Gulf region. However, its long-term potential as a source of investment remains. At the end of 2009, more than 80 SWFs, with an estimated total of $5.9 trillion in assets, could be identified.10 In 2010 alone, nearly 20 governments, mostly from emerging economies, considered or decided to establish an SWF. The positive outlook for most SWFs held firm, supported by the overall recovery in equity markets. However, total SWF-sponsored FDI in 2010 amounted to only $10.0 billion, a significant drop from 2009's $26.5 billion. The largest SWF-sponsored deals included investments in infrastructure, retail, transportation, natural resources and utilities in Australia, Canada, the United Kingdom and the United States.

While funds that invest mainly in debt instruments (e.g. government bonds) were largely unaffected by the global financial crisis, SWFs with considerable equity exposure suffered a dramatic erosion of the value of their investments. By the end of 2009, however, with the recovery of stock markets worldwide, almost all SWFs had been able to recoup their losses from 2008.

The fall in SWF-sponsored FDI in 2010 is a considerable deviation from the trend of SWFs becoming more active foreign direct investors, that started in 2005. There are two reasons for this slump. First, unlike in earlier years, in 2010 FDI by SWFs based in the Gulf region (e.g. United Arab Emirates) was almost absent. Asian and Canadian SWFs were the main investors in 2010. Second, while SWF-sponsored FDI is not necessarily pro-cyclical, the low appetite for direct investments in 2010 can be traced back to the exceptionally uncertain global financial environment of previous years. Because of that uncertainly, in 2010 SWFs directed about one-third of their FDI to acquire shares of, or inject capital into, private equity funds and other funds, rather than investing in acquiring shares issued by industry (e.g. the Canadian Pension Plan Investment Board's investment in Intoll Group, an infrastructure fund, for $3 billion).

While expenditure on FDI has declined, the fundamental drivers for stronger SWF-sponsored FDI activity remain robust. Strong commodity prices in 2010 in particular have created a positive funding environment for SWFs, including those that have been actively involved in FDI in previous years. The foreign assets of the Qatar Investment Authority, an active strategic investor, were estimated to grow from $65 billion in 2009 to $90 billion in 2010, and $120 billion in 2011. It has been suggested that the China Investment Corporation, established in 2007 with a mandate to diversify China's foreign exchange holdings, and an active investor in energy, natural resources, and infrastructure-related assets, received $100–200 billion in new funds in 2010. Other SWFs have seen strong returns in 2010, supporting policy decisions to become more proactive sponsors of FDI. Since 2009, for example, the Norwegian Government Pension Fund Global, with more than $400 billion under management and owning roughly 1 per cent of the world's equity, is now allowed to own up to 10 per cent of a listed company – the threshold to be considered FDI – making the fund a considerable potential source of FDI. Greater availability of funds, as well as policies that give SWFs more leeway to acquire larger stakes in attractive assets, together with improved in-house fund management capacity, will result in SWFs becoming more visible sources of FDI.Growing Concerns about SWFs

GROWING CONCERNS ABOUT SWFs

Increasing investments of SWFs in the banking industry have been generally welcomed in view of their stabilizing effect on financial markets. Opponents of FDI by SWFs further argue that the funds might invest in companies that were privatized in recent years and that the improvements in their efficiency from such privatizations may be rolled back as a result of SWF investment. In addition, some are sceptical about investments by SWFs from countries that lack a free market or respect for human rights and sound environmental standards. However, it should be pointed out that SWFs have to conform to national and international labour and environmental standards, and that if there is a high degree of competition in the market, SWFs have no monopoly power to control or exploit that market.But they have also aroused

TABLE 1

SELECTED LARGE FDI DEALS BY SWFS IN 2010

Value ($ million)	*Acquiring company*	*Acquiring nation*	*Target company*	*Target nation*	*Industry of the acquired company*
3 090	Canada Pension Plan Investment Board	Canada	Intoll Group	Australia	Finance
2 227	Qatar Holding LLC	Qatar	Harrods	United Kingdom	Retail
1 581	China Investment Corp	China	AES Corp	United States	Electricity, gas and water
881	Canada Pension Plan Investment Board	Canada	407 ETR Concession Co	Canada	Transport, storage and communications
800	China Investment Corp	China	Penn West Energy Trust	Canada	Mining, quarrying and petroleum
576	Ontario Teachers Pension Plan	Canada	Camelot Group PLC	U.K.	Community, social and personal service activities
400	Temasek Holdings (Pte)Ltd	Singapore	Odebrecht Oleo & Gas SA	Brazil and petroleum	Mining, quarrying
259	Caisse de Depot & Placement du Quebec	Canada	HDF(UK) Holdings Ltd	U.K.	Finance
194	GIC Real Estate Pte Ltd	Singapore	Salta Properties-Industrial Property Portfolio	Australia services	Business
100	Temasek Holdings (Pte)Ltd	Singapore	Platmin Ltd	South Africa	Mining, quarrying and petroleum
91	Canada Pension Plan Investment Board	Canada	Vornado Realty Trust	United States	Business services
43	Oman Investment Fund	Oman	Petrovietnam Insurance Joint Stock Corp	Viet Nam	Finance

Source: UNCTAD, cross-border M&A database (www.unctad.org/fdistatistics).

some negative public sentiment in several developed countries, provoking new fears of protectionism and policy moves to change legislation on FDI. In particular, concerns by developed as well as developing countries that SWFs could gain control of infrastructure and other strategic industries (e.g. energy, national defence, oil, gas and electricity supply, and other sensitive activities such as sea ports and airports) have led some governments to tighten regulations (or propose such changes) relating to investments by SWFs.

It has been argued that since SWFs could pose a threat to national security, governments should erect barriers against these investors. But most countries already reserve the right to refuse M&As for national security reasons, even if, overall, they are very open to foreign investors. National security exceptions mainly relate to economic activities in the military and other strategic sectors. A prominent example is the United States Exon-Florio provision which allows the blocking of an acquisition by a foreign entity if national security is endangered. In Japan, Germany, France, the United Kingdom and many other countries, the legal framework similarly allows the restriction or withdrawal of a foreign investment for national safety and security reasons.

The cross-border asset holdings of SWFs raise issues similar to those faced by other international market participants, including their role in global fi nancial markets. One view is that SWFs enhance market liquidity and fi nancial resource allocation. This view recognizes that SWFs, especially the larger ones, typically use a mix of well-trained in-house expertise and well-regarded international external fund managers, and have longer investment horizons that can accommodate short-term volatility. Consequently, their investment operations may dampen asset price volatility and lower liquidity risk premia, compared with a situation in which these assets were to be managed with shorter duration. Another view holds, however, that the limited publicly available information on some SWFs, their multiplicity of objectives, and a lack of clarity on their institutional structure and investment management, make it diffi cult to assess the SWFs' asset management activities and their impact on the capital markets. Without more public accountability, funds may alter their governance structures, perhaps as a result of losses, which, in turn, could lead to sharp changes in investment policies, possibly exacerbating market volatility in some asset classes. The public ownership of SWFs (and other state-owned entities) also raises questions about possible capital account restrictions initiated in recipient countries, especially to avoid certain types of foreign direct investment

As their size, number, and use grows, and as domestic and international public attention directed toward them increases, SWFs may be faced with several institutional and operational challenges, including:

(i) *Defining objectives and setting and implementing sovereign asset allocation.* A well-defined SAA within a clearly articulated investment policy is a critical operational component for public investment funds, and as new developments arise, a reassessment of existing objectives and constraints might be needed and reflected in the overall risk tolerance.

(ii) *Institutional arrangements*, including withdrawal and accumulation rules that reflect risksharing arrangements between the government and the SWF, or the central bank, and establishing responsibility for investment decisions and their outcomes. For instance, in the case of some oil-related SWFs, it is often diffi cult to determine on which institutions' balance sheet the assets appear.

(iii) *Accountability arrangements*, including fiduciary duty to citizens, the legal foundation, and the internal governance structure. In practice, the public disclosure of SWFs varies significantly in terms of the nature of information and its timeliness, providing for more or less public scrutiny of the sovereign assets.

The real danger is that sovereign wealth funds (and other forms of government-backed investment vehicles) may encourage capital account protectionism, through which countries pick and choose who can invest in what. Of course, there are always some national security limitations on what foreigners can own. But recent developments in the world suggest there may be a perception that certain foreign governments shouldn't be allowed to own what are regarded as an economy's "commanding heights." This is a slippery slope, which leads quickly and painfully to other forms of protectionism. It's important to preempt such pressures.

Sovereign funds are not likely to go away. They're based on current account surpluses and will become less important only if the countries with large surpluses begin to run prolonged current account deficits. Major countries have committed to reducing their current account imbalances, and this would limit the growth of sovereign funds. But the world economy evolves continuously in ways that make it hard to be sure current account imbalances will shrink. For example, global growth may accelerate or decelerate, and this is likely to affect commodity prices. But if commodity prices remain high, commodity exporters will have large surpluses for the foreseeable future. If commodity prices fall, the surpluses of Asian countries that export manufactures may increase.

What should the IMF do about this situation? There's no apparent reason to see the continued existence of these funds as destablizing or worrying. In fact, the IMF has strongly encouraged exporters of nonrenewable resources to build up exactly such funds in prepertion for a rainy day. Infact there's certainly no need for dramatic action. For one thing, the situation involves sensitive issues of national sovereignty. For another, at their current level of \$3 trillion, sovereign funds aren't a pressing issue. But as the level creeps closer to \$10 trillion—although even \$10 trillion isn't a huge amount of money—the phenomenon will likely attract greater attention

On the other hand, the changing investment strategy of SWFs may imply considerable opportunities as well. For example, they recycle the huge dollar inflows of the countries concerned, thereby contributing to the financing needs of the deficit countries, and therefore to stabilization of the global financial system, by injecting more capital. The passive investments of SWFs in dollar-denominated fixed assets in the past were connected with low returns; today their governments are seeking higher returns on their investments. Enhancing transparency and accountability of SWFs is important. If such conditions were to be met, there would be little reason to treat SWFs less favourably than other fund management companies, private equity groups or hedge funds.

Several initiatives are already under way to establish principles and guidelines relating to FDI by SWFs. At the multilateral level, the IMF has been called upon to develop guidelines for SWFs and has created, with some member States, the International Working Group of Sovereign Wealth Funds to agree on a common set of voluntary principles and practices for SWFs; the European Commission (EC) is exploring plans for an EU-wide law to monitor SWFs; and the OECD is developing guidelines for recipient countries. Ministers of OECD countries, at the Council at Ministerial Level on 5 June 2008, endorsed the following policy principles for countries receiving SWF investments:

> *"Recipient countries should not erect protectionist barriers to foreign investment. Recipient countries should not discriminate among investors in like circumstances. Any additional investment restrictions in recipient countries should only be considered when policies of general application to both foreign and domestic investors are inadequate to address legitimate national security concerns. Where such national security concerns do arise, investment safeguards by recipient countries should be: transparent and predictable, proportional to clearly-identified national security risks, and subject to accountability in their application".*

Clear procedures and guidelines by governments, identifying which industries are regarded as strategically important, should be established to make the investment environment more predictable. Such guidelines will have important implications for the regulatory and legal frameworks of host countries.

The size and rapid growth of Sovereign Wealth Funds is placing them front and center with regard to public attention, as well as for international financial and economic policy deliberations. Thus far, the role of SWFs in the context of the past year's turmoil in advanced economy financial markets has been notably positive. If anything, the Funds' actions have shown that they can play a shock-absorbing role in global financial markets, at least in terms of dampening short-term market volatility. This is a reflection of their typically long-term investment horizons, limited immediate redemption needs, and mainly unleveraged positions. In addition, many of these Funds' managers are highly skilled and experienced investors. As such, they understand clearly their long-term interest in preserving well-functioning, open, liquid global markets.

Nevertheless, some concerns about SWF investments have been raised in recipient countries. Worries have been expressed that SWF investments could affect national security, or that SWF investments could be based on noncommercial motives. Although it is clear that these concerns have little or no basis in the way SWFs have operated up to now, it is important to avoid negative perceptions or run the risk of a protectionist backlash. Such outcomes would be damaging for all parties concerned. It could curtail the scope for SWF investment, increase the investment risk SWFs face, and lead to retaliatory measures Also, such negative dynamics could undermine the efficient flow of global capital and even diminish the stability of the international financial and monetary system.

It is not surprising, therefore, that public and private leader in both SWF sponsor countries and recipient countries recognized that the international system would benefit from enhanced clarity regarding the principles and practices followed by both sides.The current financial crisis has given SWFs a boost in popularity—these days nations are happy to get capital from any source. The rise of sovereign wealth funds carries implications for worldwide market stability, corporate governance, and national interests. However, these concerns can be addressed by establishing the following objectives for SWFs :

(i) To invest in assets that deliver a rate of return on the basis of sound economic and financial variables that appropriately accounts for risk. Additionally, SWFs should implement transparent governance structures that clearly establish the roles and responsibilities—while enhancing the accountability—of management. These objectives establish the importance of using economic rather than political criteria as the foundation of an effective SWF investment strategy.

(ii) To comply with laws, regulations, and disclosure requirements of the countries receiving SWF investment. This critical objective identifies the important role that disclosure of a fund's investment policy, asset allocation, approach to risk management, and other financial data play in mitigating governments' and markets' uncertainty about the purpose of that fund.

(iii) To help maintain a stable global financial system and the free flow of capital. By clearly stating the need and criteria for SWFs to act as responsible players in the world's asset markets and to promote sound macroeconomic and investment policies.

Sovereign funds are not likely to go away. They're based on current account surpluses and will become less important only if the countries with large surpluses begin to run prolonged current account deficits. Major countries have committed to reducing their current account imbalances, and this would limit the growth of sovereign funds. But the world economy evolves continuously in ways that make it hard to be sure current account imbalances will shrink. For example, global growth may accelerate or decelerate, and this is likely to affect commodity prices. But if commodity prices remain high, commodity exporters will have large surpluses for the foreseeable future. If commodity prices fall, the surpluses of Asian countries that export manufactures may increase.

There's no apparent reason to see the continued existence of these funds as destabilizing or worrying. In fact, the IMF has strongly encouraged exporters of nonrenewable resources to build up exactly such funds in preparation for a "rainy day."

In sum, sovereign wealth funds are major state-owned players of the 21st century. Hedge funds, while becoming more prominent in this century, are in some sense a throw back to the end of the 19th century, when large pools of private capital moved around the world with unregulated ease—and generally contributed to a long global boom, rapid productivity growth around the world, and a fair number of crises. What happens when the 21st-century state meets the 19th-century private sector? The outcome remains to be seen.

SWFS: INDIAN PERSPECTIVE

India as a Host Country

In India, the regulatory regime governing capital inflows does not recognise SWFs as a distinct category. Hence, their investments are subject to normal regulations governing capital flows under the category of Foreign Direct Investment (FDI) and Foreign Institutional Investments (FII). In regard to some sectors, such as banking and financial market infrastructure companies, there are limits on individual holdings and the investment proposals are subject to an element of due diligence processing with regard to fit and proper requirements. For this purpose, no discrimination is made between a domestic investor and a foreign investor, or between SWFs and others, as long as the policy criteria are met.

The existing FDI policy permits investments under the 'automatic route' and the 'approval route' in most, though not all, of the activities. Under the automatic route, the investors are allowed to invest in the identified sectors up to the threshold specified for those sectors, without the need for a prior approval from regulators or the Foreign Investment Promotion Board (FIPB). In respect of the other sectors, the investors will need a prior approval of the FIPB, before undertaking any investment. The FIPB is functioning under the aegis of the Ministry of Finance and comprises representatives of various government departments, who are expected to ensure that the proposed investment addresses the administrative and other concerns before allowing investments in the concerned activity. Similarly, under the FII route, the FIIs registered with the securities market regulator (the Securities and Exchange Board of India - SEBI) can invest in the secondary market, without prior approval, subject to certain limits on individual FIIs and an overall aggregate limit for all FIIs, as a category, as well as the sectoral thresholds and other conditions applicable to FDI. SWFs can also invest directly as an FII or indirectly as a 'sub- account' of a registered FII, which include hedge funds and investment funds. Accordingly, any SWF can invest under the FDI route (automatic or approval routes, as the case may be) or under FII route either directly or indirectly. Thus, on the inflows, there is generally no discrimination on the basis of the country of origin of the foreign investor or on the basis of category of foreign investors.

The policy, however, does provide for a framework in regard to ownership and management of the entity investing in some sectors, particularly the financial sector, which is applicable equally to resident as well as non-resident investors. In respect of banks, acknowledgement from the Reserve Bank for acquisition/ transfer of shares is required for all cases of acquisition of shares which will take the aggregate holding (direct and indirect, beneficial or otherwise) of an individual or group to equivalent of 5 per cent or more of the paid-up capital of the bank. The relevant factors for 'fit and proper' assessment of the investor include the source of funds for the acquisition and, where the investor is a body corporate, its track record of reputation for operating in a manner that is consistent with the standards of good corporate governance, financial strength and integrity. The process also envisages a higher level of due diligence when the share holding of the investor exceeds 10 per cent in the investee bank's paid up capital, which includes fit and proper status of the investor entity.

An amendment to the Banking Regulation Act has been proposed which envisages prior approval of the Reserve Bank for acquisition of more than five per cent of the paid up share capital of a bank by any investor 'directly or indirectly, by himself or acting in concert with any person'. The approval will be accorded after ensuring that the investor would be 'fit and proper' from the perspective of public interest, interest of banking policy, emerging trends in banking and international best practices, and the interest of banking and financial system in India.

In the case of investments in financial market infrastructure companies, such as stock exchanges, the guidelines stipulate a desirable dispersal of ownership. Investment by individual entities, including investments by persons acting in concert, is subject to a threshold of five per cent of the equity in these companies.

In regard to Securitisation and Reconstruction Companies (SRC), the Reserve Bank conducts due diligence on the sponsors / investors before giving a certificate of registration to the SRC. Any subsequent investment by any individual entity in excess of 10 per cent of the paid up equity capital of the SRC also acquires the status of a 'sponsor' and requires prior permission of the Reserve Bank which, as the regulator, is required to satisfy itself, among other things, of the 'fit and proper' credentials of the investor.

Foreign investment in an Indian company in the financial services sector, through acquisitions, requires prior permission of the Reserve Bank which allows such investments only after ensuring that the regulatory concerns, if any, are appropriately addressed and that the bonafides of the overseas investor are satisfactory. Wherever necessary, the clearance or comments of the home country regulators of the investing entity are also sought while examining the requests.

In case of investments by foreign investors in activities other than the financial services sector, where there are security or other administrative concerns, for instance, in defence and strategic industries, and print media and broadcasting sectors, investments are allowed only under the "approval route".

In order to assess the eligibility of an entity to be registered as FII or as Foreign Venture Capital Investor, SEBI takes into account all factors relevant to the grant of a certificate and in particular the applicant's track record, professional competence, financial soundness, experience, general reputation of fairness and integrity as well as the fact whether the applicant is regulated by an appropriate foreign regulatory authority.

In brief, India is yet to consider a policy addressing investments by SWFs, except as a part of due diligence in regard to all investors.

India's as a Home Country

In India, the foreign exchange reserves are on the balance sheet of the Reserve Bank of India (RBI) and are managed as per the provisions of the RBI Act, consistent with the global best practices. The Reserve Bank adheres to appropriate prudential norms and the transparency and data dissemination standards in regard to reserves management.

Given the significant increase in the level of foreign exchange reserves, there is an increasing expectation in regard to returns. The returns on the foreign exchange reserves, under the present framework, are constrained by the mandate to the Reserve Bank of India, which understandably lays a greater emphasis on safety and liquidity.

It may, however, be possible to argue that a part of the reserves, which may be considered to be in excess of the usual requirements, be managed with the primary objective of earning higher returns. Given the limitations placed on the central bank by its mandate, it can be held that it will be appropriate to bestow this responsibility on a different sovereign entity. If and when the country considers setting up of a SWF for the purpose, one of the methodologies could be to fund SWF by purchasing the foreign exchange from the central bank, to the extent required. These foreign currency funds could then be used by the sovereign entity for seeking higher returns by investing in assets, which a central bank's mandate may not permit. As the SWF will be a public enterprise, it will be required to conform to the applicable governance, transparency and disclosure standards.

While it is possible to make a case for an Indian SWF, there are also weighty arguments for caution in this regard. First, it would be very difficult to reckon in the Indian context - as is the case with many other countries, the 'reserve adequacy' in a dynamic setting and on that basis divert a part of 'excess' reserves for a higher return from riskier assets. The current reserves management policy recognises this, based on experience during periods of both net inflows and outflows and, therefore, the overall approach to the management of India's foreign exchange reserves takes into account the changing composition of the balance of payments and endeavours to reflect the 'liquidity risks' associated with different types of flows and other requirements.

Second, while most other countries that have set up SWFs have amassed large reserves either on account of persistent current account surpluses or due to revenue gains from commodity exports, in particular of oil and gas, the Indian economy has twin deficits-a current account deficit as also a fiscal deficit. India's export basket is diversified and does not have any dominant "exportable" natural resource output, which might promise significant revenue gains at the current juncture.

Third, India has experienced consistent but manageable current account deficits barring very few years of a modest surplus. India is also having a negative international investment position (IIP) with liabilities far exceeding the assets. The large reserves have been built, over time, mostly on account of capital flows like foreign direct investments (FDI), portfolio flows through foreign institutional investors (FII), external commercial borrowing (ECB) and short-term credit. Further, the increasing reserves also reflect, in part, the lower absorption capacity of the economy, which may pick up with the economy moving on to a higher growth trajectory.

In brief, the public policy is yet to take a conscious view on the desirability of establishing a SWF.

SPV for Use of Reserves

In the context of growing developmental needs, particularly of the infrastructure sector, a step in the direction of using a small part of reserves for development has recently been taken after considerable deliberations. An announcement was made by the Finance Minister in the budget Speech 2007-2008 on February 28, 2007 to "use a small part of the foreign exchange reserves without the risk of monetary expansion" for the purpose of financing infrastructure development projects. Accordingly a scheme has been finalised which envisages the Reserve Bank investing, in tranches, up to an aggregate amount of USD 5 billion in fully Government guaranteed foreign currency denominated bonds issued by an overseas SPV of the India Infrastructure Finance Corporation Ltd. (IIFCL), a wholly owned company of Government of India. The funds, thus raised, are to be utilised by the company for onlending to the Indian companies implementing infrastructure projects in India and/or to co-finance the ECBs of such projects for capital expenditure outside India without creating any monetary impact. The lending by the SPV under the arrangement would be treated as external commercial borrowings (ECB) and would be subject to the prescribed reporting and disclosure requirements. The bonds will carry a floating rate of interest. The investment by the Reserve Bank in the foreign currency denominated bonds issued by the SPV will not be reckoned as a part of the foreign exchange reserves, but will be a foreign currency asset on the Reserve Bank balance sheet.

It is noteworthy that this arrangement is distinct in the sense that India is both a home and a host for the IIFCL's subsidiary, as it is basically a SPV for channelising foreign exchange funds for meeting the requirements of the Indian private sector for infrastructure projects in India by drawing upon the foreign exchange reserves of the country available with the central bank.

To sum up, India has not yet considered regulatory initiatives specifically addressing SWFs. Existing provisions in regard to fit-and-proper or take-over code are, however, applicable to all investors, including SWFs. Currently, the pros and cons for the establishment of an Indian SWF, as generally understood now, are still under debate. India is monitoring recent developments in regard to enhancing transparency and disclosure in respect of hedge funds, private equity and SWFs. In particular, India is watching with great interest the development of global codes, standards and practices in regard to SWFs, both in view of the presence of SWFs in the Indian financial markets and the ongoing debate on establishing an Indian SWF. The hope is that both host countries and SWFs see that their interest lies in building confidence. The hosts stand to benefit from the funds' capital. Meanshile the fund are ruled by the politics of the places where they invest. One is sovereign only at home; abroad, someone else worlds the power.

QUESTIONS

1. Define Sovereign Wealth Fund (SWFs). Critically examine the criteria to classify these funds.
2. Discuss the impact of Sovereign Wealth Funds on global financial market.
3. Critically examine the major consideration which usually guide the allocation and distribution of SWF assets.
4. Discuss the SWFs from Indian perspective.
5. Critically examine the growing concerns about Soveriegn Wealth Fund (SWFs) which need urgent consideration.
6. How are SWFs different from private equity funds? Discuss the size and structure of major SWFs.

PART VI

This Page has been intentionally left blank

36

INTERNATIONAL LONG-TERM FINANCING

INTRODUCTION

Globalisation of financial markets opens new vistas for international financial managers to raise funds across the border through flotation of debt securities and issue of new equity shares. This development, which has been described as the wave of the future, to finance world wide operations by entering in the global financial markets has significant implications since it portends a departure from the traditional patterns of financing and is clearly beyond the improvement in the risk-return trade-off established in the international financial literature. This chapter surveys the international debt securities markets and equity markets and compares their recent performance. The reasons behind the recent developments in these markets have been analysed so as to ascertain the degress of such a tendency's gaining momentum in the years ahead.

INTERNATIONAL BOND FINANCING

Eurobonds and Foreign Bonds

International bonds can be Eurobonds or foreign bonds. Again, the distinction depends on whether the borrower is a domestic or a foreign resident, and whether the issue is denominated in the domestic or a foreign currency. A Eurobond issue is underwritten by an international syndicate of banks and other financial institutions and placed (that is, sold) in countries other than the country in whose currency the issue is denominated.

The Eurobond market, which is an extension of the offshore or external financial markets, has emerged because of some of the same factors that have led to the emergence of the Eurocurrency market, or the market for short-term Eurocurrency funds. These include: (i) the absence of regulatory interference; (ii) less stringent disclosure requirements; and (iii) favourable tax status, as interest income is not subject to income and withholding tax.

A foreign bond is underwritten by a syndicate consisting of members from a single country, sold primarily within that country and denominated in its currency. The issuer (or borrower), however, is foreign. Even if the borrower is not particularly interested in the currency of the issue, the funds raised can be swapped for other currencies. Foreign bonds have nicknames: foreign bonds sold in the USA are Yankee bonds, in Japan they are Samurai bonds, and in the UK they are bulldogs.

Types of International Bond

International bonds can be of several types. These are briefly described in turn.

Straight Fixed-rate Bonds

The most common type of bonds are straight bonds on which coupons are normally paid annually or semiannually. Interest payments are a fixed percentage (determined by the coupon rate) of the par or the face value of the bond. On maturity, the bondholder receives the face value and the last interest payment.

Floating Rate Notes (FRNs)

Unlike straight bonds, FRN holders receive a variable semiannual coupon payment. The variable coupon rate is determined with reference to (by adding a margin to) a variable reference rate, such as LIBOR. FRNs came to the market as a natural outcome of the increase in interest rate volatility, which caused investors to be reluctant to hold long-maturity straight bonds.

Convertible Bonds

Convertible bonds are equity-related bonds. They resemble straight bonds with the added feature that they are convertible to equity prior to maturity at a specified price per share. This feature enables the borrower to issue debt instruments with lower coupon rates than the corresponding straight bonds. In this case, the lender is willing to accept a lower coupon rate than on a comparable straight bond because of the attractiveness of the feature of convertibility.

Bonds with Equity Warrants

These are another type of equity-related bonds. They give the holder the extra privilege of having the right (which may or may not be exercised) to buy the shares of the same company issuing the bonds. Thus warrants are like equity options except that the issuers of the bond and the warrant are the same party, unlike the case of options, in which the two issuers are different.

Zero Coupon Bonds

The holder of a zero coupon bond does not receive coupon payments prior to the maturity date. Upon maturity, the holder receives the full face value of the bond, which is initially purchased at a discount. The attractive feature of zero coupon bonds is that they are not subject to reinvestment risk, which is encountered in the case of straight bonds. With the changing level of market interest rates, the holder of a straight bond is exposed to reinvestment risk because the holder doses not know at what rate the coupon payments received prior to the maturity of the bond can be reinvested. Since zero coupon bonds offer no coupon payments prior to maturity, this kind of risk does not arise.

Multicurrency Bonds

A multicurrency bond holder receives, payments in more than one currency. One variant is a dual currency bond, which has different currency denominations for coupon payments and face value payments.

Global Bonds

Global bonds are defined as very large issues that are sold simultaneously in the world's major capital markets. Global bonds may be held and cleared through several different systems in the major geographical regions, and the securities can move freely from one system to another. The implication of these characteristics is that these bonds are highly liquid.

The Primary Market

A borrower wanting to raise funds by issuing Eurobonds to the investing public will invite an investment banker to serve as a lead manager of an underwriting syndicate that will bring the bonds to market. The underwriting syndicate is a group of investment banks, merchant banks and the merchant banking arms of commercial banks that specialise in some phase of a public issue. The lead manager usually invites co-managers to form a managing group to help negotiate terms with the borrower, assess market conditions and manage the issue. The managing group along with other banks serve as underwriters for the issue in the sense that they will commit their own capital to buy the issue from the borrower at a discount from the issue price. The discount or the underwriting spread is typically in the 2% to 2.5% range. Most of the underwriters, along with other banks, will be part of a selling group that sells the bonds to the investing public. Members of the underwriting syndicate receive a portion of the spread, depending on the number and type of function they perform. The lead manager gets the full spread, but a bank serving only as a member of the selling group receives a smaller portion.

The Secondary Market

The secondary bond market comprises market makers and brokers connected by an array of telecommunication equipment. Market makers stand ready to buy and sell for their own accounts by quoting two-way bid and ask (offer) prices. Market makers trade directly with one another, through a broker, or with retail customers, but electronic trading (online trading) is making grounds at the expense of more traditional trading.

Market makers tend to be the same investment banks, merchant banks and commercial banks that serve as lead managers in an underwriting of bond issues. Brokers accept buy or sell orders from market makers, attempting to find a matching party for the other side (they may also trade for their accounts). Brokers charge a small commission for their services to the market maker that engages them. They do not deal directly with retail clients.

Secondary market transactions require a system for transferring ownership and payment from one party to another. A clearing system would have a group of depository banks that physically store bond certificates. When a transaction is conducted, book entries are made to transfer the ownership of the bond certificates from the seller to the buyer and transfer funds from the buyer's cash account to the seller's account. Physical transfer of the bond seldom takes place.

Bonds are fixed-income securities that are regarded to be attractive investment vehicles by international investors. The following are some features of the bond market:

1. The world bond market is larger than the world stock market, offering sought-after opportunities for large institutional investors.
2. Bond markets are driven by a somewhat different mix of factors than stock markets. Therefore there are different timing patterns.
3. Bond markets offer opportunities for selective risk reduction (currency risk, sectoral risk), as well as broader portfolio risk reduction.
4. Investment in bonds can be combined with programmes aimed at currency risk neutralisation via currency derivatives.
5. Bond markets offer investors favourable liquidity due to high volume.

INTERNATIONAL EQUITY FINANCING

Unlike the case of loans and bonds, the internationalisation of equities did not take off until about 1983. International equity markets encompass primary market functions (underwriting of new equity issues) and secondary market functions (trading) of equities outside the issuer's home country. The London International Stock Exchange is the best example of an international secondary equity market, accounting for a large portion of international equity trading.

International business firms operate in international equity markets by listing their shares on foreign stock exchanges (the secondary market function) and by selling new shares to foreigners (the primary market function).

Listing on Foreign Stock Exchanges

Cross listing refers to a firm having shares listed on one or more foreign exchanges in addition to the home country stock exchange. Although cross listing is not a new concept, the increased globalisation of world equity markets has caused the amount of listing to explode in recent years. A firm may decide to cross list for the following reasons:

1. Cross listing provides a means of expanding the investor base for a firm's stock, thus potentially increasing the demand for the stock. Increased demand may boost the price and improve liquidity.
2. It establishes name recognition of the company in a new capital market, thus paving the way for the firm to source new equity or debt capital from local investors.
3. It brings the firm's name before more investors and customers. International diversification is validated if investors can trade the security on their own stock exchanges.
4. Cross listing may mitigate the possibility of a hostile takeover of the firm through the broader investor base created for the firm's shares.
5. It may be helpful in supporting a new equity issue.
6. Broadening ownership outside the national frontiers, which can be accomplished via cross listing, may help reduce price fluctuations.

Cross listing obligates the firm to adhere to the securities regulations of its home country as well as the regulations of the countries in which it is cross listed. Thus the benefits of listing on foreign stock exchanges must be balanced against the cost of the implied commitment to full disclosure. Because the disclosure guidelines of the US Securities and Exchange Commission (SEC) are more stringent than in other countries, US firms find it easier to list on foreign stock exchanges than non-US firms wishing to list on US stock exchanges. But having decided to list on a foreign stock exchange, the question arises as to where to list. The choice depends on the motive behind foreign listing. If the motive is to support a new equity issue, the target market should be the listing market. If it is to boost the firm's commercial and political visibility, the market should be the one in which the firm has significant physical operations. If the motive is to improve the liquidity of existing shares, then the market should be a major liquid market such as New York, London and Tokyo.

Selling New Shares in International Markets

A firm may sell its newly issued shares to foreign investors in one of the following ways:

1. Selling shares in a particular foreign stock market underwritten in whole or in part by institutions from the host country. It may take the form of a private placement, in which the whole issue is sold to one or a few investors, typically institutional investors such as pension funds and insurance companies.
2. Selling Euro-equity issues to foreign investors in more than one country simultaneously. The prefix "Euro" has the same meaning we came across earlier. The integration of national capital markets has led to the emergence of a Euro-equity market.
3. Selling a foreign subsidiary's shares to investors in the host country. This can lower a firm's cost of capital if investors in the host country award a higher capitalisation rate on the subsidiary's earnings than on the firm's earnings.
4. Selling shares to a foreign firm as part of a strategic alliance. This' may involve the sharing of the cost of developing new technology or pursuing complimentary marketing activities.

OTHER SOURCES OF FINANCING

There are some other means of long-term financing. These are: (i) parallel loans, (ii) credit swaps, (iii) government lending and (iv) development institution lending.

Parallel Loans

A parallel loan involves an initial exchange of funds between firms in different countries, such that the transaction is reversed some time in the future. For example, suppose that a subsidiary of a US company in Japan needs some yen funds while the subsidiary of a Japanese company in the US needs funds in US dollar. The US company then lends the Japanese subsidiary US dollar funds, while the Japanese company lends the US subsidiary an approximately equivalent amount in yen. After an agreed period of time, the US subsidiary pays the yen loan (principal plus interest) while the Japanese subsidiary simultaneously pays off the US dollar loan. Obviously, this operation doe's not involve any foreign exchange risk because no currency conversion takes place.

Parallel loans were specifically designed to circumvent foreign exchange controls. However, they have the added advantage over bank lending that the two firms can avoid transaction costs in the form of bid-offer spread in both interest and exchange rates. The problem with parallel loans is that it is difficult to find two counterparties with exactly matching needs.

Credit Swaps

A credit swap makes it possible to acquire a loan for a foreign subsidiary without having to send funds abroad. It involves the exchange of currencies between a bank and a firm, not between two firms. The procedure is best illustrated with the help of an example. A British company could place euro-denominated funds (deposited) with a German bank in Frankfurt for a certain period of time. The bank can then instruct its branch, corresponding bank or subsidiary in London to grant a British subsidiary of the German company a pound-denominated loan. On the maturity of the loan and the deposit, the bank's branch will receive the loan repayment while the British company receives the deposit.

Government Lending

Host governments of foreign investments provide financing when they believe that the underlying projects will generate jobs, provide some transfer of technology, or train local workers. Countries acting as hosts for foreign investment often provide financial incentives to foreign investors including loans, subsidies, grants and loan guarantees.

Lending by International Development Institutions

There are a number of development institutions that grant developing countries loans to finance some infrastructure projects. While these loans are granted to the host governments, the companies working there are financed indirectly.

EXTERNAL SOURCES OF FINANCE IN EMERGING MARKET ECONOMIES (EMEs)

Domestic investment still accounts for the majority of the total investment in developing and transition economies. Foreign investment can only complement this. However, each form of foreign investment plays a distinct and important role in promoting growth and sustainable development, boosting countries' competitiveness, generating employment, and reducing social and income disparities.

Foreign investors may finance their activities using a range of instruments in addition to FDI. These have different motivations, behave differently, and consequently have different impacts on development. This makes it necessary to review each instrument and the synergies between them. Differing motivations, characteristics and responses also drive different groups of investors in an enterprise – for instance, private investors (individuals, enterprises, funds etc.) and public investors (e.g. via ODA and other official finance).

Determinants of Capital Flows

The factors explaining international capital flows are categorised into 'push' factors that are external to an economy, and 'pull' factors that are internal to an economy. The push factors include parameters such as low interest rates in advanced economies, abundant liquidity, slow growth and the lack of domestic investment opportunities as also deregulation that has allowed greater global risk diversification in industrial countries. The pull factors include parameters such as the robust economic performance and the improved investment climate in EDEs, which are the results of a series of trade, financial and legal reforms. However, which factor would be dominant in a particular phase of the cycle is difficult to fathom.

Benefits and Risks of Capital Flows

In theory, free flow of capital across borders should lead to a more efficient allocation of resources between savers and investors across the world. Further, as the capital flows to capital scarce developing countries it brings along technical know-how and thus should increase growth in the recipient countries and help them to reduce the volatility in their consumption and investment in response to exogenous shocks. However, this position is not widely shared.

While there is a broad agreement among economists on the desirability of open trade in goods, there is much disagreement with respect to the virtues of financial openness. Even strong proponents of free trade have expressed skepticism about the gains from unfettered trade in financial assets. In fact, among non-industrial countries, lesser reliance on foreign capital is associated with higher growth.

Capital Controls

The sudden reversal that the EDEs had to face during the crisis of 2008 despite their good fundamentals and improved external liabilities position brought to the fore various questions on capital controls again. Capital flows have interfered with the simultaneous management of fixed/managed exchange rate peg and inflation targets – a phenomenon known as Mundell's 'Impossible Trinity'. For EDEs with flexible exchange rates, volatility of the exchange rate and the loss of trade competitiveness prompts central banks to occasionally intervene in the foreign exchange market. This increases domestic liquidity with its inflationary consequences if left unsterilised. But sterilisation has quasi-fiscal costs.

Against this backdrop, the issue of capital controls, especially the imposition of financial transactions tax, some form of Tobin Tax, is being widely debated among policy makers in multilateral forums like the G-20, and the IMF as well as in academic circles.

Significantly, the Bretton Woods institutions have relaxed their earlier position on capital controls. The IMF's own Independent Evaluation Office found that during the 1990s the Fund clearly encouraged capital account liberalisation in its bilateral policy advice to member countries. The Fund's multilateral surveillance also emphasised the benefits to developing countries of greater access to international capital flows. But following the 2008 crisis, in a policy note in February 2010 the IMF noted 'circumstances in which capital controls can be a legitimate component of the policy response to surges in capital flows'. The World Bank also recognised that 'capital controls might need to be imposed as a last resort to help mitigate a financial crisis and stabilise macroeconomic developments.' The G-20 recognised in October 2011 that 'to maintain financial stability, capital controls may be adopted or reversed as destabilising pressures abate'.

A significant uptrend in outward FDI has also been observed in the case of India in recent years. Since globaliation is a two-way process, integration of the Indian economy with the rest of the world is evident not only in term of higher level of FDI inflows but also in term of increasing level of FDI outflows. Given the trade-off between growth and instability associated with capital flows, the emphasis of the debate relating to capital flows has centered around sustainability, a country-specific approach to liberalisation of the capital account, a desirable composition and maturity profile of capital flows, and appropriate reserve management and exchange rate policies in the context of capital flows, with only occasional reference to the growth enhancing role of foreign capital in India.

FOREIGN CAPITAL FLOWS TO EMEs: RECENT TRENDS

Though gross capital flows to EDEs accelerated in the 2000s, but for the interruption in 2008 due to the global financial crisis, their external balance sheets showed greater resilience. This is reflected in changes in the components of international investment positions (IIPs) of major EDEs. The external liabilities of EDEs once were mainly debt. Now FDI and portfolio equity together dominate the stock of their liabilities. The advantage of FDI and portfolio equity flows over pure debt flows is that there is risk sharing between the lender and borrower in the case of the former. Moreover, FDI flows tend to be more stable than other forms of capital flows. A common thread running through the debt crises is that in almost all the episodes, waves of lendings were followed by a sudden stop or reversal of capital flows resulting in distress in the borrowing countries. *What lessons did the Emerging and Developing Economies (EDEs) learn from these crises?*

Gross capital inflows to EDEs rose over eight fold from US$ 200 billion in 1999 to over US$ 1,700 billion in 2007, just before the crisis in 2008. While FDI increasing steadily remained the most stable component, the acceleration was dictated by portfolio and other investment. During the crisis the gross portfolio investment inflows to these economies dropped sharply from about US$ 420 billion in 2007 to a low of about US$ 10 billion in 2008.

The long-term trend in capital flows indicates that the peaks in capital flows are often followed by sudden fall. In the 2000s, net capital flows to EDEs peaked to 4 per cent of their GDP just before the global financial crisis in 2008

The sudden reversal that the EDEs had to face during the crisis of 2008 despite their good fundamentals and improved external liabilities position brought to the fore various questions on capital controls again. Capital flows have interfered with the simultaneous management of fixed/managed exchange rate peg and inflation targets – a phenomenon known as Mundell's 'Impossible Trinity'. For EDEs with flexible exchange rates, volatility of the exchange rate and the loss of trade competitiveness prompts central banks to occasionally intervene in the foreign exchange market. This increases domestic liquidity with its inflationary consequences if left unsterilised. But sterilisation has quasi-fiscal costs.

Against this backdrop, the issue of capital controls, especially the imposition of financial transactions tax, some form of Tobin Tax, is being widely debated among policy makers in multilateral forums like the G-20, and the IMF as well as in academic circles

Significantly, the Bretton Woods institutions have relaxed their earlier position on capital controls. The IMF's own Independent Evaluation Office found that during the 1990s the Fund clearly encouraged capital account liberalisation in its bilateral policy advice to member countries. The Fund's multilateral surveillance also emphasised the benefits to developing countries of greater access to international capital flows. But following the 2008 crisis, in a policy note in February 2010 the IMF noted 'circumstances in which capital controls can be a legitimate component of the policy response to surges in capital flows'. The World Bank also recognised that 'capital controls might need to be imposed as a last resort to help mitigate a financial crisis and stabilise macroeconomic developments.' The G-20 recognised in October 2011 that 'to maintain financial stability, capital controls may be adopted or reversed as destabilising pressures abate'.

EMERGING MARKETS: A LOW-RATE BONANZA OR FUTURE WOES

Emerging market economies reap substantial benefits from capital inflows, which in general allow them to increase productive investment, extend financing terms, and reduce interest rate costs. But too rapid or imbalanced inflows often bring vulnerabilities that can include accumulations of foreign liabilities and potentially rapid increases in domestic credit and asset prices.

With interest rates remaining low, institutional fixed-income investors, such as insurance companies and pension funds, are increasing exposures to higher-risk investments, supporting demand for emerging market sovereign and corporate bonds, and pushing up inflows. Even moderate changes in portfolio allocations by institutional investors can be significant. A 2 percent increase in the portfolio share allocated to foreign assets by U.S. pension funds, from 13 to 15 percent, would result in an additional $230 billion in outflows, or about one-half of total net capital inflows to emerging market economies in 2012 (of course, not all of the additional outflow would go to emerging market economies). Amid this search for yield, capital inflows may have become more sensitive to interest rate differentials (adjusted for volatility) between developed and emerging market economies. Has the supply of emerging market assets risen to match the increase in demand? Although issuance of bonds has increased sharply over the past four years, this has, in part, substituted for the decline in syndicated loans, as European banks came under deleveraging pressure. Overall, the net new supply of assets from emerging markets to international markets was lower in 2012 than two years earlier. One important consequence of this relatively slow supply growth has been the growing share of foreign investors in key emerging market asset classes, such as sovereign bonds.

What emerging market vulnerabilities could arise as a consequence? While emerging markets benefit from favourable external financing conditions, including through reduced borrowing costs and a wider range of financing sources, excess borrowing could increase risks over the medium term. Higher corporate leverage may raise susceptibility to an adverse growth or interest rate shock, while a rise in foreign currency borrowing could increase exposure to currency or foreign financing shocks. At the same time, the crowding-in of foreign investors could lead to an asset price bubble, with prices becoming increasingly sensitive to external conditions. Inflows and low foreign interest rates may thus compound a buildup in domestic vulnerabilities, including in credit markets. Moreover, the favourable external environment might breed complacency among policymakers facing domestic financial stability challenges. Each of these possibilities is examined in turn.

How much have emerging market corporate debt fundamentals deteriorated. A combination of higher bond financing with relative stagnation in equity issuance has increased debt-equity ratios and thus corporate leverage in emerging markets. Countries that have experienced the largest increases in debt-to-equity ratios since 2007 (Turkey, the Philippines, China, Brazil, Thailand, Chile) are, in general, those that started with the highest ratios, although Korea, Mexico, and Indonesia moved in the opposite direction.

In some countries in emerging Asia, the increase in corporate debt-to-equity ratios appears related to strong domestic growth and low real interest rates, with much new debt contracted to finance infrastructure investments. There is some concern that floating-rate or short-maturity loans could represent a vulnerability when policy rates start to rise. Foreign exchange corporate borrowing generally plays a lesser role in emerging Asia, but the rise in corporate debt-to-equity ratios in Brazil appears closely related to higher issuance of foreign-currency denominated bonds. Nevertheless, Brazilian firms appear to have a lower degree of overall foreign currency exposure (including exposure through derivatives) than they did at the time of the Lehman crisis in 2008. Turkish firms, in turn, have increased leverage considerably over the last four years as borrowing from the local banking system rose from 16 percent to 28 percent of GDP. While this borrowing is collateralized and is done by firms with strong balance sheets, the rapid increase and resulting leverage warrant careful monitoring.

Overall, there has been some increase in foreign currency funding. During the past five years, total foreign-currency borrowing by emerging market businesses increased by about 50 percent. Cross-border loans plus foreign-currency-denominated bonds. In many markets the share of corporate foreign-currency debt in GDP remained substantial or even rose, amid large increases in dollar-based GDP. This trend has been complemented, in some cases, by a move away from issuing equity, which is essentially a domestic-currency liability, and toward issuing bonds denominated in foreign currency.

On top of the broad-based increases in debt-to equity ratios and foreign currency debt, some of the more speculative sectors, such as real estate companies, have seen issuance more than double in the past year. Issuance by financials has also risen more sharply than that by nonfinancial firms. A more detailed examination of the distribution of firms in Asia—excluding Japan—reveals sharper increases for the most leveraged firms. While interest coverage appears healthy on average, firms may be vulnerable to earnings or interest rate shocks. At the same time, as discussed in for many highly leveraged firms, the ratio of earnings to interest expenditures has begun to decline.

At present, corporate debt ratios and foreign currency liabilities do not appear excessive on a historical basis. But if current trends continue, corporate balance sheets could face increasing strains over time. As an illustration, should debt-equity ratios continue to rise at the same pace over the next two years as they have over the past two, the aggregate ratio for the most leveraged quarter of Asian businesses would climb from 185 to 200 percent, while that for the group of leveraged Latin American businesses would rise from 260 to 300 percent. The figures in each case would exceed recent highs, but would still be below debt-to-equity ratios for U.S. high yield issuers, which currently average about 370 percent. Similarly, extending the past year's pace of growth in foreign currency debt over the next two years would bring the ratio of corporate foreign currency-denominated debt to GDP from 10 to 12 percent for emerging markets excluding China. At such levels, financial stability risks would rise, and emerging market corporations would become significantly more susceptible to adverse shocks, such as from earnings weakness or sudden interest and exchange rate movement.

Sovereign borrowers can benefit from low rates and widening international market access, but caution is warranted. Low global rates, low volatility, and rising risk appetite have provided increased market access for a wider range of sovereign borrowers, which is certainly welcome. Foreign purchases of portfolio assets (mainly sovereign bonds and equities) in several "frontier" markets, including African markets such as Ghana, Nigeria, and Zimbabwe,

BOX-1

WHAT HAS CHINA'S LENDING BOOM DONE TO CORPORATE LEVERAGE?

Real bank lending in China has grown at double digits over the past several years, pushing the stock of loans to 130 percent of GDP by end-2012. A broader measure of credit—including trust loans, corporate bonds, and a few other sources of debt finance—has even climbed as high as 172 percent of GDP. Although much recent new lending has gone to local government entities, the corporate sector remains the largest borrower.

Leverage of the typical listed company has risen but still appears relatively contained. Based on firm-level data, the median company had financial liabilities not exceeding 55 percent of total assets at end-June 2012, up 5 percentage points since 2003. Data for a somewhat broader, but shorter, panel of firms paint a similar picture. Despite strong credit growth, many companies have managed to contain their gearing, thanks in part to years of strong profits and modest payout ratios.

Averages, however, do not tell the whole story. Some companies have geared up considerably, with debt to total assets above 80 percent for the top decile of firms, representing an increase of 10 percentage points since 2003. The industrials, materials, utilities, and real estate sectors have had the fastest increase in leverage, notably on the part of large companies, which tend to enjoy easier access to credit.

Moreover, corporate profits have failed to keep pace with the rise in interest burdens. For a 900 listed companies, the median ratio of earnings to interest expenditure fell to 2.4 by mid-2012, down from 4.4 nine years earlier. This decline reflects not only the rise in debt burdens but also the recent weakening in corporate profits. To the extent that this weakening was cyclical, a recovery should be expected. However, some sectors are likely to face persistently less favourable business conditions, as they grapple with excess capacity or rising input costs. Consequently, financial strains could become more apparent over time surged in 2012, in some cases reaching new highs. Nonetheless, the rise in dollar borrowing, including from a growing number of lower-rated issuers, suggests that developing economies need to remain mindful of their dollar exposures. A related danger is that indiscriminate demand from foreign investors could lead to policy complacency, postponing needed adjustments of large (and growing) external imbalances (e.g., Ukraine and Hungary).

External shocks could prompt a substantial increase in emerging market financing rates. Emerging market sovereign and corporate issuers have benefited greatly from favourable external conditions over the past four years, with spreads for foreign-currency-denominated debt narrowing by an average of 400 basis points since end-2008. Stimulative U.S. monetary policy and lower global risk (itself partly attributable to the actions of advanced economy central banks) together account for virtually all of the spread reduction in the emerging market bond index. The striking result that domestic conditions appear to have had little impact on spread tightening largely reflects the strong policy position of many emerging market economies before the crisis.

But what would happen if external conditions were to deteriorate? Foreign currency bond spreads are especially vulnerable to tightening in external conditions, to the extent that a combined 300 basis points effective tightening in U.S. monetary policy and 3 standard deviation rise in volatility (VIX) would wipe out the spread tightening gains of the last four years. (However, a scenario of strong global growth together with rising rates and a normalization of volatility would have a more subdued effect, as improving domestic conditions would offset some of the tightening in external conditions.) Even for local currency debt, reflecting the expanded role of foreign investors, a net sale by foreigners of 20 percent of their bond holdings would push up yields by almost 100 basis points on average, all else held constant. Many emerging markets, it appears, still face external constraints on their ability to borrow, particularly during bouts of reduced global risk appetite.

Domestic financial stability challenges are rising, partly spurred by external conditions. Several countries face stability risks from continued strong credit growth, asset price appreciation, weaker bank balance sheets, and deteriorating asset quality. Supportive monetary policy and strong private demand have bolstered domestic credit in emerging markets, pushing credit-to-GDP ratios to record highs in a number of countries in emerging Asia and Latin America. On average, bank credit expanded by 13 percent and 11 percent in Latin America and Asia, respectively, over the past year, more than twice as fast as in Eastern Europe. Capital inflows have played a role in this trend. Faced with appreciation pressures from inflows, authorities in some countries have opted to keep monetary conditions looser than they otherwise would have, for fear of becoming major carry trade destinations. While the overall credit-to-GDP ratio for emerging markets, at about 70 percent on average, remains well below the 145 percent average for advanced economies, rapid growth in this ratio has often proved to be as destabilizing as having a high ratio overall.

Household borrowing accounts for much of the overall increase in credit in Latin America, where many consumers have only recently gained access to credit markets (Table 1). However most of the total stock of credit to households in this region is not in mortgages but in non-mortgage consumer lending, typically for large durable goods such as cars. In emerging Europe, mortgage lending accounts for a much larger share of total credit, but there has been an across-the-board slowdown in all types of lending in the region. Credit growth in Asia has focused on corporate lending, consistent with the increase in corporate debt-equity ratios in the region, but there are still pockets of rapid growth in consumer lending.

Asset prices have moved up with the steady growth in credit, although no region is showing clear evidence of bubbles. Reflecting the growth in credit to households, house prices have continued to rise in Brazil, Hong Kong SAR, and Malaysia, even after adjusting for CPI inflation. In response to these developments, Hong Kong SAR, Malaysia, and Singapore have introduced fresh measures to curtail market exuberance and further reinforce financial buffers. In Korea, with the encouragement of the authorities, banks have scaled back some credit operations, responding to above trend house price growth with a small decrease in overall mortgage loans outstanding.

TABLE 1

DISTRIBUTION OF BANK LENDING AND NONPERFORMING LOANS

Region	*Share of Total Loans (in percent)*			*Share of Gross NPLs (in percent)*		*Sectoral Gross NPL Ratio (in percent)*	
	Household	*of which: Mortgages*	*Corporate*	*Household*	*Corporate*	*Household*	*Corporate*
Asia	27.5	17.7	48.9	21.9	57.1	1.4	1.7
Latin America	34.4	12.9	53.1	47.3	45.9	5.4	3.5
Eastern Europe	46.4	27.7	50.0	36.5	47.7	6.6	8.3

Sources: Annual reports; Bloomberg L.P.: and IMF staff estimates.

Note: NPL = nonperforming loan.

The figures are average values computed from the largest banks in each of the sample countries within the regions. Sample countries include Brazil, Chile, China, Hong Kong SAR, Hungary, India, Korea, Poland, Russia, Singapore, and Thailand. "Household" comprises mortgages and other consumer credits. Sectoral gross NPL ratio is computed as gross nonperforming lending to sector x/total lending to sector x.

As typically occurs after a sustained period of strong credit growth, some asset quality deterioration has begun to appear, even as nonperforming loan rates remain low on a historical basis. Some major emerging market economies, including Brazil, India, and Mexico, have seen upturns in delinquency rates for certain types of loans. While many countries have been active in adopting more stringent impaired loan recognition standards, there are concerns about asset restructuring practices and lax definition of distressed assets in some cases. The resulting risk of underestimating true asset quality problems appears particularly relevant in China and India. In China, concerns remain focused on exposures toward local government financing vehicles, but this must be weighed against the over-provisioning (some 300 percent) of recognized NPLs. In India, slowing growth and project delays have led to an increase in restructured assets, amounting to about 6 percent of total loans. In the 2008 cycle, 15 to 20 percent of similar loans turned nonperforming. Nonetheless, recent annual trends show that on average, 8.5 percent restructured loans slipped into the nonperforming category.

Despite the balance sheet expansion and moderate upturn in nonperforming loan rates, bank capital levels remain generally adequate. However, in every region (but especially in eastern Europe) there is a substantial subset of banks that may not be prepared to absorb losses from negative shocks. Even Asia's relatively high capital ratios could come under strain if growth disappoints, or, alternatively, if additional capital is required to fund rapid balance sheet expansion.

Shadow banking systems may pose additional challenges over the medium term. Informal evidence across a number of emerging markets points to rising risks from credit supplied outside bank balance sheets—sometimes described as "shadow banking." Such nontraditional lending activities include the use of pawnbrokers as a tacit source of credit, advances on cross-border wage remittances, some microcredit activities, and the use of alternative "wealth management products." China clearly stands out as having large credit creation outside the formal banking system. The striking trend toward disintermediation has accelerated in recent months. Of the 15 trillion renminbi ($2.4 trillion) in net new credit extended during 2012, some 40 percent came from nontraditional sources, notably trust funds and the corporate bond market, which expanded at high double-digit rates.

Growth in these market segments reflects regulatory arbitrage—agents finding ways to bypass restrictions on loan growth and deposit remuneration—as well as deliberate efforts by the authorities to liberalize and diversify the financial system. This diversification improves access to financial services, but it also raises fresh concerns about financial stability, as many of the new funding channels remain linked to the banking system, and most have yet to be tested in a time of market stress.

An extension of recent trends would impair financial stability in emerging markets. Lower interest rates and favourable external financing conditions have eased risks and supported growth in emerging markets, but prolongation of such conditions will likely lead to the buildup of vulnerabilities and potential instability. In responding to this environment, emerging market countries need to guard against the accumulation of too much leverage in corporate and household balance sheets, while ensuring that bank capital buffers are adequate to withstand shocks and capital flow reversals. This may require the imposition, for example, of limits on growth of very rapidly expanding credit segments. In certain circumstances, capital flow measures may be appropriate, although they should not substitute for warranted macroeconomic adjustment. At the same time, cross-border coordination of policies can help to mitigate the riskiness of capital flows. Finally, supervisors should carefully monitor sources of potential instability in the shadow banking system.

QUESTIONS

1. "Globalisation of financial markets, described as the wave of the future, opens new vistas for international financial managers in financing their worldwide operations." Critically examine the statement.
2. Discuss the factors beyond the diversification benefits which have contributed the increasing popularity of foreign equity investments with institutional portfolio managers.
3. Critically examine the recent developments in international debt securities markets.
4. "Increasing interest by investors in foreign equities portends significant implications not only for investors, but also for financial mangers of multinational firms". Discuss.
5. Critically examine the external sources of finance to developing countries in volatile financial markets.

37

COST OF CAPITAL AND CAPITAL STRUCTURE OF THE MULTINATIONAL FIRM

INTRODUCTION

Non-financial corporations regularly need to take decisions on how they finance their operations, a subject known as corporate finance. Companies can acquire the funds they need to finance long-term investments and short-term expenses in a number of ways. First, they have to decide between internal sources of finance, such as retained earnings, and external finance. Second, if a firm decides to finance its operations by raising funds from external sources, it has to choose between debt and equity finance. Third, when deciding between different forms of debt financing, companies can either issue debt securities or obtain credit from banks or other institutions.

Developments in the overall or macro-financial structure have a major impact on the corporate finance options available to non-financial corporations. In economies with well-developed capital markets, it is relatively easy for non-financial corporations to resort to financing sources other than bank loans, for instance by issuing securities. By contrast, in economies where financial intermediaries occupy a dominant position in the financial system, the corporate sector may depend primarily on loans for its external finance. Certain institutional aspects of the financial structure of an economy, such as a well-developed legal framework that protects outside investors as well as clear and transparent accounting standards, may contribute significantly to widening the sources of finance available to non-financial corporations.

The macro-financial structure of an economy can significantly affect economic growth. In general, a well-developed financial structure should improve the efficiency of financing decisions, favouring a better allocation of resources and thereby economic growth. In addition, economic growth may benefit from macro-financial structures that allow for the provision of risk capital such as venture capital by financial intermediaries.

This chapter discusses corporate finance from a theoretical perspective and the specific use of various external sources of corporate finance including a brief presentation of the concepts of the optimal capital structure and cost of capital as they apply to domestic firms and their adaptation to the multinational firms. It analyses the characteristics of corporate finance in the developed countries, namely USA, Japan and euro area along with the changes in financing patterns of Indian companies. It also considers the implications of the specific pattern of external corporate financing for monetary policy. Finally, some general conclusions are drawn.

MULTINATIONAL FINANCING OPPORTUNITIES

The objective of financial polity is to maximise the value of the firm by selecting the most appropriate mix of financing instrument,s given the firm's investment decisions. Financial policy includes decisions regarding the mix of debt and equity, the currency of denomination of debt and equity, the maturity structure of debt, the markets in which capital is raised, the method of financing domestic and foreign operations, and financial risk management.

Through its access to international financial markets, the MNC is in a unique position to minimise its cost of capital-and thereby maximise its value-by raising funds from foreign investors who are willing to pay a premium over domestic investors. If the multinational corporation can get a higher price for its debt or equity securities on international markets than in domestic markets, then or a given set of investments it can capture a lower cost of capital than a comparable domestic firm can. The option to raise funds in foreign markets is especially valuable when credit conditions are tight in the home market but not in one or more foreign markets. As with investment policy, the MNC also has more flexibility in the location and timing of its financing choices than the domestic firm has.

MULTINATIONAL OPPORTUNITIES AND FIRM VALUE

Figure-1 illustrates the potential increase in firm value provided by multinational investment and financial opportunities. The downward sloping lines in Figure-1 represent the investment opportunity set of a hypothetical domestic firm and of a comparable multinational corporation. Each firm accepts its most lucrative projects first, so expected returns falls as the capital budget is expanded; that is, as more money is spent on new investment. the expected return on the domestic corporation's initial is 20 percent along the y axis. With more attractive investment alternatives, the MNC's initial investments yield an expected return of 24 percent.

The upward sloping lines represent each firm's required return or cost of capital on investment. Firms draw on their lowest-cost sources of funds first, on each firm's cost of capital is an increasing function of the capital budget. The domestic firm has a cost of capital of 10 percent on the initial investment. With access to lower-cost funds from international sources, the MNC in Figure-1 faces a required return of only 7.5 percent on its initial investments.

The expected return on the domestic firm's initial investment exceeds its cost of capital by 10 percent, so the initial investment by the domestic firm increases shareholder wealth. Successive investments yield diminishing marginal returns. The domestic firm will continue to invest until its required return on new investment exceeds its expected return. This occurs at a capital budget of around Rs.160 crore in Figure-1.

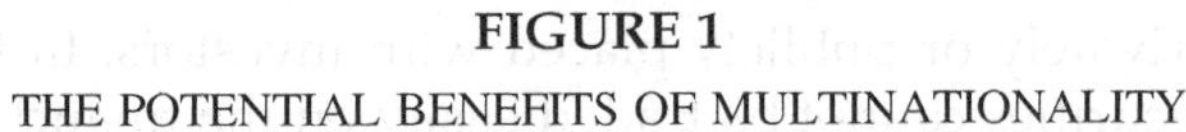

FIGURE 1

THE POTENTIAL BENEFITS OF MULTINATIONALITY

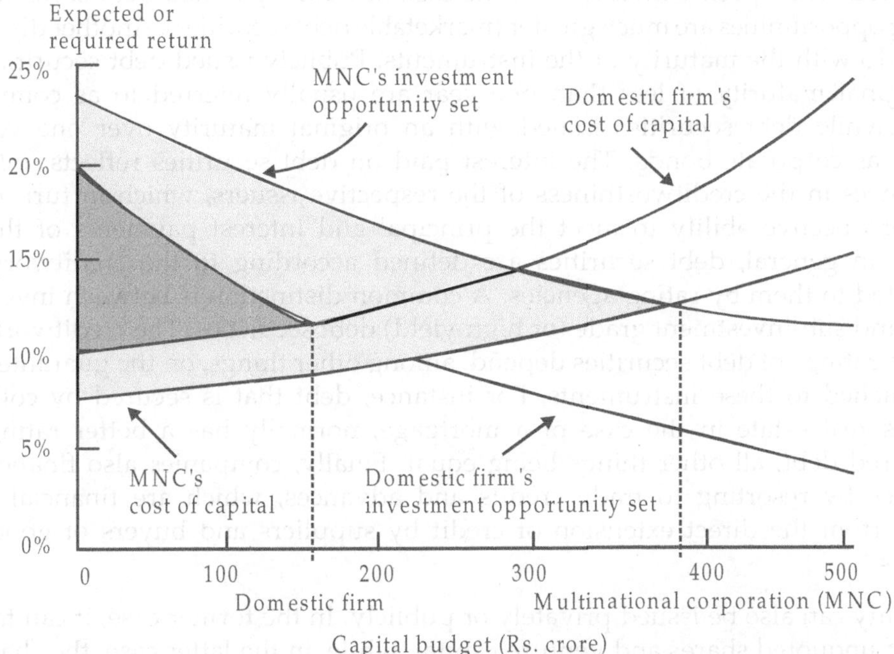

Key : Investment opportunity sets reflect expected returns on incremental amount of investment. Costs of capital reflect investor's required returns on a given amount of financing used to find that investment.

The multinational corporation in Figure-1 earns an expected return of 24 percent at a required return of only 7.5 percent along the y axis, so its initial investment increases shareholder wealth by 16.5 percent. The MNC will continue to invest until its expected return falls below its required return. This occurs at a capital budget of approximately Rs. 370 crore in Figure-1.

The market values of multinational corporations will reflect these expanded investment and financing opportunities. Although these opportunities come with additional risks, the international experience of the MNC places it in a better position than its domestic rivals to evaluate and manage these risks. If the risks are too great, of course, the multinational corporation can choose not to invest in foreign operations, It is then no worse off than its domestic counterpart.

INSTRUMENTS OF EXTERNAL CORPORATE FINANCE

The main forms of external corporate finance are debt and equity. Debt consists of financial claims of external parties that nave to be repaid by the company in specific amounts at an agreed interest rate. Equity constitutes a claim on the future profits of the firm for the providers of these funds - the shareholders. Unlike debt, equity does not have to be repaid.

The main forms of debt are loans - usually from banks - and debt securities. Debt securities can be privately or publicly placed with investors. In the case of private placements, debt securities cannot be traded easily on the financial markets, as they are placed with specific investors. In the case of publicly issued debt securities, the trading opportunities are much greater (marketable debt securities). Another distinction has to do with the maturity of the instruments. Publicly issued debt securities with an original maturity of less than one year are usually referred to as commercial paper, while debt securities issued with an original maturity over one year are known as corporate bonds. The interest paid on debt securities reflects, *inter alia*, differences in the creditworthiness of the respective issuers, which in turn reflects their prospective ability to meet the principal and interest payments of the debt issued. In general, debt securities are defined according to the creditworthiness attributed to them by rating agencies. A common distinction is between investment grade and sub-investment grade (or high-yield) debt securities. The creditworthiness and the ratings of debt securities depend, among other things, on the guarantees that are attached to these instruments. For instance, debt that is secured by collateral, such as real estate in the case of a mortgage, normally has a better rating than unsecured debt, all other things being equal. Finally, companies also finance their activities by resorting to trade credits and advances, which are financial claims arising from the direct extension of credit by suppliers and buyers of goods and services.

Equity can also be issued privately or publicly. In the former case, it can take the form of unquoted shares and venture capital, while, in the latter case, the shares are listed on a stock exchange (these are quoted shares). Private equity consists of equity investments in the unquoted securities of private and public firms. Venture capital is often provided by investors, such as specialised venture capital firms, as start-up money to finance new high-risk companies, such as those that specialise in new technologies, in return for equity ownership. Venture capitalists often obtain a seat on the boards of the firms in which they invest in order to exert influence over managerial decision-making. In order to enhance their reputation and for financing reasons, firms may decide at a given moment to substitute unquoted for quoted shares. The listing of a firm's shares on a stock exchange improves its access to the capital markets, as potential investors receive higher-quality information as a result of the improved transparency and disclosure of information required for the listing. In addition, this information often becomes publicly available at limited cost, enabling potential investors to improve their investment decisions. Furthermore, listed companies often have to meet certain financial performance criteria and accounting standards, which should increase investor confidence in the firm. Finally, once a company is listed, investors can follow its share price and consequently get a clearer picture of the company's investment potential. In most developed countries, specialised exchanges serving new or high-growth companies have been set up alongside the established stock exchanges. These new exchanges play an important role in providing high-risk capital for potentially highly successful companies that may face difficulties in obtaining funds from financial intermediaries such as banks.

There are also financial instruments which cannot be classified as equity or debt but have characteristics of both. These are called hybrid instruments. These instruments have become much more important in recent decades and some of them are also regarded as financial innovations, i.e. new financial instruments and techniques that aim to provide cheaper sources of corporate finance. Examples are convertible bonds and warrants. Convertible bonds give their owners the right to convert the bond into a certain number of shares in the issuing firm. Warrants provide their holders with the right to buy shares in a company at a certain price and are often attached to bonds. Derivatives are another type of financial innovation and have started to play an important role in corporate financing. In general, they are used by companies to hedge against market risks, such as interest rate and foreign exchange risks, or to adjust the features of their debt to the company's specific needs. The main kinds of derivatives are options, forward and futures contracts and swap agreements.

CORPORATE FINANCE AND FINANCIAL STRUCTURE

Corporate Finance at the Company Level

Decisions on how to finance the operations of non-financial corporations affect the "capital structure" of companies. This structure has been the central focus of both theoretical and empirical studies on corporate finance. The foundations of the modern theory of corporate finance were laid down by Modigliani and Miller when, in 1958, they introduced their "capital structure irrelevance" hypothesis. This theorem claimed that the market value of a firm and its cost of capital are independent of its capital structure where information is "perfect" and there are no transaction costs or taxes. In other words, any combination of debt and equity, would be as good as any other.

Following this, a large number of studies investigated the consequences of relaxing the assumptions put forward by Modigliani and Miller. This led to findings that under more realistic settings, non-financial corporations should target specific debt-to-equity ratios. For instance, in a situation where debt costs can be deducted when calculating corporate taxes, under certain assumptions specific higher debt-to-equity ratios can raise the value of the company. However, there are also limits to the level of indebtedness of a firm. In particular, where debt reaches a certain level, the potential costs of bankruptcy have to be borne in mind. Thus, these theories would suggest that for each firm there is a certain amount of debt that is optimal.

Another important development in the theory of corporate finance was the recognition that, contrary to the Modigliani-Miller assumptions, financial markets and corporate financing decisions are characterised by agency costs and asymmetric information. *Agency costs arise because of conflicts of interest between various groups of stakeholders, such as management, debt-holders, and shareholders, and affect the capital structure of the firm. Asymmetric information refers to differences in knowledge between two parties, for example borrowers and lenders, that result in one having an information advantage over the other.* The concepts of agency costs and asymmetric information are increasingly dominating the theory of corporate finance, and have become fundamental aspects of the financial decision-making process of non-financial corporations as well.

Asymmetric information may cause significant problems, referred to in the relevant literature as adverse selection and moral hazard. Adverse selection results from information asymmetries that are related to the nature of the contract to be signed by prospective lenders and borrowers. For example, a provider of funds or lender is confronted with a large set of heterogeneous borrowers, some of which may have an incentive to default on the loan. Since the lender cannot distinguish clearly between various types of borrowers in advance, its lending behaviour may be affected by this lack of information: it might refuse to provide any funds to certain borrowers, even though the borrowers offer to pay the price it requires and may be perfectly capable of repaying the funds. This problem is particularly relevant for new and high-risk companies which have not yet established stable relationships with providers of funds and which cannot be monitored closely or accurately, as objective information on these companies is not often available. For well-established companies with long track records of performance and repayment that maintain long-term relationships with lenders, adverse selection problems may be insignificant. Moral hazard arises from information asymmetries affecting the period after which a contract is signed. For example, after obtaining funds, a borrower may start to engage in risky activities that are potentially highly profitable, but which also reduce the likelihood that the funds will be repaid to the lender. In such circumstances, a lender may decide not to provide funds or to reduce the amount of funds it provides to certain borrowers.

In general, information asymmetries, such as adverse selection and moral hazard, may influence the financing decisions of non-financial corporations and thus their capital structure. For example, such asymmetries may lead to a specific capital structure being chosen by insiders that provides information on the company to outside providers of funds and which may affect the value of the firm. Furthermore, there is a *pecking order* for sources of finance: internal finance comes first, followed by external financing, which is more expensive.

Macro-financial Structure of the Economy

The theories on corporate financing decisions at the company or micro level mentioned above have been related increasingly to the macro-financial structure of an economy. *The financial structure can be defined as the whole setting of financial markets, financial instruments and financial institutions at a given point in time.* Financial structures differ from country to country and also change over time in relation to the stages of economic development. In general, they are classified in terms of the significance of financing through financial intermediaries, which are mostly banks, or through financial markets. A financial structure in which banks predominate as financial intermediaries by collecting savings through deposits and providing the bulk of external funding to the non-financial sector is called a "bank-oriented" structure. At the other end of the spectrum is a "market or securities-oriented" financial structure in which market-based funding constitutes a significant source of funds for non-financial firms. In practice, financial structures are rarely either bank-based or market-based, but a combination of the two types, although their relative importance varies from economy to economy. This is due to a large number of factors, such as regulatory frameworks, technological innovations, monetary and fiscal policies, specific legal and accounting systems and other historically determined characteristics that differ from country to country.

The link between the literature on corporate finance and the optimal capital structure for a company, on the one hand, and investigations into the macro-financial structure, on the other, has been established via models of financial intermediation, which describe the effects of information asymmetries in financial markets on the allocation of funds and corporate financing decisions. These models assert that information problems may lead to inefficiencies in financial markets that have real effects on the economy and consequently affect the source of corporate finance chosen. For example, because of adverse selection problems, investors may not be able to assess the risk profile of companies that are issuing equity or debt securities and therefore may be somewhat reluctant to invest in these securities. Consequently, only investors that are less risk-averse, such as venture capital firms, invest in securities issued by new and high-risk companies.

Furthermore, the information problems associated with financing through financial markets are an important factor in explaining why financial intermediaries exist. This is because financial intermediaries have developed the expertise to distinguish between those firms that may repay loans and those that may default, and so they can channel funds effectively and profitably from net savers to net investors. Banks and other financial intermediaries have gained experience in collecting information on prospective borrowers and in the screening and monitoring of investment projects, which mitigate costs, especially those related to adverse selection problems. At the same time, borrowers that have obtained good credit ratings may secure debt through the capital markets at lower costs than *via* financial intermediaries, as investors are willing to pay a higher price for their creditworthiness. Furthermore, financial intermediaries may be more risk-averse than those investors who attach less importance to adverse selection problems. Such intermediaries may thus refuse to provide loans to certain borrowers and force them to obtain funds through the issuance of high-yield bonds which are bought by less risk-averse investors. Thus, financial intermediaries and financial markets perform financing functions for various types of non-financial corporations according to their assessment of the costs arising from adverse selection and moral hazard problems in addition to other factors.

The prevalence of information asymmetries at the level of the macro-financial structure can be affected by various factors. For example, a well-developed accounting system combined with a relatively high degree of disclosure may encourage the use of market-based financing, as information on firms is more readily available to investors at relatively low cost. Differences in financial regulatory frameworks and legal sanctions may influence the provision of information to financial markets and consequently stimulate the development of the financial structure towards a dominance of either market-based or bank-based finance. Thus, the specific forms of corporate finance and the nature of the financial structure are influenced by various institutional characteristics of a specific economic system. This also implies that, to some extent, the financing decisions of non-financial corporations may be influenced by government policies that affect these characteristics.

THE OPTIMAL CAPITAL STRUCTURE AND COST OF CAPITAL THEORY—THE DOMESTIC FIRM

Financial theory states that for each firm there is a combination of financing encompassing debt, equity, and other forms (preferred stock) which maximise the value of the firm, while simultaneously minimisng the cost of capital. The financial manager is in constant serch for the average incremental cost of funds which the domestic firm seeks to minimise by choosing an appropriate capital structure equals:

$$k_e(1-\lambda) + i_d\lambda$$

where k_e is the stockholders' risk-adjusted required return (the cost of new equity); i_d is the after-tax cost of new debt; and λ is the firm's target debt ratio (total debt/total assets). The target debt ratio, λ, is based on the financial structure which minimises the average cost of new funds. If leverage is irrelevant in the absence of taxes, as Modigliani-Miller argue, then λ would be based on institutional constraints. The general consensus today appears to be that an optimal capital structure does exist, particularly when taxes are considered, but that the "average cost of capital curve is relatively flat over a fairly wide range of leverage ratio". Thus the cost of deviating from the optimum is likely to be minimal.

The cost-of-capital figure relevant for investment decisions is the marginal cost of capital. The marginal cost of capital will be assumed constant and hence will equal the average cost of new funds k_e $(I-\lambda) + i_d\lambda$.

COST OF CAPITAL FOR THE MULTINATIONAL FIRM

As the multinational corporation (MNC) becomes the norm rather than the exception, the need to internationalise the tools of domestic financial analysis is apparent. A key question is: *What cost-of-capital figure should be used in appraising the profitability of foreign investments*. The multinational corporation is assumed to finance its foreign subsidiaries in such a way as to minimise its incremental weighted cost of capital. As in the domestic firm, this figure will be assumed to equal the MNC's marginal cost of capital.

Further, the suppliers of capital to the MNC will be assumed to associate the risk of default with the MNC's consolidated worldwide debt ratio λ. This is primarily because bankruptcy or other forms of financial distress in an overseas subsidiary could seriously impair the parent company's ability to operate domestically. Any deviations from the MNC's target capital structure will cause adjustments in the mix of debt and equity used to finance future investments. The required adjustments and their cost implications are elaborated below:

COSTING VARIOUS SOURCES OF FUNDS

Suppose a foreign subsidiary requires I dollars to finance a new investment, to be founded as follows:

> P dollars by the parent; E_f dollars by the subsidiary's retained earnings, and D_f dollars by foreign debt with $P + E_f + D_f = I$.

In computing the subsidiary's weighted cost of capital, we will first examine the individual cost of each component as follows:

Parent Company Funds

The required rate of return on parent company funds (the rate used in capital budgeting) is the farm's marginal cost of capital. Hence, parent funds invested overseas should yield the parent's marginal cost of capital provided that the foreign investments undertaken do not change the overall riskiness of the MNC's operations.

Retained Earnings

The cost of retained earnings overseas is an issue of current concern. The existence of dividend withholding taxes, tax deferral, and transfer costs could yield specific benefits to retaining earnings abroad. With an effective foreign tax rate of t_f, each dollar of earnings abroad will provide $1—t_f$ dollars of retained earnings. If these earnings are then remitted to parent headquarters in the form of dividends, though, only $\$.52 < 1—t_f$ will get through if $t_f < .48$ and no excess foreign tax credits are available. Therefore, if the parent has a required rate of return on equity of k_e, retained earnings need yield only $(.52k_e/1—t_f) < k_e$ overseas to provide an equivalent return. On the other hand, if the parent has an effective tax rate overseas in excess of 48 per cent, then repatriated earnings will provide foreign tax credits. If these foreign tax credits can be used by the MNC, then the cost of retained earnings abroad, $.52k_e/1—t_f$ will be greater than k_e.

The question arises as to whether a company should incorporate these adjustments in computing its cost of retained earnings. The major argument against such an approach is that since MNCs typically have other, lower cost, means of shifting funds from one country to another, the use of a uniform cost of equity would be more appropriate. These transfer mechanisms include adjustments in transfer prices, dividend flows, fee and royalty charges, and intracompany loan and credit arrangements. A firm which operates through joint ventures or which has few intercorporate trade linkages will find that its ability to shift funds by means other than dividend payments is probably limited. Thus, the answer for a given firm to the question as to whether these tax adjustments should be incorporated depends upon how significant these tax and transfer cost effects are (i.e., if the cost of sending funds to headquarters is minimal, then the subsidiary's cost of equity should equal k_e; if not the cost of retained earnings should be adjusted to reflect the minimum-cost means of transferring these funds).

Depreciation

As in a purely domestic corporation, the cost of depreciation-generated funds equals the firm's incremental average cost of capital.

Local Debt

Many firms borrow locally to provide offsetting liabilities for their exposed local currency assets. The after-tax dollar cost of borrowing locally equals the sum of he interest expense plus the exchange gain or loss. If e_0 is the current dollar/local currency (LC) exchange rate, (LC1 = $\$e_0$), e_1 is the expected exchange rate at the end of one year, and r_L is the local currency interest rate, then the effective dollar interest rate equals $r_L(e_1/e_0((1–t_f)–(e_0–e_1/e_0)$ where, as before t_f is the foreign tax rate. The first term is the after-tax dollar interest cost on $LC(1/e_0) = \$1$ (paid at year-end when the exchange rate is e_1) while the second term is the gain or loss involved in repaying a local currency loan of one dollar with local currency valued at year-end at e_1/e_0 dollars. The gain or loss has no tax implications since $LC(1/e_0)$ was borrowed and $LC(1/e_0)$ repaid.

COMPUTING WITH WEIGHTED COST OF CAPITAL

With no change in risk characteristics, the parent's cost of debt and equity remains at i_d and k_e respectively. Let the subsidiary's cost of retained earnings equal k_s and its after-tax dollar cost of foreign debt equal i_f.

Since the debt ratio for parent funds P already equals λ, an additional amount of equity, E, is required to bring the corporate debt ratio back to λ where E is the solution to:

$$\frac{D_f}{D_f+E_f+E}=\lambda$$

Then $E = (D_f/\lambda)-D_f-E_f$. The opportunity cost associated with this additional equity is the difference between the cost of this equity k_eE and the parent's weighted cost of capital $[k_e(1-\lambda)+i_d\lambda]E$. By substituting and rearranging terms, this cost is seen to equal.

$$[D_f(1-\lambda) - E_f\lambda]\ (k_e-i_d).$$

If $E = 0$ (i.e., $(D_f/D_f + E_f) = \lambda$], then this term also equals 0. The incremental weighted cost of capital is then equal to

$$K_i=\frac{P}{I}[k_e(1-\lambda)+i_d\lambda]+k_s\frac{E_f}{I}+\frac{i_fD_f}{I}+(k_e-i_d)[D_f(1-\lambda)-E_f\lambda]$$

The last term is the penalty (reward) for over- (under-) leveraging abroad. If this investment changes the parent company risk characteristics, then the parent's cost of equity capital must be adjusted.

A simplified version of this formula is possible by redefining and reorganising terms. If we set $k_o = k_e(1-\lambda)+i_d\lambda$, then k_1 reduces to:

$$k_0-\alpha(k_e-k_s)-\beta(i_d-i_f)$$

where

$$\alpha=\frac{E_f}{I}\ \text{and}\ \beta=\frac{D_f}{I}.$$

This formula ignores the possibility that the optimal D/E ratio may itself be dependent on the relative costs of debts and equity. It, therefore, provides an upper bound for estimating a subsidiary's cost of capital. Furthermore, this formula is appropriate whether or not an optimal capital structure exists. If it does exist, then λ should equal the optimal debt ratio. If not, then the cost of capital measured at λ remains constant over the entire range of leverage and the leverage penalty is exactly defined.

The formula above indicates, that in those countries where the local cost of capital is high relative to an MNC's cost of funds, using the local cost of capital to evaluate investments will cause profitable ventures to be foregone. At the same time, it would be suboptimal for a multinational corporation to ignore the possibility that some of its subsidiaries may have access to lower cost funds than does the parent.

A numerical example will illustrate some of the concepts presented here. Assume that a new investment requires \$100 million. Of this total, \$20 million will be provided by parent company funds, \$25 million by retained earnings in the subsidiary, and \$55 million through the issue of new long-term debt by the subsidiary. The parent's cost of equity equals 14 per cent and its after-tax cost of long-term debt equals 5 per cent. However, this investment is expected to increase the systematic risk of the firm, thereby requiring, a rate of return of 16 per cent on new parent equity and 6 per cent after-tax on new long-term debt. With a foreign tax rate of 40 per cent and no excess foreign tax credit available, the cost of retained earnings will be set equal to 13.9 per cent. Let the nominal rate of interest on the subsidiary's debt be 16 per cent with an anticipated average annual devaluation of 5 per cent over the life of the loan. Then the effective after-tax dollar cost of this foreign debt equals 4 per cent. Assume further that the MNC's current debt/equity ratio, which is considered to be optimal, equals 3/7 with present debt equal to \$300 million and equity equal to \$700 million. Then the new corporate D/E ratio equals 355/725. To return to a D/E ratio of 3/7, additional equity in the amount of \$103 million must be raised. Ordinarily, \$31 million of this \$103 million would be in the form of debt. Thus, an opportunity cost equal to \$31,000,000 (.16 – .06) or \$3,100,000 is paid for the additional overseas leverage. The total annual risk-adjusted cost of the parent company funds equals \$20,000,000 (.16 × .7 + .06 × .3) = \$2,600,000. The annual cost of the retained earnings equals \$25,000,000 (.139) = \$3,500,000 and the total annual expected cost of the foreign debt issued is \$55,000,000 (.04) = \$2,200,000. Including the annual opportunity cost involved in over-leveraging abroad, the average incremental cost of capital (and the marginal cost equals (2.6 + 3.5 + 2.2 + 3.1/100) = 11.4 per cent. This compares with the parent company's cost of capital for this investment of 13 per cent.

SUBSIDIARY CAPITAL STRUCTURE

The question has been raised as to whether subsidiary capital structures should:

(a) conform to parent company norms;

(b) conform to the capitalisation norms established in each country; or

(c) vary, so as to take advantage of opportunities to minimise the cost of capital.

The third alternative appears to be the appropriate choice. Any accounting rendition of a separate capital structure for the subsidiary is therefore wholly illusory and should be ignored in planning foreign investments. Within the constraints set by foreign statutory or minimum equity requirements and the need to maintain a worldwide financial structure, a multinational corporation should finance its requirements in such a manner as to minimise its incremental average cost of capital.

A subsidiary with a capital structure similar to its parent may miss out on profitable opportunities to lower its cost of funds. For example, rigid adherence to a fixed debt/equity ratio may not allow a subsidiary to take advantage of government-subsidised debt or low-cost loans for international agencies. On the other hand, forcing a subsidiary to borrow funds locally to meet parent norms may be quite expensive in a country with a high-cost capital market. The cost-minimising approach would be to allow subsidiaries in low-cost countries to exceed the parent company capitalisation norm while subsidiaries in high-cost nations would have lower target debt/equity ratios. This assumes that capital markets are at least partially segmented. While there are no definite conclusions on this issue at present, the variety and degree of governmental restrictions on capital market access lend credence to the segmentation hypothesis. In addition, the behaviour of MNCs in lobbying against regulations and restrictions indicates that they believe capital costs vary significantly among countries.

A counterargument is that a subsidiary's financial structure should conform to local norms. Hence, subsidiaries based in Japan or Germany should have much higher debt/equity ratios than the U.S. parent or a French subsidiary. There are obvious advantages accruing from a localised capital structure. It permits the affiliate to be evaluated on the same basis as its local competitors, and makes foreign affiliates more acceptable by their host governing local business, rather than, for instance, operating with little equity and a high proportion of debt from local sources. Localising the capital structure also allows the firm to reap the benefits of financial leverage, where debt ratios are substantially higher than that of the parent company.

Conforming to local financial structure may cause the affiliates to operate at a higher cost of capital compared with the worldwide consolidated cost of capital of the parent. MNCs have access to international capital markets, which may enable them to raise funds at more favourable terms than in the local markets of the affiliates. They also enjoy the cost-reduction benefit of diversification. Why should they not pass these advantages to their affiliates, instead of conforming to local norms and patterns of financing? In theory, minimising the worldwide cost of capital would occur only if the overall consolidated capital structure conforms to the optimal structure.

An argument against localising capital structure is that it is purely cosmetic, even if it seemingly results in lowering the cost of capital for the affiliate. Potential lenders, particularly outside the host country, look for the firm's worldwide cash flow generation to service their loans, rather than the resources of the borrowing affiliate. Lenders realise that the parent stands behind the obligations of its affiliates, even if no direct guarantee of such loans has been given by the parent. According to this argument, an MNC has in fact an internationalised capital structure even if it departs from this norm in financing its affiliates. In addition the problem with this argument is that it ignores the strong linkage between U.S.—based multinationals and the U.S. capital market. Since most of its stock is owned and traded in the United States, it follows that firm's target debt/equity ratio is dependent on U.S. shareholders' risk perceptions. Furthermore, the level of foreign debt/equity ratios is usually determined by institutional factors which have no bearing on U.S. multinationals. For example, Japanese and German banks own much of the equity as well as the debt issues of local corporations. Combining the functions of stockholder and lender may reduce the perceived risk of default on loans to captive corporations and increase the desirability of substantial leverage. This would not apply to a wholly-owned subsidiary. However, a joint venture with a corporation tied into the local banking system may enable an MNC to lower its local cost of capital by leveraging itself, without a proportional increase in risk, to a degree that would be impossible otherwise.

A subsidiary's capital structure is relevant only insofar as it affects the parent's consolidated worldwide debt ratio. The related issues of consolidation and parent company guarantees appear to indicate that at least some MNCs believe otherwise.

PARENT COMPANY GUARANTEES AND CONSOLIDATION

Multinational firms are often thought to be reluctant to explicitly guarantee the debt of their subsidiaries even when a more advantageous interest rate can be negotiated. Their assumption appears to be that nonguaranteed debt would not be included in the parent company's worldwide debt ratio whereas guaranteed debt, as a contingent liability, would affect the parent's debt-raising capacity.

This assumption ignores certain realities. It is very unlikely that a parent company would allow a subsidiary to default on its debt, even if that debt were not guaranteed. The multinationals feel a "moral" obligation, for very practical reasons, to implicitly, if not explicitly, guarantee their subsidiaries' debt. Since an explicit guarantee will generally lower subsidiary borrowing costs, it will usually be in the parent's best interest to issue such a guarantee provided that the parent is actually committed to making good on its subsidiaries' debt.

Related to this issue of parent guaranteed debt is the belief, among some firms which do not consolidate their foreign affiliates, that unconsolidated (and nonguaranteed) overseas debt need not affect the MNC's debt ratio. Unless investors and analysts can be fooled permanently, though, unconsolidated overseas leveraging would not allow a firm to lower its cost of capital below the cost of capital for an identical firm which consolidated its foreign affiliates. Any overseas debt offering large enough to materially affect a firm's degree of leverage would very quickly come to the attention of financial analysts.

TAX AND REGULATORY FACTORS

Parent company funds, whether called equity or debt require the same rate of return. However, the appropriate ratio of parent company loans to parent equity may be a crucial decision. Loans are generally preferred to equity by MNCs for a number of reasons. First of all, parent company loans to foreign subsidiaries are often regarded as equivalent to equity investments both by host countries and local creditors. A parent company loan is generally subordinated to all other kinds of debt and does not represent the same threat of insolvency as an external loan. Given this equivalence in the eyes of potential creditors and host governments, the tax and flexibility advantages of debt could become dominant considerations. A firm typically has wider latitude in repatriating funds in the form of interest and loan repayments than as dividends or reductions in equity, since the latter fund flows are usually more closely controlled by governments.

Another reason for the use of parent company loans as opposed to equity investments is the possibility of reducing taxes. If foreign tax rates are below home rates, dividends will typically lead to increased taxes whereas loan repayments will not. For instance, in case of U.S. MNCs if foreign tax rates are above 48 per cent, and a withholding tax is assessed on dividends, paying out dividends will lead to higher taxes unless the excess foreign tax credits can be used elsewhere.

Firms, do not have complete latitude in choosing their debt/equity ratios abroad. This is frequently a subject for negotiation with the host governments. In addition, dividends are often restricted to a fixed percentage of equity. A small equity base could also lead to a high return on equity, opening up a company to charges of exploitation.

It should be reiterated here that a firm's cost of capital is not affected by whether it calls its overseas investments debt or equity. However, the cash flow from foreign investments could very well be affected by the form of this investment. U.S. multinationals usually use more equity than is required to meet government regulations. As a result, total foreign plus U.S. taxes are greater than they need be.

RISKINESS OF FOREIGN OPERATIONS

The traditional approach to international investment considers foreign operations as adding to overall firm riskiness. Foreign exchange risk, the risks of expropriation and continued governmental intervention are pointed out as increasing the political and economic risks facing any firms operating abroad. However, this view is quite limited.

According to modern capital asset pricing theory, investors must be compensated only for their securities systematic risk since nonsystematic risk can be diversified away by holding a market portfolio. Although individual foreign investments may be riskier than comparable investments in the domestic market, the diversification effect due to operating in a number of countries whose economic cycles are not perfectly in phase could reduce the variation in a firm's earnings.

Segmented Capital Markets

The cost of capital for an MNC could differ from the firm's domestic cost of funds if there are market imperfections. Such imperfections may affect the availability as well as the cost of the debt and equity components of the capital structure. Segmented capital markets are, by definition, inefficient markets which are characterised by persistent differentials in the cost of raising funds in different countries which are not offset by exchange rate movements. Segmentation arises from controls on the flow of capital across boundaries and from the varying degrees of depth and development of capital markets in different countries. It may also result from lack of accurate information on investment and lending opportunities in different markets.

Market segmentation impacts the cost of capital of the MNC upward or downward, depending on a number of factors, which include: the interest elasticity of the supply and demand for loanable funds in the domestic market, access to international sources of funds, the degree of segmentation in the home or host country capital markets, and transaction costs.

A segmented host country capital markets may provide lower cost of funds, as restrictions on capital outflow prevent these funds from seeking higher returns outside the country. In this case, an MNC's cost of capital in the host country of the project may be lower than its cost of capital at home. The management must decide in this case whether the local project should benefit from the lower cost of funds, or if it should be evaluated on the basis of the MNC's worldwide cost of capital.

More often segmentation of capital markets leads to higher cost of capital than if such markets were fully integrated. A common form of segmentation in many countries takes the form of unavailability or limited availability of equity financing. Many U.S. multinationals find it difficult to raise substantial amounts of equity capital even in many industrial countries, perhaps with the exception of the United Kingdom. Investors in many countries have an aversion to buying shares of foreign companies, and often lack sufficient information about these investments. Other determinants include controls which restrict purchase of foreign securities, difficulties of listing on foreign stock exchanges, and stiff and lengthy registration and disclosure requirements. Such requirements in the United States, for example, discourage non-U.S. multinational firms from raising equity funds in the United States.

Where the foreign investment faces a unique cost of capital due to excessive segmentation, the financial manager must make a determination as to the appropriate hurdle rate for purposes of evaluation. One possible rate is what the project should earn if it were to be competitive in its own environment.

Inflation and Exchange Risks

Foreign inflation will not affect the MNC's local currency cost of borrowing abroad. However, exchange rate changes will affect these costs. To the extent that capital markets overseas are segmented, though, the cost of borrowing abroad may not fully reflect these exchange rate expectations.

Inflation and exchange rate changes will affect the future cash flows of a project. In fact, there are systems, predictable both as to direction and magnitude. The sector of the economy a firm operates in (export, import—competing, or purely domestic) and the sources of its inputs (imports, domestic traded, or nontraded goods) are the major determinants of a firm's exchange risk.

This means that the incremental effects of changes in currency values on the parent's risk characteristics and, hence, the parent's cost of capital, can only be determined by examining the impact of variations in foreign earnings on variations in the firm's world wide consolidated earning. However, variations due to exchange rate changes will be difficult to separate out from variations due to other events such as changes in government policies, competitors' actions, etc. Nor need these exchange effects be isolated. The important factor to analyse is the simultaneous impact on firm earnings of the myriad of events to which a multinational firm is prone.

Diversification

The greater riskiness of individual projects overseas could well be offset by beneficial portfolio effects. There is little correlation between the earnings of the various national components of MNCs. To the extent that foreign cash flows are not perfectly correlated with those of domestic investments, the overall risk associated with variations in cash flows which confronts a stockholder might be reduced. Thus, the greater riskiness of individual projects overseas could well be offset by beneficial portfolio effects. However, international diversification by firms will benefit their stockholders only if there are barriers to direct international portfolio diversification by individual investors. But these barriers do exist. Neither individual nor mutual funds are broadly diversified internationally, presumably at least in part due to institutional barriers to foreign investment.

The greater the foreign involvement of a firm, the lower the covariance of its earnings per share with the earnings per share of the leading national stock index, and there is close positive correlation between the systematic risk of a firm's earnings and its stock price β. Thus higher the percentage of foreign to total earnings the lower the capitalisation rate on its earnings is reasonable. However, since multinationals are larger on average, than are non-multinationals, the reduction in earnings variability may be due to size, and a consequent increase in product diversification, rather than to the influence of foreign-source earnings. In fact while the stock price βs are slightly lower of MNCs, when corrected for size, there is no significant difference between the βs of MNCs and non-MNCs.

The earning variability is a decreasing function of foreign-source earnings even when corrected for size. The relationship between this reduction in earnings variability and a reduction in the systematic risk of an MNC's earnings, however, is not demonstrated. This is an important distinction because there is no empirical evidence to suggest a correlation between a firm's stock price β and its degree of earnings variability. The evidence available relates to a firm's systematic earnings risk. However, the risk of bankruptcy for a firm is dependent on total as opposed to only systematic earnings variability. Thus, a reduction in the total earnings variability could allow an MNC to leverage itself more highly leading to a reduction in its marginal cost of capital.

The investors recognise and reward the geographical diversification of multinationals by using a two-factor capital asset pricing model with the second factor being the percentage of foreign sales. The market behaves as if it recognises the international composition of the activities of MNCs. Taking a different approach, the dividend valuation model to measure the cost of equity capital for MNCs, it is pointed that multinationality alters a firm's perceived riskiness, MNCs that often borrow substantial amounts may be given preferential treatment by creditors, thereby reducing their cost of capital. Furthermore, their relatively large issues of stocks or bonds allow for reduced flotation costs (as a percentage of the amount of financing). Yet, this is due to their size and not to their internationalised business. That is, a domestic corporation may be given the same treatment if it is large enough. However, a firm's growth is more restricted if it is not wiling to operate internationally. Because MNCs may more easily achieve growth, they may be more able than purely domestic firms to reach the necessary size to receive preferential treatment form creditors.

Joint Ventures

Since many MNCs participate in joint ventures, either by choice or necessity, establishing the required rate of return for this form of investment is particularly important. Several problems arise. The most troublesome is the case where the MNC's required rate of return in joint venture differs from its partner's cost of capital. A complex compensation principles may be applied whereby each partner is compensated on the basis of its opportunity cost of money. This will lead to a situation where each partner tries to declare as high a cost of capital as possible. Agreement on a joint venture cost of capital using this principle will then be even less likely. One solution is to set the required rate of return for the joint venture equal to the maximum cost of capital among the participants.

The firm can use the formula presented earlier to establish its marginal cost of capital in a joint venture. There is one caveat. A joint venture partner may have access to local sources of capital which enable the joint venture to be leveraged beyond what the subsidiary would be able to do on its own. The formula presented earlier penalised a subsidiary which leverages itself more than the parent itself is leveraged. This is due to the increased risk of financial distress associated with more highly leveraged firms. However, in countries such as Japan and Germany, increased leveraged will not necessarily lead to increased financial risks due to the close relationship between the local banks and corporation. Thus, increased leverage in a joint venture in Japan, for example, may not require application of the leverage penalty. The assessment of the impact of leverage in a joint venture is a judgmental factor which requires an analysis of the partner's ties with the local financial community, particularly with the local banks.

Overcoming Cultural Differences

An English aristocrat once said, "The only trouble with going abroad is that you have to leave home to do it." True enough. People and their cultural norms vary widely around the world. The management and employees of the multinational corporation must deal with unfamiliar business and popular cultures as they seek to extend the firm's competitive advantages into new and unfamiliar markets. Being able to understand, adapt to, and manage cultural differences can make the difference between a successful and an unsuccessful international venture.

Another way to categorise differences in national business environments is according to their impact on the multinational corporation itself; in particular, along the traditional functional areas of business: marketing, distribution, personnel management, law, accounting, taxes, and finance. The following list characterises some of the differences that MNC's encounter in cross-border operations. The examples are illustrative of the costs and risks of international business, but they are not intended to be exhaustive.

i) Differences in Language

The annals of international business are replete with amusing anecdotes involving language differences. One anecdote has General Motors attempting to sell the Chevrolet Nova in Puerto Rico. Literally translated, *no va* means "it goes not". GM renamed the car Caribe for sale in Latin American countries. In another anecdote, a print advertisement for Coca-Cola in China used a set of Chinese characters that sounded like *Coca-Cola* but translated as "bite the wax tadpole." Coke's advertising slogan "Coke adds life" was literally translated into Chinese as "Coke brings you back from the dead." True to its multinational nature, Coca-Cola was quick to spot these problems and modify its Chinese advertising programme.

ii) Differences in Body Language

As if verbal language weren't enough of a barrier to communication, body language differs across cultures as well. In many settings, what we do with our bodies is even more important than what we say. (Voltaire wrote, "Words were given to man to enable him to conceal his true feelings.") Although some body language is universal, a great deal of it is an accouterment of our culture.

Eye contact is a good example. In the Western world, direct eye contact conveys confidence. Avoiding eye contact is taken as a sign of weakness and may even convey untrustworthiness. For this reason, in Western countries it is necessary for subordinates to show respect and meet the eyes of their superiors. In some Asian countries, however, subordinates show their respect by avoiding eye contact in some Arab countries, excessive eye contact between a man and woman is thought to be disrespectful to the woman. The eyes are the windows to the soul, but be careful which window you look through.

iii) Differences in Marketing

Marketing difficulties only begin with differences in language. Far more subtle are the many nonverbal differences between cultures. For example, Walt Disney owns and operates the world's most successful theme parks. At the heart of Disney's success in the United States is their appeal to the entire family. Disney tried to retain this American-style family orientation when it opened its EuroDisney theme park outside of Paris in the late 1980s. But EuroDisney was beset by a long succession of obstacles, including overoptimistic revenue forecasts, labour strife, and political and popular opposition. As if these obstacles were not enough, EuroDisney decided to follow its practice in the United States and refused to sell alcoholic beverages at the theme park. This unfortunately ensured that no self-respecting Frenchman would visit the park ("No wine with dinner? Sacre bleu!"). Fortunately for Disney, its equity stake had been kept to a minimum by bringing in a variety of European debt and equity investors in a complex project financing arrangement. Disney's reputation did take a beating, along with several classes of foreign investors and the reputation of the French government of Francois Mitterrand.

iv) Differences in Distribution Channels

A prolonged stay in a foreign country inevitably means shopping for groceries in the local community. This can be an enjoyable experience because it allows the shopper to catch the "flavour" of the local population. An observant shopper will detect many regional differences in the way foods are distributed. People in U.S. cities are accustomed to large grocery store chains that offer a wide selection of food and nonfood items. These regional and national chains keep expenses low through economies of scale and create value for their stakeholders by internalising the market for food distribution. In many other parts of the world, groceries are sold in locally owned and operated mom-and-pop stores. Large discount stores are seen as impersonal and are not trusted by shoppers. The source of the local store owners' advantage lies in their continuing relations with members of the local community. Because of these cultural differences in shopping habits, size can be seen as an advantage in one country and as a disadvantage in another country. This is just one example of how distribution channels exhibit great variation around the world.

v) Differences in Personnel Management

Multinational corporations must adapt their human resource practices and organisational structures to accommodate the types of employees they will employ in their foreign operations. Personnel management policies that work in one culture may not work in another. In other cases, personnel policies developed at home can be successfully exported.

vi) Differences in Legal, Accounting, and Tax Systems

Multinational financial managers must learn unfamiliar tax laws and tax systems, legal conventions, and business procedures to be successful in foreign countries. As an example, governments in developing countries often offer tax benefits in the form of reduced tax rates or tax holidays as an incentive for foreign direct investment. Negotiating these tax benefits and ensuring that they are not revoked subsequent to investment can be a delicate and time-consuming task for top management

vii) Differences in Financial Markets

The operations of financial markets also vary across countries. The most obvious differences are in the levels of sophistication and liquidity in national financial markets, but differences in financial market operations can be much more profound. For example, banking practices in many Islamic countries are conducted according to the teachings of the prophet Mohammed as found in the Koran and other Islamic holy scriptures. According to these Islamic banking customs, bank depositors do not receive a set rate of interest but instead share in the profits and losses of the bank. Foreign banks attempting to open branch banks or offshore banking facilities in Islamic nations must adapt their operations to such cultural and religious norms.

viii) Differences in Corporate Governance

A final difference between national business cultures lies in corporate governance—the mechanisms by which major stakeholders exert control over the corporation. The firm can be viewed as a set of contracts between various stakeholders in the firm. In this view, the corporation is defined by a legal framework of contracts. Important contracts include those with customers, suppliers, labor, debt, and equity. Because each of these contracts is executed within the laws of the society in which the firm operates, the society itself helps determine the form of these contracts and the rights and responsibilities of the various parties.

A foreign venture that does not respect the language, culture, and sensibilities of the local peoples is destined for trouble. Multinationals and their managers must learn new political systems and social behaviors, including what types of corporate behavior are punished, what types of behavior are merely tolerated, and what types of behavior can lead to fruitful partnerships with the local residents and their government.

Exposure to Country Risk

These cultural differences create additional costs for multinational operations. They also increase business risk. Risk exists whenever actual outcomes can differ from expectations. The multinational corporation has exposure to risk when its assets or liabilities can change in value with unexpected changes in business conditions. As individuals and businesses take advantage of cross-border business opportunities, they expose themselves to a wide variety of new local and global risks.

An important new risk arising from cross-border operations is country risk. Country risk is the risk that the business environment in a host country will unexpectedly change. Country risk includes the uncertainties of dealing with an unfamiliar culture, unexpected changes in the local social or political climate, unexpected changes in government regulation, financial upheavals, or natural disasters that affect the country's social, economic, political, or financial landscape. Two important dimensions of country risk for the multinational financial manager are political risk and financial risk.

Political Risk

Political risk is the risk that the business environment in a host country will change unexpectedly due to political events. Political risk is usually determined within a country as political forces exert control over the business environment Political sources of risk include unexpected changes in the operating environment arising from repatriation restrictions, taxes, local content regulations, restrictions on foreign ownership, business and bankruptcy laws, foreign exchange controls, and expropriation.

Financial Risk

Financial risk refers more generally to the risk of unexpected change in the financial or economic environment of a host country. Financial risk is partly determined by political risk, but also by a myriad of financial and economic factors that are outside the control of local political forces.

An important financial risk exposure for the multinational corporation is currency risk. The multinational corporation is exposed to currency risk (or foreign exchange risk) if an unexpected change in currency values can affect the value of the corporation's assets or liabilities. The 1970s witnessed a global increase in currency risk, largely due to the advent of floating exchange rates in 1971. Hence, an understanding of currency risk exposure, as well as the techniques used to manage that risk exposure, is essential for both large and small firms competing in today's global marketplace. Volatility in currency markets can cause the value of the multinational corporation to fluctuate in unexpected ways. Profits on overseas transactions can quickly be wiped out by unexpected changes in currency values. For this reason, financial risk management is a necessary and integral part of modern financial management.

CREATING THE TARGET CAPITAL STRUCTURE

An MNC may deviate form its target capital structure in each country where financing is obtained, yet still achieve its target capital structure on a consolidated basis. The following examples of particular foreign country conditions illustrate the motive behind deviating form a local target capital structure while still satisfying a global target capital structure.

First, consider the Country A does not allow MNCs with headquarters elsewhere to list their stock on its local stock exchange. Under these conditions, an MNC would likely decide to borrow funds through bond issuance or bank loans rather than by issuing stock in this country. By being forced to use debt financing here, the MNC might deviate form its target capital structure, which could raise its overall cost of capital. It might offset this concentration in debt by using complete equality financing in some other host country that allowed the firm's stock to be listed on the local exchange.

Consider a *second* example, in which Country B allows the MNC to issue stock there and list its stock on its local exchange. Also assume that the project to be implemented in that country will not generate net cash flows for five years. In this case, equity financing may be more appropriate. The MNC could issue stock, and by paying low or zero dividends, it could avoid any major cash outflows for the next five years. It might offset this concentration in equity by using mostly debt financing in some other host country.

As a *third* example, consider an MNC that desires financing in Country C, which is experiencing political turmoil. The use of local bank loans would be most appropriate, since local banks may be bale to prevent the MNC's operations are creditors, it is in their interest to assure that the MNC's operations are sufficiently profitable to repay its loans. These examples illustrate how the MNC's capital structure in each individual country may deviate from the global target capital structure established by the MNC.

The ideal sources of funds for all countries will not necessarily sum to match the global target capital structure. However, the parent's mix of debt and equity financing in its own country (where it has the flexibility to use either type) may be adjusted to achieve the global target capital structure.

The strategy of ignoring a "local" target capital structure in favour of a "global" target capital structure is rational as long as it is acceptable by foreign creditors and investors. However, if foreign creditors and investors monitor the local capital structure, they may require a higher rate of return on funds provided to the MNC. For example, the "local" target capital structures for the subsidiaries based in Country A (from the earlier example) and in Country C are entirely debt (unless some equity investment was provided by the parent). Creditors in these two countries may penalise the MNC for its highly leveraged local capital structure, even though its global capital structure is more balanced, because they believe that the subsidiaries in their respective countries may be unable to meet the high debt repayment levels. Their concern is valid only if the subsidiaries would not be rescued by the MNC's parent. If the parent plans to back the subsidiaries, it could guarantee debt repayment to the creditors in the foreign countries, which might reduce the risk perception and lower the cost of the debt. Many MNC parents stand ready to financially back their subsidiaries, since if they did not, their other subsidiaries would be unable to obtain financing.

CHANGES IN THE FINANCING PATTERNS OF INDIAN COMPANIES

The evolving institutional development has had an influence on the financing pattern of companies underscoring the opening up of wider choices for companies in respect of instruments for financing. This issue has been extensively discussed form the theoretical perspective, where the main focus has been on finding out what can be termed as an optimal capital structure. Indian corporate financing pattern can be studied by either using national flow of funds data, which record flows of funds between different sectors of an economy, and domestic economy and rest of the world, or the balance sheets of companies, which can be aggregated at the industry or economy level. While the flow of funds data quite comprehensively cover the transactions between sectors, these data are generally constructed form a number of sources, which are rarely consistent. Besides, they can be obtained only after considerable time lag. The company accounts data have the limitation of being based on a sample of the country's corporate sector. However, they could be reliable, if the sample is representative. Since the company finances data are compiled on the basis of information obtained from major companies, the analysis here is based on the sample of non-government public limited companies with a focus on the companies' sources and uses of funds, derived from their balance sheets.

Data on pattern of sources of funds could be broadly divided into two categories, *viz,,* internal and external. The internal sources include bonus shares, reserves and surplus (mostly retained profits) and provisions (mainly depreciation). The external sources of funds, on the other hand, comprise increase in paid-up capital (new capital issues including premium), borrowings (by way of debentures, loans and advances from intermediaries and public deposits) and trade dues.

Debt-Equity Ratio for India Companies

The debt-equity ratio, which depicts the relative importance of borrowed capital in relation to owned capital, is an important indicator of the capital structure of companies. The debt-equity ratio of companies is crucially linked to the institutional environment and the extent of development of financial markets, which, in turn, determines the financing options of corporates. A relatively high debt-equity ratio may result from under-developed domestic capital market and may create problems for corporates in serving their debt.

In the 'nineties the debt-equity ratio has witnessed a steep decline implying corporates' increased preference for equity financing. The debt-equity ratio (long-term debt to equity) of non-government non-financial public limited companies went up from 86.2 per cent in 1984-85 to 99.5 per cent in 1991-92. The ratio thereafter declined sharply. Table-2 presents the analysis of the role played by securities markets in financing the firms on the basis of Centre for Monitoring Indian Economy (CMIE) database for large firms in India. It may be observed that for the year ended March 31, 2001, the sample size (1730 companies) is small since the annual reports for many of these companies had not been released as of date. At a broad level, the two outstanding regularities in this are (a) the decline in leverage and (b) the declining importance of "other" sources of funding. The debt-equity ratio fell from 1.73 in the early nineties to 0.90 in 2001. Viewed differently, total borrowings were 2.45 times larger than the value added in 1992; this multiple came down to 1.78 times in 2001. This may reflect a combination of a decision by firms to assume lower levels of risk, a shift towards more labour intensive industries, and structural weaknesses in the market for credit.

The second feature is the shift away from debt obtained from sources "other" than Banks, FIs, and the bond market. This fell sharply from 45 per cent of debt in 1992 to 19 per cent of debt in 2001. Most of this decline was made up by growth in the proportion of debt from banks and FIs, the sum of which rose from 38 per cent in 1992 to 60 per cent in 2001. Corporate bonds also experienced growth. One factor responsible for the growth of importance of corporate bonds has been the rise of the commercial paper market, which went up from 0.16 per cent of borrowings in 1992 to 1.52 per cent in 2001.

In many countries, the corporate bond market has become very important, as a transparent and liquid alternative mechanism of debt financing, when compared with loans. Table-1 indicates that while the share of corporate bonds in total debt has risen, from 15 per cent to 21 per cent, banks and FIs have actually gained ground as a source of debt financing.

TABLE-1

DEBT FINANCING

(Rs. crore)

Characteristic	*1992*	*1993*	*2000*	*2001*
No. of firms	2,799	3,408	4,584	1,730
Gross Value Added	71,351	82,009	1,96,347	1,52,700
Total Borrowings	1,74,790	2,07,554	4,21,494	2,72,283
Debt-Equity Ratio	1.74	1.72	1.10	0.90
Source of Borrowing (per cent)				
Banks	22	26	33	37
Institutions	16	18	23	23
Corporate bonds	15	15	17	21
Others	45	39	24	19

Source: CMIE

Cross-sectional Variation in Debt Financing

While the above regularities apply for the universe of firms as a whole, there is important variation in these regularities across the size distribution of firms. In order to highlight this, the universe of firms is sorted by value added, and broken up into ten groups, each of which has an equal number of firms. These results, using the most recent accounting year (2001), are shown in Table-2. The results show a strong pattern whereby smaller firms seem to have higher debt/equity ratios. This suggests that the phenomenon of small firms suffering from credit rationing is not strongly applicable in this data set.

TABLE-2

DEBT FINANCING ACROSS SIZE DECILES (2001)

	All	*Large*	*2*	*3*	*4*	*5*	*6*	*7*	*8*	*9*	*Small*
Debt-Equity Ratio	0.90	0.76	1.06	1.42	1.44	1.08	1.20	2.82	2.52	2.61	
Sources of borrowing (percent)											
Institutions	23	17	34	42	33	26	36	29	27	35	31
Corporate bonds	21	25	15	10	10	11	6	7	4	2	11

Source: CMIE

Turning to the sources of debt financing, two strong regularities may be noted. The largest one-tenth of firms have the least dependence (17 per cent) on institutions. At the same time, they have the highest dependence on corporate bonds (25 per cent). This suggests that for the largest firms, the securities markets have become a major source of capital, and that they are able to disintermediate financial institutions by directly accessing the markets. However, as one goes beyond the top decile of large firms, the fraction of debt funding that comes from corporate bonds drops off very rapidly. This suggests that the corporate bond market is an effective venue only for the largest 10 - 20 per cent of firms. There is some evidence to suggest that in the buoyant capital market conditions, corporates substitute debt, especially borrowings form FIs, in favour of equity and *vice versa,* there is a welcome decline in the debt-equity ratio in the post-1991 period, notwithstanding the marginal reversal of trend in the recent years.

Relating the results to theory, it may be observed that the results for India (and also for other developing countries as have been observed by many studies) are quite different form the "pecking order" pattern of financing found in advanced economies. Besides, the findings have a number of implications for the stability of the financial system. The relative role of equity *versus* debt, or, in other words, the relative role of stock market and financial intermediaries, is an important issue. An important finding of the corporate finances studies has been the limited role of stock market as a source of finance, that is, capital market in general has played a secondary role in corporate financing in India, barring a few years. There is a need to take appropriate measures to correct the imbalance and develop the capital market along sound lines. In the absence of a vibrant stock market, the debt-equity ratio may be higher than what is prudentially desirable, which could create difficulties for servicing the debt by the corporates. In fact, FIs, which are a major source of long-term funds also stipulate debt-equity ratio while financing the projects. In case, the corporates are not able to raise matching equity from the market: FIs may out come forward to finance the project, thus effecting the capital formation. The liquid equity markets make equity investments less risky and more attractive as they allow savers/investors to reallocate their portfolio.

The issue of corporate governance is also crucially linked to the prevailing financing patterns in a country. Well-developed capital markets can play an important role in disciplining and guiding the management. Although banks and FIs as lenders can also play an important role in the internal mechanisms of corporate governance, they are no substitutes for market-induced corporate governance practices.

The access of corporates to different sources of finance also depends on the extent of government regulations. The financial structure may also be influenced by the tax incentives prevailing in a country. To be more specific, the financing pattern may reflect the discrimination against dividend income relative to interest income, and capital gains income relative to interest income. There is, therefore, need to remove the incentives that encourage corporates to prefer debt financing, when without such benefits corporates would have gone for equity financing.

The current financial year has witnessed reforms in the capital market regulations with far-reaching implications for the future. On the lines indicated in the Union Budget for 2001-02, significant steps have been taken to develop the debt market. The launching of the CCIL and NDS would address the need for efficient securities settlement system covering money, government securities and forex markets. The CCIL, in conjunction with NDS, is expected to facilitate extension of repo market to non-Government securities and enlargement of market participants. The introduction of floating rate bonds on uniform auction basis has also widened the scope for a flexible interest rate regime in tune with the market trends.

SOURCES OF FINANCE AND FINANCIAL STRUCTURE IN USA, JAPAN, AND IN THE EURO AREA

Differences in the Structure of Corporate Liabilities in the United States, Japan, and Euro Area

Table-3 shows national financial accounts data for non-financial corporations in the euro area and compares them with data for the United States and Japan. For the euro area, national financial accounts data have been aggregated for eight Member States. No data are included yet for Greece, Ireland, Luxembourg and Portugal. Box-1 provides an overview of the statistical concepts and the plans for developing further the statistical basis.

As can be seen in Table-3, shares and other equity (at market values) are the main liability for euro area non-financial corporations, followed by loans. Equities are also the dominant liability in the United States, while debt securities play a more important role than loans there. In Japan, loans are the most important liability. The development in shares and other equity as a percentage of liabilities depends significantly on the development of share prices. Thus, the development in this ratio is influenced by the strong rise in share prices from 1997 to 1999 in the euro area and in the United States.

As noted above, loans are the main debt financing instrument of non-financial corporations located in the euro area. The share of loans, including those granted by non-MFIs, in the liabilities of the euro area non-financial corporate sector is less important than in Japan, but significantly higher than in the United States. Within loans, those granted by euro area MFIs are the most important. As for other forms of debt financing, trade credits and advances play a relatively important role in the euro area, similar to that in Japan and the United States. Debt financing in the form of securities other than shares had, in 1999, only a small share in the total liabilities of euro area non-financial corporations in terms of amounts outstanding. By contrast, this form of financing was more important in the United States and Japan.

TABLE-3

FINANCING STRUCTURE OF NON-FINANCIAL CORPORATIONS IN THE UNITED STATES, JAPAN AND THE EURO AREA (END OF PERIOD: PERCENTAGE OF TOTAL LIABILITIES)

	United States			*Japan*	*Euro area*
	1997	*1998*	*1999*	*1999*	*1999*
Liabilities	*100.0*	*100.0*	*100.0*	*100.0*	*100.0*
Loans	30.0	27.2	23.3	5.4	38.9
of which:					
granted by euro area MFIs	21.3	19.5	16.2	—	—
granted by euro area non-monetary financial institutions	1.9	1.7	1.4	—	—
granted by either euro area sectors and by the rest of the world	6.8	6.0	5.8	—	—
Trade credit and advance payments received	10.7	9.8	8.3	7.8	12.4
Securities other than shares	3.1	2.8	2.4	10.6	9.4
Shares and other equity	51.7	56.3	62.6	70.2	33.8
of which: quoted shares	19.6	22.0	26.3	—	—
Other liabilities	4.5	3.9	3.3	6.1	5.5

Sources: ECB, Board of Governors of the Federal Reserve System and Bank of Japan.

Note: Non-consolidated data which cover all external financing instruments taken by non-financial corporations from other resident sectors including non-financial corporations and from abroad: debt securities and shares are valued at market prices.

BOX-1

CORPORATE FINANCE IN NATIONAL ACCOUNTS

Corporate finance in national accounts relates to the sector "non-financial corporations" defined in the European system (Council Regulation (EC) No. 2223/96 of June 19% on the European system of national and regional accounts in the Community (ESA 95)). This sector coven all bodies recognised as independent legal entities which are market producers and the principal activity of which is the production of goods and non-financial services.

The ESA 95 records flows and stocks in an ordered set of accounts describing the economic cycle from the generation of income to its distribution, redistribution, and accumulation in the form of assets and liabilities. The flows of assets and liabilities are seen again in the changes in the balance sheet showing the total assets, liabilities and net word) reflected in the capital account, the financial account, the other changes in the volume of assets account and the revaluation account.

Changes in assets	**Changes in liabilities**	
	Capital account	
Acquisition of non-financial assets	Internal sources of corporate finance	Saving, net Net capital transfers (receivable minus payable)

Financial account		
Net acquisition of financial assets	External sources of corporate finance (by financial instrument)	Loans Trade credit and advance payments received Securities other than shares Shares and other equity Other liabilities (deposits, insurance technical reserves and other)
Other changes in the volume of assets account and the revaluation account		

All forms of corporate finance are shown in the changes on the liabilities side of the non-financial corporations' capital and financial account. Internal sources of corporate finance relate to the change in net worth due to saving and capital transfers which are part of the capital account. External sources of corporate finance are shown under net incurrence of liabilities in the financial account. The financial account is usually broken down by financial instrument. Further breakdowns refer to the original maturity of some instruments. Major external financial instruments of non-financial corporations are loans, trade credit and advance payments received, securities other man shares and shares and other equity.

While both the capital and financial account comprise transactions, other changes to other corporate sector balance sheet may relate to mergers and acquisitions, reclassifications, or holding gains and losses. These changes are recorded under other heading "Other changes in the volume of assets account and revaluation account".

To reflect appropriately the financing structure of euro area non-financial corporations, non-consolidated data are provided. They cover all external financing instruments taken by euro area non-financial corporations, including financial resources provided by other non-financial corporations in the euro area and abroad.

To reflect appropriately the financing structure of euro area non-financial corporations, non-consolidated data are provided. They cover all external financing instruments taken by euro area non-financial corporations, including financial resources provided by other non-financial corporations in the euro area and abroad.

Finally, with respect to maturity structures, it is notable that most of the corporate lending from MFIs in the euro area is long term. In September 2000, more than 70% of all outstanding loans had an original maturity of more than one year, with more than 50% of all loans having a maturity of more than five years. Similarly high is the share of non-financial corporations' outstanding debt securities with a maturity of more than one year in their total outstanding debt securities.

Trends Over Recent Years Dominated by High Growth Rates for Loans and Debt Securities

Balance sheet data as shown in Table-3 provide a snapshot of the financing structure of non-financial corporations at a specific point in time. In particular shares and debt securities are influenced by valuation changes. For this reason, changes are best understood by looking at transactions data which do not include valuation effects (see Table-4).

The following analysis looks at these changes in more detail.

As can be seen from Table-3, some notable changes have taken place in recent years in the euro area. First, the total annual external financing flows increased significantly between 1997 and 1999. Second, the flows were particularly pronounced in debt, with the flows in loans significantly exceeding the flows in shares and other equity. Third, a considerable rise was observed in the issuance of new debt securities over the period, with the highest growth rates in the amounts outstanding of all forms of finance. Thus the flow data in Table-4 give a different picture than the changes in the balance sheet in Table-3.

TABLE-4

EXTERNAL FINANCING TRANSACTIONS OF NON-FINANCIAL CORPORATIONS IN THE UNITED STATES, JAPAN AND THE EURO AREA (EUR BILLIONS)

	Euro area			*United States*	*Japan*
	1997	*1998*	*1999*	*1999*	*1999*
Liabilities	339.3	489.2	625.0	767.0	-117.8
Loans	145.0	230.2	329.3	149.7	-113.1
Trade credit and advance payments received	58.8	63.6	68.6	165.7	-48.3
Securities other than shares	12.1	18.1	37.3	255.3	-11.1
Shares and other equity	95.5	173.9	147.2	96.5	61.7
of which: quoted shares	*62.2*	*85.8*	*89.3*	—	—
Other liabilities	27.9	3.4	42.7	99.8	-6.9

Source: ECB, Board of Governors of the Federal Reserve System and Bank of Japan.
Note: Non-consolidated data (see note to Table I); net borrowing (+), net repayments (-).

Interpreting these developments in conjunction with the information in Table-3, it can be seen that the higher recourse to loans and debt securities in recent years did not result in an increase in the share of these debt instruments in total corporate liabilities. This can be partly explained by the considerable rise in share prices between 1997 and 1999. The increase in share prices led to a substantial increase in the value of the amounts outstanding of shares and other equity which are shown in Table-3. This valuation effect resulted in a decline in the share of loans and debt securities in the overall liabilities of the corporate sector when measured at market values. Thus, while the recourse to loans and debt securities in recent years may have resulted in a higher ratio of corporate debt to GDP, it has not resulted in a rise in the debt to equity ratio of the liabilities of the euro area corporate sector measured at market values.

Debt Financing

As regards external finance in the form of loans granted by MFIs, loans to non-financial corporations increased in terms of year-on-year growth rates by between 7% and 8% in 1998 and 1999 (see Table-5). In 2000 the growth of these loans increased further, reaching 12.3% in September 2000. The trend of increasing growth of loans to non-financial corporations in this period initially reflected the decline in bank lending interest rates that the convergence leading up to Stage Three of EMU brought about in the euro area. In addition, the high growth of loans was also related to the financing of mergers and acquisitions and, after mid-1999, the strengthening of economic activity in the euro area. Most recently, it was significantly influenced by the financing of UMTS licences by telecommunications companies.

TABLE-5

MFI LOANS TO NON-FINANCIAL CORPORATIONS IN THE EURO AREA (ORIGINAL MATURITY; ANNUAL PERCENTAGE CHANGES)

		Amounts outstanding				*Annual growth rates*			
		Total	*Upto 1 year*	*Over 1 year and up to 5 years*	*Over 5 years*	*Total*	*Upto 1 year*	*Over 1 year and up to 5 years*	*Over 5 years*
		EUR tolal billions	*% of tolal amounts*	*% of tolal amounts*	*% of amounts*				
1997	Dec.	2135.1	35.8	14.5	57.4	—	—	—	—
1998	Dec.	2286.8	35.6	13.8	57.6	7.6	6.6	2.4	9.9
1999	Dec.	2419.1	35.4	15.4	57.4	7.8	7.0	11.2	7.4
2000	Sep.	2628.6	35.9	16.1	56.5	12.3	14.3	16.3	9.6

The introduction of the euro has acted as a catalyst for debt securities financing by the non-financial corporate sector. The year-on-year growth rates of debt securities issuance by non-financial corporations increased substantially in 1999 and 2000. In addition to the influence of the introduction of the euro, debt securities issuance by private non-financial corporations has been driven by the process of corporate restructuring and related merger and acquisition activity in the euro area, changes in the investment behaviour of institutional investors (which have increasingly invested in higher-yield bonds), and the robust pace of economic activity in the euro area (see Table-6). The issuance of debt securities in 2000 was also stimulated by the financing of UMTS licences, partly through non-monetary financial subsidiaries of telecommunications companies.

TABLE-6

MATURITY STRUCTURE OF DEBT SECURITIES ISSUED BY NON-FINANCIAL CORPORATIONS IN THE EURO AREA (ORIGINAL MATURITY; ANNUAL PERCENTAGE CHANGES)

	Amounts outstanding			*Annual growth rates*		
	Total EUR	*Up to 1 year % of total*	*Over 1 year % of total*	*Total billions*	*Up to 1 year amounts*	*Over 1 year amounts*
1994	275.4	19.4	80.6	3.6	-11.2	7.9
1995	284.6	17.2	82.8	3.4	-8.4	6.3
1996	285.9	18.6	81.4	0.5	8.7	-1.2
1997	289.7	19.7	80.3	1.3	7.5	-0.1
1998	297.1	20.5	79.5	2.6	6.6	1.6
1999	331.8	22.1	77.9	11.6	20.5	9.4
2000 Sep.	401.9	24.0	73.4	16.9	25.7	14.3

Equity Financing

As regards equity financing. Table-7 shows the total net amount of shares and other equity raised by non-financial corporations between 1997 and 1999. This amount increased from £95.5 billion in 1997 to € 173.9 billion in 1998, but decreased to € 147.2 billion in 1999. The latter decrease was due to a significant drop in the net issuance of unquoted shares and other equity from € 88.1 billion in 1998 to € 57.9 billion in 1999. Indeed, the net issuance of shares listed on stock exchanges (i.e. quoted shares) by non-financial corporations actually increased from € 85.8 billion in 1998 to € 89.3 billion in 1999. Thus, the data show that non-financial corporations in the euro area increasingly resorted to issuing quoted equity in 1999. In general equity issues statistics, gross issuance of quoted shares by all corporations, i.e. including financial corporations, has been growing since the mid-1990s in the euro area.

In recent years, specialised stock markets for "growth" companies have become a growing market segment for the issuance of quoted shares. In general, equity financing is particularly advantageous or even essential for the financing of innovative firms, as banks may be reluctant to provide loans due to the risk profile of these firms. Thus, for these new and high-risk firms, financing through specialised stock exchanges is of particular importance because of the existence of information asymmetries and agency costs.

TABLE-7

EQUITY FINANCING OF EURO AREA NON-FINANCIAL CORPORATIONS

(EUR billions)

	Net issuance of shares			*Memorandum Item*[1] *Gross issuance of quoted shares of all corporations*		
	Share and other equity	*of which quoted*	*of which unquoted and other equity*	*Total amount of new capital raised*	*Gross amount of new capital raised by already listed corporations*	*Gross amount of new capital raised by newly listed corporations*
1995	—	—	—	84.1	61.7	22.4
1996	—	—	—	72.0	42.6	29.4
1997	95.5	62.2	33.3	76.2	47.3	28.9
1998	173.9	85.8	88.1	146.8	96.3	50.5
1999	147.2	89.3	57.9	240.8	150.7	90.1

Source: ECB.

1) International Federation of Stock Exchanges (FIBV) data. The FIBV equities issues statistics cover approximately 97% of world stock market capitalisation and include financial corporations. The FIBV collects the number of domestic and foreign companies listed national exchanges. When a domestic company is listed on more than one national exchange. It is counted once. When a company is listed in several countries, it may he counted more than once.

The market capitalisation and the number of companies that were listed on the EURO. NM market grew from € 7 billion at the beginning of 1998 to € 167 billion in December 2000. While some of this increase can be attributed to the overall rise in share prices during this period, it is important to note that the number of listed companies continued to increase in almost every month. The total number of companies listed on the EURO. NM, which were mainly non-financial and high-tech firms, increased from 63 at the end of January 1998 to 564 at the end of December 2000.

In addition to traditional or public equity financing, venture capital financing has grown significantly in recent years, even though the overall amounts are still relatively low compared with the United States. As noted above, venture capital companies represent an important means of overcoming agency problems and information asymmetries that exist between lenders and borrowers and that are particularly significant for new and high-risk firms. Venture capital firms can collect and process information on new companies quite effectively, by using various control mechanisms, for example, gaining positions on the boards of these firms and obtaining substantial voting rights. While the data presented also include financial corporations, the amounts invested in this sector are only a small proportion of the total. The investments made by venture capitalists in euro area firms have risen more than fourfold between 1995 and 1999, with a particularly large increase, 71%, in 1999 compared with 1998. Venture capital firms actually raise more funds that they ultimately invest, although the difference between funds raised and invested decreased in 1999 compared with 1998.

In sum, there was a reduction in the share of debt as a proportion of total liabilities of non-financial corporations measured at market prices between 1997 and 1999, mainly due to the considerable rise in stock prices and despite strong growth in loans in recent years. At the same time, the non-financial corporate sector in the euro area has been acquiring a significant share of funds in the form of debt securities. Furthermore, there was a higher use of quoted shares in 1999 and it is apparent that some more specialised forms of public and private equity are being used as sources of external finance, in particular, shares listed at specialised exchanges for growth companies and venture capital. There are thus many indications of a tendency towards sophistication and diversification in the use of sources of corporate finance in the euro area. However, this process is still at an early stage and the euro area financial structure can still be considered to be dominated by bank loans and unquoted shares.

IMPLICATIONS FOR MONETARY POLICY

The relationship between corporate finance, financial structure and monetary policy is of considerable importance to the development of financial markets and economic growth, and has received much attention from both academics and policy-makers. Problems caused by asymmetric information that exist on financial markets between borrowers and lenders may force certain borrowers to seek specific forms of finance and thus influence their capital structure and the cost of capital. In practice, these information problems combined with a large number of institutional, legal and historical characteristics determine the use of specific sources of corporate finance and the development of the financial structure of an economy. It is important to stress that a bank-oriented financial structure is neither more nor less efficient than a securities-based structure. Rather, it is the complementarity of financing options that contributes to economic efficiency.

There are signs that non-financial corporations are increasingly resorting to securities-based finance, such as debt securities issuance and shares listed on both the mainstream and "high-growth" exchanges. In this development, the move towards and the introduction of the euro have acted as an important catalyst, especially with regard to the issuance of debt securities, improving the efficiency of the euro area capital markets and reducing existing information asymmetries to some extent. At the same time, loans continue to be an important source of net external financing for non-financial corporations in the euro area, in particular those extended by MFIs.

The analysis of corporate finance is of relevance to monetary policy and also has implications for financial stability. If the financing of non-financial corporations through the issuance of securities continues to grow, this may imply a larger exposure of firms to developments in financial markets, may lead to more competitive pricing of loans by banks, and could render the economy more sensitive to wealth effects. The process of monetary transmission could be affected through all these channels. The dynamics of the evolution in the external financing flows of non-financial corporations in the euro area suggest that debt securities are playing a growing role in financing, even though they started from a low base by comparison with the United States. As regards equity, quoted shares gained importance in 1999. If developments towards increased reliance on securities were to policy decisions influence the economy. Therefore it seems appropriate to reflect on their implications for monetary policy in the euro area. These include: 1) a larger exposure of firms to swings in financial markets; 2) more competitive pricing of loans by banks; and 3) a greater importance of wealth effects.

Larger Exposure of Firms to Swings in Financial Markets

The prices of financial instruments, such as corporate bonds and equities, are determined in a forward-looking manner, and, *inter alia*, incorporate the expectations of economic agents regarding future economic developments and premia for various risks. An increase in the exposure of corporations as a result of a higher share of debt securities and quoted shares would imply that companies' financing conditions might be affected more quickly by developments in financial markets than before.

More Competitive Pricing of Loans by Banks

If there are no major competitive pressures, the pricing of bank loans may not reflect market conditions. This behaviour tends to make the interest rate channel of the transmission mechanism of monetary policy weaker than in an economy where securities predominate. If a liquid market for corporate securities develops, then corporations may go directly to the market and bypass banks. This should lead to more competitive pricing by banks. In the case of the euro area, some large firms with direct access to credit have been able to obtain finance from banks at rates similar to money market races. In this context, a financial structure in which securities play a more important role in debt financing implies that changes in ECB interest rates are likely to affect bank lending interest rates more quickly.

Greater Importance of Wealth Effects

Changes in interest rates may affect the prices of assets, be they financial instruments or real assets such as property, and thus the wealth of households and non-financial corporations. The importance of wealth effects depends on the absolute value and the composition of wealth, on the impact of monetary policy and on how changes in wealth affect consumption and investment decisions. If there is a move towards a greater importance of securities, companies and households are likely to increase the share of financial assets in the form of securities in their portfolios. Thus, changes in the financial structure towards greater recourse to securities markets are likely to reinforce the importance of wealth effects, as households and non-financial corporations will probably hold a larger share of their wealth in the form of financial market instruments such as corporate bonds or equity.

ILLUSTRATIVE PROBLEMS

1. You are in charge of the capital budgeting division of a diversified multinational firm. The parent company/s cost of capital is 16.5 per cent, assuming a current borrowing interest rate of 14 per cent, a marginal tax rate of 40 per cent, and an optimal capital structure of 0.45 debt and 0.55 equity.
   You are considering an investment in a subsidiary incorporated in country X. Your firm's policy is to reflect risk of foreign undertakings in the hurdle rate, rather than to adjust projected cash flows of these projects.
   What hurdle rate would you apply to the proposed investment under each of the following situations? If no specific rate can be calculated from the data given, you may express the appropriate rate as being higher or lower than the parent's stated cost of capital, stating in each case your reasons. You are to treat each case separately, rather than cummulatively. In situations where you think that not enough information is provided, you may so state, but the missing data should be indicated in each case.
   (a) The project in country X has a risk comparable to your firm's overall risk in its domestic investments. Political risk is deemed to be insignificant, but you expect the currency of country X to depreciate by an average of 1.5 per cent annually against the U.S. dollar in the next four or five years (assume efficient exchange markets).
   (b) Same assumptions as in situation (a) except that you can borrow in local financial markets at 10 per cent, but you have reason to believe that exchange and capital markets are not efficient.
   (c) Your subsidiary in country X will be facing intense competition from local firms, which consider a 20 per cent return on investment as the minimum rate needed to attract funds from investors. (Assume) here that both the exchange and political risks are negligible.)
   (d) Your subsidiary in country X will be involved in new lines of business that are riskier, and in which your management has had no past experience. Your beta is currently 1.4, while beats of firms involved in the same activities as the project in country X is 1.8. Moreover, country X has been known to impose restrictions and blockage on transfers by affiliates to their parent firms. (Disregard the exchange risk in this case.)
   (e) The debt ratio norms for manufacturing industries in country X are radically different. For subsidiary X, a capital structure consisting of 0.65 debt and 0.35 equity would not be unusual. (Disregard both exchange and political

risks in this situation.)

(f) Cash flows to be generated by subsidiary X are negatively correlated with the company's present case flow pattern. Moreover, as stated in situation (e), the subsidiary could support a higher debt ratio than indicated in the parent's optimal capital structure. There is a small political risk involved, but in your judgment, it will be more than offset by these features. (Ignore the exchange risk in this situation.)

Solution

1. Base on the company' stated cost of capital, the cost of equity is 25.42% as shown below:

   (.45) (.40) (.14) + (.55) (x) = 0.165

   0.252 + 0.55x = 0.165

   0.252 = 0.165 – 0.0252 = 0.1398

   x = 25.42 per cent

(a) kd before tax (in country X) = 14% (1 + 0.015) + 1.5% = 15.71%

ke (in country X) = 25.42% (1 + 0.015) + 1.5% = 27.30%

k (in country X) = (.45) (.40) (0.1571) + (.55) (0.2730)

= 0.0283 + 0.1502 = 17.85%

Alternatively, k = 16.5% (1 + 0.015) + 1.5% = 18.25%

(b) This is a situation of a segmented capital market. Raising the debt funds locally would reduce affiliate X's cost of capital slightly as shown below:

kd before tax = 10% (1 + 0.015) + 1.5% = 11.65%

k = (.45) (.40) (0.1165) + (.55) (0.2730)

= 0.0210 + 0.1502 = 17.12%

(c) Although the appropriate hurdle rate for evaluating the investment in country X is about 18%, the U.S. firm should seriously consider using a hurdle rate of 20% since the subsidiary will be facing intense competition from local firms.

(d) This situation would necessiate recomputing the cost of equity (using CAPM) and making an appropriate allowance for the political risk. However, since no data on the risk free and market rates of return were given in the problem, it is not possible to calculate the new cost of equity corresponding to the higher beta of the proposed investment (as compared with U.S. firm current mix of projects). On the whole, it would seem that an upward adjustment of 2 per cent for the higher cost of equity and 5 per cent for the political risk premium is justifiable. Thus, a hurdle rate of 25% would seem appropriate.

(e) This situation would require a decision by the management of the U.S. firm on the question of whether or not they want to localise the capital structure of the subsidiary in country X (see text for merits and demerits of localising the capital structure). If the decision is in the affirmative, then the cost of capital will have to be recomputed as follows:

k (in country X) = (.65) (.40) (0.1400) + (.35) (0.2542)

= 0.0373 + 0.8900

= 12.63%

(f) If, in the judgment of the management of the U.S. firm, the firm's overall operations will derive substantial diversification benefits from the proposed project in country X, then a hurdle rate lower than the firm's cost of capital may be justifiable. However, operations in country X will have to be fairly substantial to cause a significant stabilising influence on the firm's total cash flow.

In practice, however, MNCs find it exceedingly difficult to justify a hurdle rate for a foreign project which is lower than their cost of capital at home or worldwide. When they proceed with projects that fail to meet the financial criteria of viability, they do so on strategic grounds or other motives, rather than using such factors or motives to justify lowering the hurdle rate.

2. TRW, a U.S. MNC, floated in 1991 a deutsche-mark-denominated bond issue in Germany with a coupon rate of 7.5 per cent. The issue sold at par. In 1992, the deutsche mark appreciated against the U.S. dollar by 4.5 per cent. What was the effective borrowing cost in 1992, given that TRW had a marginal income tax rate of 0.48? If at the time TRW could have sold a similar bond issue in the U.S. (denominated in U.S. dollars) at par with a coupon rate of 11 per cent, which market would have afforded TRW a lower borrowing cost? (*Hint:* The appreciation of the mark affects not only the amount of interest in terms of U.S. dollars, but also the repayment of the principal.)

Solution

Effective borrowing cost in deutsche mark-denominated bonds =

$[(0.075)(1 + 0.045) + 0.045][.52] = 6.42\%$

Cost of U.S. bonds issued at par with a coupon rate of 11% =

$(0.11)(0.52) = 5.72\%$

The U.S. bond market would have afforded TRW a lower borrowing cost than the deutsche mark bonds.

QUESTIONS AND PROBLEMS

1. Explain why a firm may issue a bond denominated in a currency different from its home currency to finance local operations. Explain the risk involved.
2. What is the advantage of using simulation to assess the bond financing position?
3. It is possible to ignore localised financial structures in estimating the cost of capital for foreign affiliates? What reasons may be advanced for ignoring them? Are there some drawbacks in taking such a position?
4. "The securities of firms with relatively large international operations are more closely related to the rest of the world market factor and less to their home country factor than the domestic firms." Do you agree. Explain why you would expect the first group to have a lower systematic risk than the second group.
5. Is investor perception or recognition of diversification opportunities necessary for improving the risk/return performance of MNCs? If these diversification effects are accurately assessed by investors should you not expect this to be reflected in higher share prices for MNCs?
6. Why has the extension of the CAPM to a world context proven to be difficult? What are the major problems which hinder a complete integration of world capital markets?
7. How does increased availability of capital to multinational firms impact their cost of capital? Does market segmentation result invariably in a higher cost of

capital for an affiliate in a segmented market?

8. Why are parent loans to affiliates often considered an equity investment? Would such a treatment distort the capital structure of the affiliate? Is such a treatment as acceptable to host governments as to multinational financial managers?
9. Could an investor benefit from an internationally diversified portfolio even if some of the foreign securities added to the portfolio have a lower yield than domestic securities which they replaced?
10. Is the risk of issuing a floating rate Eurobond higher or lower than the risk of issuing a fixed rate Eurobond? Explain.
11. Columbia corporation is a U.S. company with no foreign currency cash flows. It plans to issue either (1) a bond denominated in German marks with a fixed interest rate, or (2) a bond denominated in U.S. dollars with a floating interest rate. It estimates its periodic dollar cash flows for each bond. Which bond do you think would have greater uncertainty surrounding these future dollar cash flows? Explain.
12. Why would a U.S. firm consider issuing bonds denominated in multiple currencies?
13. Why are the artificial currency bonds popular?
14. Assume you are assessing the potential cost of financing with Eurobonds denominated in a foreign currency. What is the most critical point in time at which the exchange rate will have the greatest impact?
15. "If the parent's cost of capital is 15%, its equity investment in a subsidiary only needs to be charged to the subsidiary at 15%." Why or why not?
16. What data would you desire in order to evaluate the risk of a project in a particular country? Why would one corporation find the same level of risk acceptable while another one might reject it? Does this indicate the irrationality of corporate management?
17. How would an investing firm differ from a borrowing firm in the features (i.e., interest rate and currency's future exchange rates) it would prefer a floating rate Eurobond to exhibit?
18. Assume that RKD Group considers issuing a mark-denominated bond at its present coupon rate of 7 per cent, even though it has no incoming mark cash flows to cover the bond payments. It is attracted to the low financing rate, since dollar bonds issued in the United States would have a coupon rate of 12 per cent. Assume that either type of bond would have a four-year maturity and could be issued at par value. The Group needs to borrow $10 million. Therefore, it will issue either dollar bonds with a par value of $10 million or mark bonds with a par value of DM20 million. The spot rate of the mark is $.50. The Group has forecasted the mark's value at the end of each of the next four years, when coupon payments are to be paid:

End of Year	*Exchange rate of DM*
1	$.52
2	.56
3	.58
4	.53

Determine the expected annual cost of financing with marks. Should RKD Group Corporation issue bonds denominated in dollars or in marks? Explain.

19. Assume that Hind Motors is an Indian company that exports products to Great Britain, invoiced in Rs. It also exports products to Germany, invoiced in Rs. It presently has no cash outflows in foreign currencies, and it plans to issue bonds in the near future. It could likely issue bonds at par value in (1) Rs, with a coupon rate of 14 per cent, (2) marks, with a coupon rate of 12 per cent, or (3) pounds, with a coupon rate of 15 per cent. It expects that the mark and the pound will strengthen over time. How could Hind Motors revise its invoicing policy and make its bond denomination decision to achieve low financing costs without excessive exposure to exchange rate fluctuations?
20. Discuss the characteristics of corporate finance in the euro area.
21. Critically examine the changes in the financing patterns of Indian Companies.

38

CHANGING PATTERNS IN THE GLOBAL CORPORATE FINANCING

INTRODUCTION

The evolving institutional development has had an influence on the financing pattern of companies underscoring the opening up of wider choices for companies in respect of instruments for financing. This issue has been extensively discussed form the theoretical perspective, where the main focus has been on finding out what can be termed as an optimal capital structure. Global corporate financing patterns can be studied by either using national flow of funds data, which record flows of funds between different sectors of an economy, and domestic economy and rest of the world, or the balance sheets of companies, which can be aggregated at the industry or economy level. While the flow of funds data quite comprehensively cover the transactions between sectors, these data are generally constructed from a number of sources, which are rarely consistent. Besides, they can be obtained only after considerable time lag. This chapter presents the recent trends in the global corporate financing and the main structural determinants and the obstacles to a bottom fundamental mix in emerging markets. It also examines the key policy issues related to foreign currency maturity mismatches, the associated risks, and vulnerability indicators associated with the level of composition of corporate finance.

SOURCES OF FINANCE AND FINANCIAL STRUCTURE IN USA, JAPAN, AND THE EURO AREA

Differences in the structure of corporate liabilities in the United States, Japan, and Euro Area, presented in Table-1, show national financial accounts data for non-financial corporations. For the euro area, national financial accounts data have been aggregated for eight Member States. No data are included yet for Greece, Ireland, Luxembourg and Portugal. Box-1 provides an overview of the statistical concepts and the plans for developing further the statistical basis.

As can be seen in Table-1, shares the other equity (at market values) are the main liability for euro area non-financial corporations, followed by loans. Equities are also the dominant liability in the United States, while debt securities play a more important role than loans there. In Japan, loans are the most important liability. The development in shares and other equity as a percentage of liabilities depends significantly on the development of share prices. Thus, the development in this ratio is influenced by the strong rise in share prices from 1997 to 1999 in the euro area and in the United States.

As noted above, loans are the main debt financing instrument of non-financial corporations located in the euro area. The share of loans, including those granted by non-MFIs, in the liabilities of the euro area non-financial corporate sector is less important than in Japan, but significantly higher than in the United States. Within loans, those granted by euro area MFIs are the most important. As for other forms of debt financing, trade credits and advances play a relatively important role in the euro area, similar to that in Japan and the United States. Debt financing in the form of securities other than shares had, in 1999, only a small share in the total liabilities of euro area non-financial corporations in terms of amounts outstanding. By contrast, this form of financing was more important in the United States and Japan.

TABLE-1
FINANCING STRUCTURE OF NON-FINANCIAL CORPORATIONS IN THE UNITED STATES, JAPAN AND THE EURO AREA
(END OF PERIOD: PERCENTAGE OF TOTAL LIABILITIES)

	United States			*Japan*	*Euro area*
	1997	*1998*	*1999*	*1999*	*1999*
Liabilities	100.0	100.0	100.0	100.0	100.0
Loans	30.0	27.2	23.3	5.4	38.9
of which:					
granted by euro area MFIs	21.3	19.5	16.2	—	—
granted by euro area non-monetary financial institutions	1.9	1.7	1.4	—	—
granted by either euro area sectors and by the rest of the world	6.8	6.0	5.8	—	—
Trade credit and advance payments received	10.7	9.8	8.3	7.8	12.4
Securities other than shares	3.1	2.8	2.4	10.6	9.4
Shares and other equity	51.7	56.3	62.6	70.2	33.8
of which: quoted shares	19.6	22.0	26.3	—	—
Other liabilities	4.5	3.9	3.3	6.1	5.5

Sources: ECB, Board of Governors of the Federal Reserve System and Bank of Japan.

Note: Non-consolidated data which cover all external financing instruments taken by non-financial corporations from other resident sectors including non-financial corporations and from abroad: debt securities and shares are valued at market prices.

BOX-1
CORPORATE FINANCE IN NATIONAL ACCOUNTS

Corporate finance in national accounts relates to the sector "non-financial corporations" defined in the European system (Council Regulation (EC) No. 2223/96 of June 19% on the European system of national and regional accounts in the Community (ESA 95)). This sector coven all bodies recognised as independent legal entities which are market producers and the principal activity of which is the production of goods and non-financial services.

The ESA 95 records flows and stocks in an ordered set of accounts describing the economic cycle from the generation of income to its distribution, redistribution, and accumulation in the form of assets and liabilities. The flows of assets and liabilities are seen again in the changes in the balance sheet showing the total assets, liabilities and net word) reflected in the capital account, the financial account, the other changes in the volume of assets account and the revaluation account.

Changes in assets	**Changes in liabilities**	
	Capital account	
Acquisition of non-financial assets	Internal sources of corporate finance	Saving, net Net capital transfers (receivable minus payable)
	Financial account	
Net acquisition of financial assets	External sources of corporate finance (by financial instrument)	Loans Trade credit and advance payments received Securities other than shares Shares and other equity Other liabilities (deposits, insurance technical reserves and other)
Other changes in the volume of assets account and the revaluation account		

All forms of corporate finance are shown in the changes on the liabilities side of the non-financial corporations' capital and financial account. Internal sources of corporate finance relate to the change in net worth due to saving and capital transfers which are part of the capital account. External sources of corporate finance are shown under net incurrence of liabilities in the financial account. The financial account is usually broken down by financial instrument. Further breakdowns refer to the original maturity of some instruments. Major external financial instruments of non-financial corporations are loans, trade credit and advance payments received, securities other man shares and shares and other equity.

While both the capital and financial account comprise transactions, other changes to other corporate sector balance sheet may relate to mergers and acquisitions, reclassifications, or holding gains and losses. These changes are recorded under other heading "Other changes in the volume of assets account and revaluation account".

To reflect appropriately the financing structure of euro area non-financial corporations, non-consolidated data are provided. They cover all external financing instruments taken by euro area non-financial corporations, including financial resources provided by other non-financial corporations in the euro area and abroad.

To reflect appropriately the financing structure of euro area non-financial corporations, non-consolidated data are provided. They cover all external financing instruments taken by euro area non-financial corporations, including financial resources provided by other non-financial corporations in the euro area and abroad.

Finally, with respect to maturity structures, it is notable that most of the corporate lending from MFIs in the euro area is long term. In September 2000, more than 70% of all outstanding loans had an original maturity of more than one year, with more than 50% of all loans having a maturity of more than five years. Similarly high is the share of non-financial corporations' outstanding debt securities with a maturity of more than one year in their total outstanding debt securities.

Trends over recent years dominated by high growth rates for loans and debt securities

Balance sheet data as shown in Table-1 provide a snapshot of the financing structure of non-financial corporations at a specific point in time. In particular shares and debt securities are influenced by valuation changes. For this reason, changes are best understood by looking at transactions data which do not include valuation effects (see Table-2).

TABLE-2

EXTERNAL FINANCING TRANSACTIONS OF NON-FINANCIAL CORPORATIONS IN THE UNITED STATES, JAPAN AND THE EURO AREA (EUR BILLIONS)

	Euro area			*United States*	*Japan*
	1997	*1998*	*1999*	*1999*	*1999*
Liabilities	339.3	489.2	625.0	767.0	-117.8
Loans	145.0	230.2	329.3	149.7	-113.1
Trade credit and advance payments received	58.8	63.6	68.6	165.7	-48.3
Securities other than shares	12.1	18.1	37.3	255.3	-11.1
Shares and other equity	95.5	173.9	147.2	96.5	61.7
of which: quoted shares	*62.2*	*85.8*	*89.3*	—	—
Other liabilities	27.9	3.4	42.7	99.8	-6.9

Source: ECB, Board of Governors of the Federal Reserve System and Bank of Japan.
Note: Non-consolidated data (see note to Table I); net borrowing (+), net repayments (-).

The following analysis looks at these changes in more detail.

As can be seen from Table-1, some notable changes have taken place in recent years in the euro area. First, the total annual external financing flows increased significantly between 1997 and 1999. Second, the flows were particularly pronounced in debt, with the flows in loans significantly exceeding the flows in shares and other equity. Third, a considerable rise was observed in the issuance of new debt securities over the period, with the highest growth rates in the amounts outstanding of all forms of finance. Thus the flow data in Table-2 give a different picture than the changes in the balance sheet in Table-1.

Interpreting these developments in conjunction with the information in Table-1, it can be seen that the higher recourse to loans and debt securities in recent years did not result in an increase in the share of these debt instruments in total corporate liabilities. This can be partly explained by the considerable rise in share prices between 1997 and 1999. The increase in share prices led to a substantial increase in the value of the amounts outstanding of shares and other equity which are shown in Table-1. This valuation effect resulted in a decline in the share of loans and debt securities in the overall liabilities of the corporate sector when measured at market values. Thus, while the recourse to loans and debt securities in recent years may have resulted in a higher ratio of corporate debt to GDP, it has not resulted in a rise in the debt to equity ratio of the liabilities of the euro area corporate sector measured at market values.

Debt Financing

As regards external finance in the form of loans granted by MFIs, loans to non-financial corporations increased in terms of year-on-year growth rates by between

7% and 8% in 1998 and 1999 (see Table-3). In 2000 the growth of these loans increased further, reaching 12.3% in September 2000. The trend of increasing growth of loans to non-financial corporations in this period initially reflected the decline in bank lending interest rates that the convergence leading up to Stage Three of EMU brought about in the euro area. In addition, the high growth of loans was also related to the financing of mergers and acquisitions and, after mid-1999, the strengthening of economic activity in the euro area. Most recently, it was significantly influenced by the financing of UMTS licences by telecommunications companies.

TABLE-3

MFI LOANS TO NON-FINANCIAL CORPORATIONS IN THE EURO AREA (ORIGINAL MATURITY; ANNUAL PERCENTAGE CHANGES)

		Amounts outstanding				*Annual growth rates*			
		Total	*Upto 1 year*	*Over 1 year and up to 5 years*	*Over 5 years*	*Total*	*Upto 1 year*	*Over 1 year and up to 5 years*	*Over 5 years*
		EUR tolal billions	*% of tolal amounts*	*% of tolal amounts*	*% of amounts*				
1997	Dec.	2135.1	35.8	14.5	57.4	—	—	—	—
1998	Dec.	2286.8	35.6	13.8	57.6	7.6	6.6	2.4	9.9
1999	Dec.	2419.1	35.4	15.4	57.4	7.8	7.0	11.2	7.4
2000	Sep.	2628.6	35.9	16.1	56.5	12.3	14.3	16.3	9.6

The introduction of the euro has acted as a catalyst for debt securities financing by the non-financial corporate sector. The year-on-year growth rates of debt securities issuance by non-financial corporations increased substantially in 1999 and 2000. In addition to the influence of the introduction of the euro, debt securities issuance by private non-financial corporations has been driven by the process of corporate restructuring and related merger and acquisition activity in the euro area, changes in the investment behaviour of institutional investors (which have increasingly invested in higher-yield bonds), and the robust pace of economic activity in the euro area (see Table-4). The issuance of debt securities in 2000 was also stimulated by the financing of UMTS licences, partly through non-monetary financial subsidiaries of telecommunications companies.

TABLE-4

MATURITY STRUCTURE OF DEBT SECURITIES ISSUED BY NON-FINANCIAL CORPORATIONS IN THE EURO AREA (ORIGINAL MATURITY; ANNUAL PERCENTAGE CHANGES)

	Amounts outstanding			*Annual growth rates*		
	Total EUR	*Up to 1 year % of total*	*Over 1 year % of total*	*Total billions*	*Up to 1 year amounts*	*Over 1 year amounts*
1994	275.4	19.4	80.6	3.6	-11.2	7.9
1995	284.6	17.2	82.8	3.4	-8.4	6.3

1996	285.9	18.6	81.4	0.5	8.7	-1.2
1997	289.7	19.7	80.3	1.3	7.5	-0.1
1998	297.1	20.5	79.5	2.6	6.6	1.6
1999	331.8	22.1	77.9	11.6	20.5	9.4
2000 Sep.	401.9	24.0	73.4	16.9	25.7	14.3

Equity Financing

As regards equity financing. Table-5 shows the total net amount of shares and other equity raised by non-financial corporations between 1997 and 1999. This amount increased from £95.5 billion in 1997 to € 173.9 billion in 1998, but decreased to € 147.2 billion in 1999. The latter decrease was due to a significant drop in the net issuance of unquoted shares and other equity from € 88.1 billion in 1998 to € 57.9 billion in 1999. Indeed, the net issuance of shares listed on stock exchanges (i.e. quoted shares) by non-financial corporations actually increased from € 85.8 billion in 1998 to € 89.3 billion in 1999. Thus, the data show that non-financial corporations in the euro area increasingly resorted to issuing quoted equity in 1999. In general equity issues statistics, gross issuance of quoted shares by all corporations, i.e. including financial corporations, has been growing since the mid-1990s in the euro area.

In recent years, specialised stock markets for "growth" companies have become a growing market segment for the issuance of quoted shares. In general, equity financing is particularly advantageous or even essential for the financing of innovative firms, as banks may be reluctant to provide loans due to the risk profile of these firms. Thus, for these new and high-risk firms, financing through specialised stock exchanges is of particular importance because of the existence of information asymmetries and agency costs.

The market capitalisation and the number of companies that were listed on the EURO. NM market grew from € 7 billion at the beginning of 1998 to € 167 billion in December 2000. While some of this increase can be attributed to the overall rise in share prices during this period, it is important to note that the number of listed companies continued to increase in almost every month. The total number of companies listed on the EURO. NM, which were mainly non-financial and high-tech firms, increased from 63 at the end of January 1998 to 564 at the end of December 2000.

In addition to traditional or public equity financing, venture capital financing has grown significantly in recent years, even though the overall amounts are still relatively low compared with the United States. As noted above, venture capital companies represent an important means of overcoming agency problems and information asymmetries that exist between lenders and borrowers and that are particularly significant for new and high-risk firms. Venture capital firms can collect and process information on new companies quite effectively, by using various control mechanisms, for example, gaining positions on the boards of these firms and obtaining substantial voting rights. While the data presented also include financial corporations, the amounts invested in this sector are only a small proportion of the total. The investments made by venture capitalists in euro area firms have risen more than fourfold between

1995 and 1999, with a particularly large increase, 71%, in 1999 compared with 1998. Venture capital firms actually raise more funds that they ultimately invest, although the difference between funds raised and invested decreased in 1999 compared with 1998.

TABLE-5

EQUITY FINANCING OF EURO AREA NON-FINANCIAL CORPORATIONS

(EUR billions)

	Net issuance of shares			*Memorandum Item[1] Gross issuance of quoted shares of all corporations*		
	Share and other equity	*of which quoted*	*of which unquoted and other equity*	*Total amount of new capital raised*	*Gross amount of new capital raised by already listed corporations*	*Gross amount of new capital raised by newly listed corporations*
1995	—	—	—	84.1	61.7	22.4
1996	—	—	—	72.0	42.6	29.4
1997	95.5	62.2	33.3	76.2	47.3	28.9
1998	173.9	85.8	88.1	146.8	96.3	50.5
1999	147.2	89.3	57.9	240.8	150.7	90.1

Source: ECB.

1) International Federation of Stock Exchanges (FIBV) data. The FIBV equities issues statistics cover approximately 97% of world stock market capitalisation and include financial corporations. The FIBV collects the number of domestic and foreign companies listed national exchanges. When a domestic company is listed on more than one national exchange. It is counted once. When a company is listed in several countries, it may he counted more than once.

In sum, there was a reduction in the share of debt as a proportion of total liabilities of non-financial corporations measured at market prices between 1997 and 1999, mainly due to the considerable rise in stock prices and despite strong growth in loans in recent years. At the same time, the non-financial corporate sector in the euro area has been acquiring a significant share of funds in the form of debt securities. Furthermore, there was a higher use of quoted shares in 1999 and it is apparent that some more specialised forms of public and private equity are being used as sources of external finance, in particular, shares listed at specialised exchanges for growth companies and venture capital. There are thus many indications of a tendency towards sophistication and diversification in the use of sources of corporate finance in the euro area. However, this process is still at an early stage and the euro area financial structure can still be considered to be dominated by bank loans and unquoted shares.

TRENDS IN CORPORATE FINANCE IN EMERGING MARKETS

As many emerging markets continue to consolidate balance sheets in the aftermath of crises, and growth becomes a priority, the means and obstacles to finance corporate sector activities have taken center stage in policy discussions. Many emerging markets had completed a deleveraging process and improved their policy framework and economic fundamentals. This has increased their resilience to future crises. To reap the rewards of these adjustments, the corporate sector in emerging markets needs to be funded by a variety of sources. Also, the incentives have to be such that they prevent the reemergence of financial vulnerabilities. This requires enhanced monitoring of potential vulnerabilities in emerging markets corporates. The fact that corporate sector bond issuance has surpassed sovereign borrowing in international markets over the past three years underscores the importance of this issue.

Over the past decade, two opposing forces have determined the evolution of emerging market corporate debt. On the one hand, corporates engaged in a process of deleveraging in the late 1990s to correct some of the excesses that led to a string of crises during that period. On the other hand, the low interest rate environment of the early 2000s encouraged corporate borrowing as part of a global effort to come out of the deflationary environment that followed the bursting of the high-tech equity bubble in 2000.

With these opposing forces as background, major trends in the corporate debt in emerging markets, measured relative to GDP, show a rise from around 46 percent of GDP in 1995-97 to 62 percent in 2001-03. This increase masks important regional variations. In particular, the increase is influenced, to a large extent, by the persistent growth of bank debt to GDP in China and India. Overall the corporate debt in Asia continues to above pre-crisis levels and at a level that triples that of emerging Europe and Latin America. However, emerging Europe and Latin America show totally opposite trends: while debt ratios have increased by 10 percent of GDP in Europe relative to 1995-97, Latin American corporates have experienced a decline in total corporate debt of 5-6 percent of GDP.

Trends in corporate debt can be examined from macrodata (debt-to-GDP ratios) or from microdata (individual corporate's balance sheet information). While macrodata are much easier to obtain than microdata, the former could at times be misleading because they relate stocks to flows. For instance, while the macrodata may suggest that corporate leverage in Asia exceeds that of Latin America's corporates by a wide margin microdata on individual firm debt relative to assets—a standard measure of leverage— reveal that Asian firms are not substantially more leveraged than Latin American firms. Moreover, while in 1997 Asian corporate leverage doubled the leverage in Latin America, both ratios converged to around one-third of total assets in 2003.

Balance sheet data can also be used to assess the evolution of corporate *foreign debt* exposures. Asian firms appear to have substituted domestic for external debt after 1997. However, this trend is driven mostly by Chinese and Indian firms. Latin American firms have gradually reduced their foreign debt ratio from 35 percent of total debt in 1997 to 26 percent in 2003. More pronounced has been the drop by half in foreign debt exposure in emerging Europe in 1997-2003.

Despite the increasing importance of domestic and international bonds as a source of corporate finance, *bank lending remains* the dominant source of corporate finance for all emerging market regions. Even in Asia, where bond finance has reached almost 30 percent of GDP, bank lending dominates at around 50 percent of GDP. In Latin America, bank lending to the corporate sector was over four times the level of bond debt, while in emerging Europe, loans dwarfed the level of corporate bonds outstanding.

Bank lending to emerging market corpo-rates has increased from 40 percent of GDP in 1995 to 60 percent in 2003. However, excluding China and India, bank lending has contracted from 33 percent of GDP to 30 percent, with significant variations across regions. Moreover, while domestic bank lending to corporates has dropped to 23 percent of GDP in 2003 (from 27 percent in 1995), overall international bank lending has remained resilient at a stable 7 percent of GDP.

In Latin America, domestic bank lending to corporates has contracted the most, from 27 percent of GDP in 1995 to 17 percent in 2003, notwithstanding an increase in international lending to 8 percent of GDP in 2003 (from 6 percent in 1995). Bank credit has also declined, albeit at a more moderate pace, in Asia, because of the significant retrenchment in international lending—from 9 percent to 5 percent of GDP—that has dominated a small increase in domestic bank lending— from 41 percent to 43 percent of GDP. In emerging Europe, international and domestic bank lending increased substantially relative to the mid-1990s.

In Latin America, local banks have seen their reserves increase sharply between 1995 and 2003, a result perhaps of a tightening in regulations as well as increased risk aversion and tightened credit standards by foreign-owned banks. In contrast, Asian banks have reduced their reserves, in part because of the expansionary monetary policies in the region in the aftermath of the crisis. A persistent increase in claims on the government suggests a fair amount of crowding out in central Europe and Latin America, which contributes to low levels of intermediation. Furthermore, bank deposits have remained stagnant in Latin America, in contrast with their significant increase in Asia. However, the flattening out of the level of deposits in Asia in 2001-03 combined with the increase in corporate bond markets, suggest that bank disintermediation may be taking hold in emerging Asia. This has been accompanied by a sharp increase in bank lending to the household sector in that region.

The increase in corporate bond issuance in most of the major emerging markets has compensated, to some extent, for the decline or stagnation in corporate bank lending. This is clearly the case in Asia and, to a lesser extent, in Latin America. While the stock of corporate bonds in the emerging market universe doubled to US$320 billion in 2003, the largest share has financed Asian corporates. In contrast with their Asian counterparts, Latin American corporates have issued a larger share of international bonds—although domestic, bonds have also increased rapidly, albeit from very low initial levels.

Corporate bonds have become a relevant source of funding—that is, accounting for more than 30 percent of total corporate debt—in Korea, Malaysia, and Mexico, because of the important structural changes implemented after the crises. In Korea, corporate bonds accounted for almost 50 percent of total debt in 1998 in part because in 1997 the government raised the ceiling on corporate bond issuance from two to four times of equity capital and eliminated restrictions on investment in domestic bonds by foreign investors. Malaysia's corporate bond market is the largest among the emerging markets in relative terms (at 43 percent of GDP) and corporate bonds have grown steadily to become 45 percent of total debt in 2003. Among other measures, efforts to streamline the bond issuance process and to encourage secondary bond market activities, as well as to relax insurance companies' portfolio limits, have contributed to such growth. The growth of corporate bonds in Mexico is more recent, and they constitute 30 percent of total corporate debt. The development of a government bond yield curve that facilitated the pricing of corporate bonds and changes in the bond contracts, together with the growth of private pension funds (which were barred from investing in equities until very recently) and other institutional investors (insurance companies and mutual funds), have supported the growth of corporate bonds as a source of corporate finance.

The *overall* decline in corporate bank lending in emerging markets (exclusive of China and India) in 1995-2003, compensated only partially by an increase in domestic bond issuance, was not reciprocated by a simultaneous rebound in equity issuance. The equity issuance flows have experienced a sharp decline beginning in the last quarter of 2000, with only a moderate rebound in 2003. Even though emerging market issuance rose to just over a half of its 1999 level, it increased by about 32 percent between 2002 and 2003 and is estimated to have increased further in 2004. However, it remains to be seen if equity could become a reasonable source of funding for emerging market corporates.

Although some of the marked decline in emerging market equity issuance reflected factors specific to emerging markets, equity issuance in mature economies also saw a significant decline in flows since 2000. This was generally driven by market conditions—rising volatility and declining share prices—following the bursting of the high-tech equity bubble. Since the latter part of 2003, as economic and market conditions have improved, issuance activity has rebounded both in mature and in emerging equity markets.

To summarize, emerging market corporates have seen a stagnation or decline in bank lending, an increase in corporate bond issuance, and a decline in equity funds. While these trends are broadly in line with developments in the mature markets, it is unclear if the decline in overall funding (excluding China and India) is a result of reduced external financing needs or constraints on the sources of funding.

STRUCTURAL DETERMINANTS AND OBSTACLES

Finance matters for growth. Corporate finance theories suggest that the choice between debt and equity depends on firm-specific and institutional factors, as well as on features of the financial system in which the company operates. Recent studies show that institutional factors at the country level are more important that firm-specific differences for debt-equity ratios, and that disclosing material information is critical for improving access to equity funding.

Corporate Finance and Firm-Specific Factors

Corporate *leverage*, measured as the ratio of total debt, to assets, is somewhat higher in emerging markets than in the mature markets. The average debt ratio for emerging market corporates during 1993-2003 was 27.6 percent of assets while for the G-3 corporates, it was 23.8 percent. Further, the leverage of corporate that participate in international markets is higher than those that do not. Market participants have, on average, leverage ratios of 31.8 percent of assets, compared with 23.5 percent for non-market participants. Interestingly, market participants from Asia display higher leverage than their Latin American counterparts — with the exception of Argentina. More important, the corporates in emerging markets rely more on internal funds than external sources of funding. Internal resources, defined as cash flows generated by firm's operations divided by capital expenditures, are somewhat higher in firms in emerging markets than in mature markets, with ratios of 2.11 and 1.97, respectively. The corporate in emerging markets, especially in Asia and emerging Europe, do use internal funds more heavily and they are twice as profitable as those in the G-3 countries. Higher profitability allows the former to rely more on internal finance, but it could also reflect that they operate in riskier environments. However, market participants are less profitable than nonmarket participants, and this is consistent with the volatility of profits of the latter group (measured by the standard deviation of returns) being twice as large as the former.

Another dimension where emerging market corporates distinguish themselves from the mature market ones is the *tangibility* of firms' assets. Emerging market corporates operate in sectors where technologies are well-known and managerial decisions are easier to monitor. Thus, the more tangible the assets, the lower the scope for informational asymmetries between insiders and outsiders, allowing for higher leverage. It is noted that asset tangibility in emerging markets is 50 percent larger than in the G-3 countries, supporting a higher level of corporate leverage.

A low market-to-book ratio in emerging markets is associated with the difficulties in issuing equity securities. The *markel-to-book* ratio, which measures the difference between investors' assessment of company shares and their book value, is almost 50 percent lower in emerging markets than in mature markets. A lower market-to-book value is associated with higher corporate leverage. When the market-to-book ratio is perceived as high, firms find it advantageous to issue equity, and this has been the case more often for mature market than emerging market corporates during 1993-2003.

Even if the differences in leverage and external finance ratios between mature and emerging markets are not that significant, it is quite clear that the cost of equity capital is much higher in the latter. Estimates of the cost of equity capital (Table-6) highlight the differences in the risk assessment made by international investors across emerging and mature economies' corporations, which in turn reflects the reticence of supply equity capital to the latter. In principle, the cost of (external) capital should be a weighted average of the cost of equity and the cost of debt. Estimates of the latter are hard to obtain in a comparable basis across countries.

There are three different measures of the cost of capital, grouped into two categories. First, an ex ante measure of the cost of capital is based on expected earnings; the second category provides two measures of the cost of capital based on ex post returns. The ex ante cost of equity capital measure is derived by substituting a firm's stock price and analyst forecasts of future earnings into an equity valuation model, similar to the dividend discount model and then backing out the internal rate of return (i.e., the risk-free rate plus the equity premium) from this model. The first ex post measure looks at the relationship between stock market performance and a public sector country risk rating, while the second is based on the country's stock market volatility relative to the United States. The ex post cost of capital measures do not rely on analyst forecasts and use realized returns calculated at the country level. The first ex post measure is derived by regressing realized country-level stock index returns on the *Institutional Investor's* country. Across almost all emerging regions the cost of capital is largely higher than that found in the United States and other mature economies.

Based on the ex ante measure of the cost of equity capital, emerging market firms face a 540 basis points higher cost of capital relative to the United States (i.e., 15.6 percent versus 10.2 percent, see Table-6). As a result of the much higher cost of equity capital, the capital structure of firms in emerging markets in many cases is skewed away from equity and toward greater debt. A growing number of empirical studies have shown that this is due to institutional factors that put constraints on firms' access to equity capital (and, in some cases, also to bond financing), rather than resulting from the firm-specific characteristics of emerging market corporates outlined above.

TABLE-6

COST OF EQUITY CAPITAL ESTIMATES BY COUNTRY

(In percent)

	Cost of Capital Measures		
	Ex ante	*Ex post*	
Country	*Expected earnings*	*Country risk*	*Standard deviation*
Argentina	12.8	33.1	43.0
Brazil	20.9	22.6	33.5
Chile	12.6	15.6	21.4
Colombia	...	22.8	18.9
Mexico	15.6	17.4	24.1
Latin America	**15.5**	**22.3**	**28.2**
China	...	16.5	27.5
India	14.4	20.0	18.1
Korea	14.1	16.6	20.6
Malaysia	10.7	15.4	23.3
Thailand	13.5	17.8	21.8
Asia	**13.2**	**17.2**	**22.3**
Czech Republic	...	15.9	19.0
Hungary	...	16.2	22.6

Poland	...	17.0	32.3	
Russia	...	20.4	...	
Turkey	...	24.6	36.2	
Emerging Europe	**...**	**18.8**	**27.5**	
Emerging Markets (15)	**14.3**	**19.5**	**26.0**	
Germany	10.1	10.7	15.0	
Japan	6.2	12.5	15.5	
United States	10.2	10.5	12.3	
G-3		8.8	11.2	14.3
Average Less-Developed Economies[1]	15.6	19.8	23.7	
Average Non-U.S. Mature Economies[1]	**11.3**	**11.7**	**16.4**	

Sources: Ex ante cost of capital from Hail and Leuz (2004); ex post cost of capita! from Ibbotson Associates (2005).

[1]The number of countries in the less-developed markets average is 16 for ex ante cost of capital, and 23 for the ex post measures. There are 23 countries in all the non-U.S. average cost of capital measures.

Institutional Factors

A number of institutional factors, such as taxes, regulations, and the legal framework, are also important determinants of firms' financial decisions. In particular, the tax code in several countries favors debt over equity. Thus, firms have an incentive to increase leverage ratios up to the point where the expected costs of financial distress and bankruptcy equal the so-called "tax-shield" advantage of debt.

The tax treatment of interest and dividends is an important determinant of capital structure, and tends to favor higher debt-to-equity ratios. This is especially the case in classical tax systems, where interest expenses are deductible at the corporate level but dividends are not. Classical tax systems are used in most emerging markets, as well as in the United States and Japan. Dividend relief and dividend imputation systems attempt to reduce the distortion that favors the use of debt over equity, by reducing taxes on dividends at either the individual or the corporate level. The high corporate tax rates may be one of the factors behind relatively high leverage in Asian countries.

As firms are perceived to get closer to financial distress, the increased cost deters further debt issuance. The costs of financial distress are particularly severe in emerging markets, and are a major obstacle to issuing debt instruments. Table-7 shows that creditors' rights are much weaker in emerging markets, and this is reflected in contract enforcement and bankruptcy costs that, in many cases, are double of those in the mature markets. With the notable exceptions of Korea, Malaysia, and the Czech Republic, creditor rights are much lower than in the G-3 countries. Contract enforcement is estimated to add more than 10 percentage points to the cost of debt in our sample of emerging markets, except for countries in central Europe and Korea (Table-7). The process of bankruptcy could take up to 10 years in Brazil and India.

One of the main factors behind the reticence of investors to buy equity from emerging market corporates is the potential conflict of interest between managers and controlling shareholders (insiders) and minority shareholders—sometimes referred to as "agency costs" of insider discretion. Insiders can expropriate outside investors through higher than market salaries and perquisites, adapting investment and operations for their own benefit, or through the direct capture of assets or cash flows (referred to as "tunneling"). Investors can protect themselves against such expropriations through various mechanisms of monitoring and control, such as compensation packages that align managers' and shareholders' interests, supervision by independent directors and external committees, and the threat of takeovers.

TABLE-7

BANKRUPTCY COSTS AND LEGAL RIGHTS, 2004

Country	*Borrowers and Lenders[1] Legal Rights Index[1]*	*Contract Enforcement[2]*		*Bankruptcy Costs[3]*	
		Time (In days)	*Cost (In percentage of debt)*	*Time (In years)*	*Cost (In percent of estate)*
China	2	241	25.5	2.4	18
India	4	425	43.1	10	8
Korea	6	75	5.4	1.5	4
Malaysia	8	300	20.2	2.3	18
Thailand	5	390	13.4	2.6	38
Asia	5	286	22	4	17
Czech Republic	6	300	9.6	9.2	18
Hungary	5	365	8.1	2	23
Poland	2	1000	8.7	1.4	18
Russia	3	330	20.3	1.5	4
Turkey	1	330	12.5	2.9	8
Eastern Europe	3	465	12	3	14
Argentina	3	520	15	2.8	18
Brazil	2	566	15.5	10	8
Chile	4	305	10.4	5.6	18
Colombia	4	363	18.6	3	1
Mexico	2	421	20	1.8	18
Latin America	3	435	16	5	13
Emerging Markets	4	395	16	4	15
Germany	8	184	10.5	1.2	8
Japan	6	60	8.6	0.5	4
United States	7	250	7.5	3	8
Mature Markets	7	165	9	2	7

Source: World Bank/IFC, Doing Business database.

[1] The index measures the degree to which collateral and bankruptcy laws facilitate lending. The index ranges from 0 to 10, with higher scores indicating that collateral and bankruptcy laws are better designed to expand access to credit. This is the case when secured creditors are able to seize their collateral when a debtor enters reorganization—that is, there is no "automatic stay" or "asset freeze" imposed by the court; when secured creditors are paid first out of the proceeds from liquidating a

bankrupt firm, as opposed to other parties, such as government or workers, and when management does not stay during reorganization, but instead an administrator is responsible for managing the business during reorganization.

[2] To measure the differences in contract enforcement, the evolution of a payment dispute is analyzed. In particular, the number of days from the moment the plaintiff files the lawsuit in court until the moment of actual payment, as well as the associated cost in court fees, attorney fees, and payments to accountants and advisors.

[3] The examination of bankruptcy covers the whole process leading up to filing for bankruptcy proceedings, including the petition hearing, the court's decision, and the sale of assets. The time measure captures the average time to complete the bankruptcy procedure, including delays due to legal derailment. The cost measure includes court costs as well as fees of insolvency lawyers and accountants, as a percentage of the estate value of the bankrupt business.

The mechanisms to protect investors against these conflicts of interests are particularly costly and imperfect in emerging markets, and analysts have stressed that this factor is important in constraining not just financing choices for emerging market corporates but also, more generally, the flow of capital from mature to emerging markets. The low level of *transparency* in emerging equity markets, coupled with *weak protection of shareholders' rights* and *concentrated ownership structures*, are the main factors behind this important obstacle to achieving a better financing mix in emerging markets, in particular to financing through marketable securities.

Financial Transparency

There are two separate issues related to better corporate transparency and investor protection. The first refers to the accuracy and timeliness of financial statements. This in turn relates to the accounting and auditing standards adopted and enforced in a country, and the frequency with which financial statements are publicly disclosed. The second refers to the timely disclosure of material information, such as the release of detailed offering prospectuses, changes in ownership structure, and related party transactions, among other things.

It is generally recognized that emerging market accounting standards and their enforcement are weaker than in mature economies. Moreover, the low quality of available information was one of the main factors behind the outflow of capital during the Asian crisis. More generally, the developing countries rank on average lower than mature economies in terms of accounting standards Although major improvements have occurred in this area over the last five years or so, in particular in countries that suffered crises, much of the improvement has been in the *national* accounting and auditing standards, further it has not been in terms of comparability across countries. In the current globalized environment, investors seek investment opportunities all over the world and companies seek out capital at the best price almost anywhere. This creates a problem for investors in that national accounting differences can completely obscure their comparative assessments of various (global) investment opportunities.

As a result in part of these investors' needs, and the desire to widen the investor base available to companies seeking capital, there has been an increasing push for the international convergence of accounting standards. International organizations such as IOSCO and the Financial Stability Forum (FSF) have endorsed the use of International Financial Reporting Standards (IFRS). Indeed, many small developing countries have stopped trying to develop their own national equivalent of GAAP and have instead found it easier (cheaper) to simply adopt IFRS as their national accounting principles. Also, in a growing number of countries, the regulators allow *foreign*-listed firms to report IFRS statements rather than require them to reconcile to their national GAAP (Hong Kong SAR, Japan, Malaysia, Singapore, and Thailand, among others). However, despite more flexibility for foreign listed firms, there remains a large proportion of emerging market economies that have not adopted IFRS for *domestically* listed firms, particularly in Asia and Latin America. Table-8 shows that national accounting standards prevail over international standards in most of the major emerging markets except for the central European ones.

TABLE-8

USE OF IFRS FOR DOMESTICALLY LISTED FIRMS, BY 2005

Country	*Not Permitted*	*Permitted but Not Required*	*Required for Some*	*Required for All*
China			X	
India	X			
Korea	X			
Malaysia	X			
Thailand	X			
Czech Republic				X[1]
Hungary				X[1]
Poland				X[1]
Russia			X[2]	
Turkey		X		
Argentina	X			
Brazil	X			
Chile	X			
Colombia	X			
Mexico	X			

Source: Deloitte-Touche-Tohmatsu International Accounting Standards (www.iasplus.com).

Note: IFRS = International Financial Reporting Standards.

[1]EU and EEA member states are permitted to defer the application of IFRSs until 2007 (1) for companies that only have debt securities listed in a public securities market and/or (2) for companies whose securities are admitted to public trading in a nonmember state and, for that purpose, have been using internationally accepted standards other than IFRSs (such as GAAP) since a financial year that started prior to adoption of the European regulation.

[2]Requirement to use IFRSs being phased over 2004-07.

Corporate Governance

Even under reasonable accounting and reporting standards, conflicts of interests are likely to persist because of corporate governance problems. Generally, it is observed that stronger corporate governance significantly reduces a firm's cost of equity capital. In fact, strong external corporate governance has been shown to play an important role in mitigating the effects of financial crises. During the Asian crisis, countries that had weak external corporate governance were particularly vulnerable to a sudden loss of investor confidence displaying stronger stock market declines and exchange rate depreciations than countries with strong governance. In this case, cross-country differences in legal systems seemed to have played an equally important role as the usual macro-economic factors that contributed to the crisis. Although weak corporate governance likely did not trigger the Asian crisis, it seems to have made countries and firms in the region more vulnerable, exacerbating the crisis once it had begun.

TABLE-9

COUNTRIES WITH A CODE OF GOOD CORPORATE GOVERNANCE

Country	*Existence of Code*	*Date*	*Mandatory Compliance Level*
Latin America			
Argentina	n		
Brazil	y	June 2002	E
Chile	n		
Colombia	y	August 2003	
Mexico	y	January 1999	E
Asia			
China	y	January 2001	P
India	y[1]	April 1998	E
Korea	y	March 1999	E
Malaysia	y[2]	March 2000	P
Thailand			
Emerging Europe			
Czech Republic	y	June 2004	E
Hungary	y	February 2002	E
Poland	y	September 2002	E
Russia	y	April 2002	E
Turkey	y	June 2003	E

Sources: OECD, 2003, "White Paper on Corporate Governance in Latin America"; European Corporate Governance Institute website; and Weil, Gotshal, and Manges, 2000, "International Comparison of Corporate Governance: Guidelines and Codes of Best Practice in Developing and Emerging Markets."

Note: y = yes; n = no; E = comply or explain; P = parts of code mandated.

[1] India has incorporated directly into law many of the recommendations from various special committee reports on corporate governance.

[2] Although Thailand does not have a code for corporate governance, the Thai stock exchange does have a Code of Best Practice for Directors of Listed Companies.

In part as a result of these crises, and following recommendations from the FSF and the publication of the OECD Principles of Corporate Governance, most emerging markets have established codes of good corporate governance (See Table-9). India's equity market in recent years has benefited from the recognition that its corporate governance and transparency standards are superior to those in most emerging markets, a leading factor supporting the recent growth of primary equity markets in India.

Corporate governance measures that improve investor protection facilitate issuance by increasing the investor base, but compliance with the measures may be burdensome for small corporates and increase the cost of issuance. This is a difficult trade-off that the authorities and market participants have to assess in each country, and there are examples of the tensions in both mature and emerging markets. For instance, a number of European firms have been considering delisting from U.S. stock exchanges as a result of the costs associated with Sarbanes-Oxley provisions. Also, in 2002, the Hong Kong stock exchange (HKEx) had to back away from proposals to introduce quarterly reporting and increase the number of independent directors on companies' boards. Some respondents to the HKEx proposal noted that, quarterly reporting would sharply increase the companies' cost and lead investors to focus too much on short-term profits, while a shortage of "quality" director candidates would also make the second requirement rather costly. In the end, the HKEx left the rules unchanged but incorporated the proposals into the exchange's non-mandatory code of best practice.

Besides disclosure and the associated market discipline, there are other private sector initiatives that enhance private enforcement mechanisms for protecting minority shareholders' rights, are likely to prove quicker to implement, and are perhaps more effective than government initiatives. For example, binding arbitration dispute settlement procedures, such as the one put forward by the Brazilian stock exchange (Bovespa), would allow corporate governance enforcement mechanism to overcome weaknesses in the judicial system of some emerging markets. Other improvements in the Bovespa include the introduction of three new listing levels—Levels 1 and 2, and the Novo Mercado—that carry more stringent corporate governance standards than do basic listings, including issue-only voting stock, offer full tag-along rights, maintain a free float of 25 percent, and disclose quarterly its financial statements on a consolidated basis using either IFRS or U.S. GAAP.

One of the first things that many jurisdictions have sought to improve is the structure and responsibility of the board of directors of a corporation. Many have put in place rules that mandate a minimum number of independent directors, but there is a negative relation between firm performance and the number of outside directors, which seems to result from a firm's willingness to add directors without any regard to their expertise or qualifications. In particular, the ACGA has noted that, of the 10 large Asian markets that have a national code of best practice based on international standards, only India, Malaysia, the Philippines, and Taiwan Province of China have a truly robust definition of what constitutes an independent director. However, firms perform better when there exist various board committees (particularly audit committees), when directors from financial institutions sit on the board, and when there is a minimum number of outside directors that sit on the audit committee. Thus, there is an important role for the staff of financial and auditing institutions in providing guidance on the boards of nonfi-nancial corporations.

The introduction of "voluntary" codes of (good) corporate governance across many emerging markets, developed by public-, private-, and academic-sector groups or the local stock exchanges is another example of private sector interests enhancing the corporate governance environment. In most emerging markets, the codes are adopted by corporations, on a "comply or explain" basis. By having to note publicly which aspects of the code they do not comply with, the corporations subject themselves to market discipline and greater disclosure. In some jurisdictions, compliance with parts of the code is mandatory. For example, in June 2003, the Chinese securities commission enforced the strict compliance with their code's requirement that one-third of a corporation's board of directors be independent. This was done after the securities commission found widespread disregard for this important aspect of the code. A relatively straightforward way to further enhance the corporate governance in emerging markets would be for the authorities to mandate adherence to all or parts of their country's code.

Finally, individual firms can themselves be proactive and voluntarily institute higher governance standards in their corporate charter. In many cases firms have done so in response to active efforts by institutional investors. Examples of this are Cemex in Mexico, and Ultrapar and CCR in Brazil, whose securities have been rewarded by early actions to improve several aspects of corporate governance. Institutional investors, both local and international, have played an increasingly active role in developing better corporate governance standards, in particular in Latin America. There are several examples in Latin America of local institutional investors who held minority voting stakes in firms and were "frozen out" of many mergers and acquisition transactions, receiving little of the profits from the sale of the firms to new entities. Local institutional investors played an important role in prodding a series of legislative and private initiatives in these countries in the late 1990s and early 2000s. Some foreign institutional investors have also singled out the practice of family members issuing nonvoting shares to raise capital while retaining control as the main problem in corporate governance in Latin America, and have campaigned actively to change it.

Concentrated Ownership

A particularly detrimental effect on an emerging market firm's valuation and its ability to access capital markets result from a high degree of concentrated ownership where insiders possess control rights in excess of their proportional ownership (cash flow rights) and are able to extract private benefits from this control via tunneling or opaque related-party transactions that siphon off firm value at the expense of those shareholders that hold a minority of voting or control rights. The separation of cash flow rights and voting rights can be achieved through cross-holdings or pyramid structures in which one firm is controlled by another firm, which may itself be controlled by some other entity and so forth. Alternatively, this can be achieved via dual-class shareholding structures in which insiders (managers or controlling families) hold shares with superior (to their ownership or cash-flow) voting rights. However, concentrated ownership and poor corporate governance tend to constrain the supply of equity capital to emerging markets. Specifically, there is evidence that firms with insiders who have sufficient control rights to allow them to expropriate other investors attract significantly less U.S. equity flows, and that the impact of weak internal governance is magnified in countries with poor external governance.

Unfortunately, concentrated ownership is one of the most pervasive problems in emerging market corporate governance and one that is difficult to solve. The concentrated corporate ownership structures are hard to dismantle because of the political power they confer on their controlling shareholders, and thus are quite persistent. Indeed, the politically connected controlling shareholders of large business groups may deliberately impede the development of institutions that permit low-cost market transactions so as to preserve the status quo. Moreover, this might retard economic development in many low-income countries. In addition, these controlling shareholders tend to become entrenched in the financial and political landscape of the country, perpetuating the problem.

Financial System Design

Banks are the dominant source of debt financing in emerging markets, and although there are several reasons for this dominance, banks are likely to complement and reinforce the development of securities markets. Indeed, overcoming the institutional constraints is likely to help develop both banks and markets as complementary sources of funding for the corporate sector. Banks can do this by controlling access to distribution networks, or by encouraging regulations that increase the cost of issuance and underwriting of securities. In Japan, for instance, until 1987 the issuance conditions of corporate bonds were determined by a "Bond Committee," controlled by the major commercial banks. The bond issuance conditions were unfavorable to the development of the corporate bond market and involved the use of collateral, high management fees, and quantitative limits related to the company's equity. However, the last two decades have witnessed an expansion of securities markets everywhere, Moreover, the recent growth of corporate bond markets in the EU and Canada demonstrate that banks and markets can grow in tandem and actually support and complement each other. In Canada, corporations have increasingly become dependent on market-based financing over the 1980s and 1990s as banking legislation changes allowed banks to become increasingly involved in financial market activities such as underwriting and brokerages services. In particular, loan financing by Canadian nonfinancial corporations declined from 40-

50 percent of total funding in the early 1980s to 20 percent in 2004, as bond and equity financing increased.

In emerging markets, growth of bank corporate lending and local securities markets seem to have largely moved together — except perhaps for some cyclical episodes. Infact, the rapid growth of institutional investors has been highly supportive of market-based sources of funding. The growth of local institutional investors, and the increased participation of global institutional investors, have contributed to the development of local securities and derivatives markets. Although this impact has been mostly felt in government bond markets, corporate bond markets have started to also share the positive influence of institutional investors and their need for long-term securities.

VULNERABILITIES ASSOCIATED WITH THE LEVEL AND COMPOSITION OF CORPORATE FINANCE

In response to the constraints and obstacles to adequate and diversified sources of funding as well as to the risks of macroeconomic instability, emerging market corporates tend to rely more heavily on foreign currency and short-term debt instruments. As with the sovereign, this particular composition of liabilities in the corporate sector leads to vulnerabilities that suggest that lower leverage ratios than in the mature markets may be desirable.

Corporate Sector Currency and Maturity Mismatches

It is generally acknowledged that aggregate balance sheet mismatches pose serious problems for policy makers. Both currency and maturity mismatches can exacerbate the impact of exogenous shocks in emerging markets, increase the severity of crises, and slow down the postcrisis adjustment. Although aggregate mismatches seem to have lessened in recent years corporate sector balance sheet mismatches remain at high levels.

The excessive short-term debt, liability dollarisation, and the use of foreign jurisdictions are endogenous ways of coping with systemic risks and financial underdevelopment prevalent in emerging markets. Indeed, weaknesses in macroeconomic policies and financial market frictions contribute to higher instability of the operating environment in emerging markets compared with mature markets, complicate financial contracting, and limit the available sources of funding for local firms. *First,* the "original sin" problem prevents both emerging market sovereigns and corporates from issuing domestic currency debt abroad. (Original sin refers to the inability of emerging markets to borrow abroad in their own local currencies, which force them to issue in foreign currencies to capture foreign savings and exposes them to foreign currency risk). *Second,* the relative underdevelopment of local capital markets often prevents local firms from issuing domestic debt in long tenors or effectively hedging their currency and duration risk exposures through financial derivatives. *Third,* weak institutions and corporate governance problems limit firms' access to equity financing. Thus, an emerging market firm that is unable to obtain long-term funding locally faces a trade-off between financing long-term investments with short-term local currency liabilities, which creates a *maturity*

Assessing Corporate Credit Risk

Two approaches to assessing the overall financial health of a company are commonly used by practitioners: traditional financial ratios analysis, based on the accounting information, and the contingent claims approach, which combines the balance sheet data and the market, prices of the publicly traded securities of a firm. The financial ratios approach consists in selecting several key financial ratios that are then drawn together in one score, which provides a snapshot of the firm's financial health, for example, the Altman's Z-score. The contingent claims approach uses the well-known Black-Scholes-Merton (BSM) methodology for calculating the probability of default. The BSM method is based on the assumption that the equity value of a firm can be viewed as a European call option on the firm's assets, with the debt value as the strike price. The "distance to default" can therefore be calculated using the standard option pricing equations and interpreted as the number of standard deviations of asset growth by which the market value of assets exceeds its liabilities. Based on an analysis of the average Z-scores for the entire sample of firms, the bankruptcy (credit) risk of market participants does not appear to be significantly lower than that of nonparticipants. This suggests that the ability to borrow abroad is not necessarily associated with higher credit quality. Altman's Z-scores for emerging markets are weighted averages of the following accounting ratios: working capital/total assets, retained earnings/total assets, earnings before interest and taxes/total assets, and market value equity/book value of total liabilities. A score close to zero indicates that a company is close to bankruptcy/default.

Combining the currency mismatch indicators and bankruptcy risk measures allows the examination of the relationship between changes in currency mismatches and changes in the financial health of the corporate sector.

How well do these measures reflect the overall credit risk of the corporate sector in a particular country? Clearly, simply averaging the risk indicators by country or by industry segment does not take into account possible correlations of bankruptcy risk measures across firms, which may amplify the impact of a small number of corporate failures on the entire sector. In addition, these measures do not take into account the impact of macroeconomic factors on corporate sector vulnerability indicators as some risks for the corporate sector may be of systemic nature and, therefore, non-diversifiable. These factors also call for a more integrated assessment of corporate sector vulnerabilities.

QUESTIONS

1. Critically examine the emerging patterns in global corporate financing.
2. Discuss the sources of corporate finance and financial structure in the United States, Japan, and Euro Area.
3. Examine the recent trends in corporate finance in emerging markets.
4. "The mechanisms that protect investors against conflict of interest between creditors and shareholders, as well as between insiders (managers and controlling shareholders) and minority shareholders, are particularly imperfect and costly in emerging markets." Do you agree?
5. Critically examine the institutional obstacles to move diversified and adequate funding sources for the corporate sector in the emerging markets.
6. Discuss the key differences between emerging market corporates and their mature market counterparts—in particular, leverage ratios, and internal *versus* external funding—and the main determinants of these differences, as well as constraints to achieving a better funding mix.
7. "The firms that participate in international capital markets have higher leverage and lower profitability than non-market participants." Do you agree?

39

CHANGING INTERNATIONAL FINANCIAL REPORTING STANDARDS AND FINANCIAL RISK MANAGEMENT

INTRODUCTION

Risk management from the perspective of the financial system as a whole depends critically on the quality of information available to market participants regarding the financial condition of peers and counterparties. A smooth interface between financial, reporting standards, financial management practices in individual firms and the prudential framework can be a source of strength for the financial systems. In recent year's a number of developments have focused attention on the influence that financial reporting standards exert on decision-making by firms and investors. Market observers debated the likely impact on earnings volatility and equity valuations of listed companies in the first year of implementation of international accounting standards. Similar debates surrounded the implemention of new rules for pension plan accounting in a number of jurisdictions which are likely to have a significant impact on the asset allocation decisions and risk-taking choices of employer-sponsored pension schemes.

The development implied a shift towards greater reliance on market-based and away from historical cost valuations for balance sheet and income accounting, accounting standard setters and users focused on the possible impact on how businesses manage their risks. From the perspective of financial stability, the debate related to the economy-wide implications for the availability and use of risk capital as well as for the dynamics of asset prices.

ECONOMIC FUNCTIONS OF FINANCIAL REPORTING

A number of issues revolve around the two main economic functions of financial sporting, namely to provide information about the performance of employed resources and to facilitate their governance. Management of resources depends on proper and reliable measurement of inputs and ultimate results. Outside stakeholders, such as investors and regulators, rely on accurate and representative financial reports by the firm in forming an independent assessment of its current condition and future prospects as well as of how its performance compares to that of its peers and competitors. Moreover, formal intervention rules for the transfer of control over resources are typically based on accounting information. A case in point relates to the respective control rights of equity and debt holders in the event of default. Similarly, regulatory intervention rules are also conditioned on accounting valuations of assets and liabilities of the firm and on associated measures of risk.

A Two-way Relationship

There is a two-way relationship between accounting rules and behaviour. Accounting returns act as a focal point for outside stakeholders, including regulators, wishing to gauge the performance of a firm. As such, they inevitably condition the decisions of management. Conversely, the nexus of incentives that influences management behaviour also affects their attitude towards risk. The collective impact of changes and behaviour can in turn influence market prices and valuations. This is particularly true for those items in financial reports that include more forward-looking elements and assessments of risk.

The measurement of value is not an unambiguous scientific exercise, as it often entails judgment regarding future developments and the assessment of risk/reward trade-offs associated with a specific item. However, the capacity of financial reports' measures of value to reflect the available information has been enhanced as a result of complementary developments over the past three decades: the expansion of markets for risk transfer instruments and advances in risk measurement technology.

MARKETS FOR RISK TRANSFER

Markets for risk transfer have developed in both depth and breadth, expanding enormously the range of instruments available to facilitate the tailoring of financial risk to the specific needs and circumstances of individual market participants. Derivatives markets have blossomed, with the latest additions being those for the transfer of credit risk. Securitisation structures have increasingly been used to repackage and reallocate financial risk. Importantly, from the perspective of financial reporting, these innovations have generated readily observable market prices for an ever finer grid of risk classes. This has markedly improved the pricing of items that had hitherto been difficult to value.

Helpful as they might be in providing forward-looking valuations, market prices have a major shortcoming, namely their relative opacity as to the drivers of value. Observed prices contain risk premia that are directly related to market participants' views about the risk to future cash flows and their attitude towards risk-taking. Disentangling the relative influence of these two drivers of premia at a given point in time is a highly judgmental exercise, not least because they both vary over time. Risk assessments are subject to revisions in the light of new information. Investors' effective risk attitudes can be affected by market conditions, the availability and cost of external funding and recent performance. Hence, market price variability can reflect, at least in part, temporary shifts in risk appetite as opposed to fundamental shifts in expected cash flows. More importantly, changes in market prices may feed back to the effective risk attitude of investors and lead to a more persistent impact on valuations.

RISK MODELS

Complementing the deepening of markets for risk transfer, advances in risk measurement technology have also contributed to the accuracy of valuations for complex and illiquid balance sheet items ("marking to model"). Innovations in the pricing of derivative securities have transferred successfully to other contexts, such as the valuation of credit risk and of embedded options in financial contracts. New modelling techniques provide valuable tools for firm-wide risk measurement and management. Increasingly, investment and hedging decisions are supported by asset and liability analysis based on forward-looking models of value and risk, calibrated on observed prices but often extrapolated to cover a broader range of instruments. Regardless of their sophistication, the validity of models depends critically on the validity of the assumptions on which they rest. Moreover, model-implied valuations are not immune to the influence of the same time-varying factors as market prices, since they are based on historical relationships between observed prices and are typically calibrated to reflect recent movements in those prices. Despite these shortcomings, however, risk models offer the promise of achieving a better understanding of the drivers of risk, as they lend themselves more readily to the identification and analysis of risk premia.

VALUATION PRINCIPLES AND THEIR IMPLICATIONS

Different valuation principles rely variously on historical cost, market prices, models and internal assessments of value. By adopting different perspectives, they strike a different balance between desirable aspects of financial reports, namely accuracy, verifiability, reliability and comparability. For example, historical cost accounting produces highly predictable assessments of value over time that are tightly linked to easily identifiable past events. By contrast, valuation principles that depend on forward-looking assessments of value may be more responsive to current developments at the expense of potentially greater variation in values over time. The contrast is clearest in the case of financial securities for which daily fluctuations in market prices can at times lead to significant unrealised gains or losses if the portfolio is reported on the basis of historical acquisition costs. Moreover, while some principles allow the valuation of specific asset or liability items to depend on firm-specific inputs (eg own assessment of future benefits, discount rates based on portfolio characteristics, synergies with other assets), others such as fair value and historical cost seek to generate values that would be identical, regardless of the specific context. The greater relevance of values generated under the former principle from the viewpoint of internal decision-making comes at the cost of relatively greater dependence on internal models built around potentially opaque assumptions. The debate regarding the accounting for demand deposit liabilities of banks is a case in point.

Accounting standards strive to provide a reporting framework which is neutral with respect to economic decisions. However, as noted above, the choice of valuation principle has important implications for behaviour at the micro as well as at the macro level, especially as it relates to the treatment of risk information.

GOVERNANCE OF RESOURCES

The treatment of risk information in reporting standards has a significant influence on the governance of economic resources. The degree to which forward-looking assessments of value and risk are embedded in valuations influences the effectiveness of transfer of control rules included in the law or bilateral contracts. An obvious example is the paradoxical situation that can arise if the market value of an entity's liabilities is used to determine bankruptcy. In this case the deterioration in creditworthiness will generally increase the value of the firm since it will lead to a reduction in the value of its liabilities. Another example is given by the different implications of loan provisioning based on demonstrated signs of distress in individual loans, or on assessments of expected loss for a loan portfolio. While the former approach depends on backward-looking manifestations of risk, the latter involves forward-looking assessments of risk informed by the analysis of past experience. The nature of the adopted approach will influence reported income and capital for the bank over the business cycle and also condition the assessment of prudential authorities as to its soundness.

The importance of these influences is further magnified when examined from a systemic perspective, where the endogenous character of risk is more evident. Behaviour that is rational from the point of view of an individual firm, which perceives market prices as invariant to its actions, can lead to inefficient aggregate outcomes when the compounded effect of individual actions feeds back to market conditions. One such example is the recent compression of rates at the longer end of the UK gilt yield curve as a result of the increased demand from pension funds attempting to hedge the risk of low discount rates on the mark to market values of their liabilities. Likewise, the procyclical variation of loan provisions based on point-in-time credit risk assessments can result in lending behaviour that amplifies business cycle volatility and increases financial system vulnerability.

Lessons from Interaction between Financial Reporting and Risk Measurement and Management

An analysis of the interaction between financial reporting, on the one hand, and risk measurement and management, on the other, highlights three main messages. The first is that valuations are not unique. Value is often dependent on the perspective from which it is measured. The value contribution of the same item may differ depending on the context. Moreover, even when performed from the same perspective, valuations are subject to variations due to time-varying risk premia driven by shifting investor risk attitudes that may be only indirectly related to changes in expectations about cash flows. These issues are magnified in the case of complex instruments for which there are no deep and liquid markets. This is precisely when accounting is most relevant.

The second message is the key role played by assessments of risk. The link between risk measurement and valuations is explicit when models are used in deriving values; it is implicit when relying directly on market prices. Moreover, risk measurement and management practices have an indirect influence on reported values as they influence behaviour and asset prices. To the extent that accounting standards affect behaviour towards risk, they also influence valuations.

The final message is that a valuation approach that is best suited for one purpose might present complications for another. Given the multiplicity of external uses of financial reports, this issue can lead to tensions, including among policymakers with different objectives.

FINANCIAL REPORTING AND PRUDENTIAL POLICY

High ethical standards, adoption of high quality accounting principles, appropriate checks and balances through external and internal audits, clear division of responsibility, disclosure and transparency relate not merely to the individual firms or banks, but to the stability of the entire financial structure. In particular, it has become vital to set up firewalls against what has come to be termed as aggressive accounting practices that ultimately compromise the stake of shareholders in the corporate entity (Box-1).

BOX -1

CHANGES IN INTERNATIONAL ACCOUNTING PRACTICES

Accounting irregularities have deeply shaken public confidence in the reliability of financial reporting. The International Accounting Standards Board (IASB), based in London, began its operations in 2001 with a primary objective of " developing a single set of high quality, understandable and enforceable global accounting standards." A strong thrust towards this objective was provided by the European Union's decision to require publicly-traded companies to use International Financial Reporting Standards (IFRSs) from 2005. The IASB aims at developing, in the public interest, a single set of high quality, global accounting standards that require transparent and comparable information in general purpose financial statements. In pursuit of this objective, the Board cooperates with national accounting standard-setters to achieve convergence in accounting standards around the world.

Upon its inception the IASB adopted the body of International Accounting Standards (IASs) issued by its predecessor, the International Accounting Standards Committee. Fifteen standards that have been revised under the IAS improvement project are:

IAS 1 : Presentation of Financial Statements.

IAS 2 : Inventories

IAS 8 : Accounting Policies, Changes in Accounting Estimates and Errors.

IAS 10 : Events after the Balance Sheet Date.

IAS 16 : Properly, Plant and Equipment

IAS 17 : Leases

IAS 21 : The Effects of Changes in Foreign Exchange Rates

IAS 24 : Related Party Disclosures

IAS 27 : Consolidated and Separate Financial Statements

IAS 28 : Investments in Associates

IAS 31 : Interests in Joint Ventures

IAS 32 : Financial Instruments: Disclosure and Presentation

IAS 33 : Earnings per Share

IAS 39 : Financial instruments: Recognition and Measurement

IAS 40 : Investment Property

Some of the salient changes, especially those relating to disclosure and transparency are as follows:

- Disclosure is required of critical judgments made by management in applying accounting policies. Disclosure is required of those assumptions made by management that are important in determining accounting estimates and could cause material adjustment to the carrying amounts of assets and liabilities (IAS 1).

- The definition of related parties and the disclosure requirement for related parties have both been expanded by adding parties (e.g., joint ventures and post-employment benefit plans) and by requiring disclosure of transactions, balances, terms and conditions, and details of guarantees (IAS 24).
- Consolidation, if required, is regardless of the nature of the parent entity. Thus the requirement to consolidate controlled subsidiaries applies to parent entities that are venture capital organisations, mutual funds and unit trusts (IAS 27).
- Entities are required to disclose the compensation of key management personnel (IAS 24).
- Investments in subsidiaries, jointly controlled entities and associates, when an entity elects to present separate financial statements, are to be accounted for at cost or in accordance with IAS 39 (IAS 27).
- IAS 32 requires disclosure of information to increase users' understanding of why financial instruments are used by businesses and the associated risks. This includes information on (i) the risks associated with the entity's financial instruments; (ii) management's policies for controlling those risks; (iii) the accounting policies applied to the instruments; (iv) the nature and extent of an entity's use of financial instruments; and (v) the business purposes they serve. Improvements effected by IASB focused on reduction of complexity by clarifying and adding guidance, elimination of internal inconsistencies, and incorporation into the standards key elements.
- IAS 39 requires derivatives to be reported at their "fair" or market value rather than at cost. This overcomes the problem that the cost of a derivative is often nil or immaterial and hence if, derivatives are measured at cost, they are often not included in the balance sheet at all and their success (or otherwise) in reducing risk is not visible. In contrast, measuring derivatives at fair value ensures that their leveraged nature and their success (or otherwise) in reducing risk are reported. As in the case of IAS 32, improvements focused on reduction of complexity by clarifying and adding guidance, elimination of internal inconsistencies, and incorporation into the standards key elements.

Improvements of standards are an ongoing process. Changes in future would depend upon future experience and evolution of new instruments, markets and institutions. The revision of standards also aims to make them universally applicable. Given the diversity in financial and corporate developments in various countries, achievement of convergence of standards across countries would be a challenge that would be faced by IASB.

Source: International Accounting Standards Committee (2003).

In response to a mandate given to the OECD in 1998, a set of standards and guidelines on good corporate governance known as OECD Principles of Corporate Governance was developed and subsequently endorsed. The principles focused on the following five areas: (i) rights of shareholders; (ii) equitable treatment of shareholders; (iii) role of stakeholders in corporate governance; (iv) disclosure and transparency; and (v) responsibilities of the board.

The issue of corporate governance has assumed prominence on recent times, particularly in view of the inter-locked accounting irregularities in the US which has systemic implications. The role of auditors, investment analysts and chief executives in the irregularities highlighted the need for more stringent regulation over the functioning of these entities. Enactment of Sarbanes-Oxley Act 2002 in the US is a major step in prevention of such irregularities in future (Box-2).

BOX -2

SARBANES-OXLEY ACT

The Sarbanes-Oxley (SOX) Act, in the US, represents a response to the series of accounting irregularities in the US. The SOX Act of 2002, enacted on January 23, 2002 aims to protect investors by improving the accuracy and reliability of corporate disclosures. It recognizes the importance of sound information for improving the allocative efficiency of markets. The Act emphasizes timely and reliable public disclosure of financial statements and changes in ownership of shares due to trading activity, independence of audit committees and obligations, strengthening of criminal penalties and addressing of conflict of interest by security analysts. These elements are expected to make far reaching changes in the management of corporate entities.

The SOX Act provides for settling up of Public Company Accounting Oversight Board (PCAOB) to oversee the audit of public companies that are subject to the securities laws. The PCAOB would register public accounting firms that prepare audit reports; establish or adopt auditing quality control, ethics, independence and other standards relating to the preparation of audit reports; conduct inspection, investigations and disciplining of audit firms; and impose sanction, wherever justified, on audit firms or associated persons. Same set of standards would apply to foreign accounting firms that prepare an audit report for domestic companies.

In order to ensure auditor independence, the following provisions are made: (i) rendering of certain type of services to the same audit client by an audit firm are prohibited and PCAOB is empowered to provide exemption on a case by case basis; (ii) lead audit partner has to be rotated every 5 years; (iii) auditor is to report to the auditing committee on critical accounting policies, discussions with management officials and other material information; and (iv) audit firm whose employee during the last one year was CEO/CFO/Controller/ Chief Accounting Officer can not act as an auditor of the company.

To promote corporate responsibility principal Executive/Financial Officers would certify that the signing officer has reviewed the report, the report does not contain any untrue statement or omits a material fact, etc. Any improper influence on conduct of audits would be treated as unlawful.

The Act enhances the ambit of financial disclosures by disclosure of all material off-balance sheet transactions and other material disclosures in annual and quarterly financial reports. At least one member of the audit committee should be a financial expert. There will be enhanced review of disclosures made by certain companies and their financial statements. The Act provides for formulation of rules to eliminate conflicts of interest among analysts.

The Reserve Bank of India has progressively increased disclosure in respect of management of foreign exchange reserves. The Reserve Bank's approach with regard to transparency and disclosure closely follows international best practices in this regard. The Reserve Bank is among the 49 central banks all across the globe, which has adopted the Special Data Dissemination Standards (SDDS) templates for publication of detailed data on foreign exchange reserves. The data template provides some information on a number of parameters including currency composition, investment pattern and forward positions.

Last year, India was included in a group of 20 countries selected by IMF for preparation of country case studies in respect of management of foreign exchange reserves. The case studies, together with a summary thereof have been adopted by IMF as the accompanying document to reserve management guidelines prepared earlier by it. This document, which is now available in the public domain, contains all essential information on reserve management for the 20 participating countries, including India. Box-3 provides a summary of the present status of disclosure in respect of a cross-section of countries. As may be observed there from, only a handful of central banks, viz., Reserve Bank of New Zealand, Reserve Bank of Australia, Bank of Norway etc. have a higher level of disclosure than RBI.

Although these reforms were provoked by the trend of globalisation emerging around the same time, there was a distinct Indian flavour in their pace and sequencing. Measures to strengthen the financial sector include capital adequacy requirement, prudential norms and means to enhance transparency in the balance sheets of banks and financial institutions. Steps have been taken towards consolidated accounting and supervision and standardisation of accounting norms. Prudential norms have progressively been brought closer to international best practices and the process of convergence continues. Higher provisioning norms, tighter asset classification norms, dispersing with the concept of 'past due' for recognition of NPAs, guidelines in respect of debt restructuring/rescheduling/renegotiation, and lowering of ceiling on exposure to a single borrower are among the important measures in this area.

BOX-3

CROSS-COUNTRY POSITION IN RESPECT OF DISCLOSURE

Country/Central Bank	*Disclosures*
Reserve Bank of Australia (RBA)	• Statistical information on reserves and foreign currency transactions (monthly Bulletin) • Overview of reserves management operations and the return relative to the benchmark (annual Report) • Outline of the composition of the bench mark portfolios and discussion of the RBA's approach to risk management (annual-Annual Report)
Bank of Canada (BC)	• Operations of the Exchange Fund Account (EFA) (annual-Annual Report) • Asset Management Benchmark (annual-Annual Report) • Disaggregated reserves position (weekly –BC's website) • Comprehensive breakdown of reserves position (monthly-third business day of the following month) • Documentation of chain of authority, decision making and delegation in reserve management (BC review articles
Central Bank of Chile(CBC)	• Accounting value of reserves (weekly • Level of international reserves and foreign currency liquidity (monthly) • End-of-year value of reserves, accounting measure of absolute return measured in local currency terms, the composition of returns and the way CBC achieves the liquidity goal of reserve management (types of instruments where reserves are invested, discussion on control aspects with regard to management of risks (annual-Annual Report)

Czech National Bank (CNB)	• Regular publication of the level of reserves in the "Statistics" section of its website • Chapter on reserve management-absolute and relative performance and risk profile of reserves (annual-Annual Report)
Hong Kong Monetary Authority (HKMA)	• Bi-annual accounts of foreign exchange reserves • Headline figures for foreign exchange reserves (monthly) • Foreign currency assets (quarterly) • International reserves, analytical accounts and abridged Exchange Fund Balance Sheet and Currency Board Accounts (monthly)
Bank of Israel (BI)	• Foreign Exchange reserves (monthly) • BI's objectives, investment policy (does not include precise currency composition) and investment performance in absolute terms and relative to benchmark (annual-Annual Report)
Bank of Korea (BK)	• Size of foreign exchange reserves (twice a month) • General investment philosophy and direction (without disclosing the benchmark, currency mix, portfolio mix and portfolio returns) (annual – Annual Report) • Annual financial statement expressed in domestic currency
Reserve bank of New Zealand (RBNZ)	• Extensive disclosures in the notes to the accounts – includes risk management policies, quantitative risk exposures, net reserve management income etc., - (annual –Annual Report)
Bank of Norway	• Detailed accounts of foreign exchange reserves –includes book value, return on the total and sub portfolios in the local currency return comparison with the bench mark, currency composition etc., (annual- Annual Report)
UK (Exchange Equalisation Account	• Breakdown of assets and liabilities into broad currency blocs, SDRs and gold (quarterly) • Reserves data (IMF SDDS) (monthly) • Annual financial accounts (annual)

The need for monitoring and supervising becomes even more important systemically with the opening up of the economy. Thus, the prudential regulations were fortified by reorientation of 'on-site inspections' and introduction of 'off-site surveillance'. The focus of inspection has shifted from ensuring appropriate credit planning and credit allocation under a closed economy framework to assessment of the bank's safety and soundness and to identify areas where corrective action is needed to strengthen the institution and improve its performance.

Number of issues pertaining to financial reporting standards, relevant from a prudential policy perspective relate both to the information content of reports and to the prudential governance of financial firms. *Fistly,* the information content of reported accounts could be enhanced by the inclusion of more systematic information about risk and uncertainty. Existing standards, regardless of the degree to which they incorporate forward-looking information, are predominantly focused on giving point estimates of current value and income. This could be supplemented by two additional types of information. The first could refer to estimates of the range of potential future variation of value and income ("risk information"). Examples of such statistical summary measures include *value-at-risk* as well as the outcomes of stress tests and other sensitivity analyses. The second type could refer to measures of the uncertainty embedded in the assumptions of the valuation methodology ("measurement error information"). Clearly the importance of this latter type of information is directly related to the extent to which assumptions and models are used in the assessment of the point estimates. Thus enhanced, financial reports would give users the opportunity to form a more rounded view of the condition and prospects of the firm and avoid a false sense of precision. They would also facilitate comparisons across firms, for example by investors seeking to optimise their portfolios or by regulators in the context of financial stability.

A *second* implication for policy is the importance of seeking consistency between the treatment of accounting valuations and sound risk management principles. An example of the tensions that can arise in this context is the different treatment of demand deposits for financial reporting and for the cash arid risk management of banks. Accounting standards treat deposit liabilities on the basis of their contractual maturity. By contrast, from a bank treasury perspective, in terms of liquidity management and the associated hedging strategy, they are treated as having a longer effective maturity, which is more in line with the historical behavioural patterns of depositors.

A *third* and more general implication is that there is room for reconciling the policy objectives of prudential authorities and financial reporting standard setters based on a clearer understanding of their different perspectives. Under this approach, reporting standards would focus on providing an unbiased picture of the current financial condition of the firm and the associated risk profile, while regulatory and supervisory instruments would focus on encouraging prudent behaviour based on that picture. In practice, such a decoupling would include redesigning capital and liquidity cushion requirements on the basis of accounting returns free of intentional conservatism, applying "prudential filters" to accounting figures that incorporate risk information,and defining new triggers for regulatory intervention in the case of manifest strain.

Progress has been made in all three directions in recent years. Quantitative financial risk disclosures, such as value-at-risk measures for securities portfolios, have already been included in regulatory reporting requirements of financial firms for which this type of risk has been more important. Accounting standard setters, too, have been paying more attention to risk disclosures that are consistent with, but arguably less ambitious than, those of prudential authorities. The prescriptions of IFRS 7 are a case in point. In addition, the classification of items being valued on a fair value basis into categories indicating different degrees of estimate reliability, coupled with rough estimates of the measurement sensitivity to underlying assumptions, is an example of progress in providing measurement error information. And the close cooperation between accounting standard setters and prudential authorities in the development of standards on provisioning, the fair value option and the measurement of insurance liabilities are but the latest examples of the value added by a greater focus on risk management.

Regardless of the substantial progress made to date, the way forward needs to be based on a longer-term strategy which recognises the need to cooperate at all intermediate stages. Given the complexity of the issues and the multiplicity of stakeholders in this process, a decoupling of objectives and recalibration of policy instruments can only be a long-term goal. Over the medium term, progress can only be deliberately incremental, and appropriate safeguards should always be in place to avoid inadvertently compromising the fundamental objective of financial stability. The continuing dialogue between accounting standard setters and prudential authorities augurs well for further progress in this direction.

QUESTIONS

1. Discuss the main economic functions of financial reporting
2. Critically examine the two-way relationship between accounting rules and behaviour.
3. "Accounting standards strive to provide a reporting framework which is neutral with respect to economic decisions." Do you agree?
4. Write short note on:
   (i) Financial Reporting and Prudential Policy.
   (ii) Market for Risk Measurement and Management.
   (iii) Risk Models.
5. Discuss the main messages from the analysis of the interaction between financial reporting and the risk measurement and management.

40

COUNTRY RISK ANALYSIS

INTRODUCTION

The Oxford English Dictionary defines risk as "exposure to a peril". From a investor's point of view, risk is exposure to a loss.

> Country risk is exposure to a loss in cross-border lending, caused by events in a particular country. These events must be, at least to some extent, under the control of the government of that Country; they are definitely not under the control of a private enterprise or individual.

Country risk applies to assets and not to liabilities, although there may exist a cross-border liability risk of branch banking abroad. This liability risk, though very similar to country risk, is excluded from our definition for the sake of consistency. Among foreign assets, the definition of country risk includes only foreign loans. The risk of foreign lending is quite different from the risk of foreign direct investment, and so is the approach to the assessment of the risk. As most large banks and other institutions are exposed to both types of risk there is a case for making a clear distinction between the two by reserving the term "country risk" for the risk of foreign lending. Thus, a loan in U.S. dollars to a Bahamian borrower by the Nassau branch of a foreign bank is exposed to country risk, whereas the branch itself (the building, furniture, equipment, cash in hand, goodwill, ability to conduct business) is exposed to the risk of foreign direct investment.

WHAT IS AT RISK?

All cross-border lending in a country-whether to the government, a bank, a private enterprise or an individual-is exposed to country risk. Country risk is thus a broader concept than sovereign risk, which is the risk of lending to the government of a sovereign nation. Further, only events that are, at least to some extent, under the control of the government, can lead to the materialization of country risk. A default caused by bankruptcy is country risk if the bankruptcy is the result of the mismanagement of the economy by the government, it is commercial risk if it is the result of the mismanagement of the firm. An interesting case is that of natural calamities. If they are unforeseeable, they cannot be considered as country risks. But if past experience shows that they have a tendency to recur periodically-such as typhoons in Southeast Asia-then the government can minimize their effects. Prudent analysts also make allowance for them in their assessment of country risk. "Control by the government" is understand in the broad sense. If the government can to some extent control at least the impact of an adverse development, even though it cannot control the event itself, the possibility of that event is country risk.

COUNTRY RISK AND POLITICAL, SOCIAL AND ECONOMIC RISKS

The most frequent events that can lead to the materialization of country risk can be classified as:

Political Components

War, occupation by foreign power, riots, disorders caused by territorial claims, ideological differences, conflict of economic interests, regionalism, political polarization, etc. are the many of the critical factors of country risk analysis of political nature. Table -1 includes both domestic and international factors.The list is certainly not exhaustive.Depending on the particular type of project for which the country risk analysis is being performed, the analyst should consider more specific subcategories in some of these areas and some other important categories.

TABLE-1

POLITICAL FACTORS AFFECTING COUNTRY RISK

I. DOMESTIC

A. The Political System

1. Its Basic Strength
2. Its resiliency—capacity for change without disruptive conflict

B. The Group in Power

1. Philosophy
2. Policies
3. Government officials
   a. Ability and number of qualified officials
   b. Willingness and capability for making tough decisions
4. Strength ,capability of implementing plans

C. Opposition Groups

1. Strength
   a. Likelihood of system dirupting conflictarisng from within the country
2. Philosophy of strong opposition groups

D. The Government System

1. Efficieny
2. Red tape
3. Flexibility
4. Responsiveness

II. INTERNATIONAL

A. Likelihood of system disrupting conflict arisng from outside the country

1. Due to country's own problems
2. Due to treaty or other obligations

B. Relations with major trading partners

C. Relations of the company's home country with other countries

Socio-Cultural Components

When a company operates in a foreign country ,it must consider the possible effects of many socio-cultural variables such as civil war, riots, disorders caused by tribal strife, unequal income distribution, union militancy, religious divisions, antagonism between social classes, etc..Table-2 covers most of the major types of the socio- cultural variables, but many more can be important, especially for specific types of investments.

TABLE-2

SOCIO -CULTURAL FACTORS AFFECTING COUNTRY RISK

I. DOMESTIC

A.Social Groups

1. Homogeneity of population
   - a. Ethnic
   - b. Religious
   - c. Linguistic
   - d. Class
2. Extent of cohesiveness or divisiveness

B.General psychology of population work ethic

C. Unemployment

D. Political activism of population

E. Extent of social unrest

1. Strikes
2. Riots
3. Insurgency

II. INTERNATIONAL

A. Cross-border ties

a. Ethnic
b. Religious
c. Linguistic
c. Historical

B. Cross-border antagonism

a. Ethnic
b. Religious
c. Linguistic
c. Historical

Economic Components

Economic factors e.g. a long-term slowdown in GNP growth, strikes, rapid rise in production costs, fall in export earnings, sudden increase in food or energy imports, etc. can obviouslybe of great importance in determining the degree of country risk confronting a foreign company. Table-3 outlines many of the most important of these variables.

Among economic events, recession is an interesting case. If it is worldwide, and the government applies the appropriate countercyclical policies, it is not country risk. But if it is caused in a country by inept government policies, or if it is aggravated by such policies, it is country risk.

In this sense one can speak about political, social and economic risks. But these refer to the nature of the event that may cause a loss and they apply to all borrowers in a country; lending to a private corporation, for instance, is certainly subject to political risk. But political risk is a narrower concept than country risk, since country risk also includes social and economic risks.

TABLE-3

ECONOMIC FACTORS AFFECTING COUNTRY RISK

I. DOMESTIC

A. Economic growth,investment trends

B. Cyclicality of economy,economic diversification

C. Inflation

a. Monetary policy

b. Fiscal policy, budget deficits

D. Strength of local financial markets ,portion of total investment financed locally

II. INTERNATIONAL

A. Balance of payments

B. Internationaln trade

1. Importance of trade in GNP
2. Stability of trade earnings
   a. Diversity of exports
   b. Elasticity of export demand
   c. Elasticity of import demand
      i. capital equipmemnt
      ii. necessities
         —Degree of self- reliance in food
         —Reliance on imported energy
      iii. luxuries
3. International trade ties,proximity to major markets
4. Extent of trade controls

C. International capital

1. Currency
   a. Strength
   b. Stability
   c. Quality of exchange markets
   d. Depth of exchange markets
   e. Extent of controls over exchandge markets
2. Debt
   a.Total
   b. Short -term as share of total
   c. Debt service ratio
   d. Debt-sercvice schedule
3. International Financial Resources
   a. International reserves
   b. International borrowing capicity
      i. History of debt repayment
      ii. Credit rating
   c. Autonomous capital inflows
4. Share of total invesment financed from abroad

The risk of direct investment abroad is usually called political risk because it is mostly caused by political events. It may also be called environmental risk or even country risk. Is this the same kind of risk as the risk of lending abroad-which is this book is called country risk? What are the differences and similarities?

In principle the difference is hardly significant. Changing only a few words in the definition of country risk, one can define the risk of direct investment abroad as exposure to a loss of a real asset or business abroad as well as to a loss by a business abroad, caused by events that are, at least to some extent, under the control of the government of the host country but definitely not under the control of the owners of the asset or managers of the business.

In practice, however, there are at least six considerable differences regarding what is at risk, the time period of the exposure to the risk, the kind of events that can lead to its materialization, the probabilities of materialization, the options to avoid or minimise the risk, and the need to evaluate it.

In the case of both lending and direct investment abroad, an asset and the income produced by that asset are at risk. However, in the case of a loan, the asset is money and which directly produces income in the form of interest. In the case of direct investment - apart from the goodwill - the asset is real (plant and equipment), and the income is generated through the production and sale of goods and/or services. It is thus the plant and equipment, and the ability to use them for the production and sale of goods and/or services which are at risk (See Table - 4).

Time horizon

Loans are made from one day to a maximum of 10-12 years, and country risk evaluation encompasses these periods. It is extremely rare to contemplate a direct investment for less than five years. This is thus the minimum time horizon for risk assessment. The maximum is around 30 years, for example for oil exploration, plantations, or mining.

TABLE - 4

RISK OF LENDING AND RISK OF DIRECT INVESTMENT ABROAD

	Lending	Direct investment
What is at risk?	Money	Real assets and money
	Ability of debtor to service the debt	Ability of plant to produce and/or sell product
Maximum time horizon	12 Years	30 Years
What can go wrong?	Destruction of debtor's assets interruption of production	Destruction of subsidiary's assets interruption of production
	(Caused by war, revolution, occupation by foreign power, natural calamities, disorders, strikes)	
	Major concern in case of unguaranteed private debt where it canresult in partial or complete write-off claim.	Major concern. May result in partial or complete write-off of assets, severe losses of income, and bankruptcy.
	Rarely leads to the write-off of public sector debt. With regard to disorders and strikes, only if they are countrywide do they	

	affect the public sector's debt servicing ability.	
	Expropriation, indigenization of debtor's assets	Expropriation, indigenization of subsidiary
	Minor concern only in case of unguaranteed private debt. New owner normally honours obligations of previous owner.	Major concern. May result in substantial capital losses as well as loss of expected earnings.
	Impossibility of transferring funds	Impossibility of repatriating capital and/or remittingearnings
(Because of imposition of exchange controls by government)		
	Major concern only in case	Major Concern. of unguaranteed private debt.
	Fall of earnings, bankruptcy of debtor	Fall of earnings, bankruptcy of subsidiary
(Caused by mismanagement of the economy, credit squeeze, long-term slowdown in GNP growth, strikes, rapid rise in production costs, etc.)		
	Major concern but only in case of unguaranteed private debt	Major concern only if the plant produces mainly for the market of the host country
Deterioration of the balance of payments of debtor/host country Overextension in external borrowing by debtor/host country *(These can be caused by a great number of political, social & economic factors)*		
	Major concern in case of public debt. Concern in case of unguaranteed private debt only in as exchange controls-see above.	Concern only in as much as it can lead to exchange controls-see above. much as it can lead to
Probability of losses	Could be significant-for both capital losses and losses of expected earnings - in case of unguaranteed private debt. In case of public debt, probability of capital loss is negligible. That of expected earnings could be higher but it is usually less than in case of unguaranteed private debt.	Could be significant for both capital losses and losses of expected earnings.
Reaction to identified risk Before loan is granted, investment effected	Grant the loan or not grant it.	Go ahead with the project as planned; cancel the project; redesign the project to minimize the impact of perceived risk.

After the loan has been granted, investment effected	Virtually no possibility of minimizing the risk of outstanding loans.	Adoption of suitable strategies to minimize risk.
Need for risk evaluation	There is an international financial market and a market consensus on country risk. The lender can perform close to the market average, without country risk evaluation, just by following the market. Risk evaluation is needed only if the lender (a bank) wants to perform above the market average.	There is no international market for direct investment and no market consensus on political/environmental risk. The direct investor has to do its own risk evaluation.

Probability of losses

There are significant differences in the kind of situations that can lead to the materialization of risks and in the probability of losses. These are shown in Exhibit 1. When it lends to the private sector without government guarantee, the lender's concern are similar to those of the direct investor. The major exceptions are expropriation and indigenization which are only of minor concern to a lender. For unguaranteed private debt, the probability of capital losses and losses of earnings is also similar to that of the direct investor.

Country risk of loans to the public sector differs considerably from the risk of foreign direct investment, with respect to the situations that can lead to its materialization and the probability of capital and income losses. Taking into account the share of unguaranteed private loans in total commercial bank lending abroad, one can conclude that less than 50 percent of bank lending faces country risk similar to the risk faced by foreign direct investment.

REACTION TO RISK

Once a particular risk has been identified there are considerable differences in the options of a lender and direct investor. Assuming that for the individual bank the spread (fee for financial intermediation and compensation for risk taking) is given, the bank has only two options: to take the risk and go ahead with the loan, hoping for the best, or not to lend. Between these two extremes the potential direct investor has the additional option of redesigning the project to minimize in advance the impact of the risk. For instance, if there is the risk that the government of the host country will introduce legislation to prevent temporary redundancies, the project can be redesigned to sub-contract part of the work.

The difference in this respect is even more important if the risk is identified after the loan has been granted or the direct investment effected. The bank can do virtually nothing to minimize the risk of outstanding loans; it can only hope for the best. (It can, of course, refrain from making new loans, but this is a different matter.) Again, the direct investor can adopt suitable strategies to minimize the risk.

NEED FOR RISK EVALUATION

The need or compulsion to evaluate country risk (political risk, environmental risk) is not quite the same in the cases of lending and direct investment. Country risk assessment is a complex, tedious and costly exercise. A respectable body of opinion holds that the benefits do not justify the costs. The argument runs on the following lines:

The spread is a fee for financial intermediation and leaves a small profit margin which should cover non-interest costs plus a reward for risk taking. The fee itself does not change from one loan or one country to another. If the risk is perceived to be nil or negligible, the spread is say 3/8 percent. If the spread is more than 3/8 percent, the excess is the reward for risk taking. This reward varies, according to the market's perception of the risk, from one country to another and, within the same country, from one borrower to another.

The international financial market is near-perfect, so the argument goes, in the sense that no individual borrower or individual bank can influence the spread. Given the efficiency and speed with which information is gathered and transmitted, knowledge is near-perfect on the market. It follows that the collective unbiased risk evaluation of the marketplace, based on the best available information and reflected in the spread, cannot be surpassed in accuracy by any individual bank. Assessment of country risk is thus an exercise in futility: "The market knows best."

Events of the last decade have demonstrated that, just as the stock market, the international financial market can in the short term be disastrously wrong in its collective evaluation of country risk. Like stock market analysts in their evaluation of a company's long term prospects, individual banks can be ahead of the market in their evaluation of country risk if they have insight based on information and its interpretation as well as analytical ability superior to the market average. The purpose of country risk evaluation is to improve the individual bank's performance relative to the market average. If the bank can in the short term assess country risk more accurately than the market and can anticipate changes in the risk situation ahead of the market, it can move into countries where the risk is better than the market's perception, or where the bank perceives an improvement before its competitors, it can fund at the most favourable rates, and have smaller losses and wider average spreads than its competitors.

An individual bank can be right where the market is wrong because:

i) The market is probably less perfect than it has been thought previously. If so, spreads may not reflect an unbiased market consensus of country risk.
ii) The individual bank can have a superior insight regarding particular countries' conditions.
iii) Even without such insight, the bank can use superior techniques and develop a superior analytical ability.

At least six qualifications are required for proper assessment of country risk:

i) Conceptual awareness of factors that have a bearing on country risk.

ii) Analytical ability to assess how these factors interact in affecting debt servicing ability. (It is not enough to be aware that high and/or accelerating inflation is likely to affect debt servicing ability adversely, it is also important to know how this may happen.)

iii) In-depth knowledge of the country under scrutiny: its political and economic structure, the institutional and regulatory framework, recent political and economic developments, economic policies, strength and determination of the government to implement policies, etc.

iv) Specialized expertise to predict political variables.

v) Familiarity with economic forecasting techniques to make short and long-term projections of relevant variables: real GDP growth, inflation, balance of payments, external debt, debt service payments.

vi) Experience and skills to draw conclusions regarding debt servicing ability from observed and predicted variables, and combine these into a risk rating.

The acquisition of these qualifications requires considerable learning, training and experience. Few individuals are likely to combine all the qualifications, so country risk evaluation should be the result of cooperation, drawing on all the available expertise within, and accessible to, the bank, and should under no circumstances be left to amateurs.

EXTERNAL DEBT

Debt servicing ability can be fairly accurately forecast in short term. Uncertainty tended to increase over time, and so may the perception of the risk. The reverse may, occasionally, also be true. If, for example, a company experiences liquidity problems that are perceived to be only temporary, a short-term loan carries a higher risk than a five-year loan with a two-year grace periods.

Type of Borrower

A government is generally a better risk than the private sector because:

i) There is no transfer risk. Exchange restrictions, which create the transfer risk, are imposed by, and do not apply to, the government.

ii) The number of events or situations that may lead to the materialization of a risk is smaller than for a private borrower.

iii) In case of renegotiation the new terms will probably be less unfavourable to the bank than in the case of renegotiation of a loan to private borrower. A private corporation under financial stress will strive for conditions that will enable it to stay in business. A government is not under similar constraints because countries do not go out of business, however great their financial difficulties. Moreover, because this is known, the renegotiating country still has some credit standing left to worry about, together with its international prestige in the broader sense. Such considerations do not usually affect the negotiating position of a company.

iv) The probability of the materialization of the risk is less (although there may be exceptions to this rule). This assumptions is based on the fact that government can take measures that are not within the reach of company management to avert debt servicing difficulties. They can raise income through increasing taxes, and foreign exchange earnings throughly appropriate policy action; they can also count on other governments and international organizations to provide assistance.

Within the private sector, banks are probably better risks than non-banks because:

i) in some countries they can count on central assistance;
ii) interbank loans are usually for short terms, and can thus be recovered fairly rapidly after the flashing of the danger signal.

Purpose of the Loan

In principle, a balance of payments loan is a better risk than a budget loan to finance current government consumption. The latter, by definition, increases external indebtedness without increasing productive capacity upon which the servicing of the debt depends. This is not necessarily true for balance of payments loans.

The risk of a development loan is usually lower than that of a straight balance of payments loan (although most balance of payments loans are nowadays disguised as development loans). Almost be definition, a development loan contributes to the improvement of the country's debt servicing ability in the long term. A balance of payments loan, again by definition, implies an already precarious liquidity position. This may or may not improve, depending on external factors beyond the country's control and upon the government's ability and willingness to make good use of the time to improve its economic situation.

If the viability of a project can be assessed with greater accuracy than the viability of an economic development plan, then project financing is a better risk than development finance.

Within project financing, a project that generates its own foreign currency earnings will be a better risk than projects to improve the infrastructure or to create productive capacity to serve the domestic market.

Because there is no international market for direct investment there is no market consensus of political or environmental risk. The direct investor is on its own, and has to do its own risk evaluation. Direct investors have a much longer time horizon than lenders, but they are mainly concerned with a limited number of political variables. This is why they usually refer to the political risks of foreign investment. Lender's time horizons are much shorter but when they lend to the public sector, they have to look at all the political, social and economic variables that may affect a country's debt servicing ability. This is why they find the term political risk too restrictive and prefer country risk.

Differences in time horizons and in concerns mean that country risk evaluation from the point of view of direct investors is of limited use to lenders and vice versa.

Some countries may be good risks for setting up a plant but not quite so good for commercial bank lending; the reverse may be true for others.

More importantly, differences in time horizons and concerns require different approaches and techniques for risk evaluation.

Political risk evaluation is as old as direct investment abroad, going back at least to the East India Company in the 17th century and possibly further. Interest in country risk by banks only started with the increase in their lending to less developed countries in the late 1960s and early 1970s. It is not surprising, therefore, that non-bank multinationals are much more advanced in the art of political risk evaluation than banks in the art of assessing country risk. They use more advanced techniques, and have understood that such evaluation is not only important but expensive, because it is complicated and time consuming and requires special skills and expertise.

CLASSIFICATION OF COUNTRY RISK

Much of the conceptual confusion that surrounds country risk arises from the different criteria according to which risks can be classified. These include:

i) by the side of the balance sheet which is exposed to risk, whether assets or liabilities;

ii) in case of assets, by type of asset which is at risk: loans (country risk) vs. direct investment;

iii) geographically: Austrian, Brazilian, Chilean, etc. risk;

iv) within each country, by the nature of events that may lead to its materialization: political, social, economic, etc.;

v) regarding country risk, by type of borrower: government (or sovereign) risk, private sector risk, corporate risk, individual risk;

vi) for each type of borrower, by the action taken by the borrower that causes a loss: repudiation, default, renegotiation, rescheduling, etc;

vii) for each of these, by degree, i.e. high, low, moderate risk.

Classification by action taken by borrower

Among the various classifications, the type of action taken by the borrower is probably the most important.

Repudiation or default

In this case, the debtor notifies the creditor that he will definitely cease making any further service payments because he cannot or does not want to pay (default), or because he does not recognize the debt (repudiation). As the distinction between repudiation and default has little relevance to the lender, and because repudiation is extremely rare, we are concerned here only with default. Default as defined here is quite different from the widely used term of "technical default" (see below).

Renegotiation

Renegotiation here indicates that the lender will receive less than originally agreed because the interest rate is lowered, the spread narrowed and/or because part of the principal will not be repaid. Refinancing not covered by a penalty clause has similar consequences to the lender.

Rescheduling or moratorium

This implies that the terms of the loan are lengthened either because annual repayments of principal are lowered and spread over a great number of years than originally agreed (rescheduling) or because there will be a grace period for the repayment of principal (moratorium). The interest (or spread) remains the same as originally agreed.

There may be an opportunity loss if the lender could have relent the principal at a higher interest rate or wider spread had it been repaid as originally scheduled. There may alternatively be an opportunity gain, if the market has become more liquid in the meantime.

There will also be a loss of convenience as the schedule of the actual cash flow will be different from that of the expected cash flow. There are extra administrative costs, such as the cost of negotiating the rescheduling or the moratorium. This is usually the only measurable loss that the lender suffers as a result of rescheduling or moratorium, but even that may be recovered through a one percent penalty interest on rescheduled amounts.

Technical default

Technical default arises when the borrower fails to meet one or several terms for debt service payments because of, for example, temporary inability (or unwillingness) to pay, administrative delays, or inefficiency. The accent is on the word "temporary" : usually there is little doubt that the debtor will eventually meet his debt servicing obligations. Usually he also pays interest-sometimes at a penalty rate-on service payments due. In that case the impact from the lender's point of view is similar to that of a moratorium: there is a possibility of opportunity loss and there will be a convenience loss as well as the extra costs incurred in prompting the debtor to meet his debt servicing obligations.

Transfer risk

If prohibitive exchange restrictions have been imposed by the government, it may become impossible to transfer payments. This type of country risk can only materialize for private borrowers; if the government cannot service its own debt because it does not have the required amount of foreign exchange, the risk would come under default, renegotiation, rescheduling, moratorium or technical default.

A so-called improductive loan-a loan that is not serviced-may be a case of technical default or transfer impossibility. Depending upon how the issue is eventually resolved, it may also belong to any of the other categories.

Geographical location of risks

To which country does the risk of a given loan belong? The answer to this question is not always obvious, although it is relevant not only to the assessment of country risk but also to the setting of country exposure limits.

The risk of a loan is usually located in the country of domicile of the borrower. But if the loan is guaranteed, should it be the country of the guarantor? What about "brass plate" domiciles, where the head office is legally domiciled in a tax haven and the assets of the company are elsewhere?

As a general rule, the risk should belong to the country on which the principal protection as to the repayment of the loans depends. The risk of each loan can only be located after careful scrutiny of the overall situation, covering safeguards against loss and country jurisdiction.

The development of country risk evaluation

As sovereign lending increased, international divisions appended a one or two-page factsheet to each loan proposal or request for increase of exposure limit that went to the board for approval. These were modeled on the factsheets that accompanied requests for commercial loan approvals in domestic banking, including factors such as size, population, GNP, type of government, main exports and imports, and main trading partners.

This was soon found insufficient by the board, and country studies prepared by the economics department were added. They were essentially descriptive of structural characteristics and past performance. Later a final paragraph on country risk was added-the first attempt at the evaluation of a country's debt servicing ability.

POLITICAL RISK ANALYSIS

The most common error of the early country risk evaluations was the separate assessment of political risk and economic risk. Some country risk analysts also included attitudinal risk, business risk, financial risk, and other separately evaluated risks. It was not yet clear that country risk always refers to a financial phenomenon: the inability to make payments because of the unavailability of hard currency. Business risk may be synonymous with commercial or corporate risk, in which case it is not country risk; or it may be simply the country risk of unguaranteed loans to private enterprises. Gradually, country risk analysts came to realize that country risk materializes through the interaction of political and economic developments. It requires a comprehensive approach and cannot be broken down into separate political and economic evaluations. In particular, political developments rarely have a direct impact on debt servicing ability; they usually work through the economy. Table - 5 shows two examples of this process.

The first principle for the international manager should be "The world is my market place, and I can do business anyplace". Or, in the words of the old chinese proverb "Whether the cat is black or white makes no difference as long as he catches mice". The second principle is that you yourself are the best judge of foreign risk. Of course, there are services and consultants who can assist, but ultimately it is your product, your company, and your money that is involved. To make no decision because of unfamiliarity is a no-go decision and in the long run may turn out to be just as costly as another 'go' decision that failed.

TABLE - 5

INTERACTION OF POLITICAL AND ECONOMIC

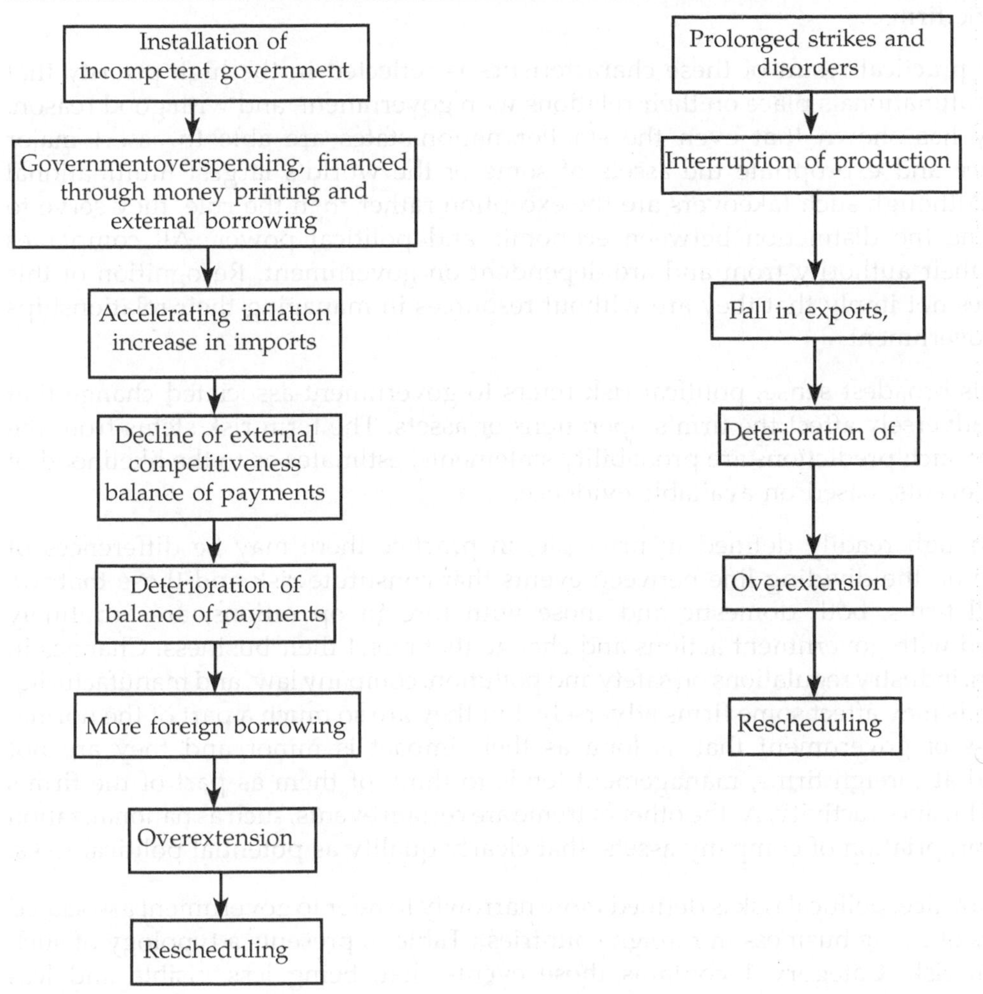

All corporate strategic planning depends on certain assumptions regarding national political conditions. Through its legislative power, government is able to influence and change the national business environment, including regulations affecting the firm's ability to compete and even the ownership of company assets.

Politics and government are particularly significant to the strategy of multinational companies. Because such companies operate within the jurisdiction of more than one government, the probability that their plans will be affected by some form of government initiative is increased. Their international mobility means that they have a certain degree of choice regarding their political environment. Unlike the domestic firm whose operations are limited to its country of origin, the strategic choice open to multinational firms includes national location and hence government. The political environment itself becomes a variable, part of management's strategic decision making. The foreign ownership links of the multinational enterprise place it in a special category in the eyes of host governments. Even though it may be incorporated under local national laws, it is classed as a foreign firm, and this often means that it is subject to special regulations and government actions not applied to domestic firms.

The practical result of these characteristics is reflected in the high priority that most multinationals place on their relations with government, and with good reason. History has shown that even the smaller nation-states are able to assert major influence and expropriate the assets of some of the world's largest multinational firms. Although such takeovers are the exception rather than the rule, they serve to underline the distinction between economic and political power. All companies derive their authority from and are dependent on government. Recognition of this fact does not imply that they are without resources in managing their relationships with government.

In its broadest sense, political risk refers to government-associated change that might adversely affect the firm's operations or assets. The term risk stems from the fact that such predictions are probability statements, estimates as to the likelihood of certain events, based on available evidence.

Although readily defined in principle, in practice there may be differences of opinion on the dividing line between events that constitute risk and those that do not. All firms, both domestic and those with foreign operations, are routinely involved with government actions and change that affect their business. Changes in taxation, industry regulations on safety and pollution, company law, and manufacturing standards may affect some firms adversely, but they are so much a part of the normal business of government that as long as their impact is minor and they are not directed at foreign firms, management tends to think of them as part of the firm's normal business activity. At the other extreme are certain events, such as nationalization and expropriation of company assets, that clearly qualify as potential political risks.

In practice, political risk is defined more narrowly to refer to government associated hazards of doing business in foreign countries. Table -6 presents a typology of such political risk. Category 1 contains those events that, being less visible and less associated with threat or force, are not always identified under the heading of political risk. Nevertheless, they merit close attention since they may have a major impact on the firm. These include special taxes falling on the products, profits, or assets of foreign firms and discrimination in government sales or purchases. Price controls have been imposed by some government on certain products of multinational firms, particularly drugs and medicines. Quite a few multinationals have found that excessive bureaucratic requirements or "red tape" represent a major obstacle to their international operations. Indigenization of management refers to government programs aimed at increasing the proportion of local nationals in the management of the firm's operations in that country.

Indigenization of capital refers to government pressure on the multinational to award an ownership stake in its operations (within the country in question) to local national investors. Finally, there are the more obvious risks associated with the loss of company assets. Note that the ordering of the risk indicated in Table - 6 does not necessarily indicate their importance on impact on the firm. Certain types of tax discrimination or price control may have a greater impact and be considered far more important than, for example, indigenization of capital or restrictions on repatriation of funds.

The purpose of political risk forecasting is to anticipate the likelihood of future events. Political risk forecasts fall into two distinct categories: predictions about evolutionary change, which unfolds with only minor deviation within the existing political system, and forecasts aimed at predicting major discontinuities in the political system itself.

Evolutionary Political Change

The emphasis here is on understanding and interpreting the existing political system, its likely future actions and directions of change. Valuable assistance toward this end may be obtained through the use of outside experts. Former political figures, diplomats, and specialized consulting firms are used by multinational companies to supplement their own efforts. However, many of the most important judgments are those that require internal knowledge of the firm, its specific circumstances and future plans, and how these may be expected to interact with future government actions. Ultimately political forecasts of this type will rely heavily on the ability of the company's own management to interpret future change in three areas: the firm's political leverage with the host government, the relationship of the firm relative to the host government's objectives and strategy, and internal change within the host government.

Forecasting Political Risk

Firm's Political Leverage. The basis of the agreement between the firm and the host government begins to change as soon as the company commits itself to the country in question. Once the investment is made and the company's facilities are in place, the firm's original bargaining position is sharply altered. Its chief bargaining lever, the freedom to commit its resources to another part of the world, has disappeared. Host governments are not unaware of this fact. The original agreement between firm and government has been aptly characterized by Raymond Vernon as an "obsolescing bargain." Unless the firm is able to forward additional contributions, in the form of prospective new investment or future contributions in the way of new technology, there will be a tendency toward progressive weakening in the firm's bargaining position. The firm's political leverage derives from its perceived future contribution. Sustained political leverage depends on the ability of the firm to offer the host government a continual prospect of future exports, new investment, employment, new technology, or other valued contributions, preferably of a type not readily duplicated by domestic firms.

One firm that manufactures containers constantly upgraded the complexity of its operations to keep a jump ahead of the capability of domestic firms. The company started its operations by producing simple cork-lined bottle caps in the host country. Subsequently it shifted to more complex plastic-lined caps, then to metal cans, and currently to aerosol cans. Continual upgrading has kept host government intervention to an extremely low level. The same phenomenon is observable in the extractive industries. In the case of oil exploration, preferential treatment is accorded companies working the more difficult, less easily duplicated areas. Offshore drilling generally is given preferential treatment compared to land-based exploration.

The government's perception of the contribution is important. Research shows that firms that initiated frequent contact with the host government, keeping it fully informed of their contribution, have significantly less government intervention in their affairs than those that do not.

TABLE-6

TYPOLOGY OF POLITICAL RISK

		Degree of "Violence" →
Government Restrictions 1. Tax Discrimination Discrimination in Govt. Sales and Purchases Price Controls Excessive Red Tape **"Indigenization" of Management** By Persuasion	Restrictions on Expatriate Managers	
2. By Persuasion	**"Indigenization of Capital** National Code on Foreign	Creeping Nationalization Investment
Government Blocks 3. Repatriation of Nationalization **Degree of "Visibility"**	**Loss of Assets** Nationalization with Partial Funds with Compensation	Expropriation/Destruction Compensation

RELATIONSHIP OF THE FIRM TO HOST GOVERNMENT OBJECTIVES AND STRATEGY

Most governments, particularly in the developing countries, are often actively engaged in setting objectives for the national economy. Multinational companies that are seen to contribute toward those objectives are generally welcome.

Infact, government attitudes toward multinational firms have become more sophisticated and pro-active. With few exceptions, they are ready to encourage investment by those firms that fit in with their own plans. In many respects, governments are thinking and planning very much like the companies themselves; they have developed strategies for attracting and managing multinational companies.

Identifying and understanding the host government's strategy is an important aid in forecasting its actions. Although no two countries will have precisely the same strategy toward foreign direct investment, it is possible to describe a number of national groups that have certain similarities in their general strategic approach toward multinationals.

Indigenous Industrialisations

A large number of developing countries are primarily interested in the contribution that multinational firms can make to the development of domestic companies and industries. Government policies are developed to ensure that foreign direct investment is largely owned and managed by nationals of he host country. A high priority is placed on the transfer of technology to national firms.

Leapfrog

Countries such as Singapore, Taiwan, Hong Kong, South Korea, and others aggressively seek international foreign direct investment to achieve a level of industrialization associated with the more advanced industrial countries. Favorable tax and other incentives (including production facilities in tariff-free zones) are provided for foreign investors, particularly companies that can contribute to the development of the country's technological and management skills. Government pressure to shift the ownership and management of multinational subsidiaries is absent or minimal.

Infant Industries

Japan is the prime example of this strategy, directed primarily at sheltering domestic companies from competition against foreign investors until they are judged able to complete effectively. Until relatively recently, incoming foreign investment was subject to severe restrictions. Only a few select firms, generally in high technology areas, were allowed into the country on the basis of 100 percent ownership. Most foreign companies that were permitted to invest did so on the basis of minority joint ventures, under the watchful eye of the government. Since the early 1970s, there has been a gradual lifting of such restrictions. They are formally terminated in 1980, though the government continues to influence the foreign investment climate.

Open Door

Foreign investors are offered equal treatment with national firms, but there is no particular drive by the central government to encourage or prohibit such investment. There are very few countries falling into this category, perhaps because foreign direct investment is a relatively minor segment of the economy.

Systematic Screening

Most countries today are selective about the type of firms that are encouraged or discouraged from establishing themselves within their boundaries. They have developed highly systematic procedures for selecting and monitoring such companies. Based on far-reaching investigations of the impact of foreign investment on the national economy, countries screen potential candidates to select those companies with attributes considered desirable and in the national interest. The screening criteria are subject to change in line with the government's economic objectives.

Change Within the Home Government

Evolutionary political change within the present system of government becomes a certainty with the passage of time. Political parties and the members comprising the national government will alter as a result of elections or other provisions for succession. Political attitudes and policies also will change in response to economic and other developments.

Japan at one time exercised stringent control over foreign investors entering the country. Industries open to foreign firms and the degree of foreign ownership were controlled in line with government strategy. Over time the country's economic situation has improved so dramatically that most of these restrictions have gradually been lifted. In other cases, the reverse happened. The 1983 fall in oil prices forced Nigeria to take measures to curtain imports and import-sensitive industries.

Forecasting internal evolutionary political change requires a close knowledge of the political pressures for change shaping the course of the current government and its likely successors. Inevitably the analysis will extend beyond the purely political. It will include cultural, economic, and institutional considerations and their influence on political events. There is no substitute for close, preferably personal, knowledge and on-the-spot contact with political trends, leaders, and institutions.

Discontinuous Change in the Political System

Major change in the political system, such as the overthrow of the established government through revolution, is viewed by some as the major source of political risk. This type of change strikes at the very foundations of the assumptions underlying all of the firm's plan and poses a threat to its continued existence in that country. There is, admittedly, an element of irrationality in viewing all such change as inevitably negative. It may be argued that every major change is bound to benefit some, even if adversely affecting others. Nevertheless, it is understandable that management would seek advance notice of impending political discontinuity and also that it would perceive such change as introducing the possibility of major adverse political events. Perhaps it would be more accurate to describe such forecasts as concerned with predicting the stability of political systems and the probability that the present rules of the game might be changed. In making such forecasts, companies rely on both subjective and quantitative assessments.

The traditional method of forecasting political change relies on expert opinion. The firm may seek the subjective judgment of people who are well informed on the national political situation, but there are obvious hazards in this approach. Experts have been proved wrong before. More to the point is conscious or unconscious bias. For example, if the expert is a member of, or closely associated with, the national government, he or she may have personal reasons for wanting to encourage foreign direct investment to help stabilize and improve the national economy. Similarly, the company's own managers will not be without individual biases. Line managers, with everything to gain from new expansion within their own jurisdiction, are known for their optimism.

Nevertheless, this approach can be effective, especially where the government structure is more a matter of personalities than established constitutional practice, as in the Middle East. This "old hands" approach can be useful in appraising the objectives and personalities of the country's current leadership, the strengths and weakness of competing political groups, and the likelihood of new legislation.

Checklists, as shown in Table - 7, are used to assist in the interpretation of political system and potential change.

Expert opinion can also be sampled on a large scale, such as with the use of Delphi techniques. A number of consulting firms that advise on political events employ a panel of experts to assess political stability. The Delphi method of using a panel of experts in successive iterations is supposed to move opinion toward a consensus view that is superior to individual estimates.

More recently, there has been a growing emphasis on quantitative methods to forecast discontinuous political change. Although they must be considered promising (and their use growing), they are still considered somewhat experimental.

In principle, the employment of such methods is not unlike the use of leading business indicators used to forecast economic change. In forecasting discontinuous political change, the objective is to arrive at a probability estimate of political upheaval through the use of certain measurable events that act as lead indicators. The variables selected are usually those thought to be causally related with drastic political change. The reasoning here is that measurable change in these variables will precede discontinuous political change.

TABLE -7

CHECKLIST OF POLITICAL RISK INDICATORS

Political Environment	*Foreign Pressures*
Form of government	Threat of war
History of government stability	Military related violence
Party fractionalization platforms	Diplomatic crisesParty political
Trade disputesVolatility of electorate	External threats to supplies
Popular support of ruling party	AlliancesRole of military
Attitude to foreign companies	*Economic Pressures*
Legal system	Per capita income

Treaties on tax and investment
State companies
Religious or ethnic splits
Internal Stability
Riots
Public demonstrations
Political strikes
Purges
Assassinations
Government crisis
History of military coups
Economic crises
Balance of payments
Inflation rate
Exchange rate volatility
Controls on repatriation of capital
National debt
Income distribution
Wealth distribution

Hans Schollhammer has developed a quantitative model that uses measures of certain causal factors to forecast political change (defined as government executives transfers and executive adjustments). The causal factors are of two types. Political causal factors include quantitative estimates of national riots, armed attacks, deaths from domestic violence, government sanctions, defense expenditures and fractionalization among political parties. Another set of measures has reference to economic causal factors, such as average per capita income, national income distribution, capital formation (as a percentage of GNP), per capita education expenditures, and available food supply measured in terms of calories per capita. Quantitative measures for these factors over time were assembled for sixty countries and adjusted for differences in population size. A statistically significant relationship was found between these factors and political change.

INTEGRATING SUBJECTIVE AND QUANTITATIVE ASSESSMENTS

Both methods have weaknesses. The more mechanical approach of the quantitative techniques is unlikely to capture unique characteristics and subtle changes in mood that may shed light on particular national situations. The expert opinion approach is subject to the problems already noted together with the fact that it is unlikely to be consistent across different national territories where assessment includes to be consistent across different national territories where assessment includes more than one country. Inevitably there will be numerous cases where the decision is not clear-cut. In these marginal cases, it may make sense to use both methods. In the words of one executive.

Rummel and Heenan conclude that political change is influenced by domestic instability, foreign conflict, political climate, and economic climate. In assessing these headings, they advocate an integrated approach combining quantitative analysis and expert qualitative judgments.

In general, the companies' systems for assessing political risk were not being used to their fullest potential. Some of their main criticisms are summarised here:

1. Delay in Preparing Report

MNC managers sometimes must make quick decisions on foreign projects, but the political risk assessment may not be completed in time. In some cases, parts of the assessment are outdated by the time the entire assessment is complete.

2. Assessments are Reactive, Not Proactive

Many political risk assessments are performed in response to a proposed project rather than in anticipation that a project proposal ma be forthcoming. This causes further delay in the political risk assessment.

3. Data Limitations

Some of the data on political variables are difficult to qualify. In addition, the assessment of political risk requires information form foreign residents in the country of concern. It is often difficult to obtain relevant information form these residents.

4. Distorted Information

From the transition of raw data on political variables to a finalised political risk assessment, the data can be come distorted. This may occur because some variables are given more or less attention than deserved, or because managers may desire to contrive the data in such a way to support their preconceived opinion.

QUANTIFYING COUNTRY RISK: A COMPREHENSIVE EXAMPLE

To develop an overall country risk rating, it is necessary to first construct separate ratings for political and financial risk which depend on a variety of factors. First the political factors can be assigned values within some arbitrarily chosen range (such as values form 1 to 5, where 5 is the best value/lowest risk. Next, the political factors are assigned weights (representing degree of importance), which should add up to 100 per cent. The assigned values of the factors times the respective weights can then be summed up to derive a political risk rating.

The process described for deriving the political risk rating can then be repeated to derive the financial risk rating. That is, values can be assigned (from 1 to 5, where 5 is the best value/lowest risk) to all financial factors. The assigned values of the factors times their respective weights can be summed up to deriven a financial risk rating.

Once the political and financial ratings have been derived, a country's overall country risk rating as related to a specific project can be determined by assigning weights to the political and financial ratings according to the perceived importance. For example, if the political risk were thought to be much more influential on a particular project than the financial risk, it would received higher weight than the financial risk rating (both weights must total to 10 percent). The political and financial ratings multiplied by their respective weights would determine the overall country risk rating for a country as related to a particular project.

As a simplified example, Exhibit 1 illustrates XYZ Company's country risk assessment of the hypothetical country Sunland. The company is assessing the establishment of a steel manufacturing plant there. From Exhibit-1, there are three political factors and five financial factors that contribute to the overall country risk rating in this example. In a realistic setting, many more factors might be included. Political risk factor A might reflect the degree of political tension within the country, political risk factor B the degree of political tension of the country with its neighboring countries, and so on. Financial risk factor A might reflect potential internal economic growth, and so on.

EXHIBIT-1

DERIVATION OF THE OVERALL COUNTRY RISK RATING BASED ON ASSUMED INFORMATION

(1)	(2)	(3)	(4) = (2) x (3)	
Political Risk Factors	*Rating Assigned by Company to Factor (Within a Range of 1-5)*	*Weight Assigned by Company to Factor According to Importance*	*Weighted Value of Factor*	
Political Factor A	4	30%	1.2	
Political Factor B	2	60	1.2	
Political Factor C	3	10	.3	
		100%	2.7	= Political risk rating
Financial Risk Factors				
Financial factor A	5	20%	1.0	
Financial factor B	4	10	.4	
Financial factor C	4	20	.8	
Financial factor D	5	10	.5	
Financial factor E	3	40	1.2	
		100%	3.9	= Financial risk rating

(1)	(2)	(3)	(4) = (2) x (3)	
Category	*Rating As Determined Above*	*Weight Assigned by Company to Each Risk Category*	*Weighted Rating*	
Political risk	2.7	80%	2.16	
Financial risk	3.9	20%	.78	
		100%	2.94	= Overall country risk rating

The number of relevant factors comprising both the political risk and the financial risk categories will vary with the country being assessed and the type of corporate operations planned for the country. The assignment of values to the factors, along with the degrees of importance (weights) assigned to the factors, will also very with the country being assessed and type of corporate operations planned for that country.

Assume the company has assigned the values and weights to the factors as shown in Exhibit-1. In this example, the company generally assigns the financial factors higher ratings than the political factors. The financial condition of the country has therefore been assessed more favourably than the political condition. Political factor B is thought to be most important, based on a weighting of 60 per cent, whereas political factors A and C receive the remaining 40 per cent weighting. Financial factor E is thought to be very important, based on its 40 per cent weighting, compared to 20 per cent weights for factors A and C and 10 per cent weights for factors B and D.

The political risk rating is determined by adding the products of assigned ratings (Column 2) and weights (Column 3) of the political risk factors. It equals 2.7, which may appear low based on the individual assigned values. yet, political factor B carries a 60 per cent weight and was assigned a low value, which explains the relatively low political risk rating.

The financial risk is computed to be 3.9, which again verifies that the financial condition of the country is better than its political condition. Once the political and financial ratings are determined, the overall country risk rating can be derived (as shown at the bottom of Exhibit-1, given the weights assigned to political and financial risk. Column 3 in the lower portion of Exhibit-1 suggests the company perceives political risk receiving an 80 per cent weight) to be much more important than financial risk (receiving a 20 per cent weight) in this country as related to the proposed project. The overall country risk rating of 2.94 may appear low given the individual category ratings. This is due to the heavy weighting to political risk, which in this example is critical, form the firm's perspective. Should XYZ Company establish a steel manufacturing plant in a country that has an overall country risk rating of 2.94 (based on a scale of 1 to 5)? The answer depends on the risk tolerance of the firm, as discussed in the following section.

Before moving on, it should be emphasised that country risk assessors have their own individual procedures for quantifying country risk assessors have their own individual procedures for quantifying country risk. The procedure described here is just one of many. Most procedures are similar, though, in that they somehow assign ratings and weights to all individual characteristics relevant to country risk assessment.

Use of Country Risk Assessment

The first step for a firm after it has developed a country risk rating is to determine whether that rating suggests the risk is tolerable. If the country risk is too high, then the firm does not need to analyse the feasibility of the proposed project any further. Some firms may contend that no risk is too high when considering a project. Their reasoning is that if the potential return is high enough, the project is worth undertaking. However, there are cases in which the degree of country risk could be to high regardless of the project's expected return. Consider a proposed development of a subsidiary that appears very profitable in Country Z. If Country Z is often engaged in war, this places a threat on the life of any employees who would be transferred to that subsidiary. In this case, Country Z should be off limits, and the proposed project should not receive further consideration.

If the risk rating of a country is in the tolerable range, any project related to that country deserves further consideration. Capital budgeting analysis would be appropriate to determine whether the project is feasible.

Incorporating Country Risk in Capital Budgeting

Country risk can be incorporated in the capital budgeting analysis of a proposed project by adjustment of the discount rate, or by adjustment of the estimated cash flows. Each method is discussed below.

Adjustment of the Discount Rate

The discount rate of a proposed project is supposed to reflect the required rate of return on that project. Thus, the discount rate could be adjusted to account for the country risk. The lower the country risk rating, the higher is the perceived risk, and the higher is the discount rate applied to the project's case flows. This approach is convenient in that one adjustment to the capital budgeting analysis can capture country risk. However, there is no precise formula for adjusting the discount rate to incorporate country risk. The adjustment is somewhat arbitrary, and may therefore cause feasible projects to be rejected or unfeasible projects to be accepted.

Adjustment of the Estimated Cash Flows

Perhaps the most appropriate method for incorporating forms of country risk in a capital budgeting analysis is to estimate how the cash flows would be affected by each form of risk. For example, if there is a 20 per cent probability that the host government will temporarily block funds form the subsidiary to the parent, the MNC should estimate the project's net present value (NPV) under these circumstances, realising that there is a 20 per cent chance that this NPV will occur. (The estimation of a project's NPV when funds are blocked is demonstrated in Chapter 21).

If there is a chance that the host government takeover will occur, the foreign project's NPV under these conditions should be estimated. Each possible form of risk has an estimated impact on the foreign project's cash flows, and therefore on the project's NPV. By analysing each possible impact, the MNC can determine the probability distribution of NPVs for the project. Its accept/reject decision on the project will be based on its assessment of the probability that the project will generate a positive NPV, as well as the size of possible NPV outcomes. While this procedure may seem somewhat tedious, it directly incorporates forms of country risk into the cash flow estimates and explicitly illustrates the possible results form implementing the project. The more convenient method of adjusting the discount rate in accordance with the country risk rating does not indicate the probability distribution of possible outcomes.

Even after a project is accepted and implemented, country risk must continue to be monitored. With a labour-intensive MNC, the host country may feel it is benefiting form a subsidiary's existence (due to the subsidiary's employment of local people), and the chance of expropriation may be low. Yet, there are several other forms of country risk that need to be considered. Decisions regarding subsidiary expansion, fund transfers tot he parent, and sources of financing can all be affected by any changes in country risk; and since country risk can change dramatically over time, periodic reassessment is required, especially for less stable countries.

MANAGING POLITICAL RISK

Although there is little a firm can do to influence national political change, this is far from suggesting that management has no power to mitigate or otherwise manage the effects of political change, whether evolutionary or discontinuous.

One method is the premium for risk approach, a form of self-insurance that the firm implements by requiring a higher rate of return in countries considered exceptionally risky. Although this is one of the best-known and most widely used methods, there are a number of hedging strategies that are often more effective. These are discussed in two categories: hedging strategies that the firm can take prior to investment in a given country and those available to it after investment. These categories are subdivided into measures internal to the firm and those that depend on passing the risk to external agencies. Exhibit-8 summarises these methods.

BEFORE INVESTING

Minimising Local Equity

An obvious way to hedge against loss is to minimize the firm's equity investment in the country. Local borrowing not only limits the company investment subject to political risk, it has the important further benefit of creating allies, local lenders who have a vested interest in the success of the firm. Furthermore, it reduces the firm's exposure to foreign exchange risk since locally generated earnings can be used to repay local capital and interest payments denominated in the same currency.

Minimizing the company's equity stake can also be achieved through local equity participation-that is, forming a joint venture with local shareholders. Participation of local shareholders will also help to build links with the local community and provide the benefit of local management advice and knowledge. Where there are local indigenization programs in effect, participation of local equity shareholders is a prerequisite rather than an option.

Equity risk may be eliminated altogether through a management contract that compensates the firm for management services provided. No company investment in ownership of facilities is involved.

International Integration

If the company established in the foreign territory is dependent on raw materials, technical skills, machinery, management, or other inputs from abroad, the government will have to think seriously before taking any measures that jeopardize the flow of such supplies. A strategy of international integration builds interdependence between the company facility in question and links with facilities in other countries. Peru's Velasco regime omitted Chrysler from its extensive program of foreign company takeovers. The Peruvian plant manufactured only some 50 percent of the Chrysler product; the remainder was imported from Chrysler plants in Detroit, Brazil, and Argentina. The Peru plant could not be operated without cooperation from Chrysler plants in these countries. Integrating production internationally with supplier plants in other countries effectively preempted a successful takeover.

The protective effect of international integration can also by achieved through control of corporate output, such as markets for the firm's products. For many years, the international oil companies operating in the Middle East were relatively immune from government takeovers because of their control over the market for petroleum products. Nationalization of the oil wells was of limited use unless the government also had the means to dispose of their production profitably.

TABLE - 8
HEDGING STRATEGIES

Before Investing
- Internal hedging
  - Minimization of local equity
    - Local borrowing
    - Local equity (joint ventures)
    - Management contract
  - International integration
    - Production integration
    - Marketing integration
    - International supply sourcing
    - External hedging
  - Government insurance
  - Private insurance
  - Host government guarantees

After Investing
- Internal hedging
  - Good citizen policy
  - Increase in technical contribution
  - Negotiation and arbitration
- External hedging
  - Private insurance
  - International investment codes
  - Divestment

Another form of international integration on the output side can be implemented through the use of international trademarks and brand names. Increasingly companies are able to register their international brand names under protective legislation in a wide number of countries. Should a government expropriate the national production facilities of a such firm, the company in question is still in a position to refuse to allow the government the right to use its brand names in other countries. This would significantly reduce the value of such assets to the expropriating government. Perhaps with this in mind, the Mexican government passed a law in 1976 that required manufacturing firms to use a local trademark in all advertising and packaging.

External Hedging

In his research into the hedging strategies for French multinationals, Bernard Marois found that the risk-reducing strategy preferred by most firms was to try to shift political risk to an external agency. Several means are available for this type of hedging.

Government and Private Insurance

Many governments in the industrial countries provide various forms of insurance for companies that invest abroad, particularly if the investment is made in the developing countries. Private insurance provided by such firms as Lloyds of London is also available to cover certain types of political risk. In both cases, whether the insurance is public or private, there are insurance premiums. The insurance covers only some portion of the assets lost by the firm in the country in question. It does not cover opportunity cost.

Host Government Guarantees

Another frequently used method is the use of host government guarantees, agreements arrived at between the firm and the host government prior to investment (when the firm's bargaining power is highest) guaranteeing certain provisions in writing. These may cover tax concessions, provisions for compensation in the event of expropriation, and other contingencies. They serve as an additional protective measure, though management will be aware that the governing power of the country will, at any time, have both the power and the authority to repudiate such agreements. This does not mean that they are without value. Many governments with an eye to the future credibility of their statements will not take such action lightly.

AFTER INVESTING

After the firm has committed itself to a particular national territory, its bargaining power is usually diminished, but is by no means without measures to influence government actions that might be against its interests.

Good Citizen Policy

Corporate behavior conforming to what is usually referred to as a good citizen policy is one of the most popular prescriptions for avoiding adverse political initiatives. A good citizen policy as applied to the behavior of a foreign firm refers to corporate initiatives such as the following:

1. Prompt response to both the letter and spirit of host government requests

These may not always be a matter of legal requirement. Governments frequently will exhort companies to embark on various measures judged to be in the national interest on a voluntary basis, such as hiring handicapped workers, purchasing goods and components from national suppliers, and setting high standards of safety.

2. Contribution to national goals

In all countries, there will be certain recognized national goals that the government hopes to forward. These may include increased exports, building up the national technological base, and developing new products. Identifying where and to what degree the company can contribute toward such goals without sacrificing its own interests is a matter of management discretion.

3. Contribution to national welfare

This refers to company support of educational institutions, hospitals, latest development and other programs that contribute to the general national welfare.

4. Developing a corporate image

A company that seeks to be recognized as a good citizen will be interested in projecting an acceptable corporate image. This is as much a matter of what it does not do as much as anything else. It is possible for any foreign firm to accentuate its international links to the point where they irritate and aggravate public relations. Especially in the developing countries, a low profile is frequently an important part of being a good citizen. Nevertheless, many firms that have qualified as good citizens have been the subject of government takeovers.

Increase in Technical Contribution

The strategy of systematic and planned increase in the firm's contribution to national technological capability is closely related to the previous point. The increased importance of technology and its near universal pursuit by government, together with the perception of the multinational as a technology transfer agent, means that the firm that can present itself in this light to the host government is in a powerful bargaining position. Negotiation and Arbitration. For the multinational firms, entry into the host country in most cases will have been the subject of negotiations with the host government. Particularly in cases involving large-scale foreign investment or investment in sensitive areas, such as those related to national defense, communications, and natural resources, normally there will have been detailed discussions between the firm and the host government in arriving at the complex arrangements and commitments that comprise the final agreement governing the conditions of entry. In the developing countries, negotiations between the investing company and the host government will apply to virtually all cases of foreign investment.

Both the company and the host government will have a degree of flexibility in terms of the entry conditions thatare considered acceptable. The final agreement reflects an area where the interests of the two parties overlap, that is, an area of mutually acceptable terms and conditions of entry.

In the case of major political change, the firm's position in the country and its relationship with the new government may have to be renegotiated. In the event of such change, prudent management will seek to establish whether such new negotiations are called for. Negotiations with the new government regarding proposed initiatives that threaten the firm can prove effective in minimizing or avoiding loss. The multinational firm inevitably will have certain bargaining counters, such as possible new investment, continued licensing of technology and the use of trade names, and provision of overseas outlets. Presented to government tactfully and effectively, these can significantly improve the company's position.

Where such negotiations fail, third-party arbitration is a possibility. Although relatively rare, the greater involvement of international agencies in developing codes of conduct for both companies and host governments offers the hope that this will become a more realistic option in the future.

Private Insurance

Even after the firm has committed its resource, it can resort to private insurance schemes to hedge against future loss. The insurance premium will be proportional to the threat of asset loss.

Investment Codes

An increasing number of international organizations are attempting to promulgate international codes providing reciprocal guarantees between multinational companies and host governments. Organization involved in such efforts include the United Nations, the International Monetary Fund, and the OECD. As yet such codes have had limited validity. However, there is hope and even expectation that in the future they may provide for international investment the sort of regulatory framework and grievance procedures currently provided for international trade.

Multilateral Investment Guarantee Agency, a member of the World Bank Group, which commenced operations in April 1988 to promote private foreign direct investment for economic development in its member countries, is expected to play an important role in: (1) Guaranteeing investments made by foreign investors against political risks in developing member countries; (ii) Producing promotional and advisory services to assist member countries in creating an alternative climate for private foreign direct investment. MIGA is a legally distinct entity from the Bank or the IFC and has its own Executive Board.

Divestment

Voluntary divestment of national assets can prove a valuable device in reducing the damage caused by government takeovers that are inevitable. Planned well in advance, divestment can be effective in extricating the firm from a situation that is no longer tenable with a minimum of damage.

The firm's ability to adjust to the constraints and conditions imposed by national government depend on its ability to anticipate and interpret political change. This refers to change within the existing political system as well as change in the system itself. Even where political developments appear to be moving against the firm, a number of hedging strategies are available that can prove effective in reducing or eliminating loss.

Outside expert opinion and forecasts may assist management in its projection and interpretation of political change. But in the final analysis, the objective will be to determine the impact of such change on the firm's own particular situation and prospects (generalizations about sweeping national political change are only a means to this end). This indicates that many of the key decisions concerning such change and the firm's reaction to it will require the judgment of internal company management.

The following guideline make up the essence of what you need to know and do in political risk analysis:

- Don't eliminate any market any place without a systematic look at it.
- Package and present your project so that the benefits to the country are easily seen by all.
- Remember in most cases you don't have to worry about confiscation or destruction but rather than the smaller changes that make doing business more costly.
- Remember political systems are always changing, which means you have continually to monitor sources of risk.
- Know why they may be picking on you, your product, or your services, or in other words know your specific sources of risk.
- Don't be a passive observer. You can influence the outcome of the pressures and minimise the risks in several ways.
- Be flexible. As they say in the East, when the wind blows north the bamboo bends northward; when the wind blows south, the bamboo bends southward. And the bamboo survives a long time.

QUESTIONS AND PROBLEMS

1. List some forms of country risk other than a takeover of a subsidiary by the host government.
2. Identify common political factors for an MNC to consider when assessing country risk. Briefly elaborate on how each factor can affect the risk to the MNC.
3. Identify common financial factors for an MNC to consider when assessing country risk. Briefly elaborate on how each factor can affect the risk to the MNC.
4. Describe the steps involved in assessing country risk once all relevant information has been gathered.
5. Describe the possible errors involved in assessing country risk. In other words, explain why country risk analysis is not always accurate.
6. Explain an MNC's strategy of diversifying projects internationally in order to maintain a low level of overall country risk.
7. Once a project is accepted, country risk analysis for the foreign country involved is no longer necessary, assuming that no other proposed projects are being evaluated for that country. Do you agree with this statement? Why or why not?
8. If the potential return is high enough, any degree of country risk can be tolerated. Do you agree with this statement? Why or why not?
9. An AMC has decided to call a well-known country risk consultant to conduct a country risk analysis on a small country in which the MNC plans to develop a large subsidiary. The MNC prefers to hire the consultant, since it plans to use its employees for other important corporate functions. The consultant uses a computer programme that has assigned weights of importance linked to the various factors. The consultant will evaluate the factors for this small country and insert a rating for each factor into the computer. While the assigned weights to the factors are

not adjusted by the computer, the factor ratings are adjusted for each particular country the consultant assesses. Do you think the MNC should use this consultant? Why or why not?

10. How could a country risk assessment be used to adjust a project's required rate of return? How could such an assessment be used to instead adjust a project's estimated cash flows?
11. Explain some methods of reducing exposure to existing country risk, while maintaining the same amount of business within a particular country.
12. Why do some subsidiaries maintain a low profile as to where their parents are located?
13. Do you think that a proper country risk analysis can replace a capital budgeting analysis of a project considered for a foreign country? Explain.
14. NYU Corporation considered establishing a subsidiary in Zenland; it performed a country risk analysis to help make the decision. It first retrieved a country risk analysis performed about one year earlier, when it had planned to begin a major exporting business to Zenland firms. Then it updated the analysis by incorporating all current information on the key variables that were used that analysis, such as Zenland's willingness to accept exports, its existing quotas, and existing tariff laws. Is this country risk analysis adequate? Explain.

41

INTERNATIONAL TAXATION

INTRODUCTION

Upon entering the global arena, an investor must also contend with multiple tax systems and multiple rates of taxation. The marginal corporate income tax rates facing a multinational can vary widely across countries furthermore, there has been variation overtime. For instance, the definition of taxable corporate income also varies across countries, depending on what costs are deductible from revenues to arrive at taxable profits. Government usually set tax rates as a function of domestic political considerations, but will sometimes treat foreign investors to the extent that they choose to encourage or discourage foreign investment. This chapter examines the international tax policies of host and home countries and the management strategies of firms to reduce total taxes paid. Specifically, we are concerned with corporate income taxes, which are generally conceived as taxes on the return to equity capital. In the discussion of multinational capital budgeting, we alluded several times to tax payments but did not present much discussion on the calculation of taxes due. This chapter completes the picture by analysing the structure of tax payments and techniques of tax management. We also considered taxes in the chapter on the cost of capital and capital structure of the multinational firm with respect to their effects on debt financing and the capital structure of a subsidiary. In this chapter, we review the basic concepts as they are comparatively straightforward and represent a natural springboard into what follows.

TAXATION AND DEBT FINANCING

We introduced taxes in previous chapters predominantly with respect to the treatment of debt financing. We examined the management implications of the deductibility of interest payments when figuring corporate income for tax purposes. Because interest on debt is a deductible expense when figuring corporate income, there is clearly a distinction between the pre-tax and the after-tax interest rate applicable to the firm. We noted that the deductibility of interest payments on debt (regardless of denomination) and the treatment of capital losses (or gains) on principal increase the present value of an investment over what it would *be* if financed entirely with equity capital. To calculate the additional benefit, we introduced the Adjusted Present Value (APV) method to figure the value of the debt-related tax shield to the corporation. Most countries also allow realised foreign exchange losses associated with debt principal denominated in appreciating currencies to be deducted from income, and also tax foreign exchange gains associated with debt principal denominated in depreciating currencies, so that uncovered interest parity is preserved.

The implications of the tax-deductibility of interest payments and the treatment of foreign exchange gains and losses on principal reflect a general principle in international taxation: the returns to debt are distinct from the returns to equity in any investment project. Interest payments are therefore separated from the rest of corporate income when figuring the corporate income tax liability, which means that the corporate income tax is designed as a tax on the returns to equity only. We discussed the implications of this tax system for the firm's capital structure. A loan from the parent to the foreign subsidiary provides an opportunity to return funds to the parent in the form of interest, which is advantageous when the parent's country has a lower tax rate than the subsidiary's country. Conversely, equity financing of foreign subsidiaries allows for reinvestment of profits and postponement of home country taxes until profits are repatriated as dividends, which is advantageous when the parent's country has a higher tax rate than the subsidiary's country. Hence, debt financing is desirable in high-tax environments and equity financing is desirable in low-tax environments. One final point is that equity financing offers added flexibility in timing repatriation.

Separation of the returns to debt from the returns to equity raises questions concerning the taxation of returns to debt. By convention, the lender is taxed on the returns to debt when he receives interest. Furthermore, the lender is usually taxed by the home government only. International debt flows, then, are really no different from domestic debt flows because the lender pays the same tax rate to the same government no matter where the capital is loaned. Hence, our analysis of international taxation will not focus on the returns to debt, but will focus instead only on the returns to equity.

INTERNATIONAL TAX POLICY

Analysing taxation of equity returns is conceptually more difficult than analysing the taxation of debt returns because there is an imbroglio of tax laws pertaining to the former. In contrast to the taxation of debt returns, equity returns are taxed in the host country, and may be taxed in the home country—possibly even at a different time. International tax policy is thus determined through often-complex interactions between host and home governments. By convention, the host government acts first and the home government determines policies vis-a-vis the host government. This section is therefore divided into two subsections, one on host government policies and one on home government policies. In reality, there is more interaction and conflict between governments than this simple outline would suggest.

Host Government Tax Policies

The general international arrangement prevailing with respect to taxation of corporate profits is that the host country gets the first opportunity—or the "first crack"—to tax income produced within its borders. Specifically, the host country gets to decide its tax rates on corporate profits first. The after-local-tax rate of return to the home country investor on direct foreign investment is therefore $r^*(1 - \tau^*)$ where r^* is the foreign rate of return and τ^* is the foreign tax rate.

In addition, however, the host country is able to set other withholding taxes, which are taxes imposed on capital paid to the parent as they are taken out of the country. The withholding taxes may be imposed on dividends or repatriation of profits, license and royalty fees, and other revenues paid, whereas these funds would escape taxation if they remained in the host country. For example, the after-tax rate of return if profits are not repatriated is $r^*(1 - \tau^*)$, but the after-tax rate of return if all profits are repatriated is $r^*(1 - r^*)(1 - \tau^*)$ where τ^* is the additional withholding tax on repatriated profits. Clearly, the withholding tax acts as an incentive to reinvest earnings in the host country.

Home Government Tax Policies

The home government's tax policies are much more complicated than those of the host government because the home country must establish tax policies relative to the previously-determined host country's policies. In particular, the home country must establish tax policy with respect to two factors: (1) treatment of foreign income and foreign taxes paid and (2) the timing of taxation. We treat these two factors separately.

In what follows, we assume that the home government's tax rate on foreign income is the same as the tax rate on domestic income. This is not necessarily the case, but generally prevails in practice. Some governments may be interested in taxing foreign profits at a different rate than the domestic rate. This practice would obviously introduce more complexities and create more distortions, but the analysis of different tax rates is just a direct extension of the kinds of analysis.

Treatment of Foreign Income and Foreign Taxes Paid

Given that there is a domestic tax rate on corporate income, there are four basic ways in which a home country government can treat foreign income and foreign taxes paid. One of the easiest possible way to treat foreign income is to *exempt* it from domestic taxation. The firm will simply not be taxed on any income that it has earned abroad, and thus the foreign tax rate governs taxes paid by the firm. The after-tax rate of return is therefore $r^*(1 - \tau^*)$, as presented previously, abstracting from withholding taxes.

A second possibility is to tax profits earned overseas at the same rate as profits earned at home, and then give a full tax *credit* for the foreign taxes paid (generally both income taxes and withholding taxes, although this need not be the case). Hence, the home tax rate generally governs taxes paid by the firm. In practice, home countries limit tax credits to the company's domestic tax liability on total foreign income, which means that the multinational enterprise pays the foreign or domestic tax rate—whichever is higher. The after-tax rate of return is therefore:

$$\min[r^*(1 - \tau^*), r^*(1 - \tau)]$$

once again abstracting from withholding taxes.

A third possibility is to tax foreign profits at the domestic tax rate but then give a *deduction* for foreign taxes paid, rather than a full credit. Foreign taxes paid therefore only reduce total taxable income. The after-tax rate of return is $r^*(1 - \tau^*)(1 - \tau)$, again ignoring the role of withholding taxes. Here, there is some double taxation of foreign income occurring. This system is therefore not often used.

The fourth possibility would be to tax foreign profits, but then give no recognition for foreign taxes paid. In other words, complete *double taxation* of foreign income occurs. The after-tax rate of return is $r^*(1 - \tau^* - \tau)$, again ignoring any withholding taxes. This is not used as a method of taxation anywhere, but is presented merely to complete the list. Hence, no matter how much multinational corporations complain about taxation, things could be worse.

Example

To illustrate these possibilities, consider a case of XYZ Co., a multinational corporation headquartered in Nide, has foreign income of $1000 million from its affiliate operating in Serendip. The government of Serendip imposes a corporate income tax of 35 percent. The government of Nide taxes domestic income at 45 percent, but has not decided what the treatment of foreign income and foreign taxes paid will be. The company therefore figures its income under all four schemes outlined previously while awaiting Nide's tax decision.

$ (in million)

	Exemption	*Credit*	*Deduction*	*Double Tax*
Foreign Income	$1000	$1000	$1000	$1000
Foreign Taxes Paid	350	350	350	350
Home Taxes Paid	0	100	293	450
Net Income	$650	$550	$357	$200

If foreign income is exempted from further taxation in Nide, the company Serendip 35 percent, so it will end up with after-tax income of $650 million. If Nide taxes foreign income at 45 percent but gives a complete credit for foreign taxes paid, the company's home tax bill is [(.45)(1000) – 350] = $100 million; after-tax income is $550 million. If Nide taxes foreign income at 45 percent and gives a deduction for foreign taxes paid, the company's home tax bill is (.45)(1000 - 350) = $293 million; after-tax income is $357 million. If Nide chooses to tax foreign income and completely ignore foreign taxes paid. the company's home tax bill is (.45)(1000 million) = 450 million; after-tax income is just $200 million. As expected, the company's prefers the tax exemption. Beyond that, the company prefers the tax credit over the tax deduction, and prefers either of these over double taxation.

Timing of Taxation

The timing of home government taxation also plays an important role in the establishment of the home country's tax policy towards foreign income. There are two major policies possible.

First, a country may choose to tax foreign equity returns during the fiscal year in which they are earned, a situation sometimes called contemporaneous taxation. This set-up exists in the United States (and most other countries) for foreign branches of multinationals. A branch is not incorporated separately from the parent and is therefore considered an extension of the parent rather than a separate entity. The profits from these branches are therefore consolidated into the parent's income statement and taxes are consequently paid when the foreign profits are earned.

Alternatively, taxation may occur at the time profits are repatriated as dividends, a situation known as tax deferral. In the United States (as well as most other countries that tax the foreign income of their multinational corporations), this set-up exists for foreign subsidiaries of multinationals. A subsidiary is an affiliate of a multinational corporation that is incorporated in the country in which it operates, and is therefore considered a separate legal entity. Thus, subsidiary profits are taxed by the home government only when they come home. The basic implication of this policy is that tax deferral encourages profits to be reinvested abroad rather than repatriated.

The first-crack principle means that the host country government sets the corporate income tax rate on returns to equity earned within its borders, as well as any withholding taxes on financial outflows. The home country government is left to react to the host country's policies by deciding the treatment of foreign income and foreign taxes paid in domestic taxation, as well as the timing of taxes. In practice, some countries exempt foreign income from taxation but most countries tax foreign income and give a full credit for foreign taxes paid. Countries could alternatively give a deduction for foreign taxes paid, or even fail to recognise foreign taxes paid altogether. Taxation can be either contemporaneous or deferred until repariation of profits occurs.

Clearly, relative tax rates affect the investment decisions of multinationls. All other things equal, the multinational prefers to invest whether taxes are lower. Economists often study the effects of taxes on the investment decisions of multinationals and on international capital flows in general. As taxes typically create distortions to the equilibrium that would otherwise prevail, they are associated with losses to global output and welfare.

GLOBAL WELFARE, TAX NEUTRALITY, AND NATIONAL WELFARE

Returns on equity are taxed in the host country, and may be taxed in the home country—possibly even at a different time. This situation may lead to distortions in equity capital allocation. We know that global welfare is maximised if capital is free to flow toward countries in which the marginal product of capital is highest. If taxes do not alter the optimum allocation of capital, taxation is said to be *neutral.* We examine below the two types of tax neutrality: *capital export neutrality* and *capital import neutrality.*

Capital Export Neutrality

Capital export neutrality, sometimes referred to as domestic neutrality, means that taxes do not distort a capital owner's choice between domestic and foreign investments. In other words, taxation is export neutral if domestic and overseas investments that earn the same pre-tax rates of return also yield the same aftertax rates of return. If capital export neutrality is violated, the capital owner will have an incentive to invest more where the tax rate is lower, thereby realising a higher after-tax rate of return.

Figure-1 illustrates a typical violation of capital export neutrality. The home country is shown on the left-hand axis, and the host country is shown on the right-hand axis. The marginal products of capital are shown by MPC and MPC* respectively, and the initial allocation of capital is at *k*. If the optimum allocation of capital is at *k'*, the home country imposes a corporate profits tax of τ while the foreign country does not impose any tax. This action introduces a distinction between the actual pre-tax marginal product of capital and the after-tax marginal product of capital, MPC(1 – τ).

As long as the home country does not tax income earned abroad, the capital owner can escape the home country's tax by investing abroad. The capital owner will therefore decide where to invest based on after-tax rates of return. At the margin, the after-tax rate of return at home, r (l – τ), will equal the rate of return abroad—viewed from the position of global welfare— resulting from the imposition of domestic taxes in the home country. After all, economic returns at home are higher than economic returns abroad, $r > r^*$. In terms of Figure-1, the loss of world welfare is given by the triangle BCD. The total tax revenue collected by the home government is area ABDE. This exhibit illustrates that when the home country has a higher tax rate than the foreign country, capital export neutrality does not hold and there is a misallocation of capital.

FIGURE-1

CORPORATE PROFITS TAX AT HOME

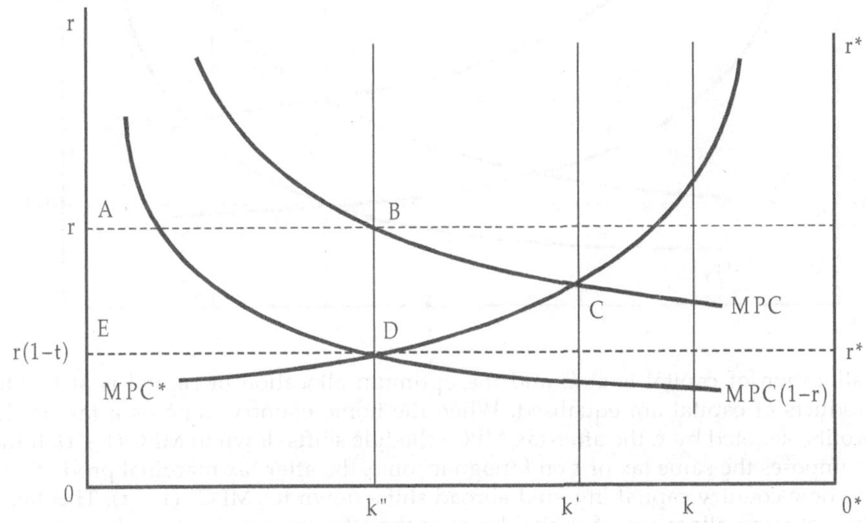

The MPC schedule and the MPC* schedule represent the demands for capital in the home and foreign countries from the origins O and O* respectively. The length of the horizontal axis represents the total quantity of capital available in the two economies and the initial allocation of capital is at *k*. The optimum allocation of capital is at *k'*, where the marginal products of capital are equalised. When the home country imposes a tax on domestic corporate profits, denoted by τ, the after-tax MPC schedule shifts down to MPC (1 – τ). This result discourages domestic investment and encourages foreign investment, so the new equilibrium is at *k"*, where the after-tax marginal products of capital are equalised. Too much capital is located abroad, and not enough capital is located at home, so there is a deadweight loss of area BCD.

One way to correct the distortion introduced in Figure-1 is for the home country to tax returns on home capital regardless of where the capital is invested. Figure-2 demonstrates the same scenario in the previous figure except both domestic and foreign returns are taxed by the home government. This shifts MPC to MPC $(1 - \tau)$ and MPC* to MPC* $(1 - \tau)$. Becuase both schedules are shifted downward by the same proportion everywhere, the intersection of the after-rax schedules preserves the optimum allocation of capital, k'. At the margin, the after-tax rates of return at home equal the after-tax rates of return abroad, $r(1 - \tau) = r^* (1 - \tau)$, so the pre-tax rate of return at home equals the pre-tax rate of return abroad, $r = r^*$. The total revenue collected by the home-country government is area ABCD, which is larger than area ABDE in Figure-1. This exhibit illustrates that if the home country taxes foreign earnings at the same tax rate as domestic earnings, capital export neutrality does hold and there is no misallocation of capital. (However, this result requires the foreign tax rate to be less than or equal to the home tax rate.)

FIGURE-2

CORPORATE PROFIT TAX AT HOME INCLUDING FOREIGN INCOME

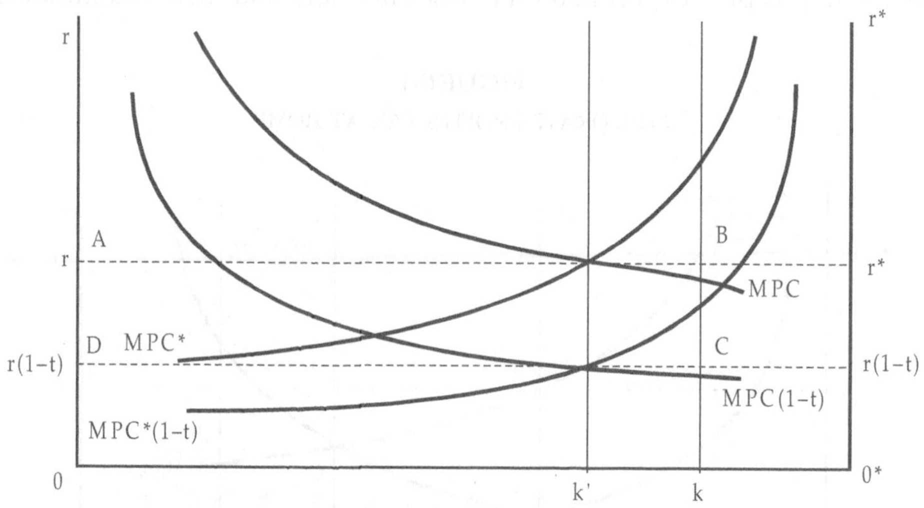

The initial allocation of capital is at k, and the optimum allocation of capital is at k' where the marginal products of capital are equalised. When the home country imposes a tax on domestic corporate profits, denoted by τ, the after-tax MPC schedule shifts down to MPC $(1 - \tau)$. If the home country also imposes the same tax of τ on foreign income, the after-tax marginal product of capital schedule on home-country capital invested abroad shifts down to MPC* $(1 - \tau)$. This tax scheme preserves the optimum allocation of capital because the after-tax marginal products of capital are identical at k'.

Capital Import Neutrality

Capital import neutrality, also known as foreign neutrality, means that taxes do not distort the after-tax returns to domestic and foreign suppliers of capital. In other words, taxation is import neutral if equal before-tax returns to competing supplies of capital translate into equal after-tax returns. This neutrality puts domestic firms and multinational corporations on an equal footing, even with respect to home country taxes.

In Figure-1, where export neutrality does not hold, import neutrality does hold. No matter where the capital comes from, it is taxed in the country in which it is invested, and nowhere else, which means that all capital invested in the home country pays only the tax rate. Similarly, all capital invested in the foreign country pays no taxes anywhere. Hence, capital import neutrality holds.

In Figure-2, however, where export neutrality does hold, import neutrality does not hold because the multinational corporation operating in the host country has a residual tax liability to the home government. This situation means that the multinational corporation is at a competitive disadvantage vis-a-vis domestic firms in the host country. After all, domestic firms have no tax bill whereas multinational firms have a tax liability to their home government. The rate of return on domestic capital invested in the host country is thus r^*, but the rate of return on foreign capital invested in the host country is $r^* (1 - \tau)$. The tax scheme may be inefficient because there could be production distortions in the host country.

In analysing the two types of tax neutrality, capital export neutrality is usually of prime concern because the distortionary effects on the allocation of capital are unambiguous. Capital import neutrality, on the other hand, is likely to be of less concern because the effects of tax disadvantages on international production and competition are not well specified. In other words, it is not obvious how much concern we should attach to the fact that different suppliers of capital receive different after-tax returns. There are distortions to the supply of capital is sub-optimal from a global perspective: one country should be supplying more capital and another should be supplying less capital.

From this analysis, several points should be evident. In general, either export or import neutrality holds—but not both. In fact, the only perfectly neutral tax system is one in which all countries have the same tax rates (and no double-taxation occurs). Finally, it should also be clear that neutrality depends on who pays the taxes—not on what government collects them.

Figures 1 and 2 depict two alternative tax philosophies. Currently, the Netherlands, Hong Kong, and France are examples of countries that exempt foreign income from domestic taxation. This practice is sometimes called the *territorial principle* of taxation, in which taxes are levied on equity returns occurring within the territory, regardless of the source of capital, and no attempt is made to tax the foreign income of domestic capital owners. Figure-1 depicts the territorial principle. The arrangement of taxing profits earned overseas exists in most home countries, such as the United States, Japan, and the United Kingdom, and is sometimes referred to as the *worldwide principle* of taxation because home governments have a claim on the firm's worldwide profits. Figure-2 depicts the worldwide principle.

GLOBAL TAX NEUTRALITY AND NATIONAL WELFARE

Up to this point, we have been concerned with global welfare and tax neutrality. We will now show that international taxation gives rise to a conflict between global welfare and national welfare because taxation alters the distribution of national gains from international investment. This conflict, in turn, can cause conflicts between home country governments and host country governments, often catching the multinational firm in the middle.

We have come to appreciate the significance of a completely neutral tax system in removing distortions from the economy. Figure-3 illustrates one such neutral tax system where both the home and host governments impose identical corporate profits taxes. This system has the effect of shifting MPC to MPC $(1 - \tau)$ and MPC* to MPC* $(1- \tau)$. As the marginal product of capital schedules shifts in the same proportion, the intersection at the optimum allocation of capital is preserved at k'. There is no misallocation of capital, so capital export neutrality holds. Because all sources of capital are taxed at the same rate, capital import neutrality also holds. There are therefore no deadweight losses to society from the tax scheme.

FIGURE-3

IDENTICAL CORPORATE PROFITS TAXES AT HOME AND ABROAD

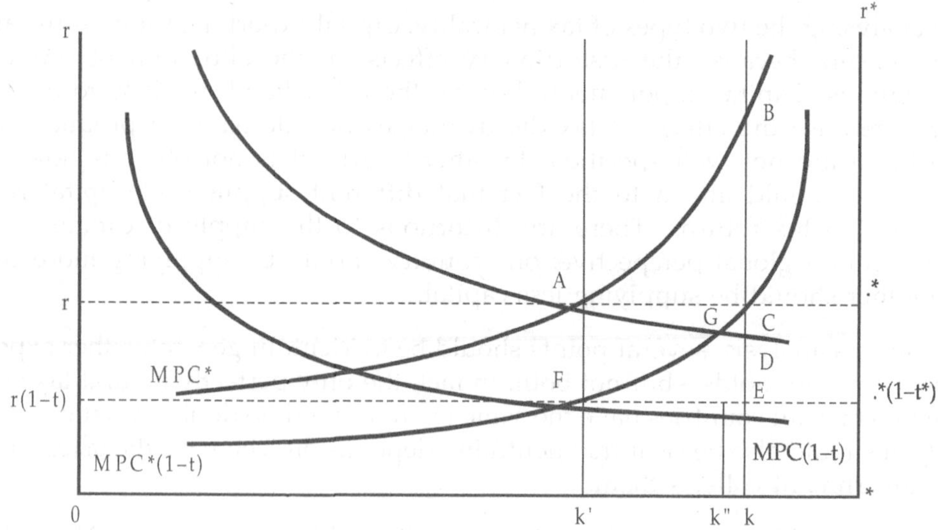

The initial allocation of capital is at *k*, and the optimum allocation of capital is at *k'* where the marginal products of capital are equalised. When the home country imposes a tax on domestic corporate profits, denoted by τ, the after-tax MPC schedule shifts down to MPC $(1 - \tau)$. When the foreign country imposes the same tax rate, denoted τ^*, corporate income, the after-tax marginal product of capital schedule on all capital invested abroad, shifts down to MPC* $(1 - \tau)$. If the home country gives a full tax credit for foreign income taxes paid, the optimum allocation of capital is preserved because the after-tax marginal products of capital are identical at *k'*. However, area ACEF represents tax revenue accruing to the foreign country that would otherwise be income to the home country. The optimum welfare for the home country is achieved when it gives a deduction for foreign income taxes paid rather than a full credit, resulting in an allocation of capital at *k"*.

Thus, there is a redistribution of welfare that does not occur in the absence of taxation. Before taxation, we know that the increase in the home country's GNP resulting from foreign investment is the triangular area ACD. The increase in the host country's GNP is the triangular area ACB. Because of taxation, however, the host country collects area ACEF in revenue from the returns to the equity capital form of direct foreign investment, and this money stays in the host country. This revenue increases the welfare of the host country such that the net increase in GNP from foreign investment is the larger area ABEF. As the tax revenue ACEF is no longer brought back into the home country, the net increase in home country GNP is area ACD minus area ACEF. As Figure-3 is drawn, there is a net decrease in GNP of area ADEF. The conclusion from Figure-3 is that the home country is likely to be a net loser from foreign investment whenever there are taxes imposed abroad.

The point the diagram illustrates is that the tax systems which maximise global welfare are not compatible with those that maximise national welfare. Viewed from the home country, over-investment abroad takes place. Conflicts between governments often arise because of each country's desire to tax multinational corporations' profits. The multinational corporation is sometimes caught in the middle.

National optimum would be reached when pretax returns domestically equal the post-tax returns abroad:

$$r = r^*(1 - \tau^*)$$

because r is the marginal benefit of investment at home and $r^*(1 - \tau^*)$ is the benefit to the home country of any foreign investment. In Figure-3, this equilibrium, $r = r^*(1 - \tau^*)$, corresponds to point G, for an allocation of capital at k''. The home government should tax both sides so as not to disrupt this marginal choice:

$$r(1 - \tau) = r^*(1 - \tau^*)(1 - \tau)$$

and it is clear that this equilibrium is achieved using the deduction method. Over-investment abroad, as viewed from the home country, will not occur if the home country provides the less-valuable tax deduction rather than a full tax credit. At the same time, however, there will not be under-investment because capital will be free to flow abroad whenever the returns are high enough to compensate for the additional taxes paid. As long as the government preserves the appropriate marginal choice, the optimum amount of investment from the home country's standpoint will be achieved. We reiterate, however, that this solution precludes the global optimum.

Some accounting activities of firms, in seeking to show profits in low-tax countries, serve to restore maximum global welfare at least temporarily. One strategy is to allocate costs to high-tax countries, thereby maximising the value of expense deductions. Another is to set prices on goods and services traded internally such that subsidiaries in high-tax countries pay high prices or receive low prices for them. The pricing of goods and services traded internally is called *transfer pricing*. In practice, the phrase has acquired negative connotations associated with firms that set prices to shift profits from subsidiaries located in high-tax countries to those in low-tax countries specifically to reduce the total tax burden.

To the extent that cost allocation and transfer pricing strategies are available, profits will indeed spring up in low-tax countries, often called *tax havens*, and disappear from high-tax jurisdictions. The profits of multinational firms are therefore mobile, at least to a certain extent. Economists often assert that cost allocation and transfer pricing strategies are economically efficient because they allow firms to produce where pre-tax returns are highest and then shift profits to low-tax jurisdictions. Production itself is not shifted — just the profits. The insight that production will not be shifted means that there will not be deadweight losses of global welfare whenever companies can effectively ignore the effects of taxation. The result, however, is that the profits transferred to the low-tax jurisdictions must generally be reinvested there. If this action represents over-investment, there will be distortions from the misallocation of capital in future periods. Hence, firms seeking to maximise their global profits serve to maximise global welfare in the current period, but if the reinvestment decisions are suboptimal there will be longer-run distortions to global welfare.

Although these accounting strategies can restore maximum global welfare, they don't necessarily remove the conflicts between governments and multinational corporations. In fact, cost allocation and transfer pricing strategies generally accentuate the conflicts between the host and home governments and the multinational corporation. Nearly every country therefore sets guidelines for these accounting activities of multinational firms. Accounting manipulation therefore becomes costly because the use of managerial time and legal fees can be high for any governmental investigation.

QUESTIONS

1. Describe various types of host government and home government tax policies.
2. Compare the effects of taxation on debt financing to the effects of taxation on equity financing.
3. Critically examine the concept of tax neutrality.
4. "Global welfare is maximised if capital is free to flow toward countries in which the marginal product of capital is highest." Do you agree?
5. "Tax system which maximise global welfare are not compatible with those that maximise national welfare." Critically examine this statement.

GLOSSARY

Additional Tier 1 capital. The sum of (1) instruments issued by banks that meet the criteria for inclusion in Additional Tier 1 capital (and are not included in Common Equity Tier 1); (2) stock surplus (share premium) resulting from the issue of instruments included in Additional Tier 1 capital; (3) instruments issued by consolidated subsidiaries of the bank and held by third parties that meet the criteria for inclusion in Additional Tier 1 capital and are not included in Common Equity Tier 1; and (4) applicable regulatory adjustments.

Advanced Basel II approaches. Basel II approach in which banks can use their internal ratings systems or models as inputs in the calculation of required capital for credit, market, and operational risks.

American Depository Receipts (ADRs). Equity-based instruments that are publicly traded in the U.S. securities markets (NYSE, AMEX, NASDAQ, OTC) and backed by a trust containing shares of non-U.S. corporations. ADRs are U.S. dollar-denominated, settle like a U.S. security, and pay dividends in U.S. dollars.

Arbitrage. Trading of financial instruments in different markets with an end towards making a profit from price differentials across markets for the same or similar instrument.

Asset manager. A financial institution that manages assets on behalf of investors.

Asset price bubble. A sharp rise in the price of an asset above its economically fundamental value over a specific period for reasons other than random shocks.

Asset restructuring. Changing the terms of payment on a loan or other lending instrument by granting a concession to the borrower. This may include: (1) the transfer from the borrower to the bank of real estate, receivables from third parties, other assets, or an equity interest in the borrower in full or partial satisfaction of the loan; (2) a modification of the loan terms, such as a combination of a reduction in an agreed-upon interest rate, an extension of the final maturity, a reduction of principal, or a reduction of accrued interest; or (3) acceptance by the bank of the conversion of the borrower's debt into equity to be held by the bank, in full or partial settlement of a debt.

Asset-backed Security (ABS). Any security, including commercial paper, that is collateralized by the cash flows from a pool of underlying assets, such as loans, leases, and receivables. When the cash flows are collateralized by real estate, an ABS may be called a mortgage-backed security (MBS); when the cash flows are divided into tranches, an ABS may be called a structured credit product.

Authorised dealer. A dealer who is authorised by the monetary authority of the country concerned to engage in certain specified foreign exchange activities. The activities are mainly concerned with exchange control.

Balance sheet exposure. This arises from the process of translating foreign currency balance sheet items into the parent-currency denominated group financial statements.

Bank letter of credit policy. Policy that enables banks to confirm letters of credit by foreign banks supporting the purchase of U.S. exports.

Banker's acceptance. Bill of exchange drawn on and accepted by a banking institution; it is commonly used to guarantee exporters that they will receive payment on goods delivered to importers.

Barter. Exchange of goods between two parties without the use of any currency as a medium of exchange.

Basel accord. Agreement among country representatives in 1988 to establish standardised risk-based capital requirements for banks across countries.

Basel Committee on Banking Supervision (BCBS). A committee of banking supervisory authorities that provides a forum for regular cooperation on banking supervisory matters. Its objective is to enhance understanding of key supervisory issues and improve the quality of banking supervision worldwide. The BCBS also develops guidelines and supervisory standards in various areas, including the international standards on capital adequacy, the Core Principles for Effective Banking Supervision, and the Concordat on cross-border banking supervision.

Basel II. A 2004 accord among national bank supervisory authorities (the Basel Committee on Banking Supervision) that revised the Committee's 1988 adequacy standards with regard to bank capital for credit risk and introduced capital requirements for operational risk. Basel II made the capital requirement more sensitive to variations in the riskiness of the bank's assets. Basel II also revised its recommended supervision processes and increased disclosure by banks. Pillar 1 of the Basel Accord covers the minimum capital adequacy standards for banks; Pillar 2 focuses on enhancing the supervisory review process; and Pillar 3 encourages market discipline through increased quantitative and qualitative disclosure of banks' risk exposures and capital adequacy.

Basel III. A comprehensive set of reform measures introduced in the aftermath of the global financial crisis to improve the banking sector's ability to absorb financial and economic shocks, enhance banks' risk management and governance, and increase banks' transparency and disclosure. These measures revise the existing definition of regulatory capital under the Basel Accord, enhance capital adequacy standards, and introduce, for the first time, minimum liquidity adequacy standards for banks.

Basis point. 1/100th of a percentage point.

Basis. The difference (or spread) between two market prices or two interest rates, for example, the difference between Euro-dollar and commercial paper rates.

Best order. An order to an agent or dealer to buy or sell an amount of foreign currency at the best Price available. No rate limit is stipulated.

Bid price. Price that a trader of foreign exchange (typically a bank) is willing to pay for a particular currency.

Bid rate. The rate of exchange at which a foreign cx change dealer will buy a currency.

Bid/ask spread. Difference between the price at which a bank is willing to buy a currency and the price at which it will sell that currency.

Bilateral netting system. Netting method used for transactions between two units.

Bill of exchange (draft). Promise drawn by one party (usually an exporter) to pay a specified amount to another party at a specified future date, or upon presentation of the draft.

Bill of lading. Document serving as a receipt for shipment and a summary of fright charges, and conveying title to the merchandise.

Blocked account. The bank account of a non-resident of a Country, where the amount of currency in the account cannot be transferred to another countr-y or currency without special permission .

Blocked funds. Funds that cannot be remitted from the subsidiary to the parent due to host government restrictions.

Brady plan. Bill intended to provide banks with the option of having some of their LDC debt replaced by the World Bank (and IMF), by trading it in at a discount.

Branch. Full-service banking office that can compete directly with other banks located in that area.

Break-even salvage value. Salvage value necessary to achieve a zero net present value for a particular project.

Brokerage. Commission charged by a broker for his services.

Business day (also baking day, clear day, market day and open day). Any day on which a foreign exchange contract can be settled, i.e. the banks at both ends of the deal must be open for business that day.

Buyer credit policy. Policy permitting banks to extend loans to foreign borrowers to purchase U.S. goods.

Buyer's option. The owner of a buyer's option can take delivery of the currency contract at any time between the dates specified in the option.

Call (put) options. A financial contract that gives the buyer the right, but not the obligation, to buy (sell) a financial instrument at a set price on or before a given date.

Capital account. Account reflecting changes in country ownership of long-term and short-term financial assets.

Capital adequacy ratio (CAR). The ratio of regulatory capital to risk-weighted assets of a financial institution. Under Basel III, regulatory capital is the sum of common equity and additional Tier 1 capital and Tier 2 capital.

Capital Requirements Directive (CRD). The Directive issued by the European Union for the financial services industry that introduced a supervisory framework reflecting the Basel II rules on capital measurement and capital standards.

Carve outs. Exceptions to the Basel II or Basel III rules.

Cash flow (or economic) exposure. This is concerned with the effect of currency changes on the parent currency value of the future cash flows generated by a company's foreign operations.

Cash management. Optimisation of cash flows and investment of excess cash.

Central counterparty (CCP). An entity that interposes itself between counterparties, becoming the buyer to sellers and the seller to buyers in what would otherwise be bilateral arrangements between sellers and buyers.

Centralised cash management. Policy that consolidates cash management decisions for all MNC units, usually at the parent's location.

Certificate of deposit (CD). Short-term financial securities issued by commercial banks that have maturities of anywhere from one month to a year.

Checklist approach. Method for evaluation involving a list of factors that are assigned ratings; used for various assessments (such as country risk assessment).

Chicago Mercantile Exchange (CME) Exchange. Exchange established to facilitate the trading of currency futures contracts.

Clearing House Interbank Payments System (CHIPS). A computerised clearing network for the transfer of international U.S. dollar payments, linking banks which have offices or subsidiaries in New York City.

Closed-end Funds (also called closed-end investment companies, publicly—traded funds, or investment trusts). After the initial offering of a limited number of shares of the fund in the market for public trading in organised exchanges, these are not redeemed (bought back by the fund) unless the fund is liquidated or when it is changed from closed-end to open-end. There are no subsequent additions of shares to the capital base o the fund unless other public offerings are made after the initial offering of stock. Unlike open-end funds, the share prices of closed-end funds are determined by supply and demand for the fund's shares rather than by the value of the portfolio of securities of the fund.

Closing exchange rate. The exchange rate prevailing at a financial reporting date.

Co-financing agreements. Arrangement in which the World Bank participates along with other agencies or lenders in providing funds to developing countries.

Collateral Assets pledged or posted to a counterparty to secure an outstanding exposure, derivative contract, or loan.

Commercial invoice. Exporter's description of merchandise being sold to the buyer

Commercial letters of credit. Trade-related letters of credit.

Commercial Paper (CP). Short-term unsecured notes issued by corporations and suppliers on international capital markets. These instruments have a maturity of less than one year.

Committee on Payment and Settlement Systems (CPSS). Committee of the Bank for International Settlements that sets standards for payment systems oversight.

Common Equity Tier 1. The sum of (1) common shares issued by a bank that meet the criteria for classification as common shares for regulatory purposes (or the equivalent for non-joint-stock companies); (2) stock surplus (share premium) resulting from the issue of instruments included in Common Equity Tier 1; (3) retained earnings; (4) accumulated other comprehensive income and other disclosed reserves; (5) common shares issued by consolidated subsidiaries of the bank and held by third parties (i.e., minority interest) that meet the criteria for inclusion in Common Equity Tier 1 capital; and (6) applicable regulatory adjustments.

Comparative advantage. Theory suggesting that specialisation by countries can increase worldwide production.

Compensation. Arrangement in which the delivery of goods to a party is compensated for by buying back a certain amount of the product from that same party.

Compensatory Financing Facility (CFF). Facility that attempts to reduce the impact of export instability on country economies.

Confirmation. This is the written document confirming the verbal foreign exchange contract agreed by telephone between dealer and dealer or dealer and client.

Consignment. Arrangement in which the exporter ships goods to the importer while still retaining title to the merchandise.

Contingency graph. Graph depicting the profit per unit to be earned on a currency option for various possible exchange rate scenarios.

Convertible bond. A bond which gives the holder the option to convert the bond into equity at a fixed conversion price.

Convertible currency. A currency which can be converted into another currency without special permission of exchange control authority.

Core Tier 1 capital ratio. The ratio of a bank's core Tier 1 capital to its total risk-weighted assets (RWA). Core Tier 1 is a similar concept to Common Equity Tier 1 in Basel III, though there are some differences, such as the inclusion of preferred shares in core Tier 1 capital and in regulatory deductions.

Countedrade. Sale of goods to one country which is linked to the purchase or exchange of goods from that same country

Counterparty risk. The risk faced by one party in a contract that the other, the counterparty, will fail to meet its obligations under the contract

Counterparty. The party on the other side of a financial transaction.

Counterpurchase. Exchange of goods between two parties under two distinct contracts expressed in monetary terms.

Country risk. Characteristics of the host country, including political and financial conditions, that can affect the MNC's cash flows.

Covered interest arbitrage. Investment in a foreign money market security with a simultaneous forward sale of the currency denominating that security

Covering. Protecting the value of the future proceeds of an international trade transaction, usually by buying or selling the proceeds in the forward market.

Credit default swap (CDS). A credit derivative whose payout is triggered by a "credit event," often a default. CDS settlements can either be "physical," whereby the protection seller buys a defaulted reference asset from the protection buyer at its face value, or in "cash," whereby the protection seller pays the protection buyer an amount equal to the difference between the reference asset face value and the price of the defaulted asset. A single-name CDS contract references a single firm or government agency, whereas CDS index contracts reference standardized indices based on baskets of single-name CDS contracts.

Credit rating. A measure of the ability of a borrower to meet its financial commitments on a timely basis. Credit ratings are typically expressed as discrete letter grades. For example, Fitch Ratings and Standard & Poor's use a scale in which AAA represents the highest creditworthiness and D the lowest.

Credit rating agency. A company that assigns credit ratings to borrowers as a measure of their ability to meet their financial commitments on a timely basis.

Credit risk. The risk that a party to a financial contract will incur a financial loss because a counterparty is unable or unwilling to meet its obligations.

Credit spread. The difference in yield between a benchmark debt security and another debt security that is comparable to the benchmark instrument in all respects except that it is of lower credit quality and hence, typically, of higher yield.

Credit value adjustment (CVA). The risk of loss caused by changes in the credit spread of a counterparty due to changes in its credit quality (also referred to as the market value of counterparty credit risk). Under Basel II, the risk of counterparty default and credit migration risk were addressed but mark-to-market losses due to credit valuation adjustments were not. Basel III introduced a CVA capital charge in addition to the default risk capital requirements for counterparty credit risk.

Credit-to-GDP ratio. A measure of domestic credit to the private sector as a proportion of gross domestic product (GDP). Domestic credit to the private sector refers to financial resources provided to the private sector, such as through loans, purchases of non-equity securities, trade credits, and other accounts receivable, that establish a claim for repayment. For some countries these claims include credit to public enterprises.

Cross exchange rate. Exchange rate between currency A and currency B, given the values of currencies A and B with respect to a third currency

Cross-border factoring. Factoring by a network of factors across borders. The exporter's factor can contact correspondent factors in other countries to handle the collections of accounts receivable.

Cross-sectional analysis. Analysis of relationships among a cross-section of firms, countries, or some other variable at a given point in time.

Cumulative Translation Adjustment (CTA) Account. Account used by FASB- 52 for capturing translation gains and losses.

Currency call option. Contract that grants the right to purchase a specific currency at a specific price (exchange rate) within a specific period of time.

Currency cocktail bond. Bond denominated in a mixture (or cocktail) of currencies.

Currency correlation. Measurement of the relationship between movements of two currencies.

Currency futures contract. Contract specifying a standard volume of a particular currency to be exchanged on a specific settlement date.

Currency put option. Contract granting the right to sell a particular currency at a specified price (exchange rate) within a specified period of time.

Currency swap. Agreement to exchange one currency for another at a specified exchange rate and date. Banks commonly serve as intermediaries between two parties who wish to engage in a currency swap.

Current account. Broad measure of a country's international trade in goods and services.

Current exchange rate. The exchange rate ruling at the balance sheet date or during the income statement period.

Current/Non-current method. A foreign currency translation method: current balance sheet items denominated in foreign currencies are translated at current exchange rates and long-term items at historical rates.

Dealer (or trader). Specialist in a bank or Corporation who is authorised to effect exchange transactions. He usually attempts to keep his book in balance but may be allowed to take a Position.

Dealer-banks Term used to identify a set of large financial institutions that are significant dealers in securities and over-the-counter (OTC) derivatives. Dealer banks may have conventional commercial banking operations, and they might also have significant activities in investment banking, asset management, and prime brokerage. They typically operate under the umbrella of holding companies.

Debt-equity swap. Exchange of a bank's debt (loans) held in return for an equity investment in the borrower's assets; this type of swap was used by commercial banks to reduce their amounts of debt owed by less developed countries.

Debt-to-equity ratio (D/E). A financial ratio that measures the extent of leverage in a company and indicates the relative proportion of debt used to finance the company's assets, compared with shareholders' equity.

Default fund. A pool of funds established by a central counterparty (CCP), contributed by clearing members to absorb the costs of clearing member nonperformance when the failed clearing member's margin contributions and the CCP's first-loss contribution are exhausted.

Deferred tax assets. The amounts of income taxes recoverable in future periods in respect of deductible temporary differences, the carry forward of unused tax losses, and the carry forward of unused tax credits.

Deleveraging. The reduction of the leverage ratio, or the percentage of debt in the balance sheet of a financial institution.

Delphi technique. Collection of independent opinions without group discussion by the assessors who provide the opinions; used for various types of assessments (such as country risk assessment).

Dependent variable. Term used in regression analysis to represent the variable that is dependent on one or more other variables.

Depreciation. Decrease in the value of a currency

De-risking. Management actions that reduce or lower risk in a firm.

Derivative. A financial instrument with a value dependent on the expected future price of its underlying asset, such as a stock or currency. Examples of derivatives include stock options, currency and interest rate swaps, and credit default swaps.

Difference-in-differences A method used for estimating the impact of a policy on an outcome by computing a double difference, one over time (before- after) and one across subjects (between beneficiaries and nonbeneficiaries). In its simplest form, this method requires only aggregate data on the outcome variable; no covariates or micro-data are strictly necessary.

Direct loan programme. Programme in which the Eximbank offers fixed-rate loans directly to the foreign buyer to purchase U.S. capital equipment and services.

Direct quotation. A rate of exchange quoted as n units of foreign currency per one unit of the home currency,

Dirty float. Exchange rate system in which exchange rates are allowed to fluctuate without set boundaries; yet, governments do intervene as they wish.

Discounting. Where a sale is to be settled by bill of exchange, the seller can 'discount' with a financial institution and receive payment before the receivable settlement date.

Documentary collections. Trade transactions handled on a draft basis.

Documents against acceptance. Situation in which the buyer's bank does not release shipping documents to the buyer until the buyer has paid the draft.

Documents against payment. Shipping documents that are released to the buyer once the buyer has paid for the draft.

Dodd-Frank Act. U.S. law sponsored by Senator Christopher Dodd and Representative Barney Frank and passed on July 21, 2010, designed to improve regulation of the banking sector and prevent a recurrence of a financial crisis in which banks would once again have to be bailed out by taxpayer funding.

Double-entry bookkeeping. Accounting method in which each transaction is recorded as both a credit and a debit.

Draft (bill of exchange). Unconditional promise drawn by one party (usually the exporter) instructing the buyer to pay the face amount of the draft upon presentation.

Dual-currency bonds. Long-term securities denominated in two currencies—for example, a bond with initial payment and interim coupon payments in non-U.S. dollar currency and a fixed final bullet principal payment in U.S. dollars.

Dummy variables. Variables used in regression analysis that are classified as either a zero or a one, for qualitative variables.

Dumping. Selling products overseas at unfairly low prices (a practice perceived to result from subsidies provided to the firm by its government).

Duration. A measure of the maturity of a financial instrument after adjusting for the frequency of payments associated with the instrument. Specifically, it is the weighted average maturity of all payments (coupon and principal), where the weights are the discounted present values of the payments. This concept is used by portfolio managers in assessing the vulnerability of their portfolio to interest rate isk.

Dynamic hedging. Strategy of hedging in those periods when existing currency positions are expected to be adversely affected, and remaining unhedged in other periods when currency positions are expected to be favorably affected.

Earnings before interest, taxes, depreciation, and amortization (EBITDA). A measure of a company's operating cash flow obtained by looking at earnings before the deduction of interest expenses, taxes, depreciation, and amortization. This measure is used to compare profitability of companies after excluding the accounting and financing effects from different asset and capital structures. This measure can be of particular interest to creditors, because it is the income that a company has available for interest payments.

Economic exposure. Degree to which a firm's present value of future cash flows can be influenced by exchange rate fluctuations.

Economies of scale. Achievement of lower average cost per unit by means of increased production.

Edge act corporations. Aid corporations that are involved in foreign trade; they are established by banks and can be set up across state borders.

Effective yield. Yield or return to an MNC on a short-term investment after adjustment for the change in exchange rates over the period of concern.

Efficient frontier. Set of points reflecting risk-return combinations achieved by particular portfolios (so-called efficient portfolios) of assets.

Efficient market. Market in which prices reflect all available information, so that excess risk-adjusted returns are not possible.

Equilibrium exchange rate. Exchange rate at which demand for a currency is equal to the supply of the currency for sale.

Equity multiplier. Assets divided by equity.

Equity-related bonds. Securities which include bonds with equity warrants and convertible bonds.

Eurobanks. Commercial banks that participate as financial intermediaries in the Eurocurrency market.

Eurobond. Bonds sold in countries other than the country represented by the currency denominating them.

Euro-clear. Telecommunications network that informs all traders about outstanding issues of Eurobonds for sale.

Euro-commercial paper. Debt securities issued by MNCs for short-term financing.

Eurocredit loans. Loans of one year or longer extended by Eurobanks.

Eurocredit market. Collection of banks that accept deposits and provide loans in large denominations and in a variety of currencies. The banks that comprise this market are the same banks that comprise the Eurocurrency market; the difference is that the Eurocredit loans are longer-term than so-called Eurocurrency loans.

Eurocurrency market. Collection of banks that accept deposits and provide loans in large denominations and in a variety of currencies.

Euro-currency. Currency held by non-residents and placed on deposit with banks outside the country of the Currency, e.g. US dollars owned by a Middle East country and deposited in London.

Euro-dollars. US dollars held by anyone who is not a resident of the United States and deposited outside the United States.

Euronote. A short-term note issued under a NIF or Euro-commercial paper facility.

European Financial Stability Facility (EFSF) A special-purpose vehicle set up by the euro area countries to preserve financial stability. The EFSF has the ability to issue bonds or other debt instruments in the market to raise the funds needed to provide temporary financial assistance to euro area Member States in economic difficulty.

European Stability Mechanism (ESM). An international organization that provides financial assistance to members of the euro area in financial difficulty in order to safeguard the financial stability of the euro area. The ESM is able to raise funds, for example, by issuing bonds or other debt instruments or entering into arrangements with Member States.

Ever-greening The provision by banks of additional loans to stressed borrowers to enable them to repay existing loans or interest. This can keep a loan from becoming nonperforming, but further increases a bank's exposure to a troubled borrower.

Exchange contract. A contract to exchange one foreign Currency for a given amount of another on a given date.

Exchange Rate Mechanism (ERM-II). Framework for a subset of the European Union Member States that provides currency-fluctuation band limits for their currencies against the euro. A fixed exchange rate and fluctuation band between the non-euro-area member country's currency and the euro is agreed, and the band is supported by coordinated intervention by the respective central banks. Membership in the ERM-II for at least two years is one of the preconditions for joining the euro area.

Exchange rate. Value of one currency with respect to another.

Exchange Traded Fund (ETF). An investment fund traded on stock exchanges, most commonly tracking an index, such as the S&P 500. An ETF may be attractive to investors because of its low cost and tax efficiency.

Exchange-traded products. Financial products that are traded on exchanges and other organized trading platforms.

Exercise price (strike price). Price (exchange rate) at which the owner of a currency call option is allowed to buy a specified currency; or the price (exchange rate) at which the owner of a currency put option is allowed to sell a specified currency

Export finance vehicle. A vehicle Company Set up to buy the export receivables of affiliated companies. Export finance companies perform exposure and/or liquidity management functions.

Exposure to exchange rate fluctuations. Degree to which a firm can be affected by exchange rate fluctuations; three common types of exposure are (1) transaction exposure, (2) economic exposure, and (3) translation exposure.

External exposure management techniques. Specific contractual arrangements, 'external' to the firm, which are designed to reduce or eliminate an existing exposure. Examples of external techniques are forward exchange contracts, foreign currency borrowing, discounting, factoring and government exchange risk guarantees.

Factor. Firm specialising in collection on accounts receivable; exporters sometimes sell their accounts receivable to a factor at a discount.

Factoring. Purchase of receivables of an exporter by a factor without recourse to the exporter

Fiscal sustainability The ability of a government to sustain its current spending, tax, and other policies in the long term without defaulting on its liabilities or promised expenditures.

Fisher effect. Theory that nominal interest rates are composed of a real interest rate and anticipated inflation.

Fixed exchange rate system. Monetary system in which exchange rates are either held constant or allowed to fluctuate only within very narrow boundaries.

Floating rate notes (FRNs). Provision of some Eurobonds, in which the coupon rate is adjusted over time according to prevailing market rates.

Forbearance A temporary postponement of loan payments granted by a lender or creditor. Forbearance gives the borrower time to make up overdue payments on a loan.

Forecast bias. Consistent over- or underestimating in forecasting.

Foreign bond. Bond issued by a borrower foreign to the country where the bond is placed.

Foreign exchange market. Market composed primarily of banks, serving firms and consumers who wish to buy or sell various currencies.

Foreign exchange swaps. A simultaneous purchase and sale of identical amounts of one currency in exchange for another with two different value dates.

Foreign Investment Risk Matrix (FIRM). Graph that displays financial and political risk by intervals, so that each country can be positioned according to its risk ratings.

Forfaiting. Method of financing international trade of capital goods.

Forward contract. Agreement between a commercial bank and a client about an exchange of two currencies to be made at a future point in time at a specified exchange rate.

Forward discount. Percentage by which the forward rate is less than the spot rate; typically quoted on an annualised basis.

Forward margin. The difference between the forward rate and the spot rate of a currency. The forward margin is either at a discount or a premium to the spot rate.

Forward premium. The excess of the forward rate above the spot rate.

Forward rate. Rate at which a bank is willing to exchange one currency for another at some specified date in the future

Forward/Forward Swap (or Forward Swap). A pair of forward exchange deals involving a forward purchase and a forward sale of a currency, simultaneously entered into, but of different maturities.

Franchising. Agreement by which a firm provides a specialised sales or service strategy, support assistance, and possibly an initial investment in the franchise in exchange for periodic fees.

Free cash flow. A measure of financial performance of a company, calculated as the cash flow generated by the company's operations minus capital expenditures needed to maintain or expand these operations. It represents the cash flow available for reducing debt or distributing dividends to equity holders.

Full compensation. An arrangement in which the delivery of goods to one party is fully compensated for by buying back more than 100 percent of the value that was originally sold.

Fundamental forecasting. Forecasting based on fundamental relationships between economic variables and exchange rates.

Funding. The process by which banks issue or assume liabilities associated with assets on their balance sheets.

Generalized method of moments (GMM). A generalized statistical method, used primarily in econometrics, for obtaining estimates of parameters of statistical models; many common estimators in econometrics, such as ordinary least squares, are special cases of the GMM. The GMM estimator is robust in that it does not require information on the exact distribution of the disturbances.

Global Depositary Receipts (GDRs). Equity-based instruments that are offered in the U.S. Rule 144A (private placement) market as well as in the non-U.S. markets. GDRs can be traded in several currencies and settled via global book-entry clearing through the Depository Trust Company (in the United States) as well as Euroclear, and CEDEL (in Europe).

Global Systemically Important Banks (GSIBs). Large banking institutions with global operations that have the potential to impact the financial system. The Financial Stability Board (FSB) has tentatively identified 29 global banks as GSIBs. These banks were provisionally earmarked to be subject to additional loss absorbency, or capital surcharges, from 1 percent to 2.5 percent of the ratio of Common Equity Tier 1 capital to risk-weighted assets.

Global Systemically Important Insurers (GSIIs) Insurers designated by the International Association of Insurance Supervisors as systemically important.

Gold standard. Era in which each currency was convertible into gold at a specified rate, allowing the exchange rate between two currencies to be determined by their relative convertibility rates per ounce of gold.

Goodwill. Identifiable intangible assets acquired in a business combination. It is usually the excess of the purchase price of a company over its book value.

Gross nonperforming loan ratio. This ratio is derived by dividing the value of nonperforming loans by the total value of the loan portfolio.

Group of Twenty (G20). The Group of Twenty Finance Ministers and Central Bank Governors established in 1999 as a forum for officials from systemically important advanced and emerging market economies to discuss key issues related to the global economy. It consists of leaders from the European Union and the following 19 countries: Argentina, Australia, Brazil, Canada, China, France, Germany, India, Indonesia, Italy, Japan, Mexico, Russia, Saudi Arabia, South Africa, Republic of Korea, Turkey, the United Kingdom, and the United States.

Hedge fund. An investment pool, typically organized as a private partnership, that faces few restrictions on its portfolio and transactions. Hence, compared with more regulated financial institutions, hedge funds use a wider variety of investment techniques—including short positions, derivatives transactions, and leverage—in their effort to boost returns and manage risk.

Hedging. The practice of offsetting existing risk exposures by taking opposite positions in instruments or contracts with identical or similar risk—for example, in related derivatives contracts.

Histogramming. A decision making technique which can be applied to interest rate and exchange rate fore- casting.

Historical exchange rate. The exchange rate ruling at the date an asset or liability was squired, or at the date of a subsequent change in the accounting valuation of the asset or liability.

Hostile takeovers. Acquisitions not desired by the target firms.

Hot money. Speculative bank deposits which are moved around the international money markets to take advantage of currency and interest rate movements.

Hybrid instruments. A combination of two or more different financial instruments that generally have debt and equity characteristics.

Imperfect markets theory. Theory suggesting that because there are costs to the transfer of labor and other resources used for production, firms may attempt to use foreign factors of production when they are less costly than local factors.

Import/Export letters of credit. Trade-related letters of credit.

Income statement exposure. This arises essentially from the process of translating foreign currency income-statement items into the parent-currency-denominated group financial statements.

Inconvertible currency. A currency which cannot be converted into another currency, usually, but not exclusively, because of exchange control regulations.

Independent variable. Term used in regression analysis to represent the variable that is expected to influence another (so-called "dependent") variable.

Indication rate. This rate tells the enquirer the going exchange rate, but the dealer is not necessarily prepared to deal at exactly this rate.

Indirect quotations. Exchange rate quotations representing the value measured by number of units per dollar.

Inflation-indexed bond. A bond that has its coupons and principal indexed to inflation. With an inflation- indexed bond, the real rate of return is known in advance, and the nominal return varies with the rate of inflation realized over the life of the bond. Hence, neither the purchaser nor the issuer faces a risk that an unanticipated increase or decrease in inflation will erode or boost the purchasing power of the bond's payments.

Institutional investor. A bank, insurance company, pension fund, mutual fund, hedge fund, brokerage, or other financial group that takes investments from clients or invests on its own behalf.

Intangibles. An identifiable non-monetary asset without physical substance.

Interbank market. Market that facilitates the exchange of currencies between. banks.

Intercompany trade. Trade flows between units (parent, subsidiaries) of the same corporate group.

Interest parity. The process which ensures that forward mar- gins equate the interest rate differentials on equivalent securities in the two financial centers involved.

Interest Rate Parity (IRP) line. Diagonal line depicting all points on a four-quadrant graph that represent a state of interest rate parity.

Interest rate theory of exchange rate expectations (or the fisher effect). The difference between the interest rates of two currencies should equal the expected rate of change of the exchange rate during the appropriate maturity period.

Interest rate swap. Agreement to swap interest payments, whereby interest payments based on a fixed interest rate are exchanged for interest payments based on a floating interest rate.

Intermediary company. The intermediary acts as a conduit for the transfer of funds between the parent company, its subsidiaries and/or third parties. For exposure management purposes, the two most common types of intermediary company are the export finance vehicle and the re-invoicing vehicle.

Intermediary loan programme. Programme in which the Eximbank provides fixed-rate funding to commercial banks, which extends the funds to eligible foreign buyers of exports; the banks incur the default risk on the loans.

Internal forward cover system. A system in which central treasury offers operating units guaranteed internal or 'paper' forward rates, and these 'paper' rates are used to evaluate operating management performance. Treasury is left with the decision of whether the company should actually take the market's forward rate or stay uncovered - and is evaluated on this decision.

International Association of Insurance Supervisors. International standard setter for insurance supervision and regulation.

International Banking Facilities (IBFs). A technique through which U.S. banks may use their domestic offices to offer foreign customers deposit and loan services free of Federal Reserve requirements and interest rate regulations.

International Depositary Receipts (IDRs). Equity-based instruments issued, traded and settled only in the European securities markets (through Euroclear and CEDEL).

International Fisher Effect (IFE) line. Diagonal line on a graph that reflects points at which the interest rate differential between two countries is equal to the percentage change in the exchange rate between their two respective currencies.

International Organization of Securities Commissions (IOSCO). International standard setter for securities regulation.

In-the-money. Descriptive term implying that the present exchange rate exceeds (is less than) the strike price on a currency call (put) option.

Intracompany trade. International trade between subsidiaries that are under the same ownership.

Investment- and noninvestment grade. An entity or transaction is considered investment grade if its credit rating is BBB– or better (Baa3 on the Moody's scale). Otherwise, it is considered noninvestment grade.

Investment banks. Non-deposit-taking financial institutions that, among other capital markets activities, act as intermediaries between securities issuers and investors, facilitate mergers and other corporate reorganizations, and act as brokers for institutional clients.

Investment funds. Financial institutions that pool investments and parcel them out to investors for fees.

Irrevocable letter of credit. Letter of credit issued by a bank that cannot be cancelled or amended without the beneficiary's approval.

Issuing bank. Bank that issues a letter of credit.

J curve effect. Effect of a weaker dollar on the U.S. trade balance, in which the trade balance initially deteriorates; it only improves once U.S. and non-U.S. importers respond to the change in purchasing power that is caused by the weaker dollar.

Joint venture. Venture between two or more firms in which responsibilities and earnings are shared.

Junk bonds. High-yield bonds that are below investment grade. These assets have been used for leveraged buy-outs and corporate takeovers.

Lagging. Strategy used by a firm to stall payments, normally in response to exchange rate projections.

Law of one price. Also called the absolute form of purchasing power parity (PPP), theory suggesting that prices of two products of different countries should be equal when measured by a common currency.

Leading. Strategy used by a firm to accelerate payments, normally in response to exchange rate expectations.

Lender-of-last-resort facilities. An institution, usually a country's central bank, that offers loans to banks or other eligible institutions that are experiencing financial difficulty. Lender-of-last-resort facilities aim to prevent widespread panic in the financial system.

Letter of credit (L/C). Agreement by a bank to make payments on behalf of a specified party under specified conditions.

Leverage The proportion of debt to equity (also assets to equity or capital to assets in banking). Leverage can be built up by borrowing (on-balance-sheet leverage, commonly measured by debt-to-equity ratios) or by using off-balance-sheet transactions.

LIFFE. London International Financial Futures Exchange.

LIMEAN. The average of LIBOR and LIBID at any point in time.

Liquidity Coverage Ratio (LCR). A liquidity standard introduced by Basel III. It is defined as the ratio of high-quality liquid assets to short-term liquidity needs under a specified acute stress scenario. Two types of liquid assets are included, both of which are supposed to have high credit quality and low market risk: Level 1 assets are meant to exhibit characteristics akin to the safest assets; those in Level 2 are subject to a haircut and a limit on their quantity in the overall liquidity requirement.

Liquidity risk. The risk that increases in assets cannot be funded or obligations met as they come due, without incurring unacceptable losses. *Market liquidity risk* is the risk that asset positions that are normally traded in reasonable size with little price impact can only be transacted at a substantial premium/discount, if at all. *Funding liquidity risk* is the risk that solvent counterparties have difficulty borrowing immediate means of payment to meet liabilities falling due.

Local Currency (LC). The local currency of a foreign subsidiary.

Locational arbitrage. Action to capitalise on a discrepancy in quoted exchange rates between banks.

Lockbox. Post office box number to which customers are instructed to send payment.

Logit model. A statistical binary response model in which the response probability follows a logistic distribution and is evaluated as a function of the explanatory variables.

London Interbank Bid Rate (LIBID). The rate which a bank is willing to pay for funds in the international interbank market.

London Interbank Offer Rate (LIBOR). Interest rate commonly charged for loans between Eurobanks.

Long exposure position. A net asset, net revenue and/or net cash inflow position in a currency. If the currency appreciates a foreign exchange gain is generated;

if it depreciates a loss is incurred. The opposite is true of a 'short' position.

Long forwards. Long-term forward contracts.

Long-term forward contracts. Contracts that state any exchange rate at which a specified amount of a specified currency can be exchanged at a future date (more than one year from today). Also called long forwards.

Long-term refinancing operations. Open market operations conducted by the European Central Bank to provide long-term liquidity to the financial system.

Macro-assessment. Overall risk assessment of a country without considering the MNC's business.

Mail float. Mailing time involved in sending payments by mail.

Margin. The amount that the holder of a financial instrument has to deposit (with its broker or exchange) to cover some or all of the risk associated with that instrument.

Margin requirement. Deposit placed on a contract (such as a currency futures contract) to cover the fluctuations in the value of that contract; this minimises the risk of the contract to the counter-party.

Margin. Up-front cash or collateral posted as a good-faith performance guarantee.

Marked-to-market. The situation where the entire outstanding portfolio of securities is re-valued at market closing prices.

Market liquidity. The degree to which an asset or security can be bought or sold in the market without affecting its price. Liquidity is characterized by a high level of trading activity. Assets that can be easily bought or sold are known as liquid assets.

Market maker. Member firm that can serve as a buyer or seller.

Market making. A trading activity by a bank or a broker-dealer firm that accepts the risk of holding a certain number of shares of a particular security in order to facilitate trading in that security. Each market maker competes for customer order flow by displaying buy and sell quotations for a guaranteed number of shares. Once an order is received, the market maker immediately sells from its own inventory or seeks an offsetting order.

Market-based forecasting. Use of a market-determined exchange rate (such as the spot rate or forward rate) to forecast the spot rate in the future.

Matching (or 'Natural' Matching). A process whereby a company matches its. long positions in a given currency (assets, revenues or cash inflows) with its offsetting short positions in that currency (liabilities, expenses, or cash outflows). The remaining unmatched position is the net exposure in the currency,

MATIF (Marche a terme des instruments financiers). The French financial futures market, Europe's most active futures exchange.

Maturity (or settlement) date. The date on which a foreign exchange contract is due to be settled.

Mixed forecasting. Development of forecasts based on a mixture of forecasting techniques.

Monetary Financial Institutions (MFIs). Defined by the European Central Bank as central banks, resident credit institutions as defined in Community law, and other resident financial institutions whose business is to receive deposits and/or close substitutes for deposits from entities other than MFIs and, for their own account (at least in economic terms), to grant credits and/or make investments in securities.

Monetary/Non-monetary method. A foreign currency translation method: non-monetary assets and liabilities arc translatedat their historical exchange rates and monetary items are translated at current exchange rates.

Money market funds. Investment funds that invest in short-term debt securities. Money market funds are also classifed as monetary financial institutions.

Money market hedge. Use of international money markets to match future cash inflows and outflows in a given currency.

Money Market Mutual Fund (MMMF). An open- ended mutual fund that invests in short-term debt securities such as U.S. Treasury bills and commercial paper.

Mortgage-backed Security (MBS). A security, backed by pooled mortgages on real estate assets, that derives its cash flows from principal and interest payments on those mortgages. An MBS can be backed by residential mortgages (residential mortgage-backed securities, RMBSs) or mortgages on commercial properties (commercial mortgage-backed securities, CMBSs). A private-label MBS is typically a structured credit product. RMBSs that are issued by a government-sponsored enterprise are not structured.

Multi-buyer policy. Policy administered by the Eximbank that provides credit risk insurance on export sales to many different buyers.

Multilateral netting system. Complex interchange for netting between a parent and several subsidiaries.

Multilateral netting. Each member of a corporate group offsets its receipts and payments with the rest of the group as a whole, so that a single net intercompany receipt or payment is made each period.

Negotiable bill of lading. Contract that grants title of merchandise to the holder, which allows banks to use the merchandise as collateral.

Negotiating bank. Bank that issues a letter of credit.

Net operating loss carrybacks. Practice of applying losses to offset earnings in previous years.

Net operating loss carryforwards. Practice of applying losses to offset earnings in future years.

Net Stable Funding Ratio (NSFR). The NSFR was introduced by Basel III to provide a sustainable maturity structure of assets and liabilities. It requires a minimum amount of stable sources of funding at a bank relative to the liquidity profiles of the assets as well as to the potential for contingent liquidity needs arising from off-balance-sheet commitments, over a one-year horizon. The NSFR aims to limit over- reliance on short-term wholesale funding during times of buoyant market liquidity and encourage better assessment of liquidity risk across all on- and off- balance-sheet items.

Net transaction exposure. Consideration of inflows and outflows in a given currency to determine the exposure after offsetting inflows against outflows.

Netting. Combining of future cash receipts and payments to determine the net amount to be owed by one subsidiary to another

New-Export policy. Policy administered by Eximbank that provides coverage on commercial risk defaults to new exporters.

Nonbank financial institutions. A financial institution that does not have a full banking license or is not supervised by a national or international banking regulatory agency. These institutions facilitate financial services, such as investment, risk pooling, contractual savings, and trading and brokering, and can include money market mutual funds, investment banks, finance companies, insurance firms, pension funds, hedge funds, currency exchanges, and microfinance organizations.

Non-performing Loans (NPL). Loans for which the contractual payments are delinquent, usually defined as being overdue for more than a certain number of days (e.g., more than 30 or 60 or 90 days).

Non-sterilised intervention. Intervention in the foreign exchange market without adjusting for the change in money supply

Ocean bill of lading. Receipt for a shipment by boat, which includes freight charges and title to the merchandise.

Odd date. Most contracts on the forward market are settled one, three, or six months ahead. Dates outside these standard periods (e.g. 35 days) are called 'odd' dates.

Open (or net) position. The difference between the long and short positions in a given currency.

Open account transaction. Sale in which the exporter ships the merchandise and expects the buyer to remit payment according to agreed upon terms.

Open market operations. The primary means by which a central bank is able to control the short-term interest rate and the supply of base money, and thus to implement monetary policy. They include outright securities transactions, securities transactions with repurchase agreements, and collateralized lending.

Open-end funds (also called mutual funds). A fund which pools resources from several individual investors and uses the proceeds to acquire and manage a portfolio of financial assets such as stocks, bonds and other types of publicly traded securities. Open-end funds continually issue and redeem shares to meet investor demand. Share prices change according to the market value of the fund's portfolio of securities (net asset value of the fund) at any point in time.

Optional date forward contract (or forward option contract). A forward exchange contract where the rate is fixed but the maturity is left for the company to decide subsequently, within a specified range of dates.

Options on futures contract. Contract that provides the right to purchase or sell the futures contract of a specified currency at a specified price by a specified expiration date.

Out-of-the-money. Descriptive term implying that the present exchange rate is less than (exceeds) the strike price on a currency call (put) option.

Outright Monetary Transactions (OMTs). A program of the ECB to purchase sovereign bonds in the secondary market, announced on September 6, 2012, aimed at safeguarding against monetary policy transmission throughout the euro area. Transactions will be based on the short end of the yield curve. A necessary condition for OMTs is strict and effective conditionality attached to an appropriate EFSF/ESM program.

Overhedging. Hedging an amount in a currency larger than the actual transaction amount.

Over-the-counter In the case of financial securities, those that are traded directly between two parties rather than on a financial exchange.

Over-the-counter (OTC) derivative A financial contract whose value derives from underlying security prices, interest rates, foreign exchange rates, commodity prices, or other market indices, and that is traded bilaterally rather than through an exchange.

Over-the-counter (OTC). Financial instruments traded off organised exchanges. Transactions are negotiated over the telephone on a bilateral basis. Generally, the parties must negotiate all the details of the transaction or agree to certain simplifying market conditions.

Parallel bonds. Bonds placed in different countries and denominated in the respective currencies of the countries where they are placed.

Parallel loan. Loan involving an exchange of currencies between two parties, with a promise to reexchange the currencies at a specified exchange rate and future date.

Parent (or home) currency. The currency of the parent company.

Parent country. The country in which the parent company is located.

Parity. The official rate of exchange between two currencies.

Partial compensation. An arrangement in which the delivery of goods to one party is partially compensated for by buying back a certain amount of product from the same party

Partial spin-off. The creation of an independent firm through the partial sale of an existing business of a parent firm; divestiture.

Pegged exchange rate. Exchange rate whose value is pegged to another currency's value or to a unit of account.

Perfect forecast line. A 45 degree line on a graph that matches the forecast of an exchange rate with the actual exchange rate.

Petrodollars. Deposits of dollars by countries which receive dollar revenues due to the sale of petroleum to other countries; the term commonly refers to OPEC deposits of dollars in the Eurocurrency market.

PIBOR. Paris Interbank Offered Rate.

Planned divestment. Act of phasing out a portion of business over time; commonly used by MNCs to phase out their overseas investments.

Point. The second most junior digit in currency quotations, i.e. £1 = $2.10365. The fourth place after the decimal point is 6 points.

Political risk. Political actions taken by the host government or the public that affect the MNC's cash flows.

Portal (Private Offerings, Resales, and Trading through Automated Linkages). NASDAQ's electronic trading system used in the U.S. secondary market for privately plced equity and debt. It is used for communicating bids and offers on privately placed securities trading under the provisions of SEC Rule 144A.

Preauthorised payment. Method of accelerating cash inflows by receiving authorisation to charge a customer's bank account.

Prepayment. Method which exporter uses to receive payment before shipping goods.

Price-elastic. Sensitive to price changes.

Price-to-book ratio (P/BV). Used to compare a stock's market value to its book value. It is calculated by dividing the current closing price of the stock by the recent quarter's book value per share.

Primary dealer. A financial institution that is authorized to deal directly with the central bank in the buying and selling of government securities.

Private-label securitization Securitization products not issued or backed by governments and their agencies.

Privatisation. Conversion of government-owned businesses to ownership by shareholders or individuals.

Probit model. A statistical binary response model in which the response probability follows a normal distribution and is evaluated as a function of the explanatory variables.

Product cycle theory. Theory suggesting that a firm initially establish itself locally and expand into foreign markets in response to foreign demand for its product; over time, the MNC will grow in foreign markets; after some point, its foreign business may decline unless it can differentiate its product from competitors.

Product differentiation. Development of a product that is unique; different from those produced by competitors, in order to maintain or improve market share.

Proprietary trading. Taking positions in the market using the firm's own capital.

Publicly traded. Financial instruments which are listed and traded in organised securities markets. These issues must fulfill registration and disclosure requirements stipulated by the SEC of the market in which the securities are being issued.

Quantitative Easing (QE). An expansion of a central bank's balance sheet through purchases of government securities and other assets, funded through the creation of base money (cash and bank reserve balances). The second round of quantitative easing by the Federal Reserve to stimulate the U.S. economy following the recession that began in 2007/08 was initiated in the fourth quarter of 2010 and is referred to as Quantitative Easing 2 (QE2).

Real cost of hedging. The additional cost of hedging when compared to not hedging (a negative real cost would imply that hedging was more favorable than not hedging).

Real Estate Investment Trusts (REITs). Specially designated corporations that own and/or operate properties and benefit from special tax treatment that exempts them from corporate income taxes provided that they pay out 90 percent of their income to their shareholders.

Real interest rate. Nominal (or quoted) interest rate minus the inflation rate.

Real net exports. Value of inflation-adjusted exports minus inflation-adjusted imports.

Regression analysis. Statistical technique used to measure the relationship between variables and the sensitivity of a variable to one or more other variables.

Regression coefficient. Term measured by regression analysis to estimate the sensitivity of the dependent variable to a particular independent variable.

Regulatory arbitrage Reducing regulatory capital requirements by taking advantage of differences in regulatory treatment across countries or across types of financial institutions, as well as of differences between economic risk and risk as measured by regulatory guidelines.

Reinvoicing center. Facility that centralises payments and changes subsidiaries fees for its function; this can effectively shift profits to subsidiaries where tax rates are low.

Repo (repurchase) agreement A sale of a security coupled with an agreement to repurchase the security at an agreed price at a future date. This transaction occurs between a cash borrower (or securities lender), typically a fixed-income securities broker-dealer, and the cash lender (or securities borrower), such as a money market mutual fund or a custodial bank. The securities lender receives cash in return and pledges the legal title of a security as collateral.

Repurchase agreement (Repo or RP). The seller of securities enters an agreement with the buyer to repurchase them at a fixed price on a specified date. By entering into a repo, the buyer in effect is lending funds to the seller of the securities for the period of the agreement (for example 30-180 days). Securities dealers use RPs extensively to finance their positions.

Resolution. Procedures and measures taken to solve the situation of an unviable institution. Bank resolution is a form of bankruptcy process managed by a government agency with the responsibility to manage an orderly liquidation and to avoid losses to insured retail depositors.

Revocable letter of credit. Letter of credit issued by a bank that can be cancelled at any time without prior notification to the beneficiary.

Revolving credit agreement. A commitment by a bank to provide funds to a client under predefined terms. These agreements contain contigency clauses wherein the bank can refuse to disburse the credit if there is a significant adverse change in the financial position of the borrower.

Risk premium. The extra expected return on an asset that investors demand in exchange for accepting its higher risk.

Risk reversals. Measure of the relative demand for upside/downside protection on an underlying asset, using out-of-the-money options pricing. It is estimated as the difference between the implied volatility on out-of-the-money call and put options and is also referred to as the volatility skew.

Risk-weighted assets. The total of all assets held by a bank weighted by credit, market, and operational risk weights according to formulae determined by the national regulator or supervisor. Most regulators/ supervisors adopt the Basel Committee on Banking Supervision (BCBS) guidelines in setting formulae for asset risk weights.

Roll-Over. When a forward exchange contract is about to mature a new forward 'contract' is created to extend the date when payment is due.

Scale economies. Cost advantages in a firm arising from expansion, including size.

Securities markets programme. Interventions by the Eurosystem in public and private debt securities markets in the euro area to ensure depth and liquidity in those market segments that are dysfunctional.

Securitization. The creation of securities from a portfolio of existing assets or future receivables that are placed under the legal ownership or control of investors through a special intermediary created for this purpose—a "special purpose vehicle" (SPV) or "special purpose entity" (SPE).

Semistrong-form efficient. Description of foreign exchange markets, implying that all relevant public information is already reflected in prevailing spot exchange rates.

Sensitivity analysis. Technique for assessing uncertainty whereby various possibilities are input to determine possible outcomes.

Settlement. Process involving the finalisation of legal documentation associated with a transaction in the securities market.

Simulation. Technique for assessing the degree of uncertainty Probability distributions are developed for the input variables; simulation uses this information to generate possible outcomes.

Single Supervisory Mechanism (SSM). A common banking supervision framework under the aegis of the European Central Bank for the euro area banks, as proposed by the European Commission in September 2012.

Solvency II. A Directive of the European Union (Solvency II Directive 2009/138/EC) that codifies and harmonizes insurance regulations in the European Economic Area. As part of its provisions, the directive determines the amount of capital that insurance companies must hold to reduce the risk of insolvency.

Special Drawing Rights (SDRs). Reserves established by the International Monetary Fund; they are used only for intergovernment transactions; the SDR also serves as a unit of account (determined by the values of five major currencies) that is used to denominate some internationally traded goods and services, as well as some foreign bank deposits and loans.

Specialists. Firms designated by the exchange to maintain orderly trading and manage limit orders for each currency.

Spot market. The currency market for 'immediate' delivery. Delivery is usually two working days after transaction date, though in some markets spot transactions may be executed for next day value

Spot rate. Current exchange rate of currency.

Spot/forward swaps. The simultaneous spot purchase or sale of a currency and an offsetting sale or purchase of the same currency in the forward market.

Spread. The difference between the buying and selling rate for a currency.

Standby letter of credit. Document used to guarantee invoice payments to a supplier; it promises to pay the beneficiary if the buyer fails to pay.

Sterilised intervention. Intervention in the foreign exchange market while retaining the existing money supply.

Straddle. Combination of a put option and a call option.

Structural adjustment loan facility. Facility established in 1980 by the World Bank to enhance a country's long-term economic growth through financing projects.

Supplier credit. Credit provided by the supplier to itself to fund its operations.

Swap. An agreement between counterparties to exchange periodic payments based on different reference financial instruments or indices on a predetermined notional amount. When the swap agreement is based on fixed versus floating interest rates, it is called an interest- rate swap.

Swap spread. The differential between the government bond yield and the fixed rate on an interest rate swap of the equivalent maturity.

Swaptions. Interest rate instruments that allow investors to take a view on future interest rate volatility, using options to trigger then underlying interest-rate swap agreements. A 10-year by 10-year swaption allows an investor to buy/ sell a 10-year option on an underlying interest rate swaps contract with a 10-year term.

Swingline. A short-term credit facility which can be drawn on short notice to cover the period between the offer of notes under a note issuance facility and the receipt of funds.

Syndicate. Group of banks that participate in loans.

Syndicated eurocredit loans. Loans provided by a group (or syndicate) of banks in the Eurocredit market.

Systematic risk. Risk that cannot be diversified away and is common to all firms or countries.

Target zones. Implicit boundaries established by central banks on exchange rates.

Technical forecasting. Development of forecasts using historical prices or trends.

Third-party trade. Trade between companies which are not part of the same corporate group.

Tier 1 capital. Under Basel III, Tier 1 capital or going- concern capital comprises Common Equity Tier 1 capital and Additional Tier 1 capital.

Time stries analysis. Analysis of relationships between two or more variables over periods of time.

Too Important to Fail (TITF). Financial institutions considered to be so large, interconnected, or critical to the workings of the wider financial system that their disorderly failure would destabilize both the financial system and the wider economy. Hence, public funds would be deployed to prevent such a failure.

Trade acceptance. Draft that allows the buyer to obtain merchandise prior to accepting it.

Transaction date. In the foreign exchange market, the date on which a foreign exchange contract is agreed.

Transaction exposure. Degree to which the value of future cash transactions can be affected by exchange rate fluctuations.

Transactions exposure. The exposure inherent in a foreign currency transaction, both commercial (trade receivables and payables) and financial (dividend and loan payments).

Transfer pricing. Policy for pricing goods sent by either the parent or a subsidiary to a subsidiary of an MNC.

Transfer risk. Risk associated with the possibility that the contemporary to the financial contract will not have foreign exchange available to meet it obligations.

Transferable letter of credit. Document that allows the first beneficiary on a standby letter of credit to transfer all or part of the original letter of credit to a third party.

Translation exposure. Degree to which a firm's consolidated financial statements are exposed to fluctuations in exchange rates.

Triangular arbitrage. Action to capitalise on a discrepancy where the quoted cross exchange rate is not equal to the rate that should exist at equilibrium.

Tripartite (or tri-party) repo. A repo transaction in which a custodian bank or international clearing organization (the tri-party agent) acts as an intermediary between the two parties. The tri-party agent is responsible for the administration of the transaction, including collateral allocation, marking to market, and substitution of collateral.

TSE. Tokyo Stock Exchange.

Umbrella policy. Policy issued to a bank or trading company to insure exports of an exporter and handle all administrative requirements.

Underwriting The process that financial institutions use to assess the eligibility of a customer to receive their products.

Unilateral transfers. Accounting for government and private gifts and grants.

Vienna Initiative. The European Bank Coordination "Vienna" Initiative (EBCI) was launched in January 2009 to provide a framework for coordinating the crisis management and crisis resolution that involved large cross-border banking groups systemically important in emerging Europe. The European Bank for Reconstruction and Development, the IMF, the European Commission, and other international financial institutions initiated a process aimed at addressing the collective action problem. In a series of meetings, the international financial institutions and policymakers from home and host countries met with commercial banks active in emerging Europe to discuss what measures might be needed to reaffirm their presence in the region in general, and more specifically in countries that were receiving balance of payments support from the international financial institutions.

VIX. Chicago Board Options Exchange Volatility Index that measures market expectations of financial volatility over the next 30 days. The VIX is constructed from S&P 500 option prices.

Volcker rule. Section of the Dodd-Frank Act seeking to restrict banks from using depositor funding to conduct proprietary trading and other activities that could expose banks to excessive risk.

Weak-form efficient. Description of foreign exchange markets, implying that all historical and current exchange rate information is already reflected in prevailing spot exchange rates.

Wholesale funding. The funding of banks in private markets, used in addition to deposits from customers, to finance bank operations. Wholesale funding sources include, but are not limited to, debt issuance, short- term instruments such as certificates of deposit and commercial paper, repo transactions, and interbank borrowing.

Withholding tax. Common name for a tax imposed by a host country on funds that are remitted from a subsidiary to its parent.

Writer. Seller of an option.

Yankee stock offerings. Offerings of stock by non-U.S. firms in the U.S. markets.

Yield curve The relationship between the interest rate (or yield) and the time to maturity for debt securities of equivalent credit risk. In this GFSR, the interest (term) spread between the 10-year Treasury bond and the 3-month Treasury bill.

SELECT BIBLIOGRAPHY

Abauf, Niso, "Foreign exchange options: the leading hedge", *Midland Corporate Finance Journal*, 5 (Summer 1987), pp. 51-58.

———, "The nature and management of foreign exchange risk", *Midland Corporate Finance Journal*, 4 (Fall 1986), pp. 30-44,

Adler, Michael, "'The cost of capital and valuation of a two-country firm", *Journal of Finance*, 29 (March 1974), pp.119-132.

Adler, Michael, and Bernard Dumas, "Portfolio choice and the demand for forward exchange", *American Economic Review*, 66 (May 1975), pp. 332-339.

———, International portfolio choice and corporation finance: a synthesis", *Journal of Finance*, 38 (June 1983), pp.925-984.

Aggarwal Raj, "International differences in capital structure norms: an empirical study of large European countries", *Management International Review*, 21 (1981) pp.75-88.

Agmon Tamir, and Donald Lessard, "Investor recognition of corporate international diversification", *Journal of Finance*, 32 (September 1977), pp.1049- 1055

Aliber, *Robert* Z., "The interest rate parity theorem: a reinterpretation", *Journal of Political Economy*, 81 (December 1973), pp.1451-1459.

Aliber, R.Z., and C.P. Stickney, "Accounting measures of foreign exchange exposure: the long and short of it", *Accounting Review*, L (January 1975), pp.44-57.

Babbel, David F., "Determining the optimum strategy for hedging currency exposure", *Journal of international Business Studies;* 14 (Spring/Summer 1983), pp.133-139.

Baker, James C., "Capital budgeting in West European countries", *issues in Financial Management*, 19(1981), pp.3-10.

Bhalla, V.K., *Managing International Investment and Finance*, Anmol Publication Pvt. Ltd., New Delhi, India, 1997.

———, International Economy: Liberalisation Process, Anmol Publication Pvt. Ltd., New Delhi, India, 1993.

Bhalla, V.K. and N.A. Sarme: Oct '87 Stock Markets Crach and Its Aftermath, ICRIER, 1998.

———, World Mountary and Financial System, ICRIER, 1987.

Bilson, John F.O., "Rational expectations and the exchange rate", in Jacob A. Frenkel and Harry O. Johnson, eds., *The Economics of Exchange Rates* (Reading, Mass., Addison-Wesley, 1978), pp.75-96.

Choi, Frederick D.S., Howard D. Lowe, and Reginald G. Worthley, "Accountors, accountants, and standard No.8", *Journal of International Business Studies,* 9 pp.81-87.

Cohn, Richard A., and John J. Pringle, "Imperfections in international financial markets: implications for risk premia and the cost of capital to firms", *Journal of Finance,* 28 (March 1973), pp.59-66.

Collins, J. Markham, and William S. Sekely, "The relationship of headquarters, country, and industry classification to financial structure", *Financial Management,* 12 (Autumn 1983), pp.45-51.

Dornbush, Rudiger, "Expectations and exchange rate dynamics", *Journal of Political Economy,* 84 (December 1976), pp 1161-1176.

Dufey, Gunter, "Corporate finance and exchange rate variations", *Financial Management,* 1 (Summer 1972), pp.51-57.

Dufey, Gunter, and Ian H. Giddy, "International financial planning: the use of market-based forecasts", *Califonia Management Review,* 21 (Fall 1978), pp. 58-81

———,"Innovation in the international financial markets", *Journal of inter- national Business Studies,* 12 (Fall 1981), pp.45-51.

Eaker, Mark R., "Denomination decision for multinational transactions", *Financial Management,* 9 (Autumn 1980), pp.23-29.

Eiteman, David K., Arthur I. Stonehill and Michael H. Moffett, *Multinational Business Finance,* sixth edition (Reading, Mass., Addison-Wesley, 1992), pp.493-494.

Errunza, Vihang, R., "Gains from portfolio diversification into less developed countries", *Journal of international Business Studies,* (Fall-Winter 1977), pp.83-99.

Errunza, Vihang, R. and Barr Rosenberg, "Investment in developed and less developed countries", *Journal of Financial and Quantitative Analysis,* 17/5 (December 1982), pp.741-762.

Errunza, Vihang R., and Lemma W. Senhet, "The effects of international operations on the market value of the firm: theory and evidence", *Journal of Finance,* 36 (May 1981), pp.401-417.

Errunza, Vihang R., and Etienne Losq, "International asset pricing under mild segmentation: theory and test", *Journal of Finance,* 49 (March 1985), pp.105-124.

Eun, Cheol S., and Bruce G. Resnick, "Currency factor in international portfolio diversification", *Financial Management,* 14 (Summer 1985), pp.45-53.

"Exchange rate uncertainty, forward contracts, and international portfolio selection", *Journal of Finance,* 43 (March 1988), pp.197-215.

Fama, Eugene F., "Forward rates as predictors of future spot rates", *Journal of Financial Economics,* 5 (October 1976), pp.361-377.

Flood, Eugene, Jr., and Donald R. Lessard, "On the measurement of operating exposure to exchange rates: a conceptual approach", *Financial Management,* 15 (Spring 1986), pp.25-36.

Folks, William R., Jr., "Decision analysis for exchange risk management", *Financial Management,* 1 (Winter 1972), pp.101-112.

Folks, William R., and Stanley R. Stansell, "The use of discriminant analysis in forecasting exchange risk movements", *Journal of international Business Studies,* 6 (Spring 1975), pp. 33-50.

Garman, Mark B., and Steven W. Kohlhagen, "Foreign currency option values", *Journal of international Money and Finance,* 2 (December 1983), pp.231-237.

George, Abraham M., "Cash flow versus accounting exposures to currency risk", *California Management Review,* 20 (Summer 1978), pp.50-55.

Germany, J. David, and John E. Monon, "Financial innovation and deregulation in foreign industrial countries", *Federal Reserve Bulletin,* 71 (October 1985), pp.743-753.

Giddy, Ian H., "An integrated theory of exchange rate equilibrium", *Journal of Financial and Quantitative Analysis,* 11 (December 1976), pp.863-892.

———, "Why it doesn't pay to make a habit of forward hedging", *Euromoney* (December 1976), pp.96-100.

———, "Exchange risk: whose view?", *Financial Management,* 6 (Summer 1977), pp.23-33.

Giddy, Ian H., and Gunter Dufey, "The random behavior of flexible exchange rates: implications for forecasting", *Journal of international Business Studies,* 6 (Spring 1975), pp.1-32.

Gordon, Sara L., and Francis A. Lees, "Multinational capital budgeting: foreign investment under subsidy", *California Management Review,* 25 (Fall 1982), pp.22-32.

Grauer, Frederick A., Robert A. Litzenberger, and Richard E. Stehle, "Sharing rules and equilibrium in an international capital market under uncertainty", Journal of Financial Economics, 5 (June 1976), pp.233-256.

Grubel, Herbert G., "Internationally diversified portfolios: welfare gains and capital flows", *American Economic Review,* 58 (December 1968), pp. 1299-1314.

Grubel, Herbert G., and Kenneth Fadner, "The interdependence of international equity markets", Journal of Finance, 26 (March 1971), pp.89-94.

Hekman, Christine R., "Don't blame currency values for strategic errors", Midland Corporate Financial Journal, 4 (Fall 1986), pp.45-55.

Hodder, James F., "Evaluation of manufacturing investments: a comparison of U.S. and Japanese practices", Financial Management, 15 (Spring 1986), pp. 17-24.

Hughes, John S., Dennis E. Logue, and Richard J, Sweeney, "Corporate international diversification and market assigned measures of risk and diversification", Journal of Financial and Quantitative Analysis, 10 (November 1975), pp.627-637.

Ibbotson, Roger C., Richard C. Carr, and Anthony W. Robinson, "International equity and bond returns", Financial Analysts Journal, 38 (July-August 1982), pp.61-83.

Jacquc, Laurent L., "Management of foreign exchange risk: a review article", Journal of International Business Studies, 12 (Spring/Summer 1981), pp.81-101.

Jacquillat, Bertrand, and Bruno H. Solnik, "Multinationals are poor tools for diversification", Journal of Portfolio Management, (Winter 1978), pp.8-12.

Jurgensen Report, Report of the Working Group on Exchange Market Intervention, Washington, D.C.: U.S. Treasury, 1983.

Kelly, Marie F. Wicks, and George C. Philippatos, "Comparative analysis of the foreign investment evaluation practices by US-based manufacturing multinational companies", Journal of International Business Studies, 13 (Winter 1982), pp.19-42.

Kester, W. Carl, "Capital and ownership structure: A comparison of United States and Japanese manufacturing corporations", Financial Management, 15 (Spring 1986), pp.5-16.

Khoury, Sarkis J., and K. Hung Chan, "Hedging foreign exchange risk: selecting the optimal tool", Midland Corporate Finance Journal, I (Winter 1988), pp.40-52.

Kohlhagen, Steven W., "Forward rates as predictors of future spot rates", Journal of International Business Studies', 6 (Fall 1975), pp.33-39

———, "A model of optimal foreign exchange hedging without exchange rate projections", Journal of international Business Studies, 9 (Fall 1978), pp.9-19.

Lee, Kwang Chul, and Chuck C.Y. Kwok, "Multinational corporations vs. domestic corporations: international environmental factors and determinants of capital structure", Journal of International Business Studies, 19 (Summer 1988), pp.195-217.

Lee, Wayne Y., and Kanwal S. Sachdeva, "The role of the multinational firm in the integration of segmented markets", Journal of Finance, 32 (May 1977), pp.479-492.

Lessard, Donald R. "International portfolio diversification: A multivariate analysis for a group of Latin American countries", Journal of Finance, 28 (June 1973), pp. 619-633.

———,"World, national, and industry factors in equity returns", Journal of Finance, 29 (May 1974), pp.379-391.

———,"Evaluating international projects: an adjusted present value approach", in Donald R. Lessard, ed., International Financial Management: Theory and Application (New York, Wiley, 1985), pp. 570-584.

———,"Finance and global competition: exploiting financial scope and coping with volatile exchange rates", *Midland Corporate Finance Journal 4* (Fall 1986), pp.6-29.

Levich, Richard M., "Tests of forecasting models and market efficiency in the international money market", in Jacob A. Frenkel and Harry G. Johnson, eds., *The Economics of Exchange Rates* (Reading, Mass., Addison-Wesley, 1978), pp.129-158.

———,"Analyzing the accuracy of foreign exchange forecasting services: theory and evidence", in Clas Wihlhorg and Richard Levich, eds., *Exchange Risk and*

Exposure: Current Developments in International Financial Development (Lexington, Mass., Heath, 1980), pp.99-127.

Levy, Haim, and Marshall Sarnat, "International diversification of investment portfolios", *American Economic Review,* LX (September 1970), pp. 668-675.

Logue, Dennis E., and George S. Oldfield, "Managing foreign assets when foreign exchange markets are efficient", *Financial Management,* 6 (Summer 1977), pp.16-22.

Modigliani, Franco and Merton Miller, "The cost of capital, corporation finance and the theory of investment", *American Economic Review,* XLVIII (June 1958), pp.261-297.

Oblak, David J., and Roy I. Helm, Jr., "Survey and analysis of capital budgeting methods used by multinationals", *Financial Management,* 9 (Winter 1980), pp.37-41.

Remmers, Lee, Arthur Stonehill, Richard Wright, and Theo Beekhuisen, "Industry and size as debt ratio determinants for manufacturing internationally", *Financial Management,* 3 (Summer 1974), pp. 24-32.

Robichek, Alexander A., and Mark R. Eaker, Debt denomination and exchange risk in international capital markets", *Financial Management,* 5 (Autumn 1976), pp.11-18.

Rodriguez, Rita M., "Corporate exchange risk management: theme and aberrations", *Journal of Finance,* 36 (May 1981), pp.427-439.

Rutterford, Janette, "An international perspective on the capital structure puzzle", *Midland Corporate Finance Journal,* 3 (Fall 1985), pp.60-72.

Sarathy, Ravi, and Sangit Chatterjee, "The divergence of Japanese and U.S. corporate financial structure", *Journal of International Business Studies,* 15 (Winter 1984). pp.75-89.

Sekely, William S., and J. Markham Collins, "Cultural influences on international capital structure", *Journal of International Business Studies,* 19 (Spring 1988), pp.87-100.

Shapiro, Alan C., "Exchange rate changes, inflation, and the value of the multinational corporation", *Journal of Finance,* 30 (May 1975), pp.485-501.

"Capital budgeting for the multinational corporation", *Financial Management,* 7 (Spring 1978), pp.7-16.

"Financial structure and cost of capital in the multinational corporation", *Journal of Financial and Quantitative Analysis,* 13 (June 1978), pp.211-226.

Shapiro, Alan C., and David P. Rutenberg, "When to hedge against devaluation", *Management Science,* 20 (August 1974), pp.1514-1530.

"Managing exchange risks in a floating world", *Financial Management,* 5 (Summer 1976), pp.48-58.

Solnik, Bruno H., "Note on the validity of the random walk for European stock market capital structure", *Journal of Finance,* 28 (December 1973), pp.1151 1159.

———, "The international pricing of risk: an empirical investigation of the world capital market structure", *Journal of Finance,* 29 (May 1974), pp. 365-378.

———,"Testing international asset pricing; some pessimistic views', *Journal of Finance,* 32 (May 1977), pp 503-512.

Stanley, Marjorie T., "Capital structure and cost of capital for the multinational firm", *Journal of International Business Studies,* 12 (Spring/Summer 1981), pp.103-120.

Stanley, Marjorie and Stanley Block, "An empirical study of management and financial variables in influencing capital budgeting decisions for multinational corporations in the 1980s", *Management International Review* 23 (1983), pp.61-71.

Stapleton, Richard C., and Marti Subrahmanyam, "Market imperfections, capital market equilibrium, and corporation finance", *Journal of Finance,* 32 (May 1977), pp.307-319.

Stehle, Richard F., "An empirical test of the alternative hypothesis of national and international pricing of risk assets", *Journal of Finance,* 32 (May 1977), pp.493-502.

Stonehill, Arthur, and Leonard Nathanson, "Capital budgeting and the multinational corporation", *California Management Review,* 11 (Summer 1968), pp.39-54.

Stonehill, Arthur, and Thomas Stitzel, "Financial structure and multinational corporations", *California Management Review,* 12 (Fall 1969), pp.91-96.

Stonehill, Arthur, Theo Beekhuisen, Richard Wright, Lee Remmers, Norman Toy, Antonio Pares, Alan Shapiro, Douglas Egan, and Thomas Bates, "Financial goals and debt ratio determinants: a survey of practice in five countries", *Financial Management,* 4 (Autumn 1975), pp. 27-41.

Toy, Norman. Arthur Stonehill, Lee Remmers, Richard Wright, and Theo Beekhuisen, "A comparative international study of growth, profitability and risk as determinants of corporate debt ratios in the manufacturing sector.', *Journal of Financial and Quantitative Analysis,* 9 (November 1974), pp.875-886.

UNCTC, *World Investment Report 1991: The Triad in Foreign Direct Investment* (New York, United Nations, 1991).

Turnbull, Stuart M., "Swaps: a zero sum game?", *Financial Management,* 16 (Spring 1987), pp.15-21.

Transnational Corporations and Management Division, *World In vestment Report 1992: Transnational Corporations as Engines of Growth* (New York, United Nations, 1992).

Wheelwright, Steve, "Applying decision theory to improve corporate management of currency-exchange risks", *California Management Review,* 17 (Summer 1975), pp. 41-49.

Wright, Richard, and Sadahiko Suzuki, "Financial structure and bankruptcy risk in Japanese companies", *Journal of International Business Studies,* 16 (Spring 1985), pp. 97-110.

INDEX